Majority and Minority

SECOND EDITION

Majority and Minority

The Dynamics of Racial and Ethnic Relations

EDITED BY

Norman R. Yetman
The University of Kansas

C. Hoy Steele
*North Carolina Community
Development Corporation*

Allyn and Bacon, Inc.
Boston • London • Sydney

Library of Congress Cataloging in Publication Data

Yetman, Norman R   1938–   comp.
  Majority and minority.

  Includes bibliographies.
    1. United States—Race question. 2. Minorities—
United States. 3. Race problems. 4. Minorities.
I. Steele, C. Hoy, joint comp. II. Title.
E184.A1Y4 1975   301.45′1′0973   74–34101

ISBN 0–205–04815–3

*For
Jill and Doug,
Teri, Shauna, and Greg.
With our hopes for a
more humane social order.*

Contents

part
one

part
two

vii

part three

Minorities in America: Historical Perspectives   159

part four

Intergroup Contact in America: Methods and Problems of Adjustment   223

Discrimination: Attitudinal and Institutional   357

part
five

part six

The Black Revolution and the Resurgence of Ethnicity   545

Preface

During the final week of preparing the manuscript for the first edition of *Majority and Minority,* a local Black youth was shot dead by a White policeman in Lawrence, Kansas. This event precipitated the greatest period of social unrest and tension that this city had experienced since Quantrill's raid during the Civil War. Throughout the late 1960s and into the 1970s this scenario occurred in communities throughout the nation, but its occurrence in our own city and in our own lives heightened the sense of urgency that has shaped our approach to both editions of this book.

The frequency of mass social unrest has dramatically declined in the four years since we witnessed those events. The tragic American involvement in the Indo-China War has been formally ended and the "civil disorders" that rent many American cities during that period have not recurred. Moreover, the widespread sense of commitment to social justice of only four years ago has been replaced by an indifference, even an aversion, to the problems of racial minority groups in America. Indeed, the activism of the "concerned generation" of the 1960s has been replaced by a stance of "benign neglect."

Yet, despite some highly visible changes (for example, the election of Black mayors in Los Angeles, Detroit, and Atlanta), the inequalities that spawned the civil disorders of the 1960s remain entrenched. For instance, the most recent data available at this writing indicate that not only has the income gap between Whites and Blacks widened during the past decade, but Black family income declined .2 percent while White family income increased 6.1 percent from 1969 to 1973. During the same period the ratio of Black to White income, which had risen steadily during the 1960s, declined substantially. With the problems of inflation and unemployment becoming increasingly acute, the prospect is that the inequalities between the White majority and America's racial minorities will continue to widen. In other words, the problems of majority-minority relations have not been resolved; they remain as entrenched and as potentially volatile as in 1970.

Thus it is with a continuing sense of frustration at our society's inability to confront and to alter these inequalities that we present this second edition. We remain acutely aware of the practical—as well as the theoretical—need for a more fundamental understanding of the dynamics of racial and ethnic relations. However, we remain equally convinced of the irrelevance of analysis and "understanding" that is not complemented by action to alter existing systems of inequality.

Although the mood of the country has dramatically changed in the past four years, our objectives in this book remain the same. As in the first edition, we have attempted to portray and to analyze the dynamics of racial and ethnic relations within the context of a general theoretical understanding of the broader field of majority-minority relations. While most of the articles that follow pertain to the contemporary United States, we have employed terminology and been guided by concepts that are applicable to other societies and other historical periods as well. We have tried to make our focus *both* theoretical and practical, and at once macroscopic and microscopic.

In the study of race and ethnicity, a concern for practical problems and the absence of an adequate sociological theory of majority-minority relations have frequently gone hand in hand; much research has been narrowly descriptive and conceptually uninformed. We maintain, however, that the attempt to conceptualize these phenomena on a broader and more general level is not incompatible with an interest in problem solving and action research. On the contrary, the former task is prerequisite to the latter; the manner in which data are perceived and conceptually organized is crucial to systematically effecting social change. Consequently, in the analysis of majority-minority relations, theory and problem solving are indivisible. In this book we have included several articles that provide a basis for the development of theory, and in the introductory essays to each part we have attempted to integrate the materials conceptually.

Our basic assumption is that the study of racial and ethnic relations should focus primarily upon the patterns of differential power and intergroup conflict in a society. Emphasis upon power and conflict in the analysis of majority-minority relations is a relatively recent occurrence. For many years the conventional wisdom among social scientists relative to the "problems" of race and ethnicity was dominated by approaches that ignored or underestimated the importance of the variables of conflict and power. It is an instructive commentary upon the state of sociological theory that many of the most effective critics of "order" theory have been social critics—often minority group members—outside the mainstream of the professional social scientific disciplines. Recently there has been an increasing recognition by sociological theorists of the need for a conflict model of societal functioning. Our own perspectives have been influenced less by formal sociological theory than by the changing character of the racial crisis in American society. Articulate minority spokesmen have been instrumental in graphically demonstrating the role of differential power in maintaining a racist social system and the presence of conflict as an inherent component of majority-minority relations.

As our interest in power and conflict suggests, we have placed strong emphasis upon sociological explanations of the dynamics of majority-minority relations. We feel that the fundamental determinants of these situations are to be found in the institutional structures of society, and that sociological concepts are most useful in explaining them. This orientation is, in our opinion, the most important feature of this volume. In contrast, other readers and textbooks in the field have been heavily psychological and social psychological in orientation, focusing primarily upon the phenomenon of prejudice. Although psychological concerns typically have occupied a major portion of courses dealing with minority groups,[1] we have included few materials dealing with them explicitly. The perspective that we stress is that prejudice is far less significant as an explanatory variable than institutional and structural factors, and consequently we have focused primarily on the dynamics of these phenomena.

Although the title we have chosen for this reader appears to equate the study of majority-minority relations with that of racial and ethnic relations, we feel that the variables that have traditionally been emphasized in "minority groups" courses—race, religion, nationality and ethnicity—have contributed to an overly narrow conceptualization of the terms *majority* and *minority*. Since the study of intergroup relations can be subsumed under much broader categories, we would argue for a more inclusive definition of these terms. Both concepts imply an unequal ordering of society; consequently, racial and ethnic relations should be conceived as a special case of structured social inequality or, as it has been traditionally termed, social stratification. If, as we maintain, the fundamental variable in majority-minority relations is a condition of unequal power between two more or less self-conscious groups, then a multiplicity of groups—students, women, the poor, people with long hair and beards, homosexuals, dwarfs—could in some sense be characterized as minor-

---

[1] Peter I. Rose, *The Subject Is Race: Traditional Ideologies and the Teaching of Race Relations* (New York: Oxford University Press, 1968), pp. 132–137.

ities. Although the articles in this book are devoted primarily to situations of race and ethnicity (which happen presently to comprise the minority groups of greatest national concern and interest in the United States), conceptually and thematically their implications extend beyond the specific situations they describe. We hope that this book not only illumines the dynamics of racial and ethnic relations, but that it also raises more general questions concerning the nature of human societies.

We have retained the basic structure and themes of the first edition but, reflecting the pace of societal change and the evolution of social scientific—and our own—thought, we have made several changes. We have retained nineteen articles from the first edition, two of which—Baron's "Black Powerlessness in Chicago," and Yetman and Eitzen's "Black Americans in Sports"—have been updated or substantially revised and expanded. Twenty-eight new articles, as well as an extensive statistical appendix, have been added. Each section has been expanded, and each of the introductory essays has been revised and expanded.

As we indicate in the introduction to Part Six, the impact of the Black Revolution of the 1960s is even more apparent now than four years ago. This movement provided a vital stimulus to a new sense of group identity and militancy among several other racial and ethnic groups and to the Women's Movement. Consequently, we have expanded coverage of minorities other than Blacks. However, as indicated above, we remain convinced that the basic structural conditions affecting minorities in American society have changed very little during the past four years. Thus we have substantially expanded the discussion of the mechanisms by which majority group power is maintained and perpetuated.

A number of individuals have assisted us in the preparation of this edition. We are especially indebted in this regard to Bob Antonio, Rowena Dores, Joe Horgan, Marion Howey, David Katzman, and George Ritzer. Special thanks must go to Anne Yetman and Donnalee Steele, who helped with much that was involved in this book's preparation and sustained and encouraged us throughout.

Norman R. Yetman
C. Hoy Steele

Majority and Minority

part one

Majority and Minority: Perspectives and Definitions

The term *minority group* was originally derived from the European experience, particularly after the emergence of the nation-state and the rise of nationalism in the late eighteenth and early nineteenth centuries. In that context it was used to characterize national or ethnic groups that had become subordinate to the peoples of another national group through the imposition of, or shifts in, political boundaries. Subsequently, the term was applied—by social scientist and layman alike—to a diversity of groups and social categories.

In recent usage the term has generally been restricted to groups characterized by "hereditary membership" and "endogamy"—racial, caste, and ethnic groupings.[1] However, as we argued in the Preface, since power differentiation is the distinctive feature of majority-minority relations, we prefer a more inclusive definition. Joseph B. Gittler's comprehensive definition is consistent with this approach. According to Gittler, "Minority Groups are those whose members experience a wide range of discriminatory treatment and frequently are relegated to posi-

[1] See Robin M. Williams, Jr., *Strangers Next Door: Ethnic Relations in American Communities* (Englewood Cliffs, N.J.: Prentice-Hall, 1964), p. 304; Charles Wagley and Marvin Harris, *Minorities in the New World* (New York: Columbia University Press, 1958), pp. 4–10.

tions relatively low in the status structure of a society."[2] In this definition the crucial element of the term's original meaning has been retained— the reference to a distinct group that occupies a subordinate position of prestige, privilege, and power. In this book we will devote particular attention to the power relation implied by the terms *minority* and *majority*.

Occasionally, as is the case today in South Africa (see Colin Legum, "Color and Power in the South African Situation," in Part Two of this book), in many areas of the American South, and in most colonial situations, a "minority" group will represent a majority of the total population. Numerical superiority, therefore, does not necessarily ensure majority status. Many commentators have suggested that *majority* and *minority* be replaced by the terms *dominant* and *subordinate* to represent more accurately the differences in power that differentiate one from the other. However, since *majority* and *minority* have been so widely used, we will continue to employ them here with the understanding that the crucial feature of the minority's status is its inferior social position in which its interests are not effectively represented in the political, economic, and social institutions of the society. We will employ the terms *dominant* as a synonym for *majority,* and we will use *subordinate* as a synonym for *minority*. It may well be that substantial differences in the nature of ethnic relations exist between situations in which the dominant group is a numerical minority and those in which it is in number, as well as in power, more substantial than the subordinate group. Consensus on the pertinence of these factors awaits a more elaborate cross-cultural analysis.

Many different dimensions (e.g., race, ethnicity, religion) have been employed to distinguish minority from majority. But, as Donald L. Noel argues in "The Origin of Ethnic Stratification (reprinted in this section of this book)," differences along these dimensions do not automatically generate conflict and create a system of ethnic inequality. Culturally, religiously, or racially disparate groups may coexist without this kind of structure emerging. Majority-minority relations do not appear until one group successfully imposes its will upon another. By definition, minority groups are subordinate segments of the societies of which they are a part. Once ethnic differences have been perceived and ethnic groups compete against each other, the most important variable is the differential power of one group relative to another. This power may be derived from the superior size, weapons, technology, property, education, or economic resources of the dominant group. Hence, minority groups are categories of people that possess imperfect access to positions of equal power, prestige, and privilege in the society.

Superior power is crucial not only to the establishment of a system of ethnic stratification but, as Noel points out, to its maintenance and

[2] Joseph B. Gittler, *Understanding Minority Groups* (New York: John Wiley and Sons, 1956), p. vii.

perpetuation as well. Once having obtained control of a society's institutions, the majority group generally strives to solidify and consolidate its position. The process by which this occurred in the United States has been succinctly summarized.

> . . . we are a nation of immigrants, but one in which the original dominant immigrant group, the so-called Anglo-Saxons, effectively preempted the crucial levers of economic and political power in government, commerce, and the professions. This elite group has tenaciously resisted the upward strivings of successive "ethnic" immigrant waves. The resultant competitive hierarchy of immigrants has always been highly conducive to violence, but this violence has taken different forms. The Anglo-Americans have used their access to the levers of power to maintain their dominance, using legal force surrounded by an aura of legitimacy for such ends as economic exploitation; the restriction of immigration by a national-origin quota system which clearly branded later immigrants as culturally undesirable; the confinement of the original Indian immigrants largely to barren reservations; and the restriction of blacks to a degraded caste.[3]

Although conflict is not always overt, continuous, or apparent in a social system based upon structured inequality, the potential for conflict is continually present. The extent to which conflict or stability is manifested appears to be a function of the social structural characteristics of the society in question. Pierre van den Berghe has contrasted the patterns of race relations characteristic of two structurally different types of societies. Under the *paternalistic* type, characteristic of a traditional, pre-industrial, predominantly agricultural society, race relations are highly stable and conflict is submerged—a function of both the mechanisms of social control used by the dominant group and the symbiotic nature of relations between dominant and subordinate groups. On the other hand, race relations in a *competitive* setting—an urbanized and highly industrialized society characterized by a complex division of labor—are less likely to remain stable. Overt conflict, initiated by both the dominant and subordinate groups, frequently erupts.[4]

Even in the most stable situations, minority groups are viewed as potentially threatening to the position of the dominant group. This is nowhere more apparent than in the American slave system, which exemplifies van den Berghe's paternalistic type of race relations. Proponents of the "peculiar institution" frequently justified slaveholding on the grounds of the slave's docility, dependence, improvidence, and fear of freedom.

[3] Hugh Davis Graham and Ted Robert Gurr, *Violence in America: Historical and Comparative Perspectives*. A Report Submitted to the National Commission on the Causes and Prevention of Violence (New York: Bantam Books, 1969), p. 794.

[4] Pierre van den Berghe, *Race and Racism: A Comparative Perspective* (New York, John Wiley, 1967).

Simultaneously, however, they saw slaves as "a troublesome presence,"[5] and they initiated elaborate mechanisms (e.g., patrols, passes, legal prohibition against literacy and the possession of weapons) to reduce resistance to the slave regime and employed brutal sanctions to discourage noncompliance to the prescribed subservient roles.

As the experience of the Black Revolution in America has amply demonstrated, attempts by a subordinate group to alter traditional relationships between dominant and subordinate groups and to achieve autonomy and equality of status are resisted by the majority group. Allen D. Grimshaw has summarized the history of changes in Black-White relations by pointing out that:

> The most savage oppression, whether expressed in rural lynchings and pogroms or in urban race riots, has taken place when the Negro has refused to accept a subordinate status. The most intense conflict has resulted when the subordinate minority group has attempted to disrupt the accommodative pattern or when the superordinate group has defined the situation as one in which such an attempt is being made.[6]

Efforts to alter the relative power of the majority and the minority thus inevitably involve conflict between the two groups, the subordinate group attempting to change the system of unequal rewards through a wide variety of means (including violence), the dominant group resorting to a multiplicity of techniques (also including violence—both legal and extralegal) to prevent such changes from occurring.[7] This is nowhere more graphically and tragically depicted than in the present situation in South Africa (described in Part Two by Colin Legum) or in the situation in Northern Ireland (see Robert Moore's article in Part Two).

The increasing "White tyranny" reflected in the repressive apartheid policy of the South African government was developed in response to the political awakening of Black Africa. Furthermore, according to Legum, the monopoly of power held by Whites and their intransigent resistance to basic change offer "no possibility of changing South Africa's existing power structure peacefully." Moore is equally pessimistic that the conflict in Northern Ireland can be peaceably resolved, arguing that changing the situation will require an entire new society.

In Part Five we shall consider the techniques that have (often unintentionally) become institutionalized and that effectively maintain the

---

[5] This is Kenneth M. Stampp's characterization. See *The Peculiar Institution: Slavery in the Ante-Bellum South* (New York: Vintage Books, 1956).

[6] Allen D. Grimshaw, "Lawlessness and Violence in America and Their Special Manifestations in Changing Negro-White Relationships," *The Journal of Negro History,* 44 (January, 1959): 17.

[7] For analyses that document the frequency with which violence has been used by majority or minority groups in America to deal with real or perceived efforts to initiate social change, see Graham and Gurr, *Violence in America.*

inequalities of the status quo. In Part Six we shall consider the tactics by which groups in America have most recently sought to effect or to prevent changes in the social system and the consequences of these tactics for American society.

The discussion thus far has indirectly indicated that the concept of minority group must always be considered in relation to the existence of a majority, or dominant, group. Although this may appear self-evident, a meager amount of the voluminous research on racial and ethnic relations has been devoted to the characteristics and attributes of the majority group and the mechanisms by which the relative relationships between majority and minority are created, maintained, and altered. A notable exception is the work of Robert Bierstedt. In "The Sociology of Majorities," written over twenty-five years ago, Bierstedt said:

> It is the majority . . . which sets the culture pattern and sustains it, which is in fact responsible for whatever pattern or configuration there is in a culture. It is the majority which confers upon folkways, mores, customs, and laws the status of norms and gives them coercive power. It is the majority which guarantees the stability of a society. It is the majority which requires conformity to custom and which penalizes deviation— except in ways in which the majority sanctions and approves. It is the majority which is the custodian of the mores and which defends them against innovation. And it is the inertia of majorities, finally, which retards the processes of social change.[8]

This statement by Bierstedt sets the tone for this book, since it properly places the primary emphasis in the analysis of majority-minority relations upon the dominant group.

The principal focus of inquiry should therefore be on the manner in which the institutions of the society are controlled by the dominant group rather than upon the characteristics of the minority group. As Preston Wilcox has argued, "Much of what has been written as sociology would suggest that . . . minorities suffer problems because of their unique characteristics rather than [because of] the systems which impinge upon them and the sanctioning of these systems by dominant groups."[9] As Howard Schuman shows in Part Five, this belief is widely held in America. William Ryan has termed it "blaming the victim."[10]

Lack of recognition of the importance of societal patterns of institutional control has meant that very often (as John Horton points out in this section) social problems are defined as a group's deviation from societal norms and standards; seldom are a society's institutions, values, and so-

---

[8] Robert Bierstedt, "The Sociology of Majorities," *American Sociological Review* 13 (December, 1948): 709.

[9] Preston Wilcox, "Social Policy and White Racism," *Social Policy* 1 (May/June, 1970): 44.

[10] William Ryan, *Blaming the Victim* (New York, Pantheon Books, 1971).

cial processes themselves the object of inquiry. A Violence Commission
Task Force Report has forcefully delineated the importance of an institutional approach to the analysis of mass protest in America. Mass protest,
it asserts,

> . . . must be analyzed in relation to crises in American institutions. . . .
> [It] is an outgrowth of social, economic, and political conditions. . . , and
> . . . recommendations concerning the prevention of violence which do not
> address the issue of fundamental social, economic, and political change
> are fated to be largely irrelevant and frequently self-defeating.[11]

In other words, both the sources of, and the solutions to, problems of
majority-minority conflict are institutional, and the most realistic approach
to their analysis must focus primarily upon the majority group and the
institutional structures of the society in question.

The importance of an institutional perspective can be demonstrated
through a more thorough examination of the usual approaches employed
by the majority group in responding to intergroup problems and conflict.
As noted above, recognition of the *existence* of a problem is accomplished on the majority's terms, as in the classic statement advanced by
spokesmen for the status quo in communities throughout America that
"we have no problems here. Our ———— [insert appropriate minority
group residing in the community] are happy." Whether or not one perceives social conditions as a "problem" depends on one's position within
the social structure. And, as the Violence Commission Staff Report noted,
whether or not one classifies behavior as "violent" depends upon
whether one is challenging the existing institutional arrangements or
seeking to uphold them.[12]

In an important article examining the functions of racial conflict,
Joseph S. Himes has pointed out that conflict forces the dominant group
to be aware of, come to grips with, and respond to, societal inequities.
Himes argues that organized social conflict alters traditional racial power
relations and changes the traditional etiquette of race relations. As the
minority group is able to mobilize power against the dominant group's
interest, traditional race relations are transformed to the point where
minority grievances can be more realistically discussed.[13] During the late
1950s and early 1960s, Blacks, having been denied change through legitimate channels, used mass protest to mobilize power against the dominant group's entrenched interests. Nonviolent protest and conflict were

---

[11] *The Politics of Protest,* A Staff Report to the National Commission on the Causes and
Prevention of Violence. Prepared by Jerome Skolnick (Washington: Government Printing Office, 1969), p. 3.

[12] *Ibid.,* pp. 3–4.

[13] Joseph S. Himes, "The Functions of Racial Conflict," *Social Forces* 45 (September,
1966): 1–10.

integral strategies of power in the civil rights movement. Martin Luther King, Jr., one of history's most articulate advocates of the weapon of nonviolence, perceived that it represented a means of effecting a redistribution of power:

> Non-violent direct action seeks to create such a crisis and foster such a tension that a community which has constantly refused to negotiate is forced to confront the issue. It seeks so to dramatize the issue that it can no longer be ignored.[14]

If the existence of problems is acknowledged by the dominant group, they are invariably ascribed to the characteristics of the subordinate group rather than to defects in the social system controlled by the majority group. For many years, discussion of Black-White relations in America was described as "the Negro problem," a stance explicitly challenged by Gunnar Myrdal in his classic *An American Dilemma*.[15] More recently, despite the Kerner Report's unequivocal ascription of the major responsibility for the explosive racial conditions in American cities to White racism, most White Americans still deny the role of external societal forces and agree that Blacks themselves are primarily responsible for the conditions in which they find themselves. (See Schuman's "Free Will and Determinism in Public Beliefs about Race," Part Five.) This interpretation is also implicit (as the Baratzes point out in Part Five) in the idea of *cultural deprivation*. According to this ideology, the relatively higher dropout rates, academic failures, and lower achievement levels found among many minority groups are attributable to the internal "deficiencies" and "instabilities" of the minority group itself—e.g., home and neighborhood factors—and not to the inadequacies of the schools. The result of this focus upon the characteristics of the minority group is to deflect attention from the institutional factors that impinge upon it. In short, the emphasis is upon the symptom rather than upon the disease.

Power differentials are also reflected in the resolution of inter-group conflict, for conflicts tend to be resolved within limits acceptable to the majority group. Efforts to alter the pattern of inequalities are therefore restricted to methods defined as "legitimate," or appropriate, by the majority group, a requisite that seldom poses a threat to the continued functioning of the existing system. An excellent example of this pattern can be found in Nancy Lurie's article (Part Three), which sketches the backgrounds of American Indian encounters with White Americans. In those situations, "problems" were always defined from the perspective of Whites and generally involved the refusal of Indians to accede to White demands for cultural assimilation or the ceding of their lands. The values,

[14] Martin Luther King, Jr., *Why We Can't Wait* (New York: Harper & Row, 1964), p. 81.
[15] Gunnar Myrdal, *An American Dilemma: The Negro Problem in Modern Democracy* (New York, Harper & Row, 1944).

needs, and desires of the Indians were seldom, if ever, a consideration in the solution of such confrontations. According to the humanitarian Thomas Jefferson, if Indians did not conform to White cultural patterns, the only viable solution was their forcible removal.

The role of the majority group in delimiting the context within which solutions to problems of intergroup conflict can be reached is exemplified by the 1968 analysis and recommendations of the Kerner Commission and the nation's reactions to them. The Commission charged that "White racism" was the ultimate source of the riots. It concluded that "there can be no higher priority for national action and no higher claim on the nation's conscience" than the elimination of racism from American society.[16] However, it warned that implementation of its recommendations would necessitate "unprecedented levels of funding and performance." Since implementation on these terms would be unpopular with the dominant group, the response to the Kerner Report—both officially and unofficially—has been to discredit or (perhaps more significant) to ignore its findings.

Although it was unacceptable to most White Americans, the Commission's report demonstrates our thesis that majority solutions seldom entail basic alterations of the society's institutional patterns. On the one hand, the Commission indicts American institutions as the primary source of the racism that permeates the society. On the other, most of its recommendations involve changing Blacks to conform to these institutions rather than substantially altering the institutions themselves. Such an approach—involving what Horton terms an *order* model of social problems—slights the basic institutional sources of racism in American society, a subject that we will explore more fully in Part Five.

We have argued that the concepts of majority and minority embrace a broader range of social phenomena than race and ethnicity alone. Traditionally, however, these two categories have been of greatest interest to social scientists. One of the initial problems encountered in the analysis of race relations is definitional: What is meant by the terms *racial* and *ethnic*? As a review of use of the term will reveal, *race* has been an extremely loose concept. Indeed, several scholars have chosen not to use it, preferring to subsume racially distinguished groups within the broad category of *ethnic* groups.[17] *Race* has been used in a variety of ways: to refer to a linguistic grouping (Aryan, English-speaking), to a religious grouping (Hindu, Jewish), to a national grouping (French, Italian), and to

[16] *Report of the National Advisory Commission on Civil Disorders* (Washington, D.C.: Government Printing Office, 1968), p. 2.

[17] See, for example, R. A. Schermerhorn, *Comparative Ethnic Relations: A Framework for Theory and Research* (New York: Random House, 1970), and Tamotsu Shibutani and Kian M. Kwan, *Ethnic Stratification: A Comparative Approach* (New York: Macmillan, 1965).

a mystical, quasi-scientific grouping (Teutonic). The variability of its usage is the key to its sociological significance, for definitions of race and ethnicity are social facts, matters of societal definition. A group is defined as a race by a society when certain selected physical or biologically transmitted characteristics of the group are isolated and their importance as differentiating factors is magnified.

As Ernest Barth and Donald Noel point out in the first article in Part One, the definition of a group as a *race* is not a function of biological or genetic differences between groups, but is dependent upon the society's perception that differences exist *and that they are important.* It is possible for groups to possess genetically identifiable characteristics without these traits providing a basis for racial distinctions. In addition, the criteria selected to make racial distinctions in one society may be overlooked or considered insignificant or irrelevant by another. As Julian Pitt-Rivers points out in "Race, Color, and Class in Central America and the Andes" (Part Two), in much of Latin America skin color and the shape of the lips—important differentiating criteria in the United States—are much less salient variables than hair texture, eye color, and stature. And among the Tutsi and Hutu tribes of central Africa, whose people have similar skin pigmentation, the physical characteristic of stature, not skin color, is determinative.[18]

Finally, it is possible for groups to be identified on an allegedly racial basis without their being physically distinguishable. In American society there have been significant changes in the prevailing conceptions of race. During the last decade of the nineteenth century and the first two decades of the twentieth, differences in political, social, and economic institutions among non-Anglo-Saxon groups were "scientifically" conceived to be due to biologically transmitted and relatively immutable racial traits. Thus, Senator Henry Cabot Lodge, in an 1896 Senate speech condemning continued unrestricted immigration by peoples from southern and eastern Europe, could argue that the Anglo-Saxon "capacity" for democracy was "instinctual."

> The men of each race possess an indestructible stock of ideas, traditions, sentiments, modes of thought, an unconscious inheritance from their ancestors, upon which argument has no effect. What makes a race are their mental and, above all, their moral characteristics, the slow growth and accumulation of centuries of toil and conflict. These are the qualities which determine their social efficiency as a people, which make one race rise and another fall. . . .[19]

Given these assumptions, unrestricted immigration meant the introduction of millions of culturally unassimilable people who lacked these same

[18] van den Berghe, *Race and Racism,* p. 12.
[19] Henry Cabot Lodge, Speech in the United States Senate, *Congressional Record,* 54th Cong., 2d. sess., March 16, 1896.

"instincts," the absence of which would ultimately bring about, according to Lodge, the "decline of human civilization."[20]

The conceptions of race entertained by Lodge and most other prominent social scientists at the turn of the twentieth century are drastically different from prevailing scientific notions today. The important difference resides in the understanding of the *process* by which a society's cultural characteristics are transmitted. In many societies, cultural traits are regarded as innate, inherited, and fully immutable. For Lodge and most of his contemporaries, cultural characteristics had been learned centuries ago and were then transmitted biologically to succeeding generations, with each generation adding to the inherited "stock of ideas, traditions, sentiments [and] modes of thought"; hence Lodge's reference to the acquisition of race "instincts" through a process of "slow growth and accumulation." Lodge's position, on the other hand, was that "race traits" were not unalterably fixed but that any alteration of each "race's" patterns could be effected only at a glacial pace. Thus, as George Stocking has pointed out, it was possible for individuals to be simultaneously environmentalists and hereditarians in their interpretation of the process of the acquisition of cultural, or (as Lodge termed them) "racial," traits.[21]

Many groups socially defined as *racial* are what the contemporary social scientist would refer to as *ethnic*. Social scientists today have rejected the idea that behavioral traits are transmitted genetically and argue that they are acquired through learning during the socialization process. Culture, rather than race, is conceived to be the primary determinant of behavior. The concept of culture has been of revolutionary significance in transforming the ideas of the relation of race and society entertained at the turn of the century to the contemporary conception that a group's mental, moral, and emotional traits are learned phenomena, products of social interaction. Since the culture concept is relatively recent, the social scientist's analytical distinction between culture and race may not necessarily coincide with the distinctions made by the members of the society in question, except as the members of that society themselves concur with these differences.

An ethnic group is identifiable by its distinctive *cultural* characteristics. Ethnicity, a term that will be used with great frequency throughout this volume, implies the existence of a distinct culture or subculture in which group members feel themselves bound together by common ties and are so regarded by other members of the society. Groups the social scientist would classify as *racial* may be ethnically distinctive as well (e.g., American Indians). Nationality, language, religion, and tribal identity are all ethnic categories that have been employed to distinguish between

---

[20] *Ibid.*
[21] George W. Stocking, Jr., *Race, Culture, and Evolution: Essays in the History of Anthropology* (New York: Free Press, 1968).

conflicting groups. Since the existence of cultural differences between social castes or classes is an important component of almost all theories of stratification, in its broadest sense the term *ethnic* can be used to refer to a wide range of social phenomena in the study of structured social inequality. It is possible for a group to possess racial, religious, national, and linguistic characteristics similar to those of the dominant group (e.g., the Buraku of Japan) and still identify itself and be identified as a distinct minority group on the basis of different cultural or subcultural traits.

By definition, ethnic groups differ in cultural characteristics (e.g., values, ideas, food habits, family patterns, sexual behaviors, modes of dress, standards of beauty, political conceptions, economic forms, and recreational patterns). Ethnic groups are inherently ethnocentric, regarding their own cultural traits as natural, correct, and superior to those of other ethnic groups, who are perceived as odd, amusing, inferior, or immoral. In the second article in this section, Noel suggests that ethnocentrism is a necessary, but not sufficient, condition for the emergence of ethnic stratification. According to Noel, a majority-minority relationship between two ethnocentric groups cannot be effected unless the groups are competing for the same scarce resources and, most importantly, one group possesses superior power to impose its will upon the other.

Prejudice is a form of ethnocentrism. According to Allport, prejudice refers to "an avertive or hostile attitude toward a person who belongs to a group, simply because he belongs to that group, and is therefore presumed to have the objectionable qualities ascribed to the group."[22] Prejudice is an attitudinal phenomenon that often involves an intense emotional component. Thus, many Whites in America will consciously and rationally reject the myths of Black inferiority but react emotionally with fear, hostility, or condescension in the presence of Blacks. The forms of prejudice may range from a relatively unconscious aversion to members of the out-group to a comprehensive, well-articulated, and coherent ideology, such as the ideology of racism that John Higham discusses in Part Three. In any form, prejudice provides a justification for the status quo and a means of rationalizing the disabilities to which the minority group is subject.

The relationship of prejudice to discriminatory behavior, on the other hand, is problematic. As numerous writers have pointed out, whether prejudice becomes translated into discriminatory behavior is dependent upon a multiplicity of variables. The existence of prejudicial attitudes and feelings is therefore irrelevant to the understanding of the *dynamics* of majority-minority relations unless sociological factors are also considered. Too often, prejudice has been considered a causal factor rather than—as we would argue—a dependent variable. As Schermerhorn has cogently suggested, prejudice "is a product of situations, historical situa-

[22] Gordon W. Allport, *The Nature of Prejudice*, abridged (Garden City, N.Y.: Doubleday, 1958), p. 8.

tions, economic situations, political situations; it is not a little demon that emerges in people simply because they are depraved.[23] To explain the dynamics of prejudice fully it is necessary to analyze the institutional conditions that have preceded and generated it.

It is important that prejudice not be equated with discrimination; the former refers to attitudes, the latter to behavior. Discrimination involves differential treatment of individuals because of their membership in a minority group. As traditionally employed, the term has implied the "unequal treatment of equals"[24]—the rejection of the claims of equally qualified individuals merely because of their minority status. Such discrimination may emanate from the personal prejudice of a majority group member. Often, however, discrimination is not the result of overt *individual* prejudice, but rather the result of individuals' conforming to the dictates of a racially biased society. In either case, despite the motivations or intent of the majority group members, the effects for the minority member—the denial of equal access to the society's rewards—are the same.

Discrimination by this definition refers to circumstances in which the privileges and rewards of the society are *arbitrarily* denied those whose *qualifications are equal* to majority group applicants. However, as we argue more fully in Part Five, the scope of this definition is too narrow, for it fails to come to grips with the *systematic* exclusion of minority group members by factors other than prejudice—for example, their lack of access to equal qualifications. If prejudice were eliminated overnight, inequalities rooted in the impersonal and normal operation of existing institutions would ensure that most minority group members still would not have equal access to the society's rewards. Much more attention must be directed to this form of systemic discrimination if the depth of majority-minority relations is to be fully comprehended.

The articles in this introductory section are intended to reflect the general orientation discussed above and to provide direction for the volume as a whole. Barth and Noel's "Conceptual Frameworks for the Analysis of Race Relations" is a recognition that any theory of racial and ethnic relations is merely a specific case within a broader theory of society and societal change. Barth and Noel seek to assess and to integrate the relevance of several sociological frameworks. They argue that the explanatory power of these competing frameworks varies, depending upon whether the focus of inquiry is upon the initial emergence, persistence, adaptation, or change of ethnic stratification systems.

The value of Noel's "A Theory of the Origin of Ethnic Stratification" is substantive as well as theoretical. In addition to specifying the neces-

23 Schermerhorn, *Comparative Ethnic Relations*, p. 6.
24 J. Milton Yinger, "Prejudice: Social Discrimination," in *The International Encyclopedia of the Social Sciences*, ed. David L. Sills (New York: Macmillan, 1968), 2:449.

sary and sufficient conditions for the emergence of ethnic stratification—ethnocentrism, competition, and differential power—Noel applies his theory to the genesis of American slavery.

A similar emphasis upon the importance of differential power in the establishment of a system of ethnic stratification is found in Stanley Lieberson's "A Societal Theory of Race and Ethnic Relations." Whereas Noel deals more fully with the origins of ethnic stratification, Lieberson is more concerned with the factors influencing ethnic relations once they have become established. Lieberson argues that a crucial variable determining the later patterns of majority-minority relations is the conditions under which initial contact between competing groups is established.

Finally, John Horton's article ("Order and Conflict Theories of Social Problems as Competing Ideologies") contrasts the different assumptions of two competing conceptions of majority-minority relations. As Horton points out, most analyses of racial and ethnic relations in the United States have been conceptualized within the framework of an *order* model, in which the sources of ethnic conflict are assumed to reside not within the structure of the society but within the "pathological," or "maladjusted," behavior of the minority group. The conflict model, emphasizing the roles of power and social conflict as the crucial variables in intergroup relations, is more closely congruent with the perspective that we have adopted here.

1

Conceptual Frameworks for the Analysis of Race Relations: An Evaluation*

ERNEST A. T. BARTH
DONALD L. NOEL

This paper presents a general frame of reference designed to classify and focus the major theoretical perspectives which have relevance for the sociology of race and ethnic relations. Societies and their subsystems of racial and ethnic differentiation constitute the units of analysis and the central concern is to analyze race and ethnic relations within the context of general sociological theory. The central theoretical task confronting sociology is that of explaining how order is achieved, maintained, and altered in social systems. Accordingly, a sociological analysis of race and ethnic relations must explain the observed variations in the dependent variables specified by this task.

Ernest A. T. Barth is Professor of Sociology at The University of Washington. Donald L. Noel is Associate Professor and Chairman of Sociology at The University of Wisconsin, Milwaukee.

Reprinted from *Social Forces* 50 (March, 1972):333–348 by permission of University of North Carolina Press.

* This article constitutes a summary statement of the theoretical framework which the authors are using in preparing a book on *Racial and Ethnic Differentiation in Sociological Perspective* to be published by McGraw-Hill. As the book is still in process, the authors would welcome receipt of any critical commentary that may be evoked by the present work. We are particularly indebted to William R. Catton, Jr., Nason E. Hall, Jr., and Clarence Schrag for their criticisms of an early draft of this work.

More precisely, this involves explanation of the emergence, persistence, adaptation, and change of systems of ethnic differentiation.[1] The empirical problems posed by this set of dependent variables may be stated as follows:

1. What structural conditions and processes account for the *emergence and initial stabilization* of various types of ethnic differentiation?
2. What structural conditions and processes account for the long-range *stability* of systems of ethnic differentiation?[2]
3. What structural conditions and processes account for *adaptation* in systems of ethnic differentiation through time?[3]
4. What structural conditions and processes account for *change* of systems of ethnic differentiation through time?

The major objective of any scientific theory is to explain the observed variation in the significant dependent variables. Once these variables have been identified, various theoretical frameworks may be evaluated in terms of the power and efficiency of their explanations. The independent variables which are combined to constitute the propositional base

[1] Unless the context indicates the contrary, we use the word ethnic as a generic term encompassing racial, nationality, and religious groups.

[2] Some theorists argue that the stability of social patterns is not a legitimate subject for scientific study (e.g., see Catton 1966:5, 12–14). The logic is that stability only needs to be accounted for if there are pressures for change that make it problematic. Hence, the explanation of change constitutes the fundamental scientific problem. This analysis ignores the important role of positive supports for stability (e.g., socialization) and the fact that some structures persist virtually unchanged (despite ceaseless pressures for change) for such long periods of time that social scientists have had to resort to the comparative method in order to introduce variation into what would otherwise be relatively invariant dependent variables.

[3] All societies face continual change. To the extent that such changes are predictable and recurrent (e.g., life-cycle role changes), mechanisms are evolved to facilitate the maintenance of order. Other changes (e.g., environmental) are not patterned nor subject to control. Hence spontaneous coping responses necessarily serve in lieu of culturally stylized responses. Both types of responses attempt to maintain order, which is not the same as stability, and hence they are manifestations of adaptation.

of a general theory are selected so as to provide maximum explanatory power relative to the dependent variables. The search for efficient independent variables is facilitated by classifying the potentially relevant variables, both dependent and independent, in terms of their rates of variation over different time periods. Some variables manifest relatively high rates of variation over short periods of time while others vary little in the short run, their variations being observable only over fairly long periods of time. For example, the relative economic power of black Americans changes little from year to year whereas the behavior of individual whites towards blacks fluctuates rapidly as a function of the situation (Raab and Lipset, 1962). Variables which manifest very little variation in the short run can, for all practical purposes, be considered as constants for studies limited to such time periods. On the other hand, a trend curve fitted to short-run variables frequently reveals little long-run variation. Such variables may be considered constants for purposes of long-run analysis. Hence, given the fundamental premise that a constant cannot explain a variable, nor a variable a constant, it may be concluded that the independent variables selected to explain the variation in a dependent variable should vary at roughly the same rate as the dependent variable.[4]

Selecting the relevant variables is the first step toward theory; but a theory, conceived as a set of logically interrelated propositions which explain observed phenomena, never emerges full blown. Conceptual tinkering and experimentation are vital to the emergence of a theory, and a conceptual frame of reference is the usual forerunner of a theory. The frame of reference includes a set of assumptions and postulates regarding the nature of reality, one or more empirical problems to be explained, and a cluster of interrelated concepts which define what is to be observed in order to construct a meaningful explanation. Theory exists only with the emergence of explanatory propositions, but the frame of reference significantly affects the theory which is constructed because, as Newcomb (1950:94) says, it "functions as a preceptual context which exercises a selective influence upon the way in which something is perceived."

Sociologists have elaborated a number of frames of reference for analyzing behavior. The race-cycle framework constitutes a special case of an evolutionary model of society and was developed with race relations specifically in mind. The consensus, interdependence, and conflict frameworks are derived from the three major models utilized in contemporary sociology—structural functionalism, symbolic interactionism, and conflict—and are applicable to a wide range of behavior. While each framework ostensibly provides a conceptual base for constructing a general theory of race and ethnic relations, the frameworks vary in their utility dependent upon the specific empirical problem to be explained (see Figure 1). Hence, a combination of frameworks must be utilized if we are to construct an adequate general theory. Accordingly, the present objective is to review each conceptual framework in order to delineate the implied propositions and make explicit the relevance of each framework

---

[4] This methodological rule suggests a resolution of the false problem of reductionism. Insofar as we are concerned to construct efficient explanations, comparability in the rates of variation of independent and dependent variables is a more basic consideration than selection of variables from the same discipline or level of analysis.

FIGURE 1.   *Major Conceptual Frameworks Related to the Key Problems in the Sociology of Race and Ethnic Relations*

Sociological Problem	Conceptual Framework			
	Race Cycle	Consensus	Interdependence	Conflict
Emergence	1			2
Persistence		1	2	2
Adaptation		2	1	2
Change	2	2	2	1

Key: 1 denotes area of primary contribution.
      2 denotes area of secondary contribution.

for the explanation of the major empirical problems in the field.

THE RACE-CYCLE FRAMEWORK

The race relations cycle framework is uniquely suited to the task of explaining variations in the structural patterns of emerging systems of ethnic differentiation. In essence it proposes that variations in the precontact characteristics of the groups coming into contact combine with variations in patterns of initial contact to produce predictable variations in the initial structure of ethnic differentiation. This natural history approach entails both a major strength and a major weakness as regards the analysis of race relations. On the one hand the emphasis upon process, which derives from the inherently evolutionary nature of a cycle approach, is a valuable reminder that race relations are dynamic and continuously marked by change. On the other hand, the cycle approach as initially formulated by Robert E. Park (1950) posits a unilinear evolution[5] of race relations which is quite inconsistent with their development in many societies. This defect has largely been remedied by subsequent modifications of Park's original cycle.

Unfortunately, race-cycle theorists have not capitalized on the framework's inherent emphasis on process. Rather they have analyzed discrete stages in the cycle without carefully specifying the key variables or structural conditions associated with movement from one stage to another. In addition, there has been a tendency to overextend the application of the framework. Rather than restricting it to the analysis of the emergence and initial stabilization of a particular interethnic system, proponents of the race cycle have tried to use it to explain stability, adaptation, and change also.

While the race cycle may have some relevance for these problems, other frameworks have greater power to explain the evolution of the system from an initially stabilized position. Moreover, the explanatory utility of the race cycle is largely limited to the emergence of the initial pattern of ethnic differentiation involving any two ethnic groups.[6] While the breakdown of the initial pattern of ethnic differentiation might be viewed as signaling the start of a new race cycle, subsequent patterns are much more crucially influenced by the intimate relationships and institutionalized power differentials characteristic of the prior pattern than they are by conditions of precontact and initial contact. In short, the cycle approach is most adequate to explain the emergence of the pattern of ethnic differentiation which follows initial contact.

In presenting his pioneer formulation of a race-cycle framework, Park (1950:150) observed that:

> In the relations of races there is a cycle of events which tends everywhere to repeat itself . . . the race relations cycle which takes the form, to state it abstractly, of contact, competition, accommodation and eventual assimilation, is apparently progressive and irreversible. Customs regulations, immigration restrictions and racial barriers may slacken the tempo of the movement; may perhaps halt it altogether for a time; but cannot change its direction; cannot at any rate reverse it. . . .

This is clearly a unilinear evolutionary model as it implies that there is a probability of *1.00* that each stage of the cycle will lead to and culminate in the next with assimilation–amalgamation ultimately assured. A cursory inspection of cross-cultural data, or even a careful

---

[5] The seeming contradiction involved in talking about a cycle approach which posits *unilinear* evolution is resolved as follows. When two distinct groups meet, they proceed through the stages in sequence until fusion occurs. Ultimately this new, fused group encounters another group and the process starts over —hence, a cycle.

[6] If initial contacts between peoples are viewed as primarily a consequence of the "swarming" of Europeans over the globe, it might be argued that the race-cycle framework is of limited and primarily historical explanatory value. This objection overlooks the fact that along with the forces promoting the development of a "world culture" there are also forces producing subcultural differentiation. So long as such differentiating processes continue and so long as there are pressures for people to migrate, new contact cycles will continue to occur and the cycle framework will have continuous utility.

analysis of data on American ethnic relations, reveals the weakness of this position. In cases where initial contact has led to either annihilation or mass expulsion, the cycle is obviously terminated short of assimilation–amalgamation.* In other cases, a temporary accommodation has reverted back to competition and resulted in a new form of accommodation. This is exemplified by the history of blacks in the colonies. They were reduced to the status of slaves after initially being accorded the status of bondsmen (Palmer, 1966). Thus, the initial (temporary and unstable) accommodation between any two groups may revert back to competition before generating a new accommodation and relations between groups may at any point in the cycle lead to stable outcomes other than assimilation. Indeed, there are at least five theoretically possible stable outcomes of interethnic contact:

1. Exclusion, encompassing expulsion and annihilation;
2. Symbiosis, a stable relation of more or less equally beneficial exchange between members of distinct sociopolitical systems;
3. Ethnic stratification, involving supersubordination within a single political system;
4. Pluralism, the equalitarian integration of distinct ethnic groups within a common political and economic system; and
5. Assimilation, the biological, cultural, social, and psychological fusion of distinct groups to create a new ethnically undifferentiated society.

It might be argued that exclusion, which terminates interethnic contact, is the only viable long-run alternative to assimilation inasmuch as the middle three outcomes are inherently unstable. This is perhaps true if one takes a very long-run time perspective, but from this perspective all structures (including assimilation) are inherently unstable. Moreover, it is both dubious and unfalsifiable (Lyman, 1968:18) to argue that groups which have not assimilated are nevertheless definitely going to assimilate—ultimately. The centuries-long separatism of the Jews, which

* Editor's note: See articles in Part Four and Part Six of this book.

may be duplicated by the French-Canadians and some American-Indian groups, suggests that it is more realistic to think in terms of a variety of relatively stable outcomes.

These inadequacies in Park's cycle have been largely resolved by elaborating the basic cycle. Brown (1934), for example, expanded the number of stages in the race cycle and estimated the probability of a variety of alternative succeeding steps (including three stable outcomes) at each of several stages in the cycle. More recently Lieberson (1961) has further refined the basic cycle by considering the relative power of the groups involved as a means of specifying the probability of conflict (introduced as an invariant second stage by Brown) and the predominant direction of assimilation (i.e., after the model provided by the host population or that provided by the migrants). A number of modifications of the original cycle, including hypothetical probabilities for each stage, are incorporated in Figure 2.

Given five possible stable outcomes of intergroup contact, the immediate task is to specify the conditions under which any given outcome is most likely. Three major classes of variables determine the *initial* outcome. These are the cultural and social-structural characteristics of the groups prior to contact, the characteristics of the migration—and the migrants, and the nature and context of the initial contacts. While it is highly desirable to assign relative weights to these variables, this is beyond the present level of development of the field. Hence, we must be satisfied to briefly illustrate the significance of several variables.

Among the significant precontact variables affecting the pattern of ethnic differentiation, the degree of cultural complementarity has probably been most frequently discussed. Lindgren (1938) stresses that cultural complementarity greatly facilitated the formation of stable symbiotic relations between the Tungus and Cossacks in Northwest Manchuria. Similarly, M. W. Smith (1940) indicates that the complementarity of economic interests and of marital attitudes between the Puyallup Indians and the early white migrants

FIGURE 2.   *The Race Cycle: A Specification of Stages and Outcomes*[a]

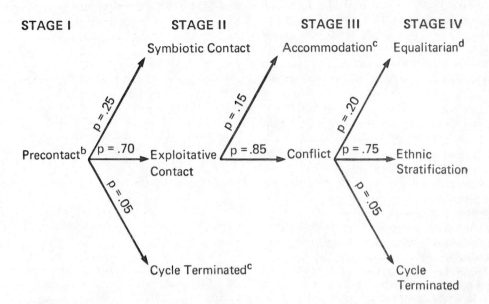

STAGE I   STAGE II   STAGE III   STAGE IV

Symbiotic Contact   Accommodation[c]   Equalitarian[d]

$p = .25$ $p = .15$ $p = .20$

Precontact[b] $p = .70$ Exploitative $p = .85$ Conflict $p = .75$ Ethnic
                                    Contact   Stratification

$p = .05$ $p = .05$

Cycle Terminated[c]   Cycle
                                                                                Terminated

[a] This schematization is a provisional one primarily intended to illustrate the logic of the race cycle. The indicated probabilities are necessarily hypothetical until an adequate sample of comparative studies is compiled.

[b] The most significant precontact variables include cultural complementarity, the patterns of migration (rate, composition,etc.), relative power, and the motives and goals of the migrants.

[c] Accommodation refers to all of the possible stable outcomes of interethnic contact, equalitarian or inequalitarian, *except* exclusion. The exclusion outcome, which includes both annihilation and mass expulsion, effectively terminates the cycle. The cycle may also be terminated by *total* assimilation but this outcome can only occur as the *culmination* of a *process* of assimilation which begins with initial contact.

[d] Equalitarian outcomes include assimilation, pluralism and symmetrical symbiosis.

facilitated a quick and peaceful pluralistic outcome. However, when whites looking for land and timber migrated with their families, contacts became strained and the undermining of the Puyallup social structure commenced. Similarly, the contradictory patterns of belief concerning land ownership which characterized the Kikuyu peoples of Kenya and the European settlers led to a long period of struggle (Leakey, 1954) which even today has not been fully resolved. Recently Mason (1970:153–154) has emphasized the relative sociocultural complexity, or stage of development, of the contacting groups as another critical determinant of the emergent pattern of ethnic differentiation.

At least three distinct aspects of the pattern of migration have been linked to variations in the initial pattern of ethnic differentiation. These are the type of migration, the causes of migration, and the characteristics of the migrants. At present, the independent effects of different aspects of migration have not been adequately isolated from their combined effects but a variety of propositions have been advanced relating the emergence of a given pattern of ethnic differentiation to such variables as the unit of migration, the goals of the migrants, the rapidity of their influx, and their specific motives for migrating (e.g., see Degler, 1971:228–232; Mason, 1970:148–152). Significant advances in this area wait further development and synthesis of typologies of migration primarily focused upon the analysis of racial and ethnic relations (e.g., see Lieberson, 1961; Price, 1969:190–213, 228–232; Schermerhorn, 1970:96–102).

The influence of the precontact variables and of the pattern of migration is focused and mediated by the structure of the initial contacts. The significance of structural influences for the subsequent development of race relations is revealed by van den Berghe's (1970:68–78) comparative analysis of acculturation and miscegenation in Africa and the Americas. Schermerhorn (1970) has also emphasized the structure of the contact situation by specifying different sequences or "recurrent historical patterns" of emergence as contexts which significantly mediate the outcome of intergroup contacts. More specifically, Noel (1968) has suggested that ethnocentrism, competition, and relative power decisively structure the contact situation and thereby provide the basis for constructing a theory of the emergence and initial stabilization of ethnic stratification. In brief, the theory holds that competition provides the motivation for stratification, ethnocentrism channels the competition along ethnic group lines, and relative power determines whether either group will be able to subordinate the other. If either ethnocentrism or competition is moderate to mild or if the power differential is small an equalitarian outcome is likely, whereas a marked degree of all three will give rise to an inequalitarian outcome. These variables affect not only the initial pattern of ethnic differentiation but all subsequent patterns.

Once a system of ethnic differentiation is established, attention shifts to the problem of maintenance of that system. All structures are eventually eroded or revamped, abandoned or overhauled; but when they have just been established the immediate concern is to forestall change. This characteristically involves an attempt to legitimate the new structure inasmuch as continued reliance upon sheer power is highly inefficient. As Park (1950: 150), observed, "The struggle for existence terminates in a struggle for status, for recognition, for position and prestige within an existing political and moral order." Hence, we need to evaluate the consensus framework as a solution to the problem of persistence.

THE CONSENSUS FRAMEWORK

Although the consensus framework has relevance for the origin, adaptation, and change of systems of ethnic stratification, its primary value inheres in the explanation it provides for the persistence of an established system. From the consensus perspective "it is a condition of the stability of social systems that there should be an integration of the component units to constitute a 'common value system'" (Parsons, 1954:388). In short, the consensus framework posits a high degree of value consensus within and between all segments of society as the crucial factor in the persistence of social structure. This explanation is rooted in both the symbolic–interactionist and the structural–functional models of society.

The structural–functional roots are revealed by the basic assumptions about the nature of man and society which underlie the framework's explanation of structural persistence. Consensus-oriented sociologists are inclined to stress that the various structural units or elements (whether concrete groups or functional subsystems) of societies are mutually dependent and therefore the well-being of the whole requires the cooperation of the parts and promotes the welfare, or interests, of the parts. This postulated identity of interests between the parts and the whole permits the assumption that stratification, which the functionalists view as a requirement of societies as social systems, is compatible with the needs of all or most of the society's component units. From the Parsonian point of view, stratification reflects the extent to which various social units adhere to the values derived from the society's basic needs or requirements. Consensus theorists argue that without common values the stratification structure would be highly unstable inasmuch as the inequitable distribution of rewards would not be perceived as legitimate. Finally, these theorists postulate that societies and their component structures tend to persist. Once established, a stratification structure may survive for generations simply because it is unchallenged. The postulate that man is a creature of habit and custom reinforces the postulate of structural persistence by affirming, as Lenski (1966:32) states, that men "accept and take for granted even those distributive arrangements which work to their disadvantage and are not essential."

The symbolic–interactionist model of society provides an additional basis for the consensus explanation of structural persistence. For interactionists, individuals interacting in a bounded situation constitute the basic unit of society. Social behavior is assumed to be organized and purposive (i.e., goal oriented); *and* stable, cooperative, goal-directed behavior requires *shared* symbols. The essence of symbolic interactionism is that men do not interact by reacting to one another's actions *per se* but rather they interpret or define each other's actions (Blumer, 1962:180). The meaning of an act is not inherent in or intrinsic to the act; hence, cooperative interaction requires that any given action (including vocal) has the same meaning for the various participants. In short, "the definition of the situation provides the frame of reference of social interaction, and . . . organized social relations presuppose the existence of a body of common definitions among the group's members" (Miyamoto, 1959:51). As men acquire shared meanings and values regarding a host of actions, objects, and persons, they acquire a culture which allows them "to predict each other's behavior most of the time and gauge their own behavior to the predicted behavior of others" (Rose, 1962:11–12; also see Blumer, 1962:183–184, 187–190). Shared definitions, rooted in shared meanings and values, are conceived as basic to stability in social relations.

The role of shared definitions is crucial in the realm of interethnic relations. Ethnicity is by no means an entirely subjective phenomenon but the social definitions of ethnicity and of appropriate intergroup behavior are highly significant. Numerous physical traits are highly visible, but in any given society few are associated with institutionalized discrimination. An individual is not assigned to a specific ethnic group because he shares certain observable characteristics with other members of the group. He is assigned because there is general agreement (consensus) that he belongs to the group regardless of whether there are actually any physical or cultural similarities. Only by acknowledging the ultimate importance of the shared social definition can we explain the fact that a physically white, obviously Caucasoid person can be classified as a Negro in the United States while a dark-skinned, obviously Negroid person may be classified as "white" (i.e., *branco*) in Brazil. When men define themselves as fundamentally alike or different, they act in accordance with this definition regardless of its veracity. As Shibutani and Kwan (1965:38) state, "What is of decisive importance is that human beings interact not so much in terms of what they actually are but in terms of the conceptions that they form of themselves and of one another."

Insofar as ethnicity is considered important, consensus regarding the ethnic identity of participants in an intergroup situation is a necessary but not a sufficient condition for stable interaction. Unless the minority and dominant participants embrace common conceptions regarding appropriate or proper behavior vis-à-vis each other, strain and/or conflict will characterize the relationship. These shared conceptions must be complementary. That is, where a white defines a black as subordinate, the black must define the white as superordinate if stress is to be minimized. Moreover, the means (form and content) of expressing deference and superiority must be agreed upon. Where this degree of consensus is achieved, stability is built into the pattern of interethnic relations and the stratification system in general. Normative consensus indicates that dominant and subordinate alike view the system as just and proper (i.e., moral) and therefore neither will seek to alter the system (Shibutani and Kwan, 1965:280). Indeed, given value consensus and the absence of incompatible structural elements, changes in interethnic or any other action patterns might well be "viewed as deriving from 'external' sources, and thus in some sense accidental" (Moore, 1960:811).

The perfect integration attendant upon complete value-consensus and structural compatibility is only approximated in any society. The postulate of perfect integration stems from the systemic theory of society. The concept of societies as social systems is a very useful heuristic device, but we must bear in mind that concrete societies are not "perfect" systems. The various structural elements are asymmetrically interdependent and thus almost inevitably unevenly integrated into the whole. Modern urban societies in particular are characterized by structural variations in dependence upon the whole. This differential autonomy generates diverse interests which are then justified by diverse (and sometimes conflicting) values. Unequal dependence and the associated diversity of interests and values is rooted in the increasing social differentiation and functional specialization of urban societies. The structural ambiguity (i.e., uncertainty in role behavior due to absent, ambiguous, or conflicting norms and values) characteristic of urban-mass societies necessarily impairs the efficiency and effectiveness of value consensus as a stabilizing mechanism. Conflicting principles of social control and social organization not only persist in urban societies, they may well be inherent in such societies in that they reflect contradictory functional requirements of social systems (Sjoberg, 1960; also see Moore, 1960:815; van den Berghe, 1963; Wagley and Harris, 1958:241–242).

This, of course, does not deny that consensus is a highly significant *factor* in the stabilization and integration of many, if not most, urban societies to say nothing of less highly differentiated societies. Value-consensus generally tends to be achieved through deliberate, rational processes and there are many such attempts in contemporary urban societies. For example, legal processes tend to create and maintain a consistent set of legal norms and the dialogue between theologians, philosophers and social critics serves the same function in the realm of moral and ethical norms. As societies urbanize, however, their stability does become increasingly based on interdependence with the result that the need for consensus *between* social units is greatly reduced. Thus, by stressing values to the exclusion of interdependence and coercive power, the consensus framework provides only a partial explanation of stability. Recent analyses of "plural societies" (e.g., M. G. Smith, 1965; van den Berghe, 1965) clearly demonstrate that a high degree of consensus is not an essential basis of societal integration and persistence.

The plural society is one characterized by fundamental differences, even incompatibilities, in the institutional systems (i.e., beliefs, values, and interaction patterns) adhered to by different segments of the society. In making value-consensus prerequisite to the existence of a stable social system, the reality of plural societies is ignored. M. G. Smith (1965:88, 86, xi) notes that "the monopoly of power by one cultural section is the essential precondition for the maintenance of the plural society" and "in order that the consensual theory may apply to the plural society, we are required to interpret all modes of subordination as willing submission, and thus as *prima facie* evidence of shared moral sentiments between the subordinate and dominant group." Clearly communication symbols must be shared between groups and there must be widespread conviction regarding the morality of the system among members of the dominant group if the plural society is to be stable. However, the critical issue is the presence or absence of consensus *between* groups on other than communication symbols. The absence of such consensus in plural societies such as South Africa and the British West Indian societies necessitates reliance upon coercion and interdependence as sources of unity and stability.

Theoretically, both interdependence (especially symmetrical) and coercion may generate consensus over time. Blumer (1966), in challenging the necessity of common values as the basis for joint action, notes that compromise, duress, mutual advantage, and sheer necessity may all motivate stable cooperation and he adds: "In very large measure, society becomes the formation of workable relations." These workable relations, even if highly inequalitarian, may eventually be redefined as traditional and accepted as right and proper by all concerned. Nevertheless, ethnically stratified societies characterized by dissensus, tension, and internal contradictions have persisted for long periods. Leaving aside the moot issue of whether consensus or conflict is more basic in social systems (for diverse viewpoints on this issue, see Adams, 1966; Horton, 1966; Williams, 1966), we conclude that:

1. The consensus framework makes its primary contribution to a comprehensive theory of intergroup relations via the explanation which it provides for the problem of stability of established patterns of ethnic relations; and
2. In general, consensus is probably the single most important and most efficient basis of maintaining ethnic patterns although it is never the only basis and in some societies it is of very little importance.

It is undoubtedly true that patterns of ethnic relations as well as total societies are invariably maintained by some combination of consensus, interdependence, sociability, and coercion (Williams, 1966; also see Blumer, 1966:538–539; van den Berghe, 1970:82–84).

THE INTERDEPENDENCE FRAMEWORK

In all societies the various component social units are interrelated and dependent upon each other to some degree. As role differentiation and specialization increase—i.e., as the society urbanizes—these interdependencies become increasingly extensive and vital to the survival of the society (Hammond, 1966). In the urban society, interdependence forces social groups or subsystems to cooperate with each other, regardless of value-consensus or dissensus, in order that each may achieve a variety of goals which they cannot achieve alone. Individuals of diverse value orientations must take each other's desires and values into account because each needs the other in order to maximize their own outcomes. As Heilbroner (1962:4) states, "We are rich, not as individuals, but as members of a rich society, and our easy assumption of material sufficiency is actually only as reliable as the bonds which forge us into a social whole."

In the rapidly changing urban environment this pervasive interdependence is highly relevant to the maintenance of order.[7] The explanation of order, defined as an arrangement of parts into a whole characterized by the capacity to function as a unit in its environment, constitutes sociology's theoretical focus because order subsumes the more heralded stability and change. The problem of adaptation, the maintenance of order, is unique precisely because it overlaps both stability and change. This unique nature must be clarified before the relevance of interdependence is analyzed.

Adaptation is an empirical problem distinct from both stability and change. As opposed to stability, adaptation requires that social systems be receptive to modifications to assure that they will not be destroyed by their own rigidity in the face of internal contradictions and environmental changes (Coser, 1956:155–157). In short, the maintenance of order is not identical to the maintenance of the status quo. Conversely, as opposed to change, adaptation envisions that only a few structures (preferably the less essential ones) be permitted to vary at any given time and these at rates not exceeding rather severely restricted limits (e.g., see Olsen, 1968:150–151). However, it is not minimal change but the minimization of change which defines adaptation. Only that degree of change which is essential

[7] Indeed, interdependence has been defined as order (i.e., determinateness as opposed to randomness) in the relationships among system elements (Parsons and Shils, 1954:107).

to the maintenance of order is adaptive. At the limit, fundamental change of one or more system elements may constitute the only possible adaptive response, but generally order is maintained via the incorporation of minor modifications within a basically unchanged system. Hence, adaptation ceases to be a distinct sociological problem only in the limiting cases. In general the difference between adaptation and stability inheres in the fact of system modification; that between adaptation and change inheres in function—the former maintains an existent order while the latter creates a new order.

From the perspective of any specific group or subsystem the adaptive problem is one of maximizing the group's outcomes. Thus we may describe a group's adaptive capacity as its ability to enhance its status relative to the other groups in a society. From the perspective of the society as a whole, however, adaptive capacity is the ability to maintain sufficient distributive justice between groups and sufficient efficiency in transactions with the environment to assure order. This requires adjustment to internal strains and external stresses without disintegration (i.e., disappearance as a distinct boundary-maintaining system). In essence, adaptation is the ability to respond to these stresses and strains with the degree of change necessary to assure the maintenance of an integrated system. This adaptive process may be a nonconscious, nondeliberative adjustment via traditional mechanisms, but in urban societies it is typically a conscious process involving contention between distinct interest groups. In either event, adaptation implies a moving equilibrium—an ordered process of change which does not disrupt ongoing social processes (see Angell, 1965:151; Parsons and Shils, 1954:107).

The relevance of interdependence for adaptation inheres in two inescapable consequences of the fact of interdependence:

1. It creates awareness throughout the system of pressures for change affecting any part of the system; and
2. It provides sanctions to curtail or eliminate these pressures.

Interdependence necessarily requires a concern with pressures for change for it implies that any "disturbance"—be it an internal strain or an external force—occurring in or impinging upon any part of the system will ramify throughout and have significant consequences for numerous parts of the system. From such a perspective, change is hardly likely to be defined as a rare and inconsequential phenomenon. Rather the interdependence perspective envisions change as a pervasive phenomenon which may be initiated at any structural point. The potential disruptiveness of change necessitates that pressures toward change be carefully observed and taken into account if order is to be maintained. If the pressures for change are internal, interdependence leads to the imposition of sanctions which must be heeded because the element seeking change is dependent upon the other elements (Olsen, 1968:151). If the pressures are external, the entire system makes an adjustive response because all of the elements are directly or indirectly affected due to their interrelatedness. In either event, the change instituted is the minimal change perceived to be consistent with the maintenance of order in the system as a whole.

Adaptive processes—pressures for change and responses to them—occur continually. This is necessarily so, short of a society which is completely insulated from the environment and characterized by perfect consensus and perfect structural compatibility. Structural imperfections—e.g., marked life-chance differentials unsupported by perfect consensus—generate many or few adaptations primarily as a function of the scope and degree of interdependence. Scope refers to the range and number of ties between elements in a system. Scope is universal (extensive) when each pair of system elements interconnect, and intensive when the interconnections between each pair of elements are multiple. The degree of interdependence refers to the variations in mutuality in the ties between any pairs of elements. Symmetry represents the ultimate degree of interdependence while highly asymmetrical interconnections represent minimal interdependence.[8]

The crucial effects of the scope and degree of interdependence upon the adaptive process are summarized in the following two propositions. First, the greater the intensive and extensive scope of interdependence between system elements (e.g., ethnic groups), the greater the number and effectiveness—other things being equal—of social change attempts initiated by the element(s) having greater functional autonomy. Second, the closer the approach to symmetrical interdependence between elements, the greater the number and effectiveness—other things being equal—of social change attempts initiated by the element(s) having lesser autonomy. In short, symmetry is positively related to "progressive" adaptations (i.e., those conducive to greater equality) while scope is negatively related. As applied to race relations this means that, with symmetry held constant, increases in the scope of interdependence work to the dominant group's advantage while decreases (e.g., via increasing separatism) work to the subordinate group's advantage. Conversely, with scope held constant, an increase in symmetry benefits the subordinate group while a decrease facilitates further imposition of inequality by the dominant group. As regards scope, the primary source of leverage is the number of opportunities to exert control; as regards symmetry, the primary mechanism is that of relative resources.

Our analysis here is compatible with van den Berghe's (1970:84) assertion that "The more economic interdependence there is, the less feasible apartheid becomes." Unfortunately, South African reality is one of highly asymmetrical interdependence: "Although it is true that the *prosperity* of the whites depends entirely on the nonwhites, the sheer day-to-day *survival* of the nonwhites depends directly on the industrial complex now controlled by the

whites" (van den Berghe, 1967:139). Willhelm (1970) maintains that in the United States, technological advance has freed whites of all economic dependence upon blacks with the result that racism can now slip the leash of economic restraint. *If* this assessment is correct (see Silberman, 1966; Terborgh, 1970 for a different assessment of technological change), our analysis suggests that increasing symmetry in other realms (e.g., political) and decreasing scope in the ties between blacks and whites are the most effective ways of minimizing the possibility of racial genocide which Willhelm foresees.

In addition to technological changes, demographic and a variety of other changes in life conditions may alter the pattern (i.e., scope and degree) of interdependence and set the adaptive process in motion (Shibutani and Kwan, 1965: 341–371). As a result of changing conditions which effect a slight change in the power balance (in either direction), new sociocultural forms which do not materially affect the existing system of ethnic stratification are institutionalized. For example, due to the now acknowledged ability of blacks to disrupt the social order, token changes have occurred in the policies and practices of many organizations including unions, political parties, and boards of education. Thus, transfer of some black students to previously all-white high schools is not intended to promote integration so much as to prevent continued disruption of the local educational system. Similarly, the removal of discriminatory clauses from union constitutions may have little effect on actual racial practices. Such changes are adaptive insofar as they represent concessions which function to maintain order and forestall more sweeping changes. Of course, order may also be maintained by introducing adaptive changes which are repressive or inequalitarian in nature. Thus, South Africa had consistently "improved" its repressive techniques while steadfastly resisting significant alteration of key elements of its social structure (Kuper, 1965:29, 68–70; van den Berghe, 1965:216, 1970:210–223).

If successful, adaptive modifications of

---

[8] The fact that interdependence is a variable, ranging from equal reliance of elements upon each other through varying degrees of asymmetrical reliance to unilateral dependence, is often overlooked with resulting errors in analysis (see Gouldner, 1959:253–254).

the existing sociocultural pattern prevent basic structural changes in the short run. They do this by repression or by partially satisfying the interests of the subordinate groups, thereby simultaneously reducing pressure upon and reinforcing the legitimacy of the established system (Dahrendorf, 1959:224–225, 233–234). Nevertheless, adaptations may be the precursors of extensive change in the long run (Coser, 1957:202). Those who benefit from the adaptive concessions may sooner or later use their new resources as a basis for launching a more sweeping protest. For example, the British-educated Indian elite played a crucial role in the emergence of mass nationalism which dominated the Indian political scene until the British withdrew (Worsley, 1964:52–64). Similarly, the better educational facilities provided for black Americans in the period 1940–52 in an effort to ward off the 1954 Brown Decision have undoubtedly been a factor in the abundance of effective leadership and organizational talent in the civil rights movement of the 1960s. The cumulative impact of negative adaptations—i.e., concessions to groups seeking to institutionalize or strengthen a pattern of inequality—may also generate significant structural change. Where positive adaptive mechanisms (e.g., mobility, political participation) are denied or severely constrained, revolt is possible. Thus, the increasingly repressive steps being taken by the Nationalist party to institutionalize apartheid in South Africa may result in violent rebellion by the black Africans and their allies (van den Berghe, 1965). However, the slim chances of successful revolt make adaptive changes more likely in the immediate future (Turk, 1967).

Adaptation thus stands between stability and change. It preserves the status quo essentially unchanged in the short run via timely concessions, but these concessions often foreshadow basic change via the gradual accretion of resources. Interdependence, as a derivative of its general unifying function, provides a crucial basis for mediating and mitigating stresses and strains that threaten social order. It generalizes sensitivity to the need for system modifications and facilitates their introduction

by providing the necessary sanctions. In spite of this adaptability, however, radical structural changes ultimately occur in all aspects of social systems. Thus, an adequate theory of ethnic differentiation must account for major changes in a given pattern of ethnic relations as well as for the pattern's origin, persistence and adaptation. To this we now turn.

THE CONFLICT FRAMEWORK

The analysis of social change inevitably engenders consideration of conflict. A conflict relationship is one in which the interacting social units are oriented toward the attainment of incompatible or mutually exclusive goals (Dahrendorf, 1959:135, 209). The goals being sought by the parties to the conflict may be the same or different. The crucial factor is simply that the participants perceive the situation as one where goal attainment by their group is inversely related to goal attainment by the other group. Conflict so conceived has relevance for each of the major theoretical problems posed in this article. It is frequently a factor in the emergence of a system of ethnic relations and it may also promote stability, once the system is established, via an uneasy equilibrium between more or less equal contenders. Conflict may also promote either adaptation or basic system change. These varied consequences indicate that conflict by itself does not automatically generate change. Nevertheless, the conflict framework has traditionally been focused upon the explanation of change and the present contention is that conflict is more useful than alternative perspectives in understanding change in established structures of ethnic relations.

With its central assumption that change is inherent in social systems the conflict perspective is necessarily oriented toward change. Social change is viewed as inherent because it is rooted in certain inevitable structural conditions. These include the fact of a changing environment but also the inevitable existence of structural incompatibilities, the inherent dysfunctional aspects of fundamental social structures (e.g., authority structures), and the existence of inequalities in power, material comforts, and other desirable rewards. Schermerhorn (1961:54–55) notes that: "the various subunits of any society—and particularly the more complex ones—are marked by disparities in numbers, cohesive organization, and resources. . . . This basic asymmetry is an essential human condition, a circumstance that sets the currents of social change in motion." These structural incompatibilities, power differentials, and other structural "flaws" inevitably generate conflict oriented toward improving the status of one's own group, be it ethnic, economic or political.

The nature of conflict—i.e., the pursuit of incompatible goals—necessarily means that to the extent that one group obtains its goals the opposing group must fail to obtain its goals. This leaves a continuing interest in change which, although it may remain latent for a time following the resolution of any specific conflict, will reemerge under certain conditions to stimulate active conflict anew. This continuing interest in change and reemergence of conflict does not guarantee change in any given instance. Nevertheless, the persistent interest of some segment of the population in change is consistent with the assumption that change is ubiquitous. The assumption is not unique to the conflict framework, nor would it constitute an explanation of change if it were, but its centrality facilitates the selection of concepts which are relevant to the analysis and explanation of change. Thus, the conflict framework stresses the concepts (i.e., variables) whose precise measurement enables social scientists to specify both the arena of conflict and the probability of change.

These concepts—e.g., vested interests, power, coercion—facilitate the derivation of two key propositions implicit in the conflict framework. First, conflict centers around vested interests—i.e., the crucial, shared values or objects in which some groups have an established claim which operates to the disadvantage of other groups. Differential vested interests assure that pressures for change will

be opposed and thereby generate a continuous struggle for power and advantage. Second, changes in the relative coercive power of the contending groups largely determine the direction and extent of social structural change. Unless the power balance has been altered no change should be expected to result from conflict.[9] The perpetuation of a traditional power balance contributes to the stability of the established system. By contrast, when the power balance is modified, fundamental change awaits only the perception of this redistribution of power and its subseqent translation into organized action (Blalock, 1967: 109–112, 126–131). Dominant groups no less than subordinate groups characteristically seek to expand and take advantage of increases in their power in order to reinforce or advance their interests (Schermerhorn, 1961:55).

While the conflict view has ancient roots its modern impetus was provided by the Marxian emphasis upon the inevitability of the clash of groups with divergent interests. While Marx emphasized social classes as the primary units of conflict, American conflict has been equally or more often structured along ethnic group lines. A few scholars (particularly Cox, 1959) have interpreted American race relations in essentially Marxian terms, but the general emphasis has been upon race *per se* as the basis of group identification, loyalty and cleavage. Until World War II the race–caste system in the United States was relatively stable precisely because the power differential between blacks and whites was so vast and stable. In the absence of major external pressure upon American society, Negroes had to be "content" with minor improvements in their status.

Since World War II the situation has changed markedly. The general international

---

[9] La Piere (1965:479–480) ignores this point and thus unwisely dismisses the conflict framework as a means of explaining change on the grounds that conflict can occur without consequent change. In truth, it is not conflict *per se* but the power balance which crucially affects the persistence and change of social patterns. Thus, the power framework (Blalock, 1967:109) or the power-conflict framework (Schermerhorn, 1970) is a more appropriate name.

situation, the emergence of the African nations and changes in the black community have resulted in a genuine shift in the power balance underlying the American race–caste system (e.g., see Isaacs, 1963). The adaptive changes of previous decades were cumulative and by the late 1940s a Negro middle class had emerged with sufficient strength to act as the decisive catalyst necessary to effectively challenge the race–caste system (Kronus, 1971:12–15). The organizational skills and leadership initially provided by the middle class generated triumphs which stimulated group pride, solidarity, and collective self-awareness which in turn stimulated mass participation in the civil rights movement. At this point there was a shift in strategy; away from litigation with its achievement of concessions —albeit increasingly significant concessions— to organized mass protest with the objective of achieving complete freedom and equality for blacks *now*. The movement is divided with respect to how extensively the fabric of American society as a whole must be changed to achieve this objective, but there is virtual unanimity as regards the primary significance of organized power as the instrument for achieving whatever basic changes are necessary (Bennett, 1964:29–35, 46; Pinkney, 1969:196–203). This power may be expressed via guerrilla warfare, peaceful (but disruptive) demonstrations, or via negotiation as a powerful (and therefore respected and accepted) pressure group participating as an equal in the traditional American political process.

Ethnicity has always been a significant factor in American politics. The enduring importance of ethnic interest groups has been masked by the cultural myth that civil rights are the rights of individuals. Now, however, the mask has been removed for, as Danzig (1964:41) says, ". . . the Negro has made us forcefully aware that the rights and privileges of an individual rest upon the status attained by the group to which he belongs—that is to say, by the power it controls and can use." Blacks are simply the most recent American minority to organize and effectively marshal

their collective power in order to protect their rights and advance their interests. The conflict and struggle so characteristic of the racial arena in contemporary America is typically a correlate of significant change in systems of ethnic stratification. Basic change is rarely smooth, automatic, and continuous. Rather it tends to be convulsive, episodic, and discontinuous for: ". . . rigidities in social structures may require opposition forces to gather momentum before they can effect adjustments [and hence] the dynamics of social structure is (sic) characterized not so much by continuously adjusted equilibrium states as by intermittent reorganizations in a dialectical pattern" (Blau, 1964:11).

The clash of opposing interests (economic, political, or otherwise) is central to basic change in the group structure of society, but this does not deny that other frameworks contribute to a comprehensive understanding of change. For example, interdependence may be interwoven with conflict in such a way that they jointly produce basic change. That is, interdependent groups may react against one another as well as in concert, and when they (Olsen, 1968: 151–152; van den Berghe, 1963:702–703) do clash basic change is usually generated. Our analysis has emphasized the primary utility of each perspective with no intent of implying a unicausal explanation of a given problem.

CONCLUSIONS

Race relations are social relations and hence they pose the same kinds of analytic problems for the sociologist as are posed by other types of social relations. Thus, in the sociological study of race and ethnic relations, the objective is to explain how patterns of ethnic differentiation emerge, how they are stabilized and maintained through time, and how they ultimately disintegrate or are transformed. Since the analytic problems or issues are the same, the sociological models which guide and inform the analysis of other aspects of the social structure should also facilitate the analysis of race and ethnic relations. In short, we contend that understanding of race and ethnic relations is most likely to be advanced by focusing on general sociological issues.

Unfortunately, sociologists have rarely dealt with the problem of the emergence of complex social patterns and this has certainly been true in regard to patterns of stratification, as Lenski (1966:ix) has reminded us. Thus our effort to understand the origin of ethnic patterns has focused upon specification and refinement of Park's pioneer race-cycle framework. (Perhaps the analysis of various contact cycles—and particularly those initiated by internal differentiation rather than migration—will provide clues useful in the development of a theory of the origin of social structures generally.) The initial contacts between peoples who differ in ways that are defined as socially significant can lead to a variety of outcomes, and the cycle framework calls attention to a number of variables which affect the outcome. In particular, we suggest that ethnocentrism, competition, and the relative power of the groups involved constitute a set of variables which are necessary and sufficient to explain the emergence of ethnic stratification, which is perhaps the most common outcome of initial contact.

Given the establishment of any system, the problem of persistence becomes crucial. Drawing from the consensus and conflict frameworks, it is clear that both common values and differential power are commonly relied upon means of assuring the continuance of a given system. Consensus makes its primary contribution in the solution of this problem but this does not necessarily mean that it is always the most important stabilizing factor. Indeed, consensus is of relatively minor importance in the stability of the "plural" societies. Nevertheless, it seems justified to conclude that while consensus may or may not be the most important or the most effective stabilizing factor, it is clearly the most efficient way to maintain a system of ethnic differentiation.

The stability of a given system is also crucially affected by the flexibility or adaptability of its various structural components.

The fact of structural interdependence both necessitates adaptability and increases the probability that it will be forthcoming. Interdependence enhances the sensitivity of the parts to the forces affecting the system as a whole and the resulting "knowledge" of the state of the whole moderates both the demands for and the resistance to change exhibited by various parts. Interdependence constitutes a major basis of societal integration and as van den Berghe (1963:697) has stated, "Relatively integrated societies can change faster than societies in a state of strain and conflict." Such adaptability promotes survival inasmuch as minor changes or concessions to structural subgroups (or the environment) constitute a safety valve capable of significantly prolonging the basic features of the status quo.

Ultimately, of course, systems do change in fundamental respects, and the cumulative impact of adaptive concessions may be a significant factor in basic structural change. However, whether such cumulation is a factor or not, radical change is generally rooted in the clash of vested interests and alterations in the power balance. Appeals to basic values (e.g., the Supreme Court's 1954 decision on school segregation) play a role in generating change but the changes resulting from such appeals are usually adaptive, not radical. If the emergence of a powerful, organized group willing to use its power (procedurally if possible, violently if necessary) against the entrenched establishment is not a prerequisite of radical change, it at least seems accurate to say that the use of such power is more effective than the appeal to legitimacy. It is also more efficient in terms of rapidity but not necessarily in terms of the human costs involved.

In assigning coercion the primary role in securing change, and consensus a major role in structural stability, we are in no sense equating consensus with stability and conflict with change. Rather we have repeatedly stressed that multiple perspectives are essential to a comprehensive explanation of each of the major empirical problems posed. This explanation is not advanced, however, by ignoring the apparent primacy of a given variable or perspective vis-à-vis a given problem. In short, we are advocating a strategy of allocation (Schermerhorn, 1970:52, 234) by applying a specific framework primarily, but not exclusively, to the explanation of a specific empirical problem. If our application of general sociological perspectives to race relations is on the right track, the next step is to engage in comparative analyses oriented toward measuring the explanatory contribution of the various frameworks, singly and in combination, much more precisely. The present general framework constitutes a schema which hopefully will facilitate the collection and organization of the comparative data necessary to achieve this increased precision.

REFERENCES

Adams, B. N. 1966. "Coercion and Consensus Theories: Some Unresolved Issues." *American Journal of Sociology* 71 (May): 714–717.

Angell, Robert C. 1965. *Free Society and Moral Crisis*. Ann Arbor: University of Michigan Press.

Bennett, Lerone, Jr. 1964. *The Negro Mood*. New York: Ballantine.

Blalock, Hubert M. 1967. *Toward a Theory of Minority-Group Relations*. New York: Wiley.

Blau, Peter M. 1964. *Exchange and Power in Social Life*. New York: Wiley.

Blumer, H. 1962. "Society as Symbolic Interaction." Pp. 179–192 in Arnold M. Rose (ed.), *Human Behavior and Social Processes*. Boston: Houghton-Mifflin.

————. 1966. "Sociological Implications of the Thought of George Herbert Mead." *American Journal of Sociology* 71(March):535–544.

Brown, W. O. 1934. "Culture Contact and Race Conflict." Pp. 34–47 in Edward B. Reuter (ed.), *Race and Culture Contacts*. New York: McGraw-Hill.

Catton, William R., Jr. 1966. *From Animistic to Naturalistic Sociology*. New York: McGraw-Hill.

Coser, Lewis. 1956. *The Functions of Social Conflict*. Glencoe: Free Press.

————. 1957. "Social Conflict and the Theory of Social Change." *British Journal of Sociology* 8(September):197–207.

Cox, Oliver C. 1959. *Caste, Class and Race*. New York: Monthly Review Press.

Dahrendorf, Ralf. 1959. *Class and Class Conflict in Industrial Society*. Stanford: Stanford University Press.

Danzig, D. 1964. "The Meaning of Negro Strategy." *Commentary* 37(February):41–46.

Degler, Carl N. 1971. *Neither Black Nor White*. New York: Macmillan.

Gouldner, A. W. 1959. "Reciprocity and Autonomy in Functional Theory." Pp. 241–270 in Llewellyn Gross (ed.), *Symposium on Sociological Theory*, Evanston: Row, Peterson.

Hammond, P. E. 1966. "Secularization, Incorporation and Social Relations." *American Journal of Sociology* 72(September):188–194.

Heilbroner, Robert L. 1962. *The Making of Economic Society*. Englewood Cliffs: Prentice-Hall.

Horton, J. 1966. "Order and Conflict Theories of Social Problems as Competing Ideologies." *American Journal of Sociology* 71(May): 701–713.

Isaacs, Harold R. 1963. *The New World of Negro Americans*. New York: Viking.

Kronus, Sidney. 1971. *The Black Middle Class*. Columbus: Merrill.

Kuper, Leo. 1965. *An African Bourgeoisie*. New Haven: Yale University Press.

La Piere, Richard T. 1965. *Social Change*. New York: McGraw-Hill.

Leakey, Louis S. B. 1954. *Mau Mau and Kikuyu*. New York: Day.

Lenski, Gerhard E. 1966. *Power and Privilege*. New York: McGraw-Hill.

Lieberson, S. 1961. "A Societal Theory of Race and Ethnic Relations." *American Sociological Review* 26(December):902–910.

Lindgren, E. J. 1938. "An Example of Culture Contact Without Conflict: Reindeer Tungus and Cossacks of Northwest Manchuria." *American Anthropologist* 40(October–December):605–621.

Lyman, S. M. 1968. "The Race Relations Cycle of Robert E. Park." *Pacific Sociological Review* 11 (Spring): 16–22.

Mason, Philip. 1970. *Race Relations*. London: Oxford University Press.

Miyamoto, S. F. 1959. "The Social Act: Re-Examination of a Concept." *Pacific Sociological Review* 2(Fall):51–55.

Moore, W. E. 1960. "A Reconsideration of Theories of Social Change." *American Sociological Review* 25(December):810–818.

Newcomb, Theodore. 1950. *Social Psychology*. New York: Dryden.

Noel, D. L. 1968. "A Theory of the Origin of Ethnic Stratification." *Social Problems* 16(Fall): 157–172.

Olsen, Marvin E. 1968. *The Process of Social Organization*. New York: Holt, Rinehart & Winston.

Palmer, P. C. 1966. "Servant into Slave: The Evolution of the Legal Status of the Negro Laborer in Colonial Virginia." *South Atlantic Quarterly* 65(Summer):355–370.

Park, Robert E. 1950. *Race and Culture*. Glencoe: Free Press.

Parsons, Talcott. 1954. *Essays in Sociological Theory*. Glencoe: Free Press.

Parsons, Talcott, and Edward A. Shils. 1954. *Toward A General Theory of Action*. Cambridge: Harvard University Press.

Pinkney, Alphonso. 1969. *The Black Americans*. Englewood Cliffs: Prentice-Hall.

Price, C. 1969. "The Study of Assimilation." Pp. 181–237 in John A. Jackson (ed.), *Migration*. London: Cambridge University Press.

Raab, E., and S. M. Lipset. 1962. "The Prejudiced Society." Pp. 29–55 in Earl Raab (ed.), *American Race Relations Today*. New York: Doubleday.

Rose, A. M. 1962. "A Systematic Summary of Symbolic Interaction Theory." Pp. 3–19 in Arnold M. Rose (ed.), *Human Behavior and Social Processes*. Boston: Houghton-Mifflin.

Schermerhorn, Richard A. 1961. *Society and Power*. New York: Random House.

————. 1970. *Comparative Ethnic Relations*. New York: Random House.

Shibutani, Tamotsu, and Kian M. Kwan. 1965. *Ethnic Stratification*. New York: Macmillan.

Silberman, Charles E. 1966. *The Myths of Automation*. New York: Harper & Row.

Sjoberg, G. 1960. "Contradictory Functional Requirements and Social Systems." *Journal of Conflict Resolution* 4(June):198–208.

Smith, Michael G. 1965. *The Plural Society in the British West Indies*. Berkeley and Los Angeles: University of California Press.

Smith, M. W. 1940. "The Puyallup of Washington." Pp. 3–36 in Ralph Linton (ed.), *Acculturation in Seven American Indian Tribes*. New York: Appleton-Century.

Terborgh, G. 1970. "Automation Hysteria and Employment Effects of Technological Progress." Pp. 361–373 in Simon Marcson (ed.), *Automation, Alienation, and Anomie*. New York: Harper & Row.

Turk, A. 1967. "The Futures of South Africa." *Social Forces* 45(March):402–412.

van den Berghe, Pierre. 1963. "Dialectic and Functionalism: Toward a Theoretical Synthesis." *American Sociological Review* 28(October): 695–705.

————. 1965. *South Africa, A Study in Conflict*. Middletown: Wesleyan University Press.

————. 1967. *Race and Racism*. New York: Wiley.

————. 1970. *Race and Ethnicity*. New York: Basic Books.

Wagley, Charles, and Marvin Harris. 1958. *Minorities in the New World*. New York: Columbia University Press.

Willhelm, Sidney M. 1970. *Who Needs the Negro?* Cambridge: Schenkman.

Williams, R. M., Jr. 1966. "Some Further Comments on Chronic Controversies." *American Journal of Sociology* 71(May):717–721.

Worsley, Peter. 1964. *The Third World*. Chicago: University of Chicago Press.

2

A Theory of the Origin of Ethnic Stratification

DONALD L. NOEL

While a great deal has been written about the nature and consequences of ethnic stratification, there have been few theoretical or empirical contributions regarding the causes of ethnic stratification.[1] It is the purpose of this paper to state a theory of the origin of ethnic stratification and then test it by applying the theory to an analysis of the origin of slavery in the United States. A number of recent contributions have clarified our knowledge of early Negro-white stratification[2] but there has been no attempt to analyze slavery's origin from the standpoint of a general theoretical framework.

Donald L. Noel is Associate Professor and Chairman of Sociology at the University of Wisconsin, Milwaukee.

Reprinted from *Social Problems* 16 (Fall, 1968):157–72, by permission of The Society for the Study of Social Problems and the author. © The Society for the Study of Social Problems.

Author's note: It should be emphasized that the present paper attempts only to explain the *origin* of ethnic stratification. The author and Ernest Barth are currently engaged in an effort to construct a general theory of ethnic stratification which answers a number of sociological questions in addition to that of origin.

[1] The same observation regarding social stratification in general has recently been made by Gerhard Lenski, *Power and Privilege*, New York: McGraw-Hill, 1966, p. ix.

[2] See Joseph Boskin, "Race Relations in Seventeenth Century America: The Problem of the Origins of Negro Slavery," *Sociology and Social Research*, 49 (July, 1965), pp. 446–455, including references cited therein; and David B. Davis, *The Problem of Slavery in Western Culture*, Ithaca: Cornell U., 1966.

The present attempt focuses upon ethnocentrism, competition, and differential power as the key variables which together constitute the necessary and sufficient basis for the emergence and initial stabilization of ethnic stratification.

Ethnic stratification is, of course, only one type of stratification. Social stratification as a generic form of social organization is a structure of social inequality manifested via differences in prestige, power, and/or economic rewards. Ethnic stratification is a system of stratification wherein some relatively fixed group membership (e.g., race, religion, or nationality) is utilized as a major criterion for assigning social positions with their attendant differential rewards.

Prior to the emergence of ethnic stratification there must be a period of recurrent or continuous contact between the numbers of two or more distinct ethnic groups. This contact is an obvious requisite of ethnic stratification, but it is equally a requisite of equalitarian intergroup relations. Hence, intergroup contact is assumed as given and not treated as a theoretical element because in itself it does not provide a basis for predicting whether ethnic relations will be equalitarian or inequalitarian (i.e., stratified). Distinct ethnic groups can interact and form a stable pattern of relations without super-subordination.[3] Factors such as the nature of the groups prior to contact, the agents of contact, and the objectives of the contacting parties affect the likelihood of an equalitarian or inequalitarian outcome but only as they are expressed through the necessary and sufficient variables.[4]

[3] A classic example is provided by Ethel John Lindgren, "An Example of Culture Contact Without Conflict: Reindeer Tungus and Cossacks of Northwest Manchuria," *American Anthropologist*, 40 (October–December, 1938), pp. 605–621.

[4] The relevance of precontact and of the nature and objectives of the contacting agents for the course of intergroup relations has been discussed by various scholars including Edward B. Reuter in his editor's "Introduction" to *Race and Culture Contacts*, New York: McGraw-Hill, 1934, pp. 1–18; and Clarence E. Glick, "Social Roles and Types in Race Relations," in Andrew W. Lind, editor, *Race Relations in World Perspective*, Honolulu: U. of Hawaii, 1955, pp. 239–262.

THE THEORY AND ITS ELEMENTS

In contrast to intergroup contact *per se,* the presence of ethnocentrism, competition, and differential power provides a firm basis for predicting the emergence of ethnic stratification. Conversely, the absence of any one or more of these three elements means that ethnic stratification will not emerge. This is the essence of our theory. Each of the three elements is a variable but for present purposes they will be treated as attributes because our knowledge is not sufficiently precise to allow us to say what degrees of ethnocentrism, competition, and differential power are necessary to generate ethnic stratification. Recognition of the crucial importance of the three may stimulate greater efforts to precisely measure each of them. We shall examine each in turn.

Ethnocentrism is a universal characteristic of autonomous societies or ethnic groups. As introduced by Sumner the concept refers to that ". . . view of things in which one's own group is the center of everything, and all others are scaled and rated with reference to it."[5] From this perspective the values of the in-group are equated with abstract, universal standards of morality and the practices of the in-group are exalted as better or more "natural" than those of any out-group. Such an orientation is essentially a matter of in-group glorification and not of hostility toward any specific outgroup. Nevertheless, an inevitable consequence of ethnocentrism is the rejection or downgrading of all out-groups to a greater or lesser degree as a function of the extent to which they differ from the in-group. The greater the difference the lower will be the relative rank of any given out-group, but any difference at all is grounds for negative evaluation.[6] Hence, English and Canadian immigrants rank very high relative to other out-groups in American society *but* they still rank below old American WASPs.[7]

Ethnocentrism is expressed in a variety of ways including mythology, condescension, and a double standard of morality in social relations. Becker has labeled this double standard a "dual ethic" in which in-group standards apply only to transactions with members of the in-group.[8] The outsider is viewed as fair game. Hence, intergroup economic relations are characterized by exploitation. Similarly, sexual relations between members of different groups are commonplace even when intermarriage is rare or prohibited entirely. The practice of endogamy is itself a manifestation of and, simultaneously, a means of reinforcing ethnocentrism. Endogamy is, indeed, an indication that ethnocentrism is present in sufficient degree for ethnic stratification to emerge.[9]

Insofar as distinct ethnic groups maintain their autonomy, mutual ethnocentrism will be preserved. Thus Indians in the Americas did not automatically surrender their

---

[5] William G. Sumner, *Folkways,* Boston: Ginn, 1940, p. 13. The essence of ethnocentrism is well conveyed by Catton's observation that "Ethnocentrism makes us see out-group behavior as deviation from in-group mores rather than as adherence to out-group mores." William R. Catton, Jr., "The Development of Sociological Thought" in Robert E. L. Faris, editor, *Handbook of Modern Sociology,* Chicago: Rand McNally, 1964, p. 930.

[6] Williams observes that "in various *particular* ways an out-group may be seen as superior" insofar as its members excel in performance vis-à-vis certain norms that the two groups hold in common (e.g., sobriety or craftsmanship in the production of a particular commodity). Robin M. Williams, Jr., *Strangers Next Door,* Englewood Cliffs, N.J.: Prentice-Hall, 1964, p. 22 (emphasis added). A similar point is made by Marc J. Swartz, "Negative Ethnocentrism," *Journal of Conflict Resolution,* 5 (March, 1961), pp. 75–81. It is highly unlikely, however, that the out-group will be so consistently objectively superior in the realm of shared values as to be seen as generally superior to the in-group unless the in-group is subordinate to or highly dependent upon the out-group.

[7] Emory S. Bogardus, *Social Distance,* Yellow Springs: Antioch, 1959.

[8] Howard P. Becker, *Man in Reciprocity,* New York: Praeger, 1956, Ch. 15.

[9] Endogamy is an overly stringent index of the degree of ethnocentrism essential to ethnic stratification and is not itself a prerequisite of the emergence of ethnic stratification. However, where endogamy does not precede ethnic stratification, it is a seemingly invariable consequence. Compare this position with that of Charles Wagley and Marvin Harris who treat ethnocentrism and endogamy as independent structural requisites of intergroup hostility and conflict. See *Minorities in the New World,* New York: Columbia, 1958, pp. 256–263.

ethnocentrism in the face of European techno-logical and scientific superiority. Indeed, if the cultural strengths (including technology) of the out-group are not relevant to the values and goals of the in-group they will, by the very nature of ethnocentrism, be negatively defined. This is well illustrated in the reply (allegedly) addressed to the Virginia Commission in 1744 when it offered to educate six Indian youths at William and Mary:

> Several of our young people were formerly brought up at Colleges of the Northern Provinces; they were instructed in all your sciences; but when they came back to us, they were bad runners, ignorant of every means of living in the woods, unable to bear either cold or hunger, knew neither how to build a cabin, take a deer, or kill an enemy, spoke our language imperfectly, were therefore neither fit for hunters, warriors, or counsellors; they were totally good for nothing. We are, however, not the less obliged by your kind offer, though we decline accepting it; and to show our grateful Sense of it, if the Gentlemen of Virginia will send us a Dozen of their Sons we will take great care of their education, instruct them in all we know, and make Men of them.[10]

Ethnocentrism in itself need not lead to either interethnic conflict or ethnic stratification, however. The Tungus and Cossacks have lived in peace as politically independent but economically interdependent societies for several centuries. The groups remain racially and culturally dissimilar and each is characterized by a general ethnocentric preference for the in-group. This conflict potential is neutralized by mutual respect and admission by each that the other is superior in certain specific respects, by the existence of some shared values and interests, and by the absence of competition due to economic complementarity and low population density.[11]

The presence of competition, structured along ethnic lines, is an additional prerequisite for the emergence of ethnic stratification.

Antonovsky has suggested that a discriminatory system of social relations requires both shared goals and scarcity of rewards,[12] and competition here refers to the interaction between two or more social units striving to achieve *the same scarce goal* (e.g., land or prestige). In the absence of shared goals members of the various ethnic groups involved in the contact situation would have, in the extreme case, mutually exclusive or nonoverlapping value hierarchies. If one group is not striving for a given goal, this reduces the likelihood of discrimination partly because members of that group are unlikely to be perceived as competitors for the goal. In addition, the indifference of one group toward the goal in effect reduces scarcity—i.e., fewer seekers enhance the probability of goal attainment by any one seeker. However, if the goal is still defined as scarce by members of one group they may seek to establish ethnic stratification in order to effectively exploit the labor of the indifferent group and thereby maximize goal attainment. In such a situation the labor (or other utility) of the indifferent group may be said to be the real object of competition. In any event the perceived scarcity of a socially valued goal is crucial and will stimulate the emergence of ethnic stratification *unless* each group perceives the other as: 1) disinterested in the relevant goal, *and* 2) nonutilitarian with respect to its own attainment of the goal.

In actuality the various goals of two groups involved in stable, complex interaction will invariably overlap to some degree and hence the likelihood of ethnic stratification is a function of the arena of competition. The arena includes the shared object(s) sought, the terms of the competition, and the relative adaptability of the groups involved.[13] Regard-

---

[10] Quoted in T. Walker Wallbank and Alastair M. Taylor, *Civilization: Past and Present*, Chicago: Scott, Foresman, 1949, rev. ed., Vol. 1. pp. 559–560. The offer and counter-offer also provide an excellent illustration of mutual ethnocentrism.

[11] Lindgren *op. cit.*

[12] Aaron Antonovsky, "The Social Meaning of Discrimination," *Phylon*, 21 (Spring, 1960), pp. 81–95.

[13] This analysis of the arena of competition is a modification of the analysis by Wagley and Harris, *op. cit.*, esp. pp. 263–264. These authors limit the concept "arena" to the objects sought *and* the regulative values which determine opportunity to compete and then partly confound their components by including the regulative values, along with adaptive capacity and the instruments necessary to compete, as part of the "terms" of competition.

ing the objects (or goals) of competition the greater the number of objects subject to competition, the more intense the competition. Moreover, as Wagley and Harris observe, "It is important to know the objects of competition, for it would seem that the more vital or valuable the resource over which there is competition, the more intense is the conflict between the groups."[14] Barring total annihilation of one of the groups, these points can be extended to state that the more intense the competition or conflict the greater the likelihood— other things being equal—that it will culminate in a system of ethnic stratification. In other words, the number and significance of the scarce, common goals sought determine the degree of competition which in turn significantly affects the probability that ethnic stratification will emerge.

The terms of the competition may greatly alter the probability of ethnic stratification, however, regardless of the intensity of the competition. The retention of a set of values or rules which effectively regulates—or moderates—ethnic interrelations is of particularly crucial significance. If a framework of regulative values fails to emerge, or breaks down, each group may seek to deny the other(s) the right to compete with the result that overt conflict emerges and culminates in annihilation, expulsion, or total subjugation of the less powerful group. If, in contrast, regulative values develop and are retained, competition even for vital goals need not result in ethnic stratification—or at least the span of stratification may be considerably constricted.[15]

Even where the groups involved are quite dissimilar culturally, the sharing of certain crucial values (e.g., religion or freedom, individualism, and equality) may be significant in preventing ethnic stratification. This appears to have been one factor in the enduring harmonious relations between the Cossacks and the Tungus. The influence of the regulative values upon the span of ethnic stratification is well illustrated by Tannenbaum's thesis regarding the differences between North American and Latin American slavery.[16] In the absence of a tradition of slavery the English had no established code prescribing the rights and duties of slaves and the racist ideology which evolved achieved its ultimate expression in the Dred Scott decision of 1857. This decision was highly consistent with the then widely held belief that the Negro "had no rights which the white man was bound to respect. . . ." By contrast the Iberian code accorded certain rights to the Latin American slave (including the right to own property and to purchase his freedom) which greatly restricted the extent of inequality between free man and slave.[17]

In addition to the regulative values, the structural opportunities for or barriers to upward mobility which are present in the society may affect the emergence and span of ethnic stratification. Social structural barriers such as a static, nonexpanding economy are a significant part of the terms of competition and they may be more decisive than the regulative values as regards the duration of the system. Finally, along with the goals and the terms of competition, the relative adaptive capacity of the groups involved is an aspect of competition which significantly affects the emergence of ethnic stratification.

Wagley and Harris assume that ethnic stratification is given and focus their analysis on the adaptive capacity of *the minority group*

---

[14] *Ibid.*, p. 263. They suggest that competition for scarce subsistence goals will produce more intense conflict than competition for prestige symbols or other culturally defined goals.

[15] Discussing the ideological aspect of intergroup relations, Wagley and Harris note that equalitarian creeds have generally not been effective in *preventing* ethnic stratification. *Ibid.*, pp. 280 ff. The operation of ethnocentrism makes it very easy for the boundaries of the in-group to become the boundaries of adherence to group values.

[16] Frank Tannenbaum, *Slave and Citizen: The Negro in the Americas,* New York: Random House, 1963.

[17] *Ibid.*, esp. pp. 49 ff. Marvin Harris has criticized Tannenbaum's thesis arguing that the rights prescribed by the Iberian code were largely illusory and that there is no certainty that *slaves* were treated better in Latin America. Harris in turn provides a functional (economic necessity) explanation for the historical difference in treatment of *free* Negroes in the two continents. See Marvin Harris, *Patterns of Race in the Americas,* New York: Walker, 1964, esp. Chs. 6 and 7.

in terms of its effect upon the span and the duration of ethnic stratification. Thus they view adaptive capacity as:

> those elements of a minority's cultural heritage which provide it with a basis for competing more or less effectively with the dominant group, which afford protection against exploitation, which stimulate or retard its adaptation to the total social environment, and which facilitate or hinder its upward advance through the socio-economic hierarchy.[18]

We shall apply the concept to an earlier point in the intergroup process—i.e., prior to the emergence of ethnic stratification—by broadening it to refer to those aspects of any ethnic group's sociocultural heritage which affect its adjustment to a given social and physical environment. The group with the greater adaptive capacity is apt to emerge as the dominant group[19] while the other groups are subordinated to a greater or lesser degree—i.e., the span of the stratification system will be great or slight —dependent upon the extent of their adaptive capacity relative to that of the emergent dominant group.

The duration, as well as the origin and span, of ethnic stratification will be markedly influenced by adaptive capacity. Once a people have become a minority, flexibility on their part is essential if they are to efficiently adjust and effectively compete within the established system of ethnic stratification and thereby facilitate achievement of equality. Sociocultural patterns are invariably altered by changing life conditions. However, groups vary in the alacrity with which they respond to changing conditions. A flexible minority group may facilitate the achievement of equality or even dominance by readily accepting modifications of their heritage which will promote efficient adaptation to their subordination *and* to subsequent changes in life conditions.

Competition and ethnocentrism do not provide a sufficient explanation for the emergence of ethnic stratification. Highly ethnocentric groups involved in competition for vital objects will not generate ethnic stratification *unless* they are of such unequal power that one is able to impose its will upon the other.[20] Inequality of power is the defining characteristic of dominant and minority groups, and Lenski maintains that differential power is the foundation element in the genesis of any stratification system.[21] In any event differential power is absolutely essential to the emergence of ethnic stratification and the greater the differential the greater the span and durability of the system, other things being equal.

Technically, power is a component of adaptive capacity as Wagley and Harris imply in their definition by referring to "protection against exploitation." Nevertheless, differential power exerts an effect independent of adaptive capacity in general and is of such crucial relevance for ethnic stratification as to warrant its being singled out as a third major causal variable. The necessity of treating it as a distinct variable is simply demonstrated by consideration of those historical cases where one group has the greater adaptive capacity in general but is subordinated because another group has greater (military) power. The Dravidians overrun by the Aryans in ancient India and the Manchu conquest of China are illustrative cases.[22]

Unless the ethnic groups involved are unequal in power, intergroup relations will be characterized by conflict, symbiosis, or a pluralist equilibrium. Given intergroup competition, however, symbiosis is unlikely and conflict and pluralism are inevitably unstable.

---

[18] Wagley and Harris, *op. cit.*, p. 264.

[19] This point is explicitly made by Tamotsu Shibutani and Kian M. Kwan, *Ethnic Stratification: A Comparative Approach*, New York: Macmillan, 1965, p. 147; see also Ch. 9.

[20] This point is made by Antonovsky, *op. cit.*, esp. p. 82, and implied by Wagley and Harris in their discussion of the role of the state in the formation of minority groups, *op. cit.*, esp. pp. 240–244. Stanley Lieberson's recent modication of Park's cycle theory of race relations also emphasizes the importance of differential power as a determinant of the outcome of intergroup contacts. See "A Societal Theory of Race and Ethnic Relations," *American Sociological Review*, 26 (December, 1961), pp. 902–910.

[21] Lenski, *op. cit.*, esp. Ch. 3.

[22] See Wallbank and Taylor, *op. cit.*, p. 95; and Shibutani and Kwan, *op. cit.*, pp. 129–130.

Any slight change in the existing balance of power may be sufficient to establish the temporary dominance of one group and this can be utilized to allow the emerging dominant group to perpetuate and enhance its position.[23] Once dominance is established the group in power takes all necessary steps to restrict the now subordinated groups, thereby hampering their effectiveness as competitors,[24] and to institutionalize the emerging distribution of rewards and opportunities. Hence, since power tends to beget power, a slight initial alteration in the distribution of power can become the basis of a stable inequalitarian system.

We have now elaborated the central concepts and propositions of a theory of the emergence and initial stabilization of ethnic stratification. The theory can be summarized as follows. When distinct ethnic groups are brought into sustained contact (via migration, the emergence and expansion of the state, or internal differentiation of a previously homogeneous group), ethnic stratification will invariably follow if—and only if—the groups are characterized by a significant degree of ethnocentrism, competition, and differential power. Without ethnocentrism the groups would quickly merge and competition would not be structured along ethnic lines. Without competition there would be no motivation or rationale for instituting stratification along ethnic lines. Without differential power it would simply be impossible for one group to achieve dominance and impose subordination to its will and ideals upon the other(s).

The necessity of differential power is incontestable but it could be argued that either competition or ethnocentrism is dispensable. For example, perhaps extreme ethnocentrism

independent of competition is sufficient motive for seeking to impose ethnic stratification. Certainly ethnocentrism could encourage efforts to promote continued sharp differentiation, but it would not by itself motivate stratification unless we assume the existence of a *need* for dominance or aggression. Conversely, given sociocultural differences, one group may be better prepared for and therefore able to more effectively exploit a given environment. Hence, this group would become economically dominant and might then perceive and pursue the advantages (especially economic) of ethnic stratification quite independent of ethnocentrism. On the other hand, while differential power and competition alone are clearly sufficient to generate stratification, a low degree of ethnocentrism could readily forestall *ethnic* stratification by permitting assimilation and thereby eliminating differential adaptive capacity. Ethnocentrism undeniably heightens awareness of ethnicity and thereby promotes the formation and retention of ethnic competition, but the crucial question is whether or not some specified degree of ethnocentrism is *essential* to the emergence of ethnic stratification. Since autonomous ethnic groups are invariably ethnocentric, the answer awaits more precise measures of ethnocentrism which will allow us to test hypotheses specifying the necessary degree of ethnocentrism.[25]

Given the present state of knowledge it seems advisable to retain both competition and ethnocentrism, as well as differential power, as integral elements of the theory. Our next objective, then, is to provide an initial test of the theory by applying it to an analysis of the genesis of slavery in the seventeenth century mainland North American colonies.

THE ORIGIN OF AMERICAN SLAVERY

There is a growing consensus among historians of slavery in the United States that Negroes were not initially slaves but that they

---

[23] See *ibid.*, esp. Chs. 6, 9, and 12; and Richard A. Schermerhorn, *Society and Power*, New York: Random House, 1961, pp. 18–26.

[24] Shibutani and Kwan observe that dominance rests upon victory in the competitive process and that competition between groups is eliminated or greatly reduced once a system of ethnic stratification is stabilized, *op. cit.*, pp. 146 and 235, and Ch. 12. The extent to which competition is actually stifled is highly variable, however, as Wagley and Harris note in their discussion of minority adaptive capacity and the terms of competition, *op. cit.*, pp. 263 ff.

[25] The issue is further complicated by the fact that the necessary degree of any one of the three elements may vary as a function of the other two.

were gradually reduced to a position of chattel slavery over several decades.[26] The historical record regarding their initial status is so vague and incomplete, however, that it is impossible to assert with finality that their status was initially no different from that of non-Negro indentured servants.[27] Moreover, while there is agreement that the statutory establishment of slavery was not widespread until the 1660's, there is disagreement regarding slavery's emergence in actual practice. The Handlins maintain that "The status of Negroes was that of servants; and so they were identified and treated down to the 1660's."[28] Degler and Jordan argue that this conclusion is not adequately documented and cite evidence indicating that some Negroes were slaves as early as 1640.[29]

Our central concern is to relate existing historical research to the theory elaborated above, *not* to attempt original historical research intended to resolve the controversy regarding the nature and extent of the initial status differences (if any) between white and Negro bondsmen. However, two findings emerging from the controversy are basic to our concern: 1) although the terms servant and slave were frequently used interchangeably, whites were never slaves in the sense of serving for life and conveying a like obligation to

their offspring; and 2) many Negroes were not slaves in this sense at least as late as the 1660's. Concomitantly with the Negroes' descent to slavery, white servants gained increasingly liberal terms of indenture and, ultimately, freedom. The origin of slavery for the one group and the growth of freedom for the other are explicable in terms of our theory as a function of differences in ethnocentrism, the arena of competition, and power vis-à-vis the dominant group or class.[30]

Degler argues that the status of the Negro evolved in a framework of discrimination and, therefore, "The important point is not the evolution of the legal status of the slave, but the fact that discriminatory legislation regarding the Negro long preceded any legal definition of slavery."[31] The first question then becomes one of explaining this differential treatment which foreshadowed the descent to slavery. A major element in the answer is implied by the Handlins' observation that "The rudeness of the Negroes' manners, the strangeness of their languages, the difficulty of communicating to them English notions of morality and proper behavior occasioned sporadic laws to regulate their conduct."[32] By itself this implies a contradiction of their basic thesis that Negro and white indentured servants were treated similarly prior to 1660. They maintain, however, that there was nothing unique nor decisive in this differential treatment of Negroes, for such was also accorded various Caucasian out-groups in this period.[33] While Jordan dismisses the Handlins' evidence as largely irrelevant to the

[26] The main relevant references in the recent literature include Carl N. Degler, *Out of Our Past*, New York: Harper and Row, 1959 and "Slavery and the Genesis of American Race Prejudice," *Comparative Studies in Society and History*, 2 (October, 1959), pp. 49–66; Stanley M. Elkins, *Slavery: A Problem in American Institutional and Intellectual Life*, Chicago: U. of Chicago, 1959; Oscar and Mary F. Handlin, "Origins of the Southern Labor System," *William and Mary Quarterly*, 3rd Series, 7 (April, 1950), pp. 199–222; and Winthrop D. Jordan, "Modern Tensions and the Origins of American Slavery," *The Journal of Southern History*, 28 (February, 1962), pp. 18–30, and *White over Black*, Chapel-Hill: U. of North Carolina, 1968. See also Boskin, *op. cit.*, and "Comment" and "Reply" by the Handlins and Degler in the cited volume of *Comparative Studies . . .*, pp. 488–495.

[27] Jordan, *The Journal . . .*, p. 22.

[28] Handlin and Handlin, *op. cit.*, p. 203.

[29] Degler, *Comparative Studies . . .*, pp. 52–56 and Jordan, *The Journal . . .*, pp. 23–27 and *White over Black*, pp. 73–74. Also see Elkins, *op. cit.*, pp. 38–42 (esp. fns. 16 and 19).

[30] Our primary concern is with the emergence of Negro slavery but the theory also explains how white bondsmen avoided slavery. Their position vis-à-vis the dominant English was characterized by a different "value" of at least two of the key variables.

[31] Degler, *Out of Our Past*, p. 35. Bear in mind, however, that slavery was not initially institutionalized in law or in the mores.

[32] Handlin and Handlin, *op. cit.*, pp. 208–209.

[33] *Ibid.* They note that "It is not necessary to resort to racialist assumptions to account for such measures; . . . [for immigrants in a strange environment] longed . . . for the company of familiar men and singled out to be welcomed those who were most like themselves." See pp. 207–211 and 214.

point and Degler feels that it is insufficient, Degler acknowledges that "Even Irishmen, who were white, Christian, and European, were held to be literally 'beyond the Pale,' and some were even referred to as 'slaves'."[34] Nevertheless, Degler contends that the overall evidence justifies his conclusion that Negroes were generally accorded a lower position than any white, bound or free.

That the English made status distinctions between various out-groups is precisely what one would expect, however, given the nature of ethnocentrism. The degree of ethnocentric rejection is primarily a function of the degree of difference, and Negroes were markedly different from the dominant English in color, nationality, language, religion, and other aspects of culture.[35] The differential treatment of Negroes was by no means entirely due to a specifically anti-Negro *color* prejudice. Indeed, color was not initially the most important factor in determining the relative status of Negroes; rather, the fact that they were non-Christian was of major significance.[36] Although beginning to lose its preeminence, religion was still the central institution of society in the seventeenth century and religious prejudice toward non-Christians or heathens was widespread. The priority of religious over color prejudice is amply demonstrated by analysis of the early laws and court decisions pertaining to Negro-white sexual relations. These sources explicitly reveal greater concern with Christian-non-Christian than with white-Negro unions.[37] During and after the 1660's laws regulating racial intermarriage arose but

for some time their emphasis was generally, if not invariably, upon religion, nationality, or some basis of differentiation other than race *per se*. For example, a Maryland law of 1681 described marriages of white women with Negroes as lascivious and "to the disgrace not only of the English but also [sic] of many *other Christian* Nations."[38] Moreover, the laws against Negro-white marriage seem to have been rooted much more in economic considerations than they were in any concern for white racial purity.[39] In short, it was not a simple color prejudice but a marked degree of ethnocentrism, rooted in a multitude of salient differences, which combined with competition and differential power to reduce Negroes to the status of slaves.[40]

Degler has noted that Negroes initially lacked a status in North America and thus almost any kind of status could have been worked out.[41] Given a different competitive arena, a more favorable status blurring the sharp ethnic distinctions could have evolved. However, as the demand for labor in an expanding economy began to exceed the supply,

---

[34] Jordan, *The Journal* . . . , esp. pp. 27 (fn. 29) and 29 (fn. 34); and Degler, *Out of Our Past*, p. 30.

[35] Only the aboriginal Indians were different from the English colonists to a comparable degree and they were likewise severely dealt with via a policy of exclusion and annihilation after attempts at enslavement failed. See Boskin, *op. cit.*, p. 453; and Jordan, *White over Black*, pp. 85–92.

[36] The priority of religions over racial prejudice and discrimination in the early seventeenth century is noted in *ibid.*, pp. 97–98 and by Edgar J. McManus, *A History of Negro Slavery in New York*, Syracuse: Syracuse U., 1966, esp. pp. 11–12.

[37] Jordan, *The Journal* . . . , p. 28 and *White over Black*, pp. 78–80.

[38] Quoted in *ibid.*, pp. 79–80 (emphasis added). Also see pp. 93–97, however, where Jordan stresses the necessity of carefully interpreting the label "Christian."

[39] See Handlin and Handlin, *op. cit.*, pp. 213–216; and W. D. Zabel, "Interracial Marriage and the Law," *The Atlantic* (October, 1965), pp. 75–79.

[40] The distinction between ethnocentrism (the rejection of out-groups *in general* as a function of in-group glorification) and prejudice (hostility toward the members of a *specific* group because they are members of that group) is crucial to the controversy regarding the direction of causality between discrimination, slavery, and prejudice. Undoubtedly these variables are mutually causal to some extent but Harris, *op. cit.*, esp. pp. 67–70, presents evidence that prejudice is primarily a consequence and is of minor importance as a cause of slavery.

[41] Degler, *Comparative Studies* . . . , p. 51. See also Boskin, *op. cit.*, pp. 449 and 454 (esp. fn. 14); Elkins, *op. cit.*, pp. 39–42 (esp. fn. 16); and Kenneth M. Stampp, *The Peculiar Institution*, New York: Knopf, 1956, p. 21. The original indeterminacy of the Negroes' status is reminiscent of Blumer's "sense of group position" theory of prejudice and, in light of Blumer's theory, is consistent with the belief that there was no widespread prejudice toward Negroes prior to the institutionalization of slavery. See Herbert Blumer, "Race Prejudice as a Sense of Group Position," *Pacific Sociological Review*, 1 (Spring, 1958), pp. 3–7.

interest in lengthening the term of indenture arose.[42] This narrow economic explanation of the origin of slavery has been challenged on the grounds that slavery appeared equally early in the Northern colonies although there were too few Negroes there to be of economic significance.[43] This seemingly decisive point is largely mitigated by two considerations.

First, in the other colonies it was precisely *the few* who did own slaves who were not only motivated by vested interests but were also the men of means and local power most able to secure a firm legal basis for slavery.[44] The distribution of power and motivation was undoubtedly similar and led to the same consequences in New England. For the individual retainer of Negro servants the factual and legal redefinition of Negroes as chattel constitutes a vital economic interest whether or not the number of slaves is sufficient to vitally affect the economy of the colony. Our knowledge of the role of the elite in the establishment of community mores suggests that this constitutes at least a partial explanation of the Northern laws.[45] In addition, the markedly smaller number of Negroes in the North might account for the fact that "although enactments in the Northern colonies recognized the legality of lifetime servitude, no effort was made to require all Negroes to be placed in that condition."[46] We surmise that the laws were passed at the behest of a few powerful individuals who had relatively many Negro servants and were indifferent to the status of Negroes in general so long as their own vested interests were protected.

The explanation for the more all-encompassing laws of the Southern colonies is rooted in the greater homogeneity of interests of the Southern elite. In contrast to the Northern situation, the men of power in the Southern colonies were predominantly planters who were unified in their need for large numbers of slaves. The margin of profit in agricultural production for the commercial market was such that the small landholder could not compete and the costs of training and the limitations on control (by the planter) which were associated with indentured labor made profitable exploitation of such labor increasingly difficult.[47] Hence, it was not the need for labor *per se* which was critical for the establishment of the comprehensive Southern slave system but rather the requirements of the emerging economic system for a particular kind of labor. In short, the Southern power elite uniformly needed slave labor while only certain men of power shared this need in the North and hence the latter advocated slave laws but lacked the power (or did not feel the need) to secure the all-encompassing laws characteristic of the Southern colonies.

There is a second major consideration in explaining the existence of Northern slavery. Men do not compete only for economic ends. They also compete for prestige and many lesser objects, and there is ample basis for suggesting that prestige competition was a significant factor in the institutionalization of slavery, North and South. Degler calls attention to the prestige motive when he discusses the efforts to establish a feudal aristocracy in seventeenth century New York, Maryland, and the Carolinas. He concludes that these efforts

[42] Handlin and Handlin, *op. cit.*, p. 210. Differential power made this tactic as suitable to the situation of Negro bondsmen as it was unsuitable in regard to white bondsmen.

[43] Degler acknowledges that the importance of perpetuating a labor force indispensable to the economy later became a crucial support of slavery but he denies that the need for labor explains the origin of slavery. His explanation stresses prior discrimination which, in the terms of the present theory, was rooted in ethnocentrism and differential power. See *Comparative Studies* . . . , including the "Reply" to the Handlins' "Comment"; and *Out of Our Past*, pp. 35–38 and 162–168.

[44] Elkins, *op. cit.*, pp. 45 (esp. fn. 26) and 48.

[45] Historical precedent is provided by the finding that "The vagrancy laws emerged in order to provide the powerful landowners with a ready supply of cheap labor." See William J. Chambliss, "A Sociological Analysis of the Law of Vagrancy," *Social Problems*, 12 (Summer, 1964), pp. 67–77. Jordan, *White over Black*, pp. 67 and 69, provides evidence that the economic advantages of slavery were clearly perceived in the Northern colonies.

[46] Elkins, *op. cit.*, p. 41 (fn. 19).

[47] By the 1680's "The point had clearly passed when white servants could realistically, on any long-term appraisal, be considered preferable to Negro slaves." *Ibid.*, p. 48.

failed because the manor was "dependent upon the scarcity of land."[48] The failure of feudal aristocracy in no way denies the fundamental human desire for success or prestige. Indeed, this failure opened the society. It emphasized success and mobility for "it meant that wealth, rather than family or tradition, would be the primary determinant of social stratification."[49] Although the stress was on economic success, there were other gains associated with slavery to console those who did not achieve wealth. The desire for social prestige derivable from "membership in a superior caste" undoubtedly provided motivation and support for slavery among both Northern and Southern whites, slaveholders and nonslaveholders.[50]

The prestige advantage of slavery would have been partially undercut, especially for nonslaveholders, by enslavement of white bondsmen, but it is doubtful that this was a significant factor in their successfully eluding hereditary bondage. Rather the differential treatment of white and Negro bondsmen, ultimately indisputable and probably present from the very beginning, is largely attributable to differences in ethnocentrism and relative power. There was little or no ethnocentric rejection of the majority of white bondsmen during the seventeenth century because most of them were English.[51] Moreover, even the detested Irish and other non-English white servants were culturally and physically much more similar to the English planters than were the Africans. Hence, the planters clearly preferred white bondsmen until the advantages of slavery became increasingly apparent in the latter half of the seventeenth century.[52]

The increasing demand for labor after the mid-seventeenth century had divergent consequences for whites and blacks. The colonists became increasingly concerned to encourage immigration by counteracting "the widespread reports in England and Scotland that servants were harshly treated and bound in perpetual slavery" and by enacting "legislation designed to improve servants' conditions and to enlarge the prospect of a meaningful release, a release that was not the start of a new period of servitude, but of life as a freeman and landowner."[53] These improvements curtailed the exploitation of white servants without directly affecting the status of the Africans.

> Farthest removed from the English, least desired, [the Negro] communicated with no friends who might be deterred from following. *Since his coming was involuntary, nothing that happened to him would increase or decrease his numbers.* To raise the status of Europeans by shortening their terms would ultimately increase the available hands by inducing their compatriots to emigrate; to reduce the Negro's term would produce an immediate loss and no ultimate gain. By mid-century the servitude of Negroes seems generally lengthier than that of whites; and thereafter, the consciousness dawns that the blacks will toil for the whole of their lives. . . .[54]

The planters and emerging agrarian capitalism were unconstrained in a planter-dominated society with no traditional institutions to exert limits. In this context even the common law tradition helped promote slavery.[55]

[48] Degler, *Out of Our Past*, p. 3. Also see Hubert M. Blalock, Jr., *Toward a Theory of Minority Group Relations*, New York: Wiley, 1967, pp. 44–48.

[49] Degler, *Out of Our Past*, p. 5; see also pp. 45–50. Elkins, *op. cit.*, esp. pp. 43–44, also notes the early emphasis on personal success and mobility.

[50] Stampp, *op. cit.*, pp. 29–33, esp. 32–33. Also see J. D. B. DeBow, "The Interest in Slavery of the Southern Non-Slaveholder," reprinted in Eric L. McKitrick, editor, *Slavery Defended: The Views of the Old South*, Englewood Cliffs, N.J.: Prentice-Hall, 1963, pp. 169–177.

[51] Stampp, *op. cit.*, p. 16; and Degler, *Out of Our Past*, pp. 50–51. Consistent with the nature of ethnocentrism, "The Irish and other aliens, less desirable, at first received longer terms. But the realization that such discrimination retarded 'the peopling of the country' led to an extension of the identical privilege to all Christians." Handlin and Handlin, *op. cit.*, pp. 210–211.

[52] Elkins, *op. cit.*, pp. 40 and 48; and Handlin and Handlin, *op. cit.*, pp. 207–208.

[53] *Ibid.*, p. 210.

[54] *Ibid.*, p. 211 (emphasis added). That the need for labor led to improvements in the status of white servants seems very likely but Degler in *Comparative Studies* . . . effectively challenges some of the variety of evidence presented by the Handlins, *op. cit.*, pp. 210 and 213–214 and "Comment."

[55] Elkins, *op. cit.*, pp. 38 (fn. 14), 42 (fn. 22), 43 and 49–52; and Jordan, *White over Black*, pp. 49–51.

Ethnocentrism set the Negroes apart but their almost total lack of power and effective spokesmen, in contrast to white indentured servants, was decisive in their enslavement. Harris speaks directly to the issue and underscores the significance of (organized) power for the emergence of slavery:

> The facts of life in the New World were such . . . that Negroes, being the most defenseless of all the immigrant groups, were discriminated against and exploited more than any others. . . . Judging from the very nasty treatment suffered by the white indentured servants, it was obviously not sentiment which prevented the Virginia planters from enslaving their fellow Englishmen. They undoubtedly would have done so had they been able to get away with it. But such a policy was out of the question as long as there was a King and a Parliament in England.[56]

The Negroes, in short, did not have any organized external government capable of influencing the situation in their favor.[57] Moreover, "there was no one in England or in the colonies to pressure for the curtailment of the Negro's servitude or to fight for his future."[58] The Negroes' capacity to adapt to the situation and effectively protest in their own behalf was greatly hampered by their cultural diversity and lack of unification. They did not think of themselves as "a kind." They did not subjectively share a common identity and thus they lacked the group solidarity necessary to effectively "act as a unit in competition with other groups."[59] Consciousness of shared fate is essential to effective unified action but it

generally develops only gradually as the members of a particular social category realize that they are being treated alike despite their differences. "People who find themselves set apart eventually come to recognize their common interests," but for those who share a subordinate position common identfication usually emerges only after repeated experiences of denial and humiliation."[60] The absence of a shared identification among seventeenth century Negroes reflected the absence of a shared heritage from which to construct identity, draw strength, and organize protest. Hence, Negroes were easily enslaved and reduced to the status of chattel. This point merits elaboration.

We have defined adaptive capacity in terms of a group's sociocultural heritage as it affects adjustment to the environment. Efficient adaptation may require the members of a group to modify or discard a great deal of their heritage. A number of factors, including ethnocentrism and the centrality of the values and social structures requiring modification, affect willingness to alter an established way of life.[61] Even given a high degree of willingness, however, many groups simply have not possessed the cultural complexity or social structural similarity to the dominant group necessary to efficient adaptation. Many Brazilian and United States Indian tribes, for example, simply have not had the knowledge (e.g., of writing, money, markets, etc.) or the structural similarity to their conquerors (e.g., as regards the division of labor) necessary to protect themselves from exploitation and to achieve a viable status in an emerging multiethnic society.[62]

By comparison with most New World Indians the sociocultural heritage of the Africans was remarkably favorable to efficient adapta-

---

[56] Harris op. cit., pp. 69–70.

[57] The effectiveness of intervention by an external government is illustrated by the halting of Indian emigration to South Africa in the 1860's as a means of protesting "the indignities to which indentured 'coolies' were subjected in Natal, ..." See Pierre L. van den Berghe, South Africa, A Study in Conflict, Middletown: Wesleyan U., 1965, p. 250.

[58] Boskin, op. cit., p. 448. Also see Stampp, op. cit., p. 22; and Elkins, op. cit., pp. 49–52.

[59] Shibutani and Kwan, op. cit., p. 42. See also William O. Brown, "Race Consciousness Among South African Natives," American Journal of Sociology, 40 (March, 1935), pp. 569–581.

[60] Shibutani and Kwan, op. cit., Ch. 8, esp. pp. 202 and 212.

[61] See the discussions in Brewton Berry, Race and Ethnic Relations, Boston: Houghton-Mifflin, 1965, 3rd ed., esp. pp. 147–149; Shibutani and Kwan, op. cit., esp. pp. 217 f; and Wagley and Harris, op. cit., pp. 40–44.

[62] Ibid., pp. 15–86 and 265–268.

tion.[63] However, the discriminatory framework within which white-Negro relations developed in the seventeenth century ultimately far outweighed the cultural advantages of the Negroes vis-à-vis the Indians in the race for status.[64] The Negroes from any given culture were widely dispersed and their capacity to adapt *as a group* was thereby shattered. Like the Negroes, the Indians were diverse culturally but they retained their cultural heritage and social solidarity, and they were more likely to resist slavery because of the much greater probability of reunion with their people following escape. Hence, Negroes were preferred over Indians as slaves both because their cultural background had better prepared them for the slave's role in the plantation system (thus enhancing the profits of the planters) and because they lacked the continuing cultural and group support which enabled the Indians to effectively resist slavery.[65] By the time the Africans acquired the dominant English culture and social patterns *and* a sense of shared fate, their inability to work out a more favorable adaptation was assured by the now established distribution of power and by the socialization processes facilitating acceptance of the role of slave.[66]

[63] *Ibid*, p. 269; Harris, *op. cit.*, p. 14; and Stampp, *op. cit.*, pp. 13 and 23.

[64] The Indians were also discriminated against but to a much lesser extent. The reasons for this differential are discussed by Jordan, *White over Black*, pp. 89–90; and Stampp, *op. cit.*, pp. 23–24.

[65] Harris, *op. cit.*, pp. 14–16, an otherwise excellent summary of the factors favoring the enslavement of Negroes rather than Indians, overlooks the role of sociocultural support. The importance of this support is clearly illustrated by the South African policy of importing Asians in preference to the native Africans who strenuously resisted enslavement and forced labor. Shibutani and Kwan, *op. cit.*, p. 126. Sociocultural unity was also a significant factor in the greater threat of revolt posed by the Helots in Sparta as compared to the heterogeneous slaves in Athens. Alvin W. Gouldner, *Enter Plato*, New York: Basic Books, 1965, p. 32.

[66] Shibutani and Kwan, *op. cit.*, esp. Chs. 10–12. Stampp observes that the plantation trained Negroes to be slaves, not free men, *op. cit.*, p. 12. Similarly, Wagley and Harris note that the Negroes were poorly prepared for survival in a free-market economic system even when they were emancipated, *op. cit.*, p. 269.

CONCLUSION

We conclude that ethnocentrism, competition, and differential power provide a comprehensive explanation of the origin of slavery in the seventeenth century English colonies. The Negroes were clearly more different from the English colonists than any other group (*except* the Indians) by almost any criterion, physical or cultural, that might be selected as a basis of social differentiation. Hence, the Negroes were the object of a relatively intense ethnocentric rejection from the beginning. The opportunity for great mobility characteristic of a frontier society created an arena of competition which dovetailed with this ethnocentrism. Labor, utilized to achieve wealth, and prestige were the primary objects of this competition. These goals were particularly manifest in the Southern colonies, but our analysis provides a rationale for the operation of the same goals as sources of motivation to institutionalize slavery in the Northern colonies also.

The terms of the competition for the Negro's labor are implicit in the evolving pattern of differential treatment of white and Negro bondsmen prior to slavery and in the precarious position of free Negroes. As slavery became institutionalized the moral, religious, and legal values of the society were increasingly integrated to form a highly consistent complex which acknowledged no evil in the peculiar institution."[67] Simultaneously, Negroes were denied any opportunity to escape their position of lifetime, inheritable servitude. Only by the grace of a generous master, not by any act of his own, could a slave achieve freedom and, moreover, there were "various legal strictures aimed at impeding or discouraging the process of private manumission."[68] The rigidity of the peculiar institution" was fixed before the Negroes acquired sufficient

[67] Davis asserts that while slavery has always been a source of tension, "in Western culture it was associated with certain religious and philosophical doctrines that gave it the highest sanction." *Op. cit.*, p. ix.

[68] Wagley and Harris, *op. cit.*, p. 124.

common culture, sense of shared fate, and identity to be able to effectively challenge the system. This lack of unity was a major determinant of the Africans' poor adaptive capacity as a group. They lacked the social solidarity and common cultural resources essential to organized resistance and thus in the absence of intervention by a powerful external ally they were highly vulnerable to exploitation.

The operation of the three key factors is well summarized by Stampp:

Neither the provisions of their charters nor the policy of the English government limited the power of colonial legislatures to control Negro labor as they saw fit. . . . Their unprotected condition encouraged the trend toward special treatment, and their physical and cultural differences provided handy excuses to justify it.

. . . [t]he landholders' growing appreciation of the advantages of slavery over the older forms of servitude gave a powerful impetus to the growth of the new labor system.[69]

In short, the present theory stresses that *given* ethnocentrism, the Negroes' lack of power, and the dynamic arena of competition in which they were located, their ultimate enslavement was inevitable. The next task is to test the theory further, incorporating modifications as necessary, by analyzing subsequent accommodations in the pattern of race relations in the United States and by analyzing the emergence of various patterns of ethnic stratification in other places and eras.

[69] Stampp, *op. cit.*, p. 22.

3

A Societal Theory of Race and Ethnic Relations

STANLEY LIEBERSON

"In the relations of races there is a cycle of events which tends everywhere to repeat itself."[1] Park's assertion served as a prologue to the now classical cycle of competition, conflict, accommodation, and assimilation. A number of other attempts have been made to formulate phases or stages ensuing from the initial contacts between racial and ethnic groups.[2] However, the sharp contrasts between relatively harmonious race relations in Brazil and Hawaii and the current racial turmoil in South Africa

---

Stanley Lieberson is Professor of Sociology at The University of Arizona.

Reprinted from *American Sociological Review* 26 (December, 1961):902–10, by permission of the author and the publisher.

[1] Robert E. Park, *Race and Culture*, Glencoe, Ill.: The Free Press, 1950, p. 150.

[2] For example, Emory S. Bogardus, "A Race-Relations Cycle," *American Journal of Sociology*, 35 (January, 1930), pp. 612–617; W. O. Brown, "Culture Contact and Race Conflict" in E. B. Reuter, editor, *Race and Culture Contacts*, New York: McGraw-Hill, 1934, pp. 34–47; E. Franklin Frazier, *Race and Culture Contacts in the Modern World*, New York: Alfred A. Knopf, 1957, pp. 32 ff.; Clarence E. Glick, "Social Roles and Types in Race Relations" in Andrew W. Lind, editor, *Race Relations in World Perspective*, Honolulu: University of Hawaii Press, 1955, pp. 243–262; Edward Nelson Palmer, "Culture Contacts and Population Growth" in Joseph J. Spengler and Otis Dudley Duncan, editors, *Population Theory and Policy*, Glencoe, Ill.: The Free Press, 1956, pp. 410–415; A. Grenfell Price, *White Settlers and Native Peoples*, Melbourne: Georgian House, 1950. For summaries of several of these cycles, see Brewton Berry, *Race and Ethnic Relations*, Boston: Houghton Mifflin, 1958, Chapter 6.

and Indonesia serve to illustrate the difficulty in stating—to say nothing of interpreting—an inevitable "natural history" of race and ethnic relations.

Many earlier race and ethnic cycles were, in fact, narrowly confined to a rather specific set of groups or contact situations. Bogardus, for example, explicitly limited his synthesis to Mexican and Oriental immigrant groups on the west coast of the United States and suggested that this is but one of many different cycles of relations between immigrants and native Americans.[3] Similarly, the Australian anthropologist Price developed three phases that appear to account for the relationships between white English-speaking migrants and the aborigines of Australia, Maoris in New Zealand, and Indians of the United States and Canada.[4]

This paper seeks to present a rudimentary theory of the development of race and ethnic relations that systematically accounts for differences between societies in such divergent consequences of contact as racial nationalism and warfare, assimilation and fusion, and extinction. It postulates that the critical problem on a societal level in racial or ethnic contact is initially each population's maintenance and development of a social order compatible with its ways of life prior to contact. The crux of any cycle must, therefore, deal with political, social, and economic institutions. The emphasis given in earlier cycles to one group's dominance of another in these areas is therefore hardly surprising.[5]

Although we accept this institutional approach, the thesis presented here is that knowledge of the nature of one group's domination over another in the political, social, and economic spheres is a necessary but insufficient prerequisite for predicting or interpreting the final and intermediate stages of racial and ethnic contact. Rather, institutional factors are considered in terms of a distinction between two major types of contact situations: contacts

[3] Bogardus, *op. cit.*, p. 612.

[4] Price, *op. cit.*

[5] Intra-urban stages of contact are not considered here.

involving subordination of an indigenous population by a migrant group, for example, Negro-white relations in South Africa; and contacts involving subordination of a migrant population by an indigenous racial or ethnic group, for example, Japanese migrants to the United States.

After considering the societal issues inherent in racial and ethnic contact, the distinction developed between migrant and indigenous superordination will be utilized in examining each of the following dimensions of race relations: political and economic control, multiple ethnic contacts, conflict and assimilation. The terms "race" and "ethnic" are used interchangeably.

DIFFERENCES INHERENT IN CONTACT

Most situations of ethnic contact involve at least one indigenous group and at least one group migrating to the area. The only exception at the initial point in contact would be the settlement of an uninhabited area by two or more groups. By "indigenous" is meant not necessarily the aborigines, but rather a population sufficiently established in an area so as to possess the institutions and demographic capacity for maintaining some minimal form of social order through generations. Thus a given spatial area may have different indigenous groups through time. For example, the indigenous population of Australia is presently largely white and primarily of British origin, although the Tasmanoids and Australoids were once in possession of the area.[6] A similar racial shift may be observed in the populations indigenous to the United States.

Restricting discussion to the simplest of contact situations, i.e., involving one migrant and one established population, we can generally observe sharp differences in their social organization at the time of contact. The indigenous population has an established and presumably stable organization prior to the

arrival of migrants, i.e., government, economic activities adapted to the environment and the existing techniques of resource utilization, kinship, stratification, and religious systems.[7] On the basis of a long series of migration studies, we may be reasonably certain that the social order of a migrant population's homeland is not wholly transferred to their new settlement.[8] Migrants are required to make at least some institutional adaptations and innovations in veiw of the presence of an indigenous population, the demographic selectivity of migration, and differences in habitat.

For example, recent post-war migrations from Italy and the Netherlands indicate considerable selectivity in age and sex from the total populations of these countries. Nearly half of 30,000 males leaving the Netherlands in 1955 were between 20 and 39 years of age whereas only one quarter of the male population was of these ages.[9] Similarly, over 40,000 males in this age range accounted for somewhat more than half of Italy's male emigrants in 1951, although they comprise roughly 30 per cent of the male population of Italy.[10] In both countries, male emigrants exceed females in absolute numbers as well as in comparison with the sex ratios of their nation. That these cases are far from extreme can be illustrated with Oriental migration data. In 1920, for example, there were 38,000 foreign born Chinese adult males in the United States, but only 2,000 females of the same group.[11]

In addition to these demographic shifts, the new physical and biological conditions of existence require the revision and creation of social institutions if the social order known in the old country is to be approximated and if

---

[6] Price, op. cit., Chapters 6 and 7.

[7] Glick, op. cit., p. 244.

[8] See, for example, Brinley Thomas, "International Migration" in Philip M. Hauser and Otis Dudley Duncan, editors, The Study of Population, Chicago: University of Chicago Press, 1959, pp. 523–526.

[9] United Nations, Demographic Yearbook, 1957, pp. 147, 645.

[10] United Nations, Demographic Yearbook, 1954, pp. 131, 669.

[11] R. D. McKenzie, Oriental Exclusion, Chicago: University of Chicago Press, 1928, p. 83.

the migrants are to survive. The migration of eastern and southern European peasants around the turn of the century to urban industrial centers of the United States provides a well-documented case of radical changes in occupational pursuits as well as the creation of a number of institutions in response to the new conditions of urban life, e.g., mutual aid societies, national churches, and financial institutions.

In short, when two populations begin to occupy the same habitat but do not share a single order, each group endeavors to maintain the political and economic conditions that are at least compatible with the institutions existing before contact. These conditions for the maintenances of institutions can not only differ for the two groups in contact, but are often conflicting. European contacts with the American Indian, for example, led to the decimation of the latter's sources of sustenance and disrupted religious and tribal forms of organization. With respect to a population's efforts to maintain its social institutions, we may therefore assume that the presence of another ethnic group is an important part of the environment. Further, if groups in contact differ in their capacity to impose changes on the other group, then we may expect to find one group "superordinate" and the other population "subordinate" in maintaining or developing a suitable environment.

It is here that efforts at a single cycle of race and ethnic relations must fail. For it is necessary to introduce a distinction in the nature or form of subordination before attempting to predict whether conflict or relatively harmonious assimilation will develop. As we shall shortly show, the race relations cycle in areas where the migrant group is superordinate and indigenous group subordinate differs sharply from the stage in societies composed of a superordinate indigenous group and subordinate migrants.[12]

[12] See, for example, Reuter's distinction between two types of direct contact in E. B. Reuter, editor, *op. cit.*, pp. 4–7.

POLITICAL AND ECONOMIC CONTROL

Emphasis is placed herein on economic and political dominance since it is assumed that control of these institutions will be instrumental in establishing a suitable milieu for at least the population's own social institutions, e.g., educational, religious, and kinship, as well as control of such major cultural artifacts as language.

Migrant Superordination

When the population migrating to a new contact situation is superior in technology (particularly weapons) and more tightly organized than the indigenous group, the necessary conditions for maintaining the migrants' political and economic institutions are usually imposed on the indigenous population. Warfare, under such circumstances, often occurs early in the contacts between the two groups as the migrants begin to interfere with the natives' established order. There is frequently conflict even if the initial contact was friendly. Price, for example, has observed the following consequences of white invasion and subordination of the indigenous populations of Australia, Canada, New Zealand, and the United States:

> During an opening period of pioneer invasion on moving frontiers the whites decimated the natives with their diseases; occupied their lands by seizure or by pseudo-purchase, slaughtered those who resisted; intensified tribal warfare by supplying white weapons; ridiculed and disrupted native religions, society and culture, generally reduced the unhappy peoples to a state of despondency under which they neither desired to live, nor to have children to undergo similar conditions.[13]

The numerical decline of indigenous populations after their initial subordination to a migrant group, whether caused by warfare, introduction of venereal and other diseases, or disruption of sustenance activities, has been

[13] Price, *op. cit.*, p. 1.

documented for a number of contact situations in addition to those discussed by Price.[14]

In addition to bringing about these demographic and economic upheavals, the superordinate migrants frequently create political entities that are not at all coterminous with boundaries existing during the indigenous populations' supremacy prior to contact. For example, the British and Boers in southern Africa carved out political states that included areas previously under the control of separate and often warring groups.[15] Indeed, European alliances with feuding tribes were often used as a fulcrum for the territorial expansion of whites into southern Africa.[16] The bifurcation of tribes into two nations and the migrations of groups across newly created national boundaries are both consequences of the somewhat arbitrary nature of the political entities created in regions of migrant superordination.[17] This incorporation of diverse indigenous populations into a single territorial unit under the dominance of a migrant group has considerable importance for later developments in this type of racial and ethnic contact.

Indigenous Superordination

When a population migrates to a subordinate position considerably less conflict occurs in the early stages. The movements of many European and Oriental populations to political, economic, and social subordination in the United States were not converted into warfare, nationalism, or long-term conflict. Clearly, the occasional labor and racial strife marking the history of immigration of the United States is not on the same level as the efforts to expel or revolutionize the social order. American Ne-

groes, one of the most persistently subordinated migrant groups in the country, never responded in significant numbers to the encouragement of migration to Liberia. The single important large-scale nationalistic effort, Marcus Garvey's Universal Negro Improvement Association, never actually led to mass emigration of Negroes.[18] By contrast, the indigenous American Indians fought long and hard to preserve control over their habitat.

In interpreting differences in the effects of migrant and indigenous subordination, the migrants must be considered in the context of the options available to the group. Irish migrants to the United States in the 1840's, for example, although clearly subordinate to native whites of other origins, fared better economically than if they had remained in their mother country.[19] Further, the option of returning to the homeland often exists for populations migrating to subordinate situations. Jerome reports that net migration to the United States between the midyears of 1907 and 1923 equalled roughly 65 per cent of gross immigration.[20] This indicates that immigrant dissatisfaction with subordination or other conditions of contact can often be resolved by withdrawal from the area. Recently subordinated indigenous groups, by contrast, are perhaps less apt to leave their habitat so readily.

Finally, when contacts between racial and ethnic groups are under the control of the indigenous population, threats of demographic and institutional imbalance are reduced since the superordinate populations can limit the numbers and groups entering. For example, when Oriental migration to the United States threatened whites, sharp cuts were executed in the quotas.[21] Similar events may be noted

---

[14] Stephen Roberts, *Population Problems of the Pacific,* London: George Routledge & Sons, 1927.

[15] John A. Barnes, "Race Relations in the Development of Southern Africa" in Lind, editor, *op. cit.*

[16] *Ibid.*

[17] Witness the current controversies between tribes in the newly created Congo Republic. Also, for a list of tribes living on both sides of the border of the Republic of Sudan, see Karol Józef Krótki, "Demographic Survey of Sudan" in *The Population of Sudan,* report on the sixth annual conference, Khartoum: Philosophical Society of Sudan, 1958, p. 35.

[18] John Hope Franklin, *From Slavery to Freedom,* second edition, New York: Alfred Knopf, 1956, pp. 234–238, 481–483.

[19] Oscar Handlin, *Boston's Immigrants,* revised edition, Cambridge, Mass.: The Belknap Press of Harvard University Press, 1959, Chapter 2.

[20] Harry Jerome, *Migration and Business Cycles,* New York: National Bureau of Economic Research, 1926, pp. 43–44.

[21] See, George Eaton Simpson and J. Milton Yinger, *Racial and Cultural Minorities,* revised edition, New York: Harper & Brothers, 1958, pp. 126–132.

with respect to the decline of immigration from the so-called "new" sources of eastern and southern Europe. Whether a group exercises its control over immigration far before it is actually under threat is, of course, not germane to the point that immigrant restriction provides a mechanism whereby potential conflict is prevented.

In summary, groups differ in the conditions necessary for maintaining their respective social orders. In areas where the migrant group is dominant, frequently the indigenous population suffers sharp numerical declines and their economic and political institutions are seriously undermined. Conflict often accompanies the establishment of migrant superordination. Subordinate indigenous populations generally have no alternative location and do not control the numbers of new ethnic populations admitted into their area. By contrast, when the indigenous population dominates the political and economic conditions, the migrant group is introduced into the economy of the indigenous population. Although subordinate in their new habitat, the migrants may fare better than if they remained in their homeland. Hence their subordination occurs without great conflict. In addition, the migrants usually have the option of returning to their homeland and the indigenous population controls the number of new immigrants in the area.

MULTIPLE ETHNIC CONTACTS

Although the introduction of a third major ethnic or racial group frequently occurs in both types of societies distinguished here, there are significant differences between conditions in habitats under indigenous domination and areas where a migrant population is superordinate. Chinese and Indian migrants, for example, were often welcomed by whites in areas where large indigenous populations were suppressed, but these migrants were restricted in the white mother country. Consideration of the causes and consequences of multiethnic contacts is therefore made in terms of the two types of racial and ethnic contact.

Migrant Superordination

In societies where the migrant population is superordinate, it is often necessary to introduce new immigrant groups to fill the niches created in the revised economy of the area. The subordinate indigenous population frequently fails, at first, to participate in the new economic and political order introduced by migrants. For example, because of the numerical decline of Fijians after contact with whites and their unsatisfactory work habits, approximately 60,000 persons migrated from India to the sugar plantations of Fiji under the indenture system between 1879 and 1916.[22] For similar reasons, as well as the demise of slavery, large numbers of Indians were also introduced to such areas of indigenous subordination as Mauritius, British Guiana, Trinidad, and Natal.[23] The descendants of these migrants comprise the largest single ethnic group in several of these areas.

McKenzie, after observing the negligible participation of the subordinated indigenous populations of Alaska, Hawaii, and Malaya in contrast to the large numbers of Chinese, Indian, and other Oriental immigrants, offers the following interpretation:

The indigenous peoples of many of the frontier zones of modern industrialism are surrounded by their own web of culture and their own economic structure. Consequently they are slow to take part in the new economy especially as unskilled laborers. It is the individual who is widely removed from this native habitat that is most adaptable to the conditions imposed by capitalism in frontier regions. Imported labor cannot so easily escape to its home village when conditions are distasteful as can the local population.[24]

[22] K. L. Gillion, "The Sources of Indian Emigration to Fiji," *Population Studies*, 10 (November, 1956), p. 139; I. M. Cumpston, "A Survey of Indian Immigration to British Tropical Colonies to 1910," *ibid.*, pp. 158–159.

[23] Cumpston, *op. cit.*, pp. 158–165.

[24] R. D. McKenzie, "Cultural and Racial Differences as Bases of Human Symbiosis" in Kimball Young, editor, *Social Attitudes*, New York: Henry Holt, 1931, p. 157.

Similarly, the Indians of the United States played a minor role in the new economic activities introduced by white settlers and, further, were not used successfully as slaves.[25] Frazier reports that Negro slaves were utilized in the West Indies and Brazil after unsuccessful efforts to enslave the indigenous Indian populations.[26] Large numbers of Asiatic Indians were brought to South Africa as indentured laborers to work in the railways, mines, and plantations introduced by whites.[27]

This migration of workers into areas where the indigenous population was either unable or insufficient to work in the newly created economic activities was also marked by a considerable flow back to the home country. For example, nearly 3.5 million Indians left the Madras Presidency for overseas between 1903 and 1912, but close to 3 million returned during this same period.[28] However, as we observed earlier, large numbers remained overseas and formed major ethnic populations in a number of countries. Current difficulties of the ten million Chinese in Southeast Asia are in large part due to their settlement in societies where the indigenous populations were subordinate.

Indigenous Superordination

We have observed that in situations of indigenous superordination the call for new immigrants from other ethnic and racial populations is limited in a manner that prevents the indigenous group's loss of political and economic control. Under such conditions, no single different ethnic or racial population is sufficiently large in number or strength to challenge the supremacy of the indigenous population.

After whites attained dominance in Hawaii, that land provided a classic case of the substitution of one ethnic group after an-other during a period when large numbers of immigrants were needed for the newly created and expanding plantation economy. According to Lind, the shifts from Chinese to Japanese and Portuguese immigrants and the later shifts to Puerto Rican, Korean, Spanish, Russian, and Philippine sources for the plantation laborers were due to conscious efforts to prevent any single group from obtaining too much power.[29] Similarly, the exclusion of Chinese from the United States mainland stimulated the migration of the Japanese and, in turn, the later exclusion of Japanese led to increased migration from Mexico.[30]

In brief, groups migrating to situations of multiple ethnic contact are thus subordinate in both types of contact situations. However, in societies where whites are superordinate but do not settle as an indigenous population, other racial and ethnic groups are admitted in large numbers and largely in accordance with economic needs of the revised economy of the habitat. By contrast, when a dominant migrant group later becomes indigenous, in the sense that the area becomes one of permanent settlement through generations for the group, migrant populations from new racial and ethnic stocks are restricted in number and source.

CONFLICT AND ASSIMILATION

From a comparison of the surge of racial nationalism and open warfare in parts of Africa and Asia or the retreat of superordinate migrants from the former Dutch East Indies and French Indo-China, on the one hand, with the fusion of populations in many nations of western Europe or the "cultural pluralism" of the United States and Switzerland, on the other, one must conclude that neither conflict nor assimilation is an inevitable outcome of racial and ethnic contact. Our distinction, however, between two classes of race and ethnic relations is directly relevant to consideration of

[25] Franklin, *op. cit.*, p. 47.

[26] Frazier, *op. cit.*, pp. 107–108.

[27] Leo Kuper, Hilstan Watts, and Ronald Davies, *Durban: A Study in Racial Ecology*, London: Jonathan Cape, 1958, p. 25.

[28] Gillion, *op. cit.*, p. 149.

[29] Andrew W. Lind, *An Island Community*, Chicago: University of Chicago Press, 1938, pp. 218–229.

[30] McKenzie, *Oriental Exclusion*, *op. cit.*, p. 181.

which of these alternatives different populations in contact will take. In societies where the indigenous population at the initial contact is subordinate, warfare and nationalism often —although not always—develops later in the cycle of relations. By contrast, relations between migrants and indigenous populations that are subordinate and superordinate, respectively, are generally without long-term conflict.

Migrant Superordination

Through time, the subordinated indigenous population begins to participate in the economy introduced by the migrant group and, frequently, a concomitant disruption of previous forms of social and economic organization takes place. This, in turn, has significant implications for the development of both nationalism and a greater sense of racial unity. In many African states, where Negroes were subdivided into ethnic groups prior to contact with whites, the racial unity of the African was created by the occupation of their habitat by white invaders.[31] The categorical subordination of Africans by whites as well as the dissolution and decay of previous tribal and ethnic forms of organization are responsible for the creation of racial consciousness among the indigenous populations.[32] As the indigenous group becomes increasingly incorporated within the larger system, both the saliency of their subordinate position and its significance increase. No alternative exists for the bulk of the native population other than the destruction or revision of the institutions of political, economic, and social subordination.

Further, it appears that considerable conflict occurs in those areas where the migrants are not simply superordinate, but where they themselves have also become, in a sense, in-

[31] For a discussion of territorial and tribal movements, see James S. Coleman, "Current Political Movements in Africa," *The Annals of the American Academy of Political and Social Science,* 298 (March, 1955), pp. 95–108.

[32] For a broader discussion of emergent nationalism, see Thomas Hodgkin, *Nationalism in Colonial Africa,* New York: New York University Press, 1957; Everett C. Hughes, "New Peoples" in Lind, editor, *op. cit.,* pp. 95–115.

TABLE 1. *Nativity of the White Populations of Selected African Countries, Circa 1950*

Country	Per Cent of Whites Born in Country
Algeria	79.8
Basutoland	37.4
Bechuanaland	39.5
Morocco[a]	37.1[c]
Northern Rhodesia	17.7
Southern Rhodesia	31.5
South West Africa[b]	45.1
Swaziland	41.2
Tanganyika	47.6
Uganda	43.8
Union of South Africa	89.7

Source: United Nations, *Demographic Yearbook,* 1956, Table 5.
[a] Former French zone.
[b] Excluding Walvis Bay.
[c] Persons born in former Spanish zone or in Tangier are included as native.
NOTE: Other non-indigenous groups included when necessary breakdown by race is not given.

digenous by maintaining an established population through generations. In Table 1, for example, one can observe how sharply the white populations of Algeria and the Union of South Africa differ from those in nine other African countries with respect to the per cent born in the country of settlement. Thus, two among the eleven African countries for which such data were available[33] are outstanding with respect to both racial turmoil and the high proportion of whites born in the country. To be sure, other factors operate to influence the nature of racial and ethnic relations. However, these data strongly support our suggestions with respect to the significance of differences between indigenous and migrant forms of contact. Thus where the migrant population becomes established in the new area, it is all the more difficult for the indigenous subordinate group to change the social order.

Additionally, where the formerly subordinate indigenous population has become

[33] United Nations, *Demographic Yearbook, 1956,* Table 5.

dominant through the expulsion of the super-ordinate group, the situation faced by nationalities introduced to the area under earlier conditions of migrant superordination changes radically. For example, as we noted earlier, Chinese were welcomed in many parts of Southeast Asia where the newly subordinated indigenous populations were unable or unwilling to fill the economic niches created by the white invaders. However, after whites were expelled and the indigenous populations obtained political mastery, the gates to further Chinese immigration were fairly well closed and there has been increasing interference with the Chinese already present. In Indonesia, where Chinese immigration had been encouraged under Dutch domain, the newly created indigenous government allows only token immigration and has formulated a series of laws and measures designed to interfere with and reduce Chinese commercial activities.[34] Thompson and Adloff observe that,

Since the war, the Chinese have been subjected to increasingly restrictive measures throughout Southeast Asia, but the severity and effectiveness of these has varied with the degree to which the native nationalists are in control of their countries and feel their national existence threatened by the Chinese.[35]

Indigenous Superordination

By contrast, difficulties between subordinate migrants and an already dominant indigenous population occur within the context of a consensual form of government, economy, and social institutions. However confused and uncertain may be the concept of assimilation and its application in operational terms,[36] it is im-portant to note that assimilation is essentially a very different phenomenon in the two types of societies distinguished here.

Where populations migrate to situations of subordination, the issue has generally been with respect to the migrants' capacity and willingness to become an integral part of the ongoing social order. For example, this has largely been the case in the United States where the issue of "new" vs. "old" immigrant groups hinged on the alleged inferiorities of the former.[37] The occasional flurries of violence under this form of contact have been generally initiated by the dominant indigenous group and with respect to such threats against the social order as the cheap labor competition of Orientals on the west coast,[38] the nativist fears of Irish Catholic political domination of Boston in the nineteenth century,[39] or the desecration of sacred principles by Mexican "zoot-suiters" in Los Angeles.[40]

The conditions faced by subordinate migrants in Australia and Canada after the creation of indigenous white societies in these areas are similar to that of the United States; that is, limited and sporadic conflict, and great emphasis on the assimilation of migrants. Striking and significant contrasts to the general pattern of subordinate immigrant assimilation in those societies, however, are provided by the differences between the assimilation of Italian and German immigrants in Australia as well as the position of French Canadians in eastern Canada.

French Canadians have maintained their language and other major cultural and social attributes whereas nineteenth and twentieth century immigrants are in process of merging into the predominantly English-speaking Canadian society. Although broader problems of

[34] B. H. M. Vlekke, *Indonesia in 1956*, The Hague: Netherlands Institute of International Affairs, 1957, p. 88.

[35] Virginia Thompson and Richard Adloff, *Minority Problems in Southeast Asia*, Stanford, California: Stanford University Press, 1955, p. 3.

[36] See, for example, International Union for the Scientific Study of Population, "Cultural Assimilation of Immigrants." *Population Studies, supplement,* March, 1950.

[37] Oscar Handlin, *Race and Nationality in American Life*, Garden City, New York: Doubleday Anchor Books, 1957, Chapter 5.

[38] Simpson and Yinger, *op. cit.*

[39] Oscar Handlin, *Boston's Immigrants, op. cit.*, Chapter 7.

[40] Ralph Turner and Samuel J. Surace, "Zoot-Suiters and Mexicans: Symbols in Crowd Behavior," *American Journal of Sociology*, 62 (July, 1956), pp. 14–20.

territorial segregation are involved,[41] the critical difference between French Canadians and later groups is that the former had an established society in the new habitat prior to the British conquest of Canada and were thus largely able to maintain their social and cultural unity without significant additional migration from France.[42]

Similarly, in finding twentieth century Italian immigrants in Australia more prone to cultural assimilation than were German migrants to that nation in the 1800's, Borrie emphasized the fact that Italian migration occurred after Australia had become an independent nation-state. By contrast, Germans settled in what was a pioneer colony without an established general social order and institutions. Thus, for example, Italian children were required to attend Australian schools and learn English, whereas the German immigrants were forced to establish their own educational program.[43]

Thus the consequences of racial and ethnic contact may also be examined in terms of the two types of superordinate-subordinate

[41] It is, however, suggestive to consider whether the isolated settlement of an area by a racial, religious, or ethnic group would be permitted in other than frontier conditions. Consider, for example, the difficulties faced by Mormons until they reached Utah.

[42] See Everett C. Hughes, *French Canada in Transition*, Chicago: University of Chicago Press, 1943.

[43] W. D. Borrie assisted by D. R. G. Packer, *Italians and Germans in Australia*, Melbourne: F. W. Cheshire, 1954 *passim*.

contact situations considered. For the most part, subordinate migrants appear to be more rapidly assimilated than are subordinate indigenous populations. Further, the subordinate migrant group is generally under greater pressure to assimilate, at least in the gross sense of "assimilation" such as language, than are subordinate indigenous populations. In addition, warfare or racial nationalism—when it does occur—tends to be in societies where the indigenous population is subordinate. If the indigenous movement succeeds, the economic and political position of racial and ethnic populations introduced to the area under migrant dominance may become tenuous.

A FINAL NOTE

It is suggested that interest be revived in the conditions accounting for societal variations in the process of relations between racial and ethnic groups. A societal theory of race relations, based on the migrant-indigenous and superordinate-subordinate distinctions developed above, has been found to offer an orderly interpretation of differences in the nature of race and ethnic relations in the contact situations considered. Since, however, systematic empirical investigation provides a far more rigorous test of the theory's merits and limitations, comparative cross-societal studies are needed.

4

Order and Conflict Theories of Social Problems as Competing Ideologies

JOHN HORTON

A recent best seller, *The One Hundred Dollar Misunderstanding*,[1] should be required reading for every student of social problems and deviant behavior. The novel makes clear what is often dimly understood and rarely applied in sociology—the fundamentally social and symbolic character of existing theories of behavior. In the novel a square, white college boy and a Lolitaesque Negro prostitute recount their shared weekend experience. But what they have shared in action, they do not share in words. Each tells a different story. Their clashing tales express different vocabularies and different experiences. Gover stereotypically dramatizes a now hackneyed theme in the modern theater and novel—the misunderstandings generated by a conflict of viewpoints, a conflict between subjective representations of "objective" reality.

John Horton is Assistant Professor of Sociology at the University of California, Los Angeles.

Reprinted from *American Journal of Sociology* 71 (May, 1966): 701–13, by permission of the author and the publisher. Copyright 1966 by the University of Chicago Press.
[1] Robert Gover, *The One Hundred Dollar Misunderstanding* (New York: Ballantine Books, 1961).

Paradoxically, this familiar literary insight has escaped many social scientists. The escape is most baffling and least legitimate for the sociologists of deviant behavior and social problems. Social values define their phenomena; their social values color their interpretations. Whatever the possibilities of developing empirical theory in the social sciences, only normative theory is appropriate in the sociology of social problems. I would accept Don Martindale's definitions of empirical and normative theory:

> The ultimate materials of empirical theory are facts; the ultimate materials of normative theory are value-imperatives . . . empirical theory is formed out of a system of laws. Normative theory converts facts and laws into requisite means and conditions and is unique in being addressed to a system of objectives desired by the formulator or by those in whose service he stands.[2]

The problem for the sociologist is not that normative theories contain values, but that these values may go unnoticed so that normative theories pass for empirical theories. When his own values are unnoticed, the sociologist who studies the situation of the American Negro, for example, is a little like the middle-class white boy in Gover's novel, except that only one story is told, and it is represented as *the* story. The result could be a rather costly misunderstanding: the Negro may not recognize himself in the sociological story; worse, he may not even learn to accept it.

One of the tasks of the sociologist is to recognize his own perspective and to locate this and competing perspectives in time and social structure. In this he can use Weber, Mills, and the sociology of knowledge as guides. Following Weber's work, he might argue that insofar as we are able to theorize

[2] Don Martindale. "Social Disorganization: The Conflict of Normative and Empirical Approaches," in Howard Becker and Alvin Boskoff (eds.), *Modern Sociological Theory* (New York: Dryden Press, 1959), p. 341.

about the social world, we must use the vocabularies of explanation actually current in social life.[3] This insight has been expanded by C. W. Mills and applied to theorizing in general and to the character of American theorizing in particular. The key words in Mills's approach to theorizing are "situated actions" and "vocabularies of motive." His position is that theories of social behavior can be understood sociologically as typical symbolic explanations associated with historically situated actions.[4] Thus, Mills argues that the Freudian terminology of motives is that of an upper-bourgeois patriarchal group with a strong sexual and individualistic orientation. Likewise explanations current in American sociology reflect the social experience and social motives of the American sociologist. Mills contends that for a period before 1940, a single vocabulary of explanation was current in the American sociologist's analysis of social problems and that these motives expressed a small town (and essentially rural) bias.[5] He interpreted the contemporary sociological vocabulary as a symbolic expression of a bureaucratic and administrative experience in life and work.[6]

Continuing in the tradition of Weber and Mills, I attempt to do the following: (1) propose a method of classifying current normative theories of deviant behavior and social problems: (2) discuss liberal and sociological approaches to the race question as an example of one of these theories; and (3) point out the implications of the normative character of theory for sociology. My general discussion of competing theories will be an elaboration of several assumptions:

1. All definitions and theories of deviation and social problems are normative. They define and explain behavior from socially situated value positions.

2. Existing normative theories can be classified into a limited number of typical vocabularies of explanation. Contemporary sociological theories of deviation are adaptations of two fundamental models of analysis rooted in nineteenth-century history and social thought. These are *order* and *conflict* models of society.

3. In general, a liberalized version of order theory pervades the American sociological approach to racial conflict, juvenile delinquency, and other social problems. I use the term "liberal" because the sociological and the politically liberal vocabularies are essentially the same. Both employ an order model of society; both are conservative in their commitment to the existing social order.

4. Alternatives to the liberal order approach exist both within the context of sociological theory and in the contemporary social and political fabric of American society. More radical versions of order models have been used by European sociologists such as Emile Durkheim; radical versions of order models are presently being used in American society by political rightists. The conflict vocabulary has been most clearly identified with Karl Marx and continues today in the social analysis of socialists and communists, while an anarchistic version of conflict theory pervades the politics of the so-called new left.

5. Current vocabularies for the explanation of social problems can be located within the social organization of sociology and the broader society. As a generalization, groups or individuals committed to the maintenance of the social status quo employ order models of society and equate deviation with non-conformity to institutionalized norms. Dissident groups, striving to institutionalize new claims, favor a conflict analysis of society and an alienation theory of their own discontents. For example, this social basis of preference for one

[3] For Weber's discussion of explanation in the social sciences see *Max Weber: The Theory of Social and Economic Organization*, trans. A. M. Henderson and Talcott Parsons (Glencoe, Ill.: Free Press, 1947), pp. 87–114.

[4] C. Wright Mills, "Situated Actions and Vocabularies of Motive," *American Sociological Review*, V (December, 1940), 904–13.

[5] C. Wright Mills, "The Professional Ideology of the Social Pathologists," *American Journal of Sociology*, XLIX (September, 1942), 165–80.

[6] C. Wright Mills, *The Sociological Imagination* (New York: Oxford University Press, 1959).

model is clear in even the most superficial analysis of stands taken on civil rights demonstrations by civil rights activists and members of the Southern establishment. For Governor Wallace of Alabama, the 1965 Selma-Montgomery march was a negative expression of anomy; for Martin Luther King it was a positive and legitimate response to alienation. King argues that the Southern system is maladaptive to certain human demands; Wallace that the demands of the demonstrators are dysfunctional to the South. However, if one considers their perspectives in relationship to the more powerful Northern establishment, King and not Wallace is the order theorist.

In sociology, order analysis of society is most often expressed by the professional establishment and its organs of publication. Alienation analysis is associated with the "humanitarian" and "political" mavericks outside of, opposed to, or in some way marginal to the established profession of sociology. . . .

THE ORDER VOCABULARY

Order theories have in common an image of society as a system of action unified at the most general level by shared culture, by agreement on values (or at least on modes) of communication and political organization. System analysis is synonymous with structural-functional analysis. System analysis consists of *statics*—the classification of structural regularities in social relations (dominant role and status clusters, institutions, etc.)—and *dynamics*—the study of the intrasystem processes: strategies of goal definition, socialization, and other functions which maintain system balance. . . .

Order theories imply consensual and adjustment definitions of social health and pathology, of conformity and deviation. The standards for defining health are the legitimate values of the social system and its requisites for goal attainment and maintenance. Deviation is the opposite of social conformity

and means the failure of individuals to perform their legitimate social roles; deviants are out of adjustment.

A contemporary example of an order approach to society and an adjustment interpretation of health and pathology has been clearly stated in Talcott Parsons' definition of mental health and pathology:

> Health may be defined as the state of optimum *capacity* of an individual for the effective performance of the roles and tasks for which he has been socialized. It is thus defined with reference to the individual's participation in the social system. It is also defined as *relative* to his "status" in the society, i.e., to differentiated type of role and corresponding task structure, e.g., by sex or age, and by level of education which he has attained and the like.[7]

THE CONFLICT VOCABULARY

Conflict theorists are alike in their rejection of the order model of contemporary society. They interpret order analysis as the strategy of a ruling group, a reification of their values and motivations, a rationalization for more effective social control. Society is a natural system for the order analyst; for the conflict theorist it is a continually contested political struggle between groups with opposing goals and world views. As an anarchist, the conflict theorist may oppose any notion of stable order and authority. As a committed Marxist, he may project the notion of order into the future. Order is won, not through the extension of social control, but through the radical reorganization of social life; order follows from the condition of social organization and not from the state of cultural integration. . . .

Conflict theory . . . implies a particular definition of health, but the values underlying this definition refer to what is required to grow and change, rather than to adjust to existing practices and hypothesized requirements for the maintenance of the social system. Health

[7] Talcott Parsons, "Definitions of Health and Illness in the Light of American Values and Social Structure," in E. Gartley Jaco (ed.), *Patients, Physicians and Illness* (Glencoe, Ill.: Free Press, 1963), p. 176.

and pathology are defined in terms of postulated requirements for individual or social growth and adaptation. Social problems and social change arise from the exploitive and alienating practices of dominant groups; they are responses to the discrepancy between what is and what is in the process of becoming. Social problems, therefore, reflect, not the administrative problems of the social system, nor the failure of individuals to perform their system roles as in the order explanation, but the adaptive failure of society to meet changing individual needs.

A growth definition of health based on a conflict interpretation of society is implicit in Paul Goodman's appraisal of the causes of delinquency in American society. Unlike Parsons, he does not define pathology as that which does not conform to system values; he argues that delinquency is not the reaction to exclusion from these values, nor is it a problem of faulty socialization. Existing values and practices are absurd standards because they do not provide youth with what they need to grow and mature:

> As was predictable, most of the authorities and all of the public spokesmen explain it (delinquency) by saying there has been a failure of socialization. They say that background conditions have interrupted socialization and must be improved. And, not enough effort has been made to guarantee belonging, there must be better bait for punishment.
>
> But perhaps there has *not* been a failure of communication. Perhaps the social message has been communicated clearly to the young men and is unacceptable.
>
> In this book I shall, therefore, take the opposite tack and ask, "Socialization to what? to what dominant society and available culture?" And if this question is asked, we must at once ask the other question, "Is the harmonious organization to which the young are inadequately socialized, perhaps against human nature, or not worthy of human nature, and *therefore* there is difficulty in growing up?"[8]

The conflict theorist invariably questions the legitimacy of existing practices and values;

the order theorist accepts them as the standard of health. . . .

The order and conflict models represent polar ideal types which are not consistently found in the inconsistent ideologies of actual social research and political practice. If the models have any utility to social scientists, it will be in making more explicit and systematic the usually implicit value assumptions which underlie their categories of thinking. In this paper as an exercise in the use of conflict-order models, I examine some of the normative assumptions which can be found in the approach of the sociologist and the political liberal to the Negro question. My thinking is intentionally speculative. I am not trying to summarize the vast literature on race relations, but merely showing the existence of an order pattern.

LIBERALS AND SOCIOLOGISTS ON THE AMERICAN NEGRO: A CONTEMPORARY ADAPTATION OF ORDER THEORY

Contemporary liberalism has been popularly associated with a conflict model of society; actually it is a variant of conservative order theory. Within the model, conflict is translated to mean institutionalized (reconciled) conflict or competition for similar goals within the same system. Conflict as confrontation of opposed groups and values, conflict as a movement toward basic change of goals and social structures is anathema.

The liberal tendency of American sociology and the essentially conservative character of contemporary liberalism are particularly marked in the sociological analysis of the Negro question. In the field of race relations, an order model can be detected in (1) consensual assumptions about man and society: the "oversocialized" man and the plural society; (2) a selective pattern of interpretation which follows from these assumptions: (*a*) the explanation of the problem as a moral dilemma and its solution as one requiring adjustment through socialization and social control; (*b*) the explanation of the minority group

8 Paul Goodman, *Growing Up Absurd* (New York: Random House, 1960), p. 11.

as a reaction-formation to exclusion from middle-class life; (c) an emphasis on concepts useful in the explanation of order (shared values as opposed to economic and political differences); an emphasis on concepts useful in the explanation of disorder or anomy within an accepted order (status competition rather than class conflict, problems of inadequate means rather than conflicting goals).

THE LIBERAL VIEW OF MAN: EGALITARIAN WITHIN AN ELITIST, CONSENSUAL FRAMEWORK: ALL MEN ARE SOCIALIZABLE TO THE AMERICAN CREED

No one can see an ideological assumption as clearly as a political opponent. Rightist and leftist alike have attacked the liberal concept of man implicit in the analysis of the Negro question: conservatives because it is egalitarian, radicals because it is elitist and equated with a dominant ideology. The rightist believes in natural inequality; the leftist in positive, historical differences between men; the liberal believes in the power of socialization and conversion.

A certain egalitarianism is indeed implied in at least two liberal assertations: (1) Negroes along with other men share a common human nature socializable to the conditions of society; (2) their low position and general inability to compete reflect unequal opportunity and inadequate socialization to whatever is required to succeed within the American system. These assertations are, in a sense, basically opposed to the elitist-conservative argument that the Negro has failed to compete because he is naturally different or has voluntarily failed to take full advantage of existing opportunities.[9]

The conservative, however, exaggerates liberal egalitarianism; it is tempered with elitism. Equality is won by conformity to a dominant set of values and behavior. Equality means equal opportunity to achieve the same American values; in other words, equality is gained by losing one identity and conforming at some level to another demanded by a dominant group. As a leftist, J. P. Sartre has summarized this liberal view of man, both egalitarian and elitist. What he has termed the "democratic" attitude toward the Jew applies well to the American "liberal" view of the Negro:

The Democrat, like the scientist, fails to see the particular case; to him the individual is only an ensemble of universal traits. It follows that his defense of the Jews saves the latter as a man and annihilates him as a Jew . . . he fears that the Jew will acquire a consciousness of Jewish collectivity. . . . "There are no Jews," he says, "there is no Jewish question." This means that he wants to separate the Jew from his religion, from his family, from his ethnic community, in order to plunge him into the democratic crucible whence he will emerge naked and alone, an individual and solitary particle like all other particles.[10]

The conservative would preserve a Negro identity by pronouncing the Negro different (inferior), the radical by proclaiming him part of the superior vanguard of the future society; but the liberal would transform him altogether by turning him into another American, another individual competing in an orderly fashion for cars, television sets, and identification with the American Creed. In their attack on the liberal definition of man, the conservative and leftist agree on one thing: the liberal seems to deny basic differences between groups. At least differences are reconcilable within a consensual society.

THE LIBERAL SOCIETY: STRUCTURAL PLURALISM WITHIN A CONSENSUAL FRAMEWORK

Thus, the liberal fate of minorities, including Negroes, is basically containment through

---

[9] For a conservative argument, see, among many others, Carleton Putnam, *Race and Reason* (Washington, D.C.: Public Affairs Press, 1961).

[10] Jean-Paul Sartre, *Anti-Semite and Jew*, trans. George J. Becker (New York: Grove Press, 1962), pp. 56–57.

socialization to dominant values. Supposedly this occurs in a plural society where some differences are maintained. But liberal pluralism like liberal egalitarianism allows differences only within a consensual framework. This applies both to the liberal ideal and the sociological description: the plural-democratic society *is* the present society.

This consensual pluralism should be carefully distinguished from the conflict variety. J. S. Furnivall has called the once colonially dominated societies of tropical Asia plural in the latter sense:

In Burma, as in Java, probably the first thing that strikes the visitor is the medley of peoples— European, Chinese, Indian, native. It is in the strictest sense a medley, for they mix but do not combine. Each group holds to its own religion, its own culture and language, its own ideas and ways. As individuals they meet, but only in the marketplace, in buying and selling. There is plural society, with different sections of the community living side by side, but separately, within the same political unit. Even in the economic sphere there is a division along racial lines.[11]

For Furnivall, a plural society has no common will, no common culture. Order rests on political force and economic expediency. For liberals and sociologists, American society has a common social will (the American Creed). Order rests on legitimate authority and consensus. The whole analysis of the Negro question has generally been predicated on this belief that American society, however plural, is united by consensus on certain values. Gunnar Myrdal's influential interpretation of the Negro question has epitomized the social will thesis:

Americans of all national origins, classes, regions, creeds, and colors, have something in common: a social ethos, a political creed. . . . When the American Creed is once detected the cacophony becomes a melody . . . as principles which ought to rule, the Creed has been made conscious to everyone in American society. . . . America is continuously struggling

[11] J. S. Furnivall, *Colonial Policy and Practice* (London: Cambridge University Press, 1948), p. 304.

for its soul. The cultural unity of the nation is sharing of both the consciousness of sin and the devotion to high ideals.[12]

In what sense can a consensual society be plural? It cannot tolerate the existence of separate cultural segments. Robin M. Williams in a recent book on race relations writes: "The United States is a plural society which cannot settle for a mosaic of separate cultural segments, nor for a caste system."[13] Norman Podhoretz, a political liberal who has written often on the Negro question has stated the issue more bluntly. In his review of Ralph Ellison's *Shadow and the Act*, a series of essays which poses a threat of conflict pluralism by asserting the positive and different "cultural" characteristics of Negroes, Podhoretz states his consensual realism:

The vision of a world in which many different groups live together on a footing of legal and social equality, each partaking of a broad general culture and yet maintaining its own distinctive identity: this is one of the noble dreams of the liberal tradition. Yet the hard truth is that very little evidence exists to suggest that such a pluralistic order is possible. Most societies throughout history have simply been unable to suffer the presence of distinctive groups among them; and the fate of minorities has generally been to disappear, either through being assimilated into the majority, or through being expelled, or through being murdered.[14]

The liberal and the sociologist operating with an order ideology positively fear the conflict type of pluralism. As Sartre rightly observed, the liberal who is himself identified with the establishment, although avowedly the friend of the minority, suspects any sign of militant minority consciousness. He wants the minority to share in American human nature and compete like an individual along with other individuals for the same values. As Podhoretz has observed, pluralism

[12] Gunnar Myrdal, *An American Dilemma* (New York: Harper & Bros., 1944), pp. 3–4.

[13] Robin M. Williams, Jr., *Strangers Next Door* (Englewood Cliffs, N.J.: Prentice-Hall, Inc., 1964), p.386.

[14] Norman Podhoretz, "The Melting-Pot Blues," *Washington Post*, October 25, 1964.

never really meant the co-existence of quite different groups:

> For the traditional liberal mentality conceives of society as being made up not of competing economic classes and ethnic groups, but rather of competing *individuals* who confront a neutral body of law and a neutral institutional complex.[15]

How then can ethnic groups be discussed within the plural but consensual framework? They must be seen as separate but assimilated (contained) social structures. Among sociologists, Milton Gordon has been most precise about this pluralism as a description of ethnic groups in American society.

> Behavioral assimilation or acculturation has taken place in America to a considerable degree. . . . Structural assimilation, then, has turned out to be the rock on which the ships of Anglo-conformity and the melting pot have foundered. To understand that behavioral assimilation (or acculturation) without massive structural intermingling in primary relationships has been the dominant motif in the American experience of creating and developing a nation out of diverse peoples is to comprehend the most essential sociological fact of that experience. It is against the background of "structural pluralism" that strategies of strengthing inter-group harmony, reducing ethnic discrimination and prejudice, and maintaining the rights of both those who stay within and those who venture beyond their ethnic boundaries must be thoughtfully devised.[16]

Clearly then the liberal vocabulary of race relations is predicated on consensual assumptions about the nature of man and society. The order explanation of the Negro problem and its solution may be summarized as follows:

1. *An order or consensual model of society.*—American society is interpreted as a social system unified at its most general level by acceptance of certain central political,

social, and economic values. Thus, the Negro population is said to have been acculturated to a somewhat vaguely defined American tradition; at the most, Negro society is a variant or a reaction to that primary tradition.

2. *Social problems as moral problems of anomy or social disorganization within the American system.*—Social problems and deviant behavior arise from an imbalance between goals and means. The problems of the Negro are created by unethical exclusion from equal competition for American goals.

3. *The response to anomy: social amelioration as adjustment and extension of social control.*—Liberal solutions imply further institutionalization of the American Creed in the opportunity structure of society and, therefore, the adjustment of the deviant to legitimate social roles.

THE RACE QUESTION AS A MORAL DILEMMA

A familiar expression of liberal-consensualism is Gunnar Myrdal's interpretation of the American race question as a moral dilemma. According to this thesis, racial discrimination and its varied effects on the Negro—the development of plural social structures, high rates of social deviation, etc.—reflect a kind of anomy in the relationship between the American Creed and social structure. Anomy means a moral crisis arising from an incongruity between legitimate and ethical social goals (for example, success and equality of opportunity) and socially available opportunities to achieve these goals. American society is good and ethical, but anomic because the American Creed of equality has not been fully institutionalized; the ethic is widely accepted in theory but not in practice.

Sidney Hook as a political liberal has likewise insisted that American society is essentially ethical and that the Negro problem should be discussed in these ethical terms:

> Of course, no society has historically been organized on the basis of ethical principles, but I

---

[15] Norman Podhoretz, as quoted in "Liberalism and the American Negro—a Round-Table Discussion," with James Baldwin, Nathan Glazer, Sidney Hook, Gunnar Myrdal, and Norman Podhoretz (moderator), *Commentary* XXXVII (March, 1964), 25–26.

[16] Milton Gordon, "Assimilation in America: Theory and Reality," *Daedalus,* XC (Spring, 1961), 280, 283.

don't think we can understand how any society functions without observing the operation of of the ethical principles within it. And if we examine the development of American society, we certainly can say that we have made *some* progress, to be sure, but progress nevertheless— by virtue of the extension of our ethical principles to institutional life. If we want to explain the progress that has been made in the last twenty years by minority groups in this country—not only the Negroes, but other groups as well—I believe we have to take into account the effect of our commitment to democracy, imperfect though it may be.[17]

THE SOLUTION: WORKING WITHIN THE SYSTEM

The liberal solution to the racial question follows from the American-dilemma thesis: the belief in the ethical nature and basic legitimacy of American institutions. Amelioration, therefore, becomes exclusively a question of adjustment within the system; it calls for administrative action: how to attack anomy as the imbalance of goals and means. The administrator accepts the goals of his organization and treats all problems as errors in administration, errors which can be rectified without changing the basic framework of the organization. Karl Mannheim has aptly characterized the bureaucratic and administrative approach to social problems. What he says about the perspective of the Prussian bureaucrat applies only too well to his counterpart in American society:

> The attempt to hide all problems of politics under the cover of administration may be explained by the fact that the sphere of activity of the official exists only within the limits of laws already formulated. Hence the genesis or the development of law falls outside the scope of his activity. As a result of his socially limited horizon, the functionary fails to see that behind every law that has been made there lie the socially fashioned interests and the *Weltanschauungen* of a specific social group. He takes it for granted that the specific order prescribed by the concrete law is equivalent to order in

general. He does not understand that every rationalized order is only one of many forms in which socially conflicting irrational forces are reconciled.[18]

The liberal administrator's solution to the Negro question entails the expansion of opportunities for mobility within the society and socialization of the deviant (the Negro and the anti-Negro) to expanding opportunities. Hence, the importance of education and job training; they are prime means to success and higher status. Given the assumption that the American Creed is formally embodied in the political structure, the liberal also looks to legislation as an important and perhaps sole means of reenforcing the Creed by legitimizing changes in the American opportunity structure.

NEGRO LIFE AS A REACTION FORMATION

Another important deduction has followed from the assumption of the political and cultural assimilation of the American Negro: whatever is different or distinct in his life style represents a kind of negative reaction to exclusion from the white society. The Negro is the creation of the white. Like the criminal he is a pathology, a reaction-formation to the problem of inadequate opportunities to achieve and to compete in the American system.

Myrdal states:

> The Negro's entire life and, consequently, also his opinions on the Negro problem are, in the main, to be considered as secondary reactions to more primary pressures from the side of the dominant white majority.[19]

More recently Leonard Broom has echoed the same opinion:

> Negro life was dominated by the need to adjust to white men and to take them into account at every turn. . . . Taken as a whole, the two

---

[17] Sidney Hook, "Liberalism and the American Negro— a Round-Table Discussion," *Commentary* XXXVII (March, 1964), p. 31,

[18] Karl Mannheim, *Ideology and Utopia* (New York: Harcourt, Brace & World, 1936), p. 118.

[19] Gunnar Myrdal as quoted by Ralph Ellison, "An American Dilemma: A Review," in *Shadow and the Act* (New York: Random House, 1964), p. 315.

cultures have more common than distinctive elements. Over the long run, their convergence would seem inevitable. . . . Because Negro life is so much affected by poverty and subservience, it is hard to find distinctive characteristics that can be positively evaluated. In the stereotype, whatever is admirable in Negro life is assumed to have been adopted from the white man, while whatever is reprehensible is assumed to be inherently Negro.[20]

CONFLICT THEORIST LOOKS AT ORDER THEORIST LOOKING AT THE NEGRO

A liberal order model—consensual pluralism, with its corollary approach to the race question as moral dilemma and reaction-formation— colors the sociological analysis of the race question. It is interesting that the fundamental assumption about consensus on the American Creed has rarely been subjected to adequate empirical test.[21] Lacking any convincing evidence for the order thesis, I can only wonder who the sociologist is speaking for. He may be speaking for himself in that his paradigm answers the question of how to solve the Negro problem without changing basic economic and political institutions. He probably speaks least of all for the Negro. The liberal sociologists will have some difficulty describing the world from the viewpoint of Negro "rioters" in Los Angeles and other cities. In any case, he will not agree with anyone who believes (in fact or in ideology) that the Negro may have a separate and self-determining identity. Such a view suggests conflict and would throw doubt on the fixations of consensus, anomy, and reaction-formation.

Conflict interpretations are minority interpretations by definition. They are rarely expressed either by sociologists or by ethnic minorities. However, a few such interpretations can be mentioned to imply that the end of ideology and, therefore, the agreement on total ideology has not yet arrived.

[20] Leonard Broom, *The Transformation of the American Negro* (New York: Harper & Row, 1965), pp. 22–23.

[21] For a recent attempt to test the American dilemma thesis see Frank R. Westie, "The American Dilemma: An Empirical Test," *American Sociological Review*, XXX (August, 1965), 527–38.

Ralph Ellison, speaking from a conflict and nationalistic perspective, has made several salient criticisms of the liberal American dilemma thesis. He has argued that Myrdal's long discussion of American values and conclusion of multiple causality have conveniently avoided the inconvenient question of power and control in American society.

All this, of course, avoids the question of power *and* the question of who manipulates that power. Which to us seems more of a stylistic maneuver than a scientific judgment. . . . Myrdal's stylistic method is admirable. In presenting his findings he uses the American ethos brilliantly to disarm all American social groupings, by appealing to their stake in the American Creed, and to locate the psychological barriers between them. But he also uses it to deny the existence of an American class struggle, and with facile economy it allows him to avoid admitting that actually there exist two American moralities, kept in balance by social science.[22]

Doubting the thesis of consensus, Ellison is also in a position to attack Mydral's interpretation of the American Negro as a reaction-formation, and assimilation to the superior white society as his only solution.

But can a people (its faith in an idealized American Creed notwithstanding) live and develop for over three hundred years simply by reacting? Are American Negroes simply the creation of white men, or have they at least helped to create themselves out of what they found around them? Men have made a way of life in caves and upon cliffs, why cannot Negroes have made a life upon the horns of the white men's dilemma?

Myrdal sees Negro culture and personality simply as the product of a "social pathology." Thus he assumes that "it is to the advantage of American Negroes as individuals and as a group to become assimilated into American culture, to acquire the traits held in esteem by the dominant white American." This, he admits, contains the value premise that "*here in America*, American culture is 'highest' in the pragmatic sense. . . ." Which aside from implying that Negro culture is not also American, assumes that Negroes should desire nothing better than what whites consider highest. But in the "pragmatic" sense lynching and Holly-

[22] Ralph Ellison, *Shadow and the Act, op. cit.*, p. 315.

wood, faddism and radio advertising are products of "higher" culture, and the Negro might ask, "Why, if my culture is pathological, must I exchange it for these?"

. . . What is needed in our country is not an exchange of pathologies, but a change of the basis of society.[23]

CONCLUSION

The hostile action of Negro masses destroying white property is perhaps a more convincing demonstration of conflict theory than the hopes of Negro intellectuals. But as a sociologist I am not really interested in raising the question of whether a conflict definition of the race question is more correct than the more familiar order model. Each view is correct in a normative and practical sense insofar as it conforms to a viable political and social experience. What indeed is a correct interpretation of the Negro problem or any social problem? The answer has as much to do with consensus as with correspondence to the facts. Normative theories are not necessarily affected by empirical evidence because they seek to change or to maintain the world, not describe it.

Whenever there is genuine conflict between groups and interpretations, correctness clearly becomes a practical matter of power and political persuasion. This seems to be the situation today, and one can expect more heated debate. If conflict continues to increase between whites and Negroes in the United States, the liberal sociologist studying the "Negro problem" had better arm himself with more than his questionnaire. A militant Negro respondent may take him for the social problem, the sociologist as an agent of white society and the scientific purveyor of order theory and containment policy.

This clash of perspectives would be an illustration of my general argument: explanations of the Negro question or any other social problem invariably involve normative theory, values, ideologies, or whatever one may care to call the subjective categories of our thinking about society. Concepts of deviation and social

[23] *Ibid.*, pp. 316–17.

problems can be discussed only in the context of some social (and therefore contestable) standard of health, conformity, and the good society. Terms like "moral dilemma," "pluralism," "assimilation," "integration" describe motives for desirable action: they are definitions placed on human action, not the action itself independent of social values.

The error of the sociologist is not that he thinks politically and liberally about his society, but that he is not aware of it. Awareness may help him avoid some of the gross errors of myopia: (1) mistaking his own normative categories for "objective" fact; thus, the liberal sociologist may mistake his belief in the consensual society for actual consensus; (2) projecting a normative theory appropriate to the experience of one group on to another group; this is what Ellison means when he says that the liberal sociologist is not necessarily speaking for the Negro. Indeed, the errors of myopia are perhaps greatest whenever the middle-class sociologist presumes to describe the world and motivation of persons in lower status. Seeing the lower-class Negro within a white liberal vocabulary may be very realistic politics, but it is not very accurate sociology.

Once the sociologist is involved in the study of anything that matters, he has the unavoidable obligation of at least distinguishing his vocabulary from that of the groups he is supposedly observing rather than converting. As a scientist, he must find out what perspectives are being employed, where they are operating in the society, and with what effect. Perhaps this awareness of competing perspectives occurs only in the actual process of conflict and debate. Unfortunately, this is not always the situation within an increasingly professionalized sociology. The more professionalized the field, the more standardized the thinking of sociologists and the greater the danger of internal myopia passing for objectivity. But outside sociology debate is far from closed; conflict and order perspectives are simultaneously active on every controversial social issue. The liberal order model may not long enjoy uncontested supremacy.

part two

Comparative
Perspectives

While there has been a dramatic surge of academic interest in the field of racial and ethnic relations during the last few decades, a salient feature of the research conducted by American scholars has been its ethnocentrism. Research and teaching in racial and ethnic relations have focused almost exclusively on the domestic scene alone. A review of intergroup research compiled in 1964 showed that 89 percent of the projects reported had been limited to research in the United States.[1] The content of *minority groups* courses has been limited in the same way, according to Peter Rose. From his survey of race relations courses, he concluded that those "which are truly cross-cultural are few and far between."[2] Richard J. Ossenberg, whose article is included in this section, notes that a similar deficiency has characterized the analysis of Canadian pluralism.

There are several reasons for this paucity of comparative research in majority-minority relations, most of which are applicable to Canada as well as to the United States. The American experience has been characterized by continuous and pervasive racial and ethnic contact involving a multiplicity of groups. Because of the large number of contact situations and the differences as well as the similarities that have character-

[1] R. A. Schermerhorn, *Comparative Ethnic Relations: A Framework for Theory and Research* (New York: Random House, 1970), p. 9.
[2] Peter I. Rose, *The Subject Is Race: Traditional Ideologies and the Teaching of Race Relations* (New York: Oxford University Press, 1968), p. 95.

ized them, the American milieu has provided an excellent laboratory from which to derive, and in which to test, generalizations regarding the nature of intergroup relations. Easy accessibility to diverse case studies of majority-minority relations may have contributed to a general disinclination to look abroad. Another factor in social scientific ethnocentrism has been the posture of the United States in world affairs. Until recently, America's experience with minority groups was exclusively domestic, since this nation had not undertaken colonial commitments comparable to those of most of the European powers.[3] Finally, because majority-minority relations in this country have had such important political and social ramifications, much social scientific research has been narrowly problem-oriented. Descriptive studies that would aid in the immediate reduction of conflict or the solution of existing "problems" have been priority items, and attempts to develop conceptual and theoretical models that possess broader applicability have been slighted.

In a sense, this book conforms to the general pattern we have criticized. Most of the articles contained herein deal with minority situations in the United States alone. And although we have attempted to place each article in a broader conceptual framework, many are devoted primarily to exposing and solving problems, rather than to the development of theory. Yet, as stated previously, we feel that for an adequate understanding of the dynamics of racial and ethnic relations in the United States—including progress toward the solution of social problems—a theoretical perspective is imperative. A comparative perspective, on the other hand, can inform both theory and the analysis of practical problems. If the study of intergroup relations is to advance in depth and sophistication, it must escape the insularity that has typified it for many years.

One important component of theory-building, particularly in a field in which theory has not been strongly emphasized, is the development of new hypotheses. The use of several cultural and social contexts from which to generate hypotheses not only provides a wider variety of data but also contributes to establishment of theoretical models on a more general and universal level. In Part One, Barth and Noel, and Lieberson all presented explicitly cross-cultural conceptual frameworks. The value of each analysis increases with the range of its applicability, for the explanatory power of theory is dependent upon the number and variety of intergroup contact situations illumined as well as the quality of the insights provided.

Edna Bonacich's lead article in this section, "A Theory of Middleman Minorities," exemplifies the value of a comparative perspective in the development of theory. She maintains that a particular type of minority group, a *middleman* minority, is found within many societies. The groups begin as "sojourners in the territories to which they move." There,

---

[3] Pierre L. van den Berghe, *Race and Racism: A Comparative Perspective* (New York: John Wiley & Sons, 1967), p. 8.

they usually occupy middleman positions between elites and masses and perform important economic functions within the host societies. Bonacich assesses the impact of additional variables in the creation of these middle groups—for example, the culture and goals of the minority groups and the hostility directed against them (from lower as well as higher status levels). In the study of majority-minority relations, attention is usually directed to the most oppressed subordinate groups; Bonacich's essay is a useful reminder, then, of the crucial role of another minority category. Obviously, the cross-cultural applicability of her discussion greatly enhances its value.

A closely related function of comparative research is to provide opportunities for testing, as well as deriving, conceptual models. The contributions of Barth and Noel, Noel, and Lieberson in Part One can be analyzed in this manner. Noel, for instance, asserts that ethnocentrism, competition, and differential power comprise the necessary and sufficient ingredients for the emergence of ethnic stratification in a given society. While he demonstrates the validity of this proposition in the case of the origins of American slavery, its applicability to the etiology of a wider range of majority-minority situations remains problematic.[4] Three articles in this section—Ulč's discussion of Czechoslovakia, Ossenberg's analysis of French Canada, and Moore's examination of Northern Ireland—provide opportunities to assess the utility of Noel's thesis, as they describe the emergence of ethnic stratification in three diverse societies.

In addition to the desire for greater conceptual sophistication in the analysis of majority-minority relations, there is the practical and urgent need to comprehend the often baffling turmoil that characterizes the American scene. Here again, a comparative perspective may be useful. In the words of Shibutani and Kwan, "Precisely because we want to understand what is happening in this country, it is desirable for us to get outside of it, since by seeing things in a broader perspective we can gain a far better comprehension of ourselves."[5] Bonacich's article, for example, suggests that the sojourner role, with its attendant economic impact, may at least partially explain the differential treatment accorded Blacks, on the one hand, and middleman (but also non-White) Japanese and Chinese, on the other, in the United States. It also indicates parallels between American Jews, Greeks, and Armenians—White middleman minorities—and the Oriental-American groups. (See, in Part Four, the following analyses of American minority groups: Sklare's article on Jews, Strodtbeck's comparison of Jews and Italians, and Lyman's discussion of Japanese and Chinese.)

---

[4] For an application of Noel's model to emergence of Mexican American subordination in Texas, see Dale S. McLemore, "The Origins of Mexican American Subordination in Texas, *Social Science Quarterly* 53 (March 1973): 656–670.

[5] Tamotsu Shibutani and Kian M. Kwan, *Ethnic Stratification: A Comparative Approach* (New York: Macmillan, 1965), p. 23.

Use of cross-cultural materials raises salient questions: What is unique to majority-minority situations in the United States, and what in these relationships is common to other nations and contexts? Are the movements occurring here also prominent around the globe? What is the international impact of events in the United States, and what is the impact of international events upon the United States? Are the models with which social scientists have conceptualized intergroup relations in this country applicable to other situations? What are some of the solutions to majority-minority conflict that have been sought elsewhere, and what have been their results? While these questions cannot be definitively answered here, they indicate some of the practical, as well as theoretical, gains that await the wider use of the comparative method in the study of intergroup conflict. The remainder of this introduction examines certain thematic trends in the comparative literature of majority-minority relations reflected in the articles in this section.

Race, traditionally one of the central categories in the study of majority-minority relations, has been described previously as an extremely loose, ambiguous concept. It is important to emphasize that racial designations are arbitrary and artificial; they serve the function of isolating and separating certain groups of people in a society based on an arbitrary selection of physical and biologically transmitted characteristics. We have distinguished *racial* from *ethnic* in that the latter refers to cultural characteristics, which may be perpetuated through several generations by socialization to prevailing cultural patterns but not by heredity (see the introduction to Part One).

Closely allied to the concept of race is that of *caste,* which refers to a particular system of separated groups within a social structure. Berreman has defined a caste system as "a hierarchy of endogamous divisions in which membership is hereditary and permanent."[6] Caste may be conceptualized as occupying one end of a continuum, its polar opposite being class. The distinction between them is that the former is, by definition, permanent and fixed, while the latter permits social mobility. While one's caste membership is ascribed, one "gets his class membership by achievement; by manifesting the criteria of membership, such as education, wealth, or a type of occupation";[7] and by surrendering any negatively sanctioned cultural characteristics that might exist, such as "peculiar" religious, dietary, or clothing habits. Tumin has observed, however, that pure caste and class systems do not exist; no systems are totally closed or totally open.[8]

[6] Gerald D. Berreman, "Caste in India and the United States," *Social Stratification in the United States,* ed. Jack L. Roach, Llewellyn Gross, and Orville Gursslin (Englewood Cliffs, N.J.: Prentice-Hall, 1969), p. 226. Italics omitted.
[7] Melvin M. Tumin, ed., *Introduction to Comparative Perspectives on Race Relations* (Boston: Little, Brown, 1969), p. 14.
[8] *Ibid.*

Racial differentiation may form the basis for construction of a caste system. However, caste distinctions are often made among groups on a basis other than hereditary physical (i.e. racial) characteristics. The Buraku (Eta) of Japan occupy a pariah position in that society, and their perceived undesirable characteristics are attributed to biological inheritance, yet no physical differences can be discerned between them and upper-caste individuals. Therefore, while it is inaccurate in the strictest sense to describe such stratification systems in terms of race, they function in a similar manner. Thus, De Vos and Wagatsuma, on the basis of their analysis of the Japanese Buraku, have claimed that "from the viewpoint of comparative sociology or social anthropology, and from the viewpoint of human social psychology, racism and caste attitudes are one and the same phenomenon."[9] This point is relevant to the analysis of one of the world's current trouble spots, Northern Ireland, as seen in Robert Moore's article in this section. Indeed, although both Catholic and Protestant groups are white, the conflict between them is often described in racial terms.

It is important that the search for regularities in intergroup relations cross-culturally not be permitted to obscure differences that may be more substantial. By the same token, superficial differences have often been overemphasized. Although slave systems undoubtedly varied somewhat throughout the Americas, more important than these differences are the underlying similarities characteristic of slavery wherever it has been established. Similarly, in his discussion of caste, Berreman disputes the idea that the caste systems of India and the United States differ substantially. "The essential similarity lies in the fact that the function of the rules in both cases is to maintain the caste system with institutionalized inequality as its fundamental feature."[10] The criterion of caste in India is religion, while in the United States it is color; but this difference is not overriding. "The crucial fact is that caste status is determined, and therefore the systems are perpetuated, by birth: Membership in them is ascribed and unalterable."[11] Berreman also disputes the notion that in India the caste system is accepted on all levels without conflict and complaint. This is the idealized view, promulgated by those of relatively high rank. The equivalents in this country are the southern White who asserts, "Our Negroes are happy," and the northern White who proudly boasts, "We have no problems here."

Different societies assign widely divergent social meanings to the visibly perceived dissimilarities between peoples. Race—meaning recognizable, inherited physical characteristics—does not always function as a criterion of caste; sometimes it is defined in terms of class. Pitt-Rivers's

[9] George De Vos and Hiroshi Wagatsuma, *Japan's Invisible Race: Caste in Culture and Personality* (Berkeley: University of California Press, 1966), p. xx. Emphasis added.
[10] Berreman, *Social Stratification,* p. 228.
[11] *Ibid.*

article in this section, "Race, Color, and Class in Central America and the Andes," illustrates this point. In Latin America, skin color is but one of several indices that constitute one's social position. While darker people generally occupy lower status positions than those of light skin, prominent men of predominantly Black and/or Indian ancestry are not infrequent. "Color is an ingredient, not a determinant of class. It can, therefore, be traded for the other ingredients." While it cannot be changed in one lifetime, it may be altered in the next generation; thus, the wives of the wealthy are generally lighter and have more "European" features than their husbands.

Pitt-Rivers notes that while certain terms are common to both the United States and Latin America, their usage varies greatly between the two areas. In Latin America, the word *Indian* denotes culture and membership in an Indian community, rather than color, while in this country "blood" quantum is the primary consideration,[12] A person called *Negro* in Georgia or Michigan might be a *White* in Peru. On the other hand, dark-hued Panamanians apply the word *Negro* only to Jamaicans, who are distinguished by their English speech and Protestant religion. Pitt-Rivers therefore urges caution in making blanket statements applicable to Latin-American "race" relations as a whole.

> Physical differences can never be obliterated, but whether they, rather than cultural or social differences, are regarded as significant is a matter each social system decides for itself. It is for this reason that the value accorded to physical appearance varies so greatly from place to place and class to class in Latin America.

He concludes, however, with the prediction that as Latin American society becomes more open—that is, as urbanization increases and isolation breaks down—the social impact of color will also change. With an enormous influx of Indians to the cities, a large, dark-skinned, urban proletariat is forming. Formerly, family background could outweigh color as a determinant of class and status. Now, however, in a mass society, "appearance takes over the function of descent in allocating social status. In a world in flux, the fact that appearance cannot be dissimulated recommends it above all other indicators." Thus, in contrast to certain other areas of the world, color is becoming more significant in Latin America, rather than less.

If social stratification in Latin America is not based primarily upon race, a stark contrast is provided by the caste system of South Africa. In

[12] In North America, Indian self-identification is more like that of Latin America, in contrast to the North American White emphasis on blood. Among the Oglala Sioux, for example, cultural criteria alone determine whether one is a *Mixedblood* or a *Fullblood*. See Murray L. Wax, Rosalie H. Wax, and Robert V. Dumont, Jr., *Formal Education in an American Indian Community*, Monograph No. 1, The Society of Social Problems (Supplement, *Social Problems* 11, no. 4, 1964).

the words of Colin Legum, author of "Color and Power in the South African Situation" (the third article in this section):

> Color is the sole determinant of power in South Africa. . . . South Africa's power structure is specifically designed to ensure that total power remains exclusively in the hands of three million whites. It not only provides for the whites' security, but also enables them to retain their position of economic and social privilege over a colored majority of thirteen millions.

Rather than being gradually deemphasized, as in many other societies, race awareness is consciously fanned and heightened; for the "irrational force of prejudice is harnessed to the rational purpose of maintaining a system of discrimination to ensure the survival of a status quo based on color."

Another article in this section offers a further contrast in societal definition of race. Otto Ulč reports that although Gypsies in Czechoslovakia are of "pure Aryan origin," they were selected, along with the Jews, for extermination in Nazi concentration camps in World War II. According to Ulč, they are conceived by Czechs and Slovaks to comprise another race; indeed, Ulč's own terminology follows racial categories, as he contrasts the Gypsies to "Whites." Discrimination and prejudicial attitudes very closely parallel the relationships between White and Black in the United States. According to Ulč's description, Gypsies occupy a pariah status and are treated by their fellow citizens as a lower caste.

Conversely, the official government ideology is assimilationist. It is critical of Whites who publicly exhibit prejudice and discrimination. However, "the stand of the [national] press is not so much the condemnation of racial bias as the defense of the integrated Gypsy." Yet the "integrated Gypsy" is a marginal man, cut off from his roots but still unacceptable to the dominant group. Thus, a disjunction exists between the essentially caste ideology of the citizenry and the class ideology of the government. The result is official satisfaction that racism—especially as contrasted with the United States—is absent within the nation, despite the reality of racially-based oppression that must be constantly endured by the minority group.

The last two articles to be discussed, Richard J. Ossenberg's "Social Pluralism in Quebec: Continuity, Change and Conflict" and Robert Moore's "Race Relations in the Six Countries: Colonialism, Industrialization, and Stratification in Northern Ireland," present fascinating contrasts, in comparison with each other as well as in comparison with other articles in Part Two discussing ethnic groups. In French Canada and Northern Ireland, each minority group derives from the same racial stock as its respective dominant group, but differs in national origin and religious belief. In Quebec, language is also a salient issue. Like the situation in South Africa, the situations in Canada and Ireland have been strongly shaped by British colonialism. In Canada, the minority group is widely divided by social class differences that have prevented unified political action; in Northern Ireland, the subordinate group is far less diverse, a fact that facilitates ethnic unity and inter-ethnic conflict. The most populous group within the Province of Quebec—French and Catholic— is the minority group within the nation-state of Canada, which is predominantly Protestant. At issue is Quebec's secession, which would turn the Protestants in the province into a minority. The Protestant majority group within the tiny state of Ulster fiercely maintains its independence from Catholic Ireland—at the expense of the Catholic minority in Ulster.

Ethnicity and caste, not race, are the critical factors here. However, Moore attempts to demonstrate that Catholic-Protestant relations in Ulster are, in fact, race relations. This is less confusing than it seems; Moore means by race relations what we have described as caste relations. (This is the opposite of the condition that Pitt-Rivers describes in South America, in which *actual* racial differences are accorded *class* significance.) On the other hand, ethnicity functions in a more complex manner in Quebec, with some castelike and some classlike characteristics. It should be noted that the willingness of the groups involved to surrender their unique identities would resolve the *ethnic* features of social stratification in each case. No such panacea is even remotely possible, however. In short, ethnocentrism does not depend on race *per se* to flourish; it thrives equally well on cultural, national, and religious differences.

Three themes are prominent among the host of issues raised in Part Two. First, the background of colonialism is apparent nearly everywhere. Most contemporary colonial settings have resulted from European expansion since the sixteenth century, producing a disproportionate number of situations in which Whites have dominated non-Whites. This background is crucial for a full understanding of the dynamics of Pitt-Rivers's discussion of Latin America and Legum's article on South Africa. Less publicized have been instances of European-European conquest, as in England's domination of Ireland. One European country's conquest of another European colonial power and subsequent domination of the latter's settlers is a variant found in French Canada. Conditions of colonialism or internal colonialism (see the introduction to Part One), which often create wide status gaps, are often propitious for the entry of middleman minorities—for example, the East Asians in Africa.

Second, economic considerations are crucial in every case. As Bonacich notes, a chief factor in the delicate position of middleman minorities is their pivotal economic role, which frequently places them in direct economic competition with business, labor, and their own clientele. In Latin America, race, ethnicity, and socioeconomic criteria together constitute one's social position. Although bias against Gypsies in Czechoslovakia "is socially rather than economically motivated," it is expressed in ways that have a negative economic effect upon the

Gypsies—for example, housing segregation. The Gypsies' low socio-economic status then serves the function of a self-fulfilling prophecy for members of the white majority, justifying in their eyes their prejudicial attitudes and discriminatory behavior.

The position of privilege occupied by White South Africans is maintained by their unyielding grip on all sources of economic and political power. According to Ossenberg, a differential sense of economic deprivation between working-class and middle-class French Canadians prevents the accession of a separatist government in Quebec. In Northern Ireland, economic discrimination experienced by Catholics led to civil rights agitation; this resulted in rioting in Londonderry in October of 1968, which, in turn, triggered the tragic chain of events that has since gripped Northern Ireland.[13]

One of the crucial economic needs of many formerly colonized nations is modernization, which includes the process of industrialization and the development and rationalization of a modern economy. Modernization is essential to these countries if they are to function independently and competitively in the international community.[14] But this goal is thwarted in part by the continued economic domination of the powerful nations (neocolonialism).[15] Ossenberg refers to the impact of United States' domination of the Canadian economy upon ethnic stratification in Quebec. Moore discusses industrialization in the evolution of Northern Ireland in the context of Britain's dominating economic influence. The role of American and European neocolonialism in South America[16] and economic support of racist regimes in South Africa and Rhodesia,[17] while beyond the scope of the articles in this section, is also significant.

[13] For an excellent complement to Moore's analysis, see Harold Jackson, *The Two Irelands: The Problem of the Double Minority—A Dual Study of Inter-Group Relations*, rev. ed., 1972. A pamphlet in the series published by Minority Rights Group, London.

[14] One long-range effect of modernization will be the hastened depletion of the world's natural resources. It can be hoped that the currently modernized (and therefore more powerful) nations will soon alter their economies in recognition of this fact, permitting the economically dependent countries to enter world markets competitively in a less wasteful manner. Unfortunately, little room for optimism in this matter exists. See "A Blueprint for Survival—Introduction: The Need for Change," *The Ecologist*, 2 no. 1 (January, 1972).

[15] See, for example, Ronald Segal, *The Race War* (New York: Viking Press, 1966).

[16] For example, American agribusiness interests throughout Latin America, with their emphasis on highly rationalized and mechanized production methods, are responsible for displacing thousands of rural agricultural workers each year. These people have nowhere to go but the cities, where they form the new and growing urban proletariat described by Pitt-Rivers. See George L. Baker, "Food Imperialism: Agribusiness Goes Multinational," *People and Land* 1, no. 2 (Winter, 1974), p. 10.

[17] On May 22, 1974, in what is probably an unprecedented action, 6,500 Black *and* White Alabama coal miners "walked off their jobs to protest imports of South African coal. Hundreds of miners also joined a demonstration that day in Birmingham. Ala., outside a stockholders meeting of the Southern Co., a major electric utility chain which has contracted for 500,000 tons of South African coal." In addition to protesting their own loss of jobs, the strikers specifically "expressed their solidarity with Black South African miners. . . ." "Times Are Changing," *New York Guardian*, June 12, 1974, p. 3.

The final theme in this section is the issue of ethnic and racial pluralism. The desire of minority groups to maintain and express their collective identity, in the face of dominant-group pressure to surrender their social and cultural distinctiveness, has been a major focus of majority-minority relations in recent history; it will remain so for years to come. The question of pluralism may be more intense in colonial situations than in others; as Lieberson observes in Part One, subordinate indigenous populations tend strongly to resist assimilation, or merger, more than subordinate migrant populations. Nevertheless, the issue is by no means restricted to colonial contexts. For example, according to Bonacich, middleman minorities "form highly organized communities which resist assimilation."

We may briefly distinguish between social pluralism and cultural pluralism, distinctions explored more fully in Part Four. *Social pluralism* refers to some separation between the social networks of majority group and minority group; members of the minority maintain a separate sphere of social institutions and primary relations, but participate to some extent in the secondary groups of the larger society. *Cultural pluralism* refers to the retention by the minority group of its traditional values, religion, and language, and to the behavior emanating from these cultural characteristics.

The salience of social and cultural pluralism is reflected in each article in this section. We have noted that, according to Pitt-Rivers, *Indian* in Latin America refers to a cultural community, and it is the retention of Indian *culture and identity*—not pigmentation—that invites discrimination. Ulč discusses the Czechoslovakian government's insistence that the Gypsies deny their cultural identity, a pressure that the Gypsies are tenaciously resisting. In South Africa, Legum reports, the minority group's freedom is circumscribed to the nightmarish extent of regulated contact (sexual and otherwise) between husband and wife. In each society mentioned, minority identity is not permitted free and full expression within the larger social context.

The degree of minority autonomy and distinctiveness that will be permitted to flourish will vary from society to society. The manifestation of this issue in the United States is explored in detail in Part Four and again in Part Six. In general, our point of view is that majority groups have defined minority deviancy in narrow terms and that intergroup conflict is reduced rather than exacerbated when social and cultural pluralism is given free expression. In Part Five, for example, some of the deleterious consequences of the denial of pluralism to minority groups in the United States are described. On the other hand, national survival would be impossible if group dissonance were allowed to take its natural course in some African societies.[18] Northern Ireland also illustrates the

---

[18] Schermerhorn, *Comparative Ethnic Relations*, p. 8.

difficulty of finding political solutions short of warfare to situations in which both the majority and the minority group will accept nothing less than complete maintenance of ethnic integrity and autonomy. For good or ill, however, the impact of social and cultural pluralism is being felt in nearly every part of the world. The rising pitch of minority protest throughout the world may indicate that it will be impossible for the demand for pluralism to be ignored much longer.

5

A Theory of Middleman Minorities*

EDNA BONACICH

Relations between groups of different race or ethnicity have taken a variety of forms. One role an ethnic group can play is that of a "middleman minority" (Blalock, 1967:79–84). Although the form has not been precisely defined, nor clearly labelled (other appelations include "middleman trading peoples," Becker, 1956:225–37, "migrant intermediation," Schermerhorn, 1970:74–6, "marginal trading peoples," and "permanent minorities," Stryker, 1959), there is a general consensus that a number of ethnic groups around the world have occupied a similar position in the social structure. Among these are the Jews in Europe (perhaps the epitome of the form), the Chinese in Southeast Asia, Asians in East Africa, Armenians in Turkey, Syrians in West Africa, Parsis in India, Japanese and Greeks in the United States, and so on. The parallel between such groups has been noted not only by social scientists, but in some instances by the people among whom they live, as shown in such designations as "the Jews of the East," and "the Jews of India."

Edna Bonacich is Assistant Professor of Sociology at the University of California, Riverside.

Reprinted from American Sociological Review 38 (October 1973), pp. 583–594, by permission of the author and publisher.

* I am indebted to Ivan Light for many valuable exchanges on this topic. In addition, thanks go to Robert Goodman, Leo Kuper, Barbara Laslett, David McElroy, John Modell, Martin Orans, and Pierre van den Berghe, for reading and commenting on an earlier draft.

One of the principal peculiarities of these groups is the economic role they play. In contrast to most ethnic minorities, they occupy an intermediate rather than low-status position. They tend to concentrate in certain occupations, notably trade and commerce, but also other "middleman" lines such as agent, labor contractor, rent collector, money lender, and broker. They play the role of middleman between producer and consumer, employer and employee, owner and renter, elite and masses. This accounts for Blalock's name for them; and although I shall question its applicability during the course of this paper, for ease of reference, I shall continue to use it.

The literature is not unanimous on the causes of this form. Most writers take the role as "given" and concentrate on the consequences of playing it. However, two prominent themes recur. The first sees the source of the pattern in the hostile reaction of the surrounding society to the cultural (including religious) and/or racial distinctiveness of these groups. They are pushed out of desirable occupations and forced to make a living in marginal lines. That they manage to escape the lowest rungs of the economic order, and sometimes acquire considerable wealth, is explained by their response to discrimination: a closing of ranks, the formation of solidary communities with considerable pride in group membership, and a special exertion to overcome handicaps (e.g. Kurokawa, 1970:131–3).

A second theme stresses the nature of the societies in which middleman groups are found. These are characterized by a "status gap" or marked division between elites and masses (Rinder, 1958–9). Examples include feudal societies with a gap between peasantry and landed aristocracy, or colonial societies with a gap between representatives of the imperial power and the "natives." Distinct ethnic minorities are seen to serve a number of functions in such societies.[1] First, since they are

[1] Note that Blalock extends the concept to include groups of mixed ancestry such as the Eurasians of Indonesia and mestizos of Brazil. This is an unusual usage, most writers reserving the comparison to distinct immigrant minorities. Clearly the "functional" advantages of foreignness are lost in the case

not involved in the status hang-ups of the surrounding society, they are free to trade or deal with anyone. In contrast, elites may feel that they lose status by dealing with the "masses" (Rinder, 1958–9:254). Second, their foreignness enables them to be "objective" in the marketplace; they do not have familistic ties with the rest of the society which can intrude on, and destroy business (Park, 1939:14). And third, they act as a buffer for elites, bearing the brunt of mass hostility because they deal directly with the latter. In a word, middleman minorities plug the status gap between elites and masses, acting as middlemen between the two.

This paper will present an alternative approach to middleman minorities. It develops a model which incorporates some of these ideas, but as part of a larger framework. The prevalent themes are found to be inadequate for two chief reasons. First, discrimination

and hostility against minorities usually has the effect of hurting group solidarity and pride, driving a group to the bottom rather than the middle of the social structure. How then can we explain the closing of ranks reaction of these particular groups, and their peculiar ability to create success out of hatred? (Or to cite cases, why [have] Japanese Americans been able to overcome racism, while Blacks have not?)

Second, the argument that middleman minorities arise in response to functional requisites may have merit. But it is clear these groups persist beyond the status gap. One finds them in post-colonial societies, after the elites have gone (e.g. the Chinese in Southeast Asia, Asians in East Africa, Parsis in India). And one finds them in modern industrial societies (e.g. the Indians in Britain, Jews in 20th century Germany, Chinese in New Zealand, Japanese in the United States).

Figure 1 outlines the relationship between the major variables of our theory. We shall follow the links of this diagram through the remainder of the paper.

---

of mixed-bloods. In addition, there is little evidence that Eurasians, for example, have concentrated in "middleman" occupations like trade (see van der Kroef, 1953:486–7).

FIGURE 1. *Schematic Representation of the Development and Perpetuation of the Middleman Minority Position*

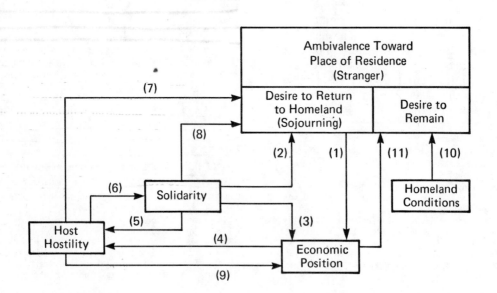

THE EFFECTS OF SOJOURNING

An empirical generalization can be formed about all the middleman groups we have examined: they begin as sojourners in the territories to which they move. They are immigrants who do not plan to settle permanently. In contrast, other ethnic minorities include indigenous peoples of colonized territories, and immigrants who are forced to sever ties with a homeland (e.g. Blacks in the new world) or choose to do so (e.g. most of the "old" European immigration to the United States, see Garis, 1927:204). While individuals may vary in initial orientation, it appears there is a general "group" orientation, undoubtedly a product of conditions in the country of emigration. Thus Loewen (1971:26–7) generalizes about an entire group:

> The early Chinese in Mississippi were not true immigrants, intending to become permanent settlers in a new homeland, but were sojourners, temporary residents in a strange country, planning to return to their homeland when their task was accomplished.

Statements of this sort abound for other middleman groups (e.g. Cator, 1936:55 on the Chinese in Indonesia; Miyamoto, 1939:85 on the Japanese in America; Mahajani, 1960:xix on the Indians in Malaya and Burma; Dotson and Dotson, 1967:81–2 on Indians in Central Africa).

The orientation of groups like Jews, Armenians, and Parsis is a bit more complicated. Certainly Jewish immigrants to the United States had no plan to return to Eastern Europe. But in all three cases there is an unusual attachment to an ancestral homeland; in the Jewish case, to Palestine. Stryker (1959:350) refers to the "continued attachment of the Parsis for their ancestral Persian home," for example. These groups are at a later stage in the cycle described by Figure 1, and their orientation toward place of residence will be taken up again later.

Sojourning is not a sufficient condition of the middleman form in that there are sojourners who do not become middlemen; but it is a necessary one, with important economic and social consequences directly related to the pattern. The economic effects (link 1) included a tendency toward thrift, and a concentration in certain occupations.

Thrift is the product of a willingness to suffer short-term deprivation to hasten the long-term objective of returning to the homeland. It is shown in excessively long hours of work, an emphasis on saving (often sending part of these savings to the homeland), and very little time or money spent on consumption. Sojourners are there to make money, not spend it, and this "future time orientation" enables them to accumulate capital. This orientation contrasts with that of settlers and "natives," who generally wish to live more rounded lives since they do not aim to live elsewhere.

Sojourning also leads the individual to select occupations which do not tie him to the territory for long periods. The sojourner wants a portable or easily liquidated livelihood. "Middleman" occupations (in the economic sense) have this characteristic, as Hoselitz points out (1963:23–4):

> [T]he capital employed by a trader or money lender turns over much faster than that used in industrial establishments. A trader may carry on his business without ever attaining property rights in the objects he deals with. If he is a broker or commission agent, he may merely lose his earnings from a transaction, but not the capital invested in it. Moreover, a money lender or banker deals in the commodity that has the widest currency, that is accepted by anyone, that can easily be transported or hidden. . . . An industrial entrepreneur usually has more property tied up in his plant for a longer time than either merchant or banker.

Middleman minorities are noteworthy for their absence from industrial entrepreneurship and investment in the kind of agriculture (e.g. cattle raising, orchards) that ties up capital. But there are other easily liquidated or transportable occupations besides trade, and these are also found among so-called "middleman" groups. Among them are the independent professions, prevalent among American Jews (Glazer and Moynihan, 1963:147); truck farming specializing in crops that have a rapid turnover, found among such diverse groups as the Chinese in New Zealand (Fong, 1959: 85), Indians in Natal (Dept. of Economics, 1961: Chapter 2), and the Japanese in California (Ichihashi, 1932:178–206); and various skilled trades, such as barbers, shoemakers, goldsmiths, jewellers, restaurant-owners, tailors, launderers, and the like, found among Armenians in Syria (Sanjian, 1965:52), Jews in Poland (Eitzen, 1971:123), and Chinese and Japanese in this country. In other words, the term "middleman minorities" is really a misnomer. The more general occupational characteristic of these groups is liquidity.[2]

The Chinese in Southeast Asia illustrate the effect of sojourning on occupational preference:

> [T]he intent of every emigrant was to work abroad in order to remit to China sums of money that would enrich his lineage when invested in land in his home village. He also intended to return home to enjoy during his old age the fruits of his arduous labours in exile. Although only a small proportion ever succeeded in this ambition, nevertheless the desire to return to China motivated the emigrants, at least at the outset, to enter a profession that would involve a minimum of fixed investment in the host country, and a maximum of liquid assets that could be returned to China (Wilmott, 1966:254).

That many sojourners do not achieve their goal of return is important, and will be dealt with later.

The principal non-economic result of sojourning is a high degree of internal solidarity (link 2). Since they plan to return, sojourners have little reason to develop lasting relationships with members of the surround-

ing host society. But they have every reason to keep deeply alive the regional and broader ethnic tie, for these relationships will persist in the future towards which the sojourner points (see Siu, 1952, for an explication of this point). Thus ethnic and regional associations are strong, mutual assistance is prevalent, and trust retained among members from the same general area. (This is not to say that sojourner communities are completely unified. On the contrary, they are often riddled with division and conflict, based on regional, linguistic, political or religious differences found in the homeland. But in relation to the host society, these differences fade before an overriding "national" unity).

In contrast, settlers have much less reason to perpetuate such ties. As Garis (1927:204) points out for the "old" immigration to the United States:

> Even though those already here objected at times to others coming in, yet once in they soon become Americans, so assimilated as to be indistinguishable from the natives; for this old immigration has consisted almost wholly of families who have come to this country with the full intention of making it their home.

Ethnic enclaves may develop among settlers out of convenience of common language; but the community tie tends to be much weaker and more likely to dissipate over time. The settler has reason to orient outwards and mix with his neighbors, while the sojourner "has no desire for full participation in the community life of his adopted land" (Siu, 1952:36).

Middleman minorities typically evince the following traits: a resistance to out-marriage, residential self-segregation, the establishment of language and cultural schools for their children, the maintenance of distinctive cultural traits (including, often, a distinctive religion), and a tendency to avoid involvement in local politics except in affairs that directly affect their group. They form highly organized communities which resist assimilation. These features, I contend are related to an orientation toward a homeland.

Communal solidarity plays an important

---

[2] Determining the liquidity or transportability of a a particular occupation may, in fact, be problematic. Undoubtedly an occupational label can encompass a variety of firms which differ in the degree to which they tie up capital. However, there is a gross difference between professionals and skilled artisans who can carry their source of income with them, and a factory owner with a major investment in heavy machinery.

role in the economic position of middleman groups (link 3). Family, regional, dialect, sect, and ultimately ethnic ties are used for preferential economic treatment. The "primordial tie" of blood provides a basis for trust, and is reinforced by multi-purpose formal and informal associations. Solidarity is interjected into economic affairs in two ways: it plays a part in the efficient distribution of resources, and helps to control internal competition. Resources distributed within the ethnic community include capital (through the use of partnerships, low interest loans, and rotating credit associations; see Desai, 1963:44–5 on Indians in Britain, and Light, 1972:23–30 on Chinese and Japanese in the United States), credit and easier terms to purchasers, information and training, and jobs and labor.

Let us concentrate on one area, the distribution of jobs and labor, for illustrative purposes. The typical middleman minority business is a family store (or truck farm), resting heavily on the use of unpaid family labor. If wage labor is needed, members of the extended family or of regional associations are preferred, and are treated like kin, sometimes living with the family behind the store. Employees work excessively long hours for low or no wages and are loyal to the owners. In exchange they are likely to become partners or to receive training and aid in setting up their own business in the same line. The middleman firm is labor-intensive but able to cut labor costs drastically through ethnically-based paternalism and thrift.

The effect of such arrangements on labor costs is shown for Japanese American laundries in San Francisco in 1909 (see Table 1). Not only did employees of Japanese firms work longer hours at less pay, but white laundry owners had to deal with a unionized work force.

The epitome of efficient distribution of resources is found in the vertical organization of a particular line, where one set of firms feeds another, within the ethnic community. Such was found in the clothing business among Jews in New York, where Jewish manufacturers sold to Jewish wholesalers who

TABLE 1. *Comparison of Labor Conditions in White, French, and Japanese Laundries, in San Francisco, 1909[a]*

	White	French	Japanese
Hours per week	49	50–63	60–72
Average wage with board and lodging per month	—	$37.69	$28.90[b]
Average wage without board and lodging per month	$69.74	$48.56	—

[a] Adapted from Millis (1915:65–6).
[b] Estimated cost of room and board for Japanese owners was $8 to $10 per month.

used Jewish retail outlets. Vertical integration exists between Indian wholesaler and retail grocers in Britain (Desai, 1963:57), and between Japanese growers, wholesalers and retailers of fruits and vegetables in Southern California before World War II (Bloom and Riemer, 1949:92–6.) Such arrangements are common among middleman minorities, and depend, in part, on the easier extension of credit within the group.[3]

Internal competition is sometimes controlled by the development of guild-like structures. Light (1972:68–70) describes a shoemakers' guild among Japanese Americans

[3] Efficient distribution of resources plus thrift have enabled middleman groups to avoid a pattern often found among disprivileged ethnic groups, i.e. debt peonage. In the early development of farming among the Japanese in California, for example, loans and credit were easily granted by suppliers of equipment, distributors of Japanese produce, and land owners, all of whom were non-Japanese (Bloom and Riemer, 1949:74). Similar arrangements have been found among black cotton farmers in the deep south (Davis, Gardner and Gardner, 1941:Chapter 15), and among the natives of Burma (Furnivall, 1956:293–4); undoubtedly crop mortgage is common around the world. Blacks and Burmans soon fell heavily into debt, the land became alienated from them, and they were reduced to a sort of serfdom. But the Japanese were able to turn the same arrangement to profit, and show a rapidly rising rate of land acquisition (Ichihashi, 1932:184, 193).

in the early part of this century which determined prices and controlled the location of shops, among other things. In the 18th century, Constantinople had seventy-two Armenian guilds (Stryker, 1959:345), while Eitzen (1971:131) records their prominence among Jewish merchants and artisans in Poland after World War 1. Chinese Chambers of Commerce serve some of the same multiple functions as guilds (e.g. Eitzen, 1971:128–9 on the Chinese in the Philippines), and both trade guilds and such chambers of commerce are found among Indians in Malaya (Sandhu, 1969:289).

In sum, middleman community organization combined with thrift, enables middleman firms to cut costs at every turn, so that they can compete effectively with other enterprises in the same line. Add to this a preference for liquidable occupations, and the result is a tremendous degree of concentration in, and domination of, certain lines of endeavor. Concentration is shown in Miyamoto's (1939:70–1) description of the Japanese in Seattle before World War II. He finds that 74 percent were in a "small shop" type of enterprise, while the community lacked a capitalist or true working class. An example of domination is provided in Table 2. In 1938 the Jews made up only five percent of the Stamford population, yet clearly dominated several business lines. Table 3 shows both concentration and domination. The degree of Chinese concentration in the "commercial" class is underestimated, in that "working class" includes employees of commercial establishments. Indeed this pattern of concentration and domination may be seen as the hallmark of "middleman minorities," and examples of it are found at various times around the world.[4] Thus in 1943, 63.6 percent of the Chinese in Jamaica were in trade compared to 2.2 percent

[4] A problem of definition can be raised: to what degree must an ethnic group be concentrated in, and dominate, certain lines before we term it a "middleman minority"? In other words, is it a discrete category or a continuum? I shall not try to deal with this problem here; but we should note that, if there is a continuum, our examples fall near the end of it.

of the total population. The Chinese made up 0.75 percent of the male wage-earning population but 22 percent of those in trade (Lind, 1958:154). In 1925, 49.3 percent of the Jews in Germany engaged in trade, commerce and peddling, compared to 9.8 percent of the rest

TABLE 2. *Comparison of Total Number of Trading and Commercial Establishments with Number Owned by Jews, for Selected Businesses, Stamford, Connecticut, 1938*[a]

	Total Number	Jewish Owned
Retail wearing apparel:		
Men's clothing stores	16	15
Children's and infants' wear	5	5
Dry goods	17	10
Women's and misses' clothing	30	22
Men's furnishings	15	13
Millineries	10	6
Corset shops	6	3
Shoe stores	19	10
Food distribution:		
Largest nonchain markets	5	5
Wholesale cattle slaughter	1	1
Wholesale produce dealers	2	2
Wholesale grocers	2	1
Butter, egg, and cheese dealers	3	2
Retail produce dealers	6	3
Wholesale meat firms	7	3
Delicatessens	9	3
Retail grocery stores	188	23
Retail package stores	51	18
Wholesale liquor dealers	7	2
Other businesses:		
Jewelry	15	13
Wholesale drug	2	2
Cut-rate cosmetics	3	2
Druggists	26	9
Furniture	25	14
Electrical supply	11	6
Hardware	11	4
Paint stores	11	3
Plumbing	5	3
Lumberyards	3	1
Department stores	7	3

[a] Adapted from Koenig (1942:210–11).

of the population (Stryker, 1959:342). In 1954, Hollingsworth (1960:1) reports that Asians in East Africa comprised one percent of the population but dominated trade. Loewen (1971:36) finds that 97 percent of the Chinese in Mississippi run grocery stores and hold a near-monopoly over the business. The list could be greatly extended. (It should be understood that domination by the group as a whole does not mean that there are no poverty-stricken members; often individuals and families do not "succeed.")

Sojourning is clearly not the only cause of the middleman form; many groups of sojourning migrant laborers do not enter small business. Almost all that do derive from Asia and the Near East. In addition, these same groups become middlemen wherever they go. Chinese, Indians, Jews, in every country show a similar occupational concentration (thus, a status gap in the receiving country cannot explain the pattern). This regularity suggests that culture of origin is an important contributory factor.

Nevertheless, sojourning is necessary to this form, as two facts demonstrate. First, the bulk of middleman minority members are not small businessmen in their homelands; they usually emanate from more deprived classes. Only in the diaspora can they improve their economic condition, a factor which prompted them to leave their homeland in the first place. Second, some of the "source" countries themselves have sojourning immigrants who dominate "middleman" lines, such as Parsis and Armenians in India (on the latter see Basil, 1969), Koreans in Japan, and Armenians in Syria. Sojourning is important in that it creates a preference for liquidity, encourages thrift, and fosters a solidary community that is cooperative internally and "free" to compete with the surrounding society.

Middleman economic behavior is closely akin to preindustrial capitalism. As described by Sjoberg (1960:Chapter 7), the multi-purpose guild of the preindustrial city maintained a monopoly over a particular economic activity, stressed particularistic (especially kinship) rather than universalistic bases of recruitment into the occupation, apprenticed extended kin with a view to setting them up on their own, controlled internal competition, pooled resources to develop capital, and performed ceremonial functions.[5] Max Weber contrasts pre-modern capitalistic forms (including the economic behavior of Jews and Parsis) with modern industrial capitalism. The distinguishing feature of the latter is "the rational capitalistic organization of (formally) free labour" (1958:21). The modern industrial capitalist treats his workers impartially as economic instruments; he is as willing to exploit his own son as he is a stranger. This universalism, the isolation of each competitor, is absent in middleman economic activity, where primordial tie of family, region, sect, and ethnicity unite people against the surrounding, often individualistic economy.

TABLE 3.   *Estimate of Chinese Economic Position in Cambodia, 1962–3*[a]

Economic Class:	Chinese No. (000s)	%	All Cambodia No. (000s)	%	Chinese as % of Total
Peasant and fisherman	0	0	4950	86	0
Working	64	15½	209	4	31
Commercial	395	84	379	6½	95
Professional and Gov't.	2	½	202	3½	1
Total	425	100	5740	100	7.4

[a] Adapted from Wilmott (1966:255).

[5] In describing commercial activity in an "economically developing" Indonesian town, Geertz (1963: Chapter 3) sees a number of the characteristics we have noted in middleman groups, including a preference for liquidity. However it is interesting that most of the traders (apart from the Chinese) hail from northern Java, and are not natives of the town. "A culturally homogeneous group, they formed a well-defined, sharply set-apart minority—*wong danang*, the Javanese word for trader, still also means 'foreigner' as well as 'wanderer' or 'tramp'—whose values deviated in major respects from those embraced by both the gentry and peasantry (Geertz, 1963:43–4).

HOST HOSTILITY

Middleman minorities are noteworthy for the acute hostility they have faced, including efforts to cut off their means of livelihood, riots and pogroms, exclusion movements and expulsion, removal to concentration camps, and "final solutions." While their treatment has varied to some extent, certain themes recur in the accusations leveled at these groups.

The middleman and the host society come in conflict because elements in each group have incompatible goals. To say this is to deny the viewpoint common in the sociological literature that host hostility is self-generated (from psychological problems or cultural traditions). Each party to the conflict has a "reasonable" point of view which arises from the interaction. I shall concentrate on the host perspective primarily because the middleman viewpoint is more commonly aired.

In middleman-host conflicts, the host society does not usually have a united set of interests. Rather, different interest groups come into conflict with the middleman group for different reasons. Indeed, in some cases the middleman's presence adversely affects the relationship or conflict between two host interest groups. That elements in the host society may form a temporary coalition against the middleman group should not obscure the fact that they do so for different reasons. This uniting of old foes has led some observers to define the hatred of middleman groups as scapegoating. It is as if some politician, trying to unite the nation, seized an innocent victim for all to hate. Such a view, I would contend, is based on a surface impression.

Conflict between the middleman and the host society arises over economic matters (link 4) and solidarity (link 5). In the first case, middleman minorities conflict with three classes: their clientele, business, and labor.

1. Conflict with Clientele—There is an inevitable conflict of interest between buyer and seller, renter and landlord, client and professional, to which middleman minorities,

because they cluster in these occupations, become heir. The Indian riots in Durban in 1949, in which Africans attacked Indian stores, homes, and persons, are an illustration. Palmer (1957:156) describes the pre-riot situation:

> [Many Africans] are forced on to land on the outskirts of town which is mostly owned by Indians. Here they erect wretched shacks made of old timbers and corrugated iron without any means of sanitation. Consequently they live in filth and overcrowded conditions. . . . Their landlords are Indians who frequently exact rack rent for the wretched little pieces of land on which the Natives build their miserable huts. The post-war years were a time of hardship in many other respects. Prices were rising and the Africans found that the Indian store-keepers with whom they dealt were demanding greatly increased prices for the flour, mealie meal, sugar, condensed milk, etc., which were so important in their diet. Therefore, there grew up among the Africans, not unnaturally, profound irritation against the Indians.

It could be argued that this is a "status gap" conflict in which Indians are merely scapegoats for the real villains, the whites. Yet the same hostility is found toward the Chinese in Thailand where there is no dominant white group:

> The Thai see the Chinese as exploiting unmercifully their advantageous economic position: the Thai are obligated to pay high prices to the Chinese for the very necessities of life, and on the other hand are forced to accept the lowest price for the rice they grow. Through deliberate profiteering, according to standard Thai thinking, this minority has driven up living costs (Coughlin, 1960:2).

2. Conflict with Business—Middleman minorities conflict with competing business groups in the settled population. These business groups may have predated the middleman's immigration, and may feel threatened by their lower-priced firms. Or they may be composed of potential businessmen who cannot compete against the entrenched middleman monopoly. This conflict occurs with both members of the superordinate group in society, as in white opposition to Indian business in South Africa, and members of subordi-

nate groups as in African business competition with Indians. (Here is an instance where two otherwise conflicting groups unite in opposition to the middleman minority. Both whites and Africans are "settled" in South Africa, and for this reason are at a disadvantage in competing with Indian firms. If whites and Africans can agree on anything in South Africa, it is on their antagonism to the Indians.)

An example of superordinate business competition is found in white relations with the Japanese on the U.S. Pacific coast. Since farming (market gardening) was an important Japanese business activity, it became an area of conflict. Competition with white farmers is described in a report prepared for the California legislature of 1919, entitled *California and the Oriental* (State Board of Control of California, 1922), with a view to passing an amended Alien Land Law (the first, enacted in 1913, having left many loopholes) which would force the Japanese off the land. The same document was submitted by the governor of California to members of the federal government in an effort to restrict further Japanese immigration:

> The working and living conditions of the Japanese farmer and farm laborer make successful competition by American farmers almost impossible. The Japanese farmers and every member in the family, physically able to do so, including the wife and little children, work in the field long hours, practically from daylight to dark, on Sundays and holidays, and, in the majority of cases, live in shacks or under conditions far below the standards required and desired by Americans. . . . American farmers can not successfully compete with Japanese farmers if the Americans adhere to the American principles so universally approved in America, including clean and wholesome living quarters, reasonable working hours, the usual Sunday rest and holiday recreation and, above all, refraining from working the women and children in the fields (State Board of Control of California, 1922:116–17).

The Chinese in Jamaica illustrate business competition with a subordinate group. According to Lind (1958:156), "The establishment of Chinese grocery shops had extended throughout the island prior to 1911 and

had thus brought vividly to the attention of the entire population that these once humble laborers were displacing the native Jamaicans as the shopkeepers of the country."

Business conflict with emerging subordinate groups has increased in post-colonial times. As liberated nations try to gain control of their economies, they come into conflict with middleman groups. In Southeast Asia and East Africa attempts have been made to curb Chinese and Indian business, to establish native peoples in lines long dominated by these groups. The efficient organization of the middleman economy makes it virtually impossible for the native population to compete in the open market; hence, discriminatory government measures (restrictions on the issuance of business licenses, special taxes, and the like) have been widely introduced.

3. Conflict with Labor—The presence of a middleman minority creates a variation of the "split labor market" (Bonacich, 1972), that is, conflict between cheap and higher priced labor. In the middleman family firm, the interests of employer and employee are not clearly distinct. Employers are paternalistic, employees willing to work long hours at low pay. The result is a cheap and loyal workforce, which threatens to disrupt the relationship between business and labor in the host society; for the latter, in trying to improve its position vis-à-vis management (with whom it has a recognized conflict), could price the business out of the market.

Host management has some interest in opposing middleman cheap labor, as we have seen. But management can use this as a weapon against labor by arguing that, if labor insists on higher wages and better work conditions, both will lose. Labor is caught in a bind: either improve its position and accept the possibility of losing the job altogether, or accept a low standard of living and middleman work conditions.[6]

---

[6] A similar competition is found with firms in other countries which use "cheap labor. The fact of a political border can enable governments to set up import duties, currency devaluations, and the like, to curb this competition, moves which cannot be used against firms in the same country.

Host workers can, of course, try to get middleman workers to join their unions. But the latter often resist, feeling more closely tied to their co-ethnic employers than to the working class of a country of impermanent residence. Besides, most see their position in the "working class" as a temporary status; a gateway to a business of their own.

Modell (1969) describes a 1937 attempt by the Retail Food Clerks, Local 770, in Los Angeles to organize the sales force in the grocery business. "Since white-run concerns could not concede a substantial advantage in labor costs to their Japanese competitors without suffering losses in trade, Local 770 believed that, if it was to organize the white portion of the industry, it could not ignore the Japanese" (Modell, 1969:198). The local appealed to Japanese workers to stand up to their employers and "fight for the American standard of living"; but the appeal was rejected, and Japanese-owned firms were black-listed and picketed by organized labor.

The host society can unite on one issue concerning middleman minorities: the solidarity of the middleman community (link 5). In all our examples, middleman groups are charged with being clannish, alien, and unassimilable. They are seen as holding themselves aloof, believing they are superior to those around them (a "chosen people"), and insisting on remaining different.

The charge of unassimilability can be broken down into at least two substantive accusations. First, middleman minorities are disloyal to the countries in which they reside. They are accused of having "dual loyalties," a familiar cry against the Jews, but also raised against others. One indicator of dual loyalty is a resistance to becoming citizens of the host country. Most works on the Chinese in Southeast Asia devote a section to the "citizenship problem," the Chinese tending not to become citizens. The same is true for Indians in East Africa, and was one of the grounds for complaint raised by President Amin in expelling the Indians from Uganda. Even when middlemen become citizens, people suspect they are acting out of expedience. Coughlin (1960:11)

describes this attitude in Thailand, where the Chinese are seen as adopting Thai ways for "protective coloration." In post-colonial societies this distrust was probably exacerbated by the fact that middleman minorities tended to be allied with the colonial masters. Indeed they have an interest in "law and order" for continued trade, hence tend to oppose disruptive political movements.

A second charge is that middleman groups drain the host country of its resources. This is epitomized by their sending money to the homeland, a point prominent in complaints against the Indians in South Africa collected by the Lange Commission in 1921 (Palmer, 1957:81). Other charges of drainage include land mining, not engaging in productive industry, and not contributing to local industries by importing necessities from the homeland. In a word, middleman groups are seen as parasites. As Amin said to the Indians of Uganda, "Some members of your community have no interest in this country beyond the aim of making as much profit as possible, and at all costs" (cited in the Los Angeles Times, August 14, 1972).

The resistance to assimilation of sojourning middleman communities would be no problem for the host society if these groups were economically isolated. Groups like the Amish, who preserve cultural distinctiveness but combine it with economic self-sufficiency, do not provoke the same concern. However middleman minorities develop great economic power in a country toward which they feel essentially alien. Such power appears devastating to host members, who believe their country is being "taken over" by an alien group.

I hope the reader is convinced that host members have reason for feeling hostile toward middleman groups. Perhaps you are saying, "Yes, there is a rational component, but the extremity of the host reaction reveals a strong irrational force at work. Middlemen may be felt to compete unfairly, they may even appear dangerously disloyal, but surely the reactions to them are out of proportion to the offense? Usually these groups are tiny minorities with little or no political power. Is it necessary to incarcerate them, as were the Japanese Americans in World War II; to expel them, as were the Asians of Uganda; or to dislocate them, as occurred in the Group Areas Act of South Africa? Surely these acts mark hysteria and deep-seated hatred?"

While some irrational elements are probably at work, even the extremity of the host reaction can be understood as "conflict" behavior. The reason is that the economic and organizational power of middleman groups makes them extremely difficult to dislodge. For example, their wealth enables them to use bribery when necessary, another charge often leveled against these groups. The Chinese in Southeast Asia illustrate the point:

> Attempts to control the Chinese have almost everywhere run into the bewildering maze of overlapping Chinese organizations which exist in every country of the area, and they have been frustrated by Chinese evasion, ability and indispensability. . . . Licensing systems have been thwarted by the willingness of inexperienced indigenous businessmen, whom they were intended to benefit, to sell their import and export permits to the Chinese who possessed what they lacked—organization, contacts, experience and capital (Thompson and Adloff, 1955:6–7).

The difficulty of breaking entrenched middleman monopolies, the difficulty of controlling the growth and extension of their economic power, pushes host countries to ever more extreme reactions. One finds increasingly harsh measures, piled on one another, until, when all else fails, "final solutions" are enacted.

EFFECTS OF HOST HOSTILITY

Briefly, the host reaction solidifies and isolates the middleman community (link 6). Voluntary segregation gives way to forced segregation. The hostility also nurtures a love of the homeland (link 7), a sentiment reinforced by communal organization (link 8) through such institutions as language and cultural schools. In addition, host efforts to undermine the group's economic influence (link 9) by laws prohibiting ownership of land, for example, restrict their alternatives and increase their occupational concentration.

AMBIVALENCE TOWARDS PLACE OF RESIDENCE

Some sojourners save enough and return to their homeland. Others, however, do not return; and it is these that come to form lasting middleman minorities. The typical middleman minority is the remnant (in some cases the majority) of a temporary movement.

The desire to remain overseas has two roots. First, political conditions in the homeland (link 10) may make an imminent return impossible. The conquest of their homeland by a foreign power has kept Jews, Armenians and Parsis in an involuntary diaspora, in two cases, for centuries. Second, sojourning produces a dialectic: it aids in business success, and that very success makes returning difficult (link 11). According to Miyamoto (1939:85) many Japanese in America did go home, but returned to America "after they failed in their native land, and found that life in Japan was harder than life over here." And doubtless failure was not required for many to realize they could not do as well in the homeland. For obvious economic reasons, removing the political barrier to a Jewish return to Israel has not led to an exodus from "Anglo-Saxon" countries.

Remaining in the land of one's sojourn can take two forms. One may relinquish his dream of the homeland and settle in the new country. This would entail engaging in more non-economic activities, joining non-ethnic organizations, intermarrying with one's neighbors, employing and being employed by persons of different ethnicity, and the like. In other words, it would mean economic and social integration; the middleman form would disappear. Such has been the fate of many individual Jews, Chinese, Indians, Japanese, and such may be the fate of whole communities.

Or, the sojourner may keep alive the desire to return.[7] His desire may appear to be mythical, finding expression in pious statements like "Next Year in Jerusalem." He may not intend to leave. Yet this orientation retains some substance in the sending of funds to the homeland, occasional visits, and continued solidarity and resistance to assimilation. Love of the homeland is kept alive by host hostility; one supports the homeland in part to have somewhere to go if things get too bad in the host country. And it helps keep that hostility alive through its economic and social consequences. The cycle is self-perpetuating, and the group becomes a permanent minority.

This ambivalence toward place of residence is captured by Simmel in his discussion of the stranger (Wolff, 1950:402–8), whom he describes "as the person who comes today and stays tomorrow. He is, so to speak, the *potential* wanderer: although he has not moved on, he has not quite overcome the freedom of coming and going." The classic example of the stranger, according to Simmel, is the Jew. Weber discusses some of the effects of a stranger or "pariah" status (1963:250):

The legally and factually precarious position of the Jews hardly permitted continuous, systematic, and rationalized industrial enterprise with fixed capital, but only trade and above all dealing in money. . . . As a pariah people, they retained the double standard of morals which is characteristic of primordial economic practice in all communities: what is prohibited in relation to one's brothers is permitted in relation to strangers.

Middleman minorities are strangers. They keep themselves apart from the societies in which they dwell, engage in liquidable occupations, are thrifty and organized economically. Hence, they come into conflict with the surrounding society yet are bound to it by economic success.

[7] The factors that determine the choice between these two alternatives will be dealt with in another paper. But briefly, one important factor seems to be changing economic conditions (the development of chain stores, super markets, etc.), making the family firm less viable, and driving the younger generations to seek employment in higher-paying non-ethnic firms.

CONCLUSION

In concentrating on the host point of view, I have not sought to justify their acts against middleman minorities, but to explain them. Indeed, the pattern we have been examining often concludes tragically. The recent Indian expulsion from Uganda has meant great personal loss. And other middleman groups have suffered worse fates. Lacking numbers and political power, in the long run they are likely to lose in their conflict with the host society.

REFERENCES

Basil, Anne. 1969. Armenian Settlements in India. West Bengal: Armenian College.

Becker, Howard. 1956. Man in Reciprocity. New York: Praeger.

Blalock, Hubert M., Jr. 1967. Toward a Theory of Minority Group Relations. New York: John Wiley.

Bloom, Leonard and Ruth Riemer. 1949. Removal and Return. Berkeley: University of California Press.

Bonacich, Edna. 1972. "A theory of ethnic antagonism: the split labor market." American Sociological Review 37 (October):547–59.

Cator, W. L. 1936. The Economic Position of the Chinese in the Netherlands Indies. Chicago: University of Chicago Press.

Coughlin, Richard J. 1960. Double Identity: The Chinese in Modern Thailand. Hong Kong: Hong Kong University Press.

Davis, Allison, B. B. Gardner and M. R. Gardner. 1941. Deep South. Chicago: University of Chicago Press.

Department of Economics, University of Natal. 1961. Studies of Indian Employment in Natal. Natal Regional Survey, Volume 11. Cape Town: Oxford University Press.

Desai, Rashmi. 1963. Indian Immigrants in Britain. London: Oxford University Press.

Dotson, Floyd and Lillian Dotson. 1967. "Indians and Coloureds in Rhodesia and Nyasaland." Pp. 77–95 in Milton L. Barron (ed.), Minorities in a Changing World. New York: Knopf.

Eitzen, D. Stanley. 1971. "Two minorities: the Jews of Poland and the Chinese of the Philippines." Pp. 117–38 in Norman R. Yetman and C. Hoy Steele (eds.), Majority and Minority (First Edition) Boston: Allyn and Bacon.

Fong, Ng Bickleen. 1959. The Chinese in New Zealand. Hong Kong: Hong Kong University Press.

Furnivall, J. S. 1956. Colonial Policy and Practice. New York: New York University Press.

Garis, Roy L. 1927. Immigration Restriction. New York: Macmillan.

Geertz, Clifford. 1963. Peddlers and Princes. Chicago: Chicago University Press.

Glazer, Nathan and Daniel P. Moynihan. 1963. Beyond the Melting Pot. Cambridge: Massachusetts Institute of Technology Press.

Hollingsworth, L. W. 1960. The Asians of East Africa. London: Macmillan.

Hoselitz, Bert F. 1963. "Main concepts in the analysis of the social implications of technical change." Pp. 11–31 in Bert F. Hoselitz and Wilbert E. Moore (eds.), Industrialization and Society. UNESCO: Mouton.

Ichihashi, Yamato. 1932. Japanese in the United States. Stanford: Stanford University Press.

Koenig, Samuel. 1942. "The socioeconomic structure of an American Jewish community." Pp. 200–42 in Isaque Graeber and S. H. Britt (eds.), Jews in a Gentile World. New York: Macmillan.

Kurokawa, Minako (ed.). 1970. Minority Responses. New York: Random House.

Light, Ivan. 1972. Ethnic Enterprise in America. Berkeley: University of California Press.

Lind, Andrew. 1958. "Adjustment patterns among Jamaican Chinese." Social and Economic Studies (University College of the West Indies) 7 (June): 144–64.

Loewen, James W. 1971. The Mississippi Chinese: Between Black and White. Cambridge: Harvard University Press.

Mahajani, Usha. 1960. The Role of Indian Minorities in Burma and Malaya. Bombay: Vora.

Millis, H. A. 1915. The Japanese Problem in the United States. New York: Macmillan.

Miyamoto, Shotaro F. 1939. Social solidarity among the Japanese in Seattle. Seattle: University of Washington Publications in the Social Sciences. 11(December):57–130.

Modell, John. 1969. "Class or ethnic solidarity: the Japanese American company union." Pacific Historical Review 38(May):193–206.

Palmer, Mabel. 1957. The History of the Indians in Natal. Natal Region Survey, Volume 10. Cape Town: Oxford University Press.

Park, Robert E. 1939. "The nature of race relations." Pp. 3–45 in Edgar T. Thompson (ed.), Race Relations and the Race Problem. Durham, North Carolina: Duke University Press.

Rinder, Irwin D. 1958–9. "Strangers in the land: social relations in the status gap." Social Problems 6(Winter):253–60.

Sandhu, Kernial Singh. 1969. Indians in Malaya. Cambridge: Cambridge University Press.

Sanjian, Avedis K. 1965. The Armenian Communities in Syria Under Ottoman Dominion. Cambridge: Harvard University Press.

Schermerhorn, R. A. 1970. Comparative Ethnic Relations. New York: Random House.

Siu, Paul C. P. 1952. "The sojourner." American Journal of Sociology 58(July):34–44.

Sjoberg, Gideon. 1960. The Preindustrial City. New York: Free Press.

State Board of Control of California. 1922. California and the Oriental. Sacramento: California State Printing Office.

Stryker, Sheldon. 1959. "Social structure and prejudice." Social Problems 6(Spring):340–54.

Thompson, Virginia and Richard Adloff. 1955. Minority Problems in Southeast Asia. Boston: Beacon Press.

van der Kroef, Justus M. 1953. "The Eurasian minority in Indonesia." American Sociological Review 18(October):484–93.

Weber, Max. 1958. The Protestant Ethic and the Spirit of Capitalism. New York: Scribner.

———. 1963. The Sociology of Religion. Boston: Beacon Press.

Wertheim, W. F. 1964. East-West Parallels: Sociological Approaches to Modern Asia. The Hague: W. van Hoeve.

Willmott, W. E. 1966. "The Chinese in Southeast Asia." Australian Outlook 20(December): 252–62.

Wolff, Kurt H. 1950. The Sociology of Georg Simmel. Glencoe, Illinois: Free Press.

6

Race, Color, and Class in Central America and the Andes

JULIAN PITT-RIVERS

The concept of *race* is unclear in Latin America. My concern here is not with what anthropologists mean by *race,* but only with what the people of Latin America think the word means when they encounter it in their daily speech. By minimal definition, it refers to a group of people who are felt to be somehow similar in their essential nature. . . .

The word *race* can, of course, be used to mark differences of ethnic identity within the nation. Sometimes awareness of any implication of heredity is so slight that a man can think of himself as belonging to a race different from that of his parents. The word clearly owes little to physical anthropology but refers, however it may be defined, to the ways in which people are classified in daily life. What are called race relations are, in fact, always questions of social structure. . . .

Terminological inconsistencies complicate from the outset discussion of race relations in Latin America. Indeed, there is not even agreement as to whether or not a "problem" of race relations exists in Latin America. The nationals of these countries often deny the

Julian Pitt-Rivers is Professor of Anthropology at the London School of Economics and Political Science.

Reprinted by permission from *Daedalus,* Journal of the American Academy of Arts and Sciences, Boston, Massachusetts, Volume 92, Number 2, pp. 253–75. The footnotes have been renumbered for this reprinting.

existence of racial discrimination. They claim from this fact a virtue that makes them, despite their supposed economic and technological underdevelopment, the moral superiors of their northern neighbor, whose "inhumanity" toward colored people they deplore. Moreover, this opinion is held not only by Latin Americans themselves, but by outside observers, the most eminent of whom is Professor Arnold Toynbee, who speaks of the Latin American's freedom from race prejudice.[1]

This point of view, in many cases a way of expressing criticism of the United States, is also held by many patriotic American citizens, including especially some who are "colored" and whose testimony, if firsthand, might be thought to suffice.[2] Nevertheless, it is not by any means held universally and is sometimes regarded as a myth. Certain critics, both national and foreign, maintain that race is as important in Latin as in North America, once it is admitted that in addition to differences in the form discrimination takes, there is a major difference: The race that is penalized is the Indian rather than the Negro. Neither of these points of view appears correct.[3] Both are confused as to the nature of the question. Yet by examining the observations upon which they are based and how they have come to hold sway, one can understand better the role ethnic distinctiveness plays in ordering the society of Latin America.

"Segregation" as it is found in the United

[1] "In Latin America happily this racial distinction is not important and this is very much to Latin America's credit." Arnold Toynbee, *The Economy of the Western Hemisphere* (Oxford, 1962), p. 4. "Here is a country [Mexico] whose population is racially diversified yet is socially and culturally united. . . . I can only hope that the Latin American and Islamic freedom from race prejudice is the 'wave of the future.'" Arnold Toynbee, "The Racial Solution," *Encounter* (September, 1965), p. 31.

[2] For example, Robert S. Browne, *Race Relations in International Affairs* (Washington, 1961), p. 22: "South and Central America have in some places developed veritable interracial societies." The qualification is vital.

[3] Juan Comas reviews some of the more scholarly versions of the two views in "Relaciones inter-raciales en America Latina, 1940–60," *Cuadernos del Instituto de Historia, serie antropologica,* No. 12 (Mexico, 1961).

States does not exist in Latin America. "Color" in the North American sense is not the basis of a classification into two statuses to which differential rights attach. Segregated schools, public facilities, transport, or restaurants do not exist in Latin America. The Negro is not formally distinguished at any point. While many institutions are devoted specifically to the Indians, the definition of Indian in this regard is not based on physical criteria. Moreover, neither color nor phenotype has sufficed in the past to debar men from prominence in the national life, as the long list of Negroid or Indian-looking men of eminence in Latin American history shows.[4]

Intermarriage is not regarded with horror. Among the upper classes and in many places among the population generally, it is, however, considered denigrating to marry someone much darker than oneself. This is so, for example, in Barranquilla, Colombia, where the greater part of the population is more or less Negroid. The idea of physical contact with darker races is nowhere considered shocking, nor is it regarded as polluting by the whites. Dark-skinned people are thought to be more sensual and therefore more desirable sexually. This is not the expression of a neurotic fear of sexual insufficiency but an accepted and openly stated commonplace. Pale-skinned people of both sexes are thought to be more frigid and proud, and less warmhearted. Mistresses tend, consequently, to be more swarthy than wives, whose pale skin indicates social superiority.

The immense majority of the population from Mexico to Bolivia are well aware of their mixed ancestry. "A touch of the tarbrush" can, therefore, never mean total social disqualification. "We are all half-castes," Mexicans commonly remark, pointing to their forearm to show the color of their skin. Still, they sometimes go on to stress that only a small percentage of their blood is Indian. National unity demands that to be truly Mexican they must have some Indian blood, but social aspirations require that they should not have too much. Color is a matter of degree, not the basis of a division into black and white.

In consequence, physical characteristics cannot be said to be socially insignificant; their significance is only different. Physical traits never account for more than part of the image that individuals present. These images are perceived in terms of what they can be contrasted with; there is no color problem where the population is homogeneous in color, whatever that color may be. Social distinctions must then be made according to other criteria. From one place to another, in greater or lesser degree, physical traits are qualified by cultural and economic indicators in order to produce that total image which accords a social identity.

Arnulfo Arias, a former president of Panamá known for his "racist" policy, is credited with the proposal to exterminate the Negroes. In a country whose capital city is predominantly Negro, he nevertheless retained sufficient popularity to be a close runner-up in the presidential elections of 1964. This is no longer curious when one realizes that the term *Negro* refers only to the population of Jamaican origins. Imported for the construction of the canal, these people have retained their English tongue and their Protestant faith. Language and religion are the significant qualifiers of color in the definition of *Negro* in Panamá.

In Barranquilla, Colombia, color is qualified by other social factors, and the term *Negro* confined to the slum-dwellers of the city. In the modern housing developments where no one is to be seen who would not qualify as a Negro in the United States, one may be told: "Only white people live here." The definition of *Negro* varies from place to place and, of course, from class to class. A man may be defined as Negro in one place, but simply as *moreno, trigueño, canela,* or even white in another. A man who would be considered Negro in the United States might, by traveling to Mexico, become *moreno* or *prieto,*

---

[4] Paez, Morelos, and Alamán looked Negroid; Porfirio Díaz, Juarez, and Melgarejo looked Indian. This can be verified from contemporary evidence. In modern popular literature and schoolbooks they are sometimes quite literally "whitewashed."

then *canela* or *trigueño* in Panamá, and end up in Barranquilla white. The definition of *Indian* presents a comparable problem once the word no longer refers to a member of an Indian community. Different places and classes use different criteria.

Skin color is merely one of the indices among physical traits that contribute to a person's total image. It is not necessarily more significant than hair type or shape of eye. The relative evaluation of different physical traits varies. The Reichel-Dolmatoffs record of a village in Northern Colombia:

> Distinctions are made mainly according to the nature of the hair and of the eyes and to a certain degree according to stature. Skin color, the shape of the lips or nose, or other similar traits are hardly taken into account. In this way, a person with predominantly Negroid features, but with long and waxy hair is often considered a "Spaniard." On the other hand, an individual with predominantly Caucasoid features and a light skin, but with straight black hair, slightly oblique eyes and of small stature, is considered an "Indian."[5]

The social structure is divided, primarily according to place of residence, into two segments—Spanish and Indian. This dichotomy, while employing a strictness which the Reichel-Dolmatoffs regard as exceptional in Colombia, allows no place for the category "Negro."

The system of classification makes what it will of the objective reality of the phenotype. The forces of the social structure utilize the raw material of phenotypical distinctions, building out of it the social statuses into which people are classified.

It has sometimes been said that the difference between Anglo and Latin American is that in the former anyone who has a drop of Negro blood is a Negro, whereas in the latter anyone who has white blood is a white.[6] The first statement is approximately true, but the second is emphatically not so. The concept of "blood" is fundamentally different in the two and has, in the past, varied from one century to another.

In Latin America, a person with non-white physical traits may be classed as white socially. A trace of European physique is, however, quite insufficient in itself to class a person as white. Although Indians with pale skin and European traits or gray hair may be found sporadically throughout Latin America, they are considered to be no less Indian on this account. In any market in the Andes one or two can usually be seen, and the *indio gringo* ("fair-skinned" or "blond" Indian) in a recognized type in parts of northern Peru. There is nothing anomalous in this description. "Indian" is not, in the first place, a physical type but a social status. The Indian is distinguished not by genetic inheritance but by birth in, and therefore membership of, an Indian community and by possession of that community's culture. This is all that is needed for the definition of an Indian, though Indians normally look "Indian." The word *Indian* has, therefore, come to mean "of Indian descent"; it is used of persons who no longer occupy Indian status, but whose physical resemblance to the Indians implies descent from them. Since Indians are the "lowest" or least "civilized" element of the population, the word in this sense means "low class." It can also be used to mean "savage," or "uncivilized," or "bad" in a purely figurative way—equivalent, say, to that of *canaille* in French. *Negro,* on the other hand, denotes a physical type that commonly carries with it the general implication of low class, but culture is usually quite subsidiary to the definition.[7]

Racial status in the United States, defined in terms of "blood" and identified purely by physical appearance, divides the population into two halves within which two parallel sys-

---

[5] G. and A. Reichel-Dolmatoff, *The People of Aritama* (Chicago, 1961), p. 138.

[6] See, for example, Albert Sireau, *Terre d'angoisse et d'espérance* (Paris, 1959), p. 22.

[7] The situation in Panamá, referred to above, is exceptional. It derives from the influx of a large number of persons of different language and culture. Some slight difference in style of speech is attributed to Negroes in certain regions.

tems of class differentiation are recognized. In Latin America, appearance is merely one indicator of social position. It is never sufficient in itself to determine how an individual should be classed. The discrimination imposed on the basis of "color" in the United States has sometimes been called a "caste" system and has been contrasted with class systems. This distinction is impossible in Latin America where color is an ingredient of total social position, not the criterion for distinguishing two racial "castes." A policy of segregation on the basis of color would, therefore, be not merely repugnant to Latin Americans but literally impossible.

Even in Panamá where the bulk of the urban population is Negro and the "oligarchy," as the traditional upper class is called, entirely European, the notion of segregation is repulsive. A member of the Panamanian upper class concluded a bitter criticism of discrimination in the United States with the remark: "After all, it's a matter of luck whether one is born black or white." It remained to be added, of course, that in Panamá it is nevertheless bad luck to be born black and good luck to be born white.

At the time of the race riots in Oxford, Mississippi, Hector Velarde, a distinguished critic, took the occasion to deplore racial discrimination in the United States in an article in a Peruvian newspaper. Why can the North Americans not learn from us the virtue of racial tolerance? he asked. He went on to illustrate his argument with the usage of the word *negrita* as a term of affection. *Negrita de mi alma* was an expression used toward a sweetheart, he said. Indeed he did not exaggerate, for *negrita* and *negra* are both forms of address that imply a certain intimacy or informality (as a diminutive the former carries the implication of a potential sexual interest the latter lacks). Velarde did not mention the Indians (who are very much more numerous in Peru than the Negroes). If he had, it would not have helped his thesis since *Indian* is never used in an equivalent fashion, though *cholo* ("civilized Indian") and *zambo* ("half-

caste") are both used as terms of affection among comrades.[8]

The implication of racial equality that he drew from his examples invites precision. Such terms do not find their way into such a context because they are flattering in formal usage, but precisely because they are not. Intimacy is opposed to respect; because these terms are disrespectful, they are used to establish or stress a relationship in which no respect is due. The word *nigger* is used in this way among Negroes in the United States, but only among Negroes. Color has, in fact, the same kind of class connotation in the Negro community as in Latin America: Pale-skinned means upper class. Hence *nigger,* in this context dark-skinned or lower class, implies a relationship that is free of the obligation of mutual respect. Velarde's example, consequently, shows that color is an indicator of class, not a criterion of caste.

Those who find no racial discrimination in Latin America take the United States as their model. They point out, correctly, that there is no color bar and that race riots do not occur. (Indian risings are a matter they do not consider.) On the other hand, those who do find racial discrimination in Latin America are concerned with the fact that there exist high degrees of social differentiation that are habitually associated with physical traits and frequently expressed in the idiom of "race." They justify their view by the racial overtones given to social distinctions. In Latin America, these critics are commonly persons of left-wing sympathy who see racial discrimination as a bulwark of class distinction and, evading all nuances, they equate the two. Taking more easily to the emotive aspects of Marxism than to its dialectic, these would-be Marxists end by finding themselves as far from reality as those colonial legislators who once attempted so vainly to control the legal status of individuals on the basis of their descent. Because there is

[8] The same is true in Ecuador. N. E. Whitten. *Class, Kinship and Power in an Ecuadorian Town* (Stanford, 1965), p. 91.

no color bar but rather a color scale that contributes only partially to the definition of status, they are pushed to an implied definition of race that is worthy of Gobineau. They speak of "racial hypocrisy" to explain why certain people claim a "racial" status to which their phenotype would not entitle them if "race" were really a matter of genes. This "false race-consciousness" if false only by the standards of a theory that would obliterate the historical evolution of the past four hundred years. History may validate these theorists if the Chinese interpretation of Marxist-Leninism acquires authority, and the class struggle, transposed to the international plane, becomes a matter of race.

The contrary opinion is usually held by persons of right-wing views. They regard class distinctions as either unobjectionable, insignificant, or at least inevitable. Once they can cite examples of people of upper-class status who show marked traces of non-European descent, they are satisfied that there is no racial discrimination in their country. (This conviction accords with the liberality of their nature and the official creed of their nation.) They are content that there is no problem if there is no "discrimination" as in the United States.

In the first case, the distinctiveness of class and color must be denied; in the second, the association between the two. The first theory ignores the individual instance; only the statistical aspect counts. The exception is evaded lest it disprove the rule. The second theory takes as significant only the chosen individual instance, overlooking the existence of a statistical norm. Indeed, no one is boycotted on account of his phenotype if his class standing is secured by the other criteria that define high status. In such a case, infrequent as it may be in Panamá, color may properly be said to be a matter of luck in the sense that it is a contingency that carries little of the weight of social definition. Economic power, culture, and community are what count.

The disapproval that Latin American visitors to the United States feel of the segregation they find there is not unconnected with the disrespectful attitude they are likely to inspire as Spanish speakers. They know that as Hispanics they are judged socially inferior in many places. Visitors from the United States, on the other hand, are often highly critical of the treatment the Indians of Latin America receive. This strikes them as much more reprehensible than the treatment of the Negroes in their own country, who have indeed much greater opportunities to improve their economic position and who, as domestic servants, are treated with more courtesy and consideration by their employers than the Indians of Latin America—a fact not unconnected with the shortage of domestic servants in the United States. Moreover, the treatment of Indians appears all the less justifiable to these visitors because Indians are not the object of discrimination throughout the greater part of North America.

Thus, comfortably blinkered by the assumptions of their own culture, each nation sees the mite in the other's eye.

In the United States one does sometimes find strong sentiments of hostility toward Indians in areas surrounding their communities; the same is sometimes true in Latin America of the Negroes (however they happen to be defined there). If Indians are not generally subject to discrimination in the United States nor Negroes in Latin America, it is in the first place due to their numerical weakness. In both countries, they pose local, not national, problems. There is roughly one Indian to fifty Negroes in the United States; in Latin America, the inverse disproportion would be greater even if one were to include only those recognized as Negro. Such a comparison can be taken no further than this, however, since the nature of social distinctions is different in the two lands.

The Indian's predicament in Latin America can be likened to that of the Negro in the United States in only one way: Both provide a major national problem at the present time. There the resemblance stops. Not only is the nature of race relations fundamentally different in the societies that evolved from the English and Spanish colonies, but Indians and

Negroes are different in their physical appearance and cultural origins. They are different above all in their place within the structure of the two societies, and have been so from the very beginning of colonial times. The Indians were the original inhabitants of the land; their incorporation or their refusal to be incorporated into colonial society hinged on the existence of Indian communities with a separate culture and a separate identity. The Negroes came in servile status and were marketed as chattel to the industrialized producers of sugar and metals. Cut off from their fellows, they soon lost their language and their original culture and became an integral part of colonial society.[9]

The Negro's status was within colonial society. The Indian's was not. To the extent that the Indian abandoned his Indian community and changed his culture, he lost his Indian identity. While the status of Negro refers to phenotype and attaches to individuals, Indian status refers to culture and attaches to a collectivity. One might speak of individual versus collective status, with all that these imply in terms of social structure. Consequently, while phenotypical differences are irrelevant to the definition of the Indian— hence the *indio gringo*—they have importance in according an individual status once he becomes "civilized." They establish a presumption as to descent, and this is an ingredient of class status. Paradoxically, the genetic background is important only in social distinctions between persons who are recognized as belonging to the same "non-Indian" race; not in the distinction between them and the Indians. "Race" is a matter of culture and community, not of genes, though class is connected with genes.

The problems of race relations in North

America and Latin America are, therefore, fundamentally different. One concerns the assimilation of all ethnic groups into a single society; the other, the status distinction between persons who have been assimilated for hundreds of years but who are still distinguished socially by their appearance. The two are comparable only at the highest level of abstraction. One may wonder, therefore, whether the word *caste,* which is so often used in reference to the status distinction between Indians and *mestizos* (or *ladinos*) in Latin American society is not something of a misnomer. It carries quite different implications in Latin as opposed to North America. It would appear that it comes into the sociological literature about Latin America on the basis of several different and all equally false assumptions which will be dealt with elsewhere.

While the value of color is somewhat similar within the Negro community of the United States and the Hispanic section of Latin America, the Negro community is separated by a *caste* distinction from a socially superior element defined by phenotype; the Hispanic population of Latin America is distinguished by language and customs, beliefs and values and habitat from an element it regards as inferior, which does not participate in the same social system and, for the most part, far from wishing to be integrated into it, desires only to be rid of the *mestizos* physically. For this reason, the aims of Indian rebellions are the opposite of the aims of race riots. The former would like to separate once and for all the two ethnic elements; the latter are inspired by the resentment at the existence of a separation. Indians rebel to drive the intruders out of the countryside; Negroes riot in towns when they are not accorded full civic privileges.

The ethnic statuses of modern Latin America vary in number from the simple division into Indian and *mestizo* found in Mexico north of the Isthmus to the four tiers of highland Peru which include *cholos* and *blancos:* (*indio, cholo, mestizo, blanco*). These "social races" have much in common with the class

[9] This loss of language and culture does not hold for parts of the West Indies and Brazil. Aguirre Beltran maintains that elements of African culture have survived in Mexico. This is true in the case of certain details of material culture and musical style, though it might be more exact to call these Caribbean rather than African. In any case, they have long since ceased to be recognized as such. See, Aguirre Beltran, *Gonzalo: La Poblacion Negra de Mexico, 1519–1810* (Mexico, 1946), p. 96.

distinctions of stratified societies. Woodrow Borah has even maintained that the ethnic distinction in Mexico is no more in essence than a matter of social class. This view raises a further problem in those areas where a regional ethnic consciousness emerges, for example among the Tlascalans, Isthmus Zapotecs, and the wealthy, educated Indians of Quetzaltenango in Guatemala.

Admitting that the class structure of Latin America carries ethnic overtones, how is this structure affected by class differences being thought about largely in the idiom of "race"? Such a view implies that classes are different in their essential nature. If the concept of "social race" teaches us to think about race in terms of social structure, we should also have a concept of "ethnic class" to remind us that class systems no longer function in the same way once class has phenotypical associations. Processes of selection come into operation that cannot exist in a homogeneous population however it is stratified.

This observation leads to a conclusion that does not altogether accord with that of Professor Wagley[10] who states: "At least, theoretically, it is only a question of time until such populations may be entirely classed as mestizo by social race and social differentiation will be entirely in terms of socioeconomic classes."[11]

In terms of his thesis continued racial intermixture produces in Latin America, unlike North America, a blurring of the distinctions among different "social races." This would be true enough, if time could be trusted to produce phenotypical homogeneity, but it ceases to be so once one introduces the notion of selection into the theory. The absence of a bar on intermarriage does not necessarily produce homogeneity.

[10] If I disagree with Professor Wagley ultimately with regard to the prospects of the future (about which wise anthropologists refrain from speculating), I do not wish to obscure my debt to Professor Wagley's thinking on this subject nor to deny homage to his admirable essay. But I would not write about this subject at all if I did not think there remains something more to be said.

[11] Wagley, "On the Concept of Social Race in the Americas," p. 540.

Distinctions of status are not always exhibited in the same ways. The castes of India are held apart by prohibitions on physical contact and commensality, and by endogamy. Feudal Europe accorded no importance to the first two and little to the third. The division of labor implied by any social distinction can bring people into either direct co-operation or segregation, depending upon the range of their ties and the basis of their "complementarity." If their status difference is assured in one way, it may prove indifferent to any other basis of distinction. For this reason the intimacy to which servants were admitted by their masters was greater in an earlier age when social distinctions were more clear-cut.

Physical differences can never be obliterated, but whether they, rather than cultural or social differences, are regarded as significant is a matter each social system decides for itself. It is for this reason that the value accorded to physical appearance varies so greatly from place to place and class to class in Latin America. But the significance of phenotype also varies greatly according to context. Political or commercial alliances are not the same as alliances through marriage. Their products are of a different order. Profits are colorless, children are not. Hence, phenotype may not matter in commercial dealings, but it is never more important than in marriage.

In Latin America today the grandchildren of a rich man who looks Indian or Negroid always appear much more European than he is himself. Color is an ingredient, not a determinant of class. It can, therefore, be traded for the other ingredients. It is not something that can be altered in the individual's life, but it is something that can be put right in the next generation. For this reason, the wives of the well-to-do tend to look more European than their husbands. In the lower classes, paler children are sometimes favored at the expense of their more swarthy siblings; their potential for social mobility is greater.

Individual motivations are ordered to produce conformity with an ideal image of ethnic class. This tends to reinforce the original image. Moreover, demographical factors reinforce this conformity in other ways—through the immigration of Europeans into Latin America and the existence of a pool of unassimilated Indians on the land. Indians are constantly abandoning their Indian identity and becoming integrated into the nation. This process is not unconnected with the current flight to the cities, for you lose Indian status once you settle in the city.[12] The result is a continual influx of persons of mainly Indian physique into the proletariat. At the same time, the immigration of Europeans into these countries has been very considerable in the last two decades, and these Europeans have almost all been absorbed into the upper classes. For demographic reasons, the correlation between class and color is increasing rather than diminishing.

Moreover, the significance of this correlation is also increasing under modern conditions. (It would be rash to say that it will go on increasing in the future, for the structure itself may well change to offset this effect.) The expansion of the open society at the expense of the local community changes the criteria whereby people are defined socially. Where known descent establishes status, color may carry little of the weight of social definition,

[12] Only exceptionally, as in the Isthmus of Tehuantepec or Quetzaltenango, can a man become integrated while retaining an Indian (or is it a pseudo-Indian?) identity. Then region replaces community as the defining unit.

but the descent must be known. It must be known whose child you are if you are to inherit the status of your father. If you have exchanged your local community for the big city, your descent becomes a matter of conjecture; you can no longer be respected because of your birth despite your Indian features. If you look Indian, it will be concluded that you were born of Indian parents. Thus, in the open society, appearance takes over the function of descent in allocating social status. In a world in flux, the fact that appearance cannot be dissimulated recommends it above all other indicators. Clothing, speech, and culture are losing force as indicators of status in the context of expanding cities, but color is becoming ever more crucial.

Although these same conditions might create an increase in social mobility that would tend to reduce the phenotypical correlation of class, it appears that the opposite is happening today. If the classification into social races is losing its precision, the ethnic aspect of class is coming to have increased importance. The social structure is changing and with it the criteria of social classification. Under modern industrial conditions, much of Latin America is moving from the systems of social race that flourished in the communities of yesterday to a system of ethnic class adapted to the requirements of the open society of tomorrow.

7

Color and Power in the South African Situation

COLIN LEGUM

I

Color is the sole determinant of power in South Africa. This distinguishes the *apartheid* republic from all contemporary societies in which serious race problems are encountered. South Africa's power structure is specifically designed to ensure that total power remains exclusively in the hands of three million whites. It not only provides for the whites' security, but also enables them to retain their position of economic and social privilege over a colored majority of thirteen millions. Security and the maintenance of privilege are held to be inseparable.

Contrary to the dominant political tendencies throughout modern societies, differences in race and color in South Africa are consciously and methodically emphasized to buttress the *status quo*. Racial and color prejudice and discrimination are embedded in the country's power structure.[1] The irrational force of prejudice is harnessed to the rational purpose of maintaining a system of discrimi-

nation to ensure the survival of a *status quo* based on color.[2]

White South Africans are among the most economically and socially privileged communities in history, but their privilege depends wholly on their ability to retain political power exclusively in their own hands. Power and privilege always go together, and it is pointless to appeal to a privileged society to abandon its power knowing that in so doing it will condemn itself to the loss of its privileges. No privileged society—white or black or brown—has ever voluntarily surrendered its privileges at one fell swoop. The greater the privileges of the society, the greater the incentive to rally to their defense. In South Africa's case, defense of white privilege is further strengthened by the white community's fear that not only their privileges but their entire security would be placed in jeopardy if they surrendered or lost power. It is futile to argue over whether they are right in holding such fears; the point is they do, and most strongly. Moreover, on objective grounds no one can honestly say that such fears are entirely groundless. After the kind of treatment black South Africans have received over three centuries, why should one suppose they will behave any better than white South Africans? One hopes they will behave better, and indeed there is evidence from the tolerant and generous attitudes displayed by African leaders like Chief Lutuli, Robert Mangaliso Sobukwe, and Nelson Mandela that they might. Will, however, the rising generation of revolutionary African leaders have much incentive, or reason, to adopt tolerant attitudes when all they have ever known has been bitterness, frustration, anger, and humiliation? To ignore this potential danger is surely a great mistake. All white South Africans clearly have a personal stake in maintaining the *status quo*. Only the most farsighted perceive the inherent

Colin Legum is associated with the London Observer.

Reprinted by permission from *Daedalus*, Journal of the American Academy of Arts and Sciences, Boston, Massachusetts, Volume 96, Number 2, pp. 483–95.

[1] Although this essay deals only with the color aspect of racial prejudice, the exploitation of prejudice between "Boer and Briton" has been an important feature of South African history.

[2] It is not helpful, therefore, to point to countries like, say, Brazil as offering useful lessons for South Africa. In Brazil the historical process—though slow and still very far from complete—has been working in precisely the opposite direction from South Africa's for the better part of a century.

fallacies in a political system that demands increasing coercion in defense of existing privilege and that progressively isolates the republic within the international community.

The general statement about the nature of South Africa's political system exposes the fallacy of the belief that color discrimination can be abolished, or even diminished in a meaningful way, without in fact jeopardizing the entire power structure. Therefore, when defenders of white supremacy argue that any political concessions made to the colored majority must inevitably lead to the abdication of white power, they more correctly reflect the realities of the situation than those advocates of gradualist reform who think it possible to diminish prejudice and discrimination without necessarily undermining the entire structure on which white supremacy rests. These two attitudes mark the division between the major white political parties—the ruling Afrikaner National Party, which holds to the view that there must be no relaxation of white power, and the United Party, which favors economic concessions and some measure of social and political reform.

II

There have been periods in South Africa's history when white supremacy was not tantamount to white tyranny; this is no longer so. It is valid to describe the present political setup in the republic as a white tyranny in strictly non-pejorative terms for two reasons: First, the ideology of the ruling party is based on the belief that total control over the sources of power must be retained in the hands of an exclusive group distinguishable only by their color; and second, the belief that this objective justifies any coercive means necessary to secure it.

An eighteenth-century Dutch governor reporting on the attitudes of the early settlers said: "They describe themselves as humans and Christians, and the Kaffirs and Hottentots as heathens; and by believing in this they permit themselves everything." Although pres-

ent-day white attitudes are usually expressed in a more sophisticated way, this assessment remains an adequate description of the general attitude of the white electorate in whom all constitutional power resides. Only those deemed by law to be, and officially registered as being, white are allowed to participate in government (whether as voters, legislators, administrators, or judges); in the armed forces; in controlling positions within the economy; or in labor organizations. The distribution of power is exercised through an elaborate system of laws, based solely on color and specifically designed to debar Africans, coloreds,[3] or Asians from free political or labor associations, free movement, free speech, free ownership of land and property, free access to education. This authoritarian construction of laws is taken to the ultimate extreme of refusing to recognize that Africans have a legal right to live anywhere in the country, and that Africans resident in urban areas may not have wives or families living with them except under certain prescribed conditions. An Orwellian position is reached when a married woman living in Reserves *may* be permitted to visit her husband in urban areas for a period of up to fourteen days for the specific purpose of conception. The exercise of even this privilege is vested in the hands of white bureaucrats answerable not to the Courts or to Parliament, but to the Minister of Bantu Affairs alone.

South Africa is, of course, not the only tyranny in the world. It is not even the only racial tyranny. What distinguishes it from other tyrannies, however, is that it is a white tyranny that exists in the African continent in the middle of the twentieth century. It is this paradox that holds the seeds of race war.

III

White supremacy, with its roots in the seventeenth century, was converted into white

---

[3] *Coloreds* in this context refers to the 1,200,000 South Africans of mixed racial origins.

tyranny after World War II in response to internal pressures by an increasingly educated and articulate African elite who reflected the "colored awakening" in the rest of the world. White South Africans came to feel that the *status quo* was in danger. Suspicions of the "sickly liberalism" of the segregationist policies of Field Marshall Smuts turned into open hostility. Feelings of uncertainty about the future were translated into demands for clear-cut policies and uncompromising leadership to "turn back the black flood." So long as the white society had felt itself securely based, it was willing to consider ways of easing traditional segregationist practices—especially in industry and education, though not in the franchise. Once, however, it began to feel its security challenged, it moved rapidly away from compromise toward policies offering to defend the traditional "white *laager*."[4]

The condition of a *laager* society is essentially paranoidal. Rooted in circumstances of persecution, it survives by persecuting those it fears. South Africa's "*laager* mentality" is not an isolated phenomenon; it is an essential characteristic of every frontier society. South Africa's modern frontiers lie, however, on the Limpopo River beyond which stretches a "hostile" black continent. At its back it has always felt the solid support of the Western world of which, historically, the white society regards itself as an outpost in the African continent. After World War II the *laager* felt itself threatened by two complementary developments—the weakening influence of its traditional Western ally in Africa and the strengthening of its "black enemy" through the rise of independent African states and their new role in international affairs, especially in the United Nations. The *laager's* reaction to these developments moved the center of white political power much farther to the right of the predominantly English-speaking United

Party. This reaction secured Afrikanerdom[5] its first electoral victory in the immediate postwar elections in 1948. Over the next nineteen years its strength continued to grow steadily through four subsequent elections.

IV

The victory of Afrikanerdom highlights another facet of the South African dilemma. Unlike other "settler communities" in the continent, South Africa's is substantial in numbers. It has enjoyed a long tradition of independence from the metropolitan colonial countries, and has created a characteristic indigenous national group—the Afrikaners—with its own language, culture, and history. It owes no allegiance to any other country; its roots are firmly planted in African soil. For such a society, survival means survival in Africa. There is no easy line of retreat by emigration as was the ultimate course open to other settler communities. Its total involvement in and commitment to Africa is a stubborn reality. The South African situation, therefore, differs markedly from that of other colonial situations in that an acceptable settlement must fulfill two fundamental requirements: the establishment of representative government involving colored emancipation; and the guaranteeing of white survival in an independent African state with the present *herrenvolk* stripped of its power.

Attempts to find ways of dealing with these problems have produced a number of irreconcilable sets of proposals. That of the African Nationalists—supported by other colored groups and by white liberals—is for undiluted majority rule with the white minority adapting itself as best it can to a politically nonracial society with guarantees of equal rights of citizenship. A second approach offered by the major white-opposition groups is for gradual evolution, but without proposing

---

[4] In South African history the *laager* was a circle of wagons, their wheels bound by thick thorn branches, within which the frontiersmen gathered their families. This served as a fortress from within which they could concentrate their fire on the unmounted black *impis* before they could come within *assegai*-throwing range.

[5] Afrikanerdom is the systematic expression of an exclusively Afrikaans-speaking political, cultural, and social movement committed to preserving its uniqueness by establishing its hegemony over the whole country. Its political instrument is the Afrikaner National Party.

either a time-scale or a concept of what kind of society it wants South Africa ultimately to become. This approach assumes that economic forces will compel increasing racial integration within the economy, and that economic integration will, in time, diminish rigid color differences and thus eventually make possible acceptable political compromises. A third approach is the traditional white policy that rests essentially on the presumption of white *baaskap*—the "white man boss." A fourth approach—an important variant on the theme of *baaskap*—is the Verwoerd policy of Separate Development.

The adoption in 1947 of the policy of *apartheid* by Afrikanerdom appeared at first sight only to provide a more programmatic approach to the maintenance of *baaskap*. As originally conceived, *apartheid* was defined as "a policy which sets itself the task of preserving and safeguarding the racial identity of the white population of the country; of likewise preserving and safeguarding the identity of the indigenous peoples as separate racial groups, with opportunities to develop into self-governing national units; of fostering the inculcation of national consciousness, self-esteem and mutual regard among the various races of the country." It endorsed "the general principle of territorial segregation of the Bantu[6] and the whites." This broad statement of principles disguised a much deeper division of opinion within Afrikanerdom. On the one side stood the dominant group, reflecting the wishes of the mass of the white electorate, which interpreted *apartheid* as a way of enforcing *baaskap*. This was the attitude of the first two *apartheid* prime ministers, Dr. D. F. Malan and Mr. J. G. Strijdom. This was not, however, the attitude of the other side led by the third prime minister, Dr. H. F. Verwoerd.

V

Verwoerd was in many ways a radical thinker. He was the first influential white politician to

6 Bantu is the official white terminology to describe the African peoples. *African* is rejected as an imprecise and "liberalistic" term.

originate a fresh approach to South Africa's color problems. His starting point was the acceptance of "the scientific fact" that Africans are not inherently inferior to whites. Hitherto only liberals in South Africa had held this view. Verwoerd's thinking led him, however, to the opposite conclusion from that of the liberals. Whereas they argued that the potential equality between races justified the notion of an integrated multi-racial society, he argued that this fact only increased the danger to white survival. Another of Verwoerd's radical conclusions was that while "many derogatory things were said about black nationalism in particular, world history showed that the desire of a group or nation to become free could not be frustrated forever." If the whites were justified in not wishing to be dominated by blacks, the blacks were equally justified in wishing not to be dominated by whites. This reasoning led him to the decisive step of rejecting the policy of white supremacy or *baaskap*.

These ideas were obviously heretical to the majority of white South Africans. Verwoerd's psycho-political skills warned him not to put forward his new ideas boldly in the political arena. Instead, they were carefully rehearsed among small groups of Afrikaner intellectuals and Dutch Reformed Church leaders and set out in a calmly reasoned way in *Has the Afrikaner Volk a Future?*, written by one of Verwoerd's closest colleagues, G. D. Scholtz. The logical conclusion drawn from this radical rethinking was that white South Africa's future lay in territorial separation, or even in complete partition. When, however, this proposal was launched publicly at a congress of the Dutch Reformed Church in 1951, both Malan and Strijdom (Verwoerd's immediate predecessors) denounced it as politically unrealistic.

While some of Verwoerd's colleagues insisted that the logic of partition must be preached from the rooftops, he recast his ideas into a policy of Separate Development that would provide for the creation of seven autonomous Bantustans within the "historical boundaries" of the Native Reserves. These cover only 13 per cent of the country. In this way he sought to allay the fears of the whites that they might have to lose a part of their present land to make territorial separation feasible.

Verwoerd's new proposals split the Afrikaner intellectuals. Those of his former supporters who believed uncompromisingly in genuine territorial partition were greatly strengthened when Verwoerd's own planning team—the Tomlinson Commission—reported in 1951 that even under optimal conditions the proposed Bantustans would be incapable of absorbing the existing African population, let alone its natural increase. By 2000 A.D. there would be ten million Africans instead of the present seven million in the "white areas" of the country. Thus "white South Africa" would continue to become blacker.

Verwoerd was, however, not to be stopped. Having rejected territorial separation except as "a very long-term objective," he stubbornly clung to his plan to establish seven viable Bantustans that, in time, could become independent states within a new "South African Commonwealth."

The practical difficulties in getting his ideas implemented were made even harder by his failure to persuade his own party either to provide the finances for the schemes needed to get the Bantustans going or to accept the eventual objective of allowing them to evolve into independence. So far only one Bantustan —the Transkei—has been launched, and its results have been depressingly negative. Verwoerd knew, perhaps better than any other white political leader, the danger of allowing the vested interests of his white electorate to obstruct radical changes within the *status quo* which, at least nationally, could be held to offer a promise of some equity to the colored majority. Yet, even though he was intellectually the outstanding Afrikaner of his day and politically by far the most powerful, he failed to influence his own Afrikaner people to understand and accept the kinds of constitutional changes he believed essential for white survival.

VI

The nub of the dilemma that faced Verwoerd —that faces any radical South African reformer—can be simply stated. Effective political power lies in the hands of a white electorate. The voting power of this electorate is so distributed as to give a predominant voice to the Afrikaner voters in the platteland.[7] These voters—educationally the most backward in the white community—stand to lose the most from any fundamental change in the present political setup. They, therefore, constitute the strongest bulwark against change in the country.

Their stubborn opposition to change has been frequently discussed in Afrikaner newspapers. Here is one typical editorial comment from *Die Transvaler*[8]:

> It is a tragedy that there are still so many whites who have not the vaguest idea about the change in Africa and who do not realise the need for adaptation. . . . Are the whites prepared for this degree of adaptation, or do they place their economic interests higher than their survival as a people?

Despite the inspired leadership of Verwoerd, the electorate has shown thus far no sign of a willingness to sacrifice immediate economic interests for longer-term survival. Their inflexible attitude, even against proposals made by their own most trusted leaders, makes peaceful change impossible to foresee, especially since the degree of sacrifice posed by the concept of Verwoerd's territorial partition is relatively minor compared to that which would be involved in an abdication of exclusive political power over the whole country. The electorate has shown no evidence of being prepared to countenance even that much.

While resisting change, the white electorate has strongly supported the build-up of the country's security and military strength in the

[7] The rural areas.

[8] This newspaper was founded, and at one time edited, by Dr. Verwoerd.

belief that the white minority can, in the long run, defend itself effectively from internal sabotage and external pressures. In the nineteen years of *apartheid* rule the republic's internal situation has changed dramatically from a predominantly nonviolent political society to an increasingly violent one. Until 1960, the year of Sharpeville, the colored nationalist movement, traditionally led by the African National Congress, held to belief in the necessity of nonviolent methods of opposition. This is no longer so. Violent opposition is now one of their accepted methods of struggle. Although the first waves of sabotage were easily crushed, more sophisticated movements relying on violent methods are in the making. For example, an undisclosed number of South Africans—probably exceeding one thousand—are being trained in African and Communist countries for an armed liberation struggle.[9] The first active group of trained guerrillas began to operate in Ovamboland in the north of Southwest Africa in 1966. In October of that year the first white South African died in his home at the hands of armed guerrillas.[10] The violent change in the political climate is illustrated by the introduction of the "Sabotage Act"[11] in 1963; by the enactment of eighteen different kinds of detention and banishment orders; and by a series of Draconian measures depriving the courts of their normal functions as typified by the notorious "180 Days Detention Law," which enables the police to hold

suspects in solitary confinement for as long as they think necessary.

It is clearly a mistake to minimize either white South Africa's capacity for resistance or its determination to resist. Still, although the whites have the will and the capacity to impose their great power, they do not possess sufficient moral authority over the colored majority to enable them to enlist their willing co-operation. They can rule, and they do; but only by force. On the other side, the colored peoples are able to challenge white authority, but lack the power to break it despite their superiority in numbers.

Such a situation offers no possibility of changing South Africa's existing power structure peacefully. The whites have power without authority or consent; the non-whites have the potentialities of power, but without the possibility of realizing them by peaceful means. This raises two major questions: How much violence will accompany change when it finally comes, and will this violence assume the proportions of a race war? Since conflicting forces within South Africa hold the country in political deadlock, the answers to these two questions must lie largely with the role of external forces.

VII

The African states are committed to the destruction of white supremacy. In terms of foreign policy, this is Africa's top priority. National priorities cannot, however, always be fulfilled; even the super-powers sometimes find that their power is insufficient to fulfill their priorities. Nevertheless, the failure to achieve a specific priority should not be interpreted as an abandonment of the priority or a weakening of the resolve to meet it. African leaders are aware of their weakness and of the consequent difficulties it poses for them. This is best illustrated by extracts from a statement made by Tanzania's President Nyerere about the Rhodesian confrontation, but applicable with even more force to South Africa:

---

[9] Today, South Africa's security system and army ranks with the strongest among the minor powers of the world. Annual military expenditure now runs to almost $500 million, more than six times as much as the 1960 allotment.

[10] After the reported capture of fifty-six "terrorists" in Ovamboland, the South African Commissioner of Police, General J. M. Keevy, disclosed that "a special unit has been established to safeguard South Africa's northern border. This unit has been trained in guerrilla warfare and is equipped with helicopters, two-way radios, provisions, vehicles and arms. The establishment of such a unit has become a necessity since terrorist activities were intensified in Ovamboland and other northern frontier territories." (*Rhodesia Herald*, December 12, 1966.)

[11] General Law Amendment Act.

In considering the future it is necessary to face up to Africa's weakness. By itself Africa does not at the present time have either the military force or the economic resources to defeat the Smith regime alone. It is necessary for Africa to find and use allies. The Communist Powers, for their own purposes, are sympathetic with Africa's position in Rhodesia. But their active military support, even if it were forthcoming, would introduce the Cold-War conflict into the heart of Africa. While the possibility remains of Africa's objective being achieved without direct Cold-War confrontation in the heart of Africa, we should aim at avoiding such confrontation. This means that, for the time being, we have to exert all our efforts to get the Western Powers themselves to act.

What of the role of the international community as represented by the United Nations? On December 15, 1965, the General Assembly drew the attention of the Security Council to the threat to international peace and security posed by the situation in the Republic of South Africa. Under Chapter VII of the Charter, the General Assembly resolved that action was essential in order to solve the problem of *apartheid*. The voting on this resolution was significant. Eighty nations voted in favor, only two (South Africa and Portugal) voted against, and sixteen abstained. The Security Council itself subsequently endorsed a resolution describing the situation in the republic as likely to "disturb" world peace.

Because the power of the United Nations rests on the willingness of its members to contribute to making its decisions effective and, ultimately, on the contribution of the superpowers, its effectiveness is determined by world power and power politics. Since the Russians have repeatedly voted in favor of direct U.N. intervention in South Africa, the crucial missing factor in mobilizing the U.N. behind its existing political commitments on South Africa is that of the Western powers.

Economic and strategic interests are usually given as the two reasons for the Western powers' failure to commit themselves to more effective action against South Africa. At present, strategic interests are of very little account; economic interests are undoubtedly important, but only in Britain's case are they crucially important.

There are, however, two other actors inhibiting Western action. First, the major Western powers have not yet become convinced that the objective of transferring power in South Africa, more or less peacefully, can be achieved through international action. It is, of course, easier to argue the case for international action than to guarantee its successful outcome; few governments can be expected to commit themselves to huge enterprises without being reasonably convinced that the objectives are realizable. Here, perhaps, is the major area of weakness in the case of international interventionists. The ability to demonstrate more convincingly the effectiveness of international action could make a major contribution toward reducing Western inhibitions. But this alone would not be enough. The Western powers are reluctant to act because of a second major factor—they do not yet believe their national interests to be directly involved in what is happening in South Africa.

No major power—white, black, or brown; Communist, capitalist, or nonaligned—has committed its resources to a warlike enterprise purely out of moral conviction. Nations undertake the use of force, military or economic, only when their national interests are threatened or can be greatly enhanced. So long as the West's national interests are not actively threatened by the situation in South Africa, it cannot be supposed that any of the major Western powers will favor U.N. intervention in support of enforcement action under Chapter VII.

The major Western powers may be ready to intervene in South Africa once the situation in Africa as a whole produces a direct threat to their national interests. By then the situation might well have become not an incipient but an active threat to world peace. Unfortunately, such a situation will arise only when violence begins to occur on a large and mounting scale and involves the rest of Africa. Violence of such dimension might well set off a race war before the U.N. could act. It would certainly embitter relations between the races in South Africa to an extent that would make it more difficult, if not impossible, to reconcile the races after power had passed from white hands.

Nobody stands to gain anything by violence on this scale. Yet opponents of *apartheid* are left without any alternative. They cannot produce peaceful change within South Africa's existing power structure, and Western policy is unwilling to unlock U.N. power until a situation of violence makes actual a threat to world peace and to Western national interests.

VIII

The foregoing analysis of the situation in South Africa leads to the following broad conclusions:

Power inside South Africa cannot be transferred peacefully to the majority.

The transfer of power will result from the application of force either inside the republic or by external forces, or perhaps by a combination of both. Such external forces might be collectively applied by the Organization of African Unity and its allies, or by the U.N.; or they might be applied by Communist countries in support of national liberation movements.

Collective action through the U.N. will only become possible when the major Western powers are willing to support it; this depends on whether an actual threat to world peace already exists, or whether their national interests are being actively threatened.

Pressures to change the direction of Western policies can only come from the African states and from the exercise of force by the opponents of *apartheid* inside South Africa. This is the crucial dilemma created by the policies of the South African government and the Western powers.

Whatever the means and whatever the time-scale, it is now clear that South Africa is set on a collision course. It is, moreover, the only area in the world where color is so bitterly and stubbornly engaged that it threatens to entangle the world community in a race war—unless prophylactic action becomes possible.

8

Communist National Minority Policy: The Case of the Gypsies in Czechoslovakia

Otto Ulč

The gipsies have interesting legends about the birth or creation of white, black and brown races by God. Their legend says that God baked the first men and women in an oven. By mistake some were kept too long in the oven and they turned out too dark and thus was born the dark race. Next time God opened the door of the oven rather too early and the image was not properly baked and not quite ready. This was the blond race. The third time God produced images baked to the right color and they were the Indians (ancestors of the gypsies) . . . thus, finally perfect human beings were formed.

Chamal Lal, *Gipsies—Forgotten Children of India*, p. 8.

Gypsies are believed to originate from the Punjab in Northwestern India. Restless wanderers for a millennium, spread throughout the continents, dejected and rejected, subjected but unassimilated, they have remained Cinderellas of world attention and conscience, with no state, organization or any medium to articulate their identity. Their pure Aryan origin notwithstanding, they were singled out with the Jews for Nazi genocide.

Otto Ulč is Associate Professor of Political Science at the State University of New York at Binghamton.

Reprinted from *Soviet Studies* 20 (April, 1969):421–43, by permission of *Soviet Studies* and the author.

The world population of Gypsies is estimated at six million, with their major concentration in Eastern Europe. Whereas, according to the 1930 census there were only some 32,000 Gypsies in Czechoslovakia—0.2% of the total population—the first postwar census of 1966 which included the Gypsies registered a sevenfold increase. Their concentration is highest in the east. The total of 221,525 Gypsies constitutes 1.55% of Czechoslovakia's population but 3.72% in Slovakia. In the province of Eastern Slovakia the percentage is 7.33. In the District of Roznava it is 10.11, in the District of Rimavská Sobota 12.51 and in 60 communities—which are not Gypsy settlements but 'normal villages'—they have a majority.

Kulturni tvorba observes with noticeable lack of enthusiasm that Czechoslovakia has become 'the fourth world Gypsy power,' surpassed only by Bulgaria, Hungary and Rumania. According to a foreign source, however, Czechoslovakia, as at 1968, exceeds all its neighbours with 220,000, as against 200,000 in both Hungary and Bulgaria, 105,000 in Rumania, 70,000 in Yugoslavia and 30,000 in Poland. The question of primacy fades in face of gloomy prophecies: it is estimated that by 1970 the Gypsies in Czechoslovakia will reach the figure of 300,000 and by the turn of the century an ominous one million.

In short, this Slavonic republic in the very centre of Europe has lost its mono-racial status. It is the purpose of this study to analyse the impact of this change, the policies undertaken to cope with the dilemma, and the resulting trials and errors. Emphasis will be laid on the fact that the task of integration has proceeded in a welfare state of a totalitarian variety. The implications are manifold, ranging from ideological embarrassment over the Gypsies' lack of responsiveness to Marxist deterministic formulae, to the imposition of measures inconceivable within the framework of Western democratic practices. The policy of the Czechoslovak government towards this minority has been rather inconsistent in the last two decades: a blend of condescension and impatience, of benevolent inactivity and calls for radical solutions.

. . .

RACIAL PREJUDICE AND WHITE BACKLASH

For us, racial theories are a laughable matter. Emilia Horváthová, member of the Slovak Academy of Sciences on Bratislava Radio, 28 March 1960.

In our case it is a fact that in the eastern part of Czechoslovakia there live 'white people' and 'black people'—with all the aftereffects resulting from such a division. . . . Racial prejudice still survives among us in some places.

Literárni noviny, 1965, no. 44, p. 3.

They live among us, but yet they are lonely and inwardly closed. They are like us, and yet they are different.

Svobodné slovo, 20 October 1967.

History has not subjected Czechoslovak society to such trials as to make it racist. Neither has the past offered the experience through which tolerance and anti-racist attitudes could have been tested. The Gypsies, owing to their substantial numerical increase and partial dispersal throughout the country, do now provide such a test.

The sudden emergence of racial difference on a serious scale caught the white citizen unprepared, confused, impatient and prone to turn his back on the newcomer in a manner that at some time in the future may well be embarrassing. At present he defines *discrimination* solely in 'apartheid terms,' that is as a legally sanctioned and enforced bias. He regards colour-blind laws as the exclusive test of racial equality. Racial attitudes are illegal and therefore do not exist. Ignorant of the Gypsy culture, the public gladly accepts the government's easy explanation of the past, exculpating the white man and relegating the responsibility for the Gypsies' plight to the distant, anonymous, deposed capitalist order.

The government is critical of biased whites who sneer at Gypsies in public, referring to them not by name but only as 'that Gypsy' (*ten cikán*), question them patronizingly as to whether they are proud of being literate, and who find these people socially unacceptable. However, one detects a significant qualification in this criticism: the emphasis and the tone of the argument is not geared to the refutation of prejudice *per se*, but rather to the point that the public generalizes and behaves poorly towards all Gypsies, including the 'good' ones. The stand of the press is not so much the condemnation of racial bias as the defence of the integrated Gypsy, who deserves to be accepted. A Gypsy's responsiveness to the integrative pressures is the criterion as to whether hostility of the public is called racial bias or legitimate criticism articulated by a culturally more advanced citizen.

The racial consciousness of Czechoslovak people is manifested in many forms. A Gypsy orphan would not be likely to find adoptive parents. Interracial marriages are rare and, when a Gypsy girl manages to find a white husband, the union will suffer, if it survives at all, owing to non-acceptance by the white world. In a way, the heaviest impact of prejudice is felt by those Gypsies who have done their utmost and have succeeded in breaking away from their historical identity. The Gypsy professionals—lawyers, physicians, artists, rare as they are—are alienated from their native environment, but not accepted by the new one. Their life is one of solitude, without friends or an opportunity to find a suitable marital partner.

The white bias is socially rather than economically motivated. The Gypsy employee, given his poor educational background and left with the most unattractive kind of manual labour, does not represent any economic challenge. It is not the place of work but of education where imposed physical proximity brings about a conflict situation. All schools are state owned and operated with no choice by the citizen but to enrol his child in the designated neighbourhood institution. Parents protest against integrated education on all grounds—

ethical, hygienic, educational. They forbid their children to fraternize with Gypsy class-mates, and petition the principals to arrange for segregated classes so as to protect their offspring from the lice-infested intruders. It cannot be stated that the teachers are always unresponsive to such pleas.

Racial prejudice must be held co-respon-sible for the less than illustrious results of the government policy to bring up literate, edu-cated Gypsy youth. These children enter the school at a disadvantage, ignorant of the lan-guage of instruction, and accepted as equals by no one. No wonder that a thoughtful ob-server calls such an experience for a Gypsy child a 'psychological massacre.' The all-too-well known story of members of minority groups, who in a racially mixed setting re-pudiate their own physical characteristics, was conceded:

> At school a Gypsy child hears insults such as black snout, thief, etc. The inferiority complex is accompanied by timidity instead of a healthy drive and ambition; thirteen- to fourteen-year olds are ashamed of their dark skin and they argue as to which of them has a lighter skin . . . they avoid the sun so as not to get tanned.

The degree of exposure to Gypsies condi-tions the level of white backlash responses in employment practices and education. Both issues are overshadowed by conflicts over housing. The danger of racial pollution of a white neighbourhood is prone to turn a Czech liberal into an unqualified bigot. The housing shortage in Czechoslovakia is universal, affect-ing Prague as much as it does the last forgot-ten village. The Gypsy intruder is resented by competing applicants for an apartment and is ostracized by the white tenants. Equally, the local administrations—the People's Com-mittees—which are in charge of allocating housing space, constitute an institutionalized bastion of anti-Gypsy bias. The Committees are in the crossfire of integrative pressure from above and segregationist pressure from below. In a rare exception to the rule of local government functioning as an extended arm of the central power, where Gypsies are con-cerned the Committees, instead of siding with Prague, reflect both in words and deeds the sentiments of their communities. The local politico preaches bias both as a representative of the people and as a private citizen. Unlike other countries, Czechoslovakia cannot offer a refuge to safe suburbia. A hard-fought-for apartment is a cherished prize to be kept for life, and both an ex-bourgeois and a party zealot are in agreement on keeping their neighbourhood clean. To the People's Com-mittees the Gypsy is unwelcome for other rea-sons too, notably out of fear of a rising crime rate. Social welfare hand-outs worry local officialdom less since this money comes from the state treasury.

Prague and the localities do not mince words in the conflict over the Gypsy issue. The centre charges bigotry and the addressees re-taliate by referring to the centre's ignorance: 'There with you on the top, it is very easy to talk the way you do, but have you any idea what kind of people the Gypsies are? A scourge, and no one can manage them at all.'

The list of infractions by the People's Com-mittees is long: the Gypsy is denied a resi-dence permit, is chased out of the community, is denied a building permit, is excluded from issuance of the tenancy decree, is refused the sale of used bricks, contrary to explicit govern-mental instruction, etc. The committee men argue that allowing one Gypsy into the com-munity is to open the gate to an unmanageable flood. As a result, the Gypsy whose hamlet was demolished has no other choice than to build a new ghetto on the site of the old one. The white public petitions the Committees to pre-vent Gypsies moving into the neighbourhood, and the wish of the toiling masses is granted. 'We demolished their hamlet but we did not accept them among us; where should they go?'

To sum up, the prejudicial attitudes of the whites in general, and discriminatory housing practices in particular, are the main grievance of the Gypsies, overshadowing by far the occasional complaint about unfair employment policies.

In Czechoslovakia the anti-Gypsy senti-ment is of grass-roots origin and not condoned above the district level of the People's Committees. A racist appeal penetrates the press only through a letter to the editor. Thus, for example, a group of workers recommended a one-way ticket for Gypsies back to India at the expense of the state. Another, rather bizarre opinion appeared in the respectable *Kulturni tvorba* (Cultural Creation):

> There are developing countries whose population is approximately on the same level [of civilization] as our Gypsies are. Would it not be worthy of our consideration to solve the Gypsy solution through a resettlement of a substantial part of the Gypsy population in a certain territory within the framework of the community of socialist countries and with the assistance of the United Nations? Our state would undertake material aid to the country willing to accept the Gypsies. This measure, as proposed, would be humane for both parties.

No Czechoslovak leader, of the Stalinist, neo-Stalinist or anti-Stalinist variety, has openly advocated such a remedy. Yet, it may be contended that the party and the government in their basic concept of integrating the Gypsy population have exhibited attitudes of white socialist superiority. As just laws are no guarantee of their just implementation, neither is imposed integration a guarantee of a fair deal.

THE CORE OF INTEGRATION: A ONE-WAY DIALOGUE

> *Under socialism it is totally unthinkable to build some 'socialist and national' Gypsy culture from the fundaments of something which is very primitive, backward, essentially often even negative and lacking in advanced tradition. . . . The question is not whether the Gypsies are a nation but how to assimilate them.*
>
> Demografie, 1962, no. 1, pp. 80–81.

> *In my opinion, the embarrassing failure in solving the so-called Gypsy question is due to the fact that the Gypsies themselves or at least people with imagination have little say in the matter. . . .*
>
> Jiři Pištora, in *Literárni noviny,* 3 July 1965, p. 12.

Compared to the record of the prewar bourgeois republic, the totalitarian state, with coercive powers at its disposal, affected more markedly the Gypsy way of life. Also, compared to the successful failure of the 1958 programme, the programme of 1965 appears, so far, a failing success. The emphasis is laid on dispersal of the Gypsies and their resettlement in urban areas—the measure believed to be most conducive to integration. Some of the weaknesses of the programme, such as its heavy bureaucratization and questionable voluntarism, have been mentioned. According to this writer the following measures, not employed so far, could be of some help: recruitment of assimilated Gypsies as intermediaries between their less responsive brethren and the state; integration backed by monetary incentives; intelligent, coordinated utilization of the armed forces as a socialist melting pot; less emphasis on the destruction of Gypsy kinship ties; adequate financing of homes for Gypsy orphans; court prosecution of practitioners of racial discrimination; last, but not least, some cross-national cooperation and exchange of thoughts with the fraternal countries which, too, have to cope with Gypsies of their own.

The great weakness is the overriding concept of integration, conceived as the Gypsies' unconditional surrender to the white majority. With assimilation a goal, no legitimacy is left to the preservation of Gypsy ethnic identity. The old recipe of Soviet nationalities policy—'socialist in content, national in form'—is not permitted to apply. During the sixties Czechoslovakia 'rehabilitated' the Gypsies as an existing *entity* (i.e., a Gypsy is a Gypsy and not a Slovak of Gypsy ancestry) with, however, no title to its survival. Constitutional minority guarantees affect, for example, the Poles and Ukrainians in Czechoslovakia, but not the numerically stronger Gypsies. Even the writers who stand up in defence of the Gypsies dismiss the eventuality of this self-preservation as deceptive nonsense. These are, it is argued, primitive, backward people, and, to some degree, degenerate ones, whose only hope is to abandon their identity, with no qualifications, and the sooner the better. Some misgivings, however, cannot be suppressed. As one writer put it, in this clash between the values of the Gypsies and of the whites, we are destroying their values without supplanting them with our own, with the net result of impoverishing rather than enriching their lives.

The white socialist bias, the air of presumed superiority is easy to detect. The entire programme of the integration of Gypsies has never been conceived or practised with their own participation. No Gypsy as a Gypsy, no matter how educated and assimilated a professional, has been recruited to take part in helping his less adjustable people. The individual's integration reads as the acceptance of the white man's image and his way of life. Once this is achieved, the beneficiary of the transformation becomes an adoptive child of white civilization with no right to articulate the interests of the group of his heritage, to be its leader, or even an intermediary, a transmission belt between the white and dark world. He is confined to the role of an anonymous textbook figure worthy of emulation. Gypsy children learn nothing at school about their heritage except for superficial references to their historical mishap which the present socialist order is about to terminate. The Gypsy remains an object and not a subject participating in local affairs, even if his people are the majority in the community. As one police commander in charge of a Gypsy settlement put it, these people are like small children whom one has to keep under constant control. Unabashed, the paternalistic manipulators burst with indignation about the plight of the American Negro. The case of these two minorities is radically different, and incomparable, it is maintained. 'Negroes struggle for an integration which is denied to them, whereas the Gypsies do not want, or are incapable of, integration.' It's as simple as that.

The integration process never left the bounds of a one-way dialogue, with the white spokesman badly qualified to pontificate instant remedies. It is admitted that the local officials in charge of the Gypsies do not bother to learn—as they are supposed to—about their history, culture and attitudes. The gravity of this failure is, perhaps, ameliorated by the fact that there is not much available in Czechoslovakia to facilitate learning about the Gypsies. The government demands the extinction of the ethnic identity of 1.5% of its total population without any serious background analysis of these people.

In short, the formation of policy concerning Gypsies without Gypsies puts the decision-makers' claim of their racial magnanimity in some doubt.

PROSPECTS

The Gypsy question is both a very complex and sensitive one. It will be beyond the powers of one, even two generations to cope with the problem.

Obrana lidu, 14 October 1967, p. 9.

The government has learned on several occasions that inauguration of a plan is no guarantee of its fulfilment. The reformers of the Gypsy people, wiser through successive failures, now shun wild promises. Sobriety is the mood of the day. No specific deadline for the completion of integration is now offered. About two-thirds of the Gypsies in Czechoslovakia have so far remained out of reach of the moulding hand of the state.

Economic imperatives do not invite much optimism. The New Economic Mode is designed to curtail state welfarism and mediocrity in performance. Provided the USSR will not veto the NEM *in toto*, a rational manager will not hire but fire the marginal, undisciplined labour force motivated by nothing but the collection of the family allowances. No matter how colour-blind the reformers will be, the Gypsies will be among their prime victims.

The integration programme will be further impeded by constitutional changes. Czechoslovakia is the country of two nations, the Czechs and the Slovaks, and whereas for the former the liberalization of 1968 was understood as a renaissance of personal freedoms, for the latter it meant primarily autonomy, federalization—a change which has been implemented despite the August 1968 invasion. Integration of Gypsies, as indicated earlier, implies the need for a transfer and resettlement from Slovakia to the Czech lands. With the Slovaks obtaining their long-coveted home rule, communication and cooperation with Prague on any issue will not be enhanced.

In the 1968 wave of rehabilitation of individuals, organizations, concepts, beliefs and the better part of the national tradition, the Gypsies were omitted. However, a group of professionals of Gypsy origin, it was reported, petitioned the government for recognition of the legitimacy of their national existence. All they have succeeded in so far is the establishment of the Union of Czechoslovak Gypsies, whose future is about as uncertain as that of the entire country.

Without delving into idle speculation, this much can be said: the racially homogeneous Czechoslovaks once took racial tolerance for granted. When they were put on trial in the postwar years, they failed the test. They failed, and refused to admit this failure. Racism of the unaware rather than of the hypocritical type prevailed.

Time is still required for a realization that racial prejudice is not a monopoly of the capitalist order. The socialist sky is capable of casting the same ugly shadow. Once fully cognizant of his prejudices the Czechoslovak white man may start to overcome them, to the benefit of all concerned.

9

Social Pluralism in Quebec: Continuity, Change and Conflict

RICHARD J. OSSENBERG

PLURALISM AND METHODOLOGY

The complexity of social pluralism in Canada is best illustrated in the case of Quebec, which could be considered as a situation of *double pluralism*. In many ways, Quebec is a plural society within a plural society, consisting not only of the widely recognized differences which separate English-speaking Canadians and French Canadians, but also, and of equal importance, the pervasive and enduring differences which separate French Canadians from each other.

The existence of severe schisms within the French Canadian population, based essentially on social class differences, largely accounts for the apparent ambiguities, inconsistencies, and contradictions which have marked the evolution of Quebec. Social scientists as well as the Canadian public generally have been perplexed by developments in Quebec largely because of their lack of recognition of the internal dynamics in the evolution of the French Canadian population.

The general image of the French Canadians is that they are of one culture, sharing geographical, linguistic, historical and general "style of life," similarities which clearly distinguish them from English-speaking Canadians. This image, interestingly, is held by many English-speaking Canadians *and* French Canadians. Among the latter group, it is especially those associated more or less directly with Quebec's Quiet Revolution and the separatist movement who find the façade of a "common front" to be compatible with ideological goals.

It cannot be denied that the image of French Canadians as one culture has a certain degree of validity. The "boundaries" of the French Canadian population, consisting essentially of geographical concentration in Quebec Province, and linguistic homogeneity, place them in considerable contrast to the English-speaking Canadian population generally. But the emphasis on this obvious contrast has obscured the existence of a myriad of factors which have always fragmented the French Canadian population in Quebec and continue to plague their search for cultural identity.

Why have the schisms within the French Canadian population been considered as relatively negligible in comparison to those which separate French Canadians and English-speaking Canadians generally? Canadians of all ethnic origins, similar to people throughout the world, tend to think of cultural and ethnic differences in terms of "we" and "they" contrasts, thereby exaggerating the cultural homogeneity of both "groups." Social scientists have largely incorporated this imagery with regard to studies of ethnic relations, although anthropologists have been somewhat more alert to the existence of internal differences within all ethnic groups than have sociologists, by virtue of their more direct and sustained contact with minority groups. There has been a general tendency, especially marked among sociologists, to over-emphasize the cultural homogeneity of minority ethnic groups, although there have been exceptions, including the studies of Wirth[1] and Cayton and St. Clair Drake.[2]

Richard J. Ossenberg is Associate Professor of Sociology at Queens University, Ontario.

From *Canadian Society: Pluralism, Change and Conflict.* Reprinted by permission of Prentice-Hall of Canada, Ltd.

[1] Louis Wirth, *The Ghetto* (Chicago: University of Chicago Press, 1929).

[2] Horace Cayton and St. Clair Drake, *Black Metropolis* (Chicago: University of Chicago Press, 1947).

There are, of course, many situations which tend to bring about relatively high degrees of cultural homogeneity and mutual identity among members of minority groups, including competition and conflict with other ethnic groups, sometimes resulting in "nativistic" or "revivalistic" movements which maximize internal social cohesion and solidarity and thereby reduce or eliminate internal divisiveness. However, these social situations have not yet ameliorated the schisms within the French Canadian population which are deeply rooted, and virtually "institutionalized" because of the peculiar nature of Quebec's double pluralism.

But it is not only the existence of social pluralism within Quebec that has accounted for difficulties in the analysis of that Province; it is also the perpetuation of long established historical patterns which continue to be relevant to an understanding of contemporary developments. The imperative need for analysis of social-historical materials in the scientific study of societies, especially those characterized by ethnic pluralism, has been recognized[3] but generally ignored by social scientists, especially functionalists who believe that group dynamics can be understood on the basis of structural conditions alone. Many of the fallacies of this assumption have been pointed out by van den Berghe.[4]

Two theoretical problems involved in the study of Quebec, which are applicable also to the general study of Canadian society, have thus far been discussed; the general absence among Canadian social scientists of a systematic conceptual model of Canada as a plural society, and their general neglect of historical considerations upon both of which I have elaborated elsewhere.[5] A third problem re-

mains: the lack of a comparative framework in the analysis of Canadian pluralism. Similar to their colleagues in the United States, Canadian social scientists have only rarely attempted to analyze their society in terms of contrasts with, or similarities to, other societies. Even those few attempts which have been made to do so, including those by Lipset and Naegele, have been very general and impressionistic. . . .

My purpose in this chapter is to analyze the social evolution of Quebec and some of its contemporary dynamics. Most of the discussion hinges heavily on a theoretical framework of social pluralism in Quebec, social-historical considerations, and, finally, a comparative analysis.

QUEBEC: A CASE OF DOUBLE PLURALISM

The most basic and enduring difference among French Canadians has been that of social class. Although English-speaking Canadians have been "elitist" in their relationships with French Canadians, emphasizing Anglo Saxon cultural, economic, and political superiority, there has also been a strong elitist tradition within the French Canadian population. Social class differences between French Canadians are no less severe than those social class differences between French Canadians and English-speaking Canadians generally. The existence of general social class inferiority among the French Canadians compared to the Anglo Saxon population of Canada, and even relatively recent non-Anglo Saxon immigrant groups, has long been recognized by people "in the know," and increasingly being acknowledged by Canadians everywhere. The relative disadvantages of the French Canadians with regard to their comparative social class standing in both Quebec and Canada generally, has been documented by Hughes,[6] Porter, [7] and

---

[3] See entire issue of *Annals of the New York Academy of Science,* XXXCIII, No. 5 (January, 1960). Most of the articles contained therein point out the importance of historical factors in an understanding of ethnic pluralism in the Caribbean.

[4] Pierre L. van den Berghe, "Toward a Sociology of Africa," *Social Forces,* XLIII, No. 1 (October, 1964), 11–18.

[5] Richard J. Ossenberg, "The Conquest Revisited: Another Look at Canadian Dualism," *Canadian Journal of Sociology and Anthropology,* IV, No. 4 (November, 1967), 201–218.

[6] Everett C. Hughes, *French Canada in Transition* (Chicago: University of Chicago Press, 1943), esp. Chapter vii.

[7] John Porter, "The Economic Elite and the Social Structure in Canada," *Canadian Journal of Eco-*

The Royal Commission on Bilingualism and Biculturalism.[8] Studies in Quebec, conducted by French Canadian scholars, including de Jocas and Rocher,[9] and Dofny[10] have also demonstrated the existence of generally low social class standing among French Canadians. The evidence is irrefutable: French Canadians stand, and have stood, at the lower rungs of the Canadian social class system. This is the fact of Canadian social structure which has been central to the debates, issues, and controversies concerning Canadian confederation both inside and outside of Quebec. It has added credence and viability to the separatist movement.

The social class inequalities within the French Canadian population, especially in Quebec, while of the same magnitude of those separating French Canadians and English-speaking Canadians generally, have been ignored, played down, or obscured by the "larger" issues of Canadian confederation. The objective evidence for these internal French Canadian social class differences has been presented[11] and there can be no debate over their existence. Yet, these internal social differences have not been systematically studied in an attempt to analyze the essence of Canadian pluralism.

The French Canadians, as a minority group in Canada, have experienced the development of an internal social class stratification system in much the same way as many minority groups in plural societies undergo the process of an internal stratification system which, more or less, is distinct from the strati-

fication system of the dominant ethnic group(s)[12] This stratification system within the minority French Canadians has basically inhibited the emergence of a strong ethnic identity and solidarity, and thereby weakened the appeal of the separatist ideology—an ideology which, at least until very recently, has been peculiar to the relatively new French Canadian middle class.[13] Internal stratification systems among minority groups are detrimental to them because status differences tend to encourage internal rivalries and conflicts, which would under conditions of ethnic solidarity and union be focussed on the dominant groups.

Although there are similarities between the French Canadians and minority groups found in other societies, there are also significant differences. It appears probable, for example, that the internal social class cleavages among French Canadians have been and remain more severe than those found among minority groups elsewhere. For various reasons, to be discussed presently, the high degree of internal cultural and economic differentiation among French Canadians, beginning with the latter phase of the colonial era of New France, distinguishes them from other minority groups in different colonial situations which tended to encourage greater solidarity among themselves.[14]

Before turning to a consideration of the historical roots of contemporary pluralism in Quebec, and how it might be compared to the pluralism found in other societies, I shall briefly outline what I think are the major dimensions and profiles of social class differences between French Canadians today.

In the last decade, the most "visible" social class within French Canada, from the

---

nomics and Political Science, XXIII, August, 1957, 377–394.

[8] Report of the Royal Commission on Bilingualism and Biculturalism, Book III.

[9] Yves de Jocas and Guy Rocher, "Inter-Generation Mobility in the Province of Quebec," *Canadian Journal of Economics and Political Science*, XXIII, February, 1957, 58–66.

[10] Jacques Dofny and Muriel Garon-Audy, "Mobilités professionnelles au Quebec," *Sociologie et Sociétés*, I, No. 2 (November, 1969), 277–301.

[11] *Ibid.* See also Jacques Dofny and Marcel Rioux, "Social Class in French Canada," in *French Canadian Society*, eds. Marcel Rioux and Yves Martin (Toronto: McClelland and Stewart, 1964), I, 307–318.

[12] See George M. Foster, *Traditional Cultures and the Impact of Technological Change* (New York: Harper, 1962), p. 41, and entire issue of *Annals of the New York Academy of Sciences*, XXXCIII, No. 5 (January, 1960).

[13] See Guindon, "Two Cultures," pp. 57–59.

[14] For evidence relating to the greater solidarity among minority groups in other plural societies, see Franklin Frazier, *Race and Culture Contacts in the Modern World* (New York: Alfred Knopf, 1957), pp. 294–295.

point of view of both academic and popular interest, has been "the new middle class." The French Canadian "new middle class" is both real and, at the same time, a product of the mass media. It is real in the sense that, especially since World War II, an increasing proportion of French Canadians have entered into the world of white collar occupations, ranging from clerical to academic.[15] The "new middle class" has been a product of the mass media in the sense that its sympathies toward separatist movements have ben identified with the French Canadian population generally, while the anti-separatist sentiments of the majority of French Canadians in lower social class positions have been obscured.

The "new middle class" of French Canadians has been properly identified as the main thrust behind the contemporary separatist movement.[16] The "hard-core" of this group is found among the intelligentsia, especially students and faculty at the University of Montreal. But the separatist sentiments are diffusing to French Canadians generally found in the upper level white-collar occupations, especially in the Montreal area—where the clash of economic interests, ethnic differences, and a sense of "relative-deprivation" are far more pronounced than they are in more static areas such as Quebec City.

This new French Canadian middle class, with some exceptions to be discussed later in this chapter, is relatively isolated from the other two major social class status groups— the old French Canadian elite, and the majority lower class French Canadians.

The relatively small old-elite French Canadians consist of persons generally of long-standing professional status (physicians, lawyers, merchants, chartered accountants, corporate directors, some university professors) some of whom could trace their heritage to their progenitors of the old days of the seigniorial estates. This group also includes members of the higher Catholic clergy who, like their colleagues, shared a somewhat con-

servative orientation toward the problems of the lower-class French Canadians. As a group, the old-elite French Canadians generally held power within the French Canadian population and received considerable deference from the Anglo Saxon elite. Since the Quiet Revolution of Quebec, which is most frequently traced to the election of Jean Lesage as Provincial Premier in 1962, the old-elite are becoming increasingly marginal, in view of the great advances made, both economically and politically, by members of the "new middle class." . . . The French Canadian old-elite are being forced into a position of ambivalence and compromise because of their need for maintaining favourable relations with the Anglo Saxon elite as well as French Canadian clientel.

Of special interest to my analysis is the relatively large French Canadian lower class (about 50 per cent).[17] This group has experienced a large degree of "apartheid" from both upper status French Canadian classes, the old-elite, and the new middle class. Meaningful social relations and political rapport between the French Canadian lower classes and members of the upper status groups have been as minimal as that between French and English Canadians generally. It has been the lower class French Canadians who have inhibited, thus far, the growth and influence of the new middle class based separatist ideology. The political behaviour of the lower class French Canadians, generally contradictory to the aspirations of the new middle class, including the 1970 provincial election, has been amply documented.[18] Very recent developments suggest the potential for these historically-based social class differences to become modified,

---

[15] Dofny and Garon-Audy, "Mobilités professionnelles. . . ."

[16] Guindon, "Two Cultures," pp. 57–59.

[17] This is a very crude estimate based on my impression of figures presented by de Jocas and Rocher, "Inter-Generation Mobility," and the considerable upward mobility of the French Canadians since the time of this study (see footnote 16).

[18] For evidence pertaining to this general pattern, but not including the 1970 election, see Pinard, "Working Class Politics," *passim*. Concerning the 1970 elections, analysis of the votes in various social class differentiated ridings indicated the continuation of the traditional differences in party preference, although not as sharply as before.

thereby assuring an unprecedented degree of social solidarity among French Canadians generally. These developments, among others, will be discussed following an exploration of the historical antecedents which gave rise to the double pluralism of Quebec.

CHANGE AND CLASS DYNAMICS IN THE EVOLUTION OF THE FRENCH CANADIANS

The French settlers in North America during the French colonial regime, lasting from about 1608 until the British conquest of 1759, were a highly differentiated group of people. The evolution of New France was dynamic, and had far reaching consequences for all classes of its population. Social stability in the colony may have been an aspiration, especially among members of the higher Catholic clergy, but never a reality.[19] The basic economic and social conditions of the colony could not possibly have given rise to the stable and socially integrated society which has been at the center of the images of New France portrayed by both English-speaking and French Canadian scholars alike.[20]

There was never one dominant economic system throughout the entire history of New France which could conceivably have led to general social integration. The system of seigniorial estates, which had been intended to be the primary economic resource in the French colony, has been interpreted by contemporaries[21] as well as subsequent analysts[22]

as a failure and, at best, a severely limited success. The seigniorial system, roughly modelled from the already antiquated quasi-feudal system of land tenure in France, had little potential of success in the new colony. Both economic and social factors mitigated against it. On the economic level, the seigniorial estate system, which was intended primarily to offer the basic economic sustenance of the French colonists and, coincidentally, to provide the basis for social integration among them,[23] offered virtually no economic rewards in comparison to the rapidly developing North American fur trade. The French Canadian *habitants* (often considered to be the approximate equivalents of feudal vassals, and the bulwark of French Canadian traditionalism) had no particular allegiance to the feudal landlords, the seigniors. Consequently, mobility of the *habitants* from one seigniorial estate to another, in response to the expectation of greater economic and social rewards, was a common pattern.[24] Moreover, there were numerous instances of habitants breaking their contractual obligations to remain on seigniorial estates in order to become more directly associated with the lucrative fur trade by specializing" as *voyageurs* or *coureurs de bois*.[25] In contemporary sociological parlance, the *voyageurs* and *coureurs de bois* were the ideal male "role-models" for French colonial youth throughout the entire history of New France. . . .

Not only was the fur trade the dominant economic system in New France; it also was so extensive and lucrative, that a number of social historians have suggested that French colonial merchants, engaging in the fur trade, had far more influence in the French court, by the time of the British conquest of 1759, than the elite of the *ancien regime*, including the higher clergy of the missionary Church.[26]

---

[19] See S. D. Clark, *The Social Development of Canada* (Toronto: University of Toronto Press, 1942), pp. 76–94, *passim*.

[20] Ossenberg, "The Conquest Revisited."

[21] Concerning the analysis of contemporary documents attesting to the failure of the seigniorial estates, see Victor Coffin, *The Province of Quebec and the Early American Revolution* (Madison: The University of Wisconsin, 1896).

[22] William B. Munro, *The Seigniorial System in Canada* (New York: Longmans, Green, 1907). See also Guy Frégault, *Canadian Society in the French Regime*, Historical Bulletin No. 3 (Ottawa: Canadian Historical Association, 1954).

[23] See Munro, *ibid*.

[24] Fregault, "Canadian Society"; see also, Edgar McInnis, *Canada: A Political and Social History* (New York: Rinehart, 1959), pp. 1–140, *passim*.

[25] *Ibid*.

[26] See Munro, *The Seigniorial System*, esp. 42–45.

It is also of interest to note that the fur trade was conducted largely on the basis of illegal enterprise, consisting mainly of sales to the English colonists in the south, in sharp contradiction to the officially proclaimed bans on such enterprise. . . . [This illegal trading] is at direct variance with the generally assumed deferential and conforming behaviour of the lower status French Canadian settlers.

The dynamics and relative chaos of the French colonial economic system was reflected in other social institutions. The general image of the stable and tradition-oriented French colonial family, at all status levels, is at variance with the objective historical facts. The family and kinship system in New France could hardly be considered a system at all. Not only was there extensive (and officially banned) cohabitation between French Canadian males and Indian females, but even the "approved" marital arrangements left some doubt as to their contribution to a stable and socially integrated French colonial culture. The economic inducements offered for marriage and the bearing of children encouraged marriages of convenience, and had little to do with the desire for perpetuation of lineage. . . .

. . . Garigue, who has expressed his view that the French Canadian family throughout the evolution of Quebec was the main integrating and stabilizing institution, has also stated that the French colonial family, in contrast to the traditional French family, was rather "nuclear" in structure and was characterized by generally liberal and democratic relations between husband and wife, parents, and children.[27]

The social and economic conditions of New France did not encourage the formation of a highly stable kinship system; the rapid expansion of the fur trade, involving an increasing number of *habitants*, the increasing geographical decentralization because of the fur trade, and the extensive sexual relations

and arrangements between colonists and Indian mates or mistresses[28] were among the most important factors.

The authority and influence of Catholicism during the colonial era were also considerably eroded because of the rapid social and economic changes. Additional factors, not yet fully studied, entered into the picture. It is rarely recognized, for example, that "until 1627 Canada welcomed Catholics and Protestants alike and the latter exercised an important economic influence."[29] These Protestants, who were most likely Huguenots, may have had considerable influence in encouraging the developing "Protestant ethic" capitalist motivation which appeared to provide much of the attraction of the fur trade. This hypothesis remains to be tested.

Quite apart from the role that the Huguenots may have played in the decline of Catholic authoritarianism and traditionalism, there appears to be considerable evidence attesting to the pattern of secularization of the colonial society. Expressions of concern by the clergy over the generalized disobedience and rebellious behaviour of the *coureurs de bois*, *voyageurs*, and *habitants* proliferated during the latter half of the life of New France.[30] Moreover, there is considerable evidence indicating the existence of conflict, both within the clerical hierarchy, especially between younger and older clergy, and between the clergy generally, and colonial administrators and the military cadres.[31]

These extensive changes in the colonial social institutions brought about a situation whereby the *ancien regime*, consisting of clergy, military, and colonial administrators, was virtually powerless in exercising social control over the general colonial population by the time of the British conquest of 1759.[32]

[27] Philippe Garigue, "The French Canadian Family," in *Canadian Dualism*, ed. Mason Wade (Toronto: University of Toronto Press, 1960), pp. 181–200.

[28] See Clark, *The Social Development of Canada*, pp. 22–44, *passim*.

[29] Frégault, *Canadian Society in the French Regime*, p. 3.

[30] Ossenberg, "The Conquest Revisited."

[31] *Ibid.*

[32] *Ibid.*

Not only were the social institutions of New France undergoing massive disruption; significant demographic changes, all of which tended toward the secularization of the colonial population, were also relevant. Population expansion because of the fur trade correlated with increasing population concentration in the major cities of Montreal, Three Rivers, and Quebec, where merchants and tradesmen conducted their enterprise— either in connection with the fur trade or with the developing shipbuilding and forest industries.[33]

THE BRITISH CONQUEST: COLONIAL PLURALISM, ELITIST COLLUSION, AND CLASS CONFLICT

The British conquest of New France in 1759, the subsequent emphasis on colonial ethnic pluralism, and collusion between elite of the French *ancien regime* and British colonists resulted, in effect, in the termination and, in some ways, the reversal of social changes that had been taking place in New France. But the general sense of deprivation and frustration among the majority of the French population, because of these factors, led to extensive insurrections and near open rebellion, initially directed against the French *ancien regime* and, later, against the British colonial system.

Before going into the evidence for these interpretations, I will outline, briefly, some typical colonial policies which have characterized the nature of ethnic relations in other plural societies, in order to place the British conquest, and its aftermath, in a comparative context.

There are many different ways in which colonial powers have related to conquered and subordinated groups. Generally, two contrasting categories of colonial policy have been identified; the policy of *direct rule*, whereby the goal is for the social, economic and political absorption of the conquered peoples, and the policy of *indirect rule*, where the emphasis is on ethnic pluralism, involving institutional separation between the colonial power and the subordinated groups, in an attempt to either reinforce or endorse the traditional elite group among the conquered peoples.[34] It is this latter form of colonial contact which is of relevance to my analysis of French-English relations following the British conquest. It was the form of colonial contact which characterized almost all of the British colonies,[35] and the situation in Canada was no exception.

It is therefore of some interest to discuss some of the essential characteristics of this typical British colonial policy in order to discuss its ramifications with regard to relations with the French.

There remains some disagreement over the motivations of colonial powers, such as Britain, in encouraging indirect rule or pluralism. On the one hand, it is argued that indirect rule, with its recognition of the traditional authority figures in the subordinated group, enhances administrative efficiency and, coincidentally, minimizes ethnic conflict because of its recognition of the cultural traditions of the conquered peoples.[36] On the other hand, the motivations for the colonial policy of indirect rule have been viewed as an effort to assure the social, economic, and political superiority of the colonial power. This is the interpretation which, I believe, has the greater logical and empirical support, especially in its application to the Canadian scene. With regard to this interpretation, Brown bluntly states the essence of its relevance:

The European prefers the native to remain native, realizing that a collapsing native culture means Europeanized natives who will inevitably demand status in the European system

[33] See Frégault, *Canadian Society in the French Regime*, p. 12; and Philippe Garigue, "Change and Continuity in Rural French Canada," in *French Canadian Society*, eds. Rioux and Martin, p. 125.

[34] For a discussion of these different kinds of policies, see Franklin Frazier, *Race and Culture Contacts*, pp. 52, 185.

[35] *Ibid.*, p. 52.

[36] For a discussion of this point of view and others, see Raymond Kennedy, "The Colonial Crisis and the Future," in *The Science of Man in the World Crisis*, ed. R. Linton (New York: Columbia University Press 1945), 306 ff.

. . . The white man wants the services of the native, but resents him as a co-participant in the social order.[37]

It was the Quebec Act of 1774 which symbolized the application of this typical British colonial policy in Canada. In essence, the Quebec Act specified conditions of ethnic pluralism in the future evolution of Canada; specifically, it put back into power members of the French colonial elite, including the Catholic clergy and the seigniors and, in addition, provided them, at least theoretically, with more power than they had ever enjoyed throughout the history of New France.[38] Thus, the *ancien regime,* which had little control over or respect from the French colonists, was restored.

. . . My argument has been, and remains, that the policy of pluralism [symbolized by the Quebec Act] resulted in extensive reactions among the majority of the French Canadian population, ranging from universal instances of *habitants* revolt on the seigniorial estates, extensive cooperation given by the *habitants* to the American colonial expeditions in Canada, and, finally, the Papineau rebellions of 1837–38. It is my thesis that all of these reactions had in common the popular basis of resentment and frustration among the majority of the French Canadian population. More specifically, these resentments were directed largely against the French authority figures, notably the seigniors and the clergy. The evidence of collusion between Catholic clergy and the British colonial administrators is extensive.[39] Evidence for the disaffection of habitants from the control of the Church, at least up to the Papineau rebellions, is equally impressive.[40]

The almost immediate manifestation of conflict among the French Canadians following the conquest can then be seen as attributable to two essential factors: On the one hand, it represented the continuation of class conflict which, as I have suggested, marked the history of New France; on the other hand, this historical conflict was intensified and sharpened by virtue of the consequences of the Quebec Act. On a comparative basis, therefore, the policy of pluralism in Canada was far less successful than the same policy when it was applied to other colonial situations, at least over the short run. The essential difference between the Canadian situation and that of other colonial situations where the British encouraged pluralism, was that the colony of New France had a comparatively high degree of economic and social change and, consequently, no continuous or pervasive leadership structure.

These were some of the historical factors which, I believe, still influence the nature of "double pluralism" in Quebec. Internal French Canadian social class differences have survived and continue to plague French Canadian solidarity.

Developments since the several decades following the conquest until the 1940's are beyond the scope of this paper. However, there is increasing, albeit still limited, evidence attesting to the survival of internal French Canadian conflicts, manifested in different ways. The usual image of the tranquility of French Canadian parish life, with the emphasis on "cow-church-and-state" orientations of the inhabitants, is being challenged by more recent reconstructions which indicate that authority figures, such as the parish priest, were far less relevant to the values and aspirations of French Canadians than has generally been assumed.[41] . . .

---

[37] W. O. Brown, "Culture Contact and Race Conflict," in *Race and Culture Contacts,* ed. E. B. Reuter (New York: McGraw-Hill, 1934), 43.

[38] For a more extended discussion of the provisions of the *Quebec Act,* see Ossenberg, "The Conquest Revisited."

[39] See Coffin, *The Province of Quebec.*

[40] *Ibid.* and Gustave Lanctot, *Canada and the American Revolution, 1774–1783,* trans. Margaret M. Cameron (Toronto: University of Toronto Press, 1967). It is interesting that these authors, who are

diametrically opposed in their interpretation of the meaning of the mass disaffection of French Canadians, both agree about its extent.

[41] See, for example, Philippe Garigue, "Change and Continuity in Rural French Canada," in *French Canadian Society,* eds. Rioux and Martin, pp. 123–136. While Garigue's notions have been criticized

THE PERPETUATION OF DOUBLE PLURALISM IN QUEBEC

Since the 1920's, Quebec and French Canadians in particular have experienced massive social and economic changes. Urbanization has been one of the obvious changes. The emergence of the Quiet Revolution has been another manifestation of contemporary social dynamics. Yet, in spite of these developments, with their far-reaching consequences, some of the historical patterns, especially as they apply to internal social schisms among the French Canadians, continue to have considerable influence.

The early post-war period in Quebec was marked by a rapid transition from some of the long sustained traditions, but intermingled with this transition were some of the forms of social coercion and constraint which had marked the nature of pluralism since the conquest.

For the first time in Quebec, the frustrations of the lower class French Canadians found some outlet through the syndicated Catholic labour unions, which provided at least a partial organizational basis for economic and political action, a basis which had been absent before. It is not surprising, therefore, that the latent long-term protest of the French Canadian lower class, found, at least temporarily, some political expression which was mobilized by the *Bloc Populaire* in 1944.[42]

The historical influence of Anglo-French elitism and collusion, at the expense of the lower class French Canadians, could be seen even during this rapid post-war transitional period. The very fact of the involvement of the Catholic Church in the labour unions symbolized the carry-over of historical patterns which continued to have influence until at least the beginning of the Quiet Revolution in the 1950's and early 1960's.

Although there was a carry-over of at least the attempt of the Catholic clergy to exercise control over the French Canadian population, there were also very significant threats to the basis for its power. Urbanization, with its inevitable weakening of traditional social institutions, was the most pervasive factor in this threat. Another factor was the increasing manifestation of internal conflict within the Church, especially between the older and younger clergy. While this internal conflict had marked the entire evolution of the French Canadian Catholic hierarchy, it was during the rapid transitional post-war period that it found its fullest and most explicit expression.

Social reform programs related specifically to the problems of the French Canadian lower classes were increasingly and actively supported by renegade priests. Referring to the initially reformist *Bloc Populaire* Party, Wade states: "But if the *Bloc Populaire* found little favour with Cardinal Villeneuve and Archbishops Charbonneau and Vachon of Montreal and Ottawa, it was clearly welcomed by the lower clergy."[43]

Archbishop Charbonneau's later support for the causes of the French Canadian lower classes occurred only a short time after his expression of anti-reformist sentiments. And Charbonneau's change of orientation was in connection with the most significant manifestation of social unrest among French Canadian workers during the first decade of the post-war period; the Asbestos strike of 1949. The Asbestos strike, lasting for several months, was not only an expression of economic grievance; it was also an expression of lower-class resentment against *both* Anglo-Saxon Canadian *and* American domination of the Quebec economy; in a sense, it was thus an even more "sophisticated" expression of French Canadian nationalism than that found in the separatist ideology of the "new middle class" which was to emerge later. Speaking of the Asbestos strike, and social and economic conditions, generally, Charbonneau, during a

---

by colleagues, his reconstruction of parish life appears to have as much merit as the conventional interpretations held by his detractors.

[42] See Pinard, "Working Class Politics," p. 22.

[43] Mason Wade, *The French Canadians: 1760–1967* (Toronto: Macmillan of Canada, 1968), II, 956.

sermon he gave in 1949, stated: "The working class is a victim of a conspiracy which wishes to crush it, and when there is a conspiracy to crush the working class, it is the duty of the Church to intervene."[44]

But even during this period of rapid change, ideological realignments, and social conflicts, Charbonneau's sentiments were too *avant-garde* to be considered compatible with the elitist vested interests of his colleagues in the higher Catholic clergy. An increasingly militant French Canadian lower class, especially in Montreal, posed definite threats to the maintenance of cohesion, stability, and loyalty, all of which are conditions that the institutional Church depends upon for existence everywhere. It was not surprising, therefore, that the Church, with the active support of the provincial government, "evicted" Charbonneau by transferring him to the British Columbia hinterland, where his conversion to lower class insurgency could pose a threat only to the king of beasts.

The continuing collusion between Anglo Saxon elites and French Canadian elites was perhaps best illustrated by the Duplessis regime. Although it is now widely held that the Duplessis regime in Quebec was riddled with corruption and was economically and culturally retrogressive, it is not so widely known that collusion between the Anglo Saxon industrial elite and the Union Nationale, under Duplessis, was responsible for this condition. Speaking about the Duplessis regime (especially its activities in 1945), Wade has observed:

> Meanwhile the Union Nationale's electoral war chest fattened, as non-French Canadian companies sought and won, at a price, the right to exploit Quebec's immensely rich natural resources, the great pool of unorganized or weakly organized labour accustomed to a lower standard of living than English-speaking North Americans, and the manifold advantages of an accommodating government in an era elsewhere characterized by extensive governmental regulation of business.[45]

[44] Quoted in *ibid.*, pp. 1108–1109.
[45] *Ibid.*, p. 1107.

The reciprocal support between the Duplessis regime and the Catholic Church[46] was but another indication of the perpetuation of the elitist tradition.

EMERGING TRENDS: THE FUTURE OF DOUBLE PLURALISM IN QUEBEC

During the time of the rapid social changes occurring in the immediate post-war period of Quebec, the basis for Quebec's most visible expression of discontent—separatism—was evolving. The "new middle class" was being formed through a combination of factors; first, increasing urbanization and industrialization in Quebec "opened" or "widened" the middle class white collar, clerical, and administrative categories among French Canadians, thereby somewhat "softening" the theretofore rigid French Canadian class distinctions. Although the upward social mobility of the French Canadians during that time was not as extensive as that for English-speaking Quebeckers, there can be no doubt that it did occur.[47] Secondly, the educational institutions of Quebec became increasingly secularized and geared to an urban-industrial economy, giving rise to an increasing group of intellectual elite. Through extensive upward mobility and the consequent feeling of "relative-deprivation" among the French Canadian new middle class —vis-à-vis their English-speaking counterparts —the Quiet Revolution gathered momentum.

The election of Jean Lesage as Provincial Premier in 1962, with his reformist economic policies and "Québec pour les Québecois" slogans, reflected the changing social structure of Quebec, especially that of the French Canadian population. The policies of Lesage were

[46] For some views indicating the existence of this relationship, as well as some reservations concerning its extent, see the diversity of interpretations provided by several observers, reprinted in Cameron Nish, ed., *Quebec in the Duplessis Era* (Toronto: The Copp Clark Publishing Company, 1970), pp. 105–123.
[47] See Dofny and Garon-Audy, "Mobilités Professionnelles."

directly geared to the newly discovered aspirations, as well as deprivations of the French Canadian middle class.

But even the Quiet Revolution did not escape the influence of the historical French Canadian internal pluralism, especially with respect to social class differences. The economic reforms of the Liberal Lesage government were extensive, including the government takeover of Quebec Hydro, but these reforms were apparently not seen by members of the French Canadian lower classes, either rural and urban, as having any particular relevance to or benefits for them. The Union Nationale, under Premier Daniel Johnson, was re-elected in 1966, largely through the massive support of the French Canadian lower class.

The Quebec provincial elections of 1970, with the Liberals again returning to power under Robert Bourassa, reflected still further changes in the dynamics of French Canadian pluralism. However, the situation then and now is far more complex than ever before. The considerable support for the separatist *Parti Quebecois*, which won only seven seats but received 24 per cent of the popular vote (closer to one-third of the popular vote if the French Canadian voters are considered as a separate grouping), suggested a degree of French Canadian nationalism not realized before. This contemporary nationalism also reflects a softening of the internal social class differences in the French Canadian population, for an analysis of the voting patterns suggests that separatist candidates were elected in four east-Montreal French Canadian lower class ridings; ridings which had been characterized by conservative voting histories. Therefore, it would apear that there is an increasing correspondence between the traditionally divided French Canadian social classes.

With regard to these developments, it would seem that the double pluralism in Quebec is disappearing, and being replaced by a single dualism, based on French Canadian and English-speaking Canadian differences and conflicts. In other words, it would appear that the long-established French Canadian internal differentiations are increasingly being ameliorated by contemporary social and economic factors.

It would seem to me that such an assumption would be somewhat misleading in the face of the pervasiveness of the differences which have divided French Canadians historically. Some of these internal tensions continue to be of relevance to an analysis of the contemporary scene in Quebec. Before discussing these factors, I wish to refer to contemporary conditions which appear to be building a bridge between the French Canadian social classes.

The first factor is that of the massive educational explosion, especially the enormous increase in French Canadians exposed to higher education. Many, if not most, of the French Canadians entering into institutions of higher learning are of lower social-class background. Dofny has estimated that approximately 37 per cent of the French Canadian students attending the University of Montreal are of lower class background, compared to about 17 per cent of English-speaking lower class background at McGill University.[48] Moreover, the newly founded but rapidly expanding system of C.E.G.E.P.S. (the equivalent of junior colleges, or university preparation programs) is catering to a predominantly French Canadian student population. The many branches of the University of Quebec are likewise designed essentially for French Canadian students.

Some of the ideological consequences of this French Canadian educational explosion appear obvious. Basically, it would appear that a conversion to new middle class values, including the ideology of separatism, is occurring among these upwardly mobile French Canadian students of lower class origins. There is some evidence that this conversion is taking place. Among the students at the University of Montreal, only the most conservative estimate would figure the pro-separatist sentiment at 90 per cent of the student population. Guindon, through a survey of first year stu-

---

[48] Jacques Dofny, *pers. comm.*

dents at *Ecole des Hautes Commerciales de Montréal* figures that 75 per cent of the students demonstrated a clear preference for *Le Parti Québecois*.[49] It would be surprising if the magnitude of this French Canadian student support of new-middle class ideologies was not found also in the C.E.G.E.P.S. and University of Quebec, where staff are mostly graduates of the University of Montreal.

There are other indications of the relationship between the upward social mobility of the French Canadians and the conversion to separatism, thereby softening the middle class–lower class differences. Studies of the 1962 and 1966 provincial elections in Quebec have clearly shown the affinity between French Canadian youth and the separatist ideology.[50] There was shown to be a direct correlation between the percentage of young French Canadians in each of Montreal's 29 electoral districts and the strength of support for separatist candidates. Also, between both election years, the percentage of French Canadians in favour of separatism more than doubled, including almost half of a representative sample of young French Canadians from all income groups. The same studies also found that the more knowledgeable the French Canadian youth was about provincial politics, the more likely he was to support the separatist cause. If this latter finding is applied to the upward educational mobility among increasing numbers of lower class French Canadians, it would appear that conversion to the values of the French Canadian new middle class is very extensive.

Have the increased educational opportunities for French Canadians correlated with increased occupational opportunities? While the exact nature of this relationship is difficult to assess, a recent study by Dofny[51] would indirectly suggest the existence of this rela-

tionship. In a comparison of upward social mobility patterns of English-speaking Quebeckers and French Canadians, Dofny found that the previously documented gap between the two groups was decreasing; that, indeed, the French Canadians were experiencing an unprecedented degree of upward occupational mobility. While Dofny attributed this upward mobility to basic structural changes in the Quebec economy, as opposed to the increasing competitive advantages of the French Canadians vis-à-vis the English-speaking Quebeckers, there can be no doubt that an increasing number of French Canadians are experiencing a "new middle class" way of life and are being at least exposed to, if not converted to, the separatist ideology resident in this group in recent years.

There is, however, evidence of the continuation of French Canadian pluralism, expressed in the historical internal social class differences. Whereas it is true that the proportion of lower class voters who supported *Le Parti Québecois* increased, in comparison to their support for separatist candidates in previous elections, and thereby also apparently conforming to the middle-class pattern, it is also true that the majority of lower class French Canadians were anti-separatist. Expressions of hostility toward separatists and the French Canadian middle class generally, were very extensive during my daily visits to St. Henri, a lower class French Canadian area in Montreal where, over a period of three months in early 1970, I attempted to assess some aspects of social changes occurring there.

During my research visit to Montreal, it also became clear that the view of the French Canadian intelligentsia toward the French Canadian lower class was essentially a patronizing one, and consisted basically of the need to "politicize" the working and lower social classes; there was, however, little or no sense of social rapport or solidarity with the lower classes.

It is difficult to assess the role that the militant Confederation of National Trade

---

[49] Hubert Guindon, *pers. comm.*

[50] These studies, conducted by Pierre Guimond and Serge Carlos, both graduate students at the University of Montreal at the time, were reported in a number of newspapers, including *The Montreal Star*, July 26, 1966.

[51] Dofny and Garon-Audy, "Mobilités Professionnelles."

Unions (C.N.T.U.) has played in bridging the gap between the French Canadian social classes. On the one hand, the massive support that its membership gave to Lévesque and his *Le Parti Québecois* in the 1970 elections, would suggest that increasing organization among French Canadian workers would increase their sympathies for the aspirations of the new middle class. On the other hand, it has been suggested that most of the new members of the C.N.T.U. are affiliated with white collar occupations,[52] thereby making the argument somewhat redundant.

In any event, it does not appear that the C.N.T.U. has thus far provided the organizational vehicle for the problems and aspirations of the French Canadian lower classes. Its militant ideological basis, attempting to appeal to both middle and lower classes, is too diffuse and, I believe, too suspect to draw massive support from the lower classes.

What will be the future of internal French Canadian conflicts and their implications for Canadian confederation? The answer depends on social, economic, and political changes within Quebec, and on the reaction of Canadians elsewhere to these changes.

THEORETICAL CONSIDERATIONS OF ALTERNATIVES

One of the most penetrating analyses of internal social class conflicts among French Canadians has been provided by Pinard.[53] Pinard suggests that in the evolution of Quebec during the past forty years, the French Canadian lower classes and middle class have acted in contradiction to each other in terms of political behaviour. In some ways, the French Canadian middle classes over this period, including the recently emergent new middle class, have demonstrated more conservatism and self imposed cultural encapsulation, than have the French Canadian lower class who, in generally supporting economic reformist

parties (as opposed to parties calling primarily for national unity), have demonstrated their own severe sense of economic deprivaton and, coincidentally, suspicion of the French Canadian middle class.

Pinard's analysis is important in terms of the future evolution of Quebec. If a political movement in Quebec combines both the economic concerns predominant in the lower classes—with the aspirations for cultural identity, without over-emphasizing either of these components, an ideological merger between lower and middle class French Canadians would appear likely.

Perhaps Guindon's portrayal of Quebec's bureaucratic revolution[54] provides a key to the potential for such a merger to appear. Guindon suggests that the massive bureaucratic expansion of Quebec industry poses a dilemma for French Canadians. On the one hand, increasing participation of French Canadians in occupations associated with large bureaucratic organizations appears inevitable. On the other hand, bilingualism within these corporations is now being encouraged. Therefore, both the sheer impersonality of bureaucracy—its contractual, as opposed to cultural or traditional basis of operation, threaten to emasculate the cultural identity especially of middle class French Canadians. Moreover, and in adding to Guindon's thesis, the exclusive use of the French language within these bureaucratic organizations would be discouraged by the very nature of their associations with enterprise outside of Quebec, thereby further weakening French Canadian cultural identity which could better survive in the context of small-scale and localistic enterprise. Given such structural dilemmas, and their inevitable dilution of cultural traditions, it would appear that convergence between lower class and middle class French Canadians would increase, based essentially on common concerns of economic deprivation instead of cultural identity.

Extensive economic deprivation among French Canadians of all social classes could bring about a merger which would virtually

---

[52] Hubert Guindon, *pers. comm.*
[53] Pinard, "Working Class Politics."

[54] Hubert Guindon, "Language, Careers and Formal Organizations," research in progress.

guarantee a separatist government in Quebec within the next decade. On the other hand, the absence of such a sense of economic deprivation among the French Canadians generally would tend to perpetuate the double pluralism of Quebec which in many ways has been the most important factor in the preservation of Canadian confederation.

The reaction of the Federal Government and the English-speaking population to the manifestation of the social, economic, and political problems of the contemporary colony of Quebec will likely influence the interplay of these considerations and determine the fate of Confederation. French Canadians, similar to minority groups throughout the world, have attained temporary high levels of social solidarity and separatist sentiments in reaction to autocratic and symbolically racist policies and behaviour of the central government supported by majority ethnic groups. The use of arbitrary military force in reaction to the anti-conscription sentiments of the French Canadians during both World Wars and against the workers during the Asbestos strike of 1949 has been typical of the entire history of French-English relations. But this policy has only contributed to the developing spirit of self-determination among French Canadians of all social classes. The use of the War Measures Act in response to the kidnappings and terrorism of the Front de Libération du Québec in October, 1970 can only accelerate the development of the separatist ideology among *les Québecois*, for it will remind them of their common heritage as victims of the double pluralism and elitist collusion which has marked their entire history.

10

Race Relations in the Six Counties: Colonialism, Industrialization, and Stratification in Ireland

ROBERT MOORE

This paper falls into four sections. The first deals with the history of English colonialism in Ireland and tries to show the way in which Irish society was stratified under colonial rule. The second section examines the effects of industrialization in Ireland and the extent to which stratification derived from industrial relations has modified that derived from the colonial period. In this section the focus of the discussion is narrowed, so that thereafter we concentrate on an analysis of the situation in the six counties of Northern Ireland only. We look also at the relationship between social class and sectarianism in twentieth-century conflicts. The fourth section is the key section in terms of the major objectives of the paper: here we ask if the social relations of Northern Ireland, and especially the class relations modified by sectarianism, are, in fact, race relations. The fourth and final section examines

Robert Moore is Senior Lecturer in Sociology at the University of Aberdeen.

The author would like to thank Mike Lyon for his comments on an early draft of this paper and Owen Dudley Edwards for criticisms of the paper as read at the University of Lancaster Conference on 'Conflict in Northern Ireland'. Neither is at all responsible for shortcomings of this discussion. This paper was completed before the resumption of direct rule from Westminster.

Reprinted from *Race* 14 (July, 1972) by permission of the author.

the policy implications of this being the case. The immediate problems of violent conflict in Northern Ireland, the role of the army, and the I.R.A. groups are not examined in this article, which is an attempt to set up an interpretive model of Northern Ireland society.

I. BRITISH COLONIALISM IN IRELAND[1]

(i) *Political*

Political considerations seem to have been at least as important as economic in England's domination of Ireland. English governments have always seen Ireland as not only a centre of native intrigue but as a potential springboard for European aggression. Thus from Tudor times one of the main objects (if not *the* main object) of English policy was to secure Ireland politically and militarily. Economic exploitation followed, thus the sequence of 'the flag following trade' seems to have been reversed in Ireland.

Henry VIII adopted a system of indirect rule in Ireland by making the Irish ruling class dependent upon the Crown through the 'surrender and re-grant' of land in Ireland. Henry also ignored the Irish system of land tenure, and his grants made land heritable, rather than tenable for life only, according to the Irish custom. This initiated changes in the tradition of Irish social structure that were to be effective until Gaelic culture was eventually destroyed.

As Henry's objectives were political, it was more important for him to maintain the settlement than to enforce the Reformation in Ireland. But in 1580 there was an insurrection with minor Spanish support which turned into a cruel guerrilla war. This strengthened the equation of Roman Catholics with traitors, which had been made by the Bull of Pius V, excommunicating Elizabeth in 1570.

One way to subdue the disloyal Irish was to replace them with loyal Englishmen. Mean-

[1] This section relies heavily on Professor J. C. Beckett's *A Short History of Ireland* (London, Oxford University Press, 1958).

while English population pressures could be relieved by migration to Ireland. Thus a policy of settlement, or plantation, was adopted. This early attempt at settlement was carried out through middlemen who largely vitiated the intention of the scheme by accepting Irish native tenants at very high rents for settlement.

Nonetheless the land settlements further undermined traditional Irish ways of life and in response to this, in 1590 in Ulster, the O'Neil revolted against the English. He submitted in 1603, and with his submission, according to Beckett, Gaelic Ireland was finished. The revolt of a Tudor nobleman was clearly more serious than a native rebellion, and it thus demanded a more radical peace. The 'flight of the Earls' in 1607 provided opportunities for extensive confiscations in Ulster. Protestant English nobles, gentry, and officials were seeking land and were thus allocated forfeited land. But, more radically, proletarian settlers were transported to Ireland. This insured a new kind of settlement rather than a change of landlords. By 1628, 2,000 British families had been resettled in the six planted counties alone.

James I sought not only to secure the loyalty of Ireland but to increase his revenues from plantations. He obtained land for planting through reviving dormant royal claims, finding flaws in titles to land, and reclaiming land settled in excess of original grants in Ulster.

Extensive forfeitures also followed the insurrection of 1641, the occasion for which was the Civil War and the consequential weakening of the government's position in England. Because they feared the aggressive Protestantism of the Long Parliament the Roman Catholic lords and gentry of the Pale sided with the Ulster insurrectionists. Ireland was re-conquered with great savagery by Cromwell and Ireton between 1649 and 1652. It was a total conquest, executed with the assistance of a Scots army under Munro. The conquest was followed by extensive changes of proprietorship, the new settlers including officers from the commonwealth army. The

majority of landlords were now Protestants rather than Roman Catholics. This political and economic shift was accompanied by an aggressive nationalism based on the assumption that 'Roman Catholics could never be loyal to the English interest.'

It would be wrong to regard Ireland as simply divided into Protestants and Catholics. The English were divided into the Old English and the new settlers; there were Roman Catholics and Protestants among them. There were also newer settlers and the old Irish nobility. From the 1680s however, Irish society consisted of three main sectors; Anglicans (the dominant group), Protestant Dissenters (mainly Scots), and Roman Catholics (the mass of the population).

The battle of the Aughrim in 1689 represented conquest for the Protestants in Ireland. The Protestant ascendancy which followed originated from the colonial garrison and was extended by penal policies against Roman Catholics and dissenters.

In 1801 the Union of Great Britain and Ireland was formed as a military necessity due to the threat from France. The Protestants had some fears of this union as it was likely to result in the spreading of English reform to the Catholic masses in Ireland. Whilst the Protestant ascendancy may thus have been destroyed in the long run, power nevertheless remained with the landlords and Church. The fear of Catholicism brought the established Church and the Ulster Presbyterians together by about 1840 and the Union with England was maintained by coercion.

(ii) *Economic*

Economic relations with Ireland were originally of a fairly minor importance compared with the political. Economic exploitation was largely a matter of private enterprise. The Irish woodlands were cut down in the late sixteenth and early seventeenth centuries, both for military purposes and for the export of timber. Under Wentworth (1633–40) Ireland was kept economically dependent on England. Ireland was deliberately underdeveloped.

There was to be no competition with English wool and Ireland was to remain a market for English wool. Thus the wool industry was restricted, and eventually destroyed in 1699. In the 1660s the export of cattle to England was banned. Irish brewers had to buy their hops from England only and an Act of 1748 forbade the export of glass from Ireland. Ireland was also treated as a colony with respect to the Navigation Acts. Thus British policy was essentially mercantilist. Ireland also had to maintain a standing army from its surplus, the balance of which reverted to the English state.

The largest source of economic exploitation was the land. Absentee English landlords extracted rents from their Irish estates and the Crown maintained numerous sinecures on Irish revenue.

The landlords collected their rent through middlemen who engaged in rent-racking. The Irish tenants lacked security, both as a result of the policy of the middlemen and as a result of the penal laws restricting leases for Roman Catholics. No tenant could afford to invest capital in his land and no landlord needed to do so for as long as he received rent. Ireland thus suffered from a chronic shortage of capital. This is a classic colonial situation; the colonisers have no interest in *developing* a colony, only in *exploiting* it.

The exception to this situation is Ulster. The manufacture of linen had been encouraged since Wentworth's administration and had grown mainly in Ulster. Linen offered no competition with English products although the export of coloured linen was banned in the eighteenth century. The influx of French Huguenots after the revocation of the Edict of Nantes also gave a considerable boost to the linen industry, as well as strengthening Protestantism. Whether land was held in Ulster under the 'Ulster custom,' which gave security of tenure and rights in tenure, or not, the Ulster tenant believed that he had these rights and acted accordingly. Thus on the basis of manufacturing and secure agriculture Ulster was able to develop economically, because capital could be accumulated and circulated.

There is no doubt, none the less, that Ireland was a British colony; dominated for England's political and economic advantage. The political security provided by the state also provided the opportunities for private economic activities, and the political loyalty of those with economic interests in Ireland reinforced the British Government's political power.

(iii) *Stratification*

Let us now examine the main features of social stratification and segregation in Ireland. We have seen that the English dominated Ireland; the English formed a ruling class of Anglican landlords and officials; they were educated in England, married amongst the English, and sat in English parliaments. The English also enacted penal legislation against both dissenters and Roman Catholics. As early as 1366 The Statutes of Kilkenny forbade Anglo-Irish intermarriage. From 1692 Catholics were excluded from office and from politics and restrictions were placed upon their acquisition and inheritance of land. This policy drove the Irish middle class abroad, thus leaving the Catholic clergy as the leaders of the Irish natives. The vast mass of the Catholics were poor or impoverished tenant farmers or farm labourers more concerned with survival than potential deprivation of office. The High Church regime of Queen Anne also forbade Catholics to worship in their own forms, under pain of severe penalties.

Charles II had also forbidden the Presbyterian Ministers to preach or administer any rites. He partially recanted in 1672 (in order to secure the loyalty of the Presbyterians) but continued to keep a watch on the Ulster Presbyterians' connection with Scotland. The Test Act excluded Presbyterians from office in the early eighteenth century and thus deprived Ulster of many officials, including a number of ardent loyalists of the 1689 period. As a result Protestants predominated in the emigration to America in the 1720s and 1730s. The Presbyterians created their own culture in Ulster, and amongst them there grew up a professional middle class largely educated at Scottish Universities. The Presbyterians did not marry Catholics. Thus we have a tripartite division of Ireland; Anglican landlords and officials; Presbyterian Scots manufacturers and professionals; and a Roman Catholic Irish peasantry. . . .

. . . The granting of the franchise . . . began the firm polarization of Irish society. With the vote restored to the Catholics in 1793, the policy of Irish reform became transmuted into republicanism. Resistance to reform meant union with Great Britain. The Anglicans had been able to dominate and deprive the dissenters, knowing that if the Catholics rose, the dissenters would need Anglican support. But now that the Catholics had the vote, Anglicans and Presbyterians drew together. Orange Societies were formed from 1795 onwards and by the end of the century Ireland was on the verge of civil war.

Catholic emancipation was granted in 1829, . . . but whilst formal disabilities were thus removed from the Catholics, power still lay in the Protestant control of the economy, the magistracy, and grand juries. Protestant rule remained coercive. For example, between 1847–57 the Union Parliament passed twelve measures suspending normal civil liberties in Ireland.

We see that an alliance was formed between previously subordinate and superordinate sections of society against the common threat of a numerically larger third section. This was a response to the growing political power of the Catholics; their power had grown through factors outside the control of the Protestant settler population, namely political considerations in the imperial government. The Protestants none the less claimed not to hate the Catholics; like the Boer farmer, the Protestants loved the native; in the late eighteenth century Henry Grattan said: 'I love the Roman Catholics, I am the friend of his liberty, but only in as much as his liberty is entirely consistent with your ascendency, and an addition to the strength and freedom of the Protestant community.' . . .[2]

[2] Cited in ibid., p. 124.

Thus prior to independence we have a situation in which the Protestant inheritors of the conquest were exploiting Ireland mainly through rents; meanwhile their political grip was weakening as a result of imperial concessions to local political demands. The Protestants occupied ruling positions or were landlords, professionals, officials, or businessmen; class and occupational considerations thus reinforced the practice of avoiding intermarriage, which also rested on a religious basis.

For Catholics, mixed marriages were explicitly forbidden in 1908. Catholics and Protestants were also divided on the basis of language and culture. Crucially, Protestants saw Catholics as disloyal to the Union. Thus, as a result of colonialism, Ireland had a population fragmented by religion and national origin and accorded different treatment thereby.

The partition of Ireland was achieved with considerable violence and bloodshed; the details of these events and the political background do not directly concern us here. . . .*

II. INDUSTRIALIZATION

Our discussion has centred so far on the social relations of a colonial, settler society. But parts of Ireland, notably the north east, were industrializing. This industrializing sector of Ireland was linked to the British economy through raw material supplies and markets; it was not oriented to the remainder of Ireland. The English economic connection also entailed the integration of the Northern Ireland economy into the British imperial economy, shipping being an especially important item. In the industrial situation we might expect to find new kinds of social relations developing, which are quite different from those of the colonial settlement, and which we might ex-

* Editor's note: The six northern counties were separated from the rest of Ireland in 1921 and remained under partial British political control, while the rest of Ireland, with its Roman Catholic majority, achieved independence.

pect to find modifying the relations of colonial domination. . . .

As in South Africa, so in Northern Ireland, there was a nascent class movement within the dominant order.[3] The Belfast Protestant Association was such a Protestant working-class organization, but its commitment to Protestantism prevented it from being a party of all working classes, or indeed truly of the Protestant working class, and its loyalty to the Unionist party (whatever this entailed in terms of social and economic policy) could be ensured by offering the threat of Catholic domination. Organizations such as Ulster Protestant Action have been formed among the working class to protect Protestant workers from unemployment, and in so doing have denied class as a basis for working-class organizations in favour of religion.

In 1933 there was an apparent rise of working *class* activity in response to the depressed state of trade in Northern Ireland. Members of the Ulster elite (Lord Craigavon and Sir Basil Brooke) appealed directly to sectarian interests in openly advocating discrimination in employment against Catholics. Brooke (later Lord Brookebrough) appealed in July 1933: 'Many in this audience employ Catholics, but I have not one about my place. Catholics are out to destroy Ulster with all their might. . . . I would appeal to Loyalists therefore, whenever possible, to employ good Protestant lads and lasses.' And in March 1934: 'I recommend people . . . not to employ Roman Catholics, *99% of whom are disloyal.*'[4] The message was obvious, only employ Catholics when there are not enough Protestants to fill jobs. The appeal has many analogies in race relations situations. The appeal also suggests to the Protestant working class that they stand to gain more by being loyal to the Unionist order than by combining with Catholic workers to challenge the employers. Brooke was assuring Protestant workers, as they have often been reassured since, that

however badly they may fare, Catholics will be worse off. Thus the Protestant could be related to the Catholic in the same way as the poor white to the Negro in the Southern States, where marginal status differences between members of the same depressed class loom large in the political consciousness of the poor whites. In turn the Government has refused to recognize the Irish Congress of Trade Unions because of its connection with the Republic. But in so doing it also refuses to recognize nonsectarian working-class organization.

It is easy to pretend that religious belief is merely an expression of something else—underlying material conflicts, bourgeois propaganda, and so on. But in Ireland we do have to account for the effects of religion as such. Nineteenth-century Irish Protestantism was deeply evangelical and thus Protestants believed that the Catholic was wrong at the theological level; in this context the possibility of converting the Catholic was not excluded. The convert was fully acceptable in Protestant society, in a way that a Negro Christian in the States would have not been socially acceptable in white Christian society.

None the less the events of the early 1930s came nearest to fulfilling a simple Marxist analysis. The bourgeoisie used religious factors to create false consciousness amongst the Ulster proletariat. The attempt to foment sectarianism was deliberate. But the success of the attempt depended on its drawing on deeply rooted traditional antipathies. The poor Protestant, perhaps a countryman before migrating to Belfast, believed himself the successor to the triumphs of Derry, Aughrim, and the Boyne and he celebrated these triumphs and his dominance first at his mother's knee and then every year on the streets cheering the Orange Lodges.

The 'false consciousness' was to a degree turned into 'true consciousness' of real interests. The Protestant workers were not to remain only the poor members of the richest and most powerful part of Northern Irish society, into which they were born; they achieved real benefits. Thus systematic discrimination in employment, the gerrymander-

[3] John Rex, 'The Plural Society: The South African Case,' *Race* (Vol. XII, No. 4, 1971).

[4] Liam de Paor, *Divided Ulster* (Harmondsworth Penguin, 1970), pp. 114–15. Emphasis added.

ing of elections, and later the discriminatory allocation of council housing and local authority jobs have been used to bring tangible rewards to Protestant workers for loyalty to the Unionist regime.[5] Legislation in England has to be matched by parallel legislation in Northern Ireland. Thus the advent of the welfare state in England has provided opportunities, not for the development of equal social rights based on citizenship, but patronage for the reinforcement of existing inequalities.

Discrimination in employment in Northern Ireland does not operate in the gross manner found in South Africa, nor in the relatively exclusive way found historically in the American deep south. Barritt and Carter, Richard Rose, and the Cameron Commission all suggest that both Catholics and Protestants are found at all levels of Northern Irish society, but not in proportion to their numbers in the population.[6] Thus few Catholics are found in senior administrative posts at provincial level. At the local level administrative posts are distributed by religious patronage, as are local authority manual and clerical jobs. Thus both Catholic and Protestant local authorities control very important sources of employment patronage, and use this to the advantage of their own religious community.[7]

Amongst private firms one finds a wide range of patterns of discrimination: total exclusion of one group, the employment of one group only when others are not available, and then solely in low-paid jobs. Some firms employ both Protestants and Catholics, but only promote Protestants to supervisory posts, others segregate on a departmental basis. The rationale of exclusion is familiar to students of race relations; customers are thought not to like being served by Catholics/Protestants, men will not work under Catholic supervisors and so on. In some cases trade unions have

actually threatened to strike if, for example, Catholics were employed in supervisory or skilled posts. Skilled and professional Catholics seem to be more discriminated against than unskilled workers.[8]

The simplest demonstration of the way in which segregation in employment works overall to the disadvantage of Catholics, can be found in the migration figures which show that between 55 and 60 per cent of Northern Ireland's emigration is accounted for by Catholic migration. This large migration from the Catholic third of the population has the effect of keeping the Catholics and Protestant populations roughly in proportion. Thus something like one in ten Catholics have to seek opportunities for work outside the province, compared with something like one in twenty-five of Protestants.

Whether class affiliation could have begun to replace sectarian affiliations to any extent in the first half of the century, we cannot know. It was too clearly in the interests of the ruling elite to divide and rule the workers for a situation to develop in which class would emerge as an important basis of conflict. We could argue similarly that racial hostility may not have increased in England in the 1960s if a policy of *laissez-faire* had been adopted, but it was too much in the political interests of certain groups and individuals to exacerbate racial hostilities for the unlikely experiment to have been tried.

What kind of society did we have in Northern Ireland at the beginning of the present phase of the conflict? Catholics and Protestants were living in relatively segregated localities; they had their separate systems of religion and education, differential access to jobs and housing; they played different sports and seldom intermarried. Every year they celebrated their difference in Easter and Orange parades and the ceremonial closing of Derry's gates. The Orange parades were also annual celebrations of the Protestant domination in which battles and massacres, sieges, and rescues were remembered with the fervour of the

---

[5] H.M.S.O. Belfast, *Disturbances in Northern Ireland*, Cmd. 532, 1969 ('The Cameron Commission') chapter 12.

[6] Denis F. Barritt and Charles F. Carter, *The Northern Ireland Problem* (London, Oxford University Press, 1962).

[7] R. Rose, *Governing Without Consensus*, (London, Faber and Faber, 1971).

[8] Ibid., p. 289; and Barritt and Carter, op. cit., chapter 6.

Children of Israel looking back to their days in the wilderness (or the trek Boer looking back to the trek and Blood River). This spirit is succinctly expressed in a letter to the *Belfast Telegraph,* cited by Rose,[9] the writer writes of 12 July: 'Orangemen that day not only commemorate a very significant military and political victory, but a great deliverance from Roman slavery, in much the same way as the Jews each year commemorate their deliverance from bondage in Egypt.' The Orange Societies which organize these annual celebrations also provide the core leadership of the ruling Unionist party, and constitute the most important constituency within Unionism. To some extent the Orange Order also provides vertical integration of Protestant society.[10]

At the same time, Protestants and Catholics are integrated into the economy of Northern Ireland and both belong to the one state, although many Catholics belong unwillingly.

. . . Unlike the South African whites the Protestants have not been able to confine the Catholic workers to factory compounds, nor have they been able to reduce them to total slavery. This has been prevented by both political and economic factors: (i) the proximity of Great Britain and the need to comply with Westminster legislation. The continued support of the Westminster Government is the *sine qua non* of the Northern Ireland state. Therefore, the Unionist Government has at least to appear to grant all its population equal rights based on citizenship, such as are granted in England. (ii) The institutions of domination and division are sufficiently strong to prevent the Catholics becoming a threat, so long as British support can be assured. Catholics are effectively deprived of political power largely as a result of their numerical minority, but also because of their minority status. Thus Catholics form a political opposition which cannot aspire to power within the parliamentary system. Only

in certain localities can Catholics exercise the monopoly powers of a majority. (iii) The existence of a pool of labour both in the poorer western (Catholic) areas of Northern Ireland, and the Republic, ensure the depression of wages without the use of political force. (iv) Discontented or unemployed Catholics can migrate to Great Britain. . . .

The Catholic birth-rate remains higher than the Protestant; the fear of being out-bred has, according to de Paor, been the cause of riots and pogroms in Belfast. The effects of these riots have been to drive Catholics out of areas of housing and out of certain jobs. . . .

Some small representations of class interests have, however, emerged, most notably from amongst the middle class. This might be seen as a minority non-sectarian movement drawn from among the people who have most to lose if rioting spreads to the suburbs. These groupings stand for compromise and peace, but have suffered the fate of most third parties in Northern Ireland. This interest is also to some degree represented in the Civil Rights movement itself. The Civil Rights movement was not entirely devoted to the protection of the glass in suburban windows however. It also represented the objectives of a Catholic middle class which had enjoyed educational and economic advance but was denied both social standing and political power in the province. An end to discrimination was clearly in their interest. The Civil Rights campaigners . . . became identified by the Protestant working class as pro-Catholic. In a sense Civil Rights movements are pro-Catholic as the privileges of the Protestant working class are founded upon the denial of citizenship rights to the Catholics. The Protestants do not need to challenge the *status quo* in Northern Ireland. . . .

Northern Ireland is a society in which social stratification derived from the social relations of an industrial society is found within the major religious groups. Attempts have been made to organize on a *class* basis across these groups but these have always been defeated by playing upon the hostilities and fears derived from the colonial past and expressed in modern sectarianism. These fears and

[9] Rose, op. cit., p. 258.

[10] See David A. Roberts, 'The Orange Order in Ireland,' *British Journal of Sociology* (Vol. XXII, No. 3, 1971); Barritt and Carter, op. cit., p. 46; R. S. P. Elliot and John Hickie (pseudonyms), *Ulster: A Case Study in Conflict Theory* (London, Longman, 1971), p. 37.

hostilities have been deliberately used by groups in power to prevent the emergence of class organization, and thus to preserve their own power. Over all there is a situation in which the Protestants collectively have a clear monopoly of political power and significant economic and social advantages over the Catholics. Why then is Northern Ireland apparently so politically unstable? Is the instability derived only from the general disruption caused by the elite taking divisive steps to maintain their power?

Recent Changes

The present conflict has derived in part from economic developments in the two parts of Ireland. In the North traditional heavy industries have declined and attempts have been made to encourage new industries to the region. The South has also embarked upon a policy of industrialization and has sought foreign capital in order to pursue this policy. The rise in living standards in Ireland and the increasing orientation of England to European markets makes it desirable for Northern Ireland to find markets in the South. Whilst the landlord elites remain powerful, in both the North and the South, new business interests have arisen to compete with them. . . . The interests of the Southern and Northern industrialists are similar and they plainly stand to profit by private and state collaborative activities. . . . The changing nature of the imperial interest and the growth of a European economic orientation have accelerated the need for a *détente* and loosened the economic power of the old elite. The likely success of this *détente* as enhanced (especially in Protestant eyes) by the oecumenical and liberal outlook of Pope John. . . .

Conventional theories of industrialization assume that one condition of industrialization is the rationalization of the labour market through the removal of traditional restraints on work. In a fully industrialized society one finds, ideally, "the complete absence of appropriation of jobs and opportunities for earnings by workers and, conversely, the absence

of appropriation of workers by owners. This involves free labour, freedom of the labour market, and freedom in the selection of workers.[11] But as the example of South Africa shows, an unfree labour market is not inconsistent with capitalist development.[12] Religious discrimination is irrelevant to the industrialization of the North; that is to say, the North can industrialize with or without the practice of religious discrimination in economic and political affairs. Thus, it is unlikely that either party . . . had any ambitions to rationalize the labour market. But if the Republic was not interested in the rights of the Northern Catholics, the Civil Rights organizations were.

We do not need to rehearse the events which followed the situation we have described; Protestant fears were aroused and expressed in hostility against Catholics. Catholic fears were re-aroused. Northern Irish society polarized, to the extent of re-segregating partially de-segregated housing. Violence became a prominent feature of the situation and city centres started to burn. The British Army arrived to restore order, but in default of a political change in Northern Ireland could only enforce the *status quo ante*. The British Army is thus seen as being engaged in a continuation of the oppression of the Catholics; in so far as this is the case it is engaged in a colonial role. Whilst the British Government suggests reform, the Northern Ireland Government sees such reform as unpopular and open to out-flanking by Protestant radicals.[13]

The Northern Ireland regime is thus in a bind. Economic developments would seem to demand economic and social changes in relations between the North and South, but if these were put into operation, they would undermine the basis of the regime's power. It is doubtful, in fact, whether such changes

[11] Max Weber, *Theory of Social and Economic Organisation*, edited by Talcott Parsons (New York, Free Press, 1964), p. 275.

[12] See H. Adam, *Modernising Racial Domination* (Berkeley, University of California Press, 1971).

[13] This point is also made by Elliot and Hickie, op. cit., pp. 46–7.

could be effected against Protestant opposition.[14]

III. RACE RELATIONS

De Paor begins his book with the assertion: 'In Northern Ireland, Catholics are blacks who happen to have white skin.'[15] Much of what we have said about post-colonial Northern Ireland points, at least superficially, to what might conventionally be regarded as a race relations situation.

If we only treat Northern Ireland as a fragment of Western capitalist society, we encounter difficulties in understanding the power structure—and, crucially, the allocation of occupational roles. Working-class roles, access to the employment market, to housing, and political power seem to be based on religion rather than ability or need. The relationship between social class, and other bases of social differentiation is sociologically problematic and historically unfixed. Certainly power and privilege do not seem to be so exclusively based on social class as in other European capitalist societies. . . .

The existence of simple segmentation does not constitute a race relations situation, nor does the simple domination of one group by another. If a structure of social relations is one of race relations we would find: (1) two or more identifiable groups, (2) a high degree of conflict in which ascriptive criteria are used to mark out the conflicting groups, and (3) the implicit or explicit use of 'some kinds of deterministic theory' to justify the ascription of roles.

On these criteria is the Northern Ireland situation one of race relations?

(1) There are two or more identifiable groups. Catholics and Protestants can be identified by their position in the economy, by their housing situation and by the schools their children go to. To some extent they can be identified by their family size. Some wear badges to show religious affiliation and every year large masses celebrate their membership of one group or another with parades, bands, banners, sashes, singing, and prayers (and now in their funerals). It is also said that you can tell a Catholic from a Protestant, 'just by looking at them.'[16] There may be some marginal validity in this contention given a long period of intermarrying within Scots, English, and Irish populations respectively. It is also known that anti-Semites are better at identifying Jews than others; similar skills might be found with respect to religious affiliation in Northern Ireland. The two groups can be identified, most obviously, by the church they attend on Sundays. The Northern Ireland population consists of more assiduous church-goers than any other part of Great Britain; there is a sense in which religion is political conflict carried on at the expressive level.[17] The Protestant identification is also peculiarly national; many identify with the Scots, this identification is seen in the use of Scots pipe bands in Orange parades, the Orange Order's direct connection with Scotland, and the popularity of Portrush for Glaswegian holidays. Edward Carson in rallying support for the Ulster Protestant cause in Glasgow before the first world war made a direct use of the kith and kin argument.[18] More recently the Scottish connection has been underlined in Ian Paisley's demand for Scots troops to be sent to Northern Ireland.

(2) There is plainly a high degree of conflict. The conflicting groups are marked out by ascriptive *religious* criteria. In Northern Ireland one is born a Catholic or a Protestant and changes of religion are rare.[19] Intermarriage, especially when accompanied by conversion to the other religion, causes considerable family conflict and is very rare (4 per cent according to Rose). The mixed marriage, like agnosticism, has no place in Northern Ire-

---

[14] Conor Cruise O'Brien, 'Violence in Ireland. Another Algeria?,' *New York Review of Books* (Vol. XVII, No. 4, September 1971), pp. 17–19.

[15] De Paor, op. cit., p. 13.

[16] Barritt and Carter, op. cit., p. 52.

[17] Rose, op. cit., p. 264.

[18] H. Montgomery Hyde, *Carson* (London, Heinemann, 1953), p. 323.

[19] Rose, op. cit., p. 268.

land society, in which everyone is ascribed to either Protestantism or Catholicism.

(3) The implicit or explicit use of 'some kind of deterministic theory' to justify the ascription of roles: it is not easy to find current explicit and recognizably racist justifications of the ascription of roles. As we saw above, the Scots connection is seen to be important and this comes out in nineteenth and twentieth century statements on racial distinctions. . . .

A Catholic recently interviewed for the *Sunday Times* by Pauline Peters seemed to recognize racial elements in the conflict, and to echo de Paor when he said: 'It's racial difference between us. Religion never comes into it. They've got their government in power which gives them money in their pockets. We're the blacks.'[20]

The popular English notion of the slow and indolent Mick raising a large family on social security, also seems to have an implicit and familiar racial determinism about it.

Religious theories also have a deterministic aspect. Northern Irish Protestant demonology identifies Rome (the Roman Catholic Church) with the Whore of Babylon (drunk on the blood of the Martyrs). It is Rome's historical and inevitable role to mislead, corrupt, and pervert; only the forces of the true (Protestant) gospel have stood and stand against Rome.

> When a Protestant is intolerant he is false to his principles . . . but for a Roman Catholic intolerance is in considerable measure an accepted principle . . . the Roman Catholic Church is a world-wide religious organisation that seeks to gain control of the institutions of mankind and of public life generally; it is not merely a church, it is a political organization.[21]

The Protestants are, in Ian Paisley's words, 'engaged in the great battle of Biblical Protestantism against popery.' The argument which has a cosmic significance is derived from scriptures and is elaborated in a theology that ascribes unchanging characteristics to Roman Catholicism and Roman Catholics. To some degree this outlook is reinforced by the history of Catholic revolt in Ireland, and Catholic intolerance from the Reformation onwards. For the Protestant especially however it is a selective history.

It would be a mistake to present a picture of Northern Ireland as a scene of continual hostility. Many of the people interviewed by Rose in the late 1960s expressed tolerant, 'live and let live' attitudes. These are attitudes common to working-class communities. Respondents also had friends of the other religion, worked alongside them, and exchanged friendly services with them. None the less social distance was maintained (crucially in the question of marriage) and intolerance was always latent and likely to express itself in conflict and violence, as recent events have shown. Of Rose's Protestant respondents, 51 per cent endorsed the use of violence to maintain Northern Ireland's constitutional position whilst 36 per cent of the whole population endorsed violence as a means to changing or maintaining the constitutional position.[22]

We might also suggest that deterministic political theory is to be found in Northern Ireland. This theory assumes that '99 per cent' of Catholics are traitors or potential traitors, that they reject the Northern Ireland constitution, that they will always use 'their might and power' to overthrow the Protestant order. By virtue of being born Catholics, they are born disloyal.

All of these considerations, when taken together point to the existence of a considerable body of deterministic theory about Catholics. It also means that the conflict in Northern Ireland is truly race conflict.

IV.   DISCUSSION

Why was it necessary to develop an elaborate analysis in order to tie a 'race relations' label to

---

[20] Pauline Peters, 'In Belfast they ask: But is there a life *before* death?' *Sunday Times* (9 January 1972), p. 6, cols. 6 and 7.

[21] Barritt and Carter, op. cit., p. 29.

[22] Rose, op. cit., chapter V.

the Northern Ireland conflict? Much of what has been said so far might have been thought to be self-evident, and the label of minor interest. We can only justify this discussion if it can be shown that race relations are peculiar situations, and that their special features have specific implications for sociology and social policy. This final discussion examines the policy implications for Northern Ireland on the assumption that the race relations analysis has been sustained. We are assuming, for the sake of discussion, that an end to violence and discrimination is a legitimate goal of policy even though our analysis so far might, in fact, lead us to think that 'solutions' are sociologically meaningless and that only continued conflict is likely.

Westminster policies towards Northern Ireland have been based on the tacit assumption that the conflicts were based on economic factors overlaid and exacerbated by a traditional system of stratification inherited from a colonial past. . . . If one accepts this analysis one may adopt an assimilationist policy. Assimilation would be encouraged by removing the causes of conflict and this might be aided by a period of positive discrimination in favour of Catholics in education, housing, employment, and so on. In other words, administrative means could be found to bring peace to Northern Ireland. Such an administrative programme could entail the allocation of substantial economic aid to the province and the setting up of machinery to ensure the equitable distribution of benefits. Then, in the absence of economic conflict (i.e. 'real' conflict), Roman Catholics and Protestants would be assimilated to one another, working harmoniously in a single prosperous economy. An analogy could be drawn with a model of Irish and Welsh workers in England, who, after facing initial hostility became part of the English working class and the trade union movement.

In the long term, presumably, the most likely outcome of such a solution would be the emergence of some sort of working-class movement. The political structures would approximate to those typical to Western capitalist societies: class conflict mediated and reduced through the collaboration of workers and employers in trade union bargaining institutions and social democratic parties.

Some of these beliefs are epitomized in the demands of the civil rights movement and in the Government's response to them. The civil rights demands were one man one vote, an end to gerrymandering, laws against discrimination and a complaints procedure, fair allocation of council housing, the repeal of the Special Powers Act and the disbanding of the 'B' Specials. One man one vote has been granted and the Government has started investigating electoral boundary changes, an ombudsman and Community Relations Commission have been established and housing has been placed under a new executive authority. The 'B' Specials were disbanded and proposals for reform of the police accepted. An investment policy was advocated to create new jobs in the province, and the Government offered to start constitutional discussions. This latter offer was rejected by opposition M.P.s who demanded an end to internment as a precondition of talks. Many of these proposals have been overtaken by increased violence and political polarization. . . .

What these kinds of reform proposals ignore is that if successful they would probably entail the destruction of the basis of Unionist power. These proposals are those of the politician who thinks, in Mansergh's words, 'he can deal out abstract justice without reference to forces around him.' They are not politically feasible proposals. In the first place such solutions ignore the fact that the Ulster Unionist party is an extension of the English Conservative party and from time to time holds vital voting power in the Westminster Parliament. (The support of the Ulster Unionists was, for example, crucial in the Common Market vote in February 1972.) There would be some reluctance therefore, especially on the part of Conservatives, permanently to alienate the Unionists. Secondly it ignores the wider political relationship between Westminster and Stormont. This relationship is nicely summed up by Rose in the final chapter of his *Governing Without Consensus* in a comparison of Northern Ireland and the American deep south: the price paid by a central government for maintaining the loyalty of the majority in peripheral territories and the coherence of a political union, is that it does not ask many questions about what goes on within those territories. Minority appeals seldom reach the central government in a way that cannot be ignored, but when they do, the central government tries to play the role of 'honest broker.' If the central government does enforce changes, they are likely to be changes to the advantage of the minority. Those changes provoke the ultras amongst the majority and threaten the coherence and stability of the union.

For the majority, their privileges are paramount and these are based on racial considerations—which are more salient than the economic. The liberal approach, typified by Barritt and Carter, underestimates the social reality of race; it treats it as irrational or epiphenomenal, to be bought off with economic benefits. The liberal solution is thus one which would not be feasible without direct metropolitan rule and considerable application of force. The force would be used against those who have traditionally been loyalists and on whom the stability of the regime depended.

The liberal or the Fabian, like the 'white middle-class liberal' in conventional race relations situations, assumes that he is dealing with a basically unitary society in which something has gone wrong that can be put right by rational policies. He has a harmonious society 'in his head' and assumes that this is the reality which men of good will can realize. It is an ahistorical and non-political analysis which takes no account of the depth and permanence of the divisions and conflict which constitute race relations. The possibility of realizing even the degree of value-consensus necessary for peace—which would presumably emerge from the social relations of the market—is remote given the political function of dissensus. Fundamental value-consensus is an absurd notion, given the nature of religious beliefs.

Could then the creation of a 'plural society' become an object of policy? This would involve the integration of the two communities in the economy and equal distribution of social rights, but cultural separation on a voluntary basis. Segregation would continue in 'kinship, education, religion . . . recreation and certain sodalities,'[23] but all would live under one government. This may seem an attractive solution to liberal 'realists' but it assumes that either all communities accept the legitimacy of the government or that the domination of one community continues. But, even supposing all communities in Northern Ireland were to accept this solution, the situation would remain highly unstable. Firstly: it would only be stable if there were no economic changes that might effect the social arrangements. This is an unlikely condition; it is arguable that economic changes were the occasion for the start of the immediate conflicts today. Secondly stability could only be assured if the oecumenical movement and movements of national liberation throughout the world were not going to affect the province. There is no evidence to support this contention. But above all it is the failure to understand the *active* role of racism that renders the plural solution nugatory.

The parties to a race relations situation believe that certain behaviour by others is inevitable; in Northern Ireland for example, this includes the imputation of treacherous intentions towards the religious and political institutions of the majority on the part of Catholics. The majority also believe that because of such characteristics it is legitimate to assign Catholics to certain occupational roles and housing situations. The members of the minority would enjoy the benefits of the society only residually, not by right (even though *de jure* rights might have been granted by the metropolitan government). By virtue of being born Catholic the minority has no claim to the legal, political, and social rights that are summed up in the notion of 'citizenship.'

[23] M. G. Smith, *The Plural Society in the British West Indies* (Berkeley, University of California Press, 1965), p. 82.

The minority would respond on the basis of similar distrust by rejecting the legitimacy of the social order. In other words, the ideological basis of the social order would itself be the active source of conflict. The basis of order lies not in economics, but beliefs about others held individually and collectively by members of the society.

In Northern Ireland there has been a plural society of the kind we have just described since partition; its instability and tendency to develop open conflicts have been plain to see. Perhaps as a footnote to this discussion we could also say that from the settlers' point of view colonialism still seems to be political rather than purely economic. Although economic factors are important within the political framework, the prime role of the majority is none the less to dominate the minority. It may be that we are seeing the development of a situation in which the economic elite need to change their style of domination in order to advance their economic interests, but are unable to do so because such a change affects their relationship with the majority of the Northern Ireland population, on whom their continued dominance depends.

During the period in which the separate province of Northern Ireland was being created there was a powerful rationale for the establishment of the province. On the basis of shipbuilding and linen, it was a viable economic entity which could be removed from the remainder of Ireland in the way in which Katanga was later to be removed from the Congo. But the independence of the north is now an economic absurdity.

If race relations is regarded as a social problem it is perhaps one of the most intractable of social problems. In Northern Ireland we have a situation in which solutions in terms of pacifying the present situation are not solutions at all, as the basic structure of inequality, discrimination, and distrust would remain. This much seems to be recognized by the Westminster Government, but it is only able to frame a political solution in terms of civil rights legislation, thus ignoring the nature of race relations.

Even if, rather simplistically, we regard the race relations situation as the creature of an elite conspiracy, devised to divide and rule the masses, we would have to note that the conspiracy has succeeded and that furthermore racism has taken on a life of its own. The elite themselves could not eliminate racism now, even if they wanted to. Racism is, as it were, in the streets, no one's property, a weapon which can be used by Unionist radicals wishing to arouse public opinion in order to outflank the Government. If we may mix metaphors: the creature of the elite is a tiger, which they have ridden but cannot dismount.

There is a sense in which there can only be a Protestant or Catholic solution to the problem of Northern Ireland. A Protestant solution would entail the use of further force to dominate and intimidate the Catholics. The extent to which direct violence could be used depends in part on the province's geographical position as part of liberal Western Europe (and a potential member of the E.E.C.) and its relationship to Southern-Irish and American-Irish opinion and pressure.

One Catholic solution would involve union with the Republic; if this was militarily possible, and welcomed by the Republic, Ireland would still be faced with a minority problem. But within Northern Ireland as at present constituted it is not possible to create a society, with the present distribution of power unchanged, in which Catholics have anything to gain.

We conclude therefore that simple solutions are not possible; and that *any* solution that does not assume and achieve fundamental changes in the power structure of Northern Ireland is impossible. The dominant groups— or those of good will amongst them—are thus unable to offer solutions in their own terms.

Conor Cruise O'Brien has put forward (in a liberal style) what are, in fact, very radical proposals for Northern Ireland. His proposals entail a fundamental shift in the power structure of the province. Running down internment and transfering security to Westminster would undermine the plausibility of the Unionist party and exacerbate current conflicts within the party. A fair employment policy would reduce Protestant working-class privileges, and proportional representation would give Roman Catholics some realistic hope of participating in government. These are not proposals for solving the problem of Northern Ireland, they are proposals for a new society.

11

Ethnic Relations in Israel[1]

Yochanan Peres

INTRODUCTION

Students of Israeli society are sometimes so fascinated by unique characteristics that they fail to relate their studies to similar situations and processes elsewhere. Through this failure, two vital benefits are lost: social problem solving in Israel is not stimulated by ideas from abroad, and Israel is not used as a social laboratory in which sociological knowledge (deriving predominantly from studies made in America) can be reconsidered.

In the case of Israel, ethnic relations, like almost any social topic, must be discussed in relation to the overwhelming problem confronting Israel: the all-involving conflict with the surrounding Arab world. No simple cause-effect relationship can be postulated between the external struggle and internal structure. Clearly, Israeli society in general and ethnic group relations in particular are deeply influenced by the Arab-Israeli conflict. On the other

Yochanan Peres is Senior Lecturer in the Department of Sociology at Tel-Aviv University, Israel.

Reprinted from American Journal of Sociology 76 (May, 1971): 1021–1047, by permission of the author and the publisher. Copyright © 1971 by the University of Chicago Press.

[1] The author would like to thank S. N. Eisenstadt and S. Herman of the Hebrew University for their guidance and encouragement. The loyal and resourceful assistance of Nira Davis is gratefully acknowledged. Limitations of space prevent me from mentioning individually my many young Jewish and Arab colleagues who worked under extremely tense and difficult conditions to make this study possible.

hand, there is obviously a feedback; social features which developed during two decades of external struggle have by now become actively engaged in this struggle. The characteristics of the opponents and the nature of their conflict have become parts of one undividable system.

On a more specific level, we should note that Israel's ethnic relations can be best described and analyzed in terms of two major relationships: (1) between European and non-European Jews (the latter will be referred to below as "Orientals"); (2) between Jewish and non-Jewish (predominantly Arab) citizens. This is admittedly an oversimplification. Both the European and the non-European Jewish groups are divided into many subgroups which differ in language, level of education, income, life-style, and many other characteristics. The non-Jewish population is also ethnically subdivided. (One non-Jewish group [the Druzes] are well known for assuming a position favoring the Jews and opposing the Arabs.)

Although the division of the Israeli population into three groups (European Jews, Oriental Jews, and Arabs) does not correspond to demographic reality, this simplistic division does organize meaningfully the complex ethnic attitudes and relationships. (Tables 1 and 2 give the actual distribution of Jews and Arabs.)

Popular images of ethnic differentiation always embody crude categorization. In this way the three "blocs" emerged in the minds of most Israelis. In private conversation, newspaper articles, and even in the parliament, "Europeans," "Orientals," and "Arabs" are referred to as the three main components of Israeli society.

RELATIONS BETWEEN EUROPEANS AND ORIENTAL JEWS

The most remarkable feature of this relationship is its tranquility. Apart from one isolated incident in which shops were looted and a few passersby attacked, there were no ethnic riots during Israel's two-decade history. All attempts to establish ethnic political parties failed. While one to three representatives of such parties occupied seats in the first, second, and third Knesset (Israeli parliament), in the last four elections no ethnic party was even in existence. (It should be noted that Israel has a multi-party system, in which about ten to fifteen parties, most of them very small, compete for the 120 seats in the Knesset.)

This tranquility is astonishing if one considers that almost all leadership positions in the country are occupied by Europeans, that

TABLE 2. *Non-Jewish Groups in Israel in 1967*

Group	Population
Muslims	287,000
Christians	71,000
Druze and others	33,000
Total	391,000*

Source: Statistical Abstract of Israel, 1968, p. 45.
* Includes the population of East Jerusalem, about 66,000.

European per capita income is about twice that of Orientals, and that the European cultural tradition and style of life dominate the society. A careful analysis will show that the relation between these two segments of the Jewish community in Israel is the product of a rather complicated balance of forces, some disintegrative, driving the ethnic groups apart, others integrative. The outcome of these countervailing forces is not a simple positive relationship but rather a sensitive equilibrium in which a sense of mutual responsibility and common loyalty coexist with covert hostility and underlying tensions.

TABLE 1. *Ethnic Distribution of the Jewish Population in Israel**

Country of Descent	Percentage
Jewish citizens of European descent:	
USSR	13
Poland	17
Rumania	11
Bulgaria, Greece	4
Central Europe (Germany, Austria, Czechoslovakia)	6
Western Europe (Britain, France, Benelux, Spain, Italy)	2
Other European countries	1
Total	54
Jewish citizens of American descent:	
USA, Canada	0.5
South and Central America	0.5
Total	1.0
Jewish citizens of Asian descent:	
Iraq	11
Yemen, Aden	6
Turkey	4
Iran	2.5
Other Asian countries	2.5
Total	26.0
Jewish citizens of African descent:	
Morocco	9
Algeria, Tunisia	3
Libya	2
Egypt	2
Other African countries	0.5
Total	16.5

Source: Statistical Abstract of Israel, 1968, p. 43.
* Total Jewish population: 2,500,000.

Factors Impeding the Integration of Jewish Ethnic Groups

Dissimilarity. Compared with other countries, the variation between Jewish ethnic groups in Israel seems to be extremely great: although all Jews have the same religion, they differ in all other aspects: language, dress, and they relate differently to each other and have a variety of socialization patterns and family structures. An extreme example is that there are some Jewish mountain tribes that emigrated from inland Morocco and Tunisia. The term "primitive society" would not be an exaggeration. Even the men were illiterate. They lived in caves in Morocco; some of them dug new caves for themselves in Israel, using their houses for storage space. Their religious beliefs and practices include many archaic superstitions. By contrast, American and western European Jews belong to the most advanced middle class of their Western societies. This is admittedly an extreme example, for most Orientals are much closer to a modern style of living, and many Europeans left environments only in the beginning stages of modernization, such as the rural Ukraine.

Considerable overlap between ethnic background and economic and demographic characteristics. In Israel, issues which would be defined in ethnically homogeneous societies as class differences have implicit ethnic elements. The majority of Europeans emigrated prior to 1949 (the last large group of European immigrants were survivors of the holocaust who came immediately after the state was established), while the overwhelming majority of Orientals arrived after 1949. Those who came first had the opportunity to obtain most of the prestigious positions as well as to occupy the more desirable housing. Newfounded towns and villages in the south or far north are predominantly Oriental, while the best neighborhoods in cities such as Tel Aviv and Haifa are predominantly European. The advancement to leadership positions is quite selective. In political positions (mayors of towns, local labor union leaders) in which leaders are directly accountable to their constituents, Orientals are found in increasing proportions. They are less prominent in national politics, although it has become customary to reserve two seats in the government and about thirty seats in the Knesset for Oriental representatives (who are never officially identified as such.) There is not one Oriental in the high ranks of the army, and very few have influential academic positions.

Emigration to Israel is perceived as emancipation from minority status. Jews are known to be extremely sensitive to any indication of prejudice or discrimination. One of the main incentives for emigration to Israel is the attempt to rid oneself of an inferior status and to become part of a dominant majority. For the Oriental Jew in Israel, immigration has only created new frustration because they have not become a part of the dominant group in Israel's ethnic stratification. "In Morocco, we were considered Jews, and here we are called Moroccans," is a frequently heard complaint.

The cultural resemblance of Orientals and Arabs. The majority of non-European Jews in Israel originated from Arabic-speaking, predominantly Moslem societies. They were naturally influenced by Arab and Muslim culture, and they incorporated many of its elements into their own social and individual behavior. There exists in Israel a certain contempt and hostility toward everything which symbolizes the Arab world. Arab music is never broadcast on the radio; Arab art is not displayed, and most people would feel uneasy if they spoke Arabic in public places. While no one identifies Oriental Jews with the external Arab enemy, it is important that much of the cultural heritage and life style of Oriental Jews is explicitly rejected, not only by Europeans, but also by the central institutions of Israeli society.[2]

Factors Promoting the Integration of Jewish Ethnic Groups

The cultural and ideological factor. In *American Dilemma*, Myrdal (1962) ponts out that most Americans subscribe to a full integration of Negroes (and other ethnic groups) into the mainstream of society. One could say that Israel is even more committed ideologically to absolute and egalitarian integration of all Jewish subgroups.

The dominant political ideologies in Israel are socialism in its several versions and liberalism. There is no conservative party in Israel, and no discriminatory ideology toward any Jew has ever been promulgated. The horrible confrontation between the Jewish people and the racist Nazi regime made reference to "natural superiority" or any official announcement of prejudice distasteful to most Israelis.[3]

[2] Egyptian films are a noteworthy exception.

[3] K. Katzenelson (1964) is an exception to this rule. Here the author tried to develop an ideology of European superiority. His book, however, was violently denounced by all segments of the public. I cannot recall one favorable response to the book.

In addition, the central role which Jewish religious symbols play in Israeli culture and education has a unifying effect. Obviously the meanings which Israelis of different backgrounds attach to mythological events like the Exodus from Egypt or to rituals like fasting on Yom Kippur are quite different, but whatever the nature of observance, the same symbols are meaningful to everyone.

Zionist ideology adds another dimension. Zionism sets forth a special interpretation of Jewish history in which Jews are considered to owe allegiance to each other rather than to the nations in which they live as a minority.[4] Israel addressed itself directly to integration, proclaiming it as one of the most important assignments on the national agenda. Intermarriage between different ethnic groups is not only accepted but highly valued. Teachers, physicians, and social workers are encouraged to settle among people they serve, and signs of prejudice are denounced not merely as unethical but as unpatriotic.

Socioeconomic factors.   While the overlap between socioeconomic status and ethnic background aggravates ethnic relations, dynamic developments in the Israeli economy and stratification system contribute to ethnic integration. It should be kept in mind that Israel's short history is a period of rapid expansion. The Jewish sector in Palestine increased four times in population, but other resources, for example, land, capital, expertise, and power expanded even more. The absorption of immigrants was and still is considered to involve some sacrifice by the absorbing society, as if the inhabitants were sharing their homeland with the newcomers. However, economic surveys show that, indeed, in the fifties, the old-timers actually increased their standard of liv-

ing more than did the immigrants. The gap diminished in the sixties. In any case, established Israelis of predominately European origin did not lose economically in sharing with the immigrants but actually prospered in the process; due to the enormous increase in resources, the economics of ethnic relations in Israel was not a zero sum game.[5]

The gain of Jews of European origin from the influx of Oriental Jews was not only economic. As the newcomers took over the lowest positions, more powerful and rewarding roles opened up for the old-timers. Furthermore, the establishment of the state with all of its branches and agencies (army, foreign office, public health, and state-sponsored science) provided new careers for which the better-educated and more-experienced Europeans were the favored candidates.

The national security factor.   Israel's involvement in its short history in a fierce struggle for survival has obviously had a unifying effect.[6]

---

[4] S. N. Herman (1970) has systematically investigated the degree to which Jewish and Zionist values have been successfully taught. Herman's empirical findings indicate that a definite majority of Israeli youth has a strong and positive Jewish identity and a sense of responsibility and attachment toward other Jews all over the world. This evidence contradicts the conclusions influenced by the insightful although unsystematic observations of scholars such as Spiro (1967) and Friedman (1967).

[5] G. Hanoch (1961) and R. Klinov-Malul (1969), two Israeli economists, both established and interpreted these facts through an interesting exchange. Hanoch reported that the income gap between immigrants and old-timers was increasing over time and explained this tendency by the growing income differentiation between manual workers and professions. He predicted that, if no far-reaching measures were taken, social and economic gaps would increase and find political expression. Klinov-Malul cited later findings which indicated that after 1958 income gaps were gradually decreasing. Responding to this challenge, Hanoch (1969) offered a new explanation: the growing gap in incomes should be understood as a result of the increase in the untrained labor force. (This increase is not exactly synonymous with immigration, as a year or two usually elapses between the arrival of immigrants and their full participation in the labor market.) Unskilled labor and skilled labor are complementary factors of production. Therefore, salaries for unskilled workers decreased relative to incomes of more professional workers. This tendency was less marked in the sixties when the increase in unskilled labor supply leveled off. In addition to that, more young immigrants achieved better training. While income differentiation between professionals and non-professionals still increased somewhat, this tendency was more than offset by more advanced skills attained by the immigrants so that the overall gap between immigrants and old-timers tended to decrease (but see original exchange in Eisenstadt 1966).

[6] J. T. Shuval (1962) raised the following considerations: Whether the threats expressed by several

This unifying effect can be subdivided into three components. (1) *Interdependence of fate:* It is clear that military defeat is perceived as a threat to the interests of all Israeli Jewish ethnic groups. (2) *A common goal:* While interdependence of fate may be passive, like the dependence of a whole village on rain, it can also be active. A common interest can be achieved by coordinated efforts. This kind of active interdependence is even more unifying if individuals or groups feel that their survival depends upon their cooperation. (3) *An outlet for aggression:* If the common goal happens to be the defense against a common enemy, an additional unifying element exists—antagonistic and aggressive impulses now have a legitimate outlet and target.

Theoretically, it seems reasonable to claim that Israel has a good chance to avoid the explosive consequences that can result from ethnic differences. This notion is based on three postulates. The tendency toward ethnic integration is increased if (1) a body of cultural symbols exists with which everyone can identify; (2) if societal resources are in a state of rapid expansion; (3) if a threat originating from a common enemy is perceived. While this summary contains an optimistic prediction, it also indicates the price a society is likely to pay. A full evaluation of this price is beyond the scope of this paper. I should like only to hint at it in a very general sense.

The unifying function of religious and national symbols might lead to an overemphasis of these symbols beyond the level that most individuals would consider appropriate. Politically, this is likely to affect those groups most closely identified with these symbols, to diminish the status of those not associated with these symbols, and to reduce their participation in public life.

A society may become "addicted" to the continuous growth of resources—immigration, manpower, land, or most important, capital. A

pause in growth may create severe intergroup problems along with the economic problems.

Finally, the position of a society toward its enemies and opponents might tend to harden beyond what would have been expected on the basis of rational self-interest.

Of course each of these problems is likely to arouse resisting forces which are just as deep-rooted in Israeli society and culture. Nevertheless, these are potentialities of which anyone concerned about Israeli society should be aware.

RELATIONS BETWEEN JEWS AND ARABS

It is a commonplace that the relationship between Israeli Jews and Arabs as ethnic groups has to be understood in the context of the wider Arab-Israeli conflict. Israeli Arabs do not deny their familial, cultural, and religious ties to the belligerent Arab states; they are enemy-affiliated minorities. There also exist some unique circumstances shaping the relations between the two peoples. First, Arabs in Israel are a recent minority. Until 1948, there was statistically a clear majority of Arabs in Palestine, although they had no sovereign power. While a minority within Israel's borders, Arabs constitute the overwhelming majority in the surrounding region. They are a minority without a political and cultural elite, a village population which had been accustomed to following the leadership of towns such as Jaffa, Haifa, Nablus, and Beirut. The 1948 war emptied some of these towns and severed the connections with the rest. The resulting lack of trained and accepted leadership increased the vulnerability of the Arabs to Jewish economic and cultural influence.

While Arabs feel a deep resentment against the Jews they are also attracted to them by a combination of cultural and practical motives. Palestine was not merely the meeting place of two national movements but also of two different life-styles. The modern and sometimes socially innovating Jewish sector confronted a largely rural and tradi-

Arab leaders to destroy Israel and kill or expel its citizens were real or propagandistic is irrelevant for our purpose. The unifying function is due to the perceived threat, whether real or not.

tional community. While they are perceived as the main source of the Arabs' misfortunes, Jews have provided many Arabs with the only access to an advanced technology, broadened consumption, and modern political ideologies.

Arab attitudes toward Jews and the State of Israel vary according to the degree of modernization achieved. The more traditional rural Arabs who are still organized in extended families controlled by "elders" or patriarchs view Jews mainly as bearers of a foreign way of life, as a threat to the harmony and integration of their community.

As long as the village community is left alone to pursue its own course, and Jews neither interfere in internal affairs (even in demonstrating different kinds of behavior) nor impede the immediate economic interests of the village, a modus vivendi with a Jewish regime can be found. The traditional village of the Middle East has known and outlived many regimes and has developed mechanisms for coping with them while preserving its own unique structure. This is not to imply that relations between Jews and the traditional elements are, or ever have been, idyllic. But being a small, dense, and extremely active society, the Jews did interfere in the internal life of the Arab village. Some interference was unintentional, such as displaying a modern way of life to the villages. Some was deliberately designed to bring modernity to the Arab village. Although Jewish authorities did try to cooperate with the traditional ruling elite, the impact of Jewish modernity brought about a gradual erosion of the authority of the elders.

The younger, modernized Arabs were much less concerned with the stability of traditional rural society, being themselves engaged in conflict with the traditional leadership. There is no disagreement between these Arabs and most Jews that the modernization of the Arab village is both desirable and inevitable. The only dispute is over the speed of the modernization process and the proper means to encourage it. But while the cultural element in the dispute concerning these young and progressive elements is relatively de-emphasized, the political conflict is considerably aggravated. The young educated Hebrew-speaking and European-dressed Arab whose tradition and religious symbols of identity have been eroded is, nevertheless, not admitted into Jewish society. As a result, the need has emerged for new symbols of identity. This new identification must be broad enough to include the shared experience and interests of Arabs all over the country and sufficiently narrow to differentiate Arabs from Jews. An extreme nationalistic ideology satisfied both these needs. Thus, as modernization proceeded, the cultural and economic conflict between Arabs and Jews weakened while the political conflict was re-emphasized.[7]

The attitude of Jews toward Israeli Arabs is obviously dominated by the struggle against the Arab world. The actual ties of Israeli Arabs to the external enemy are, however, exaggerated by some psychological factors. Israeli Arabs are weak and easily selected scapegoats toward which aggressive impulses can be channeled. Israeli Arabs are the first non-Jews to live under Jewish domination during the 2,000 years of Jewish history. Some of the historical fear, mistrust, and resentment toward the Gentile ("goy") is undoubtedly transferred to the Arabs. This tendency was especially marked among Jews of Middle Eastern descent who, until recently had been dominated by an Arab majority. Mistrust toward Israeli Arabs was also exaggerated sometimes by Jewish authorities in order to justify some of the measures taken against the Arab population (the military rule and the confiscation of more than 40 percent of Arab land). Thus, while defending the military rule in the Knesset, Ben-Gurion announced his "understanding" of feelings of animosity on the part of Israeli Arabs, saying that he would feel the same if he were in their position.

Finally, Arabs were regarded by Oriental Jews as a negative reference group, the kind of people, society, and culture one should get

[7] Elsewhere, I (1970) present a detailed discussion of these trends.

away from in order to be fully accepted in the European-dominated mainstream of Israeli life.

During the years 1962–67, the position of Israeli authorities toward the Arab population was considerably liberalized. This can be attributed to a combination of motives: commitment to democratic values (reinforced by increasing pressure by Israeli intellectuals), sensitivity to external public opinion, and tranquility on the borders. As a result, military rule and other limitations on free movements were abolished. But the frequency of hostile and prejudiced attitudes among the population-at-large remained almost unchanged. Jewish hostility toward the Israeli Arab was increased by the rapid succession of fear before the 1967 war and contempt immediately afterward. This negative turn in Jewish public opinion was soon reinforced by Arab belligerent activities in which some Israeli Arabs collaborated.

For Israeli Arabs, the violent confrontation between Israel and the Arab world in 1967 was a fatal blow to their carefully balanced identity. The widespread belief among Israeli Arabs that they could and should maintain a neutral position in the conflict between their country and their people was shaken. When communication between Israeli Arabs and their relatives and former friends in the occupied territories was reestablished, the Israeli Arab assumed at first the role of a guide by virtue of his long acquaintance with the Jews and with Israel. But a few months later, the positions of the guide and the guided were reversed. The leadership of West Bank towns such as East Jerusalem and Nablus reestablished its traditional authority, and many Israeli Arabs felt themselves once again integrated into a wider Arab community; the pressure on those Israeli Arabs who wanted to retain some impartiality became almost unbearable. For many young Arabs, this agonizing dilemma existed, not merely on the ideological level, but on the practical one as well. Because of their superior knowledge of Israeli geography, language, and customs, Israeli Arabs were often the focus of outside pressure to participate in these raids. Every time such a

collaboration is discovered, Jews express mistrust and outrage toward the entire Arab community, and the generalized hostility in turn discourages those Israeli Arabs who still want to remain loyal. In this way, the investments of good will which have been made by both parties in the last eight years are gradually lost in a vicious cycle of suspicion, terror, oppression, and retaliation.

METHOD AND DATA

The findings are based on several studies carried out in Israel before and after June 1967. The purpose of the studies was to delineate the structure of ethnic relations. Due to the unexpected occurrence of the war, we had the rare opportunity to test, by replicating some of our procedures, the impact of the outburst of violent conflict on the values and attitudes of both Jews and Arabs. Briefly, the projects on which we drew are:

1. A study of ethnic identity and relations among Jewish ethnic groups (Peres 1967, 1968a). The sample included 675 secondary school students of both sexes and fifty-one of their parents. Sampling procedure: 117 secondary schools were selected at random. Written questionnaires were administered to 50 percent of all eleventh graders (ages 16–17). Since the questions were too numerous, two different questionnaires had to be used. For this reason the N in the various tables may vary. Almost all items in these questionnaires were "closed ends."

2. A study of ethnic attitudes among residents of Tel Aviv (Peres 1968b). Four hundred and fifty adults were interviewed; 200 of them were interviewed twice (winter 1967 and winter 1968) and 250 only once (winter 1968). The sampling procedure was an ecological cluster sampling (certain blocks were randomly selected) with an over-representation of low-status neighborhoods in which more Jews of Oriental background are likely to live. The interviewing was based on a questionnaire which might be described as "open-ended." No preformulated categories

were read to the subjects, but once a response was given it was coded immediately. In cases of doubt, the respondent was asked (*after* giving his spontaneous reply) which of the categories would best fit his answer.

3. A study of ethnic attitudes among Israeli Arabs (Peres 1970), carried out in the summer of 1966 and the fall of 1967. The sample of 500 respondents was also clustered. First, eight predominantly Arab settlements were selected according to the following strata: religious affiliation, degree of urbanization, region, and size. Then residents of these settlements were selected according to the following categories: (1) high school students (ages 14–18; $N = 200$); (2) parents of these students (ages 35–70; $N = 100$); (3) working youth (ages 14–18; $N = 100$); (4) young adults (ages 20–35; $N = 100$). The interviews were performed by the open-ended method mentioned above.

The main problem which confronted me in all these studies was the problem of objectivity. An investigator studying ethnic relations in his own society is often identified with his group of origin. In times of political tension, he may also be suspected of collecting information for intelligence purposes. We tried to minimize the detrimental effect of these fears and suspicions (there is no way to eliminate them) by employing two principles: (*a*) the groups studied were represented in the investigating team throughout the project; (*b*) great caution was taken to ensure the confidentiality of the data, even at the risk of weakening the principal investigator's control over field work procedures.

Among students of the Hebrew University we were able to find members of different Jewish groups as well as Moslem and Christian Arabs willing to cooperate in the project. Arab interviewers performed the bulk of the interviewing of Arab respondents, but some of them also took part in every other activity of the research team, from the initial design to the final report. Confidentiality was insured by omitting the clearly identifying information. Interview reports in the Arab section did not include names or addresses, which made it impossible for the investigator to follow up the interview or check on the work of the interviewers. Among Jewish respondents, the level of suspicion was much lower, and names and addresses could be recorded.

FINDINGS

Not all the situations, relationships, and processes which were alluded to in the Introduction can be substantiated by the findings. First of all, since these findings relate to perceptions and attitudes, power relations and economic dependencies were not observed directly. Admittedly, the validity of attitude indicators is always somewhat questionable. Even in this study, we have evidence that irrelevant factors like the interviewers' nationality or attitude affected individual responses. Nevertheless, there are some good reasons to believe that the overall trends revealed by tables 3–6 indicate attitudes of various Israeli ethnic groups toward each other.

Relations among Jewish Ethnic Groups

Social distance. The more intimate and binding the social relationship in which one would agree to participate with another person, the smaller the social distance from this person. Typical examples of social distance items are the readiness to marry or live in close proximity with members of a different ethnic group[8] (see Matras 1965).

Tables 3, 4, and 5 reveal considerable social distance between Jews of European and Oriental descent, and the majority of respondents had at least some reservations about involving themselves "too closely" with the other group. It is remarkable, however, that only a small minority expressed clear antagonism to a close involvement, which suggests the existence of a powerful norm against the exclusion of other Jewish groups. While private preferences for intra-ethnic contacts are admitted, it does not seem permissible to elevate these preferences to a principle.

[8] As on the same block.

TABLE 3.   *Attitudes toward Marriage and Shared Neighborhood with Oriental Jews (Respondents: European High School Students)*

Item	Definitely Agree	Agree	Agree but Prefer Own Neighborhood	Disagree	N
Marriage	15%	24%	39%	21%	143
Neighborhood	23%	40%	35%	2%	143

Source: Peres 1968a.

TABLE 4.   *Attitudes toward Marriage and Shared Neighborhood with European Jews (Respondents: Oriental High School Students)*

Item	Definitely Agree	Agree	Agree but Prefer Own Neighborhood	Disagree	N
Marriage	30%	51%	16%	2%	195
Neighborhood	30%	55%	11%	1%	195

Source: Peres 1968a.

TABLE 5.   *Attitude toward Marriage and Renting a Room to an Oriental Jew (Respondents: Tel Aviv Adults, European)*

Item	Definitely Agree	Agree	Agree but Prefer Own Group	Disagree	N
Marriage	37%	20%	19%	24%	204
Renting a room	37%	30%	7%	16%	204

Source: Peres 1968b.

TABLE 6.   *Attitude toward Marriage and Renting a Room to a European Jew (Respondents: Tel Aviv Adults, Oriental)*

Item	Definitely Agree	Agree	Agree but Prefer Own Group	Disagree	N
Marriage	85%	10%	3%	3%	239
Renting a room	65%	25%	5%	5%	239

Source: Peres 1968b.

Social distance between Europeans and Orientals is asymmetrical: Orientals accept Europeans more than vice versa. This result is particularly evident when comparing tables 5 and 6. The outstanding difference between tables 3 and 5 and tables 4 and 6, respectively, was unanticipated and scarcely explainable. The questions about marriage asked in both studies were identical, and questions about neighborhoods were similar. Nevertheless, the distribution was quite different. This difference may be attributed to the different mode of interviewing (the interview vs. the questionnaire), to different location of the subjects (Tel Aviv vs. the entire country), or to age differences (high school students vs. adults). At present, we are unable to isolate these factors. In considering the validity of these distributions, note, however, that the percentage of those European high school students who definitely accepted intermarriage with Orientals exactly equals the percentage of mixed couples in the entire population of Jewish married couples (see Matras 1965, tables 2 and 5).

By using similar social distance questions, we found that, among Europeans from different countries of origin, social distance is considerably smaller than the above-mentioned distances, while, among Orientals of different countries of origin, it tends to be even larger than the distance between Oriental and European Jews.

In interviews or in written comments added to questionnaires, some respondents tried to explain their attitudes. Refusal to intermarry with Orientals is usually justified on grounds of a cultural gap or a different mentality, rather than explicitly in terms of racial inferiority. Typical reactions would be, "I prefer to marry somebody of my own background because of the importance of having the same mentality," or "I wouldn't want to have a cultural gap in my family," or, more specifically, "I can't see myself married to a man who wants to have about twelve children."

Sometimes prejudicial overtones are revealed while arguing for a favorable attitude: "I will marry the one whom I love, even if he is Oriental." Most Orientals accept intermarriage; some even prefer it. One outspoken respondent said, "I wouldn't only agree, but would even prefer it [to marry a European]. First of all, if I marry a girl of my own community, this will not contribute anything to bringing the communities closer. Second, I believe marriage with a European would result in better children."

Stereotypes and prejudices. The possible specific indications of generally prejudiced attitudes are many. In order to diminish the arbitrariness of selecting a few of them, we chose two very broad items, one claiming that unfavorable evaluations of Orientals are, according to Allport's well-known term, "earned," that is, reflect reality. The second claims that, although the current backwardness of non-Europeans may be reduced, it can never be totally abolished.

In order not to employ only abstract stereotypes, we added a concrete claim (that Oriental neighborhoods are dirty), which is also well known in the literature on prejudice and stereotypes. In order to overcome possible reluctance on the part of respondents to express prejudiced attitudes, we added the phrase, "Some people say," to each claim. This was also intended to disengage the interviewer from these prejudiced statements. Our pretest indicated that none of these stereotypes was attributed to Europeans, so we had to use a special item which stated that Europeans are emotionally "cold and unresponsive—the shortcoming most frequently ascribed to Europeans in our preliminary unstructured interviews.

Table 7 shows that prejudice against Orientals is, on the average, as strong among Orientals as among Europeans. This might be interpreted as a certain degree of self-contempt on the part of the Orientals, probably originating from an acceptance of European prejudices.[9] It should be remembered, however, that many Orientals think of *other* Orientals (not only different individuals but different subgroups) when expressing this kind of prejudiced attitude (table 8). (This tendency will be discussed later in detail.) Table 8 shows that even the relatively mild allegation against Europeans is rather rare; only a quarter of the Orientals express prejudice, and Europeans reject it altogether. Thus the asymmetry which was found in

[9] Shuval (1966) reports on the actual manifestations of self-rejection.

TABLE 7. *Prejudice against Orientals*

Question	Ethnic Group	Definitely Agree	Agree	Disagree	Strongly Disagree	N
Some people say that, for prejudices to be abolished, Orientals must rid themselves of their shortcomings. What's your opinion?	Orientals	26%	17%	34%	23%	246
	Europeans	23%	20%	39%	18%	204
Some people say that, even though Orientals may progress a lot, they will never reach the level of Europeans. What's your opinion?	Orientals	18%	16%	30%	37%	246
	Europeans	8%	17%	39%	35%	204
Some people say that neighborhoods where Orientals live seem always to be dirty. What's your opinion?	Orientals	27%	38%	21%	14%	246
	Europeans	20%	39%	29%	12%	204

Source: Peres 1968*b*.

analyzing social distance recurs here. Europeans are perceived by Orientals more as a guide or reference group than as an "oppressing majority."

Feelings of interdependence. In most studies of ethnic relations, negative aspects are carefully explored, while such positive feelings as mutual attraction and interdependence somehow escape the attention of the interviewers. In most studies, the most extreme positive attitude a respondent could have is to regard people of a different background "simply as human beings," that is, to disregard their ethnicity. Our findings indicate that in Israel social distance and prejudice are at least partially balanced by a sense of interdependence and by the desire for a fully integrated society in the future. When asked whether it would be better for the country if there were fewer of the other group, a clear majority of both Europeans and Orientals said "no."[10] Again, the Orientals' attitude toward the Europeans was more favorable than vice versa.

[10] R. M. Williams (1964, p. 410) adapted this item as an indicator of prejudice.

Some of the justification referred to the need to have more Jews in Israel, whatever their background. Some, however, referred to characteristics of the other group which seemed constructive.

"If the Europeans hadn't founded this country, we would have had nowhere to come," one Oriental woman said. Another simply stated, "We need the Europeans; they are the brain." A European respondent said, "The Orientals coming in their great numbers saved the state and its European old-timers. If they hadn't come, we would be now a negligible enclave in an Arab ocean."

The desire for integration. Ethnic attitudes should be analyzed in the context of their time perspective. Are current characteristics and relationships perceived as enduring and permanent, or are they flexible, developing toward a more egalitarian (or possibly less egalitarian) solution? Many observers view prejudice as an attitude not only negative but rigid, as an expression of an eternal truth for the past which will continue to apply in the future.

Since, in Israel, the common historical root (ancient Israel) is always emphasized,

TABLE 8.   *Prejudice against Europeans*

Question	Ethnic Group	Definitely Agree	Agree	Disagree	Strongly Disagree	N
Some people say that Europeans are emotionally cold and unresponsive. What's your opinion?	Orientals	13%	14%	26%	47%	246
	Europeans	3%	8%	41%	48%	204

Source: Peres 1968*b*.

the notion of inherited inferiority is extremely rare. Ethnic differences are perceived as cultural, acquired in the various societies of exile. When considering the future, most Israelis view ethnic differences as something which can and should eventually disappear. A majority disagreed with the prediction that Orientals will never be able to close the gap between themselves and the Europeans. Our subjects tend both to expect and endorse the reduction of inter-ethnic differences. These responses do not lend any support to the notion that Orientals in Israel are "forcefully Westernized."[11] As a matter of fact, Orientals are slightly more eager to abolish differences, while Europeans are slightly more concerned about preserving ethnic traditions.

We encouraged interviewees to elaborate the kinds of ethnic tradition they would like to preserve. The positively evaluated differences were almost always stated: "Everybody can keep his traditional life-style at home. In public places, however, an individual should behave just like everyone else." But even at home, special traditions are endorsed in peripheral or aesthetic issues: "We have some old and extremely nice folkways. It would be a pity to lose them." Another typical quotation is, "Why shouldn't everybody keep his own tradition, as long as he doesn't interfere with other people's rights?" As already emphasized, even

this partial nostalgia is a minority attitude. The majority of Orientals want complete assimilation and explicitly cite the Europeans as a desirable model. "I wish we Persians could overcome all our superstitions and be more like the Europeans—educated, industrious, and clean." Others urge the development of a new tradition which would be national and non-ethnic: "I hope a new and unified Israeli tradition will emerge."

Jewish Attitudes toward Arabs

Hostility and social distance. The levels of hostility and social distance increase considerably when Arabs are mentioned. Actually, it was difficult to formulate differentiating questions. During the pretest, the overwhelming majority of the sample tended to concentrate in the negative categories of each question. In some cases, we tried to add another extremely negative category, so that degrees of hostility toward Arabs could be differentiated. Tables 9, 10, and 11 reveal the severity of anti-Arab feelings.

Perhaps the most interesting finding was a tendency for Orientals to be more hostile than Europeans toward Arabs. At first, this discovery seems to be astonishing. It might have been assumed that the Orientals, with close ties to the Arab culture, could serve as mediators between European Israelis and Arabs. However, this is clearly not the case.

Many Oriental respondents sought to explain their negative feelings toward Arabs by referring to previous unpleasant experiences under Arab domination. This explanation

[11] M. Seltzer (1967) stresses the argument that Orientals are Westernized against their will and that their specific culture is deliberately destroyed. He implies that the majority of Orientals want to preserve ethnic differences. However, he fails to present any data to that effect.

TABLE 9.   *Social Distance from Arabs: A Comparison between Oriental and European Respondents*

Item	Ethnic Group	No Data	Definitely Agree	Agree	Agree but Prefer a Jew	Do Not Agree	Strongly Disagree	Total
Readiness for marriage	Orientals	1	0	2%	6%	24%	67%	192
	Europeans	0	0	11%	13%	29%	56%	139
Readiness for friendship	Orientals	2	0	4%	23%	34%	38%	192
	Europeans	1	3%	10%	27%	32%	27%	139
Readiness for neighborhood	Orientals	2	1%	7%	32%	27%	32%	192
	Europeans	0	4%	12%	32%	27%	25%	139

Source: Peres 1968*a.*

TABLE 10.   *Prejudice against Arabs: A Comparison between Oriental and European Respondents*

Item	Europeans	Orientals
It would be better if there were fewer Arabs	91%	93%
Every Arab hates Jews	76%	83%
Arabs will not reach the level of progress of Jews	64%	85%
Disagree to rent a room to an Arab	80%	91%
Disagree to have an Arab as a neighbor	53%	78%
Total	204	246

Source: Peres 1968*b.*

TABLE 11.   *Social Distance from Arabs: A Comparison between Oriental and European Respondents*

Question	Ethnic Group	Agree	Agree but Prefer Own Group	Disagree	Total
To marry	Orientals	11%	5%	84%	246
	Europeans	9%	11%	79%	204
To rent a room	Orientals	6%	4%	91%	246
	Europeans	13%	7%	80%	204
To have as neighbor	Orientals	12%	9%	78%	246
	Europeans	26%	21%	53%	204

Source: Peres 1968*b.*

seems insufficient to account for the extreme hostility revealed in the findings. The antagonism of Orientals toward Arabs should be seen in the context of their present illusion as well as a result of past experience. The Orientals feel that they must reject the remaining traces of their Middle Eastern origin to attain the status of the dominant European group. By expressing hostility to Arabs, an Oriental attempts to rid himself of the "inferior" Arabic elements in his own identity and to adopt a position congenial to the European group which he desires to emulate.

If this line of reasoning is correct, then those Orientals most resembling Arabs should be more hostile than others. With this hypothesis in mind, we instructed the interviewers in our second study (Peres 1968b) to record the degree of resemblance of each Oriental respondent to Arabs on two criteria: appearance and accent. We found that hostility (as expressed in the agreement to two prejudicial statements) increases slightly when resemblance to Arabs (as reported by the interviewers) increased. While the findings were not statistically significant, they did seem to be rather consistent. The slightness of the differences may stem from a ceiling effect: the ratio of anti-Arab prejudice is high in all the categories of resemblance to Arabs and therefore cannot increase greatly. If we accept this as an indication of the validity of our hypothesis, we may conclude that hostility between Arabs and Jews of Middle Eastern origin exists, not in spite of, but partially because of their many similarities.

Effects of the Six-Day War. As a result of the Six-Day War, social distance and hosility toward Arabs increased even more. Four out of five indications of anti-Arab attitudes increased between 1967 and 1968. It is noteworthy that these data were collected before Israeli-Arab participation in terror raids became known. As you may recall, most Arabs adopted a passive neutrality during the war. Small fringe groups performed very ineffective anti-Israeli activities, while other small groups

expressed their loyalty to Israel by actively helping in the war effort. At the time, the latter received much more publicity than the former. It may thus be concluded that the behavior of Israeli Arabs had no effect on the increase of Jewish hostility. This hostility resulted from the overall political situation rather than from local interaction. Generally speaking, the position of an enemy-affiliated minority is endangered when a violent clash breaks out, whatever their attitudes or actual behavior might be. The situation of the Israeli Arab seems to be no exception to this rule.

Arab Attitudes toward Jews

Social distance. Table 12 reveals that considerable rejection of social contact with Jews does exist among Israeli Arabs. Note that "friendship" is consistently conceived as less binding than neighborhood, as more respondents accept friendship than neighborhood. Some respondents explained that friendship is selective and individual; you can choose your friend personally, but not your neighbor, and neighborhood also involves the entire family. Many Arab respondents, while being quite prepared to have contact with Jews, were anxious not to allow any such contacts to the female members of their families.[12] In an Arab rural environment, most people live in their own homes, which are built by or for the family. A family rarely changes its home during the lifetime of one generation. The lack of cars and telephones and the confinement of the women and younger children to the home intensifies contact with nearby residents. Thus, neighbors are extremely important.

On the other hand, "friendship" is offered freely to every casual acquaintance. A villager is expected to invite almost every person he meets to eat or at least have coffee with him. If

[12] Note that all our Arab respondents were male. Early attempts to interview Arabs of both sexes failed almost completely. A typical reply a female interviewer received when asking to see one of the respondent's four daughters was, "Sorry, but I have no daughters."

TABLE 12.   *Social Distance from Jews*

Israeli Arabs	Agree to Make Friends with Jews	Agree to Live in Jewish Quarter	Agree to Live in House with Jews	N
All respondents	58%	42%	30%	464
Students	53%	42%	31%	181
Parents	69%	36%	22%	98
Young adults	57%	44%	36%	90
Working youth	56%	44%	32%	95

Source: Peres 1970.

such an invitation is accepted, both men will define themselves as "friends," and will exhibit a pleasant although uncommitted attitude toward each other. This friendship is less selective and less personal than in Western societies.

If these arguments are valid, then we should predict that traditional parents would be more inclined than their more modernized sons to make friends with Jews but *less* inclined to accept Jews as neighbors. Table 12 substantiates this prediction. While the rejection of social contact with Jews is, as I have said, considerable, it is significantly lower than the Jews' rejection of Arabs. Again, we observe asymmetry in the relations between a dominant and a minority group. The minority member may feel that he may gain by interaction with the majority, while majority members will tend to exclude outsiders because, among other things, they are perceived as potential competitors.

Attitudes toward the State of Israel. Attitudes which Israeli-Arabs display toward Israel as a political entity seem to constitute a much more severe problem than do their attitudes toward Jews as individuals. Even societies with a long tradition of institutionalized dissent seem to confront a dilemma if dissenters come to question the legitimacy of the society's very existence or the validity of its ultimate values. This dilemma is particularly severe if

the society has recently been established and if its continuous existence is not absolutely secure.

As table 13 shows, the right of Israel to exist is not absolutely accepted by our Arab sample. The interesting category is, of course, "Yes, with reservations." The main reservations concern (as one might expect) Israel's treatment of the Palestinian Arabs. About half of those who chose this response explicitly mentioned repatriation of the refugees as a condition for Israel's right to exist. Others emphasized mainly the granting of full first-class citizenship to those Arabs now residing in Israel. Comparing the subgroups in the sample, the most striking difference is between students and parents. (The parents are the fathers of the students who were interviewed, so that the differences cannot be attributed to different family background.)

The tendency of the young Israeli-educated Arab to display extreme nationalistic and sometimes hostile attitudes calls for special attention. These young people are relatively similar to their Jewish counterparts in most nonpolitical respects, a similarity which draws them closer to Jewish individuals. They are also much better equipped (and more positively motivated) to live among Jews. The traditional village became too small for the wider perspectives and higher aspirations of these young Arabs, so some of them sought acceptance into the Jewish community, but were soon rebuffed. Their experience discouraged others. The second possible alternative for expanding an individual's horizons beyond the confines of the village would be an identification with the surrounding Arab world. Our data indicated that students, and to a degree other young people, feel relatively more "at home" in an Arab country, while parents tend to feel more comfortable in Israel.

The impact of the war. The impact of the war on the Arab population in Israel should be understood in the light of the expectation of any Arab victory by the overwhelming majority. The Arab defeat thus shocked them

TABLE 13. *Has the State of Israel a Right to Exist?*

Israeli Arabs	Yes	Yes, with Reservations	Refuse to Answer	No	N
All respondents	31%	49%	4%	16%	470
Students	24%	49%	3%	24%	192
Parents	51%	41%	2%	3%	96
Young adults	25%	61%	4%	10%	89
Working youth	29%	44%	6%	20%	93

Source: Peres 1970.

almost as much as it did the Arabs across the border (see table 14). The humiliation of defeat could be met only with new pride, and the despair of the defeated Arab populations aroused stronger sympathy and loyalty. Thus we observe in table 15 that the war served to increase the Arabs' hatred rather than their respect for the State of Israel. While table 15 deals with the respondent's perception of a change over time, the change is better recorded by comparing responses to identical questions posed to Arab respondents before and after the war. Table 16 indicates that *more* Arabs now feel at home in the Arab world and fewer feel at home in Israel. Similarly, according to table 17, fewer Arab respondents tend to see their future as positively bound with Israel.

CONCLUSION

Ethnic relations do not exist in a vacuum, but are interwoven with other facets of social structure and environment. This general perception is specifically true about Israel, a country in which some ethnic problems seem to be very close to solution while others may be close to explosion. This contrast can be explained in fact by the distinctive functions which the Oriental Jews and the Arabs perform for Israeli society.

After the diminution of European Jewish immigration to Israel, the mass immigration from the Middle East reestablished the young state's movement toward its declared goals. Orientals occupied the vacant land and houses

abandoned by the escaping Arabs, joined Israel's armed forces, and provided a sound justification for mobilizing economic, cultural, and political aid from world Jewry. In short, Orientals contributed to Israel's survival and progress in ways that Israeli Arabs were in no position to do. Even the most moderate and loyal individuals among them could not fully identify with the country's Zionist zeal, with its commitment to Jewish immigration, and, most important, with its struggle against the Arab world. These different backgrounds were further polarized when the three main ethnic

TABLE 14. *Expected Results of the War: When the War Broke out, Who Did You Think Would Win?*

The Arabs	No one	Israel, but a Less Decisive Victory	Israel	N
67%	18%	5%	9%	457

Source: Peres 1970.

TABLE 15. *The Perceived Influence of the War on the Arabs' Attitude toward Israel: How, in Your View, Did the War Influence the Arabs' Evaluation of the State of Israel?*

Attitude	Rose	Remained the Same	Fell	N
Respect	43%	17%	40%	299
Despair	52%	34%	13%	282
Hatred	73%	23%	4%	291

Source: Peres 1970.

TABLE 16. *Feeling More at Home in Israel or in an Arab Country before and after the June War (High School Students Only)*

Attitude	1966	1967
More at home in Israel	23%	57%
No difference	14%	12%
More at home in an Arab country	23%	57%
N	117	188

Source: Peres 1970.

TABLE 17. *Political Future Perspectives, before and after the War: What Would You Like the Future of the Israeli Arab to Be? (High School Students Only)*

Response	1966	1967
They will become part of the Jewish public	6%	...
A separate but equal people within the state of Israel	81%	53%
They will be in a separate state of their own	13%	17%
An Arab state will arise in the *entire* territory of Palestine	Not asked	19%
N	116	191

Source: Peres 1970.

groups (European Jews, Oriental Jews, and Arabs) began to interact. The Orientals aspired to full integration into the mainstream of Israeli life. This meant a movement away from their Middle Eastern (that is, Arab) background and toward the dominant European group. Arabs became for the Oriental Jews a "marking-off" group which symbolized everything resented and dispensable in their own background. The threat of surrounding Arab hostility became a catalyst for increasing unity among Israeli Jews, while the nonviolent but intense hostility against the Arab minority was a negative manifestation of this otherwise encouraging unity.

From the Arab minority's point of view, the need for full participation in the country's social, economic, and political life became more urgent, while the prospects for such participation did not increase. Thus, the most dynamic and competent individuals who might have been the pioneers of integration under different circumstances became the most outspoken advocates of political hostility. One of the most tragic aspects of the conflict between Israel and her Arab neighbors is that the two groups who could be potential mediators—the Israeli Jews of Middle Eastern background and Arabs of advanced Israeli education—are the least motivated to strive for reconciliation.

REFERENCES

Eisenstadt, S. N., ed. 1966. "Mizug Edot." Symposium of Hebrew University. [In Hebrew.]

Friedman, G. 1967. *The End of the Jewish People?* New York: Doubleday.

Hanoch, G. 1961. "Income Differences in Israel." In *The Fifth Annual Report.* Jerusalem: Falk Institute.

———. 1969. "Comments." In *The Integration of Immigrants from Different Countries of Origin in Israel,* edited by S. N. Eisenstadt. Jerusalem: Magnus Press. [In Hebrew.]

Herman, S. N. 1970. *Israelis and Jews.* New York: Random House.

Katzenelson, K. 1964. *The Ashkenazic Revolution.* Tel Aviv: Anach. [In Hebrew.]

Klinov-Malul, R. 1969. "Income Gaps between Immigrants and Old Timers." In *The Integration of Immigrants from Different Countries of Origin in Israel,* edited by S. N. Eisenstadt. Jerusalem: Magnus Press. [In Hebrew.]

Matras, J. 1965. *Social Change in Israel.* Chicago: Aldine.

Peres, Y. 1967. "Ethnic Identity and Ethnic Relations in Israel." Report submitted to the U.S. Office of Health, Education, and Welfare.

———. 1968a. "Ethnic Identity and Ethnic Relations in Israel." Unpublished Ph.D. thesis. Jerusalem. [In Hebrew.]

———. 1968b. "Ethnic Relations in the Tel-Aviv Area." Unpublished research report, Tel-Aviv University.

————. 1970. "Modernization and Nationalism in the Identity of the Israeli Arab." *Middle East Journal* (Fall).

Seltzer, M. 1967. *The Aryanization of the Jewish State*. New York: White.

Shuval, J. T. 1962. "Emerging Patterns of Ethnic Strain in Israel." *Social Forces* 40(4):324.

————. 1966. "Self Rejection among North African Immigrants to Israel." *Israel Annals of Psychiatry*, vol. 4(1).

Spiro, M. E. 1967. *Children of the Kibbutz*. New York: Schocken.

Williams, R. M. 1964. *Strangers Next Door*. Englewood Cliffs, N.J.: Prentice-Hall.

part three

Minorities in America: Historical Perspectives

Although many of the articles in other sections of this book are explicitly historical, we have felt that inclusion of a separate section emphasizing the historical dimension of racial and ethnic relations in the American experience was important for three reasons. First, a historical emphasis can provide a broader perspective from which to view current majority-minority conflict. Reporting on their examination of the historical patterns of violence in Europe and America, Graham and Gurr concluded that "probably all nations are given to a kind of historical amnesia or selective recollection that masks unpleasant traumas of the past."[1] Americans appear to be no exception to this generalization; most have lacked a historical perspective concerning contemporary racial and ethnic conflict, regarding it as a historical anomaly or aberration. However, the articles in this section indicate that racial and ethnic conflict has been an enduring, persistent, and pervasive phenomenon throughout the American experience. Through distortion or omission, this fact has been obscured in the reconstruction of the nation's past. Prejudice, discrimination, conflict, and violence are not new in the United States; they are, indeed, as "American as apple pie," as the reports to the Violence Commission confirm.[2]

[1] Hugh Davis Graham and Ted Robert Gurr, *Violence in America: Historical and Comparative Perspectives,* A Report Submitted to the National Commission on the Causes and Prevention of Violence (New York: Bantam Books, 1969), p. 792.
[2] *Ibid.*

Secondly, analysis of the historical dimension of racial and ethnic relations is essential to an understanding of the development of the institutional structures that form the basis for contemporary intergroup relations. Contemporary racial and ethnic conflict has important historical roots, and present patterns of inequality are based upon, and derived from, systems of intergroup relations initiated in the past. They did not emerge full-blown overnight, despite the perennial claims by majority-group spokesmen throughout the nation—prior to the outbreak of riots—that their communities were devoid of racial tensions. These tensions have always been present in America, whether or not the majority group chose to recognize them. During recent years, as minority claims for full equality have become more insistent, more strident, and more effectively organized, the majority has been forced to confront these historically rooted inequalities. As we will argue in Part Six, adequate analysis of the dynamics of these changes is inherently historical; therefore, considerable attention must be devoted to the operation of historical forces.

Finally, our primary objective in this book, as its subtitle would indicate, is the examination of the dynamics of racial and ethnic relations. Whether these phenomena occur in contemporary American society, in another society, or in the distant past is irrelevant to this aim; historical instances of racial conflict, as well as contemporary events, provide settings in which the validity of general theoretical and conceptual approaches can be assessed. This is ably demonstrated by Noel's use of the question of the genesis of American slavery to provide an initial test of his theory of the origins of ethnic stratification. Thus, analysis of historical phenomena can suggest new ways of conceptualizing data. Roy Simón Bryce-Laporte's penetrating analysis of the slave plantation and his suggestion that it be considered in reference to other "total institutions" illumines not only the nature of the institution of slavery, but the nature of the other social institutions to which it is compared as well.

However, our emphasis upon the importance of examining the historical dimension of intergroup relations should not be permitted to obscure the significance of social-structural conditions in the present society. Too often, historical "explanations" of a society's patterns of inequality deflect attention from the extent to which these patterns are reinforced and perpetuated by contemporary institutions. For instance, the disabilities that are encountered by Blacks, Chicanos, Puerto Ricans and American Indians in the United States today are not merely a function of racism and oppression in the past, but of those same factors operating in the present. The implications of this fact are moral as well as analytical. Responsibility for the existence of unequal rewards, prestige, and power in a society cannot be relegated to the sins of one's forefathers; rather it rests with all those who participate in the society and benefit from existing institutional arrangements.

Given the broad objectives stated above, it would be impossible to provide even a brief overview of the history of majority-minority conflict in the United States in this section. Consequently, we have not attempted to be inclusive. Our primary concern in the selection of articles was not that the historical dimensions of the experience of each American minority group be detailed, but that the articles chosen provide continuity, substantively as well as conceptually, to the volume. The primary focus of the articles in this section is upon majority-group reaction to minority-group presence. In Part Four we will consider more fully the different ways in which various minority groups responded to the external (i.e. majority group) pressures they confronted.

The conflict experienced by Oriental migrants to this country is discussed by Stanford Lyman ("Contrasts in the Community Organization of Chinese and Japanese in North America) in Part Four. Although the Chinese and Japanese differed dramatically in culture and social organization, the majority response to their presence was basically identical— derogation; educational, political, social, and legal discrimination; and, ultimately, restriction of further immigration.

The initial migration of Chinese into North America began, as Bonacich (in Part Two) and Lyman note, during the middle of the nineteenth century. The Chinese came as unskilled laborers, filling a vacuum created by the California Gold Rush, and were initially welcomed. However, as their numbers grew, the Chinese were perceived as an economic threat to native labor, and racist sentiment increased. Chinese were subjected to a variety of discriminatory legislation, including laws (such as a Queue Ordinance, which placed a tax on pigtails) designed specifically to harass them. Finally, in response to anti-Chinese agitation in California, Congress, in 1882, passed the Chinese Exclusion Act, the first federal immigration restriction in the United States. It was nearly half a century before similar explicit restrictions were placed upon European immigration.[3]

The spectre of the "yellow peril," which pervaded the hysteria over Chinese immigration, was revived in the response to the later immigration of the Japanese. Despite the fact that they represented an extremely small proportion of the total population of both California and the nation as a whole, their presence generated intense hostility. An international incident was precipitated in 1908 when the San Francisco Board of Education attempted to place all Japanese children, native and foreign born, in a segregated Oriental school in Chinatown. Immediate protests from the Japanese ambassador ultimately led the school board to rescind its order. However, the *quid pro quo* was a gentlemen's agreement obtained

[3] For discussion of the Chinese in America, see Francis L. K. Hsu, *The Challenge of the American Dream: The Chinese in the United States* (Belmont, Calif.: Wadsworth Publishing Co., 1971) and Stanford M. Lyman, *Chinese Americans* (New York, Random House, 1974).

by President Theodore Roosevelt by which Japan pledged that it would halt further immigration of its citizens (other than family members of those who had previously migrated) to the United States. Because wives continued to enter after the agreement, federal legislation was enacted in 1924 to restrict all Oriental immigration into the United States. The anti-Japanese agitation drew support from the same "scientific" sources that (as John Higham points out in this section) led to the respectability of racist thought.[4] Ultimately, however, this fear of the Yellow Peril culminated in the forcible evacuation and relocation of over 100,000 Japanese Americans (more than half of them American citizens) by the federal government during the Second World War.[5]

Analysis of the historical backgrounds of conflicts encountered by Spanish-speaking Americans—those of Mexican, Puerto Rican, and Filipino descent—focuses upon Mexican Americans, the largest Spanish-speaking group. Alvarez's "Psycho-Historical and Socioeconomic Development of the Chicano Community in the United States" (in this section) and Joan Moore's "Colonialism: The Case of the Mexican Americans" (in Part Four) illuminate the historical dimension of the Chicano experience. While Alvarez generalizes about broad historical periods of the Chicano experience, Moore shows that, as a consequence of historical differences in settlement and migration, different forms of Anglo dominance occurred in different geographical areas. Just as Lieberson (Part One) has argued that initial forms of contact will influence the nature of later interactional patterns, so Moore demonstrates that initial contacts resulted in considerable difference in Anglo-Chicano relations in Texas, New Mexico, and California. However, Moore and Alvarez agree that the effects of Anglo-Chicano interaction were similar in all areas—the consequence invariably was the relative powerlessness of Chicano communities throughout the Southwest—even in New Mexico, where the greatest Anglo concessions to Chicano culture and political organization were made.

The analyses of Moore and Alvarez also provide useful data for assessing Noel's thesis concerning the origins of ethnic stratification in much the same way as Noel used the establishment of slavery as a vehicle by which to present his model. Alvarez demonstrates that in initial con-

---

[4] See Fred H. Matthews, "White Community and 'Yellow Peril,'" *Mississippi Valley Historical Review* 50 (March, 1964): 612–633.

[5] For discussion of this phenomenon, see Dorothy Swaine Thomas and Richard S. Nishimoto, *The Spoilage: Japanese American Evacuation and Resettlement* (Berkeley: University of California Press, 1969); Morton Grodzins, *Americans Betrayed: Politics and the Japanese Evacuation* (Chicago: University of Chicago Press, 1966 [reprint of 1956 edition]); Allen R. Bosworth, *America's Concentration Camps* (New York: W. W. Norton & Co., 1967); Harry H. L. Kitano, *Japanese Americans: The Evolution of a Subculture* (Englewood Cliffs, N.J.: Prentice-Hall, 1969); and Roger Daniels, *Concentration Camps USA: Japanese Americans and World War II* (New York: Holt, Rinehart & Winston, 1972).

tacts, despite their ethnocentrism, Anglos and Mexicans coexisted, co-operated, and even fought a common enemy—the Mexican central government. It was only after competition for land and resources had become intense and Anglos had gained a power advantage, with the decline of support for Mexican Americans by the Mexican government, that Mexican Americans became relegated to an inferior caste position that has persisted. It is for this reason that Alvarez argues that the subjugation experience of the "creation generation" after the Mexican War was formative, in much the same sense that Bryce-Laporte characterizes slavery as "the contextual baseline of Black American experience." Although a substantial proportion of the Chicano population is derived from the migrant generation that paralleled the surge of European immigration into the United States during the early twentieth century, the situation of Chicano immigrants differed substantially from that of European immigrant groups because Chicanos entered a society that had already adopted a clearly defined lower-caste role for them, a result of the mid-nineteenth century conquest patterns of subordination.

There has recently been a surge of research interest in the institution of slavery, as Noel's discussion of the origins of American slavery would indicate.[6] The importance of the American slave system for the analysis of majority-minority relations in the United States is not merely that, as Bryce-Laporte points out, "antebellum race relations still constitute the basis of black behavior and black-white relations in the United States today." Its larger significance for the social scientist resides in the fact that slavery, although characterized in antebellum America as the nation's "peculiar institution," was *not* peculiar but conceptually must be considered in terms of its similarities to other sociological phenomena. Unfortunately, there has been a dearth of social scientific attention directed

[6] See for example: David Brian Davis, *The Problem of Slavery in Western Culture* (Ithaca, N.Y.: Cornell University Press, 1966); Stanley M. Elkins, *Slavery: A Problem in American Institutional and Intellectual Life*, 2nd ed. (Chicago: University of Chicago Press, 1968); Eugene D. Genovese, *The Political Economy of Slavery: Studies in the Economy and Society of the Slave South* (New York: Random House, 1965); Eugene D. Genovese, *The World the Slaveholders Made: Two Essays in Interpretation* (New York: Pantheon Books, 1969); Winthrop D. Jordan, *White over Black: American Attitudes toward the Negro, 1550–1812* (Chapel Hill, N.C.: University of North Carolina Press, 1968); Herbert S. Klein, *Slavery in the Americas: A Comparative Study of Cuba and Virginia* (Chicago: University of Chicago Press, 1967); Norman R. Yetman, ed., *Voices from Slavery: Personal Accounts from the Slave Narrative Collection* (New York: Holt, Rinehart & Winston, 1970); John W. Blassingame, *The Slave Community: Plantation Life in the Antebellum South* (New York: Oxford University Press, 1972); George P. Rawick, *From Sundown to Sunup: The Making of the Black Community* (Westport, Conn.: Greenwood Press, 1972); Gerald W. Mullin, *Fight and Rebellion: Slave Resistance in Eighteenth Century Virginia* (New York: Oxford University Press, 1972); Eugene D. Genovese, *Roll, Jordon, Roll: The World the Slaves Made* (New York: Pantheon, 1974); Robert William Fogel and Stanley L. Engerman, *Time on the Cross*, vol. 1, *The Economics of American Negro Slavery* (Boston: Little, Brown, 1974).

to the analysis of slavery as a social institution and to the more general question of the nature and effects of institutional regimentation.[7] The implications of an analysis of slavery in America, therefore, might be extended to examine the dynamics of other *total institutions* and other dominant-subordinate relationships (e.g., serfdom, caste systems, racial or ethnic ghettos, and various Indian reservation systems) that have not yet been considered in these terms.

If one closely considers Noel's arguments, one questions whether the important feature of Black-White relations in the United States was slavery *per se*. Instead one sees that the crucial factors are the features that undergirded the "peculiar institution": the conception of Black inferiority and the capacity of the dominant group to restrict Blacks to a permanent subordinate position. While slavery represented the most extreme form of institutionalized inequality between Black and White in America, Leon Litwack has pointed out that the rights and privileges of Blacks were severely circumscribed throughout the entire society.[8] Racial oppression of Blacks was not restricted to the South or to slaveholders, but was a virus that infected the entire society. Throughout the North the freedoms, rights, and privileges of free Blacks were severely curtailed; at no time did the status of free man or freedom mean the same thing to Blacks as to Whites. Blacks were confronted at every turn by severe legal proscriptions. In many states barriers to voting were initiated for Blacks at the same time restrictions for whites were being liberalized or eliminated. Court testimony and the formation of legal contracts and lawsuits by Blacks were also forbidden in many states. Several states prohibited immigration, while others required Blacks to carry identification passes (as in contemporary South Africa). Excluded from public schools, Blacks were generally denied the benefits of formal education. In addition to these officially imposed liabilities, Blacks in most areas were subjected to ridicule, harassment, and occasional mob violence.[9]

The most salient feature of Black-White relations in the United States, therefore, was that Blacks—whether they were slave or free—occupied a lower caste status, and severe sanctions were employed to restrict their freedoms. The American slave, therefore, had to contend with the sanc-

---

[7] The most notable exception is Erving Goffman's perceptive essay delineating the characteristics of *total institutions*, the concept upon which Bryce-Laporte has based his analysis of the slave population. Although the striking feature of total institutions is the polar inequality that characterizes relations between superordinate and subordinate, Goffman has not anywhere considered the implications of his analysis for the study of racial and ethnic relations. Moreover, his analysis is notably ahistorical, as revealed by the omission of slavery from among those phenomena included within the rubric of total institutions. The omission is especially revealing since some of the features of total institutions are described metaphorically in terms of slavery. See Erving Goffman, *Asylums* (New York: Doubleday, 1961).

[8] Leon Litwack, *North of Slavery: The Negro in the Free States, 1790–1860* (Chicago: University of Chicago Press, 1961).

[9] *Ibid.*

tions and effects of two inferior statuses—slave and lower caste—both of which were mutually reinforcing. Unlike many other slave societies, manumission was difficult, and freedmen could not anticipate assimilation into the society on an equal basis.

After the Civil War, the reality of caste persisted and, in many areas, was even strengthened. Patterns of Black-White relations formed under slavery were not automatically supplanted by emancipation. The freedmen's roles became well defined and tightly circumscribed; the new legal status conferred by emancipation and the Reconstruction Amendments did little to alter the patterns of social relations or to promote the acquisition of new values, habits, and attitudes by either Black or White. Caste sanctions—including intimidation and violence in the form of lynching and terrorism—assured that the subservient status of Blacks persisted long after slavery had been abolished. Writing in 1929, Charles S. Johnson, a pioneer Black sociologist, noted the continuity between the slave plantation and rural Macon County, Alabama, during the 1920s.

> There have been retained, only slightly modified, most of the features of the plantation under the institution of slavery. . . . The Negro population of this section of Macon County has its own social heritage which, in a relatively complete isolation, has had little chance for modification from without or within. Patterns of life, social codes, as well as social attitudes, were set in the economy of slavery. The political and economic revolution through which they have passed has affected only slightly the social relationships of the community or the mores upon which these relations have been based. The strength and apparent permanence of this early cultural set have made it virtually impossible for newer generations to escape the influence of the patterns of work and general social behavior transmitted by their elders.[10]

In a sense, then, the term *slavery* has been too narrowly construed in common parlance. As traditionally employed, slavery has referred to a system of *legal* oppression of a group of people. But elimination of the legal underpinnings of the patterns of dominance and subordination involved in the master-slave relationship provide no assurance that these patterns will not persist for many years thereafter.[11] If slavery is considered merely one form of total institution, the durability of Black-White caste patterns and the history of Indian-White relations (see Nancy Lurie's article in this section) suggest that the modern ghetto or barrio situation and the Indian reservation system are more comparable to the slave

---

[10] Charles S. Johnson, *Shadow of the Plantation* (Chicago: University of Chicago Press, 1934), p. 16.

[11] For an excellent study of this phenomenon, see Pete Daniel, *The Shadow of Slavery: Peonage in the South, 1901–1969* (Urbana: University of Illinois Press, 1972). See also the dramatic personal account of this peonage in William F. Tuttle, Jr., "Thirty-Five Years Overdue: Note on Belated Up From Slavery," *Labor History* 15 (Winter, 1974): 86–88.

situation than might be apparent at first glance. The term *ghetto,* meaning a geographically definable residential area for a minority group, has frequently been used in a broader sense. In addition to spatial restriction of a group, the term has generally referred to corollary aspects of a group's life—to its social, economic, educational, and psychological emasculation and encapsulation. Throughout the century that has passed since the Civil War, the striking feature of the situation of Black people in the northern ghettos has been "the continuance of an enervating and destructive racism, the institutionalization, in thought and action, of second-class citizenship for Black people."[12] and Lurie's analysis (as well as that of Robert Thomas in Part Five) demonstrates that in many respects the Indian reservation, like the plantation, has features of a total institution that preclude the development of effective autonomy among its members.

While prejudice and discrimination towards Blacks, Chicanos, and American Indians has been a persistent theme throughout the American experience, the intensity of both phenomena toward other ethnic groups has ebbed and flowed. Historically, America has been the primary destination of the largest human migration in history. More than seventy million people have emigrated from Europe alone since the seventeenth century; over half of these entered the United States. As a "nation of immigrants," the United States has incorporated a great diversity of ethnic groups, whose continuing presence has been a perennial source of ambivalence for the American people. The idea of America as an asylum for the oppressed, extolled in patriotic oratory and intertwined among our nation's sacred myths, is perhaps best reflected in Emma Lazarus's classic poem, "Give me your tired, your poor, your huddled masses yearning to breathe free. . . ." On the other hand, there has been a persistent concern over the impact of ethnic diversity upon the nation's social fabric. It is revealing that Lazarus's poem, inscribed upon the Statue of Liberty, further characterizes those "tired," "poor," "huddled masses" as "wretched refuse." That many immigrant groups have been perceived as "wretched refuse" has meant that, in practice, Americans have been less charitable to those who sought entrance into the society than our idealized accounts would indicate. Americans have frequently rejected ethnic differences as alien and undesirable; specific ethnic groups, in particular, have been rejected or excluded as "un-American" and unassimilable.

As John Higham has indicated in his article in this section, *nativism,* the hostility toward groups on the basis of their "foreign" or "un-Ameri-

---

[12] Gilbert Osofsky, "The Enduring Ghetto, *Journal of American History* 4 (September, 1968): 252. For a superb analysis of the persistence of caste in a northern Black ghetto, see David M. Katzman, *Before the Ghetto: Black Detroit in the Nineteenth Century* (Urbana: University of Illinois Press, 1973).

can" connections, recurred throughout the nineteenth century. Until the final quarter of the century, the primary thrust of American nativism was religious; the antipathy of the dominant Protestant population to non-Protestants was expressed in frequent violence and in the political success of the virulently anti-Catholic and anti-Irish Know-Nothing Party. Nativism reached its zenith during the late nineteenth and early twentieth centuries, when nativist thought became increasingly racist. During that period, *scientific racism* became intellectually respectable, and to the already existing conceptions of Black, Indian, and Oriental inferiority was added the concept of the inferiority of immigrant groups from southern and eastern Europe.

Moreover, during the Progressive Era the political strength that minorities did possess was eroded by Progressive electoral "reforms"—particularly the direct primary. Joan Moore notes how these reform policies undermined Chicano political interests in California. The consequences for Blacks, who had been represented in local and state political conventions and had frequently held elective office as a consequence of efforts to attain balanced tickets, were particularly disastrous, for these reforms virtually eliminated Blacks from any elective political offices. Moore contends that this was an accidental effect of the reform movement, which embodied the anti-establishment ideals of the Progressive Era. In fact, in many areas such efforts were not accidental but represented a calculated effort to insure Anglo-Saxon dominance. Regardless of the motivation, as we note more fully in Parts One and Five, the *effect* of these political actions ran counter to minority-group interests.[13]

For most of the nineteenth century, immigrants entering the United States were drawn almost exclusively from the countries of northern and western Europe, which included the British Isles, Germany, France, Scandinavia, Belgium, and the Netherlands. During the 1880s, however, an increasing proportion of immigrants admitted annually were from other European nations. Between 1895 and 1923, the number of *new immigrants* (those from southern and eastern Europe) exceeded the number of *old immigrants* (those from northern and western Europe). By 1923, the effects of the discriminatory quota legislation of 1921 were felt, and *new* immigration declined. The seemingly innocuous distinction between *new* and *old* immigrant groups was in reality an invidious one. The terms were coined in 1870 by Francis A. Walker, Director of the Census and later president of MIT, who characterized the new immigrants thus:

They are beaten men from beaten races; representing the worst failures in the struggle for existence. Centuries are against them, as centuries were

---

[13] For an account of these effects, see Katzman, *Before the Ghetto*, pp. 202–203, and William F. Tuttle, Jr., "Racism in the Progressive Era: An Essay Review," *Wisconsin Magazine of History* 8 (Spring, 1970): 228.

on the side of those who formerly came to us. They have none of the ideas and aptitudes which fit men to government.[14]

Walker's attitude toward new immigrants was far from atypical. Almost all of the leading intellectuals of the late nineteenth and early twentieth centuries believed in the inherent inferiority of non-Anglo-Saxon groups. Never before or since have racist ideologies been so pervasive and so intellectually respectable in the United States.

These racist assumptions provided the foundations for American immigration policy from 1917 to 1965.[15] The first restrictive legislation (passed in 1917) was a literacy test, which was employed because it was felt that it would materially lessen the immigration from southern and eastern Europe while permitting immigration from northern and western Europe to continue. In the ensuing decade, even more stringent restrictive measures were enacted, each one based upon the assumption of the desirability of restricting immigration to those from the countries of the *old* immigration. Because the 1917 literacy test had failed in its objective of diminishing the influx of *new* immigrants, further legislation was passed in 1921 and 1924 to try to curtail their numbers more effectively. Finally, in 1929, the national origins quota act, based (as was preceding legislation) upon the rationale of ensuring the maintenance of Anglo-Saxon racial purity, became law. The quota system limited total immigration to 150,000 annually and established quotas for each nation. Derived by a complicated means of calculation, each nation's quota was supposed to be "in proportion to its [the nation's] contribution to the American population." The measure was designed to assign the highest quotas to those nations of northern and western Europe whose racial stock was conceived to most closely coincide with that of the "original" settlers of the country. More than four-fifths of the total quota was allocated to countries of the old immigration. For instance, while Great Britain had an admissions quota exceeding 65,000, Italy was allocated less than 6,000 and Hungary less than 1,000. This policy was retained virtually intact until its repeal in 1965. The social, economic, political, and ideological factors that contributed to the rise of racist respectability during this period are the subject of Higham's discussion. In Part Four we will examine the factors that affected the adjustments of several of the ethnic groups that were included in the new immigration.

[14] Quoted in Edward N. Saveth, *American Historians and European Immigrants, 1875–1925* (New York: Columbia University Press, 1948), p. 40.

[15] As noted above, Chinese were excluded under legislation in 1882, and Japanese immigration was completely curtailed with the passage of the Johnson-Reed Act in 1924.

12

The American Indian: Historical Background

Nancy Oestreich Lurie

Thanks to work by generations of archeologists, ethnologists and historians, there is an enormous literature for intensive study of the prehistoric and historic cultures of the North American Indians and the effects of Euro-American influences on Indian life.[1] This paper seeks only to provide a brief and general chronology of significant phases in the history of Indian-white contact as a background in understanding contemporary Indian life.

Nancy Oestreich Lurie is Professor of Anthropology at The University of Wisconsin, Milwaukee.

Reprinted from *The American Indian Today,* Stuart Levine and Nancy Oestreich Lurie, eds., by permission of the publisher, Everett Edwards, Inc., and the editors.

[1] For more intensive study of the subject: William Brandon, *The American Heritage Book of Indians* (New York, 1961; paperback: Dell, 1964): more historical than ethnological. Harold Driver, *Indians of North America* (Chicago, 1961), a scholarly reference book with useful maps. Organized according to topics rather than culture areas. Wendell H. Oswalt, *This Land Was Theirs* (New York, 1966): good treatment of ten representative tribes across the country. Robert F. Spencer, Jesse D. Jennings, *et al., The Native Americans* (New York, 1965): general introductory chapters followed by culture area descriptions and accounts of specific tribes within the areas, written for textbook use. Ruth Underhill, *Red Man's America* (Chicago 1953), also a textbook, and in many ways still the best general introduction to the subject for the beginner. Wilcomb Washburn, ed., *The Indian and The White Man* (Garden City, N.Y., 1964), a fascinating compendium of documents from the period of early contact to the present day, including John Marshall's decisions of 1831 and 1832, and House Concurrent Resolution 108—the termination bill referred to in this paper.

It is commonly but incorrectly assumed that Indian societies, before Europeans arrived, were stable, and that they had existed in idyllic and unchanging simplicity since time immemorial, until Europeans made their first landfall and began disrupting and ultimately destroying native life. We now know, on the contrary, that their societies were developing and changing in important ways long before first contact. Archeological evidence reveals that prior to the discovery of America by Europeans, widespread trade routes stretched over the entire continent. Many of our important highways follow trails long familiar to the Indians. Furthermore, pottery, burial practices, grave goods, earthworks and other clues uncovered by the archeologist clearly show that new ideas arose in many different places and diffused to neighboring areas to be adapted to different natural environments, further elaborated and passed on yet again. Religion, economic practices, and artistic and utilitarian productions were all subjected to the process. By the time of significant European contact along the east coast in the late sixteenth and early seventeenth centuries, a simple hunting and gathering economy was already giving way to a food production economy in the vast area south of the Great Lakes from the Mississippi River to the Atlantic Ocean. Domesticated corn, beans, squash and possibly other food plants as well as tobacco were in a process of northward spread from the lower Mississippi valley. They had undoubtedly been introduced from Mexican sources about one A.D., but by a process and routes not yet fully understood.

When Europeans first arrived, tribes in the northern Great Lakes region had only begun to experiment with gardening as a supplement to a diet based primarily on hunting and gathering, while tribes in the Southeast had already achieved populous, permanent settlements exhibiting marked social and material complexities as natural concomitants to the development of food production. The spread of cultural complexity was paced to some extent by the gradual selection of ever hardier varieties of what has been essentially a semi-tropical plant complex, but which now had to survive even shorter growing seasons. Warmer coastal regions permitted a somewhat faster diffusion of gardening than colder inland regions and in some cases peoples already accustomed to raising crops moved northward, displacing groups still largely dependent on hunting.

The establishment of permanent European settlements along the eastern seaboard and St. Lawrence River in the early seventeenth century required the assistance of Indians in providing food, information and skills to survive the first years in a new environment. As the fur trade took on importance, and with it competition among European nations for control of North America, the Indian tribes enjoyed a good deal of bargaining power and learned to use it astutely in their own interests in regard to both commercial and military activities. For many eastern tribes, it was the long period of the fur trade and not the aboriginal past which is recalled as a golden age.

Although the popular view is that a rapid demise was the fate of all Indians, generally it was the more fully agricultural and rigidly structured tribes which went under quickly and completely in the face of early European contact. Located close to the coasts to begin with and hemmed in by mountains or hostile tribes at their backs, these societies bore the first brunt of intense white competition for desirable land. Their more populous villages and accompanying social norms had developed prior to the advent of Europeans, which may have made for a certain inflexibility in adaptiveness. It should be borne in mind that in the seventeenth century, the difference in political and technological complexity between Indians and little groups of colonists was not so great as to suggest immediately to the tribes and powerful alliances of tribes that Europeans posed a serious threat to their future. Certainly, the relatively large and compact Indian villages with their gardens and stored surpluses of food were highly vulnerable both to new epidemic diseases and scorched earth campaigns in times of open hostilities when their continued presence in the region became a nuisance to the colonists. Thus, only remnants remain of once formidable alliances of tribes along the eastern seaboard, and many tribes noted as powerful and culturally sophisticated in the early British, French and Spanish chronicles have disappeared completely.

Further inland, the tribes were less fully committed to complexities attendant upon food production. They apparently benefitted from the greater flexibility and mobility of a hunting ethos as well as from the fact that Europeans were more interested in their country for furs than for colonization. Moreover, the nascent alliances and confederacies which had begun to develop inland were influenced and shaped in response to the Europeans who sought trade and friendship. These tribes accepted, made adaptations, and recognized as inevitable and even desirable that Europeans should be on the scene. When demand for their land eventually developed, as had happened so quickly on the coast, the inland Indians had established clear patterns for looking after their own interests as societies distinct from those of Europeans, despite their long association and extensive trade and more than occasional acceptance of white in-laws.

Beyond the St. Lawrence to the Arctic Circle, there are still groups of people, Indian and Eskimo, who are essentially hunters. Even where ecological conditions might have eventually permitted aboriginal plant domestication, their contact with Europeans occurred before there was an intervening native food producing stage. In many instances, contact with outsiders has been so recent that the first encounters involved immediate introduction to features of highly industrialized society. Thus, there are Indian and Eskimo people who rode in airplanes before they even saw an automobile.[2] Some groups are still able to subsist

---

[2] A small but revealing incident, illustrative of a kind of hunter's pragmatism, occurred in the Canadian Northwest Territories. When questioned about his first airplane ride, a Slave Indian was clearly en-

largely off the land but have availed themselves rapidly and selectively of alien items to make the life of the hunter more efficient and comfortable: repeating rifles, gasoline "kickers" for canoes, even radios. Some are as fully committed to the fur trade as a way of life as the Indians of the eastern woodlands in the seventeenth and eighteenth centuries, while for others the fur trade is in its terminal stage, and they face painful adjustments experienced earlier by other groups living in a market economy.

Gardening also diffused into the Prairie and Plains region from Mississippian sources in aboriginal times, but was largely confined to river bottom lands where bone or stone implements could turn the loose soil. The people built substantial villages of timber-framed, mud covered lodges and settled down to the elaboration of existence permitted by food production. The open plains, where coarse grass matted the earth, were exploited in brief, organized forays to take buffalo in quantity by such means as driving herds over cliffs. Having only dogs as beasts of burden, Indian people found the Plains dangerous, with uncertain and widely spaced sources of water. Only scattered bands of hunters wandered there on occasion.

Important contact with European people occurred only after the Plains had been made habitable for many tribes by the introduction of the horse. As herds of wild Spanish horses spread north, techniques of horsemanship diffused from Spaniard to Indian. Raiding for tamed animals from tribe to tribe became an important and exciting aspect of existence. The great herds of buffalo which a hunter approached on foot with trepidation could not be exploited efficiently from horseback. The buffalo suddenly became an abundant and dependable food supply and source of housing, utensils and clothing as horses became available to more and more tribes. Some tribes were more or less pushed into the Plains as the

pressure of white settlement forced one Indian group against another, but the Plains clearly attracted tribes to a new and exciting way of life as well. The gaudily befringed Indian in warbonnet astride his horse is the archetype of the American Indian all over the world, and we note with wonder the spectacular history of his distinctive way of life. It was made possible by native adaptations of an animal of European origin, achieved astonishing complexity to govern and give deep psychic and esthetic satisfaction to the life of large encampments, and collapsed with the disappearance of the buffalo in the short span of less than 200 years, roughly from 1700 to 1880. By then, the repeating rifle and commercial hunting, which hastened the demise of the buffalo, the windmill, barbed wire and the steel plow transformed the Plains into a rich grazing and grain area, no longer "The Great American Desert" of the early maps, fit only for Indians.

In the Southwest, agriculture had diffused directly from Mexico and stimulated elaborations of social life even earlier than in the Southeast, beginning perhaps about 1000 B.C. Changes in climate and invasions of hunter-raiders from the North saw shifts of settlements, abandonment of old villages and building of new ones before Europeans first visited the pueblos in 1539. Archeological studies show that the settled peoples of the Southwest, pueblos and other gardening villagers, had long exchanged items and ideas among themselves. Although actual relations with the Spaniards were frequently strained, they readily took over from the Spaniards a host of new objects, skills, plants, animals and ideas to make them peculiarly their own. Learning early the futility of overt aggression against the better armed Spaniards, the pueblo peoples particularly have developed passive resistance to a fine art in dealing with strangers in their midst—even holding hordes of modern tourists at arm's length with bland pleasantries while doing a brisk trade in hand crafts and fees for taking pictures.

The pueblos' once troublesome neighbors, the former raiders today designated as Navaho and Apache, successfully incorporated ele-

---

thusiastic but not awe-struck by modern technology —"Good! See moose sign. Come back, go find moose." Personal conversation, June Helm.

ments of sedentary Indian cultures into their more mobile life in aboriginal times, and eventually they too made judicious selections from Euro-American culture, reworking and molding them to fit their own cultural predilections. The Southwestern Indians in general retain more obvious and visible symbols of their "Indianness" and for many white observers these are the only "real" Indians left. However, their modern material culture is far from aboriginal, distinctive though it may be. Like Indian groups throughout the country, the important criteria of identity rest in intangible attitudes, values, beliefs, patterns of inter-personal relations.

As in the East, native social and material elaboration in the West tended to thin out toward the North, limited by environmental factors. In the Great Basin, tiny bands of roving gatherers maintained a bare subsistence level of existence. Nevertheless, even some of the simple Basin societies were attracted by the horse-buffalo complex of the Plains and in an incredibly short time the Comanche, for example, had ventured out to become a Plains tribe *par excellence*.

North of the Basin, the relatively greater richness of the environment permitted the Plateau Indian to live much as the more favored northern hunters east of the Mississippi, even to enjoying a fur trade era, although of briefer duration. Gardening never reached this region in aboriginal times, but after contact the horse became important to many of the Plateau peoples.

In the West, there were several unusual situations where nature furnished dependable "crops" which man could harvest without first having sown. In Central California, huge stands of oak accounted for regular supplies of acorns which the Indians converted into a nutritious flour by ingenious techniques of leaching out the bitter and somewhat toxic tannic acid. On the coast, enormous shell mounds are evidence of once large permanent settlements supported in large part by easily gathered mollusks. Many of the California Indians took quite readily to the ministrations of Spanish friars who began arriving in 1769,

and set up mission compounds where they introduced the Indians to agricultural and other skills. Crowded together in the new villages, the Indians proved tragically susceptible to new diseases. The eventual discovery of gold, the influx of lawless miners, and competition by the United States for control of California, in which Indian property and rights were often identified with Hispano-American interests, contributed to a rapid and widespread disorganization and decline among many of the California groups. The picture is, in fact, strikingly similar to the rapid depopulation and disruption of native life on the east coast.

Along the Northwest Coast from Oregon to Alaska, an abundance and variety of marine life and a northerly climate mitigated by the warm Japanese Current created ideal conditions for population growth and social elaboration which could be promoted in most places only through the development of food production. The peoples in this region had regularly traded, visited and fought among themselves when first European contacts were made by sailing ships out of Russia, England and the United States in the late eighteenth century. Trade soon flourished in which sea otter and other pelts were exchanged for both utilitarian and novelty items. The Northwest Coast peoples quickly earned a reputation for sharp bargaining and scant concern for the welfare of hapless seamen wrecked on their shores as they busily plundered ships' cargoes. An impressive way of native life became further enriched. Already skilled in working cedar with simple tools and clever methods of steaming, bending and sewing boards, the Indians soon appreciated that totem poles, storage boxes, house posts, masks and other objects could be enlarged and more ornately embellished with metal tools. However, indiscriminate slaughter of the peltry animals brought a rapid close to the coastal trade. Unlike the eastern tribes which foraged further and further west for fresh beaver areas, even to pushing out the resident tribes, the Northwest Coast people had no place else to go. The arrival of Lewis and Clark in 1806 heralded the opening of overland routes of settlement from the east and encroachment of farmers, miners and loggers. The later adaptations of the Coastal Indians have tended to center in fishing both for their own support and as commercial enterprise.

If we take a broad view of the entire continent from the end of the sixteenth century until well into the nineteenth century, we find that white contact stimulated new ideas, introduced new goods and even greatly accelerated the pace of cultural change in some cases. However, whites arrived on a scene where changes, experimentation, movements of people and diffusion of goods and ideas were already taking place. For the vast majority of tribes, there was time to develop attitudes and adaptations about the presence of whites which involved negotiation and selective borrowing of items rather than absorption into white culture and society. Exposure to similar opportunities to change, furthermore, did not lead to cultural homogeneity throughout the continent, since different Indian societies in different kinds of environments made different selections and adaptations in regard to white culture. The multiplicity of languages and local cultural identity persisted. When, from place to place, the nature of contact changed to one of intense competition for right to the land, the Indians were clearly at a disadvantage. However, even as their power to bargain waned, the various Indian groups continued to adapt to maintain their ethnic integrity. Because they made massive borrowings of European material items, which tended to be similar from place to place—guns, textiles, household utensils and tools—white people generally assumed they would soon gracefully phase out their social and cultural distinctiveness. However, we are still waiting for them to vanish.

TREATIES AND RESERVATIONS

When the United States and Canada finally emerged as the national entities controlling North America, increasingly determined to re-main at peace with one another, Indian societies were obliged to deal exclusively with one or the other of these governments and were bereft of the opportunity to play the familiar game of favored nation in war and trade among competing powers—France, Spain, Britain and the young United States. Both Canada and the United States derive their Indian policies from guidelines which were already being laid down in the mid-seventeenth century in New England and Virginia. In the face of overwhelming defeat, the depleted and demoralized tribes in these areas were offered and accepted small parcels of land—the first reservations—secured to them by treaties. These guaranteed homelands and other considerations, in the way of goods and religious and practical teachings, were to be compensation for the vast domains they relinquished. The Indians, in turn, pledged themselves to peace and alliance with the local colonies in case of war with hostile tribes or European enemies. In Virginia, in 1646, the regrouped remnants of the once powerful Powhatan Confederacy agreed in their treaty to pay a small annual tribute in furs to the colony, an interesting portent of things to come for their Indian neighbors to the West, as the fur trade was just beginning to loom importantly to the British.[3]

As the scattered and often competitive British colonies began to recognize their common interests in opposition to the French in the North and both Spain and France to the South, Indian policy became more firmly structured. By 1755, negotiations with Indians, particularly in regard to land, became the exclusive prerogative of the Crown acting through properly designated representatives. A northern and a southern superintendency were set up to regulate trade and undertake necessary diplomacy with the Indians. After the American Revolution, the southern superintendency ceased to exist as a British concern and the

[3] Nancy Oestreich Lurie, "Indian Cultural Adjustment to European Civilization," in James Morton Smith, ed., *Seventeenth Century America* (Chapel Hill, 1958), 33–60, discusses the Powhatan Confederacy and notes origins of the reservation system in North America.

northern superintendency was moved from the area of New York State to Canada.

Canadian colonial governors handled Indian affairs locally until 1860 when responsibility in Ontario and Quebec was given directly to the Province of Canada. In 1867, the British North America Act placed Indian affairs under the jurisdiction of the Government of Canada. During the ensuing years, administrative headquarters were shifted between various Offices and Branches of the Government, but policy itself tended to remain relatively consistent. Whenever possible, Canada dealt with tribes by treaty, including as many tribes under a common treaty as could be induced to sign in any particular region. Reserves were located in the tribes' homelands or in nearby, ecologically similar areas, the process being repeated from region to region as national interest in regard to allocation of land expanded west and north. Canada made its last treaty with some of the far northern Indians in 1923. A system to encourage understanding of modern principles of government provides for election of a chief and headmen in each "Band," the Canadian term for locally autonomous Indian groups. The number of headmen is determined by population size, with roughly one headman per 100 people. For some bands, such as the Iroquois groups along the southern border of Canada, this system is an uncomfortable imposition on their own patterns of semi-hereditary leadership, while for bands in the northern Territories, it has given a formal structure to an old system of leadership based on individual ability. The Canadian government has always cooperated with religious denominations in sharing responsibility for Indian affairs, especially in regard to education.

A few Canadian bands were by-passed in treaty negotiations and special provisions have been made for them to qualify for "Treaty Indian" benefits as well as conform to limitations placed on full citizenship by Treaty Indian status. A basic objective has been to encourage Indian people to declare themselves "nontreaty" as individuals and be accepted as full-fledged citizens. After 1950, most of the limitations on citizenship were lifted, even for Treaty Indians, in the hope of hastening the day when Indians would become assimilated. The Canadian government, however, has been generally more tolerant than the United States of ethnic distinctiveness and more agreeable to protecting Indian rights to their lands as defined by treaties.

Eskimo affairs, until 1966, were considered a separate concern, centering more in matters of trade and welfare than in questions of land. At present an effort is underway to consolidate and regularize Indian and Eskimo administration, stressing new experiments in economic development of native communities.

Perhaps the most distinctive feature of Canadian Indian history is the explicit recognition of old communities of stabilized Indian-white mixture, designated *Metis*. This is a sociological and not an official concept; the Metis are simply an ethnic group like Ukrainians or French Canadians, sharing none of the benefits of Indian status. They are considered different from Indians both by themselves and the Indian people who also represent some white admixture in the genealogies. In some cases, the actual kinship between certain Indian and Metis families is known to both sides. Since Metis are generally found in the western Provinces and Territories, where there are large Indian populations, and suffer the same disabilities of isolation and inadequate education and perhaps even lower social status in the Canadian class system, there is an increasing tendency to group Metis and Indians in Canadian discussions of problems of poverty, employment, education and the like. The extent to which Metis and Indians themselves are interested in making common cause remains debatable.

The picture in the United States is much more complicated. In the first place there were and are more Indian people representing greater diversity of languages, cultures and ecological adaptations. Encroachment of whites on Indian land has always been a much more acute problem. After France ceased to be a consideration in the struggle for control of North America, many tribes allied themselves with the British against the Americans in the

Revolution and War of 1812, or maintained a wary neutrality during these conflicts, waiting to see how they would turn out. Few tribes declared themselves clearly on the side of the Americans. Thus, from the start, American negotiations for land frequently followed recent hostile engagements with the tribes involved. The settlers' fears of disgruntled and warlike Indians, perhaps not yet entirely convinced they were defeated, gave added impetus to a policy designed to move Indian tribes far from the lands they ceded. In Canada, the relatively smaller populations of both Indians and whites as well as a history of friendlier relationships permitted comparatively easier negotiations for land and establishing reserves close to areas opening up for settlement.

Eventually, there was no place left to move Indians and the United States was also obliged to set up reservations in tribal homelands. Added to these many complications was the fact that in time American policy had to be adjusted to old Spanish arrangements in the Southwest where land grants established Indian title, a plan analogous but not identical to the British plan of treaties and reservations.

Following British precedent, the United States made Indian affairs a concern of the central government, but actual procedures were left vague. The Third Article of the Constitution merely empowered Congress to "regulate commerce with foreign nations, and among the several states, and with the Indian tribes." At first, administration was carried out through a system of government authorized trading posts, reminiscent of the British superintendencies. The army handled problems of hostile Indians. Peace negotiations and land sales, including arrangements for reservations, were carried out by special treaty commissions appointed as need demanded. The idea prevailed, as it had since colonial times, that changes in sovereignty over land did not abrogate the rights of possession of those who occupied the land, and that Indians should be recompensed for land which they relinquished. This concept was enunciated in the Northwest Ordinance confirmed in 1789 and extended to cover the tribes in the Louisiana Purchase in 1804. By the time the United States acquired Alaska, we had begun to equivocate on this philosophy, and questions of Indian and Eskimo land remain somewhat confused.[4]

The fact that the United States pledged itself to pay Indians for their lands at a time when there was virtually no national treasury has given comfort to those historians who would see the founding fathers imbued with the noblest of ideals. Cynics point out that it was cheaper and easier than trying to drive the Indians out by force. The price paid across the continent averaged well under ten cents an acre, and the government expected to recoup quickly by sale of land in large blocks to speculators at $1.25 an acre minimum. Moreover the debt on each treaty usually was paid under an annuity plan extending over thirty years. On the other hand, many of the tribes were not entirely naive and held out for payment in specie rather than the uncertain paper issued by banks in the early days of the republic.

Although successive efforts were made to establish a firm line between Indian and white holdings east of the Mississippi River, settlement continued to encroach on the Indian area, necessitating renegotiation of the boundary. By 1824, the demands of settlers, competition from illegal, private traders, and the diminishing returns of the fur trade led the government to abandon the trading business as basic to Indian affairs and concentrate on the land business. The Bureau of Indian Affairs was set up under the Department of War. When the Department of Interior was established in 1849 and Indian affairs were placed under its aegis, most of the eastern tribes had become located much as we find them today.

A few tribes on the seaboard occupy state reservations or are simply old Indian settlements, legacies of the colonial past which could be ignored. Along the Appalachians, par-

[4] Lurie, "The Indian Claims Commission Act," *The Annals of The American Academy of Political and Social Science* (May, 1957), 56–70, reviews the question of Indian land title, with special reference to an Alaskan case, 64–65.

ticularly toward the southern end and elsewhere in the Southeast, there are isolated communities which identify themselves as Indian, such as the numerous Lumbee of North Carolina and adjoining states and the Houma of Louisiana. Their tribal affiliations are vague, because these people are the descendants of fugitive remnants of many tribes driven from the coasts, white renegades, and, in some cases, runaway Negro slaves. These people are, in effect, Metis, but popular and official thinking in the United States has tended to more rigid classification than in Canada. Thus, rejected as white and reluctant to be considered Negro, the American Metis stress their identity as Indian. Those Indian societies which maintained a clear and unbroken tradition of tribal identity and stood in the path of settlement were exhorted, negotiated with and paid to move further west during the period of the 1820's and 1830's.

The United States entered into numerous treaties with these tribes and though it tried to deal with blocs of tribes as was done in Canada, this proved inexpedient. Both tribesmen and treaty commissioners tried to outmaneuver each other by devious diplomatic ploys. The Indians could play for delay in land sales by noting boundaries which had only Indian names and were unknown to the whites, so that final settlement would depend on formal surveys. The whites attempted to play one tribe off against another, and even one subband within a tribe against another, in the hope of leaving intransigent factions so isolated and unprotected that they would be forced to capitulate when their neighbors moved out. And then the factions would rally and claim the treaty had to include all parties with an interest to the land in question. Since treaties had to be ratified by Congress and the work of the commissioners was hampered by both budget allocations for their time and the desire to get back to Washington before Congress recessed, the Indians won compromises. The commissioners could afford to be philosophical as these loose ends could always be tied up in the next round of negotiations. There is little doubt that the Indian tribes hoped to

make the best of what could only be a bad bargain, but to stick to that bargain once made, whereas the treaty makers from Washington took the treaties lightly, striving toward a final goal of general Indian removal to the less choice land west of the Mississippi acquired in the Louisiana Purchase.

Thus we find representatives of eastern tribes scattered from Nebraska to Oklahoma: Potawatomi, Winnebago, Miami, Shawnee, Kickapoo, Ottawa, Creek, Choctaw, Chickasaw, Cherokee, Seminole and others even including members of the League of the Iroquois such as Cayuga and Seneca. However, bands or small clusterings of families of many of these tribes managed to return to their old homelands or held out against removal, arguing either the illegality of the treaty under which they were to move or misrepresentation by the government as to the quality of the new land or the terms whereby they and their possessions were to be transported. In some cases, this determination led to creation of reservations for them in their homelands, as in the cases of the Eastern Cherokee and Seminoles. Others, including some of the Potawatomi and Winnebago, were granted homesteads as individuals where it was hoped that they would become absorbed into the general rural white population. Popular indignation about the injustice shown one band of Potawatomi in Michigan led to the establishment of a small reservation for them under state jurisdiction. A group of Mesquakie (Fox) picked out and purchased their own land and applied for reservation status. Perhaps the most bizarre instance was the band of Kickapoo who just kept on going west and sought sanctuary in northern Mexico where they remain to this day, preserving many features of nineteenth century woodland Indian culture. In many cases, particularly in the Southeast, little groups simply managed to maintain themselves as Indian neighborhoods on property they were able to purchase, little noticed and bothering no one.

Several Iroquois tribes or portions of them who did not flee to Canada after the Revolution were granted their reservations in New York State by treaties signed during

Washington's administration. Of these, the Oneida were induced to move to Wisconsin in the early 1830's along with the Stockbridge, a highly acculturated Algonkian group drawing its membership from remnants of coastal tribes, primarily the Mahicans. In Wisconsin, Michigan and Minnesota we find a number of tribes, Menomini, bands of Ojibwa and others who by various delaying tactics finally managed to get reservations in their homelands.[5]

There is no question that when it was a matter of the larger national interest, defined as the demands of settlers or speculators, the government made every effort to remove the Indians.[6] Humanitarians such as Jefferson expressed the hope that if Indian people conformed to the habits of rural whites they might remain in possession of what land they would need for this purpose, but if they would not change their ways, the only alternative was forceful persuasion and removal. The rationale for dispossession of the Indians has usually conformed to a logic summed up by Theodore Roosevelt in the late nineteenth century, "this great continent could not have been kept as nothing but a game preserve for squalid savages."[7] The myth of the hunter Indian, incapable or unwilling to rouse himself from the sloth of ancestral tradition in the face of new opportunities and the model afforded by civilized man, remains with us today. On close inspection, the problem seems to be less the Indian's inability to adapt than the unorthodoxy of his adaptations. Western cultures have a different history; our traditions evolved out of a stage of feudal peasantry which the In-

dians by-passed. So Indians react in unexpected but perfectly logical ways to our ideas and artifacts.

The essential problems which arise in the confrontation of different cultural systems, each changing and adapting in its own way, are well illustrated in the fate of the Cherokee, who became literate as a result of exposure to the European idea of writing, but hit upon a syllabary rather than an alphabet to best convey the vagaries of their own tongue in written symbols. By the early nineteenth century, the Cherokee and other groups in the Southeast had built upon their growing aboriginal commitment to agriculture with new crops and implements brought by the Europeans. They were successfully self-sustaining from small farmsteads to large plantations, with many acres under cultivation and large herds of horses and cattle. But they wished to maintain themselves as distinct Indian societies, while acknowledging allegiance to the United States.

Decisions sympathetic to this outlook were expressed by the Chief Justice of the Supreme Court, John Marshall, in 1831 (*The Cherokee Nation v. The State of Georgia*) and 1832 (*Samuel A. Worcester v. The State of Georgia*) but had little effect in protecting the Cherokee or any Indian tribes from private interests and states bent on their dispossession. Frontier statesmen, particularly during the administration of Andrew Jackson, could argue that Indians were different and therefore still clearly savage and a danger. Congress, as the body duly authorized to deal with Indian affairs, simply went around Marshall's decisions. It carried out the will of local states in regard to unwanted Indians, and provided for treaties and removals.

It must be noted that not all the proponents of the plan of Indian removal were motivated by selfish interests. There were missionaries and others who felt that removal of Indian tribes from the corrupting and demoralizing influences of frontier riff-raff would be in the Indians' best interest and allow them to establish a new and better life. However, even the kindest construction placed on this view must admit to its shortsightedness. Already

---

[5] The multitude of treaties in the United States and problems of boundaries are fully set forth in Charles J. Kappler, comp. and ed., *Indian Affairs, Laws and Treaties* (Washington, D.C., Vol. 2, *Treaties*, 1904); and Charles C. Royce and Cyrus Thomas, "Indian Land Cessions in the United States," *Annual Report* of the Bureau of American Ethnology, Smithsonian Institution, Vol. 18, Pt. 2 (Washington, D.C., 1896–97).

[6] *Cf.* William T. Hagan, *American Indians* (Chicago, 1961), for a discussion of Indian rights vs. national interest.

[7] Theodore Roosevelt, *The Winning of the West* (New York, 1889–1896), I, 90.

resident on the land in the west were tribes whose interests were not consulted before newcomers were moved among them. They were often considerably less than hospitable. Furthermore, it was becoming obvious that the Plains area would not remain forever the habitation of buffalo hunters. By the time pioneers were spreading out into the Plains, instead of bypassing them on the way to the gold fields or fertile valleys of the west coast, there was really no place left to move Indians. There was also the danger that the plan of one, and later two, large Indian Territories in the West would allow tribes to see the advantages of alliance and make common cause against the white man. Therefore, most of the native tribes west of the Mississippi were placed in reservations which are separated from one another yet in or near the original homelands. In contrast, large numbers of eastern Indians were clustered in Oklahoma.[8]

By 1849, when the Bureau of Indian Affairs was shifted from the Department of War to the newly created Department of the Interior, the eastern tribes had been "pacified," although troops were occasionally called in to round up returnees and get them back to their western reservations. The real problem, however, was the Plains Indians, who at this time were in the very midst of their great cultural florescence and were formidable and enthusiastic warriors. The efforts of Interior to get these tribes on reservations by negotiation, conciliation and persuasion were often confounded by the outlook of the War Department, which considered all Indians hostile, dangerous, and fair game. An unfortunate term, "ward," used by Marshall in his 1831 decision was revived. Marshall only intended a rough analogy in endeavoring to explain the responsibility of the federal government to protect Indian tribes against unauthorized usurpation of their lands: "Their relation to the United States resembles that of a ward to his guardian." Because the Bureau "sometimes

became the uneasy and unhappy buffer between Indians and the U.S. Army,"[9] it was decided in 1862 to designate the Indian tribes as "wards" of the Indian Bureau rather than let them be considered simply as "enemies" over whose fate the army would have jurisdiction to make decisions. Unfortunately, and without ever really having legal sanction, the term "ward" took on administrative connotations by which the Bureau exercised incredible control over the lives and property of individuals, much as a guardian would act for minor and even hopelessly retarded children.

THE END OF THE TREATY PERIOD

As noted, Canada took its Indian treaties more seriously from the start and has continued to respect them. In the United States, although important hostilities such as Little Big Horn and Wounded Knee were yet to come, it was apparent by 1871 that the process of "pacification" would continue at a rapid pace. The need to make treaties with so many different tribes and the embarrassment of making new treaties every time the demands of settlement required reduction of Indian acreage suggested to policy makers that Indian tribes were not really "nations" entitled to the respect and formality of treaties. Treaties required the unwieldy and expensive process of mutual agreement—albeit the United States held the greater power in dictating terms—and Senate ratification. Terms of existing treaties would be observed as long as the government found it practicable, but after 1871 no more treaties were made with Indian tribes. Instead, "agreements" were negotiated which were worded much like treaties and mistaken for treaties by many Indians, but which were administra-

---

[8] There are exceptions, however, as a few multi-tribe reservations were set up, particularly in the Northwest.

[9] *Answers to Questions About American Indians*, Bureau of Indian Affairs (pamphlet), Washington, D.C., 1965, 7. The concept of ward, an equivocal term at best, is often confused with "trusteeship" which has legal meaning and refers to land, not people, in regard to the protective role of the federal government in regard to Indian affairs.

tively more expedient and not as binding in legalistic and even moral terms as far as the government was concerned. Champions of Indians' rights long endeavored to pique the conscience of the nation by pointing to our bad faith in entering into solemn treaties, "the highest law of the land," which we did not intend to keep.

It was the period from the 1870's to the 1920's during which the worst abuses occurred in regard to administration of Indian affairs. Most Indian people were denied the vote, had to obtain passes to leave the reservation and were prohibited from practicing their own religions, sometimes by force. Leadership and management of community affairs smacking of traditional forms and functions were either discouraged or ignored as proper representations of community interest. Children were dragooned off to boarding schools where they were severely punished if they were caught speaking their own languages. While these things all happened, shortage and rapid turnover of Bureau personnel, administrative apathy and occasional enlightenment at the local administrative level meant that the regulations were not always rigorously enforced. And the Indian societies themselves took a hand in playing off administrators, missionaries and other whites against each other to keep them busy while Indian people held the line in their determination to remain Indian. The ubiquity of factionalism in Indian societies which is so regularly deplored by those people, Indian and white, who are sincerely interested in helping Indian people make a better life, may actually have acted as an important mechanism of social and cultural survival for Indian groups. No outsider could gain total dominance for his programs aimed in one way or another at reducing Indian distinctiveness. This suggestion, while admittedly speculative, seems worth bearing in mind when we turn to the contemporary scene where there seems to be a striving for common goals, in which factionalism for its own sake in avoiding undesirable goals may be giving way to what are really healthy differences of opinion based on habitual wariness in working toward positive objectives.

ATTEMPTS AT REFORM

Educated Indian people and their philanthropic white friends during the nineteenth century were generally as committed as the government to the view that the Indians' only hope was social and cultural assimilation into white society. The reservation system *per se* as well as the widespread peculation and dereliction in duty of reservation personnel were held responsible for impeding Indians in their course toward "civilization." This view tended to ignore the many non-reservation communities in the east which remained almost defiantly Indian, even where government experiments in granting stubborn "returnees" homesteads scattered among white neighbors did not automatically result in Indian assimilation or break-down of a sense of community. If their conservatism in language, religion and other aspects of culture was noted at all, it was viewed optimistically as inevitably temporary. Ironically, one of the major measures of reform promoted by humanitarians turned out to exacerbate rather than alleviate Indians' problems. This was the Indian Allotment Act of 1887. It was actually protested by some farseeing people who recognized the opportunities it afforded for a tremendous Indian landgrab, but these voices were drowned out by those who considered themselves the Indians' true friends, righteously supported by those who stood to gain from the Allotment Act as predicted by the pessimists.[10]

The idea of allotment was that Indians could be assimilated into the white rural population in the space of a generation by granting them private property. Each individual was to

---

[10] Before the general allotment act was passed in 1887, an earlier "pilot" allotment act was passed with specific reference to the Omaha Reservation in Nebraska in 1882. *Cf.* Lurie, "The Lady from Boston and the Omaha Indians," *The American West*, III, 4 (Fall, 1966), 31–33; 80–86.

receive his own acreage, usually coming to about 180 acres per family unit, and land left over after all allotments were made was to be thrown open to sale, the proceeds used to build houses and barns and to buy stock and equipment for the Indians to become farmers.

However, even by 1887, subsistence farming by individual families was giving way to large scale, single crop enterprises. Although allotments remained tax free for a period of twenty-five or thirty years, Indian people were not adequately informed nor technically prepared for managing farms. The result was that many of the allotments were lost through tax default or sold to pay debts which far-seeing whites had allowed Indians to run up against the day they would gain patents-in-fee to their land. Although the necessity for more protective provisions was soon recognized by the government, an unexpected complication rendered much of the land useless to its Indian owners. Some time between 1900 and 1910, a rapid decrease in Indian population leveled off and a steady rise set in. Original allotments were divided among increasing numbers of heirs. Given American laws of inheritance, there developed a common situation in which an individual might own forty or more acres, but as scattered fractions of land inherited from a number of ancestors who had received allotments. The easiest course was for the Indian Bureau simply to rent the land out in large parcels to white agriculturalists and stockmen and divide the proceeds among the many heirs. Some people could live on their rent money alone, often supporting less fortunate relatives as well. But, in most cases, rent money brought only a few dollars a year and a living was eked out by wage labor in planting and harvest seasons, forays to the cities to work in factories, and exploitation of the growing tourist industry in terms of sale of handcrafts and public dance performances.

As regulations on Indian movement off the reservations tended to relax, especially if people left to seek work, Indian people became increasingly better informed on the myriad opportunities to earn a living in industrial America besides the drudgery of farming.

However, Indian communities persisted even where the allotment process had drastically reduced the land base. Indian people seemed to join circuses and wild west shows, seek out areas where relatively high wages were paid for crop work, or find their way to industrial employment in the cities in a manner reminiscent of hunting, trading or war expeditions. They drifted back home periodically to seek help from relatives if they were broke or to share the spoils of the "hunt" with their kinsmen until it was necessary to forage again. They took to automobiles as enthusiastically as many had taken to ponies at an earlier time, becoming commuters to cities or other places where they could find work, returning daily or weekly or seasonally or by whatever schedule was practical. Some people spent most of their lifetimes in the city, but returned home to their tribesmen upon retirement. And these patterns persist today. Unlike the usual migrants, Indian people do not seem to perceive urban work as a break with the rural past, but merely as an extension of the peripheries of the territory which can be exploited economically. It is difficult to escape the conclusion that Indian people were "rurban" long before anyone coined the term or saw the industrial blending of city and country life as the direction in which the nation as a whole was to move.

Although Indian groups, with their characteristic close communal life, were persisting and increasing in size, the national outlook stressed rugged individualism and private enterprise. Both policy and administration of Indian affairs were oriented toward assimilating Indians as individuals into the general population. Tribal enterprises and industries were introduced only where the overwhelming argument of certain natural resources militated against allotment in severalty. Thus a few tribal forests and fishing grounds provided regular employment and income on the reservation, but even in these cases Indian people were given little voice or purposeful training in management of tribal businesses. Beyond that, a number of areas escaped allotment either because the terrain made it impractical for subsistence farming or the problems created by allotment elsewhere had become apparent and the plan was simply shelved before more remote areas were included under it.

Other efforts to reform Indian administration gradually got around to matters of practical welfare. The Indian Bureau had always been a political pork barrel, appointments to various posts being handed out to party stalwarts. The pay was poor, but there were opportunities to shave budgets for personal gain. Allotment opened more opportunities to bribe officials to declare Indians "competent" to sell their land. The scandals of peculation, the complaints of sincere employees that the uncertainty of their jobs made it impossible to carry out decent programs, and the clear evidence of honest but unqualified and emotionally callous personnel all led to demands for improvement. Doctors and teaching staffs were put on civil service in 1892, and by 1902 all Bureau employees were on civil service except the Commissioner and Assistant Commissioner.

At the time of the First World War most of the Indian population was still without the vote and also not subject to conscription, but a surprising number of young men volunteered for the armed services and were recognized for remarkable heroism. This stirred the nation from complacency about Indian problems and in 1924 the franchise was extended to all Indians. Significantly, one Indian view, which found expression among tribes all over the country, considered the right to vote a pretty shabby reward and no more than further evidence of national disregard for Indian rights as established by treaties. The implication was that Indians volunteered in America's defense as loyal allies as pledged in treaties rather than as patriotic citizens.[11]

However, few white Americans were aware of this reaction to their magnanimous gesture, and concerned people continued efforts to understand why Indians had not yet been granted their proper place as assimilated Americans and to search for better means of accomplishing this end. The results of extensive investigation of Indian affairs by the Brookings Institution were published in 1928,[12] setting forth in concise and depressing detail just how bad things really were among Indian people under the federal jurisdiction, and suggesting means of improving the situation.

Although committed to the entrenched view that assimilation of Indians was both desirable and inevitable, the Brookings Report noted that this would take time and the settling of many just grievances harbored by the tribes before trust and cooperation could be expected of them. Throughout the Report we begin to see indications of a changing perspective on Indians' problems in the recommendations reached by objective investigators. For example, in speaking of administration as "leadership," the Report says,

This phrase "rights of the Indian" is often used solely to apply to his property rights. Here it is used in a much broader sense to cover his rights as a human being living in a free country. . . . The effort to substitute educational leadership for the more dictatorial methods now used in some places will necessitate more understanding of and sympathy for the Indian point of view. Leadership will recognize the good in the economic and social life of the Indians in their religion and ethics, and will seek to develop it and build on it rather than to crush out all that is Indian. The Indians have much to contribute to the dominant civilization, and the effort should be made to secure this contribution, in part because of the good it will do the Indians in stimulating a proper race pride and self respect.[13]

Serious efforts to implement the Brookings recommendations were delayed as the nation entered the depression of the 1930's. With the election of Franklin D. Roosevelt and appointment of John Collier, Sr. as Indian

[11] This view of the vote is still found among some Indian people.

[12] Lewis C. Merriam and associates, *The Problem of Indian Administration: report on a survey made at the request of the Honorable Hubert Work, Secretary of the Interior*, The Brookings Institution (Baltimore, 1928).

[13] *Ibid.*

Commissioner, a "New Deal" was also in store for Indian people. Collier's thinking went beyond the Brookings recommendations both in revising administrative procedures and in philosophy. He endeavored to set up mechanisms for self government which would allow Indian communities to bargain as communities with the government and the larger society. He sought to teach them about a host of opportunities for community improvement and let them choose accordingly—revolving loan funds, tribal enterprises, resource development, land acquisition, tribal courts, educational programs. In many ways Collier's plan was inappropriate: too "Indian" for some tribes, not "Indian" enough for others, and characterized by unwarranted urgency and hard sell in some instances. For all that, Indian people recognized in large measure that Collier really understood what their grievances were about even if his methods were sometimes less than satisfactory or if Bureau personnel on the local level were often incapable of throwing off old habits of mind and behavior in carrying out the intent of the new administration. Where Collier and Indian people were in agreement was in the objective of restoring not the Indian culture of any past period but the kind of conditions and relationships which existed prior to the "ward" philosophy of Indian administration, a period when Indian people could still select and adapt innovations to find satisfactory patterns of their own for community life. Above all, Collier understood the need to secure an adequate land base for meaningful social experimentation and development.

Collier's administration and philosophy . . . were short-lived as views Congress would be willing to support. They were in effective operation for seven years at most. The Indian Reorganization Act was passed in 1934, time was required to inform Indian people and allow them to make decisions in regard to it, and by 1941 the nation was at war. Domestic programs, including those of the Indian Bureau, were naturally made secondary to the war effort. Wartime prosperity brought temporary alleviation of economic problems for many Indian communities. Collier remained in office until 1946, but it was becoming increasingly apparent that his administrative ideas were losing popularity with Congress.[14] After the war, when servicemen and factory workers returned home, Indian population, like that of the rest of the nation, had increased. Programs just started before the war had not been able to keep pace with the added pressures on the still limited sources of income of the reservations. Since the "Indian problem" suddenly loomed larger than ever, the easy explanation was Collier's revolutionary departure from the time-honored Indian policy of assimilation.

Because Indian people showed a marked aptitude for industrial work during the war, and it was obvious they would not succeed as farmers, the solution was simple. Relocate them in urban centers, preferably in each case as far from the home reservation as possible, and legislate the reservations out of existence so that Indian people could not run home when things got tough or share their good fortune periodically with kinsmen who lacked the gumption to get out on their own.

Like the grand scheme of 1887 to solve the Indians' problems by the simple expedient of allotment in severalty, the relocation-reservation termination plan of the 1950's was out of date for its time in terms of national social and economic trends. If the ideal of the Allotment Act was to ensconce Indian people in a kind of average, small farm middle-class, which was actually disappearing, the ideal of

---

[14] It is an open question whether the Indian Claims Commission Act, passed in 1946, represented the last of the Collier era or the beginning of the termination era. The objective of the act is to provide restitution for Indian grievance, particularly in regard to non-payment or unconscionable consideration for land. However, as sentiment grew in favor of relocation and termination, one argument was that Indian communities would disperse once grievances were settled and only the hope of payment on old debts perpetuated Indian identity. Ideally, claims payments would give Indian people the necessary stake to begin a new life as ordinary citizens far from the reservations. In actual fact, the amounts paid were relatively small on a per capita basis, and Indian communities persisted. Many tribes are still waiting for their claims to be settled.

the policy of the 1950's was primarily to get the government out of the Indian business and scant attention was paid to where Indian people might be able to fit in American life. Indian people opposed the policy of the 1950's, arguing for the alternative of community development through local industries and beefing up the long neglected educational programs. This, Indian people argued, would enable them to plan and manage intelligently in their own behalf community development and tribal enterprises. It would also make it possible for those individuals who wished to assimilate to enter the larger society at a decent economic and occupational level.

At the very time that suburbs were burgeoning, commuting was a way of life for much of the nation, and far sighted people were anticipating greater segmentation of industrial operations and dispersing them to where the people live, Indian policy was based on models of concentrating population in large urban centers. Like the rural myth of the nineteenth century, mid-twentieth century policy promoted the myth of the "melting pot," whereby the ambitious immigrant worked his way out of the poor, ethnic neighborhood by frugality and hard work. Such thinking ignored a number of facts: (1) The agonies which such groups suffered during the period when they were exploited minorities living in urban slums. (2) The loss of a sense of community which such people suffered when, sometimes after repeated moves as a group to different urban neighborhoods, they finally "spun off" into the larger society. (3) The special reliance of Indian people on group identity, group membership and group decisions, which goes beyond anything comparable which the immigrant communities were able to establish. Immigrant communities usually were not communities when they came; their ethnic identities were, to a surprising extent, constructed in America. (4) The increasing difficulty of "making it" economically and socially in an economy which has much less use today for unskilled labor, and a society which sees color so strongly that many of its members still doubt that non-caucasians are really capable of achieving middle-class standards.

The trends of social reform and legislation had taken increasing cognizance of the fact that the individual could no longer hope to go it alone, saving for the rainy days and providing for his old age. Studies of crime and mental health had begun to raise serious questions about the nature of modern, industrialized society in depriving the individual of a sense of community and meaningful engagement in life. But in the 1950's, and to a great extent in the 1960's, it is considered unrealistic, impractical and perhaps even a little silly to suggest, as the Brookings Report did in 1928, that "The Indians have much to contribute to the dominant civilization, and the effort should be made to secure this contribution."[15]

Whether or not Indian people are potential models for satisfactory community life for the nation at large, one thing became clear during the 1950's. They were not happy with the solution to their problems of poverty offered by the government. Furthermore, it was soon obvious that the policy of the 1950's, like allotment in the 1880's, tended to create more new problems rather than solve old ones. By 1960, the presidential candidates of both parties recognized the need to reassess Indian affairs and find new directions for policy. At the same time, Indian people appeared to be more vocal and concerned with exercising a positive influence in regard to legislation affecting them. . . .

[15] Merriam, *The Problem*, 22–23.

13

The American Slave Plantation and Our Heritage of Communal Deprivation

Roy Simón Bryce-Laporte

It is our principal thesis that a continuous and predominant feature of the heritage of black Americans in the continental United States, whether as individuals or as a people, has been the deprivation of their opportunity to engage fully and share equally in the determination, development, and direction of "their" community. While the history of the United States includes the emergence of experimentations with so-called free villages of black people, some of which still exist in the South, in large measure black people have been grossly underrepresented among the leadership even in communities where they constitute the majority. Moreover, as a people, they have had virtually no history of having decided for themselves *if,* *where,* and *how* they wanted to settle and what would be the prevailing *patterns* and *policies* of the larger locale in which

Roy Simón Bryce-Laporte is Director of the Research Institute on Immigration and Ethnic Studies at the Smithsonian Institution.

"The American Slave Plantation and Our Heritage of Communal Deprivation" by Roy Simón Bryce-Laporte is reprinted from *American Scientist* Vol. 12, No. 4 (March–April, 1969), pp. 2–8, by permission of the Publisher, Sage Publications, Inc.

Author's note: This is a shorter version of a paper presented at a seminar series on "The Indian and African in the Western Hemisphere" sponsored by the Council on Latin American Studies of Yale University, on October 23, 1968.

they settled. They have had few experiences in operating freely and fully in a localized societal system of common will.

THE SLAVE PLANTATION AS CONTEXTUAL BASELINE OF BLACK AMERICAN EXPERIENCE

The definite date of the first appearance of black people in the New World is really a matter of speculation and historiography. There are those who entertain the possibility that black men were settled in America before the large-scale European presence. As evidence they usually draw on the chronicles of Bishop de las Cusas. The Bishop relates the violent encounters of Vasco Nunez de Balboa with "Ethiopian tribes" as the *adelantado* crossed the Isthmus of Panama en route to the discovery of the Pacific Ocean in 1513. Notwithstanding the speculative nature of this evidence, it is known that black people were in fact among the first non-Amerindians to explore and inhabit the New World. They came as slaves and as freemen, members of the expeditions and settlements of the Spanish conquistadores. They even came to what is now known as the continental United States before the mainstream of English colonists. An unsuccessful attempt was made by one Vásquez de Allyón to establish a Spanish colony in what is today Jamestown, before the English landed there. His scheme was aborted as his African slaves revolted, assassinated him, and sailed back to Haiti. St. Augustine, Florida, the first successful European settlement in the United States, had black people among its population. Moreover, the first contingent of black people to enter the English-dominated territories of North America landed in the port of Jamestown in 1619, one year before the Pilgrim Fathers.

The actual or official beginning of slavery in the English North American colonies is also a matter of speculation and historiography. Conservative estimations put it somewhere between the 1650s and 1660s and generally agree that legal slavery was restricted to black men, even though there were white people in indentured servitude. From the time of the landing of 20 Africans in Jamestown in 1619 until the legal recognition of slavery, black men were generally considered to be indentured servants too, even though they suffered some degree of discrimination relative to their white counterparts. However, as white servitude decreased, black slavery increased until it became the predominant form of labor experience for most blacks in the colonies.

Surely, there were fluctuations in the use and spread of slave labor in American history. It is also true that all slaves did not undergo the large plantation experience. Many of them lived in cities and small towns of the North and South. And, as historians point out, most of the rural slave holders were farmers with small lots, or planters of small-scale estates with holdings of under ten slaves. However, more than half of the slaves lived on large-scale plantations, ranging from 20 to about 1,000 slaves (see Gray, 1933:529–539 and Stampp, 1957:33–38). Thus, even if the large plantation was not the statistical norm of planters and plantations, it certainly was the statistical norm for slaves. Furthermore, even if its statistical distribution is challengeable, its social normativeness is not. The influence, prestige, and power of the large plantations and the great planters in ante bellum society are indisputable. Gaines (1925:143–146), after an exhaustive study of the real versus the apparent features of the plantation, stated: "To be a great planter was the ambition of many. . . . The large plantation was *ne plus ultra* of society . . . the ideal community of the South, its laws and usages were as dominant socially as its economic influence was dominant politically."

THE SLAVE PLANTATION AS A TOPIC OF HISTORICAL-SOCIOLOGICAL STUDY

American slavery—the enslavement of black men by white men in the continental United States—has been a topic of study for Anglo-Saxons even before the final discontinuance of the system. In fact, it has been more a pastime of historians than sociologists. As historians have sought to challenge, rectify, and exonerate the celebrated treatises in defense of slavery done by many of their outstanding figures,[1] sociologists have sought to dissociate themselves from and forget the shameful fact that one of the first books in this country to use the word sociology in its title took the form of a blatant advocation of slavery (Fitzhugh, 1854). This may well be a reflection of the humanistic, value-oriented posture of historians as contrasted with the scientific, value-free position expounded by sociologists.

Historians have tended to study slavery rather than the slave plantation, and whether they studied one or the other they have tended to treat it as a *peculiar institution*. Why it is peculiar they have not fully told us, but in terms of the way they have studied it they seem to be suggesting that it was *peculiar unto itself*. This may well be a reflection of the ideographic assumptions or biases that most historians make about human events, even social phenomena. In more recent times the study of slavery by some historians has come to embrace a comparative perspective. Tannenbaum, his students, and some of his critics have attempted to compare the American slave system to Latin American and Caribbean slave systems (see Harris, 1964; Hoetink, 1967; Klein, 1967; Tannenbaum, 1963; Williams, 1960). While this latter course does not negate the claim of peculiarity of slavery per se, it at least acknowledges that the peculiarity is not limited to the American version of slavery. An even more recent trend has been initiated among historians by Elkins (1963), who attempted an analogy between the American slave plantation and the Nazi concentration camp. This last trend, in particular, not only signals a departure from the claim of the peculiarity of slavery *as a system* but throws the study of slavery on the doorsteps of sociology, inasmuch as it deals with *the slave plantation as a social institution* which is therefore

[1] For example, the various volumes which represent responses to U. B. Phillips and other advocates or apologists of slavery.

comparable to other such sociological entities. If Elkins throws the study of the American slave plantation on the doorsteps of sociologists, he sneaks it onto the working table of black sociologists. He has left us, as we shall indicate later, homework to do.

Inasmuch as the predominant methodological concerns of American sociologists, black and white, have tended to be ahistorical and synchronic in nature, the slave plantation as an historic institution—an event of the past—has drawn very little attention from them. Instead, many American sociologists and other social scientists proceed to make of contemporary conditions, problems, and behavior of black people one of their more lucrative areas of concern. They study black problems as they would study most contemporary social problems (i.e., delinquency, urbanization, mass society, etc.). They study black problems as if they were without a backlog of unique historicity, a quality which in fact complicates such problems to a point where they cannot be fully understood, much less resolved, in comparison to truly contemporary problems. When a black boy answers the question, "Why are you rioting?" with a statement, "To get Mr. Charlie off my back" or "Because you made us slaves four hundred years ago," he is not emphasizing the contemporality of his problems by any means. The problems of black people in white America are historical and so too are the problems black people have posed for white America.

The slave plantation may be a past event but, as we have argued, it is also the contextual baseline of black experience in this country. A classical, sociological concern is the relationship between the social behavior of human beings and the conditions under which they live. Black slaves, although black and slaves, were indeed human beings with patterns of social behavior. To understand them sociologically, requires an understanding of the conditions in which they lived and the relationship of such conditions to their behavioral patterns. To understand the slave plantation and the slaves sociologically is to begin to appreciate the historicity of the problems met and caused by black people in America and the value of that historicity in coping with the contemporary expressions of such problems. Our thesis is an historical claim inasmuch as it refers to experiences starting hundreds of years ago with the coming of the first blacks to what is now the continental United States. It is a sociological chore inasmuch as it seeks to relate those historical experiences to contemporary social conditions and behavior of black people. In this paper we take the position that ante bellum race relations still constitute the basis of black behavior and black-white relations in the United States today.

The sociological study of the American slave plantation—the original context in which black people were settled, socialized, and stigmatized in America—may not be a lucrative challenge but it is a necessary chore. As of now we can point to too few efforts by black or white sociologists to carry out that chore. But even if white ones do not, black ones must, and even if white ones do black ones must still do, and do more. This is the challenge which Ralph Ellison (1967), a black American writer who even though not noted as a black nationalist, presents to young black writers, especially social scientists:

> What is missing today is a corps of artists and intellectuals who should evaluate Negro American experience from inside and out of a broad knowledge of how people of other cultures live, deal with experience, and give significance to their experience. We do too little of this, rather we depend on outsiders—mainly sociologists—to interpret our lives for us.

We do not take it upon ourselves to use this article to exonerate the sociologists. For while as a professional group some sociologists have done profound work on race relations, most works of sociologists on the subject have been too limited and less effective than would be desired. Yet, some sociologists, black and white, have tried rather earnestly to express and represent the insiders. Some of us black ones will do no less, regardless of our ineffectiveness, because we are proud to be insiders. However, in reference to black slavery as a topic, there is more to compensate for than to exonerate, for while historians have committed themselves, sociologists have avoided the issue.

Like the study of slavery, the study of the plantation is not a usual area of study of sociologists. The latter has been more a concern of geographers, anthropologists, and *rural* sociologists. Of the outstanding American sociologists who have given considerable attention to the American slave plantation there is at least one point held in common. They tend to view and treat the slave plantation *as an institution.* The late E. Franklin Frazier (1949:44), a black sociologist, spoke in particular of the large slave plantations as a social institution, "a settled way of life with its peculiar traditions and culture." Edgar Thompson Jr. (1960), a senior sociologist, includes it in the same category as farms, ranches and manors, which he calls *settlement institutions.* Such institutions accommodate and settle people of diverse backgrounds on the land, pattern their relationship to the land, and largely determine how they shall live on the land and with one another.

The stress on the institutional feature of the plantation is of course a reflection of the nomothetic tendencies among sociologists, as compared to historians. Moreover, this stress calls for a recognition of the structural comparability of the slave plantation to other entities also considered institutions, which is exactly what Elkins sought to do. The common distinctions of institutions such as plantations, Frazier and Thompson suggest, are its settlement characteristic and its territorial land or property. As a consequence, it is able to develop a style of accommodation, social relations and culture *peculiar to such types of institutions.* Irving Goffman (1961) and Amitai Etzioni (1961), of a younger generation of sociologists, have expanded this category to include other than economic-agricultural institutions. Goffman uses the terms *total institution* or *establishments,* while Etzioni employs the term *broad organizations* to refer to formal-instrumental organizations which are so broad in *scope* that they embrace and control the crucial life activities of their members or inmates—i.e., prisons, asylums, convents, circuses, boarding schools, military camps, etc. It is significant in light of our charge of ahistoricism among American sociologists that Goffman, Etzioni, and other latter-day sociologists have not included the slave plantation in their repertoire of referents. We, however, shall attempt to discuss the slave plantation, the original context of black experience in white America, as a *total institution,* which according to Goffman (1961:xiii) is ". . . a place of residence and work where a large number of like situated individuals, cut off from the wider society for an appreciable period of time, together lead an enclosed, formally administered round of life."[2]

THE SLAVE PLANTATION AS A TOTAL INSTITUTION AND AN ANTICOMMUNITY

In their effort to compare, categorize, and generate "laws" sociologists have often tended to suppress crucial differences among similar forms of human organizations. This tendency is much less likely to be shared by traditional historians with their emphasis on ideographic details and narrative; although it is true that all forms of conceptualizing, especially operational conceptualizations, are arbitrary in what is included or excluded in the constructed categories. The important preoccupation in operational conceptualizing is to reach a happy medium between the degree of distortion and the degree of successful sharpening of the aspects of the phenomena being studied.

The term community is known to have been defined in innumerably different ways in the social sciences. Consequently, it may be assumed that it is conceptually problematic and that a similar degree of problems makes difficult any effort to decide what may be categorized under or equated to communities in any technical sense. It is not uncommon among sociologists to treat prisons, convents,

[2] For a more elaborate discussion see Bryce-Laporte (1968).

mining towns, etc. as communities. While we are willing to concede that members of such organizations often speak of themselves as communities, such usage is usually based not on a technical sociological understanding but rather on habit, custom, tradition, ideology, or vernacular. Technically, as we will argue, such aggregations may have some resemblances or similarities with communities, but in fact are departures from or in some cases antitheses of community.

Whereas Goffman (1961:12) finds total institutions interesting because they are *part* organization and *part* community, Hillery (1963), another contemporary sociologist, finds them interesting because they are *distinctive* from communities in terms of how and why they are organized the way they are. In contradistinction to communities, total institutions are rigidly stratified structures which are characterized by polar inequality as demonstrated in the differentiation of rights, obligations and statuses of *inmates versus staff*. Every inmate is technically subordinate to every staff member. Every inmate, but not every staff member, is totally dependent on the total institution. Every inmate but not every staff member is forcibly confined to the territorial space and property of the total institution. Every inmate must engage in some form of forced labor or exercise which usually brings him few of the normal rewards; at the same time, it is the establishment which dictates to the inmate how these rewards may be used. It further deprives him of normal responsibility (and therefore his authority and esteem) to himself and his dependents by providing for him all crucial services without concern for his desires as an individual. All inmates are treated alike; their activities are regimented and routinized; and individual and status differences among them are reduced to the barest minimum. In contradistinction to communities, total institutions are organized around very specific and specialized goals. They create their own *institutions of maintenance* (i.e., recruitment, socialization, etc.) rather than utilize established *primary groups* (i.e., families, etc.) to satisfy their goals.

Communities often rely upon permanent primary group relations for their survival and therefore tend to accommodate them or compensate for their absences. Total institutions find such primary groups threatening and discourage or replace them. Total institutions and primary groups are potential rivals for, rather than common beneficiaries of, the loyalties of their members. Total institutions are totalitarian structures which suppress rivalry and as such are *anticommunities* which deprive members of the opportunity to *share in the shaping of their own destinies*.

In the case of the American slave plantations the anticommunal assaults on the slaves or black population took place on various levels. The African recruitment process in itself involved destruction of African families and depletion of the population of many West African communities. The sale and deployment processes, by the practice of purposefully dispersing slaves with real or apparent common ties, negated whatever primary relations may have been retained from Africa or developed on the long trek from capture to sale. Then by the various structural impositions, mortification processes, and internal control systems the slave plantation had an inhibiting impact and inescapable saliency on the behavior of the slaves. The plantation staff strove to prohibit among the slaves the emergence of strong personalities, roles of true leadership and organizations which were purchase-, property-, protest-, or power-oriented. To have permitted this would have been an irrational and direct contradiction of all the purposes or ends of the slave plantation and its ideology and psychology of human nature. This would have threatened its entire structure as a total institution. Ownership of physical property among plantation slaves was almost non-existent and limited to a few household supplies, extra clothing, and the crops or stocks that they raised on land *assigned* to them. They were neither free to purchase nor work toward purchase of durable, basic property, such as land, home, etc. They were most often not able to purchase their own freedom. They could not own other persons as property or slave and whatever claims they had over their spouses, children, and parents were offset, inasmuch as in legal terms they were all mere properties of the master. The pretense of ownership, freedom, and power also reached overdetermined dimensions with some slaves (i.e., Uncle Toms and Aunt Thomasinas), who at one and the same time acted as property and as part owner of plantation and planter (in much the way as children "own" their homes and parents). In fact, white society *alone*, at least the planter class, enjoyed the privilege of decision-making and determining *if, how,* and *where,* they (and their slaves) would settle. The slaves could merely settle. They had no choice. Their presence was decided by others and their patterns of living were in large part passive reactions to the policies of the planters and their surrogates.

The conditions of control, totalness, and remoteness which characterized the slave plantation of the United States made open, sustained, collective resistance among the slaves virtually impossible. Most successful resistance was individual, isolated, and rapid. Collective resistance was generally sporadic if open, and necessarily subtle if sustained. In other words, the very conditions which made open, sustained, collective resistance unfeasible made more subtle, covert, elusive forms of group action sustainable and prevalent. The overt aspects of culture among the slaves were subservient, submissive, and largely *primary adjustment* in response to the closed, routinized, regimented, coercive, and total nature of the slave plantation. The *underlife* of the slaves, however, consisted largely of *secondary adjustments* and these adjustments were in fact subtle, elusive roles and sociocultural relations which were prevalent and sustained among them. The underlife of the slaves included prayer meetings, spirituals, prayers, folk tales, an invisible church, and an underground escape organization, among other forms. Passing as white or as free; feigning as sick and stupid; slipping away from plantations through slave country and free society; and the protecting of slaves engaged in these maneuvers represented the most daring forms

of successful resistance that American slaves were able to sustain. Limited and ambivalent as such behavior may have been they need not mean that the prevalent personality pattern among slaves was Sambo, Tom, or Thomasina. To believe that, is to equivocate the *stereotype* with *reality* and *acting* with *being*. It is this fallacy that Elkins and many other liberally persuaded scholars, are inclined to commit when they accept and thus perpetuate the negative stereotype of the self, institutions, community, and culture of the black American in their effort to explain and criticize the society. It is the task of black sociologists to expose such fallacies, challenge or counter such claims, destroy the stereotypes and stigmas associated with black people, and thus deny the system its basis of persistence.

Perpetual, psychological, and physical *flight* (rather than *direct fighting*) became the modus operandi of American slave resistance. And, a people in flight are in less of a position to set up community or assert cultural distinctiveness than a people in fight, especially if they are visible and must avoid any permanent, conspicuous concentration. Aside from its horrors, war has been one of the major occasions for tight control, communication, collective mobilization, community development, and ethnocentric assertion (Nisbet, 1962: 38–44). Flight or escape requires a different organization and role repertoire than open, sustained collective defiance. It demands more invisible and covert bonds, calls for cunningness and elusive skills, relies upon daring individuals or small groups of loosely organized individuals; rather than settlement concentration, open confrontation, and power. Thus elusive practices were not able to mobilize and organize large numbers of slaves, any more than expressive practices were able to accommodate large numbers of them into *active* slave communities. By active we mean communities *organized and controlled by the slaves for themselves and against the rest of the plantation regime.*

The internal control of the slave plantation was broad in scope and took the form of cruel sanctions as well as crucial services. The external control of the slave plantation, however, must not be overlooked if the anticommunal effects on black people are to be fully understood. The slave plantation, much as other total institutions, permeated and pervaded the outer society. In fact, as Thompson (1959) and Genovese (1966) suggested, it grew from a dependent institution to a dominant institution with other institutions supporting it as the central entity of a culture, a society, a social system. The slave plantation stigmatized the slave in order to justify his custody, and exploitation deprived him from rehabilitation and thus supported his stigma. The slave plantation dictated the laws, treatment, and status that freed blacks should enjoy. The closer the "free" black population to the plantation or sphere of influence of the planter, the less likelihood that they could live in comfort and enjoy community and security. In fact, the genesis of community, which Frazier (1949) attributes to free blacks, was mostly developed in urban cities of the South and North, not rural hinterlands of the plantation. The same patterns emerged in the rural South only after the Emancipation Proclamation.

We would dare argue even more that the pervasiveness and permeability of the slave plantation have outlived its power and presence. As the ante-bellum America became less rural and more urban, as cities appeared, plantations disappeared but Jim Crow laws and Negro quarters came to replace them. Thus, the emergent ante-bellum cities were but symbolic survivals or departures of slave plantations (see Litwack, 1961; McNamus, 1966; Wade, 1964; Snydor, 1966). And today black men in America are still suffering the stigma of their slave status much as would ex-inmates of most total institutions. In fact, in large measure they are still treated as inmates and constitute more than their proportion of most low-status and negatively labelled inmate populations of this country (i.e., prisons, asylums, hospitals, military camps, etc.). Moreover, their present conditions of life in tenant plantations, migrant camps, and urban ghettos continue to represent imposed and closed totalitarian settlements which are structured to deprive them of control and active participation in their communities. The earlier integrationist attempts by black people can be interpreted in the terms of Goffman and Tannenbaum as futile efforts of *ex-slaves, still stigmatized ex-inmates,* to enter into the larger community of Americans as *free, equal participant-citizens.* Their efforts were repelled by the overwhelming power and retarded by the disarming paternalism of white America. The frustration they suffered in that effort has resulted in a more aggressive, nationalistic mood among black Americans. A main thrust of this new mood is *an aggressive quest for black community, here or abroad, and by any means necessary.* It signals a new and more desperate phase in black America's determined effort to reconstruct its culture, revitalize its heritage, reorganize and control its communities, redefine its image, and thus remove the last vestiges of so permeable and pervasive a total institution as was the slave plantation.

REFERENCES

Bryce-Laporte, R. S. (1968) *The Conceptualization of the American Slave Plantation as a Total Institution.* Unpub. Ph.D. dissertation, Univ. of California, Los Angeles (unpub.).

Elkins, S. (1963) *Slavery: A Problem in American Institutional and Intellectual Life.* New York: Grossett & Dunlap.

Ellison, R. (1967) "A very stern discipline." Harper's 234 (March).

Etzioni, A. (1961) *A Comparative Analysis of Complex Organizations.* New York: Free Press.

Fitzhugh, G. (1854) *Sociology of the South.* Richmond, Va.: A. Morris.

Frazier, E. F. (1949) *The Negro in the United States.* New York: Macmillan.

Gaines, F. (1925) *The Southern Plantation.* New York: Columbia Univ. Press.

Genovese, E. D. (1966) *The Political Economy of Slavery.* New York: Random House.

Goffman, I. (1961) *Asylums.* Garden City, N.Y.: Doubleday.

Gray, L. (1933) *History of Agriculture in Southern United States to 1860.* Washington, D.C.: Carnegie Institute.

Harris, M. (1964) *Patterns of Race in the Americas.* New York: Walker.

Hillery, G., Jr. (1963) "Villages, cities, and total institutions." *Amer. Soc. R.* 28 (October): 779–790.

Hoetink, H. (1967) *Two Variants of Race Relations in the Caribbean.* London: Oxford Press.

Klein, H. S. (1967) *Slavery in the Americas—A Comparative Study of Cuba and Virginia.* Chicago: Univ. of Chicago Press.

Litwack, L. (1961) *North of Slavery.* Chicago: Univ. of Chicago Press.

McNamus, E. (1966) *A History of Negro Slavery in New York.* Syracuse: Syracuse Univ. Press.

Nisbet, R. A. (1962) *Community and Power.* New York: Oxford Univ. Press.

Snydor, C. (1966) *Slavery in Mississippi.* Baton Rouge: Louisiana State Univ. Press.

Stampp, K. (1957) *The Peculiar Institution.* New York: Random House.

Tannenbaum, F. (1963) *From Slave to Citizen.* New York: Random House.

Thompson, E., Jr. (1960) "The plantation cycle and problems of typology." In V. Rubin (ed.) *Caribbean Studies—A Symposium.* Seattle: Univ. of Washington Press.

——— (1959) "The plantation as a social system." In *Plantation Systems of the New World.* Washington, D.C.: Pan American Union.

Wade, R. (1964) *Slavery in the Cities: The South, 1820–1860.* London: Oxford Univ. Press.

Williams, E. (1960) "Race relations in Caribbean society." In V. Rubin (ed.) *Caribbean Studies—A Symposium.* Seattle: Univ. of Washington Press.

14

The Psycho-Historical and Socioeconomic Development of the Chicano Community in the United States

RODOLFO ALVAREZ

The closest approximation to objective knowledge can be gained from the confrontation of honestly different perspectives that subsume the same or related sets of facts. What is presented in this paper is a marshalling of historical fact from a perspective not traditionally taken into account in scholarly discourse on Mexican Americans. The objective is to confront the reality of Mexican American society as we have experienced it and from that basis to generate hypotheses for future multidisciplinary research in this area. For this purpose we identify four historical periods and describe the climate of opinion within the generation of Mexican Americans that numerically dominates the period. What I mean by a "generation" is that a critical number of persons, in a broad but delimited age group, had more or less the same socialization experiences because they lived at a particular time under more or less the same constraints imposed by a dominant United States society. Each generation reflects a different state of collective consciousness concerning its rela-

Rodolfo Alvarez is Director of the Chicano Studies Center at the University of California, Los Angeles.

Reprinted from *Social Science Quarterly* 53 (March, 1973):920–942 by permission of the publisher and the author.

tionship to the larger society; psycho-historical differences related to, if not induced by, the economic system.

We begin our analysis with the assertion that, *as a people*, Mexican Americans are a creation of the imperial conquest of one nation by another through military force. Our people were thrown into a new set of circumstances, and began to evolve new modes of thought and action in order to survive, making Mexican American culture different from the culture of Mexicans in Mexico. Because we live in different circumstances we have evolved different cultural modes; just as we are neither identical to "Anglos" in the United States nor to Mexicans in Mexico, we, nevertheless, incorporate into our own ethos much from both societies. This is because we respond to problems of existence that confront us in unique ways, distinct from the way in which Anglos and Mexicans experience them.

How, then, did we pass from being a sovereign people into a state of being compatriots with the newly arrived Anglo settlers, coming mostly from the southern United States, and, finally, into the condition of becoming a conquered people—a charter minority on our own land?

The coming of the Spaniards to Mexico began the development of a mestizo people which has come to be the largest category of Mexican society. The mestizo is the embodiment of biological, cultural and social heterogeneity. This sector of Mexican society was already numerically ascendant by the time Mexico gained its independence from Spain. Sovereign Mexico continued more or less the identical colonization patterns that had been developed by Spain by sending a cadre of soldiers, missionaries, and settlers to establish a mission and presidio where Indians were brought in and "Christianized." Once the Indians were socialized to the peculiar mixture of Indian and Hispanic-Western cultural patterns which constituted the mestizo adaptation to the locale, they were granted tracts of land, which they cultivated to support themselves in trade with the central settlement, and through that, with the larger society with its center in

Mexico City. As the settlement grew and prospered, new outposts were developed further and further out into the provinces. Thus, Mexican society, like the Spanish society before it, was after *land* and *souls* in its development of the territories over which it held sovereignty. The Indian quickly was subjugated into the lowest stratum of society to do the heaviest and most undesirable work at the least cost possible—although biologically "pure," but fully acculturated Indians frequently entered the dominant mestizo society. They also tended to marry settlers coming north from central Mexico to seek their fortunes. Light and dark skinned alike were "Mexican."

What is of historic significance here is that in the early 1800's, particularly on the land now called Texas, this imperialistic system came into direct conflict with another; that sponsored by England which resulted in the creation of the United States of America. Both systems set out aggressively to induce the economic development of the area. However, while the Hispanic system sought economic development through the acquisition of *land* and *souls*, the Anglo system that had been established on the northern Atlantic seaboard was one of acquiring *land, but not souls.* An Indian could not have been elected president of the United States as Don Benito Juarez was in Mexico. Rather, the Indian was "pushed back" as the European settlement progressed. He had to be either manifestly cooperative in getting out of the way (and later into reservations), or be exterminated. The new society in the United States was, therefore, a great deal more homogeneous than in Mexico since it was fundamentally a European adaptation to the new land and not in any way a mixture of Indian and European elements.

It should be said here, without wanting to overemphasize, that there is some evidence from correspondence between Thomas Jefferson and James Monroe that these and other key figures in the United States had intended to take the Southwest long before U.S. settlers started moving into Texas. Insofar as the stage was not yet set for this final move, the coming of United States citizens into Texas was a case study in peaceful cooperation between peoples with fundamentally different ideological perspectives. The Anglo settlers initially and publicly made the minimal necessary assertions of loyalty to Mexico—despite the fact that they did not live up to the letter of the settlement contracts which called for them to become Mexican citizens and Roman Catholic.

This cooperative experience lasted until approximately 1830–35. During this time Texas was being rapidly settled by Mexicans moving north ("rapidly," considering their form of colonization). Also, some Europeans, a few of them Roman Catholic, arrived in Galveston and settled throughout the territory. Others, in a stream that was ultimately to become the majority, came from the southern region of the United States. I call this the cooperative experience because there is historical evidence that all of these people, regardless of their point of origin, cooperated relatively well with each other. . . . Some Anglo filibustering (insurrectionist activity in a foreign country) did take place. However, there is evidence that other Anglo groups were instrumental in helping to put these activities down. The *general* tone of the times was that of inter-cultural cooperation. Each group learned from the others as they applied their resources to the economic development of the area.

Somewhere around 1835 began what I call the "revolutionary experience." This was a revolutionary experience, in the usual sense of the term, only toward the end of this phase, as was perhaps inevitable given widespread territorial ambitions in the United States (subsequently labeled "manifest destiny" by historians of the period). The conflict was exacerbated by an ideological struggle within Mexican society between federalists and centralists. These political philosophies, while based to a considerable degree on economic self-interest of the partisans of either faction, also embodied widely divergent views on the nature of man himself.

The centralists were for administrative control over all Mexican territory by the governing elite in Mexico City. The federalists, on the other hand, were idealists trying to implement in Mexico the noble political principles of the rights of man as enunciated by the United States Constitution (after which the federalist constitution of 1824 was modeled) and by French political theorists of the Enlightenment. They were for egalitarianism in practice within a culturally and racially heterogeneous society, and not only in principle within a relatively racially and culturally homogeneous society, as in the United States. The centralists were skeptical of the possibility of self-government by a heterogeneous population, the major proportion of whom they considered inferior culturally, especially so because a poor country, such as Mexico, could not invest sufficient resources to educate the masses, who were mostly Indian.

It appeared to the majority of settlers in Texas—Mexicans, as well as others—that federalism would provide the best economic outcome for them. The province of Texas became a stronghold of federalism, and the majority decided to remain loyal to the federalist Mexican constitution of 1824. Santa Ana by this time had switched his ideological stance from federalism to centralism and had taken control of the central government in Mexico City. His reaction to events in Texas was to send troops to discipline the dissident province. However, the poorly professionalized army acted badly in Texas and alienated much of the populace by the unnecessary spilling of blood. The fact that many of these settlers came from the slaveholding South probably did not make relations with Mexicans, whom they considered inferior, easier. Heightened sentiment led to hostile actions and a revolution was started. The upshot was that Santa Ana personally came to command the army that was to put down the revolution and was himself defeated. Once the chief executive and the army of the sovereign country of Mexico were defeated, there was no real pressure for the dissident province to remain a loyal entity within the mother country—even though many of the settlers had set out originally simply to attain a federalist rather than a centralist government

in Mexico. Furthermore, when the fighting broke out, adventures and fortune seekers poured from the United States into Texas to participate in the fight. Evidence that these people, as well as their friends and relatives who remained behind, had a great sense of their "manifest destiny" to acquire more land for the United States, is abundant and is illustrated by the fact that from as far away as Cincinnati, Ohio, came contributions of cannons and supplies as soon as it appeared that separating Texas from Mexico was a possibility. Once hostilities began and these people began to pour in, the federalists loyal to Mexico were outnumbered and full-blown independence from Mexico was declared. When Santa Ana was ultimately defeated, it was still not clear that Mexico would be incapable of reassembling an army and returning to discipline the dissident province. The extreme biological and cultural heterogeneity which characterized Mexico then (as it does today) was one of the bases of Mexico's difficulty in self-government. The depth of Mexico's internal disarray became apparent soon enough. Texas was absorbed into the United States, provoking armed conflict with Mexico. If Mexico had not been able to discipline Texas, it certainly was no match for the well trained and well equipped U.S. Army backed by a *relatively* homogeneous society. By 1848 Mexico had lost approximately 50 percent of its territory. It appears that perhaps Santa Ana may have personally profited by Mexico's disarray. With the signing of the Treaty of Guadalupe Hidalgo, the Mexican American people were created *as a people:* Mexican by birth, language and culture; United States citizens by the might of arms.

THE CREATION GENERATION

Following incorporation of the Southwest into the United States in the mid-1800's there developed the experience of economic subjugation, followed by race and ethnic prejudice.

Mexico . . . simply had to accept the best deal possible under the circumstances of military defeat; that deal meant that Mexico lost any respect it might have had in the eyes of the Mexicans living on the lands annexed by the United States. This rapid change must, certainly, have given them a different social-psychological view of self than they had prior to the break. The break and annexation meant that they were now citizens of the United States, but surely they could not have changed their language and culture overnight merely because their lands were now the sovereign property of the United States; thus they maintained their "Mexicanness." Because their cultural ties were to Mexico, they were, in effect, "Mexicans" in the United States. As the number of "Americans" in the region increased, "Mexicans" became an ever smaller proportion of the population. They were . . . a minority. They thought, spoke, dressed, acted, and had all of the anatomical characteristics of the defeated Mexicans. In fact, were they not still "Mexicans" from the point of view of "Americans" even though they were United States citizens by virtue of the military defeat and treaties that gave sovereignty to the United States? For all of these reasons and more, the "Mexican" minority could be viewed as the deviants onto whom all manner of aggressions could be displaced whenever the Calvinistic desire for material acquisition was in the least frustrated.

It is the psycho-historical experience of a rapid and clear break with the culture of the parent country, and subsequent subjugation against the will of the particular population under analysis—all of this taking place on what the indigenous population considered to be its "own" land—that makes the experience of Mexican Americans different from all other ethnic populations that migrated to this country in the nineteenth and twentieth centuries.

All of the factors necessary for the development of race prejudice against Mexicans, now Mexican Americans, were present after 1836 in Texas. Any bloody war will engender very deeply felt animosity between contending factions. Furthermore, in order to kill, without feelings of remorse, it may be necessary to define the enemy as being sub-human and worthy of being killed. In the case of the fight between centralist and federalist forces in Texas it should be noted that the centralist army was almost exclusively Mexican, having

been recruited deep in Mexico and brought north by Santa Ana. The federalist forces in the province of Texas, on the other hand, were a mixture of Mexican, European, and U.S. settlers. However, once the centralist forces were defeated, the hatred toward them, that had now become a hatred of Mexico and Mexicans, could easily be displaced onto settlers who in every respect could be said to be Mexicans, even though they had been federalists and had fought for Texas independence.

Second, since most of the settlers in Texas who came from the United States were from the slave-holding South, the idea of racial inferiority was not unknown to them and could easily be used to explain the hostile emotions they held toward the Mexicans, against whom they had just fought a winning fight.

A third factor making for the development of intense race prejudice against Mexican Americans was economic. Once Texas became independent it left the door wide for massive migration from the United States. Title to the land had already been parceled out under Mexican sovereignty. Through legal and extra-legal means, the land was taken away from those provincial Mexicans, who as Texans had cooperated to try to give the province a measure of autonomy. These were the betrayed people, betrayed by their fellow Texans, once Texas became fully autonomous. By 1900 even those provincial Mexicans who had owned large tracts of land and who had held commanding social positions in Texas and throughout southwestern society had been reduced to a landless, subservient wage-earner class—with the advent of a new English language legal system, masses of English speaking, land hungry migrants, and strong anti-Mexican feelings—both by force of arms and through legal transactions backed up by force of arms. Furthermore, it was the importation of race prejudice that created an impenetrable caste boundary between the dominant provincials of northern European background and the provincial Mexicans. Once race prejudice was imported and accepted on a broad scale as an adequate explanation and justification for the lower caste condition of local "Mexicans," these attitudes could spread rapidly into the rest of the Southwest, when the United States acquired a large proportion of northern Mexico. The experience of socioeconomic and political subjugation was repeated throughout the Southwest, with some variations for peculiar circumstances in specific areas, New Mexico in particular. Many of the distinctly Mexican American attitudes throughout the country today stem from the subjugation experience of this period.

THE MIGRANT GENERATION

By 1900 the socioeconomic as well as political subservience of the Mexican American throughout the Southwest was well established. At the same time, the United States population was slowly becoming urbanized and was increasing *very rapidly* in size. Instead of small farms and ranches that provided income for one family, agriculture was increasingly conducted on very large farms in order to grow massive quantities of food profitably. Despite the growing mechanization during this period (after 1900 and before World War II), the large farms and ranches of the Southwest required massive manual labor at certain periods in the growing season. Cheap Mexican labor was inexpensive and required much less care than the machines that were only then coming on the farms.

To provide the massive agricultural labor needed, recruiters were sent deep into Mexico to spread the word of higher wages on the large farms in the United States. Coincidentally with this "pull," political upheavals in Mexico created a population "push." The resulting huge waves of migrants coming north to work the fields give the name "Migrant Generation" to this period. Until the 1920's the migrant stream flowed north predominantly through Texas (where racial attitudes were imposed) and then beyond Texas to spread out over the agricultural region of the Great Lakes and western United States. It was not until after World War II that the migrant flow began to come predominantly through California. These people have been called "immigrants" by social scientists and by policy makers because they moved from one sovereign country to another. However true their "immigrant" status might have been *legally*, they were not immigrants either *sociologically* or *culturally* because of the peculiar psycho-historical experience of Mexican Americans in the Southwest prior to 1900. Even those who eventually settled around the Great Lakes and later in the Northwest usually lived for a period of time in the Southwest where they were socialized into the cultural mode of the period.

There are at least four reasons why Mexicans arriving after 1900 but before World War II should be sociologically viewed as "migrants" who simply expanded the number of people who had more or less the same consciousness of lower caste status as those Mexican Americans who were here prior to 1900. First, the post-1900 waves of Mexican nationals coming into the United States did not come into a fresh social situation where they were meeting the host society for the first time. They did not arrive with the "freedom" to define themselves in the new society in accordance with their own wishes and aspirations. Not only were they denied the social-psychological process of "role taking" among the established higher status occupations, but demands and impositions of the dominant society were such that neither could they experiment with the process of "role making"; i.e., the creation of alternative but equal status occupations. They did not arrive with the "freedom" that comes from having one's self-image and self-esteem determined almost exclusively from one's presentation-of-self to strangers, where these strangers have no prior experience with which to question or invalidate the social claims being made by the performance. Immigrants from other lands arrived in the United States, and their place in the social hierarchy was, in a sense, freshly negotiated according to what the group as a whole could do here. The social situation that the post-1900 waves of Mexicans entering the United States encountered was very different from that of immigrants from other lands. Their experience upon entering the United States was predefined by the well established social position of pre-1900 Mexican Americans as a conquered people (politically, socially, culturally, economically, and in every other respect). They came to occupy the category closest to simple beasts of burden in the expanding regional economy.

The people coming from Mexico, in very large numbers after 1900, viewed themselves and were viewed by the dominant host society as the "same" as those Mexican Americans who had been living on the land long before, during, and after the psycho-historical experience described above as resulting in the "Creation Generation." Before they came they knew they would find, and when they arrived they did find, a large, indigenous population with whom they had language, kinship, customs, and all manner of other genetic, social, cultural, and psychological aspects in common. The very interesting and highly peculiar circumstance in the case of the post-1900 migrant from Mexico is that he left a lower *class* status in Mexico to enter a lower *caste* status in the United States without being aware of it. When a critical proportion of Mexican Americans began to earn enough money to pay for their children's education and began to expect services that they saw non-Mexican American members of the society enjoying, they found out that they were not viewed just simply as members of a less affluent class, but, rather, as members of a despised caste. This was the critical test. If they had achieved skills and affluence in Mexico, race and ethnicity would have been no barrier to personal mobility into a higher socioeconomic class. It was the attempt to permeate the normative boundaries and the subsequent reaction by the larger society that brought out in the open the way they were perceived by the dominant host society. During the period designated as the "Migrant Generation," there were many isolated instances of great conflict between groups of Mexican Americans trying to alter their lower caste status, but they were locally overpowered, and a general state of acquiescence became the state of collective consciousness.

A second factor that characterized post-1900 incoming Mexicans as migrants rather than immigrants is that the land they came to was virtually identical to the land they left.

The fact that the land they came to was very similar, physically, to the land they left behind is very important because it had been part of Mexico. Thus, the post-1900 migrant from Mexico to the United States was not leaving land to which he had a deep identity-giving psychological relationship and going off to another, very different "foreign" land, to which he needed to develop another sort of identity-giving relation. The Irish immigrant, for example, experienced a great discontinuity between the land of origin and the land of destination. Furthermore, the nation-state and the culture identified with the land to which he was going had never been part of the nation-state and culture he was leaving behind. When the Irish immigrant left "Ireland" to go to "America," there surely must have been a very clear psychic understanding that he was leaving behind a land to which he had a very special relationship that made him an "Irishman." The post-1900 migrant from Mexico need not have noticed any change. He was simply moving from one part of his identity-giving land to another. The work that he was to perform on the land of destination was identical to the work he performed on the land of origin.

A third set of factors that distinguished the Migrant Generation from immigrants from other countries involves the physical nature of the border that they had to cross to come into the United States. Over large distances the border between the United States and Mexico was never more than an imaginary line. The amount of *time* that it takes to cross the border also affects the degree of anticipatory socialization that the person can engage in prior to arrival at his point of destination. The Irish immigrant spent the better part of *two weeks* crossing an enormous physical obstacle, the Atlantic Ocean. The point here is that the nature of the physical border (its overpowering size) and the time it took to traverse it made it virtually impossible for the immigrant not to be deeply conscious of the fact that he was entering a new society and therefore, a new place within the structure of that society. This was not the case with the Mexican migrant.

A fourth set of factors distinguishing Mexicans of the Migrant Generation from immigrants from other countries is the nature of their activity in coming to this country. There is undoubtedly a significant psychic impact deriving from the degree to which the individual is a free and autonomous agent in determining the course of his own behavior. The greater the degree to which the individual perceives himself as self-determining, the less his behavior will precipitate a change of his already established identity. Conversely, the more the individual perceives (and his perceptions are validated) that his behavior is significantly determined by others, the greater will be the impact of that realization on his identity. The Irish immigrant, for example, had significant others affecting his behavior in such a way that he could not avoid considering the identity that he was rejecting and the one he was assuming. The Mexican migrants, on the other hand, were "active agents," more or less in control of their own movement. It was not until the mid-1930's that the border was "closed," that is, when an official transaction was required to cross the border. By this time, however, such an enormous number of people had already crossed, and the Mexican American population, within the lower caste existing in the southwestern United States, was so large that it did not matter in terms of the conceptual argument.

The post-1900 migrants came mainly to Texas and California. There they assumed the already established lower caste position we have described, as a consequence of the prior established social structure. Socio-psychologically, the migrants, too, were a conquered people, both because their land of origin had been conquered by the United States and because the Mexican Americans, with whom they were completely commingled, had been treated as a lower caste of conquered people inside the now expanded version of the United States. As such, they were powerless appendages of the regional economy. Their manual labor was essential to the agricultural development of the area. But whenever the business cycle took a turn for the worse, they were easily forced to go back to Mexico; they were forcibly deported. Their United-States-born children were deported right along with the parents. The deportation of Mexican Americans—United States citizens—was not uncommon, since to the U.S. Border Patrol, U.S. Immigration Service ("Migra"), and the Texas Rangers there frequently seemed little or no difference between Mexican Americans and Mexican nationals; they were all simply "Mexican."

There is for Mexican Americans a very bitter irony in all of this. The irony is that the post-1900 migrants and the pre-1900 lower caste citizens of Mexican descent learned to live more or less comfortably with all of this largely because of their frame of reference. Both constantly compared themselves to Mexican citizens in Mexico. That they should have Mexico as their cultural frame of reference is understandable. The irony is, however, that they never compared themselves to other minority groups in this country, possibly because of geographic isolation. The price the Mexican American had to pay in exchange for higher wages received for stoop labor in the fields and for lower status work in the cities was a pervasive, universal subjugation into a lower caste that came about silently and engulfed him, long before he became aware of it. He became aware of his lower caste, economically powerless position only when he (or his children) tried to break out of the caste and was forced to remain in it. By that time it was too late. He had learned to enjoy a higher wage than he would have had in Mexico and to accept a degrading lower caste position. His lower socioeconomic position in the United States was never salient in his mind.

THE MEXICAN AMERICAN GENERATION

Starting somewhere around the time of the Second World War, and increasing in importance up to the war in Vietnam, there has developed another state of collective consciousness which I call the "Mexican American Generation." This generation increasingly has turned its sense of cultural loyalty to the United States. As members of this generation were achieving maturity, they began to ask their parents:

What did Mexico ever do for you? You were poor and unwanted there. Your exodus reduced the unemployment rate and welfare problems that powerful economic elements in Mexico would have had to contend with, so they were happy to see you leave. You remained culturally loyal to the memory of Mexico, and you had dreams of returning to spend your dollars there. You sent money back to your family relations who remained in Mexico. Both of these acts of cultural loyalty on your part simply improved Mexico's dollar balance of payment. And what did Mexico do for you except help labor contractors and unscrupulous southwestern officials to further exploit you? I am an "American" who happens to be of Mexican descent. I am going to participate fully in this society because, like descendents of people from so many other lands, I was born here, and my country will guarantee me all the rights and protections of a free and loyal citizen.

What the members of the Mexican American generation did not realize was that, relative to the larger society, they were still just as economically dependent and powerless to affect the course of their own progress as the members of the older Migrant Generation. If the Migrant Generation had Mexicans in Mexico as their socioeconomic reference, the Mexican American Generation, in similar fashion, did not effectively compare its own achievements to those of the larger society, but to the achievements of the Migrant Generation. This comparison was a happy one for the Mexican American Generation. They could see that they were economically better off than their parents had ever been. They could see that they had achieved a few years of schooling while their parents had achieved virtually none.

What the Mexican American Generation did not realize was that their slight improvement in education, income, political efficacy, and social acceptance was an accomplishment only by virtue of comparison to the Migrant Generation which started with nothing. The Mexican American Generation was far behind the black population as the black population was behind the Anglo on every measure of social achievement; i.e., years of education achieved, political efficacy, annual income per family, etc. But these comparisons were rarely made during this period when Mexican Americans changed from being a predominantly rural population employed in agricultural stoop labor to an urban population employed predominantly in unskilled service occupations. Today, for example, approximately 83 percent of the Mexican American population lives in cities, even though in most instances the mass media still portrays Mexican Americans as rural stoop laborers. This was the period when the first relatively effective community protective organizations began to be formed. The organizing documents are so painfully patriotic as to demonstrate the conceptualized ambitions of the membership rather than their actual living experience.

The change of Mexican Americans from a rural to an urban population was precipitated by the rapid industrialization of agriculture that was brought about initially by the production requirements of World War II (and the simultaneous manpower drain required for the military) and was subsequently sustained and enhanced by the scientific and technological revolution that followed the war. Agriculture had increasingly been organized around big farms since 1900 in order to meet the demands of an expanding population. The massive production required by World War II, in the absence of Mexican American labor— since the Mexican American population participated disproportionately in the war—led to the increasingly rapid conversion of agriculture to resemble the industrialized factory. During the initial phases of the war, much stoop labor was imported from Mexico, but later this became less necessary because machines increasingly were filling the need for all but the most delicate agricultural picking jobs. The entire economic system reached the highest development of the ideals of industrialized society. Perhaps more money and somewhat better working conditions were to be found in cities, but that was not because of any gains on the part of Mexican Americans; it was rather because of the nature of urban living and industrial production of the post-World War II era of United States capitalism. Compared to the majority, the Mexican American still had no determinative input into the economic system. Lack of unions and lack of political effectiveness meant that the Mexican American was earning less than any other group for comparable work. Lack of education meant that the Mexican American did not have sufficient understanding of the nature of the society in which he lived and its economic system to even know that he was being treated unfairly. To the extent that he became conscious of his economically disadvantaged position, he was powerless to do anything about it.

At this point it is fair to ask: If the Mexican American Generation was so poorly educated, how did it ever get the training, skills, and general awareness of things to be able to move in large numbers from the fields to the cities and survive? Here, we have to introduce another statement about socioeconomic dependency. About the time of World War II when industrialization was beginning to be felt out in the fields, a substantial proportion of the Migrant Generation was nearing old age. Older people began to move to the cities to do the lighter work that was available there. At the same time, the young people were being moved into the war effort, young men to the military and young women to work in the war production industries and the skills and technical competency that young Mexican Americans acquired in the military were directly transferable to industrial employment in the cities after the war ended.

Finally, the fact that they fought and saw their military friends and neighbors die in defense of the United States led Mexican Americans generally not to question their relative status in the economy and their lack of control over it. Little did they realize that everyone else was also experiencing both a real and an inflationary increase in economic standing; that other groups were experiencing a faster rate of economic increase because of their more effective direct participation in bringing it about. The Mexican American was only experiencing a kind of upward coasting with the general economy and was not directly influencing his own economic betterment. As a group, Mexican Americans remained at the bottom of the socioeconomic ladder.

Many Mexican Americans attempted to escape their caste-like status by leaving the Southwest to seek employment in the industrial centers of the mid-western Great Lakes region and in the cities of the Northwest. Others went to California. A high degree of industrialization and a very heterogenerous population (religiously, ethnically, and politically) have always been the factors that attenuated discrimination against Mexican Americans in California. In fact, it is in California (and of course in the Midwest to a smaller extent) that the Mexican American first began to have the characteristics of a lower *class* population on a massive scale, as opposed to the lower *caste* experience. Of course, among the southwestern states on a smaller but widespread scale, the state of New Mexico seems to have come to a condition of class as compared to caste emphasis in a prolonged, gradual manner. This was perhaps due to the fact that the experience of the Migrant Generation never took place as intensely in New Mexico. The post-1900 immigrants came in large numbers to Texas early in the period and to California later (circa W.W. II). However, New Mexico was essentially bypassed by the Migrant Generation. Furthermore, in New Mexico the experience of the Creation Generation was neither as severe nor as complete as it was in Texas and California. In New Mexico the Creation Generation experience did take place, but so-called Hispaños managed to retain some degree of political and economic control since they represented such a large percentage of the population—even with, or in spite of, all the extensive land swindles by invading Anglos. Interestingly, the fact that the Mexicans in middle and northern New Mexico were never fully subjugated into a lower caste position is reflected in the linguistic labels they use to identify themselves. It may be argued that in order to differentiate themselves from those who had been subjugated into a lower caste, the so-called Hispaños in New Mexico started calling themselves Spanish Americans some time around the First World War, despite the fact that their anatomical features were those of Mexican mestizaje and did not resemble Spaniards. At that time, their previous geographic isolation began to be ended by large numbers of Anglos from Texas who came to settle in the southeastern part of the state of New Mexico. The Texans brought with them their generalized hatred of Mexicans and their view of them as lower caste untouchables. Thus, out of self-protection, New Mexicans started to call themselves Spanish Americans and to insist that they could trace their racial and ethnic origins to the original Spanish settlements in the area. The linguistic ruse worked so well that Mexican Americans in New Mexico came to believe their own rhetoric. The point to be made here is that this linguistic device was used by a large and isolated population that had not been fully subjugated into a lower caste to maintain in New Mexico the semblance of a class position. It is in New Mexico more than in any of the other southwestern states that Mexican Americans have participated in the society as people who have had the freedom and possibility of social mobility to become members of various social classes. They did this, however, at the price of altering their identity to make themselves acceptable to stronger economic, if not political, interests in the state. Today, however, the younger members of the post-World War II period are developing a new consciousness even in New Mexico. It is the current high school and college age offspring of the so-called Spanish Americans who are using the term Chicano

and who are demanding documentation for the presumed historic culture links to Spain. What they are finding—the greater links to Mexican and to Indian culture—is beginning to have an effect on their parents, many of whom are beginning to view themselves as Mexican Americans with some measure of pride.

Some of the tensions within the Mexican American community during this period of time could be explained in terms of the generalized attempt to be more like "Anglo" citizens. Those people who were themselves born in the United States had greater legitimation for their claims of loyalty to the United States and for their psychic sense of security on the land. They in fact would, in various disingenuous ways, disassociate themselves from those whose claim to belonging could not be as well established; even parents or family elders who were born in Mexico and came over during the period described as the Migrant Generation would be viewed as somehow less legitimate. In the cities a slight distinction was made between the older Mexican Americans who now held stable working class and small entrepreneurial positions as compared to newly arrived migrants from Mexico who entered the urban unskilled labor pool. This, of course, increased the insecurity and decreased the willingness to engage in collective action among the members of the Migrant Generation. They were in a particularly insecure position psychically, economically, and in almost every other regard. They were rejected and mistreated by the dominant Anglo population and rebuffed (as somehow deserving of that mistreatment) by their offspring.

The Mexican American Generation purchased a sense of psychic "security" at a very heavy price. They managed to establish their claims as bona fide citizens of the United States in the eyes of only *one* of the social psychologically relevant populations: *themselves*. The dominant Anglo population never ceased to view them as part of the "inferior" general population of Mexican Americans. The Migrant Generation never fully believed that their offspring would be able to become "Anglos" in any but the most foolhardy dreams of aspiring youth. They had a very apt concept for what they saw in the younger person wanting to become an Anglo facsimile: "Mosca en leche!" The Mexican American who so vehemently proclaimed his United States citizenship and his equality with all citizens never realized that all of the comparisons by which he evaluated progress were faulty. Because of his psychic identification with the superordinate Anglo, he abandoned his own language and culture and considered himself personally superior to the economically subordinate Migrant Generation. The fact that he could see that he was somewhat better off educationally and economically than the Migrant Generation led the Mexican American of this period to believe himself assimilated and accepted into the larger society. He did not fully realize that his self-perceived affluence and privileges existed only in comparison to the vast majority of Mexican Americans. He did not realize that for the same amount of native ability, education, personal motivation and actual performance, his Anglo counterpart was much more highly rewarded than he. He never made the observation that even when he achieved a higher education, he still remained at the bottom of the ladder in whatever area of economic endeavor he might be employed. Individuals, sometimes with the help of protective organizations, did bring some legal action against personal cases of discrimination. But despite a growing psychic security as citizens of the United States, they did not make effective collective comparisons. The greater security that the Mexican American Generation achieved was a falsely based sense of self-worth. To be sure, because a sizable proportion of the population managed to exist for several decades with a sense of self-worth, they could give birth to what will be called the Chicano Generation in the next section of this paper. However much the Mexican American Generation may have been discriminated against educationally and especially economically, they did achieve enough leisure and economic surplus so that their offspring did not begin from a hopeless disadvantage at birth. This extra measure of protection was perhaps the

greatest indicator that the Mexican American Generation was now part of a class and not a caste system.

THE CHICANO GENERATION

In the late 1960's a new consciousness began to make itself felt among Mexican Americans. By this time the population was solidly urban and well entrenched as an indisputable part of the country's working underclass. Migration from Mexico had slowed and was predominantly to urban centers in the United States. Theories of racial inferiority were dying, not without some sophisticated revivals, to be sure, but in general the country was beginning to accept the capacity of human populations given equal opportunities and resources. Moreover, despite the ups and downs of the marketplace, it was becoming clear to all that both technological sophistication and economic potential existed in sufficient abundance to eradicate abject poverty in the United States. These conditions had not existed in the Southwest with regard to the Mexican American population since that historical period immediately preceding the Creation Generation.

The Chicano Generation is now comparing its fortunes with those of the dominant majority as well as with the fortunes of other minorities within the United States. This represents an awareness of our citizenship in a pluralistic society. It is perhaps early to be writing the history of the Chicano Generation, but already it is clear that we have gone through an initial phase and are now in a second phase. The first phase consisted of the realization that citizenship bestows upon those who can claim it many rights and protections traditionally denied to Mexican Americans. The second phase, only now achieving widespread penetration into the population's consciousness, is that citizenship also entails obligations and duties, which we have traditionally not been in a position to perform. These two perspectives are rapidly colliding with each other. The general mental health of the Chicano community is being severely buffeted by the change in comparative focus and the relative current inability to achieve measurable success according to the new standards.

The parameters of the Mexican American population had been slowly changing, until by the mid-1960's the bulk of the post–World War II baby boom had reached draftable age and now faced the prospect of military service in the war in Vietnam. As a cohort, these young Mexican Americans were the most affluent and socio-politically liberated ever. The bulk were the sons and daughters of urban working class parents. However, a small proportion were the offspring of small businessmen; and an even smaller proportion were the offspring of minor bureaucratic officials, semi-professionals, and professionals. Especially in these latter types of families, a strong sense of the benefits of educational certification and of the rights of citizenship had been developed. When the bulk of this cohort of young people reached draftable age, which is also the age when young people generally enter college, they made some extremely interesting and shocking discoveries, on which they were able to act because they had the leisure and resources to permit self-analysis and self-determining action.

Despite the fact that the Mexican American population has the highest school dropout rate of any ethnic population in the country, by the mid-1960's a larger proportion than ever before were finishing high school. These young people then faced three major alternative courses of action, all of them unsatisfactory. One course was to enter an urban-industrial labor force for which they were ill-prepared because a high school education is no longer as useful as in previous generations. And even for those positions for which a high school education is sufficient, they were ill-prepared because the high schools located in their neighborhoods were so inadequate compared to those in Anglo neighborhoods. Moreover, persistent racial discrimination made it difficult to aspire to any but lower working class positions. Another course of action, which a disproportionate number of young

men took, was to go into military service as a way to travel, gain salable skills, and assert one's citizenship, as so many Mexican Americans had done in the previous generation. But unlike the Mexican American going into the military of World War II, the young Chicano of the mid-1960's went into a highly professionalized military, the technical skills for which he found difficult to acquire because of his inadequate high school preparation. So instead of acquiring skills for the modern technical society into which he would eventually be released, he disproportionately joined the ranks of the foot soldier and was disproportionately on the war casualty list. A third course of action open to the young Mexican American leaving high school in the mid-1960's was to make application for and enter college. This alternative was unsatisfactory because colleges and universities were not prepared to accept more than the occasional few —and then only those who would be willing to abandon their ethnicity. Refusal to admit was, of course, based on assertions of incapacity or lack of preparation. The former has racist underpinnings, while the latter is class biased since poverty and the inferior schools in which Chicano youth were concentrated did not permit adequate preparation for college and eventual middle class certification.

No matter which course of action the bulk of the young people took they disproportionately faced dismal futures. The larger society in which this ethnic minority exists had become so technical, bureaucratized, and professionalized—in short, so *middle class*—that the strictly lower working class potential of the bulk of the Mexican American population was irrelevant to it. Faced with the prospect of almost total economic marginality, the Chicano Generation was the first generation since the Creation Generation to confront the prospect of large-scale failure—of, in effect, losing ground, of psychically accomplishing less than the Mexican American Generation. The low-skill, labor-intensive society into which the Migrant Generation broke from its caste-like condition and within which the Mexican American Generation had established a firm, but strictly lower working class status, was disappearing. The United States was now predominantly professionalized and middle class, with increasingly fewer labor-intensive requirements. It is in this relatively more limited context that the Chicano Generation came to have relatively higher aspirations.

With higher aspirations than any previous generation, with the prospect of a severe psychic decline compared to its parent generation, and now, because of its greater affluence and exposure, it had to compare itself to its youth counterpart in the dominant society. The broader exposure comes from many sources, including television and greater schooling in schools that, however inferior, were better than those to which prior generations were even minimally exposed. The Chicano Generation very painfully began to ask of what value its United States citizenship was going to be. At this time a significantly large proportion of the black population of this country "revolted." That may well have been the spark that ignited the Chicano movement. The Mexican American Generation had asserted its United States citizenship with great pride, asserting a relationship between economic success and their complete "Angloization" which was now shown to be false. The Chicano Generation came to realize that it was even more acculturated than the previous generation, yet it did not have any realistic prospects of escaping its virtually complete lower and working class status. Its new consciousness came into being at a time when the Chicano Generation could hardly find any older role models with certified middle class status. Comparatively, for example, out of a population of twenty-four million there are 2,200 black persons who have earned Ph.D. degrees in all disciplines combined. Among the eight million (approximately) Mexican Americans there are only 60 who have earned Ph.D. degrees, when a similar level of disadvantage would lead us to expect approximately 730. The number of Ph.D.'s in a population is used here as a sort of barometric indicator of the level and quality of technically trained and certified leadership available to a population within a predominantly middle class society. This is so because one can guess at the ratio of lawyers and doctors as well as master and bachelor degrees for each Ph.D. Thus, the Mexican American population which began to enter colleges and universities in noticeable numbers only as late as the mid-1960's is almost completely lacking in certification for middle class status.

Another indication of the lack of certified leadership that is self-consciously concerned with the welfare of the community is the lack of institutions of higher learning of, for, and by Chicanos. There are over 100 black institutions of higher learning (both privately and publicly supported, including colleges, universities, law schools and medical schools). As recently as five years ago there were no such institutions for Chicanos. Now there are a handful of schools that either have been created *ad hoc* or where a significant number of Chicanos have moved into administrative positions due to pressures from large Chicano student enrollments. The point here is that however inadequate the black schools may have been, compared to "white" schools, they provided the institutional foci within which a broad sector of the black population has been trained and certified for middle class status since prior to 1900. Mexican Americans could neither get into institutions of the dominant society, nor did we have our own alternate institutions. Thus, the difficulty of acquiring broad scale consciousness of the condition of our people is apparent, as is the insecure ethnic identification of the early few who entered "white" institutions.

The Chicano Generation has experienced the pain of social rejection in essentially the same fashion (in the abstract) that it was experienced by the Creation Generation. That is, having been ideologically prepared to expect egalitarian co-participation in the society in which it exists, it had instead been confronted with the practical fact of exclusion from the benefits of the society. Because it can no longer compare itself to its immediate predecessors (no matter what the quantity or quality of accomplishments of the Mexican

American Generation), it has to compare itself to other groups in the larger society. Relative to them it is more disadvantaged than any other ethnic group, except the American Indian with whom it has much in common both culturally and biologically. Every new demographic analysis gives the Chicano Generation more evidence of relative deprivation, which leads to the rise of a psychic sense of betrayal by the egalitarian ideology of the United States not unlike that experienced by the Creation Generation. Members of the Chicano Generation are therefore saying to the previous generation:

> So you are a loyal "American," willing to die for your country in the last three or four wars; what did your country ever do for you? If you are such an American, how come your country gives you less education even than other disadvantaged minorities, permits you only low status occupations, allows you to become a disproportionately large part of casualties in war, and socially rejects you from the most prestigious circles? As for me, I am a Chicano, I am rooted in this land, I am the creation of a unique psycho-historical experience. I trace part of my identity to Mexican culture and part to United States culture, but most importantly my identity is tied up with those contested lands called Aztlán! My most valid claim to existential reality is not the false pride and unrequited loyalty of either the Migrant Generation or the Mexican American Generation. Rather, I trace my beginnings to the original contest over the lands of Aztlán, to the more valid psycho-historical experience of the Creation Generation. I have a right to inter-marriage if it suits me, to economic achievement at all societal levels, and to my own measure of political self-determination within this society. I have a unique psycho-historical experience that I have a right to know about and to cultivate as part of my distinctive cultural heritage.

The concerns of the Chicano Generation are those which predominantly plague the middle class: sufficient leisure and affluence to contemplate the individual's origin and potential future, sufficient education and affluence to make it at least possible for the individual to have a noticeable impact on the course of his life's achievements, but not so rich an inheritance that the individual's prominence in society

is virtually assured. The Chicano Generation is the first sizable cohort in our history to come to the widespread realization that we can have a considerable measure of self-determination within the confines of this pluralistic society. Yet we are only at the threshold of this era and have hardly begun to legitimate our claims to effective self-determination, i.e., acquisition of professional-technical certification as well as establishment of relatively independent wealth. Our capacity to secure middle class entry for a sizable proportion of our population is threatened on two major fronts.

First, we are threatened by our redundancy or obsolescence at the bottom of the social structure. This has two dimensions: we cannot earn enough money to support a United States standard of living on laborers' wages; even if we were willing to do the few remaining back-breaking jobs, there would not be enough work to go around because these are being automated, and the few that are around will be taken over by cheap Mexican labor from Mexico, unless we organize factory and farmworkers effectively. Thus, in a sense, the economic bottom of our community is falling away.

Second, we are threatened because just as the middle class sector of the larger society is getting ready to acknowledge our capacities and our right to full participation, we find that the major proportion of our population does not have the necessary credentials for entry—i.e., college, graduate and professional degrees. When large corporate organizations attempt to comply with federal equal employment regulations concerning the Spanish speaking population, they do not care whether the person they hire comes from a family that has been in the United States since 1828 or whether the person arrived yesterday from Mexico or some other Latin American country. The irony is that as discrimination disappears or is minimized, those who have historically suffered the most from it continue to suffer its aftereffects. This is so because as multinational corporations have begun their training programs throughout Latin America, and especially in Mexico, a new technically skilled and educated middle class has been greatly expanded in those countries. Many of these persons begin to question why they should perform jobs in their home country at the going depressed salaries when they could come to the United States and receive higher salaries for the same work and participate in a generally higher standard of living. This, in effect, is part of the brain drain experienced by these countries from the point of view of their economy. From the point of view of the Chicano community, however, we experience it as being cut off at the pass. That is, just as the decline of prejudice and the increase in demand for middle class type positions might pull us up into the secure middle class, a new influx of people from another country comes into the United States economy above us. Because it would cost corporations more to develop Chicanos for these positions, and because we do not have a sufficiently aware and sufficiently powerful Chicano middle class to fight for the selection of Chicanos, and because of federal regulations which only call for Spanish surname people to fill jobs, without regard to place of origin, it is conceivable that the bulk of our population might become relegated into relatively unskilled working class positions. Thus, the plight of the urban Chicano in the 1970's is not only technically complicated (how do you acquire middle class expertise with working class resources), but psychically complex (how do you relate to urban middle class imigrants from Spanish speaking countries and to rapidly organizing rural Mexican Americans) at a time when the general economy of the United States appears to be in a state of contraction, making competition for positions severe. Unless we can deal creatively with these trends, we will remain at the bottom of the social structure. This, in spite of outmoded social theories that postulated that each wave of new immigrants would push the previous wave up in the socioeconomic structure.

The introspectiveness of the Chicano generation is leading to new insights. The psycho-historical links of the Chicano Generation with the Creation Generation are primarily those of collective support against a common diffuse and everywhere present danger. The threat of cultural extinction has led the Chicano to deep introspection as to what distinguishes him both from Mexicans in Mexico and from "Anglos" in the United States. This introspection has led to a deep appreciation for the positive aspects of each culture and a creative use of our inheritance in facing the future. The fight for self-definition is leading to a reanalysis of culture. For example, Anglo research has defined "machismo" as unidimensional male dominance, whereas, its multi-dimensional original meaning placed heavier emphases on personal dignity and personal sacrifice on behalf of the collectivity—i.e., family or community. This concern for the collectivity comes through again in the emphasis placed on "la familia" in activities within a Chicano movement perspective. The fight for professional and middle class certification is the fight for our collectivity to be heard. The objective is to produce enough certified professionals who can articulate and defend our peculiarly distinct culture in such a manner that educational and other institutions of the dominant society will have to be modified. Until we have our own certified savants, we will continue to be defined out of existence by outsiders insensitive to the internal dynamic of our own collectivity. The willingness to fight may be what will get us there. YA MERO!

15

Toward Racism:
The History of an Idea

JOHN HIGHAM

It need not puzzle us that Malay and Papuan,
Celt and Roman, Saxon and Tartar should mix.
. . . The best nations are those most widely
related. . . .
—Ralph Waldo Emerson, 1856

"You cannot dodge the Mendelian law, my boy.
Like begets like, but in a union of opposites we
get throwbacks. . . . You're not going to run
the risk of mongrelizing the species, are you?"
—Peter B. Kyne, 1923

Hardly any aspect of American xenophobia over its course from the eighteenth to the twentieth century is more striking than the monotony of its ideological refrain. Year after year, decade after decade, the same charges and complaints have sounded in endless re-iteration. Variously combined, formulated, and documented, adapted to different and changing adversaries, rising and falling in intensity and acceptance, nearly all of the key ideas persisted without basic modification.

But in one major respect the pattern of nativist thought changed fundamentally. Gradually and progressively it veered toward racism. Absent from the strictures of the eighteenth century nationalist, notions of racial superiority and exclusiveness appeared

John Higham is Professor of History at Johns Hopkins University.

Reprinted from John Higham, *Strangers in the Land: Patterns of American Nativism 1860–1925,* by permission of Rutgers University Press and the author. Footnotes have been omitted.

in the mid-nineteenth, but they were to undergo a long process of revision and expansion before emerging in the early twentieth century as the most important nativist ideology. Several generations of intellectuals took part in transforming the vague and somewhat benign racial concepts of romantic nationalism into doctrines that were precise, malicious, and plausibly applicable to European immigration. The task was far from simple; at every point the race-thinkers confronted the liberal and cosmopolitan barriers of Christianity and American democracy. Ironically and significantly, it was not until the beginning of the present century, when public opinion recovered much of its accustomed confidence, that racial nativism reached intellectual maturity.

Of course racial nativism forms only a segment, though a critical and illuminating segment, of the larger evolution of race consciousness in modern times. The greater part of the complex phenomenon which is now fashionably called "race prejudice" lies beyond the scope of this article; its history is tangled and still largely unwritten. What concerns us is the intersection of racial attitudes with nationalistic ones—in other words, the extension to European nationalities of that sense of absolute difference which already divided white Americans from people of other colors. When sentiments analogous to those already discharged against Negroes, Indians, and Orientals spilled over into anti-European channels, a force of tremendous intensity entered the stream of American nativism.

The whole story of modern racial ferment, nativist and otherwise, has two levels, one involving popular emotions, the other concerning more or less systematic ideas. Most of the emotions flow from a reservoir of habitual suspicion and distrust accumulated over the span of American history toward human groups stamped by obvious differences of color. The ideas, on the other hand, depend on the speculations of intellectuals on the nature of races. The distinction is partly artificial, for the spirit of white supremacy—or what may be labeled race-feeling—has interlocked with race-thinking at many points. Indeed, their convergence has given the problem of race its modern significance. But at least the distinction has the merit of reminding us that race-feelings and explicit concepts about races have not always accompanied one another. The Anglo-Saxon idea in its early form did not entail the biological taboos of race-feeling. Nor did the pattern of white supremacy, in all likelihood, depend at the outset on formal race-thinking. Traditional religious beliefs, often hardly articulated at all, served the pragmatic purposes of the English colonists who enslaved Negroes and who scourged Indians as Satanic agents "having little of Humanitie but shape." However, the evolution of white supremacy into a comprehensive philosophy of life, grounding human values in the innate constitution of nature, required a major theoretical effort. It was the task of the race-thinkers to organize specific antipathies toward dark-hued peoples into a generalized, ideological structure.

To the development of racial nativism, the thinkers have made a special contribution. Sharp physical differences between native Americans and European immigrants were not readily apparent; to a large extent they had to be manufactured. A rather elaborate, well-entrenched set of racial ideas was essential before the newcomers from Europe could seem a fundamentally different order of men. Accordingly, a number of race-conscious intellectuals blazed the way for ordinary nativists.

FROM ROMANTICISM TO NATURALISM

Two general types of race-thinking, derived from very different origins, circulated throughout the nineteenth century. One came from political and literary sources and assumed, under the impact of the romantic movement, a nationalistic form. Its characteristic manifestation in England and America was the Anglo-Saxon tradition. Largely exempt through most of the century from the passions of either the nativist or the white supremacist, this politico-literary concept of race lacked a clearly defined physiological basis. Its vague identification of culture with ancestry served mainly to emphasize the antiquity, the uniqueness, and the permanence of a nationality. It suggested the inner vitality of one's own culture, rather than the menace of another race. Whereas some of the early racial nationalists attributed America's greatness (and above all its capacity for self-government) to its Anglo-Saxon derivation, others thought America was creating a new mixed race; and, such was the temper of the age, many accepted both ideas at the same time. But whether exclusive or cosmopolitan in tendency, these romantics almost always discussed race as an ill-defined blessing; hardly ever as a sharply etched problem. During the age of confidence, as Anglo-Saxonism spread among an eastern social elite well removed from the fierce race conflicts of other regions, it retained a complacent, self-congratulatory air.

Meanwhile a second kind of race-thinking was developing from the inquiries of naturalists. Stimulated by the discovery of new worlds overseas, men with a scientific bent began in the seventeenth and eighteenth centuries to study human types systematically in order to catalogue and explain them. While Anglo-Saxonists consulted history and literature to identify national races, the naturalists concentrated on the great "primary" groupings of *Homo sapiens* and used physiological characteristics such as skin color, stature, head shape, and so on, to distinguish them one from the other. Quite commonly this school associated physical with cultural differences and displayed, in doing so, a feeling of white superiority over the colored races. On the whole, however, the leading scientific thinkers did not regard race differences as permanent, pure, and unalterable. A minority insisted that races were immutable, separately created species; but the influence of this polygenist argument suffered from its obvious violation of the Christian doctrine of the unity of mankind. For the most part, early anthropologists stressed the molding force of environmental conditions in differentiating the human family.

In the course of the nineteenth and early

twentieth centuries, the separation between the two streams of race-thinking gradually and partially broke down. Racial science increasingly intermingled with racial nationalism. Under the pressure of a growing national consciousness, a number of European naturalists began to subdivide the European white man into biological types, often using linguistic similarity as evidence of hereditary connection. For their part, the nationalists slowly absorbed biological assumptions about the nature of race, until every national trait seemed wholly dependent on hereditary transmission. This interchange forms the intellectual background for the conversion of the vague Anglo-Saxon tradition into a sharp-cutting nativist weapon and, ultimately, into a completely racist philosophy.

Behind the fusion—and confusion—of natural history with national history, of "scientific" with social ideas, lay a massive trend in the intellectual history of the late nineteenth and twentieth centuries. Hopes and fears alike received scientific credentials; and men looked on the human universe in increasingly naturalistic terms. In religion, literature, philosophy, and social theory ancient dualisms dissolved. Human affairs and values were seen more and more as products of vast, impersonal processes operating throughout nature. The Darwinian theory represented a decisive step in this direction; in the eyes of many, it subsumed mankind wholly under the grim physical laws of the animal kingdom.

While the whole naturalistic trend encouraged race-thinking and lent a sharper flesh-and-blood significance to it, Darwinism added a special edge. By picturing all species as both the products and the victims of a desperate, competitive struggle for survival, Darwinism suggested a warning: the daily peril of destruction confronts every species. Thus the evolutionary theory, when fully adopted by race-thinkers, not only impelled them to anchor their national claims to a biological basis; it also provoked anxiety by denying assurance that the basis would endure. Although most Anglo-Saxonists still identified their race with an indwelling spiri-

tual principle, now they had also to envision the bearers of that principle as combatants in the great biological battle raging throughout nature.

On the other hand, it is not true that Darwinian (and Spencerian) ideas led directly to an outburst of racial nativism or to an overriding hereditarian determinism. The whole scientific revolution of the nineteenth century merely prepared the way and opened the possibility for those developments. Actually, the evolutionary hypothesis left major obstacles to a rigidly racial creed.

First of all, the general climate of opinion in the early Darwinian era inhibited the pessimistic implications of the new naturalism. What stood out in the first instance, as the great social lesson of the theory of natural selection, was not the ravages of the struggle for survival but rather the idea of "the survival of the fittest." To a generation of intellectuals steeped in confidence, the laws of evolution seemed to guarantee that the "fittest" races would most certainly triumph over inferior competitors. And in their eagerness to convert social values into biological facts, Darwinian optimists unblinkingly read "the fittest" to mean "the best." They felt confirmed in their supremacy over the immigrants, who in turn seemed the winnowed best of Europe. Darwinism, therefore, easily ministered to Anglo-Saxon pride, but in the age of confidence it could hardly arouse Anglo-Saxon anxiety.

Secondly, Darwinism gave the race-thinkers little concrete help in an essential prerequisite of racism—belief in the preponderance of heredity over environment. Certainly the biological vogue of the late nineteenth century stimulated speculation along these lines, but the evolutionary theory by no means disqualified a fundamentally environmentalist outlook. Darwin's species struggled and evolved within particular natural settings; they survived through adaptation to those settings. This aspect of the theory ultimately impressed itself so forcefully on American social scientists that toward the end of the century one of them acclaimed the doctrine of evolution for actually discouraging racial as opposed to environmental interpretations. And while liberal environmentalists drew comfort from the new scientific gospel, it left the race-thinkers with no definite knowledge of how hereditary forces function or persist. Darwinism explained only the survival, not the appearance, of biological variations from preexisting types. The origins of and relationships among races remained obscure.

Obviously both of these difficulties would have to be overcome if the Anglo-Saxon nationalism of the 1870's was to evolve into a fully effective instrument for race-feelings. Even to begin the transition the race-thinkers would have to cast loose from Darwinian optimism, discarding the happy thought that the fittest, in the sense of the best, always win out. That done, they would still lack a strict racial determinism. To divorce race entirely from environment and to put biological purity at the center of social policy, American nationalists would need further cues from the developing natural sciences.

PATRICIANS ON THE DEFENSIVE

Americans were slow to take that second and more drastic step. Although sweeping theories and pretentious sciences or pseudosciences of race developed in continental Europe in the late nineteenth century, American intellectuals of that period knew practically nothing of them. Nor did American scientists make any contributions to race-thinking similar to those of Broca, Ammon, or Lapouge. In the United States psychologists dealt with individuals rather than groups, sociologists with institutions rather than peoples. Anthropologists immersed themselves in narrowly empirical studies of primitive folk, chiefly the Indians. The movement toward racism was an up-hill fight in democratic America.

But a number of Anglo-Saxon nationalists in the eighties and nineties did begin to break away from evolutionary optimism. At first, instead of trying to qualify or rebut the principle of the survival of the fittest, the race-thinkers simply turned from complacent con-

templation of America's Anglo-Saxon past to an anxious look at its future. This swing to a defensive outlook marks the initial phase of racial nativism. It required no fresh intellectual stimulus; it was precipitated by the general crisis in American society.

The same internal crisis that reactivated the older nativist traditions crystallized the new one. Until unrest and class cleavage upset the reign of confidence in the 1880's, the assimilationist concept of a mixed nationality had tempered and offset pride in Anglo-Saxon superiority. But when the Anglo-Saxon enthusiasts felt their society and their own status deeply threatened, they put aside their boasts about the assimilative powers of their race. They read the signs of the times as symptoms of its peril. Contrary to an impression widespread among historians, the new racial xenophobia did not originate as a way of discriminating between old and new immigrations. It arose from disturbances, within American society, which preceded awareness of a general ethnic change in the incoming stream. At the outset, Anglo-Saxon nativism vaguely indicted the whole foreign influx. Only later did the attack narrow specifically to the new immigration.

The current social scene presented a troubling contrast to the image of America that Anglo-Saxon intellectuals cherished. The tradition of racial nationalism had always proclaimed orderly self-government as the chief glory of the Anglo-Saxons—an inherited capacity so unique that the future of human freedom surely rested in their hands. But now the disorders of the mid-eighties cast doubt on the survival of a free society. The more anxious of the Anglo-Saxon apostles knew that the fault must lie with all the other races swarming to America. Did they not, one and all, lack the Anglo-Saxon's self-control, almost by definition? So, behind the popular image of unruly foreigners, a few caught sight of unruly races; and Anglo-Saxon nativism emerged as a corollary to anti-radical nativism—as a way of explaining why incendiary immigrants threatened the stability of the republic.

The explanation came out clear-cut in the

convulsion that followed the Haymarket Affair. A writer in a business magazine stated the racial lesson of the riot in the baldest terms: anarchy is "a blood disease" from which the English have never suffered. "I am no race worshipper," he insisted, "but . . . if the master race of this continent is subordinated to or overrun with the communistic and revolutionary races, it will be in grave danger of social disaster." During the same fateful summer a leading Congregational theologian equated race and unrest in words so sharp that he withheld them from publication for a year and a half. The Reverend Theodore T. Munger, an exponent of evolutionary theology, had long admired the Anglo-Saxons, the most highly developed, the most individualistic, and indeed the most Christian of races. As he surveyed the strife of 1886, he saw "anarchism, lawlessness . . . labor strikes, and a general violation of personal rights such as the Anglo-Saxon race has not witnessed since Magna Charta. . . . This horrible tyranny is wholly of foreign origin." Fundamentally, however, the problem was not just foreign. It was "physiological": how to restrict immigration "so that the physical stock shall not degenerate, and how to keep the strong, fine strain ascendant."

Compared to the common and simple attack on radical *foreigners*, the attack on radical *races* was at first a minor theme. Indeed, it did not immediately displace the older kind of race-thinking. During the eighties many Anglo-Saxonists still clung to the traditional pride and confidence in America's powers of assimilation. Josiah Strong, for example, was still celebrating the absorptive capacities of the Anglo-Saxons after he had begun to attack the immigrants as socially disruptive. And in 1890 James K. Hosmer's glowing constitutional history of the Anglo-Saxon race still conceded that racial mingling invigorated it, although Hosmer was equally certain that immigration was diluting the Anglo-Saxons' blood and subverting their social order.

During the 1890's, as the social crisis deepened, racial nativism became more de-

fined and widespread. If one may judge, however, from Congressional debates, newspapers, and the more popular periodicals, Anglo-Saxonism still played a relatively small part in public opinion. The rising flood of popular xenophobia drew much more upon conventional anti-foreign ideas.

On the whole, the Anglo-Saxon tradition in its new nativistic form still found its support within the patrician circles where it had persisted throughout the age of confidence. Now, as then, the race-thinkers were men who rejoiced in their colonial ancestry, who looked to England for standards of deportment and taste, who held the great academic posts or belonged to the best clubs or adorned the higher Protestant clergy. Some, like Frank Parsons or Albert Shaw, were active reformers, especially in the municipal field. But, in general, racial nativists worshipped tradition in a deeply conservative spirit, and in the tumult of the nineties it seemed to them that everything fixed and sacred was threatened with dissolution. Among them were Episcopalian Bishop A. Cleveland Coxe, who added the final "e" to his family name in order to re-establish its antique spelling; Woodrow Wilson, then a historian with aristocratic sympathies, a disciple of Burke and Bagehot who believed heartily in evolution because it moved so slowly; John W. Burgess, who brought from German seminars a love for "the race-proud Teutons" rather than the Anglo-Saxons and whose political science proved that racial amalgamation endangered private enterprise; and of course Henry Cabot Lodge, who mourned for the days when society venerated the old families, their traditions, and their ancestors. No one expressed the state of mind in this group better than the Presbyterian clergyman in New York who thought nature's great principle of inequality endangered by a "specious humanity," liberty-loving Anglo-Saxons beset by socialistic foreigners, and the intelligent people in the clutches of the unintelligent.

A substantial number of these patrician nativists belonged to the cultivated intelligentsia of New England, the region where the Anglo-Saxon idea was most firmly entrenched.

There the proportion of foreign-born in the total population was rising more sharply than in any other part of the country. There too the declining vitality of the native culture contributed to a defensive attitude. Brahmin intellectuals such as Lodge, Henry Adams, and Barrett Wendell knew that the historic culture of New England had entered its "Indian Summer," and the knowledge gave them added cause to see their race and region beleaguered by the alien. In other places also a pessimistic spirit was creeping into intellectual life as the century waned. What the German writer Max Nordau was calling "vague qualms of a Dusk of the Nations" darkened various minds receptive to social anxieties or to the grimmer implications of Darwinian naturalism. But New Englanders particularly succumbed to the melancholy, *fin de siècle* mood and gave it a racial form. Thus at Harvard, Barrett Wendell, whose English accent matched his Anglophile interpretation of American literature, was settling into the conviction that his own kind had had its day, that other races had wrenched the country from its grasp for once and all.

Many if not most of these men in the early nineties remained oblivious of the new immigration, assuming that the immigrants as a whole lacked the Anglo-Saxon's ancestral qualities. However, the avant-garde of racial nationalists was discovering during those years the shift in the immigrant stream. The discovery was important, because it lent a new sharpness and relevance to race-thinking. By making the simple (and in fact traditional) assumption that northern European nationalities shared much of the Anglo-Saxon's inherited traits, a racial nativist could now understand why immigration had just now become a problem. Also, the cultural remoteness of southern and eastern European "races" suggested to him that the foreign danger involved much more than an inherited incapacity for self-government: the new immigration was racially impervious to the whole of American civilization! Thus Anglo-Saxon nativism, in coming to focus on specific ethnic types, passed beyond its first, subordinate role as a corollary to anti-radical nativism. It found its own *raison d'être*, and in doing so served to divide the new immigrants from their predecessors in an absolute and fundamental way. Racial nativism became at once more plausible, a more significant factor in the history of immigration restriction, and a more precisely formulated ideology.

Three prominent intellectuals of the day illustrate this evolution in the Anglo-Saxon idea. Each of them embarked on anti-foreign agitation in the loose terms provoked by the internal events of the eighties, and each of them ended by fixing on the new immigration as constitutionally incapable of assimilation.

Nathaniel S. Shaler, the Kentucky-born geologist who presided over the Lawrence Scientific School at Harvard, was in some ways a reluctant and unlikely nativist. One of the most benign of individuals, Shaler felt a real sympathy for disadvantaged groups; and his professional training impressed upon him the large influence of the physical environment in creating human differences. But his early southern background had given Shaler an indelible race consciousness. He easily shared the belief of his Brahmin colleagues that American democracy rested on an English racial heritage. At first he stated the racial argument against immigration in class terms, contending that the immigrants threatened social stability because, as peasants, they lacked the Americans' inborn instinct for freedom. In 1894, however, he shifted to a more specific and sweeping attack on the new immigration. Instead of indicting the immigrants as a whole, he now drew a sharp racial contrast between northwestern and southeastern Europeans, maintaining that the new "non-Aryan" peoples were wholly different from earlier immigrants and innately impossible to Americanize.

Henry Cabot Lodge arrived by a similar route at the same conclusion but carried it much further. What was perhaps his earliest public attack on immigration reflected simply a nationalist reaction to the crisis within American society. At that time, in 1888, he actually repudiated the injection of racial considerations into political issues. His own Anglo-

Saxonism still conformed to the traditional eulogistic pattern. Events, however, soon turned his attention to invidious racial comparisons.* In 1891 Lodge published a statistical analysis, which cost him much time and effort, concerning "the distribution of ability" in the American population. By classifying the entries in a biographical encyclopedia, he tried to show "the enormous predominance" of an English racial strain over every other in contributing to the development of the United States. Although the figures in this study suggested the inferiority of every non-English group in America, thereafter Lodge concentrated his fire on the new immigration, arguing that it presented a supreme danger transcending political or economic considerations: it threatened "a great and perilous change in the very fabric of our race."

To support this view, Lodge went far beyond his American contemporaries in the direction of a racial philosophy of history. During a summer in France in 1895, he happened upon a new book by Gustave Le Bon, *The Psychology of Peoples*. Le Bon was a poetic social psychologist, an enemy of democracy, and a man who lived in dread of an imminent socialist revolution. His book treated nationalities as races and races as the substrata of history. Only through crossbreeding, according to Le Bon, could a race die or miss its destiny. He saw little hope for continental Europe but thought that the English, alone among European races, had kept their purity and stability. Lodge took these ideas back to the United States and repeated them practically verbatim on the floor of the Senate in 1896 in leading the fight for the literacy test. Without restriction of the new immigration, he warned, America's fixed, inherited national

character would be lost in the only way possible—by being "bred out."

Lodge was exceptional both in his direct contact with European race-thinking and in the degree to which he embraced an ideal of racial purity. It was not so easy for others to ignore the influence of environment or to understand how a supposedly backward, inferior type could overwhelm the puissant Anglo-Saxons.

A third member of the Yankee upper crust moved more cautiously into racial nativism but exerted in the long run a more telling intellectual influence. Francis A. Walker, president of the Massachusetts Institute of Technology and one of the outstanding economists of his day, was virtually the only American who made an original contribution to nativist thought in the late nineteenth century. Unlike Lodge, Shaler or the rest, Walker faced up to the key Darwinian issue of the survival of the fittest.

When he awoke to the menace of the foreign-born during the great labor upheaval of the mid-eighties, it was not race but rather the European's characteristic "insolence and savagery" that gave Walker visions of "great cities threatened with darkness, riot and pillage." He continued to think of labor unrest as the most important aspect of the foreign peril and, in fact, never indulged in comprehensive racial theorizing. But as early as 1890 he trembled at a new influx of totally unassimilable races, representing "the very lowest stage of degradation." That these were laggards in the struggle for existence Walker had no doubt. Lest anyone should still defend the old Darwinian notion of migration as a selective process bringing America the most energetic and enterprising of Europeans, Walker neatly turned the tables, declaring that natural selection was now working in reverse. Due to the cheapness and ease of steamship transportation, the fittest now stay at home; the unfit migrate. The new immigrants, he declared in phrases that rang down through the restriction debates of the next three decades, "are beaten men from beaten races; representing the worst failures in the struggle for existence. . . .

---

* In 1890, for largely partisan reasons, Lodge brought to a head a Republican drive to enact a Force Bill designed to insure Negro suffrage in the South. The attempt failed, but not before it brought down upon Lodge the condemnation of "the best people" of Massachusetts. The next year, instead of opposing racial barriers, Lodge proceeded to champion them by opening his campaign in Congress against the new immigration. See James A. Barnes, *John G. Carlisle, Financial Statesman* (New York, 1931), 188.

They have none of the ideas and aptitudes which . . . belong to those who are descended from the tribes that met under the oak trees of old Germany to make laws and choose chieftains."

But still there was the hard question: How and why can such unfit groups endanger the survival of America's strong native stock? Walker held the clue long before it occurred to him to ask the question. As superintendent of the United States census of 1870, he had noticed that the rate of population growth in America was declining. At the time and for many years afterward he interpreted the decline very sensibly as a result of urbanization and industrialization. Then, when the events of the eighties and early nineties turned his attention to the racial significance of immigration, the old problem of population growth appeared in a new light. Might not the dwindling birth rate be a prudential response by the old American stock to a Darwinian struggle with immigrants capable of underbidding and outbreeding them? With an ingenious show of statistics, Walker argued in 1891 that the reproductive decline was occurring largely among the native population and that immigration rather than domestic conditions was responsible for it. In order to compete with cheap foreign labor, he said, Americans preferred to reduce the size of their families rather than lower their standard of living. Thus the foreign-born were actually replacing the native stock, not reinforcing it; in the very act of maintaining social and economic superiority, native Americans were undergoing biological defeat. In view of the new influx from southern and eastern Europe, Walker was sure that this long process of replacement would now enter an increasingly ominous stage.

From a racial point of view, the argument had the disadvantage of resting on social and economic determinants and therefore failing to make any real distinction between immigrant types. Nevertheless, it did effectively counter Darwinian optimism while defining the foreign danger in plainly biological terms. Like Lodge's bluster about crossbreeding, Walker's birth-rate hypothesis suggested that unobstructed natural selection might insure the survival of the worst people rather than the best. The recasting of the Anglo-Saxon tradition into the mold of a gloomy, scientific naturalism was under way.

OPTIMISTIC CROSSCURRENTS

Before this naturalistic trend made further headway, in fact before nativists paid much attention to Walker's theory, events temporarily twisted race-thinking in a very different direction. The fears and forebodings that were pushing Anglo-Saxonism toward sharper, more dogmatic formulations suddenly lifted at the end of the century; a new era bright with hope and flushed with well-being relieved the need to define enemies and explain failures. At a time when every xenophobia subsided, racial nationalism softened, relaxed, and resumed once more its historic air of triumphant confidence. Yet, oddly, it flourished as never before.

Actually, two currents of racial nationalism had developed among American intellectuals during the 1890's. One was defensive, pointed at the foreigner within; the other was aggressive, calling for expansion overseas. Both issued, in large measure, from the same internal frustrations; both reflected the same groundswell of national feeling. But one warned the Anglo-Saxon of a danger of submergence, while the other assured him of a conquering destiny. By 1898 the danger and doom were all but forgotten, and the conquest was made. An easy and successful adventure in imperialism gave racial nationalism both an unprecedented vogue and a cheerful tone. In a torrent of popular jubilation over the Anglo-Saxon's invincibility, the need to understand his predicament scientifically dissolved in a romantic glow.

Imperialists happily intent on absorbing Filipinos and Puerto Ricans felt little doubt of the Anglo-Saxons' powers of assimilation. Instead of Lodge's dread of racial mixture and his insistence on the fixity of the Anglo-Saxon folk, the country now heard once more the earlier theory of John Fiske: that Anglo-

Saxons possess a unique capacity to merge with other peoples while retaining their own dominant traits. Franklin H. Giddings, the first professor of sociology at Columbia University, dressed up in scientific language the old notion that immigration was recapitulating in the United States the same blend of European strains from which the English had originally emerged. His proof that the United States was still English moved the editor of the *Ladies' Home Journal* to congratulate the home of the oppressed for its success in assimilation. Others admitted that America's racial composition was changing but insisted that its Anglo-Saxon (or Teutonic) ideals were imposed on all comers. Albert Shaw, once one of the leading racial nativists, explained his shift away from a restrictionist position by asserting that America's power to assimilate had increased. Another imperialist felt so strong a sense of national homogeneity that he gave a new definition to the term Anglo-Saxon. All who stand together under the stars and stripes and fight for what it represents, he declared, have a right to that proud designation.

Of course, there was another, less uplifting side to this frame of mind. The prime object of the imperialist ideology, after all, was to justify imposing colonial status on backward peoples. Every Anglo-Saxonist knew that the United States was taking up "the white man's burden" in extending American control over the dark-skinned natives of the Philippines, Hawaii, and Puerto Rico. Under these circumstances the Anglo-Saxon idea easily associated itself with emotions of white supremacy. In other words, while welcoming the immigrant population into the Anglo-Saxon fold, imperialists were also linking their ideal of nationality to a consciousness of color. Although a romantic idealism temporarily blurred the ideological sharpness of racial nationalism, at a deeper and more permanent level the Anglo-Saxon would henceforth symbolize the white man par excellence.

The imperialist excitement itself lasted only a short while, leaving the Anglo-Saxon tradition freighted with race-feelings and exposed again to a defensive, nativistic reaction.

Overseas adventurers lost their savor as soon as they engendered difficult moral problems and serious international entanglements. As early as 1901 the bloodshed necessary to impose United States rule on the "new-caught, sullen peoples" of the Philippines was deflating enthusiasm for expansion. And by 1905, when Japan emerged as a new world power menacing American interests in the Far East, American opinion was nervously repudiating the conquering, global destiny of a few years before. Confronted by the "Yellow Peril," the Anglo-Saxon abandoned his rampant stance and resumed a somewhat defensive posture.

There were various indications in the early years of the twentieth century that race-thinking was entering a fretful, post-imperialist phase. One very direct reflection of the change of mood came in a book published in 1905 by a United States Army surgeon on his return from a tour of duty in the Philippines. In *The Effects of Tropical Light on White Men*, Major Charles E. Woodruff passed a depressing verdict on the racial results of imperialism. The blond, blue-eyed race, he argued, is born to command and to conquer; but in expanding southward from its foggy, overcast homelands in northern Europe it always succumbs to intense sunlight, which only the brunette races can withstand. And as Woodruff glanced apprehensively at the complexion of the immigrants pouring into the United States at the time, he added a significant afterthought. Perhaps the blond Teutons cannot expect to survive even under the climatic conditions prevailing throughout most of the United States. Woodruff displayed all of the color feelings aroused by imperialism and none of its buoyant idealism. Much the same can be said of the gloomy tracts that California's leading race-thinker, Homer Lea, wrote in the next few years on the decline of American militancy and the spread of the Yellow Peril.

Among other racial nationalists the reaction from imperial euphoria brought back the vague fears of the nineties about the Anglo-Saxons' stamina. They spoke of the old stock becoming decadent and being elbowed aside, of the Anglo-Saxon race as doomed, of the native Americans suffering from all manner of moral, physical, and psychic deterioration, due in large measure to immigration. Since nativism was at a low ebb in the early years of the century, the complaints usually sounded a mournful note rather than a belligerent or defiant one. Professor George E. Woodberry, one of the old-guard literary critics, even tried to find some comfort in the dismal spectacle. Lecturing on "race power" in literature in 1903, he suggested that the dissolution of the English race would fulfill a historic, sacrificial principle by which each great race succumbs in order to bequeath its heritage to a broader humanity.

A less spiritually satisfying but more scientific explanation of the Anglo-Saxon's flagging energies could be found in Francis A. Walker's theory that immigration discouraged reproduction among the older stock. The theory was more and more widely discussed, with hardly anyone equipped statistically to challenge it. Instead of critical scrutiny, Walker's sober argument now got a popular currency as it was inflated into the more grandiose concept of "race suicide." This happened in a curiously roundabout fashion. In 1901 Edward A. Ross used Walker's ideas in an address before the American Academy of Political and Social Science to explain how unchecked Asiatic immigration might lead to the extinction of the American people. When a higher race quietly eliminates itself rather than endure the competition of a lower one, said Ross, it is committing suicide. At the time, Ross was too confident of America's powers of assimilation to write about European immigration in these terms. Before "race suicide" did become directly pertinent to the problem which Walker himself had had in mind, Theodore Roosevelt simplified it into an argument against birth control. For all of his booming optimism, Roosevelt could not entirely repress lurking doubts over the future. His nativist tendencies being in check, he discharged his anxieties through vague, thundering appeals to mothers to arrest the suicide of "the race" by having more children.

The President's campaign for fecundity popularized the notion of race suicide. During the period from 1905 through 1909 the general magazines published over thirty-five articles dealing directly with the topic. Once it became a minor national phobia, the original, nativistic implications of the idea speedily reasserted themselves. In reply to a Rooseveltian tirade, *Harper's Weekly* remarked caustically in 1905 that exhortation would have little effect on the native birth rate as long as unlimited European immigration continued to reduce it. Soon books were being written to warn that race suicide would "toll the passing of this great Anglo-Teuton people" and the surrender of the nation "to the Latin and the Hun." In the end, the whole discussion probably caused more race-thinking than reproduction. At least it brought to a wider audience the racial pessimism previously confined to a limited group of upper-class intellectuals.

It would be wrong to suppose, however, that any despairing note sounded very loudly or struck very deeply during the first decade of the twentieth century. Pessimistic anxieties crept about the fringes of American thought; at the heart of it was a supreme confidence. As the ebullience of imperialism ebbed away, much of the slack in American spirits was taken up by another enthusiasm. Progressivism inherited and sustained a good deal of the verve and exuberance which imperialism had generated. Many of the empire-builders of 1900 became apostles of social reform in the following years, their crusading élan shifting from expansion abroad to improvement at home. As long as progressivism kept that psychological tone, as long as it radiated a sense of promise and victory, it limited the impact of imperialism's other heritage of race-thinking.

Furthermore, the premises of progressive thought, as well as its optimistic spirit, blunted the force of Anglo-Saxon nativism. By renewing faith in democracy, progressivism tended to challenge belief in racial inequalities. By concentrating on environmental reconstruction, it implicitly disputed all racial determinisms. At a time when politicians, public, and intelligentsia, alike, quickened with a vision of intelligence recasting environment, the Anglo-Saxon tradition faced powerful opposing currents. If nativistic intellectuals were to capitalize on the race consciousness left in the wake of imperialism, they would have to breast the mainstream of progressive thought.

Thus the race-thinkers of the early twentieth century belonged in considerable degree to the same social minority that had sustained the Anglo-Saxon tradition during the late nineteenth. Conservative patricians were less likely than most Americans to share the prevailing optimism and environmentalism. To men like Lodge and the founders of the Immigration Restriction League, like Major Woodruff and Professor Woodberry, the crusading spirit of progressivism brought little solace. Surely reform was not restoring the more stable social order of the past, and those who above all valued family and tradition often relapsed into a gloomy view of their racial future once the appeal of imperialism faded. A number of patrician intellectuals, it is true, were caught up in the wave of social reform and surrendered some of their ethnic worries in the process. Theodore Roosevelt, for example, who had applauded Lodge's racial tirade in 1896 and rushed off to France an order for Le Bon's books, by 1904 was calling into question the whole tendency to use racial criteria in judging nationalities. But others of Roosevelt's background felt increasingly their own social displacement in a democratic age and hugged ever more tightly—in Henry James's words—"the honor that sits astride of the consecrated English tradition."

In short, when imperialism subsided, the Anglo-Saxon tradition moved again in the nativist direction it had taken during the early and mid-nineties. Yet the subsequent compulsions of empire-building and progressive reform decisively affected its course—one in a positive, the other in a negative, way. Imperialism left a heritage of race-feelings that enriched the emotional appeal of Anglo-Saxon nativism; progressivism challenged its intellectual basis. The democratic, environmentalist outlook adopted by most of the leading social scientists and historians of the Progres-

sive era weakened the intellectual respectability of the confused, ill-defined concepts of race prevalent in the nineteenth century. To vindicate its intellectual pretensions and rationalize its emotional tone, the Anglo-Saxon tradition more than ever needed restatement in the form of a scientific law. And this was exactly what happened.

ENTER THE NATURAL SCIENTISTS

In the 1890's nativist intellectuals had barely begun to think of European races as a biological threat or to associate national survival with racial purity. Even Walker's birth-rate theory offered no logical reason to suppose that the country would suffer from the replacement of old stock by new. Perhaps the most serious intellectual handicap of American race-thinkers before the twentieth century was the lack of a general scientific principle from which to argue the prepotency of heredity in human affairs. But at the turn of the century, when social science and history came increasingly under the sway of environmental assumptions, biologists advanced dramatic claims for heredity and even helped to translate them into a political and social creed.

The new science of heredity came out of Europe about 1900 and formed the first substantial contribution of European thought to American nativism after the time of Darwin. The study of inheritance suddenly leaped into prominence and assumed a meaningful pattern from the discovery of the long-unnoticed work of Gregor Mendel and its convergence with August Weismann's theory of germinal continuity. Together, these hypotheses demonstrated the transmission from generation to generation of characteristics that obeyed their own fixed laws without regard to the external life of the organism.

Amid the excitement caused in English scientific circles by these continental discoveries, Sir Francis Galton launched the eugenics movement. Galton, who was England's leading Darwinian scientist, had long been producing statistical studies on the inheritance of all sorts of human abilities and deficiencies. But it was only in the favorable climate of the early twentieth century that he started active propaganda for uplifting humanity by breeding from the best and restricting the offspring of the worst. To Galton, eugenics was both a science and a kind of secular religion. It certified that the betterment of society depends largely on improvement of the "inborn qualities" of "the human breed," and Galton preached this message with evangelical fervor. Thus he provided biologists and physicians, excited over the new genetic theories, with a way of converting their scientific interests into a program of social salvation—a program based wholly on manipulation of the supposedly omnipotent forces of heredity.

In the latter part of the 1900's the eugenics movement got under way in the United States, where it struck several responsive chords. Its emphasis on unalterable human inequalities confirmed the patricians' sense of superiority; its warnings over the multiplication of the unfit and the sterility of the best people synchronized with the discussion of race suicide. Yet the eugenicists' dedication to a positive program of "race improvement" through education and state action gave the movement an air of reform, enabling it to flourish in the backwash of progressivism while still ministering to conservative sensibilities. By 1910, therefore, eugenicists were catching the public ear. From then through 1914, according to one tabulation, the general magazines carried more articles on eugenics than on the three questions of slums, tenements, and living standards, combined.

The leading eugenicist in America was Charles B. Davenport, a zoologist of tremendous ambition and drive who established the country's first research center in genetics at Cold Spring Harbor, Long Island. Davenport's father, a descendant of one of the Puritan founders of New England, was a genealogist who traced his ancestry back to 1086, and Davenport himself often mourned "that the best of that grand old New England stock is dying out through failure to reproduce." His early experiments at Cold Spring Harbor were devoted to testing the Mendelian principles in animal breeding; by 1907 he was beginning to apply them to the study of human heredity. In 1910 he persuaded Mrs. E. H. Harriman to finance a Eugenics Record Office adjacent to his laboratory with the aim of compiling an index of the American population and advising individuals and local societies on eugenical problems. Over a course of years she poured more than half a million dollars into the agency, while Davenport—already one of America's leading biologists—gave the rest of his life to studying the inheritance of human traits and spreading the gospel of eugenics. An indefatigable organizer, Davenport was also one of the leaders of the American Breeders' Association, where the eugenics agitation first centered. Established in 1903 by practical plant and animal breeders who wanted to keep in touch with the new theoretical advances, the association enlarged its field in 1907 to embrace eugenics.

The racial and nativistic implications of eugenics soon became apparent. From the eugenicists' point of view, the immigration question was at heart a biological one, and to them admitting "degenerate breeding stock" seemed one of the worst sins the nation could commit against itself. It was axiomatic to these naïve Mendelians that environment could never modify an immigrant's germ plasm and that only a rigid selection of the best immigrant stock could improve rather than pollute endless generations to come. Since their hereditarian convictions made virtually every symptom of social disorganization look like an inherited trait, the recent immigration could not fail to alarm them. Under the influence of eugenic thinking, the burgeoning mental hygiene movement picekd up the cry. Disturbed at the number of hereditary mental defectives supposedly pouring into the country, the psychiatrists who organized the National Committee for Mental Hygiene succeeded in adding to the immigration bill of 1914 an odd provision excluding cases of "constitutional psychopathic inferiority." By that time many critics of immigration were echoing the pleas in scientific periodicals for a "rational" policy "based upon a noble culture of racial purity."

None were quicker or more influential in relating eugenics to racial nativism than the haughty Bostonians who ran the Immigration Restriction League. Prescott F. Hall had always had a hypochondriac's fascination with medicine and biology, and his associate, Robert DeCourcy Ward, was a professional scientist. They had shied away from racial arguments in the nineties, but in the less favorable atmosphere of the new century their propaganda very much needed a fresh impulse. As early as 1906 the league leaders pointed to the new genetic principles in emphasizing the opportunity that immigration regulation offered to control America's future racial development. Two years later they learned of the eugenics sentiment developing in the American Breeders' Association. They descended upon it, and soon they were dominating its immigration activities. The association organized a permanent committee on immigration, of which Hall became chairman and Ward secretary. Ward proceeded to read papers on immigration legislation before meetings of eugenicists, and for a time the two considered changing the name of their own organization to the "Eugenic Immigration League." Meanwhile they seized every occasion to publicize the dogma that science decrees restrictions on the new immigration for the conservation of the "American race."

Obviously the eugenics movement had crucial importance for race-thinking at a time when racial presuppositions were seriously threatened in the intellectual world. But basically the importance of eugenics was transitional and preparatory. It vindicated the hereditarian assumptions of the Anglo-Saxon tradition; it protected and indeed encouraged loose talk about race in reputable circles; and in putting race-thinking on scientific rather than romantic premises it went well beyond the vague Darwinian analogies of the nineteenth century. On the other hand, eugenics failed utterly to supply a racial typology. In their scientific capacity, the eugenicists—like their master Galton—studied individual traits

and reached conclusions on individual differences. When they generalized the defects of individual immigrants into those of whole ethnic groups, their science deserted them and their phrases became darkly equivocal. Indeed, the more logical and consistent eugenicists maintained that America could improve its "race" by selecting immigrants on the ground of their individual family histories regardless of their national origins.

In the end the race-thinkers had to look to anthropology to round out a naturalistic nativism. Anthropology alone could classify the peoples of Europe into hereditary types that would distinguish the new immigration from older Americans; it alone might arrange these races in a hierarchy of merit and thereby prove the irremediable inferiority of the newcomers; and anthropology would have to collaborate with genetics to show wherein a mixture of races physically weakens the stronger.

American anthropology remained cautiously circumspect on these points. The influence of the foreign-born progressive, Franz Boas, was already great; in 1911 he published the classic indictment of race-thinking, *The Mind of Primitive Man*. In the absence of interest on the part of American anthropologists, a perfected racism depended on amateur handling of imported ideas. In a climate of opinion conditioned by the vogues of race suicide and eugenics, however, it is not surprising that scientifically minded nativists found the categories and concepts they needed without assistance from American anthropologists.

Again the inspiration came from Europe. There, chiefly in France and Germany, during the latter half of the nineteenth century anthropologists furnished the scientific credentials and speculative thinkers the general ideas out of which a philosophy of race took shape. The first of the thoroughgoing racists, Count J. A. de Gobineau, reached a limited audience of proslavery thinkers in America on the eve of the Civil War and then was forgotten. His successors were even less effective. Once in a while an immigrant writer tried to translate some of this literature into terms that might appeal to an American public, but the stuff simply was not read. Not until the beginning of the twentieth century did the invidious anthropological theories which had been accumulating in Europe for over thirty years reach a significant American audience. And when they did, they were delivered in a characteristically American package.

William Z. Ripley was a brilliant young economist who had the kind of mind that refuses to stay put. In the mid-nineties, before he was thirty years old, Ripley was teaching economics at the Massachusetts Institute of Technology, while simultaneously developing a unique course of lectures at Columbia University on the role of geography in human affairs. In its conception this course reflected Ripley's conviction of the basic importance of environmental conditions in molding the life of man; but he quickly came up against the problem of race. The question led him to the controversies among continental scholars on the anthropological traits of European peoples, and he chose the locale of Europe as a crucial test of the interplay of race and environment. In *The Races of Europe*, a big, scholarly volume appearing in 1899, he anatomized the populations of the continent, pointing temperately but persistently to ways in which physiological traits seemed to reflect geographical and social conditions.

This was cold comfort to nativists, but the book had another significance apart from the author's well-hedged thesis. Ripley organized into an impressive synthesis a tripartite classification of white men which European ethnologists had recently developed. For the first time, American readers learned that Europe was not a land of "Aryans" or Goths subdivided into vaguely national races such as the Anglo-Saxon, but rather the seat of three races discernible by physical measurements: a northern race of tall, blond longheads which Ripley called Teutonic; a central race of stocky roundheads which he called Alpine; and a southern race of slender, dark longheads which he called Mediterranean. Here was a powerful weapon for nativists bent on distin-guishing absolutely between old and new immigrations, but to make it serviceable Ripley's data would have to be untangled from his environmentalist assumptions.

It is ironical that Ripley himself did some of the untangling. For all of his scholarly caution he could not entirely suppress an attachment to the Teutonic race that reflected very mildly the rampant Teutonism of many of the authorities on which he relied. In the early twentieth century the new genetic hypotheses and a growing alarm over the new immigration turned his attention from environmental to inherited influences. He began to talk about race suicide and to wonder about the hereditary consequences of the mixture of European races occurring in America.

Before abandoning anthropology completely to concentrate in economics, Ripley delivered in 1908 a widely publicized address in which he suggested an answer to the old problem of how the crossing of superior and inferior races can drag down the former. His roving eye had come upon the experiments that some of the Mendelian geneticists were making on plant and animal hybrids. Hugo De Vries and others were demonstrating how hybridization sometimes caused a reassertion of latent characters inherited from a remote ancestor. The concept of reversion was an old one, discussed by Darwin himself, but the rise of genetics brought it into new prominence. Ripley fastened on the idea and raised the question whether the racial intermixture under way in America might produce a reversion to a primitive type. In contrast to the theory of race suicide, this doctrine—torn from the context of genetics and applied to the typology of European races—provided a thoroughly biological explanation of the foreign peril. Presumably race suicide might be arrested by legislation and by education raising the immigrant's standard of living; but reversion seemed remorseless. All of the pieces from which a sweeping statement of racial nativism might be constructed were now on hand.

The man who put the pieces together was Madison Grant, intellectually the most important nativist in recent American history. All of the trends in race-thinking converged upon him. A Park Avenue bachelor, he was the most lordly of patricians. His family had adorned the social life of Manhattan since colonial times, and he was both an expert genealogist and a charter member of the Society of Colonial Wars. Always he resisted doggedly any intrusion of the hoi polloi. On his deathbed he was still battling to keep the public from bringing cameras into the zoo over which he had long presided.

In addition to a razor-sharp set of patrician values, Grant also had an extensive acquaintance with the natural sciences and a thoroughly naturalistic temper of mind. Beginning as a wealthy sportsman and hunter, he was the founder and later the chairman of the New York Zoological Society, where he associated intimately with leading biologists and eugenicists. In the early years of the twentieth century he published a series of monographs on North American animals—the moose, the caribou, the Rocky Mountain goat. He picked up a smattering of Mendelian concepts and, unlike his eugenicist friends, read a good deal of physical anthropology too. Ripley's work furnished his main facts about European man, but he also went behind Ripley to many of the more extreme European ethnologists. Thus Grant was well supplied with scientific information yet free from a scientist's scruple in interpreting it.

By 1910 Grant's racial concepts were clearly formed and thoroughly articulated with a passionate hatred of the new immigration. He showed little concern over relations between whites and Negroes or Orientals. His deadliest animus focused on the Jews, whom he saw all about him in New York. More broadly, what upset him was the general mixture of European races under way in America; for this process was irretrievably destroying racial purity, the foundation of every national and cultural value.

Grant's philippic appeared finally in 1916. It bore the somber title, *The Passing of the Great Race*, summing up the aristocratic pessimism that had troubled nativist intellectuals since the 1890's. Everywhere Grant saw

the ruling race of the western world on the wane yet heedless of its fate because of a "fatuous belief" in the power of environment to alter heredity. In the United States he observed the deterioration going on along two parallel lines: race suicide and reversion. As a result of Mendelian laws, Grant pontificated, we know that different races do not really blend. The mixing of two races "gives us a race reverting to the more ancient, generalized and lower type." Thus "the cross between any of the three European races and a Jew is a Jew." In short, a crude interpretation of Mendelian genetics provided the rationale for championing racial purity.

After arguing the issue of race versus physical environment, Grant assumed a racial determination of culture. Much of the book rested on this assumption, for the volume consisted essentially of a loose-knit sketch of the racial history of Europe. The Alpines have always been a race of peasants. The Mediterraneans have at least shown artistic and intellectual proclivities. But the blond conquerors of the North constitute "the white man par excellence." Following the French scientist Joseph Deniker, Grant designated this great race Nordic. To it belongs the political and military genius of the world, the daring and pride that make explorers, fighters, rulers, organizers, and aristocrats. In the early days, the American population was purely Nordic, but now the swarms of Alpine, Mediterranean, and Jewish hybrids threaten to extinguish the old stock unless it reasserts its class and racial pride by shutting them out.

So the book turned ultimately into a defense of both class and racial consciousness, the former being dependent on the latter. The argument broadened from nativism to an appeal for aristocracy as a necessary correlative in maintaining racial purity. Democracy, Grant maintained, violates the scientific facts of heredity; and he was obviously proud to attribute feudalism to the Nordics. Furthermore, Grant assaulted Christianity for its humanitarianism bias in favor of the weak and its consequent tendency to break down racial pride. Even national consciousness ranked second to race consciousness in Grant's scale of values.

This boldness and sweep gave *The Passing of the Great Race* particular significance. Its reception and its impact on public opinion belong to a later stage in the history of American nativism, but its appearance before America's entry into the First World War indicates that the old Anglo-Saxon tradition had finally emerged in at least one mind as a systematic, comprehensive world view. Race-thinking was basically at odds with the values of democracy and Christianity, but earlier nativists had always tried either to ignore the conflict or to mediate between racial pride and the humanistic assumptions of America's major traditions. Grant, relying on what he thought was scientific truth, made race the supreme value and repudiated all others inconsistent with it.

This, at last, was racism.

part four

Intergroup Contact in America: Methods and Problems of Adjustment

We have previously emphasized that the primary focus of inquiry in the analysis of racial and ethnic relations should be upon the dominant group. By definition, this group possesses superior societal power, including the capacity to structure, in large measure, its relationship with the minority. It is nearly always the cultural patterns, activities, habits, mores, and laws of the majority group that become normative and by which the minority group is measured and judged. Therefore, even in a section in which the principal focus is minority-group adjustment, we must begin with an analysis of the role—or roles—assumed by the majority in the process of intergroup contact. Later, we shall discuss the fact that structural and cultural features of the minority group comprise important variables to be considered as well. Thorough analysis of minority-group adjustment should center upon the interaction of majority and minority, within a particular historical, political, economic, and cultural context.

The central question confronting any society in which ethnic stratification occurs is this: What should be the nature and extent of intergroup contact? According to Milton M. Gordon, the dominant group in America has taken three approaches to the issue of minority-group adaptation.

These three central ideological tendencies may be referred to as "Anglo-conformity" . . . , "the melting pot," and "cultural pluralism." . . . we may say that the "Anglo-conformity" theory demanded the complete renunciation of the immigrant's ancestral culture in favor of the behavior and values of the Anglo-Saxon core group; the "melting pot" idea envisaged a biological merger of the Anglo-Saxon peoples with other immigrant groups and a blending of their respective cultures into a new indigenous American type; and "cultural pluralism" postulated the preservation of the communal life and significant portions of the culture of the later immigrant groups within the context of American citizenship and political and economic integration into American society. Various individual changes were rung on these three central themes by particular proponents of assimilation goals, . . . but the central tendencies remain.[1]

Gordon's categories can be placed on a continuum ranging from lesser to greater minority-group integrity and autonomy. Each of the types that Gordon delineated would merge imperceptibly with the adjacent type. (Anglo-conformity is much closer to the melting pot than to pluralism, etc.)

The typology devised by Gordon has been widely employed by social scientists who have discussed American ethnic relations. For the typology to be more inclusive and to possess wider applicability than to the American scene alone, two slight modifications are necessary. In the first place, the culture-specific term *Anglo-conformity* should be replaced by by the more general *transmuting pot,*[2] which implies that all minority groups must divest themselves of their distinctive ethnic characteristics and adopt those of the dominant group. This position, which has long characterized America's immigration policy, forms the basis of Australia's immigration policy as well. As an Australian Minister for Immigration declared:

It is cardinal with us that Australia, though attracting many different people, should remain a substantially homogeneous society, that there is no place in it for enclaves or minorities, that all whom we admit to reside permanently should be equal here and capable themselves of becoming substantially Australians after a few years of residence, with their children in the next generation wholly so. . . .[3]

Secondly, Gordon's types can be logically extended. The transmuting pot, on the one hand, and pluralism, on the other, do not exhaust all theoretical possibilities. *Genocide* and/or *exclusion* on one extreme would permit less minority autonomy, obviously, than a policy based upon

[1] Milton M. Gordon, *Assimilation in American Life: The Role of Race, Religion, and National Origins* (New York: Oxford University Press, 1964), pp. 85–86.
[2] The term is Will Herberg's. See his *Protestant-Catholic-Jew* (Garden City, N.Y.: Doubleday, 1955).
[3] Hubert Opperman, "Australia's Immigration Policy." Paper delivered to the Youth and Student Seminar, Canberra, Australia, May 28, 1966.

a conception that the process of inter-ethnic contact resembled a trans-muting pot. On the other extreme, *separatism,* or complete autonomy for the minority group, would comprise a more expansive ideology and situa-tion than would pluralism. When Gordon's types and the two additional types are placed on a continuum, the result is the following:

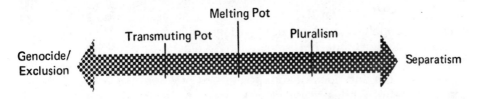

These five conceptions—with the exception of genocide—may be em-braced by either the dominant group or the subordinate group in a soci-ety. The greater the congruence between majority and minority in their assimilation ideology, the less likely that friction between the two groups will become intense.

The terms *transmuting pot* and *melting pot* imply the intermingling of majority and minority groups, while *exclusion, pluralism,* and *separatism* imply some form of minority-group separation from the rest of society. But the crucial distinctions between ideologies are not based on separa-tion or integration, but on two other variables: whether the position of the minority group within the society is voluntarily or involuntarily arrived at, whether the minority group is relatively autonomous or relatively power-less. Thus, *exclusion* refers to separation by decision of the majority, while *separatism* means that the minority group has decided to place itself apart. Likewise, *transmuting pot* or *Anglo-conformity* indicates par-ticipation in society on the terms of the dominant group, while pluralism refers to societal participation on terms essentially acceptable to the minority group. As we suggested in the introduction to Part Two, the ten-sion between the polar positions is a worldwide characteristic of majority-minority relations.

The case of the American Indians illustrates these dynamics. In the early years of the republic, U.S. policy towards the American Indian moved from genocide ("the only good Indian is a dead Indian") to ex-clusion (the reservation system). Since the late nineteenth century, the ideology of Anglo-conformity has dominated, with exclusion an accept-able alternative. For example, as Lurie observed in Part Three, the pur-pose of governmental actions such as the Indian Allotment Act of 1887 was to force the Indians to assimilate. While many Indians would have welcomed separatism, their confinement to reservations has more closely resembled exclusion, since the reservations have been almost totally con-trolled by the federal government and other extensions of white society (e.g., missionaries).

Neither Anglo-conformity nor exclusion allows for minority-group free choice. To join the larger society on the majority's terms means to cease being an Indian; to remain with family and friends on the reservation is to have one's life choices and chances severely circumscribed by powerful external forces. Yet in spite of these exigencies, there seems little likelihood that the stubbornly purposeful maintenance of Indian traditions, values, and sense of aloofness from the rest of the nation will be surrendered. Even in urban areas, where increasing numbers have migrated since World War II, Indians are resisting assimilation and forming their own ongoing communities, as Steele points out in "The Acculturation/Assimilation Model in Urban Indian Studies: A Critique."

The Black experience in America has reflected similar tensions between freedom and constriction, power and powerlessness. The ideological position of Whites toward Blacks has consistently been exclusionist (for example, the African colonization movement and, especially, segregation) with some traces of Anglo-conformity. Black response over the centuries has included at times a desire for separation—as seen, for example, in the Back to Africa campaign of Marcus Garvey and in the ideology of the Nation of Islam (Black Muslims)—but for the most part the principal goal has been to enter American society on an equal basis with Whites. For decades, until the mid-sixties, most Black self-examination, negotiation, and protest had been oriented toward obtaining the acceptance of White America and integration into the mainstream of American society. (This position is reflected in Milton Gordon's statement, written in 1961, that "the ideological attachment of Negroes to their communal separation is not conspicuous." [See the first article in this section.]) While studies have demonstrated that a significant portion of the Black populace has not wavered from that basic position, the previous consensus on this issue has dissipated (see "Black Militancy," in Part Six.) Partly in response to the lack of acceptance by White Americans, and repulsed by the fact that cultural emasculation has appeared to be a prerequisite for even limited admission into the larger society, younger Blacks in particular have increasingly assumed pluralist or separatist stances.[4]

However, American sociologists have been less exclusionist in their orientation than the society as a whole. On the other hand, they have suffered from a different myopia, according to L. Paul Metzger, in "American Sociology and Black Assimilation: Conflicting Perspectives." Metzger asserts that sociologists have consistently employed an assimilation model, which assumes that

the incorporation of America's ethnic and racial groups into the mainstream culture is virtually inevitable. . . . Successful assimilation, moreover, has been viewed as synonymous with equality of opportunity and upward mobility for the members of minority groups; "opportunity," in this

[4] This is part of the explanation of the rise of the Black Power movement offered by Stokely Carmichael and Charles V. Hamilton. For further elaboration, see their *Black Power: The Politics of Liberation in America* (New York: Vintage Books, 1967).

system, is the opportunity to discard one's ethnicity and to partake fully in the "American Way of Life"; in this sense, assimilation is viewed as the embodiment of the democratic ethos.

The assimilation model of racial interaction assumes that post–World War II newcomers to American cities—blacks, American Indians, Chicanos, and Puerto Ricans—are reenacting the processes of migration and adaptation to American cities of European and Asian immigrants earlier in the nation's history; in the words of Irving Kristol, "the Negro today is like the immigrant of yesterday."[5]

According to this perspective, the latest migrants, like previous immigrant groups, have entered urban areas basically unskilled, and because they are the most recent arrivals, they have not yet attained sufficient power in various areas of city life (schools, jobs, politics) to represent their interests. Consequently, they are subjected to the deleterious conditions (high crime and delinquency, slum housing, dependence on public welfare) encountered by previous waves of immigrants whose descendants have today improved their condition and become absorbed into the mainstream of American society. Thus the present onerous conditions of the most recent urban migrants are merely a stage in the inevitable assimilation process; it is merely a matter of time before Blacks, Indians, Chicanos, and Puerto Ricans become fully assimilated.

As indicated above, the assimiliation, or ethnic, model frequently used in the sociology of majority-minority relations is inadequate since it fails to explain both the oppression of racial minority groups and their continued separation from "mainstream" America. Consequently, many social scientists have turned to an alternative model that specifically attempts to account for these crucial variables.[6] This conceptualization—colonialism—is employed extensively in this section.[7] Robert Blauner, in "Colonized and Immigrant Minorities," specifically contrasts the colonial model to the immigrant or assimilation model. Both Blauner and Joan Moore maintain that colonialism is a major conceptual tool in the analysis of majority-minority relations in the United States. The term and its variants are also employed in Robert Moore's analysis of Northern Ireland and Ossenberg's article on French Canada in Part Two, in Thomas's description of the Sioux reservation and Allen's analysis of Black capitalism in Part Five, and in Skolnick's discussion of Black militancy in Part Six.

The concept of colonialism was not introduced to sociological dis-

---

[5] Irving Kristol, "The Negro Today is Like the Immigrant Yesterday," *New York Times Magazine,* Sept. 11, 1966, p. 50.

[6] See, for example, William J. Wilson, "Race Relations Models and Explanations of Ghetto Behavior," in *Nation of Nations: The Ethnic Experience and the Racial Crisis,* ed. Peter I. Rose (New York: Random House, 1972), pp. 259–275.

[7] This discussion draws in part on C. Hoy Steele, "American Indians and Urban Life: A Community Study." Ph.D. dissertation, University of Kansas, 1972).

cussion of race relations in the United States by sociologists, but rather by Black activists and writers. As the Skolnick Report indicates, black Americans viewed anti-colonialist activity in the Third World, particularly Africa, with intense interest; in time, anti-colonialism became an ideological tool in generating the Black Revolution and changing its thrust from a civil rights to a liberation emphasis. As American blacks came to define their status in America as a state of oppression analogous to African colonialism, an entire lexicon of *colony* terms appeared.[8] In 1962, Harold Cruse wrote of *domestic colonialism;* three years later, Kenneth Clark likened Harlem to a colony. Carmichael and Hamilton employed *internal colonialism* in their influential *Black Power.* Robert Allen followed Cruse in the use of *domestic colonialism;* he also discussed *domestic neo-colonialism* and referred to Black America as a *semicolony.*[9] Martin Luther King, Jr., Malcolm X, and Eldridge Cleaver also made use of the colonial concept.[10]

Robert K. Thomas, Robert Blauner, and Joan Moore were among the earliest social scientists to attempt to apply the concept of colonialism to the analysis of American majority-minority relations. In a companion piece to "Powerless Politics" (Part Five), Thomas characterized the Indian reservation system in America as probably "the most complete colonial system in the world. . . ."[11] But Blauner has been the dominant figure in delineating the concept of *internal colonialism,* which may be distinguished from *classic colonialism.* The latter is characterized by the outright conquest of indigenous people, who are then dominated and controlled by the imposition of alien institutions through legally established bureaucracies (e.g., the Indian reservation system). Internal colonialism, according to Blauner, is exemplified in the situation of Black people in this country. Here, the form of colonialism may be all but invisible, but the processes that occur (i.e., colonization) are similar if not identical to

[8] For a discussion of the change in meaning of *colony* words since the early part of this century, see Everett C. Hughes, "Colonies, Colonization and Colonialism," (Paper presented at the annual meeting of the American Ethnological Society, Wilmington Beach, North Carolina, March, 1973), mimeographed.

[9] Harold Cruse, *Rebellion or Revolution?* (New York: Apollo Editions, 1969); Kenneth B. Clark, *Dark Ghetto* (New York: Harper & Row, 1965); Carmichael and Hamilton, *Black Power;* Robert L. Allen, *Black Awakening in Capitalist America: An Analytic History* (Garden City, N.Y.: Doubleday, 1969).

[10] Martin Luther King, Jr., *Where Do We Go from Here: Chaos or Community?* (New York: Harper & Row, 1967); Malcolm X, *Malcolm X on Afro-American History,* Introduction by George Breitman (New York: Merit Publishers, 1967); Eldridge Cleaver, *Soul on Ice* (New York: McGraw-Hill, 1968). These and other black writers who likened black America to a colonized people are discussed extensively in Robert Loren Shelton, "Black Revolution: The Definition and Meaning of 'Revolution' in the Writings and Speeches of Selected Nationally Prominent Negro Americans, 1963–1968" (Ph.D. dissertation, Boston University, 1970), Chap. 4.

[11] Robert K. Thomas, "Colonalism: Classic and Internal," *New University Thought* 4 (1966–67): 39.

those of classic colonialism.[12] As mentioned above, attention to process is crucial to the analysis of majority-minority relations.

Blauner suggests four processes of colonization. "The first . . . is that of a forced entry into the larger society or metropolitan domain." In other words, the colonized group comes into contact with its oppressor involuntarily (cf. Lieberson, Part One).

> The second [condition] is subjection to various forms of unfree labor that greatly restrict the physical and social mobility of the group and its participation in the political arena. The third is a cultural policy of the colonizer that constrains, transforms, or destroys original values, orientations, and ways of life.

Fourth, the colonized group is "administered," "managed," and "manipulated" by the dominant power.[13] The analyses of Blauner, Moore, and Thomas illustrate these processes.

Two other processes of colonialism or colonization may be suggested. Allen argues that the colonizing power manipulates a group of the colonized to act as a buffer between itself and the main mass of the colonized and dominated group.[14] It also exploits the colonized group economically. In his article in Part Five, Allen suggests that today these two components function hand in hand with respect to Black Americans: ". . . the old Black elite of Tomming preachers, teachers, and businessmen-politicians" has given way to a new "black capitalist and managerial class . . . which will have closest contact with corporate America and which is to act as a conduit for its wishes." This program of "domestic neocolonialism"[15] was designed, according to Allen, "by America's corporate elite—the major owners, managers, and directors of the giant corporations, banks, and foundations which increasingly dominate the economy and society as a whole—because they believe that the urban revolts pose a serious threat to economic and social stability." So-called Black capitalists "administering" the ghetto, it is supposed, will siphon off ghetto anger against White society, thus protecting the economic interests of the corporate elite.

Joan Moore's analysis of *economic colonialism,* Steele's discussion of the exploitation of Indian economic resources, and Thomas's descrip-

---

[12] Blauner's initial discussion of the processes of colonialism is found in "Internal Colonialism and Ghetto Revolt," *Social Problems* 16 (1969):393–408.

[13] Blauner, "Internal Colonialism and Ghetto Revolt," p. 396. Blauner's second process of colonization, above, did not appear in the *Social Problems* article; in its place was racism, which is also discussed extensively in the essay included in this section.

[14] Allen, *Black Awakening in Capitalist America,* p. 11.

[15] Neocolonialism refers to one nation's effective control over another through economic domination rather than by occupation and formal government. Economic benefits generally accrue to the controlling nation.

tion of economic powerlessness and the problems of the tribal council system on the Pine Ridge Reservation are relevant to these last two processes of colonialism. (See also Ossenberg's mention of American neo-colonialism with respect to Canada in Part Two, and the introduction to that section).

The notion of "colonized" minority groups in America as somehow distinct from "immigrant" minorities has not been unanimously embraced by social scientists;[16] nor has the colonial model yet succeeded in supplanting the assimilation model in the social science lexicon. Like all concepts, colonialism has received legitimate criticisms. As Blauner indicates, *colonized* and *immigrant* represent two ends of a continuum. What, then, of the middle? How many characteristics of colonialism have to be present for the concept to apply—half? two-thirds? all? (Do Appalachian Whites qualify?) Furthermore, since power, an important ingredient of colonialism, is also a factor in every other type of majority-minority relationship, what purpose is served by distinctions in kind as opposed to degree? Can the advance of time change a colonized minority group to an immigrant one? What of the differences among colonized groups? Many or all of these questions may not be fully answerable; they do indicate that the concept of colonialism lacks precision in certain respects.

In response to this critique, however, it can be argued that the concept's weakness is also its strength. While its imprecision makes it unfit for micro-level distinctions, its breadth and its historical, as well as contemporary, dimensions make it appropriate for macro-level analysis. It encompasses social structural, cultural, political, and economic realms. As Blauner notes at the conclusion of his article in this section, colonialism suggests a relationship between majority-minority relations in America and this country's international activities, a relationship seldom considered in most other analyses. The term effectively emphasizes the determinative importance of differential power. It illustrates patterns and processes of intergroup contact. Finally, in our view, it delineates real and significant differences between the treatment by the dominant society of colonized and immigrant minorities in this country. These differences must be acknowledged if a thorough understanding of intergroup adjustment is to be gained.

If the assimilation model is inadequate to fully comprehend the experience of racial minorities in the American experience, nevertheless millions of Americans are not identified by race, but by ethnic characteristics based upon differences in national origin and/or religion. In Blauner's terms, these groups are *immigrant* rather than *colonized* minorities, and the nature of their adaptation to American society is important in the study of majority-minority relations. Given the assumptions of the assimi-

---

[16] See, for example, Nathan Glazer, "Blacks and Ethnic Groups: The Difference, and the Political Difference It Makes," *Social Problems* 18 (1971): 444–461.

lation model, it is surprising that cultural identity and communal separation persist among many *old* and *new* immigrant communities. On the surface, these groups seem to have lost all behavioral and cultural distinctiveness, but upon closer examination manifestations of ethnic identity persist.[17] Indeed, as we note in Part Six, the decade of the seventies has witnessed a resurgence of positive concern for ethnic identity and assertions of the importance of retaining ethnic diversity within American society.

The articles by John Cogley ("Varieties of Catholicism") and Marshall Sklare ("American Jewry . . .") in this section and by Michael Novak in Part Six indicate that the actual assimilation of white ethnic groups has been less extensive than the assimilation model would admit. This raises important questions concerning the meaning of the assimilation processes in relation to American ethnic minorities. Gordon, in the lead article in this section, "Assimilation in Amerca: Theory and Reality," argues that assimilation is a multidimensional rather than a unitary phenomenon. His thesis is tha*t behavioral assimilation,* or *acculturation*—the acquisition of the cultural characteristics of the majority group and participation in the general affairs of the entire community—has been widespread in the history of inter-ethnic contacts in America; but *structural assimilation,* involving personal and intimate relations (e.g., friendship patterns and religious and recreational ties) is far from complete. Gordon feels that structural assimilation has occurred in only two areas: in the social structure of the intellectual community, which accepts intermixture of people from different backgrounds, and among individuals from different national backgrounds who share a common religion.

The notion that the merging of the three main religious streams (Protestant, Catholic, and Jew) represents the typical direction of assimilation among whites is commonly referred to as the *triple melting pot* thesis, and it provides a helpful—if imprecise—means of conceptually ordering a complex phenomenon. From our point of view, Gordon wisely qualifies his acceptance of the triple melting pot thesis, which seems to be most applicable to urban areas containing large concentrations of ethnic groups and least useful in rural areas where the percentage of Catholics and Jews in the population is small.[18]

Another factor weighing against a conceptualization that focuses on the merging of ethnic groups is the recent recognition of the striking diversity *within,* as well as among them—an awareness reflected in several articles in this section. In "Colonialism: the Case of the Mexican Americans" Joan W. Moore shows that the specific conditions of White-

[17] See Michael Parenti, "Ethnic Politics and the Persistence of Ethnic Identification," *American Political Science Review* 61 (September, 1967): 717–726.

[18] For a critique of the triple melting pot thesis, see John L. Thomas, "The Factor of Religion in the Selection of Marriage Mates," *American Sociological Review* 16, no. 4 (August, 1951): 487–491.

Chicano contact that were crucial in the later evolution of the minority group varied significantly in the three most populous Chicano areas. The nineteenth century "conquest of New Mexico by the United States was nearly bloodless," and traditional political and social structures of the Mexican elite and masses were maintained, facilitating their continued political participation in the United States. This historical pattern may be seen today, on the one hand, in the relatively large number of Chicano legislators in New Mexico and, on the other, in the major mass movement to appear among Mexican Americans—the *Alianza Federal de Mercedes,* led by Reies Tijerina. In Texas, by contrast, majority-minority relations have been characterized by violence. Pre-conquest political structures were destroyed by the Mexican War, and political intimidation continues today. Mexican Americans in Texas have almost no representation in conventional political institutions. California resembled Texas in the early period, and in this century it has been the scene of economic exploitation of Mexican laborers, who experienced "conscious dehumanization . . . in the service of the railroad and citrus industries. . . ." Chicanos in California have participated in political structures even less than their counterparts in Texas.

Sklare describes the extreme heterogeneity among immigrant and native-born American Jews. He states:

> Since the immigration of Jews to America extends over three centuries, we would expect it to include diverse strands. But among Jews such diversity has been even sharper than with most other groups, for Jews originated in different countries, frequently with contrasting traditions.

Indeed, as in the immigration from Russia following the Communist Revolution, Jews arriving in the United States from the same country sometimes brought widely divergent values, religious beliefs, behavioral patterns, and social institutions. A variety of experiences at different times within the receiving nation has heightened the unfamiliarity of Jews to Jews and, at times, has created ambivalent feelings between Jews of relatively "old" and "new" tenure in America.

The power of the Catholic Church to mold believers from many nations into a new American ethnic group—which the Irish-dominated hierarchy may have wished for—likewise should not be overestimated. As Cogley states, "many different Catholicisms have existed side by side since the first great wave of immigrants arrived on American shores." He suggests that, through national parishes, the Church was shaped more to fit each immigrant group's conception of what it should be than the reverse. And Blauner, though primarily intent upon presenting the distinctions between colonized and immigrant minorities—and thus emphasizing the homogeneity of each type—nevertheless enjoins against the notion that the colonized minorities "are all in the same bag." Several other articles in this section present the themes of intra-ethnic and inter-ethnic diversity less directly.

Much of the previous discussion has emphasized the role of the dominant group in setting the limits within which the subordinate group may function. We have also noted in passing that influences are recipro-cal. For example, Whites relate to a specific minority group—Indians, for example—in a particular way. This evokes a response from the Indians that another group—Chicanos, for example—would not have chosen. The nature of the response, in turn, influences future White actions with respect to the minority. In other words, exclusive attention to the major-ity group will not fully explain the differential responses of oppressed minority groups. Some minorities readily adjust to majority pressures for conformity, while others prove extremely resistant to adopting the stan-dards of the dominant group. Therefore, the social institutions and cul-tural inventory of a politically unequal group (including its "backlog of unique historicity," in Bryce-Laporte's terms) are important considera-tions in any analysis of majority-minority relations.

One of the most significant variables in the ability of a minority group to adapt readily to its environing society is the extent to which its values, cultural propensities, and goal-orientations are shared with the dominant group. A second and equally significant factor is the role of the social institutions of the minority group in mediating its experiences and com-munal life within the dominant society. The crucial nature of social in-stitutions is demonstrated in "Contrasts in the Community Organization of Chinese and Japanese in North America," by Stanford M. Lyman. Al-though both groups came to America as sojourners (see Bonacich, Part Two) and met roughly the same degree and kind of racial prejudice and discrimination, their adaptations to this country have been quite different, according to Lyman. Japanese culture, including value systems, family structure (individual units as opposed to individual families), occupational propensities, belief in "the unique character structure of each genera-tional group," and other traits, facilitated much more rapid acculturation than did Chinese culture. Thus Caudill and DeVos attribute the rapid and successful adjustment of first and second generation Japanese immi-grants largely to the "significant compatibility . . . between the value systems found in the American middle class structure."[19]

In contrast to the Japanese, the Chinese manifested a greater cul-tural disparity with the dominant American values. Moreover, as Lyman points out, the Chinese established an extensive set of communal insti-

[19] William Caudill and George DeVos, "Achievement, Culture and Personality: The Case of the Japanese Americans," *American Anthropologists* 58 (1956): 1107.

tutions, including businesses, trade and guild associations, recreation and vice enterprises, "clan associations, speech and territorial clubs, and secret societies. And behind the invisible wall that separates Chinatown from the metropolis the elites of these organizations conduct an unofficial government, legislating, executing, and adjudicating matters for their constituents." These institutions served to maintain traditional Chinese culture and thus precluded extensive assimilation with American culture.

Similarly, Fred L. Strodtbeck, in "Family Interaction, Values, and Achievement," found that Jewish goals, values, and cultural norms were more closely congruent with those of the receiving society than were the goals, values, and norms of Italian immigrants. Higher achievement levels of the Jews according to the usual American criteria of economic and status mobility could thus be explained. Sklare elaborates the role of the economic institutions of American Jews, which were important vehicles for actualizing their cultural values.

The crucial mediating role of social institutions is nowhere more apparent than among many Catholic ethnic groups, who viewed ethnic pluralism, not complete assimilation with Protestant America, as the appropriate means of adjusting to American society. The separate Catholic institutional system has been instrumental in reinforcing and perpetuating the identity of several ethnic constituents. As Cogley points out, it enabled each immigrant group more effectively to maintain a pluralistic stance, "in a nation which put more emphasis on conformity than it was always ready to acknowledge." Thus the Church stood as a visible symbol around which a multiplicity of ethnic communities were organized. The institutional system that was developed—most particularly the schools, but also including hospitals, orphanages, asylums, homes for the aged, publishing houses, charitable and athletic organizations, and informal social groups—integrated these ethnic communities and served to maintain their solidarity and identity for generations.

The Irish experience in America exemplifies the dynamics of this institutional separatism. Its effects were paradoxical; while their participation in the Catholic institutional system isolated the Irish from the larger society, the system served as an agency of acculturation to that society's values. Gordon's distinction between *behavioral* and *structural* assimilation is useful at this juncture. As noted above, the former refers to the acquisition by a minority group of the values, attitudes, and life styles of the majority—what has usually been referred to as "acculturation." *Structural assimilation,* on the other hand, occurs when social equality and interaction have occurred—in voluntary associations, informal cliques, institutional activities, and intermarriage—between majority and minority group. While the church-centered institutional system impeded structural assimilation for the Irish, it facilitated behavioral assimilation; though the Irish ultimately became integrated into the mainstream of American culture, their patterns of social interaction long remained intra-tribal.[20]

As can be seen from the preceding discussion, some of the articles chosen for inclusion in this section focus specifically on the adaptations of particular groups. For the most part, however, we have been concerned in organizing Part Four to direct attention to the *processes* of minority group adjustment to American life. Since the analysis of racial and ethnic relations in American society provides specific examples of general processes, it is hoped that some of the implications of this analysis can be extended to other societies as well.

[20] Norman R. Yetman, "The Irish Experience in America," in *Irish History and Culture*, ed. Harold Orel (Lawrence: University Press of Kansas, 1975).

16

Assimilation in America: Theory and Reality

Milton M. Gordon

Three ideologies or conceptual models have competed for attention on the American scene as explanations of the way in which a nation, in the beginning largely white, Anglo-Saxon, and Protestant, has absorbed over 41 million immigrants and their descendants from variegated sources and welded them into the contemporary American people. These ideologies are Anglo-conformity, the melting pot, and cultural pluralism. They have served at various times, and often simultaneously, as explanations of what has happened—descriptive models—and of what should happen—goal models. Not infrequently they have been used in such a fashion that it is difficult to tell which of these two usages the writer has had in mind. In fact, one of the more remarkable omissions in the history of American intellectual thought is the relative lack of close analytical attention given to the theory of immigrant adjustment in the United States by its social scientists.

The result has been that this field of

Milton M. Gordon is Professor of Sociology at The University of Massachusetts at Amherst.

Reprinted by permission from Daedalus, Journal of the American Academy of Arts and Sciences, Boston, Massachusetts, Volume 90, Number 2 (Spring 1961), pp. 263–85.
Author's Note: The materials of this article are based on a larger study of the meaning and implications of minority group assimilation in the United States, which I carried out for the Russell Sage Foundation and which was published in Assimilation in American Life (New York, 1964).

discussion—an overridingly important one since it has significant implications for the more familiar problems of prejudice, discrimination, and majority-minority group relations generally—has been largely preempted by laymen, representatives of belles lettres, philosophers, and apologists of various persuasions. Even from these sources the amount of attention devoted to ideologies of assimilation is hardly extensive. Consequently, the work of improving intergroup relations in America is carried out by dedicated professional agencies and individuals who deal as best they can with day-to-day problems of discriminatory behavior, but who for the most part are unable to relate their efforts to an adequate conceptual apparatus. Such an apparatus would, at one and the same time, accurately describe the present structure of American society with respect to its ethnic groups (I shall use the term "ethnic group" to refer to any racial, religious, or national-origins collectivity), and allow for a considered formulation of its assimilation or integration goals for the foreseeable future. One is reminded of Alice's distraught question in her travels in Wonderland: "Would you tell me, please, which way I ought to go from here?" "That depends a good deal," replied the Cat with irrefutable logic, "on where you want to get to."

The story of America's immigration can be quickly told for our present purposes. The white American population at the time of the Revolution was largely English and Protestant in origin, but had already absorbed substantial groups of Germans and Scotch-Irish and smaller contingents of Frenchmen, Dutchmen, Swedes, Swiss, South Irish, Poles, and a handful of migrants from other European nations. Catholics were represented in modest numbers, particularly in the middle colonies, and a small number of Jews were residents of the incipient nation. With the exception of the Quakers and a few missionaries, the colonists had generally treated the Indians and their cultures with contempt and hostility, driving them from the coastal plains and making the western frontier a bloody battleground where eternal vigilance was the price of survival.

Although the Negro at that time made up nearly one-fifth of the total population, his predominantly slave status, together with racial and cultural prejudice, barred him from serious consideration as an assimilable element of the society. And while many groups of European origin started out as determined ethnic enclaves, eventually, most historians believe, considerable ethnic intermixture within the white population took place. "People of different blood" [sic]—write two American historians about the colonial period, "English, Irish, German, Huguenot, Dutch, Swedish—mingled and intermarried with little thought of any difference."[1] In such a society, its people predominantly English, its white immigrants of other ethnic origins either English-speaking or derived largely from countries of northern and western Europe whose cultural divergences from the English were not great, and its dominant white population excluding by fiat the claims and considerations of welfare of the non-Caucasian minorities, the problem of assimilation understandably did not loom unduly large or complex.

The unfolding events of the next century and a half with increasing momentum dispelled the complacency which rested upon the relative simplicity of colonial and immediate post-Revolutionary conditions. The large-scale immigration to America of the famine-fleeing Irish, the Germans, and later the Scandinavians (along with additional Englishmen and other peoples of northern and western Europe) in the middle of the nineteenth century (the so-called "old immigration"), the emancipation of the Negro slaves and the problems created by post–Civil War reconstruction, the placing of the conquered Indian with his broken culture on government reservations, the arrival of the Oriental, first attracted by the discovery of gold and other opportunities in the West, and finally, beginning in the last quarter of the nineteenth century and continuing to the early 1920's, the swelling to proportions hitherto unimagined of the tide of immigration from the peasantries and "pales" of southern and eastern Europe—the Italians, Jews, and Slavs of the so-called "new immigration," fleeing the persecutions and industrial dislocations of the day—all these events constitute the background against which we may consider the rise of the theories of assimilation mentioned above. After a necessarily foreshortened description of each of these theories and their historical emergence, we shall suggest analytical distinctions designed to aid in clarifying the nature of the assimilation process, and then conclude by focusing on the American scene.

ANGLO-CONFORMITY

"Anglo-conformity"[2] is a broad term used to cover a variety of viewpoints about assimilation and immigration; they all assume the desirability of maintaining English institutions (as modified by the American Revolution), the English language, and English-oriented cultural patterns as dominant and standard in American life. However, bound up with this assumption are related attitudes. These may range from discredited notions about race and "Nordic" and "Aryan" racial superiority, together with the nativist political programs and exclusionist immigration policies which such notions entail, through an intermediate position of favoring immigration from northern and western Europe on amorphous, unreflective grounds ("They are more like us"), to a lack of opposition to any source of immigration, as long as these immigrants and their descendants duly adopt the standard Anglo-Saxon cultural patterns. There is by no means any necessary equation between Anglo-conformity and racist attitudes.

It is quite likely that "Anglo-conformity" in its more moderate aspects, however explicit its formulation, has been the most prevalent ideology of assimilation goals in America throughout the nation's history. As far back as

---

[1] Allen Nevins and Henry Steele Commager, *America: The Story of a Free People* (Boston, Little, Brown, 1942), p. 58.

[2] The phrase is the Coles'. See Stewart G. Cole and Mildred Wiese Cole, *Minorities and the American Promise* (New York, Harper & Brothers, 1954), ch. 6.

colonial times, Benjamin Franklin recorded concern about the clannishness of the Germans in Pennsylvania, their slowness in learning English, and the establishment of their own native-language press.[3] Others of the founding fathers had similar reservations about large-scale immigration from Europe. In the context of their times they were unable to foresee the role such immigration was to play in creating the later greatness of the nation. They were not all men of unthinking prejudices. The disestablishment of religion and the separation of church and state (so that no religious group—whether New England Congregationalists, Virginian Anglicans, or even all Protestants combined—could call upon the federal government for special favors or support, and so that man's religious conscience should be free) were cardinal points of the new national policy they fostered. "The Government of the United States," George Washington had written to the Jewish congregation of Newport during his first term as president, "gives to bigotry no sanction, to persecution no assistance."

Political differences with ancestral England had just been written in blood; but there is no reason to suppose that these men looked upon their fledgling country as an impartial melting pot for the merging of the various cultures of Europe, or as a new "nation of nations," or as anything but a society in which, with important political modifications, Anglo-Saxon speech and institutional forms would be standard. Indeed, their newly won victory for democracy and republicanism made them especially anxious that these still precarious fruits of revolution should not be threatened by a large influx of European peoples whose life experiences had accustomed them to the bonds of despotic monarchy. Thus, although they explicitly conceived of the new United States of America as a

haven for those unfortunates of Europe who were persecuted and oppressed, they had characteristic reservations about the effects of too free a policy. "My opinion, with respect to immigration," Washington wrote to John Adams in 1794, "is that except of useful mechanics and some particular descriptions of men or professions, there is no need of encouragement, while the policy or advantage of its taking place in a body (I mean the settling of them in a body) may be much questioned; for, by so doing, they retain the language, habits and principles (good or bad) which they bring with them."[4] Thomas Jefferson, whose views on race and attitudes towards slavery were notably liberal and advanced for his time, had similar doubts concerning the effects of mass immigration on American institutions, while conceding that immigrants, "if they come of themselves . . . are entitled to all the rights of citizenship."[5]

The attitudes of Americans toward foreign immigration in the first three-quarters of the nineteenth century may correctly be described as ambiguous. On the one hand, immigrants were much desired, so as to swell the population and importance of states and territories, to man the farms of expanding prairie settlement, to work the mines, build the railroads and canals, and take their place in expanding industry. This was a period in which no federal legislation of any consequence prevented the entry of aliens, and such state legislation as existed attempted to bar on an individual basis only those who were likely to become a burden on the community, such as convicts and paupers. On the other hand, the arrival in an overwhelmingly Protestant society of large numbers of poverty-stricken Irish Catholics, who settled in groups in the slums of Eastern cities, roused dormant fears of "Popery" and Rome. Another source of anxiety was the substantial influx of Germans, who

---

[3] Maurice R. Davie, *World Immigration* (New York, Macmillan, 1936), p. 36, and (cited therein) "Letter of Benjamin Franklin to Peter Collinson, 9th May, 1753, on the condition and character of the Germans in Pennsylvania," in *The Works of Benjamin Franklin, with notes and a life of the author,* by Jared Sparks (Boston, 1828), vol. 7, pp. 71–73.

[4] *The Writings of George Washington,* collected by W. C. Ford (New York, G. P. Putnam's Sons, 1889), vol. 12, p. 489.

[5] Thomas Jefferson, "Notes on Virginia, Query 8"; in *The Writings of Thomas Jefferson,* ed. A. E. Bergh (Washington, The Thomas Jefferson Memorial Association, 1907), vol. 2, p. 121.

made their way to the cities and farms of the mid-West and whose different language, separate communal life, and freer ideas on temperance and sabbath observance brought them into conflict with the Anglo-Saxon bearers of the Puritan and Evangelical traditions. Fear of foreign "radicals" and suspicion of the economic demands of the occasionally aroused workingmen added fuel to the nativist fires. In their extreme form these fears resulted in the Native-American movement of the 1830's and 1840's and the "American" or "Know-Nothing" party of the 1850's, with their anti-Catholic campaigns and their demands for restrictive laws on naturalization procedures and for keeping the foreign-born out of political office. While these movements scored local political successes and their turbulences so rent the national social fabric that the patches are not yet entirely invisible, they failed to influence national legislative policy on immigration and immigrants; and their fulminations inevitably provoked the expected reactions from thoughtful observers.

The flood of newcomers to the westward expanding nation grew larger, reaching over one and two-thirds million between 1841 and 1850 and over two and one-half million in the decade before the Civil War. Throughout the entire period, quite apart from the excesses of the Know-Nothings, the predominant (though not exclusive) conception of what the ideal immigrant adjustment should be was probably summed up in a letter written in 1818 by John Quincy Adams, then Secretary of State, in answer to the inquiries of the Baron von Fürstenwaerther. If not the earliest, it is certainly the most elegant version of the sentiment, "If they don't like it here, they can go back where they came from." Adams declared:[6]

They [immigrants to America] come to a life of independence, but to a life of labor—and, if they cannot accommodate themselves to the character, moral, political and physical, of this country with all its compensating balances of good and evil, the Atlantic is always open to

[6] *Niles' Weekly Register*, vol. 18, 29 April 1820, pp. 157–158; also, Marcus L. Hansen, *The Atlantic Migration, 1607–1860*, pp. 96–97.

them to return to the land of their nativity and their fathers. To one thing they must make up their minds, or they will be disappointed in every expectation of happiness as Americans. They must cast off the European skin, never to resume it. They must look forward to their posterity rather than backward to their ancestors; they must be sure that whatever their own feelings may be, those of their children will cling to the prejudices of this country.

The events that followed the Civil War created their own ambiguities in attitude toward the immigrant. A nation undergoing wholesale industrial expansion and not yet finished with the march of westward settlement could make good use of the never faltering waves of newcomers. But sporadic bursts of labor unrest, attributed to foreign radicals, the growth of Catholic institutions and the rise of Catholics to municipal political power, and the continuing association of immigrant settlement with urban slums revived familiar fears. The first federal selective law restricting immigration was passed in 1882, and Chinese immigration was cut off in the same year. The most significant development of all, barely recognized at first, was the change in the source of European migrants. Beginning in the 1880's, the countries of southern and eastern Europe began to be represented in substantial numbers for the first time, and in the next decade immigrants from these sources became numerically dominant. Now the notes of a new, or at least hitherto unemphasized, chord from the nativist lyre began to sound—the ugly chord, or discord, of racism. Previously vague and romantic notions of Anglo-Saxon peoplehood, combined with general ethnocentrism, rudimentary wisps of genetics, selected tidbits of evolutionary theory, and naive assumptions from an early and crude imported anthropology produced the doctrine that the English, Germans, and others of the "old immigration" constituted a superior race of tall, blonde, blue-eyed "Nordics" or "Aryans," whereas the peoples of eastern and southern Europe made up the darker Alpines or Mediterraneans—both "inferior" breeds whose presence in America threatened, either by intermixture or supplementation, the traditional American stock and culture. The obvious corollary to this doctrine was to exclude the allegedly inferior breeds; but if the new type of immigrant could not be excluded, then everything must be done to instill Anglo-Saxon virtues in these benighted creatures. Thus, one educator writing in 1909 could state:[7]

These southern and eastern Europeans are of a very different type from the north Europeans who preceded them. Illiterate, docile, lacking in self-reliance and initiative, and not possessing the Anglo-Teutonic conceptions of law, order, and government, their coming has served to dilute tremendously our national stock, and to corrupt our civic life. . . . Everywhere these people tend to settle in groups or settlements, and to set up here their national manners, customs, and observances. Our task is to break up these groups or settlements, to assimilate and amalgamate these people as a part of our American race, and to implant in their children, so far as can be done, the Anglo-Saxon conception of righteousness, law and order, and popular government, and to awaken in them a reverence for our democratic institutions and for those things in our national life which we as a people hold to be of abiding worth.

Anglo-conformity received its fullest expression in the so-called Americanization movement which gripped the nation during World War I. While "Americanization" in its various stages had more than one emphasis, it was essentially a consciously articulated movement to strip the immigrant of his native culture and attachments and make him over into an American along Anglo-Saxon lines—all this to be accomplished with great rapidity. To use an image of a later day, it was an attempt at "pressure-cooking assimilation." It had prewar antecedents, but it was during the height of the world conflict that federal agencies, state governments, municipalities, and a host of private organizations joined in the effort to persuade the immigrant to learn English, take out naturalization papers, buy war bonds, forget his former origins and culture, and give himself over to patriotic hysteria.

[7] Ellwood P. Cubberly, *Changing Conceptions of Education* (Boston, Houghton Mifflin, 1909), pp. 15–16.

After the war and the "Red scare" which followed, the excesses of the Americanization movement subsided. In its place, however, came the restriction of immigration through federal law. Foiled at first by presidential vetoes, and later by the failure of the 1917 literacy test to halt the immigrant tide, the proponents of restriction finally put through in the early 1920's a series of acts culminating in the well-known national-origins formula for immigrant quotas which went into effect in 1929. Whatever the merits of a quantitative limit on the number of immigrants to be admitted to the United States, the provisions of the formula, which discriminated sharply against the countries of southern and eastern Europe, in effect institutionalized the assumptions of the rightful dominance of Anglo-Saxon patterns in the land. Reaffirmed with only slight modifications in the McCarran-Walter Act of 1952, these laws, then, stand as a legal monument to the creed of Anglo-conformity and a telling reminder that this ideological system still has numerous and powerful adherents on the American scene.

THE MELTING POT

While Anglo-conformity in various guises has probably been the most prevalent ideology of assimilation in the American historical experience, a competing viewpoint with more generous and idealistic overtones has had its adherents and exponents from the eighteenth century onward. Conditions in the virgin continent, it was clear, were modifying the institutions which the English colonists brought with them from the mother country. Arrivals from non-English homelands such as Germany, Sweden, and France were similarly exposed to this fresh environment. Was it not possible, then, to think of the evolving American society not as a slightly modified England but rather as a totally new blend, culturally and biologically, in which the stocks and folkways of Europe, figuratively speaking, were indiscriminately mixed in the political pot of the emerging nation and fused by the fires of

American influence and interaction into a distinctly new type?

Such, at any rate, was the conception of the new society which motivated that eighteenth-century French-born writer and agriculturalist, J. Hector St. John Crèvecoeur, who, after many years of American residence, published his reflections and observations in *Letters from an American Farmer*.[8] Who, he asks, is the American?

> He is either an European, or the descendant of an European, hence that strange mixture of blood, which you will find in no other country. I could point out to you a family whose grandfather was an Englishman, whose wife was Dutch, whose son married a French woman, and whose present four sons have now four wives of different nations. *He* is an American, who leaving behind him all his ancient prejudices and manners, receives new ones from the new mode of life he has embraced, the new government he obeys, and the new rank he holds. He becomes an American by being received in the broad lap of our great *Alma Mater*. Here individuals of all nations are melted into a new race of men, whose labours and posterity will one day cause great changes in the world.

Some observers have interpreted the open-door policy on immigration of the first three-quarters of the nineteenth century as reflecting an underlying faith in the effectiveness of the American melting pot, in the belief "that all could be absorbed and that all could contribute to an emerging national character."[9] No doubt many who observed with dismay the nativist agitation of the times felt as did Ralph Waldo Emerson that such conformity-demanding and immigrant-hating forces represented a perversion of the best American ideals. In 1845, Emerson wrote in his Journal:[10]

I hate the narrowness of the Native American Party. It is the dog in the manger. It is precisely opposite to all the dictates of love and magnanimity; and therefore, of course, opposite to true wisdom. . . . Man is the most composite of all creatures. . . . Well, as in the old burning of the Temple at Corinth, by the melting and intermixture of silver and gold and other metals a new compound more precious than any, called Corinthian brass, was formed: so in this continent,—asylum of all nations,—the energy of Irish, Germans, Swedes, Poles, and Cossacks, and all the European tribes,—of the Africans, and of the Polynesians,—will construct a new race, a new religion, a new state, a new literature, which will be as vigorous as the new Europe which came out of the smelting-pot of the Dark Ages, or that which earlier emerged from the Pelasgic and Etruscan barbarism. *La Nature aime les croisements.*

Eventually, the melting-pot hypothesis found its way into historical scholarship and interpretation. While many American historians of the late nineteenth century, some fresh from graduate study at German universities, tended to adopt the view that American institutions derived in essence from Anglo-Saxon (and ultimately Teutonic) sources, others were not so sure.[11] One of these was Frederick Jackson Turner, a young historian from Wisconsin, not long emerged from his graduate training at Johns Hopkins. Turner presented a paper to the American Historical Association, meeting in Chicago in 1893. Called "The Significance of the Frontier in American History," this paper proved to be one of the most influential essays in the history of American scholarship, and its point of view, supported by Turner's subsequent writings and his teaching, pervaded the field of American historical interpretation for at least a generation. Turner's thesis was that the dominant influence in the shaping of American institutions and American democracy was not this nation's European heritage in any of its forms, nor the forces emanating from the eastern seaboard cities, but rather the experiences created by a moving and variegated western fron-

---

[8] J. Hector St. John Crèvecoeur, *Letters from an American Farmer* (New York, Albert and Charles Boni, 1925; reprinted from the 1st edn., London, 1782), pp. 54–55.

[9] Oscar Handlin, ed., *Immigration as a Factor in American History* (Englewood, Prentice-Hall, 1959), p. 146.

[10] Quoted by Stuart P. Sherman in his Introduction to *Essays and Poems of Emerson* (New York, Harcourt Brace, 1921), p. xxxiv.

[11] See Edward N. Saveth, *American Historians and European Immigrants, 1875–1925*, New York, Columbia University Press, 1948.

tier. Among the many effects attributed to the frontier environment and the challenges it presented was that it acted as a solvent for the national heritages and the separatist tendencies of the many nationality groups which had joined the trek westward, including the Germans and Scotch-Irish of the eighteenth century and the Scandinavians and Germans of the nineteenth. "The frontier," asserted Turner, "promoted the formation of a composite nationality for the American people. . . . In the crucible of the frontier the immigrants were Americanized, liberated, and fused into a mixed race, English in neither nationality nor characteristics. The process has gone on from the early days to our own." And later, in an essay on the role of the Mississippi Valley, he refers to "the tide of foreign immigration which has risen so steadily that it has made a composite American people whose amalgamation is destined to produce a new national stock."[12]

Thus far, the proponents of the melting pot idea had dealt largely with the diversity produced by the sizeable immigration from the countries of northern and western Europe alone—the "old immigration," consisting of peoples with cultures and physical appearance not greatly different from those of the Anglo-Saxon stock. Emerson, it is true, had impartially included Africans, Polynesians, and Cossacks in his conception of the mixture; but it was only in the last two decades of the nineteenth century that a large-scale influx of peoples from the countries of southern and eastern Europe imperatively posed the question of whether these uprooted newcomers who were crowding into the large cities of the nation and the industrial sector of the economy could also be successfully "melted." Would the "urban melting pot" work as well as the "frontier melting pot" of an essentially rural society was alleged to have done?

It remained for an English-Jewish writer with strong social convictions, moved by his observation of the role of the United States as a haven for the poor and oppressed of Europe, to give utterance to the broader view of the American melting pot in a way which attracted public attention. In 1908, Israel Zangwill's drama, *The Melting Pot*, was produced in this country and became a popular success. It is a play dominated by the dream of its protagonist, a young Russian-Jewish immigrant to America, a composer, whose goal is the completion of a vast "American" symphony which will express his deeply felt conception of his adopted country as a divinely appointed crucible in which all the ethnic divisions of mankind will divest themselves of their ancient animosities and differences and become fused into one group, signifying the brotherhood of man. In the process he falls in love with a beautiful and cultured Gentile girl. The play ends with the performance of the symphony and, after numerous vicissitudes and traditional family opposition from both sides, with the approaching marriage of David Quixano and his beloved. During the course of these developments, David, in the rhetoric of the time, delivers himself of such sentiments as these:[13]

America is God's crucible, the great Melting Pot where all the races of Europe are melting and re-forming! Here you stand, good folk, think I, when I see them at Ellis Island, here you stand in your fifty groups, with your fifty languages and histories, and your fifty blood hatreds and rivalries. But you won't be long like that, brothers, for these are the fires of God you've come to—these are the fires of God. A fig for your feuds and vendettas! Germans and Frenchmen, Irishmen and Englishmen, Jews and Russians—into the Crucible with you all! God is making the American.

Here we have a conception of a melting pot which admits of no exceptions or qualifications with regard to the ethnic stocks which will fuse in the great crucible. Englishmen, Germans, Frenchmen, Slavs, Greeks, Syrians, Jews, Gentiles, even the black and yellow

[12] Frederick Jackson Turner, *The Frontier in American History* (New York, Henry Holt, 1920), pp. 22–23, 190.

[13] Israel Zangwill, *The Melting Pot* (New York, Macmillan, 1909), p. 37.

races, were specifically mentioned in Zang-will's rhapsodic enumeration. And this pot patently was to boil in the great cities of America.

Thus around the turn of the century the melting-pot idea became embedded in the ideals of the age as one response to the immi-grant receiving experience of the nation. Soon to be challenged by a new philosophy of group adjustment (to be discussed below) and al-ways competing with the more pervasive ad-herence to Anglo-conformity, the melting-pot image, however, continued to draw a portion of the attention consciously directed toward this aspect of the American scene in the first half of the twentieth century. In the mid-1940's a sociologist who had carried out an investigation of intermarriage trends in New Haven, Connecticut, described a revised con-ception of the melting process in that city and suggested a basic modification of the theory of that process. In New Haven, Ruby Jo Reeves Kennedy[14] reported from a study of intermar-riages from 1870 to 1940 that there was a distinct tendency for the British-Americans, Germans, and Scandinavians to marry among themselves—that is, within a Protestant "pool"; for the Irish, Italians, and Poles to marry among themselves—a Catholic "pool"; and for the Jews to marry other Jews. In other words, intermarriage was taking place across lines of nationality background, but there was a strong tendency for it to stay confined within one or the other of the three major religious groups, Protestants, Catholics, and Jews. Thus, declared Mrs. Kennedy, the picture in New Haven resembled a "triple melting pot" based on religious divisions, rather than a "single melting pot." Her study indicated, she stated, that "while strict endogamy is loosening, reli-gious endogamy is persisting and the future cleavages will be along religious lines rather than along nationality lines as in the past. If this is the case, then the traditional 'single-melting-pot' idea must be abandoned, and a new conception, which we term the 'triple-melting-pot' theory of American assimilation, will take its place as the true expression of what is happening to the various nationality groups in the United States."[15] The triple melting-pot thesis was later taken up by the theologian, Will Herberg, and formed an im-portant sociological frame of reference for his analysis of religious trends in American so-ciety, *Protestant-Catholic-Jew*.[16] But the triple melting-pot hypothesis patently takes us into the realm of a society pluralistically conceived. We turn now to the rise of an ideology which attempts to justify such a conception.

CULTURAL PLURALISM

Probably all the non-English immigrants who came to American shores in any significant numbers from colonial times onward—settling either in the forbidding wilderness, the lonely prairie, or in some accessible urban slum—created ethnic enclaves and looked forward to the preservation of at least some of their native cultural patterns. Such a development, natural as breathing, was supported by the later accretion of friends, relatives, and coun-trymen seeking out oases of familiarity in a strange land, by the desire of the settlers to rebuild (necessarily in miniature) a society in which they could communicate in the familiar tongue and maintain familiar institutions, and, finally, by the necessity to band together for mutual aid and mutual protection against the uncertainties of a strange and frequently hostile environment. This was as true of the "old" immigrants as of the "new." In fact, some of the liberal intellectuals who fled to America from an inhospitable political climate in Germany in the 1830's, 1840's, and 1850's looked forward to the creation of an all-German state within the union, or, even more hopefully, to the eventual formation of a sepa-

---

[14] Ruby Jo Reeves Kennedy, "Single or Triple Melting-Pot? Intermarriage Trends in New Haven, 1870–1940," *American Journal of Sociology*, 1944, 49: 331–339. See also her "Single or Triple Melting-Pot? Intermarriage in New Haven, 1870–1950," *ibid.*, 1952, 58: 56–59.

[15] Kennedy, "Single or Triple Melting-Pot? . . . 1870–1940," p. 332 (author's italics omitted).

[16] Will Herberg, *Protestant-Catholic-Jew* (Garden City, Doubleday, 1955).

rate German nation, as soon as the expected dissolution of the union under the impact of the slavery controversy should have taken place.[17] Oscar Handlin, writing of the sons of Erin in mid-nineteenth-century Boston, recent refugees from famine and economic degradation in their homeland, points out: "Unable to participate in the normal associational affairs of the community, the Irish felt obliged to erect a society within a society, to act together in their own way. In every contact therefore the group, acting apart from other sections of the community, became intensely aware of its peculiar and exclusive identity."[18] Thus cultural pluralism was a fact in American society before it became a theory—a theory with explicit relevance for the nation as a whole, and articulated and discussed in the English-speaking circles of American intellectual life.

Eventually, the cultural enclaves of the Germans (and the later arriving Scandinavians) were to decline in scope and significance as succeeding generations of their native-born attended public schools, left the farms and villages to strike out as individuals for the Americanizing city, and generally became subject to the influences of a standardizing industrial civilization. The German-American community, too, was struck a powerful blow by the accumulated passions generated by World War I—a blow from which it never fully recovered. The Irish were to be the dominant and pervasive element in the gradual emergence of a pan-Catholic group in America, but these developments would reveal themselves only in the twentieth century. In the meantime, in the last two decades of the nineteenth, the influx of immigrants from southern and eastern Europe had begun. These groups were all the more sociologically

visible because the closing of the frontier, the occupational demands of an expanding industrial economy, and their own poverty made it inevitable that they would remain in the urban areas of the nation. In the swirling fires of controversy and the steadier flame of experience created by these new events, the ideology of cultural pluralism as a philosophy for the nation was forged.

The first manifestations of an ideological counterattack against draconic Americanization came not from the beleaguered newcomers (who were, after all, more concerned with survival than with theories of adjustment), but from those idealistic members of the middle class who, in the decade or so before the turn of the century, had followed the example of their English predecessors and "settled" in the slums to "learn to sup sorrow with the poor."[19] Immediately, these workers in the "settlement houses" were forced to come to grips with the realities of immigrant life and adjustment. Not all reacted in the same way, but on the whole the settlements developed an approach to the immigrant which was sympathetic to his native cultural heritage and to his newly created ethnic institutions.[20] For one thing, their workers, necessarily in intimate contact with the lives of these often pathetic and bewildered newcomers and their daily problems, could see how unfortunate were the effects of those forces which impelled rapid Americanization in their impact on the immigrants' children, who not infrequently became alienated from their parents and the restraining influence of family authority. Were not their parents ignorant and uneducated "Hunkies," "Sheenies," or "Dagoes," as that limited portion of the American environment in which they moved defined the matter? Ethnic "self-hatred" with its debilitating psychological consequences, family disorganization,

[17] Nathan Glazer, "Ethnic Groups in America: From National Culture to Ideology," in Morroe Berger, Theodore Abel, and Charles H. Page, eds., Freedom and Control in Modern Society (New York, D. Van Nostrand, 1954), p. 161; Marcus Lee Hansen, The Immigrant in American History (Cambridge, Harvard University Press, 1940), pp. 129–140; John A. Hawgood, The Tragedy of German-America (New York, Putnam's, 1940), passim.

[18] Oscar Handlin, Boston's Immigrants (Cambridge, Harvard University Press, 1959, rev. edn.), p. 176.

[19] From a letter (1883) by Samuel A. Barnett; quoted in Arthur C. Holden, The Settlement Idea (New York, Macmillan, 1922), p. 12.

[20] Jane Addams, Twenty Years at Hull House (New York, Macmillan, 1914), pp. 231–258; Arthur C. Holden, op. cit., pp. 109–131, 182–189; John Higham, Strangers in the Land (New Brunswick, Rutgers University Press, 1955), p. 236.

and juvenile delinquency, were not unusual results of this state of affairs. Furthermore, the immigrants themselves were adversely affected by the incessant attacks on their culture, their language, their institutions, their very conception of themselves. How were they to maintain their self-respect when all that they knew, felt, and dreamed, beyond their sheer capacity for manual labor—in other words, all that they *were*—was despised or scoffed at in America? And—unkindest cut of all—their own children had begun to adopt the contemptuous attitude of the "Americans." Jane Addams relates in a moving chapter of her *Twenty Years at Hull House* how, after coming to have some conception of the extent and depth of these problems, she created at the settlement a "Labor Museum," in which the immigrant women of the various nationalities crowded together in the slums of Chicago could illustrate their native methods of spinning and weaving, and in which the relation of these earlier techniques to contemporary factory methods could be graphically shown. For the first time these peasant women were made to feel by some part of their American environment that they possessed valuable and interesting skills—that they too had something to offer—and for the first time, the daughters of these women who, after a long day's work at their dank "needletrade" sweatshops, came to Hull House to observe, began to appreciate the fact that their mothers, too, had a "culture," that this culture possessed its own merit, and that it was related to their own contemporary lives. How aptly Jane Addams concludes her chapter with the hope that "our American citizenship might be built without disturbing these foundations which were laid of old time."[21]

This appreciative view of the immigrant's cultural heritage and of its distinctive usefulness both to himself and his adopted country received additional sustenance from another source: those intellectual currents of the day which, however overborne by their currently more powerful opposites, emphasized liberalism, internationalism, and tolerance. From time to time, an occasional educator or publicist protested the demands of the "Americanizers," arguing that the immigrant, too, had an ancient and honorable culture, and that this culture had much to offer an America whose character and destiny were still in the process of formation, an America which must serve as an example of the harmonious cooperation of various heritages to a world inflamed by nationalism and war. In 1916 John Dewey, Norman Hapgood, and the young literary critic, Randolph Bourne, published articles or addresses elaborating various aspects of this theme.

The classic statement of the cultural pluralist position, however, had been made over a year before. Early in 1915 there appeared in the pages of *The Nation* two articles under the title "Democracy *versus* the Melting-Pot." Their author was Horace Kallen, a Harvard-educated philosopher with a concern for the application of philosophy to societal affairs, and, as an American Jew, himself derivative of an ethnic background which was subject to the contemporary pressures for dissolution implicit in the "Americanization," or Anglo-conformity, and the melting-pot theories. In these articles Kallen vigorously rejected the usefulness of these theories as models of what was actually transpiring in American life or as ideals for the future. Rather he was impressed by the way in which the various ethnic groups in America were coincident with particular areas and regions, and with the tendency for each group to preserve its own language, religion, communal institutions, and ancestral culture. All the while, he pointed out, the immigrant has been learning to speak English as the language of general communication, and has participated in the over-all economic and political life of the nation. These developments in which "the United States are in the process of becoming a federal state not merely as a union of geographical and administrative unities, but also as a cooperation of cultural diversities, as a

[21] Jane Addams, *op. cit.*, p. 258.

federation or commonwealth of national cultures,"[22] the author argued, far from constituting a violation of historic American political principles, as the "Americanizers" claimed, actually represented the inevitable consequences of democratic ideals, since individuals are implicated in groups, and since democracy for the individual must by extension also mean democracy for his group.

The processes just described, however, as Kallen develops his argument, are far from having been thoroughly realized. They are menaced by "Americanization" programs, assumptions of Anglo-Saxon superiority, and misguided attempts to promote "racial" amalgamation. Thus America stands at a kind of cultural crossroads. It can attempt to impose by force an artificial, Anglo-Saxon oriented uniformity on its peoples, or it can consciously allow and encourage its ethnic groups to develop democratically, each emphasizing its particular cultural heritage. If the latter course is followed, as Kallen puts it at the close of his essay, then,[23]

The outlines of a possible great and truly democratic commonwealth become discernible. Its form would be that of the federal republic: its substance a democracy of nationalities, co-operating voluntarily and autonomously through common institutions in the enterprise of self-realization through the perfection of men according to their kind. The common language of the commonwealth, the language of its great tradition, would be English, but each nationality would have for its emotional and involuntary life its own peculiar dialect or speech, its own individual and inevitable esthetic and intellectual forms. The political and economic life of the commonwealth is a single unit and serves as the foundation and background for the realization of the distinctive individuality of each *natio* that composes it and of the pooling of these in a harmony above them all. Thus "American civilization" may come to mean the perfection of the cooperative harmonies of

"European civilization"—the waste, the squalor and the distress of Europe being eliminated—a multiplicity in a unity, an orchestration of mankind.

Within the next decade Kallen published more essays dealing with the theme of American multiple-group life, later collected in a volume.[24] In the introductory note to this book he used for the first time the term "cultural pluralism" to refer to his position. These essays reflect both his increasingly sharp rejection of the onslaughts on the immigrant and his culture which the coming of World War I and its attendant fears, the "Red scare," the projection of themes of racial superiority, the continued exploitation of the newcomers, and the rise of the Ku Klux Klan all served to increase in intensity, and also his emphasis on cultural pluralism as the democratic antidote to these ills. He has since published other essays elaborating or annotating the theme of cultural pluralism. Thus, for at least forty-five years, most of them spent teaching at the New School for Social Research, Kallen has been acknowledged as the originator and leading philosophical exponent of the idea of cultural pluralism.

In the late 1930's and early 1940's the late Louis Adamic, the Yugoslav immigrant who had become an American writer, took up the theme of America's multicultural heritage and the role of these groups in forging the country's national character. Borrowing Walt Whitman's phrase, he described America as "a nation of nations," and while his ultimate goal was closer to the melting-pot idea than to cultural pluralism, he saw the immediate task as that of making America conscious of what it owed to all its ethnic groups, not just to the Anglo-Saxons. The children and grandchildren of immigrants of non-English origins, he was convinced, must be taught to be proud of the cultural heritage of their ancestral ethnic group and of its role in building the American nation; otherwise, they would not lose their

[22] Horace M. Kallen, "Democracy *versus* the Melting-Pot," *The Nation*, 18 and 25 February 1915; reprinted in his *Culture and Democracy in the United States*, New York, Boni and Liveright, 1924; the quotation is on p. 116.

[23] Kallen, *Culture and Democracy* . . . , p. 124.

[24] *Op. cit.*

sense of ethnic inferiority and the feeling of rootlessness he claimed to find in them.

Thus in the twentieth century, particularly since World War II, "cultural pluralism" has become a concept which has worked its way into the vocabulary and imagery of specialists in intergroup relations and leaders of ethnic communal groups. In view of this new pluralistic emphasis, some writers now prefer to speak of the "integration" of immigrants rather than of their "assimilation."[25] However, with a few exceptions,[26] no close analytical attention has been given either by social scientists or practitioners of intergroup relations to the meaning of cultural pluralism, its nature and relevance for a modern industrialized society, and its implications for problems of prejudice and discrimination—a point to which we referred at the outset of this discussion.

CONCLUSIONS

In the remaining pages I can make only a few analytical comments which I shall apply in context to the American scene, historical and current. My view of the American situation will not be documented here, but may be considered as a series of hypotheses in which I shall attempt to outline the American assimilation process.

First of all, it must be realized that "assimilation" is a blanket term which in reality covers a multitude of subprocesses. The most crucial distinction is one often ignored— the distinction between what I have elsewhere

called "behavioral assimilation" and "structural assimilation."[27] The first refers to the absorption of the cultural behavior patterns of the "host" society. (At the same time, there is frequently some modification of the cultural patterns of the immigrant-receiving country, as well.) There is a special term for this process of cultural modification or "behavioral assimilation"—namely, "acculturation." "Structural assimilation," on the other hand, refers to the entrance of the immigrants and their descendants into the social cliques, organizations, institutional activities, and general civic life of the receiving society. If this process takes place on a large enough scale, then a high frequency of intermarriage must result. A further distinction must be made between, on the one hand, those activities of the general civic life which involve earning a living, carrying out political responsibilities, and engaging in the instrumental affairs of the larger community, and, on the other hand, activities which create personal friendship patterns, frequent home intervisiting, communal worship, and communal recreation. The first type usually develops so-called "secondary relationships," which tend to be relatively impersonal and segmental; the latter type leads to "primary relationships," which are warm, intimate, and personal.

With these various distinctions in mind, we may then proceed.

Built on the base of the original immigrant "colony" but frequently extending into the life of successive generations, the characteristic ethnic group experience is this: within the ethnic group there develops a network of organizations and informal social relationships which permits and encourages the members of the ethnic group to remain within the confines of the group for all of their primary relationships and some of their secondary relationships throughout all the stages of the life cycle. From the cradle in the sectarian hospital to the child's play group, the social clique in high school, the fraternity and religious center

[25] See W. D. Borrie et al., The Cultural Integration of Immigrants (a survey based on the papers and proceedings of the UNESCO Conference in Havana, April 1956), Paris, UNESCO, 1959; and William S. Bernard, "The Integration of Immigrants in the United States" (mimeographed), one of the papers for this conference.

[26] See particularly Milton M. Gordon, "Social Structure and Goals in Group Relations"; and Nathan Glazer, "Ethnic Groups in America; From National Culture to Ideology," both articles in Berger, Abel, and Page, op. cit.; S. N. Eisenstadt, The Absorption of Immigrants, London, Routledge and Kegan Paul, 1954; and W. D. Borrie et al., op. cit.

[27] Milton M. Gordon, "Social Structure and Goals in Group Relations," p. 151.

in college, the dating group within which he searches for a spouse, the marriage partner, the neighborhood of his residence, the church affiliation and the church clubs, the men's and the women's social and service organizations, the adult clique of "marrieds," the vacation resort, and then, as the age cycle nears completion, the rest home for the elderly and, finally, the sectarian cemetery—in all these activities and relationships which are close to the core of personality and selfhood—the member of the ethnic group may if he wishes follow a path which never takes him across the boundaries of his ethnic structural network.

The picture is made more complex by the existence of social class divisions which cut across ethnic group lines just as they do those of the white Protestant population in America. As each ethnic group which has been here for the requisite time has developed second, third, or in some cases, succeeding generations, it has produced a college-educated group which composes an upper middle class (and sometimes upper class, as well) segment of the larger groups. Such class divisions tend to restrict primary group relations even further, for although the ethnic-group member feels a general sense of identification with all the bearers of his ethnic heritage, he feels comfortable in intimate social relations only with those who also share his own class background or attainment.

In short, my point is that, while *behavioral assimilation* or acculturation has taken place in America to a considerable degree, *structural assimilation*, with some important exceptions has not been extensive.[28] The exceptions are of two types. The first brings us back to the "triple-melting-pot" thesis of Ruby Jo Reeves Kennedy and Will Herberg. The "nationality" ethnic groups have tended to merge within each of the three major religious groups. This has been particularly true of the Protestant and Jewish communities. Those descendants of the "old" immigration of the nineteenth century, who were Protestant

(many of the Germans and all the Scandinavians), have in considerable part gradually merged into the white Protestant "subsociety." Jews of Sephardic, German, and Eastern-European origins have similarly tended to come together in their communal life. The process of absorbing the various Catholic nationalities, such as the Italians, Poles, and French Canadians, into an American Catholic community hitherto dominated by the Irish has begun, although I do not believe that it is by any means close to completion. Racial and quasi-racial groups such as the Negroes, Indians, Mexican-Americans, and Puerto Ricans still retain their separate sociological structures. The outcome of all this in contemporary American life is thus pluralism—but it is more than "triple" and it is more accurately described as *structural pluralism* than as cultural pluralism, although some of the latter also remains.

My second exception refers to the social structures which implicate intellectuals. There is no space to develop the issue here, but I would argue that there is a social world or subsociety of the intellectuals in America in which true structural intermixture among persons of various ethnic backgrounds, including the religious, has markedly taken place.

My final point deals with the reasons for these developments. If structural assimilation has been retarded in America by religious and racial lines, we must ask why. The answer lies in the attitudes of both the majority and the minority groups and in the way these attitudes have interacted. A saying of the current day is, "It takes two to tango." To apply the analogy, there is no good reason to believe that white Protestant America has ever extended a firm and cordial invitation to its minorities to dance. Furthermore, the attitudes of the minority-group members themselves on the matter have been divided and ambiguous. Particularly for the minority religious groups, there is a certain logic in ethnic communality, since there is a commitment to the perpetuation of the religious ideology and since structural intermixture leads to intermarriage and the possible loss to the group of the intermar-

---

[28] See Erich Rosenthal, "Acculturation without Assimilation?" *American Journal of Sociology*, 1960, 66: 275–288.

ried family. Let us, then, examine the situation serially for various types of minorities.

With regard to the immigrant, in his characteristic numbers and socio-economic background, structural assimilation was out of the question. He did not want it, and he had a positive need for the comfort of his own communal institutions. The native American, moreover, whatever the implications of his public pronouncements, had no intention of opening up his primary group life to entrance by these hordes of alien newcomers. The situation was a functionally complementary standoff.

The second generation found a much more complex situation. Many believed they heard the siren call of welcome to the social cliques, clubs, and institutions of white Protestant America. After all, it was simply a matter of learning American ways, was it not? Had they not grown up as Americans, and were they not culturally different from their parents, the "greenhorns"? Or perhaps an especially eager one reasoned (like the Jewish protagonist of Myron Kaufmann's novel, *Remember Me To God,* aspiring to membership in the prestigious club system of Harvard undergraduate social life) "If only I can go the last few steps in Ivy League manners and behavior, they will surely recognize that I am one of them and take me in." But, alas, Brooks Brothers suit notwithstanding, the doors of the fraternity house, the city men's club, and the country club were slammed in the face of the immigrant's offspring. That invitation was not really there in the first place; or, to the extent it was, in Joshua Fishman's phrase, it was a "'look me over but don't touch me' invitation to the American minority group child."[29] And so the rebuffed one returned to the homelier but dependable comfort of the communal institutions of his ancestral group. There he found his fellows of the same generation who had never stirred from the home fires. Some of

these had been too timid to stray; others were ethnic ideologists committed to the group's survival; still others had never really believed in the authenticity of the siren call or were simply too passive to do more than go along the familiar way. All could not join in the task that was well within the realm of the sociologically possible—the build-up of social institutions and organizations within the ethnic enclave, manned increasingly by members of the second generation and suitably separated by social class.

Those who had for a time ventured out gingerly or confidently, as the case might be, had been lured by the vision of an "American" social structure that was somehow larger than all subgroups and was ethnically neutral. Were they, too, not Americans? But they found to their dismay that at the primary group level a neutral American social structure was a mirage. What at a distance seemed to be a quasi-public edifice flying only the all-inclusive flag of American nationality turned out on closer inspection to be the clubhouse of a particular ethnic group—the white Anglo-Saxon Protestants, its operation shot through with the premises and expectations of its parental ethnicity. In these terms, the desirability of whatever invitation was grudgingly extended to those of other ethnic backgrounds could only become a considerably attenuated one.

With the racial minorities, there was not even the pretense of an invitation. Negroes, to take the most salient example, have for the most part been determinedly barred from the cliques, social clubs, and churches of white America. Consequently, with due allowance for internal class differences, they have constructed their own network of organizations and institutions, their own "social world." There are now many vested interests served by the preservation of this separate communal life, and doubtless many Negroes are psychologically comfortable in it, even though at the same time they keenly desire that discrimination in such areas as employment, education, housing, and public accommodations be eliminated. However, the ideological attachment of

[29] Joshua A. Fishman, "Childhood Indoctrination for Minority-Group Membership and the Quest for Minority-Group Biculturism in America," in Oscar Handlin, ed., *Group Life in America* (Cambridge, Harvard University Press, forthcoming).

Negroes to their communal separation is not conspicuous. Their sense of identification with ancestral African national cultures is virtually nonexistent, although Pan-Africanism engages the interest of some intellectuals and although "black nationalist" and "black racist" fringe groups have recently made an appearance at the other end of the communal spectrum. As for their religion, they are either Protestant or Catholic (overwhelmingly the former). Thus, there are no "logical" ideological reasons for their separate communality; dual social structures are created solely by the dynamics of prejudice and discrimination, rather than being reinforced by the ideological commitments of the minority itself.

Structural assimilation, then, has turned out to be the rock on which the ships of Anglo-comformity and the melting pot have foundered. To understand that behavioral assimilation (or acculturation) without massive structural intermingling in primary relationships has been the dominant motif in the American experience of creating and developing a nation out of diverse peoples is to comprehend the most essential sociological fact of that experience. It is against the background of "structural pluralism" that strategies of strengthening intergroup harmony, reducing ethnic discrimination and prejudice, and maintaining the rights of both those who stay within and those who venture beyond their ethnic boundaries must be thoughtfully devised.

17

Varieties of Catholicism

JOHN COGLEY

American Catholics have always been different from their fellow citizens. In the beginning the outstanding thing about them was that they were not Protestants, in a nation where almost everyone else was, and this led to difficulties and misunderstandings. For example, most Americans assigned tremendous importance to the Scriptures, but Catholics put notoriously little emphasis on Bible reading and when they read the Good Book at all generally shunned the standard King James edition for a version of their own. In the Protestant-shaped religious climate of the time, this was looked upon as outrageously singular for a people who called themselves Christian. Again, Catholic religious services, particularly the Latin Mass and the use of private confession, seemed exotic if not downright superstitious to many Americans brought up on the straightforward liturgy of mainline Protestantism.

The deference Catholics gave to the Pope and his representatives (made even more perturbing after 1870 by the claim that in matters of faith and morals the Pontiff is infallible) struck their neighbors as a kind of intellectual enslavement unworthy of an American's proud independence of mind. Even such a small thing as the Friday abstinence law conspicuously set off Catholics. And there were numerous other signs—the blessed medals and

John Cogley is Editor of The Center Magazine.

Excerpted from *Catholic America* by John Cogley. Copyright © 1973 by John Cogley. Used with permission of The Dial Press.

scapulars they wore around their necks, the elaborate robes and baroque titles used by their bishops, the strange clothing affected by their nuns, the all-too-graphic religious images and prints found in their homes, the plaster statues of the Virgin Mary and the Saints cluttering up their houses of worship, their custom of tipping hats or making the Sign of the Cross every time they passed a church.

Later the sources of division rested more in the realm of behavior. Long after most Americans accepted birth control as desirable and planned parenthood as even a kind of patriotic duty, Catholic clerical spokesmen continued to denounce contraception as a heinous sin, and laymen took pride in their oversized families. Though they had their own mysterious marriage courts, which granted dubious "annulments" on grounds that only a Roman canonist could understand, Catholics adamantly refused to acknowledge the benefits of divorce or the right of even an innocent party to marry again after one had been granted. Later, their unyielding position on abortion became a serious source of tension.

More than anything else perhaps, the existence of parochial schools, segregating Catholics from others in early childhood, pointed up the apparent determination of members of the Church to go their own way in a nation which put more emphasis on conformity than it was always ready to acknowledge. In turn, the schools, which were designed to relate religion to every phase of life, strengthened a whole network of separatist institutions.

Almost from the earliest days American Catholicism has maintained its own press and publishing houses, fraternal organizations, hospitals and social-service agencies, professional and academic societies. Unlike their coreligionists on the Continent, they held off from establishing sectarian labor unions and political parties, but in almost every other area of life they produced counterparts of the dominant social structures—a Catholic poetry society, a Catholic sociological society, a Catholic war veterans association, Catholic Boy Scouts, a Catholic organization dedicated to the prevention of cruelty to animals, even a society for Catholic philatelists.

There have been Catholic debutante balls presided over by the Cardinal-Archbishops of New York and Los Angeles, Catholic bowling leagues, and Catholic travel agencies sponsoring vacation tours to the shrines at Lourdes and Fatima. There have been Catholic book clubs, a Catholic theatre guild, and from time to time Catholic cookbooks have been published featuring special dishes to mark the feast days of the Church. Catholics have had their own *Nation* and *New Republic* (*Commonweal* and *America*), their own *Life* (*Jubilee*), their own *Reader's Digest* (the *Catholic Digest*), and even their own comic books.

At one time, an American Catholic who wished to do so could have enjoyed a fairly complete cultural life without venturing beyond the walls of his own religious community. Few did, however. Some managed to move in two cultural milieux, the general American and its special Catholic counterpart. But the arcane world of the Catholic subculture never actually reached more than a minority of the millions who made up the Church in the United States. Even when Catholicism appeared to be an extraordinarily cohesive force—as it no longer does—it was never really the social monolith many took it to be.

Actually, American Catholics have differed among themselves almost as much as they have from their neighbors. Liberals and conservatives, radicals and reactionaries, rich and poor, farmers and city dwellers, the highly educated and the illiterate, the devout and the lukewarm, earnest assimilationists and narrow tribalists have all found a place in the Church. Even within these subheadings, there have been significant differences. Polish workingmen of an earlier Pittsburgh, for example, would have been as baffled by the flagellant practices of the penitentes of the Southwest as their Protestant neighbors; the free and easy Sicilians of Chicago would have found the guilty puritanism of the Irish which James T. Farrell depicted in *Studs Lonigan* simply incomprehensible; the dutiful German farmers of Minnesota even today find the casual Catholicism of the Puerto Rican community something of a scandal.

Each of these groups, along with a dozen others, brought a particular national version of the many-faceted Catholic tradition to the United States, and each developed along its characteristic lines in the New World. Consequently many different Catholicisms have existed side by side since the first great wave of immigrants arrived on American shores. Some of them, tucked away in hidden corners of American life, were barely noticed, even by fellow Catholics.

The Irish created the central image and furnished most of the cultural stereotypes if only because they were the earliest to become Americanized, produced so many members of the hierarchy, the clergy, and religious orders, and were extremely vocal not only as Irishmen but precisely as Catholics. If one runs through the giants of American Catholicism, from the Carrolls to the Kennedys, Celtic names seem to predominate. Among the outstanding members of the hierarchy—England, Hughes, Ireland, Gibbons O'Connell, Spellman, and Cushing come readily to mind—the Irish have produced more than any other group. Most of the major religious orders in the American Church —Jesuits, Dominicans, Augustinians, Christian Brothers, even the cloistered Trappists— have been strongly Irish, as have the largest sisterhoods.

Among the most active laymen, the number of Irishmen who made names for themselves as journalists, writers, and controversialists is striking—from Charles Carroll to William F. Buckley, Jr. And from the earliest days to the present, Irishmen have been prominent in almost every movement within American Catholicism, as leaders of right-wing and left-wing factions, as cautious conservatives and frisky rebels, rigid clericalists and free-wheeling liberals. They have varied widely, yet one way or another all of them have helped to establish the Irish interpretation of the Catholic tradition as the cultural standard.

The Catholicism of the Irish was generally observant to a fault and comparatively steady and untroubled. It lacked the intellectuality of the French and was neither as cynical about ecclesiastics nor as relaxed about the Faith as the Italian; it was not as absolutistic or mystical as the Spanish, as orderly as the German, or as nationalistic as the Polish. Unlike other brands of Catholicism, it put a central emphasis on strict obedience to ecclesiastical law and on sexual probity. . . . Irish Catholicism—and consequently the basic thrust of American Catholicism—was tinged with a puritanism not truly consistent with basic Catholic doctrine.

Another characteristic of Irish Catholicism has been its exaggerated reverence for the clergy. In the old Ireland the best-educated and most honored men of all were those called to the priesthood. The priest was almost always a trusted man of the people who remained close to them and served as a kind of protector during the years of their political subjugation. The priest in the old country was looked to for direction and leadership in all aspects of life because of his superior education, and this dependence was carried over in American Irish communities.

One result was that for many years the Church in America was habitually looked upon as an "other"—the bishops, priests, and religious, who were encouraged to man the Catholic institutions without any "interference." The laity were brought up to mind their own affairs and leave ecclesiastical matters to their clerical betters. . . .

Finally, Irish Catholicism—which was long under threat of extinction in the homeland and in the United States later became a target of powerful Protestant militancy—was marked by a touchiness and a defensive, at times even belligerent, determination to maintain itself in a world which it took to be hostile to just about everything it stood for. This spirit —the "siege mentality" as it came to be called—led to a suspicious attitude toward others and a predisposition toward exclusiveness that cut off Catholics from full participation in the cultural life of the nation. The postconciliar ecumenical movement changed all this, however. Present-day Catholics, maybe even especially the Irish among them, have become notably less sectarian in their approach to the world beyond the borders they once defiantly set up for themselves.

The strength of the Catholicism of the Irish has been its steadiness, realism, and practicality—qualities that do not readily produce mystics and contemplatives. But for a Church still finding its way in an alien cultural atmosphere, such characteristics may have been necessary for sheer survival. Aside from their early difficulties with the French-born bishops, Irish-American Catholics were remarkably stable in their loyalty. They rallied in support of their priests and the public positions taken by the hierarchy almost as a matter of habit. They were faithful about Mass attendance, exercised great care for even minor ecclesiastical regulations, and set an abnormally high standard of observance for other national groups in doing so. They contributed generously to the incessant building drives sponsored by the Church, only rarely questioning their wisdom, and wholeheartedly supported the vast Catholic educational system that grew up in the United States.

With few exceptions, Irish priests avoided theological speculation and held on tenaciously to the doctrines they were taught in the seminary, which they passed along to laity with extraordinary tidiness. As might have been expected, they did not produce many front-rank theologians, but they were excellent catechism teachers. Under their leadership, American Catholics became not only the most law-abiding but probably the best-instructed people in the entire Church.

The Irish were notoriously unconcerned about aesthetics—the churches they built in America are generally models of mediocre architecture—but their urge toward physical expansion was remarkable from the very beginning. The Irish-American hierarchy—brick-and-mortar bishops almost to a man—had their people behind them when they built churches, seminaries, schools, colleges, universities, hospitals, and orphanages by the hundred.

Though the Irish in the United States, like those who remained in the homeland, have never been free of nationalistic excess, their outstanding loyalty to Rome gave the American Church a cosmopolitan flavor it might otherwise have lacked. There have been practically no heresies or significant threats of schism among them. Whatever the Church asked for, whether speaking from Rome through the Pope or at home through their own bishops, they offered without complaint, including their sons to the priesthood and their daughters to the convent in impressive numbers.

The traditional Irish influence has waned as Catholics in the United States have become more self-consciously "American." But the formative role it played in creating the Catholicism of the New World remained critically important for many decades.

The Germans have been numerous ever since the waves of immigration in the late nineteenth century brought hundreds of thousands of them to the United States fleeing from militarism and the anti-Catholic policies of Bismarck's *Kulturkampf.* Though German Catholics settled everywhere in the new land, their strength was in the Middle West. They dominated in such dioceses as Saint Louis, Cincinnati, and Milwaukee, whiich produced a Catholicism more staid than that found in the Irish citadels of Boston, New York, Philadelphia, and other places on the Eastern Seaboard.

The Germans, who put heavy emphasis on the intellectual side of their religion, brought with them the tradition of the parish school, where their treasured virtues of thoroughness, industry, and orderliness were studiously inculcated in the young. As early as 1835 German-American Catholics began to publish their own newspaper in Cincinnati, *Der Wahrheitsfreund.* The long-lived *Der Wanderer*—published in Saint Paul, Minne-

sota—and a dozen other publications were added later, in part to meet the challenge of Protestant missionary efforts and counteract American nativism but most of all to sustain German culture and tradition in the New World.

With their own parishes, schools, monasteries, foreign-language press, and vigorous societies of laymen, American Catholics of German descent lived in semi-isolation from mainstream Catholicism right up to the First World War. Their relations with the predominantly Irish hierarchy were not always smooth and occasionally broke out into open warfare.

In those early days, German Catholic leaders made no secret of the fact that they had little respect for Irish Catholicism, which they looked upon as arrogant, overbearing, shockingly pragmatic, and culturally inferior to their own. From time to time German bishops made it clear to Rome that they resented the Celtic dominance in America and predicted that the eagerness of the Irish leaders to acculturate the Church would eventually lead to a kind of doctrinal sell-out.

During World War I, when the nation turned bitterly and irrationally against all things Teutonic—a traumatic experience for Americans of German descent—the traditional nationalism among them cooled down somewhat; in time most of their earlier isolationism disappeared and there was a great deal of intermarriage with other Catholic groups, especially the Irish.* By the Second World War German Catholicism, with some exceptions, was comfortably integrated into the general life of the American Church.

German Catholicism in America has strong rural and monastic roots (Benedictine monks played a large part in its development). It has consequently tended to be somewhat more conservative than those versions of the

---

* In this connection, it is interesting that a number of famous "Irish Catholics" are the product of an amalgam of the two traditions, among them Senator Eugene J. McCarthy (son of Anna Baden), William F. Buckley, Jr. (son of Alois Steiner), and Fathers Daniel and Philip Berrigan (sons of Freda Fromhart).

Faith which were shaped at least in part by their reactions to the turmoil of the big cities. It has also been much less influenced by devotional fads than the Catholicism which set out to appeal to the urban masses with their sentimentality and hunger for novelty. When popular novenas (which published weekly scorecards on "prayers answered") were at their peak, the German parishes tended to put even stronger emphasis on the dignity, decorum, and inner meaning of the official liturgy; again, schools under the direction of German priests and religious were outstanding for their dedication to solid theological learning and respect for ecclesiastical tradition.

At first the German Catholics imported their clergy from the fatherland, but as time went on they were second only to the Irish in providing the Church in America with native-born priests and religious. The German clergy was never given the adulation that Irish clerics for so long took as their due, but priests and monks were solidly respected in the German communities as men set apart; anticlericalism was never a serious problem among them.

A number of the outstanding bishops of the American Church were of German origin, among them Cardinals Mundelein and Mayer of Chicago and Archbishop Rummel of New Orleans. At least until recent years, dozens of American sisterhoods were almost exclusively German, and German-Americans outnumbered other members in some important congregations of priests and brothers, notably the Redemptorist, Capuchin, Marianist, and Precious Blood orders. The great American Benedictine foundations—Saint John's in Minnesota, Saint Meinrad's in Indiana, Saint Vincent's in Pennsylvania, and Mount Angel in Oregon, among others—were originally founded by German-speaking monks. They helped set the tone for German-American Catholicism, which, aside from its early tendency to be excessively nationalistic, has always been a steadying influence on the Church.

Up until the Civil War the number of Italians in the United States was negligible. The census of 1860 listed only 10,000, most of them middle-class merchants, artisans, and artists from the north of Italy. But between 1880 and 1924, when immigration was drastically curtailed, some five million more arrived in America, most of them from the impoverished South and only a few with even a primary education. In Italy they had been farm workers with no trade or profession to fall back upon. In the United States they clustered in the big cities—New York, Philadelphia, Boston, Chicago, and elsewhere—and were doomed to the back-breaking jobs with the poorest pay that the Irish were already moving beyond. Generally they were consigned to indescribably bad living conditions in urban slums.

With the exception of a small number of Waldensians who arrived earlier seeking religious freedom, the Italians were almost all Catholic, or at least nominally so. But under the pressures of slum living, some fell away from the Church completely; others, identifying their ancestral religion with the old country and Protestantism with the New World, joined Protestant denominations, believing it the "American" thing to do; and still others, deeming themselves socialists and anticlericals, were set against all religion but particularly Catholicism.

Not until they fought their way out of poverty were the American Italians integrated into the life of the Church in America. In earlier days, almost all their priests were sent from abroad, and their Little Italies became like foreign villages set down in the metropolitan centers.

A special community of missionary priests and brothers, founded in 1877 by Bishop John-Baptist Scalabrini in Piacenza, was dedicated to working with the Italian emigrants in America. These religious, known as Scalabrinians, organized parishes in the larger Italian communities in the United States which kept the traditions of the homeland alive. Some of the well-established orders, including the Franciscans, Servites, and Salesians, also sent religious from Italy to take up the work, and a number of diocesan priests—many of them non-Italians—served other Italian-American parishes, which were almost always found in the run-down sections of town.

The most memorable of the missionaries was the extraordinary nun, Frances Xavier Cabrini, who in 1946 became the first American citizen to achieve sainthood. Mother Cabrini, a native of Lombardy, founded a community called the Missionary Sisters of the Sacred Heart, who worked as teachers and nurses in New York, Chicago, Seattle, and other places where Italian immigrants were numerous. . . .

American-Italians, however, have never been proportionately represented among the clergy or in the religious orders. For one thing, it was a long time before they encouraged their young to go into the service of the Church. In southern Italy, having a priest or nun in the family was usually looked upon as a social asset; in the land of opportunity, as often as not, it was regarded as a step backward. Again, the anticlericalism the first immigrants brought with them from Italy remained a deterrent force for many years. Finally, if the truth be told, the clerical establishment itself did little to encourage religious vocations in the Italian-American community. Italian Catholics with their effusive devotion to unknown saints, their gaudy *festas*, sublime lack of concern about ecclesiastical regulations, and disdain for the censorious emphasis of Irish Catholicism were treated as a people apart.

The piety of the Italo-Americans—which usually had little in common with the sophisticated Catholicism of Rome, Florence, or Milan but was more a reflection of the peasant faith of Sicily and the southern provinces—was characteristically explosive, sentimental, and frequently tinged with superstition. As such, it was something of an embarrassment to their more inhibited coreligionists, who were eager to conform as much as possible to American notions of sobriety and restraint in religious matters.

American Catholicism, however, was the loser. Had the Italians gained more influence in the Church in the United States, at least some of the less attractive aspects of the puri-

tanical Irish version of the Faith might have been counterbalanced by Mediterranean wit, wisdom, and *joie de vivre*.

About one out of every eight American Catholics is of Polish extraction—a large, extraordinarily cohesive group which has jealously operated its own parishes, schools, and national societies within the larger diocesan structures. In the Great Lakes dioceses of Chicago, Buffalo, Detroit, Milwaukee, and throughout Pennsylvania parishes served by Polish priests and nuns, bastions of Polish culture, have maintained only minimal contact with their Catholic neighbors. To maintain this Catholicism-within-Catholicism, American Poles still support seventeen different sisterhoods and over twenty religious communities of men who, along with some two thousand diocesan priests, operate almost eight hundred parishes, six hundred schools, and more than two hundred charitable institutions.

There have always been Poles in the United States, beginning with the volunteers who served under George Washington in the Revolutionary Army. Millions more arrived in the wave of immigration that began in 1870. Still more were added after thousands of displaced persons arrived in the United States following World War II.

The first Polish immigrants in the eighteenth century, few in number, were easily integrated into American society, but the later arrivals had to cling together for support. They established their own enclaves in the cities and towns where they found jobs as factory hands and industrial workers. Wherever they settled, they set up national parishes and parochial schools where Polish was the language of instruction and the history of the homeland occupied an honored place in the curriculum.

Catholics in Poland have traditionally made a strong identification between their religion and the mother country. Other nations have had equally strong links between Church and state but probably nowhere else in the world-wide Church is there a more patriotic Catholicism or a more Catholic patriotism, a tradition which is almost as venerable as the thousand-year-old history of the nation. It was solidly implanted in America and has been sustained primarily by the national parishes which still exist wherever Poles are numerous.

As a matter of preference, then, the Poles have played no significant role in the general life of the Church in the United States, though there have been distinguished exceptions, including Cardinal John Knol of Philadelphia, now a leader of the hierarchy, and a number of other bishops and superiors of religious orders.

Polish nationalism was at the root of the only serious schism within American Catholicism—the Polish National Catholic church, which was established in Chicago in 1895 by Father Anton Koslowski after he clashed with diocesan authorities over the question of parochial administration. Koslowski favored the trustee system of church ownership, though it had never gained a real foothold in Chicago. He won popular support for his stand against the Bishop's holding Church property in his own name, and many Poles followed him out of the Church after he organized an independent parish of his own. . . .

The vast majority of American Poles, however, have remained utterly faithful to Rome and to the local bishops, while still living in self-chosen semi-isolation. In recent years, though, there has been a growing movement among younger Poles, as among other Eastern European groups, to break with the nationalistic character of their parishes and identify with a generally American Catholicism.

The other Eastern European Catholics followed the general pattern of the Poles in maintaining their distinctive religious cultures in the New World. The Slovaks, for example, established about three hundred parishes in the United States; the Lithuanians more than one hundred; the Hungarians several dozen. Even where these groups lived in the same city neighborhoods, as they still do in Chicago, they attended separate churches and schools and strove to hold on to their national identity by means of newspapers, magazines, cutural societies, social clubs, and youth organizations. Most of them also set up their own seminaries, monasteries, and religious orders. In a few cases they even established their own institutions of higher learning.

The Ruthenians, Ukrainians, Croats, and certain other Slavic groups are Eastern-rite Byzantine Catholics, in full communion with Rome but subject to a separate canonical discipline. They follow a liturgy almost identical with that prevailing in the Orthodox Church. Most of them now have their own bishops, though before the special hierarchies were set up they were subject to the local "Latin" bishop. A great deal of dissension resulted from the earlier practice. With ample reason, the Byzantines frequently complained that the "Latin" hierarchy was showing little sympathy for their distinctive religious traditions and age-old liturgical practices. The Vatican—in an effort not to sow "confusion" by the presence of a married Catholic clergy in the United States—merely exacerbated tensions when it decreed in 1928 that in America only single men could be ordained to the priesthood, even in churches where a married clergy had always been acceptable. As a result, thousands of Eastern-rite Catholics, put off by what they took to be papal contempt for their cultural and ecclesiastical heritage, converted to the Orthodox Church, while others established their own independent churches.

As time passed, even aside from these losses, the Byzantine Catholics steadily diminished in number. In all, less than a million American Catholics now belong to one or another of the Eastern, or Uniate, churches. Many, reaching adulthood, have transferred to the Latin rite, as a result of intermarriage or simply from a desire to be identified with the more "American" Catholicism of the overwhelming majority.

Frenchmen never came to America in great numbers. Even during the years of the great immigrations, less than a half-million left France for the United States. Most Americans of French background, then, descended from the Canadians who crossed the border into New England to become United States citizens.

Franco-Americans, as they used to call themselves, followed the usual pattern of setting up ethnic parishes, in their case as much out of a distaste for the Catholicism of the Irish as anything else. The French, who made no secret of their anti-Irish feelings, from the beginning resisted the efforts of the hierarchy to integrate them into local churches. Fiercely independent, they took a particularly dim view of the demanding American-Irish clergy and made it clear they would not work with them.

Because of their unwillingness to conform, the French were long looked upon as something of a problem by the Church authorities of New England. Some of their leaders regarded every attempt to Americanize Catholicism as a shameful capitulation and scorned their coreligionists who were set on it, charging that they were motivated above all by a craven reaction to nativist mischief. In turn, the Irish made no secret of the fact that they resented the clannish ways of the French, whom they charged with strengthening the impression that Catholicism was a "foreign," divisive influence in American life.

In time, however, many of the French came around. Today, the younger generation, deliberately breaking with the cultural heritage their ancestors brought from Canada, no longer think of themselves as Frenchmen particularly but simply as Americans. French national parishes still remain but are gradually passing from the scene and the ethnic tensions of the past are slowly being forgotten.

New Orleans, a dominantly French city from the beginning, has provided the prime example of a Catholicism different in character and temperament from the Irish- or German-dominated Church found in most American cities. The tradition of the South mingled with a distinctly French interpretation of Catholic culture has given it a uniqueness that sets it off both from the rest of the Protestant South and the Catholic cities of the North.

Latin-Americans in the United States—mainly people of Mexican, Puerto Rican, and Cuban backgrounds—number in the millions. Mexican-Americans, in all about four million persons, form the largest body. One sector of this group, more properly called Hispanos, are the descendants of the Spanish colonists who originally settled the Southwest. Until fairly recent years they were almost exclusively engaged in stock raising or subsistence agriculture and lived in village societies, following folk customs handed down from father to son.

The Hispanos are characteristically devout, prayerful, and passionately Catholic, observing religious practices unknown elsewhere in the American Church. Largely isolated from their Anglo-American neighbors, they have gone their own way—a proud, impressively dignified people who have long been the victims of prejudice, economic exploitation, and racial snobbery. They have not only been cut off from the Anglo community but have suffered from the indifference of ecclesiastical authorities as well; over the years little effort was made to integrate them into the larger life of the Church. Barely represented among the clergy and shapers of lay opinion, they have never had a real voice in American Catholic life. Had they been better integrated, the Hispanos might not only have found powerful support in their search for justice but have enriched Catholicism with virtues of gentleness and sensitivity that no other group of American Catholics possesses in such abundance.

The larger group of Mexican-Americans emigrated in the twentieth century from Mexico itself. They too have suffered from discrimination and lack of education. Again, their fellow Catholics did little over the years to help alleviate the conditions under which they have been forced to live, though the bishops of the United States in 1945 organized a committee to give them special pastoral attention and twenty years later took effective action in opposing a labor-contract system which was exploiting them. In recent years, a group of militant Mexican-American (or Chicano) leaders have emerged, a few of them priests, who have not hesitated to demand full rights for their people, nor have they spared the mainstream Church in their scalding criticism of a society which has long made life intolerable for these poorest and least privileged of Americans.

Puerto Ricans and Cubans, the vast majority of whom are at least nominally Catholic, form the other large group of Latin Americans in the continental United States. The Puerto Ricans arrived in great numbers from the island after the Second World War. They settled in New York, Chicago, and other large cities—the last in the long line of ethnic groups subjected to hostility, prejudice, and segregation who found it difficult to adjust to the demands of urban living in an alien Anglo-Saxon culture.

In their case as well as in the case of the Cubans who poured into Miami fleeing the regimes of either General Batista or Fidel Castro during roughly the same years, no effort was made to set up special national parishes. With national parishes going out of style, the idea was to integrate them into existing structures. To meet their needs, many seminarians and younger members of the clergy, beginning in the 1950s, studied Spanish and attended special classes in the hope of sensitizing themselves to the cultural patterns of the newcomers.

Yet, due to ignorance of the true doctrines of the Faith, which was attributable above all to the paucity of priests on the islands, a great deal of bizarre superstition, confusingly mingled with Catholic practices, still has a strong hold on the people. It will take time to undo this, since most of them still have at best only a minimal contact with the institutional Church, and even those whom priests manage to reach find it hard to understand Catholicism in its efficient, straightforward American manifestation. Many have been won over by store-front missionaries whose peculiar "Protestant" version of Christianity —a mingling of evangelical fundamentalist fervor with corrupt Catholic devotionalism—is actually more congenial to their inherited ideas of religion than the highly structured, restrained worship available in the parish churches of New York, Chicago, or Miami.

The Negro Catholic in America has always been rare—at the present time there are somewhat fewer than 800,000, and even that small number represents a twofold increase since World War II. . . .

Until very recently, Negro Catholics were required to conform to standard liturgical uses and white patterns of thought and behavior, while they were effectively cut off from Catholic cultural life by the patterns of social segregation. The result was that no distinctive black Catholicism was ever allowed to flourish in the United States. The Church thereby deprived itself of the particular contribution Negroes might have made in theological thinking, music, and art, for example. But with more liturgical freedom and variety provided for in the postconciliar Church and a steady if still slow breaking down of racist attitudes, American Catholicism as a whole may yet be enriched by the particular genius of its still pitifully few black members.

American Catholicism, an amalgam of all these traditions, customs, national temperaments, and even liturgies has been a kind of religious United Nations, on the surface monolithic but actually perhaps more varied than any other religious denomination in the nation. In addition to the major groupings there are smaller enclaves of Portuguese, Scandinavians (who have their own Saint Ansgar's Guild), American Indians, Eskimos, Chinese, Lebanese, and numerous others, each with its very special character. If it be true, then, that "we are the Church," Catholicism in the United States speaks, and has long spoken, with many different accents. Yet only a few voices have been actually heard beyond their own ethnic boundaries. There has been an identifiable Catholic ghetto culture in America, but by and large it has been representative of a privileged group—white, fairly assimilated, and, at least in recent decades, preponderantly middle class.

18

American Jewry: Social History and Group Identity

MARSHALL SKLARE

In 1654 the first Jews, some twenty-three refugees from Brazil, arrived on American soil. Three centuries later the Jewish population of the United States totaled an estimated 5,800,000. While modest in size as a group, the impact of Jews on American life has been out of all proportion to their number and percentage of the population at large.

The significance of America's Jews must also be understood in a wider perspective. (In our usage "America" and "American" means the United States.) Here is the largest Jewish community on earth, indeed, the largest in the millennial history of the Jewish people. About 42 percent of the world's Jews live in the United States.

The importance of the United States as a center for Jews and Jewish life has been greatly increased by the impact of Nazi genocide against the Jewish people. Nazism reduced European Jewish communities to a shadow of their former importance. Only Great Britain and France survive as important centers, the latter largely because of the recent settlement of North African Jews. The importance of the United States has also been

Marshall Sklare is Ratner Professor of American Jewish Studies and Sociology at Brandeis University.

magnified by the cultural persecution of communist regimes, particularly by the government of Soviet Russia. About 2,568,000 Jews live in Soviet Russia, constituting the second largest Jewish settlement in the world. But this community exists under severe repression. For the past several decades opportunities for the expression and transmission of Jewish identity have been proscribed, fraught with grave penalties, or made difficult in other ways. While Jewish life of a sort goes on in the Soviet Union and expressions of Jewish identity make surprising appearances, this community is not to be compared to those of the free world.

The only other country with more than a million Jews is Israel. Its Jewish population of 2,365,000 (as of 1967) is even more recently arrived than that of the United States. But while only 17 percent of the world's Jews live in Israel, its significance as a center for Jews and Jewish life is little affected by its size. Israel and the United States, then, constitute the two great centers of contemporary Jewish life.[1]

While American Jewry plays a crucial role in contemporary Jewish life, it has a significance beyond the Jewish situation. In studying America's Jews, we are able to clarify the problem of the ethnic minority in modern society. While ethnic conflict in the United States centers on black–white confrontation rather than on Christian–Jewish tensions, the Jews still best exemplify the condition of being a minority group. They do so because their religion is non-Christian, and it remains so in spite of the modifications of traditional Judaism made by those Jews who have adopted prevalent cultural modes. Second, no matter how harmonious the relationship between Judaism and Christianity may appear, it is inherently a stressful relationship—the religions are closely related and historic rivals. Third, despite the current stress on pluralism, Judaism is the only significant non-Christian religion encountered in American society.

[1] For the figures see Leon Shapiro, "World Jewish Population," *American Jewish Year Book*, 69 (1968), 543–549. (Hereafter the *American Jewish Year Book* will be referred to as *AJYB*.)

The position of the Jews as the quintessential ethnic minority is reinforced by the presence of anti-Jewish prejudice and discrimination. As prejudice and discrimination are difficult to measure, differences of opinion about their extent are inevitable. Whatever the actual situation, however, present levels are sufficiently high as to imprint on Jews a feeling of minority status. Furthermore, virulent anti-Semitism is more than an ancestral memory—it is a phenomenon of the contemporary era as well as of the ancient and medieval world.

All of these factors are not sufficient to make the Jews an "ideal type": in the final analysis it is their *goal* as an ethnic minority that makes them such. Most Jews are retentivist in orientation—that is, they reject the idea that assimilation is the end toward which they should strive. Being retentivist, Jews attempt to pass their identity on to their children. Jewish efforts to retain an ethnic identity tend to be more strenuous than those of other groups and the structure of the Jewish community is consequently more elaborate. Paradoxically, because of this retentivism the Jew must separate himself from the general society while he simultaneously seeks to integrate himself into it. Since he is racially one with the dominant group and increasingly has opportunities for a dignified (in contrast to a demeaning) assimilation, his separatism—whatever its nature and extent—is an act of crucial sociological significance.

JEWISH IMMIGRATION UNTIL WORLD WAR I: GERMANS AND EAST EUROPEANS

To understand the rise of an American Jewish community we must realize that the eighteenth and nineteenth centuries were times of rapid population growth in Europe. That growth was shared by Jews. Population growth, in combination with poverty, persecution, and the changing attitudes of Jews themselves resulted in vast movements of people. Some of these movements took place within the same land, as for example the population flow from Bavarian villages to Munich or Berlin, or from Polish villages to Warsaw or Lodz. Some of it took place across frontiers. But some of it spanned continents and resulted in the establishment of new Jewish communities in Australia, Argentina, South Africa, and the United States. Immigration was to have unique meaning for Jews. With the exception of some parts of the Soviet Union, the bulk of the families remaining in traditional places of Jewish settlement on the European continent were later to be exterminated by the Nazis; only those who resettled themselves in distant places survived.

Since the immigration of Jews to America extends over three centuries, we would expect it to include diverse strands. But among Jews such diversity has been even sharper than with most other groups, for Jews originated in different countries, frequently with contrasting traditions. Conventional historical wisdom has it that there have been three waves of Jewish migration to America: the Spanish–Portuguese, the German, and the East European.[2]

During the latter part of the nineteenth century, and for several decades thereafter, some felt that differences between Jews were so sharp and immutable that the American-Jewish community would be permanently bifurcated—that it would be composed of an underclass consisting of a large and shiftless *lumpenproletariat* and an upper middle class led by a small group of aristocratic families. If this idea strikes us today as ludicrous, equally invalid is the notion that generational and place of origin differences have entirely eroded away. Differentiation traceable to the separate waves of immigration is still present despite an ever-increasing convergence with respect to class attainment, educational levels, and style of life. But such differentiation does not mean that American Jewry presently consists of two or more subcommunities, or even that it be-

[2] See Jacob R. Marcus, "The Periodization of American Jewish History," *Publication of the American Jewish Historical Society*, 47 (September 1957–June 1958), 128–130.

trays the present structure of Israeli Jewry where Oriental and Western Jews are readily distinguishable, and where certain group characteristics involve deep and abiding social problems.

American Jewry traces its origin to Sephardic Jews whose families came from the Iberian Peninsula and who lived in one or another European country (or their colonies) before journeying to America. While these seventeenth and eighteenth century Spanish–Portuguese settlers numbered only a few hundred—indeed they were no longer a majority in the American Jewish community as early as 1720—their social status and leadership role in Jewish communal affairs, together with the fact of their early arrival, has magnified their importance. Thus the synagogue that they established in Newport, Rhode Island is a national shrine. Another one of their institutions, the Spanish and Portuguese Synagogue Shearith Israel, was the first synagogue in New York City.

Ashkenazic Jews, those originating in western and eastern Europe, began coming to America in the eighteenth century. Some of the early Ashkenazim were assimilated by the Sephardim. However, by the early nineteenth century their numerical superiority had gained a cultural and institutional predominance. Until the 1880s the immigration of Ashkenazic Jews was primarily composed of individuals originating in Germany or in adjoining areas dominated by German culture. Even though the East European immigration that came afterwards exceeded the German immigration many times over, the settlement of German Jews in the nineteenth century is of more than historical and antiquarian interest—the German influence in the Jewish community is still discernible in contemporary life.

One explanation for the German-Jewish influence is their settlement throughout the length and breadth of the land: German Jews established themselves in all large- and medium-size cities and in hundreds of smaller communities as well. . . .

Geographical spread, while necessary to establish the predominance of the German Jews, would not have been sufficient. It was the spectacular rise of the German Jews into the upper reaches of the middle class, and particularly into the upper class, that brought them into positions of authority. Not only did they penetrate these class levels, but there arose in the last half of the nineteenth century a group of families whose great wealth was comparable to that of some of the richest Gentiles of the nation. These families were concentrated in New York City.[3] While they had marital and financial connections with rich merchandising families in the country at large their wealth was derived from a different source: merchant (or what we now call "investment") banking. Thus Jewish-dominated financial houses were powerful at a time when merchant banking played a crucial role in the economy.[4] However, while such banking was the cornerstone of many of the greatest German-Jewish fortunes, it was fated to decline in significance. Commercial banking, controlled almost entirely by Gentiles, grew apace and overall the banking function lost a good deal of its old significance. But by that time the position of the German Jews—as dramatized by the success of the Seligman, Loeb, Lehman, Schiff, Sachs, and Goldman families, as well as by others—had been secured both within the Jewish community as well as outside of it.

It was inevitable that the German Jews became Jewish high society. Some, like Jacob Schiff and Felix Warburg, were scions of important Frankfurt or Hamburg families and would have become members of the club in any case. But it was the social position of the thousands who came from obscure villages that was transformed by their economic success. Of course there were those whose financial rise was not very spectacular (such families tend to be overlooked by scholarly and

---

[3] This is the group celebrated by Stephen Birmingham in his book *"Our Crowd": The Great Jewish Families of New York* (New York: Harper and Row, 1967).

[4] See Barry E. Supple, "A Business Elite: German Jewish Financiers in Nineteenth-Century New York," *Business History Review*, 31, No. 2 (Summer 1957), 143–178.

popular writers alike), but even they could improve their social position by borrowing status from their more successful compatriots. In any case the new German Jews overwhelmed the ever-thinning ranks of the Sephardic (and Sephardized Ashkenazic) families who had constituted Jewish society.

The mass of America's Jews was yet to arrive. Coming between the 1880s and the World War I period, their settlement transformed the Jewish community. No longer would it be composed of a bourgeoisie that rapidly was acculturating, even if still attached to a widely admired German *Kultur*. No longer could it be confidently predicted that the group would disappear without incident into the great melting pot. In 1877 Jews were only .52 percent of the population; by 1917 they were 3.28 percent. In fact the new immigrants swamped the older element. The 400,000 Jews in the United States in 1888 were joined by 334,338 more by 1896. Thus the ratio of net migration to initial population after a mere decade was an astonishing 83 percent.

The new immigrants were East European Jews originating from Russia, Poland, Lithuania, Hungary, Rumania, and adjacent territories. They came without capital or a knowledge of the English language. Frequently they had little or no training in the occupations most common in the United States at the time. They were too numerous to spread themselves in the way the German Jews had done, and they arrived after the frontier had been settled. But in any case they lacked the desire to distribute themselves evenly. They settled in a relatively few of the largest cities, locating in conspicuously ethnic neighborhoods.

These new immigrants gave the American Jewish community a future. Their numbers made it viable demographically even as their Jewish culture did so spiritually. Nevertheless, important segments of the German-Jewish leadership viewed the new immigration as a threat to American Jewish life. It was feared that the immigrants would imperil

Jewish status, create anti-Semitism, and ultimately wreck all that had been created by the older immigrants. The solution was clear: stop, or at least reduce, the flood of immigrants. There is still some dispute as to the extent to which efforts were made in this direction, either by controlling immigration at the European source or by encouraging officials to refuse admittance to those who landed at American ports. But there is no question that at the same time the older element assisted those who settled in the United States. Much of this help was geared to speeding adjustment to the new environment. Such assistance was not always accepted in a manner that its donors deemed appropriate.

If the East European immigrants introduced a Jewish lower class to the United States and populated the first American-Jewish slums, they were nothing like the *lumpenproletariat* that the German middle and upper classes had conjured up. Although the Lower East Side of New York did have a small complement of Jewish racketeers, its streets were safe at night. Although a few Jewish husbands did not meet their family responsibilities (leading to the establishment of a social agency, the National Desertion Bureau), the Jewish family remained intact. Although relief had to be extended in some exceptional cases, the "ghettos" of the nation had a very low rate of indigence. In sum, aside from the crowded and noisome environment none of the sociological conditions associated with slum life were present in these immigrant districts.

If the East European found himself initially confined to the slum, he did not reside in tenements for very long. Moving rapidly from one newer neighborhood to another, by the 1950s the trend toward suburbia was unmistakable. And in the better suburbs Germans and East Europeans encountered each other once more. The social mobility of the East Europeans, which made this rendezvous possible, never seemed as spectacular as that of the Germans. It was not associated with the mystique of merchant banking and thus it lacked a "House of Rothschild" image. Rather, it was based on a steady rise, although sometimes temporarily halted by economic depression. The East European story is that of a group which remains in the working class for only a brief time (although long enough to make the experience of the sweatshop part of the American-Jewish saga). The majority leaves this class by the route of establishing small businesses, some of which grow into substantial enterprises in the course of time. During the past several decades East European mobility has broadened to include the practice of professional occupations as well. At present the descendants of the pre–World War I East European group are found in all segments of the middle class, as well as in the upper class.

While the social mobility of the East European Jew lacks the glamour and dizzy heights associated with the rise of the German Jew, it may be in fact a more spectacular achievement, having been accomplished against greater odds. The East European Jews could not base their success on distributing manufactured goods in a developing nineteenth century economy, because they entered the economy at a more mature phase. Also, East Europeans were too numerous to achieve success by fulfilling a single economic function. Finally, they were concentrated in a few places, rather than being widely separated and serving as a national middle class. Thus they were forced to compete against each other. As the history of the garment trades reminds us, such competition could be murderous indeed. . . .

THE CHARACTERISTICS OF THE IMMIGRANTS AND THE IMPACT OF AMERICA

The immigrants who arrived before 1917 established the basic forms of American Jewish life. It is therefore essential that we inquire who these immigrants were, together with the impact that America had on them.

With all of the adversities of life and the anti-Semitic restrictions that pressed upon

him, the immigration of the European Jew was basically elective rather than enforced.[5] As a consequence those who came did not constitute a cross section of the Jewish population. On the crucial matter of religiosity, for example, relatively few of the most learned and the most observant came to America.

The pious had in fact been forewarned. A constant theme in the reports of American correspondents who wrote for the German or Yiddish newspapers and periodicals was that whatever other virtues were esteemed in America, piety was not one of them. Letters from American immigrants to their European relatives emphasized the same theme. . . .

If the piety of the East European immigrant group has been inflated so has its social status and class position. While conceding that their families had to start from scratch when they arrived here, many present-day American Jews look upon their immigrant ancestors as having been solid and esteemed householders in the communities from which they came. In point of fact, well-established and well-regarded middle class families, not to speak of the upper classes, generally remained where they were. If they changed their place of residence they generally settled in a large city nearby. Few of those with above-average *yichus* (family reputation—by extension, social status) were motivated to make the move to the United States. Perhaps they were dimly aware of an admonition contained in Haym Salomon's letter quoted previously: "Your *yichus* is worth very little here."[6]

Selective migration allowed American Jewry to develop without the shackles of the old system of stratification. New grounds for esteem were developed; deference could now

[5] This statement is made with due regard to the pogroms, homelessness and dislocations that followed the defeat of Russia in the Russo-Japanese War and the Revolution of 1905, as well as earlier dislocations. See Lucy S. Dawidowicz, *The Golden Tradition: Jewish Life and Thought in Eastern Europe* (New York: Holt, Rinehart and Winston, 1967), pp. 69–75.

[6] Bernard D. Weinryb, "Jewish Immigration and Accommodation to America" in Marshall Sklare (ed.), *The Jews: Social Patterns of An American Group* (New York: The Free Press, 1958), p. 12.

be given where one thought deference was due. As a consequence, people of distinguished *yichus* who did come to America found that they would receive social honor only if they were successful according to the new value system. Even an august personage like Jacob Schiff, for example, made his way through his accomplishments and leadership qualities rather than on the basis of his singular *yichus*. Those who could not compete in the status marketplace were passed by.[7]

The absence of traditional constraints, the erosion of the old status structure, and the overrepresentation of the nominally Orthodox provide the backdrop for what was to be a revolutionary experience for Jews. So revolutionary was that experience—and so agreeable when measured against life in eastern Europe —that few Jews who experienced it returned home or moved to other countries. While for certain ethnic minorities return and resettlement in the motherland was a common phenomenon, for Jews emigration was exceptional.[8]

What, then, was so revolutionary about America? For the first time the fact of Jewishness became irrelevant in the public sphere. The millennial Jewish experience had been quite the opposite. Jews not only occupied a special status, but the position of the individual in the social structure was entirely determined by his Jewishness. Even when the status accorded the Jew conferred privileges as well as disabilities, it implied subordination. We should remember that no other American immigrant group, including those whose homelands were under the domination of a foreign power, had a history of subordination comparable with that of the Jews. Although they might suffer subordination if they were ruled by outsiders, other peoples lived as majorities. Their culture was the prevailing one. They possessed historical memories of their

former independence. They had faith in their ability to achieve independence once again.

America was the first new nation. It did not have to make the transition from medieval society, with its corporate structure and ascribed statuses, to modern society with its concept of individual freedom and equality. Thus there was no group in American society that had a distinctive stake in redefining the position of the Jew. And since the Jew did not have to be emancipated, there was no segment of the population seeking to restore the Jew to a *status quo ante*.[9] In sum the Jew was free, free at last. And his history meant that freedom had a special meaning for him which it did not hold for the Italian, the Pole, or the Irishman.

The meaning of freedom for the Jew can be analyzed in one way by his response to the duties of citizenship. These duties were eagerly shouldered, as for example the obligation to vote. As a leading authority has noted: "The [Lower] East Side Jews registered and voted in greater proportion than any other immigrant group, except perhaps the Irish, and they treated the franchise with greater seriousness than any other group, especially the Irish."[10] The Irish could of course afford to be relaxed—they never expected to be discriminated against at the polls. Though their power as a group depended on their getting out the vote, voting itself never became a sacred rite for them in the way it did for the Jews.

If the Jew was intoxicated with the freedom of the ballot his newly found position as a

---

[7] May N. Tabak, "My Grandmother Had Yichus," *Commentary*, April 1949, pp. 368–372, conveys some of the pathos involved.

[8] See Sidney Liskofsky, "Jewish Immigration," *AJYB*, 51 (1950), 75; and Nathan Glazer et al., *The Characteristics of American Jews* (New York: Jewish Education Committee Press, 1965), p. 19.

[9] See Ben Halpern, "America is Different," in Sklare, *The Jews*, pp. 23–39. We have, of course, oversimplified the American picture. For some of the shadings see Oscar Handlin and Mary F. Handlin, "The Acquisition of Political and Social Rights by the Jews in the United States," *AJYB*, 56 (1955), 43–98. It should be remembered, for example, that non-Protestants were denied full rights in New Hampshire until 1877.

[10] Lucy S. Dawidowicz, "From Past to Past: Jewish East Europe to Jewish East Side," *Conservative Judaism*, 22, No. 2 (Winter 1968), 20–21. For figures on the frequency of voting by Irish, Jewish, and other ethnics see Jack Elinson, Paul W. Haberman, and Cyrille Gell, *Ethnic and Educational Data on Adults in New York City 1963–1964* (New York: School of Public Health and Administrative Medicine, Columbia University, 1967), p. 155.

citizen was manifested in an even more significant area. This was in the area of education. For the East European Jew in particular the idea that Jewishness was irrelevant to one's admittance to an elementary school, to a high school, or to a municipal college or state university (and also irrelevant to how one was treated there) was astonishing. The notion that such institutions were supposed to be neutral in the area of religion was also unheard of. Accordingly, the Jewish response to public education was similar to their response to the ballot. Jews not only sent their children to school but they also made the principle of public education an article of faith. In fact loyalty to the cause of public education was so overwhelming that as late as 1917 only five small Jewish day (that is, parochial) schools had been established in the entire country.[11] Jews were simultaneously attracted to public education and suspicious of private education —they feared that the establishment of day schools would constitute disloyalty to America. Their fears were not allayed by the example of their Irish Catholic neighbors, who never doubted for a moment that they had the right to establish their own schools.

If voting was not an act that committed the Jew in any ultimate sense, his attachment to public education had more significant implications. It signified that he was prepared to render unto America that which belonged to America, and that he felt that he must reserve his Jewishness for his remaining life space. It meant that he would not be a sectarian, insisting on special rights and privileges and asking that the public order accommodate itself to his demands. It meant that he would refrain from educating his children to be sectarians. Rather, when he educated his children Jewishly he would do so on a supplementary basis so as not to interfere with public education. It meant that he would not signify his uniqueness by his manner of dress. He would don a skullcap only in the privacy of home or synagogue and thus not invade the public domain.

America offered the Jew freedom; the Jew offered America accommodation in return.

We are justified in asking whether or not America actually required accommodation as the price of freedom. Or did the Jew offer accommodation out of gratitude for his newly found status as citizen? Whichever alternative is correct not all American Jews are prepared to abide by the "social contract" established by the German and East European Jews who settled in America before World War I. Some of the immigrants who arrived later felt that the contract placed Jews at a disadvantage. And some descendants of the earlier immigrants—much more sure of themselves as Americans than were their progenitors—have come to feel that their ancestors misunderstood America, or had been too eager to please. They believe that a new contrast must be negotiated—one which will show greater fairness to Jews without doing violence to essential American doctrine.

JEWISH IMMIGRATION TO THE PRESENT

After 1921, and especially after 1924, the number of Jews arriving in the United States, particularly from eastern Europe, was severely limited by immigration restrictions. Before then, all of those who wanted to come were able, in effect, to do so. The post–World War I East European immigration was directly related to the social changes which the war brought in its wake. Some of the new immigrants had been well-established but lost everything when their communities were ravaged. But even if the old life continued intact it was no longer what it had been before the war. The small town, or *shtetl*, stagnated after World War I, losing whatever significance it had enjoyed as an economic and administrative center. Furthermore, in newly independent Poland, Jews were subject to laws and practices which were meant to displace them from middle class occupations.

One of the decisive factors motivating emigration from eastern Europe was the triumph of communism in Russia. As with other

[11] The day schools established in the early days of the Republic had closed when the public school system was established.

segments of the bourgeoisie, the revolution displaced the Jewish middle and upper class and fragmented the traditional status system. Equally significant, the triumph of communism meant that those who were not prepared to conform to the new ideology either had to leave or to suffer grave penalties. Jewish counterrevolutionary elements included religionists, Zionists, and Hebraists. Finally, those Jews who had no strong Jewish identity but whose political views deviated from the then-current version of communist ideology had every good reason to leave the Soviet Union.

All of these strands were represented among the post–World War I immigrants. Those who were Russified had little impact on American Jewish life. But this was not the case with regard to those who had a strong Jewish identity. Their influence was felt because the Jewish standards to which they were accustomed were more advanced than those that prevailed in the United States. This became evident in the field of Yiddish journalism and literature, in Hebraist circles, and in the world of Orthodoxy. But whatever their ideology, the reduced circumstances in which these new immigrants found themselves made their situation that much more poignant: they were confronted by former townsmen from the lower depths of society who had managed to raise themselves into the solid middle class or even beyond.

The most widely known of the groups that arrived between the wars were not the East Europeans, however, but those immigrants who came from Germany and Austria after 1933. This wave of immigration gave currency to the term "refugee," although some of those coming from Russia and Poland could have been similarly described. The term refugee implied that the immigrant was not moving but fleeing, that he was escaping impending catastrophe, and that under normal conditions he would never have come to America. The refugee immigration also meant that unlike their predecessors the new arrivals were drawn from a variety of class and status levels. It also meant that in contrast to the unmarried young men who had come from

Germany a century earlier, entire families arrived.

There is a stereotype that the German Jews who came to the United States after 1933 did not realize that they were Jewish until Hitler reminded them of it. This notion, which apparently emanates from East Europeans, is more a reflection of the intragroup hostilities discussed earlier than an accurate description of the social situation. In fact one segment of the German immigration was comprised of East Europeans who had settled in Germany in the recent past. Furthermore the new German immigration included individuals with very strong Jewish commitments. For example, sectarian German-Jewish Orthodoxy—hardly known in the United States—made the transition from Frankfurt to the Washington Heights section of Manhattan.[12] Additionally, Orthodox Jews who did not follow sectarian ways were also in evidence.

We would expect that those German Jews who were Orthodox—admittedly a minor segment of the group—would find little in common with their American cousins, who were mainly Reform Jews. But whatever his viewpoint on Jewish identity the new German Jew rarely integrated himself into the social world of the old German Jew. Frequently, class differences made such integration difficult. But even in cases where these differences were minimal or of little consequence and where both new and old German Jews were equally distant from traditional Jewish patterns, they found that they were separated by a cultural gulf. Generally, new German Jews of liberal conviction were devoted to German culture— or more specifically to a German-Jewish variant thereof.[13] This variant was unknown to the descendants of old German Jews. It had been relatively unfamiliar even to their immigrant ancestors, who had originated in villages and had come to America without the benefit of a university education, and in many cases without being exposed to the full curriculum

[12] See Ernest Stock, "Washington Heights' 'Fourth Reich,'" *Commentary*, June 1951, pp. 581–588.

[13] See Gershom Scholem, "Jews and Germans," *Commentary*, November 1966, pp. 31–38.

of the *gymnasium* as well. In sum, even when there was no ideological difference between old and new German Jews, the immigrants found themselves alienated from American counterparts who lacked their humanistic learning and cultural sophistication. The Jewishly committed, on the other hand, were in a less-ambiguous situation. American pluralism sanctioned the formation of sectarian associations, from which an attempt could be made to preserve the heritage of German Jewry. Or the Jewishly committed had the option of integrating themselves into East European dominated institutions where standards essentially conformed with those they had known before.

Throughout this period the immigration of East Europeans continued, some arriving even after the start of World War II. But immediately after the war such immigration became particularly noticeable. Some of the immigrants were concentration camp survivors. If the only uniqueness that they shared was their tragic life experience, they generally found whatever niche they could and attempted to reconstruct at least the semblance of a normal existence. But some of these new immigrants brought more with them: they had very strong convictions about their Jewishness. Two groups can be discerned—the Yiddishists-Bundists and the Orthodox, particulary the Orthodox sectarians.[14] The Orthodox sectarians' impact has been the most noticeable, and their example has created controversy within the minority community.

Instead of acculturating to prevailing Orthodox standards the sectarians proceeded to challenge them. They wished to preserve their form of dress, their beards and earlocks. Appearing on the streets and subways of New York, they produced highly ambivalent reactions among East European Jews whose immediate forebears had been of similar appearance.[15] In sum, the sectarians refused to abide by the social contract. Frequently they

considered themselves to be brands plucked from the fire, miraculously saved so that the way of life hallowed by tradition might be preserved. They were loath to expose their children to any substantial amount of secular education, much less to enroll them in public institutions. They proceeded to establish a network of *yeshivot*, they stimulated day school education, and they profoundly influenced the Orthodoxy of the older East European group.

Though Hasidic Jews represent only one segment of this immigration they have preempted the popular imagination. While some of the earlier East European immigrants had come from families with a Hasidic tradition, Hasidic life was never established on American shores. The courts of the *rebbaim* (plural of *rebbe*, Hasidic leader) remained in eastern Europe; immigrants of Hasidic background had only dimming memories of their special traditions. The emergence of Hasidism during World War II and shortly thereafter was made possible by the arrival of a number of *rebbaim*, together with small circles of their followers. Some refugee intellectuals were also active in creating an interest in the neo-Hasidism of Martin Buber.

Bringing the story of immigration up to date, we find that Latin America, rather than eastern or western Europe, is currently the largest source of Jewish immigration to the United States. True many such immigrants, or their parents, were born in Europe. For some their arrival in America means coming to the country that was their first choice when they or their families left eastern or western Europe, but to which they could not gain entry at the time. For others it means moving to a nation that has greater political stability than the country in which they are resident, or improved educational opportunities, or more abundant possibilities for leading a Jewish life.

All of the Jewish newcomers we have been describing, whatever the time of their immigration and the circumstances under which they came, did not need to justify their arrival either to themselves or to others. The

---

[14] For the second group see Liebman, *op. cit.*, pp. 67–89.

[15] This ambivalence is depicted in Philip Roth's well-known story that has a suburban setting: "Eli, the Fanatic," *Commentary*, April 1959, pp. 292–309.

freedom offered by America was justification enough. Whatever liberties were enjoyed (or promised) in the old society, and whatever prejudices and discriminations might be present in the new, the consensus was that America offered the Jew greater freedom and a deeper sense of belonging than he could ever possess in his homeland.

None of this holds true for immigrants who come from Israel. In recent years some 2,000 to 3,000 such persons have been admitted to the United States annually. The Hebrew term for such emigrants, *yordim* (literally, "those who descend"), provides a clue regarding their special position. Israelis are the first newcomers who must justify their immigration to themselves and to their fellow Jews. They have uprooted themselves from the Holy Land to return to the *Galut* (literally, the lands of the exile). Leaving a country where Jews constitute the majority they have resumed the age-old pattern of Jews occupying a minority group status. In a sense they have moved from a position of greater freedom to one of lesser freedom. . . .

GROUP MEMBERSHIP AND IDENTITY

If the foregoing constitutes some of the essential social history of American Jewry we must next inquire how individuals who think of themselves as Jewish assume this particular definition of their group membership.

According to *halachah* (Jewish law) the essential requirement for being Jewish is to be born of Jewish parentage, more particularly to be the offspring of a Jewish mother. Being Jewish involves two complementary aspects: membership in the ethnic group and membership in the religious community. The extent to which the individual exercises his prerogatives by participating in ethnic group affairs, and particularly in the life of the religious community, is a matter of choice. But no matter to what extent the prerogatives of birth are exercised, all Jews are essentially equal members of the ethnic group and of the religious community.

Aside from the special case of male cir-

cumcision, there is no ceremony of induction into the group or of confirmation of identity. Interestingly enough, as Jews have acculturated, and as the problem of group identity has become more complex, they have sought such ceremonial confirmation. Thus the rites of Confirmation for boys and girls and of Bat Mitzvah for girls have been developed. Furthermore, the traditional Bar Mitzvah ceremony has assumed an entirely new importance. So deep is the need to confirm identity that there are cases on record of men not having had a Bar Mitzvah at age thirteen who underwent the ceremony in adulthood. From the traditional point of view their action was superfluous, for upon attaining the age of thirteen they had automatically become fully adult members of the group.

If psychological needs make certain individuals overconform, Jewish law tends in the direction of considering that not only are all born Jews considered Jewish but that they always remain so. A question then occurs about the individual who converts to another religion. Jewish law—surprisingly enough—tends to claim him as Jewish. Jewish public opinion, on the other hand, generally does not, as became evident when the Supreme Court of Israel adjudicated the case of Brother Daniel, a Carmelite Monk who described himself as a Jew of the Catholic religion. The Court decided that Brother Daniel was not a Jew and therefore that he be denied an immigrant's certificate under the Law of the Return as well as the right to register as a Jew under the registration law. In sum, Jewish public opinion generally reserves group membership for those born of Jewish parents who either practice Judaism or who are religiously inactive in the sense that they have not converted to another faith. A religiously inactive person is thus identified as Jewish by the following rule of thumb: the religion that he does not practice is Judaism rather than Christianity.

Thus whatever the strength of the identity, one important aspect of being Jewish is the individual's resistance to accepting membership in a competing group. The bulk of American Jewry is thus the offspring of Jewish parents whose identity they have assumed. From some points of view it may seem remarkable that in an age of rapid social change so many accept their parents' identity. But actually the surprising thing about the American Jewish community is that so high a proportion of parents want their children to accept the parents' identity. Of course such a desire flows from the most profound psychological mechanisms, but also important is the fact that the life chances of children will not be severely or irretrievably modified by their taking on Jewish identity. There is clear evidence that parents have acted differently under other circumstances. Some Jewish parents in early nineteenth century Germany insisted on giving their children an identity different from their own. To be sure, their motives had pathological implications but these parents were engaged—as they saw it—in creating a better future for their children. Most American Jewish parents, on the other hand, feel that they are acting in their children's best interest when they seek to instill in them a Jewish identity. However enduring the identity on a long-range basis, only in a disordered parent-child relationship will it be rejected by the child out of hand.

All that we have said is based upon the assumption that Jewish group membership in the United States is a matter of private sentiment rather than of public commitment or legal definition. Thus the transmission of identity becomes a problem inasmuch as the state does not decide who is a Jew—persons do. This places a heavy burden upon the individual, because he must make the decision about his group identity. In theory at least, the state is not prepared to offer him any guidance. In fact, the individual is not even asked by the state to define himself for statistical purposes, as for example in connection with the decennial census.[16]

Individual decision is crucial in assuming the role of Jew. Yet these decisions are influenced by, and are dependent upon, larger entities: definitions by both the minority group and the majority. It is not enough that an individual considers himself Jewish: he must be so considered by other Jews as well as by Gentiles. In most cases all three parties are in tandem. Thus the great majority of born Jews consider themselves Jewish, are so considered by their fellow Jews, and are regarded as Jewish by Gentiles. To be sure, on occasion there are instances where discrepancies exist. For example, while many Jews would not consider members of the Hebrew Christian group to be Jewish, Hebrew Christians assert the continuing legitimacy of their former group affiliation.[17]

For every minority-group member the possibility of non-identification—that is, of assimilation—exists as either a present or remote possibility. Such assimilation may be distinguished by the degree to which it is purposive, and individuals who are assimilating could thus be arranged along a continuum of passive-active assimilators. Assimilation may be said to be complete when the individual no longer considers himself a Jew, when he is thought of as a Gentile by Jews, and when he is regarded as a Gentile by Gentiles. Of course both minority and majority are composed of diverse strands of opinion and hence may not present a unified front. A given individual might be considered Jewish by one segment of the minority or majority, while another might think of him as Gentile.

We must remember, in examining Jews as they adjust to the conditions of life in a comparatively open society such as America, that individuals move both toward the minority group as well as away from it. The process of joining the Jewish group is intriguing because students of ethnic groups generally think of movement as being in the opposite direction: from membership in the minority to membership in the majority.

As we have emphasized the dominant

---

[16] Most Jewish organizations have been against the collection of data on the basis of religion. See Marshall Sklare, "The Development and Utilization of Sociological Research: The Case of the American Jewish Community," *Jewish Journal of Sociology,* 5, No. 2 (December 1963), 169–172.

[17] See Ira O. Glick, "The Hebrew Christians: A Marginal Religious Group," in Sklare, *The Jews,* pp. 415–431.

way of joining the group is by birth. Such Jews are immediately members of an ethnic group and of a religious community. Other modes of affiliation present some ambiguities, for example those who join the group by way of conversion. Because of Judaism's minority status and its position through the centuries as a persecuted religion, its stance with respect to conversion has gone through various stages. But in the United States converts are regularly received and number several thousand each year. Such converts share the essential obligations and prerogatives of born Jews—they are religiously Jewish in the fullest sense. Because they are not born Jews, however, some Jews may consider converts to be ethnically Gentile or of indeterminate position, and may have varying degrees of self-consciousness in their relationships with them.[18] In any case when the convert changes his primary group from Gentile to Jewish he is well on the way toward assimilation into the Jewish group.

In addition to birth and conversion there is a third way of joining the group: through marriage to a Jew. While such a marriage does not make one religiously a Jew, it does mean that ethnically the person is placed in a new, and indeterminate position. If the marriage occasions severing bonds with Gentiles and joining an all-Jewish primary group, assimilation into the Jewish group is in process.

The majority of cases of conversion are in fact connected with marriage to a Jew. . . .

The fourth and final way of joining the Jewish group involves integrating oneself into a Jewish primary group. This, in effect, means changing one's ethnic loyalties. Such cases are highly exceptional and generally are encountered only in the largest cities. Frequently Gentiles of this type work in occupations that are strongly Jewish in composition. But this fourth way of joining the Jewish group is not to be compared to the previous three. Because there is no religious commitment, and because there is no ethnic commitment comparable to that of

marriage to a Jew, neither Jew nor Gentile are impelled to regard it seriously.

Our tacit assumption thus far has been that the person assimilating into the Jewish community is white. What then of the comparative handful of black Jews? Their situation has unique aspects but it also highlights the general problems encountered in the assimilation process. In the case of black Jews physical appearance raises questions as to the origin of Jewishness. The Jewish identification of some black Jews stems from family tradition, or from the usual routes of conversion and intermarriage. A more vocal, unified group claims distant descent from the *Falashas* (Ethiopian Jews), at times extending their claims of Jewishness to all American Negroes.

Until recently, identification as a Jew appeared more attractive to most black Jews than identification as a Negro. Now, however, there is pressure to identify as a Negro. Of course such pressure has always been present if only because of the existence of anti-Negro prejudice. But feelings of black pride have compounded the problem; they have created new pressures to identify as a Negro as well as to perpetuate what was to have been only a transitional arrangement: a separate black Jewish community. Finally, there is the problem of anti-Semitism. The white who is assimilating into the Jewish group is either shielded from anti-Semitism or experiences it at second or thirdhand. But the situation of the black Jew is different: he is exposed firsthand to a very direct kind of anti-Semitism in the Negro community and hence is forced to confront the problem of his own identity in a traumatic context. If he defends the Jew what kind of black is he?[19]

---

[18] Note the case of the convert in Park Forest who revealed his origin: see Herbert J. Gans, "The Origin and Growth of a Jewish Community," in Sklare, *The Jews,* p. 229.

[19] The one published study of the black Jews focuses on the group claiming *Falasha* descent. See Howard Brotz, *The Black Jews of Harlem: Negro Nationalism and the Dilemmas of Negro Leadership* (New York: The Free Press, 1964). The desire of some non-Falasha black Jews to press their claims for acceptance into the Jewish community has been complemented by the desire of some white Jews to speed such integration. Hence the establishment in New York City in 1964 of an organization known as *Hatzaad Harishon.*

Conversion, marriage, and a shift in the primary group all have their counterparts when the process moves in the opposite direction: when the individual is leaving the minority rather than joining it. Statistics on such assimilation remain elusive for several reasons. Assimilation occurs across generations rather than at a given point in time. Furthermore, the assimilated are not conscious of their state—only assimilationists are. Finally, assimilation is not widely esteemed and assimilationists tend to be conflicted about changing their group identity. Thus they are under pressure to portray themselves as different from what they are.

Whatever the numbers involved, assimilation has not been widespread enough to disorganize the American Jewish community, contrary to the expectations of an earlier generation of sociologists who saw Jews as progressing steadily from self-segregation to acculturation to assimilation. . . .

Just as prejudice and discrimination can no longer be viewed in the context of an overly hasty Jewish assimilation, so contemporary sociologists have had to grapple with the reality that Jewish identity is clearly more than a response to Gentile dislike. The efforts of both individual parents and of communal bodies to transmit Jewish identity cannot be reasonably interpreted as a "return to the ghetto." One current sociological perspective that attempts to explain the unexpected pervasiveness of ethnic identity takes the view that it results from modern man's need to protect himself from the impersonality and alienation of contemporary life. In seeking to protect himself he clings to familiar forms of social organization which go back to a more primitive stage of human culture. The critical attitudes of the analyst toward ethnic loyalties are manifest in the following statement:

> . . . the sense of ethnicity has proven to be hardy. As though with a wily cunning of its own, as though there were some essential element in man's nature that demanded it—something that compelled him to merge his lonely individual identity in some ancestral group of fellows smaller by far than the whole human race, smaller often than the nation—the sense of ethnic belonging has survived. It has survived in various forms and with various names, but it has not perished, and twentieth-century urban man is closer to his stone-age ancestors than he knows.[20]

Whether ethnic loyalties are any more characteristic of modern man's primitive past than other allegiances remains to be seen; it is doubtful that we have as yet a satisfactory theory to explain group membership and belonging. . . . But whatever the reason for the Jewish community's desire to persist, we should bear in mind that its dominant thrust is survivalist. . . .

[20] Milton M. Gordon, *Assimilation in American Life* (New York: Oxford University Press, 1964), pp. 24–25. See also Marshall Sklare, "Assimilation and the Sociologists," *Commentary*, May 1965, pp. 63–67.

19

Family Interaction, Values, and Achievement

FRED L. STRODTBECK

Unusual attainment in community service, the professions, or business, generally results in high social status. More modest advances of the order of the shift from immigrant laborer to small business operator have similar, though not identical, status consequences. There is, of course, always some difficulty in distinguishing between status which is gained by personal effort and status which accrues from family membership. When the mobility of groups is under consideration, this difficulty is somewhat less serious. For example, if one of two groups who arrived in this country at about the same time has been markedly more upwardly mobile than the other, our inability to attribute the mobility exactly to the responsible generation does not foreclose a between-group comparison. The essential strategy in a "group" approach is that it enables us to utilize an indicant of performance which arises within society itself: status. The assumption is that the abilities of the more mobile groups have been used in activities of greater social consequence. Many difficulties, such as would arise when one attempts to compare the work of a chemist and a devoted nurse, are not squarely met. So long as the values of different men, or the same men at different times, are to

Fred Strodtbeck is Professor of Sociology at The University of Chicago.

Reprinted by permission of the author from Marshall Sklare, *The Jews, Social Patterns of an American Group* (New York, Free Press, 1958), pp. 147–64.

be reconciled, it is doubtful that any fully satisfactory criterion can be found. "Relative rise in the status structure" appears to have the advantage of being a ubiquitous measure which both has application to many activities and implies the operation of a community-wide evaluation system. By this reasoning we have concluded that *status mobility* deserves serious considerations as a criterion of talented performance by groups.

This decision, made early in the research, at first seemed to create more problems than it solved. If social mobility were to be the criterion of differential talent development, how were we to get data helpful in understanding and identifying talented adolescents? Were we to be dependent in our research on the recall by adults of the attitudinal dispositions—and interpersonal relations—they believed themselves to have had as early adolescents? Since our time limitations no more permitted us to follow groups of adolescents in their status climb than in other forms of talent expression, was there an alternative to longitudinal research available? Could we not seek groups with differential mobility rates just as Durkheim had sought groups with differential suicide rates? Social group rates have the disadvantage that since they are based upon the average of acts by many persons, they ordinarily have low predictive value for particular individuals. It is nonetheless possible that theoretical understanding of factors involved in talent development may be advanced by the study of factors associated with difference in group rates. For even if group predictions fall far short of the desired predictive efficiency, the mechanisms believed to differentiate among groups may later be found to differentiate among families within particular groups and thus provide a more crucial test of our understanding.

To illustrate, there is a popular impression that Presbyterians, Quakers, and Mormons are outstandingly industrious and successful, and they are believed to have produced a disproportionately high number of public leaders and men of science. Presbyterians historically represented the prototype of ascetic Protestantism which Weber suggests is particularly consistent with the requirements for modern capitalism. Quakers and Mormons represent, in differing degrees, slight departures from ideal-type ascetic Protestantism, but there are still common emphases in the teaching of all three. From the standpoint of a research design, it would be desirable to have a classificatory typology of cultural groupings such that extreme cases could be selected with markedly different achievement rates. Hopefully, differences might be found between such groups which would clarify understanding of the requirements for achievement in particular situations. While such a design leaves much uncontrolled, it is to be considered first as a source of new hypotheses. Whatever findings result may be verified by other means.

In New Haven, where our research was to be conducted, there were only two large ethnic groups with similar periods of residence in this country: Southern Italians and Jews. Irish were also numerous, but they had been in New Haven a longer period. When it became apparent that for Italians and Jews it would be possible to locate second-generation families with early-adolescent (third-generation) sons in the public and parochial schools, an effort was made to review in detail the general demographic data relating to the time of arrival, respective economic situation upon arrival, and their subsequent socio-economic attainment. From the results of this inquiry we concluded that while Jews upon arrival had a slight advantage in terms of occupational status and urban skills, this original advantage has been appreciably widened during the period 1910–1940. Jews consistently have higher occupational status than the population at large, while, in contrast, Italians are consistently lower.

The next problem was to make decisions as to how to go about discovering what differences there might be between Italians and Jews in values, beliefs about nature, child-training practices, and family structure. To decide on research instruments, sample characteristics, and the like, it was necessary to be guided by working hypotheses suggested by the literature. Three sources were of particular importance: (a) studies of religion and social activity; (b) studies of child rearing and adult character; and (c) studies of small face-to-face group behavior. . . . [The section reprinted below follows a survey of the literature on these three topics—Editor.]

ITALIAN-JEWISH CULTURAL VALUES

It is to be assumed that the subsequent generations of Italians and Jews in this country have progressively become more acculturated and more like one another. For guidance in the formulation of hypotheses about the way in which value differences between these cultures may have influenced their differential achievement, one may turn first to the description of the original cultures from which they had emigrated. For the Southern Italian background there were some nine substantive sources (2, 3, 7, 8, 9, 10, 11, 12, 13). To the extent that they have been used in our quick overview, these sources were quite consistent. For the Jews, the relevant literature is much larger. In the present account, Zborowski and Herzog's *Life Is with People* is the primary reference (16). Their treatment of *shtetl* culture is sympathetic—perhaps idealized—but sharply focused on attitude dimensions of great relevance to Italian-Jewish contrasts.

To begin with one of the most striking differences, Jews have traditionally placed a very high value upon *education and intellectual attainment.* The Jewish parent was expected to provide education, but not in a ritualistic manner. As much education was to be provided as the sons showed themselves capable of absorbing. Learning in the *shtetl* society gave the individual prestige, respect, authority—and the chance for a better marriage. The Jewish folk saying that "parents will bend the sky to educate their sons," and the heroic stories every first-generation Jewish parent can tell of the sacrifices made by fellow-parents to educate their children, illustrate the cultural legitimation of sacrifice for education.

The legitimation of education is further bound up with prestige associated with intellectual "brainwork," and the corresponding *lack* of prestige associated with physical accomplishments. This pattern of evaluation starts early in the child's career. Traditionally, a three- or four-year-old starting *kheyder* (elementary religious school) was regarded as a serious student. Brilliant students were treated with a deference ordinarily reserved for important adults. The weight of the opinion of the young scholar is reflected by the fact that a bearded man will not be ashamed to bring a difficult Talmudic question to a boy of thirteen.

Religious learning and the satisfactions of family life were not separated as they were in monastic Catholicism. It was the custom to arrange the young scholar's marriage while he was in his middle teens. In order that such scholars might give more attention to their studies, many of the economic responsibilities of the family were assumed by the wife.

In Southern Italian culture, the traditional attitude toward education was (and is) very different. School and book-learning environments were alien and remote from everyday experiences. Priests were taken from their families and villages to be educated. To the typical Southern Italian peasant, school was an upper-class institution and potentially a threat to his desire to retain his family about him. While education might well serve for some as a means of social advancement, the peasant was disposed to believe that this avenue was not open to his children—in their case education was not functional. For each age there is a proper behavior. Family life, local political power, and other objectives were stressed as alternative goals to learning.

Even in this country, the first-generation Southern Italian parents' attitude was, in part, negative to education. As an Italian educator reports: "Mother believed you would go mad if you read too many books and father was of the opinion that too much school makes children lazy and opens the mind for unhealthy dreams." Intellectualism, in itself, was not valued in Southern Italian communities. Learned

men were of another class, or alternatively, they were men of the church. Status in the community changed slowly: property was in all cases more important. Property could be gotten faster by a trickster-trader than a scholar (1). Scholars were like monks: good men but not of the real world.

La famiglia in the Southern Italian culture was an inclusive social world. The basic mores of this society were primarily family mores—everyone outside the family was viewed with suspicion. The basic code was family solidarity, and there was strong feeling that the family should stay together—physically close together. The essence of the ethos has been most forcefully captured by Edward C. Benfield. He states the one premise from which the "family vs. all others" political orientation would seem to flow: "Choose so as to maximize the short-run advantage of the family and assume others will do likewise."

The Jewish family was traditionally a close-knit one, but it was the entire Jewish *shtetl* community rather than the family which was considered the inclusive social unit and world. Although relatives were more important than friends, all Jews were considered to be bound to each other. The primary unit was the family of procreation. Physical proximity was not so heavily stressed. Mandelbaum (6, pp. 28, 31) and Joffe (5) have pointed out that the dynamics of benefice for the Jews was not of the reciprocal exchange nature. Parents' gifts to their children are to be parallel for the next generation. In the home, as in the community, giving must move in a descending spiral. Giving serves not only to enrich the donor and succor the recipient, but it also maintains the constituency of fundamentally equal persons—and in this way enriches the community. In American Jewish communities today, the sizeable and highly publicized charitable contributions owe much to this tradition.

For the Jewish parents there was in the *Alles Für die Kinder* theme, an emphasis upon a bettered condition in the *future* which made them more willing to let children leave the community for opportunities elsewhere. Much less emphasis on the future existed in the Italian families' evaluation of alternatives.

The external world for the Jews was hostile to be sure, but it was by nature solvable. For all goods there is a proper price, for all labor there is a best way of doing it. For the Italian the equivalent phrasing is perhaps: "There is work which must be done." One might go further to say there are ways of doing the work which are more expeditious—but no matter how the work is done, there is always the chance that fate may intervene. The unpredictable intervention of fate may be for good or evil, but *Destino* is omnipresent. If a man works all his life for something which *Destino* may deny him, well then, why should men look so far ahead? There is always the present, and one might have a lucky break.

Zborowski, in his study in this country of the reactions of hospitalized Jewish and Italian veterans to pain, employs Florence Kluckhohn's well-known *time* orientation to differentiate the cultural responses (15). First, he finds that both Jews and Italians complain more about pain than "Old Americans." But, more importantly, sedation alone is enough to allay Italians. For the Jew sedation is not enough. He continues to be pessimistic and concerned about the implication of the sedation for his eventual recovery. For the Italian there is a *present-oriented* apprehension of the sensation of pain; for the Jew there is a *future-oriented* anxiety concerning the symptomatic meaning of the pain. Neither group wishes to suffer alone, neither group believes it is necessarily masculine to deny the existence of pain, and neither group believes that suffering is an end in itself.

In the use of folk medicines, belief in the "evil eye," and the like, Jewish and Italian culture shared many common irrational elements. Religious ritual was strong in both cultures. However, the complex of behavior involved in the individual's participation in his own salvation deserves separate attention.

In Italian folk theology, Catholic doctrine was popularly understood as requiring sheer obedience to arbitrary prescriptions for the sake of an arbitrary reward. Where the formula did not apply, the matter was of no real significance. Faith in the mystery of the Trinity and the timely interventions of the priest were all that was required. For the Jews, religious improvement was always possible and perfection always denied. The scholar proceeded at his own rate after becoming a rabbi. There was no one to grant the learned and respected man a more advanced degree; his job was ever undone. During the middle years he might have had to give more attention to business, but as he grew older he could spend his full time in discussion, study, and prayers.

In the East European *shtetl,* no man could occupy a position so humble that it could not in part be redeemed by his religious scholarship. Without the religious scholarship a man of means could be *prost*—simple, common, vulgar. A diploma of any type which signified learning in nonreligious fields came to be accorded respect like that accorded religious scholarship. It is important to stress that if Talmudic scholarship taught precision, juridic care, and dedication, it taught attitudes toward learning which might, with a growth of heterodoxy, be transferred to other learning. So long as the ghetto confined the area of attainment, goals of religious scholarship were highly coveted. Upon release from the ghetto, the status and financial rewards available in the disciplines of law and medicine were also attainable by work of an intellectual character similar to Talmudic scholarship. Jewish mobility has in all probability been facilitated by the transformation of a complex of behavior which had not existed for the Italians.

A peasant's mistrust of books in contrast with the veneration of learning does not exist in isolation from other attitudes. Zborowski and Herzog tell us that in the *shtetl* the hair line of babies would in some instances be shaved back so that the child would have a high forehead—hence, appear intelligent. Short, thick hands were thought to be inappropriate and ugly—*prost*. The Jewish attitude toward the body was not ascetic, the body was neither ugly nor inherently evil. It was rather that the body was a vessel for containing the spirit. Rest, food, and procreation on the Sabbath were legitimated to keep the body at full efficiency, but a specialized interest in physical development *per se* was improper. For the Jews the mind was a great tool, but ever under discipline and purposeful direction. In the early morning prayers the mind is turned to sacred matters, on the Sabbath to non-business matters—it is never a question of whether the mind can win over impulse.

It is perhaps equally true that the Italian emphasis on good food and proper relaxation is superficially similar to Jewish practice, and for that matter, to practices in many cultures. The essential difference as we perceive it is that the Italian manual worker was never ashamed of his strength; to keep his body fit was a desirable end in itself, for it was never perceived to be in competition with other necessarily more important activities.

To supplement the old-culture Italian-Jewish child training contrast there is just one comparative American study which has come to our attention. Field interviewers from the Harvard University Laboratory of Human Development contacted an area sample of families in greater Boston concerning methods of child rearing. With regard to second-generation Italians and Jews, the division of the families by social class was as follows:

	Italian	Jewish
Middle	7	64
Lower	36	15

This is consistent with the predicted differential status mobility: Jews are concentrated in the middle classes, Italians in the lower. Unfortunately, this distribution does not provide many middle-class Italian, and only relatively few lower-class Jewish families, though the frequencies for lower-class Italians and middle-class Jews are sizeable. Since this class distribution appears to be roughly "modal" for second-generation members of these ethnic groups, comparisons between these groups are of particular interest. To paraphrase slightly the language of the original manuscript, the main points made are as follows:

(a) The amount of time spent in caretaking and in affectionate interaction with the child, the warmth of the mother-child relationship, and the amount of enjoyment in childcare is not different for the two groups. Both are relatively high in infant nurturance save only for the greater severity of the Italian mothers in toilet training. For sexual play with other children, masturbation, or nudity in the home, Italians are markedly less permissive than Jews.

(b) Italians are less permissive of aggression to parents and impose more requirements on the child's table manners, conversations with adults, acting as "boy" or "girl," caution around furniture, and freedom of movement from the home than do Jews. Italians were more prone to report they followed through and demanded obedience, although in terms of authority patterns such as mother-dominant, shared, father-dominant, or divided —no differences between Italian and Jewish families were reported. Family structure from the perspective of the child is reflected indirectly in the fact that Jewish children admit deviant behavior more frequently than Italian children, and, in addition, tend to require more attention from adults.

(c) In terms of current dependency, and this is focused at about the five-year level, both groups of children are about equally dependent, but the Jewish mother is significantly more accepting of dependent behavior. In general, the emotional atmosphere of parent-child relations is somewhat warmer in Jewish than in Italian families, while at the same time Jewish families place a higher evaluation on the benefits to be gained by spanking.

(d) In terms of expected school attendance, Jews expect much longer school attendance, but there is a corresponding lesser insistence on the child's "doing well in school." Perhaps this implies a disposition to permit the child to set his own level for quality of performance.

It should be noted that there were some marked differences between the 64 middle-class Jewish and the 15 lower-class Jewish families. While this latter number is small, the lower-class families were significantly more severe in weaning and toilet-training, took less pleasure in caring for babies, interacted less, and were less warm and nurturant when the child was an infant At the current behavior level, they were also less demonstrative, much less permissive of sexual behavior, and in general more severe in their socialization practices. Italian-Jewish differences are greatly attenuated when class level is constant; hence, since class level is not controlled in the comparisons above, the exact contribution of "class" in contrast with "culture" cannot be ascertained.

Out of all this material, all too briefly summarized, we must now pick those values which appear most likely to have accounted for the differential occupational achievement of the two "old cultures" when they came to the United States. This task necessarily involves a comparison of Italian-Jewish value differences with the values we arrived at for a description of the Protestant–U.S. achievement ethic earlier [not included here—Editor]. It finally resolves itself into a comparison at five points, as follows:

(1) *Man's sense of personal responsibility in relation to the external world.* The Protestant's world was the work of God, its mysteries were profound and not to be understood by the slacker. To work to understand and transform this world was the true Christian's personal responsibility. Misfortunes have a definite place in the scheme; they are the tests which God sets before men. By such logic, hard work was understood to be behind all worldly accomplishment, but there was still no guarantee that even a lifetime of hard work would necessarily be rewarded.

For the "U.S. achiever"—the successful scientist, executive, or professional person— rational mastery of the situation has been equated with the "hard work" of the Protestants, and threat of almost continuous review of his record has been equated with anxiety over eventual salvation. There is no necessary personal deprivation which must be endured; one's accomplishment can be facilitated by "breaks," but importantly breaks are of the individual's own making. It is a matter of being available with what is needed at the right place and at the right time. Just as breaks are not given by a beneficent power, neither are failures. Whatever failure an individual has suffered could always have been foreseen and hedged against if the individual were sufficiently alert. One might commiserate with an unfortunate person, but for the "U.S. achiever" there is no legitimate excuse. His sense of personal responsibility for controlling his destiny is very great.

"Old-culture" Jewish beliefs appear to be congruent in many if not all respects with the "U.S. achiever" belief in rational mastery of the world presented above and at marked variance with that of the Southern Italian. For the "old-culture" Jew, there was the expectation that everything could be understood if perhaps not always controlled. Emphasis on learning as a means of control was strong. Religious or secular learning, once attained, unlike the Protestant's salvation and the "U.S. achiever's" status, was not in continual jeopardy. For men who were learned in trades but not specialized religious scholars, the expectations of charity to others of the community who were less fortunate was a continuing goad to keep working, but if misfortune befell a former benefactor, the community would understand. The "old-culture" sense of personal responsibility coexisted with a responsibility of the community for the individual which eases somewhat the precariousness associated with "all or none" expectations on the individual.

For the Italian, the best laid plans of man might twist awry. Misfortune originated "out there" not inside the individual. The term *destino* suggests that it has been written that a particular event will or will not come to pass. A sort of passive alertness is inculcated; no one knows when he is going to get a lucky break, but at the same time there is no motivation for a heroic rational undertaking, for such an undertaking may be *destined* to fail.

(2) *Familism versus loyalty to a larger collectivity.* The essence of familism is an emphasis on filial obedience and parental au-

thority. Calvinism was anti-familistic in its emphasis upon a first obedience to one's own soul and to God. Familistic social organization tends to involve a particular locus of activity and a hierarchy of responsibility based upon age and kinship relations rather than upon impersonal technical requirements. For this reason the "U.S. achiever" tends to be anti-familistic like the Calvinist. That is, the desire to keep two or more generations together would compete with the job and educational opportunities which require residential moves. The "U.S. achiever" moves with his wife and children on the basis of his technical qualifications to wherever he believes he can maximize his opportunities. At the early stages of his career he may even avoid the line of work where his father might help him, so as to win for himself the privilege of being judged for his own competence.

The "old-culture" Jewish pattern involved separations for business and educational reasons and a heightened consciousness that a man's first responsibility was for his children. That is, obligations were primarily from those that have more to those that have less, which, practically speaking, meant that children need not always stay to nurture parents who might be better off than they were. The Jewish pattern of weaker ties to parents is not seen to be as extreme as the pattern for the "U.S. achiever," but in some ways it contrasts sharply with the Southern Italian pattern.

Under great economic duress the Southern Italian familial organization may shrink to the nuclear unit—but this is atypical. The successful Italian wishes to draw his extended family about him, and in the process some are lifted in status just as others are secured in the status of the large-family complex.

(3) *Perfectability of man.* An aspect of Calvinism, perhaps best captured for popular consumption in *Poor Richard's Almanac* by Benjamin Franklin, is the emphasis that at every moment of every day a person should work to improve himself. "Old-culture" Jewish emphases on religious scholarship and study represented a similar belief in the responsibility for self-improvement. For the "U.S.

achiever" this perfectability requirement has, in one sense, been relaxed, but insofar as it remains, it has become even more stringent. Now, the improvement should take place in a relaxed manner with no apparent effort. The self-improvement should be "enjoyed," not "endured" as it might have been earlier. In all of these cases interest in education should be (and has been) high because it is one of the ways in which man obviously perfects himself.

For the Southern Italian there was considerable doubt as to whether man could perfect himself or, indeed, that he need try to. According to his interpretation of Catholicism, he must conscientiously fulfill his duties, but his "good works" did not form a rationalized system of life. Good works could be used to atone for particular sins, or, as Weber points out, stored up as a sort of insurance toward the end of his life, but there was no need to live in every detail the ideal life, for there was ever the sacrament of absolution. Furthermore, the Southern Italian really felt that man lived at an uneasy peace with his passions and that from time to time one had to expect them to break through. Man is really not perfectable—he is all too human, and he had better not drive himself or his mind too hard in trying to reach perfection.

(4) *Consciousness of the larger community.* The Protestants' "each man his brother's keeper" has given way in the "U.S. achiever" to a less moralistic rationale for serial consciousness based upon a recognition of the interdependencies in modern society. Just as the "old-culture" Jewish community could vicariously participate in the charities of its wealthiest members, there is a sense in which the strengthening of various aspects of American society are recognized to contribute to the common good.

The "old-culture" Jew, enabled by his success to assume a responsibility for the community, had little choice in the matter. The social pressures were great, and they were ordinarily responded to with pride and rewarded by prominence in the community forum. The identification went beyond the extended family. The giver was not to be rewarded in kind; his reward came from community recognition. Such community identification—as contrasted with family identification—was not highly developed among Southern Italians. Reduced sensitivity to community goals is believed to inhibit the near-altruistic orientations which in adolescence and early maturity lead individuals to make prolonged personal sacrifices to enter such professions as medicine or the law.

(5) *Power relations.* Analysis of the requirements for success in America suggests that insofar as differences in status may be perceived to be legitimate because the high-status person is technically more competent, then the person in the subordinate position can still give his full commitment to organizational goals without feeling or acting as if he were being dominated by his superior. Early Protestantism laid the groundwork for such limited and specific relationships by insisting that each man had a post assigned him by God so that no one should feel inferior or superior. The modern bureaucracies create for "U.S. achievers" a greatly increased number of positions in our society where a person has a specific role in a larger impersonal system to perform.

On the other hand, the "old-culture" Jew did not see power in the context of some external system of pre-established impersonal relationships. He tended, like the Protestant, to reduce power questions to other terms, to the equity of a particular bargain, for example; but unlike the Protestant, these relationships were always specific both as to persons and content involved, and *not* part of a larger system. His primary concern was to make his relationships good with others with whom he was in close contact over a particular issue. The specificity of his relations with others, including his separation of business and family matters, is also like the functional specificity of modern bureaucratic society, but again unlike it in overlooking the *system* of such functional relationships.

The "old-culture" Italian tends to see power entirely in immediate interpersonal terms and as a direct expression of who can

control the behavior of another rather than who knows more for a job in an impersonal system. He is constantly interested in "who's boss?" and with turning every relationship into a "for me-against me" or "over me-under me" polarity.

SUMMARY

Complicated though the task may be, we must now somehow integrate our empirical findings into the larger theoretical questions which lay behind our original research design. In its simplest terms, our plans started with the hypothesis that the American social system contained certain inherent requirements for the achievement of individuals in it, requirements inherited to a considerable extent from the Protestant Ethic as described by Weber, Parsons, and others, but also evolved into new forms. Then, since it was impractical to do longitudinal research, we decided to pick subcultures which had been conspicuously more and less successful in adapting *as groups* to the U.S. requirements for achievement of high status and to search their value systems and family life for clues as to why they differed in the production of achievant individuals in the United States.

Before summarizing the clues we discovered, it is necessary to stress that no one should impute an evaluative tone to our comparison of Italians and Jews—the two differentially achieving groups chosen for study. In the first place, the emphasis on status mobility as the criterion of "success" in this study should not be perceived as the only criterion by which one might recognize activities of social value. There are many alternative philosophies of life which would suggest quite different criteria of success to be investigated by the behavioral scientist. Our reason for choosing status mobility as the criterion rests primarily on the fact that it is a societal means of evaluating people which applies to a very broad range of social activities in the United States today.

Furthermore, we were not primarily

motivated by a desire to study these subcultures *per se* with the notion of predicting which groups would show the most status mobility from now on. Rather our interest was in the extent to which each of these "old cultures" was *initially* adaptive to the U.S. social setting as we analyzed it. In fact, there is considerable evidence in our data to support the notion that whatever differences in values and family interaction initially existed, they are disappearing as both groups get more assimilated into American life. For example, we found no qualitative differences in family interaction between Italians and Jews using the Bales categories, and no V-score differences in our stratified sample (with effects of socio-economic status removed). Also, while Jews were more mobility-oriented in their favorable attitudes toward higher education and prestige occupations, there was no evidence that Italians differed from the rest of the population in this respect. Finally, we know that socio-economic status affects socialization practices and power balance in the family, both of which are factors which are related to subsequent achievement. But both ethnic groups are changing in socio-economic status. To take just one possible effect of this as an illustration: more Jews are moving into high status where the fathers are more powerful and may therefore, according to our data, tend to produce sons who have values *less* conducive to upward mobility. On the other hand, more Italians may be moving into medium status where family power may be more conducive to mobility than in the lower status where many of them are now. Thus one might on this basis predict a reversal in the mobility rates of the past, with a trend toward greater mobility for the Italians in the future. So, lest the analysis be misunderstood, the interest in "old culture" differences is not at all to predict group mobility rates, but to identify clues which might have explained differences in their initial adjustment to American life.

The clues we found consist in part of the value differences based on ethnographic evidence summarized earlier, and whatever further support for them we uncovered in the empirical study. Each of these value differences was selected because we thought it should promote status mobility in the United States, and not because it was necessarily the best way of comparing Italian and Jewish subcultures. In each case, our expectations were largely confirmed by the data. Three of the five expected value differences turned up in the V-scale which differentiated Italians from Jews and which also reflected differences in past status mobility (i.e., as represented by higher scores for fathers with higher social status) and probably *future* status mobility (i.e., as represented by higher scores for over-achieving sons). There is, then, evidence from three sources that the following three values contained in the V-scale are important for achievement in the United States:

1. A belief that the world is orderly and amenable to rational mastery, and that, therefore, a person can and should make plans which will control his destiny (three items in the V-scale). By way of contrast, the notion that man is subjugated to a destiny beyond his control probably impeded Southern Italians in their early adjustment to the United States, just as it impeded boys in school or less successful fathers in their occupations in this study. Unfortunately we cannot say with any assurance whether the poor performance of the Italians and of the less successful fathers or sons was the result of the belief in fate or whether the belief in fate was the result of the poor performance. However, since we know—in the case of the Italians—that the belief was part of the "old culture" and therefore antedated their performance, we may feel justified in predicting that while beliefs and performance undoubtedly modify each other, it is the belief which came first so far as the adjustment of Southern Italians to the United States is concerned.

2. A willingness to leave home to make one's way in life. Again, by contrast, the South Italian stress on "familism" which we found evidence for in the V-scale should have interfered with upward mobility and contributed to

the lower occupational achievement of Italians as compared with Jews. Family balance of power also affects the willingness to leave home, a fact which demonstrates that one's position in life can produce a value disposition as well as the reverse. But whether the willingness to break up the family comes from an "old culture," from power balance in the family, from the father's or son's relative lack of success in job or school, it is certainly a value of importance in the "achievement complex."

3. A preference for individualistic rather than collective credit for work done. On the one item in the V-scale which dealt with this value, the Jews showed greater preference for individualistic, the Italians for collective rewards, as one would perhaps expect from the greater "familism" of the Italians. We have argued [in a section not reproduced here— Editor] that some loyalty to an abstract system of relations—to a collectivity—is essential in modern bureaucratic organizations. Hence, the greater collective emphasis of the Italians here would appear to have *favored* their quick adaptation to American life (although perhaps more now when bureaucracies are better developed than earlier). On the other hand these same bureaucracies stress individualistic rewards and impersonal relations between superiors and subordinates, both of which do not fit very well with the Italian emphases on *non-individualized* collateral loyalties and on very personal dominance-striving in face-to-face relationships. Although the questionnaire does not provide much information on this point, it is also clear that while the Jewish emphasis on individualized rewards *is* adaptive to the bureaucratic system, it also contains an element which does not fit the system so well—i.e., the stress on *personal* rather than impersonal individualistic relationships. But again, our main concern is not with Italian-Jewish differences, but with the elements in those differences which may explain their differential achievement. Here it seems to be the stress on individualistic reward among the Jews, although the case is not so clear-cut as

with the other values in the V-scale, because there is only one item and because there are at this point elements in both "old cultures" working both for and against quick adaptation to the U.S. social system.

Aside from the V-scale results, which are most impressive because they reflect differential achievement of cultures (Jews over Italians), of fathers (high over low SES) and of sons (over- vs. under-achievement in school), there are two facts from the larger questionnaire study which relate to a fourth expected value difference between Italians and Jews— namely, the value placed on the *perfectability of man*. The Jews definitely had higher educational and occupational expectations for their sons. Practically speaking, this would appear to mean they believed that man could improve himself more by education and that one should not readily submit to fate and accept a lower station in life, the way the Italians were more prepared to do.

The fifth and final expected Italian-Jewish value difference had to do with power relationships. We had been led to believe by ethnographic reports and other studies that Italians would be more concerned than Jews with establishing dominance in face-to-face relationships, and such turned out to be the case. Both in the boys' reports of who was dominant at home and in the actual decision-winning in the 48 homes we studied intensively, the Italians showed greater variations from equality of power than the Jews. While this finding is probably of lesser importance than those presented above, it nonetheless sharpens our curiosity about what effects the power balance through time in particular families will have on the son's achievement. Is it possible that when relatively equalitarian relations persist in the home, the son can move to new loyalties in larger systems of relationships such as those provided by college or a job without an outright "rupture" of family controls? Or conversely, is such an adjustment to new institutions outside the home harder the more the home has tended to be dominated by one parent or the other? Furthermore, what would be the cost of such a rupture to the son in terms of performance and motivation to continue on his own? Would the conflict not be less, the frustration less, when the break came, and consequently the emotional and intellectual adjustment more efficient if he had come from a home where controls were already diffuse and equalitarian as they are in many situations in life? The present design involved only a single visit with the families; in subsequent research it is to be hoped more can be arranged as the child is growing up, so that one can follow the effects of power balance on the child's adjustment inside the family and subsequently to life outside it.

REFERENCES

1. Brown, N. O. *Hermes the thief.* Madison: Univer. Wisc. Press, 1947.
2. D'Alesandre, J. J. Occupational trends of Italians in New York City. *Italy American Monthly*, 1935, 2, 11–12.
3. Guilds' Committee for Federal Writers Publications. *The Italians of New York.* New York: Random House, 1938.
4. Homans, G. C. *The human group.* New York: Harcourt, Brace, 1950.
5. Joffe, N. F. The dynamics of benefice among East European Jews. *Social Forces*, 1948–49, 27, 239–247.
6. Mandelbaum, D. G. *Change and continuity in Jewish life.* Glencoe, Ill.: Oscar Hillel Plotkin Library, 1955.
7. Mangione, J. *Mount Allegro.* New York: Houghton Mifflin, 1942.
8. ———. *Reunion in Sicily.* New York: Houghton Mifflin, 1950.
9. Mariano, J. H. *The second generation of Italians in New York City.* New York: Christopher, 1921.
10. Pellegrini, A. *Immigrant's Return.* New York: Macmillan, 1951.
11. Radin, P. *The Italians of San Francisco: their adjustment and acculturation*, Monographs 1 and 2, S.E.R.A. Project, Cultural Anthropology, San Francisco, 1935.
12. Sangree, W. and Hybleum, M. A study of the people of Middletown of Sicilian extraction with special emphasis on the changes in their values resulting from assimilation into the Middletown community. Unpublished Master's thesis, Wesleyan Univer., 1952.
13. Sartorio, E. C. *Social and religious life of Italians in America.* New York: Christopher, 1918.
14. Snyder, C. R. Culture and sobriety. *Quart. J. Studies on Alcohol*, 1955, 16, 101–177, 263–289, 504–532; 1956, 17, 124–143.
15. Zborowski, M. Cultural components in responses to pain. *J. Social Issues*, 1952, 8, 16–30.
16. Zborowski, M. and Herzog, E. *Life is with people.* New York: International Univer. Press, 1952.

20

Contrasts in the Community Organization of Chinese and Japanese in North America*

Stanford M. Lyman

Race relations theory and policy in North America have for the most part been built upon examination of the experiences and difficulties of European immigrants and Negroes. As a result contrasting ideas and programmes, emphasizing integration for the latter and cultural pluralism for the former, have been generated primarily in consideration of each group's most manifest problems.[1] However, relatively little work has been done to ascertain the conditions under which an ethnic group is likely to follow an integration-oriented or a pluralist-oriented path.[2] Two racial

Stanford M. Lyman is Professor of Sociology and Chairman of the Department on the Graduate Faculty of the New School for Social Research.

Reprinted from *The Canadian Review of Sociology and Anthropolgy*, 5:2(1968), by permission of the author and the publisher.

* Revised version of a paper presented at the University of California under the sponsorship of the Committee for Arts and Lectures, August 23, 1966. I am indebted to Herbert Blumer, Jean Burnet and Marvin Scott for criticisms of earlier versions of this paper.

[1] Cf. Horace M. Kallen, *Culture and Democracy in the United States* (New York, 1924) with Gunnar Myrdal, *An American Dilemma* (New York, 1944).

[2] See Clyde V. Kiser, "Cultural Pluralism", *The Annals of the American Academy of Political and Social Science*, 262 (March 1949), 118–29. An approach to such a theory is found in William Petersen, *Population* (New York, 1961), pp. 114–49.

groups found in North America—the Chinese and the Japanese—are likely candidates for the focus of such research, since they have superficially similar outward appearances, a long history as victims of oppression, discrimination, and prejudice, but quite different developments in community organization and cohesion.[3] In this paper an attempt is made to ascertain the distinctive feature of the culture and social organization of the two immigrant groups that played significant roles in directing the mode of community organization in North America.

There is sound theoretical ground for reconsidering the role of Old World culture and social organization on immigrant communities in North America. Even in what might seem the paradigm case of cultural destruction in the New World—that of the Negro—there is evidence to suggest at least vestiges of cultural survival.[4] In those ethnic communities unmarred by so culturally demoralizing a condition as slavery, there survives what Nathan Glazer calls elements of a "ghost nation", so that despite its fires social life goes on at least in part "beyond the melting pot".[5] American ideology has stressed assimilation, but its society is marked by European, Asian, and some African survivals; Canadian ideology has stressed the "mosaic" of cultures, but at least some of its peoples show definite signs of being Canadianized. The immigrants' cultural baggage needs sociological inspection to ascertain its effects on community organization and acculturation. Fortunately, the Chinese and Japanese communities provide opportunities for this research because of new knowledge

[3] For an extended analysis see Stanford M. Lyman, "The Structure of Chinese Society in Nineteenth-Century America" (unpublished Ph.D. dissertation, University of California, Berkeley, 1961).

[4] Melville Herskovitz, *The Myth of the Negro Past* (Boston, 1958). See also Charles Keil, *Urban Blues* (Chicago, 1966), 1–69.

[5] Nathan Glazer, "Ethnic Groups in America: From National Culture to Ideology", in Morroe Berger, Theodore Abel, and Charles H. Page, Editors, *Freedom and Control in Modern Society* (New York, 1954), pp. 158–76, Nathan Glazer and Daniel Patrick Moynihan, *Beyond the Melting Pot: The Negroes, Puerto Ricans, Jews, Italians and Irish of New York City* (Cambridge, 1963).

about the Old Asian World[6] and extensive material on their lives in North America.

THE CHINESE

In contrast to the Japanese and several European groups, the Chinese in Canada and the United States present an instance of unusually persistent social isolation and preservation of Old World values and institutions.[7] To the present day a great many Chinese work, play, eat, and sleep in the Chinese ghettos known throughout North America as "Chinatowns". The business ethics of Chinatown's restaurants and bazaars are institutionalized in guild and trade associations more reflective of nineteenth-century Cathay than twentieth-century North America. Newly arrived Chinese lads work a twelve- to sixteen-hour day as waiters and busboys totally unprotected by labor unions. Immigrant Chinese mothers sit in rows in tiny "sweatshops" sewing dresses for

downtown shops while infants crawl at their feet. In basements below the street level or in rooms high above the colorfully-lit avenue, old men gather round small tables to gamble at *fan t'an, p'ai, kop piu,* or other games of chance. Above the hubbub of activity in the basements, streets, stores, and sweatshops are the offices of clan associations, speech and territorial clubs, and secret societies. And behind the invisible wall that separates Chinatown from the metropolis the élites of these organizations conduct an unofficial government, legislating, executing, and adjudicating matters for their constituents.

Not every Chinese in Canada or the United States today recognizes the sovereignty of Chinatown's power élite or receives its benefits and protections.[8] At one time San Francisco's "Chinese Six Companies" and Vancouver's Chinese Benevolent Association could quite properly claim to speak for all the Chinese in the two countries. But that time is now past. Students from Hong Kong and Taiwan and Chinese intellectuals, separated in social origins, status, and aspirations from other Chinese, have cut themselves off from their Chinatown compatriots. Another segment of the Chinese population, the Canadian-born and American-born, who have acquired citizenship in the country of their birth, not only exhibits outward signs of acculturation in dress, language, and behaviour, but also grants little if any obeisance to Chinatown's élites. Some of this generation now find it possible to penetrate the racial barrier, and pass into the workaday world of the outer society with impunity. Others still work or reside in Chinatown but are too acculturated to be subject to its private law. Still a few others are active in the traditional associations seeking power and status within the framework of the old order.

[6] The "knowledge explosion" on China has been prodigious since 1949 despite the difficulties in obtaining first-hand field materials. Much research was inspired by interest in the Chinese in Southeast Asia. See Maurice Freedman, "A Chinese Phase in Social Anthropology", *British Journal of Sociology,* 16, 1 (March 1963), 1–18.

[7] Sources for the material reported are Lyman, "The Structure of Chinese Society in Nineteenth-Century America", *passim;* Leong Gor Yun, *Chinatown Inside Out* (New York, 1936), 26–106, 182–235; Calvin Lee, *Chinatown, U.S.A.: A History and Guide* (Garden City, 1955); Stuart H. Cattell, *Health, Welfare and Social Organization in Chinatown, New York City* (New York, August 1962), pp. 1–4, 20–68, 81–185. For the origins of organized labour's hostility to the Chinese see Herbert Hill, "The Racial Practices of Organized Labor—The Age of Gompers and After", in Arthur Ross and Herbert Hill, Editors, *Employment, Race, and Poverty: A Critical Study of the Disadvantaged Status of Negro Workers from 1865 to 1965* (New York, 1967), pp. 365–402. For a detailed description of Chinese games of chance see the several articles by Stewart Culin, "Chinese Games with Dice" (Philadelphia, 1889), pp. 5–21; "The Gambling Games of the Chinese in America", *Publications of the University of Pennsylvania, Series in Philology, Literature, and Archaeology,* I, 4, 1891; "Chinese Games with Dice and Dominoes", *Report of the United States National Museum, Smithsonian Institution,* 1893, pp. 489–537. The sweatshops of San Francisco's Chinatown are described in James Benet, *A Guide to San Francisco and the Bay Region* (New York, 1963), pp. 73–74.

[8] See Rose Hum Lee, *The Chinese in the United States of America* (Hong Kong, 1960), pp. 86–131, 231–51, 373–404. See also *Chinese Students in the United States, 1948–1955: A Study in Government Policy* (New York, March 1956). For a Canadian–Chinese view of his own generation's adjustment to Chinese and Canadian ways of life see William Wong, "The Younger Generation", *Chinatown News,* 11, 13 (March 18, 1964), 6–7.

That North America's Chinatowns are not merely creatures of the American environment is indicated by the relatively similar institutionalization of Chinese communities in other parts of the world.[9] The diaspora of Chinese in the last two centuries has populated Southeast Asia, the Americas, Europe, and Africa with Oriental colonies. Should the tourists who today pass along Grant Avenue in San Francisco, Pender Street in Vancouver, and Pell and Mott Streets in New York City, peering at exotic food and art, and experiencing the sights, sounds, and smells of these cities' Chinatowns, be whisked away to Manila, Bangkok, Singapore, or Semarang, or suddenly find themselves in Calcutta, Liverpool or the capital of the Malagasy Republic, they would discover, amidst the unfamiliarity of the several national cultures, still other "Chinatowns" not unlike their North American counterparts. Recognition of the recalcitrance of overseas Chinese to their surroundings takes different forms in different places. In the United States sociologists marvel at their resistance to the fires of the melting pot; in Indonesia the government questions the loyalty of this alien people; in Malaysia native farmers and laborers resent the vivid contrast between their own poverty and Chinese commercial affluence; in Jamaica Chinese are urged to quit their exclusiveness and become part of the larger community. But everywhere the issue is acculturation. Despite more than a century of migration, the Chinese have not fully adopted the culture, language, behaviour—the ways of life—of the countries in which they have settled. Their cultural exclusiveness—especially as it finds its expression in geographically compact and socially distant communities within the host societies' cities—is a world-historical event deserving far more discussion and research than it has yet been given.*

THE JAPANESE

The rapid acculturation of the Japanese in North America has been a source of frequent discussion. The fact that "Japan-town" is not as familiar a term to North Americans as "Chinatown" is an unobtrusive measure of this difference between the two peoples. Such local names as "Li'l Tokyo" or "Li'l Yokohama" have been short-lived references for Japanese communities isolated through discrimination, but these have rarely been characterized by such peculiar institutions and private government as are found in the Chinese quarter. Japanese-owned businesses are not organized on the basis of guilds or *zaibatsu;* prefectural associations exist primarily for nostalgic and ceremonial purposes, playing no effective part in political organization in the community; and secret societies like those so prominent among the Chinese are not found in North American Japanese communities. Neither sweatshops nor gambling houses are established institutions of Japanese-American or Japanese-Canadian communities. Indeed, in the geographic sense, the North American Japanese communities show increasing signs of disintegration.

Although overseas Chinese communities exhibit the characteristics of colonization with

[9] Material for the following is drawn from Maurice Freedman and William Willmott, "Southeast Asia, with Special Reference to the Chinese", *International Social Science Journal*, 13, 2 (1961), 245–70; Victor Purcell, *The Chinese in Southeast Asia* (London, 1965), Second edition; Jacques Amyot, S. J., *The Chinese Community of Manila: A Study of Adaptation of Chinese Familism to the Philippine Environment* (Chicago, 1960); Richard J. Coughlin, "The Chinese in Bangkok: A Commercial-Oriented Minority", *American Sociological Review*, 20 (June 1955), 311–16; Maurice Freedman, *Chinese Family and Marriage in Singapore* (London, 1957); Donald Willmott, *The Chinese of Semarang: A Changing Minority Community in Indonesia* (Ithaca, 1960); Shelland Bradley, "Calcutta's Chinatown", *Cornhill Magazine*, 57 (September 1924), 277–85; Christopher Driver, "The Tiger Balm Community", *The Guardian* (January 2, 1962); Tsien Tche-Hao, "La vie sociale des Chinois à Madagascar", *Comparative Studies in Society and History*, 3, 2 (January 1961), 170–81; Justus M. van der Kroef, "Chinese Assimilation in Indonesia", *Social Research*, 20 (January 1954), 445–72; Leonard Broom, "The Social Differentiation of Jamaica", *American Sociological Review*, 19 (April 1954), 115–24.

* Editor's note: See Bonacich's "A Theory of Middleman Minorities" in Part Two.

a superordinate organization to represent them to the larger society, the Japanese are organized on patterns closer to that of a reluctant minority group.[10] The earliest associations among immigrant Japanese emphasized defense against prejudice and support for the larger society's laws and customs, and these organizations have been supplanted by even more acculturation-oriented organizations in the second generation. Japanese are the only ethnic group to emphasize geo-generational distinctions by a separate nomenclature and a belief in the unique character structure of each generational group. Today the third and fourth generations in North America (*Sansei* and *Yonsei*, respectively) exhibit definite signs of a "Hansen effect"—that is, interest in recovering Old World culture—and also show concern over the appropriate allocation of their energies and activities to things American or Canadian and things Japanese. Ties to a Japanese community are tenuous and find their realization primarily in courtship and marriage and in recreational pursuits.

Although the situation is by no means so clear, overseas Japanese communities outside North America exhibit some patterns similar to and some quite different from those of the continental United States and Canada. In the most extensive study of acculturation among Japanese in pre-war Kona, Hawaii, the community appeared organized less along Japa-

nese than Hawaiian–American lines. Other studies of Japanese in Hawaii have emphasized the innovative food habits, decline of the patriarch, and changing moral bases of family life. On the other hand, Japanese in Peru, where Japan's official policy of emigration played a significant role in establishing the colony and supervising its affairs, had maintained a generally separate though financially successful and occupationally diversified community until 1942; postwar developments indicate that the Peruvian-born Japanese will seek and obtain increasing entrance into Peruvian society and further estrangement from all-Japanese associations. In Brazil, a situation similar to that of Peru developed: sponsored migration reached great heights during the period of Japan's imperialist development, and, although Brazil welcomed Japanese until 1934, a policy of coerced assimilation motivated by suspicion of Japanese intent led to a closing of many all-Japanese institutions before the outbreak of World War II. In the postwar period, Brazilian-born Japanese indicated a greater interest than their parents had in integration into Brazilian society. In Paraguay, where the first Japanese colony began in La Colmena as recently as 1936, signs of acculturation and community break-down have been reported by cultural geographers surveying the area.[11] Generally, this cursory

[10] Material for the following is based on Michinari Fujita, "Japanese Associations in America", *Sociology and Social Research* (January–February 1929), pp. 211–28; T. Obana, "The American-born Japanese," *Sociology and Social Research* (November–December 1934), pp. 161–5; Joseph Roucek, "Japanese Americans", in Francis J. Brown and Joseph S. Roucek, Editors, *One America: The History, Contributions, and Present Problems of Our Racial and National Minorities* (New York, 1952), pp. 319–84; Forrest E. la Violette, "Canada and Its Japanese", in Edgar T. Thompson and Everett C. Hughes, Editors, *Race: Individual and Collective Behavior* (Glencoe, 1958), pp. 149–55; Charles Young, Helen R. Y. Reid and W. A. Carrothers, *The Japanese Canadians* (Toronto, 1938), edited by H. A. Innis; Ken Adachi, *A History of the Japanese Canadians in British Columbia* (Vancouver (?) 1958); T. Scott Miyakawa, "The Los Angeles Sansei", *Kashu Mainichi* (December 20, 1962), Part 2, 1; Harry Kitano, "Is There Sansei Delinquency?", *Kashu Mainichi* (December 20, 1962), Part 2, 1.

[11] For the Japanese in Hawaii, see John Embree, "New and Local Kin Groups Among the Japanese Farmers of Kona, Hawaii", *American Anthropologist*, 41 (July 1939), 400–7; John Embree, "Acculturation Among the Japanese of Kona, Hawaii", *Memoirs of the American Anthropological Association*, No. 59; Supplement to *American Anthropologist*, 43, 4:2 (1941); Jitsuichi Masuoka, "The Life Cycle of an Immigrant Institution in Hawaii: The Family", *Social Forces*, 23 (October 1944), 60–64; Masuoka, "The Japanese Patriarch in Hawaii", *Social Forces*, 17 (December 1938), 240–8; Masuoka, "Changing Food Habits of the Japanese in Hawaii", *American Sociological Review*, 10 (December 1945), 759–65; Masuoka, "Changing Moral Bases of the Japanese Family in Hawaii", *Sociology and Social Research*, 21 (November 1936), 158–69; Andrew M. Lind, *Hawaii's Japanese, An Experiment in Democracy* (Princeton, 1946). For the Japanese in Peru see Toraji Irie: "History of Japanese Migration to Peru", *Hispanic–American Historical Review*, 32 (August–October, 1951) 437–52, 648–64; (February 1952), 73–82; Mischa Titiev, "The Japanese Colony in

survey of overseas Japanese communities suggests that when such communities are not governed by agencies of the homeland and where, as the researches of Caudill and de Vos indicate,[12] Japanese values find opportunity for interpenetration and complementarity with those of the host society (as in the United States and Canada), the speed with which community isolation declines is accelerated.

Contrasts between the Chinese and Japanese have been noticed frequently but rarely researched.[13] As early as 1909 Chester Rowell, a Fresno, California journalist, pointed to the Japanese refusal to be losers in unprofitable contracts, to their unwillingness to be tied to a "Jap-town", and to their geniality and politeness; in contrast he praised the Chinese

subordination to contracts and headmen, their accommodation to a ghetto existence, and their cold but efficient and loyal service as domestics. Similar observations were made by Winifred Raushenbush, Robert Park's assistant in his famous race relations survey of the Pacific coast. More recently the late Rose Hum Lee has vividly remarked upon the contrast between the two Oriental groups. Professor Lee asserts that the *Nisei* "exhibit within sixty years, greater degrees of integration into American society, than has been the case with the Chinese, whose settlement is twice as long". Other sociologists have frequently commented on the speed with which Japanese adopted at least the outward signs of Occidental culture and attained success in North America. Broom and Kitsuse summed up the impressive record of the Japanese by declaring it "an achievement perhaps rarely equalled in the history of human migration". More recently, Petersen has pointed to the same record of achievement and challenged sociologists to develop a theory which could adequately explain it as well as the less spectacular records of other ethnic groups.

Although the differences between the Chinese and Japanese in North America have excited more comparative comment than concrete investigation, an early statement by Walter G. Beach deserves more attention than it has received. In a much neglected article[14] Beach observed the contrast between the speed of acculturation of Chinese and Japanese and attributed it to those conditions within and extrinsic to the ethnic groups which fostered either segregation and retention of old world culture traits or rapid breakdown of the ethnic community. Noting that ethnic cultures were an important aspect of the kind of community an immigrant group would form he pointed out that the Chinese came to America "before Chinese culture had been greatly influenced by Western civilization". More specifically, he suggested that "they came from an old, conservative and stationary social organization

Peru", *Far Eastern Quarterly*, 10 (May 1951), 227–47. For Japanese in Brazil see J. F. Normano, "Japanese Emigration to Brazil", *Pacific Affairs*, 7 (March 1934), 42–61; Emilio Willems and Herbert Baldus, "Cultural Change Among Japanese Immigrants in Brazil in the Ribeira Valley of Sao Paulo", *Sociology and Social Research*, 26 (July 1943), 525–37; Emilio Willems, "The Japanese in Brazil", *Far Eastern Quarterly*, 18 (January 12, 1949), 6–8; John P. Augelli, "Cultural and Economic Changes of Bastos, a Japanese Colony on Brazil's Paulista Frontier", *Annals of the Association of American Geographers*, 48, 1 (March 1958), 3–19. For Paraguay see Norman R. Stewart, *Japanese Colonization in Eastern Paraguay* (Washington, D.C., 1967).

[12] William Caudill, "Japanese American Personality and Acculturation", *Genetic Psychology Monographs*, 45 (1952), 3–102; George de Vos, "A Comparison of the Personality Differences in Two Generations of Japanese Americans by Means of the Rorschach Test", *Nagoya Journal of Medicine*, 17, 3 (August 1954), 153–265; William Caudill and George de Vos, "Achievement, Culture and Personality: The Case of the Japanese Americans", *American Anthropologist*, 58 (December 1956), 110–226.

[13] Materials in this section are based on Chester Rowell, "Chinese and Japanese Immigrants—a Comparison", *Annals of the American Academy of Political and Social Science*, 24, 2 (September 1909), 223–30; Winifred Raushenbush, "Their Place in the Sun", and "The Great Wall of Chinatown", *The Survey Graphic*, 56, 3 (May 1, 1926), 141–5, 154–8; Rose Hum Lee, *The Chinese in the United States of America*, p. 425; Leonard Broom and John I. Kitsuse, "The Validation of Acculturation: A Condition of Ethnic Assimilation", *American Anthropologist*, 57 (1955), 44–8; William Petersen, "Family Structure and Social Mobility Among Japanese Americans". Paper presented at the annual meetings of the American Sociological Association, San Francisco, August, 1967.

[14] Walter G. Beach, "Some Considerations in Regard to Race Segregation in California", *Sociology and Social Research*, 18 (March 1934), 340–50.

and system of custom-control of life; and that the great majority came from the lower and least independent social stratum of that life". By contrast, he observed that the Japanese "came at a time when their national political system had felt the influence of Western thought and ambitions". He went on to say: "Japan was recognized among the world's powers, and its people were self-conscious in respect to this fact; their pride was not in a past culture, unintelligible to Americans (as the Chinese), but in a growing position of recognition and authority among the world's powers". It was because of these differences in culture and outlook, Beach argued, that Japanese tended to resist discrimination more vigorously and to adopt Occidental ways more readily, while Chinese produced a "Chop-suey culture" in segregated communities. Stripped of its ethnocentrism, Beach's analysis suggests that acculturation is affected not only by the action of the larger society upon immigrants, but also, and more fundamentally, by the nature and quality of the immigrant culture and institutions.

The present study specifies and clarifies the features of Japanese and Chinese culture which Beach only hinted at, and details the interplay between Old-World cultures and North American society. Certain key conditions of life in China and Japan at the times of emigration produced two quite different kinds of immigrant social organization. The responses of the American economy and society to Chinese and Japanese certainly had their effects. But these alone did not shape Chinese and Japanese life. Rather they acted as "accelerators" to the direction of and catalysts or inhibitors of the development of the immigrants' own culture and institutions.[15] Prejudice and discrimination added considerable hardship to the necessarily onerous lives of the immigrating Orientals, but did not wrench away their culture, nor deprive them completely of those familial, political, and social institutions which they had transported across

[15] See the discussion in Lyman, "The Structure of Chinese Society in Nineteenth-Century America", pp. 370–77.

the Pacific.[16] The Chinese and Japanese were never reduced to the wretchedness of the first Africans in America, who experienced a forcible stripping away of their original culture, and then a coercive assimilation into selected and subordinated elements of white America. Thus, although both Chinese and Japanese share a nearly identical distinction from the dominant American racial stock, and although both have been oppressed by prejudice, discrimination, segregation and exclusion, a fundamental source of their markedly different rates of acculturation is to be found in the particular developmental patterns taken by their respective cultures[17] in America.

[16] One difference with respect to hostility toward the Chinese and Japanese had to do with whether either was perceived as an "enemy" people. Although the Chinese were occasionally accused of harboring subversive intentions toward America—(see, e.g. P. W. Dooner, Last Days of the Republic (San Francisco, 1880))—it was the Japanese who suffered a half-century of such suspicions. See Jacabus tenBroek, Edward N. Barnhart, and Floyd Matson, Prejudice, War and the Constitution (Berkeley, 1954), pp. 11–99; Forrest E. La Violette, The Canadian Japanese and World War II (Toronto, 1948). Undoubtedly these deep-seated suspicions led Japanese to try very hard to prove their loyalty and assimilability. In this respect see Mike Masaoka, "The Japanese American Creed", Common Ground, 2, 3 (1942), 11; and "A Tribute to Japanese American Military Service in World War II", Speech of Hon. Hiram Fong in the Senate of the United States, Congressional Record, 88th Congress, First Session, May 21, 1963, pp. 1–13; "Tributes to Japanese American Military Service in World War II", Speeches of Twenty-four Congressmen, Congressional Record, 88th Congress, First Session, June 11, 1963, pp. 1–16; Senator Daniel Ken Inouye (with Lawrence Elliott), Journey to Washington (Englewood Cliffs, 1967), pp. 87–200.

[17] In the tradition of Max Weber, religion might properly be supposed to have played a significant role in the orientations of overseas Chinese and Japanese. However, certain problems make any adoption of the Weberian thesis difficult. First, although Confucianism was the state religion of China, local villages practiced syncretic forms combining ancestor worship, Buddhism, Christianity, and homage to local deities. Maurice Freedman, Lineage Organization in Southeastern China (London, 1958), p. 116. Abroad Chinese temples were definitely syncretic and functioned to support a non-rationalist idea of luck and the maintenance of merchant power. See A. J. A. Elliott, Chinese Spirit Medium Cults in Singapore (London, 1955), pp. 24–45; Stewart Culin, The Religious Ceremonies of the Chinese in the Eastern Cities of the United States (Philadelphia, 1887); Wolfram Eberhard,

EMIGRATION

The conditions of emigration for Chinese and Japanese reflected respectively their different cultures. The Chinese migrated from a state that was not a nation, and they conceived of themselves primarily as members of local extended kin units, bound together by ties of blood and language and only secondarily, if at all, as "citizens" of the Chinese empire.[18] Chinese emigration was an organized affair in which kinsmen or fellow villagers who had achieved some wealth or status acted as agents and sponsors for their compatriots. Benevolently despotic, this emigration acted to trans-

"Economic Activities of a Chinese Temple in California", *Journal of the American Oriental Society*, 82, 3 (July–September 1962), pp. 362–71. In the case of Japanese, the Tokugawa religion certainly facilitated a limited achievement orientation. Robert Bellah, *Tokugawa Religion: The Values of Pre-industrial Japan* (Glencoe, 1957), pp. 107–132. But both in Japan and the United States, Japanese exhibit a remarkable indifference to religious affiliation, even countenancing denominational and church differences within the same nuclear family and relatively little anxiety about religious intermarriage. See Kiyomi Morioka, "Christianity in the Japanese Rural Community: Acceptance and Rejection", *Japanese Sociological Studies. The Sociological Review*, Monograph X (Sept. 1966), 183–98; Leonard D. Cain, Jr., "Japanese-American Protestants: Acculturation and Assimilation", *Review of Religious Research*, 3, 3 (Winter 1962), 113–21; Cain, "The Integration Dilemma of Japanese-American Protestants", Paper presented at the annual meetings of the Pacific Sociological Association, April 5, 1962.

[18] For information on nineteenth-century Chinese social organization in the provinces from which North America's immigrants came, see Maurice Freedman, *Chinese Lineage and Society: Fukien and Kwangtung* (New York, 1966); Kung-Chuan Hsiao, *Rural China: Imperial Control in the Nineteenth Century* (Seattle, 1960). On the Chinese as sojourners see Paul C. P. Siu, "The Sojourner", *American Journal of Sociology*, 8 (July 1952), 32–44 and Siu, "The Isolation of the Chinese Laundryman", in Ernest W. Burgess and Donald Bogue, Editors, *Contributions to Urban Sociology* (Chicago, 1964), pp. 429–42. On the role of immigrant associations, see William Hoy, *The Chinese Six Companies* (San Francisco, 1942); Tin-Yuke Char, "Immigrant Chinese Societies in Hawaii", *Sixty-First Annual Report of the Hawaiian Historical Society* (1953), pp. 29–32; William Willmott, "Chinese Clan Associations in Vancouver", *Man*, 64, 49 (March–April, 1964), 33–7.

fer the loyalties and institutions of the village to the overseas community. In the village, composed for the most part of his kinsmen, the individual looked to elders as leaders; in emigrating the individual reposed his loyalty and submitted his fate to the overseas representative of his clan or village. Loans, protection, and jobs were provided within a framework of kin and language solidarity that stretched from the village in Kwangtung to the clan building in "Chinatown". Emigrants regarded their journey as temporary and their return as certain. Abroad the Chinese, as homeless men, never fully accepted any permanence to their sojourn. They identified themselves with their Old-World clan, village, dialect grouping, or secret society whose overseas leaders were recognized as legitimate substitutes for homeland groups. These institutional leaders further insinuated themselves into the overseas immigrant's life by acting as his representative to white society, by pioneering new settlements, and by providing badly-needed goods and services, protection against depredations, and punishments for wrongdoing.

The Japanese emigrant departed from an entirely different kind of society.[19] Japan was a nation as well as a state, and its villages reflected this fact. Village life had long ceased to be circumscribed by kinship, and the individual family rather than the extended kinship group was the locus of loyalty and solidarity. When children departed their homes they left unencumbered by a network of obligations. Unless he had been born first or last, a Japanese son was not obligated as was a Chinese to

[19] Material for the following is based on George B. Sansom, *Japan: A Short Cultural History* (New York, 1943); Taskashi Koyama, "The Significance of Relatives at the Turning Point of the Family System in Japan", *Japanese Sociological Studies. Sociological Review*, 10 (September 1966), 95–114; Lafcadio Hearn, *Japan: An Interpretation* (Tokyo, 1955), pp. 81–106; Ronald P. Dore, *City Life in Japan: A Study of a Tokyo Ward* (Berkeley, 1958), pp. 91–190; Irene Taeuber, "Family, Migration, and Industrialization in Japan", *American Sociological Review* (April, 1951), pp. 149–57; Ezra F. Vogel, "Kinship Structure, Migration to the City, and Modernization", in R. P. Dore, *Aspects of Social Change in Modern Japan* (Princeton, 1967), pp. 91–112.

remain in the home of his parents. After 1868 emigration was sometimes sponsored by the government and certainly encouraged. When Japanese departed the homeland they, like the Chinese, expected only to sojourn, but they were not called back to the home village by the knowledge that a long-patient wife awaited them or that kinsmen fully depended on their return. Moreover, the men who inspired Japanese emigration were not pioneer leaders but exemplary individuals whose singular fame and fortune seemed to promise everyone great opportunity abroad. They did not serve as overseas community leaders or even very often as agents of migration, but only as shining examples of how others might succeed.

MARITAL STATUS

The respective marital situation of these two Asian peoples reflected fundamental differences in Chinese and Japanese kinship and profoundly influenced community life overseas. Custom required that a Chinese man sojourn abroad without his wife. A man's return to hearth and village was thus secured, and he laboured overseas in order that he might some day again enjoy the warmth of domesticity and the blessings of children. Abroad he lived a lonely life of labour, dependent on kinsmen and compatriots for fellowship and on prostitutes and vice for outlet and recreation. When in 1882 restrictive American legislation unwittingly converted Chinese custom into legal prohibition by prohibiting the coming of wives of Chinese labourers it exaggerated and lengthened the separation of husbands from wives and, more significantly, delayed for nearly two generations the birth in America of a substantial "second generation" among the immigrant Chinese. Canadian immigration restrictions had a similar consequence.[20] Barred from intermarriage by custom and law and unable to bring wives to Canada or the United States, Chinese men sired children on their infrequent return visits to China, and these China-born sons later partially replenished the Chinese population in North America as they joined their fathers in the overseas venture. Like their fathers the sons also depended on Chinatown institutions. Their lack of independence from the same community controls which had earlier circumscribed the lives of their fathers stood in sharp contrast to the manner of life of the Canadian and American born.

Neither custom nor law barred the Japanese from bringing wives to Canada or America.[21] Within two decades of their ar-

[20] For discussions of United States restrictive legislation see Mary Coolidge, *Chinese Immigration* (New York, 1909), pp. 145–336; S. W. Kung, *Chinese in American Life: Some Aspects of Their History, Status, Problems and Contributions* (Seattle, 1962), pp. 64–165. A discussion of both American and Canadian restrictive legislation will be found in Huang Tsen-ming, *The Legal Status of the Chinese Abroad* (Taipei, 1954). See also Tin-Yuke Char, "Legal Restrictions on Chinese in English Speaking Countries, I", *Chinese Social and Political Science Review* (January 4, 1933,) pp. 479–94. Careful analyses of Canadian legislation are found in Duncan McArthur, "What is the Immigration Problem?", *Queen's Quarterly* (Autumn 1928), pp. 603–14; three articles by H. F. Angus, "Canadian Immigration: The Law and its Administration", *American Journal of International Law*, 18, 1 (January 1934), 74–89; "The Future of Immigration into Canada", *Canadian Journal of Economics and Political Science*, 12 (August 1946), 379–86; Jean Mercier, "Immigration and Provincial Rights", *Canadian Bar Review*, 22 (1944), 856–69; Hugh L. Keenleyside, "Canadian Immigration Policy and Its Administration", *External Affairs* (May 1949), pp. 3–11; Bora Laskin, "Naturalization and Aliens: Immigration, Exclusion, and Deportation", *Canadian Constitutional Law* (Toronto, 1960), pp. 958–77. In general see David C. Corbett, *Canada's Immigration Policy: A Critique* (Toronto, 1957).

[21] For Japanese immigration see Yamato Ichihashi, *Japanese in the United States* (Stanford, 1932), pp. 401–9; Dorothy Swaine Thomas, Charles Kikuchi, and J. Sakoda, *The Salvage* (Berkeley, 1952), pp. 3–18, 571–626; H. A. Millis, *The Japanese Problem in the United States* (New York, 1915); K. K. Kawakami, *The Real Japanese Question* (New York, 1921); T. Iyenaga and Kenosuke Sato, *Japan and the California Problem* (New York, 1921); Iichiro Tokutomi, *Japanese–American Relations* (New York, 1922), pp. 65–88 (translated by Sukeshige Yanagiwara); R. D. McKenzie, *Oriental Exclusion* (Chicago, 1928). For Japanese immigration to Canada see Young, Reid, and Carrothers, *The Japanese Canadians*; A. R. M. Lower, *Canada and the Far East—1940* (New York, 1941), pp. 61–89; H. F. Angus, *Canada and the Far East, 1940–1953* (Toronto, 1953), pp. 99–100. For a statement by a pessimistic *Nisei* see Kazuo Kawai, "Three Roads,

rival the Japanese had brought over enough women to guarantee that, although husbands might be quite a bit older than their wives, a domestic life would be established in America. Japanese thus had little need for the brothels and gambling halls which characterized Chinese communities in the late nineteenth century and which, not incidentally, provided a continuous source of wealth and power to those who owned or controlled them. Japanese quickly produced a second generation in both Canada and the United States, and by 1930 this *Nisei* generation began to claim a place for itself in North America and in Japanese–American and Japanese–Canadian life. The independence and acculturation of the *Nisei* was indicated in their social and political style of life. They did not accept the organizations of their parents' community and established *ad hoc* associations dedicated to civil rights and penetration beyond Canada's and America's racial barrier. Some Japanese immigrants educated one of their children in Japan. These few Japan-educated offspring (*Kibei*) did not enjoy the same status in North America as *Nisei*, and in their marginality and problems of adjustment they resembled the China-born offspring of Chinese immigrants. Educated in Canadian or American schools and possessed of Canadian or American culture and values, the *Nisei* found that prejudice and discrimination acted as the most significant obstacle to their success.

---

and None Easy", *Survey Graphic*, 56, 3 (May 1, 1926), 1964–6. For further discussions see Tsutoma Obana, "Problems of the American-born Japanese", *Sociology and Social Research*, 19 (November 1934), 161–5; Emory S. Bogardus, "Current Problems of Japanese Americans", *Sociology and Social Research*, 25 (July 1941), 562–71. For the development of new associations among *Nisei* see Adachi, *A History of the Japanese in British Columbia, 1877–1958*, pp. 11–14; *Better Americans in a Greater America*, booklet published by the Japanese American Citizens' League, undated (1967), 24 pp. For an ecological analysis of the distribution and diffusion of achievement orientations among Japanese in America see Paul T. Tagaki, "The Japanese Family in the United States: A Hypothesis on the Social Mobility of the Nisei", revision of an earlier paper presented at the annual meeting of the Kroeber Anthropological Society, Berkeley, California (April 30, 1966).

OCCUPATIONS AND LOCATIONS

Jobs and settlement patterns tended to reinforce and accelerate the different development patterns of Chinese and Japanese communities in America.[22] Except for a small but powerful merchant élite the Chinese began and remained as wage labourers. First employed in the arduous and menial tasks of mining and railroad-building, the Chinese later gravitated into unskilled, clerical and service work inside the Chinese community. Such work necessitated living in cities or returning to cities when unemployment drove the contract labourers to seek new jobs. The city always meant the Chinese quarter, a ghetto set aside for Chinese in which their special needs could be met and by which the white population could segregate itself from them. Inside the ghetto Old-World societies ministered to their members' wants, exploited their needs, and represented their interests. When primary industry could no longer use Chinese and white hostility drove them out of the labour market and into Chinatown, the power of these associations and their merchant leaders was reconfirmed and enhanced. The single most important feature of the occupations of Chinese immigrants was their tendency to keep the Chinese in a state of dependency on bosses, contractors, merchants—ultimately on the merchant élite of Chinatown.

The Japanese, after a brief stint as labourers in several primary industries then on the wane in western America, pioneered the cultivation of truck crops.[23] Small-scale agri-

---

[22] For information on occupations and settlement patterns see Lyman, "The Structure of Chinese Society in Nineteenth-Century America", pp. 111–27; Milton L. Barnett, "Kinship as a Factor Affecting Cantonese Economic Adaptation in the United States", *Human Organization*, 19 (Spring, 1960), 40–6; Ping Chiu, *Chinese Labor in California: An Economic Study* (Madison, 1963).

[23] For the Japanese as agriculturalists see Masakazu Iwata, "The Japanese Immigrants in California Agriculture", *Agricultural History*, 36 (January 1962), 25–37; Thomas *et al.*, *The Salvage*, pp. 23–5; Adon Poli, *Japanese Farm Holdings on the Pacific Coast* (Berkeley, 1944). For farming and fishing communities in Canada see Tadashi Fukutake,

culturalists, separated from one another as well as from the urban anti-Orientalism of the labor unions, Japanese farmers did not retain the kind of ethnic solidarity characteristic of the urban Chinese. Whatever traditional élites had existed among the early Japanese immigrants fell from power or were supplanted. In their place *ad hoc* associations arose to meet particular needs. When Japanese did become labourers and city dwellers they too became segregated in "li'l Tokyos" presided over by Old-World associations for a time. But the early concentration in agriculture and the later demands of the *Nisei* tended to weaken the power even of the city-bred immigrant associations.

COMMUNITY POWER AND CONFLICT

Finally, the different bases for solidarity in the two Oriental communities tended to confirm their respective modes of social organization. The Japanese community has remained isolated primarily because of discriminatory barriers to integration and secondarily because of the sense of congregation among fellow Japanese. The isolated Chinese community is, to be sure, a product of white aversion and is also characterized by congregative sentiments, but, much more than that of the Japanese, it rests on communal foundations. Political life in Chinatown has rarely been tranquil.[24] The

traditional clans and *Landsmannschaften* controlled immigration, settled disputes, levied taxes and fines, regulated commerce, and meted out punishments. Opposition to their rule took the form it had taken in China. Secret societies, chapters of or modeled after the well-known Triad Society, took over the functions of law, protection, and revenge for their members. In addition the secret societies owned or controlled the gambling houses and brothels which emerged to satisfy the recreational and sex needs of homeless Chinese men and displayed occasional interest in the restive politics of China. Struggles for power, blood feuds, and "wars" of vengeance were not infrequent in the early days of Chinatown. These conflicts entrenched the loyalties of men to their respective associations. More important with respect to non-acculturation, these intramural fights isolated the Chinese from the uncomprehending larger society and bound them together in antagonistic cooperation. Since the turn of the century, the grounds of such battles have shifted on to a commercial and political plane, but violence is not unknown. Chinatown's organizational solidarity and its intra-community conflicts have thus acted as agents of non-acculturation.

POSITION AND PROSPECTS
OF THE ORIENTAL IN NORTH AMERICA

The conditions for the political and economic integration of the Chinese appear to be at hand now.[25] This is largely because the forces

---

Man and Society in Japan (Tokyo, 1962), pp. 146–79. For the rise and decline of urban ghettos among Japanese in the United States see Shotaro Frank Miyamoto, *Social Solidarity Among the Japanese in Seattle,* University of Washington Publications in the Social Sciences XI, 4 (December 1939), 57–129; Toshio Mori, "Li'l Yokohama" *Common Ground,* 1, 2 (1941), 54–6; Larry Tajiri, "Farewell to Little Tokyo", *Common Ground,* 4, 2 (1942) 90–5; Robert W. O'Brien, "Selective Dispersion as a Factor in the Solution of the Nisei Problem", *Social Forces,* 23 (Dec. 1944), 140–7.

[24] On power and conflict in Chinatown see Lyman, "The Structure of Chinese Society in Nineteenth-Century America", pp. 272–369. For secret societies see Stanford M. Lyman, "Chinese Secret Societies in the Occident: Notes and Suggestions for Research in the Sociology of Secrecy", *Canadian Review of Sociology and Anthropology,* 1, 2 (1964), 79–102; Stanford M. Lyman, W. E. Willmott, Berching Ho,

"Rules of a Chinese Secret Society in British Columbia", *Bulletin of The School of Oriental and African Studies,* 27, 3 (1964), 530–9. See also D. Y. Yuan, "Voluntary Segregation: A Study of New Chinatown", *Phylon Quarterly* (Fall 1963), pp. 255–65.

[25] For an extended discussion of the progess in eliminating discrimination in Canada and the United States see Stanford M. Lyman, *The Oriental in North America* (Vancouver, 1962), Lecture No. 11: "Position and Prospects of the Oriental since World War II". On immigration matters to 1962 see S. W. Kung, "Chinese Immigration in North America", *Queen's Quarterly,* 68, 4 (Winter 1962), 610–20. Information about Chinese in Canada and the United States is regularly reported in the *Chinatown News,* a Vancouver, B.C. publication and in

which spawned and maintained Chinatown are now weakened. The near balancing of the sex ratio has made possible the birth and maturation in America of second and third generation Chinese. Their presence, in greater and greater numbers, poses a serious threat to old-world power élites. The breakdown of discriminatory barriers to occupations and residency brought about by a new assertion of civil rights heralds an end to Chinatown economic and domestic monopoly. The relative openness of Canadian and American society to American-born and Canadian-born Chinese reduces their dependency on traditional goods and services and their recruitment into communal associations. Concomitantly, the *casus belli* of the earlier era disappears and conflict's group-binding and isolating effect loses force. What remains of Chinatown eventually is its new immigrants, its culturally acceptable economic base —restaurants and shops—and its congregative value for ethnic Chinese. Recent events in San Francisco suggest that the young and newly-arrived immigrants from Hong Kong and Taiwan and the American-born Chinese school drop-outs are estranged from both the Chinatown élites and white America. Many of their activities resemble those of protesting and militant Negro groups.

The Japanese are entering a new phase of relations with the larger society in North America. There is a significant amount of anxiety in Japanese circles about the decline of Japanese values and the appearance of the more undesirable features of Canadian and American life—primarily juvenile delinquency but also a certain lack of old-world propriety which had survived through the *Nisei* generation—among the *Sansei* and *Yonsei*.[26] Moreover, like those Negroes who share E. Franklin Frazier's disillusion with the rise of a black bourgeoisie, some Japanese-Americans are

questioning the social and personal price paid for entrance into American society. Scholars such as Daisuke Kitagawa have wondered just how *Nisei* and *Sansei* might preserve elements of Japanese culture in America. At the same time one European Japanophile has bitterly assailed the Americanization of the *Nisei*.[27] Nothing similar to a black power movement has developed among the Japanese, and, indeed, such a movement is extremely unlikely given Japanese–American and Canadian material success and the decrease in social distance between Japanese and white Americans. At most there is a quiet concern. But even such mild phenomena are deserving of sociological attention.

THEORETICAL CONSIDERATIONS

This survey of Oriental community organization suggests the need to take seriously Robert Park's reconsideration of his own race relations cycle. Park at first had supposed that assimilation was a natural and inevitable outcome of race contact marked off by stages of competition, conflict, and accommodation before there occurred the eventual absorption of one people by another.[28] In addition to its faults as a natural history, a criticism so often discussed by other sociologists,[29] Park's original statement of the cycle took no account of what, in a related context, Wagley and Harris refer to as the "adaptive capacity" of the immi-

---

East–West, a San Francisco Journal. For problems of recent Chinese immigrants see *San Francisco Chronicle* (March 18, 1968) 2; for those of American born, *ibid.* (March 19, 1968), 42.

[26] On April 15, 1965, in response to a rash of teenage burglaries among Japanese in Sacramento, parents and other interested adults met and discussed how the community might act to prevent delinquency.

[27] Daisuke Kitagawa, "Assimilation of Pluralism?" in Arnold M. Rose and Caroline B. Rose, *Minority Problems* (New York, 1965), pp. 285–7. Fosco Maraini has written "The *ni-sei* has generally been taught to despise his Asian roots; on the other hand, all he has taken from the west is a two-dimensional duralumin Christianity, ultra-modernism, the cultivation of jazz as a sacred rite, a California veneer." *Meeting with Japan*, New York, 1960 (translated by Eric Mosbacher), p. 169.

[28] Robert E. Park, "Our Racial Frontier on the Pacific", *Survey Graphic*, 56, 3 (May 1, 1926), 196.

[29] Seymour Martin Lipset, "Changing Social Status and Prejudice: The Race Theories of a Pioneering American Sociologist", *Commentary*, 9 (May 1950), 475–9; Amitai Etzioni, "The Ghetto—A Re-evaluation", *Social Forces*, 37 (March 1959), 255–62.

grant group.[30] However, Park himself reconsidered the cycle and in 1937 wrote that it might terminate in one of three outcomes: a caste system as was the case in India; complete assimilation, as he imagined had occurred in China; or a permanent institutionalization of minority status within a larger society, as was the case of Jews in Europe. Park concluded that race relations occur as phases of a cycle "which, once initiated, inevitably continues until it terminates in some predestined racial configuration, and one consistent with the established social order of which it is a part".[31] Park's later emphasis on alternative outcomes and his consideration of the peculiar social context in which any ethnic group's history occurs implicitly recall attention to the interplay between native and host society cultures. As Herskovitz's researches on West African and American Negro cultures indicate, the immigrant group, even if oppressed *in transitu*, does not arrive with a cultural *tabula rasa* waiting to be filled in by the host culture. Rather it possesses a culture and social organization which in contact with and in the several contexts of the host culture will be supplanted, inhibited, subordinated, modified or enhanced. Kinship, occupations, patterns of settlement and community organization are each factors in such developments. Assimilation, or for that matter pluralism, is not simply an inevitable state of human affairs, as those who cling to "natural history" models assert, but rather is an existential possibility. Social factors contribute to the state of being of a people and to changes in that state. The Chinese and Japanese communities in America illustrate two modes of development and suggest the need to refine even further our knowledge of the factors which affect whatever mode of development an immigrant group chooses.

[30] Charles Wagley and Marvin Harris, *Minorities in the New World* (New York, 1958).

[31] Robert E. Park, "The Race Relations Cycle in Hawaii", *Race and Culture* (Glencoe, 1950), pp. 194–5. For an extended discussion of the race cycle see Stanford M. Lyman, "The Race Relations Cycle of Robert E. Park", *Pacific Sociological Review* 11, 1 (Spring 1968), 16–22.

21

Puerto Ricans in Perspective: The Meaning of Migration to the Mainland

Joseph P. Fitzpatrick

It is now twenty-two years since the large scale migration of Puerto Ricans to the United States Mainland began to develop after World War II. In the year 1946 the net outmigration from Puerto Rico to the Mainland was about 40,000. It reached a peak of almost 70,000 in 1953. It has fluctuated sharply from year to year but continues to be substantial. In the year 1966, the net outmigration was close to 29,000; in 1967, it was more than 26,000. The movement backward for permanent resettlement on the Island is considerable, but still does not compare with the movement to the Mainland. Clarence Senior[1] is certainly correct when he insists that the migration of Puerto Ricans should be considered as part of the internal migration of American citizens. Nevertheless, Puerto Ricans come from a cultural background very different from that of the Mainland United States and, despite the benefits of citizenship, they face the problems of language difference, cultural difference and cultural adjustment which are the common

---

Joseph P. Fitzpatrick is Professor of Sociology at Fordham University.

Reprinted from *International Migration Review* 2 (Spring, 1968): pp. 7–19, by permission of the Center for Migration Studies of New York, Inc. Most footnotes have been deleted, and the remaining footnotes have been renumbered.

[1] Clarence Senior, *The Puerto Ricans* (Chicago: Quadrangle Books, 1965), chap. 3.

experience of migrating people throughout the world. This large scale experience, therefore, has a universal meaning. This paper seeks to examine what it is particularly in the perspective of their experience in New York City.

This article will first examine the unique characteristics of the Puerto Rican migration; secondly, it will study the process of assimilation particularly in relation to the search for identity which presents a number of special problems to the Puerto Ricans. It will analyze one of the special problems of identity which consists in a shift from an emphasis on culture to an emphasis on power as the basis for the establishment of a strong Puerto Rican community. Finally it will seek to interpret the experience of the Puerto Ricans as part of the human effort and suffering inevitably involved in the continuing creative achievement of New York City. In the historical perspective of the past migrations to the City it is reasonable to be optimistic about the present one.

NEW VARIATIONS ON AN OLD THEME

The Puerto Rican migration can be initially understood only by perceiving it as the continuation of the experience which New York City has always had with newcomers. It is not a new or unusual occurrence for New York City that Puerto Ricans should be coming in large numbers. Rather, it would be a new and unusual experience if the City did not have them, or millions of other strangers, in her midst. It is precisely the presence of the stranger that has given New York many of its unique characteristics. Furthermore, by coming into the City, the Puerto Ricans face an experience that is neither new nor unusual. They inherit the role of strangers and re-live that painful but exciting drama of adjustment, the source of suffering and challenge out of which the strangers have consistently emerged as a new and greater people.

There are new dimensions, however, to this migration as there are new dimensions to the City's life. The Puerto Ricans have come for the most part as the first great air-borne migration of people from abroad. They are decidedly newcomers of the aviation age. A Puerto Rican can travel from San Juan to New York in less time than it took a New Yorker to travel from Coney Island to Times Square a century ago. They are the first group to come in large numbers from a different cultural background, but who are, nevertheless, citizens of the United States. They are the first group of newcomers who bring with them a cultural practice of widespread intermingling and intermarriage of people of different color. They are the first group of predominantly Catholic migrants who have not had a native clergy to accompany them. These and other characteristics make the migration of Puerto Ricans unique.

Finally they come to New York City when many characteristics of the City make their experience different. Change has always been part of the City's life. But change today is more mild than before and more extensive. Communication through radio and television has created a context in which people are in immediate, almost instantaneous contact; in which news in all its visual detail is available in the home of a Puerto Rican migrant as soon as it happens. In a world of telephones, people in Brooklyn and the Bronx can be neighbors more intimately than people, separated by a city block, could have been neighbors a century ago. The City is older and much of its real estate is decrepit and is being replaced on an enormous scale. The Puerto Ricans come to New York when nearly a million and a half Blacks are citizens of the City and the Civil Rights movement and the movement for "Black Power" are at their height. They come when automation is creating a new kind of economy, and when jobs which once were the great channels of immigrant advancement are being eliminated by the hundreds of thousands. They come when the City and Federal Governments provide a wide range of public services from public housing to welfare, which did not exist a century ago. Thus the coming of the Puerto Ricans is not just a repetition of the past, because the past no longer exists;

and no people quite like the Puerto Ricans have ever come before. Therefore any interpretation of the meaning of the migration must be related to these unique characteristics of the Puerto Rican people and the unique characteristics of New York City in the 1960's.

THE PROCESS OF ASSIMILATION: THE PROBLEM OF IDENTITY

In the presence of the circumstances just mentioned, the Puerto Ricans face the process of becoming part of the life of New York City. Central to this process is the problem of identity: "Who are we," and the effort to answer this question largely determines the direction and dynamics of assimilation. The Puerto Ricans face a unique experience in their search for identity; they face some particular problems in relation to the three basic factors on which the identity of other groups was firmly anchored, namely: nationality, color, and religion.

In the first place, the Puerto Ricans have been struggling with a problem of identity on the Island itself. The question "who are we?" has been a critical one for many years. A confident sense of who they are and where they belong, a deep-rootedness in a culture and tradition of long standing which most immigrants had before they came, this sense of secure identity has been weakening on the Island, if indeed it ever existed. This can be seen in the rapid convergence of three developments.

a) *The Problem of Political Status.* Puerto Rico is neither independent nor is it a state. It is a Free Associated State, a political status in which it enjoys a great deal of autonomy while still being part of the United States. For years, the problem of status has been a public debate around which the three major political parties are organized: the Popular Party which created the status of a Free Associated State continues to promote it as a permanent condition; the Statehood Party explicitly seeks to make Puerto Rico the fifty-first state of the Union; the Independence Party seeks complete Independence. In July, 1967, a plebiscite was held to determine the preference of the electorate. The status of Free Associated State gained 60% of the votes; Statehood was second with 38%; Independence ran a poor third with 2%. Despite the vote, however, the problem of uncertainty remains. When asking themselves politically, "who are we?", large numbers of Puerto Ricans are not so sure.

b) *The Problem of Economic development.* For the past twenty years, Puerto Rico has been passing through a period of rapid economic development. In fact, the movement, called "operation bootstrap," is considered the best example of the rapid economic development of an economically underdeveloped area in the world.

This development has had a massive impact on the traditional culture of the Island. The social and cultural adjustments to industrialization are evident everywhere, and the distress associated with them is deeply and widely felt. Almost ten years ago, the guiding spirit of economic development, Luis Munoz Marin began calling for a strong effort to preserve the traditional way of life. He wanted "operation serenity," as he called it, to be more parallel with "operation bootstrap." It is doubtful that "operation serenity" will be very effective in slowing down the cultural upheaval on the Island. From many points of view, Puerto Ricans have been culturally uprooted before they leave the Island.

c) *Changing Religious Conditions:* since Puerto Rico became an American possession, the Island has relied increasingly on the religious care of priests, sisters and brothers from the Mainland. This has been an extremely generous effort, but it brought a decidedly mainland style of Catholic life to the Island. In much of their religious life, Puerto Ricans have been conscious of dependence on a "foreign" clergy. They did not have that penetrating sense of Catholic identity which comes from a deeply rooted and untroubled folk attachment to Catholicism; there is nothing

among Puerto Ricans, for example, comparable to Our Lady of Guadalupe among the Mexicans. Nor did many have a mature conscious loyalty to the Church as an organization. There was an ambiguity even in their religious experience. As a result, the sense of identity which was the basis around which ethnic loyalties crystallized in the lives of other immigrants, was weak in the Puerto Ricans before they came.

When they arrived in New York, the problem of identity became further complicated particularly around the problem of color. Puerto Ricans range from completely white to completely black with every mixture in between. They are certainly sensitive to color in Puerto Rico, but neither color consciousness nor prejudice nor discrimination focus on color the way they do on the Mainland. Conscious of the disadvantage of color in the Mainland, they have used various devices to protect themselves against it, emphasizing that they were "Puerto Rican" and not American Negro; clinging to Spanish in the hope that language would protect them from identification as American Negroes.[2] During the nineteen fifties when the civil rights movement was pressing strongly for integration, the movement created a dilemma for Puerto Ricans. They were integrated already, biologically and socially. A completely Puerto Rican school would be a completely integrated school. Consequently they were bewildered about their relationship to the civil rights movement.[3] Literally, they did not know where they were at.

Secondly, the religious parish, more specifically the Catholic parish, which was the basis for the identity of earlier immigrant

---

[2] For a remarkable account of the struggle of one colored Puerto Rican to determine his identity, see Piri Thomas, *Down These Mean Streets,* New York, Knopf, 1967.

[3] When the boycotts against the Public Schools were first started in 1964 by Civil Rights leaders to demand integration of Blacks and whites, the Puerto Ricans supported them. Shortly afterward, they withdrew and established their own National Association of Puerto Rican Civil Rights.

groups and the basis for the development of a strong immigrant community, has not fulfilled the same functions for Puerto Ricans. Early in the migration, the authorities of the New York Archdiocese adopted a policy of integrated parishes, that is Spanish speaking priests were added to existing parishes which had served and continued to serve older populations, and special services in Spanish were introduced into the parishes; but no separate churches devoted entirely to a Spanish speaking population were planned, and efforts were to be made to integrate the Spanish speaking with the older congregations. There are a number of serious reasons for this kind of policy. But it makes difficult, if not impossible, the establishment of a strong Puerto Rican community around a center of religious identification and practice. Wide dispersal in New York and the policy of integration in Public Housing projects also make it difficult for Puerto Ricans to form those tightly knit neighborhoods of older immigrant groups where immigrant communities were strong and supporting to their people in the process of adjustment, and which contributed psychologically to the sense of identity which gave many of the immigrants a sense of cultural and personal strength. The response of many Puerto Ricans to the Pentecostal and Evangelical sects, to the style of religious practice of the store front church, have been interpreted as one effort of Puerto Ricans to find the satisfaction and sense of belonging and identity which they have not achieved in the large, highly organized parishes of either the Catholic or Protestant faiths. The number of Puerto Ricans, however, who are seriously involved in the religious sects is very small. There is some speculation that the Island itself may be fulfilling the function which the immigrant community fulfilled for earlier immigrants. Travel back and forth to the Island is enormous; it consists mainly of Puerto Ricans moving in either direction to visit, to spend vacation, to escape problems, to seek financial or family help or to find work. In any event, they know that their home town on the Island is only three hours away. They have the sense of not being far

removed, of always being able to return if life in New York proves too difficult.

FROM COMMUNITY BASED ON CULTURE TO COMMUNITY BASED ON POWER

It is clear from the foregoing that many of the factors which contributed to the strong sense of community and identity of earlier immigrant groups, will not be able to contribute in the same way to a sense of community and identity among Puerto Ricans. However, new developments have been taking place in recent years and a decided change has appeared in a shift from an emphasis on culture as the basis for community to an emphasis on power. This transition could best be expressed by a brief description of the experience of the Puerto Rican Community Development Project. This was a proposal, prepared by the Puerto Rican Forum and submitted to the Office of Economic Opportunity (the agency administering the Anti-Poverty Program) for a comprehensive, city-wide coordinating agency which would promote, integrate and supervise a system of projects designed to assist the Puerto Ricans in New York. The explicit philosophy of this proposal was presented in a lengthy chapter entitled "Rationale for a Culturally Based Project" which indicated the need to develop a project which would enable the Puerto Ricans to develop a strong sense of identity, and a strong sense of community. From this position of strength, they would be able to move more securely toward integration with the larger society of New York City. The proposal, in other words, reflected the theory of cultural pluralism, current until recently, which indicated that the preservation of traditional cultures was the best basis for a strong sense of community among immigrants. This proposal was turned down, particularly by city officials, who insisted, among other things, that they could not fund this kind of ethnic-based proposal; that it was administratively unsound; that it would duplicate what other programs were doing; that it was not practical enough—it emphasized an intangible thing like "sense of community" instead of getting down to the "nuts and bolts" of jobs. The proposal was funded sometime later when city officials expressed their confidence that it was in the hands of practical people instead of impractical intellectuals. It has since taken a decidedly political orientation and it illustrates the shift to an emphasis on power which has become the central issue in relation to Puerto Ricans and all other racial and ethnic minorities in the Country.

The shift in emphasis from culture to power as the basis for community has resulted from a number of influences which have been growing stronger during the past fifteen years. One of the most important has been the influence of Saul Alinsky in community organizing. Alinsky, a very controversial figure, has always insisted that a sense of community strength is best developed around issues in which conflicts of interest are evident. He insists that the poor regularly suffer because they do not recognize that social institutions are organized and function for the protection of the interests of the people who control them, and at the expense of the interest of the poor. He first seeks to bring the poor to an awareness of their own interest which is involved, to make explicit the conflict of interest which is implicit, and to encourage the poor to marshal their strength, organize themselves to press for a change in the structure or function of the institutions in which they are at a disadvantage. Alinsky insists that the poor must bargain from a position of strength; that, if they can do this, they can participate as equals in a resolution of conflict, and an accommodation of interests in which they will have a decisive role to play in determining whose interests will be served and in what way. According to Alinsky, this growing self-awareness, definition of community needs, the marshalling of forces to promote community interests, and the maintaining of a strong position for the protection of community interests, all these contribute to an increase in the sense of community and of identity which enable the poor to lead a much more human existence. This is not the occasion for a detailed evaluation of Alinsky's theory or method. His influence had led people to recognize that community strength may lie, not in an emphasis on the preservation of a culture in a pluralistic society, but in the organizing of resources to promote a common interest.

In their book *Beyond the Melting Pot*, Nathan Glazer and Daniel Moynihan presented a theory of assimilation which, in its general lines, is somewhat similar to the theory of Alinsky. They indicated that, in the intermingling of people of many nationalities in a City like New York, the melting pot had never actually melted. In fact, they say, the ethnic group has not disappeared; it has become a new social form. Instead of people defining their interests around nationality background as they did when they first came to the United States, they now define their interests around race or religion. In brief, the ethnic groups have now become large scale interest groups. What the United States now faces, according to Glazer and Moynihan, is not the assimilation of people of different cultural backgrounds into one predominant culture, but rather the accommodation of conflicting interests in a politically unified society. A basic theme in this analysis of immigrant experience is the strategic use of political and economic power by the ethnic groups to promote their interests in a democratic society. The significant theme is not the achievement of identity by preserving traditional cultural forms; but by participating as an effective force in the important decisions of the larger society.

Meantime, from quite a different perspective, scholars began to call attention to the culture of the poor, not so much as a traditional form which they should preserve in a pluralistic society and from which they should move with security and strength toward assimilation into the larger society; but rather as the focus of interest of the poor around which they should marshal their political strength. Walter B. Miller[4] for example, insisted that

[4] Walter B. Miller, "Implications of Lower Class Culture for Social Work," *Social Service Rev.* V (33), Sept. 1959, pp. 219–36.

the poor should not be looked upon as "deviant" from the dominant American way of life. It is important, Miller insisted, to view the behavior of the poor from within the context of their own lives. In this way, their culture, or style of life can be seen as a positive thing, possessing its own strengths and values; it represents a creative response of the poor to cope with the kinds of challenges they must face. Social service policy, therefore, should not take the form of trying to impose the dominant culture upon the poor; but to enable them, within the context of their own strengths and values to identify their needs, marshal their own resources, and create their own response and adaptation to American life and experience. Miller is not saying that the poor should never become part of the dominant culture; neither is he saying what the traditional position of the cultural pluralists implied. Miller is saying that the culture of the poor whom he studied in the Roxbury Community in Boston was, within their disadvantaged situation, an understandable creative response to the pressures of the dominant society in which their interests were not being served. Their culture, in other words, was their effort to create a system in which they pursued their own interests in the framework of a dominant society in which they were at a disadvantage. Although Miller never spells it out, his position implies that the particular culture of the poor reflects a massive conflict of interest between the poor and the more affluent members of their society; if they can organize and bargain from a position of strength about the accommodation of their interests, the cultural differences may begin to disappear. In the extensive literature about "cultural deprivation," particularly around education and mental health, this same position is reflected.

The concept of the "culture of poverty" which Oscar Lewis first presented in *Five Families*, and which he sought to explore in *La Vida, a Puerto Rican Family in the Culture of Poverty in San Juan and New York*, also reflects this same position. Lewis never advocates the perpetuation of the culture of poverty; he sees it as a condition which is often destructive of the human personality. But he does recognize it not simply as behavior that is deviant from that of the dominant culture, but as a positive thing, a style of life with its own strengths and values, which represents a creative response of people who are marginal to a developing or developed industrial and commercial world; and who cannot find their way up the channels to advancement and the enjoyment of the privileges of an affluent society. Lewis is struck by the lack of organization in the lives of the people in the culture of poverty. In other words, according to Lewis, the culture of poverty develops among people who seek to pursue their interests in this style of life in the framework of a dominant society in which they are at a great disadvantage. Lewis seems to imply, without explicitly stating it, that if the poor were organized to participate as equals in the processes of the dominant society, the culture of poverty would disappear.

This type of thinking about culture has become quite common during the past ten years. What converted it into a significant political force was the shift among the Black Americans from an emphasis on civil rights and integration to an emphasis on Black Power. Explicit in the movement for Black Power is the insistence that Black people must find a positive strength and value in the color that gives them their identity; must define their interests as Black people; marshal their resources and bargain from a position of strength about the conditions of the society in which they expect to live. Central to the movement is the remarkable development of a sense of pride in their color among Black people. But also important has been the creation of a sense of community solidarity out of their effort to organize their strength for the promotion of their own interests; community identity and strength are not seen as something which emerged from the preservation of a cultural tradition, but from the political effort to press for a realization of their interests. This emphasis on power has expressed itself in many areas of the lives of Black Americans. As it has done so, it has created an impact on the lives of poor Puerto Ricans. The response of the Puerto Ricans has affected the problem of community and identity which are such an important issue in their lives.

In view of both the theory and the practice described above, it would seem that, if Puerto Ricans can organize around an effort to promote their political interests, the achievement of identity and community strength may advance despite the particular problems of identity which Puerto Ricans face on the Island or in New York. There is some indication that this may be taking place. In the first place the aggressiveness and success of the Black citizens in anti-poverty programs has resulted in a realization among Puerto Ricans that they must do likewise. As a result a great deal of aggressiveness is appearing in areas where many Puerto Ricans are located; indeed, so much aggressiveness has appeared in one area of the Bronx that it has provoked the intervention of City level authorities to try to maintain some balance between Black persons and Puerto Ricans on a Community Corporation. Furthermore, as indicated above, the Puerto Rican Community Development Project has been marked by the presence on its staff and Board, of politically interested and politically active people who see the need for political involvement if the Project is to remain strong. At the present time there is great open hostility between Puerto Ricans and Black citizens, particularly about control over public schools and anti-poverty programs.

At this moment, it is not possible to predict what effect the present developments will have on the adjustment of Puerto Ricans to the City of New York. It is possible that their militancy around their interests in anti-poverty programs, education, public welfare, housing, etc. may enable them to develop a sense of identity and a community solidarity which, thus far, they have found it difficult to achieve. If this does take place, it will support the validity of the new theories of the adjustment of migrants to a new and strange city. They will integrate from a position of strength, but the strength will rest not on the continuation of a traditional culture in the form of an immigrant community, but on the solidarity which results from organizing their efforts for the pursuit of group interests in the political arena.

THE PERSPECTIVE OF THE CITY'S HISTORY

It is possible, however, at the present time to assess the development among the Puerto Ricans in the light of the history of previous migrations to the City. The present conflicts are distressing, not only to Puerto Ricans, but to all residents in the City. Nevertheless, difficult as the situation may be, it is very doubtful if it can compare with the distress of the City a century or more ago. New York has always been a troubled city, sometimes a violent one, because the City has always insisted on accepting newcomers, on enabling them to become part of her own life. The pain of the newcomer as well as the pain of the older resident take on a great meaning when they are seen in the perspective of the creative achievement to which the City has been dedicated since its beginning. Achievement cannot be gained without a cost in effort and suffering, and the creation of what may be the greatest city man has built has certainly involved enormous costs. In a century and three quarters, it has absorbed millions of immigrants, from dozens of different cultural backgrounds as different as that of Iroquois Indians to Russian Emigrés. To cope with this variety, to achieve a common life, to provide advancement, to create an economic, educational and political system which would enable the immigrants to develop themselves and participate actively in the City's life, is little less than a social miracle. The fact that it was attended by suffering is not a mystery; the mystery is that it was done at all.

In the perspective of that history, it is quite clear that the experience of the City is a continuing thing today. The actors change; the process appears to be the same. New York is again re-making itself, physically and socially. Together with millions of people, older and newer residents from a variety of backgrounds, the City now numbers an estimated 1,400,000 Black people among its citizens, making it the City with the largest Black population in the world; it numbers an estimated 700,000 Puerto Ricans, making it the largest Puerto Rican city in the world. The process continues of receiving newcomers, of enabling them to become part of the City's life. This time the creative effort is particularly difficult since it involves the integration of Black citizens into the life of the City. But the same process of upheaval, distress, and rapid change will be part of the life of the citizens today as it was of generations past.

At the center of this distress has been the political struggle to accommodate conflicting interests, to restrict corruption, to prevent the manipulation of the political system for purely partisan gains. It is clear from the analysis of Glazer and Moynihan, that political conflict has been a means by which most earlier groups entered into active participation in the City's life. The fact that the process of increasing participation is now involving Blacks and Puerto Ricans in intense political conflict can reasonably be interpreted as a sign that, at last, they have arrived.

From this perspective of the City's history, the difficulties which Puerto Ricans must face are not signs of deterioration or decay; they may be recognized as part of the continued creative effort of the achievement of New York City. In this perspective they have a definite meaning. This point of view is strongly resisted by many New Yorkers as unrealistic and over-optimistic. They are convinced, many of them, that the City has reached a critical moment in its life, quite unlike anything that has happened before, that disorder and the fear of personal attack are signs of widespread social disorganization rather than the pains of creative growth. This conviction can easily be turned into an accusation against Blacks and Puerto Ricans as the responsible parties. But this conviction of decay is not new. It is found at every moment of the City's history, and the lamentations about

the decline of the City are not nearly as serious today as they were in previous generations.

The resistance of many Puerto Ricans to the optimistic point of view takes a different form. They are generally appalled at the extent and intensity of suffering which they see their people facing in New York. Understandably, they attribute the problem not to the Puerto Rican people, but to the City. They project into a judgment on New York, the same judgment many of them make about the rapid industrialization of the Island. They see New York as the most evident example, not only of all that is right about an advanced technological age, but of all that is wrong with it also. It is impersonal, materialistic, secular, and it makes impossible that kind of personal relationships which characterize the culture of Puerto Rico. This point of view does not perceive the City in decay, but as too highly developed to permit the kind of human existence to which Puerto Ricans are adapted.

The objective of the present paper is not to attempt to prove or disprove any of the above positions. They all involve prophecy, and only history will prove which, if any of them, was right. The objective of this paper is simply to seek the meaning of the Puerto Ricans' migration, in the only sources from which the meaning of any migration to New York can be sought, that is, in the history of the migrations of the past. In this sense, the statement is not a matter of prophecy. It is clear that, what many knowledgeable people considered to be signs of decay and deterioration, were actually the pains of creative growth. In that perspective, as the experience of the past appears to be repeating itself, it is reasonable to interpret the distress of the Puerto Ricans as another period involving the pain of creative growth. In this perspective, the problem of identity, whether sought by an emphasis on their traditional culture or by an emphasis on political power, is simply part of the problem of becoming New Yorkers, of participating in the turbulent social process which has issued in the life of the world's greatest city.

22

The Acculturation/ Assimilation Model in Urban Indian Studies: A Critique

C. HOY STEELE

INTRODUCTION

Since World War II, American Indians have been migrating from rural to urban areas faster than any other ethnic or racial group. U.S. Census figures reveal that between 1960 and 1970 Native Americans moved to cities at a rate 4⅓ times that of Blacks and 11½ times that of Whites (U.S. Bureau of the Census, 1972:262).[1] Approximately half the nation's one million Indians now live in cities, a situation somewhat at odds with the popular image of rural, culturally isolated peoples.

Social scientists who have studied this demographic phenomenon have recognized that such an extensive ethnic population shift raises the possibility of significant alterations in cultural adaptation and social organization.

Theoretically, the range of these changes is almost infinitely broad; many scholars have proceeded on the *assumption,* however, that the inevitable overall result of Indian urbanization is acculturation or assimilation—that is, absorption—into the larger, non-Indian society.

This is an important issue for at least two reasons. First, Indians have been objects of public interest for several years now—at least to the extent that the media cover militant Indian actions and books on American Indian history are popular. However, virtually nothing is known about the nature of contemporary Indian communities or the character and substance of Indian-non-Indian relations. Social scientists are but a few steps ahead of the general populace in this regard. Urban Indians were especially ignored until around 1960, and since then only a trickle of studies has appeared. Literally for centuries, Indians have been expected to disappear into the White population. Will the rapid urbanization of the last quarter of a century finally accomplish this, as the acculturation/assimilation model predicts? Or, on the other hand, are other issues more crucial?

The second reason that the nature of Indian urbanization is important is that *acculturation, assimilation,* and related terms are frequently employed in the lexicon of the social sciences for the study of ethnic and racial groups of all types. Thus, critical examination of the limitations of these concepts with respect to American Indians may have implications for the study of other minority groups and the general analysis of majority-minority relations.[2] In this article I shall present ethnographic data that seriously question assumptions underlying the acculturation/assimilation model.

C. Hoy Steele is Director of the North Carolina Community Development Corporation.

This is an extensively revised version of a paper presented at the annual meeting of the American Ethnological Society, Wilmington Beach, North Carolina, March 10, 1973.

[1] Between 1950 and 1960 the number of Indians in cities almost tripled, and in the next ten years the urban Indian population more than doubled (U.S. Bureau of the Census, 1969:29; 1972:262).

[2] The study of Indian urbanization offers potential rewards to the researcher in other areas as well—for example, urbanization per se, inter-ethnic relations among minority groups (see the article by Barbaro in Part Six of this volume), and the effectiveness of urban social institutions in relating to a new group of constituents (see Steele, 1972: Chapter 6).

ACCULTURATION OR ASSIMILATION—
A CONCEPTUAL TANGLE

Use of the concepts of acculturation and assimilation has been marked by considerable confusion. Anthropologists have focused on acculturation, while sociologists have been preoccupied with assimilation. This reflects the traditional emphases of anthropology and sociology on the analytically separable but intimately related concepts of culture and social structure, respectively. By and large, however, both sets of scholars have been discussing the same phenomenon—the extent to which a minority group dissolves into the majority group. Since anthropologists have exhibited greater interest in Indians, it is not surprising that acculturation is the more frequently used term for Indian social and cultural change.

More recently, acculturation generally has been felt to comprise but one aspect of assimilation. Gordon (1964:71) has developed a schema of seven assimilation variables, of which three—acculturation, structural assimilation, and amalgamation—appear most crucial and have commanded the greatest attention (e.g., see Parenti, 1967). Gordon's usage is paralleled by Roy (1972) and by White and Chadwick (1972), with minor terminological differences. Acculturation, which Gordon also labels cultural or behavioral assimilation, refers to the adoption by one group of the culture traits of another. Structural assimilation, on the other hand, denotes the merger of the social networks of two groups, including their primary groups and social institutions. Finally, amalgamation, which Gordon also calls marital assimilation, denotes biological merger or intermarriage.

According to Gordon, acculturation does not necessarily lead to structural assimilation, but the latter inevitably produces the former. Indeed, once structural assimilation has occurred, all other forms of assimilation follow. "Structural assimilation, then, rather than acculturation, is seen to be the keystone of the arch of assimilation" (Gordon, 1964:81).

In this paper, *assimilation* refers to Gordon's structural assimilation, and *acculturation* corresponds to his cultural or behavioral assimilation. Although I agree with Gordon that assimilation (his structural assimilation) is probably more fundamental, in this discussion I am using the words together (acculturation/assimilation) in recognition of the predominance of the former term in research on American Indians.

THE ACCULTURATION/ASSIMILATION MODEL

Two basic assumptions appear to underlie the acculturation/assimilation model. The first is that once Indians move to cities, the process of acculturation/assimilation inevitably occurs. This assumption seems to be based on three factors: (1) the small number of Indians in relation to the rest of the urban population; (2) the assumed contrast between reservation and urban life; and (3) the phenomenon of intermarriage between Indians and non-Indians. The second and most important assumption, closely related to the first, is that Indians *must* acculturate/assimilate if their adaptation to urban life is to be successful.

Indians Will Acculturate/Assimilate

1. The social scientist who begins to examine the phenomenon of Indian urbanization immediately confronts the obvious numerical discrepancy between non-Indians and Indians in the city. Sheer weight of numbers, then, provides one rationale for assuming that movement from a reservation to an urban area necessarily or automatically implies a corresponding change, both in consciousness and behavior, from Indian to White. One scholar, writing about Indians in Spokane, Washington, states, "The assumption made in this study is that the smaller American Indian society will be assimilated into the larger white society . . ." (Roy, 1972:227; see also Price, 1968; White and Chadwick, 1972). It is anticipated that Indians will become absorbed by

the dominant society as a teaspoonful of strawberry milkshake becomes absorbed in a large glass of vanilla milkshake. As will be shown below, however, this absorption process is far from automatic.

2. An implicit emphasis in many studies upon the contrast between reservation and urban life may be a second factor influencing the adoption of the acculturation/assimilation model. *Reservation* implies both *rural* and *folk* life. In the literature of the social sciences, these terms frequently are placed in opposition to *urban* (see Redfield, 1947). Most reservations are, in fact, rural by customary standards, and their residents probably exhibit as many traits of folk societies as can be found in this country. These obvious ecological contrasts between reservation and city, however, tend to obscure equally important linkages. Most significant is the fact that the economic and social systems in which Indians participate include both reservation and city.

The economic aspect of the acculturation/assimilation model is as follows: Indians have failed to adopt normative values of thrift, hard work, and deferred gratification and have remained outside the social patterns of American life; thus, they have failed to develop the economic potential of their reservations. Acculturation (changing their values) and assimilation (participating within the economic system) will, it is thought, result in development.

Joseph Jorgensen (1971) and others—notably Indian political activists—have challenged this view of Indian economic problems. According to Jorgensen, Indian reservations are not isolated from the economic mainstream, but are totally integrated within it through economic exploitation. Even the most isolated Indian reservation is joined with an urban center or centers through the urban center's economic control. The economic problem of the reservation, Jorgensen asserts, is that Indians are indeed "integrated into the national political economy"—as "super-exploited victims" (1971:68–69, emphasis deleted; 84). He cites Bureau of Indian Affairs

statistics for 1968 showing that non-Indians received 75 percent, or 127.4 million dollars, of the gross from reservation agriculture, a total of 170 million dollars. They paid Indians only *12 percent* (16 million dollars) of their gross "for exploitation of Indian lands" (1971:82). Indian mining and timber resources are exploited in similar fashion.

As a consequence of the fact that Indians do not control the economic resources on their reservations, they live in chronic poverty. A corollary is that many reservation Indians must either commute to urban areas or make semipermanent migrations to find work. The circle is complete: commercial enterprises with urban headquarters or markets exploit Indian land, siphoning off economic benefits; reservation residents are thus forced to make a choice between moving to urban areas or commuting long distances.

We turn to the sociocultural dynamics of this situation—the social systems in which urban Indians participate. Does the acculturation/assimilation model adequately describe them? Here, we may turn to a case study (Steele, 1972) that focused on Prairie City (pseudonym), Kansas, a city of 125,000 people, and two small reservations less than fifty miles away, Prairie Band Pottawatomi and Kickapoo respectively.

Indians on these reservations are poor; jobs are virtually non-existent; and most reservation land is owned or leased by Whites. Many reservation residents commute daily to work in Prairie City and in the large industrial plants located just outside the city limits. Many former reservation residents now reside in Prairie City. They comprise approximately three-fourths of the one thousand Indians living there.

This situation has resulted in a complex social structure on a primary-group level. Residence in Prairie City rarely removes an Indian from the influence of the reservation, where a high level of locally based tribal participation is maintained. This includes three active native religious groups, annual Pow Wows, frequent dinners and other events, and a high degree of informal visiting. The proximity of the reservations to Prairie City facilitates convenient participation in these events by the urban Indians. Indeed, many Indians in Prairie City have indicated a strong preference for reservation life, but feel they must reside in the city for economic reasons. Likewise, much of the social life of the Prairie City Indian community also includes reservation residents. On Friday nights, for example, one of the most likely places to find a Pottawatomi—young or old, male or female, reservation or urban—is at either of two bowling alleys in Prairie City.

We have seen, then, that the acculturation/assimilation model makes false assumptions about both economic and social systems in which Indians participate. It assumes that underdevelopment, caused by a failure of acculturation/assimilation, is the economic problem of the reservations and that Indians who migrate to cities to look for jobs are probably planning to leave behind their cultural and social patterns. The fact is, however, that the principal economic problem of reservations is exploitation, which results from unequal power, not social and cultural distinctiveness.

The acculturation/assimilation model also assumes that the city is the total environment of the urban Indian, and conversely, that the reservation Indian is not influenced by the city. The fallacies of these notions have been demonstrated with respect to one city and its nearby reservations. Pressures upon an urban Indian to assimilate and acculturate are greatly lessened by the proximity (psychological as well as spatial) of his reservation.

3. If one assumes that Indians in cities inevitably become absorbed by the predominantly White population, one may naturally wish to look for ways of documenting this fact. One indicator of acculturation or assimilation used for many urban Indian studies is intermarriage. Little attention is paid to the non-Indian spouse, since—the reasoning seems to go—Whites are numerically dominant and therefore it is the Indian partner who will lose

his or her ethnic identity.[3] This assumption requires closer scrutiny if a poor research design is to be avoided. Indian marriage to non-Indians *may* reflect assimilation/acculturation by the former. This is an empirical question to be determined by research, however; its veracity is not evident *a priori*. Gordon grants that widespread intermarriage (amalgamation) implies prior structural assimilation. "However," he warns,

> a vastly important and largely neglected sociological point about mixed marriages, racial, religious, or national, apart from the rate, is in what social structures the intermarried couples and their children incorporate themselves. If Catholic-Protestant intermarried couples live more or less completely within either the Catholic social community or the Protestant social community, the sociological fact of the existence of the particular religious community and its separation from other religious communities remains. [1964: 130, emphasis deleted]

We may easily substitute "Indian-White" for "Catholic-Protestant."

Most Indians, reservation or urban, are constantly exposed to non-Indians. Indeed, any minority group that receives unequal treatment at the hands of a dominant group must not only be exposed to it but must also learn to adapt to many different kinds of majority-minority interactions. Furthermore, the dominant group controls all forms of mass media. Thus, an Indian marrying a White already knows a great deal about the customs, habits, expectations and values of his or her new partner. A White marrying an Indian, on the other hand, may experience extensive resocialization into a more or less separate subsociety; almost certainly, he or she will have to internalize new norms and meanings.

Let us turn again to our case study. Sufficient data were obtained to comment on eighteen interracial marriages between Indians

---

[3] One survey of urban Indian studies (Petit, 1969: 156–157) found that only one of the works examined mentioned the possibility that intermarriage could lead to non-Indian as well as Indian assimilation.

and non-Indians[4] in and around Prairie City. Three such couples seem to be entirely non-Indian in orientation; in each case both partners appear to have adopted White values, life styles, and primary relations. Six couples are split along racial lines—that is, the Indian partner is more or less active within the Indian community while his or her partner is not. Of the remaining nine couples, five are participants in both the non-Indian and Indian communities. The full extent of their participation in the non-Indian society is unknown, but they are fairly active in the Indian community on a primary group level. For example, a Chicano man whose wife is a well-known Indian dancer sells Indian craft and art work at Pow Wows and is known to many Indians. A White woman and her Pottawatomi husband are inveterate participants in weekend Indian social activities, and she occasionally performs Indian dances.

The remaining four couples present striking examples of non-Indian acculturation and assimilation to *Indian* ways.[5] A Chicano man has been the head of the Pottawatomi Education Committee since its inception. He has demonstrated a thoroughgoing emotional, as well as physical, involvement in the problems of the reservation. He stated once (only half-humorously, I thought) that he wished he were an Indian. A second man, a White, has been learning Pottawatomi from his father-in-law. To his wife's embarrassment, he is more fluent in the language than she. He has also been the more vigorous proponent of their

children's participation in Indian dancing. He is widely known and respected by Indians throughout the area.

The other two non-Indians are young White women recently married to young Indian men. Both have immersed themselves in the Indian community; one seems to have cut off most of her relationships with former White associates, while the other has very little remaining family and almost no ties outside the Indian community. Two of these four couples have recently moved from Prairie City to the Pottawatomi reservation, while a third lives just outside the city. The fourth also resides on the Pottawatomi reservation.

Indians Must Acculturate/Assimilate

If one major assumption of many urban Indian studies is that Indians who move to cities *will* become absorbed into the White urban mass, a second seems to be that survival in the city is possible by no other means—that assimilation and acculturation are *prerequisite* to successful urban adjustment (e.g., see Price, 1968; Roy, 1972; White and Chadwick, 1972).

One difficulty with this perspective is that it places the burden of successful adjustment totally on Indians themselves. Implicit is the notion that the city—that is, the dominant society and its institutions—bears no responsibility for facilitating adjustment. Whatever difficulties Indians experience are of their own making. The logic employed is of the type that holds that poor people themselves—not the political and economic institutions of the society—are responsible for poverty. Just as liberal social scientists spoke glibly of "the Negro problem" a decade ago, now we have "the urban Indian problem," if on a smaller scale.

Rarely, in urban Indian studies, are urban social institutions subjected to critical scrutiny. What are realistic possibilities for employment at a living wage in the city? How extensive is discrimination, and what forms does it take? What kinds of agencies and orga-

---

[4] Two-thirds of the Indians are married to Whites; the remainder are married to Chicanos. The extent of non-Indian acculturation/assimilation is unrelated both to these ethnic differences and to race-sex correlations. Three marriages between Indians and Blacks are not included because they present a special case. (See Steele, 1972: 113–114, 211.)

[5] As Hallowell (1972) has observed, a strict definition of acculturation refers to culture change of groups rather than of individuals. The latter phenomenon is designated *transculturalization* by Hallowell. I have chosen to use the former term because of its greater familiarity and general usage. To my knowledge, no one has yet suggested a term for (structural) assimilation on an individual, rather than a group, basis.

nizations provide meaningful assistance to low-income urban immigrants or residents of whatever ethnic group? Another parallel may be drawn with Black-White relations of the volatile sixties. The Kerner Report (Report of the National Advisory Commission on Civil Disorders, 1968) included bold assertions about the racist nature of the society; but its major recomendations amounted to changing Black people instead of restructuring the society. Similarly, the chronic poverty and attendant social problems of American Indians are widely deplored; no other mistreated ethnic group evokes greater sympathy. Yet social scientific and social policy ideologies simultaneously require conformity to Anglo, middle-class patterns as the price for inclusion of Indians in society's rewards.

Even accepting as reality the intransigence of the dominant group's social institutions and the cultural and class intolerance of the society as a whole, the question must still be asked whether acculturation and assimilation *actually* provide the only roads to successful adaptation to the city. This question leads to consideration of the internal life of the urban Indian population, which most studies fail to examine. It is my belief that this arena can provide a far richer source of social scientific knowledge than the investigation of questions of acculturation and assimilation. Those inquiries, by the nature of the issues posed, neglect more important questions. For example, are traditional Indian values retained in the city? To what extent are primary relations among urban Indians limited to the ethnic group? Does an urban Indian organizational life exist? Is there such a thing as an Indian "community" within the urban world?

My participant observation study of Prairie City, which lasted over a year, revealed interesting answers to these questions, at least for that city. In the remainder of this paper I shall comment upon Indian values, group life, and community in regard to the Indian population of Prairie City.

Repeatedly, and in a variety of ways, Indian people residing in Prairie City expressed adherence to values that they interpreted as uniquely "Indian" and that they advanced as credentials of Indianness. These include the legal criteria of Indian identity set forth by the U.S. Bureau of Indian Affairs—namely, certifiable membership in a recognized tribal group, which is in turn dependent upon blood descent of specified degree (usually one-fourth) from other members of the group. In addition to the legal requirements, there are informal credentials of "Indianness," including strong emphasis upon family life and obligations (especially in regard to the extended family), adherence to the ethic of mutual aid (especially to kin but also to other tribal members and other Indians), and participation in a variety of Indian ceremonies. "Indian" physiognomy and skin color, along with a high percentage of Indian "blood," ability to speak a native language, and observation of matters of etiquette in personal relationships (such as noninterference in the affairs of others) are also valued. Other criteria include rejection of what are commonly regarded as peculiarly Anglo traits of acquisitiveness, some forms of competition, and an exploitative attitude toward nature.[6]

People who share these values come together in a variety of formal and informal activities. I shall discuss only the formal ones. They include a Pow Wow club, a smaller Indian singing and dancing group, all-Indian bowling teams, softball teams and basketball teams, an Indian (mission) Protestant Church as well as Indian religious groups on the reservations, and an Indian Center with numerous programs that have an impact upon, and involve, many Indian people within the city. These are Indian activities by virtue of the fact that, with few exceptions, Indian people are the only participants. For many, primary relations in Prairie City are totally restricted to these formal groups and to informal association with other Indians. In short, an Indian subsociety exists within Prairie City.

A substantial minority of the Indian

---

[6] This list of values is closely paralleled by the finding of other researchers (cf. Gearing, 1970; McFee, 1972b; M. Wax *et al.*, 1964; R. Wax and Thomas 1961).

population of Prairie City—approximately 25 percent—did not come from nearby reservations but migrated from Oklahoma, Nebraska, the Dakotas, the Southwest, or more distant points. These non-Kansans[7] tend to possess relatively few credentials of Indianness in the eyes of local Indian people.[8] On the other hand, substantial numbers of individuals within this diverse category are rather adept at dealing with White society; thus, they are especially useful to several Indian organizations. The Indian Center of Prairie City, for example, which became the hub of urban Indian activity while I was engaged in field work there, effectively integrated both local and nonlocal constituencies, at leadership levels as well as participant-client levels.

A final factor contributing to the sense of Indian ethnic identity and community in Prairie City is the existence of a network of parallel activities in neighboring towns, cities, and states that provide occasions for Indian people to come together from a wide geographical area. All-Indian bowling, basketball, and softball tournaments are held frequently in neighboring cities, especially in Oklahoma. Pow Wows in the summer and dinner dances during the rest of the year occur throughout the plains states and stimulate frequent travel to distant and nearby places. Every organized group is part of some kind of regional or national network, or both.[9] These networks, added to the factors already mentioned (particularly ties to local reservations)

further reinforce Indian identity and a sense of community within the local geographic unit. They are especially useful in helping Indian migrants from states outside Kansas to become part of the Prairie City Indian community.

It is important in this context to clarify the meaning of the term *community*, which may be defined as "a self-conscious social unit and a focus of group identification" (Theodorson and Theodorson, 1969:63).

> Community also implies a certain identification of the inhabitants with the geographic area, . . . a feeling of sharing common interests and goals, a certain amount of mutual cooperation, and an awareness of the existence of the community in both its inhabitants and those in the surrounding area. [Theodorson and Theodorson, 1969: 64][10]

According to this definition, not all persons within the Indian *population* can be considered part of the Indian *community*. The excluded aggregate consists of those who, either by choice or circumstance, do not participate in the life of the Indian community—that is, they do not associate with other Indians. However, the wide range of Indian activities and the possibility of selective participation in them provide considerable flexibility, which is further enhanced by two facts relating to the earlier discussion of Indian values. First, no single individual can fulfill to the maximum all the criteria for Indian identity. Thus, at some point, everyone is vulnerable to the charge of not being totally Indian. On the other hand, some flexibility of lifestyle has to be recognized, and, in fact, standards often are not applied rigorously. Second, even more important to Indian identity than the possession of acceptable credentials (for example, a high percentage of Indian "blood" or the ability to speak a native language) is participation in the life of the community. This participation, more than anything else, identifies someone as

[7] Two small, contiguous reservations are located on the Kansas-Nebraska border. These reservations (one, Sac and Fox, the other, Iowa) are almost depopulated. People from these tribes living in Prairie City are so few that they are excluded from this discussion.

[8] Pottawatomis and Kickapoos are closely related in origin, have lived as neighbors in Kansas for more than a century, and maintain a high rate of intermarriage. They participate in overlapping social systems and, except for minor differences, share a common culture.

[9] A conflict over land between the Pottawatomi tribe and the BIA arose in 1970 and continues at this writing. The Pottawatomi have received aid from Indians of other tribes and from other Indian organizations. The Indian network, in other words, has a political dimension as well as social and cultural dimensions.

[10] These tests, which the Indian population meets, are more important than the standard of economic independence, which it cannot meet, in specifying the existence of a community (Theodorson and Theodorson, 1969:64).

"Indian," for it is a public statement of, and pride in, belonging.[11]

CONCLUSION

We have seen that the acculturation/assimilation model is an inadequate conceptual tool in examining the Indian community of Prairie City, Kansas. This model fails to encompass the total environment of the Indian community, which includes two reservations as well as the city. Its assumptions that Indians will and must become absorbed by the non-Indian urban population have been seriously questioned. The acculturation/assimilation model neglects the role of non-Indians and of urban institutions in the adaptation of Indian people to urban life. Finally, it does not allow for the possibility of the existence of an ongoing urban Indian community, much less aid in its examination.

This study alone does not provide a firm basis for generalizing broadly about the dynamics of majority-minority relations. It suggests, however, that the acculturation/assimilation model be subjected to critical scrutiny prior to its use as a device for understanding minority group adaptation.[12] Future studies hopefully will be more alert to the flexibility and complexity of ethnic identity. As McFee (1972a) has suggested, ethnicity is not a zero-sum game. In the case of the Blackfeet, whom he studied, accommodation to White society did not destroy Blackfeet identity in many cases but produced a "150 percent man," capable of functioning equally well in both Indian and White social systems.

Levy's study (1973) supplies further evidence that ethnicity may be much more dynamic than has been assumed in the past.

[11] For example, a Kickapoo man once spoke approvingly of a woman who "acted and talked Indian" even though she could pass for a fullblood White and was married to a White.

[12] Other articles in Part Four, as well as those in other sections of this book, provide further evidence that caution is required.

She found a remarkable ability among the Lubovitcher Hassidim in Brooklyn to manipulate the symbols of their ethnic identity as situationally required. When it is to their advantage to do so, Lubovitchers utilize the benefits of the larger society, but avoid activities that would set them beyond the ethnic boundary. Residence, clothing, the practice of ritual, and especially "the successful manipulation of kinship, marriage, educational institutions, and other types of social relations [can] promote individual goals while simultaneously preserving the image of Lubovitch to the larger society" (Levy, 1973:29). It also appears likely that ethnic identity may be rekindled after a period of apparent dormancy.[13]

Turning more specifically to the issue of contemporary Indian communities, it is probable that the dynamics of Indian life in and around Prairie City are representative of the hundreds of relatively small urban areas near reservations in which Indians reside (for example, see White's study [n.d.] of Rapid City). Even in major urban areas like Chicago or Oklahoma City, where the Indian population is counted in thousands rather than hundreds, communities probably exist within the Indian population in considerably greater measure than most researchers have noted (see Krutz's study [1973] of Kiowas in San Francisco).

Native Americans probably have little to fear from White culture or the seductiveness of White primary groups and other social institutions; in this generation, too, the predicted Indian demise will be proven wrong. Indeed, Indians frequently assert the superiority of their own cultural and social orientations. What Indians have to fear is White political and economic power. Perhaps scholars interested in the maintenance of Indian identity, particularly those who see that identity as valuable for Indians and non-Indians alike, will recognize this fact, and begin to turn their research sights on governmental institutions and corporate power as they are brought to

[13] See Novak's article in Part Six.

bear upon Indian communities. Field work at Dow Chemical, anyone?[14]

BIBLIOGRAPHY

Akwesasne Notes. 1973. "Pueblo Is Not for Sale." Early Summer, pp. 38–39.

Gearing, Fred. 1970. *The Face of the Fox.* Chicago: Aldine Publishing Company.

Gordon, Milton M. 1964. *Assimilation in American Life: The Role of Race, Religion, and National Origins.* New York: Oxford University Press.

Hallowell, A. Irving. 1972. "American Indians, White and Black: the Phenomenon of Transculturalization." In *Native Americans Today: Sociological Perspectives,* edited by Howard M. Bahr, Bruce A. Chadwick, and Robert C. Day, pp. 200–225. New York: Harper and Row. Reprinted from *Current Anthropology* 4 (December, 1963): 519–531.

Jessepe, Lester L. 1972. "Our Story: The Prairie Band Pottawatomi Indians (How to survive when the government tries to steal everything you have)." Mayetta, Kans. Mimeographed.

Jorgensen, Joseph G. 1971. "Indians and the Metropolis." In *The American Indian in Urban Society,* edited by Jack O. Waddell and O. Michael Watson, pp. 66–113. Boston: Little, Brown and Company.

Kemnitzer, Luis S. 1969. "Reservation and City as Parts of a Single System: the Pine Ridge Sioux." Unpublished paper presented at meetings of the Southwestern Anthropological Association. Mimeographed.

Krutz, Gordon V. 1973. "Compartmentalization as a Factor in Urban Adjustment: The Kiowa Case." In *American Indian Urbanization,* edited by Jack O. Waddell and O. Michael Watson, pp. 101–116. Lafayette, Ind.: Purdue Research Foundation.

Levy, Sydelle. 1973. "Shifting Patterns of Ethnic Identification." Unpublished paper presented at the annual meeting of the American Ethnological Society, Wilmington Beach, North Carolina, March. Mimeographed.

McFee, Malcolm. 1972a. "The 150% Man, a Product of Blackfeet Acculturation." In *Native Americans Today: Sociological Perspectives,* edited by Howard M. Bahr, Bruce A. Chadwick, and Robert C. Day, pp. 303–312. New York: Harper and Row.

———. 1972b. *Modern Blackfeet: Montanans on a Reservation.* New York: Holt, Rinehart and Winston.

Paredes, J. Anthony. 1971. "Toward a Reconceptualization of American Indian Urbanization: A Chippewa Case." *Anthropological Quarterly* 44 (October): 256–271.

Parenti, Michael. 1967. "Ethnic Politics and the Persistence of Ethnic Identification." *American Political Science Review* 61 (September): 717–726.

Petit, Patrick F. 1969. "A Preliminary Investigation of the Migration and Adjustment of American Indians to Urban Areas" (M.A. thesis, Department of Sociology, University of Kansas, Lawrence, Kans.)

Price, John A. 1968. "The Migration and Adaptation of American Indians to Los Angeles." *Human Organization* 27 (Summer): 168–175.

Redfield, Robert. 1947. "The Folk Society." *American Journal of Sociology* 52 (January): 293–308.

Report of the National Advisory Commission on Civil Disorders. 1968. Washington, D.C.: U.S. Government Printing Office.

Roy, Prodipto. 1972. "The Measurement of Assimilation: The Spokane Indians." In *Native Americans Today: Sociological Perspectives,* edited by Howard M. Bahr, Bruce A. Chadwick, and Robert C. Day, pp. 225–239. New York: Harper and Row. Reprinted from the *American Journal of Sociology* 67 (March, 1963): 541–551.

Steele, C. Hoy. 1972. "American Indians and Urban Life: A Community Study" (Ph.D. dissertation, Department of American Studies, University of Kansas, Lawrence, Kans.)

Theodorson, George A., and Theodorson, Achilles G. 1969. *A Modern Dictionary of Sociology.* New York: Thomas Y. Crowell Company.

United States Bureau of the Census. 1969. *Statistical Abstract of the United States,* 90th ed. Washington, D.C.: U.S. Government Printing Office, p. 29.

---

[14] The Dow Chemical Company is "developing" Zuni Pueblo. For an excellent, in-depth analysis of governmental and corporate exploitation of one Indian tribe (Tesuque Pueblo), see *Akwesasne Notes* (1973). For an account of the Pottawatomis' struggle with the Bureau of Indian Affairs, see Jessepe (1972).

————. 1972. Census of Population: 1970. *General Population Characteristics. Final Report PC(1)—B1 United States Summary.* Washington, D.C.: U.S. Government Printing Office, p. 262.

Wax, Murray L.; Wax, Rosalie H.; and Dumont, Robert V., Jr. 1964. *Formal Education in an American Indian Community.* Supplement to *Social Problems,* Spring.

Wax, Rosalie H., and Thomas, Robert K. 1961. "American Indians and White People." *Phylon* 22 (Winter): 305–317.

White, Lynn C., and Chadwick, Bruce A. 1972. "Urban Residence, Assimilation and Identity of the Spokane Indian." In *Native Americans Today: Sociological Perspectives,* edited by Howard M. Bahr, Bruce A. Chadwick, and Robert C. Day, pp. 239–249. New York: Harper and Row.

White, Robert A. n.d. "The Development of Collective Decision-Making Capacity in an American Indian Community: The Politics of an Urban Indian Ethnic Community." Unpublished manuscript. Mimeographed.

23

American Sociology and Black Assimilation: Conflicting Perspectives[1]

L. PAUL METZGER

INTRODUCTION

The failure of sociologists to anticipate and direct their research attention to new developments in American race relations during the 1960s has been acknowledged by Hughes (1963) and Pettigrew and Back (1967, pp. 714–16). Rossi (1964, pp. 125–26) noted that "it is sadly ironic that as the pace of change in race relations stepped up in the past four years, the volume of social science research has declined during the same period." With the exception of projects sponsored by the federal government—most notably, the so-called Coleman and Moynihan reports (Coleman 1966; Rainwater and Yancey 1967)—significant in terms of their potential impact on national policy but resting on the theoretical foundations of an earlier period of basic research (Tumin 1968, pp. 118–19), the pic-

L. Paul Metzger is Associate Professor of Sociology at the State University College, New Paltz, New York.

Reprinted from the *American Journal of Sociology* 76 (Jan., 1971), pp. 627–647, by permission of the author and the publisher. Copyright 1971 by the University of Chicago Press.

[1] I wish to express my appreciation to Mrs. Saundra Hudson for her assistance in providing background material for this article, and to Vassar College for a grant which helped to make its preparation possible. Appreciation is also due Lilo Stern and James Moss for their comments on an earlier draft.

ture Rossi sketched remains relatively unchanged; his call for research into the black movements, the political aspects of racial change, and the role of ethnicity in American life has been met by only a handful of sociologists. Despite two recent studies by Bell (1968) and Levy (1968), the civil rights movement of the early sixties remains largely uncharted by sociologists. Similarly, the black-power and nationalist movements which succeeded it, as distinct from the earlier Muslim movement (about which there are able accounts by Lincoln [1961] and Essien-Udom [1962]), remain virtually *terra incognita* within the sociological profession.

As an explanation for this failure, Hughes suggests that the concern with professionalism among sociologists has impaired their capacity to empathize with the movements of lower strata; Pettigrew and Back (1967, p. 706) refer to the timidity of foundations, the obstacles placed in the way of race-relations research by diehard white segregationists, and "a sociological bias in race relations toward studying the static and segregation-making elements." It is the thesis of this paper that the failure can be attributed in part to the theoretical framework through which most American sociologists have viewed race relations in the United States. This framework, it is believed, rests essentially on the image of American society which has been set forth by American liberalism, wherein the minority problem is defined in the narrow sense of providing adequate, if not equal, opportunity for members of minority groups to ascend as individuals into the mainstream culture. America, in this view, is the land of opportunity through competitive struggle in the marketplace; it can, and will, provide opportunities for all to gain just rewards for their individual merit. (American liberalism differs with American conservatism largely over the issue of whether the opportunities already present are adequate and takes its reformist cast from its recognition that they are not.)

Sociologists, by and large, have accepted this image of Horatio Alger in the Melting Pot as the ideal definition of American society.

Although they have repeatedly documented the discrepancy between social reality and cultural myth in America, they have also taken the view that the incorporation of America's ethnic and racial groups into the mainstream culture is virtually inevitable. (Similar tendencies can be discerned in the field of social stratification, according to Pease, Form, and Rytina 1970.) Successful assimilation, moreover, has been viewed as synonymous with equality of opportunity and upward mobility for the members of minority groups; "opportunity," in this system, is the opportunity to discard one's ethnicity and to partake fully in the "American Way of Life"; in this sense, assimilation is viewed as the embodiment of the democratic ethos.

The convergence of liberal and sociological thought in the area of race relations is striking and raises serious questions about the "value-free" character of sociological inquiry in this area.[2] This is particularly the case since the equation of assimilationist with democratic values in minority-majority relations is by no means universal even within Western culture (Schermerhorn 1959). The right of national self-determination has played a significant role in the liberal-democratic movement in Europe, and as Myrdal (1944, p. 50) noted, "the minority peoples of the United States are fighting for status in the larger society; the minorities of Europe are mainly fighting for independence from it."

Equally remarkable perhaps, is the fact that assimilationist values, with their connotations of elitism and a monocultural society, have come under as little attack as they have from either liberal or radical social criticism in the United States. The philosophy of democratic cultural pluralism has had, in fact, able spokesmen in America, most notably during the period of World War I (Bourne 1964) and the twenties (Kallen 1924), but the issue of ethnic pluralism has not been a central preoccupation of the American Left until the recent emergence of the black-power movement. This can be traced, perhaps, to the ascendancy in the thirties of Marxian modes of thought in Left circles and the resulting preoccupation with economic and political questions, on one hand, and working-class solidarity, on the other.

The aim of this paper is to examine some of the major arguments which have appeared in the sociological literature in support of the view that the outcome of race relations in the United States will be the integration or assimilation[3] of the Negro into the American mainstream. The widespread and uncritical acceptance of these arguments by sociologists, it is believed, has contributed heavily to the void in race-relations research which has been noted above, as well as to the tendency to regard black-nationalist movements as "extremist" (Glazer and Moynihan 1963, p. 78), "escapist" (Morsell 1961, p. 6), and essentially deviant-pathological phenomena.[4] It will be pointed out that some of the components of a revised perspective on American race relations can already be found within the sociological literature and that a new perspective will include (1) abandoning the idea that racial assimilation in the form of gradual absorption of black Americans into the middle-American main-

---

[2] Horton (1966) has stated that "the liberal tendency of American sociology . . . is particularly marked in the sociological analysis of the Negro question. . . . The liberal fate of minorities, including Negroes, is basically containment through socialization to dominant values" (pp. 707–8). He goes on to argue that "contemporary liberalism . . . is a variant of conservative order theory" (p. 707).

[3] The terms "integration" and "assimilation" are not necessarily synonymous. Integration, especially as it was used in the fifties, can have the limited meaning of "desegregation" (particularly de jure) and, sociologically, need not be followed by assimilation in the usual sense of cultural merger. Most sociologists have seemingly assumed, however, that desegregation would be followed by the gradual movement of blacks into mainstream American culture, and that racial characteristics would gradually lose their significance as determinants of social status and identity, and it is this assumption which is called into question here (see also Gordon 1964, pp. 246–47). The tendency for sociologists to use the two terms interchangeably is apparent in the writings of Hauser (1966a, 1966b).

[4] For a different view, see Gregor (1963, p. 431), who writes that "Negro proletarian radicalism has stood, largely mute, beyond the pale of American intellectual life." An effective rationale for the study of such movements has been made by Record (1956).

stream is necessarily either inevitable or desirable from the standpoint of democratic values, (2) a recognition that forces producing ethnicity as well as forces favoring assimilation are operative in American society today and that a realistic analysis of the ethnic and racial situation will take both into account, (3) a more balanced view of "black pluralism" (Killian 1968, p. 135) than has thus far appeared in the work of most sociologists. In short, it is argued that a rethinking of the theory of eventual assimilation will open up prospects for a more pertinent and realistic assessment of minority problems, particularly race problems, in the United States.

The arguments favoring eventual assimilation will be grouped under two headings: (1) those which rest on assertions about the nature of the dominant white American society, (2) those which rest on assertions about the nature of minority groups and experience within this society.

ARGUMENTS FROM THE NATURE OF THE DOMINANT WHITE SOCIETY

Central to the view of those sociologists who have taken the position that racial assimilation is the key to the American racial problem are certain beliefs about the nature of modern society in general, and American society in particular, which imply that prejudice, discrimination, and racist institutions are incompatible with the major features of modern social organization and hence will eventually "wither away." These assertions have taken various forms, but the common thread running through them has had several consequences: (1) the liberal optimism of most sociologists with respect to the possibility of peaceful and orderly change in the direction of racial integration;[5] (2) the belief that the

major locus of institutional racism lay in the South, as a kind of underdeveloped area, the modernization of which would remove most of the institutional supports of racism; (3) the belief that the vestigial remains of racism in the urbanized and industrialized North would disappear as the educational, economic, and occupational status of both blacks and whites improved in the direction of greater affluence and security for all. Clearly, this perspective ill equipped sociologists for the racial crises of the sixties, a period of rapid economic growth and high prosperity which nonetheless witnessed heightened racial tension, urban ghetto violence on an unprecedented scale, and marked racial polarization (National Advisory Committee on Civil Disorders 1968).[6]

---

[5] Even in the sixties, after the appearance of solidly organized white resistance in the South (Vander Zenden 1959a, 1959b, 1965) sociologists gave voice to this optimism in uninhibited terms. Rose, for example, wrote (1965, p. 7) "there could be no doubt that the races were moving rapidly toward equality and desegregation by 1964. . . . The change had been so rapid . . . that this author ventures to predict—if current trends continue—the end of all legal segregation and discrimination to a mere shadow in two decades. These changes would not mean that there would be equality between the races within this time . . . but the dynamic social forces creating inequality will, if the present trends continue, be practically eliminated in three decades."

[6] The emergence of the black movement in the sixties and the racial crises which followed forced sociologists to acknowledge, ex post facto, the resistance of American society to racial integration. They were quick to apply the retrospective wisdom that social change entails strain and conflict and that racial conflict may have positive functions (Himes 1966). Mounting black pressure was accounted for, again ex post facto, by an application of reference-group theory in the form of the notion of "relative deprivation" (Pettigrew and Back 1967, pp. 694–96). It should be noted that insofar as this theory assumes that the black movement is the product of actual *gains* made by blacks since World War II, it is open to question since the extent of black gains, especially vis-à-vis whites, in this period is not clear. On the negative side, for example, residential segregation increased in American cities between 1930 and 1960 (Hauser 1966b, pp. 76–77), and there was virtually no change in the ratio of nonwhite to white family income between 1947 and 1964 (Fein 1966, p. 122). Moynihan points out (1966, p. 189) that the acknowledged growth of the black middle class may not be accompanied by improvement in the condition of the black lower-class majority and, in *The Negro Family: The Case for National Action*, claims that the black family is in a state of decline (Rainwater and Yancey 1967). Wright (1967), citing comparative data from the U.S. Census, disputes the notion of the rapid socioeconomic advance of the Negro since World War II. Finally, Wilhelm and Powell (1964) find the roots of the black movement not in Negro advance, but *retrogression:* "With the

Robert E. Park and the Race Relations Cycle

In 1926, one of the most famous and influential statements of the theory of eventual assimilation was made by Robert E. Park (1950, pp. 149–50): "In the relations of races there is a cycle which tends everywhere to repeat itself. . . . The race relations cycle which takes the form . . . of contacts, competition, accommodation and eventual assimilation, is apparently progressive and irreversible. . . . Racial barriers may slacken the tempo of the movement, but cannot change its direction. . . . The forces which have brought about the existing interpenetration of peoples are so vast and irresistible that the resulting changes assume the character of a cosmic process." The universality and inevitability of this "cosmic process" along with other formulations of race-relations cycle theories have long since been questioned by many sociologists,[7] but the acceptance of some form of melting-pot theory as descriptive of American society has been strongly maintained nonetheless.[8]

An ambiguity with respect to Park's (1950) views on the eventual assimilation of the American Negro should be noted. In 1913, for example, he wrote:

Under conditions of secondary contact, that is to say, conditions of individual liberty and individual competition, characteristic of modern civilization, depressed racial groups *tend to assume the form of nationalities* [italics mine]. A nationality, in this narrower sense, may be defined as the racial group which has attained self-consciousness, no matter whether it has at the same time gained political independence or not. . . . The fundamental significance of the nationality movement must be sought in the effort of subject races to substitute, for those supplied to them by aliens, models based on their racial individuality and embodying sentiments and ideals which spring naturally out of their own lives. . . . In the South . . . the races seem to be tending in the direction of a bi-racial society, in which the Negro is gradually gaining a limited autonomy. [Pp. 219–20]

Frazier (1947, p. 269) noted that even up to "about 1930, Park's sociological theory in regard to race relations did not go beyond the thesis of a bi-racial organization." Hence, if Park believed in the eventual assimilation of races in the United States, his attention as an observer in the contemporary situation was strongly focused on the emergence of a black "national consciousness." Insofar as he regarded the growth of such a consciousness as a stage in the process leading to eventual assimilation, however, his cycle theory can be regarded as one of the more potent influences in the direction of viewing assimilation as a natural and inevitable process in the evolution of modern society.[9]

An American Dilemma

If Gunnar Myrdal (1944) was critical of the "do-nothing (laissez faire)" presuppositions which he detected in the work of American

---

onset of automation, the Negro is moving out of his historical state of oppression into uselessness. . . . He is being removed from economic participation in white society"; and his nascent nationalism constitutes a "quest for identity" (pp. 3–6). In short, the theory of relative deprivation as an account of black unrest has yet to be adequately tested.

[7] Berry (1958, pp. 128–49) provides a useful and critical survey of Park and others' cycle theories. Etzioni (1959) presents a systematic critique of Park's views in the context of his review of Wirth's *The Ghetto* (1928). He points out that there is no a priori reason for regarding assimilation as the inevitable outcome of culture contact, and that Park's theory, because it fails to specify the temporal span of and conditions producing each phase, can accommodate any observation and hence is untestable.

[8] For a statement of the theory of the "triple melting pot," which presents the case for the disappearance of the ethnicity of the white immigrant groups within the wider structure of American religious pluralism (itself compromised by the ecumenical movement and a shared commitment to the "American Way of Life" as a quasi-religious ideal), see Herberg (1955, particularly chap. 2).

[9] The fact that an earlier generation of American sociologists did not regard the assimilation of the American Negro as anything like an immediate prospect and viewed the emergence of a sense of collective unity as an outcome of the Negro's status in American society is apparent in E. B. Reuter's *The American Race Problem* (1927). In chap. 16, Reuter traces the history of, and analyzes the "growth of race consciousness," and concludes that "the continued growth of a Negro nationalistic spirit in America is perhaps inevitable" (p. 429).

sociologists (including Park) and the subsequent tendency of the latter to "ignore practically all possibilities of modifying—by conscious effort—the social effects of the natural forces" (p. 1050), his classic opus remained very much within the assimilationist tradition. The author of *An American Dilemma* wrote that "we assume it is to the advantage of American Negroes as individuals and as a group to become assimilated into American culture, to acquire the traits held in esteem by the dominant white Americans" (p. 929).[10]

Myrdal discerns no structural impediment in American society to the realization of an assimilationist program: the race problem is a moral problem "in the heart of the American" (p. xlvii); and "America is free to choose whether the Negro shall remain her liability or become her opportunity" (p. 1022). This decidedly nonsociological approach to the problem is justified, according to Myrdal, because "there is evidently a strong unity in this nation and a basic homogeneity and stability in its valuations. Americans . . . have something in common: a social ethos, a political creed. It is difficult to avoid the judgment that this "American Creed" is the cement in the structure of this great and disparate nation" (p. 1). Furthermore, "the conquering of color caste in America is America's own innermost desire. . . . The main trend in its history is the gradual realization of the American Creed" (p. 1021).[11] The creed is carried, Myrdal believed, by the "huge institutional structures" of the society, through which "a constant pressure is brought to bear on race prejudice, counteracting the natural tendency for it to spread and become more intense. . . . The ideals thereby gain fortifications of power and influence in society. This is a theory of social self-healing that applies to the type of society we call democracy" (p. 80).

Despite his hortatory tone and his call for national planning, social legislation, and social engineering on the part of an enlightened leadership, however, Myrdal had relatively few concrete suggestions for policy with respect to the race problem beyond his faith in the power of concerted educational effort (pp. 48–49) to break down the already-crumbling walls of the "caste beliefs and valuations" which he believed lay at the heart of white racism.[12] The race problem would be solved simply by moving the society further in the course on which it was already set—that of welfare capitalism —which would require no major reorganization of its economic and political institutions. In the process, the South, as the major locus of the racial problem and "itself a minority and a national problem" (p. 1010), would take its place in the mainstream of the American polity.[13]

[10] It is to the credit of Myrdal that he recognized that this assumption was indeed a "value premise" (p. 929) and not the statement of a "natural force" or an "inevitable social process." This distinction frequently is blurred in the sociological literature, as, for example, when Herberg (1955, p. 23) writes that the "perpetuation of ethnic differences is altogether out of line with the logic of American reality." This "logic" would seem to amount to little more than the power of an entrenched social myth.

[11] For a critique of Myrdal's view that the "strain toward consistency" produced by the psychological and moral discomforts of the dilemma is a major motive force in the direction of realization of the American creed, see Medalia (1962).

[12] In his emphasis on beliefs and attitudes, Myrdal's analysis had an affinity with the social psychological interpretation of race relations which has been so pronounced in American social science. Blumer (1958b) refers to this interpretation as the "prejudice-discrimination axis" and characterizes it as follows: "It rests on a belief that the nature of relations between racial groups results from the feelings and attitudes which these groups have toward each other. . . . It follows that in order to comprehend and solve problems of race relations it is necessary to study and ascertain the nature of prejudice" (p. 420). It is probable that the search for the determinants of prejudice and discrimination in attitudinal sets, personality structure, or role-specific behavior has inhibited the development of a social structural perspective on race relations in American sociology. The work of Lohman and Reitzes (1952, 1954) offered some corrective, but the lead they offered has not been followed.

[13] Ralph Ellison (1966, pp. 298–99) writes that *"An American Dilemma . . .* sponsored by a leading capitalist group . . . is the blueprint for a more effective exploitation of the South's natural, industrial, and human resources. . . . In the positive sense, it is the key to a more democratic and fruitful usage of the South's natural and human re sources; and in the negative, it is the plan for a more efficient and subtle manipulation of black and white relations—especially in the South."

At the level of social determinants, Myrdal suggested that the forces of modernization in the South—industrialization, urbanization, the spread of literacy—were themselves powerful mechanisms for the elimination of racism in America. This theme frequently recurs in the post-Myrdal writings on race, and is especially emphasized by Arnold Rose (1956, p. 75): "The conditions which led to the development of the caste system in the nineteenth century are no longer with us. . . . New forces have arisen which make the caste system increasingly less desirable and useful to the dominant white group in the South or any other section of the country: These include industrialization, automation, the leadership of the United States in the free Western world, rising educational levels among both whites and Negroes. . . . These changes . . . *have made a mere hollow shell of tradition*" (italics mine).[14]

Hence, the belief that racism is incompatible with the major features of modern social organization has roots which go far deeper than Myrdal's liberal optimism and ethical-philosophical idealism. It is, in fact, rooted in what is perhaps the major theme of modern sociological theory—the shift, in Cooley's terms, from "primary" to "secondary" relations as the basis of social order.

The Sociological Tradition

In the course of their presentation of the case for the inevitability of desegregation, Simpson and Yinger (1959, p. 389) note that "in the

approach to desegregation that we are taking, one can perceive a major recurring theme of sociological theory. Here is Sir Henry Maine's idea of the shift from status to contract. Here is an illustration of the perceptiveness of Simmel's work . . . concerning the influence of a money economy. Here is much of Toennies and Weber and Durkheim. Parsons and others who use the structural-functional approach have caught this fundamental orientation in such a way as to make it more readily applicable to such . . . problems as the one with which we are concerned."[15]

Thus, it is no surprise that Parsons (1966, p. 739) states that the major theoretical reason for asserting that conditions are ripe in America for the full "inclusion" of the Negro is that "the universalistic norms of the society have applied more and more widely. This has been true of all the main bases of particularistic solidarity, ethnicity, religion, regionalism, state's rights, and class. . . . Today, more than ever before, we are witnessing an acceleration in the emancipation of individuals of all categories from these diffuse particularistic solidarities." Whether phrased in terms of the Parsonian pattern variables, the older formulations of Durkheim, Cooley, or Toennies, or Myrdal's American creed, it is clear that this tradition of sociological theory views ethnicity as a survival of primary, quasi-tribal loyalties, which can have only a dysfunctional place in the achievement-oriented, rationalized, and impersonal social relationships of the modern, industrial-bureaucratic order.

That the tenets of this theoretical tradition necessarily imply the inevitable disappearance of "particularistic solidarities," however, has been put to a major theoretical

[14] Similar statements can be found in Simpson and Yinger (1954, 1958, 1959) and Rose (1965). The hypothesis that urbanization constitutes a major impetus to racial integration and equalization has been challenged on theoretical grounds by Killian and Grigg (1966) and Howard and Brent (1966); Blalock (1959) found little support for it in an analysis of Southern census data and comments that "urbanization in the South has at least in part taken a form which is compatible to that developed in certain colonial territories. . . . It is . . . entirely possible that as the South continues to urbanize, at least in the early stages . . . non-whites may remain in the most unskilled positions. . . . A constant or even an increasing gap may be maintained" (pp. 147–48).

[15] Greeley (1964), a proponent of the view that the ethnic group, which he defines as a "semi-gemeinschaft collectivity" (p. 108), remains a significant element in modern social structure, suggests that the gemeinschaft-gesellschaft tradition poses a "danger that sociologists, impressed with the tremendous increase in gesellschaft, would rule out the possibility of the survival of gemeinschaft, at least beyond the level of the nuclear family" (p. 107).

test in the recent work of Van den Berghe (1967). Rather than assuming, with the Myrdal-Parsons school, that race relations per se tend to disappear in gesellschaft-like societies, he asserts that they merely shift their form from "paternalistic" to "competitive." In the latter case, there is declining contact between racial castes, segmentation into ghettoes, and economic competition between racial groups. Although Van den Berghe (1967) asserts that racial cleavages in competitive societies "constitute one of the major sources of strain and disequilibrium in such systems" (p. 30), he makes no judgment as to their ultimate disappearance and states that a possible outcome is the "Herrenvolk democracy . . . in which the exercise of power and suffrage is restricted, *de facto* and often *de jure*, to the dominant group" (p. 29).

Van den Berghe's formulation is one of the few attempts in the literature to link the persistence of racial cleavages in competitive modern societies to the essential structure of such societies, and thus represents a major theoretical departure from the tradition discussed in this section. It is a departure which permits the description of America as a "socially pluralistic" society along racial lines despite its *cultural* homogeneity (pp. 34–36), which views racial cleavage and conflict as inherent in the nature of competitive society (pp. 30–31) and sees racism[16] as central to, rather than a "hollow shell" within, the Western cultural tradition (pp. 11–18). As such, it provides a perspective for the analysis of racial consciousness and conflict which is lacking in the orthodox Myrdal-Parsons schema.

White Gains and White Resistance

Mounting white resistance, North and South, to the black movement in the sixties forced sociologists to reassess the role of racism in the American social fabric, and, in doing so,

they have introduced (or reapplied) concepts which echo Van den Berghe's theoretical analysis. Killian (1968), for example, in *The Impossible Revolution?* writes that "the theme of white supremacy has always been an integral and pervasive feature of the American system" (p. 16)[17] and adds, "it is the challenge to white dominance that will require the greatest adjustment in the social order and that provides the greatest revolutionary potential" (p. 22). By virtue of his exclusion from a "white man's country" (p. 26), the black, says Killian, is "in the process of becoming an ethnic group" (p. 137), a development which is a radical challenge to the assimilationist ideal in America and which, hence, is fraught with the potential for a revolutionary confrontation.

The notion that specifiable "gains" accrue to whites by virtue of the subordination of blacks was introduced by Dollard (1937) and suggests that white resistance to racial change rests on something more than cultural lag or Myrdalian moral schizophrenia. As such, it is a valuable corrective to the notion that racism is "dysfunctional" or "deviant" within the wider culture. Heer (1959) and Glenn (1963, 1965, 1966) have offered both theoretical and empirical support for this notion, and Glenn writes: "Negro-white antagonism in the United States is and will long remain a matter of realistic conflict. Negroes cannot advance without the loss of traditional white benefits and it is unlikely that most of the whites who benefit . . . will willingly allow Negro advancement. This is not to say that race prejudice and social discrimination are strictly or even largely an expression of economic rationality [1966, p. 178] . . . nor should the many known and possible dysfunctions of

---

[16] Van den Berghe defines racism as "any set of beliefs that organic, genetically transmitted differences are intrinsically associated with the presence or absence of certain socially relevant abilities or characteristics" (p. 11).

[17] Westie (1965, pp. 537–38) also notes that "a wealth of sociological evidence suggests that in many social situations in America, it is not the person who behaves in a prejudiced manner who is deviant, but rather, the non-prejudiced person who refuses to discriminate. . . . People with no dilemma in Myrdal's sense seem to experience another type of dilemma; a conflict between their endorsement of democratic action and yet another normative system, which exists in the majority of American local communities; the system which says that one ought to be prejudiced and ought to discriminate."

discrimination be overlooked. However . . . the tradition of discrimination against Negroes apparently receives continuous reinforcement from the present self-interests of the majority" (1963, pp. 447–48). To the extent, however, that the theory of white gains conceives of white resistance in terms of benefits to individuals, or categories of individuals, it tends to find its place within a social psychological rather than a social structural perspective. Hence, there is not, as yet, a systematic exploration by American sociologists of the possibly latent and positive functions of racism in sustaining the "equilibrium" of the American social system.

Summary

Two perspectives on the features of modern society as they bear on the question of racial assimilation have been presented here. The first, which has occupied the place of a conventional orthodoxy in American sociology since World War II, takes the position that racism is a carry-over from the past which is bound to wither and decay and that, as a consequence, the gradual assimilation of the races can be expected. In the sense that the American creed is viewed as normatively constituent of American society, this perspective suggests a consensus model of racial change and relegates the stresses and strains of the process to a secondary place, as a kind of by-product of inevitable and healthful social trends—the rearguard response of a dying tradition. The second perspective suggests that racism is integral in American society, that it is central to the culture and interests of the white majority, and that its breakdown will only occur through a protracted process of social conflict and at least some degree of restructuring of the existing institutional arrangements of the society. The gradual emergence of the elements of such a perspective can be noted in the sociological literature in the sixties, although there is little doubt that the first perspective continues to hold sway as a kind of official orthodoxy within the sociological establishment (see, e.g., Parsons 1966, Hauser 1966a, and

Pettigrew 1969). An earlier prototype of the second perspective has been present in the Marxian analysis of the race problem.[18]

The affinity of these two perspectives with liberal and radical ideological stances, respectively, on the race problem is apparent (Horton 1966). Our purpose here, however, is neither to claim more abstract-truth value for one or the other (although we believe that the credibility of the first has been seriously put to the test by the racial events of the sixties) nor to condemn both on grounds of their ideological "contamination."[19] Like many sociological theories, these perspectives are schema which serve to point to differing aspects of a complex and probably contradictory reality. What is problematic, we believe, is the overwhelming acceptance, until recently, of the assimilationist perspective among sociologists and the claim that it is supported by social science evidence (Pettigrew 1969) in a way in which the second perspective—which can be referred to as "pluralistic"—is not. In our view, neither the accumulated evidence of social science research nor developments in American race relations in the sixties can support this view. Moreover, the acceptance of the assimilationist perspective has played a large

[18] For an effective, if neglected, analysis of American race relations in the Marxian tradition, see Cox (1948). As noted above, Marxism failed to supply a corrective to the assimilationist bias of both American social science and American social criticism. In fact, the overall impact of Marxian thought has been to relegate ethnicity to the status of "false consciousness"; national and ethnic sensibility is viewed as an outgrowth of the culture of capitalism and as a stratagem of the bourgeoisie for dividing and weakening the working-class movement. For the orthodox Marxist, minorities and minority problems, as such, will disappear with the cessation of class oppression. The strengths of the Marxian interpretation of racism lie in its linking of this pattern to the total structure of the society of which it is a part and its insistence that the race problem has determinants in the economic institutions and the struggle for power and privilege in the society. The viable elements of the Marxian perspective can be retained even as the simplistic account of the race problem as a reflex of the class struggle has been, correctly, rejected.

[19] We agree with Horton (1966, p. 713) when he writes that "the error of the sociologist is not that he thinks politically and liberally about his society, but that he is not aware of it."

role in shaping the direction of empirical research on race relations[20] and in inhibiting the development of research efforts pertinent to the last decade. Beyond pointing to the ideologically liberal presuppositions which have permeated this perspective, the further specification of factors which can account for its acceptance is a problem in the sociology of knowledge, which is beyond the scope of this paper.

ARGUMENTS FROM THE NATURE OF AMERICAN MINORITY GROUPS

If sociologists who have favored the assimilation-integration perspective have taken a benign view of the capacity and willingness of American society to achieve racial assimilation, they have also supported their position through a common set of assumptions about American minorities in general and blacks in particular. These assumptions can be stated as follows: American minorities (especially blacks) desire assimilation into mainstream America. As far as the white ethnic immigrant groups are concerned, there have been no insuperable obstacles in either their sociocultural characteristics or their ideologies which have prevented their assimilation; in this respect, their most relevant traits have been those which they shared with lower-class groups in American society as a consequence of their having entered the society at the lower rungs of the class hierarchy. They have shared the majority commitment to the American creed, and the rate of their assimilation is directly proportional to their access to the socializing agencies of the dominant culture. The conventional position on the assimilation of white ethnics was well stated by Warner and Srole (1945, p. 295) when they wrote: "The future of American ethnic groups seems to be quite limited; it is likely that they will be quickly absorbed. When this happens, one of

[20] The main trends of this research prior to the 1960s have been thoroughly summarized in the invaluable papers of Drake (1957) and Blumer (1958*b*).

the great epochs of American history will be ended, and another, that of race, will begin" (p. 295).

With the exception of the distinctiveness of his castelike position in the South and his unique visibility, the position of the Negro, it has been believed, is similar. In the words of Kristol (1966), "the Negro today is like the immigrant yesterday," and if his special history and status in American society have subjected him to unusually severe barriers to full participation, his absorption can be expected nonetheless. The remainder of this section will discuss some questions which arise concerning this view of black assimilation in the light of the recent reassessment by social scientists of the assimilation process and the nature of black culture in American society.

The Assimilation of White Ethnic Immigrants

If the assimilation of blacks is predicted on the analogy of their position with that of the white ethnic groups, serious problems arise if the assimilation of the latter has been, in fact, much less extensive than has been commonly supposed. Such is the conclusion of recent analyses of ethnicity in American society. As early as fifteen years ago, Glazer (1954, p. 172) noted that a kind of ethnic consciousness, part "nostalgia" and part "ideology," was observable among the descendants of immigrant groups, which consciousness performs "some functions, and even valuable functions, in American life." Gordon (1964) distinguishes between structural assimilation (participation in the dominant society at the primary group level) and acculturation (acquisition of the culture of the dominant group). He argues that the latter process has been rapid on the part of minorities in American society, but that the former has not and will remain limited for the foreseeable future (except in the "intellectual sub-society"). In the sense that primary social participation for most people remains limited by ethnic boundaries, the United States, argues Gordon, can be described as structurally pluralistic along ethnic, racial, and religious lines. Glazer and

Moynihan (1963) note the differential response and resistance of diverse minorities to Americanizing influences and state that the ethnic group is more than a survival of traditional immigrant culture; it is, they claim, a product of the impact of American life on such culture, a "new social form" (p. 16). They go beyond Gordon in emphasizing the ethnic influence in secondary (occupational, political) as well as primary spheres. Greeley (1969, p. 7) doubts that even the acculturation process has been as thorough as Gordon claims and has called for (1964) a reassessment of the ethnic group as a source of identity, interest-group formation, and subcultural differentiation in American society.

In view of the emphasis placed by these writers on ethnicity in contemporary American society, it is surprising, perhaps, that they have not explicitly addressed themselves to a reassessment of the assimilation-integration perspective as it applies to the black American. If the white minorities have legitimately preserved an ethnic identity, should not the blacks propose to do the same? In this connection, the views of these writers are squarely in the assimilationist tradition. Glazer and Moynihan (1963, p. 52), for example, write that "it is not possible for Negroes to view themselves as other ethnic groups viewed themselves . . . . because the Negro is only an American, and nothing else. He has no values and culture to guard and protect." In a similar vein, Gordon (1964, p. 114) writes of the black community that "dual social structures are created solely by the dynamics of prejudice and discrimination rather than being reinforced by ideological commitment of the minority itself." Both these studies, in short, are concerned with the survival or transformation of *prior* ethnic identities in America rather than with the generation of *new* ones, or, in Singer's (1962) terms, "ethnogenesis." Moreover, they fail to raise the question of what the meaning and content of racial assimilation can be in a society which remains ethnically plural. In the words of Harold Cruse (1967, p. 9), "Although the three main power groups—Protestants, Catholics, and Jews—

neither want nor need to become integrated with each other, the existence of a great body of homogenized, inter-assimilated white Americans is the premise for racial integration. Thus, the Negro integrationist runs afoul of reality in pursuit of an illusion, the 'open society'—a false front that hides several doors to several different worlds of hyphenated Americans."

The Problem of Black Culture

If the American Negro has been considered "100 percent American" by sociologists, the divergence of his culture from the middle-class norm has at the same time been heavily examined and documented. The prevailing sociological view was stated by Myrdal (1944, p. 928): "American Negro culture is not something independent of general American culture. It is a distorted development, or a pathological condition of the general American culture." The view that the race problem is a white man's problem here becomes coupled with the view that the black has been unable to create an authentic subculture in America, owing to his oppression and powerlessness, and, hence, that his condition is to be diagnosed as one of a pervasive social pathology.

It is beyond the scope of this paper to review the reassessment of this perspective which is currently under way in the social sciences, but two observations can be made. First, this reassessment, no doubt stimulated by the efforts of black intellectuals (e.g., Ellison 1966; Cruse 1967) to question the "social pathology" interpretation of black culture, has been mainly evident in the work of the so-called urban anthropologists rather than that of sociologists. Their application of ethnographic techniques to the study of the culture of the black ghetto contrasts with the usual practice of sociologists of compiling statistical indexes of social disorganization. Particularly notable in this respect have been the works of Keil (1966) and Hannerz (1969), as well as the theoretical attack mounted by Valentine (1968) on the theory of the "culture of poverty." Recent essays by Blauner (1969) and

McCarthy and Yancey (this issue, pp. 648–72) make an overdue shift of sociological attention in this direction. Ellison's (1966, p. 302) comment that "in Negro culture, there is much of value for America as a whole. What is needed are Negroes to take it and create of it the uncreated consciousness of their race" might well serve as a major leitmotiv of this reassessment on the part of both the scholarly and the black communities.

Second, the sociological emphasis on the pathologies of the black community produced a tendency among sociologists in the sixties to view the major barriers to racial integration as residing in the sociocultural characteristics of the black minority itself rather than in the racism of the dominant society. Whether phrased in the form of demographic characteristics (Hauser 1966b)[21] or the social disorganization which is believed to spring, in part, from these and, in part, from the "heritage" of prejudice and discrimination (rather than from the current institutional functioning of the society itself), these views have harmonized nicely with the benign orthodox analysis of American society outlined earlier. They have led to considerably less optimistic prognoses for the rapid assimilation of the Negro than were characteristic of the fifties (e.g., Broom and Glenn 1965, pp. 187–91) and have led to charges, especially on the part of black activists, that social scientists were simply providing a new apologia for the racial status quo in America. In any case, the view that black culture contains positive elements that can form the basis of a black ethnic consciousness which can and should be preserved is a challenge of major dimensions to the orthodox sociological image of the black community and black culture in America.

Note on the Caste Hypothesis

Through the work of Dollard (1937), Davis, Gardner, and Gardner (1941), and Warner

[21] The hypothesis that there is a direct correlation between economic discrimination and Negro population increase have been put to empirical test by Blalock (1956) and Glenn (1963), whose data do not clearly support it.

(1936), the concept of caste became, during the forties, an almost standard tool for the analysis of American race relations. The caste hypothesis acknowledged that the race problem could not be regarded as merely another instance of the minorities problem in the United States, owing to the unique position of the Negro in the overall system of stratification. Moreover, at least in the statement of Warner, the caste hypothesis viewed racial development (especially in the South) as tending toward "parallelism" (Warner 1936, p. 235), or, in Park's terms, a "biracial society." Within the conventional sociological literature, then, there has been available a conceptual framework which was not assimilationist in its premises but which has not been adequate to account for or foresee the racial crisis of the past decade.

Several reasons for the failure of the caste hypothesis in this respect can be noted. First, it described a system of racial accommodation in which the permanent status subordination of the black caste was believed to lie in a system of folkways and mores which both castes accepted as inevitable and unalterable. Hence, it was attacked by both Myrdal (1944) and Cox (1948) for failing to take into account the dynamic forces which were altering the traditional Southern pattern of "race etiquette," for exaggerating the extent of black compliance with this system, and for neglecting the role of force and violence in maintaining it. Second, the thesis of a biracial society was incompatible with the liberal-assimilationist ethos and (if only implicitly) was rejected by those sociologists who shared this ethos and feared the possibility—which Warner, in his 1936 statement, neglected—of the interracial conflict which was latent in a structure of caste parallelism. Finally, the caste concept was applied, even by the Warner school, largely to the South; hence it was compatible with the view of the Northern Negro as the "new immigrant" whose problems, in their essentials, were no different from those of the earlier white immigrants whose assimilation was proceeding apace.

An urgent need in the current analysis of

American race relations is a conceptual framework which recognizes, as the caste hypothesis does, the unique status of the black in America but which views this status, as the caste hypothesis does not, as a dynamic force with the potential for transforming the black community and black personality in the direction of becoming a major-change agency in American society. Singer's (1962, p. 423) concept of "ethnogenesis . . . the process whereby a people, that is, an ethnic group, comes into existence" remains the major effort along these lines in American sociology.

CONCLUSION

Three major conclusions emerge from this survey of the role of the assimilation-integration perspective in the study of American race relations:

1. The belief that racial assimilation constitutes the only democratic solution to the race problem in the United States should be relinquished by sociologists. Beyond committing them to a value premise which compromises their claim to value neutrality, the assimilationist strategy overlooks the functions which ethnic pluralism may perform in a democratic society. Suggestions as to these functions are found in the writings of Gordon (1964, pp. 239–41), Greeley (1964; 1969, pp. 23–30), and Etzioni (1959, pp. 260–62). The application of this perspective to the racial problem should result in the recognition that the black power and black nationalist movements, to the extent that they aim at the creation of a unified and coherent black community which generates a sense of common peoplehood and interest, are necessarily contrary neither to the experience of other American minorities nor to the interests of black people. The potential for racial divisiveness—and in the extreme case, revolutionary confrontation—which resides in such movements should also be recognized, but the source of this "pathological" potential should be seen as resting primarily within the racism of the

wider society rather than in the "extremist" response to it on the part of the victimized minority.

2. To abandon the idea that ethnicity is a dysfunctional survival from a prior stage of social development will make it possible for sociologists to reaffirm that minority-majority relations are in fact group relations (Blumer 1958a) and not merely relations between prejudiced and victimized individuals. As such, they are implicated in the struggle for power and privilege in the society, and the theory of collective behavior and political sociology may be more pertinent to understanding them than the theory of social mobility and assimilation. Although general theories of minority-majority relations incorporating notions of power and conflict can be found in the writings of sociologists (e.g., Schermerhorn 1964; Lieberson 1961), it is only recently, in the work of Killian (1968) and Oppenheimer (1969), that such perspectives have found their way into sociologists' analyses of the American racial situation.

3. To abandon the notion that assimilation is a self-completing process will make it possible to study the forces (especially at the level of cultural and social structure) which facilitate or hinder assimilation or, conversely, the forces which generate the sense of ethnic and racial identity even within the homogenizing confines of modern society. On the basis of an assessment of such forces, it is certainly within the province of sociological analysis to point to the possibilities of conscious intervention in the social process (by either the majority or the minority group) to achieve given ends and to weigh the costs and consequences of various policy alternatives. These functions of sociological analysis, however, should be informed by an awareness that *any* form of intervention will take place in a political context—that intervention itself is in fact a political act—and that the likelihood of its success will be conditioned by the configuration of political forces in the society at large. Without this awareness—which is nothing more than an awareness of the total societal context within which a given minority problem has its

meaning—sociological analysis runs a very real risk of spinning surrealistic fantasies about a world which is tacitly believed to be the best of all possible worlds. Whether the call of sociologists for racial assimilation in American society as it is currently organized will fall victim to such a judgment remains to be seen.

REFERENCES

Bell, Inge Powell. 1948. *CORE and the Strategy of Non-Violence.* New York: Random House.

Berry, Brewton. 1958. *Race and Ethnic Relations.* New York: Harper & Row.

Blalock, H. M., Jr. 1956. "Economic Discrimination and Negro Increase." *American Sociological Review* 21 (October):584–88.

———. 1959. "Urbanization and Discrimination." *Social Problems* 7 (Fall):146–52.

Blauner, Robert. 1969. "Black Culture: Myth or Reality?" In *Afro-American Anthropology,* edited by Norman E. Whitten, Jr. and John F. Szwed. New York: Free Press.

Blumer, Herbert, 1958a. "Race Prejudice as a Sense of Group Position." *Pacific Sociological Review* 1 (Spring):3–7.

———. 1958b. "Research on Racial Relations: The United States of America." *International Social Science Bulletin* 10 (1):403–47.

Bourne, Randolph S. 1964. *War and the Intellectuals: Collected Essays, 1915–19,* edited by Carl Resek. New York: Harper & Row.

Broom, Leonard, and Norval D. Glenn. 1965. *Transformation of the Negro American.* New York: Harper & Row.

Coleman, James S., et al. 1966. *Equality of Educational Opportunity.* Office of Education, United States Department of Health, Education, and Welfare (OE 38001). Washington, D.C.: Government Printing Office.

Cox, Oliver C. 1948. *Caste, Class, and Race.* New York: Doubleday.

Cruse, Harold. 1967. *The Crisis of the Negro Intellectual.* New York: Morrow.

Davis, Allison, Burleigh B. Gardner, and Mary R. Gardner. 1941. *Deep South.* Chicago: University of Chicago Press.

Dollard, John. 1937. *Caste and Class in a Southern Town.* New Haven, Conn.: Yale University Press.

Drake, B. St. Clair. 1957. "Recent Trends in Research on the Negro in the United States." *International Social Science Bulletin* 9 (4): 475–94.

Ellison, Ralph. 1966. *Shadow and Act.* New York: New American Library.

Essien-Udom, E. U. 1962. *Black Nationalism: The Search for Identity in America.* Chicago: University of Chicago Press.

Etzioni, Amitai. 1959. "The Ghetto: A Re-evaluation." *Social Forces* 37 (March):255–62.

Fein, Rashi. 1966. "An Economic and Social Profile of the Negro American." In *The Negro American,* edited by Talcott Parsons and Kenneth B. Clark. Boston: Houghton Mifflin.

Frazier, E. Franklin. 1947. "Sociological Theory and Race Relations." *American Sociological Review* 12 (June):265–70.

Glazier, Nathan. 1954. "Ethnic Groups in America." In *Freedom and Control in Modern Society,* edited by Morroe Berger, Theodore Abel, and Charles H. Page. New York: Van Nostrand.

Glazer, Nathan, and Daniel Patrick Moynihan. 1963. *Beyond the Melting Pot: The Negroes, Puerto Ricans, Jews, Italians and Irish of New York City.* Cambridge, Mass.: M.I.T. Press.

Glenn, Norval D. 1963. "Occupational Benefits to Whites from Subordination of Negroes." *American Sociological Review* 28 (June): 443–48.

———. 1965. "The Role of White Resistance and Facilitation in the Negro Struggle for Equality." *Phylon* 26 (June):105–16.

———. 1966. "White Gains from Negro Subordination." *Social Problems* 14 (Fall):159–78.

Gordon, Milton. 1964. *Assimilation in American Life.* New York: Oxford University Press.

Greeley, Andrew M. 1964. "American Sociology and the Study of Immigrant Ethnic Groups." *International Migration Digest* 1 (Fall):107–13.

———. 1969. *Why Can't They Be Like Us?* New York: Institute of Human Relations Press.

Gregor, A. James. 1963. "Black Nationalism: A Preliminary Analysis of Negro Radicalism." *Science and Society* 27 (Autumn):415–32.

Hannerz, Ulf. 1969. *Soulside.* New York: Columbia University Press.

Hauser, Philip M. 1966a. "Next Steps on the Racial Front." *Journal of Intergroup Relations* 5 (Autumn):5–15.

————. 1966b. "Demographic Factors in the Integration of the Negro." In *The Negro American,* edited by Talcott Parsons and Kenneth B. Clark. Boston: Houghton Mifflin.

Heer, David M. 1959. "The Sentiment of White Supremacy: An Ecological Study." *American Journal of Sociology* 64 (May):592–98.

Herberg, Will. 1955. *Protestant, Catholic, and Jew.* New York: Doubleday.

Himes, Joseph. 1966. "The Functions of Racial Conflict." *Social Forces* 45 (September):1–16.

Horton, John. 1966. "Order and Conflict Theories of Social Problems as Competing Ideologies." *American Journal of Sociology* 71 (May): 701–13.

Howard, Perry, and Joseph Brent III. 1966. "Social Change, Urbanization, and Types of Society." *Journal of Social Issues* 22 (January):73–84.

Hughes, Everett C. 1963. "Race Relations and the Sociological Imagination." *American Sociological Review* 28 (December):879–90.

Kallen, Horace. 1924. *Culture and Democracy in the United States.* New York: Boni & Liveright.

Keil, Charles. 1966. *Urban Blues.* Chicago: University of Chicago Press.

Killian, Lewis M. 1968. *The Impossible Revolution?* New York: Random House.

Killian, Lewis M., and Charles Grigg. 1966. "Race Relations in an Urbanized South." *Journal of Social Issues* 22 (January):20–29.

Kristol, Irving. 1966. "The Negro Today is Like the Immigrant Yesterday." *New York Times Magazine,* September 11, p. 50.

Levy, Charles J. 1968. *Voluntary Servitude: Whites in the Negro Movement.* New York: Appleton-Century-Crofts.

Lieberson, Stanley. 1961. "A Societal Theory of Race and Ethnic Relations." *American Sociological Review* 26 (December):902–10.

Lincoln, C. Eric. 1961. *The Black Muslims in America.* Boston: Beacon.

Lohman, J. D., and D. C. Reitzes. 1952. "Note on Race Relations in Mass Society." *American Journal of Sociology* 58 (November):240–46.

————. 1954. "Deliberately Organized Groups and Racial Behavior." *American Sociological Review* 19 (June):342–44.

Medalia, Nahum Z. 1962. "Myrdal's Assumptions on Race Relations: A Conceptual Commentary." *Social Forces* 40 (March):223–27.

Morsell, John A. 1961. "Black Nationalism." *Journal of Intergroup Relations* 3 (Winter):5–11.

Moynihan, Daniel Patrick. 1966. "Employment, Income, and the Ordeal of the Negro Family." In *The Negro American,* edited by Talcott Parsons and Kenneth B. Clark. Boston: Houghton Mifflin.

Myrdal, Gunnar. 1944. *An American Dilemma.* New York: Harper & Bros.

Oppenheimer, Martin. 1969. *The Urban Guerrilla.* Chicago: Quadrangle Books.

Park, Robert E. 1950. *Race and Culture.* Glencoe, Ill.: Free Press.

Parsons, Talcott. 1966. "Full Citizenship for the Negro American?" In *The Negro American,* edited by Talcott Parsons and Kenneth B. Clark. Boston: Houghton Mifflin.

Pease, John, William Form, and Joan Rytina. 1970. "Ideological Currents in American Stratification Literature." *American Sociologist* 5 (May):127–37.

Pettigrew, Thomas F. 1969. "Racially Separate or Together?" *Journal of Social Issues* 25 (January):43–69.

Pettigrew, Thomas F., and Kurt W. Back. 1967. "Sociology in the Desegregation Process: Its Use and Disuse." In *The Uses of Sociology,* edited by Paul F. Lazarsfeld, William H. Sewell, and Harold L. Wilensky. New York: Basic.

Rainwater, Lee, and William L. Yancey. 1967. *The Moynihan Report and the Politics of Controversy.* A Trans-Action Social Science and Public Policy Report. Cambridge, Mass.: M.I.T. Press.

Record, Wilson. 1956. "Extremist Movements Among American Negroes." *Phylon* 17 (March):17–23.

Report of the National Advisory Commission on Civil Disorders. 1968. New York: Bantam.

Reuter, Edward B. 1927. *The American Race Problem.* New York: Crowell.

Rose, Arnold. 1956. "Intergroup Relations vs. Prejudice: Pertinent Theory for the Study of

Social Change." *Social Problems* 4 (October): 173–76.

———. 1965. "The American Negro Problem in the Context of Social Change." *The Annals* 357 (January):1–17.

Rossi, Peter. 1964. "New Directions for Race Relations Research in the Sixties." *Review of Religious Research* 5 (Spring):125–32.

Schermerhorn, R. A. 1959. "Minorities: European and American." *Phylon* 20 (June):178–85.

———. 1964. "Toward a General Theory of Minority Groups." *Phylon* 25 (September): 238–46.

Simpson, George E., and J. Milton Yinger. 1954. "The Changing Pattern of Race Relations." *Phylon* 15 (December):327–46.

———. 1958. "Can Segregation Survive in an Industrial Society?" *Antioch Review* 18 (March):15–24.

———. 1959. "The Sociology of Race and Ethnic Relations." In *Sociology Today,* edited by Robert K. Merton, Leonard Broom, and Leonard S. Cottrell, Jr. New York: Basic.

Singer, L. 1962. "Ethnogenesis and Negro Americans Today." *Social Research* 29 (Winter): 419–32.

Tumin, Melvin M. 1968. "Some Social Consequences of Research on Racial Relations." *American Sociologist* 4 (May):117–23.

Valentine, Charles A. 1968. *Culture and Poverty.* Chicago: University of Chicago Press.

Van den Berghe, Pierre L. 1967. *Race and Racism: A Comparative Perspective.* New York: Wiley.

Vander Zenden, James. 1959a. "Desegregation and Social Strains in the South." *Journal of Social Issues* 15 (4):53–60.

———.1959b. "A Note on the Theory of Social Movements." *Sociology and Social Research* 44 (September–October):3–8.

———. 1965. *Race Relations in Transition: The Segregation Crisis in the South.* New York: Random House.

Warner, W. Lloyd. 1936. "American Caste and Class." *American Journal of Sociology* 32 (September):234–37. .

Warner, W. Lloyd, and Leo Srole. 1945. *The Social Systems of American Ethnic Groups.* New Haven, Conn.: Yale University Press.

Westie, Frank R. 1965. "The American Dilemma: An Empirical Test." *American Sociological Review* 26 (August):527–38.

Wilhelm, Sidney M., and Elwin H. Powell. 1964. "Who Needs the Negro?" *Transaction* 1 (September–October):3–6.

Wirth, Louis. 1928. *The Ghetto.* Chicago: University of Chicago Press.

Wright, Nathan. 1967. "The Economics of Race." *American Journal of Economics and Sociology* 26 (January):1–12.

24

Colonialism: The Case of the Mexican Americans*

JOAN W. MOORE

American social scientists should have realized long ago that American minorities are far from being passive objects of study. They are, on the contrary, quite capable of defining themselves. A clear demonstration of this rather embarrassing lag in conceptualization is the current reassessment of sociological thought. It is now plain that the concepts of "acculturation," of "assimilation," and similar paradigms are inappropriate for groups who entered American society not as volunteer immigrants but through some form of involuntary relationship.[1]

The change in thinking has not come because of changes within sociology itself. Quite the contrary. It has come because the minorities have begun to reject certain academic concepts. The new conceptual structure is not given by any academic establishment

but comes within a conceptual structure derived from the situation of the African countries. In the colonial situation, rather than either the conquest or the slave situation, the new generation of black intellectuals is finding parallels to their own reactions to American society.

This exploration of colonialism by minority intellectuals has met a varied reaction, to say the least, but there have been some interesting attempts to translate these new and socially meaningful categories into proper academic sociologese. Blauner's (1969) article in this journal* is one of the more ambitious attempts to relate the concept of "colonialism" as developed by Kenneth Clark, Stokely Carmichael and Eldridge Cleaver to sociological analysis. In the process, one kind of blurring is obvious even if not explicit: that is, that "colonialism" was far from uniform in the 19th Century, even in Africa.[2] In addition, Blauner (1969) makes explicit the adaptations he feels are necessary before the concept of colonialism can be meaningfully applied to the American scene. Common to both American internal colonialism of the blacks and European imperial expansion, Blauner argues, were the involuntary nature of the relationship between the two groups, the transformation or destruction of indigenous values, and, finally, racism. But Blauner warns that the situations are really different: "the . . . culture . . . of the (American black) colonized . . . is less developed; it is also less autonomous. In addition, the colonized are a numerical minority, and furthermore, they are ghettoized more totally and are more dispersed than people under classic colonialism."

But such adaptations are not needed in order to apply the concept fruitfully to America's second largest minority—the Mexi-

Joan W. Moore is Associate Professor of Urban Affairs and Sociology at the University of Southern California.

Reprinted from *Social Problems* 17 (Spring, 1970), pp. 463–472 by permission of The Society for the Study of Social Problems and the author. Copyright 1970 by The Society for the Study of Social Problems.

* I would like to thank Carlos Cortes for his very helpful comments on an earlier draft of this paper.

[1] Oddly enough it now appears that the nature of the introduction into American society matters even more than race, though the two interact. I think this statement can be defended empirically, notwithstanding the emergence of, for example, Japanese-American *sansei* militancy, with its strong race consciousness (see Kitano, 1968).

* Editor's note: This article, "Internal Colonialism and Ghetto Revolt," is included in Blauner's book, *Racial Oppression in America*, from which his related chapter, "Immigrant and Colonized Minorities," which is included in this section, is derived. See also the Introduction to Part One.

[2] For a good analysis of the variation, and of today's consequences, see the collection of papers in Kuper and Smith, 1969.

can Americans.[3] Here the colonial concept need not be analogized and, in fact, it describes and categorizes so accurately that one suspects that earlier "discovery" by sociologists of the Mexican Americans, particularly in New Mexico, might have discouraged uncritical application of the classic paradigms to all minorities. The initial Mexican contact with American society came by conquest, not by choice. Mexican American culture *was* well developed; it *was* autonomous; the colonized *were* a numerical majority. Further, they were —and are—less ghettoized and more dispersed than the American blacks. In fact, their patterns of residence (especially those existing at the turn of the century) are exactly those of "classic colonialism." And they were indigenous to the region and not "imported."[4]

In at least the one state of New Mexico, there was a situation of comparatively "pure" colonialism. Outside of New Mexico, the original conquest colonialism was overlaid, particularly in the 20th century, with a grossly manipulated voluntary immigration. But throughout the American Southwest where the approximately five million Mexican Americans are now concentrated, understanding the Mexican minority requires understanding both conquest colonialism and "voluntary" immigration. It also requires understanding the interaction between colonialism and voluntarism.

In this paper I shall discuss a "culture trait" that is attributed to Mexican Americans both by popular stereotype and by social scientists—that is, a comparatively low degree of formal voluntary organization and hence of organized participation in political life. This is the academic form of the popular question: "What's wrong with the Mexicans? Why can't they organize for political activity?" In fact, as commonly asked both by social scientist and

popular stereotype, the question begs the question. There is a great deal of variation in three widely different culture areas in the Southwest. And these culture areas differ most importantly in the particular variety of colonialism to which they were subjected. In the "classically" colonial situation, New Mexico, there has been in fact a relatively high order of political participation, especially by comparison with Texas, which we shall term "conflict colonialism," and California, which we shall term "economic colonialism."[5]

NEW MEXICO

An area that is now northern New Mexico and parts of southern Colorado was the most successful of the original Spanish colonies. At the beginning of the war between the United States and Mexico, there were more than 50,000 settlers, scattered in villages and cities with a strong upper class as well as a peasantry. There were frontier versions of Spanish colonial institutions that had been developing since 1600. The conquest of New Mexico by the United States was nearly bloodless and thus allowed, as a consequence, an extraordinary continuity between the Mexican period and the United States period.[6] The area became a territory of the United States and statehood was granted in 1912.

Throughout these changes political participation can be followed among the elite and among the masses of people. It can be analyzed in both its traditional manifestations and

---

[3] Mexican American intellectuals themselves have persistently analyzed the group in the conquest frame of reference. For a significant example, see Sánchez (1940).

[4] "Indigenous" by comparison with the American blacks. Spanish America itself was a colonial system, in which Indians were exploited. See Olguín (1967), for an angry statement to this effect.

[5] Of course, we are not arguing that colonialist domination—or for that matter the peculiar pattern of voluntary immigration—offers a full explanation of this complex population, or even of the three culture areas which are the focus of this paper. Mexican Americans and the history of the region are far too complexly interwoven to pretend that any analytic thread can unravel the full tapestry. For other theses, see the analyses developed in Grebler *et al.* (1970).

[6] This account draws on González (1967); Lamar (1966); Holmes (1964); and Donnelly (1947). Paul Fisher prepared a valuable analytic abstract of all but the first of these sources while a research assistant. I have used his document extensively here.

in contemporary patterns. In all respects it differs greatly in both level and quality from political participation outside this area. The heritage of colonialism helps explain these differences.

On the elite level, Spanish or Mexican leadership remained largely intact through the conquest and was shared with Anglo leadership after the termination of military rule in 1851. The indigenous elite retained considerable strength both in the dominant Republican party and in the state legislature. They were strong enough to ensure a bilingual provision in the 1912 Constitution (the only provision in the region that guarantees Spanish speakers the right to vote and hold office). Sessions of the legislature were—by law—conducted in both languages. Again, this is an extraordinary feature in any part of the continental United States. Just as in many Asian nations controlled by the British in the 19th century, the elite suffered little—either economically or politically.

On the lower-class level, in the villages, there was comparatively little articulation of New Mexican villages with the developing urban centers. What there was, however, was usually channeled through a recognized local authority, a *patrón*. Like the class structure, the *patrón* and the network of relations that sustained him were a normal part of the established local social system and not an ad hoc or temporary recognition of an individual's power. Thus political participation on both the elite and the lower-class levels were outgrowths of the existing social system.

Political participation of the elite and the *patrón* system was clearly a colonial phenomenon. An intact society, rather than a structureless mass of individuals, was taken into a territory of the United States with almost no violence. This truly colonial situation involves a totally different process of relationship between subordinate and superordinate from either the voluntary or the forced immigration of the subordinate—that is, totally different from either the "typical" American immigrant on the eastern seaboard or the slave imported from Africa.

A final point remains to be made not about political participation but about protopolitical organization in the past. The villages of New Mexico had strong internal organizations not only of the informal, kinship variety but of the formal variety. These were the *penitente* sects and also the cooperative associations, such as those controlling the use of water and the grazing of livestock.[7] That such organizations were mobilized by New Mexican villagers is evidenced by the existence of terrorist groups operating against both Anglo and Spanish landowners. González (1967) mentions two: one functioning in the 1890's and one in the 1920's. Such groups could also act as local police forces.

Let us turn to the present. Political participation of the conventional variety is very high compared to that of Mexican Americans in other states of the Southwest. Presently there is a Spanish American in the United States Senate (Montoya, an "old" name), following the tradition of Dennis Chavez (another "old" name). The state legislature in 1967 was almost one-third Mexican American. (There were no Mexican American legislators in California and no more than six percent in the legislature of any other Southwest state.) This, of course, reflects the fact that it is only in very recent years that Mexican Americans have become a numerical minority in New Mexico, but it also reflects the fact that organized political participation has remained high.

Finally, New Mexico is the locus of the only mass movement among Mexican Americans—the *Alianza Federal de Mercedes*, headed by Reies Tijerina. In theme, the *Alianza*, which attracted tens of thousands of members, relates specifically to the colonial past, protesting the loss of land and its usurpation by Anglo interests (including, most insultingly, those of the United States Forest Service). It is this loss of land which has

---

[7] González (1967:64) concludes that *moradas*, or *penitente* organizations, "were found in most, if not all, of the northern Spanish settlements during the last half of the 19th Century and the first part of the 20th."

ultimately been responsible for the destruction of village (Spanish) culture and the large-scale migration to the cities.[8] In the light of the importance of the traditional village as a base for political mobilization, it is not really surprising that the *Alianza* should have appeared where it did. In content the movement continues local terrorism (haystack-burning) but has now extended beyond the local protest as its members have moved to the cities. Rather than being directed against specific Anglo or Spanish land-grabbers, it has lately been challenging the legality of the Treaty of Guadalupe Hidalgo. The broadening of the *Alianza's* base beyond specific local areas probably required the pooled discontent of those immigrants from many villages, many original land grants. It is an ironic feature of the *Alianza* that the generalization of its objectives and of its appeal should be possible only long after most of the alleged land-grabbing had been accomplished.

TEXAS

Mexican Americans in Texas had a sharply contrasting historical experience. The Mexican government in Texas was replaced by a revolution of the American settlers. Violence between Anglo-American settlers and Mexican residents continued in south Texas for generations after the annexation of Texas by the United States and the consequent full-scale war. Violence continued in organized fashion well into the 20th Century with armed clashes involving the northern Mexican *guerilleros* and the U.S. Army.

This violence meant a total destruction of Mexican elite political participation by conquest, while such forces as the Texas Rangers were used to suppress Mexican American participation on the lower status or village levels. The ecology of settlement in south Texas re-

mains somewhat reminiscent of that in northern New Mexico: there are many areas that are predominantly Mexican, and even some towns that are still controlled by Mexicans. But there is far more complete Anglo economic and political dominance on the local level. Perhaps most important, Anglo-Americans outnumbered Mexicans by five to one even before the American conquest. By contrast, Mexicans in New Mexico remained the numerical majority for more than 100 years after conquest.

Texas state politics reflect the past just as in New Mexico. Mexican Americans hold some slight representation in the U.S. Congress. There are two Mexican American Congressmen, one from San Antonio and one from Brownsville (at the mouth of the Rio Grande river), one of whom is a political conservative. A minor representation far below the numerical proportion of Mexican Americans is maintained in the Texas legislature.

It is on the local level that the continued suppression is most apparent. As long ago as 1965 Mexican Americans in the small town of Crystal City won political control in a municipal election that electrified all Mexican Americans in Texas and stirred national attention. But this victory was possible only with state-wide help from Mexican American oganizations and some powerful union groups. Shortly afterward (after some intimidation from the Texas Rangers) the town returned to Anglo control. Some other small towns (Del Rio, Kingsville, Alice) have recently had demonstrations in protest against local suppressions. Small and insignificant as they were, the demonstrations once again would not have been possible without outside support, primarily from San Antonio. (The most significant of these San Antonio groups have been aided by the Ford Foundation. The repercussions in Congress were considerable and may threaten the future of the Ford Foundation as well as the Mexican Americans in Texas.)

More general Mexican American political organizations in Texas have a history that is strikingly reminiscent of Negro political organization. (There is one continuous difference:

---

[8] González (1967:75) analyses the *Alianza* as a "nativist" movement, and suggests that its source is partly in the fact that *"for the first time* many elements of Spanish-American culture are in danger of disappearing" (emphasis added).

whites participated in most Negro organizations at the outset. It is only very recently that Anglos have been involved with Mexicans in such a fashion. In the past, Mexicans were almost entirely on their own.) Political organization has been middle class, highly oriented toward traditional expressions of "Americanism," and accommodationist. In fact, the first Mexican American political association refused to call itself a political association for fear that it might be too provocative to the Anglo power structure; it was known as a "civic" organization when it was formed in Texas in the late 1920's. Even the name of this group (LULAC or the League of United Latin American Citizens) evokes an atmosphere of middle-class gentility. The second major group, the American G.I. Forum, was formed in an atmosphere of greater protest, after a Texas town had refused burial to a Mexican American soldier. In recent years, increasing politicization has been manifested by the formation of such a group as PASSO (Political Association of Spanish Speaking Organizations). But in Texas, throughout the modern period the very act of *ethnic* politics has been controversial, even among Mexican Americans.[9]

CALIFORNIA

The California transition between Mexican and American settlement falls midway between the Texas pattern of violence and the relatively smooth change in New Mexico. In northern California the discovery of gold in 1849 almost immediately swamped a sparse Mexican population in a flood of Anglo-American settlers. Prior to this time an orderly transition was in progress. Thus the effect was very much that of violence in Texas: the indigenous Mexican elite was almost totally excluded from political participation. A generation later when the opening of the railroads repeated this demographic discontinuity in

[9] This discussion draws on Guzmán (1967) and Cuéllar (forthcoming).

southern California the Mexicans suffered the same effect. They again were almost totally excluded from political participation. The New Mexico pattern of social organization on a village level had almost no counterpart in California. Here the Mexican settlements and the economy were built around very large land holdings rather than around villages. This meant, in essence, that even the settlements that survived the American takeover relatively intact tended to lack internal social organization. Villages (as in the Bandini rancho which became the modern city of Riverside) were more likely to be clusters of ranch employees than an independent, internally coherent community.

In more recent times the peculiar organization of California politics has tended to work against Mexican American participation from the middle and upper status levels. California was quick to adopt the ideas of "direct democracy" of the Progressive era. These tend somewhat to work against ethnic minorities.[10] But this effect is accidental and can hardly be called "internal colonialism," coupled as it was with the anti-establishment ideals of the Progressive era. The concept of "colonialism," in fact, appears most useful with reference to the extreme manipulation of Mexican immigration in the 20th Century. Attracted to the United States by the hundreds of thousands in the 1920's, Mexicans and many of their U.S.-born children were deported ("repatriated") by welfare agencies during the Depression, most notably from California. (Texas had almost no welfare provisions; hence no repatriation.) The economic expansion in World War II required so much labor that Mexican immigration was supplemented by a contract labor arrangement. But, as in the Depression, "too many" were attracted and came to work in the

[10] Fogelson (1967) gives a good picture of political practices which had the latent consequence of excluding Mexicans from Los Angeles politics—a fact of great importance given the very large concentrations of Mexican Americans in that city. Political impotence in Los Angeles has affected a very significant fraction of California's Mexican Americans. Harvey (1966) give a broader picture of California politics.

United States without legal status. Again, in 1954, massive sweeps of deportations got rid of Mexicans by the hundreds of thousands in "Operation Wetback." New Mexico was largely spared both waves of deportation; Texas was involved primarily in Operation Wetback rather than in the welfare repatriations. California was deeply involved in both.

This economic manipulation of the nearly bottomless pool of Mexican labor has been quite conscious and enormously useful to the development of California extractive and agricultural enterprises. Only in recent years with increasing—and now overwhelming—proportions of native-born Mexican Americans in the population has the United States been "stuck" with the Mexicans. As one consequence, the naturalization rate of Mexican immigrants has been very low. After all, why relinquish even the partial protection of Mexican citizenship? Furthermore the treatment of Mexicans as economic commodities has greatly reduced both their motivation and their effectiveness as political participants. The motivations that sent Mexican Americans to the United States appear to have been similar to those that sent immigrants from Europe. But the conscious dehumanization of Mexicans in the service of the railroad and citrus industries in California and elsewhere meant an asymmetry in relationship between "host" and immigrant that is less apparent in the European patterns of immigration. Whatever resentment that might have found political voice in the past had no middle class organizational patterns. California was structurally unreceptive and attitudinally hostile.

Thus in California the degree of Mexican political participation remains low. The electoral consequences are even more glaringly below proportional representation than in Texas. There is only one national representative (Congressman Roybal from Los Angeles) and only one in the state legislature. Los Angeles County (with nearly a million Mexican Americans) has no Supervisor of Mexican descent and the city has no Councilman of Mexican descent. Otherwise, the development of political associations has followed the Texas

pattern, although later, with meaningful political organization a post–World War II phenomenon. The G.I. Forum has formed chapters in California. In addition, the Community Service Organization, oriented to local community political mobilization, and the Mexican American Political Association, oriented to state-wide political targets, have repeated the themes of Texas' voluntary association on the level of the growing middle class.

How useful, then, is the concept of colonialism when it is applied to these three culture areas? We argue here that both the nature and extent of political participation in the state of New Mexico can be understood with reference to the "classical" colonial past. We noted that a continuity of elite participation in New Mexico from the period of Mexican rule to the period of American rule paved the way for a high level of conventional political participation. The fact that village social structure remained largely intact is in some measure responsible for the appearance of the only mass movement of Mexicans in the Southwest today—the *Alianza*. But even this movement is an outcome of colonialism; the expropriation of the land by large-scale developers and by federal conservation interests led ultimately to the destruction of the village economic base—and to the movement of the dispossessed into the cities. Once living in the cities in a much closer environment than that of the scattered small villages, they could "get together" and respond to the anti-colonialist protests of a charismatic leader.

Again following this idea, we might categorize the Texas experience as "conflict colonialism." This would reflect the violent discontinuity between the Mexican and the American periods of elite participation and the current struggle for the legitimation of ethnic politics on all levels. In this latter aspect, the "conflict colonialism" of Texas is reminiscent of black politics in the Deep South, although it comes from different origins.

To apply the colonial concept to Mexicans in California, we might usefully use the idea of "economic colonialism." The destruction of elite political strength by massive immigration and the comparative absence of local political organization meant a political vacuum for Mexican Americans. Extreme economic manipulation inhibited any attachment to the reality or the ideals of American society and indirectly allowed as much intimidation as was accomplished by the overt repression of such groups as the Texas Rangers.

To return to Blauner's use of the concept of "internal colonialism": in the case of the Mexicans in the United States, a major segment of this group who live in New Mexico require no significant conceptual adaptation of the classic analyses of European overseas colonialism. Less adaptation is required in fact than in applying the concepts to such countries as Kenya, Burma, Algeria, and Indonesia. Not only was the relationship between the Mexican and the Anglo-American "involuntary," involving "racism" and the "transformation . . . of indigenous values," but the culture of the Spanish American was well developed, autonomous, a majority numerically, and contained a full social system with an upper and middle as well as lower class. The comparatively non-violent conqest was really almost a postscript to nearly a decade of violence between the United States and Mexico which began in Texas.

The Texas pattern, although markedly different, can still be fitted under a colonialist rubric, with a continuous thread of violence, suppression, and adaptations to both in recent political affairs.

The Mexican experience in California is much more complicated. Mexicans lost nearly all trace of participation in California politics. Hence, there was no political tradition of any kind, even the purely negative experience in Texas. Then, too, the relationship between imported labor and employer was "voluntary," at least on the immigrants' side. The relationships were much more asymmetrical than in the "classic colonial" case.

If any further proof of the applicability of the idea of "colonialism" were needed, we have the developing ideology of the new *chicano* militants themselves. Like the black

ideologies, *chicanismo* emphasizes colonialism, but in a manner to transcend the enormous disparities in Mexican American experience. Thus one of the latest versions of the ideology reaches out to a time *before* even Spanish colonialism to describe the Southwestern United States as "Aztlán"—an Aztec term. "Aztlán" is a generality so sweeping that it can include all Mexican Americans. Mexican Americans are the products of layer upon layer of colonialism and the overlay of American influence is only the most recent. That the young ideologues or the "cultural nationalists" (as they call themselves) should utilize the symbols of the first of these colonists, the Aztecs (along with Emiliano Zapata, the most "Indian" of Mexican revolutionaries from the past), is unquestionably of great symbolic significance to the participants themselves. But perhaps of more sociological significance (and far more controversial among the participants) is the attempt to legitimate *chicano* culture. This culture comes from the habits, ideas, and speech of the most despised lower-class Mexican American as he has been forced to live in a quasi-legal ghetto culture in large Southwestern cities. These symbols are all indigenous to the United States and are neither Mexican, nor Spanish, nor even Aztec. But they *do* offer symbols to all Mexican Americans, after a widely varying experience with Americans in which, perhaps, the ideologues can agree only that it was "colonialist."

REFERENCES

Blauner, Robert. 1969. "Internal colonialism and ghetto revolt." Social Problems 16 (Spring, 1969):393–408.

Cuéllar, Alfredo. Forthcoming. "Perspective on politics." In Joan W. Moore with Alfredo Cuéllar, *Mexican Americans*. Englewood Cliffs, N.J.: Prentice-Hall, Inc.

Donnelly, Thomas C. 1947. *The Government of New Mexico*. Albuquerque: The University of New Mexico Press.

Fogelson, Robert M. 1967. *The Fragmented Metropolis: Los Angeles, 1850–1960.* Cambridge, Mass.: Harvard University Press.

González, Nancie L. 1967. *The Spanish Americans of New Mexico: A Distinctive Heritage.* Advance Report 9. Los Angeles: University of California, Mexican American Study Project.

Grebler, Leo *et al.* 1970. *The Mexican American People.* New York: Free Press.

Guzmán, Ralph. 1967. "Political socialization." Unpublished manuscript.

Harvey, Richard B. 1966. "California politics: Historical profile." In R. B. Dvorin and D. Misner (eds.), *California Politics and Policies.* Reading, Mass.: Addison-Wesley, Inc.

Holmes, Jack E. 1964. *Party, Legislature and Governor in the Politics of New Mexico, 1911–1963.* Ph.D. Dissertation, Chicago: University of Chicago.

Kitano, Harry H. L. 1968. *The Japanese Americans.* Englewood Cliffs, N.J.: Prentice-Hall, Inc.

Kuper, Leo and M. G. Smith (eds.). 1969. *Pluralism in Africa.* Berkeley and Los Angeles: University of California Press.

Lamar, Howard Roberts. 1966. *The Far Southwest, 1845–1912: A Territorial History.* New Haven: Yale University Press.

Olguín, John Phillip. 1967. "Where does the 'justified' resentment begin?" New Mexico Business offprint, July 1967.

Sánchez, George I. 1940. *Forgotten People.* Albuquerque: The University of New Mexico Press.

25

Colonized and Immigrant Minorities

Robert Blauner

During the late 1960s a new movement emerged on the Pacific Coast. Beginning at San Francisco State College and spreading across the bay to Berkeley and other campuses, black, Chicano, Asian, and Native American student organizations formed alliances and pressed for ethnic studies curricula and for greater control over the programs that concerned them. Rejecting the implicit condescension in the label "minority students" and the negative afterthought of "nonwhite," these coalitions proclaimed themselves a "Third World Movement."[1] Later, in the East and Middle West, the third world umbrella was spread over other alliances, primarily those urging unity of Puerto Ricans and blacks. In radical circles the term has become the dominant metaphor referring to the nation's racially oppressed people.

As the term *third world* has been increasingly applied to people of color in the United States, a question has disturbed many observers. Is the third world idea essentially a rhetorical expression of the aspirations and political ideology of the young militants in the black, brown, red, and yellow power movements, or does the concept reflect actual socio-

Robert Blauner is Associate Professor of Sociology at the University of California, Berkeley.

logical realities? Posed this way, the question may be drawn too sharply; neither possibility excludes the other. Life is complex, so we might expect some truth in both positions. Furthermore, social relationships are not static. The rhetoric and ideology of social movements, if they succeed in altering the ways in which groups define their situations, can significantly shape and change social reality. Ultimately, the validity of the third world perspective will be tested in social and political practice. The future is open.

Still, we cannot evade the question, to what extent—in its application to domestic race relations—is the third world idea grounded in firm historical and contemporary actualities? To assess this issue we need to examine the assumptions upon which the concept rests. There are three that seem to me central. The first assumption is that racial groups in America are, and have been, colonized peoples; therefore their social realities cannot be understood in the framework of immigration and assimilation that is applied to European ethnic groups. The second assumption is that the racial minorities share a common situation of oppression, from which a potential political unity is inferred. The final assumption is that there is a historical connection between the third world abroad and the third world within. In placing American realities within the framework of international colonialism, similarities in patterns of racial domination and exploitation are stressed and a common political fate is implied—at least for the long run. I begin by looking at the first assumption since it sets the stage for the main task of this chapter, a comparison and contrast between immigrant and third world experience. I return to the other points at the end of the essay.

The fundamental issue is historical. People of color have never been an integral part of the Anglo-American political community and culture because they did not enter the dominant society in the same way as did the European ethnics. The third world notion points to a basic distinction between immigration and colonization as the two major processes through which new population groups are incorporated into a nation. Immigrant groups enter a new territory or society voluntarily, though they may be pushed out of their old country by dire economic or political oppression. Colonized groups become part of a new society through force or violence; they are conquered, enslaved, or pressured into movement. Thus, the third world formulation is a bold attack on the myth that America is the land of the free, or, more specifically, a nation whose population has been built up through successive waves of immigration. The third world perspective returns us to the origins of the American experience, reminding us that this nation owes its very existence to colonialism, and that along with settlers and immigrants there have always been conquered Indians and black slaves, and later defeated Mexicans—that is, colonial subjects—on the national soil. Such a reminder is not pleasant to a society that represses those aspects of its history that do not fit the collective self-image of democracy for all men.

The idea that third world people are colonial subjects is gaining in acceptance today; at the same time it is not at all convincing to those who do not recognize a fundamental similarity between American race relations and Europe's historic domination of Asia and Africa. (I discuss how U.S. colonialism differs from the traditional or classical versions toward the end of the chapter.) Yet the experience of people of color in this country does include a number of circumstances that are universal to the colonial situation, and these are the very circumstances that differentiate third world realities from those of the European immigrants. The first condition, already touched upon, is that of a forced entry into the larger society or metropolitan domain. The second is subjection to various forms of unfree labor that greatly restrict the physical and social mobility of the group and its participation in the political arena. The third is a cultural policy of the colonizer that constrains, transforms, or destroys original values, orientations, and ways of life. These three points

organize the comparison of colonized and immigrant minorities that follows.*

GROUP ENTRY AND FREEDOM OF MOVEMENT

Colonialism and immigration are the two major means by which heterogeneous or plural societies, with ethnically diverse populations, develop. In the case of colonialism, metropolitan nations incorporated new territories or peoples through processes that are essentially involuntary, such as war, conquest, capture, and other forms of force or manipulation. Through immigration, new peoples or ethnic groups enter a host society more or less freely. These are ideal-types, the polar ends of a continuum; many historical cases fall in between. In the case of America's racial minorities, some groups clearly fit the criterion for colonial entry; others exemplify mixed types.

Native Americans, Chicanos, and blacks are the third world groups whose entry was unequivocally forced and whose subsequent histories best fit the colonial model. Critics of the colonial interpretation usually focus on the black experience, emphasizing how it has differed from those of traditional colonialism. Rather than being conquered and controlled in their native land, African people were captured, transported, and enslaved in the Southern states and other regions of the Western hemisphere. Whether oppression takes place at home in the oppressed's native land or in the heart of the colonizer's mother country, colonization remains colonization. However, the term *internal colonialism* is useful for

---

* There is another aspect of colonization which I do not deal with in this essay: the experience of being managed and manipulated by outsiders in terms of ethnic status. This is derived from the fact that the lives of colonized people tend to be administered by representatives of the dominant political and legal order. Immigrant groups experienced a considerable degree of such control, but less intensely and for a shorter period of time. They achieved a relative community autonomy earlier and gained power in a wider range of institutions relevant to them. See Chapter 3 for further discussion.

emphasizing the differences in setting and in the consequences that arise from it.[2] The conquest and virtual elimination of the original Americans, a process that took three hundred years to complete, is an example of classical colonialism, no different in essential features from Europe's imperial control over Asia, Africa, and Latin America. The same is true of the conquest of the Mexican Southwest and the annexation of its Spanish-speaking population.

Other third world groups have undergone an experience that can be seen as part colonial and part immigrant. Puerto Rico has been a colony exploited by the mainland, while, at the same time, the islanders have had relative freedom to move back and forth and to work and settle in the States. Of the Asian-American groups, the situation of the Filipinos has been the most colonial. The islands were colonies of Spain and the United States, and the male population was recruited for agricultural serfdom both in Hawaii and in the States. In the more recent period, however, movement to the States has been largely voluntary.

In the case of the Chinese, we do not have sufficient historical evidence to be able to assess the balance between free and involuntary entry in the nineteenth century. The majority came to work in the mines and fields for an extended period of debt servitude; many individuals were "shanghaied" or pressed into service; many others evidently signed up voluntarily for serflike labor.[3] A similar pattern held for the Japanese who came toward the end of the century, except that the voluntary element in the Japanese entry appears to have been considerably more significant.[4] Thus, for the two largest Asian groups, we have an original entry into American society that might be termed semicolonial, followed in the twentieth century by immigration. Yet the exclusion of Asian immigrants and the restriction acts that followed were unique blows, which marked off the status of the Chinese and Japanese in America, limiting their numbers and potential power. For this reason it is misleading to equate the Asian experience with the European immigrant pattern. Despite

the fact that some individuals and families have been able to immigrate freely, the status and size of these ethnic groups have been rigidly controlled.

There is a somewhat parallel ambiguity in the twentieth-century movement from Mexico, which has contributed a majority of the present Mexican-American group. Although the migration of individuals and families in search of work and better living conditions has been largely voluntary, classifying this process as immigration misses the point that the Southwest is historically and culturally a Mexican, Spanish-speaking region. Moreover, from the perspective of conquest that many Mexicans have retained, the movement has been to a land that is still seen as their own. Perhaps the entry of other Latin-Americans approaches more nearly the immigrant model; however, in their case, too, there is a colonial element, arising from the Yankee neocolonial domination of much of South and Central America; for this reason, along with that of racism in the States, many young Latinos are third world oriented.

Thus the relation between third world groups and a colonial-type entry into American society is impressive, though not perfect or precise. Differences between people of color and Europeans are shown most clearly in the ways the groups first entered. The colonized became ethnic minorities *en bloc*, collectively, through conquest, slavery, annexation, or a racial labor policy. The European immigrant peoples became ethnic groups and minorities within the United States by the essentially voluntary movements of individuals and families. Even when, later on, some third world peoples were able to immigrate, the circumstances of the earlier entry affected their situation and the attitudes of the dominant culture toward them.

The essentially voluntary entry of the immigrants was a function of their status in the labor market. The European groups were responding to the industrial needs of a free capitalist market. Economic development in other societies with labor shortages—for example, Australia, Brazil, and Argentina—

meant that many people could at least envision alternative destinations for their emigration. Though the Irish were colonized at home, and poverty, potato famine, and other disasters made their exodus more of a flight than that of other Europeans, they still had some choice of where to flee.[5] Thus, people of Irish descent are found today in the West Indies, Oceania, and other former British colonies. Germans and Italians moved in large numbers to South America; Eastern Europeans immigrated to Canada as well as to the United States.

Because the Europeans moved on their own, they had a degree of autonomy that was denied those whose entry followed upon conquest, capture, or involuntary labor contracts. They expected to move freely within the society to the extent that they acquired the economic and cultural means. Though they faced great hardships and even prejudice and discrimination on a scale that must have been disillusioning, the Irish, Italians, Jews, and other groups had the advantage of European ancestry and white skins. When living in New York became too difficult, Jewish families moved on to Chicago. Irish trapped in Boston could get land and farm in the Midwest, or search for gold in California. It is obvious that parallel alternatives were not available to the early generations of Afro-Americans, Asians, and Mexican-Americans, because they were not part of the free labor force. Furthermore, limitations on physical movement followed from the purely racial aspect of their oppression, as I stressed in Chapter 1.

Thus, the entrance of the European into the American order involved a degree of choice and self-direction that was for the most part denied people of color. Voluntary immigration made it more likely that individual Europeans and entire ethnic groups would identify with America and see the host culture as a positive opportunity rather than an alien and dominating value system. It is my assessment that this element of choice, though it can be overestimated and romanticized, must have been crucial in influencing the different careers and perspectives of immigrants and colonized in America, because choice is a necessary condition for commitment to any group, from social club to national society.

Sociologists interpreting race relations in the United States have rarely faced the full implications of these differences. The *immigrant model* became the main focus of analysis, and the experiences of all groups were viewed through its lens.[6] It suited the cultural mythology to see everyone in America as an original immigrant, a later immigrant, a quasi-immigrant or a potential immigrant. Though the black situation long posed problems for this framework, recent developments have made it possible for scholars and ordinary citizens alike to force Afro-American realities into this comfortable schema. Migration from rural South to urban North became an analog of European immigration, blacks became the latest newcomers to the cities, facing parallel problems of assimilation. In the no-nonsense language of Irving Kristol, "The Negro Today Is Like the Immigrant of Yesterday."[7]

THE COLONIAL LABOR PRINCIPLE IN THE UNITED STATES

European immigrants and third world people have faced some similar conditions, of course. The overwhelming majority of both groups were poor, and their early generations worked primarily as unskilled laborers. The question of how, where, and why newcomers worked in the United States is central, for the differences in the labor systems that introduced people of color and immigrants to America may be the fundamental reason why their histories have followed disparate paths.

The labor forces that built up the Western hemisphere were structured on the principle of race and color. The European conquest of the Native Americans and the introduction of plantation slavery were crucial beginning points for the emergence of a worldwide colonial order. These "New World" events established the pattern for labor practices in the colonial regimes of Asia, Africa, and Oceania during the centuries that followed. The key equation was the association of free labor with people of white European stock and the association of unfree labor with non-Western people of color, a correlation that did not develop all at once; it took time for it to become a more or less fixed pattern.

North American colonists made several attempts to force Indians into dependent labor relationships, including slavery.[8] But the native North American tribes, many of which were mobile hunters and warrior peoples, resisted agricultural peonage and directly fought the theft of their lands. In addition, the relative sparsity of Indian populations north of the Rio Grande limited their potential utility for colonial labor requirements. Therefore Native American peoples were either massacred or pushed out of the areas of European settlement and enterprise. South of the Rio Grande, where the majority of Native Americans lived in more fixed agricultural societies, they were too numerous to be killed off or pushed aside, though they suffered drastic losses through disease and massacre.[9] In most of Spanish America, the white man wanted both the land and the labor of the Indian. Agricultural peonage was established and entire communities were subjugated economically and politically. Either directly or indirectly, the Indian worked for the white man.

In the Caribbean region (which may be considered to include the American South),[10] neither Indian nor white labor was available in sufficient supply to meet the demands of large-scale plantation agriculture. African slaves were imported to the West Indies, Brazil, and the colonies that were to become the United States to labor in those industries that promised and produced the greatest profit: indigo, sugar, coffee, and cotton. Whereas many lower-class Britishers submitted to debt servitude in the 1600s, by 1700 slavery had crystallized into a condition thought of as natural and appropriate only to people of African descent.[11] White men, even if from lowly origins and serflike pasts, were able to own land and property, and to sell their labor in the free market. Though there were always anomalous exceptions, such as free and even slave-owning Negroes, people of color within the Americas had become essentially a class of unfree laborers. Afro-Americans were overwhelmingly bondsmen; Native Americans were serfs and peons in most of the continent.

Colonial conquest and control has been the cutting edge of Western capitalism in its expansion and penetration throughout the world. Yet capitalism and free labor as Western institutions were not developed for people of color; they were reserved for white people and white societies. In the colonies European powers organized other systems of work that were noncapitalist and unfree: slavery, serfdom, peonage. Forced labor in a myriad of forms became the province of the colonized and "native" peoples. European whites managed these forced labor systems and dominated the segments of the economy based on free labor.[12] This has been the general situation in the Western hemisphere (including the United States) for more than three out of the four centuries of European settlement. It was the pattern in the more classical colonial societies also. But from the point of view of labor, the colonial dynamic developed more completely within the United States. Only here emerged a correlation between color and work status that was almost perfect. In Asia and Africa, as well as in much of Central and South America, many if not most of the indigenous peoples remained formally free in their daily work, engaging in traditional subsistence economies rather than working in the plantations, fields, and mines established by European capital. The economies in these areas came within the orbit of imperial control, yet they helped maintain communities and group life and thus countered the uprooting tendencies and the cultural and psychic penetration of colonialism. Because such traditional forms of social existence were viable and preferred, labor could only be moved into the arenas of Western enterprise through some form of coercion. Although the association of color and labor status was not perfect in the classical colonial regimes, as a general rule the racial principle kept white Europeans from becoming slaves, coolies, or peons.

Emancipation in the United States was followed by a period of rapid industrialization in the last third of the nineteenth century. The Civil War and its temporary resolution of sectional division greatly stimulated the economy. With industrialization there was an historic opportunity to transform the nation's racial labor principle. Low as were the condition and income of the factory laborer, his status was that of a free worker. The manpower needs in the new factories and mines of the East and Middle West could have been met by the proletarianization of the freedmen along with some immigration from Europe. But the resurgent Southern ruling class blocked the political and economic democratization movements of Reconstruction, and the mass of blacks became sharecroppers and tenant farmers, agricultural serfs little removed from formal slavery.* American captains of industry and the native white proletariat preferred to employ despised, unlettered European peasants rather than the emancipated Negro population of the South, or for that matter than the many poor white Southern farmers whose labor mobility was also blocked as the entire region became a semi-colony of the North.

The nineteenth century was the time of "manifest destiny," the ideology that justified Anglo Expansionism in its sweep to the Pacific. The Texan War of 1836 was followed by the full-scale imperialist conquest of 1846–1848 through which Mexico lost half its territory. By 1900 Anglo-Americans had assumed economic as well as political dominance over most of the Southwest. As white colonists and speculators gained control (often illegally) over the land and livelihood of the independent Hispano

farming and ranching villages, a new pool of dependent labor was produced to work the fields and build the railroads of the region.[15] Leonard Pitt sums up the seizure of California in terms applicable to the whole Southwest:

In the final analysis the Californios were the victims of an imperial conquest. . . . The United States, which had long coveted California for its trade potential and strategic location, finally provoked a war to bring about the desired ownership. At the conclusion of fighting, it arranged to "purchase" the territory outright, and set about to colonize, by throwing open the gates to all comers. Yankee settlers then swept in by the tens of thousands, and in a matter of months and years overturned the old institutional framework, expropriated the land, imposed a new body of law, a new language, a new economy, and a new culture, and in the process exploited the labor of the local population whenever necessary. To certain members of the old ruling class these settlers awarded a token and symbolic prestige, at least temporarily; yet with that status went very little genuine authority. In the long run Americans simply pushed aside the earlier ruling elite as being irrelevant.[16]

Later, the United States' economic hegemony over a semicolonial Mexico and the upheavals that followed the 1910 revolution brought additional mass migrations of brown workers to the croplands of the region. The Mexicans and Mexican-Americans who created the rich agricultural industries of the Southwest were as a rule bound to contractors, owners, and officials in a status little above peonage. Beginning in the 1850s, shipments of Chinese workmen—who had sold themselves or had been forced into debt servitude—were imported to build railroads and to mine gold and other metals. Later other colonized Asian populations, Filipinos and East Indians, were used as gang laborers for Western farm factories.[17] Among the third world groups that contributed to this labor stream, only the Japanese came from a nation that had successfully resisted Western domination. This may be one important reason why the Japanese entry into American life and much of the group's subsequent development show some striking paral-

* This pattern was not unique to the United States. The emancipation of slaves in other societies has typically led to their confinement to other forms of unfree labor, usually sharecropping. In this context Kloosterboer cites the examples of the British West Indies, South Africa, the Dutch West Indies, the Dutch East Indies (Java), Portuguese Africa, Madagascar, the Belgian Congo, and Haiti.[13] The great influx of European immigration to Brazil also followed the abolition of slavery, and the new white Brazilians similarly monopolized the occupational opportunities brought by the industrialization that might have otherwise benefited the black masses.[14]

lels to the European immigrant pattern. But the racial labor principle confined this Asian people too; they were viewed as fit only for subservient field employment. When they began to buy land, set up businesses, and enter occupations "reserved" for whites, the outcry led to immigration restriction and to exclusion acts.[18]

A tenet central to Marxian theory is that work and systems of labor are crucial in shaping larger social forces and relations. The orthodox Marxist criticism of capitalism, however, often obscures the significance of patterns of labor status. Since, by definition, capitalism is a system of wage slavery and the proletariat are "wage slaves," the varied degrees of freedom within industry and among the working class have not been given enough theoretical attention. Max Weber's treatment of capitalism, though based essentially on Marx's framework, is useful for its emphasis on the unique status of the free mobile proletariat in contrast to the status of those traditional forms of labor more bound to particular masters and work situations. Weber saw "formally free" labor as an essential condition for modern capitalism.[19] Of course, freedom of labor is always a relative matter, and formal freedoms are often limited by informal constraint and the absence of choice. For this reason, the different labor situations of third world and of European newcomers to American capitalism cannot be seen as polar opposites. Many European groups entered as contract laborers,[20] and an ethnic stratification (as well as a racial one) prevailed in industry. Particular immigrant groups dominated certain industries and occupations: the Irish built the canal system that linked the East with the Great Lakes in the early nineteenth century; Italians were concentrated in roadbuilding and other construction; Slavs and East Europeans made up a large segment of the labor force in steel and heavy metals; the garment trades was for many years a Jewish enclave. Yet this ethnic stratification had different consequences than the racial labor principle had, since the white immigrants worked within the wage system whereas the third world groups tended to be clustered in precapitalist employment sectors.[21]

The differences in labor placement for third world and immigrant can be further broken down. Like European overseas colonialism, America has used African, Asian, Mexican and, to a lesser degree, Indian workers for the cheapest labor, concentrating people of color in the most unskilled jobs, the least advanced sectors of the economy, and the most industrially backward regions of the nation. In an historical sense, people of color provided much of the hard labor (and the technical skills) that built up the agricultural base and the mineral-transport-communication infrastructure necessary for industrialization and modernization, whereas the Europeans worked primarily within the industrialized, modern sectors.* The initial position of European ethnics, while low, was therefore strategic for movement up the economic and social pyramid. The placement of nonwhite groups, however, imposed barrier upon barrier on such mobility, freezing them for long periods of time in the least favorable segments of the economy.

Rural Versus Urban

European immigrants were clustered in the cities, whereas the colonized minorities were predominantly agricultural laborers in rural areas. In the United States, family farming and corporate agriculture have been primarily white industries. Some immigrants, notably German, Scandinavian, Italian, and Portuguese, have prospered through farming. But most immigrant groups did not contribute to

---

* I do not imply a perfect correlation between race and industrial type, only that third world workers have been strikingly overrepresented in the "primary sector" of the economy. Unlike in classical colonialism, white labor has outnumbered colored labor in the United States, and therefore white workers have dominated even such industries as coal mining, non-ferrous metals, and midwestern agriculture.

the most exploited sector of our industrial economy, that with the lowest status: agricultural labor. Curiously, the white rural proletariat of the South and West was chiefly native born.

Industry: Exclusion from Manufacturing

The rate of occupational mobility was by no means the same for all ethnics. Among the early immigrants, the stigmatized Irish occupied a quasi-colonial status, and their ascent into a predominantly middle-class position took at least a generation longer than that of the Germans. Among later immigrants, Jews, Greeks, and Armenians—urban people in Europe—have achieved higher social and economic status than Italians and Poles, most of whom were peasants in the old country.[22] But despite these differences, the immigrants as a whole had a key advantage over third world Americans. As unskilled laborers, they worked within manufacturing enterprises or close to centers of industry. Therefore they had a foot in the most dynamic centers of the economy and could, with time, rise to semiskilled and skilled positions.*

Except for a handful of industrial slaves and free Negroes, Afro-Americans did not gain substantial entry into manufacturing industry until World War I,[24] and the stereotype has long existed that Asians and Indians were not fit for factory work. For the most part then, third world groups have been relegated to labor in preindustrial sectors of the nonagricultural economy. Chinese and Mexicans, for example, were used extensively in mining and building railroads, industries that were essential to the early development of a national capitalist economy, but which were primarily

prerequisites of industrial development rather than industries with any dynamic future.**

Geography: Concentration in Peripheral Regions

Even geographically the Europeans were in more fortunate positions. The dynamic and modern centers of the nation have been the Northeast and the Midwest, the predominant areas of white immigration. The third world groups were located away from these centers: Africans in the South, Mexicans in their own Southwest, Asians on the Pacific Coast, the Indians pushed relentlessly "across the frontier" toward the margins of the society. Thus Irish, Italians, and Jews went directly to the Northern cities and its unskilled labor market, whereas Afro-Americans had to take two extra "giant steps," rather than the immigrants' one, before their large-scale arrival in the same place in the present century: the emancipation from slavery and migration from the underdeveloped semicolonial Southern region. Another result of colonized entry and labor placement is that the racial groups had to go through major historical dislocations within this country before they could arrive at the point in the economy where the immigrants began! When finally they did arrive in Northern cities, that economy had changed to their disadvantage. Technological trends in industry had drastically reduced the number of unskilled jobs available for people with little formal education.[25]

Racial Discrimination

To these "structural" factors must be added the factor of racial discrimination. The argument that Jews, Italians, and Irish also faced prejudice in hiring misses the point. Herman Bloch's historical study of Afro-Americans in New York provides clear evidence that immi-

---

* Even in the first generation, immigrants were never as thoroughly clustered in unskilled labor as blacks, Mexicans, and Chinese were in their early years. In 1855, when New York Irishmen dominated the fields of common labor and domestic service, there were sizable numbers (more than a thousand in each category) working as blacksmiths, carpenters, masons, painters, stonecutters, clerks, shoemakers, tailors, food dealers and cartmen.[23]

** Of course some Europeans did parallel labor in mining and transportation construction. But since they had the freedom of movement that was denied colored laborers, they could transfer the skills and experience gained to other pursuits.

grant groups benefited from racism. When blacks began to consolidate in skilled and unskilled jobs that yielded relatively decent wages and some security, Germans, Irish, and Italians came along to usurp occupation after occupation, forcing blacks out and down into the least skilled, marginal reaches of the economy.[26] Although the European immigrant was only struggling to better his lot, the irony is that his relative success helped to block the upward economic mobility of Northern blacks. Without such a combination of immigration and white racism, the Harlems and the South Chicagos might have become solid working-class and middle-class communities with the economic and social resources to absorb and aid the incoming masses of Southerners, much as European ethnic groups have been able to do for their newcomers. The mobility of Asians, Mexicans, and Indians has been contained by similar discrimination and expulsion from hard-won occupational bases.[27]

Our look at the labor situation of the colonized and the immigrant minorities calls into question the popular sociological idea that there is no fundamental difference in condition and history between the nonwhite poor today and the ethnic poor of past generations. This dangerous myth is used by the children of the immigrants to rationalize racial oppression and to oppose the demands of third world people for special group recognition and economic policies—thus the folk beliefs that all Americans "started at the bottom" and most have been able to "work themselves up through their own efforts." But the racial labor principle has meant, in effect, that "the bottom" has by no means been the same for all groups. In addition, the cultural experiences of third world and immigrant groups have diverged in America, a matter I take up in the next section.

CULTURE AND SOCIAL ORGANIZATION

Labor status and the quality of entry had their most significant impact on the cultural dynamics of minority people. Every new group that entered America experienced cultural conflict, the degree depending on the newcomers' distance from the Western European, Anglo-Saxon Protestant norm. Since the cultures of people of color in America, as much as they differed from one another, were non-European and non-Western, their encounters with dominant institutions have resulted in a more intense conflict of ethos and world view than was the case for the various Western elements that fed into the American nation. The divergent situations of colonization and immigration were fateful in determining the ability of minorities to develop group integrity and autonomous community life in the face of WASP ethnocentrism and cultural hegemony.

Voluntary immigration and free labor status made it possible for European minorities to establish new social relationships and cultural forms after a period of adjustment to the American scene. One feature of the modern labor relationship is the separation of the place of work from the place of residence or community. European ethnics were exploited on the job, but in the urban ghettos where they lived they had the insulation and freedom to carry on many aspects of their old country cultures—to speak their languages, establish their religions and build institutions such as schools, newspapers, welfare societies, and political organizations. In fact, because they had been oppressed in Europe—by such imperial powers as England, Tsarist Russia, and the Hapsburg Monarchy—the Irish, Poles, Jews, and other East Europeans actually had more autonomy in the New World for their cultural and political development. In the case of the Italians, many of their immigrant institutions had no counterpart in Italy, and a sense of nationality, overriding parochial and regional identities, developed only in the United States.[28]

But there were pressures toward assimilation; the norm of "Anglo-conformity" has been a dynamic of domination central to American life.[29] The early immigrants were primarily from Western Europe. Therefore, their institutions were close to the dominant pattern, and assimilation for them did not involve great conflict. Among later newcomers from Eastern and Southern Europe, however, the disparity in values and institutions made the goal of cultural pluralism attractive for a time; to many of the first generation, America's assimilation dynamic must have appeared oppressive. The majority of their children, on the other hand, apparently welcomed Americanization, for with the passage of time many, if not most, European ethnics have merged into the larger society, and the distinctive Euro-American communities have taken on more and more of the characteristics of the dominant culture.

The cultural experience of third world people in America has been different. The labor systems through which people of color became Americans tended to destroy or weaken their cultures and communal ties. Regrouping and new institutional forms developed, but in situations with extremely limited possibilities. The transformation of group life that is central to the colonial cultural dynamic took place most completely on the plantation. Slavery in the United States appears to have gone the farthest in eliminating African social and cultural forms; the plantation system provided the most restricted context for the development of new kinds of group integrity.[30]

In New York City, Jews were able to reconstruct their East European family system, with its distinctive sex roles and interlocking sets of religious rituals and customs. Some of these patterns broke down or changed in response, primarily, to economic conditions, but the changes took time and occurred within a community of fellow ethnics with considerable cultural autonomy. The family systems of West Africans, however, could not be reconstructed under plantation slavery, since in this labor system the "community" of workers was subordinated to the imperatives of the production process. Africans of the same ethnic group could not gather together because their assignment to plantations and subsequent movements were controlled by slaveholders who endeavored to eliminate any basis for group solidarity. Even assimilation to American kinship forms was denied as an alternative, since masters freely broke up families when it suited their economic or other interests.* In the nonplantation context, the disruption of culture and suppression of the regrouping dynamic was less extreme. But systems of debt servitude and semifree agricultural labor had similar, if less drastic, effects. The first generations of Chinese in the United States were recruited for gang labor; they therefore entered without women and children. Had they been free immigrants, most of whom also were male initially, the group composition would have normalized in time with the arrival of wives and families. But as bonded laborers without even the legal rights of immigrants, the Chinese were powerless to fight the exclusion acts of the late nineteenth century, which left predominantly male communities in America's Chinatowns for many decades. In such a skewed social structure, leading features of Chinese culture could not be reconstructed. A similar male-predominant group emerged among mainland Filipinos. In the twentieth century the migrant work situation of Mexican-American farm laborers has operated against stable community life and the building of new institutional forms in politics and education. However, Mexican culture as a whole has retained considerable strength in the Southwest because Chicanos have remained close to their original territory, language, and religion.

Yet the colonial attack on culture is more than a matter of economic factors such as labor recruitment and special exploitation. The colonial situation differs from the class situation of capitalism precisely in the importance of culture as an instrument of domination.[31] Colonialism depends on conquest, control, and the imposition of new institutions and ways of thought. Culture and social organization are important as vessels of a people's autonomy

---

* I do not imply here that African culture was totally eliminated, nor that Afro-Americans lived in a cultural vacuum. A distinctive black culture emerged during slavery. From the complex vicissitudes of their historical experience in the United States, Afro-American culture has continued its development and differentiation to the present day, providing an ethnic content to black peoplehood.

and integrity; when cultures are whole and vigorous, conquest, penetration, and certain modes of control are more readily resisted.[32] Therefore, imperial regimes attempt, consciously or unwittingly, either to destroy the cultures of colonized people or, when it is more convenient, to exploit them for the purposes of more efficient control and economic profit. As Mina Caulfield has put it, imperialism exploits the cultures of the colonized as much as it does their labor.[33] Among America's third world groups, Africans, Indians, and Mexicans are all conquered peoples whose cultures have been in various degrees destroyed, exploited, and controlled. One key function of racism, defined here as the assumption of the superiority of white Westerners and their cultures and the concomitant denial of the humanity of people of color, is that it "legitimates" cultural oppression in the colonial situation.

The present-day inclination to equate racism against third world groups with the ethnic prejudice and persecution that immigrant groups have experienced is mistaken. Compare, for example, intolerance and discrimination in the sphere of religion. European Jews who followed their orthodox religion were mocked and scorned, but they never lost the freedom to worship in their own way. Bigotry certainly contributed to the Americanization of contemporary Judaism, but the Jewish religious transformation has been a slow and predominantly voluntary adaptation to the group's social and economic mobility. In contrast, the U.S. policy against Native American religion in the nineteenth century was one of all-out attack; the goal was cultural genocide. Various tribal rituals and beliefs were legally proscribed and new religious movements were met by military force and physical extermination. The largest twentieth-century movement, the Native American Church, was outlawed for years because of its peyote ceremony.[34] Other third world groups experienced similar, if perhaps less concerted, attacks on their cultural institutions. In the decade following the conquest, California prohibited bullfighting and severely restricted other popu-

lar Mexican sports.[35] In the same state various aspects of Chinese culture, dress, pigtails, and traditional forms of recreation were outlawed. Although it was tolerated in Brazil and the Caribbean, the use of the drum, the instrument that was the central means of communication among African peoples, was successfully repressed in the North American slave states.[36]

American capitalism has been partially successful in absorbing third world groups into its economic system and culture. Because of the colonial experience and the prevalence of racism, this integration has been much less complete than in the case of the ethnic groups. The white ethnics who entered the class system at its lowest point were exploited, but not colonized. Because their group realities were not systematically violated in the course of immigration, adaptation, and integration, the white newcomers could become Americans more or less at their own pace and on their own terms. They have moved up, though slowly in the case of some groups, into working-class and middle-class positions. Their cultural dynamic has moved from an initial stage of group consciousness and ethnic pluralism to a present strategy of individual mobility and assimilation. The immigrants have become part of the white majority, partaking of the racial privilege in a colonizing society; their assimilation into the dominant culture is now relatively complete, even though ethnic identity is by no means dead among them. In the postwar period it has asserted itself in a third-generation reaction to "overassimilation"[37] and more recently as a response to third world movements. But the ethnic groups have basically accepted the overall culture's rules of "making it" within the system, including the norms of racial oppression that benefit them directly or indirectly.

The situation and outlook of the racial minorities are more ambiguous. From the moment of their entry into the Anglo-American system, the third world peoples have been oppressed as groups, and their group realities have been under continuing attack. Unfree and semifree labor relations as well as the undermining of non-Western cultures have deprived the colonized of the autonomy to regroup their social forms according to their own needs and rhythms. During certain periods in the past, individual assimilation into the dominant society was seen as both a political and a personal solution to this dilemma. As an individual answer it has soured for many facing the continuing power of racism at all levels of the society. As a collective strategy, assimilation is compromised by the recognition that thus far only a minority have been able to improve their lot in this way, as well as by the feeling that it weakens group integrity and denies their cultural heritage. At the same time the vast majority of third world people in America "want in." Since the racial colonialism of the United States is embedded in a context of industrial capitalism, the colonized must look to the economy, division of labor, and politics of the larger society for their individual and group aspirations. Both integration into the division of labor and the class system of American capitalism as well as the "separatist" culture building and nationalist politics of third world groups reflect the complex realities of a colonial capitalist society.*

The colonial interpretation of American race relations helps illuminate the present-day shift in emphasis toward cultural pluralism and ethnic nationalism on the part of an increasing segment of third world people. The building of social solidarity and group culture is an attempt to complete the long historical project that colonial domination made so critical and so problematic. It involves a deemphasis on individual mobility and assimilation, since these approaches cannot speak to the condition of the most economically oppressed, nor fundamentally affect the realities of colonization. Such issues require group action and

---

* These two poles of the pendulum, integration and nationalism, have long been recognized as central to the political dynamics of American blacks. As early as 1903 in *The Souls of Black Folk* W. E. B. Du Bois analyzed the existential "twoness" of the American Negro experience which lies behind this dilemma. However it is a general phenomenon applicable to all third world people in the United States, to the extent that their history has been a colonial one.

political struggle. Collective consciousness is growing among third world people, and their efforts to advance economically have a political character that challenges longstanding patterns of racial and cultural subordination.

CONCLUSION: THE THIRD WORLD PERSPECTIVE

Let us return to the basic assumptions of the third world perspective and examine the idea that a common oppression has created the conditions for effective unity among the constituent racial groups. The third world ideology attempts to promote the consciousness of such common circumstances by emphasizing that the similarities in situation among America's people of color are the essential matter, the differences less relevant. I would like to suggest some problems in this position.

Each third world people has undergone distinctive, indeed cataclysmic, experiences on the American continent that separate its history from the others, as well as from whites. Only Native Americans waged a 300-year war against white encroachment; only they were subject to genocide and removal. Only Chicanos were severed from an ongoing modern nation; only they remain concentrated in the area of their original land base, close to Mexico. Only blacks went through a 250-year period of slavery. The Chinese were the first people whose presence was interdicted by exclusion acts. The Japanese were the one group declared an internal enemy and rounded up in concentration camps. Though the notion of colonized minorities points to a similarity of situation, it should not imply that black, red, yellow, and brown Americans are all in the same bag. Colonization has taken different forms in the histories of the individual groups. Each people is strikingly heterogeneous, and the variables of time, place, and manner have affected the forms of colonialism, the character of racial domination, and the responses of the group.

Because the colonized groups have been concentrated in different regions, geographical isolation has heretofore limited the possibilities of cooperation.* When they have inhabited the same area, competition for jobs has fed ethnic antagonisms. Today, as relatively powerless groups, the racial minorities often find themselves fighting one another for the modicum of political power and material resources involved in antipoverty, model-cities, and educational reform projects. Differences in culture and political style exacerbate these conflicts.

The third world movement will have to deal with the situational differences that are obstacles to coalition and coordinated politics. One of these is the great variation in size between the populous black and Chicano groups and the much smaller Indian and Asian minorities. Numbers affect potential political power as well as an ethnic group's visibility and the possibilities of an assimilative strategy. Economic differentiation may be accelerating both between and within third world groups. The racial minorities are not all poor. The Japanese and, to a lesser extent, the Chinese have moved toward middle-class status. The black middle class also is growing. The ultimate barrier to effective third world alliance is the pervasive racism of the society, which affects people of color as well as whites, furthering division between all groups in America. Colonialism brings into its orbit a variety of groups, which it oppresses and exploits in differing degrees and fashions; the result is a complex structure of racial and ethnic division.[38]

The final assumption of the third world idea remains to be considered. The new perspective represents more than a negation of the immigrant analogy. By its very language the concept assumes an essential connection between the colonized people within the United States and the peoples of Africa, Asia, and Latin America, with respect to whom the idea of *le tiers monde* originated. The communities of color in America share essential conditions with third world nations abroad: economic underdevelopment, a heritage of colonialism and neocolonialism, and a lack of real political autonomy and power.[39]

This insistence on viewing American race relations from an international perspective is an important corrective to the parochial and ahistorical outlook of our national consciousness. The economic, social, and political subordination of third world groups in America is a microcosm of the position of all peoples of color in the world order of stratification. This is neither an accident nor the result of some essential racial genius. Racial domination in the United States is part of a world historical drama in which the culture, economic system, and political power of the white West has spread throughout virtually the entire globe. The expansion of the West, particularly Europe's domination over non-Western people of color, was the major theme in the almost five hundred years that followed the onset of "The Age of Discovery." The European conquest of Native American peoples, leading to the white settlement of the Western hemisphere and the African slave trade, was one of the leading historical events that ushered in the age of colonialism.* Colonial subjugation and racial domination began much earlier and have lasted much longer in North America than in Asia and Africa, the continents usually thought of as colonial prototypes. The oppression of racial colonies within our national borders cannot be understood without considering worldwide patterns of white European hegemony.

The present movement goes further than simply drawing historical and contemporary parallels between the third world within and the third world external to the United States. The new ideology implies that the fate of colonized Americans is tied up with that of the colonial and former colonial peoples of the world. There is at least impressionistic evi-

---

* The historical accounts also indicate a number of instances of solidarity. A serious study of the history of unity and disunity among third world groups in America is badly needed.

* The other major event was instituting trade with India.

dence to support this idea. If one looks at the place of the various racial minorities in America's stratified economic and social order, one finds a rough correlation between relative internal status and the international position of the original fatherland. According to most indicators of income, education, and occupation, Native Americans are at the bottom. The Indians alone lack an independent nation, a center of power in the world community to which they might look for political aid and psychic identification. At the other pole, Japanese-Americans are the most successful nonwhite group by conventional criteria, and Japan has been the most economically developed and politically potent non-Western nation during most of the twentieth century. The transformation of African societies from colonial dependency to independent statehood, with new authority and prestige in the international arena, has had an undoubted impact on Afro-Americans in the United States; it has contributed both to civil rights movements and to a developing black consciousness.*

What is not clear is whether an international strategy can in itself be the principle of third world liberation within this country. Since the oppression, the struggle, and the survival of the colonized groups have taken place within our society, it is to be expected that their people will orient their daily lives and their political aspirations to the domestic

---

* In the early 1970s Pan-Africanism seems to be gaining ground among black American militants and intellectuals. The most celebrated spokesman has been Stokely Carmichael who has virtually eschewed the struggle in the United States. The *Black Scholar* devoted its February and March (1971) issues to Pan-Africanism. Afro-American organizations have been challenging the South African involvements of U.S. business and government, as, for example, in the action of black employees against the Polaroid Corporation. Chicano groups have been taking an active political interest in Mexico and Latin America. On some university campuses Asian militants have taken the lead in protesting American imperialism and genocide in Southeast Asia. Whereas only recently black and brown nationalists tended to see antiwar protest as a white middle-class "trip," the third world perspective has led to an agressive condemnation of the war in Indochina and a sense of solidarity with the Vietnamese people.

scene. The racial minorities have been able to wrest some material advantages from American capitalism and empire at the same time that they have been denied real citizenship in the society. Average levels of income, education, and health for the third world in the United States are far above their counterparts overseas; this gap will affect the possibility of internationalism. Besides which, group alliances that transcend national borders have been difficult to sustain in the modern era because of the power of nationalism.

Thus, the situation of the colonized minorities in the United States is by no means identical with that of Algerians, Kenyans, Indonesians, and other nations who suffered under white European rule. Though there are many parallels in cultural and political developments, the differences in land, economy, population composition, and power relations make it impossible to transport wholesale sociopolitical analyses or strategies of liberation from one context to another. The colonial analogy has gained great vogue recently among militant nationalists—partly because it is largely valid, partly because its rhetoric so aggressively condemns white America, past and present. Yet it may be that the comparison with English, French, and Dutch overseas rule lets our nation off too easily! In many ways the special versions of colonialism practiced against Americans of color have been more pernicious in quality and more profound in consequences than the European overseas varieties.

In traditional colonialism, the colonized "natives" have usually been the majority of the population, and their culture, while less prestigious than that of the white Europeans, still pervaded the landscape. Members of the third world within the United States are individually and collectively outnumbered by whites, and Anglo-American cultural imperatives dominate the society—although this has been less true historically in the Southwest where the Mexican-American population has never been a true cultural minority.[40] The oppressed masses of Asia and Africa had the relative "advantage" of being colonized in their own land.* In the United States, the more total cultural domination, the alienation of most third world people from a land base, and the numerical minority factor have weakened the group integrity of the colonized and their possibilities for cultural and political self-determination.

Many critics of the third world perspective seize on these differences to question the value of viewing America's racial dynamics within the colonial framework. But all the differences demonstrate is that colonialisms vary greatly in structure and that political power and group liberation are more problematic in our society than in the overseas situation. The fact that we have no historical models for decolonization in the American context does not alter the objective realities. Decolonization is an insistent and irreversible project of the third world groups, although its contents and forms are at present unclear and will be worked out only in the course of an extended period of political and social conflict.

NOTES

1. For accounts of this movement at San Francisco State, see James McEvoy and Abraham Miller, eds., *Black Power and Student Rebellion* (Belmont, Calif.: Wadsworth, 1969), especially the articles by Barlow and Shapiro, Gitlin, Chrisman, and the editors; and Bill Barlow and Peter Shapiro, *An End to Silence* (New York: Pegasus Books, Division of Bobbs-Merrill), 1971.

2. In addition to its application to white-black relations in the United States—see for exam-

* Within the United States, Native Americans and Chicanos, in general, retain more original culture than blacks and Asians, because they faced European power in their homelands, rather than being transported to the nation of the colonized. Of course the ecological advantage of colonization at home tends to be undermined to the extent to which large European settlements overwhelm numerically the original people, as happened in much of Indo-America. And in much of the Americas a relative cultural integrity among Indian peoples exists at the expense of economic impoverishment and backwardness.

ple, Stokely Carmichael and Charles Hamilton, *Black Power* (New York: Vintage, 1967), esp. chap. 1—the concept of internal colonialism is a leading one for a number of students of Indian-white and Indian-mestizo relations in Latin America. Representative statements are Pablo Gonzalez Casanova, "Internal Colonialism and National Development," Rodolfo Stavenhagen, "Classes, Colonialism, and Acculturation," and Julio Cotler, "The Mechanics of Internal Domination and Social Change in Peru," *Studies in Comparative International Development*, vol. 1, 1965, no. 4, vol. 1, 1965, no. 6, vol. 3, 1967–1968, no. 12. The Stavenhagen and Cotler papers are found also in Irving L. Horowitz, ed., *Masses in Latin America* (New York: Oxford University Press, 1970). See also André Gunder Frank, *Capitalism and Underdevelopment in Latin America* (New York: Monthly Review Press, 1967), and Eugene Havens and William Flinn, eds., *Internal Colonialism and Structural Change in Colombia* (New York: Praeger, 1970).

3. Gunther Barth, *Bitter Strength, A History of the Chinese in the United States, 1850–1870* (Cambridge: Harvard University Press, 1964).

4. Harry H. L. Kitano, *Japanese-Americans: The Evolution of a Subculture* (Englewood Cliffs, N.J.: Prentice-Hall, 1969).

5. Oscar Handlin, *Boston's Immigrants* (Cambridge: Harvard University Press, 1959), chap. 2.

6. A crucial treatment of the model of immigration and assimilation is Oscar Handlin, *The Uprooted* (New York: Grosset & Dunlap, 1951).

7. *New York Times Magazine* (September 11, 1966), reprinted in Nathan Glazer, ed., *Cities in Trouble* (Chicago: Quadrangle, 1970), pp. 139–157. Another influential study in this genre is Edward Banfield, *The Unheavenly City* (Boston: Little, Brown, 1970). For a critical discussion of this thesis and the presentation of contrary demographic data, see Karl E. Taueber and Alma F. Taueber, "The Negro as an Immigrant Group: Recent Trends in Racial and Ethnic Segregation in Chicago," *American Journal of Sociology*, 69 (1964), 374–382. The Kerner Report also devotes a brief chapter to "Comparing the Immigrant and Negro Experience," *Report of the National Advisory Commission on Civil Disorders* (New York: Bantam, 1968), chap. 9.

8. W. C. Macleod, *The American Indian Frontier* (London: Routledge & Kegan Paul, 1928).

9. For a discussion of these differences in ecological and material circumstances, see Marvin Harris, *Patterns of Race in America* (New York: Walker, 1964), esp. chaps 1–4. Compare also John Collier, *The Indians of the Americas* (New York: Mentor, 1947), pp. 100–103.

10. H. Hoetink, *The Two Variants of Race Relations in the Caribbean* (London: Oxford University Press, 1967), presents a strong argument on this point.

11. For an historical account of this development, see Winthrop Jordan, *White over Black* (Chapel Hill: University of North Carolina Press, 1968), chap. 2.

12. Pedro Carrasco, cited in Sidney W. Mintz, "The Plantation as a Socio-Cultural Type," in Pan American Union, "Plantation Systems of the New World," *Social Science Monographs*, 7 (1959), 52–53.

It is an equally regular feature of the absorption of colonial peoples into the wider capitalistic system, that such absorption has often been limited to the introduction of the minimum changes necessary for production of staples required by the Western economy, while otherwise leaving practically untouched the non-capitalistic economic system prevalent in the colonial areas. The sharp separation of worker and employer classes and the colonial status of plantation areas, that is, the limited social and political absorption of plantation populations are the usual correlates of the limited economic absorption.

The systems of labor by which these colonial populations come to participate in the world capitalist system are usually described in terms of a dichotomy of compulsory versus free labor which generally results in a typological and developmental continuum: slavery, forced or conscripted labor of subject populations, various forms of contract labor with elements of compulsion such as indentured labor or peonage, and finally free labor.

Also see W. Kloosterboer, *Involuntary Labour Since the Abolition of Slavery* (Leiden: Brill, 1960), for a general account and a specific analysis of 13 different societies. This survey found the racial principle to be the prevailing rule with the following exceptions: the forced labor camps in the Soviet Union during the Stalin era, the peonage of white laborers by Maine lumber companies around 1900, and two situations where people of African descent oppressed unfree black labor, Haiti and Liberia. In addition, Portuguese have at times served as semifree agricultural workers in Brazil and the Caribbean.

13. *Ibid.*

14. F. Fernandes, "The Weight of the Past," in John Hope Franklin, ed., *Color and Race* (Boston: Beacon, 1969), pp. 283–286.

15. See Carey McWilliams, *The Mexicans in America, A Student's Guide to Localized History* (New York: Teacher's College, Columbia University Press, 1968), for a summary discussion.

16. Leonard Pitt, *The Decline of the Californios, A Social History of the Spanish-Speaking Californians, 1846–1890* (Berkeley and Los Angeles: University of California Press, 1970), p. 296.

17. Carey McWilliams, *Factories in the Fields* (Boston: Little, Brown, 1934), and *Ill Fares the Land* (Boston: Little, Brown, 1942). See also McWilliams, *North from Mexico* (Philadelphia: Lippincott, 1948). Recently two papers have applied the colonial model to Mexican-Americans. See Joan W. Moore, "Colonialism: The Case of the Mexican Americans," *Social Problems*, 17 (Spring 1970), 463–472; and Mario Barrera, Carlos Muñoz, and Charles Ornelas, "The Barrio as Internal Colony," in Harlan Hahn, ed., *Urban Affairs Annual Review*, 6 (1972).

18. Roger Daniels and Harry Kitano, *American Racism* (Englewood Cliffs, N.J.: Prentice-Hall, 1970), pp. 45–66. See also R. Daniels, *The Politics of Prejudice* (Berkeley and Los Angeles: University of California Press, 1962). The most comprehensive study of American racist attitudes and practices toward the Chinese is Stuart Miller, *The Unwelcome Immigrant: The American Image of the Chinese, 1785–1882* (Berkeley and Los Angeles: University of California Press, 1969).

19. Max Weber, *General Economic History* (New York: The Free Press, 1950), p. 277.

20. John Higham, *Strangers in the Land* (New York: Atheneum, 1969), pp. 45–52.

21. In a provocative paper which contains a comparison of black and European immigrant experience, Melvin Posey argues that Afro-Americans were never permitted to enter the nation's class system. "Toward a More Mean-

ingful Revolution: Ideology in Transition," in McEvoy and Miller, eds., *Black Power and Student Rebellion, op. cit.*, esp. pp. 264–271.

A contrast between Mexican and European immigrant patterns of work and settlement, and their consequences for social mobility is found in Leo Grebler, Joan W. Moore, and Ralph C. Guzman, in *The Mexican-American People* (New York: The Free Press, 1970), chap. 5.

22. Analyzing early twentieth-century data on European immigrant groups, Stephen Steinberg has found significant differences in occupational background, literacy, and other mobility-related factors. The Jews were consistently advantaged on these points, Catholic ethnic groups such as Poles and Italians disadvantaged. S. Steinberg, "The Religious Factor in Higher Education," Doctoral dissertation, Department of Sociology, University of California, Berkeley (1971).

23. Robert Ernst, *Immigrant Life in New York City, 1825–1863* (Port Washington, N.Y.: Friedman, 1965), pp. 214–217.

24. Robert Starobin, *Industrial Slavery in the Old South* (New York: Oxford University Press, 1970), and Leon Litwack, *North of Slavery* (Chicago: University of Chicago Press, 1961). For a recent interpretation, see Harold M. Baron, "The Demand for Black Labor: Historical Notes on the Political Economy of Racism," *Radical America*, 5 (March–April 1971), 1–46.

25. *Report of the National Advisory Commission on Civil Disorders, op. cit.*

26. Herman Bloch, *The Circle of Discrimination* (New York: New York University Press, 1969), esp. pp. 34–46. That discrimination in the labor market continues to make a strong contribution to income disparity between white and nonwhite is demonstrated in Lester Thurow's careful study, *Poverty and Discrimination* (Washington, D.C.: Brookings, 1969).

27. As far as I know no study exists that has attempted to analyze industrial and occupational competition among a variety of ethnic and racial groups. Such research would be very valuable. With respect to discrimination against Asians and Mexicans, Pitt, for example, describes how white and European miners were largely successful in driving Chinese and Mexican independent prospectors

out of the gold fields. *The Decline of the Californios, op. cit.*, chap. 3.

28. Humbert S. Nelli, *Italians in Chicago 1880–1930: A Study in Ethnic Mobility* (New York: Oxford University Press, 1970).

29. Milton Gordon, *Assimilation in American Life* (New York: Oxford University Press, 1964).

30. Beltran makes the point that the plantation system was more significant than enforced migration in affecting African cultural development in the new world. "This system, which had created institutionalized forms of land tenure, work patterns, specialization of labor, consumption and distribution of produce, destroyed African economic forms by forceably imposing Western forms. . . . Negro political life along with African social structure, was in a position of subordination." Gonzalo Aguirre Beltran, "African Influences in the Development of Regional Cultures in the New World," in Pan American Union, *Plantation Systems of the New World, op. cit.*, p. 70.

31. According to Stokely Carmichael, capitalism exploits its own working classes, while racist systems colonize alien peoples of color. Here colonization refers to dehumanization, the tendency toward the destruction of culture and peoplehood, above and beyond exploitation. S. Carmichael, "Free Huey," in Edith Minor, ed., *Stokely Speaks* (New York: Vintage, 1971).

32. An historical study of Brazilian coffee plantations illustrates how African cultural institutions were the focal point for the slave's resistance to intensified exploitation. Stanley Stein, *Vassouras* (Cambridge: Harvard University Press, 1957), pt. 3.

33. Mina Davis Caulfield, "Culture and Imperialism: Proposing a New Dialectic," in Dell Himes, ed., *Reinventing Anthropology* (New York: Pantheon, 1972).

34. Collier, *op. cit.*, pp. 132–142.

35. Pitt, *The Decline of the Californios, op. cit.*, pp. 196–197.

36. Janheinz Jahn, *Muntu* (New York: Grove, n.d.), p. 217:

The peculiar development of African culture in North America began with the loss of the drums. The Protestant, and often Puritan, slave owners interfered much more radically with the personal life of their slaves than did their Catholic colleagues in the West Indies or in South America. . . . And to forbid the drums was to show a keen scent for the essential: for without the drums it was impossible to call the orishas, the ancestors were silent, and the proselytizers seemed to have a free hand. The Baptists and Methodists, whose practical maxims and revivals were sympathetic to African religiosity quickly found masses of adherents.

Thus the long-term interest of many Afro-American youth in the playing of drums, as well as the more recent and general embracing of African and black cultural forms, might be viewed as *the return of the repressed*—to borrow a leading concept from Freudian psychology.

For a discussion of the attack on culture in the context of classical colonialism, see K. M. Panikkar, *Asia and Western Dominance* (New York: Collier, 1969); H. Alan C. Cairns, *The Clash of Cultures: Early Race Relations in Central Africa* (New York: Praeger, 1965), originally published in England as *Prelude to Imperialism,* and my brief introduction to Part 2 of this book.

37. The standard discussion of this phenomenon is Will Herberg, *Protestant-Catholic-Jew* (Garden City, N.Y.: Doubleday, 1955).

38. The ethnic and racially "plural society" is another characteristic colonial phenomenon. See J. S. Furnivall, *Colonial Policy and Practice* (New York: New York University Press, 1956), and M. G. Smith, *The Plural Society in the British West Indies* (Berkeley and Los Angeles: University of California Press, 1965).

39. The connection has been cogently argued by Dale L. Johnson, "On Oppressed Classes and the Role of the Social Scientist in Human Liberation," in Frank Cockcroft and Dale Johnson, eds., *The Political Economy of Underdevelopment in Latin America* (Garden City, N.Y.: Doubleday, 1971), and by William K. Tabb, *The Political Economy of the Black Ghetto* (New York: Norton, 1970), esp. chap. 2.

However, the international perspective on American racial problems is by no means new. W. E. B. Du Bois was one of its early exponents, and in more recent years Malcolm X placed domestic racism and strategies of liberation in a worldwide context. For a discussion of the internationalizing of Malcolm's politics, see Robert L. Allen, *Black Awakening in Capitalist America* (Garden City, N.Y.: Doubleday, 1969), pp. 31–34.

40. McWilliams, *North From Mexico, op. cit.*

Discrimination: Attitudinal and Institutional

In the Introduction to Part One, we advocated an approach to the analysis of racial and ethnic relations that focuses special attention upon the role of the dominant group in creating and sustaining a subordinate group's position in a society. It follows that in the study of racial and ethnic relations considerable emphasis should be placed upon the majority group and the systems of control and power that it possesses. In this section we shall examine more fully the crucial role of American institutions in the dynamics of intergroup relations. Accordingly, the primary question with which we shall be concerned is: What are the mechanisms by which inequalities, once established, are maintained and perpetuated?

It was also observed previously that the traditional view of majority-minority conflict has been that its reduction, or "solution," requires that the subordinate group adjust to the system. Thus, in the face of conflict, dominant-group policy may vary from extremely repressive measures (e.g., lynching, systematic persecution or harassment, pogroms) to the establishment of well-intentioned social service programs (e.g., Head Start, VISTA). The underlying objective, in most cases, is to change the minority group so that the society can continue to function in its accustomed manner. It should be obvious that this approach does not exhaust all the possibilities for conflict reduction in majority-minority relations. Implicit, and at times explicit, in this section is the suggestion that satisfactory solutions to the problems discussed might be best achieved by changes in a society's institutional structures, which are controlled by the majority. In other words, the adjustments called for should come from the dominant group as well as from the subordinate one.

It would be erroneous to imply that social scientists have entirely failed to recognize the crucial role of the majority group in their analysis of racial and ethnic relations in the United States. During the past few decades, social scientists' understanding of the role of the majority group in intergroup relations has undergone several important changes. Prior to 1960, investigators were primarily interested in racial *attitudes,* because *prejudice* was thought to be the key to the problem.[1] In the civil rights era, the early sixties, it was recognized that attitudes are less important than behavior. Accordingly, *discrimination* became the greatest concern. In keeping with this focus were the prodigious efforts undertaken to secure the passage of the 1964 Civil Rights Bill and the 1965 Voter Registration Act. It was not until *after* these legislative victories had been won, however, that the greatest racial unrest of the postwar period erupted. Once again it was clear that a more adequate analysis was required. Today, we are told—by the Kerner Commission, among others—that *racism* is the chief villain in intergroup relations. If anything, this term is the most imprecise and confusing yet employed. The ambiguity of its usage by the Kerner Commission has served as an excuse for one president to ignore the Commission's findings and for his successor to condemn them[2]—conveniently but tragically avoiding the hard truths presented.

Although we concur in the Kerner Commission's conclusion that the ultimate responsibility for the racial disorders of the 1960s should be attributed to white racism, the term is in urgent need of clarification if its significance in American society is to be fully understood. First, it is apparent that *racism* is a general term, subsuming several analytically distinct phenomena, namely *prejudice* and several forms of *discrimination.* In attempting to clarify the nature of these components, Carmichael and Hamilton distinguished between *individual* and *institutional* racism.[3] Subsequent discussions have emphasized the manner in which racism in America is embedded in the society's institutional structures, thereby operating independently of individuals.[4] Yet despite the utility of this ap-

[1] J. Milton Yinger, "Prejudice: Social Discrimination," *The International Encyclopedia of the Social Sciences,* ed. David L. Sills (New York: Macmillan and The Free Press, 1968), vol. 12, p. 449.

[2] See Richard Nixon's response to the Kerner Report's conclusions. *New York Times,* March 7, 1968, p. 1.

[3] Stokely Carmichael and Charles V. Hamilton, *Black Power: The Politics of Liberation in America* (New York: Vintage Books, 1967), p. 4.

[4] United States Commission on Civil Rights, *Racism in America and How to Combat It,* Clearinghouse Publication, Urban Series No. 1 (Washington, D.C.: Government Printing Office, 1970); Louis L. Knowles and Kenneth Prewitt, eds., *Institutional Racism in America* (Englewood Cliffs, N.J.: Prentice-Hall, 1969); Samuel Friedman, "How Is

proach, most analyses have been conceptually deficient in that they have failed to distinguish adequately between the role of psychological and sociological variables, a situation we will attempt to remedy below.

A further problem in the use of the word *racism* is that although it is inclusive, lumping together all forms of racial oppression, it is not a generic term; it does not encompass majority-minority situations based upon criteria other than race—e.g., religion, tribal identity, ethnicity, or sex. We feel that greater conceptual clarity will be provided by focusing attention upon several components instead. Therefore, in the following discussion we shall attempt to define racism carefully, but then avoid use of the word itself. We feel that this approach has practical as well as theoretical importance, since effective solutions to problems of inter-group relations are dependent upon analytical clarity.

Howard Schuman, in "Free Will and Determinism in Public Beliefs about Race," offers a commonly accepted definition of racism:

> . . . the term racism is generally taken to refer to the belief that there are clearly distinguishable human races; that these races differ not only in superficial physical characteristics, but also innately in important psychological traits; and finally that the differences are such that one race (almost always one's own, naturally) can be said to be superior to another. More simply, white racism is the belief that white people are inherently superior to Negroes in significant ways, but that the reverse is not true.

In other words, racism traditionally has referred to the conscious or unconscious in-group *belief* that out-group individuals are innately inferior. By this definition, racism is a form of prejudice. It is this definition that Higham uses in his discussion of "scientific" racist thought in late nineteenth- and early twentieth-century America (Part Three).

Schuman observes that racism as an ideology has declined markedly in recent years. In 1942, only 42 percent of a national sample of Whites reported that they believed Blacks to be equal to Whites in innate intelligence; since the late fifties, however, around 80 percent of White Americans have rejected the idea of inherent Black inferiority. Schuman therefore faults the Kerner Report for having been misleading in lumping all White antipathy toward Blacks into the category of racism. Rather than believing that Blacks are genetically inferior, the dominant White ideology is that of free will: anyone can "better himself" if he is not too lazy to

Racism Maintained?" *Et Al.* 2 (Fall, 1969): 18–21; Walter W. Stafford and Joyce Ladner, "Comprehensive Planning and Racism," *Journal of the American Institute of Planning* 35 (March, 1969): 68–74; James M. Jones, *Prejudice and Racism* (Reading, Mass.: Addison-Wesley, 1972); William J. Wilson, *Power, Racism, and Privilege: Race Relations in Theoretical and Sociohistorical Perspectives* (New York: Macmillan, 1973); and Nijole Benokraitis and Joe Feagin, "Institutional Racism: A Critical Assessment of Literature and Suggestions for Extending the Perspective," in *Black/Brown/White Relations,* ed. Charles V. Willie (New Brunswick, N.J.: Transaction Books, 1975).

make the effort. This belief is not inherently racist but rather a general judgment about the nature of man, one that may be applied to all sorts of human conditions or groupings. However, when applied to Black Americans, the belief system of free will is racist in that it refuses to recognize or acknowledge the existence of external impingements and disabilities (e.g., prejudice, discrimination) and instead imputes the primary responsibility for Black disadvantage to Blacks themselves. Blacks, by this definition, are still considered inferior people, else they would be like Whites. It becomes, as we shall note more fully below, a form of cultural discrimination.

But if the term *racism* referred merely to prejudicial beliefs alone and not to behavior or action, its relevance for the study of race relations would be limited. To restrict the meaning of racism to ideology alone would be to ignore the external constraints and societally imposed disabilities—rooted in the power of the majority group—that confront a racial minority. As Noel pointed out in Part One, if one group does not possess the power to impose its belief system upon another, ethnic stratification cannot occur. When Whites charged that the ideology of Black Power was "racism in reverse," Black spokesmen pointed out the Whites' failure to consider the component of differential power that enabled the ideology of White supremacy to result in White domination.

> There is no analogy—by any stretch of definition or imagination—between the advocates of Black Power and White racists. Racism is not merely exclusion on the basis of race but exclusion for the purpose of subjugating or maintaining subjugation. The goal of the racists is to keep Black people on the bottom, arbitrarily and dictatorially, as they have done in this country for over three hundred years.[5]

Therefore, the most crucial component of a definition of racism is behavioral and implies the idea of differential power held by the dominant racial group. Racism in its most inclusive sense must refer to actions on the part of a racial majority that have discriminatory effects—i.e., that effectively prevent members of a group from securing access to prestige, power, and privilege.[6] These actions may be intentional or unintentional. Racism therefore entails discrimination as well as an ideology that proclaims the superiority of one racial grouping to another.

Having already discussed the ideological components, let us now turn to a more elaborate analysis of the concept of discrimination. We feel that the conceptual distinctions that follow have important practical,

---

[5] Carmichael and Hamilton, *Black Power,* p. 47.

[6] Michael Banton suggests a distinction between *racism*—an ideology or belief system of racial superiority/inferiority—and *racialism,* which refers to behavior based upon racist beliefs (what we have defined in this section as attitudinal discrimination). Michael Banton, *Race Relations* (New York: Basic Books, 1967), pp. 7–8.

Table 1. *Types of Discrimination**

	Attitudinal Discriminatory practices attributable to or influenced by prejudice		**Institutional** Discriminatory practices not attributable to or influenced by prejudice	
Type	*Individual*	*Adaptive*	*Structural*	*Cultural*
Source of Discrimination	Internalized prejudicial attitudes	Acquiescence to prejudicial attitudes of others or to cultural stereotypes	Social structures (e.g. economic and political)	Cultural belief and value systems

* A similar typology is developed in Benokraitis and Feagin, "Institutional Racism"

as well as theoretical, implications, since different forms of discrimination necessitate differing strategies for effecting change.

As noted in Part One, discrimination refers to the differential treatment of members of a minority group. Discrimination in its several forms comprises the means by which the unequal status of the minority group and the disproportionate power of the majority group are preserved. In the ensuing discussion, we have distinguished between *attitudinal discrimination,* which refers to discriminatory practices attrbutable to or influenced by prejudice, and *institutional discrimination,* which cannot be attributed to prejudice but instead is a consequence of a society's normal functioning. Both of these types may be further elaborated according to the sources of the discriminatory behavior. In reality, these types are at times interrelated and seldom is discrimination against a minority group member derived from one source alone. Table 1 depicts the categories of discrimination as we have conceptualized them.

ATTITUDINAL DISCRIMINATION

The term *discrimination* has traditionally referred to circumstances in which the privileges and rewards of society are *arbitrarily* denied minority group members whose *qualifications are equal* to those of the majority group (e.g. the refusal to employ a qualified Puerto Rican or to sell a home to a Black who is able to meet the stipulated price). The most blatant form and the one for which many White Americans would probably deny responsibility is *individual discrimination,* which refers to actions motivated by personal prejudice or bigotry. In the hypothetical example above, if the primary reason that minority group members were not hired or were unable to purchase a home was because the personnel manager or the realtor was a racist—i.e., he held feelings of personal prejudice toward individuals who were Puerto Rican or Black—it would be a case of individual discrimination. Our emphasis at this point is upon the relationship between the individual's personal feelings and his actions, but we are not concerned in this book with the etiology of his prejudice—whether it arises because of the actor's psychological needs, because he is conforming to relatively well defined cultural definitions, or because of a combination of both.

As Schuman points out, consciously bigoted attitudes have declined substantially among Americans during recent years, or at least it has become less fashionable to publicly express racial prejudice. However, it is not easy to determine whether there has been a similar decline in discrimination. Overt forms of individual discrimination are now condemned, most frequently through public opinion and the law. Yet subtle, overt forms of discrimination are still prevalent.

But discrimination is not necessarily a function of individual prejudices. As Robert Merton has pointed out, it may occur without personal malice from the discriminating individual merely because he may conform to existing cultural patterns or acquiesce to the dictates of others who are prejudiced.[7] *Adaptive discrimination*[8] involves actions that can be attributed to the actor's conscious or unconscious perception of the negative effects nondiscriminatory behavior will have for him. In our hypothetical example above, the personnel manager or realtor placed in a position of having to hire or sell may genuinely disclaim any personal prejudice for having refused the minority group member the desired job or home. The grounds for his discriminatory behavior could have been other than prejudicial. Perhaps he felt himself constrained by the negative sanctions of his peers or by the fear of alienating customers. In this case, the discriminatory actor's judgment would have been based upon the existence of prejudicial attitudes of a powerful reference group (i.e. his customers). Although the "heart and mind" of the actors in our hypothetical situations may be devoid of any personal prejudice, the *effects* or *consequences* of their action—no job, no home—for the minority-group applicant are no different than they would be if they were old-fashioned, dyed-in-the-wool bigots.

Examination of several articles in this section indicates that attitudinal discrimination is still an important component of intergroup relations. There is perhaps no more volatile issue today in Black-White relations than that of birth control. The controversy has deep historical roots, for throughout American history Whites have manifested a fascination for, and anxiety over, Black sexuality, and there have been

---

[7] Robert K. Merton, "Discrimination and the American Creed," in R. M. MacIver, *Discrimination and National Welfare* (New York: Harper & Brothers, 1949), pp. 99–126. Merton characterizes this kind of individual as an "unprejudiced discriminator" or "fair-weather liberal."

[8] In the first edition of *Majority and Minority* we used the term *institutionalized* to refer to what we have here termed *adaptive*. Given the extensive use of the term institutional here and elsewhere, we have changed it to avoid terminological confusion.

numerous examples of White attempts to intrude upon the sexual and family lives of Blacks.[9] Revelations that Black teenage girls have been unknowingly sterilized by a federally funded family planning clinic and that the U.S. Public Health Service used Black males with syphilis as human guinea pigs, leaving them untreated as part of a medical research study conducted at Tuskegee, plus revival of legislative proposals for mandatory sterilization of welfare mothers or mothers with illegitimate children have contributed to charges that family planning efforts represent majority attempts at genocide of Blacks. Kammeyer, Yetman, and McClendon's analysis of the distribution of family-planning centers provides a strong inferential case that racial factors, not (as is frequently asserted publicly) socioeconomic factors, have been instrumental in accounting for the differential distribution of family-planning clinics in American communities. Precisely what motivations led to the highly disproportionate placement of family-planning centers in areas of high Black population cannot be determined in each case, but given the previous history of White concern in this area, the conclusion that these programs were not all established with the interests of Blacks foremost in mind seems inescapable.

Yetman and Eitzen conclude that, while the general public perceives the world of sports to be devoid of racism, attitudinal discrimination still persists there. Although there have been very substantial—even overwhelming—changes in the racial composition of sports teams during the past quarter of a century, the persistence of racial *stacking,* the omission of Blacks from leadership and outcome-control positions, and the relative dearth of Blacks in second-team positions indicate that discrimination is still a factor in player selection. The effects of individual and adaptive discrimination are even more pronounced at management levels—while Blacks are disproportionately overrepresented in player roles, there is a dearth of Black executives, managers, coaches, scouts, and officials.

The mass media provide one of the most important means by which negative images of minority groups are (often unconsciously) perpetuated. Popular magazines and children's literature have been among the most conspicuous purveyors of racial stereotypes. Although social scientists have pointed out the racially biased nature of these publications for decades, a study conducted in 1965 found that of 5,206 children's trade books published from 1962 through 1964, only 349, or 6.7 percent, included one or more Blacks.[10] Similarly, by omission, distortion, or mis-

---

[9] For a more elaborate discussion of these efforts and the debate among Blacks over use of family planning techniques, see Robert G. Weisbord, "Birth Control and the Black American: A Matter of Genocide?" *Demography* 10 (November, 1973): 571–590.

[10] Nancy Larrick, "The All-White World of Children's Books," *Saturday Review,* Sept. 11, 1965, pp. 63–65, 84–85. See also Bernard Berelson and Patricia J. Salter, "Majority and Minority Americans: An Analysis of Magazine Fiction," *The Public Opinion Quarterly* 10 (1946): 168–190; Otto Klineberg, "Children's Readers: Life Is Fun in a Smiling,

representation, the role of racial and ethnic minorities has been slighted in the nation's history books.[11] According to Tom Engelhardt's analysis, the cultural stereotypes in American movies reinforce those found in other media forms. All positive, humanitarian virtues remain with Whites; even if they represent the dregs of Western society, "any White is a step up from the rest of the world." Non-Whites, on the other hand, are depicted as alien intruders, helpless, dependent, or less than human. When they do assume center stage they do so as villains—"the repository for Evil." Whether undertaken consciously or unconsciously, intentionally or unintentionally, perpetuation of these racially biased roles serves to reflect and reinforce cultural beliefs in the racial inferiority on nonwhites.

INSTITUTIONAL DISCRIMINATION

Both forms of attitudinal discrimination defined above are reducible ultimately to psychological variables; either the actor is himself prejudiced or the actor defers to, or is influenced by, the sanctions of a prejudiced reference group or by the norms of a racially biased culture. The third and fourth types of discrimination—*structural* and *cultural discrimination*—are closely interrelated and parallel the distinction we emphasized in Part Four between the social structural and cultural dimensions—that is, between structural and cultural pluralism. Both can be subsumed under the category of *institutional*. Neither can be attributed to prejudicial attitudes—except, as Noel points out, in the original establishment of ethnic stratification.

Institutional discrimination refers to the effects of inequalities that are rooted in the system-wide operation of a society and have little relation to racially related attitudinal factors or the majority group's racial or ethnic prejudices. It involves "policies or practices which appear to be neutral in their effect on minority individuals or groups but which have the effect of disproportionately impacting upon them in harmful or negative ways."[12]

Fair-Skinned World," *Saturday Review,* Feb. 16, 1963; and Bob Teague, "Charlie Doesn't Even Know His Daily Racism Is a Sick Joke," *New York Times Magazine,* Sept. 15, 1968, pp. 36–37, 142–156. Sex-role stereotyping is also pervasive in children's literature. See Lenore J. Weitzman, Deborah Eifler, Elizabeth Hokada, and Catherine Ross, "Sex-Role Socialization in Picture Books for Pre-School Children," *American Journal of Sociology* 77 (May, 1972): 1125–1150.

[11] See Jeannette Henry's critique of the treatment of native Americans in "Our Inaccurate Textbooks," *The Indian Historian* 1 (December, 1967). For blacks, see Kenneth M. Stampp et al., "The Negro in American History Textbooks," *Negro History Bulletin* 31 (October, 1968): 13–16.

[12] Task Force on the Administration of Military Justice in the Armed Forces. *Report* (Washington, D.C.: U.S. Government Printing Office, 1972), p. 19. The Task Force uses the term *systemic* to refer to what we have characterized as *Institutional* discrimination.

The existence of institutional inequalities that effectively exclude substantial portions of minority groups from participation in the dominant society has seldom been considered under the category of discrimination. According to Yinger, discrimination refers to "the persistent application of criteria that are arbitrary, irrelevant, or unfair by *dominant standards,* with the result that some persons receive an undue advantage and others, *although equally qualified,* suffer an unjustified penalty."[13] The underlying assumption of this definition is that if all majority-group members would eliminate "arbitrary, irrelevant, and unfair criteria," discrimination would, by definition, cease to exist. However, as we mentioned above, if prejudice—and individual and adaptive forms of discrimination that emanate from it—were eliminated overnight, the inequalities rooted in the normal impersonal operation of existing institutional structures would remain. Because of the unequal distribution of rewards in the society, Puerto Ricans and Blacks are less likely than other groups to possess the *qualifications* for skilled jobs and the economic resources to purchase a home. Therefore, the crucial issue is not the equal treatment of those with equal qualifications but the accessibility of minority group members to the qualifications themselves. Moreover, even though the action is impersonal it has the same discriminatory *effect* for the minority group member who aspires to obtain the abundance promised by American society as it does when he is the object of individual or adaptive discrimination. Friedman has characterized what we have termed institutional discrimination this way:

> . . . a pattern of action in which one or more of the institutions or organizations of society has the power to throw on more burdens and give less benefits to the members of one race than another on an on-going basis, or in so doing support another institution or organization, and use their power in this manner. This means . . . that decisions are made, agendas structured, issues defined, beliefs, values, and attitudes promulgated and enshrined, commitments entered into, and/or resources allocated, in such a way that nonwhites are systematically deprived or exploited. It should be emphasized that under this definition the intentions of the actors, or the formal statements of the relevant norms, laws, and values, are irrelevant. . . . What counts is whether its actions in fact distribute burdens and rewards in a racially biased fashion. . . .[14]

Our definition of *institutional* has subsumed two analytically distinct, though interrelated and frequently mutually reinforcing, kinds of discrimination. The first, *structural discrimination,* refers to action resulting

---

[13] Yinger, *The International Encyclopedia of the Social Sciences,* vol. 12, p. 449. Emphasis added.

[14] Friedman, "How Is Racism Maintained?" p. 19. Friedman uses the term *structural* to define this phenomenon. As will be indicated below, our use of the term differs slightly from his.

from the normal operation of social structures, particularly the political and economic. For Black Americans especially, the historical roots of social inequalities are found in the rigid caste system that has ensured White dominance. While caste distinctions today still function to preserve inequality, they are diminishing in importance, but the ongoing effects of the caste system persist. Thus, although individual and adaptive discrimination in the economic sphere still continue, they are not necessary to maintain inequality; structural discrimination alone could maintain it indefinitely. This has been succinctly phrased in Wilhelm and Powell's statement that the situation of Blacks has changed "from an economics of exploitation to an economics of uselessness,"[15] a situation reflected in the disastrously high Black unemployment rates, particularly among young adult males. (See Statistical Appendix).

Black and Puerto Rican labor was once needed and was therefore exploited; now it is not exploited because there is no longer a need for a vast reservoir of unskilled labor. According to Herbert Hill, automation has brought about a situation in which unskilled and semi-skilled jobs are "disappearing at the rate of 35,000 a week or nearly two million a year."[16] The lower echelons of the work force are therefore a burden rather than an aid to the economy, as Robert Allen notes in his critique of business efforts to develop a new class of Black capitalists. This situation is crucial, Allen argues, for

> the pace of mechanization and automation . . . cannot be halted because of the competitive need of individual corporations to increase efficiency and reduce costs in order to maintain profits and growth, and improve their relative standing *vis-a-vis* other companies. On the contrary, it can be expected that the pace of automation will accelerate, putting more minority group and other workers without special skills out of work.

The consequence of this action, dictated by impersonal, rational market decisions, is that "the great mass of Negroes [and Puerto Ricans] are locked into a permanent condition of poverty."[17]

Both Allen and Rabin point out the close interrelationship of jobs, income, and housing. One of the most important trends in this regard has been the suburban movement of business and industry, the effect of which is to further isolate inner-city residents from access to job opportunities. The suburbanward movement of business and industry follows the trends of residential movement of the past quarter of a century, the consequence of which has been the growing racial polarization of

[15] Sidney M. Wilhelm and Edwin H. Powell, "Who Needs the Negro?" *Trans-Action* 1 Sept.–Oct., 1964): 3.

[16] Herbert Hill, "Racial Inequality in Employment: The Patterns of Discrimination," *The Annals of the American Academy of Political and Social Science* 357 (January, 1965): 31.

[17] *Ibid.*

American metropolitan areas. Individual and adaptive discrimination (in the form of informal agreements, restrictive covenants, and blockbusting practices that served to exclude racial minorities) contributed substantially to this pattern. But even if these practices had not been employed, federal governmental practices would have ensured that the suburban population would be overwhelmingly White and that Blacks would be relegated primarily to the inner cities. Most important was the governmental decision to permit private enterprise to meet the great demand for housing that had built up during the depression and World War II. As a result, suburban housing was built almost exclusively for those who could afford to pay, while people unable to meet financing requirements were forced to accept housing vacated by those moving to the suburbs. Low-cost, governmentally subsidized housing, on the other hand, which attracted a primarily Black clientele, was constructed primarily in center cities rather than in suburbs.[18]

Because housing is so integrally related to access to jobs and schools, efforts have been made to construct subsidized housing in suburban areas or to challenge the legality of zoning ordinances that have the effect of excluding minorities. However, these have almost uniformly met with bitter resistance from suburban residents. In "Highways as a Barrier to Equal Access," Rabin shows the inherently discriminatory effects of the federal highway program, which has failed to protect equal access to the benefits of development such as housing and employment.

The interdependent effects of the nation's housing and transportation policies have also had an impact on another institution—education. In the historic case of *Brown v. Board of Education,* the Supreme Court established the principle of equality of educational opportunity. Since 1954, when the decision was announced, and especially since the mid-1960s, there has been substantial dismantling of previously segregated school systems. However, residential patterns in many communities across the country have caused students to attend *de facto* segregated schools; because of migration from central cities to the suburbs, schools in many areas have become more, rather than less, segregated since the Court's 1954 *Brown* decision. The question has therefore arisen whether *de facto* segregated schools can fulfill the Court's mandate for equal educational opportunity.

One of the practical and legal remedies for eliminating *de facto* school segregation resulting from residential patterns has been busing. In *Swann v. Charlotte-Mecklenburg Board of Education* (1971) the Supreme Court unanimously supported the constitutionality of busing as a mechanism for eliminating vestiges of intra-district school segregation. However, in the case of *Bradley v. Milliken* (1974) the Court, in a narrow 5 to 4

---

[18] For an excellent discussion of these factors, see Eunice and Scott Grier, "Equality and Beyond: Housing Segregation in the Great Society," *Daedalus* 95 (Winter, 1965): 77–87.

decision, denied busing as a remedy, despite demonstration of extensive and continuing state-supported discriminatory action in policies affecting pupil placement in the Detroit metropolitan area.

By 1970, public schools in Detroit were 64 percent Black while those in the suburbs adjoining the city were 95 percent White, a pattern typical of many American metropolitan areas. In a case brought by Black parents who charged discrimination within the Detroit school system, Federal District Judge Stephen Roth found evidence of substantial discrimination by state agencies. Moreover, he ruled that because of the substantial proportion of Blacks among the Detroit public school population, integration of Detroit schools alone would only hasten White flight to the suburbs and thus would be an ineffective remedy to the Supreme Court's mandate of achieving desegregation "to the greatest degree possible." Consequently, he ordered integration plans that would involve metropolitan-wide busing of students between schools in the city and suburbs.

Important in terms of our discussion of the interrelated and cumulative nature of institutional discrimination were the district judge's findings of the mechanisms by which discriminatory housing policies served to impede access to equal educational opportunities for Blacks.

The city of Detroit is a community generally divided by racial lines. Residential segregation within the city and throughout the larger metropolitan area is substantial, pervasive and of long standing. Black citizens are located in separate and distinct areas within the city and are not generally to be found in the suburbs. While the racially unrestricted choice of Black persons and economic factors may have played some part in the development of this pattern of residential segregation, it is, in the main, the result of past and present practices and customs of racial discrimination, both public and private, which have and do restrict the housing opportunities of Black people. On the record there can be no other finding.

Governmental actions and inaction at all levels, federal, state and local, have combined, with those of private organizations, such as loaning institutions and real estate associations and brokerage firms, to establish and to maintain the pattern of residential segregation throughout the Detroit metropolitan area. . . . The policies pursued by both government and private persons and agencies have a continuing and present effect upon the complexion of the community—as we know, the choice of a residence is a relatively infrequent affair. For many years FHA and VA openly advised and advocated the maintenance of "harmonious" neighborhoods, i.e., racially and economically harmonious. The conditions created continue. While it would be unfair to charge the present defendants with what other governmental officers or agencies have done, it can be said that the actions or the failure to act by the responsible school authorities, both city and state, were linked to that of these other governmental units. When we speak of governmental action we should not view the different agencies as a collection of unrelated units. Perhaps the most that can be said is that all of them, including the school authorities, are, in part, responsible for the segregated condition which exists.[19]

Although the Supreme Court rejected the remedy of inter-district busing that Judge Roth had found warranted by discriminatory actions of Michigan state agencies and officials, the vigorous dissents to the majority decision by Justices Marshall, Douglas, and White indicate the controversial—and highly political—nature of busing as a means of implementing equality of educational opportunity. The Civil Rights Commission document "Your Child and Busing" addresses several objections that have been raised to what has become one of the nation's most volatile political issues—particularly within the White Community. Among many Blacks, as well, there is substantial skepticism of the assumption expressed in the Civil Rights Commission document that "the only way to make sure that Black Americans receive an equal educational opportunity is to put them into the same classroom with Whites."

The impact of structural discrimination is nowhere more apparent than in the political and legal system. J. Skelly Wright, in "The Courts Have Failed the Poor," quotes Anatole France's wry statement, "The law, in all its majestic equality, forbids the rich as well as the poor to sleep under bridges on rainy nights, to beg on the streets and to steal bread." That is, in Wright's words, "a law may be consistently and evenly applied, yet systematically work a hardship on a particular class." This is readily apparent in the fact that poor people do not have money to post bond or hire able lawyers. The Supreme Court has declared that indigent defendants must be provided with a lawyer, but this ruling holds only if the charge is a felony in criminal cases, not in civil suits. "Even the indigent fortunate enough to have a lawyer and win his lawsuit will be the loser in many cases because his legal fees will swallow up his modest recovery."

Wright demonstrates how structural discrimination may work to the advantage of those who consciously seek to exploit the poor. Unscrupulous retail merchants, for example, knowingly extend credit to poor people for purchase of goods they cannot afford. Later, the merchant will legally reclaim not only the items, but also the security that had been required at the time of purchase, and he keeps the portion of the price already paid. Thus, the supposedly equalitarian legal system has not been constructed to take into account the superior ability of those with more wealth, sophistication, and power to manipulate the law to the detriment of those with less.

The most important function of adaptive and structural discrimination is the preservation of the existing power imbalance between majority and minority. As Harold M. Baron observes in his article "Black Power-

[19] 338 *Federal Supplement*, pp. 586–587.

lessness in Chicago," "Negroes remain second-class citizens partly because of the discrimination of individual whites, but mainly because of the way whites control the major institutions of our society." Baron's investigation of the decision-making apparatus of the city of Chicago in 1965 led him to conclude that although Blacks comprise 20 percent of the population, they "really hold less than 1 percent of the effective power in the Chicago metropolitan area. Realistically, the power structure of Chicago is hardly less white than that of Mississippi." Since these inequities are built into the system, they are extremely resistant to change. And since those in positions of power benefit from these inequities, they are unlikely to cooperate with minority-group efforts to redistribute the rewards of the society.

Baron's postscript, written nearly a decade after his original study, indicates that although the Black population of Chicago had increased to 36 percent of the total, "the accession of Blacks to established positions of decision-making authority [had] not increased sufficiently to cause an important shift in racial power relations."[20] This is not to imply that there had been no change in the status of Blacks in that decade; Collins's analysis indicates that in the unionized construction industry, at least, there had been substantial governmental efforts to effect changes in its racial composition, and that those efforts had had some impact in increasing the number and percentages of Blacks. However, efforts at expanding economic opportunities for minorities had, as Collins suggests, been directed disproportionately at worker, as contrasted to management, positions. Collins demonstrates that the increase in the percentage of Black construction workers greatly outdistanced the increase in the percentage of black college and university faculty and administrators. Moreover, Egerton's survey ("Black Executives in Big Business") shows that positions of authority and power in the business world are almost exclusively white. In 1970, only three of 3,182 directorships of major American corporations were held by Blacks. A follow-up survey two years later showed an increase of Black directors from three to sixty-four, or a total slightly better than 2 percent.[21] In 1974, a *Time* magazine survey found that seventy-two Blacks were serving on the boards of major corporations, still far from parity.[22] Similarly, Yetman and Eitzen note the anomaly of a situation in which more than one-third of the players in each of the three major professional team sports are Black while Blacks are virtually excluded from such positions of authority, leadership, and power as managers, owners, administrators, and officials.

---

[20] A similar study of the distribution of blacks in policy-making positions in Milwaukee found that their exclusion from positions of power, especially in the business sector, was more pronounced than in Chicago. Karl H. Flaming et al., "Black Powerlessness in Policy-Making Positions," *The Sociological Quarterly* 13 (Winter, 1972): 126–133.

[21] "Blacks on Corporate Boards Multiply," *Race Relations Reporter,* November 6, 1972, p. 2.

[22] "America's Rising Black Middle Class," *Time,* June 17, 1974, p. 20.

If efforts were genuinely designed to redistribute power, then the representation of Blacks and other minorities in leadership positions would more closely approximate their proportion of the population. But despite increases in the number of Black officeholders since 1965 (see Statistical Appendix), and especially the election of Black mayors in the major cities of Atlanta, Detroit, and Los Angeles, a 1974 survey by the Joint Center for Political Studies found that Blacks held only slightly over one-half of one percent (0.57%) of the more than 521,000 elective offices throughout the country, a striking contrast with the 11.1 percent of the population they comprised.[23]

Thus it is problematic whether the changes that have occurred have effected any redistribution of power. Both Baron and Allen argue that there has been little substantial change; the system has been modified, but its essentials remain intact. As Barth and Noel indicated, ". . . generally order is maintained via the incorporation of minor modifications within a basically unchanged system."

The other component of institutional discrimination, *cultural discrimination,* is a function of cultural pluralism in a multicultural society. All groups, as we pointed out in Part One, tend to be ethnocentric concerning their own values, norms, attitudes, and ways of defining and interpreting reality. What transforms ethnocentrism into cultural discrimination is the differential *power* of the majority group to define *their* cultural attributes—their values, beliefs, and definitions of reality—as the standards and criteria for evaluation for the entire society and to exclude alternative perceptions or interpretations. James M. Jones has pointed out that cultural discrimination "is the appropriate label for the act of requiring that . . . cultural minorities measure up to White standards in order to participate in the economic and social mainstream of this country."[24] Thus, many of the majority's beliefs, values, and norms are not inherently discriminatory against racial minorities—or even directed toward them— but have the effect of excluding them and in so doing provide legitimation of the existing system of racial and ethnic stratification.

Cultural discrimination as used here does *not* refer to values, beliefs, and ideas explicitly related to racial and ethnic minority groups. Throughout American history the ideology of White supremacy was integral to the cultural inventory of White Americans and was transmitted as a normal part of the socialization process. Engelhardt's analysis of the stereotyped movie roles ascribed to Whites and non-Whites describes one of the subtle mechanisms by which racial distinctions have (sometimes unconsciously) been reflected and reinforced.[25] However, as we have previously

---

[23] *Focus,* April, 1974, p. 3.

[24] Jones, *Prejudice and Racism,* p. 159.

[25] Others have used the term *cultural racism* somewhat more broadly than we have here. Jones and Bromley and Longino have included the ideology of White supremacy, invidious racial stereotypes, and various other explicitly racial or ethnic distinctions

noted, because prejudice is integral to such cultural stereotypes, they fall under the category of attitudinal discrimination. Thus cultural discrimination does not entail beliefs concerning the characteristics of any specific minority groups; rather it refers to the fact that requirements for participation in American society are based on certain general assumptions rooted in cultural values and beliefs of the majority.

Cultural discrimination is most apparent as a consequence of perspectives or ideologies that attribute the causes of inequality to cultural deficiencies (i.e. *pathologies*) in the minority group, not recognizing them as cultural differences. Although we have emphasized the import of this phenomenon throughout, it is nowhere more clearly manifested than in the ideology of *cultural deprivation,* or what Baratz and Baratz call a *social pathology* or *deficit* model. Such characterization is predicated on the desirability of cultural homogeneity (what we referred to in Part Four as the transmuting pot conception) and the belief that deviations from standard cultural norms of the dominant group indicate personal and group inadequacy. Baratz and Baratz, expressing a position embraced by both Horton (Part One) and Metzger (Part Four), have described what we have characterized as cultural discrimination this way:

> Social science research with Negro groups has been postulated on an idealized norm of "American behavior" against which all behavior is measured. This norm is defined operationally in terms of the way White middle-class America is supposed to behave. The normative view coincides with current social ideology—the egalitarian principle—which asserts that all people are created equal under the law and must be treated as such from a moral and political point of view. The normative view, however, wrongly equates equality with sameness.

Cultural discrimination occurs when, as Schuman points out, the ideology of free will is invoked and the external disabilities and constraints imposed upon minority group members are ignored. It also occurs when the majority group does not recognize or dismisses nuances in a minority group's cognitive and linguistic styles and restricts access to power to those who conform to the dominant group's cultural values.

The tendency of the majority group to overlook or to dismiss the significance of subtle cultural differences is at the center of the heated controversy surrounding the issue of intelligence testing, since a crucial assumption of advocates of these tests is that what they measure is relatively uninfluenced by cultural differences and that they reflect a fixed, innate ability level in the individual. However, numerous critics have

---

transmitted culturally (for example, White standards of beauty) within the category of cultural racism. See Jones, *Prejudice and Racism,* 147–157, and David G. Bromley and Charles F. Longino, Jr., *White Racism and Black Americans* (Cambridge, Mass.: Schenkman Publishing Co., 1972), pp. 8–10.

pointed out that the skills correlated with success in the middle-class world and those measured on intelligence tests are a function of an individual's contact with the dominant culture. "When used to compare groups with different cultural backgrounds, the Stanford-Binet IQ test is less a comparative measure of ability than an index of enculturation into the ways of the American middle class."[26] It is, to use Jane Mercer's word, *Anglocentric.*[27] It was recognition of this arbitrary quality, Collins notes, that led the Supreme Court in the *Griggs* case to rule that tests and examinations given by an employer must have some demonstrated relevance to job performance, even if they are not overtly discriminatory, since they frequently provide artificial barriers uncorrelated with job performance. Samuda's article, "Cultural Discrimination through Testing," provides an overview of mental testing and its uses.

[26] C. Loring Brace and Frank B. Livingstone, "On Creeping Jensenism," *Race and Intelligence* (Washington, D.C.: 1971), p. AS8.

[27] Jane R. Mercer, "I.Q.: The Lethal Label," *Psychology Today* 6 (September, 1972): 44–57, 95–97.

26

Free Will and Determinism in Public Beliefs about Race

Howard Schuman

The most controversial legacy of the 1968 report of the National Advisory Commission on Civil Disorders was its assertion that "White racism is essentially responsible for the explosive mixture which has been accumulating in our cities. . . ."

To many black Americans this statement seemed painfully obvious, although it was good to hear it said officially by Americans of the commissioners' prestige. Most white Americans, however, did not like being called racists; and even among those who may have felt that the idea behind the words needed saying, there were some who considered "racist" an unnecessarily loaded way of characterizing white beliefs.

Howard Schuman is Professor of Sociology at The University of Michigan.

Published by permission of Transaction, Inc., from *Trans*-action Vol. 7 #2, Dec. 1969, Copyright © 1969, from Transaction, Inc.

Author's note: This is essentially a copy of an article entitled "Sociological Racism," appearing in *Trans*-Action, Vol. 7, No. 2, December, 1969, pp. 44–48. The title used by *Trans*-Action was not the author's, however, and has been corrected here. In addition, several other minor corrections have been made, a table omitted by *Trans*-Action has been restored, and one new paragraph has been added. The latter attempts to take account of an insightful question raised by Guy E. Swanson about an earlier version of this paper. More generally the paper has been influenced by my fruitful collaboration with Angus Campbell on the larger study of which this is one report. The study was financed by the Ford Foundation and carried out through the Survey Research Center of the University of Michigan.

The heated discussion over whether most Americans are or are not racists turns out, however, to be largely irrelevant to the way the general white public actually thinks about race today. Social scientists take for granted the deterministic assumption common to most science that all events (in this case, human behavior) can be traced to antecedent causes. The scientific debate revolves around which set of determinants "cause" people (for example, people of a particular race) to behave the way they do—primarily, whether heredity or environment or some particular combination of the two is the determining factor in some aspect of human behavior. In this sense, current social science thinking and older theories of racism are both deterministic. But the main premise of the ·average white American is that people are free to do as they will. The logic of causal inquiry, we will see, plays little or no part in public thinking about white and black differences in status and achievement.

THE DECLINE IN POPULAR RACISM

"White racism" is nowhere defined in the Kerner Commission Report, but the term racism is generally taken to refer to the belief that there are clearly distinguishable human races; that these races differ not only in superficial physical characteristics, but also innately in important psychological traits; and finally that the differences are such that one race (almost always one's own) can be said to be superior to another. More simply, white racism is the belief that white people are *inherently* superior to Negroes in significant ways, but that the reverse is not true.

Questions designed to tap white racism have been asked in national surveys for the past 25 years. The major finding of these surveys has been a dramatic *decrease* in beliefs in white racial superiority over Negroes. The most relevant and consistently measured topic has been white beliefs about racial differences in intelligence. In 1942 a National Opinion Research Center survey asked respondents: "In general, do you think Negroes are as intelligent as white people—that is, can they learn just as well if they are given the same education?" Only 42 percent of a national sample of white Americans said they believed Negroes to be as intelligent as whites. Later surveys, however, showed a continuing rise in the belief in equal intelligence, so that by 1956, 78 percent of a NORC national sample answered the same question in the affirmative. The percentage seemed to stabilize at that point and more recent surveys have continued to show that about four out of five white Americans reject the notion that white people are born with higher mental capacity than Negroes.[1]

The comparatively rapid decline of racist beliefs in this key area, the relatively small proportion of whites who still hold such beliefs, and the fact that the holdouts are disproportionately from the old South, all suggest that racism—at least in the more open forms that can be measured in surveys—is a minor and disappearing phenomenon in this country. This, of course, implies little or nothing about the disappearance of discrimination or racial hostility or other aspects of black-white inequality in America. It merely indicates that attempts to buttress anti-Negro feeling with beliefs about biological racial inferiority are no longer much resorted to by white Americans.

Social scientists tend to see in these opinion trends not only the disappearance of "racist" beliefs, but also growing white acceptance of contemporary environmental explanations of the Negro's low status and achievement in America. This tendency assumes a change in public belief paralleling changes in social science itself. The ideas about psychogenetic racial differences that played such a large role in American social science in the early part of the century have gradually been replaced by assumptions of environmental determinism. Some of these environmental explanations focus on the obvious in the American racial structure: segregation, discrimination, and the domination of Negroes by whites. Other explanations emphasize cultural and culturally induced psychological phenomena, such as the burden that lower class or rural background places on the ability to compete for urban middle-class rewards; the assumed disruptive effects of family instability and lack of successful male models; the disabling experience of growing up in a minority in a society where one's ethnic identity is both permanently fixed and negatively evaluated by the majority. Whatever the particular environmental theory, however, the important point is that an explanatory social science looks for causal variables that are independent of, yet can be said to produce, the "facts" that need explaining.

WHAT THE PUBLIC ACTUALLY BELIEVES

Projection of the logic of science onto the thinking of the general public, however, leads to paradoxical results. For it is clear that although most of the American public reject racist beliefs, unlike social scientists they do not emphasize environmental explanations of racial differences. In the study "Racial Attitudes in Fifteen American Cities," directed by Angus Campbell and myself, the following question was asked early in 1968 of a probability sample of 2,584 urban white Americans: "On the average, Negroes in this city have worse jobs, education, and housing than white people. Do you think this is due mainly to Negroes having been discriminated against, or mainly due to something about Negroes themselves?"[2]

---

[1] These figures are reported in Mildred A. Schwartz. *Trends in White Attitudes Toward Negroes*, National Opinion Research Center, Chicago, 1967.

[2] For a general report of the study and a more detailed description of the sample, see Angus Campbell and Howard Schuman, "Racial Attitudes in Fifteen American Cities," in *Supplemental Studies for the National Advisory Commission on Civil Disorders*, July, 1968, U.S. Government Printing Office, Washington, D.C. (Reprinted by Frederick A. Praeger, Publishers, New York, 1968, and by the Institute for Social Research, Ann Arbor, 1969.) The sample discussed here is of the white population, ages 16–69, in the combined 15 cities. The cities are: Baltimore, Boston, Brooklyn, Chicago, Cincinnati, Cleveland, Detroit, Gary, Milwaukee, Newark, Philadelphia, Pittsburgh, San Francisco, St. Louis, and Washington. Results from two suburban areas (around Cleveland and Detroit) are essentially the same.

More than half the sample—54 percent —believes that the inferior economic and educational status of Negroes is due mainly to Negroes themselves. (See Table, Question A.) Only 19 percent places the blame mainly on discrimination, while another 19 percent sees the cause as a mixture of discrimination and "Negroes themselves." It is interesting to note that 4 percent of the sample spontaneously denied the initial assumption of the question, claiming that in their city Negroes have jobs, education, and housing equal to or better than that of whites. This is another indication of how misleading it is for social scientists to assume public knowledge and acceptance of the findings of social science—in this case descriptive findings rather than explanatory ones. Finally, 4 percent of the sample gave "don't know" answers to the question.

The term "discriminated against" was used in the question as a simple way of representing certain environmental causes of Negro behavior, but it may have failed to provide sufficient opportunity for other environmental views, such as the stress on Negro lower-class background. However, a general follow-up question (discussed further below) encouraged respondents to explain their ideas in their own words, and another 18 percent could be identified as giving some sort of apparent environmental explanation, principally the lower education of Negroes, although lower education was already built into the question as part of the problem to be explained. It may well be that many whites giving this answer would attribute the cause of low education to Negroes themselves, but even if we assume an emphasis on environment in this response and add this 18 percent to the 19 percent who mentioned discrimination explicitly, we still find only 37 percent of the total sample attributing Negro disadvantage to causes outside Negroes themselves. More than half the sample places the responsibility for Negro disadvantage mainly or entirely on Negroes.

Somewhat similar results are reported from a July 1968 Gallup Opinion Survey with a national sample. The Gallup question reads: "Who do you think is *more* to blame for the present conditions in which Negroes find themselves—white people, or Negroes themselves?" Only 24 percent of the white population blamed "itself"; 54 percent blamed "Negroes themselves"; and 22 percent had no opinion.

Our results appear at first to contradict the NORC trends that show a sharp drop in white beliefs in Negro racial inferiority in intelligence. If Negro problems are attributed mainly to "something about Negroes themselves," doesn't this imply a racist explanation? The answer may be yes to the scientific determinist, but it is not necessarily yes to the general public.

The situation is considerably clarified by the follow-up questions we asked of the 73 percent of the sample (1,886 cases) who attributed lower Negro achievements to Negroes themselves or to a mixture of Negroes themselves and discrimination. We inquired first, "What is it about Negroes themselves that makes them have worse jobs, education, and housing?" and recorded the responses *verbatim*. (See Table, Question B.) No matter what the answer, we then asked: "Do you think Negroes are just born that way and can't be changed, or that changes in the Negro are possible?" Skipping over the free answer question for the moment, we found to our surprise that whatever the faults Negroes were seen as having, only 8 percent of the respondents saw these limitations as inborn and unchangeable, while 88 percent believed "changes in the Negro are possible." (See Table, Question C.)

We thus find that a considerable portion of the white urban population believes that the source of Negro hardships lies within Negroes themselves, but denies that this source is inborn and unchangeable. The white public therefore appears simultaneously to accept and to reject racist beliefs.

"THEY DON'T TRY"

The resolution of this paradox is suggested by the free answers to the question: "What is it about Negroes themselves that makes them have worse jobs, education and housing?" These answers were coded into the most meaningful categories inherent in the data, with the following results: Only 8 percent of those asked the question speak in terms that imply or strongly suggest biological or genetic differences—e.g., "low mental ability," "low morals"—between Negroes and whites, and the number mentioning low intelligence as such is even smaller. This certainly does not contradict the NORC trend data presented earlier, but only accentuates it. Answers that lean in an environmental direction—e.g., "lack of education," "poverty cycle," but *not* "discrimination"—are given by a somewhat larger portion (25 percent) of the follow-up sample. By far the largest category of response, however, does not point clearly in either a genetic *or* an environmental direction, but is best termed "lack of motivation"; 57 percent of those attributing Negro problems to Negroes themselves give such a response clearly, and another 10 percent offer related responses having much the same implication. Some examples from the interviews of "lack of motivation" responses are the following:

Well, they don't try to better themselves. I've come up through the ranks. I've worked at just about everything. And now I'm at a job where I'm happy and just about making top money. And they can do the same. Get out and look.

They have the same advantages the whites have but don't use them. They quit school. They quit work.

They pity themselves too much. We have Negro friends from the service; one is a hard worker and he has made something of himself. Many don't try to better themselves.

Responses like these outnumber responses focusing on mental or other lack of capacity by about seven to one.

We now have three interlocking clues to the kinds of reasoning about racial differences that most white Americans are engaged in. First, the cause of low Negro status is perceived to lie mainly within Negroes themselves, rather than in the external constraints imposed by American social structure or by the

prejudice of white Americans. Second, this internal factor is seen as a matter of motivation or will, not as a matter of capacity or ability. And third, it is not seen as either immutable or ineluctable, but rather as something that can readily be changed.

Changed by whom? For much of the white public, the implicit answer is: by individual Negroes themselves. Evidently a great many white Americans believe in a naive form of free will. Negroes can get ahead at any time, whites feel, simply by setting their sights higher and putting their shoulders to the wheel. The philosophical problem of free will is rarely mentioned, to be sure, but free will is clearly what the general public takes to be an explanation of how individual men and entire ethnic groups can, do, and should achieve success in America.

FREE WILL AND ITS BASIS

There is really nothing surprising in public commitment to the assumption of free will. It must in some form be built into every society, since elders and authorities usually feel it necessary to impress upon children and citizens that they are responsible for their own actions. While it may be that a person fails to live up to an important social norm only because of the way he was brought up or only because of the way his endocrine system functions, others in the society will not wish him to attribute his deviant behavior too easily to such causes. They will want him to hold himself responsible for his actions, and to believe that he can change if he wants to and tries hard enough.

Beyond this universal social need to hold individuals responsible for their actions, in America the emphasis on free will has an additional and very powerful cultural source in the belief that each immigrant group has started at the bottom and proceeded by ambition and effort alone to work its way toward the top. The second, third, or n-th generation descendants of immigrants are usually ready to recount vivid tales of ancestral initiative and industry. Told that Negroes have come from unskilled backgrounds, lack capital and connections, face prejudice and discrimination, many a white American will assert with pride that all this was true of his own parents as well, or of his grandparents, or of at least an uncle or two. He will point out that despite tremendous obstacles his forebears succeeded in America, and that is exactly why they now have their house in the suburbs, their children in college, and the respect of their neighbors. He will assure the listener that Negroes can do as much at any point if only they will exert the effort.

This explanation of why white Americans succeed and black Americans do not, while apparently satisfactory to the white public, will be dissatisfying to the social scientist. It explains nothing about how a motivational difference between white and black Americans, if indeed there is one, has come about. To get at deeper public explanations, social scientists can of course formulate more survey questions for the general population. By pushing a good deal we may force some respondents to assert a genetic-like explanation ("they must be born that way"), others to opt for a family structure explanation ("I guess it's the way their mothers and fathers brought them up"), and so forth. But such responses to probes are given mainly to satisfy the pressure of the interviewer—not because the average respondent himself feels that an explanation assuming free will leaves anything to be desired.

There may be a still more basic paradox underlying the oversimplification of public beliefs about race. In the struggle against earlier public conceptions of Negro inferiority, Negro leaders and white social scientists understandably stressed the essential similarity of Negroes and whites. Discrimination and lack of opportunity were presented as the primary, if not only, barriers to racial equality in achievement: remove these barriers, the implication went, and black performance will automatically and quickly equal that of whites. Insofar as the public accepted this not very subtle view of black disadvantage, it looked for

immediate results wherever equality of opportunity began to be approximated. In a sense, the average white person could say: "All right, Negroes have the same potential as whites. But then they should do as well in school, have no higher crime rate, achieve as well occupationally. If many continue to behave in undesirable ways and it is not because of lack of potential, then it must be lack of will, lack of desire." Given the invisibility of much discrimination, and the difficulty of appreciating its long-term psychological effects, the simplistic social science emphasis on immediate discrimination as the sole cause of black disadvantage leads to the simplistic free will interpretations of the public.

THE TERMS OF PUBLIC DISCUSSION TODAY

Our findings make it clear that much of the white public not only does not think in scientific terms about race; it does not even think in pseudoscientific terms. Whites do not look for deeper causes of black-white inequality because they assume this inequality can be overcome at any time by the very people suffering from it. Arguments over types of determinism are really irrelevant to this substantial part of the public, for they feel quite comfortable in thinking about race in the same simple free will terms that they use in thinking about individuals: those who really want to get ahead can do so.

Thus from one standpoint—certainly the black standpoint—the phrase "white racism" appears wholly appropriate. Most white Americans may not be racists in the more technical sense, but nothing said above suggests that they are willing to accept past or present responsibility for prejudice, discrimination, and general inequality in the spread of opportunities. In espousing free will, white Americans deny the reality of the problems faced by black Americans and thus place the whole burden of black disadvantage on blacks themselves. The distinctions concerning the definition of racism made here are, from such a standpoint, distinctions that do not make much of a difference.

In addressing white Americans today, however, it may be essential to take account of exactly the distinction drawn here between deterministic and free will viewpoints. What is more true, and more useful, to realize about the white American public than its supposed racist beliefs is the limited and naive perspective from which it views race and race relations. White Americans are, of course, caught up in their own lives and see the world from their own personal and limited perspective.

Not having experienced the world as black Americans have—a self-evident but nonetheless overwhelmingly important fact—the average white American simply has no conception of how heavily public institutions, values, and actions press down upon black Americans and work to convince them that no matter how great their efforts they will not be rewarded in American society. Most of all, white Americans do not understand that individual free will operates and has its beneficial effects only within institutional contexts that give it efficacy and purpose.

Questions and Responses Bearing on Free Will and Determinism

A. "On the average, Negroes in this city have worse jobs, education, and housing than white people. Do you think this is due mainly to Negroes having been discriminated against, or mainly due to something about Negroes themselves?"

	Percents
Mainly due to discrimination	19
Mainly due to Negroes themselves	54
A mixture of both	19
Denied Negroes have worse jobs, education, and housing—refused question	4
Don't know	4
	100 (2,584 cases)

B. "What is it about Negroes themselves that makes them have worse jobs, education, and housing?" (Asked only of those replying "mainly Negroes themselves" or "mixture" to Question A.)

	Percents
Responses that suggest genetic explanations of Negro disadvantage (e.g., "low mental ability")	8
Responses that may indicate environmental explanations (other than discrimination) of Negro disadvantage (e.g., "lack of education")	25
Responses that suggest lack of motivation as explanation of Negro disadvantage—no indication of genetic or environmental cause	57
Don't know, not ascertained	10
	100 (1,886 cases)

C. "Do you think Negroes are just born that way and can't change, or that changes in the Negro are possible?" (Asked only of those asked Question B.)

	Percents
Born that way and can't be changed	8
Changes are possible	88
Don't know	4
	100 (1,886 cases)

27

Black Powerlessness in Chicago

Harold M. Baron

Until recently, the three principal targets of the civil-rights movement in the North were discrimination and inferior conditions in (1) housing for Negroes, (2) jobs for Negroes, and (3) the education of Negroes. But after failing to bring about major changes, many Negroes realized that one reason the status quo in housing, jobs, and education continues is that *the black community lacks control over decision-making.* Negroes remain second-class citizens partly because of the discrimination of individual whites, but mainly because of the way whites control the major institutions of our society. And therefore the fourth major goal of Negro organizations and the civil-rights movement has become the acquisition of power.

It was because of this concern with power for black people that, more than two years ago, the Chicago Urban League—a social-welfare organization dedicated to changing institutions so as to achieve full racial equality—started to study the decision-making apparatus in Cook County, Ill., and particularly how it affects or ignores Negro citizens. (Cook County takes in the city of Chicago, and two-thirds of the population of the surrounding

Harold M. Baron is Director of the Urban Studies Program for the Associated Colleges of the Midwest.

suburban ring included in the Chicago Standard Metropolitan Statistical area.) Among the questions we posed were:

- What is the extent of Negro exclusion from policy-making positions in Chicago?
- Where Negroes *are* in policy-making positions, what type of positions are these, and where are Negroes in greatest number and authority?
- Do Negroes in policy-making positions represent the interests of the Negro community? and
- How might an increase in the percentage of Negro policy-makers affect socio-economic conditions for Negroes in general?

What we found was that in 1965 some 20 per cent of the people in Cook County were Negro, and 28 per cent of the people in Chicago were Negro. Yet the representations of Negroes in policy-making positions was minimal. Of the top 10,997 policy-making positions in the major Cook County institutions included in our study, Negroes occupied only 285—or 2.6 per cent.

In government (see Table 1), out of a total of 1088 policy-making positions Negroes held just 58. This 5 per cent is about one-fourth of the percentage of Negroes in the total county population. Of the 364 elective posts in the survey, however, Negroes occupied 29, or 8 per cent, indicating that the franchise has helped give Negroes representation. Yet Negroes had the most positions, percentagewise, on appointed supervisory boards, such as the Board of Education and the Chicago Housing Authority. There they occupied 10 of the 77 policy-making positions, or about 13 per cent.

Negroes were better represented on appointed supervisory boards and in elected (nonjudicial) offices than they were in local administrative positions, or in important federal jobs based in Chicago. Thus, Negroes held 12 per cent of the nonjudicial elected posts in Chicago's government, but only a little over 1 per cent of the appointive policy-making positions in the city administration. The same anomaly appears at the federal level. There is one Negro out of the 13 U.S. Congressmen

TABLE 1. *The Exclusion of Negroes from Government: Policy-Making Positions in the Cook County Public Sector (1965)*

	Policy-making positions	Positions held by Negroes	%
1. Elected officials			
U.S. House of			
Representatives	13	1	8
State legislature	120	10	8
Cook County—			
nonjudicial	34	3	9
Chicago—nonjudicial	59	7	12
Cook County—			
judicial	138	8	6
Total:	364	29	8
2. Appointive supervisory boards			
Total:	77	10	13
3. Local administrative positions			
City of Chicago	156	2	1
Chicago Board of Education	72	7	9
Metropolitan Sanitary District	7	0	0
Cook County government	13	1	8
Total:	248	10	4
4. Federal government			
Civil service	368	8	2
Presidential appointments	31	1	3
Total:	399	9	2
Grand total:	1088	58	5

TABLE 2. *The Exclusion of Negroes from Private Institutions: Policy-Making Positions in the Cook County Private Sector (1965)*

	Policy-making positions	Positions held by Negroes	%
1. Business corporations			
Banks	2258	7	a
Insurance	533	35	6
Nonfinancial corporations	4047	0	0
Total:	6838	42	a
2. Legal profession			
Total:	757	0	0
3. Universities[b]			
Total:	380	5	1
4. Voluntary organizations			
Business and professional	324	3	1
Welfare and religious	791	69	9
Total:	1115	72	6
5. Labor unions			
Internationals	94	15	16
District councils	211	20	9
Locals	514	73	14
Total:	819	108	13
Grand total:	9909	227	2
Grand total for public and private sectors:	10,997	285	2

[a] Below 1 per cent.
[b] Includes the University of Illinois, which is a public body.

from Cook County (8 per cent), but Negroes held only one out of 31 Presidential appointments (3 per cent), and eight of the 368 top federal civil-service posts (2 per cent).

Nonetheless, Negroes have—proportionately—two-and-half-times as many important posts in the public sector as they have in the private sector. As Table 2 indicates, Negroes are virtually barred from policy-making positions in the large organizations that dominate the private institutions in the Chicago area. Out of a total of 9909 positions, Negroes fill a

mere 227. This 2 per cent representation is only one-tenth of the proportionate Negro population.

The whitest form of policy-making in Chicago is in the control of economic enterprises. Out of 6838 positions identified in business corporations, Negroes held only 42 (six-tenths of 1 per cent). Thirty-five of these were in insurance, where Negroes occupy 6 per cent of the 533 posts. But all 35 were in two all-Negro insurance firms. The other seven positions were in four smaller banks. In banks in general, Negroes occupied three-tenths of 1 per cent of the policy posts. There were no

Negro policy-makers at all in manufacturing, communications, transportation, utilities, and trade corporations.

Out of the 372 companies we studied, the Negro-owned insurance companies were the only ones dominated by blacks (see Table 3). And if we had used the same stringent criteria for banks and insurance companies that we used for nonfinancial institutions, there would have been no black policy-makers in the business sector at all.

Now, amazingly enough, Chicago has proportionately more Negro-controlled businesses, larger than neighborhood operations, than any other major city in the North. Therefore, similar surveys in other Northern metropolitan areas would turn up an even smaller percentage of Negro policy-makers in the business world.

The legal profession, represented by corporate law firms, had no Negroes at high policy levels. We are convinced that the same situation would be found in other professions, such as advertising and engineering.

The very prestigious universities—the University of Chicago, Northwestern University, Loyola University, DePaul University, Roosevelt University, the Illinois Institute of Technology, and the University of Illinois (the only public university of the seven)—had a negligible 1 per cent Negro representation. Most of these universities had few Negro students, faculty members, or administrators. Five of the seven had no Negro policy-makers. The University of Illinois had one. Roosevelt University, the sole institution that had a number of Negroes at the top, was the newest, and the one with the least public support. When this university was founded, its leaders had made a forthright stand on racial questions and a firm commitment to liberal principles.

We included these major universities in our survey because other institutions—public and private—have been placing increasingly greater value on them. Every year hundreds of millions of dollars in endowment and operating funds are given to the Chicago-area schools. After all, their research activities, and their training of skilled personnel, are con-

TABLE 3. *The Exclusion of Negroes from Private Establishments: Percentage of Negro Policy-Makers in the Cook County Private Sector by Establishment (1965)*

	Total establish-ments	None	Percentage of Negro policy-makers			
			1–5%	6–15%	16–50%	51% +
1. Business corporations						
Banks	102	98	0	4	0	0
Insurance	30	28	0	0	0	2
Nonfinancial corporations	240	240	0	0	0	0
2. Legal professions	54	54	0	0	0	0
3. Universities[a]	7	5	0	2	0	0
4. Voluntary organizations						
Business and professional	5	3	2	0	0	0
Welfare and religious	14	2	4	7	1	0
5. Labor unions						
Internationals	4	0	1	1	2	0
District councils	23	13	0	5	5	0
Locals	33	14	2	8	7	2
Total:	512	457	9	27	15	4

[a] Includes the University of Illinois, which is a public body.

sidered a key to the region's economic growth. One indication of the tremendous influence these universities have is that they have determined the nature of urban renewal more than any other institutional group in Chicago (aside from the city government). Without a doubt, the universities have real—not nominal—power. And perhaps it is a reflection of this real power that only five out of 380 policy-making positions in these universities are held by Negroes.

The exclusion of Negroes from the private sector carries over to its voluntary organizations: Negroes are found in only 1 per cent of the posts there. It is in the voluntary associations that it is easiest to make symbolic concessions to the black community by giving token representation, yet even here Negroes were underrepresented—which highlights the fundamental norms of the entire sector.

The sectors and individual groups in the Chicago area with the highest Negro representation were those with a Negro constituency—elective offices, supervisory boards, labor unions, and religious and welfare organizations. These four groups accounted for 216 of the posts held by Negroes, or 75 per cent, although these four groups have only 19 per cent of all the policy-making positions we studied. Labor unions had a larger percentage—13 per cent—than any other institution in the private sector. In welfare and religious organizations, whose constituents were often largely Negro, Negroes occupied 8 per cent of the positions, the same percentage of the elected public offices they held.

Now, either the black constituency elected the Negroes directly (in the case of elective offices and trade unions); or the Negroes were appointed to posts in an operation whose clients were largely Negro (principal of a Negro school, for example); or Negroes were given token representation on bodies that had a broad public purpose (like religious organizations). By "token representation," we mean—following James Q. Wilson—that "he is a man chosen because a Negro is 'needed' in order to legitimate [but not direct] whatever decisions are made by the agency."

Of the three ways a black constituency had of getting itself represented, the most important was the first. The statistics clearly show the importance of the Negro vote. The elected political offices and the elected trade-union offices account for only 11 per cent of all the policy-making positions in Cook County. Yet almost half of all the Negro policy-makers were found in these two areas—137 out of 285.

Nonetheless, even in the major areas where Negro representation was the greatest—labor unions, elective offices, supervisory boards, and religious and welfare organizations—many institutions still excluded Negroes from positions of authority.

There are, of course, few Negroes in the building-trade unions, most of which bar Negroes from membership. Only two out of the 12 building-trade-union organizations we studied had even one Negro in a decisive slot. These two Negroes made up a mere one and a half per cent of the policy-making positions in the building-trade unions.

The greatest degree of black representation was found in the former C.I.O. industrial unions. Only one-fourth of these units in the survey totally excluded Negroes from leadership. In almost half, the percentage of Negro policy-makers was over 15 per cent—which is above token levels.

The former A.F. of L. unions (not including those in the building trades) had a higher rate of exclusion than those of the C.I.O. Two-fifths of these A.F. of L. unions had no Negroes at all in policy-making posts. But one-third of this group had leaderships that were 15 per cent or more Negro. And the only two black-controlled locals large enough to be included in this study were in A.F. of L. unions.

In elective offices, the Negro vote certainly does give Negroes some representation—though far below their proportionate number. In public administration, however, where advancement to policy-making offices comes through appointment and influence, Negroes are all but excluded from decisive posts, at both the federal and local levels. Although a very high percentage of all Negro professionals are in public service, they do not reach the top.

The only major governmental operation that had a goodly number of Negroes at the upper level of the bureaucratic hierarchy was the public-school system. Nine per cent of the top positions were occupied by Negroes. This unique situation is the result of some fairly recent appointments, made as concessions after an intense civil-rights campaign directed at the Chicago Board of Education. In this instance, one can consider these civil-rights actions as a proxy for Negro votes. Still, this high-level representation in the Chicago school hierarchy did not seem to reflect any uniform policy of including Negroes in management. At the level of principalship, which was not included as a policy-making position in this study, only 3 per cent of the positions were occupied by blacks.

The voluntary welfare and religous associations that were sufficiently important to be included in the study usually had at least a few Negro policy-makers. Only two out of 14 bodies had no Negroes in policy positions (see Table 3), while four organizations had token representation—below 5 per cent. None had a Negro majority in the key posts. Only the Chicago Urban League (with 43 per cent) had Negroes in more than 15 per cent of its policy slots. If individual religious denominations had been among the organizations counted in the survey, there would have been some black-dominated groups. As it was, Negro representation in the United Protestant Federation, which *was* included, came largely from the traditionally Negro denominations. It is of interest to note that, in recent years, Protestant groups have provided some of the few instances in which Negroes have been elected to important offices by a constituency that was overwhelmingly white.

Not only were Negroes grossly under-represented in Chicago's policy-making posts, but even where represented they had less power than white policy-makers. The fact is that *the number of posts held by Negroes tended to be inversely related to the power*

vested in these positions—the more powerful the post, the fewer the black policy-makers.

As we have seen, Negroes were virtually excluded from policy-making in the single most powerful institutional sector—the business world. In *all* sectors, they were generally placed in positions in which the authority was delegated from a higher administrator, or divided among a board. Rarely were Negroes in positions of ultimate authority, either as chief executive or as top board officer.

When Negroes ran for a board or for a judicial office on a slate, their number had been limited by the political parties apportioning out the nominations. The percentage of Negroes on such boards or (especially) in judicial offices tended to run lower than the number of Negroes in legislative posts, for which Negroes run individually.

It is also true that no Negro has *ever* been elected to one of the key city-wide or county-wide executive positions, such as Mayor, City Clerk, or President of the Cook County Board. These are the positions with the greatest power and patronage.

In welfare agencies, where Negroes have token representation, they are virtually excluded from the key posts of executive director. Only five of the 135 directors of medium and of large welfare agencies were Negro.

Now, it was in the trade-union sector that the highest percentage of Negroes had policy posts— 13 per cent. We asked several experts on the Chicago trade-union movement to list the number of Negroes among the 100 most powerful trade unionists in the area. Among the 100 people they named, the number of Negroes ranged from two to five. This did not surprise us, for it was compatible with our general knowledge of the number of Negroes with truly powerful posts in other sectors.

A RULE OF THUMB ON NEGRO POWER

All in all, then, we would suggest the following rule of thumb: *The actual power vested in*

Negro policy-makers is about one-third as great as the percentage of the posts they hold.

Thus when Negroes elected other Negroes to office, these officers tended to represent small constituencies. For example, the greatest number of Negroes in legislative posts came from relatively small districts that happen to have black majorities. Indeed, according to Cook County tradition, Negroes simply do not hold legislative posts in city, state, or federal government *unless* they represent a district that is mostly black. No district with Negroes in the minority had a Negro representative, even when Negroes constituted the single largest ethnic group. And some districts with a Negro majority had a *white* representative.

Then too, the smaller the district, the more likely it would be homogeneous, and the greater the chances of its having a black majority that could return a Negro to office. In the Chicago area, consequently, Negroes were best represented on the City Council, which is based on 50 relatively small wards, each representing about 70,000 people; Negroes were represented most poorly in the U.S. House of Representatives, for which there are only nine rather large districts in Chicago, each representing about 500,000 people.

Most of the government policy-making posts that Negroes had been appointed to were in operations that had a large Negro clientele, if not a majority—as in the case of the Chicago public schools; or in operations that had largely Negro personnel, as in the case of the post office. On the appointed supervisory boards, in fact, those with as many as two Negro members were the Chicago Board of Education and the Board of Health, both of which serve very large numbers of Negroes.

This limiting of Negro policy-makers to Negro constituencies was quite as evident in the private sector. Three of the four banks with Negroes in policy-making posts were in Negro neighborhoods; and two were the smallest of the 102 banks we studied, and the other two were not much larger. The two insurance firms had mainly Negro clients, and

were among the smallest of the 30 studied. In the voluntary organizations, the more they served Negroes, the higher the percentage of Negroes on their boards (although representation was by no means proportionate). Thus, the five Negro executive directors of welfare organizations we studied headed all-Negro constituencies: Three directed moderate-sized neighborhood settlements in the ghetto; one directed a virtually all-Negro hospital; and one directed an interracial agency that had traditionally had a Negro executive.

Still another way of limiting the power of Negro policy-makers, we discovered, was by "processing" them. Public and private institutions, as indicated, tend to have a token representation of Negroes. And many Negroes in these positions have totally identified with the traditional values and goals of the institution, regardless of what they mean to the mass of Negroes. Some of these Negro policy-makers, because of their small numbers and lack of an independent source of power, are neutralized. Others, if they are firm in representing the needs and outlook of the black community, are isolated. The two Negro members of the Chicago Board of Education represented these extremes. Mrs. Wendell Green, a longtime Board member and the elderly widow of a former judge, had been the most diehard supporter of Benjamin Willis, the former Schools Superintendent, through all of his fights against the civil-rights movement. The other Negro—Warren Bacon, a business executive— sympathized with the campaign against inferior, segregated housing and, as a result, has been largely isolated on the Board. He was rarely consulted on critical questions. His vote was usually cast with a small minority, and sometimes alone.

The fact is that the norms and traditions of *any* organization or enterprise limit the amount of power held by black policy-makers. It is no longer bold to assert that the major institutions and organizations of our society have an operational bias that is racist, even though their *official* policies may be the opposite. The Negro policy-maker in one of these institutions (or in a small black-controlled organization dependent upon these institutions, such as the head of a trade-union local) has a certain degree of conflict. If he goes along with the institution, from which he gains power and prestige, he ends up by implementing operations that restrict his minority group. Edward Banfield and James Q. Wilson have neatly pinpointed this dilemma in the political sphere:

> Not only are few Negroes elected to office, but those who are elected generally find it necessary to be politicians first and Negroes second. If they are to stay in office, they must soft-pedal the racial issues that are of the most concern to Negroes as Negroes.

This pattern is seen in the failure of William Dawson, Cook County's one Negro Congressman, to obtain many Presidential appointments or top federal civil-service posts for Negroes. Theoretically he is in a more strategic position to influence government operations than any other Chicago-based Congressman, since he has 23 years' seniority and holds the important chairmanship of the Government Operations Committee. Yet in 1965 Negroes held only 2 per cent of the top federal jobs in Chicago.

Any examination of the real power of Negroes in Chicago requires an examination of the strongest single organization in the Negro community—the Democratic Party. Wilson's study, *Negro Politics*, points out that the strength and cohesiveness of the Negro Democratic organization is largely dependent upon the strength of the total Cook County Democratic organization. The Negro organization is a "sub-machine" within the larger machine that dominates the city. The Negro sub-machine, however, has basically settled for lesser patronage positions and political favors, rather than using its considerable strength to try to make or change policy. Therefore, this Negro organization avoids controversial questions, and seeks to avoid differences with the central organization on such vital issues as urban renewal and the schools.

In short, then, not only are Negroes underrepresented in the major policy-making positions in Cook County, but even where represented their actual power is restricted, or their representatives fail to work for the long-term interests of their constituency. It is therefore safe to estimate that Negroes really hold less than 1 per cent of the effective power in Chicago metropolitan area. Realistically, the power structure of Chicago is hardly less white than that of Mississippi.

From these figures it is clear that, at this time, Negroes in the Chicago area lack the power to make changes in the areas of housing, jobs, and education. The basic subjugation of the black community, however, would not end if there were simply more Negroes in policy-making posts. We have seen the prevalence of tokenism, of whites' choosing Negro leaders who are conservative, of their boxing in Negro leaders who are proved to be liberal, of their giving these leaders less actual power than they give themselves.

Our analysis suggests that the best way to increase both the number *and* the power of Negro policy-makers is through unifying the black constituency. Access to policy-making positions could come through both the development of large, black-controlled organizations, and through getting Negroes into white-dominated organizations. If the constituency lacks its own clear set of goals and policies, however, things will surely remain the same. For success depends not just upon formal unity, but upon the nature of the goals set by the black community. In this situation, the overcoming of black powerlessness seems to require the development of a self-conscious community that has the means to determine its own interests, and the cohesiveness to command the loyalty of its representatives. We can safely predict that more and more Negroes will be moved into policy-making positions. The fundamental conflict, therefore, will take place between their co-optation into the established institutions and their accountability to a black constituency.

POSTSCRIPT–1974*

Almost a decade has passed since the base year (1965) of the study "Black Powerlessness in Chicago." At that time the successes of the civil-rights movement had already generated considerable uncertainty among business and government leadership regarding their essentially status quo racial strategies. The massive black uprisings from Watts in 1965 to those following the assassination of Dr. Martin Luther King, Jr. gave a sharp acceleration to this shift in establishment posture. Military repression of these uprisings was accompanied by a rapid increase in the granting of concessions to black people. Concomitantly, through their involvement in the struggles of the 1960's, black people gained a sense of self-consciousness and self-confidence which heightened their identification as a community seeking to control its own destiny.

In spite of these dramatic developments, the accession of blacks to established positions of decision-making authority has not increased sufficiently to cause an important shift in racial power relations. Although there has been a noticeable growth in the numbers of black occupants of decision-making positions, the qualitative gain in terms of these persons' ability to exercise the full potential of power formally vested in the offices has not been as great. The black proportion of the population has also grown in this interval so that it now comprises about 36 percent of the city of Chicago and 23 percent of Cook County. While the proportion of black holders of policy positions has increased at a somewhat greater rate than that of the population, the ratio of these two proportions for Cook County has at most shifted from 1 to 10 to 1 to 7.

Within the business sector the exclusion of blacks is still the most marked. A study of the largest 106 Chicago corporations, con-

---

* The major source of data for this postscript is the files of *The Chicago Reporter*, published monthly by the Community Renewal Society. This postscript appears here for the first time. It was not included in the original article that appeared in *Trans*-action.

ducted by Russell Barta, showed that in 1972 there was only one black out of a total of 1355 officers. On the more honorific boards of directors there were five out of 1341 members. It is noteworthy that the majority of these black directorships were for the three largest public utilities, which are regulated by governmental commissions. Black-controlled business enterprises have expanded enough so that currently more qualify for inclusion under the original study's criteria. In addition to the two insurance companies included in 1965, two banks and two industrials are now large enough and would add 40 to 50 additional black decision-makers to the totals. The reader should keep in mind that the relative scale of black business is still miniscule. For the nation as a whole, the top 100 black businesses taken together are only as large as the two hundred sixty-second largest white firm.

The legal field, as an example of the professions that service the business community, is just as exclusive as its clients. A survey of the 17 most prestigious Chicago law firms revealed one black in a total of 676 partners.

The largest proportionate increase in blacks occupying positions of power took place in elective political offices. Of the present 58 Chicago elected officials, 16 are black (15 Aldermen plus the City Treasurer). There are now two black members of the U.S. House of Representatives and 18 state legislators from the city. In addition, movement has taken place into top positions within the legislative bodies—President Pro-tem of the City Council and Democratic minority leader in the Illinois Senate. On the Circuit Court of Cook County, blacks now comprise 10 percent of the sitting judges. Starting from a lower base in 1965, there has been approximately a tripling of black holders of top public administrative posts. Most of this growth has occurred in areas with a large black clientele, notably the Chicago Board of Education, with a 56 percent black student body, and in city agencies administering war on poverty-type programs.

In private voluntary organizations, the biggest shift has been in board memberships. A 1973 survey of six major universities revealed nine blacks out of 280 trustees. The proportion among top administrators was smaller. The united welfare fund-raising operation, the Community Fund, has nine blacks out of its 50 board members and one out of its six key staff officers. Five percent of their appropriations go to minority-controlled projects. The five largest philanthropic foundations have a single black among their 54 trustees, and four percent of their allocations go to minority-controlled operations. Although we do not have a recent study on trade unions, no new black leader has emerged to major prominence within the Chicago labor movement.

As in 1965 the bulk of black incumbency in policy positions occurs where blacks have some kind of electoral involvement in the process of selection or constitute a mobilizible clientele. Otherwise, black inclusion in policy-making positions is largely on a symbolic or honorific basis. Even where tokenism was not a manifest intent in their appointment, the blacks on boards usually do not have an independent power base from which they can bargain or threaten in conflict situations. In the same vein, elected black office holders have not forged an independent bloc in either the city council or the state legislature.

Overall, blacks are hardly nearer the command posts of power than they were in 1965. It is true that more blacks are now involved in the making of operating decisions to meet the pre-established maintenance and aggrandizement goals of major institutions, but they have not been able to lever their positions for the implementing of new strategies predicated upon goals generated from the black community.

The gains the black community has made in its ability to determine its future have been accomplished through a much more diffuse process than that of a significant move into the established power structures. The means for accomplishing this increase in the power of black people have been such factors as: political and social mobilization; legal maneuvering; the challenging of the ideological hegemony of white America; and the willingness of the black working class and dispossessed to resort to extra-legal protest. Although this strengthening of the black community has been very incomplete and uneven, it has provided directly or indirectly the major impetus for whatever improvement has taken place. This increased power is not of the sort to set national and regional priorities or to chart the strategies of dominant social and economic institutions. However, it has operated to widen the hold on stable, well-paid working-class employment, to create entree to technical and lower-level management jobs, to lower the level of tolerated black unemployment, to raise the amounts of government transfer payments to the mass of unemployed black people, and to increase the quantity and quality of the housing stock.

28

Black Executives
in Big Business

JOHN EGERTON

A STOCKHOLDER: *Mr. Chairman, you have lied about your record of progress. You have told the shareholders about the 100,000 employees, black employees, of General Motors but you have not said that none of them are in top management positions. You have not told them that none of them are members of GM's Board of Directors. You have not told them that of 13,000 GM dealerships, ten of them, if that many, are black. Why are there no blacks on GM's Board of Directors?*

MR. ROCHE: *Because none have been elected.*

STOCKHOLDER: *I want an answer to that question. Why are there no blacks on your Board of Directors?*

MR. ROCHE: *No black has been nominated and no black has been elected.*

STOCKHOLDER: *Why have none been nominated?*

MR. ROCHE: *I can't answer that.*

STOCKHOLDER: *Is GM not a racist corporation, is that what you are telling us?*

MR. ROCHE: *GM is not a racist corporation.*

STOCKHOLDER: *Then why have no blacks been elected to GM's Board of Directors?*

MR. ROCHE: *I have answered the question. I have nothing further to say.*

John Egerton is a reporter for the Race Relations Reporter.

Reprinted from *Race Relations Reporter* 17 (October 1, 1970) by permission.

STOCKHOLDER: *You have not answered the question.*

MR. ROCHE: *I have given you the answer. No black to my knowledge has ever been nominated, and, of course, if they are not nominated they can't be elected.*

STOCKHOLDER: *Why are there no women on your Board of Directors?*

MR. ROCHE: *Our directors are selected on the basis of their ability to make a contribution to the success of General Motors. There would be no bar to women who were nominated and had the qualifications that the stockholders believed were essential to helping direct the (company's) affairs.*

STOCKHOLDER: *Then why have you voted against Proposal No. 5 which nominates Mr. Phillips, a black man, a qualified one, and Betty Furness, a representative of consumers?*

MR. ROCHE: *Let's get on with the meeting.* Exchange between GM Chairman James M. Roche and a stockholder at the 1970 annual meeting of the corporation, as reported in the Washington Post (*July 10, 1970*).

General Motors and its beleaguered chairman are not alone in their exposure to the charge of discrimination at the top. In the executive suites and board rooms of 50 of the nation's largest corporations, there are 3,182 senior officers and directors. Only three of them are black men.

The 50 corporations are the pillars of American capitalism. They include the 23 largest industrial corporations, the six largest commercial banks, the six largest life insurance companies, the five largest retailing companies, the six largest transportation companies, and the four largest utilities. The almost total absence of blacks in their highest offices has been confirmed by a telephone survey just completed by the Race Relations Information Center and the Community News Service, a New York-based reporting agency.

Representatives of the 50 corporations were asked to indicate whether any blacks were among their senior executives and board members who are listed in the 1970 edition of

The nation's 23 largest industrial corporations are run by 880 senior executives and 238 others who serve as directors. NONE of them are black. The corporations are:

General Motors	Standard Oil of
Standard Oil	Calif.
(N.J.)	Ling-Temco-Vought
Ford	Du Pont
General Electric	Shell
IBM	Westinghouse
Chrysler	Electric
Mobil Oil	Standard Oil (Ind.)
Texaco	General Telephone
IT&T	Goodyear
Gulf	RCA
Western Electric	Swift
U. S. Steel	McDonnell Douglas

Poor's Register of Corporations, Directors, and Executives. The answers showed that there were no blacks among the 2,522 executives named in the register, and only three blacks among the 660 others named as directors.

While the number of women in these categories was not tabulated, a casual perusal of the listings indicates that their representation is also miniscule.

There are 836 top executive officers and 118 other directors in the nation's six largest banks. Only ONE of them—a director of the Chase Manhattan Bank—is black. The other five banks are:

BankAmerica
First National City Corp.
Manufacturers Hanover Corp.
J. P. Morgan
Western Bancorporation

The three blacks now serving as corporation directors are Thomas A. Wood at Chase Manhattan Bank, Robert C. Weaver at Metropolitan Life Insurance Co., and Clifton R. Wharton Jr. at Equitable Life Assurance Society of the United States. Wood is the president of TAW International Leasing, Inc. Weaver was Secretary of Housing and Urban Development in the Johnson administration, and later president of Bernard Baruch College, and Wharton is the president of Michigan State University.

The corporations included in the survey were taken from the top of *Fortune* magazine's annual listing of the nation's 750 largest industrial, banking, insurance, retailing, trans-

The six largest life insurance companies in the nation are in the leadership hands of 355 senior officers and 126 other directors. TWO of the directors—one at Metropolitan Life and one at Equitable Life—are black. The other four companies are:

Prudential   John Hancock
New York Life   Aetna

portation, and utilities corporations. Together, the 50 corporations in the survey have assets of over $420 billion dollars and employ more than 6.5 million people.

In most instances, answers to the survey questions were provided by corporate officials in the public relations or personnel divisions of the organizations. Only two of the corporations—General Electric and International Telephone and Telegraph—refused to participate. Larry Vaber, a public relations official at General Electric, said there were no blacks on the corporation's board of directors, but said he was not authorized to release employment figures by race. When he was told that almost all of the corporations were co-operating in the survey, Vaber said he would try again to get approval to release the information. He called back later to say he had been told "it is a hard and fast rule that we release this information only to the government." At IT & T, numerous inquiries by phone and letter resulted finally in a statement from John Fitzpatrick, director of public information, saying that "since the information is available from the U.S. Government, we usually don't participate in surveys of this kind."

(The information is not, in fact, available from the government. Under existing law, corporations are required to submit an annual report on employment by race. The report includes "white collar" employees in five categories: officials and managers, professional, technicians, sales workers, and office and cler-

> *104 top executive officers and 39 other directors run the five largest retailing companies in the nation. NONE of the executives or directors are black. The five companies:*
>
> Sears, Roebuck   J. C. Penney
> A&P
> Safeway
>   Kroger

ical. These categories are too broad to identify just the senior corporate executives. The corporations are not required to submit data on their board members, who are not classified as employees. Thus, no public record exists containing the information sought in this survey.)

After all attempts to get the data from General Electric and IT&T had failed, the Race Relations Information Center checked a number of unofficial sources and got what one of the sources called "virtual assurance" that none of the top corporate officers or board members of the two corporations are black.

Results of the survey were related to William H. Brown III, chairman of the federal

> *NONE of the 251 senior executives and NONE of the 86 others who serve as directors of the six largest transportation companies in the U.S. are black. The companies are:*
>
> Penn Central   Trans World Airlines
> United Air Lines   Pan American
> Southern Pacific   American Airlines

Equal Employment Opportunity Commission. Through an aide on his staff, Brown said, "These statistics corroborate what EEOC has found again and again in its studies and in its hearings: that systems of discrimination and tokenism are entrenched throughout American industry. EEOC will become an effective force to combat such systems of discrimination only when we are granted enforcement powers by the Congress. The statistics cited provide a clear-cut example of why this commission should be granted such enforcement powers."

The EEOC is the only federal regulatory agency without the authority to issue cease-and-desist orders when violations of its regulations are detected. A bill to give the agency

that authority is now pending in Congress, but its passage is not considered likely before adjournment.

Responding further to the corporation

> *NO blacks are among the 96 top officers or the 53 others on the boards of directors of the country's four largest utilities. The companies:*
>
> American Telephone & Telegraph
> Consolidated Edison
> Pacific Gas & Electric
> Southern California Edison

survey, Brown said, "The fact that this blatant discrimination is concentrated at the highest levels of American industry makes suspect the widely heralded protestations of good faith by business and labor leaders."

Brown's predecessor as chairman of EEOC, Clifford Alexander, said the results of the survey were "about what I expected. White America says continually to black America that it wants blacks to participate in the American dream, yet these statistics show that to succeed in that dream world, you have to be white. You still hear all the same excuses, but blatant, overt discrimination continues, and you just can't describe it as anything else.

"The executive suites and board rooms are like social clubs, and all the while these corporations are projecting a public relations image of awareness and involvement. They've succeeded in convincing the hard hats that blacks are getting preferential treatment, but black people know better, and this survey documents the fact that at those levels where the real power is, the seats are still reserved for whites only."

Alexander was appointed chairman of the EEOC in 1967 by President Johnson. He resigned in 1969 with a blast at the Nixon administration for lack of commitment to equal employment opportunities for minorities.

Congressman William Clay (D-Mo.), one of nine black members in the House of Representatives and a frequent critic of discrimination in employment, said in reaction to the corporation survey that it "may be revealing to white Americans, but black America already knew it. It's indicative of the hypocrisy that exists in this country." Clay said that "at the top corporate levels, we are still in a period of pre-tokenism." Of the three black men who now serve on corporate boards of directors, Clay said he deplored any reference to them as "tokens" or "house niggers." "They should be commended for their willingness to serve," he said, "and the effort should be to increase their number. When there's only one black man on a board, he can make a motion—but there may not be anyone there to second it."

The 23 industrial corporations in the survey responded variously to the request for racial data. As indicated previously, two of them declined to answer at all. Of the remainder, most simply answered "no," without elaboration, and indicated a reluctance to discuss the matter further. At a few corporations, the requested information and additional data were freely volunteered.

Among the six commercial banks and the six life insurance companies surveyed, there appeared to be more black involvement at the corporate level than in the other types of corporations. The three black directors identified in the survey are all on bank or insurance company boards. In addition, several of the 12 institutions reported having black executives at the assistant vice president level, and one of them—Metropolitan Life Insurance Co.—said a black man now serves as a staff vice president at the corporate level and thus is one of the company's principal executive officers.

The Bank of America reported that one of the vice presidents of its New York subsidiary, Bank of America International, is E. Frederick Morrow, a Negro who formerly served as an administrative assistant to the late President Eisenhower. Aetna Life Insurance Co.'s mutual fund, a subsidiary operation, has a black on its board of directors in the person of Hobart Taylor, a lawyer and former administrative assistant to President Johnson, and the Prudential Insurance Co. had a black member of its board of directors until recently, when Samuel R. Pierce Jr. resigned to take an appointment in the Nixon administration.

Most of the banks and insurance companies also provided information on minority representation in their total work forces, and the figures they presented indicate that the percentages are above average. Chase Manhattan Bank, for example, said 31 per cent of its 21,000 domestic employees are from minority groups (22 per cent of them black).

The 15 corporations in the other three categories surveyed—retailing, transportation, and utilities—reported with little or no elaboration that their board of directors and top corporate executive positions include no blacks.

29

Powerless Politics

ROBERT K. THOMAS

To the average American, mention of the Sioux Indians brings to mind a picture of the classic, noble red man; a feathered warrior on horseback; the warrior chiefs—Crazy Horse and Sitting Bull; the conquerors of Custer finally receding before advancing civilization. And, in a large sense, there is a truth to this stereotyped picture.

The Sioux people today live on reservations in the northern plains states and they are still a warrior people. Eighty years of reservation life has been too short a time to bring about basic changes in the Sioux outlook. One of the most vital, colorful, and energetic bands of the Sioux, the Oglala, was settled on the Pine Ridge reservation in South Dakota. They are yet a vital, colorful, energetic people. They are yet warriors; but as one author put it, they are now warriors without weapons. The Bureau of Indian Affairs, one of America's oldest and most powerful bureaucracies, controls the destiny of the Oglala Sioux and has controlled it for these eighty years. As trustee of Sioux lands and resources it administers the affairs of the Pine Ridge Sioux. It provides needed social services like schools, roads, social welfare, etc. And it is entrusted by the Congress with the responsibility of promoting programs and innovations which will prepare the Sioux for eventual entry into "the mainstream of

Robert K. Thomas is Associate Professor at Monteith College of Wayne State University.

Reprinted from New University Thought 4 (Winter, 1966–67), pp. 44–53, by permission of the author and publisher.

American life." It is paradoxical that so capable a people as the Pine Ridge Sioux with such superior technical help provided by the federal government should so universally be considered a "problem" and evidence such social maladjustments as poverty, low level of education, alcoholism, juvenile delinquency, etc. It is my purpose in this paper to show why this is not paradoxical and why the "cause" of social problems is to be found in looking at the total system of relationships on the Pine Ridge Reservation, particularly at Pine Ridge's relation to the federal government, and the context of these relationships. Further along in the paper I am going to suggest that more and more of America is coming to resemble an American Indian reservation in terms of social problems and the relationship of the local community to the federal government (city slums and Appalachia are only two examples), and suggest that this process is perhaps coming about in many large nation-states in the world.

Of course, Pine Ridge is a "whole" and one must start an analysis of the total system of relationships at some point; one must have a "hook" to hang one's analysis on, an entry into this total system. I am arbitrarily choosing to look at "political" behavior, although I know that in an integrated society like Pine Ridge there are no such categories in people's experience.

I would like to describe political behavior among the Pine Ridge Sioux, or at the very least, to give a glimpse of and some understanding of their political behavior. But before I get into the main body of my paper I would like to tell something about the way I will proceed and some of the conceptual tools I will use to present this vignette of the Pine Ridge Sioux. As an anthropologist I want to take in as much of the total social situation as I can. I could look at the intersection of two social systems on the Pine Ridge reservation—on the one hand, the Sioux community, and on the other hand, the Bureau of Indian Affairs. One could learn a lot about political behavior just by looking at this intersection of the two social systems. However, I prefer to look at the Sioux community and to try to explain behavior in terms of the relationships in that community and to look at the intersection of the two social systems only in so far as it influences behavior within the Sioux community.

I will look at the Sioux community as a system of social relations rather than a social structure (a system of roles and statuses) because this allows me to focus on the relational aspect of interaction; on the meaning and content of interaction as well as the form. I can thus, for my purposes, make the bridge between the social and the cultural more easily. In other words, we can go from interaction to meaning; from form to content; from social system to culture; from behavior to perception. Further, in this paper, you will read of institution quite a bit. For my purposes, I would like to define institution as a set of social relations which come into being to do a particular task; a task that relates the community to some part of its environment. It follows from this narrow definition that kinship behavior as such will be excluded from my definition of institution. It may very well be the case that in urban society the "family" is an institution in the sense I am using it, but in a tribal society like the Sioux kinship relations are the basis of the society. A Sioux is a kinsman, by definition. Kin relations regulate such a society and permeate all tasks and activities. In aboriginal times, institutional forms were built upon the kinship system so that even in institutional contexts kinsmen dealt *as* kinsmen with other kinsmen. Kinship relations are implicitly a part of modern Sioux life.

Now let us look at the Sioux themselves. The Sioux tribe in the 1600's were living in the forests of Minnesota. They lived a style of life very much like the Chippewa of that same period. They were forest hunters whose social relations were regulated by a generational kinship system. Political and economic institutions were rudimentary. In the 1700's the Sioux began to move out on to the plains and there developed into the warriors and buffalo hunters par-excellence in North America. They borrowed many customs, traits, and institutions from the Earth Lodge people which

allowed them to meet their new environment successfully. A highly complex set of institutions, Chief's Council, warrior societies, the Sun-dance, etc., which were built on this generational kinship structure.

With the coming of the white man the situation changed drastically. The buffalo were exterminated, and the proverbial rug was pulled out from under the Sioux, at least economically speaking. The Sioux were conquered by force of arms and confined to reservations. They were in a large sense prisoners of war who were dependent upon their captors for the very food for their families. The Ghost Dance, an intense nativistic reaction in the 1890's, was their last protest against this new, uncomfortable and disruptive situation.

From around 1900 to 1920, Sioux society entered a period of stability. To the older Sioux living today this was a golden age. Tribal peoples generally look for cues outside of themselves to tell them what to do; traditional rules. Since traditional cues and traditional institutions had failed the Sioux, they now looked to authority in the place of tradition—in this case, the representatives of the powerful, benevolent, quasi-sacred, "Washington."

The Bureau of Indian Affairs during this period indeed provided a structure and a stability. The Bureau used those native institutions which still existed such as the Chief's Council to deal with the local community. They introduced the Sioux to cattle raising. This occupation was compatible with the Sioux personality. Kin groups worked their cattle together and the Bureau of Indian Affairs supervised the sale of the cattle to whites. In fact, the Bureau, during this period, not only provided cues for the Sioux community internally, but they handled the relations of the Sioux, as a total community, with white society as a whole. Individual Sioux did have relationships with whites, however. Ranchers and cowboys set the tone for the surrounding white society in that time and individual Sioux were very well able to relate (and still are) to these carriers of American cowboy culture. Life in this period was very satisfying.

ADMINISTRATION OF THE PINE RIDGE SIOUX

The Pine Ridge Sioux of today find themselves in an entirely different situation. Nearly all their former institutions on the local level have disappeared. The small Sioux community is hardly even a community in the strict sense of the word. It is a kin group without the aboriginal institutions which once related them to their environment, and no substitute institutions have developed in their place. New institutions have been preempted by outsiders. The old Chief's Council is non-functional. The warriors societies have long since disappeared and the local police force is seen as a foreign and illegitimate coercive force. Thus, few (practically no) means of social control are left to local Sioux community. There are no local school boards—the schools are run by the federal government. Their churches are controlled by an outside religious hierarchy. Economic institutions are virtually non-existent. The only really functional institutions are the old native religious groups which have carried over from aboriginal times and more recent community arrangements for putting on local Indian dances, "give-aways," celebrations, and the like. It is in these last contexts that Sioux leaders are developed.

Administration of a community's affairs by outsiders over a long period of time will naturally cause a decay or disappearance of no longer functional institutions as well as loss of effective social control in the community. But life built upon a strong network of kin relations can be satisfying. Lack of these institutional learning experiences does mean, however, that the Sioux were deprived of any ways of coming to grips themselves with their environment and learning about it. *And* the major part of the modern Sioux environment which cannot be experienced or perceived in this situation is modern America.

A more urban people in the situation of the Sioux would resist such a condition of life. Urban middle-class Americans, at least, must feel responsible for their own individual actions. They only come into "being" by their own behavior and the consequences of their choices. Such a condition for urban Americans would erode their very self images and cause personality breakdown. The Sioux, like most tribal peoples, do not need this kind of individual responsibility for self creation. They resist restriction of individual action and authoritarian relations but they look outside of themselves for definition and cues for action from other Sioux kinsmen and traditional ways of behaving. The Bureau of Indian Affairs is supposed to "take care of the Sioux" and the Sioux does not object to the Bureau's role, only if they do not do it according to Sioux ideas of how this role should best be carried out.

Thus, the over control of Sioux life by outsiders did not by itself "cause" any social pathology. True, institutions did decay and the Sioux are unable to learn about modern America because of this, but two other factors coupled with this last deprivation of experience brought social breakdown to the Sioux community. One, white neighbors began to communicate to the Sioux people that the Sioux were looked upon by whites as an incompetent, impotent, and inferior people. To the older Sioux these attitudes were not especially damaging or important, for whites were a strange order of being, almost like a being from another planet, powerful and mysterious, but hardly important in the *social* universe of the Sioux. To the modern Sioux, however, who see whites as prestigeful fellow Americans, such negative judgements, to a people who look outside of themselves for definition, are devastating. And, inexperienced in dealing with modern America and powerless to get that experience, they are unable to display competence and worth as a people to whites or to themselves.

Two, the Bureau of Indian Affairs has, because of its mandate from Congress to integrate the Sioux into the general society, tried to introduce new programs, ideas and institutions into the Sioux community for Sioux "betterment." Since 1930 this trend has accelerated.

A major "institution," introduced in recent years into the community by federal authorities, is the tribal government. From the viewpoint of the country Sioux, this new institution is "The Tribe." In many ways they look at it in the same way that many urban working class look at the police force and city government. They see it as a foreign coercive feature in their daily lives. To the older Sioux, the tribal government gets in the way of their personal approach to the powerful and benevolent federal government. The country Sioux certainly do not see the tribal council as representing them nor as making decisions for them. Tribal councilmen are elected to "get something" from the Bureau of Indian Affairs. The country Sioux are poor people and being in tribal government pays well so there are always volunteers for these offices. The criterion for selection of tribal councilmen by those few Sioux who do vote in an election is not that the tribal councilman can represent them or their opinion, but because they feel that a particular person knows how to handle whites and can "get something" for the Sioux. A tribal councilman thus may be tremendously competent or incompetent, socially responsible or irresponsible. Invariably, they are marginal to the community and sometimes even personally disliked. No sooner does the new tribal administration go into office than charges of dishonesty and "half-breeds" are hurled at them by the country Sioux, and in the next election they usually "turn the rascals out." Some few councilmen who are more representative of their communities "weather the storm," but most Sioux politicians come into office for one or two terms, are retired for a term for a new set of men, and then come back into office—a revolving personnel of political officers.

GOVERNMENT WITHOUT POWER

But let us take a look at this institution from an outside viewpoint. In form, this is an urban American institution. Such procedures as majority rule, representative government, and voting are evidence of this. Many of these forms and procedures are very foreign to Sioux life. Even the voting districts which have been laid out do not correspond to any meaningful social units. This, of course, is not an overwhelming handicap since many tribal peoples all over the world today are learning to operate and function in institutions which are urban in form. The tribal government is, however, called upon to make more decisions in the economic sphere than is usual in urban America.

But the main difference between Sioux tribal government and government in other American communities is that the Sioux tribal government is, in effect, without power. Most of the day to day decisions about Sioux life, about roads, schools, relief, are made by Bureau personnel. And information about such decisions is in Bureau files. Further, what decisions the tribal council makes are subject to approval by the Secretary of the Interior.

Local whites are very well aware of who holds the power and the purse strings on the Pine Ridge Indian reservation. And when local whites come to Pine Ridge on business they first go to see the local superintendent. A white banker or a mayor of a small town literally has no way to relate to the tribal council and usually no real reason to enter into a relationship. Ranchers and cowboys no longer set the tone for white society in this area. It is now the judgements of the small town middle-class that the Sioux must face. It is hard for these people to see the Sioux as anything but incompetent. They see Sioux affairs being run for them by a federal bureaucracy; and they perceive the Sioux leaders as perpetually haranguing and "wheedling" the government for special privilege.

In a larger sense, the tribal government is an arm of the Bureau of Indian Affairs. The local police chief, when I was on Pine Ridge Reservation, was a member of another tribe and a federal employee, not responsible either to the tribal government nor to his constituency. One only has to look at the layout of the town of Pine Ridge to see how much tribal government is an adjunct of the local Bureau.

The town of Pine Ridge is divided into two sections. The east side of town in 1957 was an area of tumble-down shacks in which the Sioux lived. The west side of town was the Bureau "compound." It was in this area along with other Bureau facilities that the tribal buildings were located.

Let us now look at the dynamics of this institution of tribal government. As I mentioned above, from the point of view of the country Sioux, the tribal council is there not to make decisions for the Sioux, rather to get something from powerful whites. But in urban America, we have a tendency to name something; to accept a definition which goes along with the very word itself; and to act on that premise. To the local Bureau employees, the tribal government is by definition a decision making body, and they approach it with suggestions about programs which would be beneficial to the Sioux. The tribal councilman may indeed share with the representatives of the federal government the assumption that he is a decision maker; or he may very well know that this is not the way his constituents perceive him. Even if it is the latter, he will listen very intently to the "suggestions" of the people who hold the power and the purse strings because he must establish his credit with them as a responsible leader in order to "get something for the Sioux." In any case, these suggestions are listened to very closely because everyone knows very well that the final decision of a tribal council's action is approved or disapproved by the Secretary of Interior. Most of the programs suggested to the tribal council are unfamiliar to them and are usually couched in terms which, from the viewpoint of an anthropologist, seems very well fitted for a middleclass American community but at wide variance with the Sioux. Enough has been said about these kinds of programs in other parts of the world, and the lack of fit they have to another culture. These programs naturally fail to reach their desired ends and this adds to the Sioux feelings of incompetence and impotence.

Now let's take a look at the reaction from the other end—the country Sioux. Very few governmental actions are initiated in the country Sioux community. One could say that so far as decision making is concerned, except in the religious sphere, the Sioux community lies inert. When a decision of the tribal council such as setting up a tribal program for cattle raising begins to be heard of in the local community, the Sioux react. Since the program is unfamiliar and basically one which is fitted for a white community, the Sioux see it as un-Sioux, as dishonest; and one hears a cry raised by a majority of the people against the "half-breeds" on the tribal council who are frittering away Sioux money and lining their own pockets. The marginal people in the community who share many things with whites, of course see the program as beneficial and respond to it. Also, they are the ones who are in the position to most benefit from a basically American white program which is unfamiliar to the majority of the Sioux. This is the basis for factionalism among the Pine Ridge Sioux —how one responds, as a Sioux, to action initiated from outside the community.

Now this seems a rather bleak picture I've painted and of course the picture is not this bleak; and even if it were this would not be all of Sioux life. Perhaps the very way I went about analyzing the situation results in such a vignette. I suppose when anyone analyzes political behavior, factions and the like in a strife torn community, the picture comes out looking rather bleak. I could mention briefly the fact that the tribal council is indeed an educative mechanism for many Sioux and that Sioux leaders are developing into master politicians in this environment. Further, as many more Sioux get experience off the reservation in the general society, come to an understanding of that society, return to the reservation, and take a responsible post in the tribal government, hopefully the situation will ease.

Nevertheless, the fact remains that the Pine Ridge reservation is a parody of the American Indian reservation system. The huge Bureau compound on Pine Ridge has an almost fort-like quality. One gets the impression from Bureau employees, as one visiting anthropologist put it, that the Sioux have just been "brought in" to the reservation and settled, several thousand of them, in little warrior camps over the reservation. The behavior of very competent middle-class bureaucrats and technicians on Pine Ridge has the quality of the British officials who dressed for dinner in equatorial Africa. The Bureau of Indian Affairs is *the* economic and political force in Pine Ridge reservation. The Bureau is ever present in the lives of the Sioux. Bureau personnel attended most public meetings and usually call them to get the Sioux to agree to some program or other, *and* direct them as well. The school teachers are federal employees in the Bureau. The local Indian who drives the school bus is a Bureau employee. The social worker who calls at an Indian home is part of the same federal bureaucracy. Tribal projects are supervised by Bureau officials. One could play this same theme through most of the daily life of the average Sioux. After living on the Pine Ridge reservation for a few months one cannot help falling into the habit of looking back over one's shoulder now and then.

The Sioux have social problems galore but the fact that they have survived at all as a community with any semblance of social health is a tribute to their vitality and greatness as a people. If one needed a case history to write a handbook on how to destroy a community one need only look at the history of Pine Ridge.

The Pine Ridge reservation is, as are most American Indian reservations, an example of a very complete colonial system—an internal colonial system; a system set up and continued with the best of benevolent intentions, to be sure; but a colonial system none the less. A colonial structure has been a common method in the world by which urban European people have structured their relationships with tribal peoples of differing cultural backgrounds. And the relations between North American Indians and incoming Europeans have followed this common pattern. The control and administration of a people's affairs and destiny by outsiders from another culture is the prime characteristic of a colonial model and American Indian reservations are an ideal type of this model.

If I had chosen to start with "economic" relations rather than political relations the system might become clearer to most readers. The Bureau of Indian Affairs is the most powerful economic force on Pine Ridge reservation. It finances the tribal government and tribal projects. It provides the money for social services and social welfare. It builds the roads and hires the workers. In fact, the only well-paying jobs for local Indians are lower echelon Bureau jobs—school bus driver, janitor, construction and road work, etc. By virtue of the fact that Sioux land is held in trust by the federal government the Pine Ridge Sioux as a tribe and as individuals do not have free security with which to get loans from banks and private sources. Small businesses find it hard to survive in such a poverty stricken area. Large outside capital does not wish to move into an area where all the land and resources are held in trust and controlled by a federal bureaucracy. The few small industries which have been "enticed" into the area by the Bureau of Indian Affairs are not accountable to the Sioux, but to the Bureau. The main physical resource of the Sioux, their land, is leased out to large white ranches. Only a few of the Sioux are fortunate enough to have well-paying Bureau jobs. Most of them are migrant workers, recipients of social welfare, or unskilled workers in low-paying government and tribally subsidized small industries. This structure, no doubt unwittingly, keeps the Sioux out of the mainstream of our economy, exploits their land resources, and keeps the Sioux people as a reservoir of unskilled migrant workers for the neighboring area. From an economic point of view, these are the classic symptoms of a colonial system and these few examples cited should make the case.

At times, the Pine Ridge Sioux, as do other American Indians, "chafe" under the over-control of their affairs. When they do the Congress only too happily volunteers to withdraw their very costly bureau altogether. Reservation leaders fear, not without some basis in fact, exploitation by their white neighbors. They feel they need some legal protections. They also know they cannot get along without much needed social services and they fear the state in which they live cannot or will not provide them these services. Further, the relationship between their tribes and the federal government is a symbolic one which guarantees the survival of their communities. (Of course, it is also to the advantage of tribal politicians to maintain the status quo.) Thus, Indian leaders are then placed in the position of defending the status quo and suffering the over-control to get legal protection, social services, and symbolic comfort. Unfortunately, many technicians and administrators in the Bureau feel they need this control in order to do their jobs and on the local reservation level press for more programs and ever more control.

THE COLONIALISM-ASSIMILATION DICHOTOMY

It should be obvious by this point in my analysis that the Pine Ridge reservation is more than just a colonial system. It is that certainly, but no European colonial service was given the job of selling or mildly coercing their "people" into accepting programs which would bring about their acceptance of European culture and their integration into European society. The two conflicting purposes are self defeating.

In recent years the Congress has tried to circumscribe the power of the Bureau of Indian Affairs by turning some of its functions over to other bureaucracies. Several years ago Indian hospitals were turned over to the U.S. Public Health Service and recently the Office of Economic Opportunity has become involved in "self-help" programs on Indian reservations. This situation has caused the differing bureaucracies to compete for power and influence on

the local and national levels and finally to increase the power of the total bureaucratic unit on the reservation. Needless to say, the colonial situation has been accentuated.

The above point illustrates a trend in modern America. More and more the federal government is taking over the responsibility of integrating deviant communities into the general society, on middle-class terms, and appointing federal bureaucracies to do that job. In the process, we are creating new "national groups" with a new identity and a new consciousness of themselves—Ozarkians, Appalachians, The Poor; even as we helped create the American Indian from among the diverse aboriginal tribal nationalities of the U.S. The relationship between these new federal bureaucracies and deviant groups looks very much like the relationship between the Bureau of Indian Affairs and the Pine Ridge Sioux—a semi-colonial structure set up to bring about directed acculturation and total assimilation.

I would suggest this trend is a symptom of a more general process in the American social system—the centralization of economic and political power in our society; the closing up and bounding of the "system"; the exclusion of deviant minorities except for limited entry into the system by individuals.

CENTRALIZED POWER

I would suspect that such is the case in many of the large nation-states of the world. Certainly many modern countries seem to be turning over the integration of deviant communities into their national societies to central governmental agencies. I would guess this to be the case in the Soviet Union, Mexico, China, India and even parts of Africa.*

The United States was the first major country in the world to try to integrate a deviant minority by turning over its affairs to a governmental bureau and charging that

* Editor's note: See, for example, Ulč's article discussing Czechoslovakian policy toward Gypsies in Section Two.

agency with the task of integration and accul-turation. That experiment failed, and, in fact, wreaked havoc in the life of the subordinate community. Now it seems that this policy is being further implemented, on a large scale in the U.S. and other nation-states. Whether it will succeed or whether it will only bring about further tensions in these already tension ridden large societies remains to be seen, but from the data at hand one would predict that this policy will increase tensions: perhaps to the point that major unforeseen changes will be brought about in our own country and other large nation-states in the near future.

30

Race and Public Policy: Family Planning Services and the Distribution of Black Americans

KENNETH C. W. KAMMEYER
NORMAN R. YETMAN
McKEE J. McCLENDON

Although the family planning movement has been in existence for many decades, most observers have noted that the 1960s brought great changes in American policies and practices regarding the control of fertility (Jaffe, 1967:145). After decades of silence, or even opposition, American political leaders at all levels, from the president to local city and county officials, have become increasingly supportive of the idea of family planning. Public family planning services were initially provided primarily through affiliates of nongovernmental organizations such as Planned Parenthood. However, during the last half of the 1960s such services were often made available through county health departments

Kenneth C. W. Kammeyer is Professor and Chairman of Sociology at The University of Maryland. Norman R. Yetman is Associate Professor of American Studies and Sociology and Chairman of American Studies at The University of Kansas. McKee J. McClendon is Assistant Professor of Sociology at The University of Akron.

This is a revised version of an article published in Social Problems 21, no. 5 (Summer 1974). Reprinted by permission of The Society for the Study of Social Problems.

and county hospitals. After the initiation of the War on Poverty, some funds for family planning services were provided by the Office of Economic Opportunity as well.

This paper will attempt to shed some light on factors that may have contributed to, or influenced, the decision of local units in the United States to provide public family planning services. We believe it will be possible to demonstrate that family planning services in the United States were provided more frequently where there were Black Americans in the population than in other areas. In other words, we will make a strong inferential case that reactions to the racial composition of the population have influenced decisions to provide family planning services.

THE RATIONALE OF THE FAMILY PLANNING MOVEMENT

Organizations that have fought and worked for family planning in the United States, from Margaret Sanger's American Birth Control League to the present day Planned Parenthood and Office of Economic Opportunity programs, have been quite consistent about their aims. The stated objective has always been to enable the poor to have the same ability to control family size as the more affluent.

As the position has recently been expressed:

> The 55 percent difference in fertility rates between poor and non-poor seems to stem largely from [the] considerable difference in the means of fertility control to which the poor have had access.
>
> The objective of national policy is to remedy this inequity by providing low-income couples with effective access to the same modern methods of fertility control which higher income Americans enjoy. [Planned Parenthood/Office of Economic Opportunity, 1969: 4]

If family planning services are made available in accordance with this rationale it might be supposed that those communities with the largest number of people who are poor would be the most likely to have such services. Such a supposition can be stated in the form of a hypothesis and labelled the *poverty* hypothesis: the availability of family planning services will be positively related to the prevalence of poverty in the population.

The family planning movement may also be viewed as activity aimed at reducing perceived high or excessive fertility. By providing contraceptive information and materials to couples who have large families, high fertility levels could be greatly reduced. Following this objective, family planning services would be initiated wherever fertility is high. If transformed into a hypothesis to explain the availability of family planning services, this may be called the *high fertility* hypothesis: the availability of family planning services will be positively related to the fertility levels found in the population.

Yet another explanation of the distribution of family planning services, but one that does not emanate from the ideology of the family planning movement, is what demographers have labelled the *diffusion* hypothesis. This hypothesis holds that birth-control methods, techniques and knowledge will be found first in urban centers and will then diffuse through more rural segments of the society. While Carlsson (1966) has made a notable attack on the diffusion hypothesis, it must be considered in this study because it may account for the distribution of family planning services in the United States.

On the basis of the *poverty* and *high fertility* hypotheses, one should find the availability of family planning services in the United States to be closely related to the amount of poverty in the population and to the fertility rate. The *diffusion* hypothesis would lead us to expect family planning services to be more frequently found in urban areas. However, there is another factor that might explain the distribution of the family planning services, one having nothing to do with the rational objectives of the family planning movement or the diffusion of ideas from urban to rural areas. That factor is the racial and ethnic composition of the population. Of course, the idea that family planning services

would be provided more frequently when there are racial or ethnic minorities in the population is repugnant to the leadership of the family planning movement. But the objectives of the leaders of the family planning movement and the implementation of these objectives in local communities throughout the nation are quite different matters. It may be that communities, through their leaders, see the need for helping to control fertility among their poor, but they perceive this need more clearly if those poor are also racial or ethnic minorities. In simple terms, the racial or ethnic characteristics of the population may create higher *visibility* for the *need* to provide fertility control services.

The proposition that family planning services will be more likely to be made available if there are racial or ethnic minorities in the population may be labelled the *racial* hypothesis. Stated in the form of a hypothesis we may say: the availability of family planning services in the United States will be positively related to the presence of racial or ethnic minorities in the population.

The idea that birth control or family planning services are directed toward racial or ethnic minorities did not emerge from a vacuum.[1] Even in the early days of Margaret Sanger's work, critics of the family planning movement charged that it was directed at particular groups. Since Sanger's efforts at that time were often concentrated among the impoverished immigrant Jews, she was charged with operating a clinic that "was intended to do away with the Jews" (Jaffe, 1968:234–235). Today a frequent charge against the family planning movement is that it is directed toward Black Amercans. Charles Willie has asserted that "many people in the Black community are deeply suspicious of any family planning program initiated by Whites" (Willie, 1971:1). There is considerable empirical evidence to support Willie's description of black perceptions of the family planning movement. Darity, Turner, and Thiebaux (1971) questioned a sample of Blacks from a

[1] For analysis of the historical dimensions of this idea, see Weisbord (1973).

medium-sized New England city and found that 29 percent of the males and 5 percent of the females aged thirty or younger agreed with the statement that "all forms of birth control are designed to eliminate Black Americans." In this same study, a less strong statement said, "Encouraging Blacks to use birth control is comparable to trying to eliminate this group from society." Forty-seven percent of males aged thirty and under agreed with this statement, while 20 percent of females in this age group agreed. Among those over thirty, 24 percent agreed (27 percent of the males, 23 percent of the females). (Darity et al., 1971:6–7)

But what do these figures prove? Only that among a substantial portion of Black Americans, particularly males, there is some acceptance of the idea that the family planning movement is directed toward them and has the objective of reducing their numbers in the population. Perhaps Black Americans have developed an ultra-sensitivity to racism in general, and thus see it at every turn; perhaps it is a simple misinterpretation of the facts. The editors of the Population Reference Bureau (1971), who published Professor Willie's remarks, adopted the latter explanation. They noted:

> Government activity in the field of population thus far has been confined largely to bringing to the poor that same ability to control individual family size, in terms of contraceptives and information, that is available to the rest of society. Inevitably, this has meant that *official birth control centers have concentrated in poor communities, a disproportionate share of which are black.* [Emphasis ours] This concentration has led some militant blacks to proclaim that family planning programs are aimed at Black "genocide." [p. 1]

This position on the issue argues that if Black Americans are more often the targets of family planning programs it is because they are more often poor, and the aim of the family planning movement is only to give the poor the same opportunity as the nonpoor to choose the number of children they want. This interpretation is, of course, a restatement of the poverty hypothesis presented earlier. The argument is that the distribution of family planning services is determined by the distribution of poverty. If family planning services are also found where there are disproportionate numbers of Black Americans it is due to the positive correlation between race and poverty.

The research that follows will test the racial hypothesis as an explanation of the distribution of family planning services. The poverty, high fertility, and diffusion hypotheses will be considered as alternative explanations.

THE STUDY

In 1969, Planned Parenthood and the Office of Economic Opportunity issued a report on the availability of family planning services in the United States (Planned Parenthood/Office of Economic Opportunity, 1969). The research for this report was conducted by the Center for Family Planning Program Development of Planned Parenthood. The purpose of the study was to provide the Office of Economic Opportunity, as well as other interested agencies and individuals, with some baseline information on the availability of family planning services in the United States. Using several data-gathering methods, information was collected on the 3,072 counties of the United States. The report provided a county-by-county breakdown on the availability of family planning services, along with a variety of other measures reflecting demographic, social welfare, and medical conditions in each county. We have used the data presented in this report as the best available information on the distribution of family planning services in the United States in 1968.

The report revealed that, in 1968, exactly twelve hundred of the 3,072 counties had *some* family planning services available to the public. Specifically, this meant that at least one of the following four services was available: (1) The county health department was providing family planning services; (2) the county hospital was providing family planning services; (3) a Planned Parenthood affiliate was providing family planning services; or (4) the Office of Economic Opportunity was providing funds for some agency to provide family planning services.

Our overall strategy in this study has been to treat the racial hypothesis as the primary hypothesis to be tested. If the expected relationship is found between the minority group, or racial, composition of the counties and the availability of family planning services, then the variables reflecting the alternative hypotheses (poverty, high fertility, and urbanism) will be introduced as control variables. More specifically, using product-moment correlation, the zero order correlation between all independent variables and the dependent variables will be examined first. Then a partial correlation analysis will be undertaken. Finally, the same data will be analyzed with a cross-classification procedure, using gamma as measure of association.

The Dependent Variable—Availability of Family Planning Services

The Planned Parenthood/O.E.O. study identified all United States counties that were providing some family planning services "either by public or voluntary hospitals, health department, Planned Parenthood affiliates or other agencies" (Planned Parenthood/Office of Economic Opportunity, 1969:5). While the Planned Parenthood study sought to establish a measure that would indicate that the percent of need for family planning services was being met by each county, this study did not have the same objectives. Our aim was to identify those counties where public or quasi-public family planning services had been made available. The study tries to determine what differentiates those counties that had taken some action from those that had apparently taken none. The dependent variable in this analysis is therefore a dichotomous classification that distinguishes those counties where some family planning services had been provided by 1968 from those counties where none had been provided.

This measure of family planning services does not mean that a county was providing for all its family planning needs, but only that

some kind of action had been taken in the county by some people—very likely those who had some degree of responsibility and power in the county. Even if, as is sometimes argued, potential users of family planning services should have initiated the request for those services, someone in a position of authority had to decide to provide it. The question that this research attempts to answer is: To what factors did the county officials respond? Was it poverty, high fertility, or race?

The Independent Variable—Racial and Minority Group Composition of Counties

Using data from the *County and City Data Book, 1967* (U.S. Bureau of the Census, 1967), United States Census reports (U.S. Bureau of the Census, 1961), and the Planned Parenthood report (1969) referred to above, we obtained demographic data so that each county could be described in the following terms:

1. Percentage of the county population Black
2. Percentage of the county population Black and Indian
3. Percentage of the county population Spanish-speaking and Indian
4. Percentage of the county Black and Spanish-speaking
5. Percentage of the county population Black, Indian, and migrant-farm laborer
6. Percentage of the county population Black, Indian, migrant-farm laborer, and Spanish-speaking
7. Percentage of the county population Black, Indian, migrant-farm-laborer, Spanish-speaking, and foreign born.

An earlier analysis revealed that the first of these indicators, percentage of the county population Black, was the strongest independent variable (Kammeyer, Yetman, and McClendon, 1972). For the United States as a whole, and in four of the five regions of the country, "percentage Black" always correlated more highly with the availability of family planning services than any combination of minority groups. Since other combinations of minority groups only diminished the relationships, it is our judgment that the introduction of other groups only confounds the issue. In individual states, certain unique combinations of minority groups in the population might prove to be stronger. However, in the remainder of this paper our independent variable will be the percentage of the population Black.

The Control Variables—Poverty, High Fertility, and Urbanism

The primary hypothesis to be tested is that the percentage of the county population that is Black will be positively related to the availability of family planning services. However, the alternatives, the poverty, high fertility, and diffusion hypotheses, call for measures of these factors that can be controlled while we examine the racial hypothesis. Also for reasons that will be discussed below, we will examine the relationships separately for different regions of the country.

Providing family planning services is, as noted above, often justified on the basis of the economic need of the population. When the population is poor there is a presumed need for public or quasi-public family planning services. Therefore, if the influence of minority groups in the population is to be shown, the poverty level of the population must be held constant. In this analysis the poverty level of counties was measured in two ways: first, by using the "percentage of the families in the county with an income under $3,000 per year," and second by using the percentage of women aged 15–44 in the county population who were medically indigent and in need of family planning services (Planned Parenthood/Office of Economic Opportunity, 1969).

The first of these two poverty measures uses the generally accepted 1960s poverty level of $3,000 yearly income per family. One might expect that it would be a satisfactory index of the poverty level of women in the childbearing years. However, the second measure is more appropriate since it focuses on medically indigent women in need of subsidized family planning. This measure was developed by Planned Parenthood researchers, who used it to estimate the number of women

in need in 1966, for all United States counties. The measure of "medically indigent women in need" was described as follows:

> . . . all fertile women who are exposed to the risk of unwanted pregnancy and who cannot afford medical care. It consists of all women who are: (a) medically indigent; (b) fertile; (c) exposed to pregnancy; (d) and not currently pregnant or seeking a desired pregnancy. [Planned Parenthood/Office of Economic Opportunity, 1969:238]

The similarity of these two measures of poverty is revealed by the fact that they were highly correlated ($r=.934$) (see Table 1). If the poverty hypothesis is to account for the distribution of family planning services in the United States, this measure should be highly correlated with the availability of family planning services. Or as a partialling variable it should reduce correlations of other correlated measures. The latter method is the principal way in which we will employ this variable.

The high-fertility hypothesis calls for some indication of fertility in the county. We used both the county fertility rate for 1966 (the number of births per one hundred women aged fifteen to forty-four in 1966) and the county crude birth rate (the number of births per 1,000 population). These variables, as control variables, will be discussed more fully below.

The diffusion hypothesis calls for a measure of the level of urbanism in each county. Since Blacks are now concentrated in urban places (Price, 1969:11), it is important to control for the effects of urbanism. When we examine the racial hypothesis, the measure of urbanism used in the analysis is the percent of the population living in places of 2,500 or more. This measure of urbanism follows the Census Bureau classification, and, while it may seem somewhat simplistic as a measure of urbanism, it does correlate very highly with much more elaborate urbanism measures. (See Queen and Carpenter, 1953:38–43.)

Finally, since Blacks are unevenly distributed throughout the United States, and their rural-urban distribution varies from one geographical region to another, it is also necessary to control for region. It is especially important to ensure that the concentration of Blacks in southern states and the preponderance of family planning services in the South do not produce a spurious relationship for the nation as a whole between "percent Black" and family planning services. Moreover, examining the regions individually permits us to examine whatever regional variations there may be in the relationships being examined.

The Findings

A correlation matrix showing the zero order correlations between the major independent, dependent, and control variables is presented in Table 1. Matrix A is for the entire United

TABLE 1.   *Correlation Matrices Showing the Zero Order Correlation between the Independent, Dependent and Control Variables for the United States and Five Regional Areas*

Correlation Matrix A, United States	(1)	(2)	(3)	(4)	(5)	(6)	(7)
(1) Available Family Planning Services	1.000						
(2) Percent Black	.428	1.000					
(3) Percent Families with Income under $3,000	.174	.479	1.000				
(4) Percent of Women in Need of Subsidized Fam. Plan.	.235	.508	.934	1.000			
(5) Fertility Rate	.076	.144	−.029	−.017	1.000		
(6) Crude Birth Rate	.151	.125	.051	−.102	.655	1.000	
(7) Urbanism	.209	−.050	−.540	−.429	.080	.140	1.000

Correlation Matrix B, Region 1, West*	(1)	(2)	(3)	(4)	(5)	(6)	(7)
(1) Available Family Planning Services	1.000						
(2) Percent Black	.466	1.000					
(3) Percent Families with Income under $3,000	−.007	−.187	1.000				
(4) Percent of Women in Need of Subsidized Fam. Plan.	.039	−.126	.714	1.000			
(5) Fertility Rate	.075	.077	.106	.068	1.000		
(6) Crude Birth Rate	.131	.165	.101	−.219	.378	1.000	
(7) Urbanism	.418	.439	−.390	−.177	.022	.110	1.000

* Washington, Oregon, California, Idaho, Nevada, Montana, Wyoming, Utah, Colorado, Arizona, and New Mexico.

Correlation Matrix C, Region 2, North Central*	(1)	(2)	(3)	(4)	(5)	(6)	(7)
(1) Available Family Planning Services	1.000						
(2) Percent Black	.324	1.000					
(3) Percent Families with Income under $3,000	−.268	−.141	1.000				
(4) Percent of Women in Need of Subsidized Fam. Plan.	−.215	−.080	.980	1.000			
(5) Fertility Rate	.162	.029	−.200	−.220	1.000		
(6) Crude Birth Rate	.250	.093	−.368	−.383	.927	1.000	
(7) Urbanism	.372	.338	−.670	−.609	.124	.284	1.000

* North Dakota, South Dakota, Nebraska, Kansas, Minnesota, Iowa, Missouri, Wisconsin, Illinois, Michigan, Indiana, Ohio.

TABLE 1. (*continued*)

Correlation Matrix D, Region 3, Northeast*

	(1)	(2)	(3)	(4)	(5)	(6)	(7)
(1) Available Family Planning Services	1.000						
(2) Percent Black	.409	1.000					
(3) Percent Families with Income under $3,000	−.447	−.279	1.000				
(4) Percent of Women in Need of Subsidized Fam. Plan.	−.367	−.197	.960	1.000			
(5) Fertility Rate	−.030	−.055	.166	.163	1.000		
(6) Crude Birth Rate	.053	.006	−.002	−.029	.880	1.000	
(7) Urbanism	.596	.499	−.693	−.572	−.069	.016	1.000

* New York, Pennsylvania, Vermont, New Hampshire, Massachusetts, Connecticut, Rhode Island, New Jersey, Maine.

Correlation Matrix E, Region 4, West-South-Central*

	(1)	(2)	(3)	(4)	(5)	(6)	(7)
(1) Available Family Planning Services	1.000						
(2) Percent Black	.009	1.000					
(3) Percent Families with Income under $3,000	−.043	.344	1.000				
(4) Percent of Women in Need of Subsidized Fam. Plan.	.019	.408	.955	1.000			
(5) Fertility Rate	−.015	.103	−.047	.003	1.000		
(6) Crude Birth Rate	.022	.110	−.110	−.049	.977	1.000	
(7) Urbanism	.306	−.029	−.497	−.368	.183	.246	1.000

* Oklahoma, Texas, Arkansas, Louisiana.

Correlation Matrix F, Region 5, South*

	(1)	(2)	(3)	(4)	(5)	(6)	(7)
(1) Available Family Planning Service	1.000						
(2) Percent Black	.277	1.000					
(3) Percent Families with Income under $3,000	.006	.301	1.000				
(4) Percent of Women in Need of Subsidized Fam. Plan.	.038	.291	.850	1.000			
(5) Fertility Rate	.138	.426	.133	.140	1.000		
(6) Crude Birth Rate	.177	.339	.005	−.064	.866	1.000	
(7) Urbanism	.219	−.009	−.614	−.467	.009	.085	1.000

* Kentucky, Tennessee, Mississippi, Alabama, West Virginia, Virginia, North Carolina, Georgia, South Carolina, Florida, Maryland, and Delaware.

States, while matrices B, C, D, E, and F are for the five regional areas separately.

For the United States as a whole, matrix A shows the correlation between "percent Black" and the availability of family planning services. The correlation coefficient is .428.

Neither the percentage of families below the poverty level in the county nor the percentage of women in need of subsidized family planning is as highly correlated with the availability of family planning. The respective correlation coefficients are .174 and .235. The two measures of fertility are even less highly correlated with the availability of family planning. The fertility rate is correlated .076, and the crude birth rate .151. Urbanism is correlated .209.

It appears that for the United States as a whole, neither the poverty hypothesis, the excessive fertility hypothesis, nor the diffusion hypothesis accounts for the distribution of family planning services as well as the racial hypothesis. However, this conclusion needs to be assessed further.

Regional Differences

In different regions of the country there are differences in the way "percent Black" is related to the availability of family planning services. There is some correlation between "percent Black" and family planning services in all regions of the country except the West-South-Central region, which therefore requires some special attention. The West-South-Central region is made up of Oklahoma, Arkansas, Texas and Louisiana. In 1968, Louisiana and Texas had very few counties providing family planning services (9.4 percent of the Louisiana counties, 12.2 percent of the Texas counties). Since Louisiana, in particular, has a substantial Black population (32 percent of the total), it is understandable that no high correlation between "percent Blacks" and family planning services was observed. Louisiana, in 1968, stood out as a clear exception to the other deep south states, since the overwhelming majority of the counties in the remaining southern states were providing some family planning services. Probably the Catholic heritage of southern Louisiana accounts for this dissimilarity. However, it is of interest to note that by the time of a 1969 re-survey by Planned Parenthood, Louisiana resembled the rest of the southern states in providing family planning services. By 1969, Louisiana had gone from the six counties of a year earlier to fifty-five counties providing family planning services. The latter figure represents 86 percent of the Louisiana counties, a proportion comparable to most other southern states, and

far greater than the percentage in non-southern states. Texas increased its percentage of counties providing family planning services in 1969 to about 21 percent, so while the West-South-Central region did not support the racial hypothesis in 1968, it might well have in 1969 after Louisiana had made such substantial changes.

Among the remaining regions of the country, the West showed the highest correlation between the "percent Black" and family planning services. The correlation in the West was .466. It was followed by the Northeast with .409, the North-Central with .324, and the South with .277.

By contrast, there was no region of the country in which poverty was correlated highly enough with the availability of family planning services that it could account for the distribution of such services. In the West, the West-South-Central and the South, the correlations between the two measures of poverty and the availability of family planning services tended to hover around zero. In the North-Central and Northeast the correlations between poverty and availability of family planning services were not even positive; they were negative. In these two regions, the greater the level of poverty in a county the less likely it was to have family planning services. In the Northeast, the high negative correlations (−.477 and −.367) might be accounted for by the fact that available family planning was highly correlated with urbanism (r=.596). Since urbanism was negatively correlated with poverty (0.572 in the Northeast and −.693 in the North Central), it would follow that poverty would not be positively correlated with family planning. Whatever the explanation, it is clear from both the low correlations in the West, West-South-Central and the South, and the negative correlations in the North-Central and Northeast, that the existence of poverty does not explain the availability of family planning services.

Measures of fertility (the fertility rate and the crude birth rate) fared equally badly as correlates of the availability of family planning services. In the Northeast and West-

South-Central regions, the correlations were around zero; in the West, the correlations were .075 and .131; in the South, they were .138 and .177; while in the North-Central, they were .162 and .250. Only in the North-Central region did high fertility seem to have the expected positive correlation with the availability of family planning services, but, it might be noted, the correlation was still lower than the correlation between "percent Black" and family planning services.

While neither the poverty nor high-fertility hypotheses explained much of the variance in the availability of family planning, either in the United States or the separate regions, urbanism was always positively related. The correlations ranged from .219 in the South to .596 in the Northeast. This suggests that urbanism could be a factor accounting for a substantial proportion of the relationship between the distribution of Blacks and available family planning services. However, this is only likely to be true for certain regions of the country, namely those where urbanism is in fact related to percent Black. As Table 1 shows, the positive correlation between urbanism and "percent Black" in the West, North-Central and Northeast is not found in the South or in the West-South-Central. There is also not a positive relationship for the total United States, apparently owing to the preponderant influence of the southern regions. We used a partial correlation analysis for the United States and for the several regions to examine the correlation between the percentage of Blacks in the county and availability of family planning services while controlling for poverty, fertility, and urbanism.

For the poverty variable we will use "women in need of subsidized family planning," since this variable correlated most highly with available family planning services. It is also a measure of poverty that has a logical affinity to the idea that it is the poor in their reproductive years who are the natural targets of family planning programs.

As an index of fertility we will use the crude birth rate of the county rather than the fertility rate. This may seem unusual since the fertility rate, which is based on the number of women in the childbearing ages rather than upon the total population, is usually assumed to be a more refined measure of fertility. There are three reasons for our decision. First, crude birth rate correlated more highly with the available family planning services than did the fertility rate. In that sense it is more likely to be able to diminish or "wash out" the correlation between "percent Black" and family planning services.

The second reason for using crude birth rate rather than the fertility rate is somewhat more complex. One critical comment on an earlier version of this paper suggested that perhaps the poverty level of a county does not reduce the correlation between "percent Black" and available family planning services because the age structure of the "White-poor" counties is different from the age structure of the "Black-poor" counties. Specifically, it was suggested that the "White-poor" counties were more likely to be made up of many more *old* poor people than the "Black-poor" counties (Williams, 1972). If age structures of "White-poor" and "Black-poor" counties differed in this way, it would mean that the "White-poor" counties would have much less need for family planning services. In effect, this is another perspective on the high-fertility hypothesis, since it is being argued that the "Black-poor" counties would have more people in the childbearing ages than the "White-poor" counties. Since the crude birth rate *is* affected by the structure of the population, it turns out to be a better control variable for fertility in the present case.

The third reason for using crude birth rate over fertility rate is that the percentage of babies in the total population would be more closely related to the services that the county must provide for children. A high crude birth rate would put a heavy demand on public services, while a high fertility rate wouldn't necessarily do so if there were only a small number of fecund women in the population. Also, a high crude birth rate is more likely to be visible to public officials than a high-fertility rate.

Two additional points are necessary before presenting the partial correlation analysis. First, while we will report here only the partials for "women in need" (poverty control) and crude birth rate (high-fertility control) the results are the same (indeed, usually more supportive of our conclusion) when the alternative control variables for poverty (percent of families with less than $3,000 income) and high fertility (fertility rate) are used. Limiting the number of control variables in this part of the analysis is done only in the interest of brevity and clarity. Second, while we argued above that crude birth rate can be used as a surrogate control for the age structure of the population, we did control for the age structure directly (women in the country population aged fifteen to forty-four) with the same result.[2]

The Partial Correlation Findings

Table 2 shows the partial correlations between "percent Black" in the county population and the availability of family planning services. The variance accounted for by the effects of

[2] Readers interested in the full set of partial correlations or any specific partials may contact the authors directly.

several crucial control variables has been removed, both singularly and in combination. Again the correlations are shown for both the United States as a whole and for the five regions separately. The West-South-Central region, of course, still shows no correlation between family planning services and the distribution of Blacks, so the discussion will focus on the United States as a whole and on the remaining four regions.

In general, neither the poverty variable (women in need) nor the fertility measure (crude birth rate), taken separately, substantially reduced the zero-order correlations. Even when the two measures were controlled simultaneously, not much of the correlation between "percent Black" and available family planning services was washed out. For the United States as a whole, this second-order partial dropped the correlation from .428 to .345. For the regions, the reduction produced by the combined effect of these variables was generally even less. With "women in need" and crude birth rate controlled, the correlation in the West changed hardly at all, going from .466 to .464. In the North-Central region it went from .324 to .309, in the Northeast from .409 to .370, and in the South from .277 to .231. In

TABLE 2. *Partial Correlation Coefficients between Percentage of the Population Black and the Availability of Family Planning Services, Controlled for "Women in Need of Subsidized Family Planning," Crude Birth Rate, and Urbanism, for the Total United States and Five Regions.*

			Region			
	United States	West	North-Central	North-east	West-South-Central	South
Zero Order Correlation Between Percent Black and Available Family Planning Services	.428	.466	.324	.409	.009	.277
Control Variables	*Partial Correlation Coefficients*					
Women in Need	.370	.475	.315	.369	.002	.278
Crude Birth Rate	.417	.454	.312	.409	.007	.234
Urbanism	.449	.346	.227	.161	.019	.286
Women in Need and Crude Birth Rate	.345	.464	.309	.370	−.001	.231
Women in Need, Crude Birth Rate, and Urbanism	.301	.347	.223	.168	−.042	.204

essence, controlling for effects of poverty and high fertility (as well as indirectly for age structure) resulted in only a modest diminution of the correlations between "percent Black" and available family planning.

By contrast, the third control variable, urbanism, had considerably more effect. It had a substantial effect when it was the only control variable, especially in the Northeast, and also in the third order partials when it was combined with the poverty and high fertility variables.

For the total United States, having partialled out the effects of urbanism, poverty, and high fertility (and age structure with the crude birth rate) there was still a correlation of .301 between the percentage of Blacks in the county population and whether or not the county had some family planning services available.

In four of five regions in the country as a whole, the third-order partials, which controlled for the effects of poverty, high fertility, and urbanism simultaneously, produced correlations that were about 30 percent less than the original zero-order correlations. In the Northeast, the reduction was even greater. In this region the correlation between "percent Black" and available family planning services decreased by about 60 percent (from .409 to .168). This was, of course, due to the high correlation between urbanism and family planning services in the Northeast.

In the four regions of the country, still excluding the West-South-Central, the third-order partial correlations were .349 (West), .233 (North-Central), .168 (Northeast), and .204 (South). In terms of the variance explained, these are not dramatically large correlations, though it can be noted again that compared to the poverty and high fertility variables, "percent Black" was much more strongly correlated with the availability of family planning services. Only by putting it in the position of the primary causal variable and subjecting *it* to the test of spuriousness do we diminish its explanatory power. If we had conversely treated the poverty and high fertility variables as the primary causes of the distribution of family planning services, *as they are generally assumed to be,* and subjected them to the same tests of spuriousness, of course we would have reduced their power also. Indeed, we would have virtually eliminated their correlation with the dependent variable.

By contrast, urbanism, reflecting the diffusion hypothesis, does often show an equally high, or higher, correlation with family planning services when the data are examined regionally. That was not the case for the country as a whole, where the correlation for "percent Black" was .428 and the correlation for urbanism was .209.

Cross-Classification Analysis

While the correlation analysis indicates in a single coefficient the degree of the relationship between the racial composition of counties and the availability of family planning, the same relationship may be examined in a cross-classification analysis and displayed by means of bar graphs. We did this by dividing the several continuous distributions into categories and cross-classifying them with the already dichotomous dependent variable. The independent variable "percent Black" was divided into five categories, ranging from those counties with no Blacks to those counties with more than 50 percent Blacks.

Figures 1 through 7 are selected bar graphs that show clearly the consistent and strong relationship between the percentage of county populations Black and the availability of family planning services.

For example, Figure 1 shows that of all United States counties that had no Blacks, only 11.8 percent had family planning services. There were 1,227 such counties. At the other extreme there were 142 counties where more than 50 percent of the population was Black, and 83.1 percent of those counties had some family planning services. The counties with intermediate percentages of Blacks had proportionately large percentages providing family planning services.

Figures 2 through 7 consistently show

FIGURE 1.   *The relationship between the percent of the county population Black and the availability of family planning services in all counties in the continental United States.*

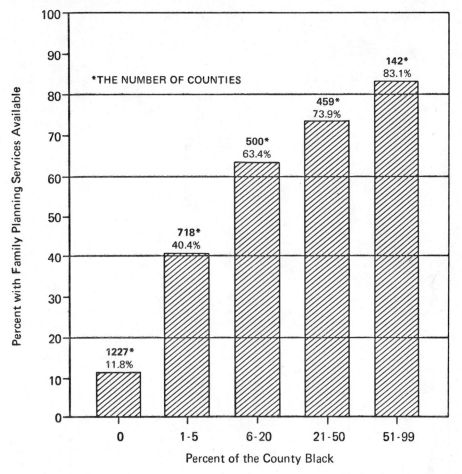

the same pattern. Whenever the percentage of Blacks increases, the proportion of the counties providing family planning services increases. The categories shown graphically in these figures were not selected because they were the most impressive data available, but rather they were thought to be the most interesting. For example, Figure 2 shows the one-third of the U.S. counties with the highest crude birth rates. Figure 3 shows the counties with the highest percentage of "women in need," and Figure 4 shows the most heavily urban counties. In all cases the relationship

between "percent Black" and available family planning services is clearly evident.

In Figure 4, as in Figures 6 and 7, there were some categories of "percent Black" that had fewer than ten cases. Whenever this occurred we combined that category with an adjacent one. These combinations are shown with double width columns.

Figure 5 shows the relationship for those counties that had both a high crude birth rate and a high proportion of "women in need." While there is a slight disruption of the pattern in the first columns, there is still a clearly

FIGURE 2.   *The relationship between the percent of the county population Black and the availability of family planning services in all counties with a crude birth rate of 19 or greater.*

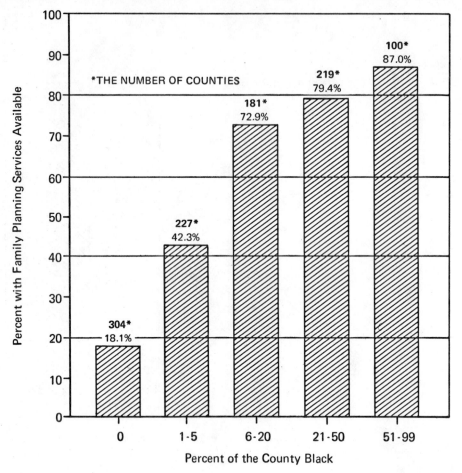

evident relationship between "percent Black" and available family planning services.

Figures 6 and 7 show the same two categories of counties, but now divided into the least urban and most urban also. In other words, Figures 6 and 7 show the relationship while holding three variables constant simultaneously. Again the relationship is shown, even though the number of cases in Figure 7 is very small.

Since there is still the possibility that we might have been selective in the choice of data for Figures 1 through 7, some additional sum-

mary information may be supplied. Each bar graph is drawn from a 2×5 table (family planning services available: yes or no; percent Blacks in the county divided into five categories ranging from zero percent to more than fifty percent). For purposes of comparison, the coefficient of association gamma was calculated for each 2×5 table. While gamma is designed for ordinal data, it may be used even for the dichotomous or nominal attributes if the order is kept the same throughout. Here we use it primarily to indicate the strength and consistency of relationships. In the cross

FIGURE 3. *The relationship between the percent of the county population*
Black and the availability of family planning services in all counties with
women in need higher than 24 percent.

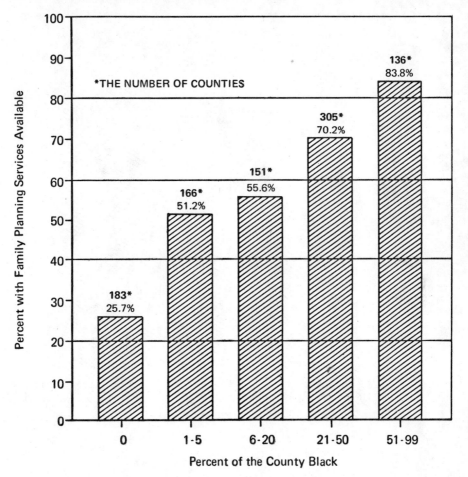

tabulation tables that produced Figures 1 through 7, the gamma values were, respectively, .71, .70, .53, .67, .45, .45, and .60. These values of gamma are only average or below average compared to the sets from which they come.

If we use gamma as an indication of the consistency of the relationship between "percent Blacks" and available family planning services, we can show very clearly that the relationship holds under almost all conditions of poverty, fertility, and urbanism. To illustrate, when we divided each of the three con-

trol variables into three categories (low, medium, and high), the result was twenty-seven ($3 \times 3 \times 3$) combinations that represented particular combinations of the characteristics of poverty, fertility, and urbanism. When we examined the relationship between "percent Black" and available family planning services for every combination there was only one table out of the twenty-seven that had a gamma with a negative sign. It happened to be for a set of thirty-eight counties (low-urban, low-poverty and medium-crude birth rate) where only one county had family planning services,

FIGURE 4. *The relationship between the percent of the county population Black and the availability of family planning services in all United States counties with 50 percent or more of the population urban.*

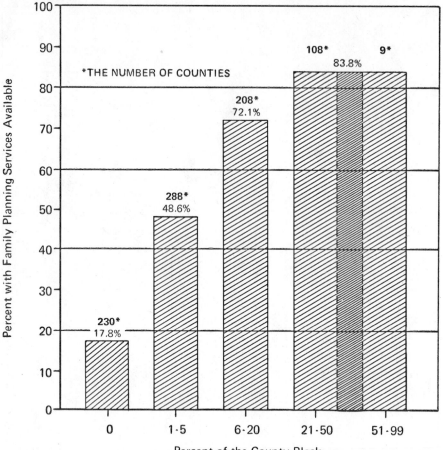

Percent with Family Planning Services Available

*THE NUMBER OF COUNTIES

230*
17.8%

288*
48.6%

208*
72.1%

108*
83.8%

9*

Percent of the County Black

0   1-5   6-20   21-50   51-99

and it was a county with no Blacks. However, since thirty-three of these thirty-eight counties had no Blacks, there was little chance for the relationship to be revealed in any case. The remaining twenty-six gammas were in the positive direction, with the average gamma value of .58.

A similar kind of cross-classification analysis was carried out for the five separate regions of the United States. Controlling for three categories of poverty and three categories of fertility for all five regions we had a total of forty-five (3×3×5) cross-classifications between the percentage of Blacks in the county and available family planning services. Fourteen of these tables had fewer than twenty cases, so we arbitrarily eliminated them from consideration. Of the remaining thirty-one tables, twenty-eight had a positive relation between "percent Black" and available family planning services. Three had negative relationships. Two of these three were in the West-South-Central region, which, as we have noted, did not show the relationship in the cor-

FIGURE 5. *The relationship between the percent of the county population Black and the availability of family planning services in all counties with a crude birth rate of 19 or higher and women in need greater than 25 percent.*

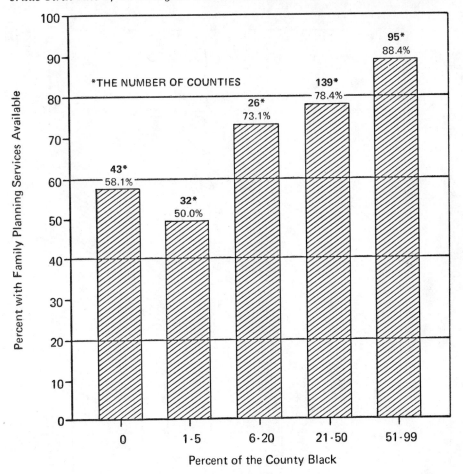

relation analysis. The remaining deviant case was in the North-Central region where the "women in need" variable was high but crude birth rate was low. Again this was a set of counties where sixty-eight of the eighty-one counties had no blacks, and only two of the eighty-one counties had family planning services. As before, this gave little opportunity for the relationship between "percent Black" and family planning services to be seen.

In general, the cross-classification analysis revealed, just as the correlational analysis had shown, that there is a fairly strong and persistent relationship between family planning services in United States counties and the presence of Blacks in the population. The percentage of Blacks in the county was the single strongest independent variable for explaining variation in the availability of family planning services. Support for the racial hypothesis was clearly greater than for either the poverty or fertility hypotheses. Further, even when controlled for urbanism, poverty, fertility, and indirectly age structure, the relationship be-

FIGURE 6. *The relationship between the percent of the county population Black and the availability of family planning services in all counties with a crude birth rate of 19 or higher, women in need greater than 24 percent, and no percent of the population urban.*

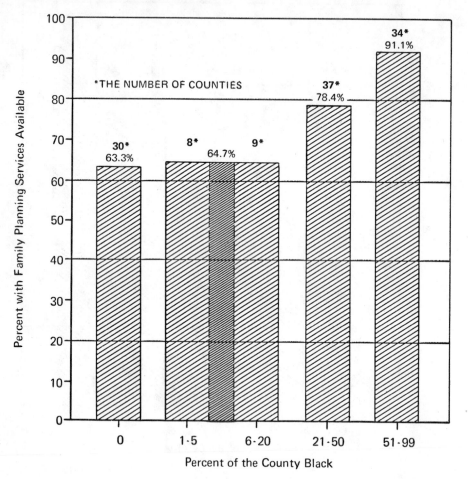

tween "percent Black" and available family planning services did not disappear.

CONCLUSION

There are several perspectives from which the findings of this research may be viewed. First, it must be emphasized that the unit of analysis in this study is the county. The act is one of making family planning services available to the population of that county. This research has demonstrated that counties that have made family planning services available are more likely to have a higher percentage of Blacks in the population than the counties that have not. We do not know which people in these counties took what precise action, and we certainly do not know from these data what motivated them to do what they did. We only know that in most regions of the country, in poor counties and rich counties, in rural and urban counties, the same pattern appears:

FIGURE 7.   *The relationship between the percent of the county population Black and the availability of family planning services in all counties with a crude birth rate of 19 or higher, women in need greater than 24 percent, and more than 50 percent of the population urban.*

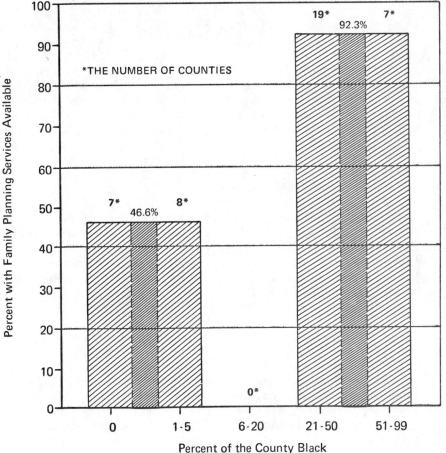

family planning is more likely to be available if there are Black Americans in the population.

Why have family planning services been established first in areas with high concentrations of Black Americans? Our findings are subject to alternative interpretations. On the one hand, our data make it clear that the claim of many Black Americans that family planning has been selectively directed toward them is not a totally unfounded and irrational perception. Whether such programs represent deliberate, conscious, systematic efforts by mem-

bers of the majority group to curtail Black fertility, or whether they reflect a genuine concern for the health and well-being of Black Americans, the *effect* of the many individual decisions has been the same: populations with a higher proportion of Blacks are more frequently the target of such programs. This fact gives apparent substance to charges that such programs are designed not simply to assist the poor, but to control the growth of the Black population.

Given the prevalence of racism in this

country, such an interpretation of these data is not implausible, nor should it be summarily dismissed as purely ideological. Racism in America has been extremely pervasive and has often been uncovered in many subtle and unsuspected forms in the most benign institutions. Black Americans have understandably come to regard new activities with suspicion and cynicism, and often search for latent rather than manifest functions of any programs that purport "to do something for" them. This suspicion derives from the perception that governmental agencies are alien and that programs of governmental assistance for minority groups do not reflect the interests of Black people. On the contrary, they often reflect the concern of the majority group to maintain and perpetuate its own power and privilege.

To view the matter from a contrary view, the data of this study could be seen as revealing a pattern of preference for assistance to Black Americans. This pattern could be interpreted as discriminatory against Whites, who have been systematically excluded from the benefits of family planning services. Certainly if we had found an opposite pattern—one in which there was an inverse, rather than a direct, correlation between family planning centers and percentage of Blacks in the population—an alternative but equally plausible case of racism might have been made. For had this been found, it could have been said that Blacks had been systematically excluded from services available to other Americans.

It may be that public officials have been more responsive to pressures by Black poor, who in the past decade have been more strident and insistent in their demands for equal justice. Thus, higher "visibility" of Black poor may have been a function not of higher fertility or of the salience of race, *per se*, as by the fact that Blacks had made their demands for equal justice and for programs of governmental assistance more keenly felt in the minds of officials responsible for making decisions. Thus, the patterns we discerned could be attributed to a responsiveness of those in power to the needs of poor Black Americans.

A problem with this "responsive" interpretation is that, given the relative dearth of Black political power in most local communities in the United States, the "success" of obtaining family planning services would appear to be an anomaly. Even if there were Black pressures for the establishment of such programs (and how frequently this occurred is problematic), in order for them to be implemented some person or persons in power in each county had to make the decision. That would raise the question of why local officials agreed on *this* particular issue. Why were officials likely to attempt to institute this particular program "to do something for" Blacks?

Since the family planning movement continues to grow, it would appear that most places in the country will have some family planning services within a few years. The Planned Parenthood/Office of Economic Opportunity follow-up study of 1969 (eighteen months after the original survey) revealed that there had been a 20 percent increase in the number of counties providing services, even in that short period of time (Planned Parenthood/Office of Economic Opportunity, 1972). This could be interpreted to mean that our findings have only transitory historical significance. However, we feel that this research is important not only for the substantive issue investigated, but also for what it reveals about public policy formation. This study indicates that race may be a crucial latent determinant of policies and programs in which it is generally assumed that such considerations are absent.

REFERENCES

Carlsson, Gosta. 1966. "The Decline of Fertility: Innovation or Adjustment Process." *Population Studies* 20: 149–174.

Darity, William A.; Turner, Castellano B.; and Thiebaux, H. Jean. 1971. *Race Consciousness and Fears of Black Genocide.* Population Reference Bureau Selection No. 37 (June), pp. 5–12.

Jaffe, Frederick S. 1967. "Family Planning, Public Policy and Intervention Strategy." *The Journal of Social Issues* 23 (July):145–163.

————. 1968. "Family Planning and Public Policy: Is the 'Culture of poverty' the New Cop-Out?" *Journal of Marriage and the Family* 30 (May):228–235.

Kammeyer, Kenneth C. W.; Yetman, Norman R.; and McClendon, McKee J. 1972. "Family Planning Services and the Distribution of Black Americans." Paper presented at the annual meetings of the Population Association of America in Toronto, Ontario, Canada.

Kelly, Francis J.; Beggs, Donald L.; and McNeil, Keith A. with Tony Eichelberger and Judy Lyon. 1969. *Multiple Regression Approach.* Carbondale and Edwardsville: Southern Illinois University Press.

Nunally, Jim C. 1967. *Psychometric Theory.* New York: McGraw-Hill.

Planned Parenthood/Office of Economic Opportunity. 1969. *Need for Subsidized Family Planning Services: United States, Each State and County, 1968.* Washington, D.C.: U.S. Government Printing Office.

Planned Parenthood/Office of Economic Opportunity. 1972. *Need for Subsidized Family Planning Services: United States, Each State and County, 1969.* Washington, D.C.: U.S. Government Printing Office.

Population Reference Bureau. 1971. *Perspectives from the Black Community.* Selection No. 37. Washington, D.C.: U.S. Government Printing Office.

Price, Daniel O. 1969. *Changing Characteristics of the Negro Population.* A 1960 Census Monograph. Washington, D.C.: U.S. Government Printing Office.

Queen, Stuart A., and Carpenter, David A. 1953. *The American City.* New York: McGraw-Hill.

U.S. Bureau of the Census. 1961. *U.S. Census of Population: 1960. General Population Characteristics.* Final Report PC (1)-B. Table 28. Washington, D.C.: U.S. Government Printing Office.

U.S. Bureau of the Census. 1967. *County and City Data Book, 1967.* Washington, D.C.: U.S. Government Printing Office.

Weisbord, Robert G. "Birth Control and the Black American: A Matter of Genocide." *Demography* 10 (November, 1973): 571–591.

Williams, Roberta. 1972. Population Reference Bureau, Personal Communication.

Willie, Charles V. 1971. "A Position Paper" Presented to the President's Commission on Population Growth and the American Future. Washington, D.C.: Population Reference Bureau Selection No. 37 (June), pp. 1–4.

31

Mexican Americans and the Administration of Justice: Bail

U.S. COMMISSION ON
CIVIL RIGHTS

Under long-standing concepts bail in criminal cases is designed to permit the release of an accused person from custody with the assurance that he will appear for trial. The eighth amendment to the Constitution of the United States prohibits excessive bail and the Federal Rules of Criminal Procedure guarantee a person's right to bail in noncapital cases before conviction. The constitutions of all five Southwestern States discussed in this report[1] also guarantee the right to bail before conviction in noncapital cases, in addition to prohibiting the imposition of excessive bail.

IMPROPER USE OF BAIL AGAINST MEXICAN AMERICANS

Allegations were made that the bail system in the Southwestern States frequently was used more severely against Mexican Americans than others. Some persons alleged that discriminatorily high bail was set for Mexican American suspects; others alleged that exces-

Reprinted from *Mexican Americans and the Administration of Justice in the Southwest.* A Report of the United States Commission on Civil Rights (March, 1970), pp. 48–52. Most of the footnotes have been omitted.

[1] Arizona, California, Colorado, New Mexico, and Texas.

sive bail or denial of an opportunity to post bail was used by law enforcement officials to retain custody of accused Mexican Americans or to harass them rather than assure appearance at trial. In one area there were allegations that the misuse of bail by local authorities had created a situation resembling involuntary servitude or peonage.

A Mexican American school teacher in Los Angeles, arrested with 12 others on a felony charge of conspiracy to commit a misdemeanor in connection with a school walkout by Mexican American high school students, complained that the timing of the arrests late on a Friday night and the setting of excessive bail were designed to keep him and the other defendants in jail over the weekend. Bail was set at $1,200 each. Unable to raise bail in this amount, they had to wait until Monday morning for a hearing on a petition for reduction of bail. On Monday the court reduced the bail to $500 each. Subsequently this was lowered to $250 and eventually changed to release on their own recognizance.

In Texas a number of complaints were heard regarding excessive bail and improper bail procedures used by law enforcement officials in Starr County during the United Farm Workers Organizing Committee (UFWOC) strike in 1966–67. In May 1967, the Texas State Advisory Committee to the United States Commission on Civil Rights held a meeting in Starr County to gather information about these allegations. Eugene Nelson, a staff organizer for the UFWOC told the Advisory Committee that he was arrested for allegedly threatening the life of a Texas Ranger; his bail was set at $2,000, the maximum fine for the offense. Later that day a well known and wealthy landowner from Starr County agreed to sign a property bond to secure his release. Local authorities, however, refused to accept the property bond even though it was well known that the signer was the owner of a great deal of property in the county. The authorities demanded copies of his tax records to prove that he had enough property to cover the bond. As a result the organizer, who had been arrested on a Friday afternoon, remained in jail until

Monday because the necessary tax certificate could not be obtained until then. On Monday he was released after the tax certificate listing all the property owned in Starr County by the signer of the bond was accepted.

Other allegations concerning excessive bail were heard by the Committee. In one case the Texas Rangers arrested 11 picketers and charged them with secondary picketing (the constitutionality of the Texas law against secondary picketing is currently being challenged in the United States District Court in Brownsville, Texas). Even though the maximum fine for violation of this law was only $500, the amount of bail was set at $1,000 apiece. Later, in its report on the situation in Starr County, the Advisory Committee concluded that members of the UFWOC and others active in the organizing campaign were denied their legal rights. Among the denials of legal rights cited by the Committee was the "holding of union organizers for many hours before they were released on bond."

In December 1968, at the Commission's hearing in San Antonio, a Mexican American attorney from Starr County testified that in his opinion the amount of bail required in most cases during the labor dispute was excessive and in many cases was "way beyond what the final fine . . . or penalty would be." He also complained that the local authorities had made it extremely difficult to bail anyone out of jail by imposing unnecessary requirements in addition to the large amounts set for bail. As a result, he said, in some cases it took 7 to 10 days to get people released from jail.

Similar complaints regarding delay or inability to obtain release on bail were received in Denver. Here, several attorneys, including the director of the public defender's office, complained that Mexican Americans who were arrested without a warrant were often being held in jail from 2 to 5 days while the district attorney's office determined whether or not to file an information against them. During this period they were questioned and an investigation was conducted, but they were not eligible for release on bail. In some cases the district attorney's office would decide to release the person rather than file an information charging him with an offense.

In Albuquerque, New Mexico, a young Mexican American who had recently returned from the National Institute of Mental Health Research Center (Narcotics Treatment Center) in Fort Worth, Texas said that he was frequently picked up by the police for "investigation" and held for 24 hours. During this time he was not eligible for release on bail. He stated, however, that he was usually released without charge and he claimed that it was fairly common practice in Albuquerque. A Federal probation officer with the United States District Court in Albuquerque told the New Mexico State Advisory Committee about an incident involving a Mexican American under his supervision. The Mexican American came to Albuquerque on an errand for his employer, and visited a friend whose home was under surveillance by local law enforcement officers on the lookout for possible narcotics violators. When he left his friend's house, he was stopped by the police. The probation officer gave the following account of what occurred:

[H]e was taken out of his car, the wrecker was called, and his car was towed in and he was booked for vagrancy. He had $90 in his pocket; he had two check stubs showing that he was working . . . and he had a note saying he was authorized to pick up the pay checks and deliver them . . . to the . . . work site.

Even though it was obvious that he had a job and had cash in his pockets:

He was booked for vagrancy and the bond on his vagrancy was $10. He had $90 in his possession and they would not permit him to post bond on the vagrancy charge. He was told that he had to see certain officers who were not on duty at the time but who would come in in the morning after which they would decide whether or not he could post bond. . . . Eventually the officers did arrive and after several hours of interrogation . . . they did permit him to post the $10 bond.

In some parts of the Southwest, complaints were made that law enforcement officials did not make it clear to Mexican American defendants that their initial judicial appearance was not the trial and that they had not been found guilty of a crime. As a result, many defendants did not show up for trial and forfeited their bail, thus establishing a criminal record and leaving themselves liable to arrest at some future date for failure to appear at trial.

Henry Trujillo, an investigator for the Alamosa County District Attorney's Office in the San Luis Valley, a poor rural area of southern Colorado, told a Commission staff member that Mexican American defendants are encouraged not to appear for trial and to forfeit their bail. They are told by the local officials that it would be too much trouble and expense to appear.

The police magistrate in Monte Vista, Colorado, in Alamosa County, said that in his community many defendants forfeit their bail, but he could not explain why. The bail procedure was similarly criticized in Fort Lupton, in northern Colorado, the scene of a number of complaints about the treatment of migrant laborers by the local police and courts in the summer of 1966. There the local magistrate reportedly set bail at $75 for migrant workers charged with public drunkenness who were in town to pick sugar beets and scheduled trial for 2 months later, long after the migrant workers would have left the community.

Mr. Trujillo disclosed another and more serious problem resembling involuntary servitude or peonage.[2] He stated that during the harvest season local farmers would go to the jails in the towns of Center and Monte Vista,

Colorado on Monday mornings and inquire about the number of Mexican American laborers arrested over the weekend. The farmers would select the best workers and pay their fines for them. Upon their release the men would have to repay the farmer by working for him. According to Trujillo, in Monte Vista the men were told by the police magistrate that if they did not remain on the farm and work off the amount owed to the farmer, they would be returned to jail. In addition, he said, the police magistrate would sometimes give the farmer a "discount." If the fine was set at $40, he would only require the farmer to pay $25. The magistrate, however, would tell the worker that the fine paid by the farmer was $40 and that he owed the farmer $40 worth of work. According to Mr. Trujillo, once the worker was released from jail, he usually was at the mercy of the farmer and often was ill-treated while on the farm. The chief of police and a patrolman in Center, and the police magistrate in Monte Vista confirmed the fact that workers are bailed out of jail or have their fines paid by local farmers and are obligated to work off the ensuing debt.

THE HIGH COST OF BAIL

In the Southwest, Mexican Americans, who as an ethnic group have an average income appreciably below that of the total population in the region, frequently cannot afford to pay even modest bail and must remain in jail until trial. The cost of such a system, both to society and to the accused and his family, is enormous.[3] Some of these practices in the Federal

---

[2] Federal law provides:
§ 1581. *Peonage* . . .
(a) Whoever holds or returns any person to a condition of peonage, or arrests any person with the intent of placing him in or returning him to a condition of peonage, shall be fined not more than $5,000 or imprisoned not more than five years, or both. 18 U.S.C. § 1581 (a).
§ 1584. *Sale into involuntary servitude*
Whoever knowingly and willfully holds to involuntary servitude or sells into any condition of involuntary servitude, any other person for any term, or brings within the United States any person so held, shall be fined not more than $5,000 or imprisoned not more than five years, or both. 18 U.S.C. § 1584.

[3] Studies dissecting the bail system have been conducted for a good many years. Their uniform conclusion is that the system has not worked very well. Accused persons in large numbers in all parts of the country are forced to spend the interval between arrest and trial in jail. Most are detained only because they cannot pay the bondsman's premium, or put up the collateral he asks. They lose their jobs and their family life is disrupted. Their chances for acquittal are lowered, their opportunities for probation diminished; their quest for equal justice handicapped.

courts have been modified by the Bail Reform Act of 1966.

In both Phoenix and Tucson, Arizona, a number of people complained that Mexican American defendants were often forced to remain in jail until trial because they could afford neither the amount of money required for bail nor a bondsman's fee. An attorney in Phoenix said that many Mexican Americans are, in effect, punished in advance of their trial because they are unable to raise enough money for bail. A city councilman in Tucson complained that all attempts to lower bail bond requirements had met stiff resistance from bail bondsmen because this would lower their income.

The director of an Office of Economic Opportunity (OEO) funded job placement program in East Los Angeles also said that Mexican American youths often remain in jail because of lack of funds for bail. He asserted: "You can't get help; there's no money to get help; you have a feeling of hopelessness." In New Mexico, Commission staff members talked to a number of Mexican Americans who were arrested on major and minor charges and had to remain in jail because they could not afford bail. In a 1967 report to the Colorado General Assembly, the Colorado Commission on Spanish-Surnamed Citizens commented about the cost of bail bonds:

> The bail system clearly discriminates and punishes the poor. The affluent can easily put up their bail and buy their freedom; the poor often do not have the price of the bail bond. The average amount of bail is about $500, and the average premium for a bail bond is $25 to $50 which is 5 percent or 10 percent of the amount of the bond. Many of the Spanish-surnamed poor cannot raise this sum and must remain in jail. By remaining in jail he loses his earnings and often his job. His family suffers and may be actually pushed onto welfare. All of this happens before the man is tried.

ALTERNATIVES TO CASH BAIL

Some alternatives to the traditional cash bail system have been tried in various jurisdictions in the Southwest. These programs hold a great deal of promise, but there have been some criticisms of their operation.

One such alternative is the release of a defendant on his own recognizance. Under this procedure the defendant is released after he has promised to return for trial; no cash bail is required. This method has been used in the past by courts to facilitate the pretrial release of certain citizens known to be reliable or prominent in the community. Now many communities have extended this system to defendants who cannot afford bail, but after a brief investigation are considered to be good risks to return for trial.

In Los Angeles and Phoenix, defendants may be released on their own recognizance. A superior court probation officer and an attorney in Phoenix, however, said that Mexican Americans residing in Phoenix are not able to obtain release from custody on their own recognizance as easily as Anglos. The attorney recalled a recent example in which he had encountered a great deal of difficulty in getting a Mexican American agricultural worker, a resident of South Phoenix, released on his own recognizance although he could always obtain such releases for Anglos in similar situations. In Los Angeles, similar allegations were made.

In Artesia, New Mexico, a Mexican American whose family had resided in the area for 40 years and who had a wife and children as well as a job, told a Commission staff member that the local justice of the peace had refused to release him on his own recognizance when he was arrested for drunken and reckless driving. He obtained such a release only after a Commission attorney talked to the justice of the peace about the case.

In Denver, Under Sheriff Mose Trujillo said that prior to the establishment of a personal recognizance system in the city and county courts many people could not afford a minimum bondsman's fee to be released before trial. In his opinion, this new system had worked well and only 5 percent of the defendants released on their own recognizance had failed to appear for trial. He expressed the view, however, that standards applied to each defendant seeking release on his own recognizance were too rigid.

SUMMARY

Although the primary purpose of bail in criminal cases is to provide for the release of an accused person from custody with the assurance that he will appear for trial, the system of bail in the Southwest frequently is used more severely against Mexican Americans than against Anglos as a form of discrimination. In certain cases, Mexican American defendants are faced with excessively high bail. Defendants in other cases are held without any opportunity to put up bail or are purposely confused by local officials about the bail hearing so that they unknowingly forfeit their bail. In one area local farmers put up bail or pay fines for migrant workers and make them work off the amount in a situation resembling peonage or involuntary servitude.

Even in the absence of such abuses, the high cost of bail under the traditional bail system prevents many Mexican Americans from being released prior to their trial, while others accused of similar crimes go free merely because they can afford to pay a bail bondsman to put up their bail. In some jurisdictions, alternatives to the traditional cash bail systems are being tried including the release of defendants on their own recognizance.

32

The Courts Have
Failed the Poor

J. Skelly Wright

The twin problems of racism and poverty have
converged in our society to become the problem of the inner city itself. Where once our
cities were cultural meccas, they are now mis-
erable slums. Where once the immigrants to
our cities came from abroad with hopes for a
better, happier life, now they come from the
South, despairing if not desperate. And after
they arrive they find no escape from the cycle
of poor health, substandard housing, disori-
ented family relationships, interrupted schooling and joblessness. There are 35 million
hardcore poor who, in the richest nation the
world has ever known, earn less than $3,000 a
year, the income level defined by the Federal
Government as constituting poverty by American standards. And, particularly in the inner
city, a vastly disproportionate number of the
poor are Negroes; in addition to the misery of
poverty, they must bear the psychic brunt of
the white racism that is eating away our
society.

Ignorance, discrimination, slums, poverty, disease and unemployment—these are the
conditions that breed despair and violence. Is
it any wonder that our cities, once melting
pots, are now powder kegs? The causes of
these conditions are too many and varied for

*J. Skelly Wright is Justice of the U.S. Court of
Appeals for the District of Columbia.*

condensation here. I shall discuss only one
aspect of the general problem: how the law
and the courts have failed the inner-city poor.

The words inscribed over the entrance of
the Supreme Court Building in Washington are
"Equal Justice Under Law." And surely one of
the proudest boasts of American lawyers is
that all men stand equal before the law. But
too much of that equality turns out, upon analysis, to be of the sort that prompted Anatole
France's sarcastic remark: "The law, in all its
majestic equality, forbids the rich as well as
the poor to sleep under bridges on rainy
nights, to beg on the streets and to steal
bread."

The point is simply that a law may be
consistently and evenly applied, yet systematically work a hardship on a particular class. In
our society, the law has worked a hardship on
those least able to withstand it. Rather than
helping the poor surmount their poverty, the
law has all too frequently served to perpetuate
and even exacerbate their despair and helplessness. And now we are reaping as we have
sown. The civil disorders which have racked
our cities demonstrate an alarmingly widespread disrespect for law among those ghettoized in the inner city.

But if the law is to gain respect, it, like
everything else, must earn respect. This it has
not done. While to us, in the words of former
Attorney General Nicholas deB. Katzenbach,
"laws and regulations are protections and
guides, established for our benefit and for us
to use," to the poor they are "a hostile maze,
established as harassment, at all costs to be
avoided." As Senator Robert Kennedy put it,
the "poor man looks upon the law as an
enemy. . . . For him the law is always taking
something away."

At first glance this may seem strange or
even mistaken. Has not our Supreme Court
made great strides in equalizing the rights of
rich and poor? After all, in the landmark case
Gideon v. Wainwright it announced that in all
felony trials the indigent defendant has the
right to free legal counsel. And more recently,
in *Miranda v. Arizona*, the Court has tried to
assure equal justice at the station house as

well as in the courtroom by requiring the police to warn a suspect of his right to free counsel before interrogating him.

Though these decisions are certainly legal milestones, they bear on only an infinitesimal percentage of those instances in which the inner-city slum dweller confronts the police and the criminal law process. *Gideon* assures the right to assigned counsel only in felony cases—those that may result in a sentence of more than one year in prison. And *Miranda* cannot stop abusive treatment by the police. All the Court can do is overturn convictions if proper and humane procedures have not been followed. It cannot assure that these procedures will be followed in the thousands of investigations of innocent people that never reach court. Ironically, then, those subject to the indignity of illegal search, harassing arrest or police brutality gain nothing from the Supreme Court's decisions unless they are found guilty.

Nor can the Court do very much about the inner-city residents' other major complaint about the police—that they do not provide adequate protection. The Court cannot undertake to assign policemen to different sections of a city. This is the function of the city government and of the police department itself. But the evidence bears out the observation that frequently more policemen than necessary are assigned to the wealthy parts of a city, where the crime rate is low, while relatively fewer are assigned to the ghetto areas, where the crime rate is much higher. Could it be that we regard an assault as more serious when it is perpetrated on one of "us" than on one of "them"?

There are other areas where the local criminal courts can play a positive role but have failed miserably. I am referring to the magistrate and police courts, which, as their names imply, frequently serve as virtual arms of the police department, dispensing their own brand of justice wholesale. For example, a study of the magistrate's court in a large Eastern city said that, in 13 minutes on the morning after a local newspaper ran an editorial under the title "Get Bums Off Street and Into Prison Cells," 60 persons were tried and convicted of vagrancy by a single magistrate. In several cases, a defendant was committed after the magistrate simply called his name, looked at him and pronounced sentence—usually three months in the city jail.

Despite the presumption of innocence, the defendant in these police and magistrate courts is, prima facie, guilty. The burden is placed upon him to give a satisfactory answer to the question, "What have you got to say for yourself?" He is almost always uncounselled and sometimes he is not even informed of the charges against him until after the so-called trial. Often no records are kept of the proceedings, and in the overwhelming majority of cases these courts are, in practice, courts of last resort. The careful provisions for appeal, certiorari and habeas corpus, which look so fair in the statute books, are almost a dead letter as far as indigent misdemeanor defendants are concerned. Thus, according to Prof. Caleb Foote of the University of California at Berkeley, the "magistrate is given an almost unchecked opportunity for arbitrary oppression or careless cruelty."

And of course these police courts—not the Federal or state courts—are those with which the poor are most likely to come into contact. Consequently, it is these courts that form the image the poor will have of our system of criminal justice. This is why the criminal law is perceived by the poor not as protection for life and property, but as the establishment's tool of oppression, designed to keep them shackled to their poverty and imprisoned in the inner city. The vagrancy and public-drunkenness laws serve primarily the aesthetic function of removing from the sight of the establishment the wretchedly poor, whose condition we do nothing about but cannot bear to see. As one study points out, the only reason for many vagrancy arrests is apparently that "the appearance of the victims was not attractive."

It is in these police courts that those accused of the crimes most often associated with poverty—vagrancy, disorderly conduct and public drunkenness, the modern counterparts of sleeping under bridges or begging on the streets—are tried. In essence, these laws and the courts that administer them have made it virtually a crime to be poor in public; and to make the condition of poverty criminal is not simply uncivilized, it is also futile and self-defeating. Instead of trying to find the vagrant a means of support, we brand him a criminal, throw him in jail, then release him. His criminal record makes it even more difficult for him to find a job, and he soon winds up in jail again. The cycle of oppression continues.

Moreover, it is not only on the criminal side that the law as it bears on the poor man is foolish and self-defeating. If anything, the cards are even more formidably stacked against him in our petty civil courts. To begin with, where property rather than liberty is at stake, the indigent, under prevailing legal doctrine, has no right to a lawyer and consequently is likely to go unrepresented. Even the indigent fortunate enough to have a lawyer and win his lawsuit will be the loser in many cases because his legal fees will swallow up his modest recovery.

The concerns of the poor do not reflect this sharp distinction between civil and criminal litigation on the right to counsel. Poverty only magnifies the importance of protecting one's meager property from seizure by legal process.

A case that the Supreme Court recently declined to review provides an example of the indigent's problem. Matias and Teresa Sandoval, a poor and illiterate Mexican-American couple in Texas, were sued by a mortgage holder and lost the two-room house in which they and their nine children had lived since 1945. Two weeks before the trial, their lawyer withdrew because they could not pay his fee. They sought help from the county legal aid attorney, who apparently did not attempt to confer with them because he spoke only English and they spoke only Spanish. The lawyer never discovered that the so-called deed on which the plaintiff had based his claim to the Sandovals' land was in fact only a mortgage, which could not confer title under Texas law.

If they had had a conscientious lawyer, the Sandovals might not have lost their home.

To ameliorate the indigent's lack of counsel, many states have established special tribunals, commonly termed small-claims courts, to enable the poor to prosecute and defend minor claims—generally for not more than $200 or $300—without counsel and at minimal cost. Rules of evidence and procedure are informal and filing fees are nominal. But the promise of the small-claims courts has not been fulfilled, for in actual operation there is little correspondence between the professed aims of these courts and the ends they serve. Those who have studied them have observed that they are primarily used, not by the poor, but by business organizations seeking to collect debts. A number of these organizations handle such a large volume of claims that they have established collection departments which make routine use of the courts. Thus it is primarily the businessman, not the poor man, who reaps the advantage of the inexpensive and speedy small-claims courts.

Why has the initial purpose of these tribunals been subverted? Primarily because business concerns are aware of their rights and the poor are not. Consequently, the poor are usually the defendants, rather than the plaintiffs, in small-claims courts. The poor lack the security and capacity to assert their rights, even when they recognize the rights. Indeed, most low-income consumers are unaware of the existence of the small-claims court. They simply do not think in terms of invoking legal processes on *their* side. They have no confidence in courts. Where the low-income consumer is irate enough to take action, he is likely to stop payment as a form of retaliation and thereby worsen his position. Finally, the poor are essentially unorganized and therefore lack the unity required to exert the sort of political pressure that would force these courts to remain true to their principles.

A recent Federal Trade Commission report concerning the practices of District of Columbia retailers bears out the observation that small-claims courts have become virtual collection agencies. The report noted the frequency with which the small group of retailers catering to the poor utilized the courts to enforce their claims under installment contracts. In 1966, 11 ghetto retailers reported 2,690 court judgments, one for every $2,200 of sales. The report concluded that, while retailers generally may take legal action against delinquent customers only as a last resort, many of those who cater to the poor depend on such action as a normal order of business. And in many instances sales are made pursuant to unconscionable installment contracts with the expectation and hope that the goods sold will be repossessed so they can be resold.

Even where the small-claims courts have not been captured by business interests, the poor person is likely to be victimized by prevailing legal doctrines, which our judges have been unduly reluctant to overhaul.

Consider, for instance, the facts of *Williams v. Walker-Thomas Furniture Company.* Beginning in 1957, Walker-Thomas, a store in Washington, D.C. sold to Mrs. Ora Lee Williams, an indigent mother on relief with seven children, about $1,800 worth of appliances and furniture. These had been purchased from time to time on installment contracts, and Mrs. Williams had been paying the debts as they became due. Then, in 1962, Mrs. Williams purchased from Walker-Thomas a stereo set with a stated value of $515. At this time she had paid back all but about $170 on the $1,800 owed for goods already purchased. When Walker-Thomas sold her the stereo, they were aware of Mrs. Williams's financial straits, for on the reverse side of the contract of sale the store's manager had noted the name of Mrs. Williams's social worker and the amount of her monthly welfare stipend— $218—as her credit references. Nevertheless, with full knowledge that Mrs. Williams had to feed, house, clothe and support herself and her seven children on this amount, the store sold her the $515 stereo set.

But this is not all; when Mrs. Williams failed to make her payments on the stereo, the store did not seek simply to repossess it. It sought to take back all the other appliances it had sold her, most of which she had already paid for! The contracts under which Mrs. Williams had bought all her goods from Walker-Thomas provided, in an obscure, almost unintelligible fine-print provision, that until the balance due on *every* item had been paid in full, the unpaid balance on a single item would be distributed among all the previous purchases. In other words the debt incurred for each item was secured by the right to repossess all the items previously bought by the same purchaser.

Perhaps it was more than coincidence that Walker-Thomas sold Mrs. Williams a stereo just when she was nearing the final payment on all her previous purchases and would then own the goods outright. But even if the sale was no more than happenstance, contracts such as Walker-Thomas's, when foisted on ignorant and helpless customers, are grossly unfair and one-sided and should not be enforced by the courts. Yet both the trial and lower-appellate courts enforced the contract and ordered Mrs. Williams to return all that she had purchased since 1957. The lower courts condemned Walker-Thomas's conduct but felt that they lacked the power to refuse enforcement of the contracts because the legislature had done nothing to protect the unwary public from such one-sided bargains.

Our court reversed. We pointed out that ordinarily one who signs an agreement without full knowledge of its terms might be held to them. But we felt that when a party of little bargaining power, and hence little real choice, signs a grossly unfair and commercially unreasonable contract with little or no knowledge of its terms his consent has not even been implied and the contract should not be enforced. The failure of the legislature to live up to its responsibility was no reason for the courts not to live up to theirs. Yet our opinion in *Williams v. Walker-Thomas* was, shockingly, one of the first to hold that the courts had the power to refuse to enforce such unconscionable contracts.

And Mrs. Williams's path to judicial relief would have been even more difficult if, rather than holding her contract, Walker-Thomas had sold its rights under the agreement to a finance company. For if the finance company, rather than Walker-Thomas, had filed suit, it might have been shielded under the legal doctrine of holder in due course. One judge has termed the doctrine "the mask behind which fraud hides," and this can be an apt description. In most jurisdictions, a financial agency can purchase installment contracts free from responsibility for fraudulent or unconscionable practices perpetrated by dealers; even if the dealer skips town and never delivers the purchased goods, the consumer may be required to pay. To prevail against the finance company, the defendant who has signed a contract waiving defenses against assignees must prove that the company knew that the underlying transaction was fraudulent —a requirement almost impossible to meet.

While the holder-in-due-course doctrine may thwart the defrauded rich man as well as the poor, its effects hit the indigent much harder in many ways. When the working poor man falls behind on his installment payments, the legal machinery, which one commentator has remarked is "geared for, and used for the benefit of, the manufacturer-seller-financier complex," is likely to put him out of work and back on the relief rolls. The recurring pattern has been outlined this way:

Mr. Smith, who can barely afford to feed, house and clothe his family, is persuaded to buy a second-hand car with $500 down and three years to pay. But because Smith does not have the $500, the dealer arranges for a loan of that amount from a finance company, which takes Smith's furniture as security. After making payments for several months, Smith finds that he cannot keep them up. Besides, the car may not be running all that well. So he stops making payments. After the dealer writes Smith a few letters, Smith is likely to find one morning that his car is gone. It has not been stolen; the dealer or his agent has legally repossessed it.

But Smith is not off the hook. The dealer, after the car is resold for less than the balance due, can secure what is known as a deficiency

judgment against him. In addition, Smith may still owe the finance company, which may take his furniture and, when that is sold, secure a second deficiency judgment.

The lawsuits in which people lose their cars, their furniture and their money and have deficiency judgments taken against them are not likely to come to trial. The overwhelming majority of merchant-initiated suits—97 per cent in the case of Harlem merchants—end in a default judgment for the plaintiff because the defendant never appears or answers the summons or complaint. In many cases, this is because he never receives the summons. A common procedure of process serving has come to be called "sewer service" because, rather than serving the defendant with notice of the action against him, the merchant's process server deposits it in the nearest sewer. Of course, if the defendant is sufficiently wary, informed and resourceful, he will be able to set aside the default judgment because he has not been given adequate notice and the court has not acquired jurisdiction over him. But in the real world, where an indigent defendant is involved, the default judgment is likely to stand. In fact, the purchaser may not even be entitled to notice before judgment, for when making his purchase he may have signed a card authorizing what is known as a "confession of judgment." This card provides that as soon as he misses a monthly payment the unpaid balance becomes immediately due and any attorney or court is empowered to obtain a lien and execution on his property without even notifying him.

Once the creditor has secured his deficiency judgment, he will proceed as quickly as possible to garnishee the debtor's salary. Garnishment, of course, means that the court orders the employer to withhold a certain amount from an employee's earnings—as much as one-half in many states—and turn it over to the creditor to satisfy the judgment. The employee often learns about the judgment when he receives his first diminished paycheck.

The process of wage garnishment has been termed "a modern parallel to debtors' prison." And it is, in many ways, not only as iniquitous, but also as ridiculous and self-defeating as the debtors' prisons were. The employee whose salary is being garnisheed is not simply going to be taking home less money; he is also likely to find himself without a job. This is because employers find the procedure of withholding employees' wages such a bother that many simply fire the employees. Just as the debtor in prison is not going to be able to pay his debts, neither will the unemployed indigent subject to garnishment be able to get and hold a job. Unless he can discharge his debts in bankruptcy—and for a number of reasons this may be impossible—his salary will again be garnisheed if he finds other employment. Again the oppressive pattern of joblessness and relief.

There are several things that could be done to break this debtor spiral, but I will mention just one: eliminate wage garnishments altogether. Three states—Florida, Texas and Pennsylvania—have already done just this, and experience shows it has helped not only debt collections but business in general. Moreover, as one commentator concludes, the elimination of wage garnishments would provide "a new kind of security to millions of Americans who live in dread of being fired. They would know that their job was safe from creditors and that the money needed to feed their families [would] be there. The welfare rolls would be reduced by the number of families forced into unemployment because their bosses wanted to eliminate [bookkeeping] expense."

It is not only in his role as consumer that the poor man finds the courts oppressive rather than redemptive. Consider the plight of the indigent tenant. To begin with, his apartment, even though it will probably be run-down, dirty and lacking in adequate services, will not be cheap. The inner-city Negro who is forced by segregation to live in the over-crowded slums may pay as much as middle-class white tenants may pay for garden-type apartments in the suburbs. And public housing is not nearly adequate to meet current needs.

Yet there is no effective mechanism for change. In view of the appalling housing shortage in our major cities, slumlords feel little economic pressure to keep their low-income housing repaired and habitable or to rehabilitate badly deteriorated buildings. They are able to make enormous profits, even on unfit and dilapidated units.

And the housing codes have not proved a spur to reform. Where housing inspctors discover violations, the landlord is notified and given a grace period to remedy defects. In a report commissioned by the Office of Economic Opportunity, Mrs. Patricia Wald, a former member of the District Crime Commission in Washington, said that in New York "the average wait for cases examined by the building department was almost five months." In the District of Columbia grace periods and extensions may postpone repairs up to a year and a half. If the problem ever reaches the prosecuting authorities, they try what Mrs. Wald calls "friendly collaboration and gentle persuasion," which may delay matters three months more. The ultimate coercive weapon in the District is a sentence of 10 days in jail or a $300 fine. But in no case has a landlord spent even one day in jail. Though the landlord's crime is far more detrimental to society than a poor man's vagrancy, as a "white collar" criminal he is handled with kid gloves by our courts. The indigent does not fare so well.

Poor tenants, even if they are somehow able to find out where and to whom they should complain, hesitate to do so, for if the landlord finds the source of the complaints "retaliatory evictions" may follow. Slum tenants are usually not protected by a lease, and their tenancies can be terminated in a summary procedure on 30 days' notice without cause. Here, then, is another area where the courts have failed the poor; they have in effect become parties to persecution by aiding the landlord in his retaliatory and antisocial purpose.

A case decided by our court is illustrative. In March, 1965, Mrs. Yvonne Edwards rented an apartment in the District of Columbia. Shortly thereafter she complained to the Department of Licenses and Inspections of sanitary-code violations which her landlord had failed to remedy. The ensuing investigation uncovered more than 40 such violations, which the department ordered the landlord to correct. Instead of fixing them, the landlord told the department to forget about the violations because he was going to evict Mrs. Edwards for making her complaint.

The landlord then gave Mrs. Edwards, who did not have a lease, 30 days' notice to vacate the premises. Mrs. Edwards fought the eviction on the ground that the notice to vacate had been in retaliation for her complaints to the housing authorities. The court ruled that evidence of retaliatory motive was irrelevant. It ordered Mrs. Edwards to vacate. The lower appellate court affirmed. As in the Walker-Thomas Furniture Store case, it deplored the plaintiff's actions but felt that the task of protecting indigent tenants seeking to exercise their First Amendment right to speak freely and to petition the government for redress of grievances belonged to the legislature, not the courts.

Our court reversed the judgment of the lower court and for the first time denied a landlord's right to evict a tenant for invoking the help of housing authorities in having her premises repaired. The fact that this is a landmark case shows that the courts have preyed on the poor. Until now the courts in every jurisdiction have not merely refused to intercede to halt retaliatory evictions, but have actually placed their imprimaturs on such evictions by enforcing them.

And not only when he is evicted will the indigent tenant find the courts of no avail. He will meet with little or no judicial success when he is displaced by the burgeoning urban-renewal programs prevalent in most of our major cities. Here displacement is likely to be on a grand scale. For example, the Detroit Housing Commission Quarterly reported in 1964 that 5,530 families had been uprooted by Detroit's 10 redevelopment projects.

Relocation typically brings no amelioration of the overcrowded living conditions common among the urban poor; in many cases the situation is made worse. Instead of replacing the slums with low-cost public housing which the poor can afford, the projects often lead to the construction of luxury-apartment buildings for the benefit of the affluent. Even worse, the slums may not be replaced with housing units at all; the sites may be used for highways, parking lots or office buildings, again for the benefit of affluent suburban commuters. As a consequence, there is likely to result a substantial rent hike in the remaining slums as low-income housing is bulldozed away.

Yet when, contrary to the promise of the Housing Act of 1949, the slum dweller is threatened with permanent displacement and turns to the courts for help, he is likely to be rejected without even a hearing. His remedies in the state courts are agreed to be inadequate and, to date, the Federal courts have denied the private citizen the right to enforce the relocation requirements of the Housing Act. It is now past time for the courts to begin to hear these cases. Newark and New Haven—two cities which have large urban-renewal programs—were among those hit by ghetto riots last summer. In both, urban-renewal projects have been cited as factors contributing to the frustration and outrage which finally exploded.

Under these circumstances, judicial review could serve a valuable and creative function. Today most cities have the resources to continue redevelopment *and* honor our national promise of relocation. Judicial review would assure that the resources were in fact used for rehousing to the fullest extent possible. Where such resources are not available, judicial review would force into the open the contradictions within the program. "By enjoining displacement where adequate rehousing was not available," said a recent article in the Yale Law Journal, "the courts not only would be supporting a sound public policy, but also would be generating pressures that could lead to a legislative solution."

The last area I shall discuss in which the courts have failed the poor is welfare. For too long our welfare programs have embodied the degrading theory that welfare is a form of charity and that dependency is the fault of the individual. Welfare recipients are watched with suspicion and their use of welfare money is hedged with limitations. There are frequent investigations to prevent the misuse of public funds. "In their zeal," says Prof. Charles Reich of Yale, "public agencies have claimed and exercised the privilege of entering recipients' homes at any hour of the day or night—the law literally pursues recipients into the bedroom." There is an insistence that, because a man is on welfare, the authorities have a right to concern themselves with his family's affairs and morality. But as Professor Reich has pointed out, "such invidious laws and the general pattern of bureaucratic supervision, investigation and control conspire to increase dependency by preventing those who need welfare from leading normal lives or achieving independence and self-esteem." The program is self-defeating in that its effect is too often to destroy rather than restore the dignity of the recipient.

Now a new philosophy of social welfare is struggling for acceptance in this country. This modern school of thought considers dependency a condition ordinarily beyond the control of the individual and seeks to establish the status of welfare benefits as rights, based on the notion that everyone is entitled to a share of the common wealth. This conception of welfare seems justified in view of all the others in our society who receive government subsidies and largess, not as a matter of privilege or charity but as a matter of entitlement. For example, the transportation industry is dependent on public assistance; airlines are subsidized on short hauls; shipping is directly subsidized and indirectly aided by laws favoring American-flag vessels; trucking is aided by public roads. Second-class mail rates are essentially a subsidy to the magazine industry. Home-owners are given many types of financial guarantees and assistance, while farmers have been beneficiaries of public-assistance programs for many years. Other subsidies are less obvious. Docks and airports are supplied to the shipping and airline industries at public expense; channels of the radio and television spectrum are given without charge to the broadcast industry. Intellectual activity, espe-

cially scientific research, is also subsidized. Perhaps the biggest subsidies of all are some of our tax exemptions.

Despite the pervasiveness of public assistance throughout our economy, only the welfare recipient is singled out for special, degrading supervision and control. When a farmer receives Government subsidies, the payments are not presented as relief but as an attempt to restore an imaginary balance in the economy, thrown out of kilter by large anonymous forces depressing agricultural prices. In some instances the payments are made to appear as "transactions" in which the Government has purchased commodities from the farmer. Once payments pass to the farmer, they cease to be public funds whose use the Government is entitled to investigate and supervise. The farmer's private life remains his own. Thus in broad outline the payments are designed to preserve the farmer's self-esteem and independence. Throughout our economy, business subsidies follow this general pattern.

It is absolutely essential that we cease treating the welfare recipient as society's child and, instead, bring him back into the mainstream so that he and society can be relieved of the burdens of welfare. Legal recognition and sanction of this emerging philosophy could be one of the most significant advances of our time. But it has not happened. And the courts are again partly to blame. For they, like society in general, have adopted a double standard, one for aid to business and the farmer and a very different one for welfare. Says Reich: "It is a double standard from the moral point of view and a double standard from the legal point of view. There is a law for the poor and a law for the rest of us. Receipt of government aid by the poor carries a stigma, whereas receipt of government aid by the rest of the economy has been made into a virtue."

The effect of this double standard has been to deny welfare recipients the values and protection that the rest of the publicly supported private economy enjoys. The courts could provide some of that protection but, for the most part, have not. Because they continue to view welfare as a gratuity rather than a right, courts have refused to enjoin governmental invasion of privacy, which would not be tolerated except for our degrading conception of the poor as second-class citizens. In disputes involving welfare recipients, the courts have refused to enforce the procedural safeguards long established in connection with many other types of public benefits. A free television license can be revoked only after the most scrupulous observance of due process in a hearing and review procedure, but a poor man's welfare payments can be cut off without any hearing whatever.

While the courts have not created the problems of the inner city, they have not acted to alleviate them and, in many instances, have actually exacerbated the plight of the poor. They have had a hand in what Richard Nixon has called white America's attempt to buy off the Negro and keep him out of sight in the ghetto. As the consensus report of the Assembly on Law and the Changing Society concludes, the cluster of problems known as the urban crisis "arises partly from basic weakness in social, economic and political institutions and partly from weakness in the machinery of justice itself." Even if the courts cannot solve the problems that beset the inner city, they and the legal system as a whole can and should play a significant part in that endeavor. Professor Reich of Yale has put it this way: "All too often, law is used as an excuse for maintaining an unjust status quo. . . . But no form of law is ever necessary or inevitable. Law is the servant of social policy, not a determinant of it. It is our policy that must change." The courts can and must participate in bringing about that change by changing the law, at least in the areas where judges made the offending law in the first place.

As Roscoe Pound said, law is social engineering, "and it must be judged by the results it achieves . . . not by the beauty of its logical processes." I have suggested a number of areas in which, by this criterion, the law must be judged a failure. Though our most pressing social, moral and political imperative is to liberate the urban poor from their degradation, the courts continue to apply ancient legal doctrines which merely compound the plight of the poverty-stricken. These doctrines may once have served a purpose, but their time has passed. They must be modified or abandoned.

33

Minority Income and Employment: Issues and Efforts

A. Michael Collins

Examination of minority employment patterns provides clear illustrations of the typology of discrimination developed by Yetman and Steele, as well as some lessons in combating discrimination. More than a decade of government legislation and intervention has produced mixed, sometimes contradictory results and bitter debate over future policies.

Defenders of Nixon administration policies and those who are sometimes called *neoconservatives* point to indicators of non-white economic progress: black families with male heads under thirty-five years of age who reside outside the South have achieved income parity with comparable white families, and the median family income of nonwhite families has risen from 54.3 percent of that of whites in 1950 to 63.7 percent in 1970 (Table 1).[1]

Critics point out that the income parity of young Black northern families is explained not by income equality but by the higher participation rate of Black wives in the labor force; while the ratio of Black to White family income has risen, it is still low, and the gap in terms of dollars has actually widened (U.S.

A. Michael Collins is Director of the Operating Engineers Dual Enrollment Program.

This article is published here for the first time.

[1] The so-called neoconservative label is often used to refer to the group of scholars presently associated with the magazines *The Public Interest* and *Commentary*.

Bureau of Census, 1973:112). The Bureau of Census figures for 1971, which include Spanish-surnamed individuals, reveal that incomes are still very unequally distributed along racial lines (Bryce, 1974:19). (See Table 2.)

Non-White unemployment also continues to be highly disproportionate. Since 1966, only in 1970 and 1971 were non-White unemployment rates even slightly less than double White unemployment rates.[2] The lowest yearly average for non-White unemployment in the decade 1964–1973 (6.4 percent) exceeds the highest White yearly average (5.4 percent), and current unemployment figures show that the gap is not narrowing.

Underemployment is perhaps even more serious than unemployment in aggregate terms. The Kerner Commission, using 1966 data, reported that if non-White employment were upgraded proportionately to the level of White employment, about $4.8 billion in additional income would be produced, compared to $1.5 billion in additional income that would be gained if non-White unemployment were to be reduced to the level of White unemployment (quoted in Knowles and Prewitt, 1969:20).

In assessing patterns of employment discrimination and the efforts made to change them, one must keep in mind the many interdependencies of the economic system. Structural employment policies, which are aimed at specific groups, must operate within the context of general economic conditions. The greatest barrier to increasing non-White employment is economic decline, which tends to negate structural efforts. Not only does a shrinking job market make it more difficult to increase non-White employment, but the recession of 1973 and 1974 has caused a disproportionately rapid rise in non-White unemployment.

Racial discrimination in employment practices has been a pervasive characteristic in American industry. Following the counter-reconstruction, Jim Crow reigned virtually un-

[2] Current employment statistics may be found in U.S. Department of Labor, *Monthly Labor Review*.

TABLE 1. *U.S. Median Family Income, 1950–1970*

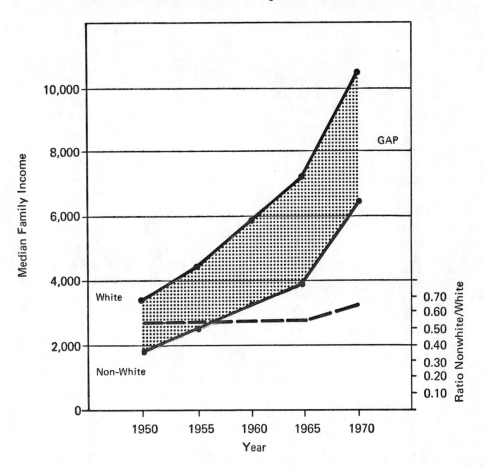

challenged until the 1930s.[3] The decade of the 1940s marked the first time in this century that a national political party, and the president himself, publicly affirmed the idea that the federal government has a responsibility

actively to seek improvement in the status of Black people. President Roosevelt's 1941 executive Order establishing the Fair Employ-

[3] Five general surveys of the Black wage earner are Charles H. Wesley, *Negro Labor in the United States, 1850–1925* (1927; reprint ed., New York: Russell & Russell, 1967); Sterling D. Spero and Abram L. Harris, *The Black Worker* (New York: Atheneum Publishers, 1968); W. E. B. Du Bois, *The Negro Artisan* (1902; reprint ed., Millwood, N.Y.: Kraus Reprint Co.); Lorenzo J. Greene and Carter G. Woodson, *The Negro Wage Earner* (1930; reprint ed., New York: Russell & Russell, 1969); and F. Ray Marshall, *The Negro and Organized Labor* (New York: John Wiley & Sons, 1965).

TABLE 2. *Family Incomes and Earnings— 1971*

Race	Median Income	Percent of Families with Incomes	
		Under $5,000	$15,000 or more
White	$10,672	16.2	25.4
Spanish	7,548	30.4	10.3
Black	6,440	38.6	10.6

ment Practices Commission was a first step in that direction, but widespread and effective action to combat job discrimination did not occur until nearly a quarter of a century later, after passage of the Civil Rights Act of 1964.

Title VII, the employment section of the Civil Rights Act, created the Equal Employment Opportunity Commission (EEOC). Under Title VII, any person discriminated against on the grounds of race, religion, or national origin can lodge a complaint with the EEOC. After investigation, the EEOC can initiate court action against the discriminating employer, often on behalf of all persons in situations similar to that of the original complainant, in a class action suit. Remedies can include employment or promotion of the person discriminated against, payment of the back pay that the person would have earned had he not been discriminated against, and "affirmative action" by the employer to rectify past patterns of discrimination.

The Johnson administration established no particular pattern of prosecution of employment discrimination cases, but the Nixon administration launched an effort that focused on the unionized construction industry. There were several reasons for that focus.

First, the unionized construction industry was highly visible. Construction projects were noticeable—often too noticeable for those who lived or worked near them. Construction was booming in the late sixties, with an expanding work force and manpower shortages caused in part by the expansion of the Vietnam War. Much construction took place in urban areas, often near predominantly non-White neighborhoods. In 1972, Herbert Hill, National Labor Director for the NAACP, suggested the following reasons for the "unique importance" to Black workers of the construction industry:

- The industry is large, growing, and visible.
- Many projects are in or near large Black communities.
- Wages are high.
- The industry is comparatively dependent on public funds.
- "Jobs in the building trades are for men. In the highly important symbolic sense as well

as for practical considerations, construction jobs are 'manly' jobs" (Hill, 1972:5).

Second, discrimination in the construction industry was relatively clear-cut. Civil rights groups had already exposed many examples of blatant racism, particularly within the building trades. Few reliable data are available for the period before 1967, but the 1960 Census reported that only 2 percent of those listed as union apprentices were non-White, and many local unions barred Blacks from membership.

Finally, the construction industry was politically vulnerable. While construction contractors are predominantly Republican, they tend to make their greatest efforts in local and state politics and (except for Robert Mardian, indirectly) no construction industry representatives were found in high positions in the Nixon administration. As for the unions, Nixon owed them no favors when he assumed office in 1969.

The construction industry provides the only extensive case study to date of the effects of government efforts on job discrimination. The construction industry, one of the least understood sectors of the American economy, is in many ways unique. Construction accounts for about 13 or 14 percent of the gross national product, and the industry employs some 5 or 6 percent of the nation's labor force.[4] The industry is characterized by many relatively small firms; no contractor does as much as 1 percent of the United States' construction work by volume (Mills, 1972:ch. 1). The predominant image of the construction industry held by the average person is of unionized building and heavy construction projects. Although, in fact, less than half of the construction industry is unionized (and residential construction is overwhelmingly nonunion), the unionized sector is more visible because it has the well-known high-paying jobs and is concentrated in major cities.

The unionized construction industry is unusual in that workers often find jobs through a local union rather than an employer

---

[4] See current issues of *Construction Review*, U.S. Department of Commerce, Business and Defense Services Administration.

because of the rapidly changing requirements and temporary nature of construction projects. Many building trades local unions are referral unions, which means that they operate a hiring hall from which workers are dispatched to jobs. Although employers have the contractual right to reject workers dispatched from the hiring hall, employment is in fact controlled more by the union than by the employer. Thus, employment policies must take into consideration the roles played by both labor and management.

Until the depression of the 1930s and the founding of the Congress of Industrial Organizations (CIO) in 1935, the record of organized labor with respect to Blacks was largely negative. Only a few unions, notably the Knights of Labor in the 1880s and the United Mine Workers after 1890, made any serious efforts to recruit Black members. While the American Federation of Labor (AFL) consistently espoused nondiscrimination in principle, its constitution after 1902 sanctioned issuance of Jim Crow chapters to all-Black unions, and the AFL never enforced its nondiscriminatory policy on member unions. Thousands of Black workers were effectively denied the advantages of union organization, and their employment as strike-breakers sharpened the animosities between Black and White workers.[5] By 1940, however, the CIO's vigorous campaign to recruit Blacks had brought some 200,000 into its constituent unions, and Blacks had become an important part of the American labor movement, although they were disproportionately represented in lower-skilled jobs and industrial unions.

Since the predominant source of manpower in the unionized construction industry is the hiring hall of the referral trade union, the racial composition of union membership has become the yardstick by which progress is measured. Objective data were for a long time practically nonexistent and are still unsatisfactory. Referral unions were required to sub-

mit data on the color, sex, and ethnic makeup of their membership to the EEOC beginning in 1967.[6]

The percentage of male, non-White workers in the United States labor force remained almost constant at about 10.0 percent during the late 1960s and early 1970s, providing a convenient benchmark for achievements in the construction industry (*Manpower Report of the President*, 1973: 129–130). In 1967, 12.9 percent of construction workers were non-White, but there was a wide variation among trades. While the laborers, roofers, and trowel trades, traditionally open to minorities, had 35.7 percent minority membership, the mechanical trades had only 3.1 percent, and the miscellaneous construction trades 5.6 percent.[7]

Construction employment practices provide abundant examples of all the types of discrimination delineated by Yetman and Steele. Individual discrimination was often effected through formal or informal exclusion of non-Whites from union membership, or

[5] See the vivid description of this conflict in William F. Tuttle's *Race Riot* (New York: Atheneum Publishers, 1971), especially chapter 4, "Labor Conflict and Racial Violence."

[6] The surveys are called EEO-2, survey of apprentices, and EEO-3, survey of union membership. Caution is required in interpretation. Before Title VII, unions were prohibited from keeping the figures required by EEO-2 and 3. Union membership figures (EEO-3) are particularly suspect, as shown by more intensive surveys done in specific areas, usually during court cases. The sample of reporting unions and apprenticeship programs is far from complete and is inconsistent from year to year, reducing the comparability of data. Matched samples are generally unavailable. Also, EEO-3 covers only referral unions, which comprise less than 60 percent of the construction work force. Many union researchers charge that the surveys are poorly designed and executed. Nevertheless, the data are the best available. Other statistics are collected by the United States Department of Labor, but often they do not cover exactly the same sector of the industry. For a discussion of data problems, see Hammerman, 1972.

[7] The building trades are grouped as follows—laborers, roofers, and trowel trades: bricklayers, laborers, plasterers and cement masons, and roofers; mechanical trades: boilermakers, electrical workers, elevator constructors, iron workers, plumbers and pipefitters, and sheet metal workers; miscellaneous construction trades: asbestos workers, carpenters, lathers, marble polishers, operating engineers, painters, and decorators. There are also wide variations of non-White membership within groups, from 1.6 percent (asbestos workers) to 36.4 percent (laborers). EEOC, Local Union Report EEO-3, 1967.

through segregated local unions, non-Whites being relegated to inferior jobs and lower pay. Many companies had segregated lines of seniority (a practice more prevalent in manufacturing than construction, where seniority is usually informal). Non-Whites were often denied access to training opportunities.

Many local unions are dominated by members of one European ethnic group (especially in the East), and were themselves formed to combat past discrimination against immigrant groups (the New York Irish plumbers union to which George Meany belongs is an example). Some of these local unions have been among the most resistant to desegregation.

Adaptive discrimination is a particular problem in construction. Local unions are political institutions with elected leaders; turnover is frequent. As is so often the case where racial discrimination exists, in labor unions the bigots tend to be noisier than those who are not prejudiced, while those who are excluded have no vote within the union. Regardless of their personal feelings, union officials find it easier to do little or nothing. When job opportunities are limited, there are almost insurmountable pressures not to expand union membership; when the job market is expanding, many members expect their relatives and friends to have the first opportunities.

The AFL-CIO has formally opposed discrimination within its affiliated unions, supported equal rights legislation (including the Civil Rights Act of 1964), and sponsored many activities designed to overcome discrimination. Yet it has been a party to adaptive discrimination by inaction, placing considerations such as the need to maintain a national labor federation, the autonomy of affiliates, and internal politics ahead of the need to end discrimination.

The position of contractors illustrates the importance of making anti-discrimination regulations universal in application. Affirmative action against discrimination in construction involves substantial costs for recruitment, training, and other activities. As long as construction contracts are awarded by competitive bidding, contractors are not willing to assume costs not borne by all other contractors—costs which will put them at a competitive disadvantage. In this case, a contractor does not do well by doing good.

During the sixties, the attention of Congress and civil rights organizations was focused on attitudinal discrimination, so the greater weight of judicial and administrative action fell on those types. Formal segregation of unions and separate racial seniority lines were struck down in early court cases under the Civil Rights Act. The courts developed a guideline for the finding of discrimination: a *prima facie* case of discrimination can be made on the basis of comparison of the number of minority workers on a job and the number residing in that area. The burden is then placed on the employer to explain the disparity (Gould, 1972:380 ff.).

One frequent component of court decisions is to require the hiring of more minority journeymen, often using a quota basis (for example, every other man dispatched from the hiring hall) until the minority composition of union membership equals that of the population. The courts ruled this could be done even when the referral methods in use at the time were not themselves discriminatory, because their operation tended to perpetuate the effects of past discrimination (Gould, 1972:389–390; Hill, 1972a:247 ff.). This was an early step against discrimination.

In early 1969, the Nixon administration announced the Philadelphia Plan, the first of a series of plans that, with some exceptions, required that a minimum percentage of hours worked by each craft on a federally aided construction project be worked by minority employees. Some plans were imposed by the federal government, while others, called hometown plans, were voluntarily established by labor, management, and civil rights groups. The plans were the subject of acrimonious debate, and are generally considered to have had disappointing results in most areas, although few formal studies of them have been done. The most thorough effort to date, a study of the Indianapolis and Washington, D.C., plans by Richard Rowen, found that the achievements of the plans were chiefly attributable to two factors, the sincerity of the participants and the state of the construction job market in the area (Rowen, 1971: ch.1; see also Marshall *et al.*, 1974: ch.1).

It soon became apparent that there was an inadequate number of qualified minority craftsmen available in the unionized sector, and the courts' attention turned to patterns of entry into the industry. Construction unions typically expand their membership in three ways: through formal apprenticeship (except for laborers, a nonapprenticeable trade), through organization of nonunion journeymen, and through direct admission of unskilled persons into journeyman ranks, often working up from a helper category. Apprenticeship is the traditionally respected way of learning most of the trades, and the surest path to advancement, although less than half of all union members in the 1960s had gone through apprenticeship (Marshall et al., 1974:ch.3). Apprenticeship (jointly sponsored by labor and management) consists of three to five years of on-the-job and classroom training at a rate of pay that increases by degrees up to the journeyman rate.

Court questioning of apprenticeship practices came at a time when the perceived importance of apprenticeship to the unions was growing because of rapid technological change and greater complexity of construction process, along with a new emphasis on productivity caused by challenges from the nonunion sector. Nepotistic practices were banned in a 1969 court decision.[8]

Union and apprenticeship program admissions practices fell under the wide net of the Supreme Court's decision in *Griggs v. Duke Power Co.* (401 U.S. 424 [1971]), a landmark civil rights case potentially comparable in its effects to *Miranda* or *Brown v. Board of Education*. In the *Griggs* case, the Court held that Title VII requires removal of "artificial, arbitrary and unnecessary barriers to employment

when the barriers operate" to discriminate. Speaking for a unanimous court, Chief Justice Burger wrote:

> The Act proscribes not only overt discrimination but also practices that are fair in form, but discriminatory in operation. The touchstone is business necessity. If an employment practice which operates to exclude Negroes cannot be shown to be related to job performance, the practice is prohibited.

The implications of the above paragraph are only beginning to be realized. The Court provided a weapon that strikes to the heart of cultural discrimination. Any practice that produces a disparate effect to the disadvantage of minorities must be shown to be related to job performance, and a "business necessity," even if the practice is itself fair in form. The immediate and specific effect of the decision on construction was to strike down virtually every intelligence or aptitude test used for employment or union admission, thus removing a major barrier to minority employment.

Government and judicial action created an increased demand for minority construction workers by requiring their use of federally financed projects and by requiring affirmative-action programs with the goal of matching the percentage of minority workers with the percentage of minorities living in an area. They forced changes in the method of hiring workers and referring them to jobs, and they removed barriers that restricted access to training programs. Despite these efforts, relatively few minority workers were actually entering the construction trades, even through local unions that were fully cooperating with the new regulations. Critics claimed insincere efforts by the industry, while industry spokesmen claimed a lack of interest by qualified candidates. Both elements were undoubtedly present; the vast differences between regions, unions, and contractors makes it dangerous to generalize too freely about the construction industry.

The response to the lack of candidates was to reach another step beyond the traditional training process and create formal re-

---

[8] *Local 153, International Local Association of Heat and Frost Insulator's and Asbestos Workers v. Vogler*, 407 F. 2d 1047 (5th Cir. 1969).

TABLE 3. *Non-White Building Trades Referral Union Membership*

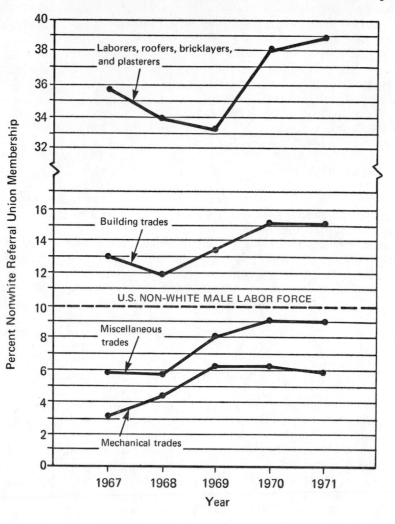

Source: EEOC Local Union Survey EEO-3

cruitment, outreach, and preparatory training programs, most supported by federal funds. The AFL-CIO has supported programs operated through the Worker's Defense League; five international unions operate Job Corps programs at thirty different sites to prepare disadvantaged high school dropouts for entry-level jobs. The Labor Education Advancement Program (LEAP) provides counseling, tutoring, and other services. Many entry-level and upgrading programs have been funded through the Manpower Development and Training Act. The experience of the construction industry demonstrates that simply removing barriers to equal employment opportunity is inadequate; vigorous (and sometimes expensive) "affirmative action" is necessary to obtain the desired results, especially in the face of continued resistance (Marshall, 1969:14–15).

By 1971, affirmative action efforts had begun to produce substantial effects. The percentage of non-Whites in building trades unions had risen to 15 percent, with the laborers, roofers, and trowel trades 38.6 percent non-White, the mechanical trades 5.7 percent non-White, and the miscellaneous trades 9 percent non-White (see Table 3). Clearly it is inappropriate to speak of the building trades as a single entity, when union minority ratios vary from 2 percent (elevator constructors) to 42.8 percent (laborers). Nor are international unions themselves monolithic in their prac-

tices, as many individual surveys have shown; they will vary in racial composition from locality to locality. For example, although 13.2 percent of building trades union members were non-Whites in 1969, 61.3 percent of building trades local unions had less than one percent Black membership, with low percentages of Black members particularly concentrated in small local unions (Hammerman, 1972:22).

Apprenticeship statistics show an even greater change (Table 4). Not only did the percentage of minority apprentices more than

TABLE 4. *Non-White apprentices as a percentage of total apprentices*

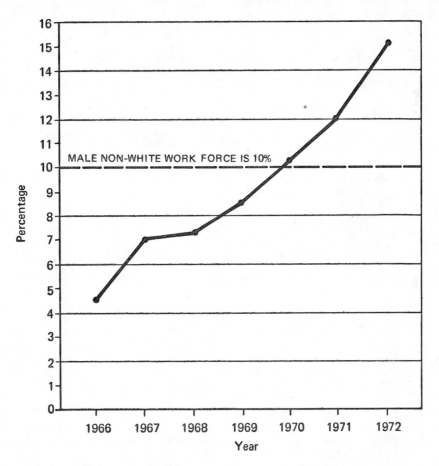

Source: Bureau of Apprenticeship and Training, U.S. Dept. of Labor: federally serviced workload as of December 31.

triple between 1966 and 1972, but non-Whites comprised 19.6 percent of the new accessions in 1972. EEOC surveys also show that non-Whites are not being dropped from apprenticeship programs at a rate higher than that for Whites (Hammerman, 1973:45).

It is interesting to compare the rise in non-White union membership to general unemployment rates in construction. Except for one year, construction unemployment rates fell steadily from 1963 through 1969 (Table 5). A relative scarcity of workers could be expected to make entry of new workers easier, and non-White union membership and apprentice membership did grow (Tables 3 and 4). Unemployment rose from 1970 through 1972, reaching a high of over 10 percent, but minority union membership rose in 1970, and minority apprentice membership continued to rise sharply throughout the period. I think this can be taken to mean that affirmative action requirements were having an effect. More non-Whites were joining unions at a time when union unemployment was rising, and the traditional "last hired, first fired" expectation for non-Whites did not take place. On the other hand, 1971 showed a slight drop in non-White union membership, indicating that earlier gains can still be imperiled by a shrinking job market.[9]

There is no consensus about the meaning

[9] Again it must be remembered that different years' samples are not the same, reducing the uses of comparisons to only the broadest trends.

TABLE 5.   *U.S. Unemployment Rates 1963–1972*

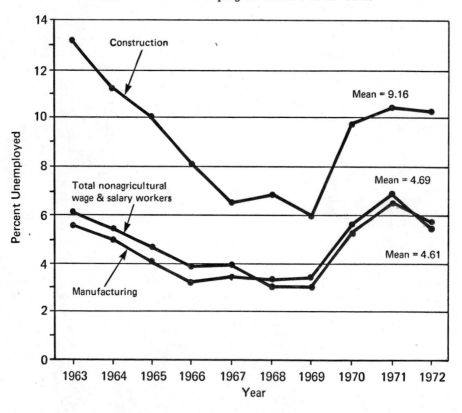

Source: Manpower Report of the President.

of the record of the last decade's efforts to increase minority employment. Union officials,
while conceding that discrimination persists in
some areas, claim that their efforts have been
sincere and their record good when compared
to problems of training, the decline in the
federal highway program, and construction
unemployment averaging 9.2 percent between
1963 and 1972. However, NAACP spokesman
Herbert Hill argues that the unions are as
recalcitrant as ever, and that whatever has
been accomplished is due to government coercion, for which Title VII has proven to be a
powerful and effective tool (Hill, 1972a:
250 ff.). Herbert Hammerman, an EEOC official, believes that the changes in minority
employment "appear to reflect a commitment
on the part of several parties, including international unions, government, and civil rights
organizations, to bring about change *within
the system as it is structured*" (Hammerman,
1973:46). Hammerman's statement brings us
to the heart of the interpretive problem. Government and voluntary efforts have had a
major impact on attitudinal discrimination.
Many forms of individual discrimination have
been ended. Government actions have been
effective against adaptive discrimination because they give the union official a scapegoat,
support those who sincerely want to end discrimination, and make contractors equal by
requiring all to support affirmative action (although unions and union contractors bitterly
criticized the Nixon administration for neglecting nonunion construction contractors in
its affirmative-action efforts).

Yet much resistance remains over measures dealing with institutional discrimination.
Unions are particularly concerned about the
possible dilution of standards for journeymen,
through the disqualification of existing ap-
prentice-selection procedures and the court-
ordered shortening and restructuring of
training programs, both apparenticeship and
nonapprenticeship. They charge that judges
and government officials are elitists, presum-
ing to restructure skilled trades they do not
understand while protecting their own professions. At a time when the unionized proportion

of the construction industry is shrinking,
unions feel that their survival depends on
offering better craftsmen than can be obtained
outside the union. AFL-CIO President George
Meany expressed his position in a speech before a building trades convention:

> There are some of these do-gooders with offi-
> cial hats, or without official hats, who feel that
> the so-called minority groups should be pro-
> vided a shortcut to attaining the skills neces-
> sary to becoming skilled building trades
> mechanics.
> Well, you and I know there is no short cut,
> and we also know there is no place in today's
> highly competitive construction industry for
> those who are not fully capable of meeting
> whatever competition there is.
> To turn out half-trained mechanics would be
> a fraud and deceit on the industry, and a fraud
> and deceit on the trainees themselves.

Meany advocates increased support for
outreach programs that will prepare minority
candidates for apprenticeship without changing existing standards (Goulden, 1972:409),
but under the *Griggs* decision all standards
must be related to successful job performance,
a phrase that has resulted in a great deal of
employment but little agreement among statis-
ticians and testing psychologists. Many apprenticeship programs have, in fact, had to
lower existing requirements for previous education and drop admissions tests.

Ray Marshall, one of the country's foremost manpower economists, has advocated
equality of opportunity for the construction
trades and projected its consequences:

> Equity would seem to require that all journey-
> men meet the same qualifications test. In other
> words, union Whites who have inferior qualifi-
> cations to nonunion Negroes should not be per-
> mitted to work without a test while Negroes
> are required to be examined simply because
> those Whites have in the past benefited from
> protection of a union which barred Negroes
> from membership. It is not discriminatory to
> require all Negroes and all Whites to meet the
> same qualification tests. In a casual industry
> like construction, we cannot assume that union
> members in a given labor market have any
> inherent right to jobs in that market, especially
> when their union has practiced racial dis-

crimination. However, we can assume that all workers who have gone through a nondiscriminatory registered apprenticeship program are qualified journeymen. [Marshall, 1970:13]

Marshall proposes performance standards for the construction trades. Some unions are actively considering performance standards for new members (some local unions have already adopted them), but elected union officials fear that testing of present members is an issue that promises political suicide for themselves; coercion would almost certainly be necessary to institute such a testing program.

Kenneth Clark, a Black educator and psychologist, has also warned against

sentimentalistic, seemingly compassionate programs of employment of Negroes which employ them on Jim Crow double standards or special standards for the Negro which are lower than those for Whites.

This is a perpetuation of racism—it is interpreted by the Negro as condescension and it will be exploited by them. Those who have been neglected and deprived must understand that they are being taken seriously as human beings. They must not be regarded as peculiar human beings who cannot meet the demands more privileged human beings can meet. [Clark, 1969:55–56].

On the other hand, S. M. Miller (1973) has outlined four moral justifications for affirmative action and other forms of "positive discrimination":

1. Compensation and rectification, "a penalty or reparation paid by society to right the wrongs it has inflicted upon particular groups" (69). Oppressed groups have accumulated disadvantages, and society has an obligation to repair the damages by giving preferences to those discriminated against, since in the past it has given preference to the dominant groups.

2. The inappropriateness of many criteria for judging qualifications (69–70). This argument parallels that of the Supreme Court in the *Griggs* decision and adds that "personnel practices ignore important abilities and experiences of disadvantaged and discriminated groups" (70).

3. Development. "The development principle argues that positive discrimination is necessary to make it possible for true equality of opportunity eventually to operate. . . . It is necessary to invest in the discriminated" (70).

4. Fairness. "The fairness principle asserts that equal opportunity cannot be thrust on discriminated people; the institutions of society and the formerly discriminated must be ready for it. . . . Since disadvantage is cumulative and not self-correcting, intervention is needed to right the situation" (71).

Miller points out that, given the goal of not merely ensuring equal opportunity but also of overcoming institutional discrimination, "it may be necessary to significantly change the structures into which the discriminated are to be integrated and from which they are to benefit." These changes include

redefinition and restructuring of tasks, reduction of wage differentials and hierarchy, participation in decisions, and different bases for recruiting and promoting people (71).

Miller's discussion raises the question of how much of an impact the law can have on society. Hill is pessimistic on this point.

While it would not be unreasonable to conclude in the light of the experience of the past six years, that if the law operated in a static society it might be possible to eliminate most racist employment practices during the next decade . . . the law functions within a rapidly changing context, where factors beyond the reach of the judicial process make it appear that the promise of equal opportunity for Black workers will not be easily realized if, indeed, it can be realized at all. Among these factors are a large-scale movement of manufacturing plants and other facilities away from urban areas, an increasingly complex technology, and a contraction of jobs in industries which had previously provided employment for large numbers of Black wage earners. . . . Moreover, racism in employment is not merely a basis for the exploitation of Black workers; it has become a culture value which is self-sustaining. To the extent that the White community continues to act upon its perceived racial interests, the institutions of society such as corporate enterprise and organized labor, in their effort to remain within the dominant racial value system, will tend to reflect that racism in its many and varied forms. Thus, a large employer may build a new plant in the suburbs for the ostensible reason of being close to a skilled labor force, among other considerations. But the new and expanding suburbs exist in large measure because of the efforts of whites to avoid residential contact with Blacks, and the employer's decision moves job opportunities away from Black workers and closer to White workers. [Hill, 1972a:265–267]*

Less pessimistic than Hill, I believe that the law has succeeded in changing mores, but that the more fundamental issues in ending discrimination have not been thoroughly aired before the majority of the American people. What we know about the attitudes of White America is somewhat contradictory and not too encouraging. On the one hand, the American public is far more liberal in its attitudes when presented with specific proposals than when queried about general ideological positions (Stewart, 1974: ch. 4). On the other hand, racial attitudes may harden as affirmative action affects a greater proportion of the economy.

In January, 1973, the Gallup organization asked reactions to the following statement:

Because they have not been given a fair chance for so long, Blacks and other minority groups should now be given special preference over others when it comes to things like jobs and being admitted into colleges and labor unions.

Eighty percent of those sampled disagreed with this argument, 15 percent agreed, and 5 percent had no opinion (Stewart, 1974:120). However, 65 percent agreed with this statement:

The only way the problems of Blacks and other minority groups can be solved is for the federal government to make an all-out effort by spending much more money on domestic problems affecting all Americans, like health, education, housing, and improving things in our cities (121).

* Editor's note: See Rabin's article, "Highways as a Barrier to Equal Access," in this section.

The poll does not suggest widespread majority-group support for affirmative action.

The future of affirmative action remains unclear. There is no overarching strategy within government or without. The course of affirmative action in construction illustrates the characteristically incremental decision-making processes of the government. The peril of incremental decision-making is that it can lead step by step down a blind corridor, eventually reaching a dead end, a discontinuity where quantitative changes become qualitative, raising issues not previously foreseen. To this malady, incremental policy is equally susceptible whether it seems to be succeeding or failing.[10]

Federal efforts became much more effective when they moved beyond the demand side of the manpower equation to include action to increase the supply of qualified workers. It is often overlooked that the unionized construction industry presents a relatively accessible (to the courts) and rationalized system of training, compared to other sectors of the economy. It is instructive to compare that industry's programs with affirmative-action programs in areas such as higher education, where efforts have been almost entirely concentrated on demand (higher rank and salaries) but very little has been done to stimulate supply: between 1968 and 1972, minority representation on college faculties increased only from 2.2 percent to 2.9 percent (American Council on Education, 1973). Similarly, the principle propounded in the *Griggs* decision, that job qualifications must be significantly related to the successful performance of those jobs, could have a revolutionary impact when applied to other sectors of the economy.

Questions fundamental to the future of our society have not been faced squarely. Should America's racial groups be evenly distributed among occupations, or is that idea a resurrection of the now-discredited melting pot

[10] For a good discussion of this point, see Amitai Etzioni's *The Active Society* (New York: Free Press, 1968).

ideal? Should the end of government policy be equality of opportunity or equality of result?

Governmental institutions have taken the lead in combating discrimination, and their efforts, if limited, have borne some fruit. But American history suggests that while the courts and government may lead for a time, they may not do so forever. An end to job discrimination must depend not only on the courts but on political action as well, and there the issue remains profoundly in doubt.

As a social goal, ending job discrimination must be linked with ending poverty. Equal access to exploitation would make the efforts of the last decade no more than another empty promise. Poverty is relative. Although non-Whites are greatly overrepresented among the poor, they are not a majority of the poor. Therefore, the interests of millions of Whites in ending institutional discrimination coincide with those of the Black underclass.

The Nixon administration's response to inflation and resource scarcity was to lower the standard of living of the average American while protecting capital. Even those non-Whites who had succeeded in gaining access to previously closed jobs found their economic position being eroded along with that of the White middle class. An end of job discrimination rests upon a much more equal distribution of the national income. In pursuit of that goal, non-Whites can become part of the new majority and exercise the power that majority brings. In this direction lies our greatest hope for a more just society.

BIBLIOGRAPHY

American Council on Education. 1973. *Teaching in Academe*. Washington, D.C.: American Council on Education.

Bryce, Herrington J. 1974. "On the Progress of Blacks." *ADA World* (April–May):19 ff.

Clark, Kenneth. 1969. Efficiency as a Prod to Social Action." *Monthly Labor Review* 92 (August): 54–56.

Derryck, Dennis A. 1972. *The Construction Industry: A Black Perspective*. Washington, D.C.: Joint Center for Political Studies.

Equal Employment Opportunity Commission. 1967–1972 (Annual) "Survey of Local Union Apprentices" (EEO-2) and "Survey of Local Union Membership" (EEO-3). Washington, D.C.: EEOC.

Gould, William B. 1972. "Racial Discrimination, the Courts, and Construction." *Industrial Relations* (October):380–393.

Goulden, Joseph C. 1972. *Meany*. New York: Atheneum.

Hammerman, Herbert. 1972. "Minority Workers in Construction Referral Unions." *Monthly Labor Review* 95 (May):17–26.

———. 1973. "Minorities in Construction Referral Unions—Revisited." *Monthly Labor Review* 96 (May):43–46.

Hill, Herbert. 1972. "Racism and Organized Labor." *The New School Bulletin*.

———. 1972a. "The New Judicial Perception of Employment Discrimination—Litigation Under Title VII of the Civil Rights Act of 1964." *University of Colorado Law Review* 43 (March):243–268.

Knowles, Louis L., and Prewitt, Kenneth. 1969. *Institutional Racism in America*. Englewood Cliffs, N.J.: Prentice-Hall.

Manpower Report of the President. 1974. Washington, D.C.: U.S. Government Printing Office.

Marshall, Ray. 1969. "The Impact of Civil Rights Laws on Collective Bargaining in the Construction Industry." *Poverty and Human Resources* 5, no. 1 (Jan.–Feb.): 5–17.

Marshall, Ray; Franklin, William S.; and Glover, Robert W. 1974. *A Comparison of Construction Workers Who Have Achieved Journeyman Status Through Apprenticeship and Other Means*. Washington, D.C.: U.S. Dept. of Labor.

Miller, S. M. 1973. "The Case for Positive Discrimination." *Social Policy* 4, no. 3 (November/December), pp. 65–71.

Mills, Daniel Quinn. 1972. *Industrial Relations and Manpower in Construction*. Cambridge, Mass.: MIT Press.

Rowen, Richard. 1971. *Gaining Entry to the Skilled Construction Trades*. Philadelphia: University of Pennsylvania Press.

Rowen, Richard, and Brudno, Robert J. 1972. "Fair Employment in Building: Imposed and Hometown Plans." *Industrial Relations* (Oct.):394–406.

Rustin, Bayard. 1971. "The Blacks and the Unions." *Harper's,* May, pp. 73–76.

Stewart, John G. 1974. *One Last Chance: The Democratic Party, 1974–76.* New York: Praeger Publishers.

U.S. Bureau of Census. 1973. *U.S. Book of Statistics and Information.* Washington, D.C.: U.S. Government Printing Office.

34

Corporate Imperialism vs. Black Liberation

Robert L. Allen

In the United States today a program of *domestic neocolonialism* is rapidly advancing. It was designed to counter the potentially revolutionary thrust of the recent black rebellions in major cities across the country. This program was formulated by America's corporate elite—the major owners, managers, and directors of the giant corporations, banks, and foundations which increasingly dominate the economy and society as a whole[1] because they

Robert L. Allen *is Associate Editor of* The Black Scholar.

[1] For an insightful recent study of corporate domination of American society, see *Who Rules America?* by G. William Domhoff (Englewood Cliffs, New Jersey: Prentice-Hall, 1967). Domhoff concludes in this carefully documented study that an identifiable "governing class," based upon the national corporate economy and the institutions nourished by that economy, exercises effective control over the national government and indeed the whole of American society.

Domhoff's conclusion is supported by an investigation of the American economy. In 1967, the most recent year for which complete figures were available, there were over one and a half million corporations active in the economy. Yet, of this corporate multitude, a mere five hundred, the top industrial companies, accounted for nearly 45 percent ($340 billion) of the total Gross National Product for that year. Economist A. A. Berle has estimated that the 150 largest corporations produce half the country's manufactured goods, and that about two-thirds of the economically productive assets of the United States are owned by not more than five hundred

believe that the urban revolts pose a serious threat to economic and social stability. Led by such organizations as the Ford Foundation, the Urban Coalition, and National Alliance of Businessmen, the corporatists are attempting with considerable success to co-opt[2] the black power movement. Their strategy is to equate black power with black capitalism.

In this task the white corporate elite has found an ally in the black bourgeoisie, the new, militant black middle class which became a significant social force following World War II. The members of this class consist of black professionals, technicians, executives, professors, government workers, etc., who got their new jobs and new status in the past two

companies. Markets for whole industries are each dominated by fewer than five corporations: aircraft engines, automobiles, cigarettes, computers, copper, heavy electrical equipment, iron, rubber, structural steel, etc. All of this places enormous economic power in the hands of a small number of semiautonomous firms. These firms in turn are controlled by largely self-perpetuating and interlocked managerial groups consisting in all of a few thousand managers and directors—the core of the corporate elite.

The fantastic economic power of these autonomous corporations has direct repercussions in the nation's political and social life. In fact, the corporations are a primary force shaping American society. Andrew Hacker, writing in *The Corporation Takeover* (New York: Harper & Row, 1964), remarked that "A *single* corporation can draw up an investment program calling for the expenditure of several billions of dollars on new plants and products. A decision such as this *may well determine the quality of life for a substantial segment of society:* Men and materials will move across continents; old communities will decay and new ones will prosper; tastes and habits will alter; new skills will be demanded, and the education of a nation will adjust itself accordingly; even government will fall into line, providing public services that corporate developments make necessary." (Emphasis added; p. 10.)

Multiply this by five hundred, and the magnitude of corporate power is immediately evident. More and more, a relative handful of firms dominate the society, yet they are not subject to the sort of democratic checks and balances which are (formally, at least) imposed on the government. These firms can decisively affect the fate of American society, but they are not controlled by that society. Consequently, bringing corporate power under social control should be a major problem listed on the public agenda.

[2] That is, to assimilate militant leaders and militant rhetoric while subtly transforming the militants' program for social change into a program which in essence buttresses the status quo.

decades.[3] They were made militant by the civil rights movement; yet many of them have come to oppose integrationism because they have seen its failures. Like the black masses, they denounced the old black elite of Tomming preachers, teachers, and businessmen-politicians. The new black elite seeks to overthrow and take the place of this old elite. To do this it has forged an informal alliance with the corporate forces which run white (and black) America.

The new black elite announced that it supported black power. Undoubtedly, many of its members were sincere in this declaration, but the fact is that they spoke for themselves as a class, not for the vast majority of black people who are not middle class. In effect, this new elite told the power structure: "Give us a piece of the action and we will run the black communities and keep them quiet for you." Recognizing that the old "Negro leaders" had become irrelevant in this new age of black militancy and black revolt, the white corporatists accepted this implicit invitation and encouraged the development of "constructive" black power. They endorsed the new black elite as their tacit agents in the black community, and black self-determination has come to mean control of the black community by a "native" elite which is beholden to the white power structure.

Thus, while it is true that blacks have been granted formal political equality, the prospect is—barring any radical changes—that black America will continue to be a semi-colony of white America, although the colonial relationship will take a new form. . . .

The urban uprisings of 1967 made it painfully obvious to America's corporate leaders that the "race problem" was out of control and posed a potential threat to the continued existence of the present society. McGeorge Bundy spoke for a significant section of American business opinion when he insisted time and time again that resolution of the race question "is now the most urgent domestic concern of this country." The endemic racism which had functioned to the advantage of an adolescent capitalism was, in this view, in dire need of serious alteration as it spawned disruption in the mature capitalist society. Blacks must be brought into the mainstream of the economy if they no longer would remain docile while confined outside of it. This did not mean that every black person should be transformed into a capitalist. Rather it implied the creation of a class of capitalists and corporate managers within the black community. The theory was that such a class would ease ghetto tensions by providing living proof to black dissidents that they can assimilate into the system if only they discipline themselves and work at it tirelessly. A black capitalist class would serve thereby as a means of social control by disseminating the ideology and values of the dominant white society throughout the alienated ghetto masses.

Speaking of the related phenomenon of tokenism, Baran and Sweezy pointedly observed:

> The theory behind tokenism, not often expressed but clearly deducible from the practice, is that the black bourgeoisie is the decisive element in the Negro community. It contains the intellectual and political elite, the people with education and leadership ability and experience. It already has a material stake in the existing social order, but its loyalty is doubtful because of the special disabilities imposed upon it solely because of its color. If this loyalty can be made secure, the potential revolutionizing of the Negro protest movement can be forestalled and the world can be given palpable

---

[3] In size this new black middle class is still quite small, although it has grown rapidly. A rough estimate of its dimensions can be gathered from the fact that in 1966 about one-eighth of all black families had annual incomes of $10,000 or more. In that same year, however, more than 70 per cent of black families received incomes of less than $7,000, and about half of these reported incomes below the poverty level. [Editor's note: By 1973 35% of black families had incomes of $10,000 or more and 48% received less than $7,000. It should be noted, however, that 65% of white families had incomes exceeding $10,000 and only 22%—less than half the percentage of black families—of white families earned less than $7,000. Although median black family income rose more than 100% during the two decades 1951–1971, the gap between median black and white incomes actually increased. See Collins' article in this section as well as the Statistical Appendix.]

evidence—through the placing of loyal Negroes in prominent positions—that the United States does not pursue a South African-type policy of *apartheid* but on the contrary fights against it and strives for equal opportunity for its Negro citizens. The problem is thus how to secure the loyalty of the black bourgeoisie.[4]

Coupled with the thrust toward black capitalism and black management is a much-touted effort to integrate black workers into the economy, particularly those whom industry designates as the "hard-core unemployed." These are persons who, when measured against normal hiring standards, simply are unemployable. They have no marketable skills. And the young among them swell the ranks of rioters. Reclamation of this group, which in 1967 numbered in the hundreds of thousands, would have the further advantage of adding about one billion dollars annually to national output, while at the same time subtracting millions from welfare costs. But, as remarked before, most of the training and retraining programs tried to date have had at best only limited success due in part to their limited scope.

Beyond opening up jobs in industry and training potential workers, some provision also must be made for those who are too old to be retrained, or are tied down by child-raising, or suffer from physical or psychosocial impairments which make it impossible for them to work. In the past this task was assigned to the welfare system. But the welfare system itself is in crisis and, as the Riot Commission's report stated, ". . . our present system of public assistance contributes materially to the tensions and social disorganization that have led to civil disorders," because the welfare system is built upon a labyrinth of federal, state, and local legislation which sometimes conflicts with itself and which requires a cumbersome inefficient bureaucracy to administer it. The Commission recommended the establishment of a simplified "national system of income supplementation," which not only would make

payments to traditional welfare recipients, such as elderly people and women with children, but which also would encompass employed persons working at substandard hours or wages and those among the unemployed for whom there are no jobs (i.e., the technologically unemployed). Backing for some type of guaranteed income scheme has been growing, and such a program quite possibly will be implemented in the foreseeable future.[5]

The emergence of corporations and corporate liberals as leaders in the effort to resolve the urban crises became apparent in August 1967 with the formation of the National Urban Coalition. Organized in Washington, the Coalition was an alliance of some twelve hundred business, labor, religious, civil rights, and government leaders. In its ranks were such corporate leaders as Roy Ash, president of Litton Industries, a major aerospace company; Henry Ford II, chairman of the Ford Motor Company; David Rockefeller, president of the Chase Manhattan Bank; Frederick J. Close, chairman of the Aluminum Company of America; and Andrew Heiskell, chairman of Time, Inc. Heiskell and New York's Mayor John Lindsay acted as co-chairmen of the group's steering committee. John Gardner, former Secretary of Health, Education, and Welfare, became chairman.

Announcing that it had committed itself "to programs instead of promises," the Coalition proceeded to set up subsidiary groups in cities around the country. Gardner called for greater black involvement in meeting the urban crisis, arguing that stability in the cities could not be achieved "until we bring into the same conversation all significant leadership elements that hold power or veto power in the life of the community." He also announced that it would take twenty-five years and perhaps two hundred billion dollars to finally solve the urban crisis.

Another major organization in the government-business partnership was the Na-

---

[4] Paul A. Baran and Paul M. Sweezy, *Monopoly Capital* (New York: Monthly Review Press, 1966), pp. 272–73.

[5] Support for a guaranteed annual income is evident among a wide range of business and political opinion. See also Robert Theobald (ed.) *The Guaranteed Income* (New York: Doubleday, 1966).

tional Alliance of Businessmen. The Johnson Administration set up NAB early in 1968, and Henry Ford II was appointed chairman. Part of its function was to act as a "one-stop service for businessmen in dealing with the federal government." Many businessmen had complained bitterly about the frustrations involved in dealing with several government agencies at once. "We had to get approval from one state and three Washington agencies for money, and this was time-consuming," said one executive. "In my opinion, no businessman has that kind of time."

NAB set high goals for itself: five hundred thousand jobs for hard-core unemployed by 1971—one hundred thousand of them by June 1969—and some two hundred thousand jobs in the summer of 1968 for youth out of school. With much fanfare, Ford began visiting other businessmen, urging them to sign pledges that they would hold a certain number of job openings for hard-core cases. The hard-core cases were to be drawn from fifty key cities which NAB listed as most in need. But despite a well-publicized beginning, NAB had to concede that its campaign to find temporary jobs for the summer of 1968 was a good bit less than successful.

In return for the businessmen's efforts, Johnson promised that 350 million dollars would be made available to cover "extraordinary" costs involved in training and supportive services.[6] He also sent to Congress a housing bill designed to subsidize the construction industry by enabling the federal government to charter construction consortiums and grant them tax concessions to bring their returns up to the level of other forms of investment.

Writing in a special issue of *Fortune* magazine devoted to "Business and the Urban Crisis" (January 1968), Max Ways discussed business's newfound interest in the racial crisis. First noting the "sluggishness and ineptitude" with which the government and most social institutions have responded to the crisis, Ways went on to write:

[6] Nixon, also, promised to provide incentives to business for training and hiring the hard-core unemployed.

. . . Since mid-year of 1967, and largely as a response to the race crisis, [the] business attitude toward the problems of the city is shifting. The ardent efforts of the nation's business institutions will be especially needed, because they have qualities demanded by the double crisis of the Negro and the city. Modern corporations are flexible and innovative. They are accustomed to sensing and meeting and evoking the changing desires of the public. Above all, they practice the difficult art of mobilizing specialized knowledge for action—i.e., the art of managing change.

Moreover, Ways wrote, business can hope to succeed where the government had failed because "Business is the one important segment of society Negroes today do not regard with bitter suspicion."

To still any remaining doubts in the minds of his businessmen readers, Ways said rehabilitation of the cities promises to open up the era of the "public market" when whole communities "will need to buy [for their residents] cleaner air and rivers, better scientific research, better techniques of learning, better traffic control." If these demands are to be met, Ways asserts, clearly the great corporations will play a large part in supplying them. "One can imagine, say, a private contractor selling an antipollution service to fifty neighboring towns and cities." This is not a far-fetched dream. There is no logical reason why the corporations cannot profitably enter the field of public works and public service on a massive and independent basis. There is a great opportunity for business here, and it appears that ghetto reorganization will be the pilot project.

One of the more vigorous units set up by the National Urban Coalition was its New York City branch. The New York Coalition was headed by Christian A. Herter, Jr., a Mobil Oil Corporation vice president. Roy Innis of CORE sat on the Coalition's board of directors. In May 1968, the organization announced plans to raise some four million dollars from private sources. Within a month the group had accumulated more than half of the amount it sought. A third of the money was to be turned over to Mayor Lindsay's Summer Program to keep the peace in the city's streets.

Part of the money was also to go to two new corporations created by the New York Urban Coalition. The corporations were to begin operations in July. One was the Coalition Development Corporation, the purpose of which was to provide managerial and technical advice to ghetto businessmen. The second was the Coalition Venture Corporation, and its purpose was to make available risk capital to ghetto businessmen. The idea for these corporations stemmed from an eighteen-page report drafted in March by the Coalition's Economic Development Task Force. "One major goal of the New York Coalition," the report began, "is to foster self-sustaining social and economic growth in the ghettos." The task force was assigned the job of determining how best to achieve this goal. "Historically," the report continued, "minority groups have been chafed and been constricted in their economic and social growth by having to live in a society where the means of generating capital frequently have been held by individuals who lived outside the minority community."

The task force concluded that ghetto businessmen are handicapped by a critical shortage of business know-how and a chronic lack of venture and operating capital. It recommended (1) that a management assistance corporation be set up "to provide managerial and other assistance to help the entrepreneurs maximize their effective use of current and future resources"; (2) that a small business investment corporation be created and licensed by the Small Business Administration "to provide equity capital and make long-term loans to ghetto entrepreneurs," and (3) the establishment of a venture capital corporation to provide funds for new investments. Within a few months the first and third proposals were implemented.

On the surface these recommendations would appear to be free of any taint of white manipulation and control. The Coalition was simply creating a mechanism for providing black entrepreneurs with the business information they required and the capital that has been denied them by the big, white banks downtown. Charges such as those leveled by Innis against Robert Kennedy's corporate endeavors in the Brooklyn ghetto would seem out of place here. Yet, when the Coalition's proposal is examined more closely, the thin but tough strings which would tie black capitalists to the corporate power structure are revealed.

In the first place, the boards of directors of each of the proposed Coalition corporations were to be the same "in order to ensure close coordination." This board would set general policy guidelines, and beneath it there would be a review committee charged with relating the guidelines to actual practice. Specifically, the review group would be concerned with establishing specific requirements for assistance, reviewing and approving (or rejecting) specific proposals, and suggesting what financial arrangements should be made. Furthermore, the review committee would have the authority to mandate the involvement of the development corporation in any projects in which it thinks this is desirable. Thus, the review group determines which ghetto businesses are funded, and it has the power to appoint what is in effect a monitor in those enterprises about which it has reservations.

The review committee itself was to consist of individuals drawn from the membership of the Coalition, representatives of financial institutions, and community representatives. Review of specific proposals would be conducted by "proposal teams" composed of five persons. The makeup of these teams is important. Two members would be drawn from the staff of Coalition corporations, two from financial institutions, and one from the community. Hence, the "proposal teams" would be securely controlled by exactly the same corporate interests which control the Urban Coalition itself, although there would be a semblance of community participation.

Investment proposals would be judged on the basis of several criteria, including location in a ghetto, providing employment opportunities to ghetto residents and "social utility."

This latter phrase was nowhere defined in the report, but some insight into its meaning is shed by the following paragraph:

> Ghetto residents complain that most of the businesses in their areas are controlled by "outsiders." . . . Real and imagined abuses and deception by the outside shopowners are major causes of discontent. This discontent implicitly or explicitly has linked "business-white-abuse" in ghetto minds so that distrust is not only of whites in business, *but of business itself. Therefore, to the extent possible, the concepts of business as a beneficial force . . . must be promoted to gain active support of the community as a whole.* [Emphasis added.]

Consequently, those proposals which, among other things, promise to help spread in black communities the corporatist mentality of business as a "beneficial force," would likely be judged by the review group as having "social utility."

Also, criteria for assessing individual applicants were listed in the task force report. In addition to criteria relating to the soundness of the applicant's business plans, the reviewers must also seek evidence of "a strong desire to succeed as an independent businessman"; evidence of a "sustained effort toward an objective, such as holding a job, accumulating savings, getting an education, or supporting a family"; evidence of the applicant's "energy and willingness to work much more than forty hours a week"; and evidence of "his understanding of his need for counseling and advice and a willingness to accept it."

In sum, it must be concluded from the foregoing that far from being a "no-strings-attached" program, the endeavors of the New York Coalition amount to a sophisticated mechanism for selecting and aiding persons in the black community who are to be programmed into the new class of black capitalists. The review group selects only those applicants who meet predetermined personal, socio-ideological, and financial standards. These standards would tend to favor those applicants who already exhibit traditional middle-class virtues of thriftiness, hard work,

and devotion to family. The development corporation then acts as a subtle means for socializing the selected individuals into the corporate world, i.e., inculcating in them those values, attitudes, and practices which are deemed desirable by the corporate groups which back the Coalition. Thus, in concrete example, can be seen how the New York corporatists' plan would generate a black capitalist buffer class firmly wedded (in both financial and ideological terms) to the white corporate structure.[7]

One of the first endeavors of the New York Coalition in this direction was the granting in late 1968 of a substantial loan to the New Acme Foundry in Harlem. The Foundry was to produce bronze, aluminum, and nonferrous metal castings for valves and fittings for the petroleum industry, bases and parts for street lamps, elevator gear blanks, parts for door locks, and medical instruments, among other products. The Foundry was expected eventually to sell shares to the Harlem community, but until that time the Harlem Commonwealth Council would be the principal shareholder. Rozendo Beasley and Donald Simmons, both HCC officers, were named, respectively, president and chairman of the board of the Foundry.

The New York Coalition makes a good example because its activities are more subtle than many other corporate efforts to penetrate and control the ghettos. The use of semiautonomous development corporations avoids the stigma of white interference and allows for maximum financial maneuverability. The more distasteful aspects of corporate manipu-

---

[7] The members of the existing black business class are not opposed to these plans so long as they are assured of "equal" status in the corporate world. Thus Berkeley G. Burrell, head of the National Business League, told a group of white business leaders in Newark in April 1968 that it was necessary to end the "system of plantationship" which white-dominated corporations have supported in the past. "What is needed," he went on, "is a positive and truly meaningful partnership of the haves and the have-nots that will place capable black men side by side with capable white men in an entrepreneur effort that can succeed."

lation and control—the kind of thing Innis complained about—are removed by one step and further glossed over by the attractive promise of community participation. However, the essential purpose for putting black power into business—the creation of a stabilizing black buffer class which will make possible indirect white control (or neocolonial administration) of the ghettos—is still guaranteed by the structure of the program.

The concept of community development corporations was given a significant boost in July 1968 with the introduction in Congress of a so-called Community Self-Determination Act. The Act enjoyed the bipartisan sponsorship of thirty-five senators and was endorsed by CORE. It calls for the inclusion of the poor into the economic system as "earners, producers, owners and entrepreneurs," and aims at "developing order, stability and participation" in the system. The Act would set up development corporations in black communities. These corporations would sell shares to local residents, and in many ways would operate as ordinary stock companies, but they would also exercise broad powers usually reserved to government agencies or indigenous community organizations. They could, for example, plan urban renewal programs and speak for the community in many areas of public policy. A National Community Corporation Certification Board would loosely supervise the development corporations, but effective control would likely rest in the hands of a professional bureaucratic elite, as was true under the antipoverty program.

At this juncture it is important to observe that the neocolonial thrust of corporate efforts in the ghetto is not necessarily correlated with the personal intentions of businessmen. Indeed, many of them are sincere reformers. Rather, this neocolonialism is an inevitable product of the structure of corporate capitalism. And one of the most significant structural aspects of modern American capitalism is the growing importance of planning by individual firms.

Some believe that black capitalism offers the best hope for achieving black self-determination. A recent report on black business in San Francisco cited a "growing consensus" that a viable, self-determined black community could be "created by the participation of black citizens in the mainstream of American economic activity and a sharing of the disposable capital which results."[8]

This belief, however, is not justified. Perhaps at the turn of the century it might have been, but, today, the American corporate economy, especially the industrial sector, is characterized by widespread planning. The free market is being replaced by a market controlled by and subservient to the large corporations. This was made necessary by the rise of modern large-scale production with its concomitant requirements of heavy capital outlays, sophisticated technology, and elaborate organization. To operate efficiently, such a complex and expensive system cannot rely on the vicissitudes of a free market. It requires careful planning, from procurement of raw materials to sale of the finished product to the consumer.

But corporate planning is antithetical to black self-determination. Corporate planning involves the subtle but nonetheless real manipulation of consumers in order to maintain and regulate demand for products. It involves corporate control of sources of supply and of labor. Genuine black self-determination would necessarily upset this process of manipulation and control, at least in the black communities (and there is a thirty-billion-dollar market in these communities alone). Consequently, if planning is to prevail (and the tendency is toward tighter and more pervasive corporate planning), then black self-determination can never be more than a chimera.

Concretely, this means that any black capitalist or managerial class must act, in effect, as the tacit representative of the white corporations which are sponsoring that class. The task of this class is to ease corporate penetration of the black communities and facilitate corporate planning and programming of the markets and human resources in

---

[8] *Black Business in San Francisco.*

those communities. This process occurs regardless of the personal motivations of the individuals involved, because it stems from the nature of the corporate economy itself and the dependent status of the fledgling, black capitalist-managerial class.

When this same process occurs between a major power and an underdeveloped country it is called neocolonialism. This latter term has been used in this study to describe corporate activities in the ghetto, because these efforts, as should by now be quite evident, are analogous to corporate penetration of an underdeveloped country. The methods and social objectives in both cases are identical. . . .

It is interesting to note that Richard M. Nixon was the first major public figure to thrust the concept of black capitalism into the public spotlight. Nixon opened the subject in a radio broadcast in Milwaukee on March 28, 1968, in which he declared that the country must give black people a better share of economic and political power or risk permanent social turbulence. "By this," Nixon said, "I speak not of black power as some of the extremists would interpret it—not the power of hate and division, not the power of cynical racism, but the power the people should have over their own destinies, the power to affect their own communities, the power that comes from participation in the political and economic processes of society. . . ."

. . . Nixon spelled out how he planned to implement his program of black capitalism. He urged that tax incentives be granted to corporations which locate branch offices or new plants in the urban ghettos, or which hire and train the unskilled and upgrade the skills of those at the bottom of the employment ladder. He asserted that new capital was needed in the ghettos. He called for expanded SBA loans, reinsurance programs to "reduce the risk of investment in poverty areas," greater use of correspondent relationships between large, white-controlled lending institutions and smaller, black-controlled ones, and he urged that churches, labor unions, and corporations doing business in poverty areas should keep some of their cash deposits in banks that serve those communities. He also called for expanded opportunities for black home ownership on the grounds that "People who own their own homes don't burn their neighborhoods. . . ."

All of this sounds terribly impressive, almost like a new beginning. But close scrutiny reveals it to be only another camouflaged effort to reassert white control over the ghettos, although that control would now be one step removed and sugar-coated with promises that blacks might "get a piece of the action. . . ."

. . . The man whom Nixon appointed to head up his newly created Council on Urban Affairs . . . Daniel P. Moynihan, believes that the cities cannot be saved by the Washington government. Instead the job will require massive local efforts which, in his view, can be brought about only by an alliance of liberals and conservatives. Moynihan's decentralism probably will work out in practice to mean that more essential social services will be turned over to business, and operated on a profit-making basis.

This privatization of government functions is advocated on the grounds that it will increase efficiency and reduce waste. While this may be possible, it is also equally likely that corporate inroads into the public sector will result in greater corporate control of ever-widening spheres of public life. The logical extension of this kind of decentralism would reduce the overt function of government to tax collector and subsidizer of corporate "urban development" programs. Put another way, the creation of Max Ways's "public market" would necessarily be accompanied by a reduction in government's ability to intervene in corporate programs and planning as they apply to that market. In the interest of expediency, corporate autonomy would take priority over democratic control. The private sector of the economy normally operates in this fashion, but to extend this mode to the public sector could well culminate in a sort of velvet-fisted corporate dictatorship of American society. However, since corporations already control or heavily influence so many aspects of American life, their open takeover of the public sector probably would be marred by only a ripple of dissent. Americans seem to adjust easily to the role of organization men.

At the apex of the new hierarchical structure being created in the ghettos is to stand the black capitalist and managerial class. This is the class which will have closest contact with corporate America and which is to act as a conduit for its wishes.

But if this new black elite is to perform its role effectively as a surrogate ruling class, then the base of the pyramid class structure being constructed in the ghetto must first be stabilized. It does no good to establish a black governing class if the foundation upon which it is built and which it is destined to rule is shaky and threatens to topple the whole edifice. The "hard-core unemployed" are especially important in this process of stabilization, because it is believed that they are a key factor in contributing to the general unrest in the ghettos. Hence, crash programs were formulated and rushed into operation to absorb at least some of these lumpenproletarians into the work force.

What are these programs to accomplish? A candid answer was given by Professor Herbert R. Northrup, chairman of the Department of Industry at the Wharton School of Finance and Commerce of the University of Pennsylvania, who did research under a Ford Foundation grant into the racial attitudes of American industry. In a magazine interview, Northrup spoke of the value of a job for an alienated black: "A job does wonders. First thing you know, he's got a mortgaged house and a mortgaged car like the rest of us—he's part of the system—and he's got to stay on the job like all the rest of us to meet the payments."[9] These few words, spoken almost casually by an intimate of "the system," nevertheless illuminate one of the many ways by which that system traps people and ties them to it. Northrup would probably term the word "trap" something of an exaggeration. He would prefer the phrase, "integrating the Negro labor

force." But this is only a euphemism which obscures a central aim of the "hard-core" programs: creating in black workers a sense of commitment or allegiance to the corporate, capitalist system.[10] Indeed, creating a sense of loyalty or indebtedness to the system appears in some instances to be much more important than actually alleviating black unemployment, the overt and much-publicized goal of these programs.

In fact, one of the criticisms leveled at government-sponsored job training programs is that they frequently tend to be unrealistic, training people for jobs which are not available and thereby unintentionally contributing to black alienation and unrest. The United States Commission on Civil Rights came close to saying precisely this in its annual report for 1967.

From the corporate point of view, a more realistic approach is that currently being taken by many companies. The Lockheed Corporation, for example, has been actively recruiting minority group workers since 1961. Unlike some companies, Lockheed is especially sensitive about being cooperative in projects that provide jobs for minorities, because it is heavily dependent on federal government contracts, which amounted to 88 percent of all Lockheed's sales between 1961 and 1967. Lockheed, therefore, became one of the first major companies to recruit and train hard-core jobless. Its experiences have become models for other corporations.

Lockheed set up its first hard-core programs at plants in Georgia and California. To qualify, a prospective trainee had to be a school dropout, out of work, with no consistent work record of any sort, and have an annual family income of three thousand dollars or less. At Lockheed-Georgia ninety-eight trainees entered the first twelve-week program. They were paid twenty to thirty dollars a week and given a transportation allowance plus five dollars per dependent. At its Sunnyvale, Cali-

---

[9] *U.S. News & World Report,* October 14, 1968.

[10] The participation of employed auto workers in the 1967 Detroit rebellion and now the Revolutionary Union Movement shows, however, that this will not necessarily be the outcome of integration programs.

fornia plant, 108 trainees signed up for two programs. In one, they were given a training allowance. In the other, they were paid the going wage of $2.40 to $2.80 per hour. Not surprisingly, the company found that those who received the higher wages were less likely to quit than those who got the low training allowance.

More surprising to company officials were other findings. The company discovered that many of the trainees had to be taught "proper standards of dress and decorum." Others had to be impressed with the necessity of reporting to work on time, and still others had to be taught the arts of verbal expression. The Lockheed counselors had to be especially patient during this orientation period.

After completing this phase, the trainees were taught basic factory skills, and then moved on to more specialized operations such as welding, sheet-metal assembly, or keypunch operation. Throughout the training period, counselors had to be adept in dealing with the trainees' personal problems such as habitual lateness, excessive drinking, or occasional jailings. But the effort was worth the trouble. Because of the solicitousness displayed by the company and its training personnel, those trainees who successfully completed the course identified with the company and became loyal employees. Their "quit" rate was substantially lower than that of workers hired normally. In short, they were "integrated" into the system.

Lockheed's experience has been corroborated by other companies which have launched similar programs. Both the Ford Motor Company and General Motors, to name two, have hired and trained hundreds of so-called unemployables and have found them to be among their more loyal employees. The explanation for this phenomenon is relatively simple. The hard-core training programs are far more than mere technical training courses. The trainee's personal habits are carefully and skillfully reshaped, and he is taught socially acceptable methods of resolving ordinary personal problems. In a word, these programs perform the same socializing function as do the public schools—of shaping and programming individuals to fit into slots in the economy and society at large. Since most, if not all, of the hard-core unemployed are school dropouts, their socialization is incomplete, and this goes a long way toward explaining their lack of motivation and inability to find and hold jobs.

If a corporation assumes the burden of completing the socialization process, then, in all likelihood, the trainee will identify with that company. The average ghetto schoolchild does not identify with the school because there is no immediate and positive reason for him to do so. School is a boring or unpleasant experience which the child must endure. But an adult in a training program receives tangible rewards in the form of a training allowance or wages and the expectation of a job at the end of the course. The rewards cannot help but facilitate the individual's identification with the company, especially in view of the low self-esteem such a person is likely to have. Thus, the training programs are the propaganda equivalent of management training courses for budding executives. Both teach requisite skills and build subtle psychological links between individual and corporation. The more sophisticated job trainee, as the more sophisticated junior executive, can be expected to identify with the corporate system as a whole, as well as the individual firm that employs him.

It goes without saying that such time-consuming training programs are expensive. If the companies had to foot the entire bill, these programs probably never would have materialized. But the federal government is picking up most of the tab, including costs for transportation services, health care, and special counseling.

Another innovation in the process of incorporating so-called unemployables into the economy is seen in special on-the-job training programs. For example, an organization known as the Board for Fundamental Education can be hired by a company to teach its low-level workers reading, writing, spelling, arithmetic, and basic English grammar with texts that relate these subjects to the employee's job. . . .

In its initial flush of enthusiasm, the business press tended to describe the new job training programs in glowing phrases. But there are long-term problems that mitigate against the eventual success of these programs to find jobs for the hard-core jobless and convince the black working class that it has a stake in the corporate system. To begin with, there is the fact that most of the programs to date are small and have only limited impact. Just to bring the black jobless rate down to the unemployment rate for whites would require finding jobs for some 350,000 unemployed blacks. In an economy which is generating new jobs at the rate of 1,500,000 per year, this may not seem like too difficult a task. But it must be borne in mind that only a very few of these jobs will be open to the average unemployed black for reasons having more to do with technological advancement than racial discrimination. And in the event of a recession, even these openings will disappear.

In June 1968, the *Wall Street Journal* made a preliminary assessment of the success of corporate efforts dealing with the racial and urban crises. The *Journal* surveyed fifty major corporations, among them the top twenty-five industrial giants, and each of the five biggest banks, insurance companies, merchandisers, utilities, and transportation companies. The survey found these companies "playing a significantly larger role in the civil rights arena than they did five, or even two, years ago," but the results were hardly anything to brag about. The *Journal* pondered the social responsibilities of corporations, but many of the executives interviewed were quite candid about this subject. "If the cities continue to deteriorate, our investments will inevitably deteriorate with them," explained Paul A. Gorman, president of the Bell System's Western Electric Company. U.S. Steel's chairman, Roger M. Blough, sternly warned that if business doesn't do something "it is a very reasonable expectation that business will experience a serious degradation of the climate which allows it to operate profitably." A chain store spokesman expressed what was probably in the backs of

the minds of many corporate executives when he said simply: "We're vulnerable."

The *Journal* survey reported on a number of instances in which corporations were aiding black businesses, hiring more black workers, and upgrading those already on the payroll. But the survey also unintentionally revealed two major problems which the corporations are incapable of handling and which threaten to subvert these efforts. Part of the reason that black unemployment is so high is that black workers have traditionally held the jobs which are now being eliminated by mechanization and computerization. At least one company in the survey reported that the percentage of blacks on its payroll had actually declined for this reason. But the pace of mechanization and automation, uneven though it is, cannot be halted because of the competitive need of individual corporations to increase efficiency and reduce costs in order to maintain profits and growth, and improve their relative standing *vis-à-vis* other companies.[11] On the contrary, it can be expected that the pace of automation will accelerate, putting more minority group and other workers without special skills out of work.

The second problem is this: In the event of a recession, most of the corporate programs would be seriously undermined. "In a serious recession, we will have a very serious problem," said James Roche, chairman of General Motors. What Roche meant was that a recession would force curtailment or complete stoppage of ghetto aid programs and cutbacks in hiring. Layoffs would probably result and, of course, blacks, who have least seniority, would be the first to go. Roche's observations reveal the precarious nature of the corporate programs, predicated as they are upon continued prosperity. But continued prosperity in the United States is heavily dependent upon the status of the international capitalist system, and this is something over which American corporations and banks do not yet have com-

---

[11] It is this factor which also precludes *socially oriented* planning in a capitalist society.

plete hegemony. Any serious dislocations in this system (e.g., monetary crises) which depleted corporate surpluses now available would sweep away black capitalism and reveal its insubstantial nature.

Even less dramatic changes in the economic climate, such as inflation-curbing spending cutbacks by the Nixon Administration, could well have serious adverse effects on embryonic black capitalism. In the past, clampdowns on inflation have been followed by recessions of greater or lesser magnitude: Unemployment rose, the stock market fell, and business went into a slump. There is no reason to believe this pattern will not be repeated, and some experts have predicted that over-all unemployment may well climb above 4 percent in 1969. Black capitalism and ghetto redevelopment, plumes on the wave of a booming economy, would be blown away by the harsh wind of recession if the wave breaks.

Assuming that no recession is in the offing, the long-term prospect still favors a critical job shortage in the cities. The Economic Development Administration, a part of the U.S. Commerce Department, said in its 1967 annual report that poverty in rural areas is getting worse. Consequently, more unskilled persons from these areas are flooding into the cities. "By 1975," the EDA reported, "the 25 largest metropolitan areas, excluding those in California, will have a potential shortage of 2.9 million jobs."

To make matters worse, there is a growing trend for industrial concerns and other businesses to move out of the cities to small towns or the suburbs. High taxes and high labor costs in the cities are what motivate this move, but the net effect is to intensify the financial crisis in the urban areas and to add to black unemployment.

Finally, there is the role of the unions. The unions have not been hospitable to training programs for the hard-core jobless as they have not been particularly friendly to black labor in general. The unfriendly attitude toward black workers supposedly stems from the period when the labor movement was in its

youth and black workers sometimes were brought in as strike breakers. This occasional scab role played by unorganized blacks fed the racism of the white workers and was used as the excuse for excluding blacks or restricting them to menial jobs. Today, with blue-collar jobs declining in some industries (notably steel) and just barely holding steady in others, the unions have adopted a tacit policy of viewing hard-core jobless, especially members of minority groups, as economic enemies. Labor leaders increasingly stress the need for protecting and preserving the existing jobs held by union members. The unemployed are seen as a great mass of potential strike breakers and scabs, ready on a moment's notice to take the union member's job and upset the wage scales for which the unions have so bitterly fought.

That this narrow-minded policy is ultimately self-destructive seemingly has not occurred to most union leaders and their rank-and-file followers. Their sole concern apparently is to protect what they have and to let the future take care of itself. The labor unions perceive the advance of automation and mechanization as a threat to their interests, but the union leaders, once militant fighters for social change, have no program other than a panicky defensive reaction for meeting this challenge. Pleas to labor leaders to organize the jobless go unheeded as the unions watch their power base eroded; the prospect of their eventual impotence seems ever more certain. . . .

To summarize: The black rebellions injected a new sense of urgency into the urban crisis and prompted the corporate elite to reassess its role in handling the problems of the cities. The strategy evolved by the corporatists calls for the establishment of a black elite which can administer the ghettos. Where possible, black workers will be reintegrated into the economy. Those blacks who can't be absorbed into the work force may be pensioned off on some type of income maintenance porgram. From the corporate viewpoint, this strategy is more efficient, less costly, and more profitable than either traditional welfare statism or massive repression. With the federal government (i.e., taxpayers) footing the bill, the corporations have all to gain and little to lose.

This strategy is fraught with difficulties and contradictions, some of which have been discussed in the preceding pages. In essence it devolves into the equivalent of a program of neocolonial manipulation, not unlike what transpires in many underdeveloped countries in the Third World. Whether it will succeed depends partly on the ability of corporate America to overcome the difficulties mentioned, and partly on the black communities themselves. In the long run, this stategy cannot help but intensify class divisions and class conflicts within the black communities. Increasingly, the majority of the black population will find itself dominated by a new oppressor class, black instead of white. . . .

35

Highways as a Barrier to Equal Access

Yale Rabin

The sprawling decentralization of this nation's metropolitan areas in the period since World War II has opened new opportunities for improved housing, employment, and schools for millions of Americans, predominantly whites, while restricting both the range of opportunities and the quality of life for blacks and other minority groups who are being relegated in steadily increasing numbers to a growing dependence on the diminishing resources of the central cities. The result is a growing polarization—racially and economically—which is persistently self-reinforcing, and which threatens to perpetuate the burdens and disadvantages which a long history of racial discrimination has produced. Many, if not most, of the great concerns generally characterized as urban problems are probably attributable to the nature of these metropolitan changes.

This polarization is a pervasive aspect of the continuing process of metropolitan decentralization and is a major condition resulting from that process. It therefore appears reasonable to assume that an effective strategy for altering this condition must deal directly with the process by which it continues to be gener-

Yale Rabin is a planning consultant based in Philadelphia, Pennsylvania.

Reprinted from *The Annals* of the American Academy of Political and Social Science 407 (May, 1973). © 1973 by The American Academy of Political and Social Science.

ated. While it is recognized that a great many diverse forces contribute to the process of decentralization, there is much evidence to suggest that transportation policies, programs, and facilities play an important role.

Based on the judgment that the effects of racial and economic polarization are grave enough to require effective remedial action, this article examines the decentralization-polarization process and those aspects of the process that are transportation related, and discusses the implications of that relationship for present and future strategies for change. The elements of the discussion are:

1. The extent of black[1] concentration in central cities, and the dispersal of whites and jobs to the suburbs, are increasing. This process has resulted, and continues to result, in reduced access to growing employment opportunities in the suburbs for inner-city blacks.

2. This reduced access is caused by both the dispersed locations of jobs in relation to black central city concentrations and the dependence for access to those jobs on automobile ownership. These in turn derive from the transportation policies and programs of the federal government, and in particular the authorization and funding of the multi-billion dollar system of metropolitan area highways, which have exerted a major influence on metropolitan dispersal.

3. State highway departments, in designing and constructing the highway systems financed by federal and state funds, have played a major role in determining the spatial distribution of suburban development. Decisions by government agencies at the federal and state levels which determine and approve the locations of highways and their points of access have been and continue to be made without regard to their impact on the redistribution of housing and employment opportunities or the comprehensively planned development of metropolitan areas.

4. In implementing these highway programs, agencies of government have, by pro-

[1] In this article the term "black" is used to describe blacks, Puerto Ricans, Mexican-Americans, and American Indians.

viding new or improved access, created billions of dollars in new land values, enriching land owners and developers, and adding substantially to the tax revenues, and consequently the amenities, of countless suburban municipalities; but have failed to take any steps to protect equal access to benefits such as housing and employment. Pending projects should be reexamined in this light.

5. While restrictive land-use controls are the most apparent obstacle to low- and moderate-income housing in the suburbs, their removal will not of itself produce housing accessible to low-income blacks, or halt the decline of central cities, or alter the pace and pattern of employment and population dispersal, or create access between existing housing and existing jobs. These changes will require a metropolitan mechanism capable of: making and implementing land-use and transportation decisions in order to locate and provide new low- and moderate-income housing in relation to and in proportion to job opportunities; channeling the growth of centers of employment and residence; and improving transportation access between those centers.

While these circumstances require changes in plans and planning, there are immediate problems that must be the concern of lawyers and lawmakers. Vigorous attempts need to be made to protect the rights of low-income and minority groups under existing transportation programs; and new laws must be enacted that enable the necessary changes in planning to take place.

It is recognized that transportation facilities and policies are not an isolated force and that other public programs have facilitated dispersed development.[2] The focus is on transportation because it is a major factor in dispersal and because transportation facilities are shaped by government policies and paid for by public funds.

It is not intended here to make a quali-

tative judgment about decentralization per se. The ecological and other considerations necessary for such an evaluation go far beyond the scope of this article. Nor is it intended to suggest that racial and economic polarization are inevitable consequences of decentralization. Decentralization, assuming the ability to alter some of the underlying forces, could conceivably result in patterns of spatial, social, and economic distribution substantially different from those that characterize the changes now taking place.

METROPOLITAN DECENTRALIZATION AND POLARIZATION

Racial Concentration

The most persistent aspect of metropolitan change is the growing concentration of blacks in the central cities and the continuing exodus of whites and jobs to the surrounding suburbs. The percentage of central city population that is black has doubled since 1950. Between 1950 and 1960, the percentage of blacks living in the central cities of Standard Metropolitan Statistical Areas (SMSAs) increased from 12 percent to 18 percent. In the decade between 1960 and 1970, in the sixty-six SMSAs having populations of 500 thousand or more, the central cities lost 1.92 million whites, while black population there increased by 2.811 million to 10.82 million. In the suburban rings, white population grew by 12.468 million to 54 million, while black population increased by 762 thousand to 2.577 million. The percentage of black population in suburban rings increased from 4.2 percent in 1960 to 4.5 percent in 1970, while the percentage of blacks in the central cities increased from 18 percent in 1960 to 24 percent in 1970. Of the 2.5 million blacks who lived in the suburbs, almost a quarter live in cities of 50 thousand or more which are located within suburban rings.[3]

---

[2] Probably the most significant of these have been the Federal Housing Administration (FHA) mortgage insurance program and the water and sewer grants program of the Department of Housing and Urban Development.

[3] U.S. Bureau of the Census, Statement of Dr. George H. Brown, Director, before the U.S. Commission on Civil Rights Hearings on Barriers to Minority Suburban Access, Washington, D.C., June 14, 1971.

In the Philadelphia SMSA, for example, the number of blacks in the suburban ring rose by 48 thousand, increasing the percentage from 6.1 percent in 1960 to 6.6 percent in 1970. However, the suburban ring in the Philadelphia SMSA includes the older cities of Burlington, Camden, and Gloucester in New Jersey; and Bristol, Chester, Coatesville, Conshohocken, and Norristown in Pennsylvania. These cities, some of which have higher rates of unemployment than does Philadelphia, accounted for almost two-thirds of the increase in black population in the seven suburban counties in the SMSA. Consequently, the black population that gained access to the newer developing communities of the suburban counties comprised less than 3 percent of the over half a million increase in those places.[4]

In the thirty-one SMSAs with a population of 1 million or more in 1970, 85.5 percent of all black households earning under $4 thousand per annum lived in the central cities. For whites, 53.6 percent of households earning under $4 thousand a year lived in the suburban ring. In the category of $10 thousand or more annually, 30.9 percent of whites and 76.8 percent of blacks remain in the central cities.[5] The high percentage of low-income white households in suburban areas is not necessarily an indication that barriers of cost do not deter whites. It is more likely the case that a substantial portion of this low-income white group are long-time residents of the older cities located within the suburban ring and not recent arrivals to the newer expanding suburban communities.

Between 1960 and 1970, the increase in the proportion of city population that is black was almost five times as great as the increase in the proportion of suburban population that is black. And, much of the small gain in the suburbs is offset by the many blacks whose new "suburban" housing is in places like Camden, New Jersey, or East St. Louis, Missouri.

[4] U.S. Census of Population, 1970.
[5] Statement of George Brown.

Dispersal of Jobs

The continuing departure of whites for the growing opportunities of the suburbs has been accompanied by a steady flow of industrial and commercial employment. In a study published in 1968, John Kain of Harvard University concluded:

> By any measure metropolitan growth, since World War II, has been rapid but unevenly distributed. Outlying portions of metropolitan areas have been growing quickly while the central areas have been growing very little and, in an increasing number of instances have actually declined. During this period, what began as a *relative* decline became an *absolute* decline for a lengthening list of central cities. Losses in retail trade and property values, declining profits for central city merchants, and falling tax bases have usually followed from these employment and population declines. Morever, depopulation was selective; the young, employed, well-to-do, and white moved to suburban areas leaving behind the aged, the unemployed, the poor, and the Negro.[6]

Kain found that between 1954 and 1963 the central cities of the forty largest metropolitan areas lost an average of 25,798 manufacturing jobs and that this loss was almost exactly offset by an average growth of manufacturing jobs in the suburbs of 25,948 jobs.[7] Significant declines were also found in retailing and wholesaling employment with the greatest percentage of decentralization occurring in wholesale employment.[8] Kain found that the data ". . . suggest an *acceleration* of postwar trends toward metropolitan dispersal."[9]

This forecast has certainly been borne out by more recent data. According to an analysis of 1970 census data published by the *New York Times,* the fifteen largest SMSAs in the

[6] John F. Kain, "The Distribution and Movement of Jobs and Industry, in *The Metropolitan Enigma,* James Q. Wilson, ed. (Cambridge, Mass.: Harvard University Press, 1968), p. 1.
[7] Ibid., pp. 19, 20.
[8] Ibid., p. 16.
[9] Ibid., p. 22.

country provided about 19 million jobs in 1960. Of these approximately 12 million were located in the central cities and 7 million in the suburbs. During the decade between 1960 and 1970, employment in the suburban areas of those SMSAs rose by over 3 million for a gain of 44 percent. During the same period, employment in the central cities declined by 836 thousand or 7 percent, and the central cities' share of total SMSA employment fell from 63 percent to 52.4 percent. By 1970, in nine of these fifteen SMSAs the number of suburban jobs exceeded the number of jobs in central cities; and for all fifteen SMSAs, 72 percent of all workers who lived in the suburbs were also working in the suburbs.[10]

When examined in greater detail, these changes are even more dramatic. In New York City between 1960 and 1970, the number of jobs dropped by almost 10 percent, a loss of almost 340 thousand, while employment in the suburbs increased by 353 thousand. In six other cities employment fell by over 10 percent. In Detroit employment within the city fell by 23 percent, or 156 thousand jobs. In the Philadelphia SMSA the number of jobs in the city fell by 98 thousand or 11.3 percent between 1960 and 1970. By contrast, jobs in the suburbs increased during the same period by 61.4 percent, a gain of 314 thousand jobs.[11]

Adjusting for the one-year difference in time, omitting the disproportionate impact of New York, and assuming conservatively that only 75 percent of the loss was in manufacturing, the average job loss in the remaining fourteen cities for the 1960–70 period was over 20 percent greater than the average job loss that Kain found for the 1954–63 period.

More recent data covering the period from January 1970 to December 1972 indicate that the trend continues unabated. In each case there has been a decline in the city's share of SMSA employment, and in each case

the rate of decline has been equal to or greater than that of the 1960–70 period.[12]

Inaccessibility

The nature and extent of racial polarization and employment dispersal are widely recognized, and disparities between the unemployment rates of blacks and whites are well known. Unemployment rates among blacks have for many years been approximately double the unemployment rates for whites. There are strong indications that, while a number of other factors including poor education, lack of skills, and racial discrimination contribute to higher unemployment rates among blacks, the inaccessibility resulting from polarization and dispersal plays an important role. Several examinations of this relationship provide compelling evidence that this is so.

Kain, in a study published in early 1968, examined these relationships for the cities of Chicago and Detroit and found that distance imposed unreasonable cost burdens on centrally located blacks, and that public transit, because it focused on the central buiness district, was badly oriented for traveling from the ghetto to outlying centers of employment.[13] He examined the effects of residential segregation on black unemployment and the effects of dispersal on black unemployment and concluded:

> While the estimates presented in this paper of Negro job loss due to housing market segregation are highly tentative, they nonetheless suggest that housing market segregation may reduce the level of Negro employment and thereby contribute to the high unemployment rate of metropolitan Negroes.[14] [Furthermore] . . . the empirical findings do suggest that postwar suburbanization of metropolitan employ-

[10] Jack Rosenthal, "Large Suburbs Overtaking Cities in the Number of Jobs Supplied, *New York Times*, October 15, 1972. These figures appear to exclude employment in state and local governments.

[11] Ibid.

[12] See U.S. Department of Labor, Bureau of Labor Statistics, *Employment and Earnings* 17, no. 9 (March 1971); ibid., vol. 19, no. 8 (February 1973).

[13] John F. Kain, "Housing Segregation, Negro Employment, and Metropolitan Decentralization, *Quarterly Journal of Economics* 82 (May 1968), pp. 180, 181.

[14] Ibid., p. 196.

ment may be further undermining the position of the Negro, and that the continued high levels of Negro unemployment in a full employment economy may be partially attributable to the rapid and adverse (for the Negro) shifts in the location of jobs.[15]

Subsequent conclusions by others have not been couched in such cautious terms.

A paper presented to the Conference on Poverty and Transportation in 1968 also acknowledged that existing public transit facilities were designed primarily to bring residents of outlying areas to the employment concentrations to be found in the central business district and then noted:

> In contrast suburban employment concentrations are being developed during an era of widespread private ownership of automobiles. They rely on their employees to commute to work by private automobile and generally are poorly serviced by transit, if at all. Central city residents, particularly low income residents and Negroes, may find suburban employment centers difficult or expensive to reach, because their incidence of private automobile ownership is relatively low. A normal expedient would be to relocate one's residence near the area of current or prospective employment. However, non-whites may be deterred from doing so by residential segregation. These factors interact so as to limit the number of job opportunities available to lower income Negroes.[16]

The author also found that distance reduced the level of information about job availability and that the scattered nature of suburban employment was a deterrent to job seeking.[17]

The National Commission on Urban Problems appointed by President Lyndon B. Johnson in 1967 examined five metropolitan areas: Baltimore, New York, Philadelphia, St. Louis, and San Francisco; and found that "commuting from the central cities of these five metropolitan areas to suburban jobs is both time consuming and costly."[18] They also found that "existing in-and-out commuter public transit systems are generally not suited to 'reverse commuting.'"[19]

A study of the Philadelphia area done at Villanova University in 1971 to examine accessibility of suburban employment by public transportation found that only 11 percent of the trips from low-income, inner-city residential zones to suburban industrial parks can be made in less than forty-nine minutes and that 42 percent would take between seventy and eighty-nine minutes. In addition, 63 percent of all trips had weekly costs between $3.50 and $8.37. The remaining 37 percent ranged in cost from $10.20 to $16.00 per week.[20] Because the rate of automobile ownership in inner-city residential zones was 11.4 persons per automobile, most residents were dependent on other means of transportation.[21] It was concluded that ". . . people who reside in low-income residential areas of Philadelphia are virtually trapped because of lack of mobility in reaching regional industrial parks."[22]

Data on distibution of employment by place of residence in the fifteen largest SMSAs for 1970 also suggest that central cities are more accessible from the suburbs than the suburbs are from the central cities. Workers who live in cities hold 70.0 percent of all city jobs and 14.4 percent of all suburban jobs, while workers who live in suburbs hold 85.6 percent of all suburban jobs and 30.0 percent of all city jobs. Suburban residents hold more than twice the proportion of city jobs that city residents hold of suburban jobs; and 70 percent of all employment-related commuting be-

---

[15] Ibid., p. 197.

[16] Edward Kalachek, "Ghetto Dwellers, Transportation, and Employment" (presented at the Conference on Poverty and Transportation, Brookline, Massachusetts, June 7, 1968), pp. 3–5.

[17] Ibid., pp. 10, 13.

[18] "Building the American City," Report of the National Commission on Urban Problems to the Congress and to the President of the United States, December 12, 1968, p. 48.

[19] Ibid.

[20] John Collura and James J. Schuster, "Accessibility of Low-Income Residential Areas in Philadelphia to Regional Industrial Parks," Institute for Transportation Studies, Villanova University, 1971, pp. 6, 7, 28, 29.

[21] Ibid., p. 41.

[22] Ibid., Abstract.

tween city and suburbs is by workers living in the suburbs. In addition, the share of city jobs held by suburban residents has increased at a much greater rate than the share of suburban jobs held by city residents.

While it is not possible here to assign specific dimensions to the role played by inaccessibility in increasing the employment disadvantages of black city residents, it appears clear that access to suburban employment opportunities is substantially reduced.

Some Related Effects

The consequences of this seemingly inexorable polarization process produces secondary effects which tend to compound and reinforce disparities in opportunity and tendencies toward dispersal. Thus the departure of commerce, industry, and middle-class residents to the suburbs may reduce the city's tax revenues. To offset this loss, new taxes are levied or rates raised, adding further to the impetus to leave. Such cities, faced with the need to spread declining tax revenues over an expanding demand for services and facilities, are unlikely to be able to compete with the more affluent suburbs for competent personnel and may be forced to hire less-qualified applicants, or reduce the number of their employees. These cutbacks result in reductions in the level and quality of services—for example, in increased classroom sizes, less frequent street maintenance, or restricted library hours.

These effects simply add to the pressure for leaving and at the same time reduce the quality of life for those who must remain. The exodus of middle-class households then hastens the further departure of retail and consumer services establishments, once again reinforcing the cycle.

The situation in the city is further compounded by the scattered successes achieved in attempts to lower suburban cost barriers. Since these have the effect of slightly lowering the income thresholds necessary for access to the suburbs, they enable some households at the upper level of the economically restricted population in the city to leave, thereby increasing the proportion of low-income households which remain.

HIGHWAYS AND DECENTRALIZATION

Highways and Suburban Development

The forces at work in the process of decentralization, while diverse, appear to fall for the most part into two general categories: (1) those that tend to create pressures to disperse and (2) those that enable or limit decentralization and influence its characteristics. The first may include, among others, lack of space for expansion, high land costs, obsolete facilities, changing transportation needs, new transportation options, high taxes, poor services, inadequate housing, poor schools, fear of violence, and racial discrimination.

The second category includes suitable and affordable land to which necessary services are available, or can be reasonably made available, and which is accessible to necessary support services such as labor, materials, markets, housing, schools, shopping, and employment.

Transportation facilities are significant factors in both categories. However, it is in the second category that they assume a dominant role; for no matter how inexpensive or suitable land may be, and no matter how adequate the supporting services and facilities may be, to make development feasible, the land must be accessible. Adequate access, or the reasonable expectation that it will be provided, is essential if development is to take place.

The relationship between land use and transportation has long been understood, and the principle that both should evolve from a planning process that fits transportation facilities to travel needs generated by planned patterns of land use is a basic element of planning theory. However, as is so often the case, practice is another matter. In metropolitan areas it is the highway system which stimulates development. The National Commission on Urban Problems was emphatic on this point:

Probably there is no more important single determinant of the timing and location of urban development than highways. Highways in effect "create" urban land where none existed before by extending the commuting distance from existing cities. The low-density pattern found in most of the Nation's suburban areas would never have been possible without the effect of high-speed highways in reducing the importance of compact urban development. As highways stretch out from existing urban areas, development quickly follows, with even the most carefully considered plans and zoning ordinances rarely providing a match for the development pressures generated. The phenomenon of strip commercial development along non-limited access roads is one example of the irresistibility of such pressures.[23]

An understanding of the development potential of highways has not been limited to planners. Highway departments across the country have, over the past twenty years, produced dozens of studies that demonstrate the "beneficial" role of highways in stimulating development and increasing land values.[24]

A striking example of highway impact is to be found in Parsippany–Troy Hills, N.J., where five highways, three of them new interstates, will intersect. Population since 1950 has increased from 15,290 to 55,112 in 1970. The value of all property in the town has risen from $107 million to $483 million in the past ten years.[25]

The principal incentive behind this growing system of metropolitan highways in the U.S. Highway Trust Fund[26] which provides about $5.5 billion annually in funds whose use is restricted by law to highway construction. These funds pay 90 percent of the costs for

highways that are elements of the interstate system and 50 percent of the cost of U.S. primary highways, state highways, and urban highways.

Between 1956 and the end of 1972, over $55 billion in Highway Trust funds had been spent on the interstate system alone. By comparison, the 1970 Urban Mass Transit Assistance Act, with its authorization of $3.1 billion over a five-year period, appears as little more than a token gesture to placate the critics of poor transportation planning.

These restricted Trust Fund subsidies, and principally the 90 percent interstate contributions, are powerful incentives to the continuing construction of highways; and in the absence of adequate funding for mass transit or control by regional plans, they are also powerful incentives for continuing uncontrolled dispersal.

Highways and Public Transit

It has already been noted that existing public transit systems are generally not capable of meeting the journey-to-work needs of those who live in the inner city who might work or seek work in the suburbs. In addition, the great volume of auto commuting generated by highway-oriented patterns of dispersal has resulted in substantial reductions in patronage on existing public transit facilities.

Public transit reached its peak patronage of 23.3 billion passengers per year in 1945. By 1970 this figure had declined to 7.3 billion, 40 percent less than the 12.1 billion passengers per year recorded in 1912.[27]

Faced with greatly reduced revenues, some transit companies have ceased to operate, thus eliminating service entirely. In most cases the result has been severe cutbacks in service and substantial increases in fares— often by as much as 400 percent since 1950— burdens that are most heavily borne by low-income inner-city residents who are most de-

[23] "Building the American City," p. 231.

[24] U.S. Department of Commerce, Bureau of Public Roads, *Highways and Economic and Social Change* (Washington, D.C.: U.S. Government Printing Office, 1964), pp. 204–21.

[25] David K. Shipler, "New Highways Shaping Future of City's Suburbs," *New York Times*, August 19, 1971.

[26] For more detailed discussion of the Trust Fund see Alan Mowbray, *Road to Ruin* (Philadelphia: Lippincott, 1969); Helen Leavitt, *Superhighway, Superhoax* (Garden City, N.Y.: Doubleday, 1970); and Ben Kelley, *The Pavers and the Paved* (New York: Donald W. Brown, Inc., 1971).

[27] Wilfred Owen, *The Accessible City* (Washington, D.C.: Brookings Institution, 1972), p. 27.

pendent on public transit for access between home and workplace.

Not only does widespread affluence intensify the traffic problem by substituting automobiles for buses but this very reaction ricochets back and intensifies the poverty problem. With the majority of the urban area residents, and practically all of the suburbanites, commuting by car, too few mass transit users remain to support good service. Thus an increase in per capita income has improved the transportation position of the majority, except perhaps in the peaks of traffic congestion but has left the poor worse off. Elderly residents, physically unable to drive, are also left worse off. . . . Simultaneously with the decline of mass transit, manufacturing, retailing, and other activities have been suburbanizing. With suburban densities far too low to support the extension of the lines of even a healthy mass transit system, the elderly, those financially unable to own a car, those unable to drive and others find that dependence on the central city mass transit system has narrowed their employment opportunities very appreciably.[28]

Highways and Planning

The planning of highways is carried out, not by metropolitan planning agencies as might be reasonably expected, but by state highway departments whose officials have repeatedly contended that they have neither the responsibility nor the authority to deal with land-use matters. Thus highway officials do not include among their considerations the developmental impacts of the routes, access points, and intersections of the systems they design.

This attitude has persisted, with the tacit approval of the Bureau of Public Roads which must approve all federally funded projects, in spite of a provision in the Federal-Aid Highway Act of 1962 that:

after July 1, 1965, the Secretary shall not approve . . . any program for projects in urban areas of more than fifty thousand population unless he finds that such projects are based on a continuing comprehensive transpor-

tation planning process carried on cooperatively by States and local communities in conformity with the objectives stated in this section.[29]

Procedures for compliance with this provision were developed by the Bureau of Public Roads, and their effect was to preserve, virtually unchanged, the prerogatives of state highway departments.

As transportation planning processes were organized in metropolitan areas, planning agencies at both local and metropolitan levels were bypassed by state highway departments which deal directly with local governing bodies and elected officials.[30]

The Bureau of Public Roads made no requirement that highway plans be consistent with land-use plans, even where such plans had been adopted by local authorities. Even the refusal of a local government to participate in cooperative planning, or to approve of highway elements within its jurisdiction, was not considered evidence that the process was ineffective, or grounds for disapproving a project. All that was required was that the state highway department make "scrupulous efforts" to obtain a local government's cooperation.[31]

Recognition of the need for comprehensive planning was not limited to the 1962 Highway Act. Subsequent highway and mass transit legislation in 1964, 1966, 1968, and 1970 has repeated and expanded the concern of Congress and instructed highway officials to coordinate roads with other forms of urban transportation, give due consideration to the impact of highways on the future development of metropolitan areas, and, in consultation with the Department of Housing and Urban Development (HUD), "assure that urban transportation systems most effectively serve both national transportation needs and the

[28] Wilbur R. Thompson, *A Preface to Urban Economics* (Baltimore: Johns Hopkins Press, 1965), p. 375.

[29] Federal-Aid Highway Act of 1962, Public Law 87-866, section 9(a).

[30] Thomas A. Morehouse, "The 1962 Highway Act: A Study in Artful Interpretation," *AIP Journal* 35, no. 3 (May 1969), p. 164.

[31] Ibid., p. 163.

comprehensively planned development of urban areas."[32]

In compliance with the 1962 Highway Act and subsequent legislation, many regional transportation agencies were established, but these were limited to advisory roles, thus leaving the authority of the state highway departments intact. All of the initiatives in the "continuing comprehensive transportation planning process" were maintained by those who allocate and spend the resources of the Highway Trust Fund. Having observed this process for several years, the National Commission on Urban Problems also found that state highway departments

. . . are able to ignore totally the desires of local officials; and no State agencies—outside the legislatures and Governors—are established to reconcile differences. The result is that State highway departments to a considerable extent go their own way, leaving local officials "holding the bag" after a poorly planned and designed highway has damaged sections of built-up areas (and left the job of relocating displacees to already hardpressed local housing officials) or completely ignored and effectively destroyed development plans. . . . In practice, then, highways are seldom used as affirmative tools for development guidance.[33]

While the Congress wisely urged comprehensive planning, the states took care to see that the light shed by planning studies should not adversely affect existing commitments. In California, for example, the legislature in compliance with the 1962 Highway Act established the Bay Area Transportation Study Commission (BATSC), but

. . . wisely provided that the Commission's existence should not interfere with or in any way impede "execution by Federal, State, or local public agencies of any projects in the Bay Area which have already been planned by such agencies, *or which might be planned during the course of the study.*"[34]

The BATSC report, issued in 1969, was frank in conceding that the highway-dominant system proposed failed to deal with problems such as the isolation of racial minorities from employment owing to lack of public transportation and low rates of automobile ownership.[35] The report explained that, "BATSC analysis and projections are based largely on extension of current policies and planning as it exists in the Bay Area."[36] The major reason for this is that "no *enforceable* general regional plan to which transportation might be fitted exists."[37]

Meanwhile, new regulations issued by the Department of Transportation in 1968 required that public hearings on highway proposals include consideration of twenty-three possible effects of highways including social, economic, and environmental impacts.[38] However, since the new regulations contained no criteria or guide lines by which these impacts were to be judged, no enforceable requirements were produced other than that these factors be "considered." During the four years that the new public hearing regulations have been in effect there is no record of a single instance in which the U.S. Department of Transportation, *on its own initiative,* rejected a highway project proposed by a state highway department because of its adverse social, economic, or environmental impact.

Approved highway plans are by definition enforceable, and their developmental consequences, in the absence of meaningful standards and enforceable regional plans, have been and continue to be determined by private developers and sanctioned by the zoning powers of local municipal governments.

Congressional concern for the comprehensively planned development of urban areas and the coordination of all forms of urban transportation is unmistakeable. It seems in-

[32] Department of Transportation Act, Public Law 89-670, 1966, section 4(g).

[33] "Building the American City," p. 231.

[34] Bay Area Transportation Study Commission, "Bay Area Transportation Report," May 1969, pp. 3, 4, emphasis added.

[35] Ibid., p. 11.

[36] Ibid., p. 74.

[37] Ibid., p. 74, emphasis added.

[38] Policy and Procedure Memorandum 20-8 BPR, January 17, 1969. Original hearing requirements relating to the interstate system required only that a hearing be held on the "economic effects" of the proposed highway.

conceivable in these circumstances that the implementation of the highway program to date can be construed as complying with their wishes. Development is guided not by plans, comprehensive or otherwise, but by private investment decisions; and a major result of the process has been the erection of massive new economic barriers to overcoming the disadvantages produced by a long history of racial discrimination.

IMPLICATIONS FOR CHANGE

Edward Banfield, writing recently in this journal, skillfully disposed of "the several factors widely held to be the principal causes of the 'urban crisis,' "[39] and concluded with a characteristic flourish:

> If these are not the principal causes of the "urban crisis," what are? My answer is that they are mainly changes in the way things are perceived, judged, and valued, and in the expectations that are formed accordingly—in a phrase, changes in the state of the public mind.[40]

While this point of view serves as a convenient rationale for the further conclusion that ". . . the 'urban crisis' is not to be solved or alleviated by government programs, however massive,"[41] it ignores both the increasing polarization which is taking place and the role played by "massive government programs" in bringing it about.

Efforts to Date

Urban economic problems, real not imagined, underlie every aspect of the "urban crisis" and are largely a consequence of the inequitable distribution of metropolitan re-

sources and opportunities. Efforts, to date, to alleviate racial and economic polarization have been directed primarily at the exclusionary barriers to the construction of low- and moderate-income housing in suburban communities. These efforts have taken several forms. There have been numerous law suits attacking the restrictive provisions of local zoning ordinances; a few states have enacted legislation that establishes procedures for overriding local zoning restrictions; a few regional planning agencies have prepared "fair share" plans for allocating low- and moderate-income housing among suburban communities; and the U.S. Department of Housing and Urban Development has revised its site location criteria in order to promote racial integration. The immediate goal of most of these efforts has been the production of moderate- rather than low-income housing.

These measures, while producing scattered instances of success, have, nevertheless, had no material effect on the gap between the growing concentrations of minority groups in central cities and the steady departure of employment opportunities to the suburban hinterland.

This is true because zoning suits generally affect only one municipality. State "anti-snob" zoning statutes depend on the initiative of developers who have been denied permission to build, and their reluctance has rendered these statutes ineffective. In New York State, a state housing agency has the authority to override local zoning and build low- and moderate-income housing; but there has been a marked reluctance to do so in wealthy suburbs of New York City such as Westchester County. Fair share plans, while they serve a useful purpose in quantifying disparities and developing allocation models, lack any authority to require compliance. New HUD site location criteria have resulted in a virtual halt to the construction of inner-city subsidized housing[42] and have resulted in the construc-

---

[39] Edward C. Banfield, "A Critical View of the Urban Crisis," *The Annals* 405 (January 1973), pp. 8–14. The factors that Banfield considers and dismisses are: overcrowding, white flight to the suburbs, the physical environment, white racism, and the multiplicity of metropolitan governments.

[40] Ibid., p. 13.

[41] Ibid., p. 14.

[42] The more recent moratorium on spending imposed by President Nixon has halted the construction of all subsidized housing for which funds had not already been committed.

tion of some units in the suburbs, the great majority of which have been occupied by whites.

Highway projects have also been challenged in the courts. And, a few of these challenges have succeeded in halting individual projects, either on the grounds that relocation resources were inadequate or that public parkland was being improperly taken. No attempt, however, has yet been made to invoke the wishes of Congress and challenge highway proposals because the auto-dominant pattern of dispersal which they generate reduces both the mobility and the basic opportunities of low-income inner-city residents. Highway proposals should be vulnerable simply on the grounds that they subvert "the comprehensively planned development of urban areas."

In the light of growing national support for mass transit, it is also important to understand that new rail transit systems such as Bay Area Rapid Transit (BART) in California and the Lindenwold Line in New Jersey are equally ineffective for improving access for inner-city residents to opportunities in the suburbs. Both systems are designed to bring suburban residents to their places of employment in the offices and stores of the central business districts. The same is also true of the rail transit systems approved for Washington and Atlanta. Both focus on the central business districts and government centers.

Metropolitan Development Policy, Equal Opportunity, and Regional Planning

While it is important that immediate attempts be made to insure that the benefits of present programs are more equitably accessible, long-range improvements will require more fundamental changes. If disparities in opportunity are to be effectively reduced, and hopefully eliminated, there must be intervention in the process itself to alter the forces that generate, shape, and sanction racial and economic polarization. Such intervention must be regional in character and must be based on a functional rather than a political definition of

the region. That is, it must not be arbitrarily restricted by state boundaries.

Regional planning agencies could effectively meet this need if granted additional authority in the context of a national urban growth policy, or more appropriately, a national metropolitan development policy. Such a policy should include, among many others, such goals as:

- the elimination of transportation barriers to and between employment and housing;
- the development of patterns of land use which can be efficiently served by public transportation;
- the development of integrated multi-mode transportation systems which fit travel mode to type and intensity of land use, and permit convenient interchange between modes;
- the provision of low- and moderate-income housing in relation to and in proportion to existing and potential opportunities for employment throughout the region.

None of the goals is in any way inconsistent with the policies set forth in existing metropolitan development and transportation legislation. Goals such as these merely express a recognition of the widespread effects of narrowly conceived programs that have been implemented in isolation from each other. Based on that recognition, they incorporate other dependent goals such as equal access to opportunity.

Such a metropolitan development policy should, of course, also include goals directed at guiding growth, protecting and improving the environment, preserving open space and natural resources, providing public services and facilities, conserving energy, and so on. All of these goals will then require the development of reasonable standards against which the performance of regional planning agencies and local governments can be evaluated.

We have both the experience and the expertise to formulate such standards. It is as feasible to establish standards for equal access to employment and housing as it is to establish standards for clean air or pupil-teacher ratios.

And, more important, we have learned through experience that the injunction to "consider," in the absence of standards, is an empty gesture which has failed to provide any protection at all. The following are a few examples of equal-opportunity related standards which might be employed in evaluating transportation proposals:

- New transportation systems and facilities should improve accessibility between centers of low-income minority-group housing and centers of employment.
- New transportation facilities must support and reinforce existing public transit systems.
- Access points to new transportation facilities may not be located within jurisdictions which do not provide housing opportunities for minority-groups and low-income households.

In order to implement such policies, regional planning agencies must be granted powers which they do not now have:

1. The planning function must be made both meaningful and objective by transference of all responsibility for the planning of transportation facilities from state highway and transportation departments to the regional planning agencies. The state agencies would of course continue to build, maintain, and operate transportation facilities and conduct research in the areas of technology and safety.

2. The regional planning agencies must be granted limited development control powers in order to meet clearly defined regional goals: as in areas where it is necessary to control growth stimulated by transportation facilities, or where low- or moderate-cost housing sites are not provided by local authorities; or to protect regional resources, provide regional facilities, or prevent the development of land not suitable for development.[43]

3. The regional planning agencies should function as regional relocation agencies to provide the maximum opportunities for access to employment-related housing for households displaced by public actions.

4. The regional planning agencies should be authorized to function as a housing authority of last resort—that is, to be able to condemn land and construct low- and moderate-income housing where local authorities fail to meet regional needs for such housing.

An early step toward the provision of improved access should be the extension of control over the locations of regional employment growth. This could be accomplished by selecting several existing suburban commercial or industrial centers which have the best access to inner-city residential areas, and which have room for expansion, and directing new development to them by restricting the further growth of the other less accessible centers. In this way a concentration of employment could be achieved which would warrant the provision of bus service to inner-city residential areas.

An analysis should also be made of land adjoining the rights-of-way of all existing rail lines in the region to identify sets of locations that have the potential for development capable of supporting rail transit service. Relocating or adding stations along existing commuter rail lines may serve to reinforce improved access policies and generate additional transit patronage. There may be instances in which relatively short extensions to these lines may serve to establish viable links between inner-city housing and suburban employment.

Current Policies Should Be Challenged

In the interim, to the continuing attacks on restrictive zoning should be added widespread efforts to bring the federal highway and transit programs into compliance with the wishes of Congress as expresed in the highway, transit,

---

[43] The political feasibility of delegating development control authority to a regional planning agency is considerably enhanced by the continuing trend toward increased revenue sharing. As long as municipal services must be financed primarily out of property taxes, local zoning prerogatives will be jealously guarded. However, the transfer of any substantial portion of this burden to revenue sharing

funds should reduce the opposition of those who view local zoning control primarily as a tool for controlling municipal expenditures.

and metropolitan development legislation of
the past ten years and the provisions of existing civil rights legislation. The restriction of
funds to financing a single mode of transportation which discriminates against low-income
persons should be challenged. Similarly, challenges should be raised to any project, road or
rail, that has the effect of reducing the travel
options of low-income persons—depriving
them of access to basic necessities such as
employment and housing. The construction of
pending projects should be halted until a
determination is made that each proposal
meets equal opportunity criteria and "most
effectively serves both national transportation
needs and the comprehensively planned development of urban areas."

It is no longer reasonable to accept the
conclusion that:

We are not yet able to plan transportation networks or systems with adequate sophistication
to preclude the occurrence of unanticipated
results in land use patterns, nor have we been
able to plan and implement land use patterns
that assure the continuing adequacy of in-
stalled or proposed transportation facilities.[44]

We have been able to do so for a long time. We
have, however, been unwilling, perhaps because "the state of the public mind" has attached insufficient importance to the burdens
imposed on some by decisions made by those
who experience only the benefits of public
programs.

[44] Max L. Feldman, "Transportation: An Equal Opportunity for Access," in *Environment and Policy*,
W. R. Ewald, Jr., ed. (Bloomington: Indiana University Press, 1968), p. 186.

36

Early Childhood Intervention: The Social Science Base of Institutional Racism

Stephen S. Baratz
Joan C. Baratz

To understand the present political and academic furor over the efficacy—and therefore the future—of such early-intervention programs as Head Start, it is necessary first to examine the basic concepts and assumptions upon which these programs are founded and then to determine whether existing data can support such an approach to the problem of educating children from black ghettoes.

This paper attempts (1) to present an overview of the interventionist literature with particular emphasis on the role of the social pathology model in interpreting the behavior of the ghetto mother, and (2) to illustrate how the predominant ethnocentric view of the Negro community by social science produces a distorted image of the life patterns of that community. The importance of this distortion is that, when converted into the rationale of social action programs, it is a subtle but pernicious example of institutional racism.

Stephen S. Baratz is a Senior Professional Associate, Institute of Medicine, National Academy of Science.

Joan C. Baratz is Director of the Education Study Center.

Reprinted from *Harvard Educational Review* 40 (Winter, 1970), pp. 29–50 by permission. Copyright © 1970 by President and Fellows of Harvard College.

This paper is concerned with the goals of intervention programs that deal with altering the child's home environment, with improving his language and cognitive skills, and most particularly with changing the patterns of child-rearing within the Negro home. These goals are, at best, unrealistic in terms of current linguistic and anthropological data and, at worst, ethnocentric and racist. We do not question the legitimacy of early childhood programs when they are described solely as nursery school situations and are not based on the need for remediation or intervention; nor do we question such programs when they increase chances for the employment of economically deprived Negroes. Finally, we do not question such programs when they are described as opportunities to screen youngsters for possible physical disorders, even though follow-up treatment of such diagnostic screening is often unavailable.

We wish to examine in more detail, however, the social pathology model of behavior and intelligence in Head Start[1] projects. We shall attempt to demonstrate that the theoretical base of the deficit model employed by Head Start programs denies obvious strengths within the Negro community and may inadvertently advocate the annihilation of a cultural system which is barely considered or understood by most social scientists. Some thirty years ago, Melville Herskovits (1938–39) made the following insightful observation when talking about culturally related behavioral differences:

[We need to recognize the existence of] . . . the historical background of the . . . behavioral differences . . . being studied and those factors which make for . . . their . . . existence, and perpetuation. When, for instance, one sees vast programs of Negro education undertaken without the slightest consideration given even to the possibility of some retention of African habits of thought and speech that might influence the Negroes' reception of the instruction thus offered—one cannot but ask

[1] We recognize that no two Head Start projects are exactly alike. Head Start is used here as a generic term for intervention programs designed for underprivileged pre-school children.

how we hope to reach the desired objectives. When we are confronted with psychological studies of race relations made in utter ignorance of characteristic African patterns of motivation and behavior or with sociological analyses of Negro family life which make not the slightest attempt to take into account even the chance that the phenomenon being studied might in some way have been influenced by the carry-over of certain African traditions, we can but wonder about the value of such work. (Herskovits, 1938–39, p. 121)

It is one of the main contentions of this paper that most, if not all, of the research on the Negro has sorely missed the implications of Herskovits' statement. Rather, research on the Negro has been guided by an ethnocentric liberal ideology which denies cultural differences and thus acts against the best interests of the people it wishes to understand and eventually help.

SOCIO-POLITICAL IDEOLOGY AND STUDIES OF THE NEGRO

Though it has seldom been recognized by investigators, it has been virtually impossible for social science to divorce itself from ideological considerations when discussing contemporary race relations. As Killian (1968) has pointed out with reference to the social science role after the 1954 Supreme Court Decision:

Because of their professional judgment that the theories were valid and because of the egalitarian and humanitarian ethos of the social sciences, many sociologists, psychologists, and anthropologists played the dual role of scientist and ideologist with force and conviction. Without gainsaying the validity of the conclusions that segregation is psychologically harmful to its victims, it must be recognized that the typically skeptical, even querulous attitude of scientists toward each other's work was largely suspended in this case. (Killian, 1968, p. 54)

Social science research with Negro groups has been postulated on an idealized norm of "American behavior" against which all behavior is measured. This norm is defined operationally in terms of the way white middle-class America is supposed to behave. The normative view coincides with current social ideology—the egalitarian principle—which asserts that all people are created equal under the law and must be treated as such from a moral and political point of view. The normative view, however, wrongly equates equality with sameness. The application of this misinterpreted egalitarian principle to social science data has often left the investigator with the unwelcome task of describing Negro behavior not as it is, but rather as it deviates from the normative system defined by the white middle class. The postulation of such a norm in place of legitimate Negro values or life ways has gained ascendance because of the pervasive assumptions (1) that to be different from whites is to be inferior and (2) that there is no such thing as Negro culture. Thus we find Glazer and Moynihan (1963) stating: "The Negro is only an American and nothing else. He has no values and culture to guard and protect" (Glazer, N. and Moynihan, D., 1963).

Billingsley (1968) has taken sharp objection to the Glazer and Moynihan statement, pointing out:

The implications of the Glazer-Moynihan view of the Negro experience is far-reaching. To say that a people have no culture is to say that they have no common history which has shaped and taught them. And to deny the history of a people is to deny their humanity. (Billingsley, 1968, p. 37)

However, the total denial of Negro culture is consonant with the melting-pot mythology and it stems from a very narrow conceptualization of culture by non-anthropologists (Baratz and Baratz, 1969). Social science has refused to look beyond the surface similarities between Negro and white behavior and, therefore, has dismissed the idea of subtle yet enduring differences. In the absence of an ethno-historical perspective, when differences appear in behavior, intelligence, or cognition, they are explained as evidence of genetic defects or as evidence of the negative effects of slavery, poverty, and discrimination. Thus, the social scientist interprets differences in behavior as genetic pathology or as the alleged pathology of the environment; he therefore fails to understand the distortion of the Negro culture that his ethnocentric assumptions and measuring devices have created. The picture that emerges from such an interpretive schema may be seen as culturally biased and as a distortion of the Negro experience.

Liberals have eagerly seized upon the social pathology model as a replacement for the genetic inferiority model. But both the genetic model and the social pathology model postulate that something is wrong with the black American. For the traditional racists, that something is transmitted by the genetic code; for the ethnocentric social pathologists, that something is transmitted by the family. The major difference between the genetic model and the social pathology model lies in the attribution of causality, *not* in the analysis of the behaviors observed as sick, pathological, deviant, or underdeveloped. An example of the marked similarity between the genetic and the social pathology perspectives can be found in the literature concerning language abilities of Negroes.

LANGUAGE ABILITIES OF NEGROES

Language proficiency is considered at length in both the social and the genetic pathology models. This concern is not accidental, but is the result of a basic assumption shared by both the social pathologists and the genetic racists that one's linguistic competence is a measure of one's intellectual capacity.

Thus we find Shaler (1890), who believed in the genetic inferiority of the Negro, writing:

> His inherited habits of mind, framed on a very limited language—where the terms were well tied together and where the thought found in the words a bridge of easy passage—gave him much trouble when he came to employ our speech where the words are like widely separated steppingstones which require nimble wits in those who use them. (Shaler, 1890, p. 23)

And later, Gonzales (1922) describes the language of the Carolina coastal Negroes called Gullahs in a similar manner:

> Slovenly and careless of speech, these Gullahs seized upon peasant English used by some of the early settlers and by the white servants of the wealthier colonists, wrapped their clumsy tongues about it as well as they could, and, enriched with certain expressive African words, it issued through their flat noses and thick lips as so workable a form of speech that it was gradually adopted by other slaves and became in time the accepted Negro speech of the lower districts of South Carolina and Georgia. With characteristic laziness, these Gullah Negroes took short cuts to the ears of their auditors, using as few words as possible, sometimes making one gender serve for three, one tense for several, and totally disregarding singular and plural numbers. (Gonzales, 1922, p. 10)

Hunt (1968) provides a similar description, but from the social pathology perspective, when he writes of the parents of Negro children:

> These parents themselves have often failed to utilize prepositional relationships with precision, and their syntax is confused. Thus, they serve as poor linguistic models for their young children. (Hunt, 1968, p. 31)

And Deutsch (1963), writing on the same subject, states:

> In observations of lower-class homes, it appears that speech sequences seem to be temporally very limited and poorly structured syntactically. It is thus not surprising to find that a major focus of deficit in the children's language development is syntactical organization and subject continuity. (Deutsch, 1963, p. 174)

Green (1964) gives us another example of the deficit orientation of social pathology thinkers:

> The very inadequate speech that is used in the home is also used in the neighborhood, in the play group, and in the classroom. Since these poor English patterns are reconstructed constantly by the associations that these young people have, the school has to play a strong

role in bringing about a change in order that these young people can communicate more adequately in our society. (Green, 1964, p. 123)

Finally, Hurst (1965) categorizes the speech of many Negro college freshmen as:

. . . [involving] such specific oral aberrations as phonemic and subphonemic replacements, segmental phonemes, phonetic distortions, defective syntax, misarticulations, mispronunciations, limited or poor vocabulary, and faulty phonology. These variables exist most commonly in unsystematic, multifarious combinations.

Because of their ethnocentric bias, both the social pathologists and the genetic racists have wrongly presumed that linguistic competence is synonymous with the development of standard English and, thus, they incorrectly interpret the different, yet highly abstract and complex, non-standard vernacular used by Negroes as evidence of linguistic incompetence or underdevelopment (Baratz, J., 1969). Both share the view that to speak any linguistic system other than standard English is to be deficient and inferior.

Since as early as 1859, when Müller (1859) wrote the *History of Ancient Sanskrit Literature*, the racist contention has been that languages (and their cognitive components) could be hierarchically ordered. Müller himself offered German as the "best" language for conceptualization, but it will not surprise anyone to learn that at various times and according to various writers, the "best" language has been the language of the particular person doing the thinking about the matter. Thus, the ethnocentrism of the social pathology model, which defines a difference as a deficit, forces the misguided egalitarian into testing a racist assumption that some languages are better than others.

THE LOGIC OF INTERVENTION

It is important, then, to understand that the entire intervention model of Head Start rests on an assumption of linguistic and cognitive deficits which must be remedied if the child is to succeed in school. The current linguistic data, however, do not support the assumption of a linguistic deficit. The linguistic competence of black children has been well documented in a number of recent investigations (Stewart, 1968; Labov and Cohen, 1967; Labov, 1969; Dillard, 1969; Baratz, 1969; Wolfram, 1969). Many lower-class Negro children speak a well ordered, highly structured, but different, dialect from that of standard English. These children have developed a language. Thus one of the basic rationales for intervention, that of developing language and cognitive skills in "defective" children, cannot be supported by the current linguistic data.

Nonetheless, the first intervention programs assumed that the causes of a Negro child's failure in school could be counteracted in those months prior to his entrance into school. Data soon became available concerning the effects of Head Start, indicating that three months was not enough time for intervention to be effective (Wolff and Stein, 1967). The social pathologists reasoned that the supposedly progressive deleterious effects of the early environment of the Negro child were so great they could not be overcome in a few months. This argument provided the basis for the extension of Head Start to a full year before school—and by extension into intervention programs which begin earlier and earlier in the child's life and which eventually call for interference with existent family and child-rearing activities.

This expanding web of concern is consistent with the deficit model. Postulation of one deficit which is unsuccessfully dealt with by intervention programs then leads to the discovery of more basic and fundamental deficits. Remediation or enrichment gradually broadens its scope of concern from the fostering of language competence to a broad-based restructuring of the entire cultural system. The end result of this line of argument occurs when investigators such as Deutsch and Deutsch (1968) postulate that "some environments are better than others."

With the recognition of failures and limitations within Head Start and like programs with a social pathology base, proponents of intervention call for earlier and earlier intervention in the child's life. This follows from an interlocking set of assumptions which they frequently make:

1. that, upon entering school, the Negro disadvantaged child is unable to learn in the standard educational environment;
2. that this inability to learn is due to inadequate mothering;
3. that the ghetto environment does not provide adequate sensory stimulation for cognitive growth.

The first premise is buttressed by the continued reports of failure of black children in our schools. Indeed, they do not benefit from the standard educational environment. (That does not, however, say anything about whether they are capable of learning generally.) The second premise is an extension of the earlier work on mothering of institutionalized children as reported by Spitz (1945), Goldfarb (1955), Rheingold (1956), and Skeels and Dye (1939). Much of this literature, however, is predicated on the total absence of a mother or mothering agent. Indeed, the Skeels follow-up study (1960) indicates that a moronic mother is better than no mother at all. The difficulty in extending this logic to the ghetto child is that *he has a mother*, and his behavior derives precisely from her presence rather than her absence.

Then too, the sensory stimulation assumption was an over-extension of the earlier work of Kretch *et al.* (1962), where animals were raised in cages with either considerable sensory stimulation or *none* at all. Again, the model was that of absence of stimulation rather than difference in type and presentation of stimulation.

THE INADEQUATE MOTHER HYPOTHESIS

It is important to understand that the inadequate mother hypothesis rests essentially on the grounds that the mother's behavior produces deficit children. It was created to account for a deficit that in actuality does not exist—that is, that ghetto mothers produce linguistically and cognitively impaired children who cannot learn. Black children are neither linguistically impoverished nor cognitively underdeveloped. Although their language system is different and, therefore, presents a handicap to the child attempting to negotiate with the standard English-speaking mainstream, it is nonetheless a fully developed, highly structured system that is more than adequate for aiding in abstract thinking. French children attempting to speak standard English are at a linguistic disadvantage; they are not linguistically deficient. Speaking standard English is a linguistic disadvantage for the black youth on the streets of Harlem. A disadvantage created by a difference is not the same thing as a deficit!

In addition, before reviewing some of the notions of the inadequate mother hypothesis, it is necessary to stress that the data presented in that literature fail to show anything more than correlations between child-rearing behaviors and school achievement. As has been discussed elsewhere (Baratz, S., 1968), these correlations cannot be utilized as if they are statements of cause and effect. Altough available data do indeed indicate that these culturally different Negro children are not being educated by the public school system, the data fail to show (1) that such children have been unable to learn to think and (2) that, because of specific child-rearing practices and parental attitudes, these children are not able (and, presumably, will never be able) to read, write, and cipher—the prime teaching responsibilities of the public school system.

Nevertheless, the inadequate mother hypothesis has proliferated in the literature of educational psychology. Of chief concern in this literature is the mother-child interaction patterns of lower-class Negroes. Despite the insistence that these patterns are the chief cause of the child's deficits, the supporting data consist almost entirely of either (1) responses to sociological survey-type questionnaires or (2) interaction situations contrived in educational laboratories. There is almost no anthropologically-oriented field work that offers a description of what actually does happen *in the home* wherein the deficit is alleged to arise.

One of the chief complaints leveled against the black mother is that she is not a teacher. Thus one finds programs such as Caldwell's (1968) which call for the "professionalization of motherhood," or Gordon's (1968) which attempts to teach the mother how to talk to her child and how to teach him to think.

The first assumption of such programs is that the ghetto mother does not provide her child with adequate social and sensory stimulation (Hunt, 1961). However, further research into the ghetto environment has revealed that it is far from a vacuum; in fact, there is so much sensory stimulation (at least in the eyes and ears of the middle-class researcher) that a contrary thesis was necessarily espoused which argues that the ghetto sensory stimulation is excessive and therefore causes the child to inwardly tune it all out, thus creating a vacuum for himself (Deutsch, C., 1968).

More recently, studies of social interaction suggest that the amount of social stimulation may be quantitatively similar for lower-class and middle-class children. Thus, the quantitative deficit explanation now appears, of necessity, to be evolving into a qualitative explanation; that is, the child receives as much or even more stimulation as does the middle-class child, but the researchers feel this stimulation is not as "distinctive" for the lower-class child as it is for the middle-class child (Kagan, 1968). Of course, it is interesting to note here that, except for those environments where social and sensory deprivation are extremely severe or total, a condition which is certainly not characteristic of the ghetto environment, there is not evidence to suggest that the ghetto child is cognitively impaired by his mother's sensory social interactions with him.

It has further been suggested that the ghetto mother manages her home in such a manner that the child has difficulty developing a proper sense of time and space—i.e. the organization of the house is not ordered around regularly occurring mealtimes and is not ruled by the White Anglo-Saxon Protestant maxim "everything in its place, and a place for everything." To the middle-class observer, such a home appears to be disorganized and chaotic, while it is merely organized differently. Thus we have data which tell what the mother does not do, but we are missing the data which describe what she does do and explain how the household manages to stay intact. Again, there is no extant research that indicates that the development of a concept of time is either helped or hindered by a child's growing up in an environment where there are regularly occurring meal- and bedtimes. There is, however, a considerable literature concerning cultural differences in the concept of time (Henry, 1965).

Further, it is continually asserted that the ghetto mother does not talk or read to her child, thus supposedly hindering his intellectual growth and language development. Despite the fact that no study has ever indicated the minimal amount of stimulation necessary for the child to learn language, and despite the fact that *the child has in fact developed language,* the ghetto mother is still accused of causing language retardation in her infant.

The mother's involvement in reading activities is also presumed to be extremely important to the child's development and future school success. The conclusions of many studies of the black ghetto home stress the absence of books and the fact that ghetto mothers rarely read to their children. Although the presence of books in the home may be quite indicative of middle-class life styles, and stories when read may very well give pleasure to all children, there appears to be no evidence which demonstrates that reading to children is essential for their learning to read, or that such reading will enhance their real language development. Although Irwin's (1960) landmark study indicates that children who are systematically read to babble more, it does not demonstrate that they are linguistically more proficient than those children who are not read to systematically.

A further factor in the mother's behavior which is continually blamed for deficits in the child is her lack of communication to him of the importance of school achievement. Although the literature presents a great many cases which illustrate that the lower-class mother verbalizes great achievement motivations concerning her children, these verbalizations are largely discredited in the eyes of some psychologists (Katz, 1968) who see little action—e.g., helping with homework, joining the PTA—underlying her statement of achievement motivation for her child. (Here, ironically, the supposedly non-verbal mother is not being penalized for her verbal behavior.) Indeed, her verbalizations tend to exhort the child to behave and achieve in class in relation to some assumed behavioral norm rather than to some educational reward; e.g., learn to read because the teacher says so, not because there are many things that one can learn from books (Hess *et al.*, 1968). Nonetheless, there do not appear to be any data which show that pre-school children resist learning, avoid schooling, or generally do not wish to achieve in the classroom; nor are there data to suggest that intrinsic motivations (learn for learning's sake) are effective for teaching reading, or that extrinsic ones (do it because I tell you) are not. In fact, the behaviorist literature tends to indicate that different sub-groups (i.e., lower-class versus middle-class) respond differently to various reinforcements (for instance, food versus praise).

The recent work of Hess, Shipman, Brophy, and Bear (1968) is sure to add considerable fuel to the inadequate mother hypothesis. Hess and his colleagues collected data on 163 black mothers and their four-year-old children. The mothers were divided into four groups: professional, skilled, unskilled-family intact, and unskilled-father absent. Social workers collected data in two extensive home interviews. Later, the mothers and children came to the university where IQ and other formal tests were administered. The mothers were also presented with theoretical situations and asked what they would do or say—e.g., what would you say to your child on his first day of school. In addition, the mothers were asked to teach their children a block-sorting task and to replicate a design on an etch-a-sketch box with their children. The Hess *et al.* data furnished a good deal of information concerning teaching styles of lower- and middle-class black women. These data, however, were undoubtedly influenced by the fact that the situations in which they were elicited (i.e., interviewing and a laboratory task) are much more typical of middle-class experiences. Nevertheless, many differences in maternal language and teaching styles appeared. It would be a mistake, however, to conclude that these differences in language and teaching style cause the child to be un-educable. What makes him appear "uneducable" is his failure in an educational system that is insensitive to the culturally different linguistic and cognitive styles that he brings to the classroom setting. The school, therefore, fails to use the child's distinct cultural patterns as the vehicle for teaching new skills and additional cultural styles.

One of the major difficulties with the work of Hess *et al.* lies in their concept of "educability." Superficially this refers to those skills which every child potentially possesses but which presumably are not developed if the mother's behavior is "restricted" and not similar to that of those middle-class mothers who produce children who succeed in school. Those skills which the child potentially possesses, however, are not defined by Hess *et al.* simply as language development, but rather more subtly as the use of standard English. Concept development is not seen as the development of language for thought (There are, of course, no languages that one cannot think in!) but rather, it is defined in terms of performance on standardized tasks or measures of verbal elaboration. Again, motivation is described not in terms of wanting to read, but rather in terms of books around the house and the use of the public library. "Educability" then, is really defined as specific middle-class mainstream behaviors rather than as the possession of universal processes through which specific behaviors can be channeled. The lower-class mother is *a priori* defined as inadequate because she is not middle-class.

In their discussions of the mothers' language behavior, Hess *et al.* rely heavily on the concepts of Basil Bernstein, who describes two different communicative styles generally used by lower- and middle-class English children. That the language and teaching behaviors of lower-class Negro mothers are different from those of middle-class mothers is beyond question. That the different behavior leads to cognitive defects has yet to be demonstrated. Carroll (1964) has discussed the methodological issue of the relationship of language style to cognition. To say that a particular language has a deleterious effect on cognitive performance, speakers of that language must be tested for cognitive ability on a non-linguistic task—such a task has yet to be developed or tested.

The Hess data, while providing considerable information on maternal behavior differences in lower- and middle-class black women, do not indicate that the children from lower-class homes are any less ready to learn than are the middle-class children, nor do they demonstrate that these children will be less able—especially if they are placed in a school that takes advantage of their experiences, as the present school curriculum does in certain crucial regards for the middle-class child. The Hess data do show, however, that the behaviors of the middle-class Negro mothers are more typically mainstream and that what these mothers teach their children is more typically within mainstream expectations; therefore, such children tend to perform better in a testing situation—and subsequently in a school situation—which requires mainstream behaviors and heuristic styles than do lower-class children, who have learned something else.

There is much to be learned about mater-

nal teaching styles and how they can be used to help the child function better in interactions with the mainstream culture. Research has indicated how unlike the middle-class mother the lower-class mother is, but there is very little description of who the lower-class mother is and what she does.

THE FAILURE OF INTERVENTION

Intervention programs postulated on the inadequacy of the mother or the lack of environmental stimulation (Shaefer, 1969; Gordon, 1968; Klaus and Gray, 1968) fail after an initial spurt in IQ scores. This appears to be an artifact of the methodology, for the first contact with mainstream educational patterns (an agent intervening in the home, a Head Start Program, kindergarten or first grade in the public school) appears automatically to cause an increase in IQ for these children. This artifact is clearly evidenced in the "catch-up" phenomenon where non-Head Start children gain in IQ apparently as a result of exposure to a school environment. The additional observation, that increases in IQ of both Head Start *and* non-Head Start children decrease after second or third grade, is a further indication that early childhood intervention is not where the answer to the failure of children in public school lies.

Interventionists argue that what is needed are school-based programs (Project Follow-Through) which maintain the "gains" of Head Start by changing the nature of the school environment. In effect, this argument is a specious one since it was the intervention program itself which was supposed to insure the child's success in the schools as they are presently constituted. For the early childhood interventionists then to turn around and say that the schools do not do their job in maintaining the increases which the school itself has generated in non-Head Start children (as well as the increases of Head Start children) is indeed to point to the crux of the matter: the failure lies in the schools, not the parents, to educate these children. This clearly indicates that critical intervention must be done, but on the procedures and materials used in the schools rather than on the children those schools service. Intervention which works to eliminate archaic and inappropriate procedures for teaching these children and which substitutes procedures and materials that are culturally relevant is critically needed. It is important to note here that such intervention procedures—e.g. the use of Negro dialect in the teaching of reading (Baratz and Baratz, 1969)—are not ends in themselves. The goal of such procedures is to have the children perform adequately on standardized achievement tests. It is the process, not the goals, of education that must be changed for these children. *The educational problems of lower-class culturally different Negro children, as of other groups of culturally different children, are not so much related to inappropriate educational goals as to inadequate means for meeting these goals.*

It is not, therefore, a particular program for early childhood intervention at a critical period which affects IQ scores. Rather it is the initial contact with mainstream middle-class behaviors that tends to raise temporarily the scores of young children. As the test items, however, begin to rely more and more heavily on the language style and usage of the middle class, these culturally different dialect-speaking children tend to decrease in test performance. Unlike the behaviors which initially raise IQ scores and which the child learns simply from contact with the middle-class system, fluency in a new language style and usage must be taught formally and systematically for it to be mastered. Indeed, this failure to teach the mainstream language styles and usage by means of the child's already existing system may well explain why the initial test gains of these children are not maintained.

The early childhood programs, as well as public schools, fail in the long run because they define educability in terms of a child's ability to perform within an alien culture; yet they make no attempt to teach him systematically new cultural patterns so that the initial

spurt in test scores can be maintained. Educability, for culturally different children, should be defined primarily as the ability to learn new cultural patterns within the experience base and the culture with which the child is already familiar. The initial test scores of culturally different children must not be mis-evaluated as evidence of educability," but rather should be viewed as evidence of the degree to which the child is familiar with the mainstream system upon which the tests are based both in content and presentation.

Because of the misconception of educability and the misevaluation of the test data, interventionists and educators create programs that are designed (1) to destroy an already functionally adequate system of behavior because it is viewed as pathological and (2) to impose a system of behavior without recognizing the existence of a functionally adequate system of behavior already in place. (Thus it is comparable to attempting to pour water into an already wine-filled pitcher.) Education for culturally different children should not attempt to destroy functionally viable processes of the sub-culture, but rather should use these processes to teach additional cultural forms. The goal of such education should be to produce a bicultural child who is capable of functioning both in his sub-culture and in the mainstream.

However, since Head Start has disregarded or attempted unknowingly to destroy that which is a viable cultural system, we should not have been surprised by its failure in attempting to "correct" these behaviors. Head Start has failed because its goal is to correct a deficit that simply does not exist. The idea that the Negro child has a defective linguistic and conceptual system has been challenged by the findings of Stewart (1964, 1967, 1968, 1969), Baratz, J. (1969), Labov (1969), and by Lesser and his colleagues (1965, 1967), who point to the structurally coherent but different linguistic and cognitive systems of these children. Indeed, the deficit model of Head Start forces the interventionist closer and closer to the moment of conception and to the possibility of genetic determination of the behavior now attributed to a negative environment. This position is plaintively described by Caldwell (1968):

> Most of us in enrichment . . . efforts—no matter how much lip service we pay to the genetic potential of the child—are passionate believers in the plasticity of the human organism. We need desperately to believe that we are born equalizable. With any failure to demonstrate the effectiveness of compensatory experiences offered to children of any given age, one is entitled to conclude parsimoniously that perhaps the enrichment was not offered at the proper time. (Caldwell, 1968, p. 81)

Elsewhere Caldwell refers to what she calls the Inevitable Hypothesis which we interpret as backing up further and further (intervene at four, at three, at one, at three months) until we are face to face with the possibility of genetic differences between Negroes and whites which forever preclude the possibility of remediation or enrichment. We are in Caldwell's debt for such a passionate statement of the real issue at hand. All educators concerned with intervention of any kind and unaware of the culture (and the alternative conceptual framework it offers) respond at a gut level to the implications which the failure of early childhood programs has for the overtly racist genetic model. The frustation due to the failure of intervention programs proposed by the social pathologists could lead to three possible lines of responses from those watching and participating in the unfolding of events. They are:

1. an increased preoccupation with very early intervention, at birth or shortly thereafter, to offset the allegedly "vicious" effects of the inadequate environment of the Negro child;
2. the complete rejection of the possibility of intervention effects unless the child is totally removed from his environment to be cared for and educated by specialists;
3. the total rejection of the environmentalist-egalitarian position in favor of a program of selective eugenics for those who seem to be totally unable to meet the demands of a technological environment—scientific racism.

Suffice it to say that recently we have seen an articulation of all three of these unfeasible positions.

The clearest line of thought currently evident comes from people such as Shaefer (1969a), Gordon (1968), and Caldwell (1967) advocating the introduction of specialists into the home who would not only provide the missing stimulation to the child, but also teach the mother how to raise her children properly. Thus, the new input is an intensive attempt to change totally the child's environment and the parent's child-rearing patterns.

But the fear is that even such a massive attempt will still fail to inoculate the child against failure in the schools. Recognizing this, Caldwell (1967) provides the model for intervention programs which take the child completely out of the home for short periods of time for the purpose of providing him with the experiences unavailable to him during his first three years of life. It is only a short distance from this position to Bettelheim's statement (*New York Times,* March 1969) advocating total removal of Negro children to kibbutz-like controlled environments in order to overcome the effects of the allegedly negative values and practices of the ghetto—in short, the annihilation of distinctive Afro-American cultural styles.

Finally, the appearance of the scholarly article recently published by Arthur Jensen (1969) in the *Harvard Educational Review* represents the attempt of a former social pathologist to deal with the failure of the intervention programs. He may find his position politically distasteful but, for a scientist who lacks a cross-cultural perspective and a historical frame of reference, it is the only way to maintain his scientific integrity. Like most scholars who come to advocate an unpopular thesis, Jensen has done his homework. His familiarity with the data indicates to him the futility of denying (1) that Negro children perform less well on intelligence tests than whites and (2) that Head Start has failed in its intent to produce permanent shifts in IQ which lead to success in the educational system. Since Jensen rejects the social pathology model but retains a concept that describes Negro behavior as defective, it is not at all surprising that he has no alternative other than a model of genetic inferiority.

However, like the social pathologists who had to create an explanation (i.e., inadequate mothering) for a non-existent deficit, Jensen is also called upon to explain the reasons for a relative theory of genetic inferiority in the American Negro. His argument, similar to those of earlier genetic racists, states that the Negroes who were brought over as slaves "were selected for docility and strength and not mental ability, and that through selective mating the mental qualities present never had a chance to flourish" (Edson, 1969). Interestingly enough, this contention was decimated almost thirty years ago by Melville Herskovits (1941) in his book, *The Myth of the Negro Past*, in which he presents historical and anthropological data to reject the notion of selective enslavement and breeding. It is precisely the absence of a sophisticated knowledge and perspective of cultural continuity and cultural change which has forced both the social pathologists and the genetic pathologists to feel that they have dealt with "culture" if they acknowledge that certain test items are "culture-bound." Such changes represent very surface knowledge of the concept of culture and, in particular, do not deal with subtle yet significant cultural differences. Many social scientists believe that they are dealing with the culture when they describe the physical and social environment of these children. One must not confuse a description of the environment in which a particular culture thrives for the culture itself.

Because historical and political factors have combined to deny the existence of a Negro culture (Baratz and Baratz, 1969), social scientists have found themselves having to choose between either a genetic deficit model or a deficit model built on an inadequate environment (the "culture" of poverty). However, our view of the current status of research on the Negro in the United States indicates that we are on the brink of a major scientific revolution with respect to American studies of

the Negro and the social action programs that derive from them. This revolution began with Herskovits and is being forwarded by the linguistic and anthropological studies of Stewart (1964–1969), Szwed (1969), Abrahams (1967), Hannerz (1969), and others. The basic assumption of this research is that the behavior of Negroes is not pathological, but can be explained within a coherent, structured, distinct, American-Negro culture which represents a synthesis of African culture in contact with American European culture from the time of slavery to the present day.

Since the pathology model of the language and thought of Negroes as it is used in intervention programs has been created by the superimposition of a standard English template on a non-standard dialect system, producing a view of that non-standard system as defective and deviant, then the data gathered in support of that pathology view must be totally re-evaluated and old conclusions dismissed, not solely because they are non-productive, but also because they are ethnocentric and distorted and do not recognize the cultural perspective. The great impact of the misuse of the egalitarian model on social science studies of the Negro must be re-examined.

As long as the social pathology and genetic models of Negro behavior remain the sole alternatives for theory construction and social action, our science and our society are doomed to the kind of cyclical (environment to genes) thinking presently evident in race relations research. Fortunately, at this critical point in our history, we do have a third model available, capable of explaining both the genetic and social pathology views with greater economy and capable of offering viable research and societal alternatives.

The major support for the assertion of a revolution in scientific thinking about the Negro comes from the discovery that the urban Negro has a consistent, though different, linguistic system. This discovery is an anomaly in that it could not have been predicted from the social pathology paradigm. This finding, if we can judge from the incredulity expressed about it by our colleagues, violates many of the perceptions and expectations about Negro behavior which are built into the assumptive base of the social pathology model. This assumptive base, it is argued, has restricted our phenomenological field to deviations from normative behavior rather than to descriptions of different normative configurations. In the present case, it would appear that the defect and difference models of Negro behavior cannot exist side by side without a growing awareness of the need for change and radical reconstruction of our modes of theorizing and conceptualizing about Negro behavior.

However, there may be resistance to adopting the cultural difference model which stems not only from the inherent methodologies of the social pathology theory, but also from the much more vague, and often unexpressed socio-political view of the particular investigator seeking to support his view of our current racial situation—views which are unarticulated and therefore unexamined. Thus, the resistance we anticipate may be intensified by the fear that talking about differences in Negro behavior may automatically produce in the social pathologist the postulation of genetic differences. This fear, so often expressed, is related to the real fact that the genetic model itself relied on behavioral differences as the basis for its conclusions about genetic determination. Three points can be made here to deal with this concern: (1) it has not and should not be the role of rational scholarly discourse to dismiss data and knowledge simply because it does not fit a particular ideological position extant at a particular moment in history; (2) differences, which indicate that learning has taken place, are not deficits; and (3) the view of the current social pathology position is in many ways prone to the same criticisms leveled at the genetic pathology model. The current scientific crisis will resolve itself solely on the basis of scholarly research and not ideology or polemic. The basic assumptions of scholarly research must be examined and models tried out that offer more successful and economical explanations.

In summary, the social pathology model has led social science to establish programs to prevent deficits which are simply not there. The failure of intervention reflects the ethnocentrism of methodologies and theories which do not give credence to the cognitive and intellectual skills of the child. A research program on the same scale as that mounted to support the social pathology model must be launched in order to discover the different, but not pathological, forms of Negro behavior. Then and only then can programs be created that utilize the child's differences as a means of furthering his acculturation to the mainstream while maintaining his individual identity and cultural heritage.

REFERENCES

Abrahams, R. *Deep Down in the Jungle,* Revised edition. Hatboro, Pa.: Folklore Associates, 1967.

Baratz, J. Language development in the economically disadvantaged child: A perspective. *ASHA,* 1968, March.

————. Linguistic and cultural factors in teaching English to ghetto children. *Elementary English,* **46,** 1969, 199–203.

————. Language and cognitive assessment of Negro children: Assumptions and research needs. *ASHA,* March, 1969.

Baratz and Shuy, R. (Eds.) *Teaching Black Children To Read.* Washington, D.C.: Center for Applied Linguistics, 1969.

Baratz, S. and J. Negro ghetto children and urban education: A cultural solution. *Bulletin of the Minnesota Council for the Social Studies,* Fall, 1968, Reprinted in *Social Education,* **33,** 4, 1969, 401–404.

————. The social pathology model: Historical bases for psychology's denial of the existence of Negro culture. APA Paper, Washington, D.C., 1969.

Baratz, S. Social science research strategies for the Afro-American. In J. Szwed (Ed.), *Black America.* New York: Basic Books, in press.

Bettelheim, B. Psychologist questions value of Head Start program. *New York Times,* March 17, 1969.

Billingsley, A. *Black Families in White America.* Englewood Cliffs, New Jersey: Prentice-Hall, Inc., 1968.

Caldwell, B. The fourth dimension in early childhood education. In R. Hess and R. Bear (Eds.), *Early Education: Current Theory, Research and Action.* Chicago: Aldine Publishing Co., 1968.

————. What is the optimal learning environment for the young child? *American Journal of Orthopsychiatry,* **37,** 1967, 9–21.

Carroll, J. *Language and Thought.* Englewood Cliffs, New Jersey: Prentice-Hall, 1964.

Deutsch, C. Auditory discrimination and learning social factors. *Merrill-Palmer Quarterly,* **10,** 1964, 277–296.

Deutsch, M. The disadvantaged child and the learning process. In Passow (Ed.), *Education in Depressed Areas.* New York: Columbia University Teachers College, 1963.

Deutsch, C. and Deutsch, M. Theory of early childhood environment programs. In R. Hess and R. Bear (Eds.), *Early Education: Current Theory, Research and Action.* Chicago: Aldine Publishing Co., 1968.

Dillard, J. L. *Black English in the United States.* New York: Random House, in press.

Dye, H. B. A study of the effects of differential stimulation on mentally retarded children. The Procedures of the American Association of the Mentally Deficient, Vol. 44, 1939, 114–136.

Edson, L. Jensenism, n. The theory that I.Q. is largely determined by the genes. *New York Times,* August 31, 1969. 10ff.

Glazer, N. and Moynihan, D. *Beyond the Melting Pot.* Cambridge, Massachusetts: MIT Press and the Harvard University Press, 1963.

Goldfarb, W. Emotional and intellectual consequences of psychological deprivation in infancy: A re-evaluation. In P. H. Hoch and J. Zobin (Eds.), *Psychopathology of Childhood.* New York: Grune and Stratton, 1955.

Gonzales, A. *The Black Border: Gullah Stories of the Carolina Coast.* South Carolina: The State Company, 1922.

Gordon, I. Research Report: Infant performance. Gainesville, Florida: Institute for Development of Human Resources, University of Florida, 1968.

Green, R. Dialect sampling and language values. In R. Shuy (Ed.), *Social Dialects and Language Learning.* Champaign, Ill.: NCTE, 1964, 120–123.

Hannerz, U. *Soulside Inquiries into Ghetto Children and Community.* Stockholm, Sweden: Almquist & Wiksele, 1969.

Henry, J. White people's time, colored people's time. *Transaction,* March–April, 1965.

Herskovits, M. The ancestry of the American Negro. *American Scholar,* 1938–39, reprinted in *The New World Negro.* Bloomington, Indiana University Press, 1966. 114–122.

————. *The Myth of the Negro Past.* New York: Harper and Brothers, 1941.

Hess, R., Shipman, V., Brophy, J. & Bear, R. *The Cognitive Environments of Urban Preschool Children.* The Graduate School of Education, University of Chicago, 1968.

Hunt, J. McV. *Intelligence and Experience.* New York: The Ronald Press Company, 1961.

————. Towards the prevention of incompetence. In J. W. Carter (Ed.), *Research Contributions from Psychology to Community Health.* New York: Behavioral Publications, 1968.

Hurst, C. G., Jr. *Psychological Correlates in Dialectolalia,* Washington, D.C., Howard University: Communities Research Center, 1965.

Irwin, D. C. Infant speech: Effect of systematic reading of stories. *Journal of Speech and Hearing Research,* 1960, **3,** 187–190.

Jensen, A. How much can we boost IQ and scholastic achievement? *Harvard Educational Review,* **39,** 1969, 1–123.

Kagan, J. His struggle for identity, *Saturday Review,* December, 1968.

Katz, I. Research issue on evaluation of educational opportunity: Academic motivation. *Harvard Educational Review,* **38,** 1968, 57–65.

Killian, L. M. *The Impossible Revolution?* New York: Random House, 1968.

Klaus, R. A. and Gray, S. W. The early training project for disadvantaged children: A report after five years. *Monograph, SRCD,* **33,** 1968.

Kretch, D., Rosenzweig, M. & Bennet, E. L. Relations between brain chemistry and problem solving among rats raised in enriched and impoverished environments. *Journal of Comparative Physiological Psychology,* **55,** 1962, 801–807.

Labov, W. The logic of nonstandard dialect. In J. Alatis (Ed.), *School of Languages and Linguistics Monograph Series, No. 22.* Georgetown University, 1969, 1–43.

Labov, W. and Cohen, P. Systematic relations of standard rules in grammar of Negro speakers. Project Literacy #7, 1967.

Lesser, G., Fifer, G. & Clark, D. H. Mental abilities of children from different social class and cultural groups. *Monograph of Society for Research in Child Development,* 1965, **30,** 647.

Malone, C. A. Developmental deviations considered in the light of environmental forces. In Pavenstedt, E. (Ed.), *The Drifters: Children of Disorganized Lower Class Families.* Boston: Little, Brown and Co., 1967.

Müller, F. M. *History of Ancient Sanskrit Literature, so far as it illustrates the primitive religion of the Brahmans.* London: Williams and Norgate, 1859.

Rheingold, H. The modification of social responsiveness in institutional babies, *Monograph of Society for Research and Child Development,* 21 (2), Serial No. 63, 1956.

Shaefer, E. Tutoring the "disadvantaged." *The Washington Post,* February 9, 1969.

———. Home tutoring, maternal behavior and infant intellectual development, APA Paper, Washington, D.C., 1969.

Shaler, N. S. The nature of the Negro, *Arena,* **3,** 1890, 23–35.

Skeels, H. Adult status of children with contrasting early life experiences. *Monograph Society for Research in Child Development,* **31,** 3, 1960, 1–65.

Skeels, H. and Dye, H. A study of the effects of differential stimulation on mentally retarded children. Proceeding of the American Association for Mental Deficiency, **44,** 1939, 114–136.

Spitz, R. Hospitalism: An inquiry into the genesis of psychiatric conditions in early childhood. *Psychoanalytic Study of the Child,* 1945, **1,** 53–74.

Stewart, W. Urban Negro speech: Sociolinguistic factors affecting English teaching. In R. Shuy (Ed.), *Social Dialects and Language Learning,* NCTE, Champaign, Ill., 1964.

———. Social dialects. In E. Gordon (Ed.), *Research Planning Conference on Language Development in Disadvantaged Children,* Yeshiva University, 1966.

———. Sociolinguistic factors in the history of American Negro dialects, *The Florida FL Reporter,* **5,** 2, Spring, 1967.

———. Sociopolitical issues in the linguistic treatment of Negro dialect. *School of Languages and Linguistics Monograph Series, No. 22.* Georgetown University, 1969, 215–223.

———. Historical and structural bases for the recognition of Negro dialect. *School of Languages and Linguistics Monograph Series, No. 22.* Georgetown University, 1969, 239–247.

———. Continuity and change in American Negro dialects. *The Florida FL Reporter,* Spring, 1968.

———. On the use of Negro dialect in the teaching of reading. In J. Baratz and R. Shuy (Eds.), *Teaching Black Children To Read.* Washington, D.C.: Center for Applied Linguistics, 1969.

37

Cultural Discrimination Through Testing

Ronald J. Samuda

INTRODUCTION

The fact that blacks score significantly lower than whites on tests of mental ability has been well documented. Several studies, ranging over the past half century, have repeatedly demonstrated that the mean score of blacks falls at one standard deviation below the mean score of whites, especially on tests which purport to measure levels of intellectual functioning. It was not the statement of those facts that angered minorities, for they have been well known to psychologists, psychometricians, geneticists, and sociologists since the introduction of mass objective-type testing during the First World War.

It was the interpretation placed on the differences between the black and white averages and the comparative distribution of scores which led to the more recent embittered controversy. For the Coleman Report (1966) had, contrary to expectations, failed to un-

Ronald J. Samuda is Associate Professor in the Department of Applied Human Development and Guidance and Assistant Dean for Program Development at Teachers College, Columbia University.

This article is based on a chapter from *Psychological Testing of American Minorities: Issues and Consequences*, by Ronald J. Samuda, copyright 1975 by Dodd, Mead & Company and used with their permission and the permission of the author.

cover any evidence that differences in IQ scores and in test results of basic academic achievement between blacks and whites were significantly related to differences in the physical facilities, curricula, and teacher characteristics of the schools. Coleman and his associates arrived at the surprising conclusion, based on careful study, that the educational provisions throughout the country were not all that different for the two ethnic groups. If the cause could not be found in the educational environment, where else, then, could it be? If the lead dictated by nurture proved to be a dead end, why not try nature? And so, the pendulum swung. Instead of environmental factors, some highly publicized papers (Jensen, 1969; Herrnstein, 1971) argued for heredity and genetic endowment as the preponderant determinant in explaining the consistent differences in obtained means between test results of blacks and whites.

To say that blacks score lower than whites because they are enslaved by genetic inferiority, or because they are victims of social, economic, and cultural deprivation, which a biased testing system helps to aggravate, is not new. Indeed, the part played by heredity, on the one hand, and the environment, on the other hand, in the test performance of black children has been investigated for a number of years. Long before Shuey (1958 and 1966) and Dreger and Miller (1960), attempts were made at compiling the existing studies of black test performance. Among the major reviewers, there were those who, like Pintner (1931), interpreted blacks' lower scores as a sign of racial inferiority, and those who, to the contrary, maintained that

The material in this publication was prepared pursuant to a contract with the National Institute of Education, U.S. Department of Health, Education and Welfare. Contractors undertaking such projects under Government sponsorship are encouraged to express freely their judgment in professional matters. Prior to publication, the manuscript was submitted to the Center for Policy Research, Columbia University, for critical review and determination of professional competence. This publication has met such standards. Points of view or opinions, however, do not necessarily represent the official view or opinions of either the Center for Policy Research or the National Institute of Education.

these differences were due to the influence of nurture and selection. In the nature versus nurture debate, Peterson (1932) reconciled both positions by recognizing that the environment as well as the race accounted for the differences between blacks' and whites' scores. Among the "equalitarian-environmentalists"—to use Shockley's term—Canady (1946) concerned himself with the problem that since tests of mental abilities had been standardized, almost without exception, on samples of white subjects, they could not be regarded as adequate measures for comparing the two groups. In his pioneer work on test bias, Klineberg (1935) found that various factors—selective migration, socioeconomic status, language, education, motivation, speed—affected to a lesser or greater degree and independently or simultaneously the scores of black children. Subsequently, his review of the literature in 1944 and North's, in 1957, led to the conclusion that there seemed to be no genetic basis for racial differences in intelligence.

It is undeniable that one had to wait until Shuey's *The Testing of Negro Intelligence,* first published in 1958 and later revised in 1966, in order to get a complete and thorough review of the intelligence test scores and studies of blacks. Her efforts command respect—over 500 studies covering a period of 50 years, drawing from books, articles, published and unpublished monographs, theses and dissertations, and using 81 different tests of intellectual ability.

The fundamental issue of the testing controversy has been well expressed by Roger Lennon at the 1969 Invitational Conference on Measurement in Education. "There is a deep-seated conviction," Lennon says, "that the performance of poor black, Puerto Rican, Mexican-American or just poverty-stricken examinees on these tests will be relatively poor; that because of this poor performance, inferences will be made as to the ability of these examinees, which inferences will lead to treatment either in school or on jobs that will in effect constitute a denial of opportunity" (p. 42). Basically, one can say that the issue has re-

mained the same over the years; yet, it seems that the Sixties and early Seventies have raised a new concern. As Lennon remarks in the above-cited address:

> The discussion has moved off the pages of educational and psychological journals onto the pages of mass media. Its forum has moved from the classroom and the psychological laboratory to City Hall and the courtroom. The tone of the discourse has become strident and emotional. The matter of bias and relevancy of test results has become political and central to a great many other concerns in the entire civil rights movement (p. 43).

The debate concerning standardized tests, and especially the interpretations placed on the results or scores of minorities, has intensified in recent years. The public has been alerted to the social, economic, educational, and psychological implications of testing which preserves the status quo and relegates black and other minorities to an inferior status in the society at large. A cadre of black, Hispanic-American, and other minority social scientists has spearheaded the attack on the testing industry and many eminent non-minority psychologists, sociologists, and educators have joined the ranks of those who claim that testing serves a gatekeeping function to keep poor people poor and minorities at the bottom of the social scale. The implications and consequences of testing are far-reaching in the areas of education, especially higher education, in industry and employment. Testing is seen by many as the chief element in retarding the social mobility of minorities and in blocking the path for the poor, the black and other minorities to share in the educational opportunities, and by extension, in the goods of society.

So far, relatively unopposed and unchallenged in its selective and censoring function, the testing industry has been subjected to a national wave of disenchantment, skepticism and hostility as evidenced in the numerous lawsuits, court rulings and in the positions taken by the Association of Black Psychologists and the American Personnel and Guidance Association.

A SOCIAL CRITICISM OF TESTING

. . . The most common individually administered instruments used to measure the intelligence of children in the United States are the Stanford-Binet Intelligence Scales and the Wechsler Intelligence Scale for Children (WISC). A brief examination of both tests will reveal that their standardization samples included no black children. Among the various U.S. versions of the Binet-Simon Intelligence Scales, the Stanford revision emerged as the standard test of intelligence. First developed at Stanford University in 1916 and later revised in 1937 by Lewis Terman in collaboration with Maud Merrill, the Stanford-Binet was standardized on a sample comprising 3,184 boys and girls ranging from 1.5 to 18 years of age, drawing from eleven states and from urban and rural, high and low socioeconomic milieux. In *Measuring Intelligence* (1937), Terman and Merrill gave the following account of their standardization sample:

> In order to secure a representative group of school children, we chose them from different sections of the country, trying to avoid selective factors due to social and economic status. We chose average schools, and, as far as possible, recruited the pre-school group from younger brothers or sisters of children already in school. *All subjects are American-born and belong to the white race.* There has been no elimination of any particular nationality groups. (p. 12)

One is, therefore, drawn to conclude, along with Kimble and Garmezy (1968) that "for this reason, the test proved to be of doubtful validity in evaluating the intelligence of foreign born or Negro children or for comparing their intelligence with that of native white children" (p. 508). A similar statement could be made in the case of the WISC for the manual put out by the Psychological Corporation in 1949 mentioned that only white children were examined. The chosen sample included 2,200 children (1,100 boys and 1,100 girls) ranging from 5 to 15 years of age and carefully screened as far as geographical

distribution and socioeconomic status were concerned. Among the researches cited by Dreger and Miller (1960) that used the WISC, Young and Bright (1954) and Caldwell (1954) when testing Southern black children encountered difficulties with the instrument and Dreger and Miller commented:

> Not surprisingly in view of its standardization, the WISC was found inappropriate for testing Southern Negro children from 10 to 13 years of age (Young and Bright, 1954, p. 367). In this investigation the suggestion is also made that cultural bias results from using the WISC, standardized as it was on a white population (Caldwell, 1954, p. 368).

Whenever tests like the Stanford-Binet and the WISC are used with subjects whose characteristics do not correspond to the sample upon which those instruments were normed, it is logical to conclude that 1) such uses are invalid as measures of the intellectual level or potential of these subjects; 2) whenever such tests are administered to subjects significantly different from the white sample, scores are expected to be relatively low; and, 3) comparisons of scores from minority subjects with majority norms have questionable validity and utility.

It is not simply the inappropriate use of these tests which is at issue. It is the consequence of such use which is even more destructive. It is a fact that blacks, as a group, repeatedly and consistently score lower than whites—as low as minus one standard deviation—when administered tests such as the Stanford-Binet and the WISC. However, it is a sad reality that, as a result, classes for slow learners, the educable mentally retarded and the mentally retarded house a significantly greater proportion of black children than white children. Coleman's study (1966) showed that at the elementary and secondary level the school attended by the average black child contains a significantly greater proportion of children in the low tracks. Dunn (1968) noted that at the national level, minorities comprise more than 50 percent of the mentally retarded. The figures issued by the Bureau of Intergroup Relations of the State Department of Education for the State of California in the fall of 1970, reveal that whereas blacks who represent 9.1 percent of the total student population of the state account for 27.5 percent of the educable mentally retarded, they constitute only 2.5 percent of the mentally gifted. Such statistics undisputedly demonstrate the existence of racial imbalance in both the classes for the retarded and the classes for the gifted. In view of the fact that minority children continue to be tested by means of instruments with recognized deficiencies and inadequacies, it seems hardly possible that such an imbalance can ever be rectified under the existing circumstances.

In an eight-year study, conducted by Jane Mercer and her associates on mental retardation in Riverside, California, the effects of the indiscriminate and harmful use of IQ results have been well documented.

It should be mentioned that Mercer's research was confined to the California environment, particularly that of the southern region. Her studies, although pertinent to the conditions of blacks and other minorities, relate more specifically to children of Chicano Hispanic-American ethnicity. Thus, she consistently referred to the concept of Anglocentricity in the value orientation and standardizations of tests used to measure the potential of children having an essentially Spanish-speaking Mexican-American cultural background.[1]

Mercer's contention is that so-called intelligence tests, as presently used, are to a large extent, "Anglocentric"; that is, they mirror the standards, values, experiences of the white Anglo-Saxon middle-class. Consequently, the results of such tests inevitably affect, to a greater degree, persons from a different cultural background and from lower socioeco-

nomic status as well as minority ethnic groups.

Among the various findings, the one which concerns us most importantly is that the public schools have been sending more children to MR classes than any of the other eight categories of organizations under consideration. Moreover, the criteria upon which selection was made in the public schools contacted included: 1) the almost exclusive reliance on IQ test scores and the almost total absence of medical diagnosis; 2) the utilization of a high cut-off score (IQ of 79 or below as compared to a recommended IQ of 69 or below) in order to draw the borderline between mental retardates and normals; 3) the failure to take into account sociocultural factors when interpreting IQ test results.

The over-representation of Mexican-Americans and blacks in MR classes is astounding. Mercer quotes four-and-a-half times more Mexican-Americans and twice as many blacks as would be expected from their proportion in the population. Yet, whenever a "two-dimensional definition" of mental retardation is used, that is, one which not only considers the intellectual performance of individuals but also assesses their adaptive behavior (one's ability to cope with one's family, neighbourhood and community), and whenever IQ scores are interpreted with the knowledge that sociocultural factors contaminate them, then Mercer shows that the racial imbalance disappears and as a consequence, approximately 75 percent of the children placed in MR classes were mislabelled. In other words, the Riverside studies revealed that the majority of those children had, in the language of the court, been wrongfully placed and suffered "irreparable harm and injury."

In the case of *Larry P. et al v. Wilson Riles et al* (1972) the plaintiffs, six black San Francisco elementary school children, charged the defendants, namely, the California State Department of Education and the San Francisco School District with having placed them in EMR classes on the basis of IQ tests alone. When the said plaintiffs were retested by certified black psychologists who used techniques

[1] Mercer has done a remarkable and commendable job, and the reader is well advised to consult the following publications upon which the subsequent summary is based: *The Meaning of Mental Retardation. Sociocultural Factors in Labelling Mental Retardates, Institutionalized Anglocentrism: Labelling Mental Retardates in the Public Schools, The Labelling Process.* (See also bibliographic references at the end of this paper.)

taking into account the cultural and experiential background of the plaintiffs, all achieved above the cut off score of 75. Accordingly, U.S. District Judge Robert F. Peckham ordered that

. . . defendants be restrained from placing black students in classes for the educable mentally retarded on the basis of criteria which place primary reliance on the results of IQ tests as they are currently administered, if the consequence of use of such criteria is racial imbalance in the composition of such classes.

In an unprecedented decision, the Court recognized the pervading cultural bias of the present tests, and the misplacement of and ensuing harm done to black children when tested by such measures. The Court's order was aimed at preventing future wrongful placement of black children in special classes, but it did not provide for the elimination of the effects of past discrimination, nor did it rule that the use of intelligence tests be suspended or that the EMR black children be released and retested for fairer placement. Yet, it cited the efforts of the New York City school system which banned group IQ tests and the Massachusetts school system (see Mass. Regulations Pertaining to Education of Certain Children, October 27, 1971) as alternative plans to be used, pending the development of appropriate tests.

USE OF IQ TESTS FOR GROUPING

The foregoing discussion has been focused specifically on the use of individually administered tests of intelligence—the WISC, the Stanford-Binet commonly used to differentiate between "normal" subjects and those who might be classified as "educable mentally retarded" into special classes. Such types of tests require special training on the part of the test administrator, and special conditions of administration, which, despite the inadequacies cited by the members of the Association of Black Psychologists and the American Personnel and Guidance Association, and demonstrated in the research and recommendations

of Jane Mercer (1971), may be less biased in terms of assessing the intelligence of minorities than that of standardized group tests.

Spawned by the same movement from which the original individual Binet-type of test sprang, group tests of mental ability were pioneered by Arthur Otis during the First World War. They represent a short-cut of the individual test and a means of administering the same test to large numbers of subjects at the same time. They are based on the same premise that it is possible, by administering a number of tasks to individuals, and by comparing performance with the average performance of the standardization sample, to estimate with some accuracy the index of intellectual functioning which in turn can predict likelihood of perforance in school or on some set of academic or employment behaviors.

Group IQ tests, or tests of academic aptitude, as they are sometimes called, represent the basic instruments used by teachers and counselors for advising students, for placement in tracks, or for selection and promotion. They exert a powerful influence on the curricular organization and social stratification within schools. At the higher levels of education, they may become the deciding criteria for acceptance or rejection of applicants for college. They are generally published as omnibus paper-and-pencil packages comprising about 70 or 80 objective-type items, often arranged spirally in terms of difficulty level. Thus, when an IQ is quoted, it is given as a number which can be interpreted in terms of relative performance compared with the average or mean.

The purpose and general orientation of the group IQ test is to provide a measure of mental functioning paralleling the individually-administered Stanford-Binet Intelligence Scale. It requires demonstration of logical reasoning, numerical ability, the manipulation of verbal concepts, and spatial reasoning.

What is significant for the purposes of this discussion is that research studies report differences in relative performance of different ethnic and socioeconomic groups on a variety of such group-administered tests yielding a global IQ score. It is on the basis of such comparisons that conclusions are drawn concerning the relative superiority or inferiority of one group to another. Such comparisons have led textbook writers in psychometrics to state that "contrary to indications in much of the popular literature, genetic factors definitely seem to have a strong relationship to IQ" (Stanley and Hopkins, 1972, p. 348).

The case of Hobson v. Hansen (1967) which attacked the tracking system then in use in the Washington, D.C., school system, posed a similar problem since the lower track or "basic track" constituted primarily of black children was placed there on the basis of a cut-off score of 75 on IQ tests. There too, cultural bias and invalidity of certain tests, as well as wrongful placement and irreparable harm and injury, were acknowledged and sanctioned. As Judge Wright put it:

> The evidence shows that the method by which track assignments are made depends essentially on standardized aptitude tests which, although given on a system-wide basis are completely inappropriate for use with a large segment of the student body. Because the tests are primarily standardized on and are relevant to a white middle-class group of students, they produce inaccurate and misleading test scores when given to lower-class and Negro students. As a result, rather than being classified according to ability to learn, these students are in reality being classified according to their socioeconomic or racial status, or—more precisely—according to environmental and psychological factors which have nothing to do with innate ability (p. 514).

If one accepts Mercer's findings, cited earlier, which show that 75 percent of the black and Mexican-American children enrolled in MR classes on the basis of IQ test results do not belong there, then one can say that "irreparable harm and injury" has been inflicted upon those children as Judge Peckham and Judge Wright admitted: "This court is thus of the view that for those students who are wrongfully placed in EMR classes, irreparable harm ensues" (Judge Peckham in Larry P. et al v. Wilson Riles et al, 1972).

The effects of grouping, especially for tracking, have been frequently disastrous. It is a well known fact that classes for low achievers offer a severely limited and low quality curriculum in which reading, spelling, and mathematics are reduced to a minimum and the stimulation of a challenging program and higher achieving peers is lacking entirely. Yet, despite the criticisms of ability grouping (Goldberg, Passow, and Justman, 1966; Goodlad, 1966; Eash, 1961; Borg, 1964), school administrators in many parts of the country still continue to process children into homogeneous groups without making any serious attempt to change the teaching process, the strategies or the use of materials employed in the teaching-learning situation. The results of such grouping are particularly marked for minority pupils who, in the main, fall at the lower end of the IQ range and are, therefore, relegated to classes for slow learners. Yet, in their extensive and thorough research summary, Findlay and Bryant (1970) concluded that: 1) separation into ability groups, *when all children are considered,* has no clear-cut positive or negative effect on average scholastic achievement; but 2) the slight trend towards improving the average achievement of high level groups is offset by a *substantial loss by average and low groups.* (Author's emphasis.)

The fact is that the use and interpretation of IQ tests in the context of the "normal" elementary and secondary schools may result in the same sort of labelling as Mercer demonstrated in her Riverside study. Thus, from the standpoint of the disequalization of educational opportunity, IQ tests can, and often do, serve a sorting and segregating function. They can and are used at all levels of the educational process as a fail-safe mechanism to ensure that those who attend desegregated schools with mixed populations become resegregated within the curricular or tracking organization of the school. That is not to say that there is a deliberate and organized effort to keep blacks poor and inferior, although the operation and effect of endemic racism and social roles entrenched in the system of education conspire to retain the stigma of inferior status for blacks and to retard their social mobility in United States society in general. The use of the IQ test and particularly the interpretation of test results are increasingly seen as the barrier to change.

Increasingly, the evidence points to the conclusion that "racist claims of Caucasian superiority contribute to the Negro's lack of intellectual self-confidence. This insecurity is especially provoked by any direct comparison with white performance" (Pettigrew, 1964, p. 114). Educators and social psychologists, among other researchers, have demonstrated the reality of Pettigrew's assertion in a number of ways, such as: a) blacks will perform lower when the situation is perceived as hostile or threatening; b) blacks will gain when the tester is of the same race; c) the IQ test often functions as a self-fulfilling prophecy; d) scoring low on an intelligence test may be a rational response to perceived danger (in the case of talented blacks); e) the language and special tasks involved in an IQ test are relatively alien to the experiences of blacks and, therefore, do not measure even present functional ability.

EXPERIMENTS RELATED TO TEST ENVIRONMENT

In a series of experimental situations, Irwin Katz and his associates have attempted to determine the effects of psychological factors in situations involving white peers and white and black authority figures on the intellectual productivity of black subjects (Katz, 1968). Of importance to the present discussion are the results of the findings as they relate to the differential conditions of the test-taking situations. In essence, these researchers have demonstrated that:

a. The testing situation, when perceived as a hostile one (i.e. where the chances of success are low), impedes the performance of any individual, especially that of blacks in a white world (p. 279).

b. Motivation is highest when the chances of success are perceived as being slightly better than even (p. 279).

c. Blacks tend to rate themselves unrealistically lower than do whites in situations demanding intellectual productivity (Katz and Benjamin, 1960).

d. When working in biracial teams, blacks tend to be passively compliant and submissive unless they are forced to assert themselves (Katz et al, 1958; Katz and Benjamin, 1960; Katz and Cohen, 1962).

e. Blacks' performance increases when a relatively simple digit symbol code is disguised as an eye-hand coordination instrument and administered by a white examiner but decreases when the same task is presented as an IQ test and administered by a white examiner (Katz et al, 1965).

f. Blacks perform significantly better when they anticipate to be compared intellectually with blacks than with whites (Katz et al, 1964).

g. Blacks strongly inhibit their feelings of hostility toward whites, and as a result of the blocking of aggressive impulses, performance is impaired (p. 281–282).

Such findings are in keeping with a mounting body of evidence that demonstrates how psychological factors related to the test-taking situation, as well as social stereotypes and roles, seriously contaminate the results of IQ tests and, in the terms of Anastasi, may introduce a "moderator variable" or systematic error into test results. Such considerations call into question the predictive validity of a black lower-class person's IQ score, especially when derived from the traditional test situation.

THE SELF-FULFILLING PROPHECY

In interpreting the results of the interaction between teacher expectations in classroom situations and examiner race and attitudes in the test taking center, Katz (1964), Clark (1963), Kvaraceus (1965), Reisman (1962, 1965) have postulated or implied the possibility of negative or positive effects on pupil

productivity as a function of teacher/exam-
iner perceptions. It is what the pupil perceives
the teacher or examiner to feel that is important in the test situation. Rosenthal and Jacobson (1968), in a widely publicized study,
attempted to demonstrate the viability of the
hypothesis that the perception and attitudes of
the experimenter, examiner, or teacher may
serve as self-fulfilling prophecies in their
interaction with pupils. However, the authors'
claims that experimenter-induced teacher expectations resulted in significant gains in students over a period of less than one year have
been subjected to critical review in terms of
the validity of their data (Snow, 1969; Thorndike, 1968). Furthermore, subsequent studies
of a similar nature failed to produce corrobo-
rating results (Fleming and Anttonen, 1970;
Gozali and Meyer, 1970; Haberman, 1970;
Jose and Cody, 1971).

However, perceived examiner attitudes
and social stereotypes are still believed to be
paramount factors influencing the results of
tests and the learning process itself. In a more
recent study, Rist (1970) reported the observations of an all black kindergarten class of
pupils who were followed up over a period of
two and a half years. It was found that the
organization of the original kindergarten in-
take of children into reading groups was
largely determined by subjectively interpreted
characteristics of the students, and that the
composition of the various groups within the
class resembled that of the social class structure of the larger society. Rist stated that
placement in one or another of the reading
groups in kindergarten was more related to the
teacher's perceptions of social stereotypes than
to the actual achievement levels. The teacher
served as the agent of the larger society to
ensure that proper "social distance" was maintained between the various strata of the society
represented by the children (p. 444). The picture that emerges from this study is one in
which "the school strongly shares in the com-
plicity of maintaining the organizational perpetuation of poverty and unequal opportunity.
This, of course, is in contrast to the formal

doctrine of education in this country to ameliorate rather than aggravate the condition of
the poor" (p. 447).

It is clear, then, that test results can
serve to reinforce social roles, and to trap poor
and minority students in a vicious circle when
they are placed in a class of poor performers at
the very beginning of their educational career.
Stigmatized as a "slow learner," the minority
student behaves accordingly, thus reinforcing
his low score and his teacher's expectations,
often determined on the basis of one inappropriate test. Instead of progressing, he steadily
falls further and further below his peers; de-
featism replaces faith and hope; motivation
disappears and stigmatization leaves its indelible mark on the black child's self-esteem and
self-concept. Doomed from the very beginning
to an inferior education, he usually drops out
of school to accept his role in the larger society
—employment as an unskilled worker, or possibly, a life dependency on public welfare.

THE EFFECTS OF LANGUAGE
DIFFERENCES ON TEST RESULTS

Every debate has at least two sides. So it is
with the controversy concerning the effects of
differences of language on the test results of
minority students in general, and blacks in
particular. On the one hand, there are those
(Bernstein, Bereiter, Engelman) who subscribe to a theory of "cultural deprivation" as
the main cause of the relatively low performance of lower-class students on academic
tasks. The basic assumption underlying the
"cultural deprivation" theory, or what is sometimes referred to as the "deficit model" (Baratz
and Baratz, 1970), is that black children live
in impoverished environments characterized
by over-crowded homes often lacking in adequate sanitary facilities, dilapidated buildings
and unaesthetic surroundings, a lack of objects, books, toys, furniture, etc., and are subjected to conditions which seriously limit and
impair growth and verbal facility.

Deutsch (1967) claims that, although

noise is a characteristic of the lower-class environment, it is not meaningfully related to the child himself. His auditory discrimination—which Deutsch found to be related to reading ability—is, thus, markedly diminished. Moreover, Hess, Shipman et al (1968) related the child's poor ability to conceptualize abstractly to maternal language style, and found a correlation between mother's language abstraction and the child's subsequent intellectual performance (p. 168). It is the contention of the "cultural deprivation" theorists that the lower-class environment does not equip the preschool child with that essential training or conditioning conducive to learning and success in school. Handicapped before he reaches school, the disadvantaged child falls victim to the "cumulative deficit" phenomenon as he progresses through school. What is necessary, therefore, is early intervention through well structured programs designed to reduce the invidious influence of the ghetto conditons (Gray and Klaus, 1965).

On the other hand, William Labov (1971) and Baratz and Baratz (1970) strongly disagree with an interpretation of differences between black children and their white middle-class peers which places primary value on middle-class norms of behavior and denies black language and culture. These writers see the "cultural deprivation" theory as "unrealistic in terms of current linguistic and anthropological data and, at worst, ethnocentric and racist" (Baratz and Baratz, 1970, p. 30).

Labov categorically refutes the deficit theory which advances verbal and sensory deprivation as the cause of low achievement in school. Such a notion, he feels, places the blame on the child for poor performance, absolves the school, and results from the work of educational psychologists "who know very little about language and even less about black children" (Labov, 1971, p. 59). Contrary to Deutsch and Bereiter, Labov finds that ghetto children are subjected to a great deal of verbal stimulation, possess the same basic vocabulary as middle-class children, the same capacity for

conceptual learning and use the same logic as any other speaker of English. He demonstrates in his research report that the ineptitude, bashfulness, and monosyllabic behavior of the black child in school represent a form of response to a threatening situation since, when the same child is at ease and operating within his own frame of reference, he is extremely verbal, assertive, and capable of dealing with complex and abstract formulations expressed in a different idiom from that of standard English. Labov and his associates have been accused of romanticizing black English. Many educators feel strongly that such a position is unrealistic in terms of the essential needs of education in the society at large.

However, the main point of the argument is that education of the black ghetto child can only proceed from a proper understanding of the individual within his own linguistic and cultural milieu so that emphasis is placed on a bi-cultural or bi-lingual perspective rather than on one which stresses the rightness of standard English and standard middle-class norms. Labov admits that there exist black English speakers who are developmentally immature in thinking process, but, on the other hand, he points to the multitude of non-standard English speakers who can and do express themselves in a black idiom and at a level of abstraction which connotes a high capacity for logical thought. There is, thus, an urgent need to distinguish between those two speakers in order to prescribe the right kind of education matched to the individual needs of the individual child. Labov calls for the teaching of standard English to black ghetto children in a manner similar to the teaching of English to a non-native student—teaching English as a foreign language. Thus, the responsibility falls upon both the teacher and the school to develop instruments matched to the child's language and thought and to provide the right social climate which will transform the seemingly monosyllabic, inept, and ignorant child into the fluent and able user of the English language.

If Labov and the Baratzes are right, then it follows that standardized IQ tests do not, and cannot as they presently exist, measure the true potential of black children whose language and life styles are largely determined by the conditions of the ghetto. For such tests depend heavily on vocabulary and language usage which place the minority child at a distinct disadvantage.

GUIDELINES, TRENDS, AND ALTERNATIVES: A SUMMARY

The attacks upon testing described in the previous sections of this paper may result in an expansion and elaboration of psychometrics rather than in an abolition of objective tests. Changes are mandatory if the makers and users of tests are to discharge their functions responsibly. The likelihood of the direction of such changes can be seen in at least six categories of responses to the exposure of the limitations of the use of standardized tests with minority students in particular and with the general application of tests to the education of any student. Those categories can, in turn, be dichotomized into two major trends: Namely, one that seeks to retain the concepts of aptitude or fitness to perform in future situations from the results on a standardized set of behavioral tasks; and the other, that emphasizes the purposes and goals of testing as essentially descriptive and prescriptive leading from an analysis of functional levels and cognitive styles to the prescription of learning experiences matched to the individual needs of each student.

The first general trend is illustrated by the response of the majority of test producers to the charge that testing serves to keep minority groups in a relatively inequitable educational situation, to label as educationally or mentally retarded many who are able to do normal work in a setting suited to their needs, and to act as the gatekeeping function to the avenues of higher education by unfairly depressing true potential of minority students through comparison with middle-class norms.

Test producers have claimed that tests have been misused because of the misconceptions of counselors, teachers, admission officers, and administrators. They claim that those who use the tests should be aware of the meaning of the results and should not interpret the scores on IQ tests as implying permanent, innate, or irremediable deficiency. For the scores merely indicate the degree of the individual's atypical level of function. They point up the unfairness of life—not the unfairness of the test. Thus, it is the job of the school to gear instruction to the special needs of the student and to bring him up to par. Such a stance predicates a certain standard of behavioral responses and emphasizes the fact that IQ tests are predictors of future achievement, and that the school does exist as a middle-class institution which trains people to fit into a certain kind of society. Thus, as long as the norms of society remain as they are, IQ tests of the individual or group variety do fulfill a necessary and vital function. The need, therefore, is to train the users to ensure that the scores are properly interpreted.

The second trend is somewhat similar to the first in that it emphasizes the need for the training and sensitization of test users in the potentialities of a variety of errors of interpretation due to technical and psychological factors which contaminate test results. Such a position has been enunciated by a Division of APA, the Society for the Psychological Study of Social Issues (Fishman et al, 1964), in the well-publicized "Guidelines for Testing Minority Group Children." The article deals specifically with three basic critical issues in the testing of minorities—lack of reliable differentiation in the range of minority group scores which tend to cluster at the lower end of the total range; lack of predictive validity when scores are compared with standardization samples of a different sociocultural background; emphasis on adequate understanding of sociocultural background of the group being tested in order to make a true interpretation of scores. Fishman and his associates call for a thorough re-examination of the "use of tests" and retraining of those who administer and interpret tests. In addition, they suggest certain modifications in the structure of existing tests, and in the procedures and test-taking situations; but the main burden of their recommendations is upon the need to interpret test results with the understanding that there exist variables extraneous to test content, that contaminate them. It is the opinion of those workers that tests continue to be used as a means of judging the performance of the minority child with that of advantaged white middle-class children in order to determine "the magnitude of the deprivation to be overcome" (Passow, 1967, p. 168). The essential philosophy of the "Guidelines" follows the lines of the cultural deprivation theory or deficit model whereby tests are seen as gauging the success of the student in overcoming the deficiencies which an unfair social system has forced upon him.

The third trend represents a focus upon measures of the environment to bolster and supplement the scores from traditional intelligence tests. The essential thesis rests in the proposition that "the addition of a measure of the environment greatly enhances the estimation of academic achievement" (Wolf, 1964, p. 102). It has been empirically demonstrated that the measurement of what parents do in the home can be used to predict school achievement with a fairly high degree of accuracy (Bloom, 1964; Wolf, 1964). Thus, by combining measures of the individual's environment with measures of his performance on standardized tests of intelligence, and employing methods of multiple correlation, it is possible to raise the coefficient of correlation to .87 which is practically the upper limit of such a correlation when the reliability of the instruments used is taken into account. Measurement of the environment, therefore, implies better indices of prediction and provides useful information for the development of "new curricula designed to help overcome identified environmental deficiencies among students. Useful information about the ingredients for programs of compensatory edu-

cation could be obtained from careful examination of the environmental measures" (Wolf, 1964, p. 103). As in the studies and interpretation of minority pupils' test results, throughout almost all of the 1960's there is a tacit and underlying acceptance of the deficit model and of the emphasis upon the environment as the principal factor in determining the deprived state of the minority person. Spawned in the period of the Kennedy and Johnson administrations, such positions typify the drive to right the balance and furnish the enrichment necessary to ameliorate the "cultural disadvantage" of an impoverished environment. Essentially, Wolf holds that since the development of the particular individual's characteristics is greatly influenced by environmental variables, one can discover how particular traits are learned, maintained, or altered systematically relating data about the individual to data about the environment.

The fourth trend, espoused particularly by Jane Mercer and her associates at Riverside, California, calls for a "pluralistic sociocultural" perspective on the testing of minorities. Such a position is consistent with the modified use of standardized measures of IQ but requires that "a culturally aware pluralistic interpretation would thus evaluate the intelligence of each person only in relation to others who have come from similar sociocultural backgrounds and who have had approximately the same opportunity to acquire the knowledge and skills to answer questions on an intelligence test designed for an Anglo-American society" (Mercer, 1971, p. 335).

The fifth trend represents a departure from traditional testing and involves the development of new measures consistent with the special language characteristics of minority individuals. This movement runs counter to that implied by the cultural deprivation or deficit model which postulates that black children fail to learn appropriately at school because they have certain developmental or maturational deficits in the areas of language, learning set, attitudes, and capacity for logical thought. Labov and the Baratzes take the position that standardized tests are, by their very nature, biased against black and other minority children and therefore make normally intelligent children look stupid when their scores are compared with white middle-class children. Although they stress a linguistic or anthropological frame of reference, this school of thought has vital implications for measurement. Those researchers hold that 1) tests which make use of standard English can only judge the abilities of those individuals who have been accustomed to using standard English; 2) the verbal-deprivation theory is bolstered by the fallacious use and interpretation of traditional tests of mental ability; 3) there is no reason to believe that any nonstandard vernacular is, in itself, an obstacle to learning; 4) the frequently monosyllabic verbal expression of black and lower class children in the school represents a form of response to a formal and threatening situation rather than a lack of verbal capacity or verbal deficit; 5) evidence of the use of formal speech patterns does not necessarily coincide with logical thought; and, 6) so long as we continue to use traditional standardized measures of mental ability with minorities and to explain the atypical results on the basis of a verbal deprivation theory, we will continue to rationalize the failure of the school and the educational system in terms of the personal deficiencies of the individual. Such a notion implies the development of new measures matched to the language style and vernacular of the individual while ensuring that the circumstances of testing are such that the minority child feels free to respond without anxiety or emotional threat. It is difficult to see how such tests can be designed in the vernacular of black English in written form, but what Labov stresses is the need to look at the logic of the child's expression in the language and form that are consistent with his sociocultural background and not merely to make judgments based on his capacity to use standard English which may only reflect the ability to be verbose

rather than to think logically and precisely. No doubt, tests of standard English will be necessary in the provision of the proper climate for optimum instruction but such test results cannot provide any true estimate of the minority child's verbal capacity or his ability to conceptualize.

The sixth trend signifies a culmination of several schools of thought and theories related to the measurement and education of minorities. It calls for an emphasis on description and prescription rather than on selection and prediction in order to facilitate equal educational opportunities (Gordon, 1971). Such a position radically departs from traditional testing particularly in the purposes of psychometrics since it focuses, essentially, on the descriptive, diagnostic, and qualitative analysis of behavioral function. It represents an integration and extension of several theoretical positions and the application of research findings to the education of minorities. Moreover, it represents an extension of educational opportunity for the mass of citizens through individualized prescriptive educational planning. Thus, instead of seeking to abolish tests, this trend regards psychometrics as a fundamental means by which we can begin to make education more accessible to the underprivileged elements of society without penalizing the individual for not belonging to the middle-class mainstream culture. The primary objective of testing becomes not just one of discovering where the individual is on a scale of attainment, or of estimating his chances of success on a particular course of study, but it consists of diagnosing in some detail what he can and cannot do so as to plan those strategies which will optimize learning. It further recognizes that in order to gear instruction to individual needs, something must be known about the verbal and cognitive style of the child. By testing within the context of the individual's linguistic frame of reference, we can gauge the level and quality of his intellectual functioning and that of his academic attainment. But judgments of mental capacity must take into account such factors as health and nutritional status, as well as the social and cultural environmental factors impinging upon academic and social development. Such a trend also implies an extension of existing tests whereby patterns of achievement in any given subject area provide qualitative descriptions or profiles in terms of the strength of skill or knowledge and an account of those particular gaps or weaknesses towards which instruction should be focused. Thus, test procedures would be directed towards the broadening of the varieties of competencies and skills, not merely through objective item-types, but additionally, through open-ended probes designed to incorporate atypical patterns and varieties of learning. Such a trend also seeks to incorporate the work of David McClelland within the corpus of psychometric technology by stressing measures of ego development and motivation which depend upon operant (of free associative) thought patterns in assessing non-academic learning such as social competence, coping skills, political and avocational skills.

In the final analysis, we need to look at our purposes for testing. If testing is to serve a selective and sorting function, and if, indeed, psychometric technology is intended to preserve an elite, then it follows that traditional procedures for measuring intelligence and scholastic aptitude, tied to a set of middle-class ethnocentric norms, will serve that function very well. However, if it is our purpose to serve the mass of citizens, and if it is our goal to make measurement more facilitative for the education of the poor, of the minority student, and of the atypical individual, then we will need to expand our research endeavours so that psychometric technology becomes the handmaiden of educational innovation in optimizing the individual's competence. Through the qualitative analysis of achievement and weaknesses, we can point the way towards the modification of patterns of instruction which will match the individual needs of individual students. It is therefore the hope of such a philosophy of testing to contribute to the achievement of optimal developmental and educational opportunity for all.

REFERENCES

Anastasi, Anne, Psychology, Psychologists and Psychological Testing, *American Psychologist,* 1967, 22, 297–306.

Baratz, S. S. and Baratz, N. G., Early Childhood Intervention: The Social Science Base of Institutional Racism, *Harvard Educational Review,* 1970, 40 (1), 29–50.

Biaggio, A., Relative Predictability of Freshman Grade-Point Averages from SAT Scores in Negro and White Southern Colleges, *Technical Report Number 7,* Research and Development Center for Learning and Re-Education, University of Wisconsin, Madison, 1966.

Black, Hillel, *They Shall Not Pass,* New York, Morrow, 1963.

Bloom, B., *Stability and Change in Human Characteristics,* New York, John Wiley and Sons, Inc., 1964.

Borg, W. R., *An Evaluation of Ability Grouping,* Coop. Res. Proj. No. 577, Salt Lake City, Utah State University, 1964.

Caldwell, M. B., *An Analysis of Responses of a Southern Urban Negro Population to Items on the Wechsler Intelligence Scale for Children,* unpublished doctoral dissertation, Pennsylvania State College, 1954.

Canady, H. G., The Psychology of the Negro, in P. L. Harriman (ed.) *The Encyclopedia of Psychology,* Philosophical Library, 1946, 65, p. 161–175.

Clark, K. B., Educational Stimulation of Racially Disadvantaged Children, in A. H. Passow (ed.), *Education in Depressed Areas,* New York, Teachers College, Columbia University, 1963, p. 142–162.

Clark, K. B. and Plotkin, L., *The Negro Student at Integrated Colleges,* New York, National Scholarship Service and Fund for Negro Students, 1963.

Cleary, A., Test Bias: Prediction of Grades of Negro and White Students in Integrated Colleges, *Journal of Educational Measurement,* 1968, 5 (2), p. 115–124.

Cleary, A. and Hilton, T. A., An Investigation of Item Bias, *Educational and Psychological Measurement*, 1968, 28 (1), 61–75.

Clemans, W. V., A Note in Response to a Request by the Editor to Comment on R. L. Williams' Article, *The Counseling Psychologist*, 1970.

Coleman, James S. et al, *Equality of Educational Opportunity*, Washington, D.C., Government Printing Office, 1966.

College Entrance Examination Board, Report of the Commission on Tests, 1, *Righting the Balance*, New York, 1970.

Darlington, Richard B., Another Look at "Cultural Fairness," *Journal of Educational Measurement*, Summer 1970, 8 (2), 71–82.

Davis, J. A. and Temp, G., Is the SAT Biased Against Black Students? *College Board Review*, 1971, 81, 4–9.

Deutsch, M., *The Disadvantaged Child*, New York, Basic Books, Inc., 1967, p. 39–57.

Dreger, Ralph M. and Miller, Kent S., Comparative Psychological Studies of Negroes and Whites in the United States, *Psychological Bulletin*, 1960, 57 (5), 361–402.

Dubois, Philip H., *Increase in Educational Opportunity Through Measurement in Educational Change: Implications for Measurement*, Princeton, N.J., Educational Testing Service, 1972.

Dunn, L. M., Special Education for the Mildly-Retarded. Is Much of It Justifiable? *Exceptional Children*, 1968, 35, 5–22.

Dyer, H. S., Is Testing a Menace to Education? in C. I. Chase and H. G. Ludlow (eds.), *Readings in Educational and Psychological Measurement*, New York, Houghton Mifflin, 1966, 40–45.

Eash, M. J., Grouping: What have we learned? *Educational Leadership*, 1961, 18, 429–434.

Ebel, R. L., Measurement Responsibilities of Teachers, in D. H. Noll and R. T. Noll (Eds.), *Readings in Educational Psychology*, 2nd edition, New York, Macmillan Company, 1968, p. 383–391.

Ebel, Robert L., The Social Consequences of Educational Testing, in Anne Anastasi (ed.), *Testing Problems in Perspective*, Washington, D.C., American Council on Education, 1966.

Findley, W. G. et al, *Ability Grouping: Status Impact and Alternatives*, Center for Educa-tional Improvement, University of Georgia, Athens, 1970.

Flaugher, Ronald L., *Some Points of Confusion in the Testing of Black Students*, AERA Symposium, February, 1973.

Fleming, E. F. and Anttonen, R. G., Teacher Expectancy or My Fair Lady, in John Pilder, *Abstracts/1:1970*, Annual meeting, paper session, Washington, D.C., American Educational Research Association, 1970, 66.

Goldberg, M. L., Passow, A. H., and Justman, J., *The Effects of Ability Grouping*, New York, Teachers College, Columbia University, 1966.

Good, W. R., Misconceptions about Intelligence Testing, 1954, in C. I. Chase and H. G. Ludlow (eds.), *Readings in Educational and Psychological Measurements*, New York, Houghton Mifflin, 1966, 177–179.

Gordon, E. W., *Qualitative Assessment of Learner Behavior and the Design of Learning Experiences*, paper delivered at the Institute for Assessment of Minorities, Educational Testing Service, Princeton, New Jersey, May 8, 1972.

Gordon, E. W. and Wilkerson, D. A., *Compensatory Education for the Disadvantaged*, New York, College Entrance Examination Board, 1966.

Gozali, J. and Meyer, E. L., The Influence of Teacher Expectancy Phenomena on the Academic Performances of Educable Mentally Retarded Pupils in Special Classes, *Journal of Special Education*, 1970, 4, 417–424.

Goslin, D. A., Standardized Ability Tests and Testing, *Science*, 1968, 159, 851–855.

Gray, F. W. and Klaus, R. A., An Experimental Pre-School Program for Culturally Deprived Children, *Child Development*, 1965, 36, 887–898.

Gross, Martin J., *The Brain Watchers*, New York, Random House, 1962.

Haberman, M., The Relationship of Bogus Expectations to Success in Student Teaching (Or, Pygmalion's Illegitimate Son), in John Pilder, *Abstracts/1:1970*, Annual Meeting, paper session, Washington, D.C., American Education Research Association, 1970, 66.

Herrnstein, R., IQ, *Atlantic Monthly*, 1971, 228, 43–64.

Hess, R. D., Shipman, V., Brophy, J. E. and Dear, R. M., *The Cognitive Environments of Urban*

Pre-School Children, Graduate School of Education, University of Chicago, 1968.

Hills, J. R., Klock, J. C. and Lewis, S., *Freshman Norms for the University System of Georgia, 1961–1962,* Atlanta, Georgia, Office of Testing and Guidance, Regents of the University System of Georgia, 1963.

Jensen, A., How Much Can We Boost IQ & Scholastic Achievement? *Harvard Educational Review,* 1969, 39, 1–123.

Jose, J. and Cody, J. J., Teacher-Pupil Interaction as It Related to Attempted Changes in Teacher Expectancy of Academic Ability and Achievement, *American Education Research Journal,* 1971, 8, 39–50.

Karmel, Louis J., *Measurement and Evaluation in the Schools,* New York, The Macmillan Company, 1970.

Katz, I., Factors Influencing Negro Performance in the Desegregated School, in *Social Class, Race & Psychological Development,* edited by M. Deutsch, I. Katz, and A. R. Jensen, New York, Holt, Rinehart and Winston, 1968, p. 254–289.

————, Review of Evidence Relating to Effects of Desegregation on the Intelligence Performance of Negroes, *American Psychologist,* 1964, 19, 381–399.

Kimble, Gregory A. and Garmezy, Norman, *Principles of General Psychology,* third edition, New York, The Ronald Press Company, 1968.

Klineberg, Otto, *Race Differences,* New York, Harper, 1935.

Klineberg, Otto (ed.), *Characteristics of the American Negro,* New York, Harper, 1944.

Kvaraceus, W. C., Disadvantaged Children and Youth: Programs of Promise or Pretense? *Proceedings of the 17th Annual State Conference on Educational Research,* California Advisory Council on Educational Research, Burlingame, California, California Teachers Association, 1965.

Labov, W., Academic Ignorance and Black Intelligence, *Atlantic Monthly,* 1971, 228, 59–67.

Lennon, R. T., *Testing and the Culturally Disadvantaged Child,* Lecture delivered at the Mackey School, Boston, February 26, 1964, New York, Harcourt, Brace and World, Inc., p. 1–40.

Lennon, Roger T., Testing: The Question of Bias, in Thomas J. Fitzgibbon (ed.), *Evaluation in the Inner City,* New York, Harcourt, Brace and World, 1970.

LeSage, W. and Riccio, A. C., Testing the Disadvantaged: An Issue of Our Time, *Focus on Guidance,* 1970, 3 (1), 1–7.

Linden, K. W. and Linden, J. D., *Modern Mental Measurement: A Historical Perspective,* Guidance Monograph Series, Series III: Testing, Boston, Houghton Mifflin, Co., 1968.

Lorge, I., *Techniques for the Development of Unbiased Tests,* 1952 Invitational Conference on Testing Problems, Princeton, N.J., Educational Testing Service, 1952.

Mehrens, William A. and Lehmann, Irvin J., *Standardized Tests in Education,* New York, Holt, Rinehart and Winston, Inc., 1969.

Mercer, Jane, Institutionalized Anglocentrism: Labeling Mental Retardates in the Public Schools. *Race, Change, and Urban Society,* 1971, 5, 311–338.

————, *The Labelling Process,* Paper presented at the John F. Kennedy Center for the Performing Arts, Washington, D.C., October 16, 1971.

————, The Meaning of Mental Retardation in *The Mentally Retarded Child and His Family,* edited by Koch, R. and Dobson, J. C., New York, Brunner Mazel, 1971.

————, Sociocultural Factors in Labeling Mental Retardates, *Peabody Journal of Education,* April, 1971, 188–203.

Messick, Samuel and Anderson, Scarvia, Educational Testing, Individual Development and Social Responsibility, *The Counseling Psychologist,* 1970, 2, 80–88.

North, R. D., *The Intelligence of American Negroes,* New York, Anti-Defamation League of B'nai B'rith, 1957.

Pasanella, Ann K., Manning, W. and Findikyan, N. *Bibliography of Test Criticism,* New York, College Entrance Examination Board, 1967.

Peterson, J., The Comparative Abilities of White and Negro Children, *Comparative Psychology Monographs,* 1923, 5, 1–141.

Pettigrew, T. F., *A Profile of the Negro American,* Princeton, N.J., D. Van Nostrand Co., Inc., 1964.

Pintner, R., *Intelligence Testing: Methods and Results,* New York, Holt, 1931.

Reissman, F., *The Culturally Deprived Child,* New York, Harper & Row, Inc., 1962.

————, Teachers of the Poor: A Five Point Plan in *Proceedings of the 17th Annual State Conference of Educational Research,* California Advisory Council of Educational Research, Burlingame, California, California Teachers Association, 1965.

Rist, R. C., Student Social Class and Teacher Expectations: The Self-Fulfilling Prophecy in Ghetto Education, *Harvard Educational Review,* August, 1970, 40, 411–451.

Roberts, S. O., *Studies in the Identification of College Potential,* Nashville, Tennessee, Department of Psychology, Fisk University, 1962 (mimeographed).

Rosenthal, Robert and Jacobson, Lenore, *Pygmalion in the Classroom: Teachers Expectation and Pupils' Intellectual Development,* New York, Holt, Rinehart and Winston, 1968.

Shimberg, B., *Testing and Opportunity,* Speech given at the Institute for Assessment of Minority Students, Princeton, N.J., Educational Testing Service, April, 1972.

Shimberg, M. E., An Investigation into the Validity of Norms, with Special Reference to Urban and Rural Groups, *Archives of Psychology,* 1929, 104.

Shuey, A. M., *The Testing of Negro Intelligence,* New York, Social Science Press, 1966.

Snow, R. E., Unfinished Pygmalion, Review of Rosenthal and Jacobson, *Pygmalion in the Classroom in Contemporary Psychology,* 1969, 14, 197–199.

Sommer, John, Response to Robert Williams, *The Counseling Psychologist,* 1970, 2, 92.

Spearman, C., *The Abilities of Man,* New York, Macmillan Company, 1927.

Standards for Development and Use of Educational and Psychological Tests (third draft), *APA Monitor,* February, 1973, 4 (2) I–XV.

Stanley, J. C. and Hopkins, K. D., *Educational and Psychological Measurement and Evaluation,* 5th edition, Englewood Cliffs, N.J., Prentice-Hall, Inc., 1972.

Stanley, J. C. and Porter, A. C., Correlation of Scholastic Aptitude Test Scores with College Grades for Negroes vs. Whites, *Journal of Educational Measurement,* 1967, 4, 199–218.

Stone, Chuck, *Testing Godfather Holds Key to Plantation,* Philadelphia Daily News, 1973, p. 10.

Terman, Lewis M. and Merrill, Maud A., *Measuring Intelligence,* London, George G. Harrap and Co., Ltd., 1937.

Thorndike, R. L., Concepts of Culture Fairness, *Journal of Educational Measurement,* 1971, 8 (2), 62–70.

————, Review of Rosenthal and Jacobson's *Pygmalion in the Classroom, American Educational Research Journal,* 1968, 5 (4), 708–711.

Turnbull, William W., *Foreword of Educational Change: Implications for Measurement,* Princeton, N.J., Educational Testing Service, 1972.

Wechsler, David, The IQ Is an Intelligent Test, in Charles D. Spielberger, Robert Fox and Bruce Masterton (eds.), Contributions to General Psychology, *Selected Readings for Introductory Psychology,* New York, The Ronald Press Company, 1968, p. 304–309.

Wesman, A. B., Intelligence Testing, *American Psychologist,* 1968, 23, 267–274.

Williams, Robert L., Abuses and Misuses in Testing Black Children, *The Counseling Psychologist,* 1970, 2, 62–73.

Wolf, R., *The Measurement of Environment, 1964 Invitational Conference on Testing Problems,* Princeton, N.J., Educational Testing Service, 1964, p. 93–106.

Young, Florence M. and Bright, H. A., Results of Testing 81 Negro Rural Juveniles with the Wechsler Intelligence Scale for Children, *Journal of Social Psychology,* 1954, 39, 219–226.

38

Toward Quality Education for Mexican Americans

UNITED STATES
COMMISSION ON CIVIL RIGHTS

In this report, the Commission has attempted to identify specific conditions and practices that bear on the failure of schools in the Southwest to provide equal educational opportunity to Mexican American students. The specific areas selected for inquiry were: curriculum; school policies on grade retention, ability grouping, and placement in classes for educable mentally retarded; teacher training; and counseling. In each of these areas the Commission has documented the inadequacies of the schools and their lack of concern for Mexican American children, who represent nearly 20 percent of the school enrollment in the Southwest. In addition, this report examined the actions of the Federal Government to see what sort of efforts had been made under Title VI of the 1964 Civil Rights Act to assure equal educational services for Chicanos.

The findings of this report reflect more than inadequacies regarding the specific conditions and practices examined. They reflect a systematic failure of the educational process, which not only ignores the educational needs of Chicano students but also suppresses their culture and stifles their hopes and ambitions. In a very real sense, the Chicano is the excluded student.

This is the concluding chapter of *Toward Quality Education for Mexican Americans* (February, 1974), United States Commission on Civil Rights, Report VI: Mexican American Education Study.

The process of exclusion is complex. Each component is strong in its own right, but in combination they create a situation which almost inevitably leads to educational failure of Mexican American students. The process involves not only the schools themselves, but all other agencies and institutions that make decisions upon public education in the Southwest—decisions regarding who will teach, what will be taught, and how it will be taught.

Mexican American children, like all children, enter school already having acquired considerable knowledge and skills. Learning does not commence when children begin school, but much earlier. By the time children enter school they have learned a language; they have absorbed a culture, and they have gained a sense of values and tradition from their families and communities.

Entrance into public school brings about an abrupt change for all children, but for many Mexican American children the change is often shattering. The knowledge and skills they have gained in their early years are regarded as valueless in the world of the schools. The language which most Chicano children have learned—Spanish—is not the language of the school and is either ignored or actively suppressed. Even when the Spanish language is deemed an acceptable medium of communication by the schools, the Chicano's particular dialect is often considered "substandard" or no language at all. English, a language in which many Chicano children are not fluent, is the exclusive language of instruction in most schools of the Southwest. Yet, with little or no assistance, Mexican American children are expected to master this language while competing on equal terms with their Anglo classmates.

The curriculum which the schools offer seldom includes items of particular relevance to Chicano children and often damages the perception which Chicanos have gained of their culture and heritage. It is a curriculum developed by agencies and institutions from which Mexican Americans are almost entirely excluded.

Chicano children also are taught primarily by teachers who are Anglo. Generally, these teachers are uninformed on the culture that Chicanos bring to school and unfamiliar with the language they speak. The teachers themselves have been trained at institutions staffed almost entirely by Anglos, and their training and practice teaching do little to develop in them the skills necessary to teach Mexican American children.

Under these conditions Chicano children are more likely than their Anglo classmates to have problems in dealing with the alien school environment. Many need guidance and advice which school counselors are supposed to provide. But only rarely are Mexican American children able to find a Mexican American counselor to confide in or one with some understanding of their background. The overwhelming majority of counselors are Anglos, trained in Anglo dominated institutions. Training programs provide little to equip them to deal sensitively and effectively with Chicano children. Moreover, the ratio of students to counselors is so high as to preclude all but the most cursory and superficial guidance. Counselors have little alternative but to advise Mexican American children on the basis of information which many recognize as inadequate and even inaccurate.

These are among the conditions and practices which serve to insure poor performance by Chicano students. Widespread assignment practices which purport to be educationally beneficial to students who are not "achieving" do little more than provide official recognition that Chicano children are failing and serve to exonerate the school from any blame. Thus, children who have not acquired sufficient mastery over the material at a particular grade level are retained in grade and separated from their promoted classmates. No special diagnosis of their problems or special help is provided. Rather, they are recycled through the same educational program that already has been proven inappropriate. Chicano children are retained in grade at more than twice the rate for Anglos.

Most of the schools in the Southwest practice some form of ability grouping—placement of students in classes based upon their perceived "ability." Although mobility between different ability groups is theoretically possible, in practice it seldom occurs. Once a child is placed in a low ability group class, he is unlikely to leave it. Chicano students are grossly overrepresented in low ability group classes and underrepresented in high ability group classes.

In some cases children are considered so deficient as to be incapable of functioning in normal classes. These children are placed in special classes for the educable mentally retarded. If it is difficult for a child placed in a low ability group class to move to a higher ability group, it is even more exceptional for a child assigned to a class for the educable mentally retarded ever to leave it. Chicano children are two and one-half times as likely as Anglos to be placed in such classes.

The criteria which govern decisions concerning these school practices necessarily work to the disadvantage of Chicano students, already severely handicapped by other school conditions and practices. Students are evaluated and assigned on the basis of the subjective judgment of teachers and counselors, nearly all of whom are Anglo, and the results of standardized tests, which carry a heavy Anglo middle class bias. A disproportionate number of Mexican American students are labeled failures and are placed in low ability groups, retained in grade, or assigned to classes for the educable mentally retarded. These practices have demonstrated their ineffectiveness as techniques to upgrade the quality of education for Mexican American students. They are, in effect, a poor substitute for the needed change in educational programs that would accomplish this result.

The process described above represents a self-fulfilling prophecy. The educational system has established a set of conditions which greatly impedes the success of Chicano children:

- Chicanos are instructed in a language other than the one with which they are most familiar.
- The curriculum consists of textbooks and courses which ignore the Mexican American background and heritage.
- Chicanos are usually taught by teachers whose own culture and background are different and whose training leaves them ignorant and insensitive to the educational needs of Chicano students.
- And when Chicano pupils seek guidance from counselors they rarely can obtain it and even more rarely from a Mexican American counselor.

Having established the conditions that assure failure, the schools then judge the performance of Chicano children, and here also, the test is generally not a fair one.

Many Mexican Americans give up the unfair competition and drop out of school before graduation. Even of those who remain, most cannot perform at grade level. In effect, the schools have predicted failure and then, by their own actions, assured that this prediction comes true.

The process of cultural exclusion, by which the needs and rights of Mexican American students are largely ignored, carries over into the area of civil rights law enforcement. Title VI of the Civil Rights Act of 1964, which prohibits discrimination in any program or activity receiving Federal financial assistance, has been an effective instrument for combatting some aspects of discrimination in public education. Under this law, the Department of Health, Education, and Welfare has attacked the problem of racial segregation in schools in the Deep South with some degree of success.

Until recently HEW ignored almost entirely the problem of the schools' denial of equal educational services to Chicano students in the Southwest. In recent years, the Department increasingly has turned its attention toward this problem and has established firmer requirements aimed at assuring equal educational opportunity for Chicanos. These efforts, however, remain far from adequate. Little in the way of HEW resources is devoted to the civil rights denials perpetrated against Mexican American students, and the Department has been slow to make use of its main enforcement weapon—termination of Federal financial assistance—even in cases involving blantant violations. For purposes of Federal civil rights enforcement, as well as in all other aspects of their education, Mexican American students are still largely ignored.

To understand fully the dimensions of the educational problems facing Mexican Americans in the Southwest, assume that these problems affected not only Mexican Americans, but all students generally.

- Forty percent of *all* students in the Southwest would fail to graduate from high school.
- Three of every five 12th graders in the Southwest would be reading below grade level.
- Sixteen percent of *all* students in the Southwest would be required to repeat the first grade for failure to perform at an acceptable academic level.

In the face of so massive a failure on the part of the educational establishment, drastic reforms would, without question, be instituted, and instituted swiftly. These are precisely the dimensions of the educational establishment's failure with respect to Mexican Americans. Yet little has been done to change the status quo—a status quo that has demonstrated its bankruptcy.

Not only has the educational establishment in the Southwest failed to make needed changes, it has failed to understand fully its inadequacies. The six reports of the Commission's Mexican American Education Study cite scores of instances in which the actions of individual school officials have reflected an attitude which blames educational failure on Chicano children rather than on the inadequacies of the school program. Southwestern educators must begin not only to recognize the failure of the system in educating Chicano children, but to acknowledge that change must occur at all levels—from the policies set in the state legislatures to the educational environment created in individual classrooms.

39

Your Child and Busing

UNITED STATES
COMMISSION ON CIVIL RIGHTS

The school bus is familiar to every American. For decades, it has been viewed as a convenience, even a necessity, for the education of the Nation's children. Whether brought up in big cities, suburbs, or rural areas, millions of Americans—at one time or another—were bused to and from school and thought little about it. Traditionally, busing has caused little upset or controversy, for everyone understood that the benefits, in the form of better educational opportunity, well warrant the minor inconvenience which a bus ride involves. Scenes of picketing and protest over busing were rare, and occurred only when parents demanded more, not less, busing.

In recent years, the situation has changed radically. The school bus has been vilified as representing a needless waste of money, a threat to the safety of children, and a health hazard. Busing has been condemned, not as a relative inconvenience but as an absolute evil.

The storm over busing is a limited one. For most purposes, busing continues and even increases with little show of concern. Handicapped children still are bused to schools with special facilities. Gifted children still are bused to schools with curriculum and teachers better suited to develop their abilities. And children in rural areas still are bused in increasing numbers as the movement toward school consolidation proceeds.

Only in the context of school desegregation has busing become an issue of emotion and controversy. For this purpose alone, the familiar school bus has aroused passionate objections, has stimulated protest marches to the Nation's Capital, and has generated acts of violence. . . .

There are many legitimate concerns about busing for desegregation: Will the quality of education suffer? Will the children be safe? Will their health be jeopardized? Will problems of school discipline increase? Will the bus rides be unreasonably long? Are the courts going beyond constitutional requirements? These and other questions demand answers that fact, not rhetoric, can provide. . . .

The Commission concedes that we, like others who have spoken on this issue, are not without a special viewpoint. Our perspective is one that we have developed over the years as individuals and through our collective experience as members of the Commission. It is fourfold.

First, we believe that the great importance the American people have placed on education is justified and that every child deserves, as a matter of right, a high quality education.

Second, we believe that the Supreme Court of the United States has been right in the several decisions it has handed down on this issue since 1954.*

Third, we believe that school desegregation is the most urgent moral imperative facing the American people; that racial justice and racial unity are essential to the Nation's future well-being and that they cannot be achieved so long as our children are educated in racial isolation.

Fourth, we are convinced that acceptance of the continuation of school segregation at this critical point in our history will leave to future generations a heritage of distrust, cynicism, and alienation which may prove irreversible.

Clearinghouse Publication No. 36 of The United States Commission on Civil Rights (May, 1972).

* Editor's note: This document was published before the Court's 1974 *Bradley v. Milliken* decision.

1. For almost as long as there has been an automobile, American children have been going to school by bus. Thousands of men and women who today hold important positions in American life went to school by bus and would not have been able to complete school otherwise. Sometimes they spent several hours on the bus each day, leaving home before daybreak and not returning until dark.

Indeed, some trips could be measured in terms of days and weeks instead of hours. Some round trips simply were too long to be made daily. Thus the pupil would leave home on Monday morning, spend the entire week at school, and return home on Friday. Blacks in Warren County, Virginia can recall making such trips as late as 14 years ago. Theirs was one of 17 Virginia counties which had no black high school, so 106 Warren County black students had to attend schools in two neighboring counties. Instead of making daily round trips of more than 100 miles, 59 of them boarded at school. Some Indian pupils spend months at boarding schools, after being flown there from hundreds of miles away. One such trip carries Alaskan youths to a boarding school in Oklahoma—a distance of more than 3,000 miles. Some of the planes go from village to village to pick up students, much as a bus picks up pupils at stops along a country road, before the students board airliners for the rest of the trip.

New Mexico has two bus routes measuring 74 miles one-way and three others of about 70 miles in each direction—none having any connection with desegregation. A bus route in the Needles, California area stretches 65 miles one-way, and the pupils spend about 3 hours a day on the bus.

Pupil transportation in the United States did not begin with the motor bus. It is nearly as old as public education itself, and student transportation at public expense goes back almost to the beginning of compulsory education. Massachusetts in 1852 became the first State to adopt compulsory education and in 1869 became the first State to provide pupil transportation at public expense. If all children had to go to school, it stood to reason that some means of transportation had to be furnished for those who lived too far away to walk. By 1919 every State had authorized the use of tax money for pupil transportation.

The earliest trips were by horse-drawn wagons or sleds. Just prior to 1920 the first motor buses were used, gradually becoming the now-familiar yellow, box-shaped vehicle that generally carries 50 or 60 young passengers.

But the tax-supported school bus isn't the only means of pupil transportation. In at least two States, Maine and Louisiana, children travel to and from school by boat. And in some remote areas at times, children have been flown to school by airplane. Many urban children use commercial buses to get to school and have done so for years, largely at their own expense. Fewer than half of the Nation's pupils get to school on foot or by bicycle.

Today busing is a national issue. But for decades, busing has been a matter of concern for Southern blacks. One concern was that the buses were used to carry children to racially separate schools, and that almost always meant a better school for white than black children. Another concern was that black children were not even provided buses until well after buses were provided for whites, and in some instances many years afterward. Busing was looked upon as an advantage—a symbol of the desire of parents and the community to provide children with the best possible schooling. Black parents were shortchanged in terms of buildings, teachers, books, and supplies—in short, in public education itself—and they were similarly deprived of pupil transportation.

Henry Marsh, a young black Virginian who is vice mayor of Richmond, recalled in a recent address that his earliest memory of school segregation was when he "walked five miles each way to a one-room school with one teacher and seven grades, while white children rode past me on the school bus to a modern, well-staffed school."

When buses were finally provided for black children in the South, the service was segregated in the same manner as the schools were segregated. Sometimes the buses were old ones that had been replaced by new buses for white children. Many Southern blacks can remember that when they were bused at all, they were bused beyond the front door of a nearby white school in order to be driven to a black school. Many pupil miles were added, at great cost to hard-pressed State and local education budgets, to bus children for long distances in order to maintain segregation.

White and minority children alike had no guarantee of attending a neighborhood school, or even the school nearest their home. Thousands of children passed each other on the way to different schoolhouses. One North Carolina county had four separate sets of schools. And in south Texas, until the recent consolidation of districts, Anglo children were bused out of a district that was predominantly Mexican American to schools predominantly white.

Before and after the 1954 *Brown* v. *Board of Education* decision, strictly segregated bus routes were laid out for segregated schools. Thus, in 1958 a white teacher in south Georgia almost lost her job because she let one of her pupils ride home on the black bus. Thousands of miles, hours, and gallons of gasoline were spent transporting children to racially separate schools.

Pupil transportation has grown rapidly over the years and neither segregation nor desegregation has been the most important factor. Aside from the steady increase in enrollment, the most important factor by far has been school consolidation, especially after the Second World War. During the War, labor and materials were scarce and non-defense construction of all kinds had to be postponed. Once the War was over, school districts set about building new consolidated schools to replace the old one- and two-room schoolhouses that were inadequate to meet growing educational needs. In the meantime, highway building, which also had been postponed by the War, became a major national undertaking—thus providing the roads that made it possible for buses to serve the new consolidated schools.

Rising educational demands and the thinning of rural populations spurred school consolidation during the fifties and sixties. In 1925 there were 163,000 one-teacher elementary schools, and at the end of the Second World War half of them were still around. By the early 1960's, however, the number of these one-teacher schools had dropped to 13,000 and today only 2,000 remain. Similarly, the number of school districts dropped from 127,000 in the early thirties to about 17,000 today.

During recent decades other factors have been at work to increase busing. Many high school students in the sprawling suburbs had to be bused, so busing became an urban as well as a rural practice. Cities used busing to relieve crowded schools. Bus service was provided for the gifted and the handicapped, enabling these children to attend schools tailored to their needs. Some parents—worried about such things as lack of subdivision sidewalks, dangerous traffic conditions, and bad weather—demanded bus service. Gradually, bus pickups became closer and closer to the pupil's home, for the convenience of both pupils and parents.

As the number of buses increased, so did the purposes for which they could be used. Many classes in nature study, art, or music, civics classes, science classes, choruses, bands and athletic teams have been transported by school bus to special events and occasions. Many trips to parks, museums, farms, concert halls, theaters, zoos, seats of government, industrial plants, and health clinics have been made possible by the school bus.

Since 1921, the number of children transported at public expense has risen from 600,000 to nearly 20,000,000. The number of vehicles has grown from about 60,000 in 1930 to about 256,000 at the beginning of the last school year. During the 1970–71 school year, school buses logged 2,200,000,000 miles at a total cost of one and a half billion dollars. From coast to coast, 43.5 percent of the public school enrollment is now bused.

Although busing has played a role in the desegregation controversy almost from the time of the *Brown* decision, busing specifically for desegregation purposes has been used across the Nation only in the last 3 or 4 years. Busing as a desegregation tool became a national issue with a series of court decisions, starting in 1966, which will be discussed below.

How much of the increase in busing has been caused by desegregation? In a letter dated March 24, 1972, Secretary of Transportation John A. Volpe quoted the National Highway Traffic Safety Administration as estimating that less than 1 percent of the annual increase in busing can be attributed to desegregation. Taken altogether, according to most published estimates, the number of children who are bused for desegregation purposes is 2 to 4 percent of those transported. While busing may seem "massive" to a community just beginning to bus to achieve desegregation, this category of busing accounts for only a small part of the national total.

Indeed, in some parts of the country desegregation has reduced the amount of busing. In 42 desegregating Georgia districts between 1965 and 1969, with enrollment up 92,000 and the number bused up 14,000, there was a decrease of 473,000 in the total number of miles traveled. Similarly, in 27 Mississippi districts at about the same time bus mileage dropped 210,000 miles although the number of students bused had increased by 2,500. It is easy to see how desegregation could reduce the amount of busing, especially in rural areas which had extensive busing for segregation purposes. In those localities, white and black children no longer are passing each other on the way to segregated schools lying in opposite directions. Bus routes are more efficient and shorter, meaning quicker rides for the children.

That a great deal of busing can be tolerated—and by deliberate choice of the parents—was illustrated by statistics on public and private school busing published in 1970 by *South Today*. The *South Today* article surveyed pupils at 10 segregated private schools and found that the number of pupils bused averaged 62 percent and that the distance averaged 17.7 miles each way. By contrast, public schools in the eight States in which these private schools were located were busing less than half the enrollment an average of 10.1 miles each way. Thus, more of the private school students were being bused, and they were traveling an average of 7.6 miles each way farther than pupils at the public schools.

To grasp the importance of the school bus to American education, one needs only to imagine the national outcry that would result if all bus service for all purposes suddenly were withdrawn. Only when busing is used for desegregation purposes is there bitter complaint.

2. Before 1954, public school segregation was lawful in the United States. In 1896, the Supreme Court ruled that States could provide separate facilities for whites and blacks, so long as the facilities were equal.

At the time of the famous 1954 *Brown* case, segregated schools were required by law in 17 States and were permitted by law in four States. Southern schools were strictly segregated, but they were seldom—if ever—equal. Much more money was spent for white education than for black education, and in some States expenditures for white pupils were several times those for black pupils.

In 1954, the Court unanimously overturned the 1896 decision, declaring that "separate educational facilities are inherently unequal." A year later, in the same case, the Court ordered desegregation to proceed "with all deliberate speed."

However, the speed with which the decision was carried out was all too deliberate. The pace of desegregation was painfully slow, each year depriving more black children of equal educational opportunity. In the mid-1960's, courts took note of the inaction and began ordering segregated school districts to take firmer steps to remove all traces of discrimination.

In the first dozen years after the *Brown* decision, courts concerned themselves with the right of individual black children to attend nonsegregated schools. Southern districts answered with elaborate freedom-of-choice plans which put the burden of desegregation on the children seeking it. In 1966, however, the Fifth Circuit Court of Appeals focused on the school system as a whole and said that formerly dual systems had to convert to "unitary," or single, systems without racial division. The court also said that freedom-of-choice plans would be acceptable only if they resulted in desegregation, and not merely in the possibility of desegregation.

Two years later, the Supreme Court held that districts have a duty to set up a unitary system and eliminate segregation "root and branch." The Court called for a school system in which there would be no white or black schools, "but just schools."

"The burden on a school board today," the Court said, "is to come forward with a plan that promises realistically to work, and promises realistically to work *now*."

These two decisions set the stage for the busing controversy. This was not because they ordered busing—the districts involved already had busing—but because they ordered elimination of "white" and "Negro" schools, and in many communities that could be done only by busing both white and black pupils.

In the meantime, a few Northern cities—Boston, Chicago, Evanston, Berkeley, Hartford, Rochester, Riverside, and others—began experimenting with busing as a means of increasing school integration. Some of these plans called for "one-way" busing—that is, transporting minority pupils to predominantly white schools. Others called for "two-way" busing, in which both white and minority children would be bused.

In 1969, in a Mississippi case, the Supreme Court declared an end to the "all-deliberate-speed" rule. "The obligation of every school district," the Court asserted, "is to terminate dual school systems at once and to operate now and hereafter only unitary schools."

In 1971, in the *Charlotte-Mecklenburg* case, the Court ruled on what kind of steps should be taken to create a unitary system. The Court held unanimously that busing is a proper means of desegregating schools.

"We find no basis for holding that the local school authorities may not be required to employ bus transportation as one tool of school desegregation," wrote Chief Justice Warren Burger. "Desegregation plans cannot be limited to the walk-in school."

The Court was careful in its handling of the busing issue. It suggested that busing should not be used if the time or distance would endanger the child's health or education. But in the case at hand, the Court saw no such danger.

Courts in the North, meanwhile, also were finding unconstitutional segregation and were ordering desegregation with the use of busing to achieve it. Involved in these decisions were cities like Pontiac, Pasadena, Detroit, and Denver. Other cities—Harrisburg, Pennsylvania, for example—acted under State law.

It can be seen from the cases just outlined that desegregation moved gradually and logically in the direction of using every available and reasonable tool, including busing. Old segregation patterns are deeply rooted and slow to give way. It became evident that many American children would never see desegregated classrooms unless positive steps were taken to break the old pattern.

Nevertheless, courts did not leap to order wholesale busing. On the contrary, busing was called for only when necessary to undo the unconstitutional wrong of segregated schools.

Despite the care with which the courts acted and despite the fact that many years had gone by since the *Brown* decision, busing drew a violent reaction during 1970 and 1971 in some communities. Busing began dominating the Nation's headlines. Two buses were overturned in Lamar, South Carolina, and buses were burned in Denver and Pontiac.

But these headline-making incidents were the exception rather than the rule. While they were happening, scores of districts were desegregating quietly. Moreover, the incidents usually have occurred at the beginning of the school year. Once the school-opening tensions and disturbances settle down, desegregation generally goes forward in orderly fashion.

Many a superintendent, board, and court has struggled to find a way to desegregate effectively without busing. They have had to conclude, in the final analysis, that there is no other way. Given the tightly segregated neighborhoods in most American communities, desegregation simply is not possible in many localities without busing and isn't likely to be for years to come. Where courts have ordered school districts to carry out desegregation plans involving busing, they have done so for a sound reason: namely, that a violation of the Constitution must have an effective remedy and some way to bring the violation to an end. Without that, the constitutional right to attend an unsegregated school is meaningless.

3. As an issue of national controversy, busing has created a forest of fears, myths, and incorrect and misleading statements. For example, busing for desegregation purposes frequently is described as "massive" busing. But, as we have seen, the number of children bused solely for desegregation purposes is relatively small.

Busing for desegregation purposes often is called "forced" busing. But, as noted previously, pupil transportation in America followed closely behind compulsory education, which "forces" children to go to school, whether on foot or by bus. Thus, any busing in a State with a compulsory attendance law could be called "forced" busing, for the child has to go to school and attend the school to which he is assigned, and the bus is his means of getting there. Moreover, as mentioned previously, bus trips to private schools—to which parents freely choose to send their children—often are much longer than trips to public schools.

Somehow the busing-for-desegregation debate has become clouded in its own language and expressions, in which the word "busing" almost always follows such labels as "massive" and "forced," and in which the defenders of busing are pictured as wanting children bused simply to have the experience of being bused.

Somehow a pattern of fears and myths has become fixed in the minds of the public, making it hard to sort out the facts and determine what is true and what is false. Let us deal, with some of the fears and myths often heard about busing:

1. A child has a right to attend a "neighborhood" school.

Long before the busing issue, there were parents who wanted the right to send their children to the school of their choice. Sometimes they wanted to send their children to the "neighborhood" school and sometimes they wanted to send their children to schools outside the neighborhood.

Parents who felt that their children should attend the same school as children in the next block wanted the say-so about which of two nearby schools would be their "neighborhood" school. Sometimes parents have felt that the route to one school would be safer than the route to another because of traffic, the lack of sidewalks or crossing guards, and so on.

At times parents have wanted to send their children to schools outside the neighborhood. Sometimes parents have felt that a school a little farther away had better teachers. Sometimes classrooms were less crowded at another school. And sometimes their children had more friends at another school.

A few parents have gone to court to force a school board to send their children to a certain school. In some of these lawsuits parents have insisted that their children be sent to the nearest—that is, the "neighborhood"—school. Courts have ruled in these cases that the school board, and not the parents, has the right to determine which school a child will attend.

A 1965 Michigan case provides an example. The local board felt that because a school was overcrowded some of the pupils should be sent to another school farther away (and keep in mind, this was several years before the busing controversy in that State). The court ruled that the board had the right to send the students to a school other than the "neighborhood" school.

For many years, of course, some States sent all pupils of one race to one school and all the pupils of another race to another school, no matter what the parents said. Often this meant going directly past the door of a nearby school to another school much farther away.

Courts backed up the boards, holding that there was no legal or sacred right to a "neighborhood" school. The courts held that boards had the right to make pupil assignments and decide to which school a child would go. In an 1876 Cincinnati case, a court used colorful language to make that point, saying that "children cannot cluster round their school like they do around their parish church."

In recent times, courts have supported the right of boards to send children to certain schools in order to reduce segregation. Courts have upheld boards which have taken the position that the best schooling is schooling which does not occur in segregated classrooms. The courts have regarded this as a sound educational position with which they should not interfere. The Pennsylvania Supreme Court went on to point out that the neighborhood-based school—made up, by and large, of children of the same race and status—is the exact opposite of the old "common" school, which is deeply rooted in American history and which brought together children from a wide variety of families and backgrounds.

Clearly parents cannot, on their own, make the final decision about where to send their children for public schooling—whether it be to the nearest school, the "best" school, the newest school, or whatever. A school district in which parents made such final decisions could hardly operate, because every parent would want to enroll his children in the "best" or most convenient school. The final decision must be made by the board, on the basis of what is best for the district as a whole, and no parent has the absolute right to send his child to a school simply because it happens to be geographically nearest.

The educational trend in recent years has been away from the neighborhood school, whose facilities are necessarily limited by size, toward larger schools which can provide better facilities and a broader curriculum. The neighborhood school was not sacred in the days of segregation, and there is no reason why it should be today. To make the neighborhood school the cornerstone of American education would be to turn the clock back educationally as well as socially.

2. Busing puts a child out of reach of his parents or neighbors when school illnesses and injuries occur.

This is a fear that seems to bother many parents more than it should. Children do have accidents and get sick at school, but not very often.

If the matter is serious, school authorities are capable of seeing that the child gets immediate attention. Some schools have small buses and automobiles that are used to transport handicapped children, and these can be used in an emergency. Of course, nearly all school officials have private automobiles handy which could be used if necessary. Some large schools employ full-time nurses or, at least, have first-aid facilities and equipment and faculty members with health and first-aid training.

Harrisburg, Pennsylvania prepared this response to questions about what would happen if a child who is bused got sick or hurt at school:

"The school nurse will be called immediately for preliminary diagnosis and treatment. A parent will be called if warranted. If a parent is unable to pick up the child, the school district will provide transportation to take the child home."

The concern is one that undoubtedly has passed through the minds of millions of parents whose children have been bused all along for reasons having nothing to do with desegregation (less than half the Nation's school enrollment walks to school). Yet the concern has not been serious enough to block such bus-related educational developments as consolidation, often requested and ardently supported by parents. It can hardly now pose a danger of major proportions for the relatively small percentage of children who are bused for desegregation purposes.

3. Buses aren't safe.

Thousands of American parents would disagree with that statement. In school districts across the country, they have been asking for more busing, not less.

The reason, of course, is the growing congestion in urban areas and the ever-increasing number of automobiles. Streets that once rarely saw an automobile, and could be used as places to play catch or touch football at practically any time of the day, now are clogged with automobiles. Streets once safe now are so heavy with traffic that they are dangerous for young children to cross.

Hence many parents have been asking for—indeed, demanding—bus service. Gradually, over the years, school districts have been providing bus service closer and closer to the children's homes. The parents who have been demanding this service regard buses as being safer than walking, rather than the reverse. Stringent State traffic laws go to great lengths to protect school buses and their young passengers.

Parents whose children are bused can take comfort in the fact that the National Safety Council regards the school bus as "the safest transportation in the United States." Says the Council: "The school bus is safer to travel in than your own automobile, an airplane, buses (other than school buses), or a passenger train."

The National Safety Council's latest statistics show that while there are 2.4 fatalities per 100 million miles of travel in private automobiles and .29 in airplanes, the figure for school buses is .06.

That children who ride buses are safer than children who walk was supported by a 6-year report compiled by the Pennsylvania Department of Education. The report found bus riding three times safer than walking—one

accident for every 280 pupils who walked to school, against one for every 898 who rode to school on a bus.

4. Fights and racial clashes occur on buses and in the desegregated schools.

Scuffling, bullying, and other childish behavior have always been a part of growing up and always will be. It occurs wherever children gather—at home, on playgrounds, at school, and on the way to and from school, whether the trip is on foot or by bus.

As far back as 1939 educators were trying to decide if busing causes an increase in disciplinary problems. The conclusion was that it does not.

Nevertheless, districts using busing have taken steps to reduce incidents on buses. The standard approach has been to place monitors on buses, as well as in the halls and schoolyards. Some parents believe their children are safer on a bus with an adult monitor than they would be walking home by themselves or in small groups.

School disorders are indeed a problem. But the fact that disorders occurred at schools and on buses before they were desegregated indicates that such incidents are not uniquely connected with busing for desegregation. Moreover, there is reason to believe that some incidents are given overblown attention—in and out of the press—if they somehow can be connected with the controversial issue of busing. Some incidents that otherwise would not even be reported are suddenly "racial" incidents.

There is considerable evidence that disorderly pupils take their cue from their elders, particularly those in the community. Students can hardly be unaffected when adults burn and bomb buses, throw up picket lines, and shout insults. If there is tension and disorder outside the school, there is bound to be tension and disorder inside.

Once the protests and demonstrations fade, so do school disorders. In Pontiac, for example, discipline returned to normal and monitors were removed after the pickets left the schools. In Pasadena, incidents in the schools have dropped to the lowest point in 6 years.

Uneasiness is to be expected at first, of course, when children are being placed in new and unfamiliar learning situations. Some districts have moved creatively to prepare schools, officials, teachers, parents, pupils, and the community for desegregation, often with successful results. Students themselves have taken steps to make the change to biracial education as orderly as possible. But when a busing program is carried out quietly and smoothly it makes very small headlines or none at all.

5. Busing forces children to spend long hours away from home, thereby taking away play and study time.

There seems little doubt in the minds of busing opponents that busing steals hour after hour from the children. The facts do not support this result as being a natural and usual consequence of busing.

Indeed, in the South the reverse can and does happen. Desegregation actually can cause many children to spend less time on the bus. This is because they are no longer bused past one segregated school to get to another; hence the trip is shorter.

In Hoke County, North Carolina, for example, the switch from segregation to integration resulted in bus runs that were 15 minutes shorter. In Georgia the number of pupils bused statewide has risen gradually from 516,000 in 1967–68 to 566,000 in 1970–71. During the same period, however, the number of miles logged by Georgia buses has dropped from 53,997,000 to 51,257,000.

Similarly, it is possible that an attendance area in a Northern district might be so drawn that a bus trip after desegregation might be quicker than the ride or walk prior to desegregation.

In most districts where pupils are being bused for desegregation, trips are rarely long. The average travel time reported seems to be 20 to 30 minutes. Trips of an hour or more would be out of the ordinary. A trip of a half hour or so would not bring the pupil home much later than if he walked from a neighborhood school.

The desegregation order for Richmond, Virginia, for example, would call for average bus rides of about 30 minutes, which is less than the current average in an adjacent county involved in the decision.

Of 11 cities surveyed recently by the Center for National Policy Review, the length of the average trip had been increased by more than 15 minutes in only two. In six cities, the average trip remained exactly the same before and after court-ordered desegregation.

The Supreme Court, in the *Charlotte-Mecklenburg* case, was mindful of the fact that children should not be subjected to bus rides "when the time or distance of travel is so great as to risk either the health of the children or significantly impinge on the educational process." Thus the Court has already taken steps to protect children against the overlong trips that concern busing opponents.

6. Minority Americans are just as opposed to busing as majority Americans.

It is true that many minority Americans are apprehensive about desegregation, but rarely because it would mean a bus ride for their children. They have more solid reasons. At times they oppose desegregation, and not without cause. Minority schools have been closed in carrying out desegregation plans while previously white schools have remained in use. Often it has been the minority senior high school that has been converted to a desegregated junior high school. Some black principals and teachers have lost their jobs or have been demoted.

Minority Americans have another concern about desegregation. They fear that their children could be abused and mistreated in a predominantly white school and swallowed up in the dominant white atmosphere. They remember the taunts and threats from Little Rock onward. Some minority parents feel that their children, therefore, would be better off in an improved school serving their own group.

Some minority Americans have been discouraged by what they sense to be white opposition to desegregation at every step of the way. In frustration and dismay, they have come to question integration.

While many minority Americans share these strong concerns, most, nevertheless, want to see the public schools desegregated. They recognize, as do most majority Americans, that ours is one Nation—not two or three—and that the Nation cannot be sure of its future until its citizens learn to live together, beginning in the classroom.

More concretely, minority Americans have long known, as the Supreme Court stated in 1954, that "separate educational facilities are inherently unequal." As one black leader put it recently, the only way to make sure that black Americans receive an equal educational opportunity is to put them into the same classrooms with whites.

In several cities, the Commission on Civil Rights has been told of inner-city schools that have been improved magically and almost overnight when the district launched a busing program. And in a letter to a Washington newspaper, a black parent from North Carolina gave her own testimony:

"Within one month, the parents of the white children who were bused managed to get the black school painted, repairs made, new electric typewriters and sewing machines, and the shelves filled with books . . .

"I contend that busing for one year will upgrade all our schools quicker than anything the President or Congress can do."

7. Busing is too expensive.

To be sure, a school bus is not an inexpensive item. The average school bus costs $8,500.

However, pupil transportation is a relatively small part of the Nation's education budget. Down through the decades, although the number of children bused has risen substantially, that part of the education budget which goes for pupil transportation has stayed about the same. In 1933, the expenditure for pupil transportation was 3.5 percent of the cost of operating public schools. In 1969–70, it was 3.6 percent.

Last year, the cost of pupil transportation was just over $1.5 billion, out of a total public school expenditure of nearly $44 billion.

When school districts talk about the high cost of busing they are speaking, generally, about capital outlay—that is, the one-time expenditure of funds to buy the necessary buses to carry out a desegregation plan. This initial expenditure can, indeed, put a severe strain on limited school funds. Past legislation has made Federal funds available to help districts buy buses, and this seems the logical answer to the initial burden of acquiring buses.

8. Instead of busing, we should spend the money on education.

This issue is at the heart of the busing debate. Some argue that learning can best be advanced in desegregated schools; others argue that learning can best be advanced by leaving children in segregated neighborhood schools and pumping catch-up funds for compensatory education into schools serving low-income areas.

For some 15 years, educators and social scientists have been debating the matter, and the debate is far from over.

In the thick of the debate is a massive 1966 Federal study called the "Coleman Report." Boiled down, the Coleman Report found that minority children from low-income families learn faster when there is racial and economic integration of classrooms. The report said family background is, by far, the most important factor in a child's education, but an integrated classroom can accelerate learning.

Other studies have found that minority students do better in integrated classrooms. A 1968 report said the evidence "is quite conclusive; i.e., integrated minority pupils recorded higher achievement gains than segregated minority pupils." Said another report: "Several studies, which compared disadvantaged Negroes in traditional compensatory education programs with Negro students transferred to majority white schools, showed integration to be superior."

The issue is not integration versus compensatory education, but whether catch-up programs can work by themselves. In 1967 the Commission on Civil Rights evaluated compensatory education programs in isolated schools in large cities and concluded that the data did not show lasting gains in achievement. Berkeley, California found that compensatory education in racially isolated schools was not closing the education gap, so Berkeley coupled compensatory education with an integration program accomplished through busing. Results to date in Berkeley show advanced achievement by both white and minority students.

Some busing opponents say desegregation is a failure because it has not yet closed the achievement gap between majority and minority pupils. This criticism overlooks the fact that widespread desegregation through the use of busing is a fairly new development. It would be unrealistic to expect a few years of desegregation to overcome the effects of generations of segregation. But in one desegregated system after another, the gap is being closed.

To repeat, it is not a question of desegregation versus compensatory education: Both are needed to bring education alive for all of the Nation's pupils. As the National Advisory Council on the Education of Disadvantaged Children said in 1969:

"School desegregation and compensatory education are not an either/or proposition, but are mutually complementary actions which can lose much of the effectiveness in isolation from each other."*

* Editor's Note: For extensive discussion of the research evaluating the effects of busing, see David J. Armor, "The Evidence on Busing," *The Public Interest* (Summer, 1972), pp. 90–126, and the rebuttal to this article by Thomas F. Pettigrew, Elizabeth L. Useem, Clarence Normand and Marshall S. Smith, "Busing: A Review of 'The Evidence,'" *The Public Interest* (Winter, 1973), pp. 88–134.

9. Busing prevents students from taking part in extra-curricular activities.

There is little reason why this should happen. Students have been riding buses for years, sometimes in remote rural areas, without surrendering after-school activities.

Districts undertaking desegregation through busing commonly have provided what is known as an "activity" bus. The "activity" bus is scheduled so that it doesn't leave until late, an hour or so after school ends for the day. Thus there is late bus service available to take students home after football and basketball practice, play rehearsals, band practice, track meets, chorus rehearsals, club meetings, and so on. . . .

10. Busing would carry children into dangerous neighborhoods where drugs, crime, and violence are commonplace.

Drugs and crime pose a very real threat to society. But the notion that they are limited only to inner-city neighborhoods simply does not square with the facts.

Recent statistics released by the Federal Bureau of Investigation show that crime respects no boundary between city and suburb. In fact, it is increasing faster in the suburbs than in the cities. Violent crime, for example, was up 13 percent in suburban areas and 9 percent in cities. As for drugs, suburban and inner-city parents alike can testify that their schools are far from being drug-free.

The job of school officials is to see that no children—whether they are bused or walk—are placed in danger. And the schools are taking the steps necessary to meet this duty. The steps include adult crossing guards, neighborhood and school monitors, and close coordination with police and municipal authorities.

The problem of safeguarding children from crime and violence is a very real one, but it has nothing to do with busing. If a neighborhood in which a school is located poses a threat to school children, the school should be closed and the children should be sent to another school. If school and municipal authorities cannot make certain that a school is safe, *no* child—black or white—should be made to attend it, whether he walks to school or gets there by bus.

In short, the answer to the very real problem of danger to school children does not lie in stopping the busing of some, but in taking steps to assure that all children can attend school in safety.

11. Busing penalizes white students by setting them back until other pupils "catch up."

No study supports this statement. On the other hand, a number of studies have found that white pupils either have gained or stayed at about the same level after integration.

Berkeley, California and Louisville, Kentucky found that both majority and minority pupils gained. Riverside, California and Denver, Colorado reported that the education of white children had not suffered. Evanston, Illinois found the same thing—adding that in the process the community "has made considerable gains in the improvement of communications between races."

Far from damaging educational opportunity for whites, busing often means better educational offerings for everyone. That is because busing frequently is the occasion for a district to reorganize its schools and make educational improvements.

At schools that previously had heavy minority enrollments, the change is especially dramatic. These schools often are given repairs, additional teachers, and general improvements during or just after desegregation —to the benefit of both white and minority pupils enrolled in them.

To experts inside and outside the field of education, desegregation is an essential part of quality education and segregation is educationally harmful to both minority and majority pupils. Dr. Michael J. Bakalis, Illinois State School Superintendent, put it this way in recent congressional testimony:

"A high price is paid by any child, be he white or black, who goes through his entire school career without ever meeting a child or teacher of another racial or ethnic background.

. . . Segregated schools can only serve to nurture prejudicial attitudes among the young and to divide us further as a people. A child who has been so isolated throughout his formative years is being educationally deprived."

12. It is not the job of the schools to cure social ills.

This statement, frequently made by busing opponents, takes an extremely narrow view of education's role.

Education is more than reading, writing, and arithmetic; education is preparation for life. Students need more than facts and problem-solving skills; they need to know how to lead full and useful lives in a complex world. In a Nation made up of a variety of races and nationalities, that means learning how to live and work with people of different skin colors and cultural backgrounds.

If one accepts this broad view of education, one cannot imagine a worse way of undertaking it than in classrooms segregated by race and national origin.

The segregated classroom stands to millions of minority Americans as proof that majority Americans do not wish to surrender the separate but unequal educational advantage that is theirs from early childhood. The segregated classroom denies millions of majority Americans the opportunity to become acquainted with minority children whose future they share.

As the president of the Pontiac PTA told a House Subcommittee recently:

"The inconvenience busing creates for the parents and the extra time students spend on the bus seem a very small price to pay to see, hopefully, our children mature into the type of American citizens that the drafters of our Constitution and the present interpreters of the Constitution must have envisioned when they included and interpreted the provisions for equality."

Few top educators would agree to a role for education insulated from the Nation's social problems. Segregated schooling might provide instruction, but it does not provide education.

CONCLUSION

We have tried to put the busing controversy into the proper light. It is not easy to separate the exaggerations about busing from what busing actually is: that is, simply one of many tools with which school districts can carry out their constitutional duty to desegregate.

Busing is a last resort and only that. But when all other tools are ineffective, school districts have the duty to use the last remaining tool to meet their constitutional obligation. . . .

For 50 years, the school bus has been a friendly figure—an accepted and vital part of the American educational picture. Without the bus, millions of Americans would have had to rely on the limited educational offerings of one-room schools. Some might never have completed school.

Now, because it is being used to carry out desegregation plans, some suddenly have cast the familiar yellow bus as a villain. It is a reversal of roles that cannot but trouble thoughtful Americans.

The basic issue is not busing but integration. Either we continue moving toward the goal of integration, or we reject it and hold onto the separate schooling outlawed in the *Brown* decision. In rejecting busing in the racially segregated situation in which most Americans live today, we also reject integration. . . .

40

Ambush at Kamikaze Pass

TOM ENGELHARDT

"Westerns" may have been America's most versatile art form. For several generations of Americans, Westerns provided history lessons, entertainment and a general guide to the world. They created or recreated a flood of American heroes, filled popcorned weekends and overwhelmed untold imaginations. It's as difficult today to imagine movies without them as to think of a luncheonette without Coca Cola. In their folksy way, they intruded on our minds. Unobtrusively they lent us a hand in grinding a lens through which we could view the whole of the non-white world. Their images were powerful; their structure was satisfying; and at their heart lay one archetypal scene which went something like this:

White canvas-covered wagons roll forward in a column. White men, on their horses, ride easily up and down the lines of wagons. Their arms hang loosely near their guns. The walls of the buttes rise high on either side. Cakey streaks of yellow, rusty red, dried brown enclose the sun's heat boiling up on all sides. The dust settles on their nostrils, they gag and look apprehensively towards the heights, hostile and distant. Who's there? Sullenly, they ride on.

Beyond the buttes, the wagon train moves centrally into the flatlands, like a spear pointed at the sunset. The wagons circle. Fires are built;

Tom Engelhardt is an editor for the Pacific News Service.

Reprinted from the *Bulletin of Concerned Asian Scholars* **3** (Winter–Spring, 1971) by permission of the author. Copyright © 1971 by Tom Engelhardt. This version has been slightly edited from the original. Footnotes have been omitted.

guards set. From within this warm and secure circle, at the center of the plains, the whitemen (-cameras) stare out. There, in the enveloping darkness, on the peripheries of human existence, at dawn or dusk, hooting and screeching, from nowhere, like maggots, swarming, naked, painted, burning and killing, for no reason, like animals, they would come. The men touch their gun handles and circle the wagons. From this strategically central position, with good cover, and better machines, today or tomorrow, or the morning after, they will simply mow them down. Wipe them out. Nothing human is involved. It's a matter of self-defense, no more. Extermination can be the only answer.

There are countless variations on this scene. Often the encircled wagon train is replaced by the surrounded fort; yet only the shape of the object has changed. The fort, like the wagon train, is the focus of the film. Its residents are made known to us. Familiarly, we take in the hate/respect struggle between the civilian scout and the garrison commander; the love relations between the commander's daughter and the young first lieutenant who-has-yet-to-prove-himself; the comic routines of the general soldiery. From this central point in our consciousness, they sally forth to victory against unknown besiegers with inexplicable customs, irrational desires, and an incomprehensible language (a mixture of pig-latin and pidgen Hollywood).

What does this sort of paradigm do to us? Mostly, it forces us to flip history on its head. It makes the intruder exchange places in our eyes with the intruded upon. (Who ever heard of a movie in which the Indians wake up one morning to find that, at the periphery of their existences, in their own country, there are new and aggressive beings ready to make war on them, incomprehensible, unwilling to share, out to murder and kill etc.) It is the Indians, in these films, who must invade, intrude, break in upon the circle—a circle which contains all those whom the film has already certified as "human." No wonder the viewer identifies with those in the circle, not with the Indians left to patrol enigmatically the bluffs overlooking humanity. In essence, the viewer is forced behind the barrel of a repeating rifle and it is from that position, through its gun sights, that he receives a picture history of Western colonialism and imperialism. Little wonder that he feels no sympathy for the enemy as they fall before his withering fire— within this cinematic structure, the opportunity for such sympathy simply ceases to exist.

Such an approach not only transforms invasion into an act of self-defense; it also prepares its audiences for the acceptance of genocide. The theory is simple enough: We may not always be right (there are stupid commanders etc.), but we are human. By any standards (offered in the film), "they" are not. What, then, are they? They are animate, thus they are, if not human, in some sense animals. And, for animals facing a human onslaught, the options are limited. Certain of the least menacing among them can be retained as pets. As a hunter trains his dog, these can be trained to be scouts, tracking down those of their kind who try to escape or resist, to be porters, to be servants. Those not needed as pets (who are nonetheless domesticable) can be maintained on preserves. The rest, fit neither for house training nor for cages, must be wiped out.

From the acceptance of such a framework flows the ability to accept as pleasurable, a relief, satisfying, the mass slaughter of the "non-human"—the killing, mowing down of the non-white, hundreds to a film and normally in the scene which barely precedes the positive resolution of the relationships among the whites. Anyone who thinks the body count is a creation of the recent Indochinese war should look at the movies he saw as a kid. It was the implicit rule of those films that no less than ten Indian (Japanese, Chinese . . .) warriors should fall for each white, expendable secondary character.

Just as the style and substance of the Indian wars was a prototype for many later American intrusions into the third world (particularly the campaigns in the Philippines and Indochina), so movies about those wars provided the prototype from which nearly every American movie about the third world derived. That these third world movies are pale reflections of the framework, outlook, and even conventions of the cowboy movie is easy enough to demonstrate. Just a few examples, chosen almost at random from the thirty or forty films I've caught on T.V. in the last few months. Pick your country: the Mexico of toothy Pancho Villan bandits, the North Africa of encircled Foreign Legionnaires, the India of embattled British Lancers, or even South Africa. One would think treatment of South Africa might be rather special, have its own unique features. But Lo! We look up and already the Boers are trekking away, in (strange to say) wagons, and, yep, there's, no . . . let's see . . . Susan Hayward. Suddenly, from nowhere, the Zulus appear, hooting and howling, to surround the third-rate wagons of this third-rate movie. And here's that unique touch we've all been waiting for. It seems to be the singular quality of the Zulus that they have no horses and so must circle the wagon train on foot, yelling at the tops of their voices and brandishing their spears . . . but wait . . . from the distance . . . it's the Transvaal cavalry to the rescue. As they swoop down, one of the Boers leaps on a wagon seat, waving his hat with joy, and calls to his friend in the cavalry, "You've got 'em running, Paul. Keep 'em running, Paul! Run 'em off the end of the earth! (*Untamed*, 1955)

Or switch to the Pacific. In any one of a hundred World War II flicks, we see a subtle variation on the same encirclement imagery. From the deck of our flagship, amidst the fleet corraled off the Okinawa coast, we look through our binoculars. The horizon is empty; yet already the radar has picked them up. Somewhere beyond human sight, unidentified flying objects. The sirens are howling, the men pouring out of their bunks and helter-skelter into battle gear. At their guns, they look grimly towards the empty sky: the young ensign too eager for his first command, the swabby who got a date with that pretty Wave, the medic whose wife just sent him a "Dear John" letter (he's slated to die heroically). A speck on the horizon, faces tense, jokes fall away, it's the Kamikaze! Half-man, half-machine, an incomprehensible human torpedo bearing down from the peripheries of fanatical animate existence to pierce the armored defenses of the forces of Western democracy. The result? Serious damage to several ships, close calls on more, several secondary characters dead, and an incredible number of Japanese planes obliterated from the sky.

That there is no feeling of loss at the obliteration of human torpedoes is hardly surprising. Even in those brief moments when you "meet" the enemy, movies like this make it immaculately clear that he is not only strange, barbarous, hostile and dangerous, but has little regard for his own life. Throwing himself on the gatling guns of the British with only spear in hand, or on the ack-ack guns of the Americans with only bomb in portal, he is not acting out of any human emotion. It is not a desire to defend his home, his friends, or his freedom. It has no rational (i.e. "human") explanation. It is not even "bravery" as we in the West know it (though similar acts by whites are portrayed heroically). Rather, it is something innate, fanatical, perverse—an inexplicable desire for death, disorder and destruction. . . .

. . . The overwhelmingly present theme of the non-human-ness of the non-white prepares us to accept, without flinching, the extermination of our "enemies" (as John Wayne commented in *The Searchers,* 1956, there's "humans" and then there's "Comanches") and just as surely it helped prepare the ideological way for the leveling and near-obliteration of three Asian areas in the course of three decades.

It is useful, in this light, to compare the cinematic treatment of the European front in World Wars I and II with that of the Pacific front. From *The Big Parade* (a silent film) on, a common and often moving convention of movies about the wars against Germany went something like this: The allied soldier finds himself caught in a foxhole (trench, farmhouse etc.) with a wounded German soldier. He is about to shoot when the young, begrimed soldier holds up his hand in what is now the

peace symbol, but at the time meant "Do you have a cigarette?" Though speaking different languages, they exchange family pictures and common memories.

The scene is meant to attest to man's sense of humanity and brotherhood over and above war and national hatred. Until very recently, such a scene simply did not appear in movies about the Japanese front. Between the American and his non-white enemy, a bond transcending enmity was hardly even considered. Instead, an analogous scene went something like this: A group of Japanese, shot down in a withering crossfire, lie on the ground either dead or severely wounded. The American soldiers approach, less from humanitarian motives than because they hope to get prisoners and information. One of the Japanese, however, is just playing possum. As the American reaches down to give him water (first aid, a helping hand), he suddenly pulls out a hand grenade (pistol, knife) and, with the look of a fanatic, tries to blow them *all* to smithereens. He is quickly dispatched (see, for instance, *In Love and War,* 1956).

The theme of alien intruders descending on embattled humans and being obliterated from an earth they clearly are not entitled to is most straightforwardly put in Science Fiction movies; for monsters turn out to be little more than the metaphysical wing of the third world. These movies represent historically events which have taken place only in the Western imagination. Thus, the themes of the cowboy (third world) movie come through in a more primeval way. An overlay of fear replaces the suspense. Metaphorically, the world is the wagon train; the universe, the horizon. (Or, alternately, the earth space-ship is the wagon train; an alien planet, the horizon.) From that horizon, somewhere at the peripheries of human existence, from the Arctic icecap (*The Thing,* 1951), the desert (*Them,* 1954), the distant past (*The Beast from 20,000 Fathoms,* 1954), the sky (*War of the Worlds,* 1953), at dawn or dusk, hooting and beeping come the invaders. Enveloping whole armies, they smash through human defenses, forcing the white representatives of the human race to fall back on their inner defense line (perhaps New York or Los Angeles). Imperiling the very heartland of civilized life, they provide only one option—destroy THEM before THEM can destroy us.

In this sort of a movie, the technical problems involved in presenting the extinction of a race for the enjoyment of an audience are simplified. Who would even think about saving the Pod People? (*Invasion of the Body Snatchers,* 1956) . . .

Unfortunately for American movie makers, Asians and others could not simply be photographed with three heads, tentacles, and gelatinaceous bodies. Consequently, other conventions had to be developed (or appropriated) that would clearly differentiate them from "humanity" at large. The first of these was invisibility. In most movies about the third world, the non-whites provide nothing more than a backdrop for all-white drama—an element of exotic and unifying dread against which to play out the tensions and problems of the white world. Sometimes, even the locales seem none-too-distinguishable, not to speak of their black, brown, or yellow inhabitants. It is not surprising, for instance, that the Gable-Harlow movie *Red Dust* (1932), set on an Indochinese rubber plantation (Gable is the foreman), could be transported to Africa without loss two decades later as the Gable-Kelly *Mogambo.* It could as well have been set in Brazil on a coffee plantation, or in Nevada with Gable a rancher. . . .

A second convention of these films concerns the pecking order of white and non-white societies when they come into conflict. It is a "united front" among whites. Often the whites portrayed are the highly romanticized third-rate flotsam and jetsam of a mythologized American society—adventurers, prostitutes, opportunists, thieves (just as the films themselves, particularly when about Asia, tend to represent the brackish backwater of the American film industry). Yet no matter how low, no matter what their internal squabbles, no matter what their hostilities towards each other, in relation to the third world the whites stand as one: Missionary's daughter and drunken ferryboat captain ("I hate the Reds," he says to her, "because they closed a lot of Chinese ports where they have dames. Chinese, Eurasian, and White Russian. . . . Somebody pinned the bleeding heart of China on your sleeve but they never got around to me." / *Blood Alley,* 1955); soldier of fortune and adventurer-journalist, natural enemies over The-Woman-They-Both-Love (They escape Canton together, avoiding the clutches of the Reds in a stolen boat / *Soldier of Fortune,* 1955); sheriff, deputies and captured outlaws (They are surrounded by Mexican bandits / *Bandalero,* 196?); or on a national level, the British, Americans and Russians (They must deal with "the chief enemy of the Western World," Mao Tse-tung / *The Chairman,* 1970). This theme is, of course, simply a variation on a more home-grown variety—the Confederates and Yankees who bury their sectional hatreds to unite against the Indians; the convicts on their way to prison who help the wagon train fight off the Sioux, bringing the women and children to safety etc. (See, for example, *Ambush at Cimarron Pass,* 1958, which combines everything in one laughable mess—a Yankee patrol and its prisoner team up with a Confederate rancher to fight off an Apache attack.)

The audience is expected to carry two racial lessons away from this sort of thing. The first is that the presence of the incomprehensible and non-human brings out what is "human" in every man. Individual dignity, equality, fraternity, all that on which the West theoretically places premium value, are brought sharply into focus at the expense of "alien" beings. The second is the implicit statement that, in a pinch, any white is a step up from the rest of the world. They may be murderers, rapists, and mother-snatchers, but they're ours.

When the inhabitants of these countries emerge from the ferns or mottled huts, and try to climb to the edges of the spotlight, they find the possibilities limited indeed. In this cinematic pick-up-sides, the whites already have two hands on the bat handle before the contest begins. The set hierarchy of roles is structured something like this: All roles of positive authority are reserved for white characters. Among the whites, the men stand triumphantly at the top; their women cringe, sigh and faint below; and the Asians are left to scramble for what's left, like beggars at a refuse heap.

There is only one category in which a non-white is likely to come out top dog—villain. With their stock of fanatical speeches and their propensity for odd tortures, third world villains provided the American filmmaker with a handy receptacle for his audience's inchoate fears of the unknown and inhuman. Only as the repository for Evil could the non-white "triumph" in films. However, this is no small thing; for wherever there is a third world country, American scriptwriters have created villain slots to be filled by otherwise unemployable actors (though often even these roles are monopolized by whites in yellowface). From area to area, like spirits, their forms change: the Mexican bandit chief with his toothy smile, hearty false laugh, sombrero and bushy eyebrows (see, f.i., the excellent *Treasure of the Sierra Madre*, 1948, or the awful *Bandalero*); the Oriental warlord with his droopy mustache and shaven head (see *The Left Hand of God*, 1955, *The General Died at Dawn*, 1936, *Shanghai Express*, 1932, *Seven Women*, 1965, etc. ad nauseam); the Indian "Khan" or prince with his little goatee and urbane manner (*Khyber Pass*, 1954, *Charge of the Light Brigade*, 1936). Yet their essence remains the same.

Set against their shiny pates or silken voices, their hard eyes and twitching mouths, no white could look anything but good. In *Left Hand of God*, Humphrey Bogart, the pilot-turned-opportunist-warlord-advisor-turned-fraudulent-priest becomes a literal saint under the leer of Lee J. Cobb's General Yang. Gregory Peck, an "uninvolved" scientist-CIA spy, becomes a boy wonder and living representative of humanity when faced with a ping-pong playing Mao Tse-tung in *The Chairman*. How can you lose when the guy you want to double-deal represents a nation which has discovered an enzyme allowing pineapples to grow in Tibet and winter wheat in Mongolia, yet (as one of the Russian agents puts it) is holding it so that the rest of the "underdeveloped" world, "90 poor, 90% peasant . . . will crawl on their hands and knees to Peking to get it." All in all, these non-white representatives of evil provide a backboard off which white Western values can bounce in, registering one more cinematic Score for Civilization.

The other group of roles open to non-whites are roles of helplessness and dependence. At the dingy bottom of the scale of dependence crouch children. Non-white children have traditionally been a favorite for screenwriters and directors. Ingrid Bergman helped them across the mountains to safety (*The Inn of the Sixth Happiness*, 1958); Deborah Kerr taught them geography (*The King and I*, 1956); Humphrey Bogart helped them to memorize "My Old Kentucky Home" (*Left Hand of God*); Carrol Baker went with them on a great trek back to their homelands (*Cheyenne Autumn*, 1964); Richard Widmark took one (a little half-breed orphan girl—sort of the black, one-eyed Jew of the tiny tot's universe) back to the States with him (55 *Days at Peking*). And so on.

Essentially, non-white children fulfill the same function and have the same effect as non-white villains. They reflect to the white audience just another facet of their own humanity. Of course, if you ignore W. C. Fields, children have had a traditionally cloying place in American films; but in the third world movie they provide a particularly strong dose of knee-jerk sentiment, allowing the white leads to show the other side of Western civilization. It is their duty not just to exterminate the world's evil forces, but to give to those less capable (and more needy) than themselves. And who more closely fits such a description than the native child who may someday grow up to emulate us.

While it is children who demonstrate the natural impulses of the white authorities towards those who do not resist them, but are helpless before them or dependent upon them, it is women who prove the point. Even within the cinematic reflection of the white world, women have seldom held exalted positions. Normally they are daughters of missionaries, sweethearts of adventurers, daughters, nurses, daughters of missionaries, wives on safari, schoolmarms, daughters of missionaries, or prostitutes. (The exceptions usually being when women come under a "united front" ruling—that is, they confront Asian men, not white men. Then, as with Anna in *The King and I*, while their occupations may not change they face society on a somewhat different footing.) Several rungs down the social ladder, non-white women are left mainly with roles as bargirls, geishas, belly dancers, nurse's aids, missionary converts, harem girls, prostitutes. In such positions, their significance and status depend totally on the generosity (or lack of generosity) of those white men around whom the movies revolve.

However "well-intentioned" the moviemaker, the basic effect of this debased dependency is not changeable. Take that classic schmaltz of the 1950's, *The World of Suzie Wong*. William Holden, a dissatisfied architect-businessman, has taken a year's sabbatical in Hong Kong to find out if he can "make it" as an artist. (It could have been Los Angeles, but then the movie would have been a total zilch.) He meets ***Susie Wong***, a bargirl who is cute as a Walt Disney button and speaks English with an endearing "Chinese" accent. ("Fo' goo'niss sakes" she says over and over at inappropriate moments.) He wants her to be his model. She wants to be his "permanent girlfriend." Many traumas later, the moviemakers trundle out their good intentions towards the world's ill-treated masses. They allow Holden to choose Susie over Kay, the proper, American, upper class woman who is also chasing him. This attempt to put down the upper classes for their prejudices towards Chinese and bargirls, however, barely covers over the basic lesson of the movie: a helpless, charming Chinese bargirl *can* be saved by the right white man, purified by association with him, and elevated to dependency on him. (Her bastard child, conveniently brought out for his pity quotient, is also conveniently bumped off by a flash flood, avoiding further knotty prob-

lems for the already overtaxed sensibilities of the scriptwriters.) It all comes across as part act of God, part act of white America.

Moving upwards towards a peak of third world success and white condescension, we discover the role of "sidekick." Indispensable to the sidekick is his uncanny ability to sacrifice his life for his white companion at just the right moment. In this, he must leave the audience feeling that he has repaid the white man something intangible that was owed to him. And, in this, we find the last major characteristic of third world roles—expendability. Several classic scenes come to mind. In this skill, the otherwise pitiful Gunga Din excelled (*Gunga Din*, 1939). Up there on a craggy ledge, already dying, yet blowing that bugle like crazy to save the British troops from ambush by the fanatic Kali-worshippers. Or, just to bring up another third world group, the death of the black trainer in *Body and Soul* (1947), preventing his white World Heavyweight Champion (John Garfield) from throwing the big fight. Or even, if I remember rightly, Sidney Poitier, Mau Mau initiate, falling on the Punji sticks to save the white child of his boyhood friend Rock Hudson (*Something of Value*, 1957). The parts blend into each other: the Filipino guide to the American guerrillas, the Indian pal of the white scout, that Mexican guy with the big gut and sly sense of humor. In the end, third world characters are considered expendable by both moviemakers and their audiences because they are no more a source of "light" than the moon at night. All are there but to reflect in differing mirrors aspects of white humanity.

While extermination, dependency and expendability have been the steady diet of these movies over the decades, American moviemakers have not remained totally stagnant in their treatment of the third world and its inhabitants. They have over the last forty years, emerged ponderously from a colonial world into a neo-colonial one. In the 1930's, the only decade when anything other than second-rate films were made about Asia, moviemakers had no hesitation about expressing an outright contempt for subjugated and/or powerless Asians; nor did they feel self-conscious about proudly portraying the colonial style in which most Westerners in Asia lived. The train in *Shanghai Express* (1932) is shown in all its "colonial" glory: the Chinese passengers crammed into crude compartments; the Westerners eating dinner in their spacious and elegant dining room. Here was the striking contrast between the rulers and the ruled and nobody saw any reason to hide it. . . .

A decade later such scenes . . . would have been gaffes. In the wake of the World War and its flock of anti-Japanese propaganda flicks (whose progeny were still alive in the early 1960's), the destruction of the British, French and Dutch empires, the success of the Communist revolution in China, the birth and death of dreaded "neutralism," and the rise of the United States to a position of preeminence in the world, new cinematic surfaces were developed to fit over old frames. In their new suits, during the decade of the 50's, cowboy-third world movies flourished as never before. A vast quantity of these low-budget (and not-so-low-budget) films burst from Hollywood to flood the country's theatres. In the more "progressive" of them, an India in chains was replaced by a struggling, almost "independent" country; the "regimental beastie" by a Nehru (-Gandhi) type "rebel" leader; the Kali-worshipping, loinclothed fanatic by Darvee, the Maoist revolutionary ("You cannot make omelettes without breaking eggs"). Yet this sort of exercise was no more than sleight of hand. The Nehru character looked just as ridiculously pompous and imitative as did Gunga Din when he practised his bugle; nor did the whites any less monopolize center stage (holding, naturally, the key military and police positions); nor could the half-breed woman (Ava Gardner) any less choose light (the British officer) over darkness (Darvee and his minions). Soon, all this comes to seem about as basic a change in older forms as was the "independence" granted to many former colonies in the real world (*Bhowani Junction*, 1956).

If any new elements were to enter these movies in the 1950's (and early 60's), it was in the form of changes in relations within the white world, not between the white and non-white worlds. These changes, heralded by the "adult westerns" of the late fifties, have yet to be fully felt in films on Asia; yet a certain early (and somewhat aborted) move in this direction could be seen in some of the films that appeared about the Korean war (not a particularly popular subject, as might be imagined)—a certain tiredness ("Three world wars in one lifetime" / *Battle Circus*, 1953) and some doubts. The WWII flick's faith in the war against the "Japs," in a "civilian" army, and in "democracy" comes across tarnished and tired. The "professional" soldier (or flyer) takes center stage. ("We've gotta do a clean, professional job on those [North Korean] bridges." / *The Bridges at Toko-ri*, 1954). There is, for instance, no analogue in your WWII movies to the following conversation in *The Bridges at Toko-ri*. Mickey Rooney (a helicopter rescue pilot) and William Holden (a flyer) are trapped (shot down) behind the North Korean lines. Surrounded, they wait in a ditch for help to arrive. During a lull in the shooting, they begin to talk:

HOLDEN: *"I'm a lawyer from Denver, Colorado, Mike. I probably couldn't hit a thing [with this gun] . . ."*

ROONEY: *"Judas, how'd you ever get out here in a smelly ditch in Korea?"*

HOLDEN: *"That's just what I've been asking myself . . . the wrong war in the wrong place and that's the one you're stuck with . . . You fight simply because you are here."*

Within minutes, they are both killed by the advancing Korean soldiers.

Yet though the white world might seem tarnished, its heroes bitter, tired and ridden with doubts, its relationship to the non-white world had scarcely changed. If anything, the introduction of massive air power to Asian warfare had only further reduced the tangential humanity of Asian peoples. For in a movie like *Toko-ri* (as at Danang today), you never even needed to see the enemy, only charred bodies.

This attempt, particularly in westerns, to introduce new attitudes in the white world, increasingly muddied the divisions between stock characters, brought to the fore the hero-as-cynic, and called into question the "humanity" of the whites vis-à-vis each other. Such adjustments in a relatively constant cinematic structure represented an attempt to update a form which the world's reality put in increasing danger of unbelievability. By the early 1960's, the "adult western" had reached a new stage—that of elegy (see, for instance, *The Man Who Shot Liberty Valence,* 1962). Superficially, such movies seem to be in a state of sentimental mourning for the closing of the frontier and the end of a mythical white frontier life. However, westerns as a form were originally created amidst industrial America partially to mourn just such a loss. The elegiac western of the 60's was, in fact, mourning the passing of itself. Today, this form has come to what may be its terminal fruition in America, the "hip" western—*Butch Cassidy and the Sundance Kid* (1969), which is a parody not of the western, but of the elegiac western, since not even that can be taken totally straight any more.

However, even in this extension of the western, one thing has not changed—attitudes towards the third world. When, for instance, Butch and Sundance cannot make a go of it in a hemmed in West, they naturally move on, "invading" Bolivia. In Bolivia, of course, it's the same old local color scene again, with one variation: instead of the two of them killing off hundreds of Bolivians in that old wagon train scene, hundreds of unidentified Bolivians band together to kill them. It all boils down to the same thing.

Whatever *Butch Cassidy* may be the end of, I think we stand at the edge of a not totally new, but nonetheless yawning abyss—the "sympathetic" film. The first of what I expect will be an onslaught of these are appearing now. They have at least pretensions towards changing how we see relationships not only within the white world itself, but between the white and Indian worlds. And what is appearing in westerns today may be the transmuted

meat of Asian or African films within the next decade.

The recent *A Man Named Horse* (1970?) is a good example. It seems to have been a sincere and painstaking attempt to make a large-scale, commercially successful movie about the Sioux (before they were overrun by the whites), to show from an Indian point of view their way of life, their rituals (recreated from Catlin's paintings) and beliefs, their feelings and fears. Yet, at every turn, the film betrays the edges of older and more familiar frameworks.

It concerns an English Lord hunting in the American West early in the 19th century. Captured by a Sioux raiding party, he is brought back to their village (where the rest of the film takes place). There he becomes a slave (horse) for an Indian woman (Dame Judith Anderson). Already a white "hero" has been slipped into this movie about Indians, betraying an assumption that American audiences could not sustain interest in a film without whites. Given the way we look at these films, he immediately becomes the center of our attention; thus, in the end, you are forced to relate to the Sioux village through his eyes; and to relate to the Sioux as they relate to him (aiding him or mistreating him). Second, by following the travails of this Lord-turned-beast of burden as he assimilates to the tribe, the movie seems to prove that old adage, "put a white man among even the best of savages and you have a natural chief." (He kills enemy Indians, goes through the sun initiation ritual, marries the chief's daughter, teaches the tribe British infantry tactics, and, in the end, his wife and adopted mother being dead, he splits for the white world.)

His girlfriend has that Ali McGraw look which probably is supposed to allow the audience to "identify" better with the Indians, but looks about as fitting as it did among the Jews of New Jersey (*Goodby Columbus*). Even a stab at righting the wrongs westerns have done to language has a similarly dismal result. The movie's makers, reacting to the common use of pidgen-Hollywood by Indian characters in normal westerns, allow the Sioux in this movie to speak their own language. As all but two of the characters are Sioux, much of the movie is conducted in the Sioux language. If this were a French movie, there would naturally be subtitles; but as these are Sioux *au naturel,* and as there is already a conveniently English-speaking character, an alternate means is called upon. Another "prisoner" is created, an Indian who spent some time with the French and speaks broken English. At the behest of the English Lord, he translates what is necessary to his and our understanding. In this way, the Indians, while retaining the dignity of their own language, are perhaps slightly less able to express themselves comprehensibly in this picture than in a normal western. More important, just as if it were the normal wagon train scenario, it forces us to see everything through white eyes.

And as long as the eyes through which we see the world do not change, so long as the old frameworks for movies about the third world are not thrown away, "intentions" go for little indeed. It is hard even to think of examples of films where sympathetic intentions are matched by deeds. Certainly one would have to venture beyond the bounds of the U.S. to find them—perhaps *The Battle of Algiers* (which, in reverse, does for the French colonizers what we were never willing to do for the Indians). Its view begins at least to accord with the brutal history of the third world; to tell a little what it means, from the colonized point of view, to resist, to fight back, to rebel against your occupiers.

American moviemakers, however, are at heart still in love with an era when people could accept the six year old Shirley Temple telling Khoda Khan not to make war on the British because "the Queen wants to protect her people and make them rich." Their main substitution in later movies being to replace the Queen with (American) technology—machine guns to mow 'em down, and band-aids to patch 'em up. This mood is best captured by Gene Tierney in *The Left Hand of God* when Humphrey Bogart says, "China's becoming a nightmare, Anne . . . What are we really doing here? . . . We belong back in the States, marrying, raising a family." She replies, ". . . There's too much work to do here . . . the things we're doing here are what they need; whether medicine or grace. And we can give it to them . . ." Of course, the historical joke of this being uttered in China's Sinkiang province in 1947, a time when the unmentioned communist revolution is sweeping through the central provinces, passed the scriptwriters by. Yet, on the whole, just this distance between the film's "message" and Chinese reality about sums up the American approach to the third world. In the end, no matter where the moviemakers may think their sympathy lies, their films are usually no more than embroideries on a hagiography of "pacification."

Within such a context, there is no possibility for presenting resistance, rebellion, or revolution by the intruded upon in a way that could be even comprehensible, no less sympathetic. Quite the opposite, the moviemakers are usually hell-bent on glorifying those Asians (or other third worlders) who allied with the Western invaders, not those who at some point resisted either the invasion or its consequences. However, there is an insoluble contradiction here. The method for judging nonwhites in these films is based on how dependent or independent they are of the white leads and the white world. To the degree to which they are dependent, they are seen as closer to humanity. To the degree to which they are independent (i.e. resist) they are seen as less liable to humanization or outrightly inhuman and thus open to extermination. ("Mitchell, we must stamp this out immediately." / *Gunga Din*). In other words, there is an inherent bias in these movies towards the glorification of those "natives" who have allied with us. Yet what makes the white hero so appealing is the audience's feeling that no matter how low he sinks, he retains some sense of human dignity. There is always that feeling (as Bogart and countless cowboy stars brought out so well) that despite appearances, *he is his own man.* Yet no movie Asians linked to the West can ever really be that. Though they can bask in the light of humanity, they can never be much more than imitation humans. In only one non-white role is this possibility open—that is the role of villain (he who refuses white help and actively opposes him). Only the villain, already placed outside the pale (sic) of humanity, can be his own man.

The result is a knotty problem. If those close to the whites are invariably dependent, they cannot but be viewed in some way with contempt, no matter how the movie makers go about trying to glorify them. On the other hand, if those most contemptible non-humans, the villains, are the only Asians capable of "independence" in these films, they are also the only Asians who are the cinematic equivalents of the white leads. Thus, we cannot help but have a sneaking respect for those who oppose us and a sneaking contempt for those who side with us. (How similar this is to the attitudes of many American soldiers in Vietnam towards ARVN and towards the NLF forces.) No doubt this is at least partly responsible for the extremes American moviemakers have gone to in glorifying one and despoiling the other. . . .

American movies about the third world should not be given more credit than is their due. Despite the impression you might get in the theatre, American moviemakers did not invent the world, nor even the version of world history they present in their films. However, they must be given full credit for developing a highly successful and satisfying cinematic form to encapsulate an existing ideological message. With this form, they have been able to relegate the great horrors of Western expansion into the rest of the world, and present-day American hegemony over great hunks of it, to another universe of pleasure and enjoyment.

They have successfully tied extermination of non-white peoples to laughable relief, and white racial superiority to the natural order of things. They have destroyed any possibility for explaining the various ways in which non-white (not to speak of white) people could resist invasion, colonization, exploitation, and even mass slaughter.

Cowboy (-third world) films are, in the end, a vast visual pacification program, ostensibly describing the rest of the world, but in fact aimed at the millions of people who for several generations have made up the American viewing audience. It's hardly a wonder that Vietnam did not sear the American consciousness. Why should it have? For years, Americans had been watching the whole scene on their screens: REV DEV, WHAM, endless My Lai's, body counts, killing of wounded enemy soldiers, aerial obliteration, etc. We had grown used to seeing it, and thrilling with pleasure while reaching for another handful of popcorn.

Such a "pacification" program is based on the inundation principle. It is not a matter of quality (probably there have been no good films on Asia since the 1930's), but quantity. So many cowboy-third world movies have rolled factory-style off the production line that the most minute change of plot is hailed as a great innovation. In the end, all the visual "choices" available to a viewer just emphasize the way in which America is strikingly a one-channel country. In fact, it might not be too far wrong to say that while pacification may have failed in Vietnam, its pilot project here in America has generally succeeded; that we are a pacified population, living unknowingly in an occupied country.

41

Black Americans in Sports: Unequal Opportunity for Equal Ability

NORMAN R. YETMAN
D. STANLEY EITZEN

Since 1947, when Jackie Robinson broke the color line in the "national game" of baseball, the idea that organized sport has escaped the pervasive effects of racism has become one of the most cherished myths in American life. This myth is confirmed for most Americans by the prominence of Blacks in the contemporary sports world. In each of the major professional sports, the percentages of Black competitors far exceed their proportion (11 percent) of the total United States population. In 1974, better than 60 percent of all professional basketball players were Black, while they comprised more than one-third of all professional football and baseball players. Their disproportionate numbers and the prominence of a Henry Aaron, a Kareem Abdul-Jabbar, or an O. J.

Norman R. Yetman is Associate Professor of American Studies and Sociology and Chairman of the American Studies Department at The University of Kansas.

D. Stanley Eitzen is Professor of Sociology at Colorado State University.

This is a revised version of an article first published in *Civil Rights Digest* 5 (August, 1972). Reprinted by permission of the authors. Copyright © 1972 Norman R. Yetman and D. Stanley Eitzen.

Research for this article was supported by a grant from the Graduate Research Fund of The University of Kansas.

Simpson have led many Americans—Black and White—to infer that collegiate and professional athletics have provided an avenue of mobility for Blacks unavailable elsewhere in American society and thus have "done something" for Black Americans.

However, an increasing number of social scientists, journalists, and Black athletes have challenged this myth, charging that Black athletes are exploited and that discrimination pervades the entire sports establishment. According to these critics, the existence of racism in collegiate and professional sports is especially insidious because the promoters of, and commentators on, athletics have made sports sacred by projecting an image of it as the single institution in America relatively immune from racism. Several aspects of the athletic world have been alleged to be racially biased—recruitment policies, the assignment of playing positions, performance expectations, and rewards and authority.

STACKING

One of the best documented forms of discrimination in both the college and the professional ranks is popularly known as *stacking*. The term refers to situations in which minority-group members are relegated to specific team roles and excluded from competing for others. The consequence is often that intra-team competition for starting roles is between members of the same race (e.g., those competing as running backs are Black, while those competing as quarterbacks are White). For example, Rosenblatt (1967) noted that while there are twice as many pitchers on a baseball team as there are outfielders, in 1965 there were three times as many Black outfielders as pitchers.

Examination of the stacking phenomenon was first undertaken by Loy and McElvogue (1970), who argued that racial segregation in sports is a function of centrality —that is, spatial location—in a team sports unit. To explain positional racial segregation in sports, they combined organizational principles advanced by Hubert M. Blalock and Oscar Grusky. Blalock has argued that:

1. The lower the degree of purely social interaction on the job . . ., the lower the degree of [racial] discrimination.
2. To the extent that performance level is relatively independent of skill in interpersonal relations, the lower the degree of [racial] discrimination. [Blalock, 1962: 246]

Grusky's notions about the formal structure of organizations are similar:

> All else being equal, the more central one's spatial location: (1) the greater the likelihood dependent or coordinative tasks will be performed and (2) the greater the rate of interaction with the occupants of other positions. Also, the performance of dependent tasks is positively related to frequency of interaction. [Grusky, 1963: 346]

Combining these propositions, Loy and McElvogue hypothesized that ". . . racial segregation in professional team sports is positively related to centrality." Their analysis of football (where the central positions are quarterback, center, offensive guard, and linebacker) and baseball (where the central positions are the infield, catcher, and pitcher) demonstrated that the central positions were indeed overwhelmingly manned by Whites, while the peripheral (noncentral) positions were overrepresented by Blacks. In baseball, 83 percent of the persons listed as infielders were White, while 50 percent of the outfielders were White. The proportion of Whites was greatest (27 of 28, or 96 percent) in the position of catcher, the most central position in baseball. In football, the positions most central on the offensive unit (center, guards, and quarterback) were 96 percent White in 1968 (Loy and McElvogue, 1970). Our own analysis of the 1971 rosters of the National Football League (NFL) demonstrated that this strong relationship between role centrality and race has persisted. We found, moreover, when comparing players who had been in the league the same length of time, that the greater the

number of years in the league, the higher the proportion of White players in central positions. Among those players in the league one to three years, 82 percent were White; four to six years, 90 percent White; seven to nine years, 96 percent White; and ten or more years, 97 percent White. (This may be a consequence of the league's having a smaller proportion of Black players in the past. A better analysis would be to follow a cohort through their playing careers.) This evidence demonstrates clearly that Blacks are the victims of discrimination.

The effects of discrimination are more devastating than just limitation to noncentral positions. In seventeen of the twenty-six pro football teams surveyed, approximately three-fourths of all 1971 advertising slots (radio, television, and newspapers) were allotted to players in central positions. Second, noncentral positions in football depend primarily on speed and quickness, which means in effect that playing careers are shortened for persons in those positions. For example, only 5.8 percent of the players listed in the *Football Register* in the three predominantly Black positions —defensive back, running back, and wide receiver (62 percent of all Black players)—were in the pros for ten or more years, while 10.4 percent of players listed in the three predominantly White positions—quarterback, center, and offensive guard—remained that long. The shortened careers for noncentral players have two additional deleterious consequences—less lifetime earnings and limited benefits from the players' pension fund, which provides support on the basis of longevity.

The Loy and McElvogue interpretation of these data rested primarily upon a position's spatial location in a team unit. However, Edwards has argued that the actual spatial location of a playing position is an incidental factor in the explanation of stacking. According to Edwards, the crucial variable involved in positional segregation is the degree of outcome control or leadership responsibilities found in each position. For example, quarterbacks have greater team authority and ability to affect the outcome of the game than do individuals who occupy noncentral positions (Edwards, 1973: 209).

Thus, the key is not the interaction potential of the playing position but the leadership and degree of responsibility for the game's outcome built into the position that account for the paucity of Blacks at central positions. This is consonant with the stereotype hypothesis advanced by Brower (specifically for football but one that applies to other sports as well):

The combined function of centrality in terms of responsibility and interaction provides a frame for exclusion of blacks and constitutes a definition of the situation for coaches and management. People in the world of professional football believe that various football positions require specific types of physically- and intellectually-endowed athletes. When these beliefs are combined with the stereotypes of blacks and whites, blacks are excluded from certain positions. Normal organizational processes when interlaced with racist conceptions of the world spell out an important consequence, namely, the racial basis of the division of labor in professional football. [Brower, 1972: 27]

In this view, then, it is the racial stereotypes of Blacks' abilities that lead to the view that they are more ideally suited for those positions labelled "noncentral." For example, Brower compared the requirements for the central and noncentral positions in football and found that the former require leadership, thinking ability, highly refined techniques, stability under pressure, and responsibility for the outcome of the games. Noncentral positions, on the other hand, require athletes with speed, quickness, aggressiveness, "good hands," and "instinct" (Brower, 1972:3-27).

Although social scientists have examined the stacking phenomenon in football and baseball, they have neglected basketball. They have tended to assume that it does not occur because, as Edwards has put it:

. . . in basketball there is no positional centrality as is the case in football and baseball because there are no fixed zones of role responsibility attached to specific positions. . . . Nevertheless, one does find an evidence of discrimination against black athletes on integrated

basketball teams. Rather than stacking black athletes in positions involving relatively less control, *since this is a logistical impossibility,* [italics added] the number of black athletes directly involved in the action at any one time is simply limited. [Edwards, 1973: 213]

However, Eitzen and Tessendorf (1974) reasoned that positions in basketball do vary in responsibility, in leadership, in the mental qualities of good judgment, decision-making, and recognition of opponents' tactics, and in outcome control. To confirm this judgment, they undertook a content analysis of instructional books by prominent American basketball coaches to determine whether there were specific responsibilities or qualities attributed to the three playing positions—guard, forward, and center—in basketball. They discovered surprising unanimity among coaches on the attributes and responsibilities of the different positions. The guard was viewed as the team quarterback, its "floor general," and the most desired attributes for this position were the mental qualities of judgment, leadership, and dependability. The center was pictured as having the greatest amount of outcome control because that position is nearest the basket and because the offense revolves around it; the center was literally the pivot of the team's offense. Unlike the traits for other positions, the desired traits mentioned for forwards stressed physical attributes—speed, quickness, physical strength, and rebounding—even to the point of labeling the forward the "animal."

Given this widespread agreement that there are varied zones of responsibility and different qualities expected of guards, forwards, and centers, Eitzen and Tessendorf hypothesized that Blacks would be overrepresented—stacked—at the forward position, where the essential traits required are physical rather than mental, and underrepresented at the guard and center positions, the most crucial positions for leadership and outcome control. Using data from a sample of 274 NCAA basketball teams from the 1970–71 season, they found that Blacks were, in fact, substantially overrepresented as forwards and underrepresented at the guard and center positions.

Whereas 32 percent of their total sample of players were Black, 41 percent of forwards were Black. But only 26 percent of guards and 25 percent of centers were. Eitzen and Tessendorf found that this pattern held regardless of whether the players were starters or second-stringers or whether they played for college or university division teams. Given these findings, it is apparent that racial stacking occurs in each of the major sports.

The paucity of Blacks in central team roles reflects the impact of wider societal stereotypes. Since it is widely assumed that Blacks are intellectually inferior to Whites and incapable of leadership and that tension will be generated by placing them in leadership positions, Blacks in sports are relegated to positions where the requisite skills are speed, strength, and quick reactions, not thinking or leadership ability. However, McPherson has challenged the notion of *centrality*, asserting that the unequal racial distribution of players occurs through a process of self-segregation; Black male youths select those positions in which Black sports heroes, who are among their leading role models, are most prominent (McPherson, 1971).

Since McPherson produced no empirical support for his explanation, Eitzen and Sanford (1973) sought to determine whether Black athletes changed positions from central to noncentral more frequently than Whites as they moved from high school to college to professional competition. Their data from a sample of 387 professional football players indicated that there had been a statistically significant shift by Blacks from central positions to noncentral ones. That Blacks in high school and college occupied positions that are occupied primarily by Whites in professional football casts doubt on McPherson's model. Athletic role models or heroes will most likely have greater attraction for younger individuals in high school and college than for older athletes in professional sports, but professional players were found distributed at all positions during their high school playing days. The socialization model also assumes a high degree of irrationality on the part of the player—it assumes that as he becomes older and enters more keenly competitive playing conditions, he will be more likely to seek a position because of his indentification with a Black star rather than because of a rational assessment maximizing his ultimate athletic success.

It is conceivable, however, that socialization variables do contribute to the racial stacking patterns in baseball and football as noted above, but in a negative sense. That is to say, given discrimination in the allocation of playing positions (or at least the belief in its existence), young Black males will consciously avoid those positions for which opportunities are (or are believed to be) low (e.g., pitcher, quarterback) and will select instead those positions where they are most likely to succeed (e.g., the outfield, running and defensive backs). Gene Washington, all-pro wide receiver of the San Francisco Forty-Niners, was a college quarterback at Stanford through his sophomore year, then switched to flanker. Washington requested the change himself. "It was strictly a matter of economics. I knew a Black quarterback would have little chance in pro ball unless he was absolutely superb . . ." (Quoted in Olsen, 1968a:29).

REWARDS AND AUTHORITY

Discrimination in professional sports is explicit in the discrepancy between the salaries of White and Black players. At first glance such a charge appears to be unwarranted. Black players rank among the highest paid in professional baseball (seven of ten superstars being paid more than $100,000 in 1970 were Black), and the mean salaries of Black outfielders, infielders, and pitchers exceed those of Whites. However, Scully (1974) reanalyzed data employed by Pascal and Rapping (1970) in an earlier study and found substantial salary discrimination against Blacks when performance levels were held constant. Blacks earn less than Whites for equivalent performance.

An obvious case of monetary discrimination becomes apparent if one considers the total incomes of athletes (salary, endorsements, and off-season earnings). Pascal and Rapping, for instance, citing the Equal Opportunity Commission Report of 1968, related that Black athletes appeared in only 5 percent of the 351 commercials associated with New York sports events in the fall of 1966 (Pascal and Rapping, 1970:40). Our own analysis of the advertising and media program slots featuring starting members of one professional football team in 1971 revealed that eight of eleven Whites had such opportunities while only two of thirteen Blacks did. Neither do Blacks have the same opportunities as Whites when their playing careers are finished. This is reflected in radio and television sportscasting, where no Black person has had any job other than providing the "color."

Officiating is another area that is disproportionately White. Baseball has had only two Black major league umpires in its history. Professional basketball has only recently broken the color line in officiating. The same is true of football, which provides another case of racial stacking. Blacks are typically found in the head linesman role—seldom in the role of head referee.

Although the percentage of Black players in each of the three most prominent American professional sports (baseball, football, and basketball) greatly exceeds their percentage of the total population, there is ample evidence that few opportunities are available to them in managerial and entrepreneurial roles. For example, data from 1974 sources (*The Baseball Register, Football Register*, and *National Basketball Association Guide*) show that of the twenty-four major league baseball managers and twenty-six National Football League head coaches, none was Black. Four of the seventeen head coaches (24 percent) in the National Basketball Association (NBA) were Black.

Assistant coaches and coaches or managers of minor league professional teams also are conspicuously white. In 1973, there were but two Black managers among more than 100 minor league professional baseball teams. During the same year, in the National Football League, which had a Black player composition of 36 percent, there were only twelve Blacks, or 6.7 percent, among the 180 assistant coaches. Finally, despite the disproportionate representation of Blacks in major league baseball, only three coaches (less than 3 percent) were Black. Moreover, Black coaches are relegated to the less responsible coaching jobs. Baseball superstar Frank Robinson, who was appointed the first Black major league field general after the conclusion of the regular 1974 season, has pointed out that Blacks are excluded from the most important roles.* "You hardly see any Black third-base or pitching coaches. And those are the most important coaching jobs. The only place you see Blacks coaching is at first base, where most anybody can do the job" (quoted in Axthelm, 1974:57).

The virtual dearth of Black coaches in professional sports is paralleled at the college and high school levels. Although many predominantly white colleges and universities have, in response to pressures from angry Black athletes, recently made frantic efforts to hire Black coaches, they have been hired almost exclusively as assistant coaches, and seldom has a coaching staff included more than one Black. As of this writing (1974), not a single major college has a Black head football coach, and only a handful of major colleges (e.g., Arizona, Georgetown, Harvard, Illinois State, and Washington State) have head basketball or track coaches who are Black. This same pattern has characterized American high schools. Blacks, historically, have found coaching jobs only in predominantly Black high schools. And, although the precise figures are unavailable, it would appear that the movement toward integration of schools dur-

---

* Robinson's appointment, coming more than twenty-seven years after the entrance of another Robinson—Jackie—into major league baseball, was the exception that proves the rule. So historic was the occasion that it drew news headlines throughout the nation and a congratulatory telegram from President Ford.

ing the 1960s has had the effect of eliminating Blacks from coaching positions, as it has eliminated Black principals and Black teachers in general. So anomalous is a Black head coach at a predominantly White high school in the South that when, in 1970, this barrier was broken, it was heralded by feature stories in the *New York Times* and *Sports Illustrated.** And the situation appears to be little different outside the South, where head coaches are almost exclusively White.

Blacks are also excluded from executive positions in organizations that govern both amateur and professional sports. In 1974, not a single major NCAA college had a Black athletic director. On the professional level, there was no Black representation in the principal ownership of a major league franchise. No Black held a high executive capacity in any of baseball's twenty-four teams, although there was one Black assistant to Baseball Commissioner Bowie Kuhn. Nor have there been any Black general managers in pro football. Professional basketball's management structure is most progressive in this regard, although it must be recalled that ownership remains white. Two of seventeen NBA clubs had Black general managers in 1973. However, it was a noteworthy event when, in 1970, former NBA star Wayne Embry was named general manager of the NBA Milwaukee Bucks, thereby becoming the first Black to occupy such a position in professional sports.

Thus the distribution of Blacks in the sports world is not unlike that in the larger society, where Blacks are admitted to lower-level occupations but virtually excluded from positions of authority, leadership, and power. Although there have been significant advances for Black athletes in the past quarter of a century, there has been no comparable access of Blacks to decision-making positions. With the exception of professional basketball, the corporate and decision-making structure of professional sports is virtually as White as it was

* See also Pat Jordan, *Black Coach* (New York: Dodd, Mead, 1971).

in 1946, before Jackie Robinson entered major league baseball.

ABILITY AND OPPORTUNITY

Another form of discrimination in sport is unequal opportunity for equal ability This means that entrance requirements to the major leagues are more rigorous for Blacks—therefore, Black players must be better than White players to succeed in the sports world. Rosenblatt was one of the first to demonstrate this mode of discrimination. He found that in the period from 1953 to 1957 the mean batting average for Blacks in the major leagues was 20.6 points above the average for Whites. In the 1958-to-1961 time period the difference was 20.1 points, while from 1962 to 1965 it was 21.2 points. He concluded that:

> . . . discriminatory hiring practices are still in effect in the major leagues. The superior Negro is not subject to discrimination because he is more likely to help win games than fair to poor players. Discrimination is aimed, whether by design or not, against the substar Negro ball player. The findings clearly indicate that the undistinguished Negro player is less likely to play regularly in the major leagues than the equally undistinguished white player. [Rosenblatt, 1967: 53]

Since Rosenblatt's analysis was through 1965, we extended it to include the years 1966–1970. The main difference between Blacks and Whites persisted; for that five-year period Blacks batted an average of 20.8 points higher than Whites.

The existence of racial entry barriers in major league baseball was further supported by Pascal and Rapping, who extended Rosenblatt's research by including additional years and by examining the performance of the races in each separate position, including pitchers. They found, for instance, that the nineteen Black pitchers in 1967 who appeared in at least ten games won a mean number of 10.2 games, while White pitchers won an average of 7.5. This, coupled with their findings that Blacks were superior to Whites in all other playing positions, led them to conclude that: ". . . on the average a Black player must be better than a White player if he is to have an equal chance of transiting from the minor leagues to the major" (Pascal and Rapping, 1970:36). Moreover, Scully's elaborate analysis of baseball performance data has led him to conclude that ". . . not only do Blacks have to outperform whites to get into baseball, but they must consistently outperform them over their playing careers in order to stay in baseball" (Scully, 1974:263).

Similarly, Brower (1973) found that the situation in professional football paralleled that in baseball and basketball. First, the most dramatic increases in the numbers of Black professional football players occurred during the middle sixties and early seventies. Table 1 shows the increasing percentages of Blacks in professional football. (Compare these data with the corresponding basketball data in Tables 2 and 3.)

Moreover, Brower (1973) found that, as in baseball and basketball, "Black . . . players must be superior in athletic performance to their White counterparts if they are to be accepted into professional football." His data revealed statistically significant differences in the percentages of Black and White starters and nonstarters. Blacks were found disproportionately as starters, while secondstring status was more readily accorded to Whites. Whereas 63 percent of Black players were starters in 1970, 51 percent of White

players were. Conversely, 49 percent of White players, but only 37 percent of Black players, were not starters in that year. These findings led Brower to conclude that "mediocrity is a White luxury" (Brower, 1973:3).

Whether Black athletes are disproportionately overrepresented in the "star" category and underrepresented in the average, or journeyman, athlete category on collegiate and professional basketball teams was the subject of our research. We also provided a historical dimension by investigating whether the racial distribution of basketball teams had changed over time. Our investigation showed that the Black predominance in basketball is a relatively recent phenomenon and that basketball, like football and baseball, was largely segregated until the late 1950s and early 1960s. There are records of Black basketball players on teams from predominantly White colleges as far back as 1908, but such instances were rare during the first half of the century. In professional sports, the National Basketball Association remained an all-White institution until 1950, three years after Jackie Robinson had broken the color line in modern major league baseball and four years after Blacks re-entered major league football after having been totally excluded since the early 1930s.

Tables 2 and 3 document the striking changes in racial composition of basketball since 1954. From the immediate post–World War II situation (1948), when less than 10 percent of collegiate squads were integrated, to 1970, when nearly 80 percent contained members of both races, there was a substantial and impressive move toward integration. Not only were more schools recruiting Blacks, but the number of Black players being recruited at each school increased dramatically. The most substantial increase among collegiate teams was during the period between 1966 and 1970, which can be partly attributed to the breakdown of previously segregated teams throughout the South.

The changes in the professional game are even more marked, for Blacks have clearly come to dominate the game—both numerically

TABLE 1. *Percentages of Blacks per Year in Professional Football*

Year	Percentage of Black players
1950	0
1954	5
1958	9
1962	16
1966	26
1970	34

TABLE 2.   *Racial Composition of NCAA Basketball Teams, 1948–1970*

Year	Number of NCAA teams pictured in Converse Yearbook	Number of Black players	% of teams with Blacks	Black players as % of total	Avg. no. of Blacks on integrated squads
1948	182	25	9.8 (18)	1.4	1.4
1954	184	83	28.3 (52)	4.5	1.6
1958	201	182	44.3 (89)	9.1	2.0
1962	239	241	45.2(108)	10.1	2.2
1966	235	381	58.3(137)	16.2	2.8
1970	253	685	79.8(202)	27.1	3.4

TABLE 3.   *Racial Composition of Professional Basketball Teams, 1954–1970*

Year	Number of teams	Number of Black players	% of teams with Blacks	Black players as % of total	Avg. no. of Blacks/per total team
NBA 1954	9	4	44 (4)	4.6	.4
1958	8	11	87 (7)	11.8	1.3
1962	9	34	100 (9)	30.4	3.8
1966	9	57	100 (9)	50.9	6.3
1970	14	94	100(14)	54.3	6.7
ABA 1970	11	80	100(11)	57.3	7.3

and, as we shall note more fully below, statistically. Although Blacks comprise approximately one-tenth (11 percent) of the total U.S. population, they account for more than one-fourth (27 percent) of the nation's collegiate basketball players and more than three-fifths of the professional players. The percentage composition of Black players on college basketball teams is even more striking when, according to the *Chronicle of Higher Education* (Jacobson, 1971:1), Blacks comprised only 6.9 percent of undergraduate students in 1970 and nearly half (44 percent) attended predominantly Black institutions. Therefore, as contrasted to nearly two decades ago, organized basketball—on both the college and professional levels—has eliminated many of the barriers that once excluded Blacks from participation. The changes in professional baseball and football, while not so dramatic, have also occurred primarily since the middle sixties.

Having determined that Black players are disproportionately overrepresented on collegiate and professional basketball teams relative to their distribution within the general population, we wanted to examine more systematically the roles Blacks played on these teams. Specifically, we wanted to determine whether they have been found disproportionately in the first five ranks (starters) and whether their average position ranking on a team has been higher than that of Whites. We also wished to utilize historical data to determine whether the positional patterns had changed significantly in the years during which the percentage of Black players had increased so dramatically.

We operationally defined the top players according to their offensive productivity as measured by their scoring average. The five players with the highest scoring averages will be referred to hereafter as the top five, first string, top players, or starters. We believe that this method represents the best single measure that could be obtained, and that there is no appreciable bias involved in its use.

We found that the same situation of unequal opportunity for equal ability that Rosenblatt, Scully, and Pascal and Rapping found in professional baseball was characteristic of college and, to a lesser extent, professional basketball. Using data from 1958, 1962, 1966, and 1970 professional and collegiate records, we found that during each year there was a progressive decline in the percentage of Blacks occupying a position as scoring average declined. This was most marked in the distribution of Black players who were leading scorers and poorest point producers. While Black players comprised no more than 29 percent of all the members of integrated teams during the years 1958–1970, in each of these years nearly half—and in some years, more than half—of the leading scorers were Black. Conversely, Blacks were disproportionately underrepresented in the lowest scoring position. Moreover, our data revealed that between 1958 and 1970 no less than two-thirds—and in some years as high as three-fourths—of all Black players were starters. These data present solid evidence that since 1958, Blacks have been found disproportionately in starting roles on college basketball teams and have been disproportionately underrepresented on second teams.

In professional basketball, where they have come to dominate the game, Blacks were slightly overrepresented in starting roles until 1970, when equal numbers of Blacks were starters and non-starters. Following Rosenblatt's approach in comparing White and Black batting averages, we compared the scoring averages of Black and White players for the four years (1957–58, 1961–62, 1965–66, 1969–70) of our analysis. Although scoring averages were identical for both races in 1957–58, Blacks outscored Whites in the remaining years by an average 5.2, 3.3, and 2.9 points, respectively. Although there remains a not insubstantial gap between the scoring averages of Whites and Blacks, the magnitude of these differences has declined as the percentage of Black players in the league has increased. This is a contrast to the situation in professional baseball, where the mean batting average for Blacks has remained 20 points greater than the average for Whites for nearly two decades.

CONCLUSIONS

Although the patterns are not so strong among pro as among college teams, these data have consistently shown that Black players in organized collegiate and professional basketball, like those in football and baseball, have been found disproportionately in starting roles. Several possible explanations for this phenomenon have been advanced. First, it has been suggested that Blacks are naturally better athletes and their predominance in starting roles can be attributed to their innate athletic superiority. As sociologists, we are inclined to reject interpretations of Black athletic superiority as genetically or physiologically based, although our stance must be an agnostic one, since there is too little evidence on the question. What is important to note here, however, is that although a genetic interpretation is a logical (if not entirely convincing) explanation of the disproportionate percentage of Blacks found on college and pro teams, it cannot explain their prevalence in *starting* roles. Even if Blacks possessed genetically based athletic superiority, they should not be systematically overrepresented in starting positions, but should still be randomly distributed throughout the entire team. As Jim Bouton (former major league baseball player who has challenged the racial composition of major league baseball teams) has written, "If 19 of the top 30 hitters are Black, then almost two-thirds of all hitters should be Black. Obviously it is not that way." (Bouton, 1970:302) An interpretation based on the natural superiority of Blacks must, therefore, be rejected.

A second possible explanation is discrimination in recruiting practices. Harry Edwards has charged that college coaches, in their recruitment of blacks, seek to obtain only those players who are almost certain to be starters.

A black athlete generally fares well in athletic competition relative to other incoming athletes at a White-dominated college. The cards are somewhat stacked for him, however, because few Black high school athletes get what are typically classified as second- and third-string athletic grants-in-aid. One simply does not find Black athletes on "full-rides" at predominantly White schools riding the bench or playing second-or-third team positions. Second-and-third third team athletic grants-in-aid are generally reserved for White athletes. [Edwards, 1969: 9–10]

This appears to be a plausible explanation of the data for both college and professional players. On the one hand, the coach may be consciously or unconsciously prejudiced and may find the idea of having Black team members repugnant, but nonetheless he may recruit Black "star" players because their presence will enhance his team's performance. In this situation the Black player who is capable, but not outstanding, is liable to be overlooked, while his White counterpart is not. In addition, coaches are sensitive to criticism of their coaching policies by powerful alumni, booster organizations, and fans. In a situation where these groups are perceived by a White coach as bigoted, even if he himself is not, it is likely that his recruitment of Black players will be calculated to minimize criticism of his coaching policies. Therefore, Black team members are more likely to be outstanding athletes, for the performance of average ballplayers would be inadequate to counterbalance the criticism their presence would create. For many years a quota system, limiting the number of Black starters, operated informally in both college and professional basketball.

The selective recruitment of only those Blacks certain to be starters may be undertaken consciously or unconsciously, but it would appear seldom to be acknowledged by a coach. However, one of the nation's most successful college coaches, one who has been acclaimed as a recruiter adept at communicating with young Black ballplayers, has advanced a sophisticated rationale for the reason three of the four Blacks on his 1970–71 squad were starters. "The ghetto environment of the Black demands that he be a star, if he is to participate at all," he explained. "He could never justify an understudy's role to himself or to the brothers he left behind in the playground. Thus there is no point recruiting Blacks who will not start" (quoted in Lipsyte, 1971: 37). Whether this impressionistic theory of Black sport role socialization is valid or merely a justification for selective recruitment must be more fully assessed.

Another explanation that has been advanced to explain the disproportionate number of Black starters is that of structural inequalities—especially educational and economic—that are found in the larger society and have disproportionate effects on Black, as contrasted to White, athletes. Thus, athletic ability, talent, and associated skills are not the only criteria by which a potential college athlete is selected. Academic ability is also a crucial factor to be weighed in the decision of whether or not to award an athletic scholarship. One of the major problems in the recruitment of an athlete to compete for a college or university is that he may be academically unqualified for the academic demands that a college athlete must face. Since the quality of elementary and secondary education received by Blacks has been demonstrated to be inferior (Coleman, 1966), a greater percentage of potential Black athletes would tend to be marginal students.

Moreover, most universities reflect a White middle-class cultural bias that represents a substantial hindrance to students from backgrounds other than White and middle class. Thus, while a coach may offer a scholarship to an outstanding player who is a marginal student or to a marginal player who is an outstanding student, he will most likely hesitate to offer a scholarship to a marginal player who is also a marginal student. These factors are important ones for the college coach to weigh, and, although racial factors may not enter into these calculations directly, the *effects* of these kinds of policies will be felt disproportionately by Blacks.

This appears to be a plausible interpretation of the data and, indeed, there are undoubtedly situations in which these kinds of considerations have operated. Fortunately, we possessed some data that enabled us to test how significant a factor this may have been in explaining our earlier findings. As part of our original request of sports information directors, we requested information on the grade-point averages (GPA's) of the players. We received information on all members of 110 integrated teams. If the argument that academic potential is a significant variable influencing the relative recruitment of marginal Black players is valid, then one would conclude that the GPA's of second-string Black players would be higher than those of first-string Blacks, for whom the academic considerations would be a less crucial factor.

We found that the average GPA's of the 106 starting Blacks in our sample was 2.26 (on a 4-point scale), whereas the average of 98 second-string players was 2.33. Although this slight difference is in the predicted direction, it did not even approach statistical significance. Thus, although these considerations may have been operative in specific cases, they must be dismissed as factors in substantially influencing the distribution of the data.

The limited access of Blacks to institutions of higher learning may also be instrumental in contributing to the patterns described above in another way. Each competing educational institution has only a limited number of athletic scholarships to dispense each year and these are awarded to outstanding players. However, often a squad will have players from the student body—*walk-ons*—who have not been recruited by the coach but who try out for the squad and make it. Because Blacks comprise an extremely small proportion of the student bodies at predominantly White institutions, most such nonscholarship athletes will be White. Thus, a team may be composed of several outstanding Black and White players on scholarship and several mediocre players who are White.

A final explanation of the disproportionate Black prowess in both college and professional basketball resides in the structural limitations to which Black children and adults are subjected. Since opportunities for vertical mobility by Blacks in American society are circumscribed, athletics may become perceived as one of the few means by which a Black can succeed in a highly competitive American society; a male Black child's and adolescent's primary role models are much more likely than a White's to be athletic heroes. And the determination and motivation devoted to the pursuit of an athletic career may therefore be more intense than for the White adolescent whose career options are greater. Jack Olsen, in *The Black Athlete,* quotes a prominent Black coach:

> People keep reminding me that there is a difference in physical ability between the races, but I think there isn't. The Negro boy practices longer and harder. The Negro has the keener desire to excel in sports because it is more mandatory for his future opportunities than it is for a White boy. There are nine thousand different jobs available to a person if he is white. [Olsen, 1968b:14]

On the other hand, James Green has questioned whether the lure of a professional career completely explains the strong emphasis on athletics among Blacks. He argues that the explanation that a Black manifests a "keener desire to excel . . . because it is mandatory for his future . . ." simply reflects the commentator's own future orientation. An alternative explanation of strong Black motivation, according to Green, is the positive emphasis in Black subculture that is placed on the importance of physical (and verbal) skill and dexterity. Athletic prowess in men is highly valued by both women and men. The athletically capable male is in the comparable position of the hustler or the blues singer; he is something of a folk hero. He achieves a level of status and recognition among his peers whether he is a publicly applauded sports hero or not (Green:1971).

Whatever the factors operating, the conclusion that Black athletes encounter discrimination in collegiate and professional basketball seems inescapable. Despite the myth to the contrary, equality of opportunity for those of equal skills is not operating. This conclusion has implications that extend beyond the sports world. If discrimination occurs in so public an arena, one so generally acknowledged to be discrimination free, and one where a premium is placed on individual achievement rather than upon ascription, how much more subtly pervasive must discrimination be in other areas of American life, where personal interaction is crucial and where the actions of power wielders are not subjected to public scrutiny.

REFERENCES

Axthelm, Pete. 1974. "Black Out." *Newsweek*, July 15, 1974, p. 57.

Blalock, H. M., Jr. 1962. "Occupational discrimination: Some theoretical propositions." *Social Problems* 9: 240–247.

Bouton, Jim. 1970. *Ball Four*. New York: World Publishing Company.

Brower, Jonathan J. 1972. "The racial basis of the division of labor among players in the National Football League as a function of stereotypes." Paper presented at the Pacific Sociological Meetings, Portland.

Brower, Jonathan J. 1973. "The quota system: The white gatekeeper's regulation of professional football's black community." Paper presented at the Annual Meetings of the American Sociological Association, New York.

Coleman, James S. 1966. *Equality of Educational Opportunity*. Washington, D.C.: U.S. Government Printing Office.

Edwards, Harry. 1969. *The Revolt of the Black Athlete*. New York: The Free Press.

Edwards, Harry. 1973. *Sociology of Sport*. Homewood, Illinois: The Dorsey Press.

Eitzen, D. Stanley and David C. Sanford. 1973. "The segregation of blacks by playing position in football: Accident or design?" Unpublished paper: The University of Kansas.

Eitzen, D. Stanley, and Irl Tessendorf. 1974. "Racial segregation by position in sports: The special case of basketball." Unpublished paper: The University of Kansas.

Green, James. 1971. Personal communication.

Grusky, Oscar. 1963. "The effects of formal structure on managerial recruitment: A study of baseball organization." *Sociometry* 26 (September): 345–353.

Jacobson, Robert L. 1971. "Black enrollment rising sharply, U.S. data show." *Chronicle of Higher Education*, October 4.

Lipsyte, Robert. 1971. "Al McGuire was in town last week." *New York Times*, March 1: 37.

Loy, John W. and Joseph F. McElvogue. 1970. "Racial segregation in American sport." *International Review of Sport Sociology* 5: 5–24.

McPherson, Barry D. 1971. "Minority group socialization: An alternative explanation for the segregation by playing position hypothesis." Paper presented at the Third International Symposium on the Sociology of Sport, Waterloo, Ontario.

Olsen, Jack. 1968a. "The black athlete—a shameful story." *Sports Illustrated* (July 22): 28–41.

Olsen, Jack. 1968b. *The Black Athlete*. New York: Time-Life Books.

Pascal, Anthony H. and Leonard A. Rapping. 1970. *Racial Discrimination in Organized Baseball*. Santa Monica, Calif.: The Rand Corporation.

Rosenblatt, Aaron. 1967. "Negroes in baseball: The failure of success." *Transaction* 4 (September): 51–53.

Scully, Gerald W. 1974. "Discrimination: The case of baseball." In Roger G. Noll, ed., *Government and the Sports Business*. Washington, D.C.: The Brookings Institution.

part six

The Black Revolution
and the Resurgence
of Ethnicity

Our objectives in this book have been twofold: to enable the reader to comprehend more fully the important role of race and ethnicity in American life and to raise more general questions concerning the dynamics of majority-minority relations. These objectives converge in the analysis of the Black Revolution and subsequent ethnic movements of recent years. On the one hand, the tide of Black militancy has been one of the most momentous and far-reaching developments in American history and therefore is itself worthy of special attention. Of more general interest to the social scientist is the fact that the Black Revolution provides an excellent case study of a social movement, an attempt to initiate change in a social system. Although we have referred to the impact of the Black Revolution, we feel that this movement is of sufficient import to consider its dynamics and consequences in somewhat greater detail.

There appears to be little doubt that the rise of Black militancy was one of the most momentous developments of the turbulent decade of the 1960s. Each year, the scale of racial conflict and violence appeared to escalate. In retrospect, the beginnings appear relatively subdued: in 1960 the most dramatic events involved drugstore sit-ins in Greensboro, North Carolina, a tactic that quickly spread throughout the South. In the intervening years, the pace and intensity of protest increased dramatically.

For several summers the nation was rent with civil disorders; cities were burned, property damage ran into the millions of dollars, and the toll of dead—primarily, although not exclusively, Blacks—numbered nearly a hundred. In the heated climate of those years, four of the most important figures in the movement for Black equality were the victims of assassins' bullets. Two of them—Malcolm X and Martin Luther King, Jr.—were Black; two—John and Robert Kennedy—were White.

Between 1960 and 1970, the goals and means of the Black protest movement underwent substantial changes. As is characteristic of much social change, yesterday's radicalism became today's moderation. Many of today's moderate ideologies and tactics would have appeared unthinkably radical to concerned individuals—Black and White—in 1960. Joseph C. Hough has characterized this as the "stretching of the extremism spectrum."

> About 1953, I had my first conversation with [a friend in the South] about race relations, and he and I agreed that while the Negro deserved a better chance in America, we must be careful to oppose two kinds of extremists —the NAACP and the Ku Klux Klan. In 1955, we had another conversation, and again we agreed that Negroes ought to be able to attend desegregated public schools, but that we should oppose two kinds of extremes— White Citizens Councils and Martin Luther King. In 1966, this same friend said to me, "If we could get the good whites and the good Negroes to support Martin Luther King, perhaps we could put the brakes on these SNCC and CORE people and also put a stop to this ridiculous revival of the Ku Klux Klan.[1]

As both Skolnick ("Black Militancy") and Lester ("Black America . . .") point out in Part Six, the civil rights movement of the 1950s and early 1960s was supplanted by a more militant Black Revolution. The civil rights movement was based essentially upon an order model of society; the primary goal was integration into the mainstream of the dominant society, and the primary means were nonviolent. The fundamental ideological thrust of the Black Revolution, on the other hand, was derived from a conflict model of societal functioning. In response to the intransigence and unresponsiveness of White America to the needs and interests of Black people, articulate Black spokesmen increasingly questioned the capacity of traditional goals and means to ensure the dignity and autonomy of Black people in a White society. Moreover, as Skolnick states, the civil rights movement "operated for the most part on the implicit premise that racism was a localized malignancy within a relatively healthy political and social order; it was a move to force American morality and American institutions to root out the last vestiges of the 'disease.' "

---

[1] Joseph C. Hough, Jr., *Black Power and White Protestants: A Christian Response to the New Negro Pluralism* (New York: Oxford University Press, 1968), pp. 224–225.

With the advent of the emphasis upon Black Power in 1966, this assumption has increasingly been questioned, resulting in the development of a broader perspective of the racial crisis in America as being rooted essentially in American institutions.

Even after the Kerner Commission's report in 1968, the sense of militancy among Black People, particularly among the young, increased. The Black protest movement, as Skolnick notes, increasingly shifted in emphasis from equality to liberation, from integration to separatism, and from dependency to the quest for power. Perhaps most important in this transition was the growing recognition that the problem was national and could not be confined to the South, that nonviolence was merely a *tactic* in a power struggle and in many instances was useless to obtain Black equality and autonomy, and that racism in America was rooted in the society's institutions. The primary efforts of the Black Revolution, consequently, were to obtain a more equitable distribution of power in the many institutional spheres of American life and ideologically to institute a "search for new forms"—to provide cultural alternatives to those of White America.

The decade of the 1960s ended as pessimistically as it had begun optimistically. In 1960, both Whites and Blacks concurred in the belief that the solution to the racial crisis confronting the nation could be achieved through the traditional operation of America's institutions. The new decade began with a country tragically divided and with the sober realization that the magnitude of the problems of racism was so overwhelming that even if the nation possessed the will and imagination to attack them, their solution would still be difficult to attain. Furthermore, the impetus of the Black Revolution had been expended. As Lester states:

> By the spring of 1970 when Cambodia was invaded by U.S. and South Vietnamese forces and the students were killed at Kent State and Jackson State, it was apparent that hardly any of the political elements which had created the political ferment of the sixties survived. King was dead and the civil rights movement passé; Carmichael was living in Guinea; Rap Brown was underground; Cleaver was in Algeria and the Panthers in disarray.

Lester's analysis of the forces leading to the fragmentation of the Black Revolution concludes with a "prognosis for the future [that] is . . . bleak."

If the sixties can be characterized as the decade of the Black Revolution, the compelling question arises as to why the Revolution occurred when it did in American history. Without dismissing the continuity of contemporory Black protest with previous efforts to challenge the injustices of a racist society, it seems apparent that the intensity, pervasiveness, and mass support of Black protest activities in the sixties were far more effective and far more disruptive in challenging the social order than ever before in American history.

It is extremely difficult to establish a historical benchmark from which to date the origins of the Black Revolution, since one's choice of events is usually an arbitrary one that leaves unanswered the questions of the conditions that elicited those events. The roots of the Black Revolution can be found deep in the experience of Black and White in America. In a sense, they are as old as the introduction of slavery into North America, since resistance to the slave system and to racist conceptions of the inferiority of Black people has been persistent throughout American history. But, as Bryce-Laporte noted (Part Three), under American slavery militancy and protest were individualistic, unorganized, and unsustained; collective resistance to the system was virtually impossible given the intractable nature of the slaveholders' monopoly of power and control.

As we noted in Part Three, the Civil War did little to alter the subservient position of Black people. The freedmen were given liberty but not the means (i.e., economic and political equality) to effectively ensure its realization. Blacks remained largely unskilled and illiterate, most of them living lives of enforced dependence upon the still dominant whites. The result was a Black peasantry dominated by an agricultural system that ensured dependence upon the land and isolation from the main currents of the larger society. In such a situation of geographical isolation and high illiteracy, Blacks found effective communication and organization—essential to a protest movement—almost impossible to achieve. Most of the protest that did occur continued to take individualistic forms that were ineffective in altering the *system* of caste relations. What was necessary to challenge the inequalities of the system was political consciousness and political action on a mass scale.

For a widespread social movement to occur, however, broad social structural and demographic changes were required. The twentieth century has witnessed far-reaching and powerful economic and political processes, whose interplay altered traditional patterns of Black-White interaction. These factors established the preconditions for the rise of the Black Revolution. Thus the emergence of Black protest activities cannot be accounted for by providing a catalogue of symbolically significant events that have often appeared to trigger a new movement or a change of direction in existing forms of protest (e.g., the Supreme Court's 1954 *Brown vs. Board of Education* decision; the 1955 Montgomery bus boycott; the sit-ins of 1960; the 1963 police brutality in Birmingham, Alabama; the passage of the 1964 and 1965 Civil Rights Acts; and the SNCC 1966 Black Power Statement). Moreover, the movement transcends, and consequently cannot be equated with, the organized groups (e.g., the NAACP, Urban League, CORE, SNCC, and Black Panthers) that have provided the leadership and organization for protest activities. Above all, the Black

Revolution is an outgrowth of sociological changes in American society, and in order fully to comprehend the depth of the movement it is necessary to consider several of these changes briefly.

One of the most important preconditions for the emergence of an organized collective protest movement in the United States was the break-up of the southern feudal system. Although substantial Black ghettos existed in many northern cities during the nineteenth century,[2] prior to 1900 the Black population was overwhelmingly southern and rural. Two of the major demographic trends in twentieth-century America have been the migration of Blacks out of the South and their movement from rural areas urbanward. In 1900, nine-tenths (89.7 percent) of the Black population was found in the South, but in 1970 the percentage was only slightly more than one-half (53 percent). In 1900, Blacks were primarily rural residents; only 22.7 percent lived in urban areas. By 1970, this percentage had increased to 81.3 percent, which meant that Blacks represented a more urbanized population than Whites. Although a substantial portion of this increase in the number of urbanized Blacks occurred in the North, it was happening in the South as well. Between 1900 and 1970, the percentage of the southern Black population residing in urban areas increased from 17.2 percent to 67.3 percent.

The sociological and psychological effects of this movement to the North and to urban areas were extremely important in the emergence of collective protest. Northern life lessened many of the sanctions of the southern caste system. The premium placed in urban areas upon freedom and impersonality, upon the development of voluntary organizations, and upon the great range of opportunities for education and mobility available to an individual diminished or destroyed the patterns of interaction that had characterized pre-twentieth-century inter-racial contact in the South. White-Black relations became less stable as racial roles and etiquette fluctuated and as Blacks came into open economic competition with Whites on a large scale for the first time. Using van den Berghe's terminology, we may characterize these conditions as producing a shift from *paternalistic* to *competitive* race relations.[3]

One of the most important consequences of the urbanward, and particularly the northward, migration of Blacks has been the increased availability of occupational and educational opportunities for them. Although discrimination has flourished in both employment and education at all levels, increasing numbers of Blacks, especially after World War II, obtained college educations and positions that permitted the expansion of a Black middle class. The Black middle class has been the object of considerable criticism from Black sociologists for emulating the most crass

---

[2] See Gilbert Osofsky, "The Enduring Ghetto," *The Journal of American History* 55 (September, 1968): 243–255.

[3] Pierre L. van den Berghe, *Race and Racism: A Comparative Perspective* (New York: Wiley, 1967).

and materialistic aspects of White middle-class life styles while rejecting many aspects of their Black heritage.[4] However, these criticisms should not obscure the fact that the creation of an educated, skilled, articulate, and upwardly mobile group of Blacks provided a pool of leadership for the protest against the racist system.

Especially in the earlier stages of the Black Revolution, members of the Black middle classes were instrumental in articulating the incongruity between America's promises and its realities. Most often, these individuals comprised the leadership of traditional protest organizations such as the NAACP and the Urban League. The primary involvement in, and support of, the Black Revolution was initially derived from disaffected members of the middle classes whose expectations had been aroused by the promise of America's ideology of equality but who had themselves been blocked in the fulfillment of these expectations. Educated, articulate members of the middle class were instrumental in mobilizing and organizing the initial protests against the system. Once initiated, however, the protest movement appears to have built upon its own inertia, deriving an ideology independent of, and increasingly critical toward, the middle-class integrationist orientation of its founders.

The presence of a significant middle class may, in fact, be a crucial variable in the creation of an ethnic protest or social movement, as suggested by several articles in this volume. Ossenberg describes the pivotal position of middle-class French Canadians in the development of a separatist French ideology in Quebec (Part Two), and Alvarez (Part Three) notes that Chicanos are losing out to Spanish-surnamed foreigners for many jobs "because we do not have a sufficiently aware and sufficiently powerful Chicano middle class. . . ." Despite important differences between Black and Indian organizations, Black organizations like the NAACP have an American Indian parallel in the National Congress of American Indians, established in 1944, which laid the groundwork for more militant pan-Indian protest groups like the American Indian Movement that arose in the 1960s. And although Indian "leaders" have frequently played the role of co-opted surrogate oppressors, as Josephy indicates in "Freedom for the American Indian" some members of this largely middle-class category have served as eloquent spokesmen for Indian protest actions.

A further fact not to be underestimated in considering the growing intensity of Black protest during the 1950s and early 1960s is that the international context within which American race relations were conducted had been substantially altered from what it had been previously. Between the end of World War II and the early 1960s, the colonial empires of most European nations had been dismantled. The transformation

---

[4] See, for example, E. Franklin Frazier, *Black Bourgeoisie* (Glencoe: Free Press, 1957), and Nathan Hare, *The Black Anglo-Saxons* (New York: Macmillan, 1970).

of former colonies into independent nation-states signaled the demise of the legitimacy of the doctrine of White supremacy in the former colonial states and gave added impetus to its decline in the United States as well, as Skolnick notes.

America's race relations became, for the first time in her history, inextricably intertwined with the conduct of her foreign affairs. The emergence of a series of newly independent Asian and African nations not only affected the psychology of Black Americans, but also forced the government of the United States to assume a stance of unequivocal support for the goals of full equality for Blacks. In light of the Cold War and the competition between the United States and the Soviet Union for the allegiances of these developing nations, the perpetuation of the traditional patterns of inequality in America became a constant source of embarrassment. Widespread international publicity surrounded every racial incident, including every affront to the diplomatic representatives of the new African and Asian nations. The appeals of American presidents for nondiscriminatory treatment were continually couched in terms of the deleterious effects of such incidents upon the nation's international posture. In a nationally televised speech explaining his decision to send federal troops to ensure the safety of Black high school students in Little Rock, Arkansas, President Eisenhower said:

At a time when we face grave situations abroad because of the hatred that Communism bears toward a system of government based on human rights, it would be difficult to exaggerate the harm that is being done to the prestige and influence and indeed to the safety of our nation and the world. Our enemies are gloating over this incident and using it everywhere to misrepresent our whole nation. We are portrayed as a violator of those standards of conduct which the peoples of the world united to proclaim in the Charter of the United Nations.[5]

Later, continued diplomatic embarrassments caused President Kennedy to appeal directly to business and civic leaders in several states to pass legislation ensuring an "immediate end" to segregation in public accommodations. The resistance of state lawmakers to these appeals to ensure free access to public accommodations gave increased impetus to the passage of such legislation by the Congress. It is problematic whether the Black Revolution would have received this important initial support from the federal government without the diplomatic pressures exerted in this manner. In this regard Isaacs has speculated that:

Maybe American democracy, pursuing its own glacial course, would have come finally to the greater fulfillment of its promises. This we will now

[5] Quoted in Harold R. Isaacs, *The New World of Negro Americans* (New York: Viking, 1964), p. 13.

never know. We will not know how far and how fast the American society would have moved itself, what new shapes of freedom it would have brought into being out of the stuff of its own making. We can only muse now on what might have happened in these years if the total world scene had not so drastically altered and brought American white supremacy so abruptly and so painfully into the full view of a world in which white supremacy had ceased to be the accepted order of things.[6]

The preceding discussion obviously does not exhaust the list of factors that contributed to the emergence of Black protest as a national movement in the United States. A definitive assessment of the conditions that generated the Black Revolution must await future historians, although the selections by Skolnick and Lester in this section provide sensitive contemporary appraisals of the vicissitudes of the movement. Moreover, these selections suggest that any serious analysis of Black protest must focus upon broad social-structural and institutional changes in American society that both generated the movement and resulted from it.

Just as the roots and dynamics of the Black Revolution remain to be examined fully, so also the movement's full impact upon American society has not yet been adequately assessed. The remaining selections in Part Six suggest that its impact has far transcended the specific problem of obtaining full citizenship for Black Americans. It appears to have generated increasing self-awareness and protest among other racial and ethnic minorities as well. Michael Novak's partly autobiographical "White Ethnic" reflects on the newly awakened desire of many White—particularly Roman Catholic—groups to resist pressures "to abandon our own traditions, our faith, our associations, in order to reap higher rewards in the culture of the national corporations. . . ." American Indians have been resisting these forces for generations. In addition, they have recently demonstrated a willingness to adopt many of the tactics of direct protest associated with the Black Revolution, such as the Trail of Broken Treaties that culminated in the occupation of the Bureau of Indian Affairs building in Washington, D.C., and the confrontation over Wounded Knee. Josephy articulates the oppressive conditions that led to such actions and recommends needed changes.

The impact of the Black Revolution has not been on racial and ethnic minorities alone. The rhetoric of the Black Revolution has provided much of the ideological content for student and anti-war protest and even for the "liberation movements" of women and homosexuals. In "Thy Neighbor's Wife, Thy Neighbor's Servant," Catherine Stimpson describes the effects of the civil rights movement on Women's Liberation. Ironically, one stimulus to that movement was the male chauvinism of many participants in the civil rights movement. In addition to drawing parallels be-

[6] *Ibid.*, pp. 20–21.

tween the statuses of Blacks and women, Stimpson suggests certain areas where analogies and comparisons are inappropriate, and where the paths of the two movements must diverge.

More generally, Herbert Gans has argued that the social protest of the sixties will have an even broader impact upon the entire society in the future. According to Gans, the protestors' demands were not designed to undermine the values of equality, liberty, and democracy that have long been held sacred by Americans, but to realize them more fully.[7]

Just as we cannot assume that the Black Revolution was "caused" by a single prior event or set of events, we do not suggest that the movements of other racial and ethnic minorities and additional protesting groups were mechanistically created by the Black Revolution. A complex interplay of forces, including the social structural conditions discussed above and specific contemporary events like the War in Indo-China, generated the ferment of the times. Furthermore, each discrete group has its own separate and unique history; examined together they present a panorama of extreme diversity. For example, Stimpson discusses the crucial impact of pro-Black reform efforts on women's movements since abolitionism. It has been argued, on the other hand, that every tactic used by Blacks in the 1960s was antedated by American Indians, the difference being that in the Indians' case hardly anyone else bothered to notice.[8] An additional variable of considerable importance is thus suggested—the willingness of the majority group and majority-controlled news media to devote attention to a minority social movement, or the ability of the movement to demand it. Ironically, while the Black Revolution undoubtedly paved the way in this regard, the refusal of the nation to face seriously the need for a thorough restructuring of its institutions, as demanded by Black militants and underscored by urban riots, may have been a significant reason for increased societal attention to *seemingly* less threatening and far-reaching reform movements like ecology, Women's Liberation, and justice for American Indians.

Another and quite different feature of inter-ethnic relations among minority groups is suggested by Fred Barbaro in "Ethnic Resentment." Barbaro describes the dynamics underlying the federal government's domestic programs during the Black Revolution. The Kennedy-Johnson programs, theoretically designed to meet the needs of all poor people in America, increasingly came to be viewed as a response to Black demands. In fact, they disproportionately benefitted Blacks to the relative exclusion of other minority groups. The funding was totally inadequate for any single group's needs, as Barbaro notes; instead of demanding more for all, however, Jews, Puerto Ricans, and Chicanos developed

[7] Herbert J. Gans, "Social Protest of the 1960's Takes the Form of the Equality Revolution," *The New York Times Magazine,* November 3, 1968, pp. 36–37, 66–76.

[8] Jack Forbes, "The *New* Indian Resistance?" *Awkesasne Notes* 4 (Late Spring, 1972): 20–22.

attitudes of rivalry and hostility toward Blacks.[9] Undoubtedly, this was a contributing factor to the failure to sustain the Black Revolution and to develop effective coalitions among minorities, as discussed by Lester and Barbaro. According to Barbaro, it "also contributed to the eradication of existing cooperative efforts among minorities."

White ethnics have also voiced resentment over what has appeared to them to be exclusive attention to Black needs on the part of government. According to Novak, this response has led many intellectuals to characterize White ethnic groups as a primary source of White racism in the society. Novak refuses to accept this easy assumption: "Racism is not our invention; we did not bring it with us; we found it here. And should we pay the price for America's guilt? Must all the gains of the blacks, long overdue, be chiefly at our expense?"

These protests raise fundamental political questions. Did the poverty programs destroy the Black Revolution? Lester asserts that Nixon did Blacks a favor by ending their dependence on the federal government. Is governmental largesse inherently divisive, inherently co-optive? According to Barbaro, more than altruism was at work in the hearts of the politicians and government officials who designed the Office of Economic Opportunity. He appears to agree with the argument that "the New Frontier-Great Society programs . . . from the start . . . were conceived and designed as a political strategy to buttress an obvious trend in Democratic politics, the importance of the big city vote." Future movements must not only beware of divisive tendencies among ethnic groups, but also must be alert to the possibility that seemingly positive responses of those in power may ultimately prove negative in their consequences for the groups themselves.

A related issue, equally crucial, concerns the role of cultural ideologies in relation to political realities. According to Allen (Part Five) and Lester, Black cultural nationalism has become a tool of bourgeois politics—it is irrelevant or even harmful in itself to the mass of Black Americans, and it forecloses coalitions with other groups. Although some of the specific needs of American Indians may be unique—namely the restructuring of their relationship with the federal government—they experience economic oppression, assimilation pressures, and exclusion from free participation in the society in common with Blacks, Chicanos, and others. Ironically, however, the strong sense of ethnic identity that has enabled them to survive may also incline them toward reticence when the subject of cooperative struggle is broached.

The "new ethnicity" of which Novak writes was born, in part, of

---

[9] The same feelings of "relative deprivation" were experienced by Asian Americans (see Bok-Lim C. Kim, "Asian Americans: No Model Minority," *Social Work* 18 [May, 1973]: p. 44) and by American Indians (see, for example, C. Hoy Steele, "American Indians and Urban Life: A Community Study" [Ph.D. dissertation, The University of Kansas, 1972], which also discusses the phenomenon of interethnic competition).

resentment against Blacks; yet White ethnics clearly are not among that upper fifth of the population that receives 45 percent of the American income.[10] They are more likely among the 69 percent reported by Gans that do not earn quite enough for the "modest but adequate" range, and some are among the desperate poor.[11] When a new movement for economic and social justice arises, whose side will they be on? The same question may be asked of the groups discussed by Barbaro—Puerto Ricans, Jews, and Chicanos—and of Blacks as well. Schermerhorn puts the matter eloquently and bluntly:

> If the meaning of ethnicity remains purely intrinsic, if it has no goal beyond itself, if it is exhausted in self-congratulation and bemused nostalgia, it will become like a stagnant pool whose lack of outlet condemns it to final pollution. If, however, it flows free, or to change the figure, if ethnicity becomes . . . an agent for larger goals, it can lose its egoistic pretensions and contribute its rich resources to the major needs of a society growing daily more desperate.[12]

Finally, what of the White majority, primarily Protestant and middle class? How will they—we—respond to the new demands for justice and freedom that will inevitably be voiced? As Lester realistically acknowledges, "the White majority . . . will always have the power to determine just how far Blacks [and other minority groups] go, just how much they get." In other words, as Lester suggests, "Perhaps the real question is, what is the current state of White America?" And what is its future?

[10] R. A. Schermerhorn, "Ethnicity in the Perspective of the Sociology of Knowledge," *Ethnicity* 1 (1974): 11.
[11] Gans, "Social Protest of the 1960's Takes the Form of the Equality Revolution."
[12] Schermerhorn, "Ethnicity in the Perspective of the Sociology of Knowledge."

42

Black Militancy

JEROME H. SKOLNICK

We begin with a number of misgivings. This is
by no means the first official commission to
investigate violent aspects of black protest in
America. On the contrary, official treatments
of the "racial problem" may be found far back
in American history, and official investigations
of racial violence have been with us since
1919. Occasionally, these investigations have
unequivocally condemned the participants in
racial disorder, both black and white, while
neglecting the importance of their grievances.
More often, their reports have stressed that the
resort to violence is understandable, given a
history of oppression and racial discrimination. All of these reports, nevertheless, have
insisted that violence cannot be tolerated in a
democratic society. Some have called for far-
reaching programs aimed at ending discrimination and racism; all have called for more
effective riot control. None of them appear to
have appreciably affected the course of the
American racial situation.

The cycle of protest and response continues. Violence occurs; it is again investigated, again understood, and again deplored.

There are grounds for skepticism, therefore, concerning yet another report on black

*Jerome H. Skolnick is Professor of Criminol-
ogy at the University of California, Berkeley.*

Reprinted from *The Politics of Protest: Violent Aspects
of Protest and Confrontation*, A Staff Report to the
National Commission on the Causes and Prevention of
Violence, Prepared by Jerome Skolnick, Director, pp.
97–135. Footnotes have been omitted.

militancy. And we are faced with a number of
more specific problems. Our subject is too vast
and complex to be dealt with adequately in a
single chapter. Black protest cannot be properly studied apart from the larger political and
social structure and trends of American society. . . .

. . . Our analysis is limited to certain
specific issues. We have avoided generalizations about the "racial problem" and its solutions. Those wishing to understand the broad
social and economic conditions of black
Americans, and the kinds of massive programs
needed to remedy those conditions, should
look to the Kerner Report and to the vast body
of literature on the subject. Much of this has
been said before, and we see little point in
saying it again. Our general aim, rather, is to
examine the events of the past several years to
understand why many black Americans believe it increasingly necessary to employ, or
envision, violent means of effecting social
change.

This chapter is divided into three main
sections. In the first, we examine the interaction between black protest and governmental response which caused many participants in the civil rights movement to reject
traditional political processes. Our analysis
considers the importance of anti-colonialism
in providing new meaning and ideological substance for contemporary black protest. We
have found it particularly important to stress
that, for many black militants, racial problems
are international in scope, transcending the
domestic issue of civil rights. The urban riots
have been a second major influence on contemporary militancy, and this section concludes with an analysis of the meaning of riots
for the black community and for black organizations.

The second section considers some major
themes in contemporary black protest, and examines their origins in the history of black
protest in America, the anti-colonial movement, and the present social situation of black
Americans. Many of these themes are most
clearly expressed in the actions of militant

youths in the schools. The final part of this section analyzes the nature and extent of this increasingly significant youth protest.

We conclude with an analysis of the extent and direction of ghetto violence since the publication of the Kerner Report, and the future implications of the political response to that violence.

Two related points should be understood. First, this chapter does not attempt to encompass the entire spectrum of black protest in America. Rather, it is concerned with new forms of political militancy that have recently assumed increasing importance in black communities. Its general outlines are fairly clear, even though, as we write, new militant perspectives are being generated. We regard what follows as an *introduction* to a phenomenon whose importance has been inadequately appreciated.

Second, it is important to keep the violent aspects of black protest in perspective. The connection between black militancy and collective violence is complex and ambiguous. There has so far been relatively little violence by militant blacks in this country—as compared to nonviolent black protest—despite the popular impression conveyed by the emphasis of the news media on episodes of spectacular violence (or threats of violence). This is true historically, and it is largely true for the contemporary situation. It must also be remembered that much of the violence involving blacks has originated with militant whites—in the case of the early race riots and the civil rights movement—or from police and troops, in the case of the recent ghetto riots. On the other hand, we cannot be optimistic about the future. Recent developments clearly indicate that black Americans are no longer willing to wait for governmental action to determine their fate. At the same time, we find little that is reassuring in the character of the present governmental response to black protest. We can only agree with the Kerner Commission that "this nation will deserve neither safety nor progress unless it can demonstrate the wisdom and the will to undertake decisive action against the root causes of racial disorder."

THE ROOTS OF CONTEMPORARY MILITANCY

> *Those who profess to favor freedom, and yet deprecate agitation, are men who want crops without plowing up the ground.*
>
> Frederick Douglass
>
> *You show me a black man who isn't an extremist and I'll show you one who needs psychiatric attention.*
>
> Malcolm X

Black men in America have always engaged in militant action. The first permanent black settlers in the American mainland, brought by the Spanish explorer Lucas Vasquez de Ayllon in 1526, rose up during the same year, killed a number of whites, and fled to the Indians. Since that time, black protest has never been altogether dormant, and militant blacks have experimented with a wide variety of tactics, ideologies, and goals. No simple linear or evolutionary model covers the complexity of those developments. It is inaccurate, for example, to suggest that black protest has moved from peaceful use of orderly political and legal processes to disorderly protest and, finally, to rejection of nonviolent means. . . .

At the same time, the use of legal argument and of the ballot is far from dead in the contemporary black protest movement. The history of black protest is the history of the temporary decline, fall, and resurgence of almost every conceivable means of achieving black well-being and dignity within the context of a generally hostile polity, and in the face of unremitting white violence, both official and private. Where black protest has moved toward the acceptance of violence, it has done so after exhausting nonviolent alternatives and a profound reservoir of patience and good faith.

This is the case today. In this section, we examine the events leading up to the most recent shift in the general direction of militant black protest—the shift from a "civil rights" to a "liberation" perspective.

Civil Rights and the Decline of Faith

From the decline of Garveyism in the 1920's until quite recently, the dominant thrust of black protest was toward political, social, economic, and cultural inclusion into American institutions on a basis of full equality. Always a powerful theme in American black militancy, these aims found their maximum expression in the civil rights movement of the 1950's and early 1960's. Today, these aims, while actively pursued by a segment of militant blacks, are no longer at the forefront of contemporary militancy. Several features of this transition stand out:

1. The civil rights movement was largely directed at the South, especially against state and local laws and practices, and, in general, it saw the federal government and courts as allies in the struggle for equality. The new movement for black liberation, while nationwide in scope, is primarily centered in the black communities of the North and West, and is generally antagonistic to both local and federal governments.

2. The civil rights movement was directed against explicit and customary forms of racism, as manifested in Jim Crow restrictions on the equal use of facilities of transportation, public accommodations, and the political process. The liberation movement focuses on deeper and more intractable sources of racism in the structure of American institutions, and stresses independence rather than integration.

3. The civil rights movement was largely middle-class and interracial. The liberation movement attempts to integrate middle- and lower-class elements in rejection of white leadership.

4. The civil rights movement was guided by the concepts of nonviolence and passive resistance. The liberation movement stresses self-defense and freedom by any means necessary.

For the civil rights movement, the years before 1955 were filled largely with efforts at legal reform, with the NAACP, especially, carrying case after case to successful litigation in the federal courts. Among the results were the landmark decisions in *Shelly v. Kraemer,* striking down restrictive covenants in housing, and the series of cases leading up to *Brown v. Board of Education,* declaring that the doctrine of "separate but equal" was inherently discriminatory in the public schools. The Supreme Court directed Southern school jurisdictions to desegregate "with all deliberate speed," but in the following years little changed in the South. The great majority of black children remained in segregated and markedly inferior schools; blacks sat in the back of the bus, ate in segregated facilities, and were politically disenfranchised through the white primary and the poll tax. Southern courts and police continued to act as an extension of white caste interests. Established civil rights organizations, lulled by judicial success in the federal courts, lapsed into a state of relative inactivity. There was a considerable gap, however, between the belief of the NAACP and other groups that major political changes were in sight and the reality of the slow pace of change even in the more "advanced" areas of the South. The gap was even greater between the conservative tactics and middle-class orientation of the established civil rights organizations and the situation of the black ghetto masses in the North.

Since the NAACP, the Urban League, and other established groups continued to operate as before, new tactics and new leaders arose to fill these gaps. In 1955, Mrs. Rosa Parks of Montgomery, Alabama, refused to give up her bus seat to a white man, and a successful boycott of the bus system materialized, led by the Reverend Martin Luther King, Jr. Around the same time, with less publicity, another kind of organization with another kind of leadership was coming into its own in the Northern ghettos. Elijah Muhammad and the Nation of Islam gained wide support among those segments of the black community that no one else, at the moment, was representing: the Northern, urban, lower classes.

Neither the direct-action, assimilationist approach of the Reverend Dr. King nor the separatist and nationalist theme of the Nation of Islam was new. Both were traditional themes which had been adopted in response to specific situations. Direct action was used by the abolitionists prior to the Civil War, by left-wing ghetto organizers in the 1930's, and by CORE in the early 1940's; it had been threatened by A. Philip Randolph in his March on Washington in 1941, but called off when President Roosevelt agreed to establish a Federal Fair Employment Practices Commission. The roots of separatism are equally deep, beyond Marcus Garvey to Martin Delaney and the American Colonization Society in the eighteenth century.

The move to direct action in the South brought civil rights protest out of the courts and into the streets, bus terminals, restaurants, and voting booths, substituting "creative disorder" for litigation. Nevertheless it remained deeply linked to the American political process and represented an innate faith in the protective power of the federal government and in the moral capacity of white Americans, both Northern and Southern. It operated, for the most part, on the implicit premise that racism was a localized malignancy within a relatively healthy political and social order; it was a move to force American morality and American institutions to root out the last vestiges of the "disease."

Nowhere were these premises more explicit than in the thought and practice of Martin Luther King, Jr. Nonviolence was for him a philosophical issue rather than the tactical or strategic question it posed for many younger activists in SNCC and CORE. The aim was "to awaken a sense of moral shame in the opponent." Such a philosophy presumed that the opponent had moral shame to awaken, and that moral shame, if awakened, would suffice. During the 1960's many civil rights activists came to doubt the first and deny the second. The reasons for this did not lie primarily in white Southern terrorism as manifested in the killing of NAACP leader Medgar Evers, of three civil rights workers in Neshoba County, Mississippi, of four little girls in a dynamited church in Birmingham, and many others. To a large extent, white Southern violence was anticipated and expected. What was not expected was the absence of strong protective action by the federal government.

Activists in SNCC and CORE met with greater and more violent Southern resistance as direct action continued during the sixties. Freedom Riders were beaten by mobs in Montgomery; demonstrators were hosed, clubbed and cattle-prodded in Birmingham and Selma. Throughout the South, civil rights workers, black and white, were victimized by local officials as well as by night-riders and angry crowds. It was not surprising, then, that student activists in the South became increasingly disillusioned with nonviolent tactics of resistance. Following the shotgun murder in 1966 of Sammy Younge, Jr., a black civil rights activist at Tuskegee Institute, his fellow students organized a protest march:

> We had no form, which was beautiful. We had no pattern, which was beautiful. People were just filling the streets, and they weren't singing no freedom songs. They were mad. People would try and strike up a freedom song, but it wouldn't work. All of a sudden you heard this, "Black Power, Black Power." People felt what was going on. They were tired of this whole nonviolent bit. They were tired of this organized demonstration-type thing. They were going to do something.

Despite the passage of civil rights legislation and legal support for integration, Southern courts continued to apply caste standards of justice. Official violence of the past—beating, shooting, and lynching—was supplemented and sometimes replaced by official violations of the law. Judges, prosecutors, and local bar officials explicitly attempted to suppress the civil rights movement, without any pretense of harmonizing competing interests within the ambit of the law. Many celebrated aspects of democracy, the jury system, for instance, worked to maintain terrorist racism instead of prosecuting and punishing it. In the same manner the constitutional inhibitions on federal intrusion into state sovereignty became from the black viewpoint a mockery of democracy instead of a keystone.

The problems of white violence and Southern judicial intransigence were compounded by political constraints on the federal government, such that it failed to move decisively toward radically altering the Southern situation. . . .

The deepest or most entrenched meaning of racism began to emerge, and it made considerable sociological as well as historic sense: a society that has been built around racism will lack the capacity, the flexibility, the institutions to combat it when the will to change belatedly appears. The major American institutions had developed standards, procedures, and rigidities which served to inhibit the Negro's drive for equality. It was as if a cruel joke had been played; the most liberally enshrined features of democracy served to block the aspirations to equality—local rule, trade unionism, referendums, the jury system, the neighborhood school. And to complete the irony, perhaps, the most elitist aspect of the constitutional system—the Supreme Court —was for a time the cutting edge of the established quest for equality, for which it came under considerable populist fire.

At the March on Washington in 1963, John Lewis of SNCC voiced the growing lack of enthusiasm for more civil rights bills. "This bill will not protect young children and old women from police dogs and fire hoses for engaging in peaceful demonstrations. . . ." Federal policy also began to show less enthusiasm for the civil rights movement. Federal government officials were often unable to obtain a strong popular or congressional consensus, even for their moderate efforts at enforcement, and responded accordingly. . . .

Faith in the political process, and especially in the traditional alliance between blacks and the liberal elements in the Democratic Party, suffered another blow in the failure to seat the Mississippi Freedom Democratic Party delegation at the 1964 Democratic convention. The MFDP represented both a re-jection of Southern white-only Democratic politics and a fundamental belief in the good offices of liberal Democrats, whose compromise offer of two seats among the regular Mississippi delegation was seen as an insult.

The MFDP episode climaxed a growing disillusionment with the white liberal. As a black commentator wrote in 1962, "Negroes are dismayed as they observe that liberals, even when they are in apparent control, not only do not rally their organizations for an effective role in the fight against discrimination, but even tolerate a measure of racial discrimination in their own jurisdictions." The recognition that civil rights laws would not suffice to bring blacks into full equality in American society furthered the search for more intractable causes of disadvantage in American institutions. Militants began to examine the reasons why discriminatory practices remained in such traditionally "liberal" institutions as labor organizations, schools, and civil service. The liberal's motives became suspect. Suspicion extended to another traditionally "friendly" institution—academic social science, and its representatives in the federal welfare "establishment." The Moynihan Report, which many blacks took as an affront, was interpreted as an attempt to place the blame for continued discrimination in the Negro community and not on the structure of racism.

The increased criticism of liberals, academics, and federal bureaucracies was part of a broader turn to a renewed critique of the situation of blacks in the North. To a large extent, and despite such evidence as the Harlem uprisings of 1935 and 1943, most white Northerners had congratulated themselves on the quality of their "treatment" of the Negro vis-à-vis that of the South. But with the explosion of Harlem again—along with several other Northern cities—in 1964, attention began shifting to the problem of institutional racism in the North, and this shift was accelerated by the Watts riot the following year. In a real sense, the riots surprised not only liberal and academic whites, but civil rights leaders as well. While undermining the moral credibility of liberal Northerners, the riots deprived most civil rights leaders of a vocabulary for expressing the deeper problems of the Northern ghettos. There was a widespread sense that civil rights leaders either could not or would not speak to the kinds of issues raised by the riots, and that a wide gulf separated those leaders—mostly of middle-class background—from the black urban masses. During the 1964 Harlem riot, for example, Bayard Rustin and other established civil rights leaders were booed and shouted down at rallies and in the streets, while crowds shouted for Malcolm X.

By the mid-1960's, then, civil rights activists had petitioned the federal government and the white liberals and found them wanting. They also found themselves increasingly out of touch with the vocal ghetto masses. At the same time, another issue began to emerge. Militants began to ask whether there was not a contradiction between the lack of action at home and American commitments overseas: "How is it that the government can protect the Vietnamese from the Viet Cong and the same government will not accept the moral responsibility of protecting people in Mississippi?" . . .

When [in 1966] Stokely Carmichael of SNCC brought the new direction of civil rights activists into the public eye with the slogan of "Black Power," it became clear that a shift of major importance had occurred.

This change of direction away from the established political process toward a critique of larger American policy at home and abroad did not occur in a vacuum. The civil rights movement had been organized on an assumption of the responsiveness of American institutions and especially of the federal government. As these assumptions were viewed more critically, as the movement began looking at the North as well as at the South, and as it became clear that racism was not simply a localized phenomenon confined to the Southern bigot, activists began to look harder in two directions: inward toward the social structure of the urban ghetto and the increasing protests of those caught within it, and outward toward American foreign policy and to the emerging anti-colonial movement. In looking inward to the urban ghetto, many civil rights activists met and merged with the voices of black, Northern, urban, lower-class protest. In looking toward the anti-colonial struggle, black militants acquired a new conception of their role in the world and new models of collective action.

The Impact of Anti-Colonialism

Throughout most of the past century the world was dominated by whites. The domination was political, economic, social, and cultural; it involved nothing less than the reclassification of the majority of the world's population as somewhat less than human. "Not very long ago, the earth numbered two thousand million inhabitants; five hundred million men, and one thousand five hundred million natives."

Today this is no longer true. The great majority of lands formerly under colonial domination have gained at least formal autonomy. The impact of this development has yet to be completely assessed, but it is clear that no discussion of the character of racial conflict in America can ignore it. . . .

The revolt against colonialism has affected American black protest in three ways. It has substantially overthrown the image of blacks as people without culture or history; it has created a host of new states run by nonwhites, whose influence in the world increases daily; and it has provided attractive models of ideology and action.

Culture

Colonialism operates on several different levels: as a political order, an economic system, and a set of cultural arrangements. In conjunction with its political and economic aims, colonialism attempted to deny, depreciate, or destroy indigenous cultures. The revolt against colonialism, therefore, is in part a revolt against cultural dispossession.

The white man's intervention in Africa and Asia was rationalized as a "civilizing mission." Thought to be lacking in history and culture, and certainly lacking in Christianity, "natives" were held to be in desperate need of cultural and spiritual tending. Colonialism was not entirely a system of raw exploitation; it is better conceived as "an association of the philanthropic, the pious, and the profitable." Like all philanthropy, the colonial concern for the native was predicated on the idea of the social and sometimes innate inferiority of the recipient vis-à-vis the donor. . . . The conception of the Negro as "a man without a past" dominated racial contacts here and abroad, and the denial that blacks possessed anything of cultural value shaped many aspects of colonial policy.

The assimilationist policy of the French, Portuguese, and Belgian colonial administrations allowed black men to attain legal rights by becoming as nearly white, in culture and manner, as possible. Thus the advancement of blacks to full legal rights in Portuguese colonies, for example, meant taking a test to prove that the candidate had transcended his cultural origins. These arrangements, and the white cultural hegemony which they reflected, have obvious parallels in the American situation, and their effects cut deeply into the self-image of blacks. The rejection of color, hair and facial features could be found wherever these policies against black people developed, in Brazil and in West Africa as well as Chicago. "The first attempt of the colonized is to change his condition by changing his skin."

A limited rebellion against this cultural and historical dispossession has long been an undercurrent of black protest in America and Africa. The concept of black self-affirmation which was present in Garveyism and Pan-Africanism came alive in the post–World War II drive for African independence. This resulted in part from the limitations of assimilationist policy itself. "The candidate for assimilation almost always comes to tire of the exorbitant price which he must pay and which he never finishes owing." The thrust toward black self-affirmation was also encouraged by questioning the monolithic character of European culture and values: ". . . as time went on, African intellectuals began to ask . . . why it should automatically be assumed that it is an unadulterated virtue to accept Western values."

The assault on the dominance of Western culture was deeply implicated in the quest for political independence from white rule. After the Second World War, African nationalist movements began a process of reconstruction of African history and reevaluation of African culture which continues today. Much scholarship is devoted to charting and analyzing the growth of early African civilizations, and affirming their high level of cultural and technological development. The strength of these efforts at cultural reconstruction reflects the pervasiveness of white stereotypes of black inferiority. Cultural autonomy is important because it has only been recently and precariously attained.

Nevertheless, the cultural impetus of anticolonialism has substantially reversed for many blacks, especially for the new militants, the negative stereotypes which suffused Western thought for centuries and which still linger in white conceptions of black culture and black achievements. The significance of black independence is inestimable. If nothing else, it has involved a reappraisal by American black militants of the potential of nonwhites, and hence of themselves. Malcolm X, a central figure in promoting the new international outlook of American black militancy, found himself deeply moved by the very existence of a technological society in Egypt: "I believe what most surprised me was that in Cairo, automobiles were being manufactured, and also buses. . . ." "I can't tell you the feeling it gave me. I had never seen a black man flying a jet."

Power

The successful revolt against colonialism has changed the structure of power in the world, and this fact has not been lost on black militants in America. It demonstrated that peoples supposed to be culturally and technologically "backward" can triumph over ostensibly superior powers; and it has developed in many militants a consciousness that, in global terms, nonwhites represent the majority.

Successful anti-colonial movements are evidence that the military and technological supremacy of the major Western powers is incapable of containing movements for national liberation. The eventual victories of such movements in Algeria and Kenya, and the inability of a massive and costly American effort to deflect the course of the national liberation movement in Vietnam, are not lost on American blacks. If nothing else, these facts demonstrate that should urban insurgency come to this country, it would require a massive and frustrating effort to control, at enormous costs to all involved. Perhaps above all, the aura of invulnerability which may have surrounded the technologically powerful white nations has substantially crumbled. . . . Perhaps most significantly, the recognition that whites are an international minority necessarily changes the meaning for many black militants of their national minority position. . . .

Beyond the question of mere numbers, the political and technological achievements of nonwhite countries produce a sense of pride and optimism: "For the Negro in particular, it has been a stirring experience to see whole societies and political systems come into existence in which from top to bottom . . . all posts are occupied by black men, not because of the sufferance of white superiors but because it is their sovereign right."

American Negroes across the political spectrum, according to one observer, uniformly showed a certain amount of pride in response to the successful explosion of a nuclear device by China. Again, the partial identification with Oriental nations is not completely new; there were elements of ambivalence among some Negroes about fighting the "colored" Japanese in World War II. What is new is the sense of pride in the growing power of the nonwhite nations.

There were four African and three Asian nations in the UN in 1945; twenty years later there were thirty-six African and fifteen Asian countries represented. The rise of these new states, especially when coupled with the exigencies of Cold War diplomacy, has meant that since World War II American leaders have been well aware that the way blacks are treated at home has important ramifications for world affairs. A number of American black militants have looked to the UN specifically as an arena for bringing black grievances before the world. Malcolm X urged African leaders to bring up the plight of Afro-Americans in UN meetings and urged American Negro leaders to visit nonwhite countries, where they "would find that many nonwhite officials of the highest standing, especially Africa, would tell them—privately—that they would be glad to throw their weight behind the Negro cause, in the UN and in other ways." As colonialism disappears, the previously unquestioned authority of the white world likewise disintegrates, and with it the capacity of a predominantly white society to maintain its privileges. Black militants are aware of this, and recognize the impact it may have: ". . . the first thing the American power structure doesn't want any Negroes to start," wrote Malcolm X, "is thinking internationally."

Politics, Ideology, and Violence

Anti-colonialism provided, directly or indirectly, a cultural resurgence and a sense of international influence among American blacks. It also provided new models of ideology and action which, with greater or lesser relevance, could be applied to the American situation. Two themes especially stand out: the politicization of conflict and the redefinition of the meaning and uses of violence.

White domination of nonwhites shared with other forms of political domination an attempt to define the situation in non-political terms. In Africa, as previously suggested, political domination was cloaked in philanthropic or religious sanctions. As a result, early expressions of anti-colonial conflict tended to take forms which were not explicitly political:

> Every colonial administration has aimed at establishing a depoliticized regime or has emphasized maximum depoliticization of all the expressions of native life. . . . Consequently, political reactions against the colonial situation were expressed indirectly at first, for example, through new syncretist religious movements loaded with revolutionary implications.

Again, the American parallels are not hard to find. Black religious movements of this kind—best typified by the Nation of Islam—have generally drawn recruits from the most oppressed sectors of the American black population.

The success of the movements for political independence in the colonial countries required a recognition that the plight of the "native" was a political problem, and that political action was the most effective vehicle of major social change. Early nationalist movements in Africa, therefore, sought to turn nearly every aspect of life into a political issue. This was especially true of the area of culture. The quests for political and for cultural autonomy had a reciprocal influence; the rebuilding of culture served as a basis of political organization. The political importance of culture lay in the fact that "natives," as people without history or culture, were also seen as people without political claims of their own, and therefore as people to be dealt with from above —benevolently or otherwise. Black culture was—and still remains—a "contested culture" whose very existence is a political issue of the greatest importance, in the United States as in Africa.

Through the same process of politicization, instances of black resistance in history were redefined as precursors of contemporary political struggles. "Native" crime was redefined as early revolutionary activity; instances of rebellion were sought in the past and their significance amplified.

In viewing history as an arena of white violence and native resistance, the anti-colonial perspective stressed the intrinsically violent character of colonial domination. Colonialism was seen as dependent on the routinization of violence, both physical and psychological, against the native. Consequently, revolutionary violence against the colonial regime was deemed not only necessary, but justifiable, on both political and psychological grounds. Colonialism, wrote Frantz Fanon, "is violence in its natural state, and it will only yield when confronted with greater violence." Further, "at the level of individuals, violence is a cleansing force. It frees the native from his inferiority complex and from his despair and inaction; it makes him fearless and restores self-respect."

Anti-colonial writers defined the situation of nonwhites as one of subordination under a political, social, economic, and cultural order intrinsically hostile to the interests of nonwhites, and therefore not susceptible to change through orderly political processes; "revolt is the only way out of the colonial situation, and the colonized realizes it sooner or later. His condition is absolute and calls for an absolute solution; a break and not a compromise." The rejection of compromise meant a corresponding rejection of the native middle class, which was seen as parasitical, timid, and generally antagonistic to the struggle of the native masses for liberation. The motive force of the anti-colonial revolution, for these writers, lay in the *lumpenproletariat* of the cities. Through revolutionary violence, Fanon wrote, "these workless less-than-men are rehabilitated in their own eyes and in the eyes of history."

THE IMPACT OF RIOTS

Although it is difficult to assess accurately the various influences on contemporary black militancy, the Northern urban riots are surely important. Whereas anti-colonialism provided, directly or indirectly, a model of cultural identity and a sense of international influence, riots both dramatized the failure of the American polity to fulfill the expectations of the civil rights movement, and demonstrated the gap between black leaders and the prevailing sentiments of their constituencies. The urban riots, then, have had important consequences for black leaders as well as for governmental action. Newer and younger faces and organizations have emerged in recent years to represent the interests of the urban lower classes, and the older representatives of the civil rights movement have been required to redefine their political programs to accommodate these new forms of militancy. . . .

The "Riffraff" Theory

Until recently, riots were regarded as the work of either outsiders or criminals. The "riffraff" theory, as it is known, has three assumptions —that a small minority of the black population engages in riot activity, that this minority is composed of the unattached, uprooted, and unskilled, and that the overwhelming majority of the black population deplores riots. This theory helps to dramatize the criminal character of riots, to undermine their political implications, and to uphold the argument that social change is possible only through lawful and peaceful means. If riots can be partly explained as the work of a few agitators or hoodlums, it is then much easier to engage wide support in repudiating violent methods of social protest.

Official investigations generally publicize the fact that normal, ordinary, and law-abiding persons do not instigate riots. According to the FBI, riots are typically instigated by a "demagogue or professional agitator" or by "impulsive and uninhibited individuals who are the first in the mob to take violent action or to keep it going when it wanes." Thus,"hoodlums" were responsible for the 1943 riot in Detroit, "marauding bands" of criminals in Watts, "a small fraction of the city's black population" in Chicago in 1968, and "self-appointed leaders, opportunists, and other types of activists" in Pittsburgh. . . . Implicit in the "riffraff" theory is the idea that riots are unilaterally violent, that public officials and agencies merely respond in defense against the violence of "irresponsible advocates," and that the riots have little wider meaning in the black community.

The "riffraff" theory has been challenged by various studies. As long ago as 1935, the Harlem Commission reported that "among all classes, there was a feeling that the outburst of the populace was justified and that it represented a protest against discrimination and aggravations resulting from unemployment." More recently, a study of participants in the Watts riot suggests that 46 percent of the adult population in the curfew zone were either actively or passively supporting the riot. The riot had a "broad base" of support and was characterized by "widespread community involvement." Although participants in the Watts riot were predominantly male and youthful, support for rioting was as great from the better-educated, economically advantaged, and long-time residents as it was from the uneducated, poor, and recent migrants.

The Kerner Report provided further evidence to contradict the "riffraff" theory, but its significance was lost in the mass of facts and figures. The most convincing attack on this theory came from Fogelson and Hill's study of participation in the 1967 riots which was published at the end of the Kerner Commission's supplemental studies. The authors found that (1) a substantial minority, ranging from 10 to 20 percent, participated in the riots, (2) one half to three quarters of the arrestees were employed in semiskilled or skilled occupations, three fourths were employed, and three tenths to six tenths were born outside the South, and (3) individuals between the ages of fifteen and thirty-four and especially those between the ages of fifteen and twenty-four are most likely to participate in riots.

Riots are generally viewed by blacks as a useful and legitimate form of protest. Survey data from Watts, Newark, and Detroit suggests that there is an increasing support, or at least sympathy, for riots in black communities.

Over half the people interviewed in Los Angeles responded that the riot was a purposeful event which had a positive effect on their lives. Thirty-eight percent of the population in the curfew area said that the riot would help the Negro cause. "While the majority expressed disapproval of the violence and destruction," writes Nathan Cohen in the Los Angeles Riot Study, "it was often coupled with an expression of empathy with those who participated, or sense of pride that the Negro has brought worldwide attention to his problem."

That riots are seen by many as a legitimate and instrumental method of protest has drastic implications for the "riffraff" theory. Fogelson and Hill ask:

> Is it conceivable that . . . several hundred riots could have erupted in nearly every Negro ghetto in the United States over the past five years against the opposition of 98 or 99 percent of the black community? And is it conceivable that militant young Negroes would have ignored the customary restraints on rioting in the United States, including the commitment to orderly social change, unless they enjoyed the tacit support of at least a sizeable minority of the black community?

Studies of riot participation suggest that "rioters" represent a cross section of the lower-class community. The young people who participate are not known to be psychologically impaired or especially suffering from problems of masculine identity. Juveniles arrested in the 1967 Detroit riot were found by a psychological team to be less emotionally disturbed and less delinquent than typical juvenile arrestees. Furthermore, the recent riots have served to mobilize the younger segments of the black community and to educate them to the realities of their caste position in American society. . . .

THE DIRECTION OF CONTEMPORARY MILITANCY

By the mid-1960's, many militant black leaders had become convinced that the aims and methods of the civil rights movement were no longer viable. The failures of the federal government and of white liberals to meet black expectations, the fact of the urban revolts, and the increasing American involvement overseas all served to catalyze a fundamental transformation in black perceptions of American society. The anti-colonial perspective, rather unique when expressed by Malcolm X in 1964, now provided many blacks with a structured world-view. For the Black Panther Party, for example, it provided the "basic definition":

> We start with the basic definition: that black people in America are a colonized people in every sense of the term and that white America is an organized Imperialist force holding black people in colonial bondage.

Many articulate black spokesmen saw the final hope of black Americans in identification with the revolutionary struggles of the Third World. Even political moderates began pointing to the discrepancy between the massive commitment of American resources abroad and the lack of a decisive commitment to end racism at home. Martin Luther King wondered why "we were taking the black young men who had been crippled by our society and sending them 8,000 miles away to guarantee liberties in Southeast Asia which they had not found in Southwest Georgia or East Harlem." He also questioned the official condemnation of the ghetto poor for their "resort to violence":

> As I have walked among the desperate, rejected, and angry young men I have told them that Molotov cocktails and rifles would not solve their problems. . . . But they asked—and rightly so—what about Vietnam? . . . Their questions hit home, and I knew that I could never again raise my voice against the violence of the oppressed in the ghettos without having first spoken clearly to the greatest purveyor of violence in the world today—my own government.

By the mid-1960s, then, criticism of fundamental American policies at home and abroad was widespread among intellectuals in the black community. The dominant themes in contemporary black protest reflect this basic mood. Three major themes stand out: self-defense and the rejection of nonviolence; cultural autonomy and the rejection of white values; and political autonomy and community control. These trends do not exhaust the content of contemporary militancy, and they are held in varying combinations and in varying degree by different groups and individuals. All of them, however, share a comon characteristic: they are attempts to gain for blacks a measure of safety, power, and dignity in a society that has denied them all three.

Self-defense

Traditionally, Americans have viewed self-defense as a basic right. The picture of the armed American defending his home, his family, his possessions, and his person has its origins in frontier life but is no less a reality in modern suburbia. In that picture, however, the armed American is always white. The idea of black men defending themselves with force has always inspired horror in whites. In some of the early slave codes, black slaves were not permitted to strike a white master even in self-defense. In the caste system of the Southern states. Negroes were expected to accept nearly any kind of punishment from whites without retaliation; openly showing aggression meant almost certain violent retaliation from whites. Still, individual blacks occasionally fought back in the face of white violence in the South; and blacks collectively resisted attacking whites in the race riots of 1917, 1919, and 1943.

The civil rights movement, under the leadership of Martin Luther King, and the sit-ins and freedom rides of the 1960's stressed nonviolence and what some called "passive resistance." As a result of the failure of local and federal officials to protect civil rights workers in the South, however, a number of activists and their local allies began to arm themselves against attacks by the Ku Klux Klan and other white terrorist groups. It was only too obvious that local police and sheriffs in the South were at best only halfheartedly concerned with the welfare of rights workers, and at worst were active participants in local terrorist groups. The latter was the case in Neshoba County, Mississippi, for example, where the local sheriff's department was deeply implicated in the killing of three civil rights workers. More often, civil rights groups found they could not depend on Southern officials for protection. In 1959, the head of the NAACP chapter in Monroe, North Carolina, had organized local blacks into a rifle club as an armed defense against repeated assaults by the Ku Klux Klan. A notable result was that "the lawful authorities of Monroe and North Carolina acted to enforce order *only after, and as a direct result of,* our being armed."

Following the bloody Southern summer of 1964, local defense groups sprang up in several black communities in the South. Their primary purpose was to protect nonviolent civil rights workers in the absence of police protection and to end white terrorism against black communities. As a rule, they favored nonviolence as a civil rights tactic, but felt that it could only operate where nonviolent demonstrators were protected from assault. A study of one such group in Houston, Texas, concluded that the overall effect of an organized showing of armed force by blacks was to decrease the level of violence in the community. White vigilantes were deterred from action, and police were forced to perform an effective law enforcement role.

During this period, the focus of attention began to shift to the ghettos of the North. The dramatic episodes of police harassment of demonstrators in the South had overshadowed, for a time, the nature of the routine encounters between police and blacks in the ghetto. The ghetto resident and those who spoke for him, however, had not forgotten the character of the policeman's daily role in the black community, or the extent of private white violence against Northern blacks in history. The writings of Malcolm X spoke from Northern, rather than Southern, experience in demanding for blacks the right to defend themselves against attack:

I feel that if white people were attacked by Negroes—if the forces of law prove unable, or inadequate or reluctant to protect those whites from those Negroes—then those white people should be able to protect themselves against Negroes using arms if necessary. And I feel that when the law fails to protect Negroes from white attack, then those Negroes should use arms, if necessary, to defend themselves.

"Malcolm X Advocates Armed Negroes!" What was wrong with that? I'll tell you what was wrong. I was a black man talking about physical defense against the white man. The white man can lynch and burn and bomb and beat Negroes—that's all right. "Have patience" . . . "The customs are entrenched" . . . "Things are getting better."

After the Watts riot of 1965, local blacks formed a Community Action Patrol to monitor police conduct during arrests. In 1966, some Oakland blacks carried the process a little farther by instituting armed patrols. From a small group organized on an ad hoc basis and oriented to the single issue of police control, the Black Panther Party for Self-Defense has grown into a national organization with a ten-point program for achieving political, social, and economic goals. In the process, the name has been condensed to the Black Panther Party, but the idea of self-defense remains basic: "The Panther never attacks first, but when he is backed into a corner, he will strike back viciously."

The Black Panther Party has been repeatedly harassed by police. After the conviction of the party's leader, Huey P. Newton, for manslaughter in the death of a white policeman, Oakland police fired into the Black Panther office with rifles and shotguns presumably because they felt that a conviction for first-degree murder would have been more appropriate. On September 4, a group of 150 whites, allegedly including a number of off-duty policemen, attacked a group of Panthers and their white supporters in the Brooklyn Criminal Court building. The confrontation between the Panthers and some elements of the police has become a feud verging on open warfare. This warfare highlights the fact that for the black citizen, the policeman has long since ceased to be—if indeed he ever was—a neutral symbol of law and order. Studies of the police emphasize that their attitudes and behavior toward blacks differ vastly from those taken toward whites. Similar studies show that blacks perceive the police as hostile, prejudiced, and corrupt. In the ghetto disorders of the past few years, blacks have often been exposed to indiscriminate police assaults and, not infrequently, to gratuitous brutality. Many ghetto blacks see the police as an occupying army; one of the Panthers' major demands is for stationing UN observers in the ghettos to monitor police conduct.

In view of these facts, the adoption of the idea of self-defense is not surprising. Again, in America self-defense has always been considered an honorable principle, and the refusal to bow before police harassment strikes a responsive chord in ghetto communities, especially among the young. In Oakland, ghetto youths emulate the Panthers; the Panthers, in turn, attempt to direct youth into constructive channels. . . .

The Black Panther Party has remained defensive and has been given credit for keeping Oakland cool after the assassination of Martin Luther King, but this has not stemmed from any desire on their part to suppress black protest in the community. Rather, it has stemmed from a sense that the police are waiting for a chance to shoot down blacks in the streets. Continued harassment by the police makes self-defense a necessary element of militant action for the Panthers and for similar groups, such as the Black Liberators in St. Louis.

Beyond this, society's failure to commit itself to ending racism leads many militants to feel that there is no end in sight to the long history of white violence and repression. Advocates of self-defense can easily point to instances of official violence employed at one time or another against a variety of groups in the United States. With the approval of the government in Washington, Southern whites militarized their entire society between 1830 and 1860, terminated the education of Negro slaves and deprived them of all human rights; restricted their movements, and punished real or alleged revolts by summary execution of suspects. Mob violence tacitly sanctioned by the government was employed with terrible effect against West Coast Chinese as well as against Southern blacks in the decades following the Civil War. Systematic political persecution by the government, using techniques of discriminatory legislation, nighttime raids, mass deportation, officially condoned mob violence, and jailing of political prisoners, was employed against rebellious political minorities like the IWW and socialists of 1917 to 1922. During the First World War, most resident Germans were suspected of disloyalty and many were physically attacked or had property destroyed by mobs; during the Second World War, virtually the entire West Coast Japanese community was removed by the United States government to concentration camps in the West. Most prominent in these allusions to violence is the 250-year campaign of suppression waged against the American Indians, the one example in United States history of official violence raised to a genocidal scale. For some militants, the history of the struggle deserves particular attention in the light of contemporary events, for it provides a scenario for massive suppression of a large racial minority. . . .

Cultural Autonomy

The strain toward black liberation mixes indigenous and international influences. The resurgence of interest in cultural autonomy reflects both of these influences, as well as the unique problems confronting black Americans during the mid-1960's. Three elements of that situation are especially significant.

First, with the rise of an international outlook and a concomitant recognition of America's role in supporting oppressive regimes overseas, black Americans found themselves in a society that appeared to be bent on suppressing nonwhite ambitions on a worldwide, as well as a domestic, scale. "A rising tide of consciousness that we are Africans," writes James Forman, "an African people living in the United States and faced with the problem of sheer survival, dominates

the thoughts of many black college students today." Looking backward at the long history of white domination in this country, and outward at American neocolonialism, militants questioned the cultural basis of American values: "I do not want to be a part of the American pride. The American pride means raping South Africa, beating Vietnam, beating South America, raping the Philippines, raping every country you've been in."

The exclusion of blacks from the mainstream of American culture has made rejection of that culture less difficult. . . . Unimpressed by the performance of this country under the dominance of white, Western culture, blacks looked to their own cultural heritage as a source of affirmation of a different set of values. "We reject the American Dream as defined by white people and must work to construct an American reality defined by Afro-Americans."

A second element of the situation was intrinsic. Supported by the revival of awareness of African history and culture accompanying the anti-colonial movement, blacks grew more and more impatient with the attempt of the American cultural apparatus—especially the schools and mass media—to enforce cultural standards which either ignored or depreciated the independent cultural heritage of Afro-Americans. . . .

In addition to demanding recognition of a rich cultural heritage, militant blacks resented the policy implications of the rejection of that heritage by whites. American social science has traditionally—with the exception of men like Herskovits—argued that the Negro is only "an exaggerated American" without values of his own; "the Negro is only an American and nothing else. He has no values and culture to guard and protect." Two corollary notions, both of which have important implications for social policy, flow from this conception. On the one hand, the current cultural arrangements become relatively immune from independent criticism by blacks; on the other hand, the distinctness of black behavior comes to be seen as pathological.

Yesterday's rural Negro may have had something like a folk culture, so the myth goes, but today's urban Negro can be found only in a set of sociological statistics on crime, unemployment, illegitimacy, desertion, and welfare payments. The social scientists would have us believe that the Negro is psychologically maladjusted, socially disorganized and culturally deprived.

This elitist perspective implies that something must be done to bring blacks up to the cultural standards of the "community" or, at the extreme, that blacks themselves have to clean their own houses—literally and figuratively—before "earning" admittance into the American mainstream. A long-term result of the denial of black culture was the entire set of conceptions centering around the notion of "cultural deprivation": black children failed in school because they came from a "cultureless" community, not because the schools did not teach. Central to this perspective was the ideology of American public welfare, with its commitment to raising the moral standards of the poor and its public intrusions into the family arrangements of ghetto blacks.

The drive toward cultural autonomy, therefore, was in part a rejection of the cultural vacuum of "welfare colonialism" into which the black community has been thrown. It was also an organizational response to the failure of white liberals to fulfill the promise of the civil rights movement of the 1950's. For the most part, white supporters of the movement for civil rights thought in assimilationist terms. Their object was to open opportunities for the Negro to enter the mainstream of American life. Many blacks, however, questioned the cost involved in aiming for inclusion on terms that were irrevocably the terms of white culture. Many whites, too, tended to assume that their function in the movement for civil rights was to guide, instruct, and otherwise lead the movement from the top. These facts, coupled with the rise of identification with nonwhites on an international basis and increased contact with the black masses in the North, led black activists to move toward limiting the role of whites in their organizations. The Student Nonviolent Coordinating Committee excluded whites from leadership positions in 1966, citing these reasons:

> The inability of whites to relate to the cultural aspects of Black society; attitudes that whites, consciously or unconsciously, bring to Black communities about themselves (western superiority) and about Black people (paternalism); inability to shatter white-sponsored community myths of Black inferiority and self-negation; inability to combat the views of the Black community that white organizers, being "white," control Black organizers as puppets; . . . the unwillingness of whites to deal with the *roots* of racism which lie within the white community; whites though individually "liberal" are symbols of oppression to the Black community—due to the collective power that whites have over Black lives.

The rejection of white leadership was mistakenly viewed as a form of "racism in reverse" by many white and some black commentators. But this rejection was not necessarily or consistently a withdrawal from whites *qua* whites. Rather, it was an assertion of the ability of blacks to control their own organizations, and a rejection of white claims, symbolic or explicit, of political leadership. As such, it represented one aspect of a general thrust toward black political independence.

Political Autonomy and Community Control

The movement of black militants toward a concern for political autonomy, with a corresponding rejection of traditional political avenues and party organizations, is a result of several influences. One we have already noted—the failure of traditional politics to play a meaningful part in the drive for black dignity and security. Passing civil rights legislation is not the same as enforcing it. Pleading for goodwill and racial justice from the relative sanctuary of Congress, the courts, or the White House is a good deal easier than committing a massive federal effort to eradicate institutional racism. On a local level, it occasions no great difficulty to appoint a few Negroes to positions of some influence; the crucial test is whether local government acts decisively to correct the problems of the ghetto and to provide a genuine avenue of black participation in community decision-making. On all of these counts, most local governments have failed or, more accurately, have hardly tried. The result is that local government has become, to those beneath it, oppressive rather than representative. Certainly, there are "differences within the system," the structure of political power in a given community is usually less monolithic than it appears from below, and there may be several loci of influence rather than an organized and cohesive "power structure." But these points are only meaningful to those who enter the system with some preestablished influence. A critical fact about the black ghettos of the cities, and of the black belt communities of the South, is their traditional lack of such a base of influence. Without this, blacks have participated in the political process as subjects rather than citizens. Traditionally, black political leaders have been less a force for black interest than middlemen in a system of "indirect rule": "In other words, the white power structure rules the black community through local blacks who are responsive to the white leaders, the downtown, white machine, not to the black populace." [See Baron's article, "Black Powerless in Chicago," in Part V.—Eds.]

The critical character of the lack of black participation in decision-making is obvious; control over the centers of decision-making means control over the things about which decisions are made. This includes, of course, such traditional civil rights issues as housing, employment, and education, as well as newer focal points of black protest like the police and the welfare apparatus. As the civil rights movements showed, blacks cannot expect major changes in their political interests when control over the speed, direction, and priorities of change is held by whites who are at best less urgently committed, and at worst openly hostile, to black aims.

A major factor influencing the thrust for black political autonomy is the fact that racism itself has created the conditions for effective black political organization. Residential segregation has meant that, in the black belt South as well as the urban North and West, blacks occupy whole districts en bloc. With the growing influx of blacks to the central cities, and the corresponding exodus of whites to the suburbs, larger and larger areas of the inner cities are developing black majorities. This fact is critical since, as the Chicago study shows, ". . . Negroes simply do not hold legislative posts in city, state, or federal government *unless* they represent a district that is mostly black. No district with Negroes in the minority had a Negro representative, even when Negroes constituted the single largest ethnic group."

In light of these facts, black political organization is both feasible and imperative. Historically, blacks have responded to their political exclusion in America in a variety of ways. There has been a traditional strain of separatism, manifested in schemes for removal to Africa or for setting aside certain areas in the United States for all-black control; several militant groups express similar aims today. For the most part, however, contemporary black protest is oriented to the idea of black community control and/or the development of independent black political bases and a black political party. The response to the idea of "Black Power" has ranged from accusations by black intellectuals of liberal pragmatism and anti-intellectualism, to white criticism of its inherent racism and retreat from the goals of integration. The Kerner Report argued that advocates of Black Power had "retreated into an unreal world," that they had "retreated from a direct confrontation with American society on the issue of integration and, by preaching separatism, unconsciously function as an accommodation to white racism." This argument constitutes a msinterpretation of American political history, of the decline of the civil rights movement, and of the goals of contemporary black protest.

The interpretation of American political history as one of peaceful and orderly inclusion of diverse groups into the polity is inaccurate. We need not recapitulate here. Many groups have used violence as an instrument of social change; some minorities have been forcibly repressed. It is highly unrealistic to depend on the mere goodwill of the larger society to meet black grievances. The idea of black political organization is based on the hard fact that no political order transfers its power lightly and that if blacks are to have a significant measure of political control they must organize into a position of bargaining strength:

> Before a group can enter the open society, it must first close ranks. By this we mean that group solidarity is necessary before a group can operate effectively from a bargaining position of strength in a pluralistic society. Traditionally, each new ethnic group in this society has found the route to social and political viability through the organization of its own institutions with which to represent its needs within the larger society.

The notion that advocates of black autonomy have "retreated from a direct confrontation" with white society "on the issue of integration" is misleading. It ignores both the fact that the decline of the goals of the early civil rights movement came about as the direct result of societal, and especially governmental, inaction, and that blacks may be expected to modify their tactics after decades of such inaction. It also fails to appreciate the fact that black protest now aims, at least in theory, at a transformation of American institutions rather than inclusion into them.

> Thus we reject the goal of assimilation into middle-class America because the values of that class are in themselves anti-humanist and because that class as a social force perpetuates racism. . . . Existing structures . . . must be challenged forcefully and clearly. If this means the creation of parallel community institutions, then that must be the solution. If this means that black parents must gain control over the operation of the schools in the black community, then that must be the solution. The search for new forms means the search for institutions that will, for once, make decisions in the interests of black people.

This is not separatism, nor is it racism. Militant leaders from Malcolm X to Huey P. Newton have stressed the possibility of coalitions with white groups whose aim is radical social change. The Black Panther Party has links with the Peace and Freedom Party, and its candidate, Eldridge Cleaver, ran for President on the Peace and Freedom ticket. For the most part, the new black stance is better described as a kind of militant pluralism, in which not whites, but traditional politics and politicians of both races, are rejected.

Militant Youth

It is for young blacks that the "new spirit of revolutionary militancy" has had special relevance. The Kerner Report observed that there was enough evidence by 1966 to indicate that a large proportion of riot participants were youths. It also suggested that "increasing race pride, skepticism about their job prospects, and dissatisfaction with the inadequacy of their education, caused unrest among students in Negro colleges and high schools." The events of 1968 support and go beyond this finding. The schools are more and more becoming the locus of a whole spectrum of youthful protest, from negotiation to violence. This section attempts to describe the nature of this phenomenon and to account for its significance and apparent increase in the last few years.

The transition from a "civil rights" perspective to a "liberation" perspective has had a profound impact on the ideology and activities of black youth. The following changes are the most significant:

1. The civil rights movement was for the most part nonviolent, directed at Southern racism, and recruited its most active members from the colleges. The new movement has shifted its focus to cities in the North and West, regards nonviolence as only one of many tactics for achieving power and autonomy, and recruits its most active members from high schools as well as colleges.

2. The civil rights movement was concerned with integrating schools, eliminating de facto segregation, and providing equal educational opportunities for blacks. The new move-

ment stresses cultural autonomy, community control of schools, and the development of educational programs which are relevant to black history and black needs.

3. During the civil rights movement, high school youth often participated in demonstrations, sit-ins, and marches. But this participation was limited in terms of activity and responsibility. In recent years, however, youth have become integrated into the liberation movement, often in leadership roles. One of the most significant features of the new militancy is the increasing political consciousness of black youth; this trend is reflected in the formation of Afro-American organizations in high schools and in the proliferation of youth chapters of militant political organizations.

Since 1960, there have been dramatic changes in the character and quantity of high school protests. Even allowing for varying fashions in news reporting and the tendency of the press to underreport nonviolent protest, it is nevertheless evident that there has been a significant increase in militant action among black (and white) high school youth. There are two significant aspects to this new militancy: first, young blacks are now engaging in collective political action and are less involved in internal gang warfare; and second, the educational system is intrinsically important to the movement for liberation because, as it is argued, cultural autonomy and black dignity are only possible if children are taught by persons responsible and sympathetic to the black community.

It is only recently that students have begun to regard themselves as potential power holders in the institutions which they attend. Youthful militants have focused on the school, for it is here that for the first time expectations are cruelly raised and even more cruelly crushed. Whereas the last year has seen increasing protests by middle-class black students in colleges and universities, the high school has been the main target of militant action for lower-class urban youth and for a significant segment of middle-class youth as well. The protests raise many issues: black

student unions, curriculum reforms, black teachers, democratic disciplinary procedures, "soul" food, bussing, boycotts, amnesty for "political" offenders, community control, police brutality, and many others.

High school protests by black students have significantly increased in the last few years. Both middle- and lower-class youth participate in such protests, often with the active support of their parents and local community organizations. The success of boycotts and other instrumental protests suggests the increasing political consciousness of youth. Although interracial violence continues in varying intensity, black and white students occasionally demonstrate more solidarity than they have in the past. "It's the youngsters versus the system," commented the Mayor of Trenton, New Jersey, after a school disorder, "rather than the students versus the students." High school activists have generally impressed school officials with the sophistication and legitimacy of their demands. Despite the general hostility of the white community and press, some ameliorative concessions have been made to black students while more fundamental disputes over school control and decentralization are still being contested.

The pervasiveness and strength of youthful militancy must be appreciated in the context of the black liberation and student movements. Traditional discussions of high school youth have invariably focused on "troublesome" and "abnormal" forms of "acting-out" behavior—disturbances at dances, athletic events, and parties, vandalism, gang fights and disputes over gang territory, etc. Much of this activity was seen as a function of youthful exuberance, or of adolescent restlessness, or of lower-class culture. Theorists and experts have shown a special interest in explaining the negative and pathological attributes of gangs, but they have rarely been concerned with examining collective youth action from a political perspective. There is a strong tendency to regard the political activities of youth in terms of "conspiracy" and "anarchy"—an attitude which underestimates the popular appeal and purposeful character of the student movement.

Similarly, much attention has been directed to the problem of why young people cause so much trouble for the schools, whereas the equally legitimate question of why schools cause so much trouble for youth has been seriously neglected. The problematic aspects of the educational process are widely attributed to students' cultural and family backgrounds, or to their inability to adjust to the demands of school life, or to their failure to cooperate with teachers and school administrators. Fighting, vandalism, truancy, disobedience, and other "disrespectful" behavior are handled as a form of psychological immaturity and cultural primitivism, commonly associated with adolescent "acting-out."

The politicization of black youth reflects the growing political interest of youth in general. More specifically . . . student militancy has its roots in the black liberation movement for political and cultural autonomy. Several years ago, school protests focused almost uniquely on the problem of de facto segregation. Black adults and their children boycotted local schools to protest their failure to comply with federal standards on integration. White crowds, particularly in the South, gathered outside newly integrated schools to jeer, harass, and even attack Negro students. Civil rights organizations engaged student support to protest segregated facilities, but always insisted on the use of nonviolent tactics. In late 1960, for example, a representative of the Southern Christian Leadership Conference predicted a widespread resumption of demonstrations against segregation: "I certainly judge from the students' activity," he said, "that they are mobilizing for a big push in the fall. They are going to find unique ways to apply the technique of nonviolence." Traditional civil rights organizations, especially the NAACP, were quick to condemn violence, even from black youths seeking revenge against white attacks.

The new directions of the black movement have influenced and in turn been influenced by urban, lower-class youth. Separatism has replaced integration as a primary objective, and nonviolence has become for many another tactic of resistance rather than a moral creed. It is the spirit and determination of black youth that moved James Forman to describe the 1960's as the "accelerating generation, a generation of black people determined that they will survive, a generation aware that resistance is the agenda for today and that *action* by people is necessary to quicken the steps of history." The militancy of youth has received considerable support from adults and community organizations. 'If we had done this twenty years ago, our children wouldn't have to be doing this today. These children will make us free."

Perhaps the most significant reason for the militancy of youth is the fact that education is central to the liberation perspective. The Nation of Islam has long recognized the importance of recruiting and socializing a whole new generation of proud and masculine youths:

The education and training of our children must . . . include the history of the black nation, the knowledge of civilizations of man and the Universe, and all sciences. . . . Learning is a great virtue and I would like to see all the children of my followers become the possessors of it. It will make us an even greater people tomorrow.

New militant leaders and students themselves have come to appreciate the value of this perspective, realizing that only through control of the educational system can they build a political movement and instill pride, dignity, self-appreciation, and confidence in black Americans.

The struggle for educational autonomy is both a cultural and political struggle. It is a cultural struggle in the sense that the school can provide youth with an education which gives proper attention to black history and black values, thus providing a positive sense of self-appreciation and identity. But it is also a political struggle, for it is widely felt that the educational system is a predominant means used by those in power to teach people to "unconsciously accept their condition of servitude." According to Edgar Friedenberg, a white sociologist who has written extensively on education, "the school is the instrument through which society acculturates people into consensus before they become old enough to resist it as effectively as they could later." Thus, local control of the educational system will provide an opportunity to build a resistance movement as well as to achieve some cultural independence from the values of white America. "We don't want to be trained in ROTC to fight in a Vietnam war," says one black youth. "We want ROTC to train us how to protect our own communities." Whatever differences may exist between militant black groups, their programs generally speak to self-defense, political independence, community control, and cultural autonomy. These themes challenge American social arrangements at a deeper level than did the movement for "civil rights," and, in doing so, they reveal problematic aspects of our national life which have been taken for granted, at least by whites. Thus, since the publication of the Kerner Report, the thrust of black protest, especially among the young, has shifted from equality to liberation, from integration to separatism, from dependency to power.

CONCLUSION

As we have pointed out, group political violence is not a peripheral or necessarily pathological feature of American political history. For many black Americans today, violent action increasingly seems to offer the only practical and feasible opportunity to overcome the effects of a long history of systematic discrimination. The events of 1968 suggest that violent racial incidents have, at least temporarily, become part of the routine course of events rather than sporadic calamities.

Martin Luther King, Jr., was killed on April 4, 1968. In the aftermath, civil disorders occurred throughout the country, following an already rising incidence of disorder in the first three months of the year. The following facts are significant: (1) The month of April *alone* saw nearly as many disorders as the entire year of 1967, and more cities and states were involved than in all the previous year. (2)

There were more arrests and more injuries in April, 1968, *alone* than in all of 1967, and nearly as much property damage; and there were more National Guard and federal troops called more times in April, 1968, than in all of 1967.

Major riots—none of which, individually, matched in dead or injured the largest riots of the past three years—took place in several cities during the month of April. In Chicago, 9 were killed and 500 injured; in Washington, D.C., 11 died, with 1,113 injuries. There were 6 deaths and 900 injuries in Baltimore, and 6 more deaths in Kansas City, Missouri. Racial violence of some degree of seriousness occurred in 36 states and at least 138 cities.

Considered in isolation, the summer itself was less "hot" than that of the previous year, but it was hardly quiet. Racial violence occurred in July, for example, in Seattle; in Paterson, New Jersey; in Jackson and Benton Harbor, Michigan; in San Francisco and Richmond, California. In Cleveland, a shoot-out between black militants and police ultimately left eleven dead, including three policemen. And any aura of relative quiet over the summer should be dispelled by the fact that racial violence in 1968 did not end with the end of the summer. The opening of schools in the fall was accompanied by an increase in school disorders; sporadic assaults on police, and by police, continue as of this writing in many cities and on college and high school campuses.

Two general points emerge in considering the extent of racial disorder in 1968. First, generally speaking, the violence began earlier and continued longer. The year 1967 also witnessed spring violence, but not to the same degree; and not all of the increase in the spring of 1968 can be attributed to the assassination of Dr. King. It has become more and more difficult to keep track of violent racial incidents.

Second, 1968 represented a new level in the massiveness of the official response to racial disorder. In April alone, as noted, more National Guard troops were called than in all of 1967 (34,900 to 27,700) and more federal troops as well (23,700 to 4,800). *Never* before in this country has such a massive military response been mounted against racial disorder. Troops in the streets of the cities are well on the way to becoming a familiar sight. In one city—Wilmington, Delaware—armed National Guard troops, enforcing a series of harsh anti-riot and curfew provisions, occupied the city from April, 1968, until January, 1969.

Although it is far too early for certainty, limited evidence suggests that the massive ghetto riot—typified by the uprisings in Watts, Newark, and Detroit—may be a thing of the past. None of the disorders of 1968 matches these in scope. The specific explanation for this is far from clear. It lies somewhere in the interaction between more massive and immediate "riot control" efforts by authorities and the apparent perception by many blacks that the "spontaneous riot," as a form of political protest, is too costly in terms of black lives. It is clear that some militant ghetto organizations, such as the Blackstone Rangers in Chicago and the Black Panther Party in Oakland, have made direct and markedly successful efforts to "cool" their communities, especially in the wake of the King assassination. These efforts have been spurred in part by the belief that a riot would provide the opportunity for police attacks on ghetto militants: "We don't want anything to break out that will give them [the police] the chance to shoot us down. They are hoping that we do something like that but we are passing the word to our people to be cool." . . . If this is a genuine trend, the decline of the large-scale riot has important analytical implications. It provides a kind of test for competing perspectives on the sources and meaning of riots. If the decline of riots means the decline of disorders in general, then the view of riots as controllable explosions rooted in black "tension" makes a good deal of sense. If, on the other hand, the decline of the riot means only a change in the character of violent black protest, then the roots of black violence may go deeper and reach more profoundly into the structure of American institutions.

The police and social control agencies increasingly view themselves as the political and military adversaries of blacks. This official militancy has even taken the form of direct attacks on black militant organizations. Black youth has become a special target for governmental and police action. Despite frequent successes in high schools, youthful militancy has often met with tough-minded programs of social control on the part of police and school officials. Most "helping" programs—job training, summer outings, athletic events, tutoring and civic pride projects, etc.—are seasonal and employ short-term recreational strategies to "keep a cool summer" and distract youths from more militant kinds of activities. Some authorities feel, for example, that "riots are unleashed against the community" from high schools and that the granting of concessions to students will only encourage further rioting.

Consistent with this policy, intelligence units are supplementing youth officers within police departments and are developing sophisticated counter-insurgency techniques of gang control. The size of the gang intelligence unit in Chicago has been increased from 38 to 200. Governmental programs on behalf of urban youth rarely involve young people in the decision-making process. A modest program of job training in Chicago which appointed local youth leaders to positions of administrative responsibility was harassed by police and discredited by a Senate investigation. Rather than increasing opportunities for the exercise of legitimate power by adolescents, public agencies have opted for closer supervision as a means of decreasing opportunities for the exercise of illegitimate power.

At the same time, it is clear that the massive national effort, recommended by the Kerner Commission, to combat racism through political and peaceful programs has not materialized and shows few signs of doing so in the near future. Despite widespread agreement with the Commission's insistence that "there can be no higher priority for national action and no higher claim on the nation's conscience," other priorities and other claims still seem to dominate the nation's budget.

43

The Current State of
Black America

Julius Lester

It is difficult to believe that a mere five years
ago the rhetoric of revolution was the language
of black America. So silent is black America
now that *Newsweek* was moved to ask in a
recent cover story: "Where is Black America?"
It is a question being asked by many in black
America, too. Few seem to know, recognizing
only that blacks are not where they were five
years ago, and perhaps will not be there any
time in the foreseeable future. The "revolution" is over; long live Shaft.

The black political movement of the previous decade went through several transforma-
tions in record historical time. In retrospect it
appears that all the political tendencies in
black history converged in the sixties, existing
simultaneously and with varying degrees of
strength, creating a literal explosion in the
American psyche. For a political movement to
begin with sit-ins against segregated public
eating facilities in dime stores in 1960 and
progress to the revolutionary fervor of the
Black Panther Party in a mere eight years is
perhaps too much psycho-historical terrain for
any people to travel so quickly. Yet that is
exactly what occurred.

The early political movement of the
sixties was limited in its political scope and
aim. There was a problem: The lunch

*Julius Lester is Professor of Black Studies at
The University of Massachusetts, Amherst.*

Reprinted from *New Politics*, Vol. X, no. 3 (Spring,
1973). Copyright 1973, NEW POLITICS.

counters were segregated. How was the problem to be solved? Sit-in demonstrations. There
are some now who characterize the sit-ins of
1960–61 as bourgeois. This is an over-simplifi-
cation, for the sit-ins were not aimed at integrating lunch counters as much as at removing the most visible manifestation of the
southern apartheid system. No people can begin to define the nature of the freedom they
want to fight for if their lives are circumscribed on every level by a system which
clearly defines what they can and cannot do,
where they can and cannot go. The sit-in
movement and freedom rides were directed at
removing an imposed prohibition, not at integrating with white people.

The young black southern college students who spearheaded the civil rights movement of 1960–61 and created the Student Non-
Violent Coordinating Committee (SNCC) were
not political sophisticates. They were simply
young men and women who had decided to
say, No more. Their political education was to
come from their own experiences and perhaps
we would not now have to wonder what happened if more of that education had also been
instruction on the dynamics of political movements and American history. It was a practical
education SNCC acquired and the most important part of it in the first year was the realization that segregation was not *the* problem as
had been thought, but only the false front of a
castle of horrors. Nothing would be solved
when blacks could choose or not choose to eat
at lunch counters. An aspect of oppression
would have been alleviated, but the main body
of that oppression would remain untouched.
Oppression emanated from a political and economic system in which blacks were denied
equal participation. Thus, the problem was for
blacks to gain access to the system through
political representation.

So began the next phase: The voter registration campaigns of 1962–64. Into the rural
South young blacks and whites went to organize blacks to register for the vote, run candidates for office and overturn the white
supremacist southern Democratic Party. In the
classical sense, there was nothing revolution-

ary about this. Indeed, even the young organizers recognized that they were functioning within the confines of the Constitution and bourgeois politics. They were not seeking to overturn the system but an aberration of it, so that the system itself might function better through the equal participation of all its citizens. This approach was in the tradition of Frederick Douglass and W. E. B. Du Bois, great protestants, but believers in America, whose protest was against a system functioning improperly and not against the system itself.

Almost simultaneous with the voter registration campaigns, however, another element of black political thought was reintroduced in the North through the personage of Elijah Muhammud and the words of his chief spokesman, Malcolm X. Black separatism, like every aspect of black political thought, has its beginning during the Abolitionist period (1830–1860), and while the separatist philosophy was never widely adhered to, its promise of relief from suffering by separation from the oppressor found a sympathetic, though often secret response from practically all blacks at one time or another. Malcolm X differed from his historical predecessors by being more than a separatist preaching an unclaimed Garden of Eden in Africa.

Malcolm's first impact was as a challenger to Martin Luther King, Jr., the philosophical legatee of Douglass and Du Bois, and his tactic of non-violence. Until Malcolm, no one had dared articulate the right of self-defense if, for no other reason than it meant stepping into the ring with King, the most revered black in American history. Malcolm dared and his challenge went ever farther, for not only did he deride King for his non-violence, he heaped scorn upon the new Moses for wanting to lead his people into the main stream of American life. Malcolm X, particularly after leaving the Nation of Islam, presented a radical analysis of the American political and economic system, and unlike King, who deserves a place on Mount Rushmore for being such a good American, Malcolm maintained that the system functioned as it was designed to function and if blacks were to have any chance at life, liberty and the pursuit of happiness, another system would have to be designed.

During his brief political career, Malcolm frightened more blacks than he attracted and his assassination in the winter of 1965 came as a welcome relief to black America. Though many blacks today would swear on a stack of red, green and black buttons that everyone loved Malcolm while he was alive, it is not true. Malcolm was the Old Testament prophet, articulating visions of Armaggedon, crying in the wilderness but listened to only in the echo of his words from the safety of martyrdom.

Among those few who heard and responded during his lifetime were many of the people in SNCC. His analysis and vigorous articulation of the essential inhumanity of the system was dovetailing neatly with the experiences of the organizers in the South, who were learning that the Federal Government was not particularly interested in having the Fourteenth Amendment upheld if it meant opposing such powerful men of the U.S. Senate as Eastland and Stennis of Mississippi, Long of Louisiana, or McClellan and Fulbright of Arkansas. What could be safer in a democracy than registering people to vote? Theoretically, nothing, but in Mississippi and throughout the South, it could cost you your life. It was to be a while before young people raised as Americans to believe in America's rhetoric, realized that the political reality was not a direct reflection of the rhetoric.

Black bourgeois politics reached its climax with the March on Washington in August, 1963. There at the temple to the Great Emancipator, looking down the Mall toward the Capitol under whose dome slave coffles had marched a mere one hundred and ten years before, Martin Luther King, Jr., delivered a classic speech of platitudinous flatulence which school children now have to learn alongside that other speech of similar nebulous content, the Gettysburg Address. There was nothing wrong with the dream King articulated, except that it revealed just how much of a classic American liberal he was, blind to the realities of a system that used people as if they were mere lumps of coal to be shovelled into the furnace to keep the ship's engines running. Less than a month later when four young girls were killed in the bombing of a church in Birmingham, Alabama, Dr. King's dream seemed like an opium-induced fantasy.

The March on Washington appeared at the time to be a new high for the civil rights movement, but it was actually the funeral, with an appropriate eulogy. Black protest came North in 1963 with demonstrations in many northern cities against *de facto* school segregation and discrimination in labor unions and hiring practices. The blacks of the urban North were a different breed from their southern counterparts who went to jail singing freedomsongs and prayed at demonstrations. The faces of northern blacks reflected a world of concrete skyscrapers, exploitative merchants, rats, roaches and filthy streets. Where the southern black had experienced oppression from whites who were descendants of slave drivers, overseers and plantation owners, the northern black had been subject to descendants of Janus, who smiled with one face while giving orders for their continued subjugation with the other. And it was these northern blacks who would move the civil rights movement from protest to revolution.

The crucial moment began the summer of 1964 at the Democratic Convention in Atlantic City, New Jersey. The civil rights organizers in the South, frustrated in their efforts to open the political system to blacks, decided to take their case to the Democratic Convention and there challenge the all-white delegation from Mississippi as unrepresentative of the state's population. Having been pledged support by politicians within the party as well as influential labor leaders, they went to Atlantic City only to be offered a compromise by the very people they were relying upon. Politics is the art of compromise, said Hubert Humphrey, Walter Reuther and Bayard Rustin, smiling with one mouth as they made deals out of the other. The Mississippi Freedom Democratic Party would accept no compromises and the SNCC workers returned South having learned a bitter lesson: The Democratic Party was in the business of power, not justice.

Having attempted to organize blacks under the umbrella of one of the dominant political parties and been rebuffed, it was but a short step to organizing an independent political party for blacks. Stokely Carmichael went into Lowndes County, Alabama, to organize the Lowndes County Freedom Organization, which took as its symbol a black panther and was dubbed by the press, the Black Panther Party.

While Carmichael and others drove the back roads of Alabama counties, the third strand of black history was introduced. Until August, 1965, most Americans thought watts denoted the intensity of light bulbs. In some remote areas it still may, but most Americans now know it as that sector of Los Angeles, Calif., where a new black protest began. For almost a week, stores were emptied of their merchandise and burned, and policemen were battled with bricks and guns.

It took black political rhetoric almost a year to catch up to Watts, but when in June, 1966 Stokely Carmichael asked a crowd in Greenwood, Mississippi, "What do you want?," and they, having been carefully prepared by SNCC organizers, shouted back, "Black Power!," a new day had come. Of all the threads of black political thought, the revolutionary one is the most tenuous. David Walker's *Appeal* (1827) was the first document calling for the violent overthrow of slavery and, though the impulse to destroy slavery by force was strong among the slaves, this was revolution aimed at a system within the American system. Once slavery was ended, most blacks settled down quickly to what would be the impossible task of getting into the system. Although black history is dotted with a few socialist thinkers and writers advocating the replacement of capitalism, their influence was small and followings were negligible.

The black revolutionary movement of the

late sixties was new in black history and was a response to an unresponsive system. The slogan, Black Power, was a shorthand articulation of what was required if the needs of the people were to be alleviated—power in the hands of blacks. Since the system had proven itself unwilling to share its power, black had to take power for themselves. That meant revolution.

Carmichael and the SNCC of 1966 were the children of Malcolm X, with whom many of them had had intimate personal contact. It was through him, as well as several trips to Africa members of the organization had taken, that changed SNCC from an organization fighting for civil rights under the law to one which saw itself and the black struggle as a part of a worldwide revolutionary struggle. But a few months before its enunciation of Black Power, SNCC had taken a bolder step when, in January 1966, it issued a statement opposing the Vietnam war and linking the liberation movement in South Vietnam with the struggle of blacks in this country.

As a philosophy, Black Power had two essential parts. The first has already been capsulized—the necessity to acquire the necessary power to make the decisions governing the lives of blacks. The second explored the black aspect of that power. Malcolm X had articulated a nationalist position, emphasizing the uniqueness of black culture and the necessity for black people to have an identity based on not only an acceptance but an exaltation of that culture. Carmichael picked up this theme and with the urban rebellions as a backdrop, it took root as it had never done before. Cultural nationalism has its roots in the thought of Martin Delaney, the 19th century Abolitionist who is considered to be "the father of black nationalism." Marcus Garvey is undoubtedly the greatest exemplar of cultural nationalism with a separatist ideology. So, Carmichael's admonition that "black is beautiful" was not new. The overwhelming response to it was, however.

Through cultural nationalism blacks had a means to express their alienation from the American psyche and their desire to establish something different. It was a psychological break with America and never again would a black poet write as Langston Hughes once had, "Let America be America again." Yet ironically, it was to be in the illusory glory of cultural nationalism that blacks were to get trapped.

Simultaneously with the rise of cultural nationalism, black revolutionary politics reached its apex in Rap Brown, Carmichael's successor as leader of SNCC, and the Black Panther Party, a California-based organization which had taken its name and symbol from the Lowndes County Freedom Organization. Organized by Huey Newton and Bobby Seale, the BPP was, at first, a self-defense group patrolling the Oakland community with shotguns as deterrents to police violence against blacks. The Party itself became the target of the police and Newton was shot and arrested on a charge of killing a policeman. With Newton in prison, leadership of the Party was assumed by Eldridge Cleaver, a recent parolee from the California prison system. Under him the Party's membership and national position increased rapidly. In their black jackets and black berets, the Panthers looked like junior guerrillas or an improvisational theater troupe. However, most policemen had had no contact with the latter and assuming they were the former, the police did as police will.

The Black Panther Party was a curious anomaly in black history, for it was the first national black Marxist-Leninist organization. With its class analysis, Marxism-Leninism had very little chance of being accepted by blacks, particularly at the historic moment when blacks were beginning to achieve a cultural identity for the first time in their history. Yet, with their little red books, the BPP preached Maoist revolution to audiences of white college students, but never found real support among blacks. Huey Newton has since acknowledged that the Party made a mistake in its strong advocacy of a Marxist-Leninist ideology and blames Cleaver for this. He is correct, for an examination of Newton's writings and Seale's *Seize the Time* reveal a very different political ideology than that espoused by Cleaver. Newton and Seale were more democratic socialists than revolutionaries, the American press to the contrary.

Cleaver's revolutionary rhetoric and posturing was unfortunate not only in and of itself, but it was contrary to the change taking place in the American political mood. By 1968 white America had tired of black protest, student rebellions, revolutionary rhetoric and police forces across the country underlined the mood in what seemed to be an organized campaign to rid America of the Panthers. Organized or not it succeeded. Members of the Party were murdered, arrested and jailed and when Cleaver faced arrest and a return to prison, he chose exile and the Party declined.

The election of Nixon brought not only repression of the Panthers but of radicals in general. A revolutionary organization, however, gathers strength and support from its successes and its ability to survive and insure the lives of its members. The Panthers and smaller black revolutionary groups were obviously unable to withstand the repression and while blacks were outraged by it, they looked upon the Panthers as fellow-sufferers, not liberators. The Panthers made it clear that the price of revolution was high. Perhaps too high. To have one's revolutionary commitment judged by one's willingness to die was more than a little macabre to a lot of blacks who, though oppressed, are as much enamored of life as anyone else.

By the spring of 1970 when Cambodia was invaded by U.S. and South Vietnamese forces and the students were killed at Kent State and Jackson State, it was apparent that hardly any of the political elements which had created the political ferment of the sixties survived. King was dead and the civil rights movement passé; Carmichael was living in Guinea; Rap Brown was underground; Cleaver was in Algeria and the Panthers in disarray.

However, cultural nationalism had survived, for it was a most effective chameleon.

Cultural nationalism is not an ideology but an apolitical attitude, which cuts across political distinctions, adapting itself to each and everyone. Unfortunately, black America, almost narcissistically glorying in its blackness, was in no mood to recognize the web of illusion in which it was garbing itself. Thus, under the guise of cultural nationalism, black bourgeois politics reasserted itself and it was stronger than ever. Enough blacks were elected to the House of Representatives that a Congressional Black Caucus was formed. Out of Chicago came a young minister who, before King was cold in his grave, was being called his successor. Rev. Jesse Jackson was articulate, handsome and forceful, and preached an economic nationalism which had its roots in Booker T. Washington. The third national leader to emerge was Immamu Baraka, a poet-playwright, who returned to his hometown of Newark, New Jersey and played a key role in organizing the election of Newark's first black mayor. Baraka was a curious nationalist, though. While politically defining himself as a Pan-Africanist and organizing a Pan-African Congress in Atlanta in 1970, he was not adverse to becoming deeply involved in local politics. It was a well-disguised bourgeois politics, but bourgeois politics it was.

The fourth, and perhaps most influential force was the quietest—the Nation of Islam, commonly called the Black Muslims. When the dust settled from the explosive sixties, blacks looked around and noticed that the only organization which had survived and even flourished was the Nation. Most important, it was the one organization with a clearly defined and viable program which it was executing. Other nationalists talked about "nation-building." The Muslims, with their supermarkets, University, schools, farms, etc., seemed to be trying to do it. Most impressive was the fact that they were doing it without the aid of press conferences and interviews in the white press.

Today, the Nation of Islam, without a doubt, remains the most important and influential organization. It satisfies the psychological need of blacks for an identity, while at the same time offering fulfillment through working to make the Nation's program concrete. Its membership numbers are secret, but they are far larger than one might think. And there are few non-Muslim blacks who do not admire the Muslims, respect them and support them spiritually.

The dominant political thought remains cultural nationalism, but except for small groups of separatists, cultural nationalism has merged with bourgeois politics to produce Shirley Chisholms and Richard Hatchers, politicians who work within the context of the Democratic Party.

What has happened follows an almost classical dynamic. The proletariat rebelled in the mid to late sixties and was suppressed by police violence. The ruling class, recognizing that some changes would be necessary if it were to continue to rule, offered reforms (Federal poverty programs, job-hiring, television shows and movies) for which only the bourgeoisie had the necessary education and skills. The bourgeoisie accepted and now, with a stake in the system, supports the American status quo. This formula breaks down, however, when one realizes that the black middle class is seriously disaffected from America. That psychological break which occurred with the acceptance of cultural nationalism was real and nowhere more real than among the black middle-class. But until a viable political philosophy and program are presented, the black bourgeoisie and its political potential will be siphoned off by bourgeois politicians.

The black college students of the Seventies are almost the exact opposite of their activist predecessors of the Sixties. Affected and shaped by the Sixties, most of them are asking with *Newsweek*, "What happened?" Because there are no answers forthcoming, they drift, wanting to do something and not knowing what. They are overripe for political exploitation and manipulation by the first demagogue who can penetrate their apathy and speak to their discontent. They represent a danger not to the system but to the black community itself.

Black bourgeois politics is doomed to be the tailend of the American political system. President Nixon's political analysts in preparing for the 1972 elections saw clearly that blacks were hopelessly disorganized and politically ineffective and could be safely disregarded. Whatever political strength blacks once had depended on the old Democratic labor-liberal-black alignment. With the demise of that, blacks are once more servants in the halls of Tara.

In the spring of 1972 there was an attempt to forge a black political unity at a black political convention in Gary. Engineered by Baraka and headed by him, the convention was hailed in the black press as being the beginning of a new day, etc., etc., etc. In the year since, such assessments have shown themselves to be the result of wishful thinking and poor political judgment. Nothing has come from the Gary meeting and nothing will, because race alone is not a basis for political unity and can never be. Unity begins with the recognition of a common problem and as long as some blacks think the problem is whites, and others are sure it's the economic system, and still others are convinced that there isn't a problem that can't be solved by one more black Congressman, any talk of unity is absurd.

Thus, black America is fragmented and less politically involved than at any time in the past fifteen years. Yet, conditions continue to worsen. The black urban communities are economically depressed; schools in these communities deteriorate, along with housing, sanitation services and the availability of jobs. With Nixon cutting back Federal domestic programs, the situation can only worsen.

This, however, is crucial. Nixon is, in a way, doing blacks a favor. Since the days of FDR blacks have looked to the Federal government for the social legislation and funds to remedy its problems. Nixon reads the mood of America correctly when he says that the government will no longer play Big Daddy. Thus, blacks are shoved out into the cold. Yet, if one looks at it another way, blacks may be forced to come out of the slough of dependency on the Federal government once and for all and devise the programs they need. Almost forty years ago, W. E. B. Du Bois advocated economic planning for the black community by blacks. And in forty years blacks have become more and more wards of State. Today, all black leaders from Baraka to the Congressional Caucus are decrying the Nixon cutbacks instead of sensing an opportunity to create a viable political and economic alternative.

The dependency relationship of blacks to the Federal government has roots deeper than FDR, however. Indeed, it is a legacy from slavery and is, perhaps, so deeply ingrained into the black psyche that most fear to see it and call it by name. It is easier to board a chartered bus and go to Washington to picket for the return of OEO than it is to organize food cooperatives within apartment houses.

But the telling point of the black political movement of the sixties, all elements of it, was how little it related programatically to the economic problems of black America. No major organization of the sixties acted in concert with the National Welfare Rights Organization. The Black Panther Party has been the one group to attempt to speak to the problem of economic deprivation but it has done so with classic liberal paternalism, providing free breakfast programs, etc., instead of creating the mechanisms within the community which will allow the people to provide for themselves. Huey Newton now calls himself "Supreme Servant of the People," but revolutions don't need Head Waiters.

The one optimistic note may be the Black Worker's Congress, based in Detroit. At least it is concerning itself with the black working class, something no organization of the sixties attempted to do in any organized way. And perhaps out of the Congress will come, in a decade or two, the basis for an actual revolutionary force as opposed to the ephemeral one of the sixties.

The prognosis for the near future is, however, bleak. There is no evident creative leadership in black America, and no one developing a revolutionary analysis. However, it is axiomatic that people revolt when there is a sign of hope. The revolutionary movement of the sixties created hope and left it unfulfilled. Nothing is more cruel than for people to have hope for significant change and be left with used sawdust. It will be a long time before anyone can talk revolution to blacks and be listened to.

In the final analysis, the fate of black America is inextricable from that of America itself. Those who maintained that blacks were the revolutionary vanguard were mistaken; they are merely the shock troops. As bitter a pill as it is to swallow, blacks cannot make a revolution alone; even more galling is the fact that the white majority has the power and will always have the power to determine just how far blacks go, just how much they get. Black revolution depends upon an American revolution. Perhaps the real question is, what is the current state of white America?

44

Freedom for the American Indian

ALVIN M. JOSEPHY, JR.

During the last few years there has been an outpouring of information on American Indians. Books and magazine articles; radio and television documentaries, discussions, and commentaries; movies; and newspaper reports and editorials have focused attention with new and more accurate perspectives on Indian cultural backgrounds, Indian-white history, and present-day Indian needs and aspirations.

One result is that non-Indian Americans today are more understanding than they have ever been of the Indian side of what happened in the *past*. The Native Americans who resisted the intruding whites from the time of Jamestown and Plymouth to the last battle on the plains are now seen as patriotic peoples who struggled righteously for their lives, lands, freedom, religious beliefs, and means of livelihood. Although Indian scholars, still to come, will add breadth and depth to the record from their own cultural and tribal insights, the long history of past shame is clear for all who will read or listen.

Despite all that has been written and said, however, what is more important to the contemporary Indian—his own problems, wants, and goals of *today*, not of the past—

Alvin M. Josephy, Jr. is a vice president and senior editor with American Heritage Publishing Company.

seems still confusing to most non-Indian Americans, not alone among the nation's opinion makers and the general public, but in the areas of the federal government that deal with Indian affairs. As a result, sound and harmonious relations between Indians and non-Indians appear to many people to be as elusive today as they were to the whites and Native Americans of the past.

The fault is often ascribed to two principal gaps in thinking, one historic and the other cultural. On the historical level, the non-Indian has become aware of what happened in the past, but he feels that that is all over and cannot be undone, and that the Indian of 1973—a full century after Custer—should "shape up" and be like everyone else. The continuation of reservations puzzles him. Are they concentration camps, or what? He is mystified by the special relationship between the federal government and the Indians that seems to perpetuate, at one and the same time, an incompetent, sometimes corrupt bureaucratic rule by Washington over the Indians, and a helpless, but apparently willing, dependence by the Indians on the federal treasury. Why does it go on? Who is at fault?

The Indians, at the same time, view history differently. Once, they knew, they were free people, thoroughly capable of governing themselves, and all of the present-day United States was theirs. The white man subjugated and dispossessed them. The small portions of land that were left to them (land that had never belonged to anyone else)—or that were given to them by the government, because all of their own territory had been stolen from them—were set aside as reservations for their sole possession and use, with guarantees made to them in solemn treaties that the federal government would protect these reservations for as long as the Indians wished. As payment for the land that was taken, the government promised services—education, health facilities, vocational training, roads, and so forth.

There are about 1,000,000 Indians in the United States today (the estimates of their pre-Columbian population in the same area range from 850,000 up to 9,800,000). About half of them live on reservations and half in urban and rural areas. But almost all of them consider themselves the descendants and inheritors of the peoples who made the treaties with the federal government. To them, not only is the history of the past very much alive, but they are the continuers of that history. Small as their numbers may be, they are the Indian past that is still running like an unbroken thread through our body politic and through many present-day concerns. The land of the reservations is all they have left, but it is still theirs and no one else's. Although it is only a token of what they once had, it is sacred to them for what it means as the repository of their tribal culture, history, and traditions; the burial grounds of their fathers; the homes of their families; the last tie they possess with their mother, the Earth, and with all of nature; the firm root of their existence as Indians and tribal peoples; and the basis of whatever prospects they have for a future as Indians. Their history, up to the present day, has been one of struggle to force the government to live up to its treaty promises and protect the reservations against the erosions and exploitation of non-Indians. Far from being concentration camps, in short, the reservations are beloved and guarded as homelands by the tribes, and the people can come and go from them as they please.

This sense of an unbroken connection with the historic past reflects the first gap of information between Indians and non-Indians. The Indian is very much aware of the details of the treaties and promises made to his ancestors; the white man, in or out of government, is not. The Indian is also aware of the details of federal-Indian relations from the time when the treaties were made. They include broken promises; zigzagging policies of different administrations in Washington; frauds, lies, and injustices by the score; stern rule by tyrannical agents, missionaries, and army officers; punishments; denial of rations; the stamping out of native languages, religion, and culture; the shanghaiing of children for enforced attendance at distant white men's schools; the smashing of tribal institutions,

values, and standards, and the substitution of alien forms; the bringing of poverty with no solutions; and, finally, prejudice, persecutions, neglect, aimlessness, and death. The Indians knew this history, year by year, on one reservation after another. The whites know it only vaguely—in stereotypes and fuzzy generalizations, no more graphic than was the list just recited. The Indian therefore knows exactly what he would like to end; the white man would agree that it should be ended, but he is not exactly sure of what—other than poverty—there is to end.

The cultural gap between Indians and non-Indians is even wider than the historical. Since 1924, Indians have been citizens of the United States. They have the vote and in almost all ways except the most important—the possession of freedom (to be discussed later)—they are considered like all other Americans. They need, use, and enjoy the material traits of modern-day civilization. Some of them are thoroughly acculturated, and even assimilated, into the white man's society. Many are truly bicultural, at home on reservations but equally able to get on in white men's cities. But almost all of them are knowingly and feelingly still Indians, possessors of cultural values, standards, and beliefs that they inherited from their peoples and that differ profoundly from those of the non-Indians.

A whole literature exists on Indian life and beliefs. They differed in some ways from tribe to tribe, but there were many samenesses. The Indians' concepts of their relations to their fellowmen, to the supernatural, and to nature and the Earth were basically somewhat similar among tribes in all areas of the Western Hemisphere. To non-Indians, with a background of Judeo-Christian religion and philosophy and Western European socioeconomic and political development, Indian ways were different and, therefore, inferior. Cooperation rather than competition; group orientation rather than personal ambition; stewardship of nature rather than its conquest; brotherhood with all creation rather than dominion over it—these were just a few among many of the

Indians' ways which were brushed aside and ignored by the white conqueror.

But they did not die. The cultural values, too, are part of the Indian thread that still runs through the United States, believed in and observed by peoples of Indian blood and background, whether they live on reservations or in cities. The proof of their ability to endure exists strikingly in the Atlantic coastal states where Indian tribes were smashed into small and powerless fragments, then overrun, absorbed, and forgotten by non-Indians long before the American Revolution Today their descendants have emerged as cohesive groups —Penobscots, Micmacs, Malecites, Passamaquoddies in Maine; Wampanoags in Massachusetts; Narragansets in Rhode Island; Niantics, Pequots, Mohegans, and others in Connecticut; Patchogues, Shinnecocks, and Montauks, among others, in New York; Chickahominys, Powhatans, and Rappahannocks in Virginia; Croatans (descendants, perhaps, of those who absorbed Raleigh's "Lost Colony" in 1587) in North Carolina; and many others—still Indians, still proud of their tribal heritages, still clinging to their ancestral cultural values—which continue to be markedly different from those of the rest of American society.   •

If those values have persisted in the East among people who have been overrun and submerged by the white man for more than two centuries, then how strong they must still be among the more recently conquered peoples, like the Sioux, Cheyenne, Navajos, and many dozens of others in the West, who continue to observe such spiritual ceremonies as the Sun Dance, use their own curers and purify themselves with the sweat bath, go on vision quests, and honor their holy men. And how impossible, it seems to imply, it has been—and will be—for the white man to eradicate them and turn the Indian fully into a white man, living in complete accordance with the white man's cultural values.

Almost all Indians (and, in fairness, some white men) have viewed such an effort as immoral and, indeed, incredibly shortsighted and self-defeating. But the drive and power of the dominant culture have shown neither interest in, nor patience with, the Indians' ways. The white man has not cared to understand Indian culture, much less consider that it could co-exist with his own, and he is totally at sea when the Indian clothes his words and actions in terms of his own culture, as he did recently in stating his purposes during the occupations of Alcatraz Island, the Bureau of Indian Affairs Building in Washington, D.C., and the region of Wounded Knee in South Dakota. There was, of course, nothing novel about the white man's reactions to each of these confrontations. He viewed them as lawless outbursts by radical minorities among the Indians and missed the point entirely that though they were desperate attempts (the only methods left to the Indians) to call the nation's attention to their terrible oppression and suffering (something many whites did understand), they were even more important as efforts to break the bonds of their yearnings to save themselves as Indians by saving their Indian cultural traditions and heritage. Not all Indians approved of the militant and violent tactics and damage at the Bureau of Indian Affairs and at Wounded Knee. But most Indians knew what it was all about, agreed with the aims of the occupiers, and prayed for their safety and success.

In a sense, those recent Indian-white confrontations, accompanied by patronization, brutal insensitivity, and lack of understanding on the part of too many whites who were involved, illuminated the depth of the historical and cultural gaps that still separate Indians and non-Indians. In a way, also, they climaxed the long centuries of a misguided white policy toward Indians that began in the first English colonies on the Atlantic. Until 1890, it was one of assimilate or die. Since then, and until today, it has been assimilate or stagnate in poverty. Both ideas, one a continuation of the other, have been at the heart of the nation's Indian policy since the first Administration of George Washington. The most benign concept of white men toward Indians has been that of saving them by turning them, as quickly as possible, into white men—Christianizing them, settling them down as farmers or mechanics, cutting their hair, clothing them as whites, educating them without reference to their own history, culture, language, or background, and getting them to disappear as white men in the white man's world. Programs changed from one administration to the next, but each was designed to speed up the assimilation process—and each, in turn, failed. As part of the process, the Indian was stripped and robbed of whatever might impede assimilation—among them, his freedom of religion, his tribal institutions, his mythology and artistic inheritance, and his land and resources. In 1934 he regained his religious freedom. But assimilation is still the aim of national Indian policy. Hobbled by the historic and cultural gaps which perpetuate his ignorance and confusion about the Indians' real needs and goal, the non-Indian American continues to view assimilation as the best—indeed, the only—destiny for the Indians. He gives this as a mandate to the federal government, which through appropriate committees in Congress and the Bureau of Indian Affairs (the executive branch's agency in the Department of the Interior charged with handling relations with the Indians), persists in trying to carry it out. In the process, Indian lands and resources, the basis for continued Indian life, are not protected (the whittling away of Indian assets increasing, of course, Indian poverty), and Indian self-determination, even though proclaimed as an Administration goal by President Nixon in July, 1970, is frustrated.

Serious as they have been as impediments blocking the non-Indians' understanding and support of Indian aims, the historic and cultural gaps obfuscated the actual mainspring of the nation's traditional Indian policy and the true motive behind the drive to force Indian assimilation. Stated bluntly, it has been —and continues to be—the acquisitive greed for Indian lands and resources. Many non-Indians undoubtedly believe that the era when the Indians were defrauded and cheated of their lands is over. But the facts are the opposite. Indians have never been permitted rest in their fight to save what they have. Today the assault against the reservations is more massive and threatening to them than at any time in the recent past. Dams are flooding the best parts of their lands. Rights-of-way for railroad lines, transmission lines, highways, and other facilities are slicing through the reservations. Leases for huge real estate developments, white men's resorts, coal strip mines, and power, gasification, and petrochemical plants are being approved for the reservations by the Department of the Interior.

All these developments, plumped down on top of the Indians, industrializing their lands, and making less of the reservation available for them, may be viewed as hastening assimilation. But that is putting the cart before the horse. The real effect is that the reservations are being taken away from the Indians and turned into white men's domains. The methods used, moreover, are the same as those of the past. The Navajos, Hopis, Crows, Northern Cheyennes, and many others have all been victimized by fraud, cheating, lies, and deceit in the leasing of their lands and resources during the last few years.

Scores of Indians are articulate today in expressing their people's needs and demands. Individuals, tribes, and regional and national Indian organizations have grown expert in using the white man's own media to try to communicate what they want. In time, they will undoubtedly bridge the historic and cultural gaps, bringing non-Indians to see their destiny as they see it. But achieving that destiny will be impossible until the mainspring of national Indian policy is, so to speak, smashed, and the taking of Indian lands and resources is checked. The only instrument with which this can be accomplished is what all Americans, save Indians, possess: freedom. Without it, as they now are, their lands, lives, decisions, and fate are at the mercy of a government primarily responsive to outside aggrandizers. Without it, their boundaries of existence narrow and their future as Indians shrivels. To the Indians, there is method in the determination of the government, up to now, to talk self-determination and freedom for them, but in practice to deny it.

What is the relation of the government to the Indians that denies them freedom? In 1934, the Indian Reorganization Act imposed on almost every tribe in the country a uniform type of government, modeled after the white man's ways, with constitutionally-elected tribal officers, a tribal council, or legislature, and tribal courts. For most tribes, it was a tragic mistake. The Indians were used to their own traditional forms of government—whether by clan leaders, traditional chiefs, councils of elders, or some other group or individual— and, in large numbers, they resented and boycotted the alien system that was foisted on them. Constitutions were accepted by small voting minorities in many tribes, and to this day the tribal governments are divisive institutions on numerous reservations, ignored by majorities of the people. Worse still, the powers of the Indian governments were limited. Over all important matters, the Bureau of Indian Affairs maintained absolute control, with the right to approve or veto. Much like the native legislatures in British colonial governments, the tribal councils became little more than ceremonial rubber stamps for the real authority that lay with the white man.

As a consequence, the tribal governments became responsive, and responsible, to the Bureau of Indian Affairs, rather than to their own people. The Bureau, in turn, being responsible to Congress for "no trouble on the reservations," ran the tribes in collusion with pliant and venal tribal officers who basked in the prestige and petty rewards of their positions. This situation, in which reservation peoples often refer to their officeholders as "Uncle Tomahawks" and "Apples" (red outside, white inside), has perpetuated dependence, dulled initiative, and made a sham of real self-determination. Though the present administration regards the tribal councils as the organs of Indian freedom, the real boss is still the Bureau of Indian Affairs.

The question of the authority of the Bureau has been muddied by its position as trustee of Indian lands and resources, a function which almost every tribe wishes it to continue to fulfill. How, asks the Bureau, can we give up ultimate authority and still act responsibly as trustee? The answer lies in an analogy. A bank can be a trustee for a white man's money or property, carry out that function with or without consultation with its client, and have no authority over any other part of that person's life. But, beginning with its trust responsibility over tribal property, the federal government, through the Bureau of Indian Affairs, has insidiously extended its governance over every other portion of an Indian's life. To be convinced, one has only to sit for a day in the outer office of a Bureau agency on any reservation and see the stream of Indians coming in, hat in hand, for advice, approval, and permission in a hundred personal and varied matters. Relatively few Indians turn to their own tribal institutions. They go to the government for approval of wills, for advice on travel, and for a weekly or monthly allowance doled out to them arbitrarily from part of the rental receipts from land leased to whites.

With great truth, Warren H. Cohen and Philip J. Mause wrote in the *Harvard Law Review* in June, 1968: "Although normal expectation in American society is that a private individual or group may do anything unless it is specifically prohibited by the government, it might be said that the normal expectation on the reservation is that the Indians may not do anything unless it is specifically permitted by the government."

This is not freedom.

As a result of the confrontations at the Bureau of Indian Affairs Building and at Wounded Knee, federal-Indian relations are today in a state of crisis. The Indians have made known their needs and demands, but Administration officials and Congress—either through lack of understanding, or because of a determination not to lose control of the Indians and their resources, have responded so far with proposals that are superficial and relatively meaningless—little more than a moving around of chairs, so to speak. None of their reactions go to the heart of relations between the Indians and the federal government, and nothing they propose can therefore succeed in satisfying the Indians or the challenges that the Indians have raised.

Yet the time for a revolutionary change in federal-Indian relations is here and now. The Indians have expressed it, and the form of that change can be stated in the following terms:

1) Within every town, city, county, and state, free Americans have local governments of their own choosing, free of interference by the federal government. Their systems of mayors, town managers, city councils, or whatever, are their own business. Federal officials or agents may be in those areas to carry out the delivery of federal programs to local citizen groups, who may be considered the clients or beneficiaries of the programs. But the local affairs of the people are not the concern of the federal personnel. If there is a local political problem, the people have the means through their own systems of government to handle it themselves. Their governments normally are responsive and accountable to the people. In times of local conflict, the federal officials sit in a corner and read a newspaper. The problem is not theirs.

The Indian tribes must attain the same level of freedom. The dominant society must stand back and enable the people of each tribe to create governments of their own choosing with the full freedom to manage and control their own affairs. If such governments are established, they will of necessity be responsive and responsible to their individual peoples and will provide the basis for what is now missing: The enforcement of the government's trusteeship obligations over lands and resources; protection of treaty rights; the design and execution of development programs that the people really want and will make succeed; educational and other institutions that have meaning for their people; contracting with nongovernmental, as well as governmental, agencies for technical assistance, credit, and services; and the effective safeguarding of their people against discrimination, abuse, and injustices.

2) Simultaneously, the Bureau of Indian Affairs must be stripped of its authority over the tribes and become, in fact as well as in theory, a service organization, limited in its functions to the delivery of expertise, services, and credit to Indian clients at their request. The present status of the Bureau, on reflection, is ludicrous. In effect, it is charged with being an entire supergovernment over the tribes, with departments and individuals supposedly expert in every phase of modern-day community activity and individual life. It must be expert on the reclamation of stripmined land, on the buying of school books, on marital problems, on water rights law, on the harvesting of timber, on corporate relations, on the hiring of a lawyer, and on tens of thousands of other matters, many of them vital to Indian concerns. All these spheres of expertise are often centered in one all-powerful bureaucrat or in a small group of his assistants, whose judgments are often autocratically imposed on the Indians, whether they are right or wrong, wanted or unwanted. It is an impossibility to be so infallible, not only in so small an agency, but in one in which mediocrity and incompetence have been hallmarks.

When a tribe needs technical assistance for its people, it should have the freedom to seek the best and, by contract underwritten by the federal government, make its own arrangements with the private, as well as the public sector. But the most important principle must be one, again, of freedom: the B.I.A. personnel, as well as all federal officials, must relate to the Indians and their governments on nontrustee affairs in the same manner in which federal agents relate to non-Indian citizens and their local governments. In Indian matters, they should no longer be permitted to take sides, and they should not have the right to interfere. Their sole duties should be to deliver services adequately funded by the federal government as guaranteed by treaties.

In such a state of affairs, with totally free governments of their own choosing, and with the right to manage and control their own lives as they see fit, Indian initiative will inevitably be unfettered. Compared with the past and present record of the white man thinking for the Indian and doing everything for him—a record replete with maladministration, petty tyranny, and failure—the future will seem like an age of miracles. Even if there are mistakes, internal conflicts, and inefficiency, it can be no worse than what has been and what is. Moreover, it will be the Indians' own business; they have the right, like everyone else, to make mistakes and, by making them, learn and gain experience. If they have truly accountable governments, with such safeguards as methods for referendums, the handling of corruption, and the protection of individual and tribal rights, all must ultimately be far superior to what now exists.

3) To carry out the trustee function, a special management-and-legal apparatus should be created within the federal government, separate from the B.I.A. service delivery organization, responsible to the Indians alone, and charged with a commitment to the trust obligation. Its functions must be the management of trustee affairs and the determined protection of tribal lands, water rights, and mineral and other resources. Its relationship to the Indians should approximate that of a bank and lawyer to their client, and it should have nothing to do with any other phase of the Indians' life.

This relationship between the federal government and the Indians would provide the underpinnings for the settling and solving of all other matters. There are numerous demands of a bewildering variety that must be negotiated between free Indians and the federal government. The Indians participating in "The Trail of Broken Treaties," which occupied the Bureau of Indian Affairs Building in October, 1972, presented the government with a set of twenty demands which should provide guidelines for such negotiations. They include, among other points, a review and rectification of broken treaties; the enforcement of treaty rights; the re-establishment of a treaty-making relationship between the tribes and the government; and the inclusion of off-reservation Indians and members of tribes not now federally recognized as recipients of programs for Indians.

What has been proposed here is not in conflict with any Indian demand. It is addressed to the non-Indian, in and out of government, who is confused about the present status of the Indian and the substance of what he wants. It calls only for Indian freedom—the prerequisite for meaningful negotiations for everything else.

45

White Ethnic

Michael Novak

Growing up in America has been an assault upon my sense of worthiness. It has also been a kind of liberation and delight.

There must be countless women in America who have known for years that something is peculiarly unfair, yet who have found it only recently possible, because of Women's Liberation, to give tongue to their pain. In recent months, I have experienced a similar inner thaw, a gradual relaxation, a willingness to think about feelings heretofore shepherded out of sight.

I am born of PIGS—those Poles, Italians, Greeks, and Slavs, non-English-speaking immigrants, numbered so heavily among the workingmen of this nation. Not particularly liberal, nor radical, born into a history not white Anglo-Saxon and not Jewish—born outside what in America is considered the intellectual mainstream. And thus privy to neither power nor status nor intellectual voice.

Those Poles of Buffalo and Milwaukee—so notoriously taciturn, sullen, nearly speechless. Who has ever understood them? It is not that Poles do not feel emotion: what is their history if not dark passion, romanticism, betrayal, courage, blood? But where in America

Michael Novak is consultant in the humanities to The Rockefeller Foundation.

is there anywhere a language for voicing what a Christian Pole in this nation feels? He has no Polish culture left him, no Polish tongue. Yet Polish feelings do not go easily into the idiom of happy America, the America of the Anglo-Saxons and, yes, in the arts, the Jews. (The Jews have long been a culture of the word, accustomed to exile, skilled in scholarship and in reflection. The Christian Poles are largely of peasant origin, free men for hardly more than a hundred years.) Of what shall the man of Buffalo think, on his way to work in the mills, departing from his relatively dreary home and street? What roots does he have? What language of the heart is available to him?

The PIGS are not silent willingly. The silence burns like hidden coals in the chest.

All four of my grandparents, unknown to one another, arrived in America from the same county in Slovakia. My grandfather had a small farm in Pennsylvania; his wife died in a wagon accident. Meanwhile, a girl of fifteen arrived on Ellis Island, dizzy, a little ill from witnessing births and deaths and illnesses aboard the crowded ship, with a sign around her neck lettered "PASSAIC." There an aunt told her of the man who had lost his wife in Pennsylvania. She went. They were married. Inheriting his three children, each year for five years she had one of her own; she was among the lucky, only one died. When she was twenty-two, mother of seven, her husband died. And she resumed the work she had begun in Slovakia at the town home of a man known to us now only as "the Professor": she housecleaned and she laundered.

I heard this story only weeks ago. Strange that I had not asked insistently before. Odd that I should have such shallow knowledge of my roots. Amazing to me that I do not know what my family suffered, endured, learned, hoped these past six or seven generations. It is as if there were no project on which we all have been involved. As if history, in some way, began with my father and with me.

Let me hasten to add that the estrangement I have come to feel derives not only from a lack of family history. All my life, I have been made to feel a slight uneasiness when I must say my name. Under challenge in grammar school concerning my nationality, I had been instructed by my father to announce proudly: "American." When my family moved from the Slovak ghetto of Johnstown to the WASP suburb on the hill, my mother impressed upon us how well we must be dressed, and show good manners, and behave—people think of us as "different" and we mustn't give them any cause. "Whatever you do, marry a Slovak girl," was other advice to a similar end: "They cook. They clean. They take good care of you. For your own good."

When it was revealed to me that most movie stars and many other professionals had abandoned European names in order to feed American fantasies, I felt only a little sadness. One of my uncles, for business reasons and rather late in life, changed his name too, to a simple German variant. Not long, either, after World War II.

Nowhere in my schooling do I recall an attempt to put me in touch with my own history. The strategy was clearly to make an American of me. English literature, American literature, and even the history books, as I recall them, were peopled mainly by Anglo-Saxons from Boston (where most historians seemed to live). Not even my native Pennsylvania, let alone my Slovak forebears, counted for very many paragraphs. I don't remember feeling envy or regret: a feeling, perhaps, of unimportance, of remoteness, of not having heft enough to count.

The fact that I was born a Catholic also complicated life. What is a Catholic but what everybody else is in reaction against? Protestants reformed "the Whore of Babylon," others were "enlightened" from it, and Jews had reason to help Catholicism and the social structures it was rooted in to fall apart. My history books and the whole of education hummed in upon that point (during crucial years I attended a public, not a parochial, school): to be modern is decidedly not be be medieval; to be reasonable is not to be dogmatic; to be free is clearly not to live under ecclesiastical authority; to be scientific is not to attend ancient

rituals, cherish irrational symbols, indulge in mythic practices. It is hard to grow up Catholic in America without becoming defensive, perhaps a little paranoid, feeling forced to divide the world between "us" and "them."

We had a special language all our own, our own pronunciation for words we shared in common with others (Augustine, contemplative), sights and sounds and smells in which few others participated (incense at Benediction of the Most Blessed Sacrament, Forty Hours, wakes, and altar bells at the silent consecration of the Host); and we had our own politics and slant on world affairs. Since earliest childhood, I have known about a "power elite" that runs America: the boys from the Ivy League in the State Department, as opposed to the Catholic boys from Hoover's FBI who, as Daniel Moynihan once put it, keep watch on them. And on a whole host of issues, my people have been, though largely Democratic, conservative: on censorship, on communism, on abortion, on religious schools . . . Harvard and Yale long meant "them" to us.

The language of Spiro Agnew, the language of George Wallace, excepting its idiom, awakens childhood memories in me of men arguing in the barbershop, of my uncle drinking so much beer he threatened to lay his dick upon the porch rail and wash the whole damn street with steaming piss—while cursing the niggers in the mill, below, and the Yankees in the mill, above: millstones he felt pressing him. Other relatives were duly shocked, but everybody loved Uncle George: he said what he thought.

We did not feel this country belonged to us. We felt fierce pride in it, more loyalty than anyone could know. But we felt blocked at every turn. There were not many intellectuals among us, not even very many professional men. Laborers mostly. Small businessmen, agents for corporations perhaps. Content with a little, yes, modest in expectation. But somehow feeling cheated. For a thousand years the Slovaks survived Hungarian hegemony, and our strategy here remained the same: endurance and steady work. Slowly, one day, we would overcome.

A special word is required about a complicated symbol: sex. To this day my mother finds it hard to spell the word intact, preferring to write "s——." Not that much was made of sex in our environment. And that's the point: silence. Demonstrative affection, emotive dances, exuberance Anglo-Saxons seldom seem to share; but on the realities of sex, discretion. Reverence, perhaps; seriousness, surely. On intimacies, it is as though our tongues had been stolen. As though in peasant life for a thousand years the context had been otherwise. Passion, yes; romance, yes; family and children, certainly; but sex, rather a minor part of life.

Imagine, then, the conflict in the generation of my brothers, sister, and myself. (The book critic for the *New York Times* reviews on the same day two new novels of fantasy: one a pornographic fantasy to end all such fantasies [he writes], the other about a mad family representing in some comic way the redemption wrought by Jesus Christ. In language and verve, the books are rated even. In theme, the reviewer notes his embarrassment in reporting a religious fantasy, but no embarrassment at all about the preposterous pornography.) Suddenly, what for a thousand years was minor becomes an all-absorbing investigation. It is, perhaps, one drama when the ruling classes (I mean subscribers to *The New Yorker*, I suppose) move progressively, generation by generation since Sigmund Freud, toward consciousness-raising sessions in Clit. Lib., but wholly another when we stumble suddenly upon mores staggering any expectation our grandparents ever cherished.

Yet more significant in the ethnic experience in America is the intellectual world one meets: the definition of values, ideas, and purposes emanating from universities, books, magazines, radio, and television. One hears one's own voice echoed back neither by spokesmen of "Middle America" (so complacent, smug, nativist, and Protestant), nor by "the intellectuals." Almost unavoidably, perhaps, education in America leads the student who entrusts his soul to it in a direction that, lacking a better word, we might call liberal:

respect for individual conscience, a sense of social responsibility, trust in the free exchange of ideas and procedures of dissent, a certain confidence in the ability of men to "reason together" and to adjudicate their differences, a frank recognition of the vitality of the unconscious, a willingness to protect workers and the poor against the vast economic power of industrial corporations, and the like.

On the other hand, the liberal imagination has appeared to be astonishingly universalist, and relentlessly missionary. Perhaps the metaphor "enlightenment" offers a key. One is initiated into light. Liberal education tends to separate children from their parents, from their roots, from their history, in the cause of a universal and superior religion. One is taught, regarding the unenlightened (even if they be one's Uncles George and Peter, one's parents, one's brothers perhaps), what can only be called a modern equivalent of *odium theologicum*. Richard Hofstadter described anti-intellectualism in America, more accurately in nativist America than in ethnic America, but I have yet to encounter a comparable treatment of anti-unenlightenment among our educated classes.

In particular, I have regretted and keenly felt the absence of that sympathy for PIGS that simple human feeling might have prodded intelligence to muster: that same sympathy that the educated find so easy to conjure up for black culture, Chicano culture, Indian culture, and other cultures of the poor. In such cases, one finds, the universalist pretensions of liberal culture are suspended: some groups, at least, are entitled to be both different and respected. Why do the educated classes find it so difficult to want to understand the man who drives a beer truck, or the fellow with a helmet working on a site across the street with plumbers and electricians, while their sensitivities race easily to Mississippi or even Bedford-Stuyvesant?

There are deep secrets here, no doubt, unvoiced fantasies and scarcely admitted historical resentments. Few persons, in describing "Middle Americans," "the Silent Majority," or Scammon and Wattenberg's "typical American voter," distinguish clearly enough between the nativist American and the ethnic American. The first is likely to be Protestant, the second Catholic. Both may be, in various ways, conservative, loyalist, and unenlightened. Each has his own agonies, fears, betrayed expectations. Neither is ready, quite, to become an ally of the other. Neither has the same history behind him here. Neither has the same hopes. Neither is living out the same psychic voyage. Neither shares the same symbols or has the same sense of reality. The rhetoric and metaphors differ.

There is overlap, of course. But country music is not a polka; a successful politician in a Chicago ward needs a very different "common touch" from the one used by the county clerk in Normal; the urban experience of immigration lacks that mellifluous, optimistic, biblical vision of the good America that springs naturally to the lips of politicians from the Bible Belt. The nativist tends to believe with Richard Nixon that he "knows America and the American heart is good." The ethnic tends to believe that every American who preceded him has an angle, and that he, by God, will one day find one too. (Often, ethnics complain that by working hard, obeying the law, trusting their political leaders, and relying upon the American Dream they now have only their own naïveté to blame for rising no higher than they have.)

It goes without saying that the intellectuals do not love Middle America, and that for all the good warm discovery of America that preoccupied them during the 1950's, no strong tide of respect accumulated in their hearts for the Yahoos, Babbitts, Agnews, and Nixons of the land. Willie Morris, in *North Toward Home,* writes poignantly of the chill, parochial outreach of the liberal sensibility, its failure to engage the humanity of the modest, ordinary little man west of the Hudson. The intellectual's map of the United States is succinct: "Two coasts connected by United Airlines."

Unfortunately, it seems, the ethnics erred in attempting to Americanize themselves, before clearing the project with the educated classes. They learned to wave the flag and to send their sons to war. (The Poles in World War I were 4 percent of the population but took 12 percent of the casualties.) They learned to support their President—an easy task, after all, for those accustomed abroad to obeying authority. And where would they have been if Franklin Roosevelt had not sided with them against established interests? They knew a little about communism, the radicals among them in one way, and by far the larger number of conservatives in another. Not a few exchange letters to this day with cousins and uncles who did not leave for America when they might have, whose lot is demonstrably harder and less than free.

Finally, the ethnics do not like, or trust, or even understand the intellectuals. It is not easy to feel uncomplicated affection for those who call you "pig," "fascist," "racist." One had not yet grown accustomed not to hearing "Hunkie," "Polack," "Spic," "Mick," "Dago," and the rest. At no little sacrifice, one had apologized for foods that smelled too strong for Anglo-Saxon noses, moderated the wide swings of Slavic and Italian emotion, learned decorum, given oneself to education American style, tried to learn tolerance and assimilation. Each generation criticized the earlier for its authoritarian and European and old-fashioned ways. "Up-to-date" was a moral lever. And now when the process nears completion, when a generation appears that speaks without accent and goes to college, still you are considered pigs, fascists, and racists.

Racists? Our ancestors owned no slaves. Most of us ceased being serfs only in the last 200 years—the Russians in 1861. What have we got against blacks or blacks against us? Competition, yes, for jobs and homes and communities; competition, even, for political power. Italians, Lithuanians, Slovaks, Poles are not, in principle, against "community control," or even against ghettos of our own. Whereas the Anglo-Saxon model appears to be a system of atomic individuals and high mobility, our model has tended to stress communities of our own, attachment to family and relatives, stability, and roots. We tend to have a fierce sense of attachment to our homes, having been homeowners less than three generations: a home is almost fulfillment enough for one man's life. We have most ambivalent feelings about suburban assimilation and mobility. The melting pot is a kind of homogenized soup, and its mores only partly appeal to us: to some, yes, and to others, no.

It must be said that we think we are better people than the blacks. Smarter, tougher, harder working, stronger in our families. But maybe many of us are not so sure. Maybe we are uneasy. Emotions here are delicate. One can understand the immensely more difficult circumstances under which the blacks have suffered, and one is not unaware of peculiar forms of fear, envy, and suspicion across color lines. How much of all this we learned in America, by being made conscious of our olive skin, brawny backs, accents, names, and cultural quirks, is not plain to us. Racism is not our invention; we did not bring it with us; we found it here. And should we pay the price for America's guilt? Must all the gains of the blacks, long overdue, be chiefly at our expense? Have we, once again, no defenders but ourselves?

Television announcers and college professors seem so often to us to be speaking in a code. When they say "white racism," it does not seem to be their own traditions they are impugning. Perhaps it is paranoia, but it seems that the affect accompanying such words is directed at steelworkers, auto workers, truck drivers, and police—at us. When they say "humanism" or "progress," it seems to us like moral pressure to abandon our own traditions, our faith, our associations, in order to reap higher rewards in the culture of the national corporations—that culture of quantity, homogeneity, replaceability, and mobility. They want to grind off all the angles, hold us to the lathes, shape us to be objective, meritocratic, orderly, and fully American.

In recent years, of course, a new cleavage has sprung open among the intellectuals. Some seem to speak for technocracy—for that alliance of science, industry, and humanism whose heaven is "progress." Others seem to be taking the view once ascribed to ecclesiastical conservatives and traditionalists: that commitment to enlightenment is narrow, ideological, and hostile to the best interests of mankind. In the past, the great alliance for progress sprang from the conviction that "knowledge is power." Both humanists and scientists could agree on that, and labored in their separate ways to make the institutions of knowledge dominant in society: break the shackles of the Church, extend suffrage to the middle classes and finally to all, win untrammeled liberty for the marketplace of ideas. Today it is no longer plain that the power brought by knowledge is humanistic. Thus the parting of the ways.

Science has ever carried with it the stories and symbols of a major religion. It is ruthlessly universalist. If its participants are not "saved," they are nonetheless "enlightened," which isn't bad. And every single action of the practicing scientist, no matter how humble, could once be understood as a contribution to the welfare of the human race; each smallest gesture was invested with meaning, given a place in a scheme, and weighted with redemptive power. Moreover, the scientist was in possession of "the truth," indeed of the very meaning of and validating procedures for the word. His role was therefore sacred.

Imagine, then, a young strapping Slovak entering an introductory course in the Sociology of Religion at the nearby state university or community college. Is he sent back to his Slovak roots, led to recover paths of experience latent in all his instincts and reflexes, given an image of the life of his grandfather that suddenly, in recognition, brings tears to his eyes? Is he brought to a deeper appreciation of his Lutheran or Catholic heritage and its resonances with other bodies of religious experience? On the contrary, he is secretly taught disdain for what his grandfather *thought* he was doing when he acted or felt or imagined through religious forms. In the boy's psyche, a new religion is implanted: power over others, enlightenment, an atomic (rather than a communitarian) sensibility, a contempt for mystery, ritual, transcendence, soul, absurdity, and tragedy; and deep confidence in the possibilities of building a better world through scientific understanding. He is led to feel ashamed for the statistical portrait of Slovak immigrants which shows them to be conservative, authoritarian, not given to dissent, etc. His teachers instruct him with the purest of intentions, in a way that is value-free.

To be sure, certain radical writers in America have begun to bewail "the laying on of culture" and to unmask the cultural religion implicit in the American way of science. Yet radicals, one learns, often have an agenda of their own. What fascinates *them* among working-class ethnics are the traces, now almost lost, of *radical* activities among the working class two or three generations ago. Scratch the resentful boredom of a classroom of working-class youths, we are told, and you will find hidden in their past some formerly imprisoned organizer for the CIO, some Sacco/Vanzetti, some bold pamphleteer for the IWW. All this is true. But supposing that a study of the ethnic past reveals that most ethnics have been, are, and wish to remain, culturally conservative? Suppose, for example, they wish to deepen their religious roots and defend their ethnic enclaves? Must a radical culture be "laid on" them?

America has never confronted squarely the problem of preserving diversity. I can remember hearing in my youth bitter arguments that parochial schools were "divisive." Now the public schools are attacked for their commitment to homogenization. Well, how *does* a nation of no one culture, no one language, no one race, no one history, no one ethnic stock continue to exist as one, while encouraging diversity? How can the rights of all, and particularly of the weak, be defended if power is decentralized and left to local interests? The weak have ever found strength in this country through local chapters of national organizations. But what happens when the national organizations themselves—the schools, the unions, the federal government—become vehicles of a new, universalistic, thoroughly rationalized, technological culture?

Still, it is not that larger question that concerns me here. I am content today to voice the difficulties in the way of saying what I wish to say, when I wish to say it. The tradition of liberalism is a tradition I have had to acquire, despite an innate skepticism about many of its structural metaphors (free marketplace, individual autonomy, reason naked and undisguised, enlightenment). Radicalism, with its bold and simple optimism about human potential and its anarchic tendencies, has been, despite its appeal to me as a vehicle for criticizing liberalism, freighted with emotions, sentiments, and convictions about men that I cannot bring myself to share.

In my guts, I do not feel that institutions are "repressive" in any meaning of the word that leaves it meaningful; the "state of nature" seems to me, emotionally, far less liberating, far more undifferentiated and confining. I have not dwelt for so long in the profession of the intellectual life that I find it easy to be critical and harsh. In almost everything I see or hear or read, I am struck first, rather undiscriminatingly, by all the things I like in it. Only with second effort can I bring myself to discern the flaws. My emotions and values seem to run in affirmative patterns.

My interest is not, in fact, in defining myself over against the American people and the American way of life. I do not expect as much of it as all that. What I should like to do is come to a better and more profound knowledge of who I am, whence my community came, and whither my son and daughter, and their children's children, might wish to head in the future: I want to have a history.

More and more, I think in family terms, less ambitiously, on a less than national scale. The differences implicit in being Slovak, and Catholic, and lower-middle class seem more and more important to me. Perhaps it is too much to try to speak to all peoples in this very various nation of ours. Yet it does not seem evident that by becoming more concrete, accepting one's finite and limited identity, one necessarily becomes parochial. Quite the opposite. It seems more likely that by each of us becoming more profoundly what we are, we shall find greater unity, in those depths in which unity irradiates diversity, than by attempting through the artifices of the American "melting pot" and the cultural religion of science to become what we are not.

There is, I take it, a form of liberalism not wedded to universal Reason, whose ambition is not to homogenize all peoples on this planet, and whose base lies rather in the imagination and in the diversity of human stories: a liberalism I should be happy to have others help me to find.

46

"Thy Neighbor's Wife, Thy Neighbor's Servants": Women's Liberation and Black Civil Rights

CATHARINE STIMPSON

Thou shalt not covet thy neighbor's house, thou shalt not covet thy neighbor's wife, nor his manservant, nor his maidservant, nor his ox, nor his ass, nor anything that is thy neighbor's.

Tenth Commandment

The optimism of politics before a revolution is exceeded only by the pessimism of politics after one. One current optimistic theory sees all the oppressed classes of America joining together to storm the citadel of their oppressor. Black liberation and women's liberation as movements, blacks and white women as people, will fight together. I respect black liberation, and I work for women's liberation, but the more I think about it, the less hope I have for a close alliance of those who pledge allegiance to the sex and those who pledge allegiance to the skin. History, as well as experience, has bred my skepticism.

That blacks and women should have a common enemy, white men and their culture, without making common cause is grievous,

Catharine Stimpson is Assistant Professor of English at Barnard College.

From Chapter 27, " 'Thy Neighbor's Wife, Thy Neighbor's Servants': Women's Liberation and Black Civil Rights," by Catharine Stimpson, of *Woman in Sexist Society,* by Vivian Gornick and Barbara K. Moran. © 1971 by Basic Books, Inc., Publishers, New York. Footnotes have been renumbered.

perhaps. They even have more in common than an enemy. In America they share the unhappy lot of being cast together as lesser beings. It is hardly coincidence that the most aggressively racist regions are those most rigidly insistent upon keeping women in their place, even if that place is that of ornament, toy, or statue. Of the ten states that refused to ratify the Nineteenth Amendment, giving women the vote, nine were southern. The tenth was Delaware. Gunnar Myrdal, in a brief appendix to *An American Dilemma,* his massive study of American blacks, tersely analyzed this peculiar national habit. Both blacks and women are highly visible; they cannot hide, even if they want to. A patriarchal ideology assigns them several virtues: blacks are tough; women fragile. However, the same patriarchal ideology judges them *naturally* inferior in those respects that carry "prestige, power, and advantages in society."[1] As Thomas Jefferson said, even if America were a pure democracy, its inhabitants should keep women, slaves, and babies away from its deliberations. The less education women and blacks get, the better; manual education is the most they can have. The only right they possess is the right, which criminals, lunatics, and idiots share, to love their divine subordination within the *paterfamilias* and to obey the paterfamilias himself.

The development of an industrial economy, as Myrdal points out, has not brought about the integration of women and blacks into the adult male culture. Women have not found a satisfactory way both to bear children and to work. Blacks have not destroyed the hard doctrine of their unassimilability. What the economy gives both women and blacks are menial labor, low pay, and few promotions. White male workers hate both groups, for their competition threatens wages and their possible job equality, let alone superiority, threatens nothing less than the very nature of things. The tasks of women and blacks are usually

[1] Gunnar Myrdal, Appendix 5, "A Parallel to the Negro Problem," *An American Dilemma* (New York: Harper and Brothers, 1944), p. 1077.

grueling, repetitive, slogging, and dirty. After all, people have servants, not simply for status, but for doing what every sensible person knows is unappetizing.

Blacks and women also live in the wasteland of American sexuality, a world which, according to W. E. B. Du Bois, one of the few black men to work for women's emancipation, "tries to worship both virgins and mothers and in the end despises motherhood and despoils virgins."[2] White men, convinced of the holy primacy of sperm, yet guilty about using it, angry at the loss of the cozy sanctuary of the womb and the privilege of childhood, have made their sex a claim to power and then used their power to claim control of sex. In fact and fantasy, they have violently segregated black men and white women. The most notorious fantasy claims that the black man is sexually evil, low, subhuman; the white woman sexually pure, elevated, superhuman. Together they dramatize the polarities of excrement and disembodied spirituality. Blacks and women have been sexual victims, often cruelly so: the black man castrated, the woman raped and often treated to a psychic clitoridectomy.

These similarities in the condition of blacks and women add up to a remarkable consistency of attitude and action on the part of the powerful toward the less powerful. Yet for a white woman to say, "I've been niggerized, I'm just a nigger, all women are niggers," is vulgar and offensive. Women must not usurp the vocabulary of the black struggle. They must forge their own idiom by showing how they are, for instance, "castrated" by a language and a tradition that makes manhood, as well as white skin, a requisite for full humanity.

Women's protest has followed black protest, which surged up under the more intense and brutal pressure. Antislavery movements preceded the first coherent woman's rights movement, black male suffrage, woman's suffrage, the civil rights movement, the new feminism. For the most part, white women

have organized, not after working *with* blacks, but after working *on behalf* of them. Feminism has received much of its impetus from the translation of lofty, middle-class altruism into the more realistic, emotionally rugged salvation of the self.

The relationship between black rights and woman's rights offers an important cautionary tale, revealing to us the tangle of sex, race, and politics in America. It shows the paradox of any politics of change: we cannot escape the past we seek to alter, any more than the body can escape enzymes, molecules, and genes. As drama, the story is fascinating. Blacks and white women begin generous collaborations, only to find themselves in bitter misalliance. At crucial moments, the faith of one in the other changes into doubt. High principles become bones of contention and strategies violate high principles. The movements use each other, betray each other, and provoke from each other abstract love and visceral hostility. The leaders are heroic—men and women of great bravery, resilience, intellectual power, eloquence, and sheer human worth whose energy is that of the Christians and the lions together. And the women of the nineteenth century, except for their evangelical Christianity, sexual reticence, and obsequious devotion to marriage, the family, home, or at least to heterosexuality, worked out every analysis the new feminism is rediscovering. . . .

A black liberation movement has been active in America since the first black arrived in Virginia; only white belief in it has been erratic. The liberal civil rights movement which began in 1960, during the Greensboro, North Carolina sit-ins and ended around 1966, during the healthy purge of white power and participation, helped to generate contemporary women's liberation. The growth of women's liberation has imitated that of modern black protest. Civil rights activity, which demands equality within a system, breeds revolutionary activity, which demands a radically new system. Civil rights and liberation groups live together, more or less uneasily, their common enemy forcing a loose loyalty. The public, in-

---

[2] W. E. B. Du Bois, "The Damnation of Women," *Darkwater* (New York: Schocken Books, 1969), p. 164.

sensitive to bold differences of ideology and tactics, thinks of them as one.

There are really no formal bridges between integrated black civil rights groups and white women's liberation groups as there were in the nineteenth century, as there are in contemporary white radical gatherings. Reliable people also think that surprisingly few of the new feminists were seriously involved in civil rights. More came out of the New Left or in response to discriminatory post-World War II work conditions. The women who were committed to black causes, if they could shake loose from the roles of Lady Bountiful, Sister Conscience, or Daring Daughter, each in its way an archetypal woman's role, gained political and personal consciousness.

For many of us, civil rights activity was only a part of the interminable process of wooing knowledge, courage, and self-esteem. Other influences on our feminism may have been the psychological and moral need to have a cause, especially an impeccable but unconventional one; emotional or intellectual insults from the masculine world; and, to an interesting degree, a mother, grandmother, or aunt who, whether she wanted to or not, rebelled against woman's business as usual. For others, civil rights activity may have been crucial. It was, I am sure, different for northerners and southerners.

All learned something about the ideal of equality and how to organize to get it. Sensing the limitless possibilities of the protest movement also made us sense the impossible limits of old sex roles. Lillian Smith talks about the genteel church ladies who organized the Association of Southern Women for the Prevention of Lynching. No feminists, the ladies still helped to corrode the iron myth that white women were chaste butterflies. They had realized "that all a woman can expect from lingering on exalted heights is a hard chill afterwards."[3]

Like their ancestors in the antislavery movement, some women in the civil rights movement felt abused. They were given work supportive in nature and negligible in influence; they were relegated to the "research library and to the mimeograph machine."[4] If they were sexually exploited, their own sexual exploits were judged according to a double standard that let men sow wild oats but told women to reap the whirlwind. Not only did movement men tend to be personally chauvinistic, but many of the movement's ideals—strength, courage, spirit—were those society attributes to masculinity. Women may have them, but never more than men. The more paramilitary, the less nonviolent, black protest became, the less women and the putative womanly virtues were honored.

Still another pressure upon women in civil rights was the virility cult of white liberals officially concerned with the "Negro Problem." In 1965 the Moynihan Report made its notorious to-do about strong women and weak men. Behind its analysis lurked a grim belief in the patriarchal family. The Report declared:

When Jim Crow made its appearance towards the end of the 19th century, it may be speculated that it was the Negro male who was most humiliated thereby; the male was more likely to use public facilities, which rapidly became segregated once the process began, and just as important, segregation, and the submissiveness it exacts, is surely more destructive to the male than to the female personality. Keeping the Negro "in his place" can be translated as keeping the Negro male in his place; the female was not a threat to anyone.

---

[3] Lillian Smith, *Killers of the Dream*, rev. (New York: W. W. Norton, 1961), p. 141.

[4] Carol Hanisch, "Hard Knocks: Working for Women's Liberation in a Mixed (Male-Female) Movement Group," Shulamith Firestone and Anne Koedt, eds., *Notes from the Second Year: Women's Liberation* (New York, 1970), p. 60. Other white women veterans of the civil rights movement have less unhappy accounts of what happened, particularly in the South. They accuse some women of themselves using sex in order to gain power. They say that at least in the beginning women were influential. A white woman was the first administrator of the Student Non-Violent Co-ordinating Committee office in Atlanta. Jobs were given out on the basis of competence. Women could not have some simply because it would have been stupid and dangerous to have a white woman appear in public with a black man.

Compounding its errors of fact and spirit, the Report went on:

> Unquestionably, these events worked against the emergence of a strong father figure. The very essence of the male animal, from the bantam rooster to the four-star general, is to strut.[5] . . .

The influence of black protest on women's liberation is more pervasive than the effect of one public event on the private lives of some valuable, interesting women. The civil rights movement scoured a rusty national conscience. Moral and political struggle against a genuine domestic evil became respectable again. The movement clarified concepts of oppression, submission, and resistance and offered tactics—the sit-ins, boycotts, demonstrations, proofs of moral superiority—for others to use to wrest freedom from the jaws of asses. Confrontation politics became middle class again as the movement helped to resurrect the appealing American tradition of rebellion. The real domino theory deals with the collapse of delusions of content. Once these delusions are exposed for one group, they tend to be obvious for others. The black became, as he had been before, the test of white good will. Being treated like blacks became proof of exploitation.

All of the women's liberation groups, even the more conservative, have drawn deeply on the inadvertent largesse of the black movement. Some women look to it for encouraging political lessons. It teaches that the oppressed must become conscious of their oppression, of the debasing folly of their lives, before change can come. Change, if it does come, will overthrow both a class, a social group, and a caste—a social group held in contempt. For those who place women's liberation into the larger context of general revolution, black people "have exposed the basic weakness of the system of white, Western dominance which we live under."[6] Brutal versions of the theory of the survival of the fittest have been refuted: the weaker can defeat the stronger. Their tactics will prove the virtue of flexibility, speed, and cunning. Those who were expelled from the civil rights movement are grateful for being forced to take stock of themselves, instead of taking stock of blacks. So isolated, they often go on to praise black models of the doctrine of separatism.[7]

Even more commonly, women use blacks to describe themselves. They draw strenuous analogies between themselves and blacks, between women's civil rights and black civil rights, between women's revolution and the black revolution. The metaphor litters even the most sensible, probing, and sensitive thought of the movement. One influential pamphlet, which I like, deploys it no less than eleven times:[8]

1. Women, like black slaves, belong to a master. They are property and whatever credit they gain redounds to him.
2. Women, like black slaves, have a personal relationship to the men who are their masters.
3. Women, like blacks, get their identity and status from white men.
4. Women, like blacks, play an idiot role in the theatre of the white man's fantasies. Though inferior and dumb, they are happy, especially when they can join a mixed group where they can mingle with The Man.

[5] "The Negro Family: the Case for National Action," in Leon Friedman, ed., *The Civil Rights Reader* (New York: Walker and Company, 1967), p. 291.

[6] Roxanne Dunbar, "Female Liberation as the Basis for Social Revolution," Firestone and Koedt, *op. cit.*, p. 48. Dunbar says the Vietnamese have also done this.

[7] The Honorable Shirley Chisholm discusses separatism: ". . . because of the bizarre aspects of their roles and the influence that nontraditional contact among them has on the general society, blacks and whites, males and females, must operate almost independently of each other in order to escape from the quicksands of psychological slavery." Her essay, "Racism and Anti-Feminism," *Black Scholar*, 1 (January–February 1970): 40–45 is a lucid account of the new feminism by an admirable black woman.

[8] Beverly Jones and Judith Brown, "Toward a Female Liberation Movement" (Boston: New England Free Press, n.d.).

5. Women, like blacks, buttress the white man's ego. Needing such support, the white man fears its loss; fearing such loss, he fears women and blacks.

6. Women, like blacks, sustain the white man: "They wipe his ass and breast feed him when he is little, they school him in his youthful years, do his clerical work and raise him and his replacements later, and all through his life in the factories, on the migrant farms, in the restaurants, hospitals, offices, and homes, they sew for him, stoop for him, cook for him, clean for him, sweep, run errands, haul away his garbage, and nurse him when his frail body alters."

7. Women, like blacks, are badly educated. In school they internalize a sense of being inferior, shoddy, and intellectually crippled. In general, the cultural apparatus—the profession of history, for example—ignores them.

8. Women, like blacks, see a Tom image of themselves in the mass media.

9. Striving women, like bourgeois blacks, become imitative, ingratiating, and materialistic when they try to make it in the white man's world.

10. Women, like blacks, suffer from the absence of any serious study on the possibility of real "temperamental and cognitive differences" between the races and the sexes.

11. The ambivalence of women toward marriage is like the ambivalence of blacks toward integration.[9] . . .

However, I believe that women's liberation would be much stronger, much more honest, and ultimately more secure if it stopped comparing white women to blacks so freely. The analogy exploits the passion, ambition, and vigor of the black movement. It perpetuates the depressing habit white people have of first defining the black experience and then of making it their own. Intellectually

sloppy, it implies that both blacks and white women can be seriously discussed as amorphous, classless, blobby masses. It permits women to avoid doing what the black movement did at great cost and over a long period of time: making its protest clear and irrefutable, its ideology self-sufficient and momentous, its organization taut. It also helps to limit women's protest to the American landscape. The plight of woman is planetary, not provincial; historical, not immediate.

Perhaps more dangerous, the analogy evades, in the rhetorical haze, the harsh fact of white women's racism. Our racism may be the curse of white culture, the oath of an evil witch who invades our rooms at birth. Or our racism may dankly unite culture and the way in which white infants apprehend their bodies, the real biological punishment in the myth of the Fall from the Garden of Eden. Whatever the cause, the virus has infected us all. One story may symbolize its work. Castration, when it was a legal punishment, was applied only to blacks during the period of Western slavery. In Barbados in 1693, a woman, for money, castrated forty-two black men. White men made the law. Their fear dictated the penalty. Yet a woman carried it out. White skin has bought a perverse remedy for the blows that sex has dealt.[10]

---

[9] It should be noted that when many contemporary feminists compare themselves to slaves, they are speaking of historical slavery, not of black American chattel slavery, of which they have no personal knowledge. They are influenced not only by Engels but by John Stuart Mill's *The Subjection of Women* (1869).

[10] Joel Kovel, *White Racism: A Psychohistory* (New York: Pantheon, 1970), p. 193, gives a brilliant analysis of the way in which biology, economics, and cultural assumptions may have come together to breed American racism. He says that while the South enjoyed the black body and the North made it taboo, for both regions it was:

the very incarnation of that fecal substance with which the whole world had been smeared by the repressed coprophilia of the bourgeois order. Here was the central forbidden pleasure that had become generalized into the pursuit of world mastery: the playing with, the reincorporation of lost bodily contents, the restoration of the narcissistic body of infancy, the denial of separation and the selfhood that had been painfully wrung from history. Here was the excremental body that had been hated, repressed, spread over the universe, but which was still loved with the infant's wish to fuse with the maternal image.

However, Kovel writes as if "man" meant both "man" and "woman," there being no difference between them, or as if writing about "man" were enough.

The racism of white women dictates more than a desire to dominate *something;* it also bears on her participation in what Eldridge Cleaver calls the "funky facts of life." For the black man she may be the sumptuous symbol of virtue, culture, and power, or she may be a sexual tempter and murderer, or she may be an object upon which revenge may fall. She may think of the black man as the exotic superstud, the magic phallus. A union with him may prove her sophistication and daring. She may perceive the black woman as a threat, a class and caste hatred rooted in sexual jealousy and fear.[11] I frankly dislike some of the assumptions about white women I find in black writers. I am neither the guiding genius of the patriarchy nor the creator of my conventional sex role nor a fit subject for rape. Being "cleanly, viciously popped," which LeRoi Jones says that I want, but which my culture provides for me only in "fantasies" of evil, is in fact evil. Yet white women do have deeply ambiguous sexual attitudes toward black people which often have very little to do with love.

My generalizations, which obviously ignore the idiosyncratic, subtle mysteries of the psychology of individual persons, may partly explain the tensions between members of the black movement and of the woman's movement. There are also political reasons for incompatibility. The logic of the ideology of separatism is one. Blacks must liberate themselves from whites, including white women; women must liberate themselves from men, including black men. Everyone's liberation must be self-won. My brief narrative of the nineteenth century surely warns us against proxy fights for freedom. The result is that black liberation and women's liberation must go their separate ways. I would be ridiculously presumptuous if I spoke for black women. My guess is that many will choose to work for the black movement. They will agree with the forceful Sonia Sanchez Knight poem "Queens of the Universe":

> . . . we must
> return to blk/men his children full and our
> women/love/tenderness/sweet/blkness ful of
> pride/so they can shape the male children into
> young warriors who will stand along side
> them.[12]

They will accept the theory that "any movement that augments the sex-role antagonisms extant in the black community will only sow the seed of disunity and hinder the liberation struggle."[13] Any black woman's movement will also have a texture different from that of a white woman's movement.

The logic of the ideologies of class improvement also makes an alliance between blacks and white women seem ultimately unstable. Both classes suffer from irrational eco-

[11] Such attitudes, once clandestine, are now much discussed in many places. Among them are Eldridge Cleaver, *Soul On Ice* (New York: Dell Publishing Co., Delta Book, 1968); E. Franklin Frazier, *The Negro Family in the United States*, rev. and abrd. ed. (Chicago: University of Chicago Press, 1966); Frantz Fanon, *Black Skin, White Masks*, trans. Charles Lam Markman (New York: Grove Press, 1967); Calvin C. Hernton, *Sex and Racism in America* (New York: Grove Press, 1966); Theodore R. Hudson, "In the Eye of the Beholder," *Negro Digest* (December 1969): 43–48; LeRoi Jones, *Dutchman and The Slave: Two Plays* (New York: William Morrow, Apollo Edition, 1964); LeRoi Jones, "American Sexual Reference: black male," *Home* (New York: William Morrow, Apollo Edition, 1966).

One of the most interesting studies of white women and black women is Archibald E. Grimké, "The Sex Question and Race Segregation," *Papers of the American Negro Academy* (Washington, D.C., December 1915). Grimké, a lawyer, writer, publicist, and diplomat, was asking white women to help create legal equality for blacks and to end the double standard which had so victimized black women. Yet he was dubious about the possibility of sexual solidarity because of the resentment white women felt toward black women. Grimké, born in 1849, was the illegitimate son of Henry Grimké, Angelina and Sarah's brother, and Nancy Weston, a family slave. After the Civil War, he left the South to educate himself in the North. His aunt Sarah, who accidentally discovered his existence and then deliberately discovered his blood relationship to her, helped him to go on to Harvard.

[12] *Black Scholar* 1 (January–February 1970): 29.

[13] Robert Staples, "The Myth of the Black Matriarchy," *Black Scholar* 1 (January–February 1970): 15. Staples, who thinks the black woman more aggressive, independent, and self-reliant than the prototypical white woman, finds the myth of the black matriarchy a "cruel hoax," which the white ruling class has imposed in order to create internal dissensions within the black community.

nomic discrimination: black men the least, black women the most. If society rights this wrong, it may only multiply the competition among the outcast for the cushy jobs. More dangerously, society may fail to change its notions of work. It must begin to assume, especially in a technological age, that ability is an asexual happenstance; that doing housework and raising children are asexual responsibilities; that the nuclear family, in which a father, whose sex gives him power, guarantees the annual income, is only one of several ways of leading the good life. Changing these notions means uprooting our concepts of sex and power. Such assumptions are axioms to members of women's liberation. Whether they are or not to members of black liberation, or any other political force, is unclear to me.

Finally, those of us in women's liberation have tasks independent of those confronting black liberation. We must do much more arduous work to persuade women to recognize the realities of their life. Few blacks still need consciousness-raising. Our job is harder because white, middle-class women have so many privileges and because the national impetus toward suburbia makes each home, embracing its homemaker, not just a castle, but a miniature ghetto. Blacks have long celebrated their culture. We must discover if women have a commonly felt, supportive culture, a fertile, if academically disdained, luster of responses and beliefs. We must also confront the moral and strategic necessity of building a revolution that rejects violence. A black man, carrying a gun, despite horrified warnings that armed blacks make white black-lashes, is effective. A woman, carrying a gun, despite the fact that women can and do shoot, is politically ineffective in America. Our culture finds it bizarre, and I, for one, find it regressive.

However, people in the black movement and in the woman's movement can work together on civil rights. Nearly everyone, except the crackers of both sexes, professes belief in civil rights. However, getting them is still a matter of hard work, imaginative administration, gritty willfulness, and often despair. Once, fighting miscegenation laws together would have been appropriate. Now raising bail money for Panther women is necessary. The movements can also form coalitions to struggle for specific ends. Such goals must appeal to the self-interest of both blacks and women. Among them might be decent day-care centers, humane attitudes toward prostitution, the organization of domestic workers, and the recognition of the dignity of all persons on welfare. Insisting upon these goals must lead to a real guaranteed annual income.[14]

What, at last, we have in common is a gift to America from its haphazard and corrupt revolution—the belief in human right that makes civil right imperative. We also share, if we are lucky, a vision of a blessed and generous and peaceable kingdom. If not for us, for our children. . . .

[14] Perhaps a transcendent ideal of modern socialism may unite elements of the two movements. However, I think that for the moment new feminism's allegiance to abolishing sexism and black liberation's allegiance to blackness are both too strong for that.

47

Ethnic Resentment

FRED BARBARO

The antipoverty and other Great Society programs were launched in a decade that was
notable for its professed altruism. The proclaimed objective was the elimination of
poverty and many of its by-products. By the
time the decade came to a close the dream had
tarnished in the wake of violence against
political leaders, civil disorders, a prolonged
war in Vietnam and police violence directed
against our youth.

Perhaps the results were predictable: as
the blacks, the most visible minority, sought to
hasten the conversion of the dream to reality,
other groups waited for their opportunities to
recoup real or imaginary losses sustained during the 1960s. It was not so easy to foretell,
however, the apparent hostility of other minorities against blacks resulting from the implementation of the Kennedy-Johnson domestic
programs. Blacks were increasingly seen as
the major beneficiaries of these programs and
quickly became the targets of other groups
frustrated by their inability to receive what
they perceived to be their fair share. As the
war effort consumed more and more resources
and the promised program expansion failed to
reach the level where these groups could be
served, anti-black sentiments increased. Non-

Fred Barbaro is Associate Professor and Assistant Director of Field Work at Columbia University School of Social Work.

Published by permission of Transaction, Inc., from Society, Vol. 11, No. 3 (1974). Copyright © 1974 by
Transaction, Inc.

black minority groups reasoned that there
would only be one pie, that it was being baked
for and consumed by blacks, and that they
must more aggressively stake their claims if
they wished to receive a slice of that pie.

Anti-black sentiment was expressed in a
variety of ways and with varying degrees of
hostility:

- A proposal for a fellowship program for
  Puerto Ricans emphasizes the educational
  gap between Puerto Ricans and blacks
  rather than the white majority.
- An agency's report on Jewish participation
  in the antipoverty program states that although officials in the program are not
  anti-Semitic, "they are unaware of Jewish
  poverty and . . . they are more interested
  in serving 'their own'."
- Mexican-Americans, the largest minority
  group in Los Angeles, express resentment
  over the channelling of most of the public
  and private aid into the black community
  of Watts.

This inter-minority rivalry not only seems
to have been a major deterrent to the development of a coalition to seek the incremental
expansion of programs to meet common
needs, but also contributed to the eradication
of existing cooperative efforts among minorities. This same rivalry has led to an intensifi-
cation of the tendency of each group to look
inward and to make its claims upon the institutions of government in conflict with, and
sometimes at the expense of, other organized
interest groups.

These ethnic group struggles are not
unique in American politics. For example, the
Irish and Italians competed for political advantage long before the blacks and Puerto
Ricans arrived in New York City in any sizable
number. Nor is there any evidence to suggest
that Jews, Puerto Ricans, blacks and Chicanos
would behave differently from other groups
under similar circumstances. However, the
confluence of political and social circumstances in the sixties shaped a situation in
which common aspirations and goals disinte-
grated in the cross-currents of individual

group demands. A review of the origin and nature of the conflict over limited program resources and the resulting tendency of each group to seek separatist solutions to its problems may be instructive as we seek clues to how these problems will be handled in the seventies.

Other groups such as the Polish-Americans and Italian-Americans were not included in this discussion because their relationship with blacks differed qualitatively from those of groups previously mentioned. Members of the Italian and Polish communities have not participated in Great Society programs in large numbers and only recently have begun to reconsider that position. In addition to not wanting to associate with what they perceived to be black-oriented programs they also knew that their participation would result in their neighborhoods being designated as poverty areas—a definition they were not willing to accept. For example, Italian-Americans in Newark would not permit the establishment of a field office of the antipoverty agency in their ward, and thereby denied themselves thousands of dollars worth of program jobs and needed services. Finally, the intensity of the feelings between these groups and blacks, and their tendency to support conservative causes, does not make them likely candidates for a liberal coalition in the near future.

BLACK PREFERENCE: FACT OR FANCY?

A common view expressed by most minority group members interviewed was that the Kennedy-Johnson programs were designed for blacks, and, in fact, blacks did reap most of the benefits from the program. This conclusion is supported by the literature on the program written by those on the task force that drafted the original legislation, administered the program on the federal and local levels or conducted studies of its operations.

At what point in time did the New Frontier-Great Society programs become black-oriented? In *Regulating The Poor*, Piven and Cloward argue that from the start they were

conceived and designed as a political strategy to buttress an obvious trend in Democratic presidential politics, the importance of the big city vote. The migration of blacks to the North and the weakening of the North-South Democratic coalition, both of which began following World War II, led to the prominence of the cities in Democratic party strategy. Although Kennedy's victory was attributable to his performance in the cities, his margin of victory was small. The full potential of the cities was not yet realized.

Since local political parties were controlled by whites and few attempts to recruit and register blacks had been made, a means to tap the repository urban black vote had to be found. The best method to nurture the black vote seemed to be the extension of municipal service to them while avoiding alienation of the urban white vote. Thus, the antipoverty programs focused on the cities.

The consequent urban bias of antipoverty programs was documented by Sar Levitan. The ten largest recipients of Community Action Program funds, fiscal years 1965–1968, were New York, Chicago, Los Angeles, Philadelphia, Detroit, St. Louis, Washington, D.C., Boston, Atlanta and Pittsburgh. Together they received almost three times the national average per person. "Illinois received $39.4 million in CAP funds in fiscal 1967, while Alabama, with almost the same number of poor people, received only $17.5 million; New Jersey and Wisconsin, despite similar poverty populations, were granted $26.4 million and $8.9 million, respectively." In addition to the political need for the urban vote there were other reasons, perhaps of equal importance. In such volatile and complex times as the sixties, it is not hazardous to speculate that social policy was the result of several demands made on the political system.

Among the most persistent demands being made at the time of the 1960 presidential election were those proposed by the black-white coalition in the civil rights movement. Although the initial cry was for "freedom," suggesting civil rights legislation as the solution, by the time of the 1963 March on Washington, the slogan included jobs, housing and education as well as freedom.

A review of John F. Kennedy's personal life and early political career would disclose little to suggest that he was prepared either intellectually or emotionally to handle the direct action stage of the movement. As a legislator he did not require black votes to win elections in Massachusetts nor did he sponsor any significant legislation in the civil rights area. Yet as a national candidate he became increasingly aware of these issues. Presidential adviser Theodore Sorensen stated, "Most Negro leaders were shrewd judges of which politicians cared deeply about their values and which cared chiefly about their votes—and while Kennedy may have initially been more influenced by the second concern, by the 1960s the first had become more and more important to him."

Kennedy's references to poverty in America during his campaign were not directed at alleviating black poverty nor is there evidence that he envisioned an attack on poverty along the lines of the 1964 act. His rhetoric was a challenge to eight years of Republican "prosperity," in spite of a 6 percent unemployment level. After his election he turned to Walter Heller, chairman of the Council of Economic Advisors, to direct his antipoverty strategy which resulted in attempts to stimulate the economy through tax deductions and other devices. But by the spring of 1963 he realized that a stimulated economy was not enough and instructed Heller to plan a broad and comprehensive war against poverty.

After he became president, Lyndon Johnson endorsed Kennedy's decision. He proceeded to skillfully engineer the passing of the Act in 1964, the Civil Rights Bill of 1964 and the Voting Rights Bill of 1965 as "living memorials" to President Kennedy. By this time few doubted that the legislative package was aimed at black America to relieve the pressure building up in the nation's streets. The President's "We Shall Overcome" speech before Congress was another attempt to lead and hopefully contain the pace of the movement. But Johnson was quickly running out of inex-

pensive measures, and although he knew that the present programs were inadequate, his sense that the country was not prepared for a bold new program to benefit blacks, prevented dramatic action. He needed time.

According to Lee Rainwater and William L. Yancey, it was Daniel P. Moynihan and Richard N. Goodwin, both holdovers from the Kennedy Administration, who persuaded Johnson that more must be done to deal with black poverty. The result of their efforts was the White House Conference, "To Fulfill These Rights," a traditional device employed by several administrations to educate the public by focusing national attention on a problem, and to buy time. Johnson's decision to announce his plans for the conference at the federally financed, mostly black, Howard University, was significant. If there were any doubts before the speech regarding who would benefit from this new thrust, there were none afterwards. The speech, written by Goodwin and Moynihan, incorporated many of the conclusions of a report prepared by Moynihan entitled, *The Negro Family: The Case for National Action*. The thesis of the report was that "freedom was not enough" and proceeded to document the "widening gulf" between black and white citizens. Moynihan's solutions were expensive, e.g., a full employment program for males and a guaranteed annual income, and the conference was designed to work out the details and gather support for the programs.

In August 1965, Watts erupted and white America felt betrayed. The controversy over the "Moynihan Report" destroyed the White House Conference. Our deepening involvement in Vietnam made it impossible to have both "guns and butter." Johnson did not follow up on the bold promises he made at Howard University and instead proposed the modest Model Cities program. A disappointed Moynihan left Washington quietly, the perfect scapegoat; he let everyone off the hook.

The motivation and the initiative taken by the executive branch in responding to black demands are clear: first political then social pressure shaped policy. Legislative intent is not always realized during the implementation stage however. What factors led to the favored status of blacks in dispersal of funds? Sar Levitan's study, previously cited to indicate the urban bias of the programs, concludes that blacks received a far greater share of the benefits from these programs than their percentage in the poor population would warrant. Levitan supports this statement by his analysis of ethnic census data gathered on various components of the program by OEO, the Department of Labor and the Bureau of the Census.

Levitan attributes the black advantage to factors related to the civil rights movement. "With almost every community eligible for CAP dollars, distribution of funds on the basis of poverty population was virtually impossible. . . . The only explanation . . . is that areas with the most effective organization and sophistication in the art of grantsmanship received the largest proportion of funds. 'Rural discrimination' was closely related to the absence of effective local organization in sparsely populated rural areas." Levitan argues that the movement "gave the Negro . . . an organizational base which was lacking among whites who were poor."

The author agrees that the civil rights experience provided blacks with a distinct advantage over other groups who lacked an organizational base on the local level, and that the antipoverty program became interwoven in the battle for black equality. But the political and social pressures on the policy-makers described above seem to contradict Levitan's contention that "those who drafted the Economic Opportunity Act in 1964 were unaware that they were drafting a civil rights law." It was the whites who were involved in the task force, supported the legislation, helped draw up guidelines, administered the program and sat on the boards of the Community Action Agencies who were responsible for the black bias of the program. Many had been associated with liberal causes for years and moved into antipoverty jobs because, as Levitan states, "it was possible to view the early O.E.O. as a potential institutional base for the second phase of the civil rights movement." Later, in

addition to battling Puerto Ricans and Chicanos for program resources, blacks would compete with these same whites for top administrative jobs and control over "their" program.

With this overview of the antipoverty program's inception and development it will be useful to examine the history of three minority groups who sought to share in the benefits of the programs and found themselves embroiled in inter-minority disputes.

THE PUERTO RICAN CASE

To the unsophisticated observer, reports of black-Puerto Rican conflict are likely to be greeted with surprise. From the earliest days of the civil rights movement the groups have been linked together in an apparently solid coalition. However, for those involved and those who monitored the scene closely, the cry for "jobs for blacks and Puerto Ricans" was more of a strategic device than a factual description of the true nature of the relationship between the groups. Puerto Rican participation in civil rights organizations and on picket lines was lower than for whites. If they did participate, they were not likely to hold leadership positions and, equally important, were not representative of the larger Puerto Rican community.

Puerto Rican leaders began seeking other arrangements to advance their cause even before the replacement of the civil rights movement with Black Power organizations. They reasoned that their participation resulted in minimal rewards and a submergence of their identity and special problems. They lacked an organizational base in local communities, and had hardly any professional organizations exclusively concerned about their problems. If they did participate in a protest action and were successful in developing 25 jobs for minority workers, for example, they had some difficulty in producing qualified applicants while the local Urban League could produce twice that number in 24 hours.

It was not easy for the Puerto Rican

leadership to break away. They were charged with racism and a desire not to associate with blacks because they ranked low on the socio-economic ladder. There was some truth to this charge among the rank and file whose cultural background and disparate life experiences made it difficult for them to identify with black aspirations. By and large it was not true of the leadership. Regardless of how well they articulated their predicament, few provided them with a sympathetic hearing. Americans who cared at all focused on black-white relations. Puerto Ricans began looking inward for their solutions.

For the Puerto Rican leadership it became a problem of attracting the nation's attention. All special interest groups face this task, and of course the fewer people affected, the more difficult it is to interest the media, legislators and the populace. After all, what does the average American know about Puerto Rico or Puerto Ricans? Puerto Rico is a vacation paradise that is somehow related politically to this country. Weren't Puerto Ricans involved in shootings directed against President Truman and members of Congress? Puerto Rican teenage gangs "rumbled" with other gangs in the 1950s. What ever happened to them? Puerto Ricans now want jobs and freedom. Every bit of knowledge was accompanied by a boat load of questions attesting to the nation's general ignorance on the subject.

Faced with this dilemma, Puerto Ricans, so accustomed to submerging black-Puerto Rican differences under the "freedom umbrella," began to emphasize their differences. Blacks already had the nation's attention and coattailing in this manner had greater potential than under the previous arrangement. Statistical evidence was presented to show that Puerto Ricans were lagging behind both blacks and whites in many areas. Soon whites were dropped from the comparison. The motivation was, as one spokesman put it, "to change the impression held by most people that because many of us are white, we are making it. This evidence should dispel that notion."

Statistics were always cited in terms of percentages, for 1.5 million Puerto Ricans (the Puerto Ricans actually claim 3 million mainland residents) could not build as strong a case when speaking in terms of absolute numbers. With 22 million to draw from, blacks could match numbers with other minority groups in the areas of poverty and its related miseries. But these kinds of arguments were pointless when one considered the fact that the funds were not adequate to even begin to meet the needs of any group. In addition, blacks could always add other variables like "justice" to bolster their claim for preferential treatment. Puerto Ricans, Chicanos and Jews could add their special grievances and the spiral would continue to climb but the main problem of insufficient funds would remain. Under these conditions equitable allocations were difficult, if not impossible.

In New York City, where almost one million Puerto Ricans live, the leadership joined the blacks in seeking a decentralized program. Few trusted City Hall to cater to their interests; in fact one of the unique features of the act was that it was possible to bypass both the state and local governments. In retrospect, some among the leaders feel that decentralization was a mistake. Twenty-six local community corporations were established, controlled mostly by blacks, while Puerto Ricans received funds for 12 citywide programs. This arrangement was based in part on the related beliefs that Puerto Ricans who lived in the designated poverty areas would receive services and that Puerto Ricans were dispersed throughout the city and needed citywide programs to serve them. It wasn't long before both beliefs were challenged.

In 1967, a study which monitored Puerto Rican residential patterns dispelled the notion that Puerto Ricans were leaving their ghettos and were moving to new locations throughout the city. "Almost without exception," the *New York Times* found, "Puerto Rican settlements appear as foothills to Negro areas." As neighbors they began a fierce competition for control of the community corporations and their jobs and services. A winner-take-all psychology

soon developed and during the early days of
the program, only the blacks were well organized enough to "take."

At the local level there was little patience
with those who lectured on power politics or
the "big picture." Puerto Ricans could understand that white suburbanites ran the banks
and corporations but they did not have access
to that action. As they saw it, the blacks were
the "haves" and they were the "have nots."
Attempts to negotiate a larger percentage of
the funds for Puerto Rican programs were
frustrated at every turn. For example, in
Newark, Puerto Ricans fought for three years
to get their only proposal for a $30,000 pro-
gram approved by the local CAA which was
allocated for more than 5 million dollars for
programs. They picketed meetings of the board
of directors and staged several "sit-ins" at the
CAA headquarters. Finally, during a heated
debate, a young Puerto Rican shouted, "do we
have to riot to get funds?" After several confrontations along these lines relationships between the groups were frozen at a civil, but
less than cordial, level.

Black administrators were not unsympa-
thetic but they had problems of their own.
Their constituencies felt that black protest was
responsible for the enabling legislation and
that they were entitled to its benefits. The
funds available did not begin to meet the needs
of the black community in terms of services or
jobs. Of equal importance was the fact that
after the original programs were funded, allocations to many of the CAAs were frozen at
the level for the preceding year. Therefore,
new programs could not be funded without
eliminating existing programs and that was
not a realistic alternative. Each program had a
built-in constituency of workers and people
served who resisted every effort to curtail,
eliminate, or even evaluate their programs.
Puerto Rican leaders understood the dilemma
faced by black administrators but that did not
make their task any easier. Understanding
slowly turned to disappointment and finally to
bitterness. It was at this point that some began
to reason that Puerto Ricans would receive

more benefits from a centralized program, administered by a white director or even City
Hall; both of which, they felt, would be more
responsive to their pressure.

Over the years Puerto Ricans in New
York City have lost two-thirds of their citywide
programs due to cutbacks. The black-Puerto
Rican struggle continues in areas like Brownsville where 40 percent of the population is
Puerto Rican but where blacks have firm control of the Community Corporation board. In
these cases, winner-takes-all means not only a
lack of jobs but a lack of services for Puerto
Ricans. As programs become identified as being black or Puerto Rican, the other group
tends not to use them. Therein lies one of the
ironies, among many, in the tragic struggle
between blacks and Puerto Ricans over programs ostensibly designed to alleviate the
misery of poverty.

THE JEWISH CASE

The Jewish case is replete with irony. For
many years Jews gave generously of their time
and resources in support of the civil rights
movement. Although the early days of the
movement were not free of tension between
the races, much of the camaraderie and good
will was genuine as blacks and whites came
together to sing, plan and act in buses, in
meeting rooms, and on picket lines. But events
beyond the control of both groups were forcing
changes in the relationship.

The precise moment the civil rights
movement died is not known. Some place the
time shortly after the enactment of the 1964
Civil Rights Act. It was clear by that time that
the fight against de jure segregation produced
the "easy" victories, for the nation was prepared to strike down such absurdities as separate drinking fountains, separate waiting
rooms in bus terminals and segregated lunch
counters. But these victories did not materially
change the living conditions of most blacks.
When it became apparent that the de facto
segregation and racism were intricately woven

into the fibers of our most cherished institutions, solutions became more elusive. Blacks were prepared to abandon the interracial coalitions that served a useful purpose during the formative years of the movement and to assume full control of their struggle.

The late David Danzig, long associated with the American Jewish Committee, explained the change in the following manner:

> . . . There are great differences between the civil rights movement and the 'Negro Revolution,' and these differences papered over so long by certain historical exigencies are now surfacing into full view. The civil rights movement was and is essentially concerned with the structure of law and social justice: its goals were equality before the law and equality of individual opportunity. As a movement it was begun by people whose aim was not to aid the Negro as such but to bring American society into closer conformity with constitutional principle. For the greatest part of its history, civil rights was the white liberal's cause. Liberals expounded the moral basis for human rights in religion and politics, developed the theory of human equality in the physical and social sciences, led the intellectual offensive against racism, and took the initiative in founding the civil rights organizations. . . .
> What changed civil rights almost overnight from a peripheral moral issue to our major domestic movement was the emergence of the Negroes themselves as a nationwide bloc.

As often is the case in sudden change, some were prepared for it and some were not. The targets of opportunity for black militants in the North were the white merchants, landlords and teachers. In certain cities Jews were disproportionately represented in these target groups. As the incidents between the groups increased some Jews felt betrayed while others felt all Jewry was under attack. If in the heat of battle an anti-Semitic remark was made, it soon overshadowed the original cause of the conflict. Thus black anti-Semitism became the issue rather than poor housing or inferior education.

It was, therefore, not surprising when the Anti-Defamation League of B'nai B'rith confirmed what many sensed: the Jewish community was turning inward away from non-Jewish affairs. A league survey among 2,500 American Jewish leaders indicated an increasing concern over the lack of public indignation toward anti-Semitic manifestations causing many Jews to concentrate on their own interests and their own security. It is within this historical context that one can understand the release of a report critical of black control of the antipoverty program by the American Jewish Congress, a report that would not have been written five years before.

The Jewish case against the antipoverty program is well stated in the report which concentrated on the New York City experience but which the authors claim is applicable to other jurisdictions. The report estimates that there were about 250,000 indigent Jews in the City, comprising 15 percent of the poor, 60 percent of which are over 60 years of age. Although the authors acknowledge the difficulty involved in identifying the Jewish poor, they state "unequivocally" that in spite of the large sums of money spent in fighting poverty, little of this money has gone to alleviate the plight of this group.

Reasons for the exclusion of Jews from the program are separated into two categories: those external to the Jewish community and those internal to it. Among those reasons external to the Jewish community the report finds:

1. The Act and Federal guidelines emphasized a decentralized system of specified poverty areas, as opposed to citywide programs. Many poor Jews do not live in these areas.
2. Agencies within the poverty areas establish their programs to serve not the entire area but one or more specific groups within the population. Jews, numerically weak, tend to be ignored.
3. Agencies have failed to reach out to serve the poor outside the pockets of poverty although they are permitted to do so.
4. Low priority is given to programs serving the aged.
5. Poverty officials are unaware of Jewish poverty and are more interested in servicing "their own."

6. The holding of elections for the governing boards of the community corporations are held on the Jewish Sabbath.
7. Fear of physical abuse.
8. None of the criteria used to designate poverty areas is descriptive of Jewish poverty.

Reasons for non-participation internal to the Jewish community pertain to the lack of organization of the aged and lack of organization on the local level. The feeling among Jewish organizations that the poverty program belonged to blacks and Puerto Ricans is given as another reason. Finally Jews have been "unable or reluctant to engage in the 'politics of poverty'. . . . The traditional Jewish abhorrence of violence and of confrontation as a political weapon" has discouraged Jews from pressing their demands.

Many of the biases described in the report are similar to objections raised by the Puerto Ricans and Mexican-Americans. Therefore it is important to note the rationale which led to some of these biases. When attempting to tackle a problem as large and as diverse in its manifestations as poverty, priorities must be established. While political considerations are important ingredients in this process, the decision to relegate programs serving the aged to a low priority status in favor of education and training programs designed to serve children and young adults resulted not only in a lack of services for several thousand indigent Jewish aged, but for millions of black senior citizens as well. Similarly the practice of stressing aid to black and Puerto Rican businessmen under Title IV of the act can only be viewed as discrimination if one disagrees with the premise that more mileage for the dollar can be realized if minority businessmen are helped to establish and expand businesses in impoverished areas where they reside. The American Jewish Congress in fact helped to legitimatize this strategy when it joined with the Urban League to establish the Interracial Council for Business Opportunities to accomplish these same goals.

Although the report disclaims any "attempt to compete with other minority groups for the meager funds presently available to fight poverty," it calls for a more equitable distribution of funds and offers several schemes to accomplish this. Since the report contains no suggestion for a liberal coalition to seek adequate financing for all, the call for a more equitable distribution of curtailed funding can only be interpreted as an attempt to join the competition for program resources.

The fact that some Jews have suffered as a result of the evolutionary changes in black-white relationships is not doubted or dismissed. But it must be stated that change is never orderly or equitable in either its rewards or penalties. This report, and the supporting evidence in the Anti-Defamation League survey, indicates that a segment of the Jewish leadership has turned inward. For years this leadership was ahead of its constituency, and indeed, ahead of the nation in preaching tolerance and justice. This belief was, in part, self-serving for it is based on the premise that only in a pluralistic society, built on tolerance and the acceptance of differences can the Jewish community avoid assimilation and exist as a separate, viable entity. Perhaps constituent pressure demanded a change or perhaps the leaders no longer believe in the creed they have lived by so long. Nevertheless, it is difficult to see how Jewish security can be achieved at the expense of the largest minority group in the United States.

THE MEXICAN-AMERICAN CASE

Historically, the relationship between blacks and Mexican-Americans has been marked by competition and tension. Unlike the Jews and Puerto Ricans, Mexican-Americans have not participated in sizable numbers in the civil rights movement although they have certainly been affected by it. Cultural factors and memories of vying for the scant amount of status, jobs, housing and other resources successfully barred them from meaningful involvement in what they perceived to be a black cause. And yet as an urban people—a little recognized fact—Chicanos were likely candidates to compete with blacks in the cities of the Southwest for the urban biased Great Society programs. Of the 5 million plus Mexican-Americans concentrated in the states of Texas, New Mexico, Colorado, California and Arizona, the overwhelming majority live in cities like Phoenix, East Los Angeles, Los Angeles, San Diego, San Francisco, Denver, Albuquerque, Austin, Corpus Christi, El Paso and San Antonio.

The infusion of program resources into black communities in the Southwest was, for many Chicanos, another example of Anglo indifference to their plight. Surely, they argued, in terms of numbers and measurements of deprivation they could rival blacks, and in some areas exceed them, in qualifying for assistance. Some examples of what they perceived as discrimination in the distribution of funds illustrate their case:

- The stepped up public and private aid channelled into Watts following the disorders there during the summer of 1965 stirred sharp resentment among Mexican-American leaders. Chicanos are the largest minority group in Los Angeles and generally regarded the Watts neighborhood superior to several of their own in this sprawling city.
- A 1971 *Business Week* report in this same city quotes the director of the Minority Enterprise Small Business Investment Company as saying that Chicanos received only 35 percent of the poverty funds and control only 25 percent of the agencies distributing these funds.
- In Santa Clara County, California, where Chicanos comprise 25 percent of the poor population and 50 percent of all the Aid to Dependent Children welfare cases, their leaders denounced the allocation of funds to the traditional service agencies in the area which they felt had a history of catering to the "less needy" blacks.

The more militant Chicano leaders soon realized that they could not compete with blacks for policy making positions because they lacked the political clout that could make

such appointments possible. President Johnson's response to Chicano demands resulted, in 1967, in the appointment of a six-member cabinet level committee to study the ways the federal government could best work with state and local governments and private industry to improve conditions for Mexican-Americans. The effort was followed by the largely unsuccessful White House Conference of Mexican-Americans that same year.

The inability to influence national policy more meaningfully soon led to disenchantment with the handful of Mexican-American elected leaders whom the militants felt had not served them well. Thus the militants were soon fighting a three front war—the Anglos, the blacks and segments of the largely conservative Mexican-American communities. The elected officials, perhaps more attuned to the sentiments of their constituents, tried to discredit the militants by making disparaging comparisons between them and the blacks. Representative Henry B. Gonzales's 1968 attack is illustrative of this tactic:

We see a strange thing in San Antonio today; we have those who play at revolution and those who imitate the militance of others—We have those who cry "brown power" only because they have heard "black power."

Undoubtedly the successes of the civil rights and Black Power movements did not go unnoticed in the Chicano communities. At times the rhetoric was similar and analogies of the struggle of the two groups were made: Chicano leaders have labelled Denver and Del Rio their "Selma" and projected that East Los Angeles will be to the Chicanos in the seventies what Watts was to the blacks in the sixties. But great pains were taken by other segments of the Chicano leadership to emphasize the differences between themselves and blacks in their respective claims for justice. Some of these leaders rejected integration as a viable policy for Mexican-Americans and began to stress their cultural heritage. A college student summed up this sentiment when he wrote:

We're not like the Negroes. They want to be white men because they have no history to be proud of. My ancestors come from one of the most civilized nations in the world.

The fact that many Mexican-Americans chose to assimilate or at least identify strongly with the dominant culture, suggests that this view may be a minority opinion strategically used to win adherents to the more militant cause. However, other observers have also noticed the reaction of the populace when the term "La Raza" is evoked. Ralph M. Kramer noted in his comparative case studies on the antipoverty programs that part of the Chicano-black strain "was related to the difference in their social goals and their feelings of cultural superiority and distinctiveness." Their problems with blacks were seen as another chapter in their historic conflict with Anglos in the Southwest.

It appears that Chicanos will continue to look inward, kindle their own anger and make their own demands. Blacks, at least for the present, will be seen as competitors rather than cohorts.

The history of each of these minorities illustrates how initial hopes of alleviating the misery of poverty turned bitter as each became involved in an anti-black competitive drive to receive its share of Kennedy-Johnson program resources. Each not only suffered the loss of jobs and services but also the opportunity to force a powerful coalition capable of obtaining aid for their common problems.

The apparent success of President Nixon's drive to unilaterally eliminate or curtail many of these programs clearly suggests how self-defeating, for all groups, the competitive behavior has been. The dissolution of the liberal coalition has foreclosed the possibility, at the present time, of mounting an effective counterattack against the President's actions. Congressional activity is largely centered on protecting its prerogatives vis-à-vis the administration rather than a concern over preserving the programs. There are many factors that would explain this change in the national mood in less than a decade but the conflict surrounding the administration of these pro-

grams is an important consideration in any analysis of the situation.

The evidence we have uncovered indicates that blacks have little interest in forming coalitions if the price they must pay is to share limited program resources for an unspecified goal of intergroup harmony. Groups join coalitions to increase, not decrease, their influence. As the largest minority group in the country, blacks are consolidating power at the municipal level and increasingly see themselves exercising power on the national level. There is little talk among blacks of the use of disruption as a viable strategy to increase the flow of federal funds. Disruption has focused the nation's attention on black problems, but it has also brought repression. Funds received in direct response to fears of civil disorders, like those for summer recreation programs, hardly begin to address black priorities.

The events of the past decade have convinced the Puerto Ricans, Chicanos and Jews that their best interests would be served if they turned inward. The former groups will attempt to build strong political and service organizations within their own communities, while the latter—having achieved these goals—will reassess past values and strategies. Most leaders spoke of a two to three year period of ethnocentric preoccupation—sufficient time, it was hoped, to heal old wounds before an enduring coalition is possible.

The seeking of strength from within is a trend, not a monolithic movement and, of course, unforeseen events may bring the groups together sooner. Even today at the height of the tension, there is some cooperation taking place. Blacks and Puerto Ricans are working together in some school districts in New York City for greater representation on local school boards. A coalition of blacks, Chicanos and liberal whites won all seven seats on the Houston Texas School Board in 1971. They almost succeeded in winning the mayoralty election, as well. There are probably many other examples of intergroup cooperation that will remain unheralded.

Recent attempts by Puerto Ricans and Chicanos to form a national alliance can be viewed as another indication of anti-black sentiment and in certain respects it is. But it is also a sign that the two groups recognize the fact that without blacks their chances to influence the political system on a national scale are diminished and this latest attempt is aimed at compensating for this weakness. Despite sharing a language and cultural background there is little reason for these groups to unite since they do not share a common experience in this country. What they do share is a need for a common national Spanish voice to bring their concerns to the nation's attention. With the Chicanos largely concentrated in the five Southwestern states and the Puerto Ricans situated mostly in the Northeast, an alliance has certain distinct advantages. The geographic distance between them also provides fewer opportunities for the groups to compete for limited resources and thus lessens the chances for eruption of intergroup hostility. It should be noted, however, that all is not calm on the Puerto Rican-Chicano front. Officials in the Office of Spanish Surnames in Washington, for instance, report competition between the two minorities over the Elementary and Secondary Schools Act's Title VII funds. These monies, designated for bilingual programs for minority school children, are the source of friction between competing Chicano and Puerto Rican groups.

On the national scene blacks are coalescing following their moderately successful national convention at Gary, Indiana. Chicanos have abandoned plans to open an East Coast office in deference to their new Puerto Rican allies. While these efforts may increase the bargaining power of these groups on minor issues, they will not be successful, working alone, in advancing goals that will realistically meet their needs. Instead of an extension of the antipoverty or the Model Cities programs, programs are needed to solve problems of structural poverty, like a guaranteed annual income, a full employment program, a vastly accelerated housing program, national health insurances and increased federal aid to education. The dissolution of the liberal coalition during the second half of the Johnson Administration and the Vietnam War foreclosed the possibility of enacting these programs but they are natural extensions of the trends started in the 1960s. Even with direct American involvement in the war at an end, Congress is not likely to entertain such broad sweeping reforms in the absence of constituent pressure. The time to begin planning for a legislative assault is now. The first step is to establish a cooperative effort among groups.

An organization like the Leadership Conference on Civil Rights must begin the dialogue. Although the Conference membership does not represent all segments of the minority community, it offers some organizational stability. Recent attempts by groups like Common Cause, consumer advocate agencies and environmental protection organizations have demonstrated that liberal reform can still attract wide support. Support from these groups will certainly be sought but at this time they lack a significant number of minority group members in their constituencies to serve as conveners of the desired forum.

There is some evidence that some black and white leaders have recognized the need for a broader coalition to advance minority goals. Senator Hubert H. Humphrey summarized the feelings of many of those who attended a gathering in honor of former President Johnson at his library in December, 1972. Senator Humphrey said:

> . . . I would argue that the civil rights movement got into trouble when more and more people came to see it as an effort to give blacks a special break that was not afforded to other groups. . . . The concept of civil rights must be broadened to include the rights and opportunities that should be available to other disadvantaged groups. Rather than a minority movement, this should be a movement based on economic enrichment of low-income and elderly people of all colors, and the minorities would benefit in the process. In the political arena there just aren't enough Blacks, Chicanos, Indians and Puerto Ricans to form an electoral majority. Overemphasis on the needs of these identifiable groups can be and has been counterproductive.

These are not new sentiments—they have been stated and tried before. The task ahead for minorities is to call a ceasefire in the inner cities and to mobilize their forces to protect their interests. Unlike the past, they now have the political power to assure that they will not have minority status within the coalition. Within this context, new and former allies will be able to join them in promoting progressive legislation.

Statistical
Appendix

GENERAL STATISTICS

TABLE 1. *Race of the Population for Regions, Divisions, and States: 1970*

United States Regions Divisions States	Total	White	Negro and other races Total	Negro	Other races Total	Indian	Japanese	Chinese	Filipino	All other	Percent distribution Total	White	Negro and other races Total	Negro	Other
United States	203 211 926	177 748 975	25 462 951	22 580 289	2 882 662	792 730	591 290	435 062	343 060	720 520	100.0	87.5	12.5	11.1	1.4
REGIONS															
Northeast	49 040 703	44 310 504	4 730 199	4 344 153	386 046	49 466	38 978	115 777	31 424	150 401	100.0	90.4	9.6	8.9	0.8
North Central	56 571 663	51 641 183	4 930 480	4 571 550	358 930	151 287	42 354	39 343	27 824	98 122	100.0	91.3	8.7	8.1	0.6
South	62 795 367	50 420 108	12 375 259	11 969 961	405 298	201 222	30 917	34 284	31 979	106 896	100.0	80.3	19.7	19.1	0.6
West	34 804 193	31 377 180	3 427 013	1 694 625	1 732 388	390 755	479 041	245 658	251 833	365 101	100.0	90.2	9.8	4.9	5.0
NORTHEAST															
New England	11 841 663	11 388 774	452 889	388 398	64 491	10 872	7 485	18 113	6 962	21 059	100.0	96.2	3.8	3.3	0.5
Middle Atlantic	37 199 040	32 921 730	4 277 310	3 955 755	321 555	38 594	31 493	97 664	24 462	129 342	100.0	88.5	11.5	10.6	0.9
NORTH CENTRAL															
East North Central	40 252 476	36 160 135	4 092 341	3 872 905	219 436	57 732	33 002	31 001	22 375	75 326	100.0	89.8	10.2	9.6	0.5
West North Central	16 319 187	15 481 048	838 139	698 645	139 494	93 555	9 352	8 342	5 449	22 796	100.0	94.9	5.1	4.3	0.9
SOUTH															
South Atlantic	30 671 337	24 112 395	6 558 942	6 388 496	170 446	67 126	17 467	19 332	23 914	42 607	100.0	78.6	21.4	20.8	0.6
East South Central	12 803 470	10 202 810	2 600 660	2 571 291	29 369	10 363	3 795	4 235	2 473	8 503	100.0	79.7	20.3	20.1	0.2
West South Central	19 320 560	16 104 903	3 215 657	3 010 174	205 483	123 733	9 655	10 717	5 592	55 786	100.0	83.4	16.6	15.6	1.1
WEST															
Mountain	8 281 562	7 798 087	483 475	180 382	303 093	235 439	20 360	9 245	4 466	33 583	100.0	94.2	5.8	2.2	3.7
Pacific	26 522 631	23 579 093	2 943 538	1 514 243	1 429 295	155 316	458 681	236 413	247 367	331 518	100.0	88.9	11.1	5.7	5.4
NEW ENGLAND															
Maine	992 048	985 276	6 772	2 800	3 972	2 195	348	206	453	770	100.0	99.3	0.7	0.3	0.4
New Hampshire	737 681	733 106	4 575	2 505	2 070	361	360	420	157	772	100.0	99.4	0.6	0.3	0.3
Vermont	444 330	442 553	1 777	761	1 016	229	134	173	53	427	100.0	99.6	0.4	0.2	0.2
Massachusetts	5 689 170	5 477 624	211 546	175 817	35 729	4 475	4 393	14 012	2 361	10 488	100.0	96.3	3.7	3.1	0.6
Rhode Island	946 725	914 757	31 968	25 338	6 630	1 390	1 093	1 761	629	1 757	100.0	96.6	3.4	2.7	0.7
Connecticut	3 031 709	2 835 458	196 251	181 177	15 074	2 222	1 621	2 209	2 177	6 845	100.0	93.5	6.5	6.0	0.5
MIDDLE ATLANTIC															
New York	18 236 967	15 834 090	2 402 877	2 168 949	233 928	28 355	20 351	81 378	14 279	89 565	100.0	86.8	13.2	11.9	1.3
New Jersey	7 168 164	6 349 908	818 256	770 292	47 964	4 706	5 681	9 233	5 623	22 721	100.0	88.6	11.4	10.7	0.7
Pennsylvania	11 793 909	10 737 732	1 056 177	1 016 514	39 663	5 533	5 461	7 053	4 560	17 056	100.0	91.0	9.0	8.6	0.3
EAST NORTH CENTRAL															
Ohio	10 652 017	9 646 997	1 005 020	970 477	34 543	6 654	5 555	5 305	3 490	13 539	100.0	90.6	9.4	9.1	0.3
Indiana	5 193 669	4 820 324	373 345	357 464	15 881	3 887	2 279	2 115	1 365	6 235	100.0	92.8	7.2	6.9	0.3
Illinois	11 113 976	9 600 381	1 513 595	1 425 674	87 921	11 413	17 299	14 474	12 654	32 081	100.0	86.4	13.6	12.8	0.8
Michigan	8 875 083	7 833 474	1 041 609	991 066	50 543	16 854	5 221	6 407	3 657	18 404	100.0	88.3	11.7	11.2	0.6
Wisconsin	4 417 731	4 258 959	158 772	128 224	30 548	18 924	2 648	2 700	1 209	5 067	100.0	96.4	3.6	2.9	0.7
WEST NORTH CENTRAL															
Minnesota	3 804 971	3 736 038	68 933	34 868	34 065	23 128	2 603	2 422	1 456	4 456	100.0	98.2	1.8	0.9	0.9
Iowa	2 824 376	2 782 762	41 614	32 596	9 018	2 992	1 009	993	614	3 410	100.0	98.5	1.5	1.2	0.3
Missouri	4 676 501	4 177 495	499 006	480 172	18 834	5 405	2 382	2 815	2 010	6 222	100.0	89.3	10.7	10.3	0.4
North Dakota	617 761	599 485	18 276	2 494	15 782	14 369	239	165	204	805	100.0	97.0	3.0	0.4	2.6
South Dakota	665 507	630 333	35 174	1 627	33 547	32 365	221	163	83	715	100.0	94.7	5.3	0.2	5.0
Nebraska	1 483 493	1 432 867	50 626	39 911	10 715	6 624	1 314	551	324	1 902	100.0	96.6	3.4	2.7	0.7
Kansas	2 246 578	2 122 068	124 510	106 977	17 533	8 672	1 584	1 233	758	5 286	100.0	94.5	5.5	4.8	0.8
SOUTH ATLANTIC															
Delaware	548 104	466 459	81 645	78 276	3 369	656	399	559	392	1 403	100.0	85.1	14.9	14.3	0.6
Maryland	3 922 399	3 194 888	727 511	699 479	28 032	4 239	3 733	6 520	5 170	8 370	100.0	81.5	18.5	17.8	0.7
District of Columbia	756 510	209 272	547 238	537 712	9 526	956	651	2 582	1 662	3 675	100.0	27.7	72.3	71.1	1.3
Virginia	4 648 494	3 761 514	886 980	861 368	25 612	4 853	3 500	2 805	7 496	6 958	100.0	80.9	19.1	18.5	0.6
West Virginia	1 744 237	1 673 480	70 757	67 342	3 415	751	368	373	722	1 201	100.0	95.9	4.1	3.9	0.2
North Carolina	5 082 059	3 901 767	1 180 292	1 126 478	53 814	44 406	2 104	1 255	905	5 144	100.0	76.8	23.2	22.2	1.1
South Carolina	2 590 516	1 794 430	796 086	789 041	7 045	2 241	826	521	1 222	2 235	100.0	69.3	30.7	30.5	0.3
Georgia	4 589 575	3 391 242	1 198 333	1 187 149	11 184	2 247	1 836	1 584	1 253	4 164	100.0	73.9	26.1	25.9	0.2
Florida	6 789 443	5 719 343	1 070 100	1 041 651	28 449	6 677	4 090	3 133	5 092	9 457	100.0	84.2	15.8	15.3	0.4
EAST SOUTH CENTRAL															
Kentucky	3 218 706	2 981 766	236 940	230 793	6 147	1 531	1 095	558	612	2 351	100.0	92.6	7.4	7.2	0.2
Tennessee	3 923 687	3 293 930	629 757	621 261	8 496	2 276	1 160	1 610	846	2 604	100.0	83.9	16.1	15.8	0.2
Alabama	3 444 165	2 533 831	910 334	903 467	6 867	2 443	1 079	626	540	2 179	100.0	73.6	26.4	26.2	0.2
Mississippi	2 216 912	1 393 283	823 629	815 770	7 859	4 113	461	1 441	475	1 369	100.0	62.8	37.2	36.8	0.4
WEST SOUTH CENTRAL															
Arkansas	1 923 295	1 565 915	357 380	352 445	4 935	2 014	587	743	289	1 302	100.0	81.4	18.6	18.3	0.3
Louisiana	3 641 306	2 541 498	1 099 808	1 086 832	12 976	5 294	1 123	1 340	1 249	3 970	100.0	69.8	30.2	29.8	0.4
Oklahoma	2 559 229	2 280 362	278 867	171 892	106 975	98 468	1 408	999	612	5 488	100.0	89.1	10.9	6.7	4.2
Texas	11 196 730	9 717 128	1 479 602	1 399 005	80 597	17 957	6 537	7 635	3 442	45 026	100.0	86.8	13.2	12.5	0.7
MOUNTAIN															
Montana	694 409	663 043	31 366	1 995	29 371	27 130	574	289	236	1 142	100.0	95.5	4.5	0.3	4.2
Idaho	712 567	698 802	13 765	2 130	11 635	6 687	2 255	498	206	1 989	100.0	98.1	1.9	0.3	1.6
Wyoming	332 416	323 024	9 392	2 568	6 824	4 980	566	292	108	878	100.0	97.2	2.8	0.8	2.1
Colorado	2 207 259	2 112 352	94 907	66 411	28 496	8 836	7 831	1 489	1 068	9 272	100.0	95.7	4.3	3.0	1.3
New Mexico	1 016 000	915 815	100 185	19 555	80 630	72 788	940	563	386	5 953	100.0	90.1	9.9	1.9	7.9
Arizona	1 770 900	1 604 948	165 952	53 344	112 608	95 812	2 394	878	1 253	12 271	100.0	90.6	9.4	3.0	6.4
Utah	1 059 273	1 031 926	27 347	6 617	20 730	11 273	4 713	1 281	392	3 071	100.0	97.4	2.6	0.6	2.0
Nevada	488 738	448 177	40 561	27 762	12 799	7 933	1 087	955	817	2 007	100.0	91.7	8.3	5.7	2.6
PACIFIC															
Washington	3 409 169	3 251 055	158 114	71 308	86 806	33 386	20 335	9 201	11 462	12 422	100.0	95.4	4.6	2.1	2.5
Oregon	2 091 385	2 032 079	59 306	26 308	32 998	13 510	6 843	4 814	1 633	6 198	100.0	97.2	2.8	1.3	1.6
California	19 953 134	17 761 032	2 192 102	1 400 143	791 959	91 018	213 280	170 131	138 859	178 671	100.0	89.0	11.0	7.0	4.0
Alaska	300 382	236 767	63 615	8 911	54 704	16 276	916	228	1 498	35 786	100.0	78.8	21.2	3.0	18.2
Hawaii	768 561	298 160	470 401	7 573	462 828	1 126	217 307	52 039	93 915	98 441	100.0	38.8	61.2	1.0	60.2

Source: U.S. Bureau of the Census, *Census of Population: 1970, General Population Characteristics*, Final Report PC(1)-B1 United States Summary, section 1, p. 293.

TABLE 2.   *Total Resident Population: 1900, 1940, 1950, 1960, and 1965 to 1973*

(Numbers in millions)

Year	Total	Black	Percent black
1900[1]........................	76.0	8.8	12
1940[1]........................	131.7	12.9	10
1950[1]........................	150.7	15.0	10
1960........................	179.3	18.9	11
1965........................	193.0	20.9	11
1966........................	195.0	21.3	11
1967........................	197.0	21.6	11
1968........................	198.9	21.9	11
1969........................	200.9	22.2	11
1970........................	203.2	22.6	11
1971........................	205.7	23.0	11
1972........................	207.8	23.4	11
1973........................	209.5	23.7	11

Note: Data are for resident population as of April 1 for each year. Data for 1965–1969, and 1971–1973 are estimates.

[1] Data exclude Alaska and Hawaii.

Source: U.S. Bureau of the Census, *Current Population Reports*, Special Studies, Series P-23, No. 48, "The Social and Economic Status of the Black Population in the United States, 1973," p. 10.

TABLE 3.   *Percent Distribution of the Population by Region: 1950, 1960, 1970, and 1972*

Subject	1950[1]	1960	1970	1972
BLACK				
United States.........millions..	15.0	18.9	22.6	22.9
Percent, total.....................	100	100	100	100
South..............................	68	60	53	52
North..............................	28	34	39	40
Northeast..........................	13	16	19	20
North Central.....................	15	18	20	20
West..............................	4	6	8	8
WHITE				
United States.........millions..	134.9	158.8	177.7	179.0
Percent, total.....................	100	100	100	100
South..............................	27	27	28	29
North..............................	59	56	54	53
Northeast..........................	28	26	25	24
North Central.....................	31	30	29	29
West..............................	14	16	18	18

[1] Data exclude Alaska and Hawaii.

Source: U.S. Bureau of the Census, *Current Population Reports*, "The Social and Economic Status of the Black Population in the United States, 1972," Series P-23, no. 46, p. 10.

TABLE 4. *United States Population of Indians, Japanese, Chinese, Filipinos, and Puerto Ricans*

	Indian	Japanese	Chinese	Filipino	Puerto Rican[2]
1890	248,253	2,039	107,448		
1900	237,196	24,236	89,863		
1910	276,927	72,157	71,531	160	
1920	244,437	111,010	61,639	5,603	
1930	343,352	138,834	74,954	45,208	
1940	345,252	126,947	77,504	45,563	
1950	357,499	141,768	117,629	61,636	301,375
1960[1]	523,591	464,332	237,292	176,310	892,513
1970[1]	792,730	591,290	435,062	343,060	1,391,463

[1] The 1960 and 1970 census data include Hawaii and Alaska.

[2] Data on persons of Puerto Rican parentage were first collected in the 1950 census.

Source: Bureau of the Census, *Historical Statistics of the United States*, p. 9; Bureau of the Census, *1970 Census of Population*, Subject Reports, American Indians, p. 5; Puerto Ricans, p. xi; Bureau of the Census, *1960 Census of Population, Characteristics of the Population*, vol. 1, part 1, p. 145.

TABLE 5. *United States Population by Race, Ethnic Origin, and Sex: March 1971*

(Numbers in thousands. Noninstitutional population)

Race and ethnic origin	Total	Male	Female	Percent distribution		
				Total	Male	Female
Total......................	202,848	98,420	104,428	100.0	100.0	100.0
RACE						
White.......................	177,626	86,420	91,206	87.6	87.8	87.3
Negro.......................	22,810	10,795	12,015	11.2	11.0	11.5
Other races.................	2,412	1,205	1,207	1.2	1.2	1.2
ETHNIC ORIGIN						
English, Scotch, Welsh...........	31,006	14,852	16,154	15.3	15.1	15.5
French.........................	5,189	2,509	2,679	2.6	2.5	2.6
German.........................	25,661	12,854	12,806	12.7	13.1	12.3
Irish..........................	16,325	7,706	8,619	8.0	7.8	8.3
Italian........................	8,733	4,351	4,381	4.3	4.4	4.2
Polish.........................	4,941	2,444	2,497	2.4	2.5	2.4
Russian........................	2,132	1,038	1,094	1.1	1.1	1.0
Spanish origin.................	8,956	4,419	4,539	4.4	4.5	4.3
Central or South American......	501	235	267	0.2	0.2	0.3
Cuban..........................	626	313	313	0.3	0.3	0.3
Mexican........................	5,023	2,562	2,461	2.5	2.6	2.4
Puerto Rican...................	1,450	655	795	0.7	0.7	0.7
Other Spanish origin...........	1,356	654	703	0.7	0.7	0.7
Other ethnic origin[1].........	84,689	40,655	44,035	41.7	41.3	42.2
Not reported..................	15,216	7,593	7,623	7.5	7.7	7.3

[1] Includes about 20 million Negroes, as well as many persons reporting more than one origin.

Source: U.S. Bureau of the Census, *Current Population Reports*, "Selected Characteristics of Persons and Families of Mexican, Puerto Rican, and Other Spanish Origin, March 1971," Series P-20, no. 224, p. 3.

TABLE 6. *Spanish Origin Population by Type and Sex, for the United States and Five Southwestern States: March 1972*

(Numbers in thousands. Includes civilian noninstitutional population of the United States and members of the Armed Forces in the United States living off post or with their families on post)

Area and type of origin	Total		Male		Female	
	Number	Percent	Number	Percent	Number	Percent
UNITED STATES						
Total, Spanish origin............	9,178	100.0	4,540	100.0	4,638	100.0
Mexican..................................	5,254	57.2	2,677	59.0	2,577	55.6
Puerto Rican...........................	1,518	16.5	754	16.6	765	16.5
Cuban.....................................	629	6.9	302	6.7	326	7.0
Central or South American...............	599	6.5	277	6.1	322	6.9
Other Spanish origin....................	1,178	12.8	530	11.7	648	14.0
FIVE SOUTHWESTERN STATES						
Total, Spanish origin............	5,429	100.0	2,712	100.0	2,717	100.0
Mexican..................................	4,549	83.8	2,323	85.7	2,226	81.9
Other Spanish origin....................	881	16.2	390	14.4	491	18.1

Source: U.S. Bureau of the Census, *Current Population Reports,* "Persons of Spanish Origin in the United States, March 1972 and 1971, Series P-20, no. 250, p. 15.

TABLE 7. *Persons of Spanish Surname as Percent of Total Population for Five Southwestern States: 1970, 1960, and 1950*

(Statistics for 1970 based on 15-percent sample; for 1960, 25-percent sample; and for 1950, 20-percent sample)

State	1970			1960			1950		
	Total population	Spanish surname		Total population	Spanish surname		Total population	Spanish surname	
		Number	Percent of total		Number	Percent of total		Number	Percent of total
Total, all 5 States	36,146,872	4,667,975	12.9	29,309,477	3,513,684	12.0	21,053,280	2,281,710	10.8
Arizona	1,770,893	246,390	13.9	1,302,161	206,904	15.9	749,587	128,580	17.2
California	19,957,304	2,222,185	11.1	15,720,860	1,456,223	9.3	10,586,223	758,400	7.2
Colorado	2,207,259	211,585	9.6	1,753,925	152,039	8.7	1,325,089	118,715	9.0
New Mexico	1,016,000	324,248	31.9	951,023	275,731	29.0	681,187	248,560	36.5
Texas	11,195,416	1,663,567	14.9	9,581,508	1,422,787	14.8	7,711,194	1,027,455	13.3

Source: U.S. Bureau of the Census, *1970 Census of Population, Subject Reports,* "Persons of Spanish Surname," PC(2)-1D, p. vii.

TABLE 8. *Immigration Rate: 1900–1972*

Year	Number of immigrants	Immigration rate per 1,000 population	Year	Number of immigrants	Immigration rate per 1,000 population
1900	448,572	5.89	1935	34,956	0.27
1901	487,918	6.29	1936	36,329	.28
1902	648,743	8.20	1937	50,244	.39
1903	857,046	10.63	1938	67,895	.52
1904	812,870	9.89	1939	82,998	.63
1905	1,026,499	12.25	1940	70,756	.54
1906	1,100,735	12.88	1941	51,776	.39
1907	1,285,349	14.77	1942	28,781	.21
1908	782,870	8.83	1943	23,725	.17
1909	751,786	8.31	1944	28,551	.21
1910	1,041,570	11.27	1945	38,119	.27
1911	878,587	9.36	1946	108,721	.77
1912	838,172	8.79	1947	147,292	1.02
1913	1,197,892	12.32	1948	170,570	1.16
1914	1,218,480	12.29	1949	188,317	1.26
1915	326,700	3.25	1950	249,187	1.64
1916	298,826	2.93	1951	205,717	1.33
1917	295,403	2.86	1952	265,520	1.69
1918	110,618	1.07	1953	170,434	1.07
1919	141,132	1.35	1954	208,177	1.28
1920	430,001	4.04	1955	237,790	1.44
1921	805,228	7.42	1956	321,625	1.91
1922	309,556	2.81	1957	326,867	1.91
1923	522,919	4.67	1958	253,265	1.45
1924	706,896	6.19	1959	260,686	1.47
1925	294,314	2.54	1960	265,398	1.47
1926	304,488	2.59	1961	271,344	1.48
1927	335,175	2.82	1962	283,763	1.52
1928	307,255	2.55	1963	306,260	1.62
1929	279,678	2.30	1964	292,248	1.52
1930	241,700	1.96	1965	296,697	1.53
1931	97,139	.78	1966	323,040	1.64
1932	35,576	.28	1967	361,972	1.82
1933	23,068	.18	1968	454,448	2.26
1934	29,470	.23	1969	358,579	1.77
			1970	373,326	1.82
			1971	370,478	1.79
			1972	384,685	1.84

Source: Executive Office of the President: Office of Management and Budget, *Social Indicators,* 1973, p. 251.

INCOME AND EMPLOYMENT

TABLE 9.   *Median Family Income, by Race of Family Head: 1947–1971*

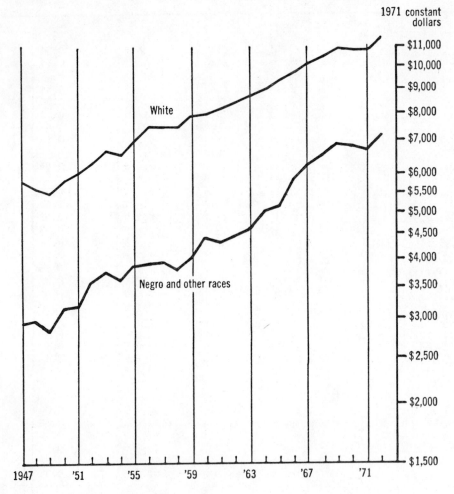

Source: *Social Indicators*, p. 153.

TABLE 10. *Median Income of Families: 1950 to 1973*

(In current dollars)

Year	Race of head			Ratio: Negro and other races to white	Ratio: Negro to white
	Negro and other races	Negro	White		
1950.....................	$1,869	(NA)	$3,445	0.54	(NA)
1951.....................	2,032	(NA)	3,859	0.53	(NA)
1952.....................	2,338	(NA)	4,114	0.57	(NA)
1953.....................	2,461	(NA)	4,392	0.56	(NA)
1954.....................	2,410	(NA)	4,339	0.56	(NA)
1955.....................	2,549	(NA)	4,605	0.55	(NA)
1956.....................	2,628	(NA)	4,993	0.53	(NA)
1957.....................	2,764	(NA)	5,166	0.54	(NA)
1958.....................	2,711	(NA)	5,300	0.51	(NA)
1959.....................	3,161	$3,047	5,893	0.54	0.52
1960.....................	3,233	(NA)	5,835	0.55	(NA)
1961.....................	3,191	(NA)	5,981	0.53	(NA)
1962.....................	3,330	(NA)	6,237	0.53	(NA)
1963.....................	3,465	(NA)	6,548	0.53	(NA)
1964.....................	3,839	3,724	6,858	0.56	0.54
1965.....................	3,994	3,886	7,251	0.55	0.54
1966.....................	4,674	4,507	7,792	0.60	0.58
1967	5,094	4,875	8,234	0.62	0.59
1968.....................	5,590	5,360	8,937	0.63	0.60
1969.....................	6,191	5,999	9,794	0.63	0.61
1970.....................	6,516	6,279	10,236	0.64	0.61
1971	6,714	6,440	10,672	0.63	0.60
1972	7,106	6,864	11,549	0.62	0.59
1973					
United States..........	7,596	7,269	12,595	0.60	0.58
South.................	6,495	6,434	11,508	0.56	0.56
North and West.......	8,943	8,378	13,049	0.69	0.64
Northeast..........	8,027	7,762	13,230	0.61	0.59
North Central......	9,076	9,109	13,128	0.69	0.69
West..............	10,208	8,233	12,661	0.81	0.65

Source: Current Population Reports, Series P-23, no. 48, p. 17.

TABLE 11. *Median Family Income in 1970, by Age of Head and Ethnic Origin: March 1971*

Age of head	Total population			Spanish origin	
	All races	White	Negro	Total	Mexican
Total.........................	$9,867	$10,236	$6,279	$7,334	$7,117
14 to 24 years old..................	7,037	7,294	5,013	5,697	5,534
25 to 34 years old..................	9,853	10,187	6,605	7,324	7,567
35 to 44 years old..................	11,410	11,790	7,569	8,345	8,058
45 to 54 years old..................	12,121	12,626	7,357	8,146	7,491
55 to 64 years old..................	10,381	10,737	6,438	7,482	7,997
65 years old and over..............	5,053	5,263	3,282	3,756	(B)
Head year-round, full-time worker:					
Median family income..............	$11,804	$12,016	$8,880	$9,309	$8,946
Percent of all families...........	64.1	65.5	51.4	57.4	57.0

B = *Base less than 75,000.*

Source: Current Population Reports, Series P-20, no. 224.

TABLE 12. *Median Earnings: 1956–1971, by Race and Sex (For Year-Round Full-Time Workers)*

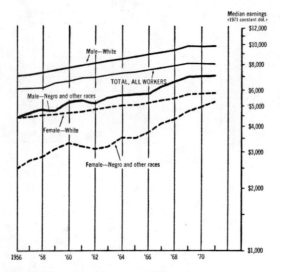

Source: Social Indicators, p. 125.

TABLE 13. *Median Earnings: 1956–1971, by Race and Sex (For Year-Round Full-Time Workers)*

(1971 constant dollars)

Year	Median earnings-- all wage and salary workers	White		Negro and other races	
		Male	Female	Male	Female
1956.....................	6,116	7,019	4,408	4,340	2,440
1957.....................	6,121	7,122	4,471	4,514	2,685
1958.....................	6,185	7,263	4,517	4,717	2,784
1959.....................	6,454	7,578	4,592	4,638	3,050
1960.....................	6,629	7,746	4,665	5,183	3,245
1961.....................	6,888	7,957	4,709	5,254	3,146
1962.....................	6,961	8,066	4,821	5,086	3,050
1963.....................	7,108	8,303	4,925	5,429	3,132
1964.....................	7,223	8,482	5,038	5,594	3,491
1965.....................	7,379	8,747	5,083	5,606	3,483
1966.....................	7,523	8,944	5,184	5,653	3,682
1967.....................	7,652	9,114	5,331	6,152	4,084
1968.....................	7,871	9,329	5,471	6,523	4,281
1969.....................	8,140	9,808	5,710	6,804	4,675
1970.....................	8,114	9,774	5,725	6,880	4,874
1971.....................	8,102	9,801	5,749	6,928	5,181

Source: Social Indicators, p. 146.

TABLE 14. *Persons Below the Low-Income Level: 1959 to 1973*

(Persons as of the following year)

Year	Number (thousands)			Percent below the low-income level		
	Negro and other races	Negro	White	Negro and other races	Negro	White
1959.....................	10,430	9,927	28,336	53.3	55.1	18.1
1960.....................	11,542	(NA)	28,309	55.9	(NA)	17.8
1961.....................	11,738	(NA)	27,890	56.1	(NA)	17.4
1962.....................	11,953	(NA)	26,672	55.8	(NA)	16.4
1963.....................	11,198	(NA)	25,238	51.0	(NA)	15.3
1964.....................	11,098	(NA)	24,957	49.6	(NA)	14.9
1965.....................	10,689	(NA)	22,496	47.1	(NA)	13.3
1966.....................	9,220	8,867	19,290	39.8	41.8	11.3
1967.....................	8,786	8,486	18,983	37.2	39.3	11.0
1968.....................	7,994	7,616	17,395	33.5	34.7	10.0
1969	7,488	7,095	16,659	31.0	32.2	9.5
1970	7,936	7,548	17,484	32.0	33.5	9.9
1971	7,780	7,396	17,780	30.9	32.5	9.9
1972	8,257	7,710	16,203	31.9	33.3	9.0
1973	7,831	7,388	15,142	29.6	31.4	8.4

Source: Current Population Reports, Series P-23, no. 48, p. 29.

TABLE 15. *Persons Below the Low-Income Level in 1970, by Ethnic Origin of Head, for the United States and Five Southwestern States: March 1971*

(Numbers in thousands)

Ethnic origin	United States		Five Southwestern States		Remainder of United States	
	Number below low-income level	Percent below low-income level	Number below low-income level	Percent below low-income level	Number below low-income level	Percent below low-income level
All persons .	25,522	12.6	4,608	12.9	20,914	12.5
White	17,480	9.9	3,626	11.3	13,854	9.5
Negro.............	7,650	33.6	852	29.8	6,798	34.2
Spanish origin.....	2,177	24.3	1,481	27.7	696	19.3
Mexican...........	1,407	28.0	1,283	29.4	124	18.6
Puerto Rican......	424	29.2	13	(B)	411	29.2
Cuban.............	86	13.7	12	(B)	74	13.2
Other	260	14.0	174	19.8	86	8.8

B = Base less than 75,000.

Source: Current Population Reports, Series P-20, no. 224, p. 8.

TABLE 16. *Major Occupation of Employed Persons, by Race and Sex: 1970 and 1960*

WHITE ☐   NEGRO AND OTHER RACES ■

Data relate to persons
14 years old and over

NUMBERS IN THOUSANDS

		Male		Female	
		White	Negro and other races	White	Negro and other races
Professional, Technical, and Kindred Workers	1970	6,198.7	317.9	3,907.5	406.6
	1960	4,158.6	144.6	2,485.3	197.4
Managers and Administrators, except Farm	1970	4,971.7	153.8	958.3	55.5
	1960	4,696.1	100.7	795.2	33.8
Sales Workers	1970	3,171.1	96.6	1909.2	90.6
	1960	2,915.2	60.7	1606.0	45.5
Clerical and Kindred Workers	1970	3,116.4	335.8	8,863.4	719.0
	1960	2,723.1	198.8	5,984.7	219.1
Craftsmen and Kindred Workers	1970	8,879.3	622.3	446.2	48.7
	1960	8,239.4	428.3	256.4	20.7
Operatives, except Transport	1970	5,339.4	756.9	3,193.8	526.1
	1960	5,112.9	573.9	2,819.5	315.9
Transport Equipment Operatives	1970	2,264.4	379.9	109.0	12.8
	1960	2,164.6	323.5	34.4	3.5
Laborers, except Farm	1970	2,345.4	599.3	220.5	48.1
	1960	2,365.9	783.2	136.2	36.5
Farmers and Farm Managers	1970	1,243.5	37.7	58.6	3.3
	1960	2,213.4	176.0	100.7	17.2
Farm Laborers and Farm Foremen	1970	637.7	145.4	108.9	31.8
	1960	947.5	291.1	171.3	76.3
Service Workers, except Private Household	1970	3,008.1	632	3,612.5	811.6
	1960	2,231.4	560.0	2,415.2	547.7
Private Household Workers	1970	22.2	17.4	533.2	519.9
	1960	31.6	29.5	758.4	898.4

NOTE: Persons with occupation not reported are excluded.

Source: Census of Population: 1970, General Population Characteristics, p. 351.

TABLE 17.   *Unemployment Rates, by Race: 1948–1972*

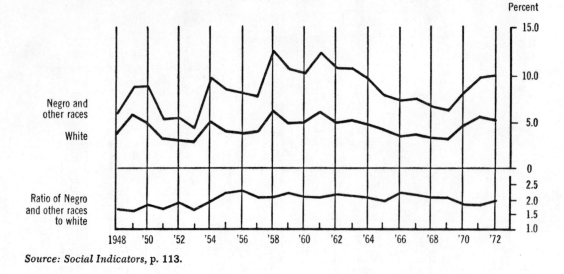

Source: Social Indicators, p. 113.

TABLE 18.   *Unemployment Rates, by Race: 1948–1972*

(Annual averages)

Year	White	Negro and other races	Ratio of Negro and other races to white
1948.....................	3.5	5.9	1.69
1949.....................	5.6	8.9	1.59
1950.....................	4.9	9.0	1.84
1951.....................	3.1	5.3	1.71
1952.....................	2.8	5.4	1.93
1953.....................	2.7	4.5	1.67
1954.....................	5.0	9.9	1.98
1955.....................	3.9	8.7	2.23
1956.....................	3.6	8.3	2.31
1957.....................	3.8	7.9	2.08
1958.....................	6.1	12.6	2.07
1959.....................	4.8	10.7	2.23
1960.....................	4.9	10.2	2.08
1961.....................	6.0	12.4	2.07
1962.....................	4.9	10.9	2.22
1963.....................	5.0	10.8	2.16
1964.....................	4.6	9.6	2.09
1965.....................	4.1	8.1	1.98
1966.....................	3.3	7.3	2.21
1967.....................	3.4	7.4	2.18
1968.....................	3.2	6.7	2.09
1969.....................	3.1	6.4	2.06
1970.....................	4.5	8.2	1.82
1971.....................	5.4	9.9	1.83
1972.....................	5.0	10.0	2.00

Source: Social Indicators, p. 136.

TABLE 19. *Unemployment Rates by Sex and Age: 1960, 1967, and 1970 to 1972*

(Annual averages)

Subject	1960	1967	1970	1971	1972
NEGRO AND OTHER RACES					
Total...........................	10.2	7.4	8.2	9.9	10.0
Teenagers.......................	24.4	26.3	29.1	31.7	33.5
Adult women.....................	8.3	7.1	6.9	8.7	8.8
Adult men.......................	9.6	4.3	5.6	7.2	6.8
WHITE					
Total...........................	4.9	3.4	4.5	5.4	5.0
Teenagers.......................	13.4	11.0	13.5	15.1	14.2
Adult women.....................	4.6	3.8	4.4	5.3	4.9
Adult men.......................	4.2	2.1	3.2	4.0	3.6
RATIO: NEGRO AND OTHER RACES TO WHITE					
Total...........................	2.1	2.2	1.8	1.8	2.0
Teenagers.......................	1.8	2.4	2.2	2.1	2.4
Adult women.....................	1.8	1.9	1.6	1.6	1.8
Adult men.......................	2.3	2.0	1.8	1.8	1.9

Source: *Current Population Reports*, Series P-23, no. 46, p. 39.

TABLE 20. *Unemployment Rates for Persons 16 to 64 Years Old, by Age, Sex, and Ethnic Origin: March 1971*

(Civilian noninstitutional population)

Age and sex	Total population			Spanish origin		
	All races	White	Negro and other races	Total	Mexican	Puerto Rican
MALE						
Total, 16 to 64 years old..	6.0	5.6	9.1	8.6	10.1	10.0
16 to 24 years old..............	13.6	12.7	20.1	15.2	14.3	25.4
25 to 44 years old..............	4.4	4.2	5.9	6.3	7.1	5.0
45 to 64 years old..............	3.9	3.9	5.5	8.0	12.2	(B)
FEMALE						
Total, 16 to 64 years old..	7.0	6.5	10.4	9.2	10.1	10.6
16 to 24 years old..............	12.5	11.2	22.4	14.4	15.5	(B)
25 to 44 years old..............	6.1	5.8	7.9	8.4	8.9	(B)
45 to 64 years old..............	3.9	3.8	4.6	4.9	5.3	(B)

B = *Base less than 75,000.*

Source: *Current Population Reports*, Series P-20, no. 224, p. 10.

EDUCATION

TABLE 21.   *Median Years of School Completed, by
Race: 1940–1970*

Persons 25 Years Old and Over

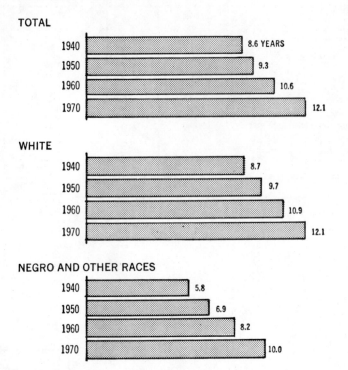

TOTAL

1940	8.6 YEARS
1950	9.3
1960	10.6
1970	12.1

WHITE

1940	8.7
1950	9.7
1960	10.9
1970	12.1

NEGRO AND OTHER RACES

1940	5.8
1950	6.9
1960	8.2
1970	10.0

Source: Census of Population, 1970, General Population Characteristics, p. 347.

TABLE 22. *The High School Educated Population: 1940–1972, by Age and Race*

Age and year	Number of persons with at least 4 years of high school (thousands)			Percent of persons with at least 4 years of high school		
	All races	White	Negro and other races	All races	White	Negro and other races
PERSONS 20 YEARS OLD AND OVER						
1940.........................	23,142	22,446	695	26.8	28.7	8.7
1950.........................	35,205	33,807	1,398	35.6	37.8	14.8
1960.........................	47,690	45,002	2,688	43.3	45.4	24.0
1962.........................	54,119	51,049	3,070	48.5	50.9	27.0
1964.........................	58,017	54,402	3,615	50.6	52.9	30.7
1965.........................	59,928	56,179	3,749	51.7	54.0	31.4
1966.........................	61,499	57,558	3,941	52.7	55.0	32.7
1967.........................	63,951	59,677	4,274	54.0	56.2	34.9
1968.........................	67,109	62,553	4,556	55.6	57.8	36.3
1969.........................	69,811	64,961	4,849	57.0	59.2	38.0
1970.........................	72,913	67,559	5,357	58.4	60.5	40.6
1971.........................	75,934	70,212	5,722	59.7	61.8	42.2
1972.........................	78,908	72,895	6,015	61.5	63.6	43.7
PERSONS 20 TO 24 YEARS OLD						
1940.........................	5,108	4,923	185	44.1	47.6	14.8
1950.........................	5,998	5,674	324	52.4	56.0	24.9
1960.........................	6,867	6,313	554	63.6	66.6	41.9
1962.........................	7,470	6,880	590	68.1	71.7	42.9
1964.........................	8,859	8,070	789	72.3	75.0	52.7
1965.........................	9,344	8,566	778	73.2	76.3	50.2
1966.........................	9,661	8,804	857	75.0	77.9	54.2
1967.........................	10,314	9,385	929	76.0	78.8	56.4
1968.........................	11,080	10,020	1,060	77.5	80.0	59.9
1969.........................	11,577	10,498	1,079	78.3	81.1	58.6
1970.........................	12,554	11,234	1,320	80.5	82.7	65.8
1971.........................	13,511	12,055	1,456	81.4	83.5	67.6
1972.........................	14,256	12,775	1,484	82.7	84.9	67.9

Source: Social Indicators, p. 100.

TABLE 23. *Undergraduate Enrollment, 18- to 24-year-olds: 1940–1972, by Race*

Year	White Number (1,000)	White Percent	Negro and other races Number (1,000)	Negro and other races Percent
1940	1,162	7.8	47	2.6
1950	1,504	10.8	80	4.4
1960	1,942	14.2	128	6.7
1967	4,293	24.5	362	14.4
1968	4,532	25.2	404	15.5
1969	4,850	26.1	469	17.0
1970	4,791	24.3	475	16.5
1971	5,097	24.8	579	18.5
1972	5,095	23.9	596	18.3

Source: Social Indicators, p. 105.

TABLE 24. *Percent of the Population 25 Years Old and Over Who Had Completed Less Than 5 Years of School or 4 Years of High School or More, by Ethnic Origin: March 1971*

Years of school completed and age	Total population All races	Total population White	Total population Negro	Spanish origin Total	Spanish origin Mexican	Spanish origin Puerto Rican
PERCENT COMPLETED LESS THAN 5 YEARS OF SCHOOL						
Total, 25 years old and over..	5.0	4.1	13.5	19.5	25.7	23.7
25 to 29 years old	1.1	1.1	1.8	5.8	6.6	9.3
30 to 34 years old	1.4	1.3	2.3	9.6	10.2	15.1
35 to 44 years old	2.6	2.3	5.4	18.1	25.5	20.3
45 to 54 years old	3.6	2.7	11.8	20.4	27.8	23.6
55 to 64 years old	5.9	4.3	22.3	38.1	54.6	49.0
65 years old and over	13.4	11.1	40.8	47.3	63.2	61.0
PERCENT COMPLETED 4 YEARS HIGH SCHOOL OR MORE						
Total, 25 years old and over..	56.4	58.6	34.7	32.6	26.3	19.8
25 to 29 years old	77.2	79.5	57.5	48.4	48.5	32.5
30 to 34 years old	72.9	75.1	53.8	41.8	41.4	21.8
35 to 44 years old	66.2	69.0	41.3	34.0	23.9	18.7
45 to 54 years old	58.7	61.7	29.1	24.5	14.9	16.3
55 to 64 years old	45.2	47.8	17.4	16.3	4.6	(B)
65 years old and over	29.3	30.8	11.3	15.1	6.7	(B)

B = Base less than 75,000.

Source: Current Population Reports, Series P-20, no. 224, p. 12.

OTHER SOCIAL INDICATORS

TABLE 25. *Life Expectancy at Birth, by Sex and Race: 1901–1971*

(Years of life)

Year	White			Negro and other races		
	Both sexes	Male	Female	Both sexes	Male	Female
1901 (1900-1902)........	49.6	48.3	51.2	33.8	32.5	35.1
1910 (1909-1911)........	51.9	50.3	53.7	35.9	34.2	37.7
1920 (1919-1921)........	57.5	56.6	58.6	47.1	47.2	47.0
1930 (1929-1931)........	60.9	59.2	62.8	48.4	47.5	49.5
1940.....................	64.2	62.1	66.6	53.1	51.5	54.9
1941.....................	66.2	64.4	68.5	53.8	52.5	55.3
1942.....................	67.3	65.9	69.4	56.6	55.4	58.2
1943.....................	64.2	63.2	65.7	55.6	55.4	56.1
1944.....................	66.2	64.5	68.4	56.6	55.8	57.7
1945.....................	66.8	64.4	69.5	57.7	56.1	59.6
1946.....................	67.5	65.1	70.3	59.1	57.5	61.0
1947.....................	67.6	65.2	70.5	59.7	57.9	61.9
1948.....................	68.0	65.5	71.0	60.0	58.1	62.5
1949.....................	68.8	66.2	71.9	60.6	58.9	62.7
1950.....................	69.1	66.5	72.2	60.8	59.1	62.9
1951.....................	69.3	66.5	72.4	61.2	59.2	63.4
1952.....................	69.5	66.6	72.6	61.4	59.1	63.8
1953.....................	69.7	66.8	73.0	62.0	59.7	64.5
1954.....................	70.5	67.5	73.7	63.4	61.1	65.9
1955.....................	70.5	67.4	73.7	63.7	61.4	66.1
1956.....................	70.5	67.5	73.9	63.6	61.3	66.1
1957.....................	70.3	67.2	73.7	63.0	60.7	65.5
1958.....................	70.5	67.4	73.9	63.4	61.0	65.8
1959.....................	70.7	67.5	74.2	63.9	61.3	66.5
1960.....................	70.6	67.4	74.1	63.6	61.1	66.3
1961.....................	71.0	67.8	74.5	64.4	61.9	67.0
1962	70.9	67.6	74.4	64.1	61.5	66.8
1963	70.8	67.5	74.4	63.6	60.9	66.5
1964.....................	71.0	67.7	74.6	64.1	61.1	67.2
1965.....................	71.0	67.6	74.7	64.1	61.1	67.4
1966.....................	71.0	67.6	74.7	64.0	60.7	67.4
1967.....................	71.3	67.8	75.1	64.6	61.1	68.2
1968.....................	71.1	67.5	74.9	63.7	60.1	67.5
1969.....................	71.3	67.8	75.1	64.3	60.5	68.4
1970	71.7	68.1	75.4	64.6	60.5	68.9
1971	71.9	68.3	75.7	65.2	61.3	69.4

Source: Social Indicators, p. 27.

TABLE 26. *Maternal and Infant Mortality Rates: 1940, 1950, 1960, and 1965 to 1972*

(Per 1,000 live births)

Year	Negro and other races				White			
		Infant				Infant		
	Maternal	Under 1 year	Under 28 days	28 days to 11 months	Maternal	Under 1 year	Under 28 days	28 days to 11 months
1940........	7.6	73.8	39.7	34.1	3.2	43.2	27.2	16.0
1950........	2.2	44.5	27.5	16.9	0.6	26.8	19.4	7.4
1960........	1.0	43.2	26.9	16.4	0.3	22.9	17.2	5.7
1965........	0.8	40.3	25.4	14.9	0.2	21.5	16.1	5.4
1966........	0.7	38.8	24.8	14.0	0.2	20.6	15.6	5.0
1967........	0.7	35.9	23.8	12.1	0.2	19.7	15.0	4.7
1968........	0.6	34.5	23.0	11.6	0.2	19.2	14.7	4.5
1969........	0.6	32.9	22.5	10.4	0.2	18.4	14.2	4.2
1970........	0.6	30.9	21.4	9.5	0.1	17.8	13.8	4.0
1971........	0.5	28.5	19.6	8.9	0.1	17.1	13.0	4.0
1972........	(NA)	29.0	20.6	8.5	(NA)	16.3	12.3	4.0

Source: Current Population Reports, Series P-23, no. 48, p. 116.

TABLE 27. *Number and Rate of Live Births: Indians and Alaska Natives in 24 Reservation States, and U.S., All Races (Calendar Years 1955–1967, Rates per 1,000 Population)*

Year	Indian and Alaska Natives		Indian (23 Res. States)		Alaska Native		U.S. All Races	
	Number	Rate	Number	Rate	Number	Rate	Number	Rate
1955	17,028	37.1	15,304	36.1	1,724	49.3	4,047,295	24.6
1956	17,947	38.0	16,040	36.9	1,907	51.5	4,163,090	24.9
1957	18,814	39.3	16,982	38.6	1,832	47.7	4,254,784	25.0
1958	19,371	39.9	17,428	39.2	1,943	48.7	4,203,812	24.3
1959	20,520	41.7	18,616	41.4	1,904	45.9	4,244,796	24.0
1960	21,154	42.5	19,188	42.2	1,966	45.6	4,257,850	23.7
1961	21,664	42.8	19,570	42.3	2,094	48.6	4,268,326	23.3
1962	21,866	42.7	19,770	42.1	2,096	48.6	4,167,362	22.4
1963	22,274	43.0	20,142	42.4	2,132	49.5	4,098,020	21.7
1964	22,782	43.3	20,794	43.1	1,988	45.7	4,027,490	21.0
1965	22,370	41.7	20,352	41.5	2,018	43.4	3,760,358	19.4
1966	21,100	38.7	19,154	38.5	1,946	41.1	3,606,274	18.4
1967	20,658	37.4	18,948	37.5	1,710	35.5	3,520,959	17.8

Source: Department of Health, Education, and Welfare, Indian Health: Trends and Services, 1969, p. 10.

TABLE 28. *Infant Deaths and Death Rates: Indians and Alaska Natives in 24 Reservation States, and U.S., All Races (Calendar Years 1955–1967, Rates per 1,000 Live Births)*

Year	Indian and Alaska Native Number	Rate	Indian Number	Rate	Alaska Native Number	Rate	U.S. All Races Number	Rate
1955	1,065	62.5	936	61.2	129	74.8	106,903	26.4
1956	1,066	59.4	900	56.1	166	87.0	108,183	26.0
1957	1,136	60.4	989	58.2	147	80.2	112,094	26.3
1958	1,123	58.0	989	56.7	134	69.0	113,789	27.1
1959	1,016	49.5	870	46.7	146	76.7	112,088	26.4
1960	1,064	50.3	914	47.6	150	76.3	110,873	26.0
1961	961	44.4	827	42.3	134	64.0	107,956	25.3
1962	967	44.2	827	41.8	140	66.8	105,479	25.3
1963	972	43.6	864	42.9	108	50.7	103,390	25.2
1964	856	37.6	747	35.9	109	54.8	99,783	24.8
1965	872	39.0	740	36.4	132	65.4	92,866	24.7
1966	822	39.0	722	37.7	100	51.4	85,516	23.7
1967	666	32.2	571	30.1	95	55.6	79,028	22.4

Source: Indian Health: Trends and Services, p. 20.

TABLE 29. *Victims of Homicide: 1940–1971, by Race and Sex*

(Rate per 100,000 population)

Year	All races	White Male	White Female	Negro and other races Male	Negro and other races Female
1940	6.3	5.0	1.4	55.5	13.0
1941	6.0	4.5	1.3	55.0	12.6
1942	5.9	4.4	1.3	53.5	12.1
1943	5.1	4.2	1.2	42.5	9.9
1944	5.0	4.0	1.2	44.1	9.7
1945	5.7	4.9	1.3	48.0	10.7
1946	6.4	4.9	1.5	54.4	12.4
1947	6.1	4.8	1.5	51.5	11.9
1948	5.9	4.5	1.5	51.0	11.7
1949	5.4	4.1	1.4	45.8	11.4
1950	5.3	3.9	1.4	45.5	11.2
1951	4.9	3.6	1.4	41.3	10.7
1952	5.2	3.7	1.3	45.4	10.8
1953	4.8	3.5	1.4	41.3	9.6
1954	4.8	3.5	1.4	40.6	9.5
1955	4.5	3.4	1.2	36.9	9.5
1956	4.6	3.3	1.3	37.1	10.3
1957	4.5	3.2	1.3	36.5	9.2
1958	4.5	3.4	1.4	34.9	9.3
1959	4.6	3.5	1.4	35.0	9.4
1960	4.7	3.6	1.4	34.5	9.9
1961	4.7	3.6	1.5	33.3	8.9
1962	4.8	3.8	1.6	35.5	8.9
1963	4.9	3.9	1.5	35.7	9.0
1964	5.1	3.9	1.6	37.4	9.2
1965	5.5	4.4	1.6	40.0	10.0
1966	5.9	4.5	1.8	43.4	10.6
1967	6.8	5.3	1.9	49.5	11.9
1968	7.3	5.9	1.9	54.6	11.7
1969	7.7	6.0	2.0	58.1	11.7
1970[1]	7.6	6.4	2.0	56.2	10.6
1971[1]	8.5	7.0	2.3	60.3	12.7

[1] Provisional data.

Source: Social Indicators, p. 66.

TABLE 30. *Households Living in Substandard Units, by Race: 1950–1970*

Race	1950	1960	1970[1]
NUMBER (thousands)			
All races..................	14,794	8,474	4,740
White.......................	12,126	6,210	3,303
Negro and other races..........	2,667	2,263	1,437
PERCENT			
All races..................	35.4	16.0	7.4
White.......................	31.8	13.0	5.7
Negro and other races..........	73.2	44.0	23.0

[1] In 1970 "Negro and other races" is limited to Negro only and "white" includes white and other races.

Source: Social Indicators, p. 207.

TABLE 31. *Black Legislators and Blacks Elected to Other Public Office: 1964, 1968, 1970, 1972, and 1974*

Subject	1964	1968	1970	1972	1974
Total....................	103	1,125	1,860	2,625	2,991
United States Senate:					
United States...............	-	1	1	1	1
South......................	-	-	-	-	-
House of Representatives:					
United States...............	5	9	13	15	16
South......................	-	-	2	4	4
State Legislature:					
United States...............	94	172	198	238	239
South......................	16	53	70	90	90
Mayors:					
United States...............	(NA)	29	81	83	108
South......................	(NA)	17	47	49	63
Other:					
United States...............	(NA)	914	1,567	2,288	2,627
South......................	(NA)	468	763	1,242	1,452

Source: Current Population Reports, Series P-23, no. 48, p. 125.